Food Substitutions

Ingredient/Amount Called For	Substitute
Baking powder, 1 teaspoon	½ teaspoon cream of tartar + ¼ teaspoon baking soda
Brown sugar, 1 cup	1 cup granulated sugar + 2 tablespoons molasses
Buttermilk, 1 cup	1 tablespoon lemon juice or vinegar + enough milk to make 1 cup
Chocolate **Unsweetened baking,** 1 oz	3 tablespoons baking cocoa + 1 tablespoon melted vegetable shortening
Semisweet chips, 1 cup	6 oz semisweet baking chocolate, chopped
Semisweet baking, 1 oz	1 oz unsweetened baking chocolate + 1 tablespoon sugar OR 1 tablespoon baking cocoa + 2 tablespoons sugar and 2 teaspoons vegetable shortening
Cornstarch, 1 tablespoon	2 tablespoons all-purpose flour
Garlic, ½ teaspoon (small clove)	⅛ teaspoon garlic powder
Fresh Herbs, 1 tablespoon chopped	1 teaspoon dried
Tomato sauce, 15-oz can	1 can (6 oz) tomato paste + 1½ cans water
Yeast, 1 package (0.25 oz)	2¼ teaspoons regular or active dry yeast
Yogurt, plain, 1 cup	1 cup sour cream

COOKBOOK

Everything You Need to Know to Cook Today

HARVEST

An Imprint of WILLIAM MORROW

GENERAL MILLS

Director, Brand Experience Creative:
Melissa Wildermuth

Manager, Brand Experience Creative—
Food Licensing, Partnerships & Ideas:
Lisa Balzo

Executive Editor/Food Editor: Cathy
Swanson Wheaton

Recipe Development and Testing:
Betty Crocker Kitchens

Photography: General Mills
Photography Studios and Tony
Kubat Photography

Photographer: ReGina Murphy

Photo Assistants: Morgan Marks,
Maren Woolhouse, Maya Bolduan

Food Stylists: Carol Grones,
Amy Peterson

Food Styling Assistant: Jerry Dudycha

Prop Stylist: Michele Joy

Inspiring America to Cook at Home™

The BIG RED Cookbook™

HARVEST

Vice President and Editorial Director:
Deb Brody

Editor: Sarah Kwak

Assistant Managing Editor:
Marina Padakis

Senior Production Editor:
Christina Stambaugh

Art Director: Tai Blanche

Cover and Interior Design: Tai Blanche

Senior Production Associate:
Kimberly Kiefer

THIRTEENTH EDITION

Library of Congress Cataloging-in-Publication Data has been applied for.

ISBN 978-0-358-40858-1

Find more great ideas at BettyCrocker.com

22 23 24 25 26 RTL 10 9 8 7 6 5 4 3 2 1

Back cover photos: Monte Cristo Quesadillas (page 64), Huli Huli Chicken with Mango Bowls (page 427), Four-Cheese Homemade Ravioli (page 198), Lemon Birthday Cake Cookies (page 552), Pork Carnitas Rice Bowls (page 413)

The content and recipes in this book have been reviewed with Registered Dietitians and nutrition experts at the General Mills' Bell Institute of Health and Nutrition. Please consult with your healthcare team for specific dietary needs and plans.

This book presents, among other things, the research and ideas of its author. It is not intended to be a substitute for consultation with a professional healthcare practitioner. Consult with your healthcare practitioner before starting any diet or other medical regimen. The publisher and the author disclaim responsibility for any adverse effects resulting directly or indirectly from information contained in this book.

Share the joy of homemade with more yummy recipes and helpful cooking tips at bettycrocker.com

Dear Makers,

Whether you're a seasoned pro or want to fake it until you make it, this book is filled with everything you need to know to cook today. Anyone can be a Betty! From the ever-present dinner-dilemma crunch to finding healthy foods your kids will actually eat or wowing your family and friends with a memorable meal, let the yummy, on-trend recipes, helpful tips and how-tos from America's most-trusted kitchens be your expert kitchen helpers for fun cooking adventures and amazing eats!

Turns out you can judge a book by its cover! This isn't your grandmother's *Betty Crocker Cookbook*. This 13th edition with a **new, larger, lay-flat and easy-to-store format** is just the beginning. With over 1,300 recipes and nearly **400 exclusive new recipes**, there's something for everyone and every occasion. You'll still find the classics, such as Banana Bread, Roast Turkey and Chocolate Chip Cookies, but also soon-to-be BFFs such as Oat and Almond Pumpkin Bread, Buffalo Cauliflower Pizza and Cuban Picadillo Tacos. Check out the **new Veggie Forward chapter** full of incredible recipes, as well as **gluten-free, vegetarian and vegan** options.

Hectic nights have met their match with the **new 5-ingredient recipes**, as well as **multi-cooker, air fryer, slow-cooker and make-ahead** dishes. Cut down on food waste with the Use It Up features—**clever ideas to use up the ingredients you already have on hand**—sprinkled throughout.

One thing hasn't changed—our standard of excellence. Every recipe has been thoroughly tested in the Betty Crocker Kitchens, giving you confidence in the kitchen, no matter what your cooking skills, so you too, can be a Betty.

Here's to great meals and happy bellies!

Betty

Contents

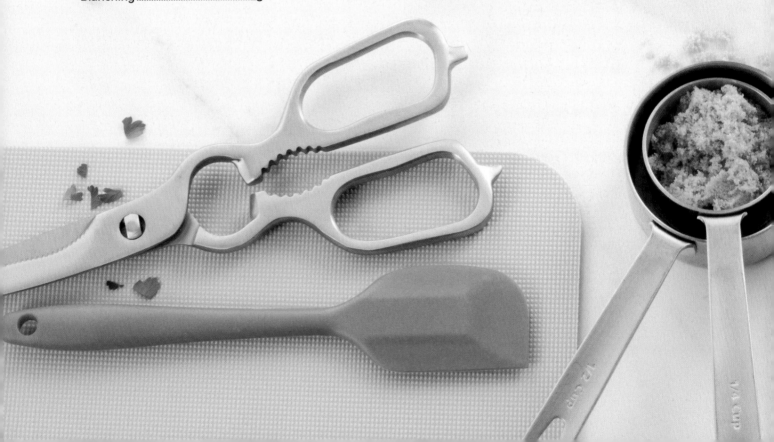

Getting Started

Getting Started Basics

Here's the information you'll need to start cooking! From organizing your kitchen to descriptions of cooking utensils, basic cooking terms and skills and how to perform them, and how long to store foods, you'll find a wealth of information here.

Kitchen Organization

Whether you are just learning to cook or to want to make cooking more inspirational or less time consuming, a little organization can be just what you need.

A PLACE IN YOUR KITCHEN CALLED HOME

Whether your kitchen is the size of a postage stamp or a sprawling ranch, make the most of your space so that cooking will be more enjoyable.

- Store items near where you use them—pans by the stove, spices where you mix, tableware where you serve.

- Keep items you use frequently in easy-to-grab-from spaces; store things you rarely use in a different spot.

- Use cabinet organizers so everything can be located quickly.

- Install roll-out shelves if you don't already have them— they make it easier to see and grab items.

- Keep your counters clutter-free so they are open for cooking.

- Add hooks to cabinet doors to hang measuring cups and spoons, and pot holders or oven mitts.

- Designate one spot in your kitchen for cookbooks.

KEEPING YOUR KITCHEN SANITY

Are you tired of looking for an item you know you have but can't locate? Use these simple organizing tips to keep things in order, and cooking will be much easier and more effortless.

- **Group similar foods together.**

- **Use prime real estate well.** Reserve the front-and-center parts of any space for the ingredients you reach for most often. Use the space around, and higher and lower shelves, for those items you use occasionally.

- **Label liberally.** Mark repackaged foods with name and date. Leave no question as to what things are and where they are stored.

- **Tame the clutter.** Use containers to keep foods together easily and neatly, such as sauce and seasoning packets or bags of pasta.

- **Use trays to prevent later cleanup.** Place raw meats in the refrigerator on trays or in containers with sides to catch meat juice drips and prevent them from dirtying shelves. Store these items separately from produce to prevent bacterial contamination.

- **Follow first in, first out.** Place newer, unopened packages behind older ones. What you buy first should be used first.

SMART AND CREATIVE STORAGE

Here are some items from around the house to upcycle for food storage.

Baby Food Jars Snacks or bulk spices

Canning Jars Individual portions of hot or cold cereal, or yogurt and fruit

Coffee Tins Flour, sugar, pasta or rice

Magazine Holders with Holes Potatoes or onions

Over-the-Door Shoe Holder Individual snacks or small bags of food

Plastic Shoe Boxes Sauce and seasoning packets, herb and spice jars

Smart Shopping Strategies

Set aside time for weekly meal planning to avoid last-minute dashes to the store or takeout splurges. It pays to be strategic about grocery shopping—you can save money and avoid wasting food. Shopping will be easier and more efficient, helping you stick to your list and budget, so you'll have the energy and time to enjoy cooking.

MEAL PLANNING

- **Start fresh.** Before you shop, do a quick cleanup and inventory of your fridge, freezer and pantry so you'll know what you have, and have to use soon.

- **Keep a running list.** As you run out of an ingredient, add it to a list on a whiteboard inside your cupboard or on your phone. Create your weekly shopping list by adding onto this one.

- **Create a chart.** Map out a chart of the week's meals, snacks and brown-bag lunches you'll need. Consider your schedule and the time you can spend cooking.

- **Strategize your list.** Plan meals that help you make use of foods you already have—especially those items you noted need to be used soon.

- **Coordinate for recipes and meals.** As you consider each meal on your chart, add the ingredients you'll need to your shopping list.

SHOP SMART

- If possible, shop alone so that you aren't distracted.

- Bring your own bags—many stores offer a reusable bag discount, or charge for their bags.

- Clip coupons ahead of time and read store ads, both print and online.

- Know what your budget is.

- Always shop with a list.

SUPERMARKET SKILLS

- Shop and cook seasonally to get the freshest foods at the best prices.

- Shop the perimeter of the store for the most healthful fresh items (dairy, produce, meats).

- Check out the discount shelves for bargains.

- Buy in bulk those items you use often.

- Check the unit price per ounce to compare package sizes or brands for the best price. Many stores offer this information on the shelf labels. If not, you can determine the unit price with this equation:

Price ÷ number of ounces = cost per unit.

Use the calculator feature on your phone to do the math.

Ingredients

See also Food Substitutions (inside front cover).

BAKING INGREDIENTS

Baking Powder A leavening mixture that, when mixed with liquid and heat, releases carbon dioxide gas bubbles, causing baked goods to rise. Cannot be a substitute for baking soda.

Baking Soda A leavening ingredient that must be mixed with an acid ingredient such as lemon juice or buttermilk for it to cause baked goods to rise.

Butter Available salted or unsalted; must contain at least 80% butterfat. Butter (not margarine) is used in recipes in this book for the best taste, texture, appearance and performance. Margarine products can vary greatly and may not provide optimum results. See page 542.

Chocolate Cocoa beans are ground into a thick paste called chocolate liquor, then processed to make the various forms of chocolate.

- **Baking Cocoa** Made from dried chocolate liquor with cocoa butter removed; unsweetened.

- **Bittersweet (Dark), Sweet (German), Milk and Semisweet Chocolate** Available in bars and chips (German chocolate in bars only) for baking and eating. **Dark Chocolate** contains a higher percentage of cocoa solids (more than 60%) and less added sugar than semisweet, with a rich, intense flavor; available as baking chocolate and chocolate bars for eating.

- **Unsweetened Chocolate** Available in bars; no sugar is added, so bitter in flavor—use just for baking.

- **White Chocolate** Contains no chocolate liquor and so it is not truly chocolate. Labeled as "white baking chips" or "vanilla baking bar."

Coconut The fruit of the coconut palm tree; available sweetened or unsweetened. Shredded coconut is moist and therefore best for baking. Dried (desiccated) flaked coconut is used mostly for decorating.

Cornstarch A thickener derived from corn; good for making clear, rather than opaque sauces.

Corn Syrup A sweetener made from corn sugar processed with acid or enzymes. Dark corn syrup has caramel-like flavor and dark color; can be used interchangeably with light corn syrup, but flavor and color of finished dish may be affected.

Cream of Tartar A dry acid ingredient that adds stability and volume when beating egg whites.

Eggs Add richness, moisture and structure to baked goods.

1

2

3

4

5

6

7

8

9

10

11

12

13

14

15

1/2 tsp [2.5 ml]

1 tsp [5 ml]

1 tsp [5 ml]

Flour A primary baking ingredient; comes in many varieties. Below are varieties of wheat flour. There are also many other non-wheat flour choices that are either gluten-free or low-gluten. Follow recipes specifically designed for these products, as they are not directly interchangeable with wheat flour.

- **All-Purpose** The most common flour; available bleached and unbleached.
- **Bread Flour** Gives more structure to bread because it's higher in protein.
- **Cake Flour** Made from soft wheat; makes tender, fine-textured cakes.
- **Quick-Mixing Flour** Processed to blend easily; used for sauces and gravies.
- **Self-Rising Flour** Combined with baking powder and salt. Not interchangeable with other flours.
- **Whole Wheat Flour** Made from the whole grain; gives foods a nutty flavor and heartier texture.
- **White Whole Wheat Flour** Whole grain flour made from white wheat, which can give baked goods the appearance and flavor of being made with all-purpose flour but with the benefits of whole grain.

Molasses Made during the sugar-refining process; available in light and dark varieties, which are interchangeable unless specified otherwise.

Salt Adds flavor, controls the growth of yeast in breads.

Spices Add flavor to baked goods.

Sugar Made from sugar beets or sugarcane.

- **Brown Sugar** Made from granulated sugar plus molasses; light or dark brown in color. Use interchangeably unless one is specified in a recipe.
- **Coarse, Decorating or Pearl Sugar** Large grained. Use for decorating.
- **Colored Sugar** Use for decorating.
- **Granulated** Available in boxes or bags, cubes and packets. **Superfine sugar** dissolves quickly and is great for beverages, meringues and frostings.
- **Powdered Sugar** Granulated sugar that has been processed to a fine powder; contains a very small amount of cornstarch to keep it from clumping.
- **Raw or Turbinado Sugar** Golden brown–colored; coarser than granulated sugar. Sprinkle on cookies, scones, muffins and pies before baking.

Vegetable Shortening Sold in sticks and cans, this solid all-vegetable product is available in regular and butter-flavored varieties. Use to grease pans, make pie pastry and as all or part of the fat in cookies and other baked goods when specified for crumb tenderness, flaky texture or a clean flavor.

Yeast A leavening ingredient used to make breads rise. There are several varieties available.

- **Bread Machine Yeast** Finely granulated yeast for bread machine recipes.
- **Fast-Acting Dry Yeast** Dehydrated yeast that allows bread to rise in less time than regular yeast.
- **Regular Active Dry Yeast** Dehydrated yeast that can also be used in most bread recipes.

DAIRY/REFRIGERATED INGREDIENTS

Butter See Butter, page 9.

Cheese See Cheese Types, page 44.

Cream Smooth, rich dairy product separated from milk; churned to make butter, and pasteurized and processed into several forms:

- **Half-and-Half** Contains 10 to 20% butterfat; does not whip. To save on fat and calories, look for fat-free half-and-half. Although not recommended for baking, it is great for soups and beverages.
- **Sour Cream** Regular sour cream contains 18 to 20% butterfat. Low-fat and fat-free varieties are available and can often be substituted for regular.

Photo (at left) 1 Brown Sugar **2** Granulated Sugar **3** Egg **4** Yeast **5** White Baking Chips **6** Coconut **7** Sweet Baking (German) Chocolate **8** Baking Cocoa **9** Chocolate Chips **10** Butter **11** Whole Wheat Flour **12** All-Purpose Flour **13** Salt **14** Ground Cinnamon **15** Baking Powder

- **Whipping Cream** Available in light and heavy varieties. Contains 36 to 40% butterfat. Doubles in volume when whipped. Ultra-pasteurized cream will have a longer shelf life than regular pasteurized cream.

Eggs See Egg Basics, page 101.

Milk Pasteurized dairy milk is available in many types. Today there are also many non-dairy options to choose from; see Dairy Milk Alternatives, page 75. Read labels to compare protein, calcium and calories.

- **Buttermilk** Fat-free or low-fat product; adds a tangy taste to baked goods.
- **Evaporated Milk** with at least half of the water removed. Available in cans, typically in the baking aisle; whole, low-fat and skim varieties.
- **Fat-Free (Skim)** Contains almost no fat.
- **Low-Fat Milk** Available as 1% milk (99% of the milk fat removed) and 2% milk (98% of milk fat removed). Recipes in this book were tested with 2% milk.
- **Sweetened Condensed Milk** A highly sweetened milk product; used mostly for baking. Available canned; whole and fat free.
- **Whole Milk** Contains at least 3.5% milk fat.

Tofu See Learn to Prepare Tofu, page 408.

Yogurt Product made from milk with healthful bacteria added. A variety of yogurts are available with a range of fat content, sugar and possibly added fruit for flavor. Look for yogurt with "live and active cultures" to be sure you are getting the most from your yogurt. Thick, creamy **Greek Yogurt** is regular yogurt with the watery whey drained off, resulting in yogurt with generally higher protein content and less sugar than regular yogurt.

PANTRY INGREDIENTS

Bouillon/Broth/Stock Bouillon is available in cubes or granules. **Broth and stock** are available in cans and boxes. **Soup Base** is a highly concentrated stock available near bouillon and broth in supermarkets.

Coffee Available as whole beans or ground and instant. See Beverage Basics, page 74.

Gelatin Colorless, tasteless thickening agent used to solidify foods when dissolved in liquid and refrigerated. Also available in sweetened fruit flavors.

Herbs and Spices See Herbs, page 500 and Spices, page 501.

Honey A liquid sweetener produced by bees. Store at room temperature.

Legumes See Bean & Legume Basics, page 269.

Maple Syrup Boiled-down maple tree sap. Maple-flavored syrup and pancake syrup are made from corn syrup and other sweeteners, with some maple syrup or maple flavor added.

Pasta See Pasta Basics, page 182.

Rice See Rice Basics, page 224.

Sun-Dried Tomatoes Available dry in bags, and packed in oil in jars; use the type specified in the recipe.

Tea Available in a variety of loose tea, tea bags and instant products; both regular and decaffeinated. See Beverage Basics, page 74.

Tortillas Fresh thin flat breads, made from corn or wheat flour. Used for sandwich wraps, tacos and burritos and in recipes.

Cooking Oil The healthiest oils are those that are high in monounsaturated and polyunsaturated fats, such as **Vegetable** and **Olive Oil**. For cooking, not all oils are equal. Choose the right oil depending on what you will use it for.

- **High-Heat Cooking** For frying and stir-frying, choose **Corn, Soybean, Peanut** or **Regular Sesame Oil**.
- **Moderate-Heat Cooking** For sautéing choose **Olive, Canola** or **Grapeseed Oil**.

Some oils don't perform well with heat, such as **Flaxseed** and **Walnut**. They can be used when no heat is required, such as in dressings or dips.

Photo (left) 1 Red Pepper Sauce **2** Worcestershire Sauce **3** Balsamic Vinegar **4** Red Wine Vinegar **5** Mayonnaise **6** and **7** Mustards **8** Salsa **9** Roasted Bell Peppers **10** Pesto **11** Capers

Salsa Sauce made from tomatoes and other vegetables and/or fruits. Make your own (page 479), or look for it in jars, ranging from mild to spicy.

Soy Sauce Asian sauce made from fermented soybeans and wheat or barley.

Vinegar Many varieties with different flavors, which can balance other ingredients in salad dressings and other recipes. Varieties include: **Apple Cider**, **Wine** (red and white), **Balsamic** (dark and white) and **Rice Vinegar**.

Worcestershire Sauce Highly flavored sauce for stews and meat dishes; contains anchovies, garlic, soy sauce, onions, molasses and vinegar.

NUTS, PEANUTS AND SEEDS

Great sources of protein, nuts and seeds also contain vitamins, minerals and other components that can contribute to good health. Great for eating out of hand or added to recipes for flavor and crunch.

They naturally contain oil, so they may spoil easily. To prevent rancidity, store tightly covered in the refrigerator or freezer. (Do not freeze cashews, as they will become soggy.) Always taste items that tend to turn rancid before adding them to a recipe; if they don't taste fresh, compost them or throw them out. See Refrigerator and Freezer Food Storage Chart, page 36, for storage times.

Almonds Available in the shell, shelled (raw and roasted, with and without salt), blanched, sliced and slivered. Also ground into almond flour and meal, and made into almond milk.

Brazil Nuts Available in the shell and shelled; shells are extremely hard. Kernels are rich and oily. Eat raw or use in trail mixes.

Cashews Available shelled; raw and roasted (with and without salt). Rich, buttery flavor. Also made into cashew milk.

Chestnuts Available fresh in the shell; shelled dried, canned (whole or pieces; in syrup) and as puree (sweetened and unsweetened). For fresh, choose firm, plump, blemish-free skin. Chestnuts need to be peeled as well as shelled. Store canned chestnuts in cool, dry place. Refrigerate shelled nuts in airtight container.

Hazelnuts (Filberts) Available whole in the shell and shelled; raw and roasted; and chopped. Use in desserts, salads, main dishes.

Macadamia Nuts Available shelled, roasted or raw; rich, buttery, sweet flavor.

Pecans Available in the shell and shelled (halves or chopped). Shells should be blemish- and crack-free and the kernels within shouldn't rattle when shaken.

CONDIMENTS, SAUCES AND SEASONINGS

For information on international condiments, sauces and seasonings, see the Global Flavors features within the recipe chapters.

Capers Unopened buds of a Mediterranean plant, with a sharp, tangy flavor; packed in vinegar brine. Use in appetizers and sauces, dressings and savory or fish dishes.

Ketchup Thick, spicy sauce made from tomatoes, vinegar and seasonings. Use as a sauce or in cooking.

Mayonnaise/Salad Dressing Creamy sauce used for salads and sandwiches. **Salad Dressing** is usually sweeter than mayonnaise. To make your own mayonnaise, see page 479.

Mustard A thick sauce in a range of colors and flavors, from bright yellow to darker, more highly flavored varieties; adds a sharp flavor to dishes.

Pesto Italian sauce made from basil, Parmesan cheese, olive oil and pine nuts. Make your own (page 480), or look for it in the refrigerated area and in jars near spaghetti sauce.

Red Pepper Sauce Spicy sauce made from hot peppers. To make your own fermented hot sauce, see page 458.

Roasted Bell Peppers Both red and yellow bell peppers are available packed in jars for salads, sandwiches, snacking and cooking.

Pine Nuts From the pine cones of several varieties of pine trees. Their pungent flavor overpowers some foods. Use in pesto.

Pistachios Available in the shell (partially open), tan (natural), red (dyed) or white (blanched), and shelled, raw, roasted, salted and unsalted.

Pumpkin Seeds (Pepitas) Available with or without hulls, raw, roasted and salted. Delicious, delicate flavor; common in Mexican cooking.

Sesame Seed Available golden, brown, white or black. Used in many cuisines around the world; they add a nutty flavor and texture to dishes. Traditionally sprinkled over stir-fries, or Asian cold noodle dishes; but also added to salad dressings or marinades, smoothies or baked goods.

Sunflower Seeds Available in or out of shells, roasted plain or salted. Good for snacking, in salads, sandwiches, baked goods.

Walnuts English (most common) and black varieties, in the shell or shelled. Walnuts should have shells free from cracks or holes; shelled walnuts should be crisp and meaty, not shriveled.

Photo (below) 1 Almonds **2** Brazil Nuts **3** Cashews **4** Chestnuts **5** Hazelnuts (Filberts) **6** Macadamia Nuts **7** Pecans **8** Pine Nuts **9** Pistachios **10** Walnuts **11** Pumpkin Seeds (Pepitas) **12** Sunflower Seeds

The Right Tool for the Job

Just imagine trying to cut a lawn with a pair of scissors—it wouldn't be easy, quick or enjoyable, right? Similarly, having the right tools in the kitchen can help make cooking easier, quicker and a lot more fun! Don't worry— you won't necessarily need everything listed. Start by stocking your kitchen with items you'll use often or that can slash prep time. As you expand your cooking abilities, you can continue to add to your kitchen tool collection.

COOKING TOOLS AND HANDY GADGETS

Baster Use to keep meat and poultry moist when roasting. The bulb draws up liquid into the stem. Squeeze the bulb again to release the liquid over the meat.

Bowls (large, medium and small) Use for mixing ingredients.

Photo (right) 1 Colanders and Strainers **2** Pancake Turner **3** Graters and Wood Turner **4** Spoons **5** Timer **6** Kitchen Towel **7** Salad Spinner **8** Cooling Racks **9** Zester **10** Offset Metal Spatula **11** Basting Brushes **12** Whisk **13** Rolling Pin **14** Pastry Blender **15** Jar Opener **16** Ruler **17** Citrus Reamer **18** Scrubbing Brush **19** Silicone Mat **20** Rubber Spatulas **21** Bowls **22** Meat Mallet **23** Potato Masher **24** Silicone Pot Holder **25** Kitchen Scissors

Brushes A wide variety of sizes and materials is available. Keep brushes used for pastry separate from those used on meat.

Can Opener Available in handheld (manual) and electric versions.

Citrus Reamer and Juicer Both remove juice easily from citrus fruits; juicer also keeps the seeds from getting in the juice.

Cheese Servers Sets of **Cheese Knives** are available: Use **Spreaders** for spreadable cheese, **Thin-Blade Knife** or **Cheese Knife with Holes** for soft cheese, a **Cheese Plane** or **Slicer** for shaving semihard or hard cheese and **Cheese Cleaver** or **Cheese Spade** for cutting firm, hard cheeses into pieces.

Colanders and Strainers Use colanders for draining pasta and vegetables. Use strainers to drain liquid from canned goods and to separate out solids from liquids.

Cooling Racks Use to cool baked goods so that air can get underneath hot pan or food.

Fat Separator Looks like a liquid measuring cup with a special spout so that as fat rises to the top, juices can be poured off, leaving the fat behind; perfect when making gravy.

Graters Many styles with a variety of hole sizes for grating or shredding. A handheld **Plane Grater** is very sharp, with many small holes.

Jar Opener Aids in opening jars and bottles.

Kitchen Towels Dish and hand towels should be absorbent; those made for drying stemware and cutlery should not scratch or leave lint.

Kitchen Twine Food-safe, oven-safe cotton string used to tie meat or poultry together before roasting, for even cooking.

Meat Mallet Breaks down tough meat fibers for more tender meat; flattens meat so it's the same thickness, for even cooking.

Oven Mitt/Pot Holder Use to remove hot pans from oven or stove-top. **Barbecue Mitts** cover more of your forearm when grilling.

Pastry Blender Handy for making pastry, but you can substitute a potato masher or fork.

Potato Masher Handheld tool for mashing potatoes, cooked vegetables and apples for applesauce; can be used for making pie pastry.

Rolling Pin Use for rolling cookies, pastry and bread dough. Look for one with sturdy, easy-to-hold handles.

Ruler Use to measure dough and in other recipes that require food to be shaped to a certain size for even cooking; also use to determine pan sizes.

Salad Spinner Quickly removes the water from lettuce and leafy herbs after washing.

Scrubbing Brush Aids in pan and dish washing to remove stuck-on food.

Silicone Mat Use to line cookie sheets when baking cookies or pastries, for easy removal, and as an alternative to waxed or cooking parchment paper or floured surface for rolling out pie pastry.

Rubber Spatula or Scraper A must-have for folding, stirring and scraping food from bowls, jars and saucepans. Look for those that are heat resistant to use when cooking.

Spatula and Pancake Turner Use to turn foods such as burgers or pancakes, remove cookies from sheet and serve desserts. Use **Offset Metal Spatulas** to spread frosting on baked goods while keeping fingers from marking the frosted surface.

Spoons Use to stir thick batters and doughs. Use wooden spoons for hot items on the stove, such as soups and sauces; won't scratch nonstick cookware. **Slotted Spoons** allow liquid to drain away from food.

Timer Lets you know when cooking or baking time is finished; also for timed directions in recipes.

Tongs Use to handle raw cuts of meat without touching them, to turn foods when cooking or serving and to toss and serve green salads. (Do not let tongs that have touched raw meat contact the cooked meat or other foods until thoroughly washed.)

Vegetable Peeler Used to peel almost any vegetable or fruit and to make vegetable ribbons and chocolate curls.

Whisk Use to beat air into eggs, sauces and dressings and to smooth lumpy batters.

Zester Use to remove peel from citrus fruit, leaving the bitter pith below it.

KNIVES AND RELATED TOOLS

An integral part of cooking, a good set of knives is a worthwhile investment. Since you'll use them daily, invest in the best quality you can afford. Wash them by hand. Keep them sharp and they will last many years. Choose knives that feel good in your hand. Look for stainless-steel blades with sturdy, durable handles.

Chef's Knife Use for chopping, slicing and dicing foods. Choose an 8- or 10-inch blade for your first chef's knife; later add shorter-blade versions for specific tasks.

Carving Knife The long, thin blade of this knife makes it the perfect choice for carving meat and poultry and for slicing cooked meats.

Kitchen Scissors Great for snipping herbs, cutting up chicken or cutting fat from chicken pieces.

Paring Knife The short, small blade of this knife is great for peeling vegetables or fruits, removing the seeds of fruit and cutting small food items, such as halving grapes.

Photo (right) 1 Carving or Utility Knife **2** Chef's Knife **3** Sharpening Steel **4** Serrated Utility Knife **5** Paring Knife **6** Boning Knife **7** Steak Knives **8** Bread Knife **9** Kitchen Scissors **10** Cutting Boards

10

3

2

1

10

9

4

5

6

7

8

10

Santoku Knife Similar in size to a chef's knife but with a different-shaped blade for a slightly different cutting action. Typically has a thinner, sharper blade, which gives more precise control for slicing dense food such as carrots as well as other tasks.

Serrated (Bread) Knife Use longer-blade serrated knife to cut bread or angel food cake without tearing or compressing it.

Sharpening Steel A quick way to occasionally sharpen knives by gently scraping the blade back and forth across several times; rinse and wipe the blade before using.

Steak Knife Use to cut meat into bite-size pieces while dining.

Utility Knife Smaller than a chef's knife, larger than a paring knife. Used for many kitchen tasks when these other knives aren't the right size.

---

3 ESSENTIAL KNIVES

If you can't afford an entire set of knives, have these essentials in your kitchen:

- Chef's knife
- Paring knife
- Serrated (bread) knife

COOKWARE

A variety of cookware is essential for cooking. Often, you are able to purchase sets of cookware with an assortment of pieces to provide for basic cooking needs. The best heat conductors are copper and aluminum, so buying pans made of these materials ensures better cooking results. Avoid purchasing uncoated aluminum pans, as the aluminum can react with acidic foods, causing off flavors in the food as well as discoloring the pans. Also avoid pans made entirely of stainless steel, as they can get hot spots when heated, causing food to cook unevenly.

Dutch Oven A large pot with a tight-fitting lid. Sides are shorter than a stockpot. Use for moist slow-cooking methods such as braising and stewing, or for large batches of chili or soup if you don't have a stockpot.

Griddle Large, heavy, flat pan with very short (if any) sides; great for pancakes, bacon, sandwiches and fried potatoes. Regular griddles are used on the stove-top; electric versions are also available.

Grill Pan Heavy pan with shallow sides and ridged cooking surface that allows fat to drain away from food as it cooks and leaves grill marks on food. Regular grill pans are used on the stove-top; electric versions are also available.

CUTTING TECHNIQUES

Chop: Gather food into close custer. Hold down top of knife with fingers from one hand while holding knife handle in other hand. Manipulate knife (holding tip of knife on board) up and down over food, until evenly chopped.

Slice: Hold food with fingers of one hand, tucking fingers under. Slice with knife held in the other hand.

Julienne: Slice long, thin, uniform strips of food, using slicing method first and then slicing again into thin strips.

Dice or Cube: Hold food with fingers of one hand, tucking fingers under. With knife in other hand, cut into strips; rotate strips, then cut into small squares.

CUTTING BOARD SMARTS

- Have at least 2 cutting boards: one for raw meats and poultry and one for vegetables and fruit.

- Hard plastic or glass cutting boards are the best choices for raw meat, poultry and seafood, as they are less porous than other materials such as wood, keeping meat juices from leaking into any small cracks, which can harbor bacteria.

- Do not cut cooked meat or poultry with the unwashed knife and board used to cut them when raw.

Saucepans Come in a range of sizes from 1 to 4 quarts; should have a tight-fitting lid. Having a variety of sizes will ensure you have the right size for cooking or reheating food; using the wrong size can be a reason a recipe isn't successful.

Sauté Pan Similar to skillets, sauté pans generally have sides that are a little higher. The sides can be straight or slightly sloped. In addition to a long handle, these pans may have a loop handle on the other side so the pan can be easily lifted. Used to brown and cook meats as it can cut down on spattering.

Skillet Available in 8-, 10- and 12-inch sizes. Skillets generally have low, gently sloping sides that allow steam to escape. Use for panfrying or quick-cooking methods where food is often stirred or turned.

Stockpot Large pot with tall sides; perfect for making stocks and soups or cooking pasta.

Wok A round- or flat-bottomed pan with high sloping sides; popular in Asian cooking for stir-frying, steaming and deep-frying. Electric woks are also available.

Photo (below) 1 Baking Dish **2** Rectangular Baking Pan **3** Square Baking Pan **4** Round Cake Pan **5** Rectangular Baking Dish **6** Roasting Pan with Rack **7** Loaf Pans **8** Fluted Tube Cake Pan **9** Pie Plate and Pie Pan **10** Silicone Muffin Pan **11** Broiler Pan and Rack **12** Tart Pan **13** 15x10x1-inch pan **14** Cookie Sheet

BAKEWARE

Bakeware is available in many materials, including aluminum, glass, ceramic and terracotta (clay). For the recipes in this book, *pan* refers to shiny metal and *baking dish* refers to heat-resistant glass or ceramic.

Baking Dish Made of heat-resistant glass or ceramic; usually round, square or rectangular. Use for desserts, egg bakes, casseroles and other main dishes.

Baking Pans Metal baking pans available in a variety of sizes and in round, square, rectangular and loaf shapes. Use for cakes, breads and desserts. See below for specific types of cake pans.

Cake Pans

- **Angel Food (Tube) Cake Pan** Round metal pan, 10 inches wide, with hollow tube in the middle. The bottom is usually removable, making it easy to remove the cake from the pan. Use for angel food, chiffon and sponge cakes.

- **Fluted Tube Cake Pan** Round pan with patterned or indented side; typically metal, with center tube. Use for cakes and coffee cakes.

Rectangular Baking (Jelly Roll) Pan The 15x10 pan has 1-inch sides and is used for baking thin, flexible cakes for jelly rolls and for roasting vegetables. It's also referred to as a **Sheet Pan** when used to make entire meals. While this pan could be used for baking cookies, the sides can cause cookies near the edges to brown more quickly and can make it harder to remove the cookies without damaging them, so it's not recommended. Other size rectangular pans are available. Check recipe for specific size, as it can affect the cook time and doneness.

Casserole Deep glass or ceramic dish for baking and serving food; may come with a matching cover.

Cookie Sheet Flat rectangular aluminum sheet with very short side on one or more edges; comes in various sizes. The open sides allow for good air circulation while baking cookies, biscuits, scones, shortcakes or bread.

Custard Cups or Ramekins Deep glass or ceramic **Custard Cups** are small, heatproof 6- or 8-oz baking dishes. **Ramekins** are similar; however, they have flat bottoms and come in a variety of shapes (short and shallow or tall and deep) and sizes, and made of a variety of materials. Use for baking custards or other desserts, or savory dishes, in individual portions.

Muffin Pan One pan with 6, 12 or more individual cups; for baking muffins or cupcakes. Cups can range from miniature to jumbo.

Pie and Tart Pans

- **Pie Plate or Pan** Glass **Pie Plates** are designed for baking pies with a flaky or crumb crust; a **Pie Pan** is the metal version. Regular and deep-dish versions are available. See Picking Pie Pans, page 606.

- **Tart Pan** Available in a variety of shapes and sizes, typically metal with removable bottom.

Pizza Pan Flat, round metal pan with no side, or low side for deep-dish pizza. Some are perforated to help crisp the crust. A **Pizza Stone** is typically flat and preheated in the oven. The unbaked pizza is slid onto the hot stone to help crisp the crust.

Popover Pan Similar to muffin pan, but with 6 or 12 individual extra-deep cups; especially designed for baking popovers.

Soufflé Dish Round open dish with high side, designed for baking soufflés.

Springform Pan Round, deep pan in various sizes, with removable side. For cheesecakes and desserts that can't be turned upside down for removal from pan.

OTHER OVENWARE

Broiler Pan and Rack has slits to allow fat to drip away from meat as it cooks, falling into the pan below. For easier cleanup, line pan and rack separately with foil; cut through foil over rack slits with knife.

Microwavable Cookware Specifically made and designated to be used in the microwave. Use only dishes labeled "microwavable" in the microwave.

Roasting Pan Large, rectangular pan with short sides so that as much of the heat from the oven as possible can reach the food. Typically comes with a roasting rack to elevate the food and allow the fat to drain away from the food as it cooks. Use to roast whole poultry and tender cuts of meat with little or no liquid.

MEASURING UTENSILS

Using the correct measuring equipment can make a difference in how a recipe turns out.

- **Glass Measuring Cups** Use to measure liquids. To measure accurately, pour liquid to desired mark on cup; set on counter and read from the side at eye level.

- **Plastic and Metal Measuring Cups** Use to measure dry ingredients. Spoon dry ingredient into cup; level off with metal spatula or the flat side of a knife.

- **Measuring Spoons** Use to measure small amounts of liquid, such as extracts or food color, and dry ingredients such as salt, baking soda and baking powder. *For dry ingredients*, fill and level off as for dry ingredients above. *For liquid ingredients*, fill to rim.

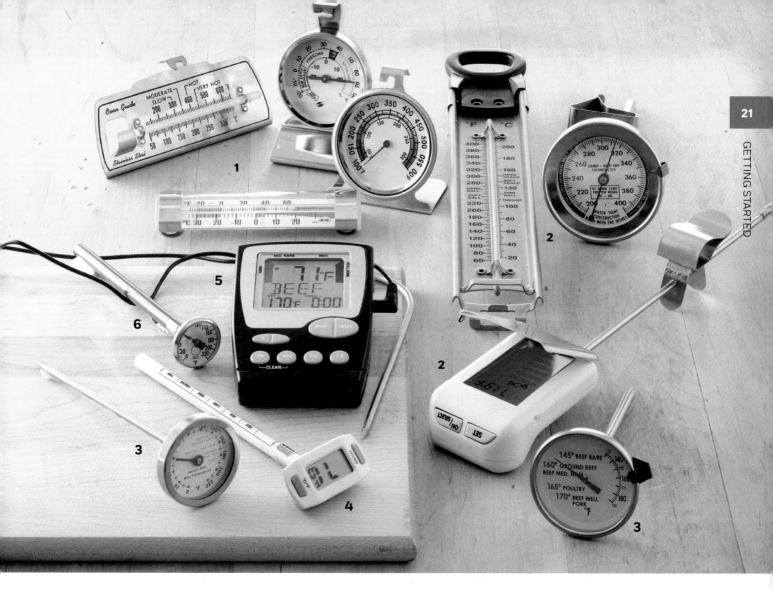

THERMOMETERS

Look for a variety of thermometers in discount or larger grocery stores and kitchen specialty stores.

Candy/Deep-Fry Thermometer Use to check temperature of candy mixture while it cooks and temperature of oil when deep-frying.

Digital Oven Probe Thermometer Temperature read-out goes on counter or oven door; long cord with a probe allows it to measure temperature of food inside without opening oven door. Set the temperature you wish to cook food to, and an alarm will sound when it reaches that temperature.

Instant-Read Thermometer Gives an accurate reading of food's temperature in seconds. Use to check internal temperature of meat and baked goods, and temperature of liquid for bread making. Not heat-safe, so don't leave in oven or grill while cooking.

Photo (above) 1 Oven and Refrigerator/Freezer Thermometers **2** Regular and Digital Candy/Deep-Fry Thermometers **3** Ovenproof Meat Thermometer **4** Digital Instant-Read Thermometer **5** Digital Oven Probe **6** Instant-Read Thermometer

Oven Thermometer Helps you determine if your oven is heating to the proper temperature. Ovens can run hot or cool over time; if your oven is at the wrong temperature, it can affect the success of a recipe. Nudge the oven heat control up or down as needed to get the temperature to where it needs to be.

Ovenproof Meat Thermometer Heat safe, so can be left in food while in the oven.

Refrigerator/Freezer Thermometer Helps you determine if these appliances are at the correct temperature.

IS MY THERMOMETER ACCURATE?

Thermometers can lose accuracy over time. To check whether your food thermometer is reading accurately, heat 2 cups water to boiling in a 1-quart saucepan. Immerse the stem of the thermometer 2 inches into the boiling water; it should read 212°F after 30 seconds. If the thermometer is off a few degrees, calibrate it according to the manufacturer's directions, or allow for this adjustment when measuring the temperature of food. Check thermometers once or twice a year for accuracy.

SMALL ELECTRIC APPLIANCES

Some appliances are necessary if you want to make a recipe—making waffles is impossible if you don't have a waffle iron, for example. Many times, small appliances aren't essential, but they certainly can make your time in the kitchen easier, quicker and a lot more enjoyable. As you think about equipment for your kitchen, consider purchasing these items as you need them.

Air Fryer Bakes and roasts using a powerful fan to create crispy food with less oil.

Blender Use to mix, liquefy and puree. An **Immersion Blender** is a handheld appliance used to puree soups and sauces right in the pan. A **Personal Blender** makes enough for one serving. **Power Blenders** have strong motors to easily blend harder foods.

Bread Machine Mixes, kneads, rises and bakes bread; can also be used to easily make dough to shape for other foods such as rolls and pizza crust to bake in your oven.

Coffee Grinder Quickly grinds whole beans for making coffee.

Coffee Maker Brews coffee automatically; available in models for making coffee a cup at a time to a full pot, or with options for both.

Food Processor Handles a host of prep tasks quickly: chopping, slicing, mixing, shredding, pureeing and kneading.

Photo (below) 1 Electric Hand Mixer **2** Food Processor **3** Stand Mixer **4** Waffle Maker **5** Mini Chopper **6** Blender

Hand Mixer Use to whip and mix liquid foods or thin batters quickly. Not good for heavy batters or dough.

Mini Chopper A small version of food processor. Use to chop small amounts of food or grind whole dried spices quickly.

Multi Cooker A combination of slow cooker and pressure cooker with the ability to sauté; for some recipes, can save you more cleanup, steps and time than using separate equipment and methods.

Pressure Cooker Steam builds up pressure inside the cooker, causing the temperature to rise above what it can be when cooking conventionally, so food cooks faster.

Rice Cooker Cooks rice and keeps it warm until ready to serve; may also be used to steam food if it comes with a steamer basket.

Slow Cooker An easy way to make meals with little preparation, as the food cooks for long periods with little attention, electricity or without heating up your kitchen. Great for less-tender cuts of meat.

Stand Mixer Preferred by professional chefs over hand mixers for ease of use (hands free) and power (heavy duty, quicker). Handles thick, stiff mixtures such as bread dough.

Toaster or Toaster Oven For toasting bread, bagels and frozen waffles, a **Toaster** is what you need. As well as toasting, a **Toaster Oven** can heat up, broil and bake foods (such as garlic bread and frozen snacks) quicker and with less energy than the regular oven.

Waffle Maker Bakes waffles; available in a variety of shapes and sizes.

Cooking Technique How Tos

We've gathered the best ways we've found to tackle the most-used cooking skills you'll need to know. Refer back to this feature any time you come across a technique that's unfamiliar; it's an easy way to build your cooking prowess. Many techniques have more in-depth instructions elsewhere in the book. See the index for specific techniques. See also Cooking Terms, starting on page 26.

BASTING

Brushing food with liquid adds flavor to the food while also keeping it moist during cooking.

BEATING SOFT AND STIFF PEAKS

Soft Peaks Beat just until peaks form but curl over.

Stiff Peaks Continue beating until peaks stand upright.

BLANCHING

Immerse food in boiling water to loosen skins, partially cook or brighten color.

Immediately immerse food in ice water to stop cooking process.

BOILING AND SIMMERING

Boil Bubbles continuously rise and break surface of liquid.

Simmer Liquid is at a slightly lower temperature than boiling; bubbles rise slowly and break just below the surface.

BROILING

Cook food directly under heated broiler element at a specified distance. Used when grilling isn't feasible, and to brown the tops of foods.

CORING FRUIT

Using Paring Knife Cut fruit into quarters; cut out core with knife.

Using Corer Pierce fruit at stem end with corer; twist into fruit and pull out with core.

Cooking Technique How Tos *continued*

CRUSHING

Place food in resealable plastic bag; seal. Roll rolling pin over bag until food is in small, even pieces.

CUTTING IN

Work fat (such as butter) into dry ingredients with a fork, potato masher or pastry blender until clumps formed are the size of small peas.

DEEP-FRYING

Heat oil to temperature directed in recipe. Carefully lower food into hot oil; do not crowd.

Drain fried food by transferring to paper towel–lined cookie sheet with slotted spoon.

DRIZZLING

Using Spoon Drop glaze in a thin stream while moving slowly over food.

Using Bag Fill small resealable plastic bag with glaze. Cut tiny (⅛-inch) corner; squeeze glaze slowly over food.

FOLDING

Gently combines ingredients without losing airy texture of whipped foods. Cut spatula down into center of bowl, pull it toward the side and turn it over the top; repeat until evenly mixed.

HULLING

Gently press huller into fruit. Squeeze huller, not fruit, while twisting and pulling hull away from fruit.

MEASURING CORRECTLY

Dry Ingredients Spoon into dry measuring cup; level off using a flat-edged utensil such as knife or metal spatula.

Brown Sugar Spoon into dry measuring cup; firmly pack with back of spoon; level off as for dry ingredients.

Liquids Pour into liquid measuring cup; check amount by placing cup on work surface and reading from the side at eye level.

Small Amounts Dry ingredients: dip measuring spoon into ingredient; level off. Liquid ingredients: fill measuring spoon to rim.

PEELING

Cut into skin at top of fruit or vegetable with peeler or paring knife. Turn food, carefully removing skin in strip(s).

SNIPPING AND CUTTING WITH KITCHEN SCISSORS

Snip Place small items in small cup. Cut with scissors until uniform size.

Cut Use scissors to cut small pieces of food into smaller similar-shaped pieces.

SKIMMING

Use a slotted or regular cutlery spoon to scrape off and remove just the top layer from mixture.

STRAINING

Pour food through strainer to drain away liquid and separate out unwanted solids. If directed in recipe, use back of spoon to press liquid through.

Cooking Terms

See also Cooking Technique How Tos, starting on page 23.

Al Dente Describes texture of pasta or other food cooked just enough, neither underdone nor too soft (overcooked).

Bake To cook food in oven with dry heat. Bake uncovered for a dry, crisp top, or covered to keep food moist.

Baste To add liquid or fat over surface of food during cooking to keep food moist, using a spoon, brush or bulb baster.

Batter Mixture of flour, eggs, liquid and other ingredients that is thin enough to be spooned or poured.

Beat To mix ingredients vigorously with spoon, fork, whisk or electric mixer. When electric mixer is specified, mixer speed is included. See Learn to Beat, Whip & Fold, page 592.

Blanch To place food in boiling water briefly to preserve color, partially cook or remove skin. Food is then placed in ice water to stop cooking process. See Learn to Blanch, page 145.

Blend To mix ingredients thoroughly using spoon, whisk, rubber spatula, blender or food processor.

Boil To heat liquid or food to a temperature that causes bubbles to rise continuously and break the surface.

Braise To first sear large cuts of meat, then cook them slowly in liquid in a covered pan to make them tender. See Learn to Braise, page 332.

Bread or Coat To cover food before frying or baking, usually by dipping in or brushing with liquid (such as beaten egg or milk), then coating with bread crumbs, cracker crumbs or cornmeal.

Broil To cook food directly under a heat source in oven. See Broiling Meat, page 311, and Learn to Broil, page 368.

Brown To cook quickly, usually over high heat, causing surface of food to turn brown; adds color and flavor to finished dish.

Caramelize To melt sugar slowly over low heat until golden brown and syrupy. Sugar can be caramelized on top of food with a kitchen torch or by placing it under the broiler. Onions and other vegetables that naturally contain sugar may also be caramelized by slow cooking.

Chill To place food in refrigerator until thoroughly cold.

Chop To cut food into coarse or fine pieces of irregular shapes, using knife, food processor or mini chopper.

Core To remove the inedible center of a fruit (apple, pear, pineapple).

Crisp-Tender Describes doneness of cooked vegetables when they are between raw (hard and crunchy) and completely soft.

Crush To smash into very small pieces or crumbs using a rolling pin (crackers), the side of a knife blade (garlic), a meat mallet (peppercorns) or a mortar and pestle (dried herbs and seeds).

Cube or Dice To cut food with knife into uniform pieces. Cubed pieces are ½ inch or larger on all sides; diced are smaller than ½ inch, typically ¼ inch.

Cut In To work butter or shortening into dry ingredients. Use a pastry blender, potato masher or fork, lifting it up and down with rocking motion, until particles are of desired size.

Cut Up To turn foods into smaller pieces of irregular sizes, using knife or kitchen scissors. Also, to separate a large food, such as a whole chicken, into smaller pieces (legs, breast, thighs, wings, etc.).

Dash An ingredient amount of less than ⅛ teaspoon.

Deep-Fry To cook in hot fat that fully covers the food being fried. See also Fry and Panfry (below) and Learn to Deep-Fry, page 70.

Deglaze To add a small amount of liquid to a pan after food has been cooked, to loosen the flavorful browned bits. See Deglazing the Pan, page 303.

Dip To moisten or coat food by submerging it completely in a liquid or batter.

Dissolve To stir a dry ingredient such as salt, sugar or gelatin into a liquid until dry ingredient disappears.

Dot To drop small pieces of an ingredient (such as butter) randomly over the top of another food.

Dough A stiff but pliable mixture of flour, liquid and other ingredients that can be dropped from a spoon, rolled or kneaded.

Drain To separate liquid from solids by pouring food through a colander or strainer to save only the solids. To drain fat from meat, place strainer over an empty can or heatproof bowl to hold fat so it does not damage sink plumbing.

Drizzle To pour a thin stream of liquid over food from the tip of a spoon, squeeze bottle or liquid measuring cup or resealable food-storage plastic bag.

Dust To sprinkle a work surface or food lightly with flour, sugar or baking cocoa.

Flake To break apart layers of a food with a fork.

Flute To squeeze pie pastry with fingers to make a decorative edge.

Fold To gently mix ingredients without losing volume. See Learn to Beat, Whip & Fold, page 592. Also, to bend food over itself.

Fry To cook in hot fat over medium to high heat. See also Deep-Fry (above) and Panfry (below).

Garnish A decorative, edible accessory added to a dish before serving, to enhance its appeal with color, flavor and/or texture; can be placed under, around or on top of finished dishes.

Glaze To spread, drizzle or brush an ingredient on hot or cold food to add thin, glossy coating.

Grate To rub a hard-textured food across the holes of a grater to make small particles.

Grease To coat the bottom and sides of a pan with shortening, using a pastry brush or paper towel, to prevent food from sticking; cooking spray can sometimes be used. Do not use butter unless specified in the recipe, as it can make some foods stick.

Grease and Flour After greasing pan (above), to sprinkle it with a small amount of flour; shake pan to distribute evenly on bottom and sides. Turn pan upside down over sink and tap bottom to remove excess flour.

Grill To cook directly over a heat source. See Grilling Basics, page 420.

Hull To remove stem and leaves from strawberries with a paring knife or huller.

Husk To remove leaves and silk from ears of fresh sweet corn.

Juice To extract the liquid contained in fruits and vegetables. See Learn to Juice, page 88.

Julienne Describes long, thin matchstick-like pieces, usually 1 ½x¼x¼ inches.

Knead To press dough with your hands to develop its structure and texture. See Learn to Knead Yeast Dough, page 522.

Marinate To soak meat, fish or vegetables in a flavorful liquid (called a marinade) to infuse with flavor and/or tenderize.

Melt To turn a solid into a liquid or semiliquid by heating.

Microwave To cook, reheat or thaw food in a microwave oven. See Microwave Cooking, page 33.

Mince To cut food with knife into very fine pieces that are smaller than chopped but bigger than crushed.

Mix To combine ingredients to distribute evenly.

Panfry To cook food in a small amount of fat in an uncovered skillet. See Learn to Sear and Panfry, page 302. See also Deep-Fry and Fry (above).

Peel To removed outer covering of fruits and vegetables with paring knife, vegetable peeler, citrus zester or fingers. Also refers to the outside (colored) layer of citrus fruit, containing aromatic oils.

Poach To cook gently in simmering liquid just below the boiling point.

Process To use a blender, food processor or mini chopper to liquefy, blend, chop, grind, mix or knead food.

Puree To make smooth. See Learn to Puree, page 177.

Reduce To boil off liquid from a dish as it cooks to thicken it and/or intensify the flavor.

Roast To cook meat, poultry or vegetables in the oven in a shallow, uncovered pan to achieve a brown exterior and moist interior. See Roasting More-Tender Cuts, page 311; Learn to Roast Vegetables, page 254.

Roll To flatten dough into a thin, even layer, using a rolling pin. Also, to shape food into balls; to turn food over in all directions to coat it.

Roll Up To form a flat food into a log shape; the food may be spread with a filling or have filling at one end. Begin at one end or side and fold the food up and over itself continuously while pushing.

Sauté To cook food over medium-high heat in a small amount of fat, frequently tossing or turning it.

Score To cut shallow lines, about ¼-inch deep, through surface of food such as meat or bread dough to decorate or tenderize, or to allow fat to drain away as the food cooks or bakes.

Sear To cook meat over high heat to brown it and form a flavorful crust. See Learn to Sear and Panfry, page 302.

Season To add flavor with salt, pepper, herbs, spices or seasoning mixes.

Shred To cut food into thin strips using a knife or food processor fitted with a shredding disk. Also, to pull apart cooked meat using two forks.

Simmer To cook liquids or foods in liquid just below the boiling point, so bubbles slowly rise and break under the surface. See Learn to Simmer, page 219.

Skim To remove fat or foam from soup, broth, stock or stew, using a spoon, ladle or skimmer (a flat, small-holed utensil with a long handle).

Slice To cut into flat pieces of about the same size.

Smoke To cook foods while exposing them to smoke from burning wood that imparts its flavor. See Smoking Basics, page 446.

Snip To cut into very small pieces with kitchen scissors.

Soft Peaks Describes egg whites or whipping cream beaten until peaks curl over when beaters are lifted from bowl. See Learn to Beat, Whip & Fold, page 592.

Steam To cook food in a steamer basket or steamer pan insert placed over boiling or simmering water in covered pan.

Stew To cook meat slowly in covered pot, pan or casserole in just enough liquid to cover; similar to braising (above), for less-tender cuts of meat. Also name for dish where small, uniform-size pieces of less-tender meats are cooked slowly with vegetables in a thickened broth or gravy.

Stiff Peaks Describes egg whites or whipping cream beaten until peaks stand up straight when beaters are lifted from bowl. See Learn to Beat, Whip & Fold, page 592.

Stir To mix ingredients with a circular or figure-eight motion until thoroughly blended.

Stir-Fry To cook small, similar-size pieces of food in small amount of hot oil in a wok or skillet over high heat while stirring constantly.

Strain To pour food through a strainer (and/or cheesecloth) to separate out unwanted solids; may also be done to puree a mixture.

Tear To break into pieces with your fingers.

Toast To brown baked goods, nuts or seeds lightly in toaster, oven, broiler or skillet.

Toss To gently combine ingredients by lifting and dropping them, using hands or large utensils.

Whip To introduce air into ingredients, to increase volume until they are light and fluffy. See Learn to Beat, Whip & Fold, page 592.

Helpful Nutrition and Cooking Information

We provide nutrition information for each traditional recipe; this includes calories, fat, cholesterol, sodium, carbohydrate, fiber, protein and carbohydrate choices so that you can decide what foods and/or servings fit into your eating plan. See also Cooking Gluten Free or Vegan, page 31.

CRITERIA USED TO CALCULATE NUTRITION INFORMATION

- Whenever a choice is given (such as ½ cup sour cream or plain yogurt), the first ingredient was used.

- Whenever a range is given (such as 3- to 3 ½-pound cut-up whole chicken), the first ingredient amount was used.

- Whenever a range of servings is given (such as 4 to 6 servings), the first serving number was used.

- "If desired" ingredients were not included. Recipe variations were not calculated.

- Only the amount of a marinade or frying oil that is estimated to be absorbed by the food during preparation or cooking was calculated.

CRITERIA USED TO CALCULATE LOWER-CALORIE RECIPES

Recipes designated as Calorie Smart were determined using the following guidelines (per serving).

- Main dishes: 350 calories or less

- Chilies, stews, plain meats: 250 calories or less

- Soups, breads, side dishes, appetizers: 175 calories or less

- Desserts: 200 calories or less

- Condiments, beverages, dips, sauces, dressings: 80 calories or less

INGREDIENTS USED IN RECIPE TESTS AND NUTRITION CALCULATIONS

- The ingredients used represent those that the majority of consumers use in their homes: large eggs, 2% milk, 80% lean ground beef and canned ready-to-use chicken broth, unless otherwise indicated.

- Fat-free, low-fat or low-sodium products were not used unless indicated.

- Solid vegetable shortening was used to grease pans unless otherwise indicated.

EQUIPMENT USED IN RECIPE TESTING

We used equipment that the majority of consumers use in their homes. If a specific piece of equipment (such as a whisk) is necessary for recipe success, it is listed in the recipe.

- Cookware and bakeware without nonstick coatings were used unless otherwise indicated.

- No dark-colored, black or insulated bakeware was used.

- When a pan is called for in a recipe, a metal pan was used; "baking dish" or "pie plate" means ovenproof glass was used. See page 20.

- An electric hand mixer was used when mixer speed is specified in the recipe directions. If a stand mixer is necessary, the recipe calls for that appliance. When a mixer speed is not given, a spoon, spatula or fork was used.

Recipe Icons

Recipes in the book are flagged with these icons if they meet the respective criteria:

Easy 5 ingredients or fewer (not including water, salt or pepper, or "if desired" ingredients) and 15 minutes or less prep time.

Fast 30 minutes or less total time to prepare the recipe.

Make Ahead Entire recipe or a significant portion can be made ahead.

Air Fryer Main recipe or variation has air fryer directions for preparing the recipe.

Multi Cooker Main recipe or variation has multi-cooker directions for preparing the recipe.

Slow Cooker Main recipe or variation has slow-cooker directions for preparing the recipe.

Calorie Smart Calorie counts per serving:

- Complete Meals/One Dish Meals (protein from meat, poultry, fish or legumes with veggies and potatoes, rice or other grains): 550 calories or less
- Main Dishes/Plain Meats/Main Dish Salads/ Soups/Stews/Chilies/Cereals/Pancakes/Waffles: 400 calories or less
- Sides/Side Dish Salads/Snacks/Breads/Appetizers: 200 calories or less
- Desserts: 200 calories or less
- Beverages/Smoothies/Sauces/Condiments/ Dressings: 150 calories or less

Gluten Free See Gluten-Free Cooking, page 31, for details.

Vegetarian See Vegetarian and Vegan Cooking, page 32, for details.

Vegan See Vegetarian and Vegan Cooking, page 32, for details. All vegan recipes are also vegetarian.

Health and Nutrition

What is healthy eating? Eating foods that are good for you—but also enjoying them. Trendy diets come and go, and nutrition research changes frequently, leaving a haze of questions. Bottom line: Common sense and balance are the pillars of good health; good food choices can have a positive effect on our health.

SMALL BUT MIGHTY CHANGES

Start with small changes to build positive habits. Try these easy ways based on www.choosemyplate.gov to up your healthy-eating game.

Don't skip meals. When you miss meals, it's harder to maintain even blood glucose levels, making it easy to overeat at the next meal or overindulge in *anything*, just to take away the hunger. Stick to your food plan; if you don't have time for a meal, have satisfying snacks on hand.

Plan meals and snacks. Planning what you eat might seem a little over-the-top at first, but in time you'll become aware of what foods keep you satisfied and when your hunger tends to hit, so you can be armed with healthy foods that keep you on track. Plan to grocery shop when you aren't hungry, with a list of the healthy foods you need, so you won't be tempted to purchase foods that aren't part of your plan.

Make half your plate fruits and vegetables. Focus on whole fruits, rather than juice. Use fresh, frozen, canned or dried fruits to satisfy your sweet tooth instead of cookies or candies and as a healthy dessert choice. Vary your veggies to include greens and other varieties that include green, red and orange choices. Add veggies to salads, sides and main dishes as a way to increase your consumption.

Reduce sugar, saturated fat and sodium. The USDA Dietary Guidelines recommend consuming less than 10% of calories per day from added sugar, less than 10% of calories per day from saturated fats and less than 2,300 milligrams (mg) per day of sodium. Guidelines are based on gender and age. To find out more information, visit https://www.dietaryguidelines. gov/sites/default/files/2020-12/Dietary_Guidelines_ for_Americans_2020-2025.pdf. One way to do this is to prepare your veggies without sauces or glazes, to help keep the sodium, saturated fat and added sugars you consume in check.

Make half your grains whole grains. Choose whole grain foods, such as oats, whole wheat flour and popcorn, over refined grains for at least half of the grains you eat each day. Read Nutrition Facts labels and ingredient lists on packages to be sure foods are whole grain.

Move to low-fat and fat-free dairy. Choose low-fat or fat-free milk and yogurt and low-fat varieties of cheese rather than full-fat varieties.

Vary your protein routine. Mix up your protein choices to include seafood, beans, nuts, seeds, soy foods, eggs, lean meats and poultry. Eat fish and seafood twice a week. Add beans or peas, unsalted nuts or seeds and soy foods to main dishes and snacks to add protein. (See Soy Foods, page 406.)

Food Safety

America's food supply is one of the safest in the world. Farmers, ranchers, food processors, supermarkets and restaurants must follow strict rules and regulations when getting food to you. But once food leaves the grocery store, you must take care to keep it safe.

Why worry about food safety? Because most illnesses reported from "bad food" are caused by bacterial contamination. Nearly all cases can be linked to improper food handling—and could have been prevented.

Microorganisms are always with us: They are on us and on animals, in the air and water and on raw food. Some bacteria are useful, like those used to make cheese or ferment beer. But other bacteria, called pathogens, cause foods to spoil or cause food-borne illness.

Bacteria that can cause food to *spoil* can grow even at refrigerator temperatures (at or below 40°F). They usually make the food look or smell bad, raising a red flag that it should be thrown out. *Food-borne illness* bacteria grow at temperatures between 40°F and 140°F—temperatures between chilled and hot-from-the-oven. These pathogens you can't always see, smell or taste; if eaten, they may lead to illness, disease or even death.

To prevent this type of bacteria from becoming harmful, you must stop them from multiplying. When contaminated food is eaten, people most often get sick within 4 to 48 hours. But it's not always easy to determine if the problem is the flu or food-borne illness. Call a doctor or go to a hospital immediately if symptoms are severe.

BASIC FOOD SAFETY RULES

WASH YOUR HANDS

Proper hand washing could eliminate nearly half of all causes of food-borne illness. Always wash hands

- Before handling food and utensils, and before serving and eating food.

- After handling food, especially raw meat, poultry, fish, shellfish and eggs.

- Between jobs like cutting up raw chicken and making a salad.

- After using the bathroom, blowing your nose, changing diapers, touching pets, and handling garbage, dirty dishes, hair, dirty laundry and phones.

- If you have any kind of skin cut or infection on your hands, wear protective plastic or rubber gloves.

KEEP IT CLEAN

- Wash all utensils and surfaces with hot, soapy water after contact with raw meat, poultry, fish or seafood. Use paper towels when working with these foods.

- Bleach and commercial kitchen-cleaning agents are the most effective at killing bacteria. Hot water and soap or hot water alone may not kill all strains of bacteria that are present.

- Keep dishcloths and sponges clean and dry because when these materials are wet, they harbor bacteria and may promote their growth. Wash them often in hot water in the washing machine; for added safety, sanitize them three times a week by soaking them in a mixture of ¾ cup bleach to 1 gallon water.

- Keep refrigerator surfaces clean, inside and out. Sort through perishable foods each week, tossing out anything past its prime.

- Keep pets out of the kitchen and away from food.

SAFE PICNICS AND PACKED LUNCHES

- Pack lunch in an insulated lunch bag or small cooler, with a freezer pack, frozen juice box or frozen small plastic bottle of water to keep the food cold. Keep out of the sun. Perishable foods packed in an uninsulated bag should be refrigerated when they reach their destination.

- Wash thermal containers and rinse well with boiling water after each use. Be sure hot foods are boiling when poured into these containers. For cold foods, dry and cool to room temperature before filling.

- Wash fruits and vegetables before packing.

- Chill picnic food before packing it in thermal or insulated bags or an ice-filled cooler. Because beverage coolers will be opened more frequently, use one cooler for beverages and another for perishable food.

- Tightly wrap raw meat, poultry, fish and seafood to be cooked when you get there, or pack them in a separate cooler, to keep them from dripping on other foods. Bring along hand sanitizer for cleaning hands after handling raw poultry, meat, fish or seafood, if running water and soap won't be available.

DON'T CROSS-CONTAMINATE

Cross contamination happens when cooked or ready-to-eat foods pick up bacteria from other foods, hands, cutting boards and/or utensils. Working with raw meat, poultry, shellfish, fish and eggs requires special handling to keep them from contaminating other foods.

- Keep them separate from cooked or ready-to-eat foods in your grocery cart.

- Prevent leaks by repacking leaky packages and by thawing foods in the refrigerator on a tray with sides to catch any juices.

- It's best to have at least two cutting boards: one for raw meats, poultry and seafood and one for vegetables and fruit. Don't cut raw meat on wooden boards, as the raw juices can get into the wood, where bacteria can grow.

- Don't put cooked food on an unwashed plate that was used for raw meats.

- Wash sinks and sink mats with hot, soapy water if they've come in contact with raw meat or its juices.

KEEP HOT FOOD HOT

- Don't leave hot foods at room temperature for more than 2 hours, including preparation and cooling time. Keeping food hot means keeping it at 140°F or higher.

- Don't partially cook perishable foods, then set them aside or refrigerate to finish them later. It's okay to cook them with one appliance, then immediately complete them with another; grilling recipes will frequently use this technique.

- Keep cooked food hot or refrigerate until ready to reheat and serve. This includes carryout foods, too.

- Reheat leftovers, stirring often, until steaming hot (165°F), using a cover to get the food hot in the center and retain moisture. Heat soups, sauces and gravies to a rolling boil, then boil 1 minute, stirring frequently, before serving.

KEEP COLD FOOD COLD

- Don't leave cold food at room temperature for more than 2 hours, including preparation time. Keeping food cold means keeping it at 40°F or lower.

- When shopping, put perishable foods (eggs, milk and dairy, seafood, fish, meat and poultry, and items that contain them, such as deli salads) in your cart last. Make sure they are cold to the touch when you select them. Put packages that can leak into plastic bags to prevent dripping on other foods in your cart.

- Perishable foods should be taken home and refrigerated immediately. If the trip is longer than 30 minutes or it is a hot day, bring freezer shopping bags or a cooler with freezer packs for these items to prevent them from reaching unsafe temperatures.

- Purchase frozen foods that are free from ice crystals; visible ice crystals may mean the food had been partially thawed and refrozen.

- Foods will chill faster if they are stored in small, shallow containers and there is space between them in the refrigerator or freezer.

- Never thaw foods at room temperature; thaw only in the refrigerator or microwave following the manufacturer's directions. If you thaw food in the microwave, cook it immediately.

SAFE BUFFETS

Serve food in family-size dishes rather than larger catering-size ones. Put out new dishes of food as they become empty.

- Keep foods hot (at least 140°F) by using slow cookers, chafing dishes, fondue pots or a warming tray. Use warming units heated by electricity or canned cooking fuel, not candles, as they don't get hot enough to keep foods safe.

- Chill salads made with seafood, poultry, meat or dairy products and the dishes you'll serve them in, so they will stay cold longer.

- Hot or cold foods shouldn't stand at room temperature for more than 2 hours. Throw it out if you are in doubt how long it's been out.

- At restaurants or potlucks, salad bars and buffets should look clean. Make sure cold foods are cold and hot foods are steaming before putting them on your plate.

Cooking Gluten Free or Vegan

Many recipes in this book are gluten free, vegetarian or vegan. Follow these guidelines to understand how to cook for those who are gluten sensitive or following a vegan diet.

GLUTEN-FREE COOKING

WHAT IS GLUTEN?

Whether you are celiac or have a gluten sensitivity, or you just choose to avoid gluten, here's what you need to know to cook or bake gluten free. Gluten is a protein that naturally occurs in grains such as wheat, barley, rye and some oats. But foods that are naturally gluten free can contain gluten if they have been processed in a plant where gluten-containing foods are made or made in a kitchen with utensils that have been used with foods containing gluten and not thoroughly washed. That's where it can get a little tricky.

IS IT GLUTEN FREE?

In the gluten-free recipes in this book, we've specifically called for gluten-free versions of ingredients if they might not be naturally gluten free. Many products will say "gluten free" somewhere on the label, but many do not—and you can't be sure if those contain gluten. *Always read labels to make sure each recipe ingredient is gluten free. Products and ingredient sources can change.* If you're unsure if it's gluten free—call the manufacturer.

COOKING TIPS

Keep Separate For those who are gluten sensitive, keeping things separate matters because it's hard to completely remove all gluten residue from kitchen prep areas. It's necessary to keep dedicated spaces for storing and working with gluten-free ingredients, including cutting boards and utensils such as rubber scrapers and metal spatulas. Gluten-free foods can easily become contaminated with gluten by even the tiniest bit left on a utensil or countertop—and that can have detrimental effects to those who are sensitive.

Pan Prep Grease pans with gluten-free solid shortening, or spray with cooking spray *without* flour.

Liquid Absorption Gluten-free doughs may absorb liquids differently than wheat-based dough, so follow recipe directions carefully.

Dough Handling Gluten-free doughs tend to be sticky. Wet or grease your hands to prevent the dough from sticking.

Determining Doneness Gluten-free baked goods often look done before they actually are, so follow the doneness directions given, in addition to bake time.

VEGETARIAN AND VEGAN COOKING

There are several types of vegetarian diets that focus on veggies, fruits, whole grains and calcium-rich foods while restricting various combinations of fish, meat, poultry, fish, eggs and dairy products. A *Flexitarian* diet is an alternative to vegetarianism, where you focus on veggies, fruits, whole grains, legumes and nuts but you occasionally enjoy meat. A *vegan* diet follows the strictest vegetarian diet while also omitting eggs and any products made from ingredients that are animal based, such as honey, or made using animal products in their manufacture.

IS IT VEGAN?

We call for specifically vegan ingredients if there are options available that aren't vegan, as they may use an animal-based ingredient:

- **Nondairy yogurt** may contain gelatin.
- **Nondairy Parmesan cheese** may be made using an animal rennet.
- **Nondairy sour cream** may contain gelatin.

Always read labels to make sure each recipe ingredient is vegan. Products and ingredient sources can change. Recipes labeled "Vegan" in this book are also, by default, vegetarian. Look for vegetarian and vegan recipes throughout the book.

Cooking at Higher Elevations

At elevations of 3,500 feet or higher, there are unique cooking challenges. Air pressure is lower, so water has a lower boiling point and liquids evaporate faster. That means recipes for conventional and microwave cooking may need to be adjusted.

SPECIFIC HIGH-ELEVATION COOKING ADJUSTMENTS

Slow-Cooker Cooking Meats may take twice as long as specified to get tender. To shorten meat cooking times, use High heat setting. For vegetables, cut into smaller pieces than the recipe specifies, so they cook more quickly.

Deep-Fried Foods May brown too quickly on the outside before the center is cooked. Reduce oil temperature by 3°F for every 1,000 feet of elevation and increase fry time, if necessary.

Cooked Sugar Mixtures Any cooked sugar mixtures, such as boiled candy or cooked frostings, will concentrate faster because water evaporates quicker. See Cooking at High Elevation, page 567.

MORE HIGH-ELEVATION COOKING HELP

If you're new to high-elevation cooking, go to the USDA website, https://www.fsis.usda.gov/food-safety/safe-food-handling-and-preparation/food-safety-basics/high-altitude-cooking.

Or visit the Colorado State University website, https://extension.colostate.edu/docs/comm/highaltitude.pdf.

Unfortunately, no set of rules applies to all recipes; sometimes the only way to make improvements is through trial and error. Here are some guidelines to help you with high-elevation cooking challenges.

- **Boiling foods** such as pasta, rice and vegetables will take longer.
- **Candy Making** See Cooking at High Elevation, page 567.
- **Microwave cooking** may require more liquid, and foods may need to be microwaved longer; the type and amount of food, its water content and the exact elevation may affect how much.
- **Meat and poultry cooking** when braising (see page 332) or boiling takes longer—possibly up to twice as long. Cooking large meat cuts such as roasts and turkeys in the oven also takes longer.
- **Grilling foods** will take longer.
- **Baked goods** made with baking powder or baking soda (but not yeast) can be improved with one or more of these changes:
  - Increase oven temperature by 25°F.
  - Increase liquid.
  - Decrease baking powder or baking soda.
  - Decrease sugar and/or use larger pan.
- **High-fat baked goods** such as pound cakes will turn out better if you decrease the fat. Quick breads and cookies usually don't require as many adjustments.
- **Yeast bread dough** may need less flour, as flour dries out more quickly at high elevations. Use the minimum amount called for or decrease the amount by ¼ to ½ cup. Dough rises faster at high elevations and can easily overrise; let dough rise just until doubled in size.

Microwave Cooking

Convenient to use and great for many tasks, the microwave oven is an indispensable, time-saving appliance for any kitchen. It's perfect to use for reheating but it can be used to cook many food items with little time or fuss. Look here to get great microwave tips and a chart for cooking a variety of foods.

MICROWAVING TIPS

- You may need additional cooking time than what is stated in the chart below if you increase the amount of food.

- Check food at the minimum time to avoid overcooking; microwave longer if necessary.

- Stir food from the outer edge to center so food cooks evenly.

- If food cannot be stirred or the microwave doesn't have a turntable, rotate the dish a quarter- to half-turn during cooking.

- Foods that contain high amounts of sugar, fat or moisture may cook more quickly than other foods in the microwave or done with other cooking methods. If some of the ingredients in the dish seem to be getting done too quickly, reduce the power of the microwave before continuing to cook.

- Small pieces of food cook faster than larger pieces.

- For even cooking, arrange food in a circle with thickest parts toward the outside of the dish.

- Use standing time to help finish cooking and distribute heat through food.

- To microwave vegetables, see the Fresh Vegetable Cooking Chart, page 246.

MICROWAVE TESTING FOR THIS BOOK

Recipes in this book that are cooked or heated in a microwave oven were tested in consumer ovens with 800 to 1200 watts of power. Find the wattage of your microwave inside the door or unit on a label or on the back near the UL tag, or in the Use and Care Manual. Adjust your cooking times if the wattage of your oven is more or less than ours.

MICROWAVE COOKING AND HEATING CHART

At-a-glance times for cooking, warming and softening many favorite foods. Be sure to use microwavable dishes, paper towels and plastic wrap. Follow any directions that specify times for stirring or standing.

FOOD, UTENSIL AND TIPS	POWER LEVEL	AMOUNT	TIME
Bacon (cook) Place on plate or bacon rack lined with paper towels. Place paper towels between layers; cover with paper towel. Microwave until crisp.	High	**1 slice** **2 slices** **4 slices** **6 slices** **8 slices**	30 seconds to 1½ minutes 1 to 2 minutes 2 to 3 minutes 3 to 5 minutes 4 to 6 minutes
Brown Sugar (soften) Place in glass bowl; cover with damp paper towel, then plastic wrap.	High	**1 to 3 cups**	1 minute Let stand 2 minutes until softened. Repeat heating once or twice.
Butter (melt) Remove wrapper. Place in glass bowl; cover with paper towel.	High	**1 to 8 tablespoons** **½ to 1 cup**	10 to 50 seconds 60 to 75 seconds
Butter (soften) Remove wrapper. Place on small plate.	Very Low (20%)	**1 stick (½ cup)**	1 minute
Caramels (melt) Remove wrappers. Place in a 4-cup glass measuring cup, uncovered.	High	**1 bag (11 oz) plus 2 to 4 tablespoons milk**	2 to 3 minutes, stirring once or twice.
Baking Chocolate (melt) Remove wrappers. Place in glass dish; cover.	Medium (50%)	**1 to 3 oz**	1½ to 2½ minutes, until it can be stirred smooth.
Chocolate Chips (melt) Place in glass bowl, uncovered.	Medium (50%)	**½ to 1 cup**	2 to 3 minutes, until they can be stirred smooth.

FOOD, UTENSIL AND TIPS	POWER LEVEL	AMOUNT	TIME
Coconut (toast) Place in pie plate, uncovered.	High	¼ to ½ cup **1 cup**	1 ½ to 2 minutes 2 to 3 minutes Stir every 30 seconds.
Cream Cheese (soften) Remove from wrapper or tub; place in glass bowl, uncovered.	Medium (50%)	**8-oz package** **8-oz tub**	1 to 1 ½ minutes 45 to 60 seconds
Fruit, Dried (soften) Place in 2-cup glass measuring cup; add ½ teaspoon water for each ½ cup fruit. Cover with plastic wrap, turning back a corner or ¼-inch edge to vent steam.	High	¼ to ½ cup ½ to 1 cup	30 to 45 seconds 45 to 60 seconds Let stand 2 minutes.
Fruit, Frozen (thaw) Place in glass bowl.	Medium (50%)	**16-oz bag**	3 to 5 minutes Thaw until most of the ice is gone, stirring or rearranging twice.
Fruit, Refrigerated (warm) Place on turntable or floor of microwave.	High	**1 medium** **2 medium**	15 seconds 20 to 30 seconds Let stand 2 minutes.
Honey (dissolve crystals) Fill glass measure large enough to hold honey jar about ⅓ full with water.	High	½ to 1 cup	Heat water 30 seconds to 1 minute, or until very warm. Place opened jar of honey in water, stirring occasionally until crystals dissolve.
Ice Cream (soften) Leave in original container; remove any foil.	Low (10%)	**½ gallon**	2 to 3 minutes Let stand 2 to 3 minutes.
Muffins or Rolls, small to medium (heat) Place on plate, napkin or in napkin-lined nonmetal basket, uncovered.	High	**1** **2** **3** **4**	5 to 10 seconds 10 to 15 seconds 12 to 20 seconds 20 to 30 seconds
Muffins, large to jumbo (heat) Place on plate or napkin, uncovered.	High	**1** **2** **3** **4**	10 to 20 seconds 20 to 30 seconds 30 to 40 seconds 40 to 50 seconds Let stand 1 minute.
Nuts, Chopped (toast) Place in glass measuring cup, uncovered; add ¼ teaspoon vegetable oil for each ¼ cup nuts.	High	¼ to ½ cup ½ to 1 cup	2 ½ to 3 ½ minutes 3 to 4 minutes Stir every 30 seconds until light brown.
Snacks, Popcorn, Pretzels, Corn or Potato Chips (crisp) Place in paper towel–lined nonmetal basket, uncovered.	High	**2 cups** **4 cups**	20 to 40 seconds 40 to 60 seconds
Syrup (heat) Place in glass measuring cup or pitcher, uncovered.	High	½ cup **1 cup**	30 to 45 seconds 45 to 60 seconds Stir every 30 seconds.
Water (boil) Place in glass measuring cup, uncovered.	High	**1 cup**	2 to 3 minutes

Entertaining Basics

Great food and your favorite people are the perfect ingredients for a memorable event! From holiday celebrations to backyard cookouts, dinner parties to birthday parties, there are many reasons to gather friends and family. Food is the ultimate connector—people relax, laugh, and stay and chat when there's food involved.

EASY ENTERTAINING STRATEGIES

The secret to throwing a successful gathering starts with a relaxed host or hostess. Use these strategies to entertain with minimal fuss so you can enjoy the party, too.

- Select a few "wow" recipes to make that will make a delicious statement, then fill in the menu with store-bought prepared foods.

- Consider local delis, specialty bakeries, gourmet shops, international grocers and organic food stores as your behind-the-scenes food providers. Scope them out ahead of time, making sure any unusual items you are interested in will be available when you need them, not just on certain days or for certain occasions.

- Consider asking guests to bring a food item to the party. It's a great way to slash the cost of entertaining if you are on a budget. People are happy to bring something because you are doing the work of hosting.

- Specify what you'd like them to bring or give them a little guidance, such as "please bring an appetizer or sweet treat to share." Many people have a recipe they are known for—they'd be tickled if you ask them to bring it. It's easy to know how to round out the meal if you know what everyone is bringing.

- Cheese boards (page 44) or snack boards (page 42) are perfect for entertaining, as an appetizer or dessert—easy to assemble and sure to please. From simple and inexpensive to impressive showstoppers, the cheeses and other foods you select for a board are limitless.

Food Storage

STORING FOOD IN THE REFRIGERATOR AND FREEZER

Use these charts as a guideline for how long you can store food to still be at its best quality until you're ready to use it. If you won't use the food within the refrigerator time, freeze it for later use.

REFRIGERATOR AND FREEZER FOOD STORAGE CHART

FOODS	REFRIGERATOR (35°F TO 40°F)	FREEZER (0°F OR BELOW)
Baked Products		
Breads (quick and yeast), Coffee Cakes, Muffins Cool completely; wrap tightly. Let any frosting set at room temperature, then freeze item uncovered before wrapping to freeze long-term.	5 to 7 days Refrigerate bread during hot, humid water or if it contains perishable ingredients like meat or cheese.	2 to 3 months Freeze tightly wrapped in resealable freezer plastic bags. Thaw by loosening wrap and let stand at room temperature 2 to 3 hours.
Cakes (unfrosted or frosted) Cool completely; wrap tightly. Do not freeze cakes with fruit filling.	3 to 5 days Refrigerate cakes that contain dairy products in the filling (such as custard filling) or frosting.	3 to 4 months (unfrosted) 2 to 3 months (frosted) Cakes filled and frosted with plain sweetened whipped cream can be frozen. Freeze unwrapped on a plate. When frozen, wrap and freeze longer-term. Thaw by loosening wrap. Thaw unfrosted cakes at room temperature; for frosted cakes, place in refrigerator overnight.
Cheesecakes (baked) Cool completely; wrap tightly.	3 to 5 days	4 to 5 months Thaw, wrapped, in refrigerator 4 to 6 hours.
Cookies (baked) Place delicate or frosted cookies between layers of waxed paper. Do not freeze meringue, custard-filled or cream-filled cookies.	Only if stated in recipe	Up to 12 months (unfrosted) Up to 3 months (frosted) Thaw most cookies, covered, in container at room temperature 1 to 2 hours. Crisp cookies: remove from container to thaw.
Pies (unbaked or baked fruit pies, baked pecan and baked pumpkin pies) Thaw *frozen baked fruit* pies unwrapped at room temperature or unwrap and thaw at room temperature 1 hour, then heat in 375°F oven 35 to 40 minutes or until warm. Thaw *frozen baked pecan or pumpkin pies* unwrapped 3 to 4 hours in refrigerator.	*Baked pumpkin, pecan, lemon meringue and custard pies*, 3 to 4 days. *Fruit pies at room temperature*, 1 to 2 days or refrigerated up to 7 days.	Up to 4 months (unbaked and baked fruit pies, baked pecan pies) Up to 1 month (baked pumpkin pie) To bake frozen unbaked fruit pies: unwrap and cut slits in top crust. Bake at 425°F for 15 minutes. Reduce oven to 375°F; bake 30 to 45 minutes longer until juices begin to bubble through slits.
Dairy Products		
Cottage Cheese, Creamy Ricotta	Up to 10 days	Not recommended
Hard Cheese	3 to 4 weeks If hard cheese is moldy, trim ½ inch from the affected area and rewrap tightly.	6 to 8 weeks Thaw wrapped cheeses in refrigerator. Texture will be crumbly; use in baked goods.
Buttermilk, Cream and Milk	Up to 5 days	Not recommended Unsweetened and sweetened whipped cream can be frozen: Drop small mounds onto waxed paper, freeze and store in airtight container. To thaw, let stand at room temperature about 15 minutes.
Sour Cream and Yogurt	Up to 1 week	Not recommended

FOODS	REFRIGERATOR (35°F TO 40°F)	FREEZER (0°F OR BELOW)
Eggs		
Fresh Eggs (in shell)	2 weeks	Not recommended
Cooked Eggs (in shell)	1 week	Not recommended
Fats and Oils		
Butter	No longer than 2 weeks	No longer than 2 months
Margarine and Spreads	No longer than 1 month	No longer than 2 months
Mayonnaise and Salad Dressing	No longer than 6 months	Not recommended
Meats		
If wrapped in butcher paper, rewrap tightly in plastic wrap or foil, or place in resealable freezer plastic bag.		
Chops (uncooked)	3 to 5 days	4 to 6 months
Ground (uncooked)	1 to 2 days	3 to 4 months
Roasts and Steaks (uncooked)	3 to 5 days	6 to 12 months
Cooked Meats	3 to 4 days	2 to 3 months
Cold Cuts	3 to 5 days (opened)	Not recommended
	2 weeks (unopened)	1 to 2 months
Bacon, Cured	5 to 7 days	3 months
Hot Dogs	1 week (opened)	1 to 2 months
	2 weeks (unopened)	1 to 2 months
Ham, Whole or Half (cooked)	5 to 7 days	1 to 2 months
Ham Slices (cooked)	3 to 4 days	1 to 2 months
Nuts		
Store nuts in an airtight container.		
	6 months	1 year
Poultry		
See Chicken & Turkey Basics, page 318, for wrapping, storing and thawing directions.		
Whole, including Game Birds, Ducks and Geese (uncooked)	1 to 2 days	No longer than 12 months
Cut up (cooked)	5 to 7 days	No longer than 9 months
Cooked Poultry	3 to 4 days	1 to 2 months
Seafood		
See Fish Basics, page 354, for wrapping and storing fish.		
Fish (uncooked)	1 to 2 days	3 to 6 months
Fish (breaded, cooked)	Store in freezer	2 to 3 months
Cut up (uncooked)	1 to 2 days	3 to 4 months
Shellfish (cooked)	3 to 4 days	1 to 2 months

Appetizers
& Snacks

Appetizer & Snack Basics

Whether you're looking to host an unforgettable party or eat more smaller meals throughout the day, or need a quick fix for your late-night craving, appetizers and snacks will be a perfect choice.

Planning an Appetizer Party

A great way to host a party is by serving an array of appetizers. The casualness of little bites puts everyone at ease so that the conversation can flow. A little planning will help set the tone for a fun and memorable party.

TIPS FOR SELECTING APPETIZERS

- Unless it is a sit-down occasion, choose appetizers that are easy to pick up and handle.
- Choose a variety of flavors and textures as well as colors and shapes.
- Choose a selection of hot, cold and room temperature recipes for variety, but also to make it easier to serve them.
- Serve at least three different appetizers for variety, adding more types for more guests and doubling or tripling recipes to have enough.
- Allow for 12 pieces per person for an appetizer party (or 6 if serving dinner after). Double or triple recipes to accommodate larger groups.
- Stage baking and serving trays of hot appetizers throughout the evening, so that there will always be hot appetizers available, rather than baking them all for the beginning of the party.

SUCCESSFUL PARTY SECRETS

- Map out a timeline of how many guests will be at the event, what you want to serve and how many batches of each recipe you'll need.
- Consider your theme and who will attend, then decorate and set the table or buffet area ahead of time. Think about serving—will the event require equipment such as a fondue pot, slow cooker, or hot plate?
- Choose a place for the food that has easy access for guests. For a large gathering, set up several areas with different appetizers so guests can browse at their leisure while mixing and mingling.
- Offer cutlery bundles wrapped in paper or cloth napkins for foods that require utensils, and place where they are easy to grab. Add small trays for guests to gather appetizers—often beverages will fit on these trays too.
- Make recipes or parts of recipes ahead as much as possible. Often you can prep individual ingredients and wrap them separately to assemble quickly at the last minute.

- Serve foods in interesting containers—pretty plates or bowls, or hollowed-out loaves of bread or other foods such as bell peppers or pumpkins. Line plates with fresh lettuce leaves for color and texture and add garnishes to foods.

The Benefits of Snacking

Smart snacking can fuel your body and brain throughout the day. Choosing foods that combine protein, high-fiber carbs and healthy fats can help you feel fuller longer and provide nutrients to give you the energy your body craves. Work fresh veggies and fruits into your snacks, as they offer nutrients and antioxidants while bulking up the volume and keeping the lid on calories.

If possible, plan your snacks ahead of the hangries to keep you from making poor food choices and overeating. Pack snacks in the morning to take with you or have healthy options on standby for those times you'd grab just about anything. Plant-forward snacks can satisfy your hunger for munching while keeping the calories at bay. Try one of these plant-forward snacks when you want a homemade, satisfying snack.

Plant-Forward Snacks

Swirled Harissa Yogurt Dip (page 41) with carrot sticks

Dill Pickle Dip (page 41) with cucumbers and bell pepper sticks

Guacamole (page 50) with whole grain tortilla chips

Spicy Green Bean Fries (page 51)

Roasted Beans 3 Ways (page 55)

Cheesy Jalapeño-Cauliflower Tots (page 55)

Roasted Sweet Potato Miso Hummus (page 49) with whole wheat pita wedges

Dill Pickle Dip

Swirled Harissa Yogurt Dip

Dill Pickle Dip

Pickles come in different varieties and flavors. Feel free to use your favorite for this dip.

PREP 15 Minutes **TOTAL** 1 Hour 15 Minutes • *2½ cups*

1 container (7.5 oz) chive-and-onion cream cheese	1 cup diced kosher dill pickles
½ cup sour cream	4 teaspoons chopped fresh dill weed
2 tablespoons dill pickle juice	Pretzels, potato chips or fresh vegetables, if desired
¼ teaspoon garlic powder	

1 In medium bowl, beat cream cheese, sour cream, pickle juice and garlic powder with electric mixer on medium speed until blended and smooth.

2 Stir in pickles and dill. Cover and refrigerate at least 1 hour before serving to blend flavors. Serve with pretzels, chips or vegetables. Store covered in refrigerator up to 3 days.

2 Tablespoons Calories 45; Total Fat 4g (Saturated Fat 2.5g, Trans Fat 0g); Cholesterol 15mg; Sodium 120mg; Total Carbohydrate 0g (Dietary Fiber 0g); Protein 1g **Carbohydrate Choices:** 0

Swirled Harissa Yogurt Dip

PREP 10 Minutes **TOTAL** 2 Hours 10 Minutes • *1½ cups*

1½ cups plain whole milk Greek yogurt	¼ teaspoon garlic powder
3 tablespoons finely chopped fresh basil leaves	3 tablespoons mild harissa (from 10-oz jar)
2 teaspoons fresh lemon juice	Additional fresh basil leaves, if desired
1 teaspoon honey	Gluten-free pita chips or cut-up fresh vegetables, if desired
½ teaspoon salt	

1 In small bowl, mix yogurt, 3 tablespoons of the basil, lemon juice, honey, salt and garlic powder.

2 Into small serving bowl, spoon half of yogurt mixture. Spread 2 tablespoons of the harissa over yogurt; top with remaining yogurt. Cover and refrigerate 2 hours to blend flavors.

3 To serve, top with remaining 1 tablespoon harissa. With spoon or table knife, gently swirl harissa and yogurt. Garnish with basil. Serve with pita chips or vegetables.

2 tablespoons Calories 35; Total Fat 1.5g (Saturated Fat 1g, Trans Fat 0g); Cholesterol 0mg; Sodium 150mg; Total Carbohydrate 2g (Dietary Fiber 0g); Protein 2g **Carbohydrate Choices:** 0

Tzatziki Dip

Tzatziki is a yogurt sauce made with cucumber and other ingredients. Frequently used with Greek dishes, it's a flavorful appetizer dip or topping for meat or chicken, salad or bowls. The cool dairy flavor pairs well with spicy or highly seasoned foods.

PREP 10 Minutes **TOTAL** 2 Hours 10 Minutes • *2 cups*

1½ cups plain Greek yogurt	1 teaspoon olive oil
⅔ cup finely chopped seeded peeled English (hothouse) cucumber	½ teaspoon salt
	Additional fresh mint leaves, if desired
3 tablespoons finely chopped fresh mint leaves	Pita (pocket) breads, cut into wedges, if desired
1½ teaspoons fresh lemon juice	Fresh vegetables, if desired

1 In medium bowl, gently mix yogurt, cucumber, chopped mint, lemon juice, oil and salt until blended. Cover and refrigerate 2 hours to blend flavors.

2 Garnish with mint leaves. Serve with pita wedges and vegetables.

2 Tablespoons Calories 20; Total Fat 1g (Saturated Fat 0g, Trans Fat 0g); Cholesterol 0mg; Sodium 85mg; Total Carbohydrate 1g (Dietary Fiber 0g); Protein 2g **Carbohydrate Choices:** 0

EASY SNACK BOARDS

Also known as charcuterie, snack boards are a wonderful and easy way to nibble! They can be as simple as leftover tidbits you collect from your fridge and pantry to a fancy spread made from global meats and cheeses. Use them as a snack when watching TV, as a fun, interactive dinner or as the main event at a cocktail party.

You can make a themed board around a celebration, such as a baby shower or the Fourth of July. You could also create a board around one food and its toppings or accompaniments, such as a sandwich board with meats, cheeses, breads, and spreads; a hot chocolate board, with stir-ins and toppings; or a cookie board with assorted cookies, fruit and dips.

Tips for Great Snack Boards

- For several people, use a large cutting board or two, shallow trays or baking pans with short sides to place the foods on. For just a few people, use a large plate or small cutting board. You can even create a snack board for one on a small plate or in a shallow bowl or jar!

- Look for foods that add color, texture, shape for interest.

- Arrange foods by type in one area of the snack board to keep it from getting too busy.

- Break up sections of foods with small shallow bowls of sauces or other condiments, accompaniments such as pickles or olives or other small foods such as nuts, dried fruit, or small candies. They are functional as well as eye-catching.

USE UP THE LEFTOVERS CUP (FOR ONE)

Make a snack for one in a shallow cup.

- Deli meats
- Cheeses
- Mustard
- Sliced fruit or grapes
- Coleslaw
- Bread, crackers

BLOODY MARY BOARD

Serve up this board when you're serving Bloody Marys to a crowd.

- Cheese cubes and balls
- Small pickles
- Olives
- Shrimp, sliders, cocktail wieners
- Crisply cooked bacon slices
- Bloody Mary salt
- Lime wedges
- Skewers

MOVIE NIGHT BOARD

Create a board to nibble on during a movie.

- Strawberries
- Caramel corn
- Assorted movie candies
- Popcorn
- Cheese and crackers
- Licorice
- Hot dogs

BURRITO BOARD

Everyone gets to customize their own burritos when these add-ons are served.

- Shredded cooked chicken
- Black beans
- Cheese
- Chopped tomatoes
- Sliced avocados
- Tortillas
- Sour cream
- Pico de gallo

Rye Bread

Round Candy-Coated
Chocolate-Flavored
Candies

Sugar Snap
Peas

Pistachios

Cheddar
Cheese
Sticks

Pretzel
Sticks

Salami

Pimiento-Stuffed
Green Olives

Cucumber
Slices

Crackers

Corned
Beef

Pastel-Colored Mint
Candy Drops

Swiss Cheese
Cubes

Purchased
Cookies

Creating a Cheese Board

- Use at least 3 types of cheese; for larger groups or buffets, add more varieties and/or larger quantities. Plan on at least 2 oz per person when other foods are served or more if this is the only offering.

- Aim for a variety of flavors and textures. Many specialty grocery stores and cheese shops can provide samples for you to try, as well as offer flavor suggestions.

- Cheese is easier to cut when cold but tastes better at room temperature. Remove it from the refrigerator and unwrap 30 to 60 minutes before serving.

- Arrange cheeses on a board or platter with room in between for cutting/serving. Provide butter knives or servers appropriate to each type (see Cheese Servers, page 16).

- Offer crackers and/or bread to go with the cheeses. Consider adding other foods that provide color, texture and flavor, such as dried and/or fresh fruits, nuts, olives, preserves, mustard, chutneys and/or honey for drizzling.

- Wine is the perfect partner for cheese. Ask your wine and cheese shop for suggestions on pairings.

Cheese Types

VERY HARD (GRATING)

- **Asiago** Mild when young; nutty and moderately sharp when aged. Melts best when grated. Use with pasta, potatoes, rice salads, vegetables.

- **Cotija** Ranges from firm, dry and crumbly to semisoft; salty, sharp flavor. **Cotija Añejo** (aged) is firmer and harder than regular Cotija. Both will soften but not change shape when heated. Crumble over salads or Mexican-style dishes such as tacos or refried beans.

- **Parmesan** Sharp, savory, salty; flavor intensifies with age. Melts best when grated. Use in salads, cooked dishes, casseroles and on pizza.

- **Pecorino Romano** Sharp, robust: similar to but richer than Parmesan. Made from sheep's milk. Melts best when grated. Use in pasta, soups, salads, egg dishes, stuffings or on pizza.

HARD

- **Cheddar** Rich, nutty flavor, ranging from mild to full bodied; sharp cheddar also has a bite. **Smoked cheddar** is flavored with hardwood smoke. Other ingredients may be added.

- **Edam** Mildly salty, nutty. Melts best when shredded. Use in sandwiches, salads, soups and snacks.

- **Emmentaler** Similar to Swiss; mild, nutty, buttery. Melts well. Use in sandwiches, sauces, snacks.

- **Gouda** Mellow, rich caramel flavor. **Smoked Gouda** is flavored with hardwood smoke. Melts best when shredded. Use in sandwiches, soups, salads, snacks.

- **Gruyère** Mellow, buttery, nutty. Melts well. Use in fondues, baked dishes, onion soup.

- **Halloumi** Firm unripened cheese of Mediterranean origin. A mixture of goat's and sheep's milk; can be fried or grilled and will hold its shape.

- **Jarlsberg** Similar to Swiss. Slightly sweet, nutty. Use in baked dishes, sandwiches, snacks.

- **Manchego** Creamy, mildly nutty; a Spanish version of cheddar. Melts well. Serve at any meal course on its own or in sandwiches, salads, baked dishes, snacks.

- **Swiss** Mellow, buttery, slightly nutty. Melts well. Use in baked dishes, fondues, sandwiches or salads.

SEMISOFT

- **Blue Cheese** Rich, robust, salty with a lingering tang. Melts best when crumbled. Use in vegetable, green, fruit, and pasta salads; spreads, dressings, dips; soufflés; or with grilled meats.

- **Cheese Curds** Mild and milky, with a rubbery texture. Use as a snack or as a topping.

- **Feta** Very sharp, salty flavor. Melts best in sauces when crumbled. Use in salads, Greek-style dishes, eggs, hot or cold pasta dishes.

- **Fontina** Delicate, nutty with a hint of honey flavor. Melts well. Use in sandwiches, baked dishes, snacks.

- **Gorgonzola** Italian blue cheese; spicy flavor becomes more pronounced as it ages. Melts best when crumbled. See Blue Cheese for uses.

- **Havarti** Buttery, mild yet tangy. Melts best when shredded. Use in sandwiches, egg dishes and salads. Other ingredients such as caraway seed may be added.

- **Paneer** Indian cheese similar to Queso Blanco. Mild, fresh, mozzarella-like flavor. Not aged; holds its shape when heated. Customarily diced and used in a variety of Indian-style dishes including vegetables and salads.

- **Queso Blanco** Fresh (unripened) with a crumbly, curdy texture. Commonly fried. Softens but holds its shape when heated. Use in soups, salads, stuffings, snacks.

- **Roquefort** French blue cheese made from sheep's milk. Similar in flavor to blue cheese with a melt-in-your-mouth texture. See Blue Cheese for uses.

SOFT

- **Brie** Rich, buttery. Softens and flows when heated. Use as an appetizer, heated and topped with sauce; in sandwiches and snacks.

- **Burrata** Fresh curd stretched, kneaded, filled with a center of mozzarella and cream that oozes when cut.

- **Chèvre (Goat)** Creamy, fresh, mildly tangy. Made with goat's milk. Softens but holds its shape when heated. Use in appetizers, salads, baked dishes, sauces.

- **Cottage Cheese (Dry or Creamed)** Mild, milky. Use in baked dishes and salads.

- **Cream Cheese** Rich, slightly tangy. Melts best in sauces. Use in baked dishes, cheesecakes, fruit or gelatin salads, snacks, spreads. Other flavoring ingredients may be added.

- **Fresh Mozzarella** Creamy, soft texture, with a delicate, milky flavor. Use in salads, sandwiches, as an appetizer and pizza topping.

- **Mascarpone** Very soft, sweet, mild with a buttery texture. Melts best in sauces. Use in fillings, toppings, dips, spreads, sauces.

- **Queso Fresco** Spongy, fresh (unripened), with a grainy texture. Slightly acidic flavor. Softens but holds its shape when heated. Crumble over enchiladas or refried beans.

- **Ricotta** Mild, slightly sweet. Use in fillings, stuffings, spreads and cheesecakes.

Jarlsberg

Gouda

Queso Fresco

Emmentaler

Chipotle Cheddar

Gruyère

Manchego

Cotija

Cotija Añejo

Smoked Gouda

Horseradish Havarti

Cottage Cheese

Ricotta

Smoked Cheddar

Tomato-Basil Cheddar

Havarti

Edam

Queso Blanco

Mascarpone

Sharp Cheddar

Dill Havarti

Blueberry Cheddar

Mozzarella

Colby

Blue

Gorgonzola

Fontina

Cream Cheese with Chives

Garden Vegetable

Cream Cheese

Romano

Roquefort

Pearl Mozzarella

Feta

Parmesan

Curds

Brie

Chèvre (Goat)

Asiago

FAST • CALORIE SMART • VEGETARIAN

Greek Layered Dip

To make your own pita chips, heat oven to 350°F. Split 2 whole wheat pita (pocket) breads horizontally to make 2 rounds. Cut each round into 6 wedges. Arrange on ungreased large cookie sheet, rough surface up. Generously spray with cooking spray. Bake 8 to 10 minutes or until golden brown and crisp. Cool.

PREP 10 Minutes **TOTAL** 10 Minutes • **3 cups**

- 1 container (8 oz) plain hummus (for homemade hummus, see page 48)
- 1 container (6 oz) plain Greek yogurt
- 1 tablespoon chopped fresh parsley
- 1 teaspoon lemon juice
- ⅛ teaspoon pepper
- 1 medium plum (Roma) tomato, seeded, chopped
- ⅓ cup pitted kalamata or ripe olives, quartered
- ⅓ cup finely chopped seeded cucumber
- 1 cup crumbled feta cheese (4 oz)
- 4 medium green onions, chopped (¼ cup)
- 1 tablespoon olive oil
  Pita chips, cucumber slices and red bell pepper strips, if desired

Spread hummus on shallow serving platter or in pie plate. In small bowl, mix yogurt, parsley, lemon juice and pepper; spread evenly over hummus. Top with tomato, olives, chopped cucumber, cheese and onions. Drizzle with oil. Serve with pita chips, sliced cucumber and bell pepper strips.

2 Tablespoons Calories 45; Total Fat 3g (Saturated Fat 1g, Trans Fat 0g); Cholesterol 5mg; Sodium 110mg; Total Carbohydrate 3g (Dietary Fiber 0g); Protein 2g **Carbohydrate Choices:** 0

LIGHTER DIRECTIONS: To reduce the fat and calories in this recipe, use plain fat-free Greek yogurt. Reduce feta cheese to ½ cup and olive oil to 1 teaspoon.

MAKE AHEAD • CALORIE SMART

Cheese Ball

PREP 15 Minutes **TOTAL** 10 Hours 45 Minutes •
16 servings (2 tablespoons each)

- 2 packages (8 oz each) cream cheese
- 1 cup shredded sharp cheddar cheese (4 oz)
- ¾ cup crumbled blue, Gorgonzola or feta cheese (3 oz)
- 1 small onion, finely chopped (½ cup)
- 1 tablespoon Worcestershire sauce
- ½ cup chopped fresh parsley
  Assorted crackers, if desired

1 Place cheeses in medium bowl; let stand at room temperature about 30 minutes or until softened. Add onion and Worcestershire sauce. Beat with electric mixer on low speed until blended. Beat on medium speed 1 to 2 minutes, scraping bowl frequently, until fluffy. Cover and refrigerate at least 8 hours until firm enough to shape into ball.

2 Shape cheese mixture into large ball. Roll in parsley. Place on serving plate. Cover and refrigerate about 2 hours or until firm. Serve with crackers.

1 Serving Calories 160; Total Fat 14g (Saturated Fat 9g, Trans Fat 0g); Cholesterol 45mg; Sodium 240mg; Total Carbohydrate 2g (Dietary Fiber 0g); Protein 6g **Carbohydrate Choices:** 0

LIGHTER DIRECTIONS: For 3 grams of fat and 65 calories per serving, use fat-free cream cheese and reduced-fat cheddar cheese.

CRANBERRY–BLUE CHEESE BALL: Omit cheddar cheese, onion and Worcestershire sauce. Increase blue cheese to a 5-oz package. Add 2 tablespoons honey, ¼ teaspoon ground red pepper (cayenne) and ½ teaspoon salt with the cheeses. After mixing in Step 1, stir in ½ cup each chopped sweetened dried cranberries and chopped toasted pecans. Cover and refrigerate 2 hours or until firm enough to shape into a ball. After rolling in parsley, ball will be ready to serve.

Greek Layered Dip

Cheese Ball

PEPPER JACK CHEESE BALL: Substitute ¾ cup shredded pepper Jack cheese for the blue cheese. Omit Worcestershire sauce. Substitute cilantro for the parsley.

PIZZA CHEESE BALL: Substitute 2 cups shredded mozzarella cheese for the cheddar and blue cheeses. Omit Worcestershire sauce. Add ½ cup each chopped drained sun-dried tomatoes in oil, chopped pitted ripe olives and chopped thinly sliced pepperoni, ½ teaspoon dried oregano leaves and ½ teaspoon pepper with the onion. Substitute ⅓ cup chopped fresh chives for the parsley.

CALORIE SMART • VEGETARIAN • VEGAN

Classic Baba Ghanoush

Tahini (see page 48) gives this Middle Eastern dip its distinctive smoky, creamy flavor.

PREP 10 Minutes **TOTAL** 1 Hour 35 Minutes • *1½ cups*

1 large eggplant (about 1½ lb)*	½ teaspoon ground cumin
2 tablespoons sesame tahini paste	⅛ teaspoon pepper
1 tablespoon olive oil	Pomegranate seeds and chopped fresh parsley, if desired
1 tablespoon fresh lemon juice	Toasted baguette slices or pita wedges, if desired
1 clove garlic	
¾ teaspoon salt	

1 Heat oven to 450°F. Line 15x10x1-inch pan with foil. Pierce eggplant in several places with tip of sharp knife; place on pan. Roast uncovered 45 to 55 minutes, turning once, until skin is blackened and inside begins to soften. Let stand until cool enough to handle, about 30 minutes.

2 Cut eggplant lengthwise in half. Scoop out flesh and place on several layers of paper towel to absorb excess moisture. In food processor, place eggplant, tahini, oil, lemon juice, garlic, salt, cumin and pepper. Cover and process until smooth.

CHARRING EGGPLANT

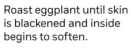
Roast eggplant until skin is blackened and inside begins to soften.

Scoop out flesh and place on several layers of paper towel to absorb excess moisture.

---

3 Spoon into serving bowl. Sprinkle with pomegranate seeds and parsley. Served with toasted baguette slices or pita wedges.

2 Tablespoons Calories 45; Total Fat 2.5g (Saturated Fat 0g, Trans Fat 0g); Cholesterol 0mg; Sodium 150mg; Total Carbohydrate 4g (Dietary Fiber 2g); Protein 1g **Carbohydrate Choices:** 0

*Choose dark purple, smooth, glossy, taut-skinned eggplant that is free from blemishes and rust spots. Caps and stems should be intact and free of mold.

CALORIE SMART • GLUTEN FREE

Pico de Gallo

This fresh condiment is delicious on its own as a dip with chips, or use it to top your favorite tacos, enchiladas, grilled vegetables, scrambled eggs or burgers.

PREP 15 Minutes **TOTAL** 2 hours 15 Minutes • *2½ cups*

2 large ripe tomatoes, seeded, chopped	3 tablespoons finely chopped seeded jalapeño chile (1 large)
¼ cup chopped red onion	2 tablespoons chopped fresh cilantro
¼ cup chopped green bell pepper	2 tablespoons fresh lime juice
	¼ teaspoon sea salt

In medium bowl, mix all ingredients. Cover and refrigerate at least 2 hours to blend flavors.

2 Tablespoons Calories 5; Total Fat 0g (Saturated Fat 0g, Trans Fat 0g); Cholesterol 0mg; Sodium 30mg; Total Carbohydrate 1g (Dietary Fiber 0g); Protein 0g **Carbohydrate Choices:** 0

FAST • GLUTEN FREE

Buffalo Chicken Dip

PREP 20 Minutes **TOTAL** 20 Minutes • *4½ cups*

1 cup chunky blue cheese dressing	2 packages (8 oz each) cream cheese, softened
2 tablespoons gluten-free Buffalo wing sauce	**DIPPERS, IF DESIRED**
3 cups chopped cooked chicken	Carrot and celery sticks, bell pepper strips or gluten-free crackers

1 In large microwavable bowl, mix dressing and sauce. Stir in chicken and cream cheese. Cover; microwave on High 5 minutes. Stir; cover, and continue to microwave on High 6 to 8 minutes, stirring after every minute (bowl will be hot) or until at least 165°F.

2 Spoon dip into serving dish. Serve with dippers.

2 Tablespoons Calories 280; Total Fat 22g (Saturated Fat 8g, Trans Fat 1g); Cholesterol 45mg; Sodium 430mg; Total Carbohydrate 10g (Dietary Fiber 1g); Protein 9g **Carbohydrate Choices:** ½

HEIRLOOM → NEW TWIST

HEIRLOOM

FAST • CALORIE SMART • VEGETARIAN • VEGAN

Hummus

Tahini, a thick paste made from ground sesame seed, gives this dip its distinctive flavor. Look for tahini in the condiment, international foods or pickle aisle.

PREP 5 Minutes **TOTAL** 5 Minutes • *2 cups*

- 1 can (15 oz) chick peas (garbanzo beans), drained, ¼ cup liquid reserved
- ½ cup sesame tahini paste*
- ¼ cup olive oil
- 2 cloves garlic, finely chopped
- 3 tablespoons lemon juice
- 1 teaspoon salt
- ⅛ teaspoon pepper
  Chopped fresh parsley, if desired
  Pita (pocket) bread wedges, crackers or fresh vegetables, if desired

1 In blender or food processor, place chick peas, reserved liquid, tahini, oil, garlic, lemon juice, salt and pepper. Cover and blend on high speed, stopping occasionally to scrape sides, until smooth.

2 Use immediately or cover and refrigerate up to 5 days. Spoon into serving dish. Garnish with parsley. Serve with pita bread wedges.

2 Tablespoons Calories 110; Total Fat 8g (Saturated Fat 1g, Trans Fat 0g); Cholesterol 0mg; Sodium 210mg; Total Carbohydrate 7g (Dietary Fiber 2g); Protein 3g **Carbohydrate Choices:** ½

*½ cup sesame seed can be substituted for the tahini, but the hummus will not be smooth.

CUMIN HUMMUS: Add ¼ teaspoon ground cumin with the salt and pepper. Omit parsley. Sprinkle with cumin seed, if desired.

ROASTED GARLIC HUMMUS: Stir 1 to 2 tablespoons Roasted Garlic (page 188) into blended mixture.

SUN-DRIED TOMATO HUMMUS: Stir ⅓ cup chopped drained sun-dried tomatoes (packed in oil) into blended mixture.

Clockwise from top: Tzatziki Dip (page 41), Baba Ghanoush (page 47), Hummus

Roasted Sweet Potato
Miso Hummus

NEW TWIST

MAKE AHEAD • CALORIE SMART • VEGETARIAN • VEGAN

Roasted Sweet Potato Miso Hummus

There's no end to what this hummus tastes good on. Use it as a sandwich spread with roasted veggies or turkey, or add a scoop to a salad or grain bowl.

PREP 15 Minutes **TOTAL** 3 Hours 25 Minutes • *3 cups*

1 large orange-fleshed sweet potato (12 to 14 oz)

4 cloves garlic in skins

1 can (15 oz) chick peas (garbanzo beans), drained, rinsed

¼ cup sesame tahini paste

2 tablespoons fresh lemon juice

2 tablespoons extra-virgin olive oil

1 tablespoon white miso

1 tablespoon soy sauce

¼ teaspoon salt

2 tablespoons coarsely chopped fresh cilantro

½ teaspoon toasted sesame seed

Pita wedges or chips, if desired

1 Heat oven to 400°F. Line rimmed cookie sheet with foil; spray with cooking spray. Place sweet potato on cookie sheet and poke all over with fork. Add garlic cloves to pan. Bake 20 minutes, then remove garlic; set garlic aside to cool. Continue to bake sweet potato 40 minutes to 1 hour 5 minutes longer or until sweet potato is completely tender when pierced all the way through with fork. Let stand about 10 minutes or until cool enough to handle.

2 Peel cooked sweet potato and garlic; place in large food processor. Add chick peas, tahini, lemon juice, olive oil, miso, soy sauce and salt. Cover; process until smooth. If needed, add water 1 tablespoon at a time to desired consistency. Cover and refrigerate at least 2 hours to allow flavors to blend.

3 To serve, spoon hummus onto serving platter. Top with cilantro and sesame seed. Serve with pita wedges or chips.

2 Tablespoons Calories 50; Total Fat 3g (Saturated Fat 0g, Trans Fat 0g); Cholesterol 0mg; Sodium 120mg; Total Carbohydrate 5g (Dietary Fiber 1g); Protein 1g **Carbohydrate Choices:** ½

Guacamole

Ripe avocados yield to gentle pressure. To ripen, let stand at room temperature in a closed paper bag.

PREP 15 Minutes **TOTAL** 15 Minutes • *2 cups*

- 1 small jalapeño chile or 1 tablespoon canned chopped green chiles
- 2 ripe large avocados
- 2 tablespoons fresh lime or lemon juice
- 2 tablespoons finely chopped cilantro
- 2 tablespoons finely chopped red onion
- ¼ teaspoon salt
  Dash pepper
- 1 small tomato, seeded, chopped (½ cup)
- 1 small clove garlic, finely chopped
  Tortilla chips, if desired

1 Remove stems, seeds and ribs from chile; finely chop chile. Cut avocados lengthwise in half; remove pit and peel. In medium glass or plastic bowl, mash avocados with fork. Gently stir in chile and remaining ingredients except tortilla chips until mixed.

2 Serve with tortilla chips. Press and smooth plastic wrap directly on surface of leftover guacamole to help prevent discoloration.

2 Tablespoons Calories 35; Total Fat 2.5g (Saturated Fat 0g, Trans Fat 0g); Cholesterol 0mg; Sodium 40mg; Total Carbohydrate 2g (Dietary Fiber 1g); Protein 0g **Carbohydrate Choices:** 0

COTIJA GUACAMOLE: Stir in ½ cup crumbled Cotija cheese with remaining ingredients in Step 1.

LOADED GUACAMOLE: Top guacamole in striped sections with crumbled chèvre (goat) cheese, finely chopped fresh mango, tomato, red onion and pumpkin seeds (pepitas).

CUTTING AN AVOCADO

Cut avocado lengthwise through skin around pit.

With hands, slowly twist both sides to separate.

Slide flatware tablespoon under pit to remove.

Make cuts or slices through flesh; slide spoon between skin and flesh to remove.

Guacamole

Hot Artichoke Dip

PREP 10 Minutes **TOTAL** 35 Minutes • *About 1½ cups*

- ½ cup mayonnaise or salad dressing (for homemade mayonnaise, see page 479)
- ½ cup grated Parmesan cheese
- 4 medium green onions, chopped (¼ cup)
- 1 can (14 oz) artichoke hearts, drained, coarsely chopped
  Crackers or cocktail rye bread, if desired

1 Heat oven to 350°F. In small bowl, stir mayonnaise and cheese until well mixed. Stir in onions and artichoke hearts. Spoon into ungreased 1-quart casserole.

2 Cover and bake 20 to 25 minutes or until hot. Serve warm with crackers.

2 Tablespoons Calories 100; Total Fat 8g (Saturated Fat 2g, Trans Fat 0g); Cholesterol 5mg; Sodium 180mg; Total Carbohydrate 3g (Dietary Fiber 1g); Protein 2g **Carbohydrate Choices:** 0

MICROWAVE DIRECTIONS: In 1-quart microwavable casserole, mix all ingredients except crackers. Cover with microwavable plastic wrap, folding one edge or corner back ¼ inch to vent steam. Microwave on Medium-High (70%) 4 to 5 minutes, stirring after 2 minutes, until hot.

LIGHTER DIRECTIONS: For 1 gram of fat and 20 calories per serving, use ⅓ cup plain fat-free yogurt and 3 tablespoons reduced-fat mayonnaise for the ½ cup mayonnaise.

HOT ARTICHOKE-SPINACH DIP: Increase mayonnaise and Parmesan cheese to 1 cup each. Stir in 1 box (9 oz) frozen chopped spinach, thawed (squeeze thawed spinach to drain; spread on paper towels and pat dry). Spoon into ungreased 1-quart casserole. Bake as directed.

HOT ARTICHOKE-CRAB DIP: Gently stir in 1 can (6 oz) drained crabmeat with onions and artichoke hearts in Step 1. Continue as directed.

Hot Artichoke Dip

FAST • VEGETARIAN

Spicy Green Bean Fries

Thai chile paste is a blend of red chiles and Thai spices. Serve these fries with any of your favorite condiments.

PREP 10 Minutes **TOTAL** 25 Minutes • *4 servings*

1½ lb fresh green beans, trimmed	¾ cup plain panko crispy bread crumbs
1 tablespoon all-purpose flour	3 tablespoons grated Parmesan cheese
2 eggs	½ teaspoon salt
2 tablespoons Thai chile paste (from 6.5-oz jar)	

1 Heat oven to 425°F. Spray 15x10-inch baking pan bottom and sides with cooking spray. In 1-gallon resealable food-storage plastic bag, place flour. Add beans; shake until well coated.

2 In shallow bowl, beat eggs and chile paste until well mixed. In another small bowl, mix bread crumbs, Parmesan cheese and salt. Working in batches of 6 or 7 beans at a time, dip beans in egg mixture; shake off excess. Roll in bread crumb mixture to coat. Place beans in a single layer in baking pan. Lightly spray beans with cooking spray.

3 Bake 10 to 14 minutes or until crisp and golden brown.

1 Serving Calories 210; Total Fat 5g (Saturated Fat 1.5g, Trans Fat 0g); Cholesterol 95mg; Sodium 660mg; Total Carbohydrate 30g (Dietary Fiber 4g); Protein 10g **Carbohydrate Choices:** 2

Spicy Green Bean Fries

EASY • MAKE AHEAD • CALORIE SMART • GLUTEN FREE • VEGETARIAN • VEGAN

Quick Pickled Red Onions

Enjoy these fermented onions with appetizers or as an accompaniment to sandwiches or your favorite bowls or salads.

PREP 15 Minutes **TOTAL** 3 Hours 15 Minutes • *8 servings* (about ¼ cup each)

1 large red onion, thinly sliced (about ¾ lb)	2 teaspoons salt
1½ cups vegan white wine vinegar	8 to 10 black peppercorns
½ cup water	6 cloves garlic, thinly sliced
2 tablespoons pure maple syrup	

1 In two 1-pint (16-oz) jars, evenly divide onions. In 1½-quart saucepan, heat remaining ingredients to boiling over high heat. Carefully pour mixture over onions. Use a spoon to press onions into vinegar mixture so all the onions are covered.

2 Let stand uncovered 1 hour. Cover and refrigerate at least 2 hours. Store covered in refrigerator up to 3 weeks.

1 Serving Calories 25; Total Fat 0g (Saturated Fat 0g, Trans Fat 0g); Cholesterol 0mg; Sodium 600mg; Total Carbohydrate 6g (Dietary Fiber 0g); Protein 0g **Carbohydrate Choices:** ½

Quick Pickled Red Onons

USE IT UP
CARAMELIZED ONIONS

If your onions are about to spout, make Caramelized Onions with the slow-cooker method (opposite) or on top of the stove (page 67). Store them in the refrigerator up to 1 week. The rich, buttery flavor will turn your dishes into something spectacular.

CARAMELIZED ONION BACON BURGERS Top burgers with sliced American cheese, crisply cooked bacon, and caramelized onions.

QUICK PHILLY CHEESESTEAKS Stir-fry sliced bell peppers and sliced mushrooms with a little steak seasoning; add caramelized onions and heat through. Heat thinly sliced roast beef in skillet; top with sliced provolone cheese. Layer in hoagie buns.

CARAMELIZED ONION HUMMUS Stir chopped caramelized onions and fresh thyme leaves into hummus. Top with additional caramelized onions. Serve with pita wedges, crackers, or veggies.

VEGGIE OMELETS Sauté mushrooms; add grape tomato halves and caramelized onions during the last few minutes of cooking. Fill omelets with veggies.

CARAMELIZED ONION, PROSCIUTTO AND ARUGULA PIZZA Finely chop prosciutto and sauté until crisp. Brush partially baked pizza crust (see page 205) with olive oil; sprinkle with 2 finely chopped garlic cloves. Top with prosciutto, caramelized onion, and shredded mozzarella cheese. Bake as directed. Top with arugula tossed lightly with balsamic vinaigrette.

Caramelized Onion Dip

PREP 20 Minutes TOTAL 10 Hours 20 Minutes •
24 servings (2 tablespoons dip and about 3 toasts each)

DIP

- 8 cups thinly sliced sweet or yellow onions (about 3 lb)
- 2 tablespoons butter, melted
- ½ teaspoon salt
- ½ teaspoon pepper
- 2 packages (8 oz each) cream cheese, cubed, softened
- 1 tablespoon soy sauce
- ½ cup mayonnaise
- 1 tablespoon chopped fresh parsley leaves
- 1 teaspoon chopped fresh thyme leaves, if desired

TOASTS

- 1 loaf (16 inches) baguette French bread, cut into ¼-inch slices
- ¼ cup butter, melted

1 Spray 5-quart slow cooker with cooking spray. Mix onions, 2 tablespoons melted butter, salt and pepper in slow cooker. Cover; cook on Low heat setting 10 to 12 hours or until onions are very tender and browned.

2 Drain onion mixture; discard liquid or reserve for another use. Return onions to slow cooker. Stir cream cheese and soy sauce into onions.

3 Cover; cook on Low heat setting 15 minutes. Stir in mayonnaise; top with parsley and thyme.

4 Meanwhile, heat oven to 325°F. Brush baguette slices on both sides with melted butter. On ungreased cookie sheet, place half the bread slices in single layer. Bake 6 to 8 minutes, turning once, until golden brown and crispy. Repeat with remaining bread slices. Serve with dip.

1 Serving Calories 170; Total Fat 13g (Saturated Fat 6g, Trans Fat 0g); Cholesterol 30mg; Sodium 250mg; Total Carbohydrate 11g (Dietary Fiber 1g); Protein 2g **Carbohydrate Choices:** 1

USE YOUR COOKING LIQUID!

If you're using the slow-cooker method for caramelizing onions, the cooking liquid can be used to add flavor to soups, stews and broths in place of equal amounts of water. Store it covered in the refrigerator 1 week or up to 3 months in the freezer.

FAST

Nachos

PREP 5 Minutes TOTAL 10 Minutes • *4 servings*

- 28 tortilla chips
- 1 cup shredded Monterey Jack or cheddar cheese (4 oz)
- ¼ cup canned chopped green chiles, if desired
- 2 tablespoons sliced ripe olives, well drained
- ⅓ cup sour cream
- ¼ cup salsa

1 Heat oven to 400°F. Line cookie sheet with foil. Spread out tortilla chips on cookie sheet. Sprinkle with cheese, chiles and olives.

2 Bake about 4 minutes or until cheese is melted. Top with sour cream and salsa. Serve hot.

1 Serving Calories 260; Total Fat 18g (Saturated Fat 8g, Trans Fat 0g); Cholesterol 35mg; Sodium 370mg; Total Carbohydrate 15g (Dietary Fiber 1g); Protein 9g **Carbohydrate Choices:** 1

BEEF NACHOS: Sprinkle 1 cup shredded cooked beef over tortilla chips after placing them on the cookie sheet. Continue as directed.

CHICKEN NACHOS: Sprinkle 1 cup shredded cooked chicken over tortilla chips after placing them on the cookie sheet. Continue as directed.

Caramelized Onion Dip

Nachos

Air Fryer Success

It's like a convection oven for your countertop. Rather than using hot oil to crisp and/or cook, air fryers circulate hot, dry air, cutting down on calories and mess! Use these tips to have success when using an air fryer.

What Can I Cook in an Air Fryer?

GOOD

Air fryers work well on these types of foods:

- Foods that are that are usually roasted, baked or deep fried
- Vegetables, bite-size appetizers, wings, pastries, steaks, chops, burgers, shrimp, fish fillets, cookies and cakes
- Frozen packaged foods like pizza rolls and empanadas

BAD

Choose another cooking method if cooking these types of foods, as the air fryer won't give good results for these:

- Foods that require wet heat cooking like boiling, braising and steaming

Tips for Using an Air Fryer

- **Use an Instant-Read Meat Thermometer** When cooking meats and frozen packaged items, use an instant-read meat thermometer to check that items are thoroughly heated.

- **Grease the Basket** Fry baskets have a nonstick coating, but to ensure that your food won't stick, rub it with a little vegetable oil or spray with cooking spray before filling it with the food to cook.

- **Don't Overcrowd the Basket** Or the food will be prevented from crisping and browning.

- **Cook Food in Batches** For small items such as fries, open the air fryer and shake the basket every few minutes. For larger items, cook in single layer (don't stack the food); use silicone tongs to flip the food.

- **Check Food During Cooking** Opening the air fryer will cause it to pause temporarily, but it will resume cooking at the same temperature once the basket is placed back inside.

- **Help Food Stay Crisp** Use vegetable oil in an oil mister or cooking spray to help foods crisp if they don't already contain a lot of fat. Spray items before placing them in the air fryer.

- **Prevent Smoking** Fat can collect in the fryer base when cooking foods high in fat. To prevent smoking, pour a small amount of water into the fryer base before cooking high-fat foods.

Cheesy Jalapeño-Cauliflower Tots

Roasted Beans 3 Ways

Cheesy Jalapeño-Cauliflower Tots

If you prefer, you can drop the cauliflower mixture by tablespoonfuls onto the cookie sheet and then flatten slightly. This will give the tots a flatter shape, but you won't have to individually shape them.

PREP 25 Minutes **TOTAL** 50 Minutes •
6 servings (5 tots each)

3 cups cauliflower florets, cooked (page 247)	¼ teaspoon salt
1 cup shredded pepper Jack cheese (4 oz)	1 egg, beaten Cooking spray Chipotle-Lemon Tartar Sauce (page 484) or French Fry Dipping Sauce (page 482)
⅓ cup all-purpose flour	
2 medium green onions, finely chopped (2 tablespoons)	

1 Heat oven to 375°F. Line cookie sheet with cooking parchment paper. In food processor, place cooked cauliflower florets. Cover; process with on-and-off pulses until cauliflower has rice-like texture. Press cauliflower between clean kitchen towels or paper towels to squeeze out as much liquid as possible.

2 In large bowl, place cauliflower. Add remaining ingredients except cooking spray and sauce. Using wet hands (mixture will be sticky), shape about 1 tablespoon of cauliflower mixture into tot shape; place on cookie sheet. Repeat with remaining cauliflower mixture. Spray tots with cooking spray.

3 Bake 20 to 25 minutes or until golden brown. Serve with tartar sauce.

1 Serving Calories 230; Total Fat 18g (Saturated Fat 6g, Trans Fat 0g); Cholesterol 55mg; Sodium 490mg; Total Carbohydrate 11g (Dietary Fiber 2g); Protein 7g **Carbohydrate Choices:** 1

AIR FRYER DIRECTIONS: Spray air fryer basket with cooking spray. Place one layer of unbaked tots, sides not touching, in air fryer basket. Spray tots with cooking spray. Set to 350°F. Cook 6 to 8 minutes or until golden brown. Repeat with remaining tots.

Roasted Beans 3 Ways

Be sure to bake the beans for the minimum time and add more time if necessary. The beans may pop open and jump in the pan a bit, so use pot holders when stirring. To check for doneness, remove a few beans from various locations in the pan; cool slightly and test for desired crunch and texture. You can always pop them back in the oven until you get the crunch you like. Keep in mind that larger beans will take longer to crisp.

PREP 10 Minutes **TOTAL** 1 Hour 30 Minutes •
5 servings (about ⅓ cup each)

BEANS

2 cans (15 oz each) chick peas (garbanzo beans), butter beans or cannellini beans, rinsed, drained	½ teaspoon ground cumin
2 tablespoons vegetable oil	

EASY INDIAN SEASONING BLEND

2 teaspoons garam masala
½ teaspoon salt

SMOKY MEXICAN SEASONING BLEND

1 teaspoon ground chipotle chile pepper
1 teaspoon lime zest
½ teaspoon salt

ITALIAN HERB SEASONING BLEND

2 teaspoons gluten-free Italian seasoning
½ teaspoon garlic salt

1 Heat oven to 400°F. Place drained beans on several thicknesses of paper towels and blot dry.

2 In medium bowl, stir together vegetable oil and the ingredients for one of the seasoning blends. Stir in beans until evenly coated. Spread out beans in single layer on 15x10-inch baking pan with sides.

3 Bake 45 to 60 minutes, stirring every 15 minutes, until beans are deep golden brown, dry and crunchy. Let cool in pan at least 15 minutes. Store at room temperature in bowl loosely covered with waxed paper up to 5 days.

1 Serving (Smoky Mexican Chick Peas) Calories 210; Total Fat 9g (Saturated Fat 1g, Trans Fat 0g); Cholesterol 0mg; Sodium 500mg; Total Carbohydrate 25g (Dietary Fiber 7g); Protein 7g **Carbohydrate Choices:** 1½

Loaded Kimchi Fries

Patting the chicken dry before adding to the hot skillet not only helps it brown nicely, but it will release easier rather than sticking, too.

PREP 30 Minutes **TOTAL** 55 Minutes •
8 servings (about 1 cup each)

- 1 bag (32 oz) frozen crinkle-cut French-fried potatoes
- ½ cup mayonnaise (for homemade mayonnaise, see page 479)
- 2 tablespoons gochujang (Korean chile paste)
- 1 tablespoon lime juice
- 3 tablespoons butter
- 1 cup thinly sliced kimchi, drained and patted dry
- 1 package (20 oz) boneless skinless chicken thighs, cut into ½-inch strips
- 6 medium green onions, cut diagonally in ¼-inch pieces, white and green parts separated
- 1 tablespoon soy sauce
- 2 cups shredded sharp cheddar cheese (8 oz)
- 1 tablespoon fresh cilantro leaves

1 Heat oven to 425°F. Spray 18x13x1-inch half-sheet pan with cooking spray. Spread frozen potatoes in a single layer in pan; bake 35 to 40 minutes or until crisp on edges and golden brown.

2 Meanwhile, in small bowl, beat mayonnaise, 1 tablespoon of the gochujang and the lime juice with whisk until mixed; set aside.

3 Then, in 10-inch skillet, melt 1 tablespoon of the butter over medium-high heat; add kimchi. Cook 3 to 5 minutes or until it begins to brown. Transfer to another small bowl; cover with foil to keep warm.

Loaded Kimchi Fries

4 Pat chicken dry with paper towels. Add remaining 2 tablespoons butter to skillet; melt over medium-high heat. Add chicken; cook without stirring 4 minutes. Stir chicken; stir in green onion whites, soy sauce and remaining 1 tablespoon gochujang. Cook 4 to 6 minutes, stirring occasionally, until chicken is no longer pink in center. Drain; discard cooking liquid.

5 Push potatoes close together in pan. Top with 1 cup of the cheese, followed by chicken mixture, then the remaining cheese. Top with kimchi. Bake 3 to 5 minutes or just until cheese is melted. Drizzle with mayonnaise mixture; top with green onion greens and cilantro.

1 Serving Calories 480; Total Fat 34g (Saturated Fat 12g, Trans Fat 0.5g); Cholesterol 115mg; Sodium 1040mg; Total Carbohydrate 22g (Dietary Fiber 3g); Protein 23g **Carbohydrate Choices:** 1½

EASY • **MAKE AHEAD** • **CALORIE SMART** • **GLUTEN FREE**

Deviled Eggs

Deviled eggs are a great appetizer choice, no matter what the occasion. From fresh herbs to assertive wasabi, you can flavor the egg yolk filling in so many ways, appealing to any taste. Knowing how to make hard-cooked eggs with bright yellow yolks ensures excellent results.

PREP 15 Minutes **TOTAL** 40 Minutes •
12 servings (1 egg half)

- 6 eggs
- 3 tablespoons mayonnaise, salad dressing or half-and-half (for homemade mayonnaise, see page 479)
- 1 teaspoon prepared mustard (any flavor) or ½ teaspoon ground mustard
- ⅛ teaspoon pepper

1 In 2-quart saucepan, place eggs in single layer. Cover with cold water at least 1 inch above eggs. Cover saucepan; heat to boiling.

2 Immediately remove from heat; let stand covered 15 minutes for large eggs, 12 minutes for medium eggs and 18 minutes for extra-large eggs.

3 Drain. Immediately place eggs in cold water with ice cubes, or run cold water over eggs until completely cooled.

4 To peel, gently tap egg on countertop until entire shell is finely crackled. Roll gently between hands to loosen shell. Starting at large end, peel egg under cold running water to help remove shell.

5 Cut lengthwise in half. Slip out yolks into small bowl; mash with fork. To prevent eggs from tipping on serving plate, cut a thin slice from bottom of each egg white half before filling. Or to stand eggs upright, cut crosswise slice about ⅔ from top of narrow end of egg to remove yolk; cut thin slice from bottom of wide end of egg white to rest on serving platter.

Spicy Sriracha Deviled Eggs

MAKING DEVILED EGGS

Cut a thin slice from bottom of each egg half so eggs can sit on platter.

Spoon prepared filling into egg halves or use cookie scoop to fill eggs.

6 Add mayonnaise, mustard and pepper to yolks and mash until smooth. Fill whites with egg yolk mixture, heaping it lightly. Serve or cover and refrigerate up to 24 hours.

1 Serving Calories 60; Total Fat 5g (Saturated Fat 1g, Trans Fat 0g); Cholesterol 95mg; Sodium 60mg; Total Carbohydrate 0g (Dietary Fiber 0g); Protein 3g **Carbohydrate Choices:** 0

LIGHTER DIRECTIONS: For 1 gram of fat and 25 calories per serving, mash only 6 yolk halves in Step 6 (reserve remaining yolks for another use or discard). Use fat-free mayonnaise. Stir in ⅓ cup finely chopped zucchini.

AVOCADO DEVILED EGGS: Omit mustard. Add ½ ripe avocado, 1 teaspoon fresh lemon juice and ⅛ teaspoon salt to the yolks in Step 6. Sprinkle with chopped chives before serving.

BACON-CHEDDAR DEVILED EGGS: Mix 2 or 3 slices crumbled crisply cooked bacon and 2 tablespoons finely shredded cheddar cheese into yolk mixture. Garnish with additional crumbled bacon or chopped fresh chives or parsley.

BLUE CHEESE DEVILED EGGS: Omit mustard. Mix ¼ cup crumbled blue cheese into yolk mixture. Garnish with coarse ground black pepper and small celery leaves.

CHIPOTLE DEVILED EGGS: Omit mustard. Mix 1½ to 2 teaspoons finely chopped chipotle chiles in adobo sauce (from 7-oz can), drained, and 1 thinly sliced green onion into yolk mixture. Garnish with whole or chopped cilantro leaves.

CURRIED DEVILED EGGS: Omit mustard. Mix 2 tablespoons mango chutney (finely chop larger pieces of fruit if needed) and ¼ teaspoon curry powder into yolk mixture. Garnish with cashews or dry-roasted peanuts.

FRESH HERB DEVILED EGGS: Mix 1 teaspoon each chopped fresh chives, parsley and dill into yolk mixture. If desired, substitute basil or marjoram for the dill. Garnish with additional fresh herbs.

SPICY SRIRACHA DEVILED EGGS: Increase mayonnaise to ¼ cup and mustard to 1½ teaspoons. Omit pepper. Drizzle Sriracha sauce over egg yolk mixture; garnish with chopped cilantro leaves.

ZESTY DEVILED EGGS: Mix ½ cup finely shredded cheddar cheese, 2 tablespoons chopped fresh parsley and 1 to 2 teaspoons prepared horseradish into yolk mixture. Garnish with additional cheese or parsley.

58

Cheddar-Stuffed
Pretzel Nuggets

Curry Beef Empanadas

Cheddar-Stuffed Pretzel Nuggets

PREP 45 Minutes TOTAL 1 Hour 15 Minutes •
48 servings (1 pretzel nugget and 2 teaspoons dip)

PRETZELS

- 3¾ to 4¼ cups all-purpose flour
- 1 tablespoon sugar
- ½ teaspoon table salt
- 1 package (¼ oz) regular active or fast-acting dry yeast (2¼ teaspoons)
- 1½ cups very warm water (120°F to 130°F)
- 1 tablespoon butter, melted
- ½ cup shredded cheddar cheese (2 oz)
- 4 slices bacon, crisply cooked, crumbled
- 2 tablespoons finely chopped seeded jalapeño chiles (about 2 medium)
- 2 cans or bottles (16 oz each) American-style lager beer
- 2 tablespoons baking soda
- 1 egg, beaten
- 1 tablespoon coarse (kosher or sea) salt

BEER CHEESE DIP

- 1 package (8 oz) cream cheese, cut into cubes, softened
- ¾ cup American-style lager beer (reserved from 1 can above)
- 2 cups shredded cheddar cheese (8 oz)

1 Line two large cookie sheets with cooking parchment paper. In large bowl, mix 3¾ cups of the flour, the sugar, table salt and yeast. Add warm water and butter; beat with electric mixer on medium speed 3 minutes, scraping bowl frequently and adding additional flour, ¼ cup at a time, until dough is soft and leaves side of bowl. Divide dough into 4 equal portions.

2 On lightly floured surface, one dough portion at a time, roll portion into 12x4-inch rectangle. On one long side of rectangle, sprinkle 2 tablespoons cheddar cheese, 2 teaspoons bacon and 1½ teaspoons jalapeño. Starting at same long side, roll up dough; firmly pinch edges to seal. Cut each roll into 12 (1-inch) pieces; pinch ends to seal. Place on cookie sheets. Repeat with remaining dough, cheese, bacon, and jalapeño. Cover with plastic wrap; let stand 30 minutes.

3 Heat oven to 425°F. Reserve ¾ cup of the beer for dip. In 3-quart saucepan, heat remaining 3¼ cups beer and the baking soda to boiling; reduce heat to low. Gently place 4 or 5 dough pieces in beer; cook about 20 seconds, turning once, until dough is slightly puffed. Remove with slotted spoon; return to cookie sheets. Repeat with remaining dough pieces. Brush with egg; sprinkle with coarse salt. Bake 8 to 10 minutes or until golden brown.

4 Meanwhile, in 2-quart saucepan, cook cream cheese and reserved beer over medium heat 6 to 7 minutes, stirring frequently, until cream cheese is melted. Stir in cheddar cheese a little at a time; cook about 4 minutes, stirring frequently, until all cheese is melted and sauce is smooth. Serve warm pretzel nuggets with warm dip.

1 Serving Calories 90; Total Fat 4.5g (Saturated Fat 2.5g, Trans Fat 0g); Cholesterol 15mg; Sodium 320mg; Total Carbohydrate 8g (Dietary Fiber 0g); Protein 3g **Carbohydrate Choices:** ½

MAKE-AHEAD DIRECTIONS: You can make these delicious party snacks well in advance. Place baked cooled pretzel nuggets in a resealable freezer plastic bag; freeze up to 2 weeks. To reheat, place on cookie sheets and bake at 350°F 12 to 14 minutes or until hot. Make the dip while they bake.

MAKE AHEAD • CALORIE SMART

Curry Beef Empanadas

PREP 50 Minutes **TOTAL** 1 Hour 10 Minutes •
20 servings (1 empanada and 2 teaspoons sauce each)

EMPANADAS

- ½ lb ground beef (at least 80% lean)
- ½ cup chopped onion
- 2 cloves garlic, finely chopped
- ¼ cup mango chutney (from 9-oz jar)
- 2 teaspoons curry powder
- ¼ teaspoon salt

Pie Pastry for Two-Crust Pie (page 607), prepared through Step 2, or 1 box (14.1 oz) refrigerated pie crusts, softened as directed on box

- 1 egg, slightly beaten

SOUR CREAM CHUTNEY DIP

- ¾ cup sour cream
- 2 tablespoons finely chopped green onions
- 2 tablespoons mango chutney (from 9-oz jar)
  Sliced green onion, if desired

1   Heat oven to 400°F. Line large cookie sheet with cooking parchment paper. In 10-inch nonstick skillet, cook beef, onion and garlic over medium-high heat 5 to 7 minutes, stirring occasionally, until thoroughly cooked. Remove from heat; drain. Stir in ¼ cup chutney, the curry powder and salt; set aside.

2   Roll 1 pie pastry round into 12-inch circle. With 3½-inch round cutter, cut circles from pastry. Repeat with second pastry round, rerolling dough to get 20 circles.

3   Place about 1 tablespoon beef mixture on center of each round. Brush edges with beaten egg. Fold dough over filling; pinch edges firmly together and press with fork to seal. Place empanadas on cookie sheet about ½ inch apart. Prick tops with fork to allow steam to escape. Brush with beaten egg.

4   Bake 13 to 15 minutes or until golden brown. Remove from cookie sheet to cooling rack. Cool 10 minutes.

5   Meanwhile, in small bowl, mix dip ingredients except green onion until well blended. Sprinkle with green onion. Serve warm empanadas with dip.

1 Serving Calories 130; Total Fat 8g (Saturated Fat 4.5g, Trans Fat 0g); Cholesterol 45mg; Sodium 120mg; Total Carbohydrate 11g (Dietary Fiber 0g); Protein 3g **Carbohydrate Choices:** 1

MAKE-AHEAD DIRECTIONS: Freeze baked empanadas tightly covered. To reheat, place on cookie sheet and bake at 350°F about 10 minutes.

Thai Peanut-Chicken Wonton Cups

CALORIE SMART

Thai Peanut-Chicken Wonton Cups

Smaller shreds of carrots fit better in these bite-size appetizers, and are easier to eat. You can quickly shred your own carrot, or if you purchase matchstick carrots, coarsely chop them first.

PREP 20 Minutes **TOTAL** 40 Minutes • *24 cups*

- 24 wonton wrappers (about 3¼-inch square; from 12-oz package)
- ¼ cup unsweetened coconut milk (from 14-oz can; not cream of coconut) •
- 1 tablespoon packed brown sugar
- 1 tablespoon soy sauce
- 2 tablespoons creamy peanut butter

- 2 teaspoons red curry paste
- 2 teaspoons finely chopped gingerroot
- 2 cups chopped cooked chicken
- ⅓ cup finely shredded carrot
- 2 tablespoons chopped fresh cilantro
  Lime wedges, if desired

1   Heat oven to 375°F. Spray 24 mini muffin cups with cooking spray. Carefully press 1 wonton skin into each cup, allowing wrapper edges to extend above edge of cups; spray wonton wrappers lightly with cooking spray.

2   In medium bowl, mix coconut milk, brown sugar, soy sauce, peanut butter, curry paste and gingerroot with whisk until blended. Add chicken; stir to coat. Fill each wonton cup with a heaping tablespoon of chicken mixture.

3   Bake 17 to 19 minutes or until filling is hot and wontons are crisp and golden brown. Top with carrots and cilantro. Serve warm with lime wedges.

1 Cup Calories 60; Total Fat 2g (Saturated Fat 1g, Trans Fat 0g); Cholesterol 10mg; Sodium 75mg; Total Carbohydrate 6g (Dietary Fiber 0g); Protein 4g **Carbohydrate Choices:** ½

The Magic of Meatballs

Whip up a batch of meatballs and keep them on hand for easy appetizers or meals at your fingertips! Totally customizable, they can be made with whatever ground meat you have—ground beef, chicken or turkey. See page 63 for the basic meatball recipe plus lots of variations, or use what you have on hand to create your own meatball flavor.

Change the Size

Mini meatballs make great one-bite appetizers. Serve them with toothpicks so they are easy to grab. Or skewer them with bite-size pieces of veggies, brush with a sauce such as barbecue or chili sauce and bake at 350°F 15 to 20 minutes or until veggies are tender.

Regular-size meatballs are great for dinner recipes. Use them to fill slider buns or hot dog buns for a quick sandwich or serve with cooked pasta or stir-fried veggies for a quick meal.

Change the Flavor

Try changing the flavor of the bread crumbs or adding different seasonings or change the sauce they are served in.

Change the Shape

Make square meatballs and skip the rolling step! In 13x9-inch pan, pat uncooked meatball mixture into a rectangle either 1½ inches thick for regular meatballs or 1 inch thick for mini meatballs. Using knife dipped in water, cut mixture into squares, but do not separate. Bake as directed. Cool slightly and separate meatballs by cutting them apart with knife.

Serve 'em Up

There are endless ways to use cooked meatballs! Try one of these delicious ideas.

Hawaiian Meatball Flatbread Toss turkey or chicken meatballs in teriyaki or sweet-and-sour sauce. Spread pizza sauce over purchased flatbread; top with meatballs, chopped green onions, shredded mozzarella cheese, drained pineapple tidbits and crumbled crisply cooked bacon. Bake as directed on flatbread package.

Sweet Chili Meatball Skewers Thread mini meatballs, small whole fresh mushrooms, and bell pepper strips on bamboo skewers. Place on cookie sheet; brush with sweet chili sauce. Bake 15 to 20 minutes or until vegetables are crisp-tender and meatballs are hot.

Asian Meatball Bowl Heat meatballs in teriyaki sauce until hot. Spoon hot cooked rice into individual serving bowls and top with meatballs and stir-fried veggies. Sprinkle with sesame seed, if desired.

Meatball Heros Heat meatballs in ketchup with Sriracha sauce to taste. Spoon meatballs into hero buns and top with slices of American cheese. Broil 2 to 3 minute or until cheese is melted.

Barbecue Meatballs Alfredo Heat meatballs in barbecue sauce. Toss hot cooked noodles with Alfredo sauce and top with meatballs. Sprinkle with chopped parsley.

MAKING MEATBALLS

Shape mixture into 1- or 1½-inch balls. Place in pan.

Bake until no longer pink in center and instant-read thermometer reads correct temperature for meat used.

MAKING SQUARE MEATBALLS

Skip rolling the meatballs by making them square.

Sweet Chili
Meatball Skewers

5-INGREDIENT RECIPE

American Cheese

Steak Sauce

Ground Beef

ORIGINAL STEAK SAUCE
FOR STEAKS, PORK AND CHICKEN
NET WT 8.5 OZ (241g)

Quality Foods.
PROGRESSO
PANKO
CRISPY BREAD CRUMBS
PLAIN

PER 1/4 CUP SERVING
100 CALORIES 0 SAT FAT 55 SODIUM <1g TOTAL SUGARS

PROGRESSO
PANKO
CRISPY BREAD CRUMBS

Egg

Panko Crumbs

Steakhouse Cheeseburger Meatballs

5-INGREDIENT RECIPE

CALORIE SMART

Steakhouse Cheeseburger Meatballs

Hello, easiest appetizer ever! Spiked with bold steakhouse seasoning and plenty of cheese, these meatballs are greater than the sum of their parts and guaranteed to win big.

PREP 30 Minutes **TOTAL** 1 Hour 30 Minutes • *20 meatballs*

1 lb ground beef (at least 80% lean)	½ teaspoon salt
¼ cup plain panko crispy bread crumbs	¼ teaspoon pepper
	1 tablespoon water
3 tablespoons steak sauce	5 slices (¾ oz each) American cheese, each cut in 4 squares
1 egg	

1 In medium bowl, mix beef, bread crumbs, 1 tablespoon of the steak sauce, the egg, salt and pepper. Shape mixture into 20 (1½-inch) meatballs. Refrigerate 1 hour.*

2 Heat 12-inch nonstick skillet over medium heat. Add meatballs. Cook 12 to 14 minutes, turning frequently, until brown on all sides and instant-read meat thermometer inserted in center reads 160°F. Remove from heat. Add remaining 2 tablespoons steak sauce and the water, and gently stir to coat. Top each meatball with cheese square; cover 1 to 2 minutes or until cheese melts.

1 Meatball Calories 70; Total Fat 4.5g (Saturated Fat 2g, Trans Fat 0g); Cholesterol 30mg; Sodium 200mg; Total Carbohydrate 2g (Dietary Fiber 0g); Protein 5g **Carbohydrate Choices:** 0

*Refrigerating meatballs helps them hold their shape during cooking.

CALORIE SMART

Meatballs

PREP 15 Minutes **TOTAL** 40 Minutes • *20 meatballs*

1 lb ground beef (at least 80% lean)	½ teaspoon Worcestershire sauce
½ cup unseasoned dry bread crumbs	¼ teaspoon pepper
¼ cup milk	1 small onion, finely chopped (½ cup)
½ teaspoon salt	1 egg

1 Heat oven to 400°F. In large bowl, mix all ingredients. Shape mixture into 20 (1½-inch) meatballs. In ungreased 13x9-inch pan or on rack in broiler pan, place meatballs.

2 Bake uncovered 20 to 25 minutes or until no longer pink in center and instant-read meat thermometer inserted in center reads 160°F. If not using immediately, cool completely and cover and refrigerate 3 to 4 days or freeze 2 to 3 months. Reheat in desired homemade or bottled sauce such as teriyaki, cocktail or sweet-and-sour.

1 Meatball Calories 60; Total Fat 3g (Saturated Fat 1g, Trans Fat 0g); Cholesterol 25mg; Sodium 95mg; Total Carbohydrate 2g (Dietary Fiber 0g); Protein 4g **Carbohydrate Choices:** 0

MINI MEATBALLS: Shape beef mixture into 1-inch balls. Bake 15 to 20 minutes. Makes 3 dozen appetizers.

SKILLET MEATBALLS: Prepare as directed—except after Step 2, cover and refrigerate meatballs 1 hour. In 10-inch skillet, cook meatballs over medium heat about 20 minutes, turning occasionally, until no longer pink in center and instant-read meat thermometer inserted in center of meatball reads 160°F.

TURKEY OR CHICKEN MEATBALLS: Substitute 1 lb ground turkey or chicken for the ground beef. (If using ground chicken, reduce milk to 2 tablespoons.) To bake, spray 13x9-inch pan with cooking spray before adding meatballs; bake until no longer pink in center and instant-read meat thermometer inserted in center reads at least 165°F. To cook in skillet, heat 1 tablespoon vegetable oil over medium heat before adding meatballs; cook until no longer pink in center and meat thermometer inserted in center reads at least 165°F.

PORK MEATBALLS: Substitute 1 lb ground pork for the ground beef, or substitute ½ lb ground pork for ½ lb of the ground beef.

ITALIAN MEATBALLS: Substitute Italian-style bread crumbs for the plain bread crumbs.

NASHVILLE HOT CHICKEN MEATBALLS: Substitute ground chicken for the beef, increase bread crumbs to ⅔ cup and omit Worcestershire sauce and pepper. Add 2 tablespoons original cayenne pepper sauce, ¼ teaspoon ground red pepper (cayenne) and 2 cloves chopped garlic. In 2-quart saucepan, mix ¼ cup butter, 2 tablespoons packed brown sugar, 2 tablespoons original cayenne pepper sauce , 1 teaspoon paprika and ½ teaspoon each ground red pepper (cayenne) and salt. Cook over medium heat until butter is melted and brown sugar is dissolved. Add cooked meatballs; toss to coat. Reduce heat to medium-low. Cover and cook 1 to 2 minutes or until meatballs are hot.

MAPLE-GLAZED MEATBALLS: In 2-quart saucepan, mix ¾ cup barbecue sauce and ¼ cup maple-flavored or pure maple syrup. Heat over medium heat, stirring frequently, until hot. Add cooked meatballs; cover and simmer 1 to 2 minutes or until meatballs are hot.

QUICK QUESADILLAS

Quesadillas are a great go-to when you're looking for a hearty snack, light meal or dinner in a snap. Try one of these yummy filling combinations, or use up what you have in your fridge.

Quesadilla Fillings

BEEF AND MUSHROOM

Pizza cheese, cooked boneless beef, cooked sliced mushrooms

BUFFALO CHICKEN

Mozzarella cheese, leftover chopped boneless Buffalo chicken and celery, blue cheese crumbles

HAM AND SWISS

Swiss cheese, ham, green onions

SHRIMP AND AVOCADO

Pepper Jack cheese, chopped cooked shrimp, avocado

VEGGIES AND CHEESE

Cheddar cheese, chopped cooked veggies

How to Cook Quesadillas

Use these directions to cook quesadillas.

BRUSH tortillas lightly with butter on one side.

PLACE one tortilla, buttered side down, on griddle or large skillet.

SPRINKLE lightly with shredded cheese.

TOP with finely chopped other fillings.

SPRINKLE lightly with more cheese.

TOP with another tortilla, buttered side up.

COOK over medium-low heat until bottom has golden-brown spots; carefully turn. Cook until bottom has golden-brown spots and cheese is melted. Cut into wedges with pizza cutter or knife.

Serve with a Dipping Sauce

Raid your fridge for a sauce such as barbecue or chili sauce, salsa or ranch dressing to serve with the quesadilla wedges or try one of these.

Any pesto (for homemade, see page 480)

Chipotle-Lemon Tartar sauce (page 484)

Fish Taco Sauce (page 483)

French Fry Dipping Sauce (page 482)

Yum Yum Sauce (page 485)

FAST • CALORIE SMART

Monte Cristo Quesadillas

PREP 20 Minutes TOTAL 30 Minutes •
18 servings (1 wedge and about 1 tablespoon preserves)

¼ cup mayonnaise (for homemade mayonnaise, see page 479)
2 teaspoons Dijon mustard
6 (6-inch) flour tortillas
6 very thin slices cooked ham (3 oz)
6 very thin slices cooked turkey (3 oz)
3 slices (¾ oz each) Swiss cheese, cut in half diagonally
2 eggs
2 tablespoons milk
1 cup plain panko crispy bread crumbs
2 tablespoons butter, melted
1 tablespoon powdered sugar
1 cup raspberry preserves

1 Heat oven to 425°F. Line large cookie sheet with cooking parchment paper.

2 In small bowl, mix mayonnaise and mustard until well blended. Spread about 2 teaspoons on one side of each tortilla to within ¼ inch of edge. Divide ham, turkey and cheese on one half of each tortilla. Fold tortillas in half over fillings; press lightly. Cut each tortilla into 3 wedges.

3 In small bowl, beat eggs with fork; stir in milk until well blended. In another small bowl, toss panko crumbs and melted butter until well mixed. One at a time, dip tortilla wedges in egg mixture; shake off excess. Dip in panko mixture, pressing crumbs lightly into tortilla; place on cookie sheet.

4 Bake 8 to 10 minutes, turning after 5 minutes, until wedges are golden brown and cheese is melted.

5 Sprinkle with powdered sugar. Serve with raspberry preserves.

1 Serving Calories 170; Total Fat 7g (Saturated Fat 2.5g, Trans Fat 0g); Cholesterol 35mg; Sodium 230mg; Total Carbohydrate 22g (Dietary Fiber 0g); Protein 4g **Carbohydrate Choices:** 1½

Monte Cristo Quesadillas

Mini Pork Carnitas Tacos

If using ribs, they may be too lean to render enough fat to get brown and crisp. If you don't see any fat in the skillet after the water has evaporated in Step 1, add 1 tablespoon vegetable oil. Continue as directed.

PREP 45 Minutes **TOTAL** 1 Hour 45 Minutes •
20 servings (3 tacos each)

CARNITAS

- 2 lb boneless pork shoulder or butt, or country-style ribs, cut into 1-inch pieces
- 1 small onion, chopped (½ cup)
- 3 cloves garlic, finely chopped
- 1 teaspoon dried marjoram leaves
- 1 teaspoon dried thyme leaves
- ¾ teaspoon salt
- ¼ teaspoon pepper

GREEN SALSA CREMA

- ⅔ cup crema (Mexican-style cream) or sour cream
- ⅔ cup green tomatillo salsa

TACOS

- 15 flour tortillas (10- to 12-inch)
- 3 cups shredded iceberg lettuce
- 2 ripe medium avocados, peeled, pitted, each cut into 15 slices
- 1¼ cups crumbled Cotija or queso fresco cheese
- 1 jar (24 oz) roasted red bell peppers, drained, cut into ¼x½-inch strips

1 In 12-inch skillet, place meat in single layer. Add cold water until meat is almost but not completely covered (about 1½ cups). Add remaining carnitas ingredients. Heat to boiling; reduce heat to medium. Cook uncovered 35 to 45 minutes or until liquid has evaporated and meat begins to brown.

2 Meanwhile, in small bowl, mix crema and salsa; cover and refrigerate until serving time. Using 4-inch round cookie or biscuit cutter, cut 4 mini tortillas out of each tortilla. Cover with plastic wrap to prevent drying out; set aside.

3 Heat oven to 425°F. Into 15x10x1-inch pan, spoon meat mixture, pan juices and any browned bits from skillet. Bake uncovered 10 to 15 minutes or until pork is brown and edges are crisp. Drain fat if necessary; scrape any browned bits from pan and set aside. Cut meat into ¼-inch pieces; place in medium bowl. Mix in browned bits.

4 To assemble tacos, spoon 1 tablespoon pork down center of each mini tortilla; top each with 1 tablespoon lettuce, 1 avocado slice, about 3 roasted pepper strips and 1 teaspoon cheese. Drizzle each with about 1 teaspoon green salsa crema.

1 Serving Calories 310; Total Fat 16g (Saturated Fat 6g, Trans Fat 0.5g); Cholesterol 40mg; Sodium 690mg; Total Carbohydrate 27g (Dietary Fiber 2g); Protein 14g **Carbohydrate Choices:** 2

Mini Pork Carnitas Tacos

Mini Hot Dog–Pimiento Cheese Bites

3 Cut each slice of bread into 3 rectangular pieces with sharp knife. Place a sausage on one end of each rectangle; roll up. Place rolls, seam side down, on cookie sheet. In small bowl, mix butter and dill weed; brush over each roll.

4 Bake for 7 to 8 minutes or until edges are golden brown. Meanwhile, stir milk into remaining cheese mixture.

5 Just before serving, microwave cheese mixture uncovered on High 30 seconds to warm. Serve dip with bites.

1 Serving Calories 90; Total Fat 8g (Saturated Fat 3.5g, Trans Fat 0g); Cholesterol 15mg; Sodium 130mg; Total Carbohydrate 0g (Dietary Fiber 0g); Protein 2g **Carbohydrate Choices:** 0

CALORIE SMART

Buffalo-Barbecue Chicken Wings

PREP 20 Minutes **TOTAL** 55 Minutes •
12 servings (2 wing pieces each)

12 chicken wings (about 2 lb)	½ teaspoon Cajun seasoning
2 tablespoons butter	¼ teaspoon ground cumin
½ cup all-purpose flour	1 cup blue cheese dressing, if desired (for homemade, see page 148)
½ teaspoon salt	
¼ teaspoon pepper	
1 cup barbecue sauce	Celery, carrot and zucchini sticks, if desired
1 tablespoon red pepper sauce	

1 Heat oven to 425°F. Cut each chicken wing at the joints to make 3 pieces; discard tip. Cut off and discard excess skin.

2 In 13x9-inch pan, melt butter in oven. In 1-gallon resealable food-storage plastic bag, mix flour, salt and pepper. Add chicken; seal bag tightly. Shake until chicken is completely coated with flour mixture. Place chicken in pan.

3 Bake uncovered 20 minutes. In small bowl, mix barbecue sauce, pepper sauce, Cajun seasoning and cumin. Turn chicken. Pour sauce mixture over chicken; toss until evenly coated with sauce. Bake 10 to 12 minutes longer or until juice of chicken is clear when thickest part is cut to bone (at least 165°F).

4 Serve with dressing and vegetables.

1 Serving Calories 110; Total Fat 3.5g (Saturated Fat 1.5g, Trans Fat 0g); Cholesterol 20mg; Sodium 430mg; Total Carbohydrate 13g (Dietary Fiber 0g); Protein 6g **Carbohydrate Choices:** 1

FAST • CALORIE SMART

Mini Hot Dog–Pimiento Cheese Bites

You can use any soft bread to make these bites. A sandwich loaf bread is more rectangular in shape, making less waste when the crusts are trimmed. Use the crusts to make dry bread crumbs for topping egg and vegetable dishes or even salads.

PREP 20 Minutes **TOTAL** 30 Minutes •
12 Servings (1 bite and 1 tablespoon dip each)

PIMIENTO CHEESE

1 cup shredded cheddar cheese (4 oz)	5 drops red pepper sauce
¼ cup mayonnaise (for homemade mayonnaise, see page 479)	1 tablespoon milk
	BITES
2 tablespoons drained chopped pimiento (from 2-oz jar)	4 slices soft sandwich bread
2 oz (from 8-oz package) cream cheese, softened	12 cocktail-size smoked link sausages (from 14-oz package)
	1 tablespoon butter, melted
	¼ teaspoon dried dill weed

1 Heat oven to 400°F. Line cookie sheet with cooking parchment paper. In small microwavable bowl, mix all pimiento cheese ingredients except milk.

2 Cut crusts from bread; flatten with rolling pin. Spread each slice with a generous tablespoon of the pimiento cheese; reserve remaining pimiento cheese for dip.

Caramelized Onion, Nectarine and Bacon Flatbread

PREP 50 Minutes **TOTAL** 1 Hour 10 Minutes • *12 slices*

FLATBREAD

Pizza Crust
(page 204)

CARAMELIZED ONIONS

2 tablespoons butter

2 large sweet onions or
yellow onions, sliced
(4 cups)

2 teaspoons chopped
fresh or ½ teaspoon
dried thyme leaves

¼ teaspoon salt

¼ teaspoon pepper

TOPPING

1 container (8 oz)
soft spreadable
cream cheese

½ cup crumbled chèvre
(goat) or blue cheese
(2 oz)

1 ripe nectarine, pitted,
thinly sliced

2 tablespoons
crisply cooked,
crumbled bacon

Chopped fresh thyme,
if desired

1   Make pizza crust as directed in recipe—except after resting, divide dough into 3 equal portions. Reserve 1 portion for another use.

2   While the dough is resting, in 12-inch nonstick skillet, melt butter over medium-high heat. Stir in onions, thyme, salt and pepper. Cook uncovered 15 to 20 minutes, stirring frequently, until deep golden brown.

3   Heat oven to 425°F. Line large cookie sheet with cooking parchment paper. Pat each dough portion into 12x6-inch rectangle. Place crusts on pan, about 2 inches apart. Prick crusts with fork every few inches to prevent air bubbles. Bake 9 to 11 minutes or until crusts are golden brown. Cool 5 minutes.

4   Spread cream cheese to within ½ inch of edge of each crust. Sprinkle evenly with goat cheese. Arrange caramelized onions and nectarine slices evenly over cheese. Sprinkle with bacon and thyme.

5   Bake 4 to 5 minutes or until topping is heated through. Cut each flatbread crosswise into 6 slices.

1 Slice Calories 200; Total Fat 12g (Saturated Fat 6g, Trans Fat 0g); Cholesterol 25mg; Sodium 310mg; Total Carbohydrate 20g (Dietary Fiber 1g); Protein 5g **Carbohydrate Choices:** 1

MAKE-AHEAD DIRECTIONS: The unused dough can be shaped and baked as directed in Step 3, for a quick snack or appetizer any time. After cooling, place in resealable freezer plastic bag, removing all air. Freeze up to 3 months. Thaw at room temperature before topping with your favorite toppings and heating.

CARAMELIZED ONION AND GRAPE OR PEAR FLATBREAD: Prepare as directed—except substitute 1 cup green or red seedless grape halves or a sliced ripe pear (any variety) for the nectarine.

PESTO CAPRESE FLATBREAD: Heat oven to 375°F. Place 1 baked crust on baking sheet. Spread 2 tablespoons pesto over flatbread. Arrange 8 oz sliced fresh mozzarella and 2 medium tomatoes, sliced, over pesto. Bake 4 to 5 minutes or until toppings are warm. Sprinkle with ⅛ teaspoon coarse salt, ⅛ teaspoon coarsely ground pepper and 1½ teaspoons balsamic vinegar. Drizzle with 1 tablespoon pesto.

CARAMELIZED ONION AND BLUEBERRY FLATBREAD: Prepare as directed—except substitute about 1 cup fresh blueberries for the nectarine. Omit bacon.

CARAMELIZED ONION, APPLE AND PROSCIUTTO FLATBREAD: Prepare as directed—except substitute thinly sliced apple for the nectarine and chopped prosciutto for the bacon.

CARAMELIZED ONION AND CRANBERRY-POMEGRANATE FLATBREAD: Prepare as directed—except spoon ⅔ cup whole cranberry sauce over cheeses. After topping flatbreads with caramelized onions, top with ¼ cup fresh pomegranate seeds and the bacon. Omit nectarine and thyme.

CARAMELIZING ONIONS

Melt butter; add thinly sliced onions and seasonings. Cook, stirring frequently, until deep golden brown.

Caramelized Onion, Nectarine and Bacon Flatbbread

Crispy Panfried Panko Shrimp

Most fresh shrimp at grocery stores have been frozen and thawed already, so purchasing frozen shrimp and thawing them yourself most likely will be a cheaper option.

PREP 20 Minutes **TOTAL** 30 Minutes • *4 servings*

¼	cup all-purpose flour	3	tablespoons vegetable oil
½	teaspoon salt		Chopped fresh chives, if desired
⅛	teaspoon ground red pepper (cayenne)	1	lemon, halved
2	eggs		Tartar sauce (for homemade, see page 484), cocktail sauce, or pasta sauce (for homemade, see page 201), if desired
¾	cup plain panko crispy bread crumbs		
12	uncooked jumbo shrimp (¾ lb), thawed if frozen, peeled (with tail shells left on), deveined		

1 In shallow dish, stir together flour, salt and red pepper. In another shallow dish, lightly beat eggs. In another shallow dish, place bread crumbs.

2 Pat shrimp dry with paper towels. Coat shrimp with flour mixture. Dip into eggs; shake off excess. Coat well with crumb mixture.

3 In 12-inch skillet, heat oil over medium-high heat. Add shrimp in a single layer; immediately reduce heat to medium. Cook 3 to 6 minutes, turning once, until shrimp are pink and coating turns golden brown. Garnish with chives and serve with lemon and sauce.

1 Serving Calories 290; Total Fat 14g (Saturated Fat 2.5g, Trans Fat0g); Cholesterol 190mg; Sodium 420mg; Total Carbohydrate 23g (Dietary Fiber 0g); Protein 18g **Carbohydrate Choices:** 1½

SMOKY PANKO SHRIMP: Add 1 teaspoon smoked paprika to flour mixture.

Cheesy Pull-Apart Garlic Bread

You can use one piece of heavy-duty foil from a wide roll or two 24-inch-long regular pieces of foil, overlapping, for the bread.

PREP 20 Minutes **TOTAL** 50 Minutes • *16 servings*

1	round loaf (about 1 lb) crusty bread (sourdough, Italian, rustic wheat)	1	tablespoon finely chopped fresh rosemary or 1 teaspoon dried rosemary leaves
½	cup butter, softened	3	cloves garlic, finely chopped
¼	cup grated Parmesan cheese	10	slices provolone cheese (from 8-oz package)

1 Heat oven to 350°F. Cut bread vertically in 1-inch slices to within ½ inch of bottom of loaf; do not cut through loaf. Give bread a quarter turn; cut bread vertically again in 1-inch slices to create 1-inch square sticks that are connected at bottom of loaf. Place 18x24-inch piece foil on cookie sheet; place bread in middle of foil.

2 In small bowl, mix butter, Parmesan cheese, rosemary, and garlic until well blended. Open cuts gently with one hand and spread butter mixture between slices and over top of loaf using small spatula or table knife.

3 Cut 5 of the cheese slices in half; cut each remaining cheese slice into 8 wedges. Arrange cheese halves in the first row of cuts. Place a cheese wedge in each of the remaining spaces. Spray foil with cooking spray around bread loaf. Wrap loaf in foil to seal.

4 Bake 20 minutes. Open foil; bake 5 to 10 minutes longer or until cheese is melted. Serve warm.

1 Serving Calories 180; Total Fat 10g (Saturated Fat 6g, Trans Fat 0g); Cholesterol 25mg; Sodium 330mg; Total Carbohydrate 15g (Dietary Fiber 0g); Protein 7g **Carbohydrate Choices:** 1

Crispy Panfried Panko Shrimp

Cheesy Pull-Apart Garlic Bread

Shrimp–Pimiento Cheese Toast

CALORIE SMART

Shrimp–Pimiento Cheese Toast

Shredding your own cheese and using an electric hand mixer to beat the cheese mixture ensures a creamy spread.

PREP 25 Minutes **TOTAL** 40 Minutes • *20 slices*

- 1 loaf ciabatta bread (about 14 oz)
- 2 tablespoons mayonnaise
- 2 teaspoons pickled jalapeño juice (from 12-oz jar pickled jalapeño slices)
- 1 teaspoon Dijon mustard
- ¾ teaspoon lemon juice
- ¾ teaspoon soy sauce
- 5 oz extra-sharp cheddar cheese, shredded (1⅓ cups)
- 1 oz Colby cheese, shredded (⅓ cup)
- ¾ cup coarsely chopped peeled cooked shrimp, thawed if frozen
- ¼ cup finely chopped red bell pepper
- 2 teaspoons chopped pickled jalapeño slices (from 12-oz jar pickled jalapeño slices)
- 1 jar (2 oz) diced pimientos, drained
- 1 medium green onion, thinly sliced (1 tablespoon)

  Additional thinly sliced green onion, if desired

1 Heat oven to 375°F. Line 15x10x1-inch pan with cooking parchment paper.

2 Cut bread crosswise in half using serrated knife. Cut each half horizontally; place cut side up on pan. Bake 15 minutes or until edges are light brown.

3 Meanwhile, in medium bowl, mix mayonnaise, jalapeño juice, mustard, lemon juice and soy sauce until well blended; add cheeses. With electric mixer, beat on medium speed about 2 to 3 minutes or until mixture is creamy and spreadable. Stir in remaining ingredients except additional onion.

4 Spread cheese mixture evenly over cut sides of bread. Bake about 10 minutes or until cheese is melted. Top with green onion; let stand 5 minutes before cutting. Cut each piece crosswise into 5 slices. Serve warm.

1 Slice Calories 110; Total Fat 4.5g (Saturated Fat 2g, Trans Fat 0g); Cholesterol 25mg; Sodium 220mg; Total Carbohydrate 10g (Dietary Fiber 0g); Protein 6g **Carbohydrate Choices:** ½

LEARN TO DEEP-FRY

Cooking food in enough hot oil to cover is called "deep-frying." If you are a fan of crispy foods, then you will want to master deep-frying.

Start with fresh oil—neutral-flavored oils such as canola, peanut, safflower and sunflower work best. These choices also have a high smoke point, which means that they can be heated to a fairly high temperature without breaking down or smoking. Olive oil is not a good choice for deep-frying, because it generally has a fruity flavor that clashes with the food being fried, and a lower smoke point than other oils.

A deep-fry thermometer is a must for perfecting this cooking technique. It rests on the edge of pan, in the cooking oil, to monitor the temperature of the oil. Be sure to cook the food at the temperature listed in the recipe you are using. The temperature of the oil can fluctuate as cold, uncooked foods are added to it and as food cooks. Work quickly in batches, adjusting the heat level if necessary, to keep the oil at the desired temperature for your recipe.

Use a deep fryer or large saucepan with a heavy bottom for frying. The cooking vessel should have tall enough sides to accommodate the oil while allowing at least 4 inches between the top of the oil and the top of the pot. Plan for the oil to rise and bubble as the food cooks. Follow these basic steps for crisply cooked food.

- Pour oil into cold pot.
- Heat oil to desired temperature, using thermometer for accuracy.
- Be sure food to be fried is dry; pat with paper towels if necessary.
- Carefully drop food into hot oil using metal slotted spoon; do not crowd.
- Remove cooked food from oil with slotted spoon.
- Drain fried food on paper towel–lined plate or platter.
- Allow oil to return to desired temperature before adding additional batches.

When cooked at the desired recipe temperature, deep-frying produces a deliciously crispy exterior, and the inside food should be nearly free of any sign of oil. Try this recipe for Shrimp Egg Rolls and enjoy!

Shrimp Egg Rolls

Shredded cooked chicken or pork can be substituted for the shrimp in this home-cooked version of a favorite take-out food. Thaw frozen egg roll skins at room temperature.

PREP 1 Hour 15 Minutes TOTAL 1 Hour 15 Minutes •
8 egg rolls

1 teaspoon cornstarch	½ teaspoon grated gingerroot
¼ teaspoon five-spice powder	½ cup finely chopped peeled cooked shrimp
4 teaspoons soy sauce	Vegetable oil for frying
1 tablespoon vegetable oil	8 egg roll skins (from 1-lb package)
4 cups coleslaw mix (from 16-oz bag)	1 egg, beaten
1 cup fresh bean sprouts	Sweet-and-sour sauce, if desired
2 medium green onions, sliced (2 tablespoons)	

1 In small bowl, mix cornstarch, five-spice powder and soy sauce until well blended; set aside.

2 In large skillet or wok, heat 1 tablespoon oil over medium-high heat until hot. Add coleslaw mix, bean sprouts, onions and gingerroot; cook 3 to 4 minutes, stirring constantly, until tender. Add shrimp and cornstarch mixture; cook 1 to 2 minutes, stirring constantly, until mixture is thoroughly coated. Remove from skillet; cool to room temperature.

3 In deep fryer or 4-quart Dutch oven, heat 3 to 4 inches oil to 350°F.

4 Meanwhile, place 1 egg roll skin on work surface with one corner facing you. (Cover remaining skins with damp paper towel to prevent drying out.) Place ¼ cup of the coleslaw mixture slightly below center of egg roll skin. Fold corner of egg roll skin closest to filling over filling, tucking point under. Fold in and overlap right and left corners. Brush remaining corner with egg; gently roll egg roll toward remaining corner and press to seal. (Cover filled egg roll with damp paper towel to prevent drying out.) Repeat with remaining egg roll skins and coleslaw mixture.

5 Fry egg rolls a few at a time in hot oil 4 to 6 minutes, turning once, until golden brown. Drain on paper towels. Serve with sweet-and-sour sauce.

1 Egg Roll Calories 220; Total Fat 11g (Saturated Fat 2g, Trans Fat 0g); Cholesterol 60mg; Sodium 220mg; Total Carbohydrate 22g (Dietary Fiber 2g); Protein 8g **Carbohydrate Choices:** 1½

OVEN-FRIED EGG ROLLS: Heat oven to 400°F. Spray cookie sheet with cooking spray. Place uncooked egg rolls, seam sides down, on cookie sheet. Lightly spray tops and sides of egg rolls with cooking spray. Bake 15 to 20 minutes or until golden brown.

FORMING EGG ROLLS

Fold corner of egg roll wrapper over filling, tucking in corner.

Fold in and overlap left and right corners of egg roll wrapper.

Brush remaining corner with egg; gently roll egg roll toward remaining corner and press to seal.

Beverages

Beverage Basics

The world of beverage choices has evolved beyond standard coffee, tea and lemonade. While those beverages never go out of style, our discerning taste buds sometimes long for more excitement. From Ginger Water and 10-Minute Oat "Milk" to Spirit-Free Margaritas, Sangría Slushies and Kombucha, you'll find thirst-quenching recipes here for every occasion.

Coffee Anytime

Coffee is grown in more than 50 countries around the world in tropical climates, at high altitudes and in rich soil. The most common, highest quality, most expensive variety is Arabica coffee, a descendant of the original coffee beans grown in Ethiopia hundreds of years ago, with the very best Arabica coming from very high altitudes. Robusta is another coffee variety that is becoming more common, particularly in blends and instant coffees. This coffee has a higher caffeine level than Arabica.

There are many methods for brewing coffee, and a large selection of coffeemakers to choose from. You might choose an automatic drip coffeemaker, a French press, percolator or even a cappuccino machine—the method and equipment chosen will depend on your needs and unique coffee preferences. However you make coffee, here are tips for great coffee:

- **Purchase coffee in small amounts** that can be used in a few days.
- **Store unopened coffee** packages in the freezer for no more than 1 month.
- **Grind just before brewing,** if possible.
- **Use the right grind for the job.** Matching the right grind to the brewing method is key to a good cup of coffee. If coffee is bitter, it may be too finely ground. If it is flat tasting, the grind may be too coarse. Check with professionals where you purchase beans for the correct grind. Here are some general guidelines:
  - **Automatic Drip:** medium grind
  - **Espresso Maker:** fine grind
  - **Percolator:** coarse grind
  - **French Press:** coarse grind
- **Use good water** for best flavor—filtered or bottled water are good choices.
- **Measure**
  - **Regular Coffee:** 1 tablespoon coffee for 6 oz water
  - **Stronger Coffee:** 2 tablespoons coffee for 6 oz water

Tea for Relaxation

From afternoon tea in England to a tea ceremony in Japan, the consumption of tea is steeped in rich history and tradition. This simple beverage is the most commonly consumed beverage in the world because it is delicious, healthful, easy to make and just plain relaxing. All tea plants belong to the same species, *Camellia sinensis*. The thousands of different varieties of tea vary by where it is grown, the time of year it is picked and how it is processed. Black and green teas contain a good amount of antioxidants. Some common varieties of tea include:

- **Black Tea:** This common tea contains the most caffeine of all tea, 50 to 65 percent of the amount in coffee. This tea is processed by crushing and fermenting the leaves. Some common black teas include Darjeeling, English Breakfast and Lapsang Souchong.
- **Green Tea:** Pale green with a light, fresh flavor, green tea is favored in Asia. This tea is steamed and dried but not fermented. Varieties of this tea include Gunpowder and Tencha.
- **White Tea:** Pale in color with a light, sweet flavor, white tea is the least processed of all teas; it is simply steamed and dried. It contains very little caffeine. Familiar varieties include Silver Needle and White Peony.
- **Oolong Tea:** Partially fermented and a cross between black and green teas, this is also known as Chinese restaurant tea. Oolong is full bodied, with a sweet aroma. Imperial oolong is prized for its honey flavor and Formosa oolong tastes a bit like peaches.
- **Herbal Teas:** Because these teas do not contain any leaves from the *Camellia* plant, they are sometimes referred to as tisanes. These combinations consist of herbs, flowers and fruits.

For brewing tea, here is equipment you might want on hand:

- Teakettle for boiling water
- Teapot for brewing
- Tea press for brewing
- Infuser for holding tea leaves in a teapot
- Strainer for pouring (if there is no infuser)

To brew tea:

- Start with cold water in a teakettle. For black or oolong tea, bring water to a boil. For green or white tea, water should be between 170°F and 190°F.

- Warm a teapot by filling it with hot water and letting it stand for a few minutes; drain.
- Place desired tea in teapot; use about 1 teaspoon loose tea or 1 teabag for each ¾ cup water. Pour boiling or hot water over tea; steep 3 to 5 minutes.
- Pour tea into cups; use a strainer to catch loose tea leaves.

There Is More to Milk

It used to be that milk was only found in a few varieties—whole, skim or reduced fat. Now there are other types to choose from. Look for organic milk, lactose-free milk (for those that cannot drink regular milk) and milk with additional calcium or omega-3 fatty acids added. Goat's milk is also available and is easy to digest, has less lactose than cow's milk and is less allergenic.

But for those who cannot drink dairy milk, there are many tasty dairy-free choices, many of which are vegan; some are perfect for those with nut or soy allergies.

DAIRY MILK ALTERNATIVES

- **Soymilk:** Made from soybeans, this alternative milk is very popular. Look for it unsweetened, sweetened and flavored. It has a nutrition profile with protein content like dairy milk and is usually fortified with vitamins. Similar in flavor to low-fat milk.

- **Nut Milks:** Made from almonds, cashews, macadamia nuts, hazelnuts or peanuts; although these alternatives have less protein than dairy milk, they do have as much (or more) calcium and vitamin D. These products are made with ground nuts, water and sweetener. Creamy with a hint of nut flavor.

- **Grain Milks:** Made by soaking rice, oats, quinoa or other grains in water. Oat and rice milk tend to be well tolerated by those with food allergies or intolerances. Look for grain milk that is calcium fortified. Flavor depends on what grain was used.

- **Coconut Milk:** This alternative beverage is the closest to dairy milk in texture and is fairly high in fat content. This is often a good choice for those with multiple food allergies; it does not contain soy or gluten. It has fewer calories, less protein and less calcium than dairy milk, and a hint of coconut flavor.

- **Pea Protein Milk:** This milk is less impactful on the land than almond milk and has more protein than dairy or soy milk. Creamy, smooth flavor.

- **Hemp Milk:** Made with the seeds of the hemp plant (which don't contain any CBD), hemp milk is high in protein and calcium (more calcium than dairy milk) as well as other nutrients. Nutty flavor and similar in texture to almond or soy milk.

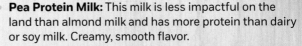

Cold Brew Coffee

PREP 10 min **TOTAL** 18 hr • *4 servings*

1⅓ cups coarse-ground regular or decaffeinated coffee (4 oz)	Ice cubes
	Paper coffee filters or cheesecloth
4 cups water	

1 Place ground coffee in medium bowl or large jar. Add water; stir gently. Cover; refrigerate at least 12 hours, but no longer than 18 hours.

2 Place several paper coffee filters or 2 layers of cheesecloth in fine-mesh strainer; place strainer over top of pitcher. Pour coffee and grounds into strainer; strain well but do not stir. Discard solids or save for another use. (See Use It Up: Coffee Grounds, below.)

3 Fill 4 large glasses with ice cubes; pour ¾ cup coffee into each glass. Store any remaining coffee covered in refrigerator for up to 3 days.

1 Serving Calories 5; Total Fat 0g (Saturated Fat 0g, Trans Fat 0g); Cholesterol 0mg; Sodium 5mg; Total Carbohydrate 1g (Dietary Fiber 1g); Protein 0g **Carbohydrate Choices:** 0

BUTTERSCOTCH SPICE COFFEE COOLER: Prepare Cold Brew Coffee as directed in Step 1—except in 4-cup glass measuring cup, microwave ½ cup of the water uncovered on High about 30 seconds or until boiling. Stir in 1 teaspoon ground cinnamon and ¼ teaspoon ground cloves; stir in remaining 3½ cups cold water. To serve, spoon 2 tablespoons vegan butterscotch caramel topping into bottom and down sides of each of 4 large glasses. Fill glasses with ice cubes. Mix coffee and 3 tablespoons packed organic brown sugar until sugar is dissolved. Pour ¾ cup coffee into each glass; top each with ½ cup 10-Minute Oat "Milk" (page 87) or almond milk. Top with nondairy whipped topping, drizzle with additional butterscotch topping and sprinkle with ground cinnamon, if desired.

Iced Caramel Cashew Latte

PREP 10 min **TOTAL** 10 min • *2 servings*

½ cup ground espresso or French roast coffee	2 teaspoons vegan caramel or chocolate fat-free topping
1½ cups water	Ice cubes
2 cups unsweetened cashew milk	Organic sugar, if desired

1 Using drip coffeemaker, brew coffee with water as directed by coffeemaker manufacturer.

2 In heatproof pitcher, stir together coffee and cashew milk.

3 Drizzle topping over insides of 2 large glasses. Fill glasses with ice cubes. Pour cashew milk mixture over ice. Sweeten to taste with sugar.

1 Serving Calories 45; Total Fat 2g (Saturated Fat 0g, Trans Fat 0g); Cholesterol 0mg; Sodium 190mg; Total Carbohydrate 6g (Dietary Fiber 0g); Protein 1g **Carbohydrate Choices:** ½

ICED VANILLA SOY LATTE: Substitute vanilla soy milk for the cashew milk.

ICED VANILLA ALMOND LATTE: Substitute almond milk for the cashew milk.

⟳ USE IT UP
COFFEE GROUNDS

COWBOY COFFEE RUB: Page 424

ODOR ELIMINATOR: Rub on hands after chopping onions or garlic

PAN SCRUB: Use to loosen stuck-on foods from regular pans (not nonstick)

FERTILIZER: Sprinkle in garden soil or compost bin

STRAINING COFFEE

Strain cold brew coffee by pouring it through several layers of cheesecloth in a fine mesh strainer to catch all coffee bean pieces.

Cold Brew Coffee

DECORATING CAPPUCCINO

Using small spoon, place ⅛ teaspoon cinnamon in 3 areas on frothed milk.

Drag end of toothpick lightly through cinnamon areas and frothed milk.

Hazelnut Cappuccino

EASY • FAST • CALORIE SMART • GLUTEN FREE • VEGETARIAN

Hazelnut Cappuccino

PREP 10 min **TOTAL** 10 min • *2 servings* (1 cup each)

½ cup ground espresso or French roast coffee	¼ cup hazelnut-flavored coffee syrup
1½ cups water	⅛ teaspoon ground cinnamon
¾ cup whole milk	

1 Brew coffee according to coffeemaker manufacturer's directions, using ground coffee and water.

2 Place milk in 2-cup microwavable jar with lid. Microwave milk uncovered on High about 45 seconds or until hot (do not boil). Place lid on jar; using pot holder, shake jar vigorously until milk is foamy.

3 To serve, pour coffee and coffee syrup into 2 (10-oz) mugs. Add hot milk (pour by holding spoon against edge of jar to hold foam). Spoon foam on top. Sprinkle each cup with cinnamon. Serve immediately.

1 Serving Calories 140; Total Fat 3g (Saturated Fat 1.5g, Trans Fat 0g); Cholesterol 10mg; Sodium 45mg; Total Carbohydrate 25g (Dietary Fiber 1g); Protein 3g **Carbohydrate Choices:** 1½

FROTH IT YOUR WAY

There are many ways to get froth for your coffee drinks!

Microwave milk on High in 4-cup microwavable glass measuring cup for 2 to 3 minutes or until hot (do not boil). Use one of the methods shown below to create foam.

Immersion Blender Pour milk to be frothed into a tall, narrow container.

Whisk It will take a little time; use frothed milk quickly, as it tends to disappear faster with this method.

Frother (Battery-Operated Mini "Whisk") Great for mixing hot chocolate, too!

Electric Mixer Use for larger quantities.

Easy Iced Tea

Brew a pot of tea, using double the amount of tea bags. Remove the tea bags and pour into a heatproof pitcher. Cool the tea before refrigerating to eliminate cloudiness. Refrigerate until very cold. To sweeten iced tea, add Simple Syrup (page 95), or use honey, agave nectar or sugar.

FAST • CALORIE SMART • GLUTEN FREE • VEGETARIAN

Chai

PREP 10 min TOTAL 10 min • *4 servings*

2 cups water	2 to 4 black peppercorns, crushed
¼ cup loose Darjeeling tea leaves or 5 tea bags black tea	Pinch of ground cinnamon
2 cups milk	¼ cup sweetened condensed milk or 4 teaspoons sugar
⅛ teaspoon ground cardamom	
2 whole cloves, crushed	

1   In 2-quart saucepan, heat water to a rapid boil over medium-high heat; reduce heat to low. Add tea leaves; simmer 2 to 4 minutes to blend flavors. (If using tea bags, remove and discard.)

2   Stir in remaining ingredients except condensed milk. Heat just to boiling, but do not let boil over. Remove from heat; stir in condensed milk. Strain tea through strainer into cups.

1 Serving Calories 130; Total Fat 4g (Saturated Fat 2.5g, Trans Fat 0g); Cholesterol 15mg; Sodium 85mg; Total Carbohydrate 17g (Dietary Fiber 0g); Protein 5g **Carbohydrate Choices:** 1

FAST • CALORIE SMART • GLUTEN FREE • VEGETARIAN • VEGAN

Fresh Citrus Green Tea

PREP 10 min TOTAL 10 min •
4 servings (about 1 cup each)

4 cups boiling water	¼ cup vegan orange juice
4 tea bags green tea	2 tablespoons lemon juice
¼ teaspoon ground cinnamon	2 orange slices, cut in half
6 whole cloves, broken into pieces	
¼ cup organic sugar	

1   Place tea bags in teapot or other heatproof container. Pour boiling water over tea bags. Add cinnamon and cloves. Cover; let steep 3 to 5 minutes.

2   Remove tea bags from teapot; strain tea through strainer to remove cloves. Add sugar, orange juice and lemon juice to tea; stir to mix. Place orange slice half in each cup. Pour tea over orange slices in cups.

1 Serving Calories 70; Total Fat 0g (Saturated Fat 0g, Trans Fat 0g); Cholesterol 0mg; Sodium 0mg; Total Carbohydrate 16g (Dietary Fiber 0g); Protein 0g **Carbohydrate Choices:** 1

EASY • FAST • CALORIE SMART • GLUTEN FREE • VEGETARIAN • VEGAN

Hot Spiced Cider

A slow cooker is a great way to keep this cider warm after it's made.

PREP 5 min TOTAL 15 min • *6 servings*

6 cups vegan apple cider	¼ teaspoon ground nutmeg
½ teaspoon whole cloves	3 sticks cinnamon

1   In 3-quart saucepan, heat all ingredients to a boil over medium-high heat. Reduce heat to low; simmer uncovered 10 minutes.

2   Strain cider mixture through strainer into hot-beverage carafe or pitcher to remove cloves and cinnamon. Serve hot with additional cinnamon sticks, if desired.

1 Serving Calories 120; Total Fat 0g (Saturated Fat 0g, Trans Fat 0g); Cholesterol 0mg; Sodium 10mg; Total Carbohydrate 28g (Dietary Fiber 0g); Protein 0g **Carbohydrate Choices:** 2

HOT SPICED CRANBERRY CIDER: Substitute 2 cups vegan cranberry juice cocktail for 2 cups of the cider. Add ½ cup packed organic brown sugar. Increase cloves to 1½ teaspoons. Omit nutmeg and add 1 thinly sliced orange with other ingredients. Remove orange slices with other ingredients as directed.

EASY • FAST • CALORIE SMART • GLUTEN FREE • VEGETARIAN • VEGAN

Very Berry Iced Tea

For a special touch, freeze fresh raspberries in ice cubes and add them to each serving. Top glasses with fresh fruit on skewers.

PREP 10 min TOTAL 10 min •
8 servings (about 1 cup each)

4 cups Easy Iced Tea (at left)	3 cups vegan red raspberry juice blend, chilled
	½ cup fresh raspberries

1   In 2-quart pitcher, mix iced tea and the juice blend. Stir in raspberries.

2   Fill glasses with ice; pour tea mixture over ice.

1 Serving Calories 60; Total Fat 0g (Saturated Fat 0g, Trans Fat 0g); Cholesterol 0mg; Sodium 5mg; Total Carbohydrate 16g (Dietary Fiber 0g); Protein 0g **Carbohydrate Choices:** 1

RASPBERRY LEMONADE TEA: Substitute refrigerated vegan raspberry lemonade for the raspberry juice blend.

Hot Chocolate

PREP 10 min **TOTAL** 10 min • *4 servings* (¾ cup each)

2 tablespoons sugar	½ cup half-and-half
2 tablespoons unsweetened baking cocoa	¼ cup semisweet or dark chocolate chips
2½ cups milk	½ teaspoon vanilla

1 In 2-quart saucepan, mix sugar and cocoa. Using whisk, gradually stir in milk and half-and-half until well blended. Cook over medium heat, stirring constantly, until thoroughly heated (do not boil). Remove from heat.

2 Add chocolate chips; stir constantly until chips are melted and mixture is smooth. Stir in vanilla. Pour into cups.

1 Serving Calories 230; Total Fat 12g (Saturated Fat 7g, Trans Fat 0g); Cholesterol 25mg; Sodium 75mg; Total Carbohydrate 23g (Dietary Fiber 1g); Protein 6g **Carbohydrate Choices:** 1½

LIGHTER DIRECTIONS: For 160 calories and 4 grams of fat per serving, substitute fat-free (skim) milk and fat-free half-and-half.

DOUBLE-CHOCOLATE HOT CHOCOLATE: Substitute chocolate milk for regular milk.

Chocolate–Peanut Butter Protein Shake

Make it special by topping with a fresh strawberry garnish.

PREP 10 Minutes **TOTAL** 10 Minutes • *1 serving*

6 tablespoons gluten-free vegan chocolate protein powder (1 scoop)	1 tablespoon peanut butter
1 tablespoon unsweetened baking cocoa	1 frozen banana, chopped
1 cup milk	1 tablespoon ground flaxseed meal

1 In blender, place all ingredients. Cover; blend on high speed until smooth.

2 Pour into large glass. Serve immediately.

1 Serving Calories 510; Total Fat 16g (Saturated Fat 4.5g, Trans Fat 0g); Cholesterol 10mg; Sodium 290mg; Total Carbohydrate 51g (Dietary Fiber 7g); Protein 40g **Carbohydrate Choices:** 3½

VEGAN CHOCOLATE–ALMOND BUTTER PROTEIN SHAKE: Substitute almond milk for the milk and almond butter for the peanut butter.

Hot Spiced Cider, Chai, Hot Chocolate

Very Berry Iced Tea

Chocolate–Peanut Butter Protein Shake

Powdered sugar

Cranberry juice

Frozen yogurt

Strawberries

Fresh Strawberry Shake

5-INGREDIENT RECIPE

Fresh Strawberry Shake

PREP 5 min **TOTAL** 5 min •
3 servings (about 1 cup each)

1 pint (2 cups) fresh strawberries	2 cups strawberry fat-free frozen yogurt (from 1.75-quart container) or strawberry fat-free ice cream
½ cup cranberry juice cocktail	
2 tablespoons powdered sugar	

1 In blender, combine all ingredients. Cover; blend on high speed until smooth.

2 Pour into 3 large glasses. Serve immediately.

1 Serving Calories 220; Total Fat 0g (Saturated Fat 0g, Trans Fat 0g); Cholesterol 0mg; Sodium 90mg; Total Carbohydrate 48g (Dietary Fiber 2g); Protein 6g **Carbohydrate Choices:** 3

STRAWBERRY-BANANA SHAKE: Reduce strawberries to 1½ cups. Add 1 medium peeled banana with the strawberries.

PEACH-ORANGE SHAKE: Substitute 2 cups frozen peach slices for the strawberries. Substitute orange juice for the cranberry juice cocktail and vanilla yogurt for the strawberry yogurt.

EASY • FAST • MAKE AHEAD • GLUTEN FREE
• VEGETARIAN • VEGAN

Fresh Lemonade

PREP 10 min **TOTAL** 10 min • *8 servings* (1 cup each)

6 cups cold water	Ice cubes
2 cups fresh lemon juice (8 to 10 lemons)	Lemon slices, if desired
1 cup organic sugar	

1 In large pitcher, combine water, lemon juice and sugar; stir until sugar is dissolved. Refrigerate about 3 hours or until chilled, if desired.

2 Fill glasses with ice cubes. Pour lemonade over ice. Garnish with lemon slices.

1 Serving Calories 115; Total Fat 0g (Saturated Fat 0g, Trans Fat 0g); Cholesterol 0mg; Sodium 15mg; Total Carbohydrate 29g (Dietary Fiber 0g); Protein 0g **Carbohydrate Choices:** 2

GINGER LEMONADE: In 3-quart saucepan, heat water, sugar and 10 to 12 slices fresh gingerroot (¾ to 1 inch) to boiling. Remove from heat; stir in lemon juice. Cool 15 minutes; remove gingerroot. Refrigerate at least 3 hours to chill. Garnish with lemon slices.

WATERMELON LEMONADE: Substitute 2 cups pureed watermelon for 2 cups of the water.

FRESH LIMEADE: Substitute lime juice for the lemon juice and lime slices for the lemon slices.

SPIRIT-FREE LEMONADE-ORANGE SPRITZER: Reduce water to 1 cup. Substitute ½ cup fresh orange juice (about 1 large orange) for ½ cup of the lemon juice. Refrigerate 2 hours or until chilled. In Step 2, before serving over ice, stir 5 cups lemon-flavored sparkling water into lemon mixture. Garnish with lemon and orange slices.

GRATING LEMON ZEST AND JUICING LEMONS

To get the most juice from a lemon, let it stand at room temperature 10 minutes or microwave on High for 30 seconds before squeezing.

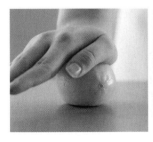   

Before squeezing, roll lemon back and forth, pressing down with firm pressure, to soften the cell walls that hold the juice.

Cut lemon in half crosswise. Using a citrus reamer or the back of a soup spoon, press and twist in center of cut side of lemon to squeeze out juice. Strain juice through fine mesh strainer.

Hand-held Plane Grater: Use to grate tiny pieces of citrus zest or whole nutmeg.

Paring Knife or Zester: Pull across peel, pressing lightly to remove zest, but not the bitter white pith below.

LEARN TO MAKE KOMBUCHA

Kombucha is a fermented tea produced by using a mushroom-like fungus host, called a SCOBY, that transforms the tea into fizzy, thirst-quenching kombucha. Our delicious recipes are on page 97.

What Is a SCOBY?

SCOBY is an acronym for Symbiotic Culture of Bacteria and Yeast. Start with a USDA organic SCOBY to ensure success. SCOBYs can be purchased online or found in some natural food stores. Purchase a live starter culture kit (15 oz), which contains a SCOBY pellicle in at least 12 fluid oz of starter tea liquid. PH strips can also be purchased online.

When ready to make kombucha, pour the starter kit (both SCOBY and liquid) into a bowl and inspect the SCOBY. A healthy SCOBY is white to light tan in color. There may be streaks of brown and black on it, which is just leftover tea. A healthy SCOBY may or may not float. It is normal for the SCOBY to sink to the bottom of the jar during fermentation. Do not use if the SCOBY has any mold on it. Do not discard the liquid—you need it to start the fermentation.

It is normal for the SCOBY to grow during fermentation. There may be stringy brown bits coming off it and sediment in the bottom of the jar. It is not harmful to consume sediment. You can filter it after the initial fermentation, if you like (see Adding Flavor and Fizz).

FILTERED WATER

You'll want to use water that has been filtered to remove chorine. You can use water from home if it's been through a filtration system or use spring, purified or distilled water purchased from a store.

FERMENTING

The Ideal temperature for the fermentation process is 70-80°F. Temperatures at the upper end of this range will quicken the fermentation process. Fermenting at temperatures below 70°F may cause mold issues with the mixture.

PH IS CRITICAL

Using the pH strips is critical to determining that your kombucha is safe for drinking. Follow the directions on the package to determine the pH of your kombucha. Before starting the fermentation process, the pH should be 4.2 or below. (If the pH is higher than 4.2, stir in 1 tablespoon of distilled white vinegar.) After the initial fermentation process is complete, the pH of the kombucha must be in the range of 2.5-4.2 to be safe to drink.

SAVE THE SCOBY

Once the initial fermentation is complete, you can save your SCOBY for future batches of kombucha. Using a slotted spoon, remove it from the finished kombucha to another smaller, clean, dry jar. Add 1½ cups of the finished kombucha to the jar. Stir occasionally to make sure the top of the SCOBY doesn't dry out.

Cover the jar with a paper coffee filter; securing it with a rubber band. Store in a cool, dark place until ready to make another batch of kombucha. Once the SCOBY grows to about an inch thick, it can be pulled apart horizontally to create a second SCOBY. Discard all contents in jar if any mold is evident.

ADDING FLAVOR AND FIZZ

Once the initial fermentation is complete and the SCOBY is removed (See SAVE THE SCOBY), the kombucha can be filtered to remove sediment and add flavor and fizz. Strain the kombucha through a fine mesh strainer or cheesecloth. Additional ingredients for flavor can then be added (for ideas, see recipe below). After ingredients are added, let the mixture ferment (this is called the secondary fermentation) an additional 1 to 3 days in a warm place out of direct sunlight until the kombucha is the desired fizziness and flavor. There is no SCOBY needed for the secondary fermentation.

STORING KOMBUCHA

The finished kombucha (either plain or flavored and having gone through the secondary fermentation) can be poured into clean and dry plastic or glass bottles, leaving 1 to 2 inches headspace in each bottle. Screw on lids. Refrigerate until ready to use. Carbon dioxide will build up in the bottles during this fermentation, so remove the lids daily to release this pressure.

EQUIPMENT FOR MAKING KOMBUCHA

1-gallon-size glass jar with lid (cleaned and dried)	Filtered water
	Paper coffee filter
15-oz USDA organic live SCOBY starter culture kit (see above)	Rubber band
	Room thermometer
	pH strips

USE IT UP
LEMONS

84

Lemon Zest

QUICK BREADS: Add grated zest to blueberry muffins or scones, zucchini or apple quick bread, pancakes or waffles.

COCKTAILS: Twist a piece of lemon peel over a cocktail to release the flavor and aroma from oils in the peel. Cut long strip of peel using citrus peeler or paring knife; twist into a spiral to garnish cocktails.

Whole Slices

Freeze in a single layer on cooking parchment paper–lined cookie sheet, covered lightly, until frozen. Transfer slices to a resealable freezer plastic bag. Add frozen slices to lemonade, iced tea, water, punch or cocktails.

Lemon Juice

VINAIGRETTE: In small jar, place ¼ cup olive or vegetable oil, 2 tablespoons lemon juice and ¼ teaspoon red pepper sauce. Cover and shake until well blended.

BRIGHTEN BEVERAGES: Add a little to your favorite fruit-based cocktails or smoothies to brighten the flavor.

FREEZE JUICE: In ice cube trays; move cubes to a resealable freezer plastic bag. Thaw and use in recipes calling for lemon juice.

Ginger Water

PREP 10 min **TOTAL** 40 min •

14 servings (2 tablespoons concentrate each)

GINGER CONCENTRATE

- 1 cup water
- 1 cup honey
- ¼ lb fresh gingerroot, cut into ¼-inch slices
- 2 teaspoons grated lemon peel
- 2 tablespoons fresh lemon juice

WATER AND ICE

- Ice cubes
- Sparkling water or water, chilled

1 In 2-quart saucepan, mix water, honey and gingerroot. Heat over medium heat 5 minutes, stirring frequently until honey is dissolved. Remove from heat; stir in lemon zest and lemon juice. Let stand 30 minutes.

2 Pour ginger mixture through fine-mesh strainer; discard gingerroot or reserve for another use. Transfer ginger concentrate to 2-quart pitcher. Store covered in refrigerator up to 2 weeks. Stir concentrate before each use.

3 To make 1 glass of ginger water, add ice to glass; mix 2 tablespoons of the ginger concentrate with 1 cup water. To make a pitcher of ginger water, in 2-quart pitcher mix 1 cup of the ginger concentrate with 6 cups water. Serve over ice.

1 Serving Calories 80; Total Fat 0g (Saturated Fat 0g, Trans Fat 0g); Cholesterol 0mg; Sodium 0mg; Total Carbohydrate 20g (Dietary Fiber 0g); Protein 0g **Carbohydrate Choices:** 1

MANGO-MINT GINGER WATER: In glass, place 3 mango slices, 2 lemon slices and 2 or 3 mint leaves, pressing against sides with spoon; add ice. Pour 1 cup chilled sparkling water and 2 tablespoons ginger concentrate over ice; mix gently.

JALAPEÑO-BASIL GINGER WATER: In glass, place 3 jalapeño slices, 2 lime slices and 2 or 3 fresh basil leaves, pressing against sides with spoon; add ice. Pour 1 cup chilled sparkling water and 2 tablespoons ginger concentrate over ice; mix gently.

♻ **USE IT UP**

COOKED GINGERROOT

After making the ginger concentrate, strain ginger and freeze for later use.

BEVERAGES: In hot tea, lemonade or sparkling water

BAKED GOODS: Chop; add to gluten-free muffins or scones.

MAIN OR SIDE DISHES: Chop; add to gluten-free stir-fries, Asian sauces/dressings or hot, cooked rice.

Mango-Mint Ginger Water

Jalapeño-Basil Ginger Water

MAKING OAT "MILK"

Resist the temptation to press the oats when straining, as pressing can result in oat milk with an undesirable texture. Use the oat milk for drinking just as it is, or in cold drinks such as smoothies or shakes. Pour it over cereal or use it in pancakes or muffins. Without any added ingredients, it will thicken as it's heated, so avoid using it for hot beverages. This dairy-free, gluten-free "milk" can be stored up to 3 days in the refrigerator. Be sure to shake it well or stir before using.

10-Minute Oat "Milk" with Coconut Berry Smoothie and Mint Mocha

Raspberry Brunch Punch

Fruity Green Smoothies

EASY • FAST • CALORIE SMART • GLUTEN FREE •
VEGETARIAN • VEGAN

10-Minute Oat "Milk"

PREP 10 min **TOTAL** 10 min •
4 servings (about ¾ cup each)

4 cups water	1 tablespoon pure maple syrup
1 cup gluten-free rolled oats	⅛ teaspoon salt
	Cheesecloth

1 In blender container, place water, oats, maple syrup and salt. Cover; blend on medium speed 20 to 30 seconds or until well blended. Do not overblend.

2 Line fine-mesh strainer with cheesecloth; place over large bowl. Pour oat mixture into strainer; strain well but do not press oat mixture to release more liquid. Discard cheesecloth and oat mixture. Transfer oat milk to 1-quart glass jar; cover and refrigerate. Shake well before using.

1 Serving Calories 90; Total Fat 1.5g (Saturated Fat 0g, Trans Fat 0g); Cholesterol 0mg; Sodium 85mg; Total Carbohydrate 17g (Dietary Fiber 2g); Protein 2g **Carbohydrate Choices:** 1

COCONUT-BERRY SMOOTHIE: In blender, place 1 cup oat milk, 1¼ cups frozen mixed berries, ¼ cup sweetened flaked coconut and ¼ teaspoon ground cinnamon. Cover; blend on high speed about 30 seconds or until smooth, stopping blender to stir with spoon if necessary. Garnish with additional coconut, if desired.

MINT MOCHAS: Brew coffee using ½ cup ground French roast coffee and 1½ cups water, and adding ½ cup chopped mint leaves. Meanwhile, in 1-cup glass measuring cup, stir together 1 cup oat milk, 2 tablespoons vegan chocolate-flavored syrup and 2 teaspoons organic sugar. Microwave on High 1 to 2 minutes, until heated through. To serve, pour brewed coffee into 2 mugs. Top with oat milk mixture; garnish with nondairy whipped topping and additional chocolate syrup, if desired.

EASY • FAST • CALORIE SMART • GLUTEN FREE •
VEGETARIAN • VEGAN

Raspberry Brunch Punch

For a party-ready presentation, add frozen lemon slices and frozen raspberries to keep the punch cold and look sensational!

PREP 5 min **TOTAL** 5 min • *24 servings* (½ cup each)

3 cups vegan red raspberry juice blend, chilled	concentrate (from 12-oz can)
¾ cup frozen (thawed) lemonade	1 bottle (2 liters) ginger ale, chilled

In beverage server, punch bowl or large pitcher, mix raspberry juice blend and lemonade concentrate. Stir in ginger ale. Serve immediately.

1 Serving Calories 60; Total Fat 0g (Saturated Fat 0g, Trans Fat 0g); Cholesterol 0mg; Sodium 10mg; Total Carbohydrate 15g (Dietary Fiber 0g); Protein 0g **Carbohydrate Choices:** 1

SUBSTITUTION: Try using vegan raspberry juice instead of the juice blend.

PEACH-MANGO PUNCH: Substitute vegan peach-mango juice blend for the red raspberry juice blend.

EASY • FAST • CALORIE SMART • GLUTEN FREE •
VEGETARIAN • VEGAN

Refreshing Green Juice

See Learn to Juice, page 88.

PREP 10 min **TOTAL** 10 min • *2 servings*

8 large leaves fresh green kale (6 oz)	¼ bunch fresh cilantro (1 oz)
1 medium Bartlett pear (9 oz), unpeeled	½ medium lemon, peeled

1 Cut ½ inch off stem ends of kale; discard. Turn juicer on. Alternate adding ingredients to juicer a little at a time, until fruits and vegetables are processed into juice.

2 Stir juice well; pour into 2 glasses. Serve immediately. Discard pulp.

1 Serving Calories 140; Total Fat 1g (Saturated Fat 0g, Trans Fat 0g); Cholesterol 0mg; Sodium 45mg; Total Carbohydrate 29g (Dietary Fiber 6g); Protein 3g **Carbohydrate Choices:** 2

RASPBERRY-LIME JUICE: Substitute 2 unpeeled sweet red apples, 1 (6-oz) package fresh raspberries and ½ medium peeled lime for the kale, pear, cilantro and lemon.

EASY • FAST • CALORIE SMART • GLUTEN FREE

Fruity Green Smoothies

PREP 10 min **TOTAL** 10 min • *2 servings* (1 cup each)

½ cup almond milk	1 tablespoon honey
3 cups packed fresh baby spinach leaves	1 frozen banana, chopped
2 tablespoons lemon juice	½ cup ice cubes

1 In blender, place all ingredients. Cover; blend on high speed until smooth.

2 Pour into 2 glasses. Serve immediately.

1 Serving Calories 130; Total Fat 1g (Saturated Fat 0g, Trans Fat 0g); Cholesterol 0mg; Sodium 75mg; Total Carbohydrate 27g (Dietary Fiber 3g); Protein 2g **Carbohydrate Choices:** 2

SUBSTITUTION: If you are not a fan of almond milk, try using soymilk or rice milk instead.

MANGO-SPINACH SMOOTHIES: Substitute ⅔ cup frozen mango chunks for the frozen banana.

TROPICAL GREEN SMOOTHIES: Substitute 3 tablespoons orange juice for the lemon juice and ⅔ cup frozen pineapple chunks for the frozen banana.

LEARN TO JUICE

Juicing is an easy way to incorporate more fresh produce into your diet. And a diet that is rich in produce can make you feel fabulous, with an added plus that it is fun to blend your own flavors together. If you frequent juice bars you might find the menu items pricey, so that is another great reason to start making your own juices.

When you start juicing, be aware of the calorie and sugar content in the concentrated mixtures after the bulk and much of the fiber are removed from fruits and vegetables. Juices should not replace fruits and vegetables in your diet but should complement the foods you are already eating.

TYPES OF JUICERS

There are two main types of juicers, each with unique features:

- **Slow Juicer:** Also known as an upright juicer, this type uses a single auger to crush and squeeze produce and extract juice. Don't be fooled by the name—this juicer takes just a few minutes longer than the other type. Juice from a slow juicer will be fairly thick and a pretty color, with a small amount of foam.

- **Centrifugal Juicer:** Sometimes called a high-speed juicer, this juicer separates juice from pulp with high-speed spinning. A centrifugal juicer will remove more pulp and fiber from the juice than a slow juicer, and there will be more foam. This appliance is great for making juice in larger quantities.

PREPPING PRODUCE

- Choose vibrant, fresh produce—juice will only be as good as the produce it is made from.

- Wash produce before cutting.

- Cut produce into pieces that will fit in the feed tube. Most fruits and veggies can be juiced with the peel, stems and leaves left on, if they are scrubbed and have not been chemically treated. Peels can add color and boost nutrients in the juice.

- Roll leaves like lettuce and kale into tight balls before adding.

- Remove pits from foods, and rind from melon, pineapple and citrus.

- Wrap herbs around other produce before adding so that they are evenly incorporated.

- Have all produce ready before you start juicing so that it is easy to alternate adding different produce pieces to the juicer in small batches.

TIPS FOR SUCCESS

- Start by purchasing small amounts of produce so that you can experiment to see what flavor combinations you like best. Then you can purchase larger amounts.

- If you are new to juicing, start with fruit-based combinations and slowly work into more vegetables.

- For the best flavor, add at least a little fruit to vegetable mixtures. Apples and pears can play a great supporting role in vegetable juices.

- Think about the colors of the produce and what colors they will create when mixed, as eye appeal makes a difference.

- Alternate adding different produce pieces to the juicer in small batches. If a piece of produce is stuck in the juicer, add a little of the juice that has already been made to help it through the juicer.

- Stir juice after processing and just before serving.

Refreshing Green Juice (page 87)

Drink Basics

Whether you are a cocktail lover, wine drinker or beer aficionado, having a good selection of bar ingredients at hand for gatherings will make you a hosting superstar. Start with a sampling of liquors, wines and beers plus a variety of mixers and nonalcoholic beverages and build from there. You can check with guests ahead of time to see if they have preferences, getting a heads-up on what you might want to have ready to serve. Having the right bar tools is also important, making it a cinch to whip up those drinks with confidence.

Tools for the Bar

- Blender
- Bottle opener
- Coasters
- Cocktail napkins
- Cocktail shaker
- Corkscrew
- Ice bucket and tongs
- Mini measure (shot glass)
- Muddler
- Pitcher
- Stir sticks and toothpicks

GLASSWARE

All-purpose wine glasses (stemmed or not stemmed): Used for white or red wine

Beer mugs Used for beer, to keep it cold

Highball tumblers Used for gin and tonics, Tom Collins, coolers, spritzers, iced tea and soft drinks (10- to 14-oz)

Margarita glasses Used for margaritas, daiquiris and some frozen or slushy drinks

Martini/cocktail glasses Used for martinis, Manhattans and some iced and frozen drinks

Old-fashioned (rocks or lowball glasses) Used for Scotch or other on-the-rocks drinks and old-fashioned cocktails (6- to 10-oz)

Shot glasses Used to measure spirits for cocktails or to drink straight liquor

Tulip glasses Used for champagne

Cocktail Mixology

Another term for mixing drinks, mixology is all about making good drinks, understanding what goes into drinks and using quality ingredients. Most classic cocktails have a basic formula, with differences in flavor coming from the brand of liquor, the mixer, the glass or garnish used. For cocktail mixing, keep basic spirits stocked, but also be sure to check your recipes before a gathering, in case you need ingredients you don't have. Then have some fun mixing cocktails!

SPIRITS TO STOCK

- Beer
- Bourbon and/or whiskey
- Brandy or cognac
- Gin
- Scotch
- Tequila
- Various liqueurs, as desired
- Vermouth
- Vodka
- Wine (red and white)

MIXERS TO STOCK

- Aromatic bitters
- Club soda
- Cola
- Drink mixes (bloody Mary, margarita, daiquiri)
- Ginger ale
- Lemon-lime soda
- Lime and lemon juice
- Simple Syrup (page 95)

Garnishes are part of the fun of mixology, so be sure to have a variety of choices when making cocktails. Most cocktails will suggest a certain garnish, but you can mix it up a bit if you like. Using decorative toothpicks to spear garnishes like cherries, olives and fruit is great for eye appeal as well as keeping them from sinking to the bottom of the glass. Showcase your garnishes in small containers for a festive and practical way to mix cocktails for a group.

- Black pepper
- Celery sticks
- Coarse salt
- Fresh fruit (lemons, limes, oranges, berries)
- Fresh mint or basil
- Granulated, coarse and powdered sugar
- Maraschino cherries
- Sliced fresh jalapeños or cocktail onions
- Stuffed cocktail olives
- Whole hazelnuts

Shaken Cocktails

The best shaken cocktails are always served refreshingly cold, with a very thin layer of ice floating on the surface. Equally important are the garnishes—they add flavor as well as make the drinks look special. Knowing a few tips will make cocktails an easy task and just might make you legendary.

1 **Chill glasses** in the freezer.

2 **Measure correctly** the amounts of chosen cocktail ingredients.

3 **Use a cocktail shaker** with a strainer insert, allowing the drink mixture to move around the ice cubes while shaking, chilling it well.

4 **Strain the drink immediately** after mixing so that ice will chill the drink but not dilute it.

5 **Keep garnishes ready** to add quickly to finished cocktails.

6 **Serve shaken drinks immediately.**

SHAKING COCKTAILS

Place ice in shaker. Add cocktail ingredients; cover and shake vigorously to blend and chill.

Remove shaker cover; place strainer over top of shaker. Pour drink into glass, straining out ice.

About Beer

Although the major ingredients of beer are simple (grain, hops and yeast), the explosion of different flavors of craft beer has made this simple beverage an art, with craft breweries sprouting up virtually everywhere. It is truly remarkable that the United States now has more beer styles and brands than any other place in the world, and even non-beer drinkers are enjoying the fun!

Craft breweries are often relatively small and independently owned. Their beers will be based on ale or lager or a combination of the two but will have other ingredients that make them individual—and the beer from their breweries might fall in the specialty category. Each brewer will have their own style and a one-of-a-kind beer menu.

Here are the basic categories of beer with some varieties (or flavors) you might like to sample:

Ales: Often higher in alcohol than lagers, ales tend to be sweet, tasty beers. Some of the more well-known varieties include the following:

- **Belgian pale ale:** copper colored with a malty, somewhat spicy flavor
- **Berliner weisse:** wheat based and very pale with a refreshingly sour flavor
- **Brown ale:** generally mellow but flavorful with a caramel-like flavor
- **IPA (India pale ale):** comes in a range of styles ranging from fruity to bitter (hoppy)
- **Lambic:** wheat based with a complex sour flavor
- **Oatmeal stout:** dark ale, full bodied and malty with a slight oatmeal flavor
- **Saison/Farmhouse ale:** refreshing fruity ale with mild to moderate tartness

Lagers: Most of the mass-produced beers are lagers, but there is a large variety of styles available. Here are some of the more well-known varieties:

- **American pale lagers:** light in color with delicate sweetness; should be served very cold
- **Bock beer:** dark and somewhat strong with an intense malty flavor
- **Doppelbock:** dark with a malty rich flavor and high alcohol content
- **Pilsner:** very aromatic with a crisp, refreshingly bitter flavor

Specialty: In this category, you will find the beers that do not fit in the other categories. They often have flavors from fruits, herbs and spices to make them unusual, interesting and delicious, and often quite memorable. Here are some flavors that you might see:

- **Fruit beers:** usually light- to medium-bodied lagers or ales that have fruit extract or real fruit added, resulting in sweet-flavored beers

- **Herb and spice beers:** flavor will resemble the ingredients that are added
- **Smoked beers:** flavor and aroma are derived from added smoky flavoring

Wine Primer

Wine has been enjoyed all over the world for centuries. Three things determine the flavor of wine: the type of grapes, where the grapes were grown and how the grapes were processed for the wine. Whether you are serving it with a meal or with appetizers, the choice of wine is mostly personal. For suggestions on serving and what to buy, wine stores can be very helpful and provide guidance. Experimenting with different wines will be helpful too, as in the end it is what you like and what tastes good!

Varietal is a term describing wines primarily made from one grape. Within each varietal, different brands will taste different, but here are some general flavor guidelines.

WHITE GRAPE VARIETALS

- **Chardonnay:** rich and creamy, with a buttery, full flavor that often has vanilla overtones
- **Chenin blanc:** light and fruity, often with a spicy peach flavor
- **Pinot gris/pinot grigio:** refreshing, with a little spice and fruity overtones
- **Riesling:** crisp and fresh, with a delightful fruity flavor and notes of peach, apple or apricot
- **Sauvignon blanc or fumé blanc:** often slightly acidic, with citrus and herb overtones

RED GRAPE VARIETALS

- **Cabernet sauvignon:** bold with a velvety texture and rich flavor often reminiscent of chocolate, coffee, blackberries and plums
- **Malbec:** dark red with rich flavor
- **Merlot:** fruity flavor with a medium body and overtones of blackberry and plum
- **Pinot noir:** light-bodied wine, often spicy with the flavors of cherries, blackberries and currants
- **Syrah/shiraz:** dark red, bold and spicy with overtones of dark fruit like blackberries and plums
- **Zinfandel:** spicy red with earthy overtones of berries and peppers

ROSÉ/BLUSH WINES

Not truly red wine. The pink color comes from minimal contact with the red grape skins, which differentiates them from whites. Blush, rosé and pink generally used interchangeably.

OTHER WINES

Sparkling wines include Asti Spumante and champagne. Fortified wines have added liquor and include Madeira, Marsala, port and sherry. Aromatic wines such as vermouth are flavored with herbs and spices.

STORING AND SERVING WINE

- Store wine in a cool, dry location away from light. Lay bottles with a real cork on their sides (do not stand them upright) so the corks do not dry out and shrink, which can allow air to enter and spoil the wine. If bottles have screwcaps, glass or plastic corks, bottles can be stored either upright or on their sides for storage space efficiency.
- Serve white and sparkling wines between 45°F and 55°F. Reds should be a bit warmer, at 55°F to 60°F, for the best flavor.
- Wine glasses are designed to maximize aromas and flavors of wine. A set of all-purpose glasses for both red and white wines is a good place to start.
- If you have wine left over, place the cork back into the bottle, seal the bottle with a wine plug or pour the wine into a clean bottle with a screw top. Refrigerate for up to 3 days.

HEIRLOOM *AND* NEW TWIST

HEIRLOOM

EASY • FAST • GLUTEN FREE •
VEGETARIAN • VEGAN

Classic Margarita Cocktails

PREP 5 min TOTAL 5 min • *2 servings*

Margarita salt or
kosher (coarse) salt

4 cups ice cubes

½ cup silver tequila

½ cup fresh lime juice

¼ cup Simple Syrup
(page 95)

¼ cup orange-flavored
liqueur (such as triple
sec or Cointreau)

2 lime slices

1 Rim 2 (12-oz) margarita glasses as directed on this
page, using salt. Add 1 cup ice to each glass.

2 Place remaining ice in cocktail shaker or pitcher.
Add tequila, lime juice, simple syrup and liqueur.
Shake or stir until blended and chilled.

3 Strain into glasses. Garnish with lime slices.

1 Serving Calories 310; Total Fat 0g (Saturated Fat 0g, Trans Fat 0g);
Cholesterol 0mg; Sodium 400mg; Total Carbohydrate 32g
(Dietary Fiber 0g); Protein 0g **Carbohydrate Choices:** 2

PINEAPPLE MARGARITA: Substitute organic sugar
for the salt. Reduce lime juice to 2 tablespoons and
omit liqueur. Add ¾ cup pineapple juice with the tequila.
Garnish with pineapple wedges, if desired.

CILANTRO-JALAPEÑO MARGARITA: Add 5 jalapeño
slices and 2 tablespoons coarsely chopped cilantro to
shaker before shaking. Garnish with jalapeño slices and
cilantro sprigs.

NEW TWIST

FAST • GLUTEN FREE • VEGETARIAN • VEGAN

Spirit-Free Margaritas

PREP 5 min TOTAL 5 min • *2 servings*

Margarita salt or
kosher (coarse) salt

4 cups ice cubes

2 orange wedges

½ cup fresh lime juice

¼ cup agave nectar
or Simple Syrup
(page 95)

1 cup club soda, chilled

2 strips orange zest

1 Rub rims of 2 (12-oz) glasses with water; dip rims of
glasses into salt. Fill each glass with 1 cup ice.

2 Squeeze juice from orange wedges into cocktail
shaker or pitcher. Add orange wedges, lime juice and
agave nectar; using cocktail muddler or wooden spoon,
press down and twist. Add remaining ice to shaker. Shake
or stir until blended and chilled.

3 Strain into glasses. Top with club soda; stir. Garnish
with orange peel.

1 Serving Calories 160; Total Fat 0g (Saturated Fat 0g, Trans Fat 0g);
Cholesterol 0mg; Sodium 430mg; Total Carbohydrate 40g
(Dietary Fiber 0g); Protein 0g **Carbohydrate Choices:** 2½

92

BETTY CROCKER COOKBOOK

Pineapple and
Cilantro-Jalapeño
Margaritas

RIMMING THE EDGE OF GLASS

Wet rim of glass with citrus
wedge or dip into lemon or
lime juice or water on small
plate; shake off excess

Dip wet rim into coarse
(Kosher) salt, sugar,
decorator sugar or candy
sprinkles on small plate.

Spirit-Free
Margaritas

Manhattan Cocktails

**EASY • FAST • GLUTEN FREE •
VEGETARIAN • VEGAN**

Manhattan Cocktails

PREP 5 min **TOTAL** 5 min • *2 servings*

- 2 vegan maraschino cherries
- ¼ cup small ice cubes or shaved ice
- ⅓ cup bourbon or whiskey
- ⅓ cup vegan sweet vermouth
- 2 dashes aromatic bitters

1 Chill 2 (3-oz) martini glasses in freezer.

2 Place cherry in each chilled glass. Place ice in cocktail shaker or pitcher. Add bourbon, vermouth and bitters; shake or stir to blend and chill. Pour into glasses, straining out ice.

1 Serving Calories 160; Total Fat 0g (Saturated Fat 0g, Trans Fat 0g); Cholesterol 0mg; Sodium 0mg; Total Carbohydrate 7g (Dietary Fiber 0g); Protein 0g **Carbohydrate Choices:** ½

**EASY • FAST • CALORIE SMART •
VEGETARIAN • VEGAN**

Martini Cocktails

PREP 5 min **TOTAL** 5 min • *2 servings*

- 2 pimiento-stuffed green olives or lemon twists
- ¼ cup small ice cubes or shaved ice
- ⅓ cup gin
- ⅓ cup vegan dry vermouth
- 2 dashes aromatic bitters

1 Chill 2 (3-oz) martini glasses in freezer.

2 Place olive in each chilled glass. Place ice in cocktail shaker or pitcher. Add gin, vermouth and bitters; shake or stir to blend and chill. Pour into glasses, straining out ice.

1 Serving Calories 150; Total Fat 0.5g (Saturated Fat 0g, Trans Fat 0g); Cholesterol 0mg; Sodium 65mg; Total Carbohydrate 5g (Dietary Fiber 0g); Protein 0g **Carbohydrate Choices:** ½

CHOCOLATE MARTINI COCKTAILS: Omit all ingredients except ice. Swirl about 1 tablespoon vegan chocolate syrup inside 4 chilled glasses. Add ⅓ cup chocolate-flavored liqueur, ⅓ cup vegan dairy-free Irish cream liqueur, ⅓ cup vanilla-flavored vodka and ⅓ cup vegan crème de cacao to ice in cocktail shaker; shake or stir. Pour over swirled chocolate into each glass.

COCONUT RUM MARTINI COCKTAILS: Omit all ingredients except ice. Add ½ cup pineapple juice, ½ cup coconut rum and ⅓ cup dark rum to ice in cocktail shaker; shake or stir, as directed. Pour into two 6-oz glasses. Garnish each cocktail with a pineapple wedge and vegan maraschino cherry.

MANGO MARTINI COCKTAILS: Omit all ingredients except ice. Puree 5 slices mango and 5 tablespoons syrup from 1 jar (24 oz) refrigerated organic mango slices in extra light syrup. Add ½ cup of the mango puree, ½ cup peach-flavored vodka, ¼ cup orange-flavored liqueur and 2 tablespoons fresh lime juice to ice in cocktail shaker; shake or stir, as directed. Pour into two 6-oz glasses. Garnish each cocktail with a slice of mango and slice of lime, if desired.

POMEGRANATE MARTINI COCKTAILS: Omit all ingredients except ice. Wet rim of each glass by rubbing with lime wedge; dip into colored organic sugar. Add 1 cup pomegranate juice, 3 tablespoons citrus-flavored vodka, 2 tablespoons orange-flavored liqueur and 1 tablespoon fresh lime juice to ice in cocktail shaker; shake or stir, as directed. Pour into two 6-oz glasses.

SWEET MARTINI COCKTAILS: Substitute vegan sweet vermouth for the vegan dry vermouth.

MAKING A CITRUS TWIST

With a vegetable peeler or small paring knife, cut strip of orange or lemon peel; twist as desired for corkscrew shape. Wring peels close to the surface of drinks so the fruit oil can add flavor and fragrance.

Martini Cocktails

Classic Bloody
Mary Cocktails

Hibiscus Fizz

FAST • CALORIE SMART • GLUTEN FREE

Classic Bloody Mary Cocktails

Bloody Mary cocktails are very easy to make at home. It helps to start with chilled ingredients. Store vodka in the freezer; it won't freeze but will be icy cold. Rim glasses with bloody Mary salt (below) for extra flavor.

PREP 10 min **TOTAL** 10 min • *4 servings*

1 cup vodka	Hot pepper sauce, if desired
¾ cup chilled tomato juice	Ice cubes
¼ cup fresh lemon juice	Garnishes, if desired: celery stalks, pickle spears, cucumber spears, gluten-free beef jerky sticks, lime or lemon wedges
¼ teaspoon celery salt	
¼ teaspoon pepper	
¼ teaspoon Worcestershire sauce	

1 In 4-cup glass measuring cup, mix vodka, tomato juice, lemon juice, celery salt, pepper and Worcestershire sauce until well blended. Add pepper sauce to taste.

2 Fill 4 glasses with ice. Pour tomato juice mixture over ice. Garnish as desired.

1 Serving Calories 140; Total Fat 0g (Saturated Fat 0g, Trans Fat 0g); Cholesterol 0mg; Sodium 220mg; Total Carbohydrate 3g (Dietary Fiber 0g); Protein 0g **Carbohydrate Choices:** 0

MAKE-AHEAD DIRECTIONS: Mix all ingredients as directed—except vodka. Cover and refrigerate until serving time. When ready to serve, add vodka and continue as directed.

EASY • MAKE AHEAD • CALORIE SMART • GLUTEN FREE • VEGETARIAN • VEGAN

Hibiscus Fizz

Rim the glasses with additional sugar for a festive presentation.

PREP 10 min **TOTAL** 1 hr 40 min • *4 servings*

2 cups water	Ice cubes
4 hibiscus-flavored tea bags	1 cup vegan prosecco or sparkling white wine, chilled
1 tablespoon organic sugar	Fresh berries or hibiscus flowers, if desired
1 -inch piece fresh gingerroot, peeled, thinly sliced	

1 In 2-quart saucepan, bring water to a boil. Add tea bags, sugar and gingerroot; stir to mix. Let steep 5 to 7 minutes. Pour tea mixture through strainer into small pitcher. Cool 15 minutes. Refrigerate at least 1 hour 15 minutes to chill tea completely.

2 Fill 4 large glasses with ice. Pour ½ cup tea over ice in each glass; top each with ¼ cup wine. Garnish with fresh berries.

1 Serving Calories 60; Total Fat 0g (Saturated Fat 0g, Trans Fat 0g); Cholesterol 0mg; Sodium 0mg; Total Carbohydrate 5g (Dietary Fiber 0g); Protein 0g **Carbohydrate Choices:** ½

MAKE-AHEAD DIRECTIONS: Prepare the tea as directed in Step 1; cover and refrigerate up to 5 days. When ready to serve, continue with Step 2.

SPIRIT-FREE HIBISCUS-GINGER FIZZ: Substitute vegan nonalcoholic ginger beer for the prosecco.

 USE IT UP
PROSECCO

MIMOSA: Equal parts chilled juice and prosecco

SANGRÍA: Sub (with 1 cup ginger ale) for the dry white wine in White Sangría (page 95)

SPARKLING COCKTAILS: Sub for vegan sparkling wine or champagne

Simple Syrup

Use this syrup instead of granulated sugar to sweeten drinks. It works especially well in cold drinks since it's a liquid—no gritty sugar! Instead, use 1 tablespoon per drink, or more if you have a sweet tooth.

PREP 5 min TOTAL 5 min • **48 servings**
(1 tablespoon each)

2 cups organic sugar
2 cups water

In 2-quart saucepan, stir sugar and water. Heat over medium heat, stirring frequently, until sugar is dissolved. Store covered in refrigerator up to 1 month.

TRIPLE BERRY SIMPLE SYRUP: Make as directed—except add 3 cups frozen mixed berries, thawed. After removing from heat, let stand 30 minutes. Strain through fine-mesh strainer; discard berries or reserve for another use.

STRAWBERRY-RHUBARB GINGER SIMPLE SYRUP:
In 3-quart saucepan, mix 2 cups chopped fresh or frozen rhubarb, 2 cups sliced fresh strawberries and 2 tablespoons chopped peeled fresh gingerroot with the sugar and water. Heat to boiling; reduce heat. Simmer uncovered 10 minutes, stirring occasionally. Remove from heat; let stand 30 minutes. Strain through fine-mesh strainer; discard solids or reserve for another use.

GINGER SIMPLE SYRUP: Make as directed—except add 8 oz fresh gingerroot, peeled and cut into ¼-inch slices. After removing from heat, let stand 30 minutes. Strain through fine-mesh strainer; discard gingerroot.

DILL SIMPLE SYRUP: Make as directed—except add 1½ cups lightly packed fresh dill weed. After removing from heat, let stand 30 minutes. Strain through fine-mesh strainer; discard dill.

⊙ USE IT UP
STRAWBERRY-RHUBARB COOKED FRUIT

Use the cooked fruit from the Strawberry-Rhubarb Ginger Simple Syrup to make Strawberry-Rhubarb Muffins: Prepare Blueberry Muffins (page 507) as directed—except stir in cooled cooked fruit from the Strawberry-Rhubarb Ginger Simple Syrup with the milk, oil and egg. Substitute 1 cup sliced fresh strawberries for the blueberries.

Sangría

PREP 10 min TOTAL 10 min • **8 servings**

⅔ cup fresh lemon juice (from 3 to 4 lemons)
⅓ cup fresh orange juice (from 1 large orange)
¼ cup organic sugar
1 lemon, cut into thin slices
1 orange, cut into thin slices
1 bottle (750 ml) vegan dry red wine
Ice cubes, if desired

In 2-quart glass pitcher, combine lemon juice, orange juice and sugar; stir until sugar is dissolved. Add lemon and orange slices. Stir in wine and ice.

1 Serving Calories 130; Total Fat 0g (Saturated Fat 0g, Trans Fat 0g); Cholesterol 0mg; Sodium 0mg; Total Carbohydrate 14g (Dietary Fiber 0g); Protein 0g **Carbohydrate Choices:** 1

ROSÉ SANGRÍA: Substitute vegan rosé/blush wine for the red wine. Substitute peach or strawberry slices for the lemon and lime slices.

WHITE SANGRÍA: Substitute vegan dry white wine such as chardonnay or sauvignon blanc for the dry red wine.

SPIRIT-FREE SANGRÍA: Substitute spirit-free vegan red wine for the alcoholic red wine.

SANGRÍA SLUSHIES: Freeze wine in ice cube trays at least 10 hours or up to 24 hours. Place wine ice cubes in blender with lemon juice, orange juice and sugar. Cover and blend about 30 seconds or until no large ice chunks remain. For sweeter slushies, stir in additional sugar to taste. Serve with sliced fruit.

Rosé Sangría and White Sangría

HEIRLOOM

MAKE AHEAD • GLUTEN FREE

Eggnog

For food safety, our eggnog is made with a cooked egg custard instead of raw eggs.

PREP 35 min TOTAL 2 hr 35 min • *10 servings*

CUSTARD

- 3 eggs, slightly beaten
- ⅓ cup granulated sugar
  Dash salt
- 2½ cups milk
- 1 teaspoon vanilla

EGGNOG

- 1 cup whipping cream
- 2 tablespoons powdered sugar
- ½ teaspoon vanilla
- ½ cup light rum, brandy or whiskey*
  Ground nutmeg

1 In 2-quart saucepan, stir eggs, granulated sugar and salt until well mixed. Gradually stir in milk. Cook over medium heat 10 to 15 minutes, stirring constantly, until mixture just coats a metal spoon; remove from heat. Stir in 1 teaspoon vanilla. Place saucepan in cold water until custard is cool. (If custard curdles, beat vigorously with hand beater until smooth.) Cover and refrigerate at least 2 hours but no longer than 24 hours.

2 Just before serving, in chilled medium bowl, beat whipping cream, powdered sugar and ½ teaspoon vanilla with electric mixer on high speed until stiff.

3 Gently stir 1 cup of the whipped cream and rum into custard. Pour custard mixture into small punch bowl. Drop remaining whipped cream in mounds onto custard mixture. Sprinkle with nutmeg. Serve immediately. Store covered in refrigerator up to 2 days.

1 Serving Calories 200; Total Fat 11g (Saturated Fat 7g, Trans Fat 0g); Cholesterol 90mg; Sodium 70mg; Total Carbohydrate 12g (Dietary Fiber 0g); Protein 4g **Carbohydrate Choices:** 1

*2 tablespoons rum extract and ⅓ cup milk can be substituted for the rum.

LIGHTER DIRECTIONS: For 120 calories and 3 grams of fat per serving, for the custard, substitute 2 whole eggs plus 2 egg whites for the 3 eggs and 2¼ cups fat-free (skim) milk for the milk. For the eggnog, substitute 2 cups frozen (thawed) reduced-fat whipped topping for the beaten whipping cream, powdered sugar and vanilla.

BOURBON-MAPLE EGGNOG: Make eggnog as directed except substitute ½ cup real maple syrup for the granulated sugar in the custard and add 2 tablespoons real maple syrup with the whipping cream. Substitute bourbon for the rum. If desired, dip rims of glasses or mugs in eggnog and coat in finely chopped, crisply cooked gluten-free bacon.

NEW TWIST

MAKE AHEAD • CALORIE SMART • GLUTEN FREE • VEGETARIAN • VEGAN

Double-Vanilla Vegan "Eggnog"

PREP 10 min TOTAL 1 hr 15 min •
8 servings (½ cup each)

- 4 pitted whole dates
- ½ cup hot tap water
- 3½ cups vanilla almond milk
- 1 can (13.55 oz) coconut milk (not low-fat)
- 2 teaspoons vanilla
- ½ teaspoon ground nutmeg
- ½ teaspoon ground cinnamon
- 1 vanilla bean
- ½ cup rum or 1 teaspoon rum extract

  Toppings, if desired: refrigerated nondairy whipped topping, cinnamon sticks

1 In small bowl, soak dates in hot water 5 minutes to soften. Drain well; discard water.

2 In blender, place dates and remaining ingredients except vanilla bean, rum and toppings. Split vanilla bean in half lengthwise; scrape seeds into blender. Discard pods. Cover; blend on high speed 2 to 3 minutes or until well blended. Cover and refrigerate at least 1 hour.

3 Just before serving, stir rum into almond milk mixture until well blended; pour into pitcher or small punch bowl. Top each serving with toppings.

1 Serving Calories 150; Total Fat 10g (Saturated Fat 8g, Trans Fat 0g); Cholesterol 0mg; Sodium 80mg; Total Carbohydrate 6g (Dietary Fiber 1g); Protein 1g **Carbohydrate Choices:** ½

MAKE-AHEAD DIRECTIONS: Can be prepared through Step 2; cover and refrigerate up to 48 hours. Continue as directed in Step 3.

Eggnog

Double-Vanilla Vegan "Eggnog"

Kombucha

PREP 15 min **TOTAL** 1 week • *29 servings* (½ cup each)

14½ cups filtered water, room temperature

1 cup organic sugar

6 black or green tea bags

1 kombucha starter kit containing 1 SCOBY and

1½ cups starter liquid, room temperature (see Learn to Make Kombucha, page 82)

1 (1-gallon) glass jar with lid, pH strips, coffee filter and rubber band

1 In medium saucepan, bring 2 cups of the filtered water to a boil; remove from heat. Stir in sugar; add tea bags. Allow tea to steep about 1 hour or until mixture reaches room temperature.

2 Remove tea bags. Pour tea into clean, dry 1-gallon glass jar. Stir in remaining 12½ cups filtered water and 1½ cups starter liquid from starter kit (discard any remaining starter liquid). Test the pH. (See pH Is Critical, page 82.)

3 Add SCOBY to jar with slotted spoon; gently stir. Secure coffee filter over top of jar with rubber band. Place in warm spot (70°F to 80°F) out of direct sunlight. Let stand undisturbed for 7 days.

4 Test pH using a pH strip. For safe consumption, the pH of the kombucha must be in the range of 2.5 to 4.2. If pH is within the appropriate range, taste for desired

sweetness and fizziness. If pH is outside desired range or if you prefer it less sweet and more fizzy, let mixture ferment up to 3 days longer. Test pH of kombucha for appropriate range before consuming.

5 Remove SCOBY and 1½ cups of the kombucha (see Save the SCOBY, page 82). If any solid material is apparent, remove by pouring kombucha through fine-mesh strainer or cheesecloth. Store finished kombucha in glass jar covered with lid in refrigerator for up to 2 weeks.

1 Serving Calories 20; Total Fat 0g (Saturated Fat 0g, Trans Fat 0g); Cholesterol 0mg; Sodium 0mg; Total Carbohydrate 5g (Dietary Fiber 0g); Protein 0g **Carbohydrate Choices:** ½

STRAWBERRY-RHUBARB KOMBUCHA: In 1-quart glass jar, mix 3½ cups of the finished kombucha and ½ cup Strawberry-Rhubarb Ginger Simple Syrup (page 95). Secure coffee filter over top of jar with rubber band. Place in warm spot (70°F to 80°F) out of direct sunlight. Let stand 1 to 3 days until mixture reaches desired fizziness and flavor. Test pH for safe consumption level of 2.5 to 4.2. Strain kombucha, if necessary. Store finished kombucha, covered with lid, in refrigerator.

PEACH KOMBUCHA COCKTAIL: In small bowl, toss 4 frozen peach slices, partially thawed, with 1 teaspoon organic sugar. Fill 2 glasses with ice cubes; top with peaches and sweetened liquid from peaches. For each serving, pour ¼ cup bottled peach juice, 1 teaspoon fresh lemon juice, 2 tablespoons vodka (1 oz) and ⅓ cup finished kombucha over peaches in each glass. Top each with vegan maraschino cherry.

Peach Kombucha Cocktail and Strawberry-Rhubarb Kombucha

Breakfast
& Brunch

Breakfast & Brunch Basics

Set the stage for a great day by filling your "tank" with a satisfying breakfast. Not only is it good to get your metabolism off to a great start, but it's a loving thing you can do for yourself and family. Whether it's a grab-and-go breakfast or a sit-down-and-savor brunch, you'll find recipes for every way you do breakfast.

Planning for Hectic Morning Breakfasts

- Make a list before you grocery shop, so you'll remember to stock your kitchen with quick and easy breakfast options and ingredients for recipes your family enjoys.
- When possible, pull together breakfast the night before and have it ready to grab on your way out the door.

Quick Breakfast Ideas

SWEET

Mango and Pistachio Overnight Oats (page 119)

Overnight Chia Seed Breakfast Pudding (page 121)

Apple Pie–Zucchini Breakfast Cookies (page 118)

SAVORY

Hard-Cooked Eggs (page 102)

Hearty Breakfast Sandwiches (page 104)

Mini Veggie Quiches (page 107)

Planning for a Leisurely Brunch

- Plan brunch for a time of the morning that allows you to enjoy the gathering. The types of foods can vary with the time of day you choose. If it is an early brunch, you might serve a make-the-night-before item like **Overnight Everything Bagel Breakfast Casserole** (page 103) with a bowl of mixed fruit. For a late morning brunch, you might choose **Spinach-Mushroom Eggs Benedict Enchiladas** (page 106) with a tossed green salad.
- Choose a variety of foods that include one or two main dishes, fresh fruit and/or vegetable salads and a choice of sweet or savory breads and/or a dessert. Beverages can be as simple as coffee, tea and juices. Make it special with **Ginger Water** (page 85) or **Classic Bloody Mary Cocktails** (page 94)!
- Plan for some foods that can be served at room temperature or chilled, if possible.
- Write your menu down so that you can check items off as you get things ready.
- Set the table or buffet with the centerpiece and gather plates, napkins and other serving utensils the night before.

Egg Basics

Eggs are a fast and easy way to get a nutritious breakfast on the table in minutes! With the snap of your fingers, you can even make an easy dinner when your fridge is practically empty—a quick fried egg sandwich, or scrambled egg burritos. Or top salads with poached or hard-cooked eggs for extra protein and interest.

EASY • FAST • CALORIE SMART

Scrambled Eggs

PREP 10 Minutes **TOTAL** 10 Minutes • *4 servings*

6 eggs	⅛ teaspoon pepper, if desired
⅓ cup water, milk or half-and-half	1 tablespoon butter
¼ teaspoon salt	

1 In medium bowl, beat eggs, water, salt and pepper thoroughly with fork or whisk until well mixed.

2 In 10-inch skillet, heat butter over medium heat just until butter begins to sizzle. Pour egg mixture into skillet.

3 As mixture begins to set at bottom and side, gently lift cooked portions with metal spatula so the thin uncooked portion can flow to bottom. Avoid constant stirring. Cook 3 to 4 minutes more or until eggs are thickened throughout but still moist.

1 Serving Calories 140; Total Fat 11g (Saturated Fat 4.5g, Trans Fat 0g); Cholesterol 285mg; Sodium 260mg; Total Carbohydrate 0g (Dietary Fiber 0g); Protein 9g **Carbohydrate Choices:** 0

MEXICAN SCRAMBLED EGG BURRITOS: In 10-inch skillet, cook ½ lb chorizo sausage links, cut lengthwise in half, then sliced, ½ cup chopped green or red bell pepper and ½ cup chopped onion over medium-high heat about 5 minutes, stirring frequently, until sausage is no longer pink; drain. Cook eggs in skillet as directed, adding sausage mixture to eggs before cooking the last 3 to 4 minutes in Step 3. Spoon mixture down center of 4 flour tortillas; top with salsa, shredded cheese and sour cream, if desired, and roll up.

MAKING FRIED EGGS

Carefully slide each egg from custard cup into pan.

Cook until film forms over top and whites and yolks are firm, not runny.

EASY • FAST • CALORIE SMART • GLUTEN FREE • VEGETARIAN

Fried Eggs, Sunny Side Up

PREP 15 Minutes **TOTAL** 15 Minutes • *4 servings*

2 tablespoons butter	4 eggs

1 In 10-inch skillet, melt butter over medium-high heat. Break 1 egg into custard cup or small glass bowl. Carefully slide egg from cup into skillet. Repeat with remaining 3 eggs. Immediately reduce heat to low.

2 Cook uncovered 5 to 7 minutes, frequently spooning butter from skillet over eggs, until film forms over top and whites and yolks are firm, not runny.

1 Serving Calories 130; Total Fat 11g (Saturated Fat 5g, Trans Fat 0g); Cholesterol 200mg; Sodium 110mg; Total Carbohydrate 0g (Dietary Fiber 0g); Protein 6g **Carbohydrate Choices:** 0

LIGHTER DIRECTIONS: Omit butter and use nonstick skillet. Add eggs to skillet as directed. Cook over low heat about 1 minute or until edges turn opaque. Add 2 teaspoons water for each egg. Cover and cook about 5 minutes longer or until film forms over top and whites and yolks are firm, not runny.

LEARN WITH BETTY SCRAMBLED EGGS

Ideal Scrambled Eggs: These eggs are fluffy and moist with large curds and no visible liquid egg remaining.

Undercooked Scrambled Eggs: These eggs haven't been cooked long enough, as liquid egg remains.

Overcooked Scrambled Eggs: These eggs are dry with small curds. Brown spots will affect the flavor.

EASY • FAST • CALORIE SMART • GLUTEN FREE • VEGETARIAN

Poached Eggs

PREP 10 Minutes TOTAL 15 Minutes • *4 servings*

4 eggs

1 In 10-inch skillet or 2-quart saucepan, heat 2 to 3 inches water to boiling. Reduce heat so water is simmering (see page 23).

2 Break 1 egg into custard cup or small glass bowl. Holding cup close to water's surface, carefully slide egg into water. Repeat with remaining 3 eggs.

3 Cook uncovered 3 to 5 minutes or until whites and yolks are firm, not runny. Carefully remove eggs with slotted spoon.

1 Serving Calories 80; Total Fat 5g (Saturated Fat 1.5g, Trans Fat 0g); Cholesterol 185mg; Sodium 60mg; Total Carbohydrate 0g (Dietary Fiber 0g); Protein 6g **Carbohydrate Choices:** 0

EASY • FAST • CALORIE SMART • GLUTEN FREE • VEGETARIAN

Hard-Cooked Eggs

PREP 10 Minutes TOTAL 30 Minutes • *6 eggs*

6 eggs

1 In 2-quart saucepan, place eggs in single layer; cover with cold water at least 1 inch above eggs. Cover and heat to boiling. Immediately remove from heat. Let stand 15 minutes for large eggs, 12 minutes for medium or 18 minutes for extra-large.

2 Drain. Immediately place eggs in cold water with ice cubes or run cold water over eggs until completely cooled.

3 To peel, gently tap egg on countertop until entire shell is finely cracked. Roll gently between hands to loosen shell. Starting at large end, peel egg under cold running water to help remove shell.

1 Egg Calories 80; Total Fat 5g (Saturated Fat 1.5g, Trans Fat 0g); Cholesterol 185mg; Sodium 60mg; Total Carbohydrate 0g (Dietary Fiber 0g); Protein 6g **Carbohydrate Choices:** 0

MAKING POACHED EGGS

Carefully slide egg into water.

Cook until whites and yolks are firm, not runny.

FAST • CALORIE SMART • GLUTEN FREE

Potato, Bacon and Egg Scramble

Precooking the potatoes in boiling water helps them cook faster, turning this scramble into a 20-minute meal.

PREP 10 Minutes TOTAL 20 Minutes • *5 servings*

1 lb small red potatoes (6 or 7), cubed	2 tablespoons butter
6 eggs	4 medium green onions, sliced (¼ cup)
⅓ cup milk	5 slices gluten-free bacon, crisply cooked, crumbled
¼ teaspoon salt	
⅛ teaspoon pepper	

1 In 2-quart saucepan, heat 1 inch water to boiling. Add potatoes. Heat to boiling; reduce heat to medium-low. Cover and cook 6 to 8 minutes or until potatoes are tender; drain.

2 In medium bowl, beat eggs, milk, salt and pepper with fork or whisk until well mixed; set aside.

MAKING HARD-COOKED EGGS

Place eggs in single layer, covering with at least 1 inch of water above eggs.

Gently tap egg until entire shell is finely cracked.

Starting at large end, peel under running water to help remove shell.

Potato, Bacon and Egg Scramble

Cauliflower-Tofu Scramble

3 In 10-inch skillet, melt butter over medium-high heat. Add potatoes; cook 3 to 5 minutes, turning occasionally, until light brown. Stir in onions. Cook 1 minute, stirring constantly.

4 Pour egg mixture into skillet. As eggs begin to set at bottom and side, gently lift cooked portions with spatula so that thin uncooked portion can flow to bottom. Avoid constant stirring. Cook 3 to 4 minutes or until eggs are thickened throughout but still moist. Sprinkle with bacon.

1 Serving Calories 250; Total Fat 14g (Saturated Fat 6g, Trans Fat 0g); Cholesterol 245mg; Sodium 380mg; Total Carbohydrate 18g (Dietary Fiber 2g); Protein 13g **Carbohydrate Choices:** 1

CHORIZO, POTATO AND EGG SCRAMBLE: Omit bacon. In 8-inch skillet, crumble ½ cup bulk gluten-free chorizo sausage; add ½ cup chopped green bell pepper. Cook and stir until sausage is no longer pink; drain. Stir into eggs at end of cook time. Garnish each serving with 1 to 2 tablespoons salsa.

FAST • CALORIE SMART • VEGETARIAN • VEGAN

Cauliflower-Tofu Scramble

PREP 15 Minutes **TOTAL** 15 Minutes •
6 servings (about ¾ cup each)

1 package (12 oz) extra-firm tofu, drained	1 cup frozen riced cauliflower (from 10-oz bag)
1 tablespoon vegetable oil	¾ teaspoon garlic salt
½ cup chopped red bell pepper	¾ teaspoon turmeric
4 medium green onions, sliced (¼ cup)	¼ teaspoon pepper

1 Place tofu in a medium bowl. Using a fork, crumble into large curds.

2 In 12-inch skillet, heat oil over medium-high heat. Add bell pepper and onions; cook 1 to 2 minutes, stirring occasionally. Stir in tofu and remaining ingredients. Cook, stirring occasionally, 4 to 5 minutes or until mixture is hot and bell pepper is crisp-tender. Serve immediately.

1 Serving Calories 70; Total Fat 4.5g (Saturated Fat 1g, Trans Fat 0g); Cholesterol 0mg; Sodium 130mg; Total Carbohydrate 3g (Dietary Fiber 1g); Protein 5g **Carbohydrate Choices:** 0

CAULIFLOWER-TOFU BREAKFAST BURRITOS: Spoon your favorite guacamole down the center of each of 6 (7- or 8-inch) flour tortillas; top with cooked mixture. Roll up and place on plates. Garnish with cilantro and serve with salsa.

MAKE AHEAD • CALORIE SMART

Overnight Everything Bagel Breakfast Casserole

For an extra flavor kick, use spicy pork sausage.

PREP 25 Minutes **TOTAL** 5 Hours 20 Minutes • **12 servings**

1 lb bulk pork sausage	12 eggs
4 everything bagels, cut into 1-inch cubes (8 cups)	1½ cups half-and-half
	½ teaspoon salt
	¼ teaspoon pepper
8 medium green onions, chopped (½ cup)	2 cups shredded sharp cheddar cheese (8 oz)
½ cup chopped red bell pepper	

1 Spray 13x9-inch (3-quart) baking dish with cooking spray. In 10-inch nonstick skillet, cook sausage over medium-high heat, stirring occasionally, until no longer pink; drain.

2 In baking dish, toss sausage, bagel cubes, onions and bell pepper until well mixed. Set aside.

3 In large bowl, beat eggs, half-and-half, salt and pepper with whisk until well blended. Stir in 1 cup of the cheese; pour evenly over bagel mixture. Cover with foil; refrigerate at least 4 hours but no longer than 24 hours.

4 Heat oven to 375°F. Uncover baking dish. Bake 30 to 40 minutes or until golden brown and knife inserted in center comes out clean. Sprinkle with remaining 1 cup cheese. Bake about 5 minutes longer or until cheese is melted. Let stand 10 minutes before serving.

1 Serving Calories 340; Total Fat 21g (Saturated Fat 9g, Trans Fat 0g); Cholesterol 230mg; Sodium 580mg; Total Carbohydrate 21g (Dietary Fiber 1g); Protein 18g **Carbohydrate Choices:** 1½

Pimiento Cheese
Breakfast Casserole

Pimiento Cheese Breakfast Casserole

Pimiento cheese is practically a staple in the southern United States. There are many styles and everyone has their own recipe. It's typically served as a dip or spread. Shredding your own block cheese makes it easier to blend it into a creamy pimiento cheese.

PREP 20 Minutes **TOTAL** 1 Hour 25 Minutes • *8 servings*

PIMIENTO CHEESE

- 1 block (8 oz) sharp cheddar cheese, shredded
- ½ cup mayonnaise
- 2 jars (4 oz each) diced pimientos, well drained
- 1 can (4.5 oz) chopped green chiles
- 8 medium green onions, thinly sliced (½ cup)
- 2 tablespoons finely chopped jarred pickled jalapeño chiles
- 2 teaspoons Worcestershire sauce
- ¼ teaspoon ground red pepper (cayenne), if desired

CASSEROLE

- 10 eggs
- 1 package (20 oz) refrigerated shredded hash brown potatoes
- 2 cups chopped cooked ham
- Chopped Italian (flat-leaf) parsley, if desired

1 Heat oven to 350°F. Spray 13x9-inch (3-quart) baking dish with cooking spray.

2 In large bowl, beat pimiento cheese ingredients with electric mixer on medium speed 1 to 2 minutes or until creamy.

3 In another large bowl, beat eggs with whisk; stir in pimiento cheese mixture. Add potatoes and ham; stir until well mixed. Pour mixture into baking dish.

4 Bake 43 to 48 minutes or until edges are golden brown and center is set. Let stand 15 minutes; top with parsley before serving.

1 Serving Calories 440; Total Fat 29g (Saturated Fat 10g, Trans Fat 0g); Cholesterol 285mg; Sodium 1020mg; Total Carbohydrate 19g (Dietary Fiber 2g); Protein 24g **Carbohydrate Choices:** 1

FAST • MAKE AHEAD • CALORIE SMART

Hearty Breakfast Sandwiches

PREP 30 Minutes **TOTAL** 30 Minutes • *4 sandwiches*

- 4 pork breakfast sausage patties (from 12-oz package)
- 4 eggs
- ¼ teaspoon pepper
- ¼ cup shredded cheddar or mozzarella cheese (1 oz)
- 4 English muffins or bagels, split

1 Cook sausage patties as directed on package. Keep warm.

2 In small bowl, beat eggs and pepper until well blended. Spray 10-inch skillet with cooking spray. Heat over medium heat until hot. Pour egg mixture into skillet. Reduce heat to low; cook until eggs are almost set but still moist, stirring occasionally from outside edge to center, allowing uncooked egg to flow to bottom of skillet.

3 Sprinkle with cheese. Cover; remove from heat. Let stand 1 minute or until cheese is melted. Meanwhile, toast English muffins. Place 1 sausage patty on bottom half of each English muffin. Top each patty with one fourth of the eggs. Cover with top half of English muffin.

1 Sandwich Calories 390; Total Fat 23g (Saturated Fat 8g, Trans Fat 0g); Cholesterol 220mg; Sodium 700mg; Total Carbohydrate 26g (Dietary Fiber 2g); Protein 18g **Carbohydrate Choices:** 2

MAKE-AHEAD DIRECTIONS: Wrap individual cooled sandwiches in plastic wrap; refrigerate up to 4 days. To reheat, unwrap sandwich and place on microwavable plate. Cover with paper towel. Microwave on Medium (50%) 1 minute or until hot.

MEXICAN BREAKFAST BURRITOS: Substitute 8 breakfast sausage links for patties and 4 (7- or 8-inch) flour tortillas for English muffins. In Step 3, place 2 cooked links on each tortilla; top with eggs and drizzle with red pepper sauce. Roll up tortillas, tucking in sides.

MAKE AHEAD • CALORIE SMART

Ham and Cheddar Strata

PREP 15 Minutes **TOTAL** 1 Hour 35 Minutes • *8 servings*

- 12 slices bread
- 2 cups cut-up cooked smoked ham (about 10 oz)
- 2 cups shredded cheddar cheese (8 oz)
- 8 medium green onions, sliced (½ cup)
- 6 eggs
- 2 cups milk
- 1 teaspoon ground mustard
- ¼ teaspoon red pepper sauce
- Paprika, if desired

1 Heat oven to 300°F. Spray 13x9-inch (3-quart) glass baking dish with cooking spray.

2 Trim crusts from bread. Arrange 6 of the slices in baking dish. Layer ham, cheese and onions on bread in dish. Cut remaining 6 bread slices diagonally in half; arrange on onions.

3 In medium bowl, beat eggs, milk, mustard and pepper sauce with fork or whisk; pour evenly over bread. Sprinkle with paprika.

4 Bake uncovered 1 hour to 1 hour 10 minutes or until center is set and bread is golden brown. Let stand 10 minutes before cutting.

1 Serving Calories 380; Total Fat 20g (Saturated Fat 9g, Trans Fat 0g); Cholesterol 190mg; Sodium 970mg; Total Carbohydrate 25g (Dietary Fiber 2g); Protein 25g **Carbohydrate Choices:** 1½

MAKE-AHEAD DIRECTIONS: Prepare recipe as directed through Step 3; cover and refrigerate up to 24 hours. Increase bake time by 5 to 10 minutes if necessary.

FAST • CALORIE SMART • GLUTEN FREE

Basic Omelet

Omelets are a great way to start your day or a natural go-to when it's dinnertime and there aren't many groceries in the refrigerator.

PREP 20 Minutes TOTAL 20 Minutes • **4 omelets**

8 eggs	8 teaspoons butter
Salt and pepper, if desired	

1 For each omelet, in small bowl, beat 2 of the eggs until fluffy. Add a dash of salt and pepper. In 8-inch nonstick omelet pan or skillet, heat 2 teaspoons of the butter over medium-high heat just until butter is hot and sizzling. As butter melts, tilt pan to coat bottom.

2 Quickly pour eggs into pan. While rapidly sliding pan back and forth over heat, quickly and continuously stir with spatula to spread eggs over bottom of pan as they thicken. Let stand over heat a few seconds to lightly brown bottom of omelet. Do not overcook; omelet will continue to cook after folding. If desired, add filling before folding.

3 To remove from pan, first run spatula under one edge of omelet, folding about one-third of it to the center. Transfer to plate by tilting pan, letting flat, unfolded edge of omelet slide out onto plate. Using edge of pan as a guide, flip folded edge of omelet over the flat portion on the plate.

4 Repeat with remaining butter and eggs. If desired, omelets can be kept warm on platter in 200°F oven while preparing remaining omelets.

1 Omelet Calories 220; Total Fat 18g (Saturated Fat 8g, Trans Fat 0g); Cholesterol 395mg; Sodium 180mg; Total Carbohydrate 1g (Dietary Fiber 0g); Protein 12g **Carbohydrate Choices:** 0

LIGHTER DIRECTIONS: For 8 grams of fat and 130 calories per omelet, substitute ½ cup fat-free egg product for 2 eggs.

CHEESE OMELET: Before folding each omelet, sprinkle with ¼ cup shredded cheddar, Monterey Jack or Swiss cheese, or ¼ cup crumbled blue cheese.

DENVER OMELET: Before adding eggs to pan for each omelet, cook 2 tablespoons chopped cooked ham, 1 tablespoon finely chopped bell pepper and 1 tablespoon finely chopped onion in butter about 2 minutes, stirring frequently. Continue as directed in Step 2.

HAM AND CHEESE OMELET: Before folding each omelet, sprinkle with 2 tablespoons shredded cheddar, Monterey Jack or Swiss cheese and 2 tablespoons finely chopped cooked ham.

MAKING AN OMELET

Stir eggs with spatula to spread over bottom of pan.

Fold about one-third of omelet over other side.

Use edge of pan to flip folded edge of omelet onto plate.

Denver Omelet

HEIRLOOM

FAST • CALORIE SMART

Eggs Benedict

As one story goes, Delmonico's restaurant in New York City was the birthplace of this classic brunch dish. In the late 1800s, when regular patrons Mr. and Mrs. LeGrand Benedict complained of nothing new on the lunch menu, the chef created this now-famous dish and named it after them.

PREP 30 Minutes **TOTAL** 30 Minutes • *6 servings*

Hollandaise Sauce (page 495)	6 thin slices Canadian bacon or cooked ham
3 English muffins, split, toasted	6 eggs
7 teaspoons butter, softened	Paprika, if desired

1 Prepare Hollandaise Sauce; keep warm.

2 Spread each toasted muffin half with 1 teaspoon of the butter; keep warm.

3 Poach eggs in 12-inch skillet, using method for Poached Eggs, page 102.

4 Meanwhile, in 10-inch skillet, melt remaining 1 teaspoon butter over medium heat. Cook bacon in butter until lightly browned on both sides.

5 Place 1 slice bacon on each muffin half; top with 1 poached egg. Spoon hollandaise sauce over eggs. Sprinkle with paprika.

1 Serving Calories 380; Total Fat 28g (Saturated Fat 15g, Trans Fat 1g); Cholesterol 345mg; Sodium 550mg; Total Carbohydrate 14g (Dietary Fiber 1g); Protein 16g **Carbohydrate Choices:** 1

NEW TWIST

Spinach-Mushroom Eggs Benedict Enchiladas

If you prefer, you can make hollandaise sauce using 1 package (1.25 oz) hollandaise sauce mix, 1 cup water and ¼ cup butter. Prepare according to package directions.

PREP 25 Minutes **TOTAL** 45 Minutes • *6 servings*

1 tablespoon butter	Hollandaise Sauce (page 495)
2 cups sliced fresh mushrooms (about 5 oz)	3 cups loosely packed fresh baby spinach leaves (from 5-oz package), chopped
6 eggs	
⅓ cup water	1 tablespoon water
¼ teaspoon salt	½ cup shredded Monterey Jack cheese (2 oz)
⅛ teaspoon pepper	
¾ cup diced cooked ham	¼ cup chopped tomato
6 (6-inch) flour tortillas	

1 Heat oven to 350°F. Spray 11x7-inch (2-quart) glass baking dish with cooking spray. In 10-inch nonstick skillet, melt butter over medium heat. Add mushrooms; cook 3 minutes, stirring frequently. Remove from skillet.

2 In medium bowl, beat eggs, ⅓ cup water, salt and pepper with fork or whisk. Pour egg mixture into same skillet; sprinkle with ham. Cook over medium heat. As mixture begins to set on bottom and side, gently lift cooked portions so that thin uncooked portion can flow to bottom. Avoid constant stirring. Cook 3 to 4 minutes or until eggs are thickened throughout but still moist. Remove from heat.

Eggs Benedict

Spinach-
Mushroom
Eggs Benedict
Enchiladas

3 For each enchilada, spoon slightly less than ½ cup egg mixture down center of tortilla; top with about 2 tablespoons mushrooms. Roll up; place enchiladas, seam sides down, in baking dish. Cover; bake 15 minutes.

4 Wipe out skillet. On high heat, toss spinach and 1 tablespoon water 1 to 2 minutes or until spinach is wilted.

5 Pour hollandaise sauce over enchiladas. Spoon spinach, cheese and tomatoes down center of enchiladas. Bake uncovered 5 minutes or until cheese is melted.

1 Serving Calories 420; Total Fat 31g (Saturated Fat 17g, Trans Fat 1g); Cholesterol 340mg; Sodium 820mg; Total Carbohydrate 16g (Dietary Fiber 1g); Protein 17g **Carbohydrate Choices:** 1

⟳ USE IT UP
SPINACH

SOUPS, STEWS OR PASTA DISHES Stir in during the last few minutes of cooking, just until it wilts.

SALAD SUBSTITUTE Mix it with other greens in salads when making lettuce salads.

GREEN SMOOTHIES Add it with fruit in smoothies for a boost of nutrition.

SANDWICHES Add to sandwiches in place of lettuce.

SPINACH PESTO Prepare as directed on page 480. Use as a sandwich spread, to toss with pasta or serve on top of eggs.

CALORIE SMART • VEGETARIAN

Mini Veggie Quiches

PREP 30 Minutes **TOTAL** 1 Hour • *10 quiches*

Pie Pastry for One-Crust Pie (page 607)

4 oz (half of 8-oz package) cream cheese, softened, cut into 10 cubes

3 eggs

2 cloves garlic, finely chopped

½ teaspoon Italian seasoning

¼ teaspoon salt

¼ teaspoon pepper

2 cups lightly packed fresh baby spinach leaves (from 5-oz bag), chopped

½ cup chopped red bell pepper

½ cup finely shredded sharp cheddar cheese (2 oz)

5 medium green onions, sliced (about ⅓ cup)

1 Heat oven to 425°F. Prepare pastry as directed, rolling into 12-inch round. With 3½-inch round cookie cutter, cut into 10 rounds, rerolling scraps as necessary. Press 1 round in bottom and up sides of each of 10 regular-size muffin cups. Place 1 piece of cream cheese in center of each muffin cup; slightly pressing into dough. Set aside.

2 In medium bowl, beat eggs, garlic, Italian seasoning, salt and pepper with fork or whisk. Stir in remaining ingredients until well blended. Spoon about 2 tablespoons of the mixture into each crust-lined muffin cup.

3 Bake 16 to 20 minutes or until filling is set and edges are light golden brown. Cool 10 minutes. Remove from pan; sprinkle with Parmesan cheese. Serve warm. Cover and refrigerate any remaining quiches.

1 Quiche Calories 200; Total Fat 14g (Saturated Fat 6g, Trans Fat 0g); Cholesterol 75mg; Sodium 270mg; Total Carbohydrate 12g (Dietary Fiber 0g); Protein 5g **Carbohydrate Choices:** 1

Mini Veggie Quiches

GLOBAL FLAVORS

Middle Eastern

**Take a trip to the other side of the world without even leaving your kitchen!
Explore the variety of flavors and diversity of Middle Eastern cuisine. Try Classic Shakshuka, page 110, for a taste of the Middle East.**

DATES

The fruit of the date palm. Very sweet; contain a long, narrow seed. Available dried, or fresh in late summer through mid-fall.

FIGS

Fresh figs can be found May to December, depending on the variety, which can range in color and flavor. Dried figs are available year round.

FLATBREAD

There are many varieties that vary slightly in ingredients and technique. Flatbread is used at nearly every meal to scoop up meat, vegetables and rice and to sop up sauces and dips. **Pita** rounds can be split horizontally to form a pocket that is used to stuff ingredients for sandwiches. **Naan** is traditionally baked in a tandoor oven to achieve its characteristic smoky flavor. **Sabaayed** is a grilled Somali flatbread that has a crispy outside and flaky interior.

HARISSA

A spicy-hot sauce, both green and red; use as accompaniment for couscous and to flavor soups, stews and other dishes. Available canned or jarred. To make your own, see page 457.

POMEGRANATES

Inside the leathery skin of this fruit are hundreds of juicy, tart seeds packed in sections separated by membranes. Typically available August through December; also look for fresh pomegranate seeds, which eliminates peeling and separating the fruit.

POMEGRANATE MOLASSES

Pomegranate juice reduced to thick, tart-sweet syrup, used as a marinade for grilled meats or in everything from dips to stews.

PRESERVED LEMONS

A staple in Moroccan cooking, these lemons have been preserved in salty lemon juice brine—possibly with cinnamon, cloves or other spices—giving them a silky texture and unique flavor.

SUMAC

Ground dried berries found in Middle Eastern markets, this brick- to dark-purple spice adds fruity, astringent flavor to meat, fish and vegetables.

TAHINI

A MIddle Eastern staple, this thick paste is made from ground sesame seed. Available in many grocery stores near the international ingredients.

ZA'ATAR

Both a native spice of the Middle East with flavors reminiscent of marjoram, oregano and thyme and also the name of a popular dry spice blend containing toasted sesame seed, marjoram and sumac. Mix with olive oil and salt and drizzle over warm bread or use to season meat and vegetables.

Pomegranate

Preserved Lemons

Sabaayed

Pomegranate Molasses

Olive Oil

Sumac

Dates

Honey

Almonds

Fresh Dates

Figs

Dried Pineapples

Olives

Dried Apricots

Dried Mangos

Ground Turmeric

White Sesame Seeds

Ground Ginger

Za'atar

Egyptian Roomi Cheese

Gingerroot

Tahini

Feta

Fresh Turmeric

Saffron

Cinnamon

Red Harissa

Green Harissa

Whole Allspice   Ground Allspice   Whole Coriander   Ground Coriander   Cumin Seed   Ground Cumin   Caraway Seed   Ground Caraway

Potato Nugget
Breakfast Cups

Classic Shakshuka

CALORIE SMART

Potato Nugget Breakfast Cups

PREP 30 Minutes **TOTAL** 1 Hour 55 Minutes • *12 servings*

12 **dozen (144) frozen mini potato nuggets (from 28-oz bag)**	4 **eggs, slightly beaten**
1 **cup shredded sharp cheddar cheese (4 oz)**	¼ **teaspoon salt**
	½ **lb bulk breakfast sausage**
¼ **cup milk**	1 **small onion, diced (½ cup)**

1 Heat oven to 400°F. Place foil baking cup in each of 12 regular-size muffin cups; spray foil baking cups with cooking spray.

2 Place 6 potato nuggets in each muffin cup; bake 30 minutes. Remove from oven; cool 5 minutes. Using two paper towels, gently press potatoes into cups to create a base. Evenly sprinkle cheese over potatoes in each muffin cup.

3 In small bowl, mix milk, eggs and salt; set aside.

4 In 10-inch nonstick skillet, cook sausage and onion over medium-high heat 5 to 7 minutes, stirring frequently, until browned. Cool 2 minutes. Spoon evenly over potato nugget base in each cup. Pour egg mixture evenly over sausage mixture. Top each cup with 6 more potato nuggets; gently press into mixture.

5 Bake 32 to 34 minutes or until mixture is set and potato nuggets are golden brown. Cool 15 minutes.

1 Serving Calories 220; Total Fat 14g (Saturated Fat 4.5g, Trans Fat 0g); Cholesterol 80mg; Sodium 490mg; Total Carbohydrate 15g (Dietary Fiber 1g); Protein 8g **Carbohydrate Choices:** 1

CALORIE SMART • GLUTEN FREE • VEGETARIAN

Classic Shakshuka

Here is our version of a Middle Eastern favorite.

PREP 25 Minutes **TOTAL** 50 Minutes • *6 servings*

2 **tablespoons olive oil**	1 **teaspoon sugar**
1 **medium onion, chopped (1 cup)**	1¼ **teaspoons salt**
1 **medium red bell pepper, chopped (1 cup)**	¼ **teaspoon pepper**
3 **cloves garlic, finely chopped**	¼ **teaspoon crushed red pepper flakes**
2 **teaspoons ground cumin**	6 **pasteurized eggs***
1 **teaspoon paprika**	¾ **cup crumbled feta cheese (3 oz)**
1 **can (28 oz) crushed tomatoes, undrained**	**Chopped fresh cilantro or chives, if desired**
	Crusty bread, if desired

1 Heat oven to 350°F. In 12-inch ovenproof skillet, heat oil over medium heat. Add onion, bell pepper and garlic; cook about 8 minutes, stirring occasionally, until tender. Add cumin and paprika; cook 1 minute, stirring once. Stir in tomatoes, sugar, salt, pepper and pepper flakes.

2 Heat to simmering; remove from heat. With back of spoon, make 6 (3-inch-wide) indentations in tomato mixture. Break eggs, one at a time, into custard cup or small glass bowl; carefully slide egg into each indentation. Place skillet in oven.

3 Bake uncovered 20 to 25 minutes or until whites are firm but yolks are still slightly runny. Bake longer for firm yolks, if desired. Sprinkle with cheese and cilantro. Serve with bread.

1 Serving Calories 220; Total Fat 14g (Saturated Fat 5g, Trans Fat 0g); Cholesterol 205mg; Sodium 960mg; Total Carbohydrate 13g (Dietary Fiber 2g); Protein 10g **Carbohydrate Choices:** 1

*Use only pasteurized eggs in this recipe to prevent the risk of foodborne illness that can result from eating raw or undercooked eggs. They can be found in the dairy case at large supermarkets.

USE IT UP
COOKED SAUSAGE CRUMBLES

Keep cooked breakfast, pork or turkey sausage in a freezer container to have on hand to add bulk, flavor and protein to your recipes.

BREAKFAST BURRITOS
Add while making Scrambled Eggs (page 101). Place mixture in center of tortilla with any other toppings such as shredded cheese, black beans, avocado and/or salsa; roll up. And serve more on top with syrup and berries.

FRUITY SAUSAGE PANCAKES OR WAFFLES Add to batter with blueberries or chopped strawberries before cooking.

SAUSAGE SLOPPY JOES Omit Step 1 of Sloppy Joes (page 289). Substitute the cooked crumbles for ground beef in Step 2.

MEATY CHILI OR SOUP Stir into chili or soup before reheating. Heat until hot.

SAUSAGE-MUSHROOM FLATBREAD Top your favorite flatbread with cooked mushrooms, thyme, sausage crumbles, sliced red onion, chopped bell pepper and fontina cheese. Bake as directed on flatbread package.

111

Moroccan-Style Breakfast Bowl

FAST • CALORIE SMART • GLUTEN FREE • VEGETARIAN

Moroccan-Style Breakfast Bowl

To streamline this recipe even more, you can prepare the Moroccan chick peas, quinoa and hard-cooked eggs ahead and refrigerate. Warm the chick peas and quinoa just before assembling the bowls.

PREP 15 Minutes **TOTAL** 15 Minutes • *2 servings*

MOROCCAN CHICK PEAS

- 1 cup chick peas (garbanzo beans; from 15-oz can), drained, rinsed
- 2/3 cup chunky-style salsa
- 3 tablespoons water
- 1/2 teaspoon chili powder
- 1/2 teaspoon garam masala
- 1/8 teaspoon salt

BOWL

- 1 cup lightly packed baby arugula leaves
- 1 teaspoon olive oil
- 1 teaspoon fresh lemon juice
- 1 cup cooked quinoa, warmed (page 212)
- 2 hard-cooked eggs (page 102), peeled and cut in half, or poached eggs (page 102)
- 6 thin slices avocado
- 1/4 cup hummus (for homemade hummus, see page 48)
- 1/4 cup crumbled feta cheese (1 oz)
- Red pepper flakes and additional salsa, if desired

1 In 10-inch skillet, heat all Moroccan chick peas ingredients over medium heat to boiling, stirring occasionally. Cook uncovered 2 minutes, stirring frequently.

2 To assemble bowls, toss arugula with oil and lemon juice; place half of the arugula to one side of each serving bowl. Place half of the quinoa and half of the chick pea mixture in each bowl. Top each with 2 hard-cooked egg halves, and half of each of the avocado slices and hummus. Sprinkle each with feta cheese and red pepper flakes. Serve immediately with additional salsa.

1 Serving Calories 550; Total Fat 27g (Saturated Fat 6g, Trans Fat 0g); Cholesterol 205mg; Sodium 1610mg; Total Carbohydrate 54g (Dietary Fiber 12g); Protein 23g **Carbohydrate Choices:** 3½

CALORIE SMART

Oven-Baked Bacon

This is a terrific way to cook bacon when you are cooking a large batch or when you want to add seasonings. If you want to cook just a few plain pieces, see our microwave directions on page 33.

PREP 5 Minutes **TOTAL** 40 Minutes • *12 slices*

- 12 slices bacon

1 Heat oven to 350°F. Line 15x10x1-inch pan with foil. Place oven-safe cooling rack on foil, making sure rack fits within interior of pan so drippings don't fall to bottom of oven. Arrange bacon in single layer on rack.

2 Bake 20 minutes. Turn bacon over. Bake 10 to 15 minutes longer or until crisp and golden brown. Remove from rack to paper towels. Serve warm.

1 Slice Calories 60; Total Fat 3g (Saturated Fat 1g, Trans Fat 0g); Cholesterol 10mg; Sodium 135mg; Total Carbohydrate 5g (Dietary Fiber 0g); Protein 2g **Carbohydrate Choices:** ½

BALSAMIC AND BROWN SUGAR BACON: In small bowl, mix ¼ cup packed brown sugar and 2 tablespoons balsamic vinegar. Make bacon as directed—except after turning bacon over, brush slices with balsamic mixture.

HERB-SEASONED BACON: In large resealable food-storage plastic bag, place 3 tablespoons salt-free herb blend. Separate bacon slices and place in bag; seal and shake to coat. Arrange bacon in single layer on rack. Bake as directed.

HONEY-MUSTARD BACON: Brush both sides of bacon with ⅓ cup honey mustard. Arrange bacon in single layer on rack. Bake as directed.

PEPPERED BROWN SUGAR BACON: In large resealable food-storage plastic bag, mix ½ cup packed brown sugar, 1 teaspoon coarse ground black pepper and ¼ teaspoon ground red pepper (cayenne). Separate bacon slices and place in bag; seal and shake to coat. Arrange bacon in single layer on rack. Bake as directed.

PRALINE BACON: In small bowl, mix ¼ cup packed brown sugar and ¼ cup finely chopped pecans. Make bacon as directed—except after turning bacon over, sprinkle evenly with pecan mixture.

Pancakes

This classic pancake recipe has appeared in every Betty Crocker cookbook since 1950. Pancakes are a breakfast tradition, and are so easy to make. Our recipe calls for regular milk, but we also give a variation to use buttermilk. Top either version with maple syrup or fresh fruit.

PREP 25 Minutes **TOTAL** 25 Minutes • *9 pancakes*

1 egg	¼ teaspoon salt
1 cup all-purpose or whole wheat flour	¾ cup milk
1 tablespoon sugar	2 tablespoons vegetable oil or melted butter
3 teaspoons baking powder	

1 In medium bowl, beat egg with whisk until fluffy. Stir in remaining ingredients just until flour is moistened (batter will be slightly lumpy); do not overmix or pancakes will be tough. For thinner pancakes, stir in 1 to 2 tablespoons additional milk.

2 Heat griddle or skillet over medium-high heat (375°F). (To test griddle, sprinkle with a few drops of water. If bubbles jump around, heat is just right.) Brush with vegetable oil if necessary.

3 For each pancake, pour slightly less than ¼ cup batter onto hot griddle. Cook 2 to 3 minutes or until bubbly on top and dry around edges. Turn; cook other side until golden brown.

1 Pancake Calories 100; Total Fat 4g (Saturated Fat 1g, Trans Fat 0g); Cholesterol 20mg; Sodium 240mg; Total Carbohydrate 13g (Dietary Fiber 0g); Protein 2g **Carbohydrate Choices:** 1

BERRY PANCAKES: Stir ½ cup fresh or frozen (thawed and well drained) blackberries, blueberries or raspberries into batter.

BUTTERMILK PANCAKES: Substitute 1 cup buttermilk for ¾ cup milk. Reduce baking powder to 1 teaspoon. Add ½ teaspoon baking soda.

ORANGE-CRANBERRY PANCAKES: Substitute orange juice for milk. Stir in ¼ cup dried cranberries and ¼ cup chopped dried apples after mixing ingredients in Step 1.

WHOLE GRAIN STRAWBERRY PANCAKES: Make pancakes with whole wheat flour. Top each serving with ¼ cup strawberry yogurt and ½ cup sliced fresh strawberries.

Grain-Free Pancakes

Stir up these grain-free pancakes for breakfast when you want a quick and filling meal. Try topping with your favorite berry!

PREP 20 Minutes **TOTAL** 20 Minutes • *15 pancakes*

¾ cup blanched almond meal	4 eggs, slightly beaten
¼ cup coconut flour	2 tablespoons virgin coconut oil, melted
¾ teaspoon baking soda	Additional coconut oil for griddle
1 container (5.3 oz) plain yogurt (⅔ cup)	

1 Heat griddle or skillet over medium heat or electric griddle to 350°F. (Surface is ready when a few drops of water sprinkled on it dance and disappear.)

2 In small bowl, mix almond meal, coconut flour and baking soda. In medium bowl, beat yogurt, eggs and melted coconut oil with whisk until well blended. Stir flour mixture into yogurt mixture until blended.

3 Brush griddle with coconut oil. For each pancake, pour or scoop about 2 tablespoons batter onto hot griddle. Cook 1 to 2 minutes or until pancakes are browned. Turn; cook other side until golden brown. Remove pancakes from griddle to serving plate. Repeat with remaining batter. If not serving immediately, remove pancakes to oven-safe cooling rack placed on cookie sheet; keep warm in 200°F oven.

1 Serving Calories 80; Total Fat 6g (Saturated Fat 2.5g, Trans Fat 0g); Cholesterol 50mg; Sodium 90mg; Total Carbohydrate 3g (Dietary Fiber 1g); Protein 3g **Carbohydrate Choices:** 0

Pancakes

Grain-Free Pancakes

Smashed Pea-Zucchini Pancakes with Golden Syrup

Apple Oven Pancake

Broccoli and
Mushroom–
Stuffed Potato
Pancakes

Smashed Pea-Zucchini Pancakes

If you don't have a vegetable spiralizer, you may find spiralized zucchini at some grocery stores. Otherwise, substitute 1 cup shredded zucchini for spiralized zucchini and stir into the pancake batter just before cooking.

PREP 30 Minutes **TOTAL** 30 Minutes •
7 servings (2 pancakes each)

2 small zucchini or 3 cups spiralized zucchini	½ teaspoon onion powder
1⅓ cups almond milk	¼ teaspoon ground red pepper (cayenne)
1 tablespoon olive oil	¼ teaspoon pepper
2 eggs	1 cup frozen peas, thawed
1¼ cups brown rice flour	About 1 cup Golden Syrup (page 466) or maple-flavored syrup, if desired
1 cup almond flour	
2 teaspoons gluten-free baking powder	
½ teaspoon salt	

1 If using whole zucchini, cut off ends. Cut zucchini with spiralizer according to manufacturer's directions and measure about 3 cups; set aside.

2 In blender container, place almond milk, oil and eggs. Cover; blend on medium speed 10 seconds until well mixed. Add remaining ingredients except peas and syrup. Cover; blend on medium speed 30 seconds, stopping blender to scrape sides if necessary, until smooth. Add peas. Cover; pulse 3 to 5 times or just until peas are broken up.

3 Heat griddle or skillet over medium heat or electric griddle to 350°F. Brush with oil if necessary.

4 On large plate or work surface, make 14 mounds of zucchini using ¼ cup (do not pack) zucchini spirals for each mound, breaking spirals apart as necessary.

5 For each pancake, pour about ¼ cupful batter on hot griddle. Immediately top each pancake with a mound of spirals, pressing lightly with spatula. Cook 2 to 3 minutes or until bubbly on top and dry around edges. Turn; cook other side until golden brown. Serve with Golden Syrup.

1 Serving Calories 270; Total Fat 13g (Saturated Fat 1.5g, Trans Fat 0g); Cholesterol 55mg; Sodium 370mg; Total Carbohydrate 30g (Dietary Fiber 4g); Protein 9g **Carbohydrate Choices:** 2

TURNING PANCAKES

Pancakes are ready to turn when they are puffed and bubbles form on top.

Apple Oven Pancake

Part pancake, part popover, it puffs up high around the edges when it's done. Serve it quickly, before it sinks.

PREP 10 Minutes **TOTAL** 45 Minutes • *4 servings*

- 2 tablespoons butter
- 2 tablespoon packed brown sugar
- ¼ teaspoon ground cinnamon
- 1 cup thinly sliced peeled baking apple (1 medium)
- 2 eggs
- ½ cup all-purpose flour
- ½ cup milk
- ¼ teaspoon salt

  Lemon juice and powdered sugar, if desired

1. Heat oven to 400°F. In 9-inch glass pie plate or cast-iron skillet, melt butter in oven; brush butter over bottom and side of pie plate. Sprinkle brown sugar and cinnamon over the melted butter; arrange apple over sugar.

2. In medium bowl, beat eggs slightly with whisk. Stir in flour, milk and salt just until flour is moistened (do not overbeat or pancake may not puff). Pour into pie plate over apples.

3. Bake 30 to 35 minutes or until puffy and deep golden brown. Serve immediately, sprinkled with lemon juice and powdered sugar.

1 Serving Calories 200; Total Fat 9g (Saturated Fat 5g, Trans Fat 0g); Cholesterol 110mg; Sodium 240mg; Total Carbohydrate 24g (Dietary Fiber 1g); Protein 6g **Carbohydrate Choices:** 1½

CAST-IRON SKILLETS

It's worth digging out your heavy cast-iron skillet from the back of your cupboard or, if you're lucky enough to find one, picking one up at a garage sale. What makes cast iron so special? It holds the heat like no other pan material, so it's the perfect choice for the Apple Oven Pancake to help it puff and give it its crispy texture.

A cast-iron skillet is also terrific for meats that need a great sear (see page 302) before being braised, delivering a beautiful brown crust. Also oven-safe, it makes delicious roasted veggies with perfectly golden-brown, crispy edges. It's the secret weapon for amazing fried chicken, producing crispy chicken while the deep side helps cut down on oil spatters.

Broccoli and Mushroom—Stuffed Potato Pancakes

PREP 55 Minutes **TOTAL** 55 Minutes • *8 pancakes*

POTATOES

- 2 lb medium russet potatoes, peeled, cut into large pieces
- 1 tablespoon butter, softened
- ¾ cup all-purpose flour
- 4 medium green onions, chopped (about ¼ cup)
- 2 tablespoons grated Parmesan cheese
- ½ teaspoon salt
- ¼ teaspoon pepper

FILLING

- 6 tablespoons butter
- 2½ cups fresh baby portabella mushrooms, finely chopped (about 6 oz)
- ¾ cup fresh broccoli florets, finely chopped
- 2 cloves garlic, finely chopped
- 1½ teaspoons chopped fresh thyme leaves
- ¼ teaspoon crushed red pepper flakes
- ¼ teaspoon pepper
- ¼ teaspoon salt

  Sour cream and additional chopped fresh thyme leaves, if desired

1. In 3-quart saucepan, place potatoes; add enough water to just cover potatoes. Heat to boiling; reduce heat. Cover and simmer 15 to 20 minutes or until potatoes are tender when pierced with a fork; drain. Return potatoes to pan; shake over low heat to dry. Mash potatoes and 1 tablespoon butter in pan with potato masher or electric mixer until no lumps remain. Stir in flour, onions, Parmesan cheese, salt and pepper until well mixed; set aside.

2. Meanwhile, in 12-inch nonstick skillet, melt 2 tablespoons of the butter over medium heat. Add mushrooms and broccoli; cook, stirring occasionally, 3 to 5 minutes or until mushrooms and broccoli are tender. Remove from heat; stir in remaining ingredients except sour cream and additional thyme.

3. Using ¼ cup potato mixture for each pancake, shape into 16 (3½-inch) pancakes. Spoon about 2 tablespoons filling in center of 8 of the pancakes. Top with remaining pancakes. Reshape into 3½-inch pancakes, pinching edges to seal.

4. In same skillet, melt 2 tablespoons of the butter over medium-high heat. Add 4 of the potato pancakes; cook 2 to 4 minutes on each side or until golden brown and slightly crisp. Repeat with remaining 2 tablespoons butter and pancakes. Serve with sour cream and fresh thyme.

1 Pancake Calories 240; Total Fat 11g (Saturated Fat 7g, Trans Fat 0g); Cholesterol 30mg; Sodium 330mg; Total Carbohydrate 31g (Dietary Fiber 2g); Protein 4g **Carbohydrate Choices:** 2

Waffles

PREP 35 Minutes **TOTAL** 35 Minutes • *6 (7-inch) round waffles*

2 **eggs**	¼ **teaspoon salt**
2 **cups all-purpose or whole wheat flour**	1¾ **cups milk**
1 **tablespoon sugar**	½ **cup vegetable oil or melted butter**
4 **teaspoons baking powder**	**Syrup or fresh berries, if desired**

1 Heat waffle maker. (Waffle makers without a nonstick coating may need to be brushed with vegetable oil or sprayed with cooking spray before batter for each waffle is added.)

2 In large bowl, beat eggs with whisk until fluffy. Beat in remaining ingredients except syrup just until smooth.

3 Pour slightly less than ¾ cup batter onto center of hot waffle maker. (Check manufacturer's directions for recommended amount of batter.) Close lid of waffle maker.

4 Bake about 5 minutes or until steaming stops. Carefully remove waffle. Serve immediately. Top with syrup or berries. Repeat with remaining batter.

1 Waffle Calories 380; Total Fat 22g (Saturated Fat 4.5g, Trans Fat 0g); Cholesterol 70mg; Sodium 480mg; Total Carbohydrate 38g (Dietary Fiber 1g); Protein 8g **Carbohydrate Choices:** 2½

LIGHTER DIRECTIONS: For 7 grams of fat and 255 calories per waffle, substitute ½ cup fat-free egg product for eggs, use fat-free (skim) milk and reduce oil to 3 tablespoons.

Sunny Breakfast Waffle-Wiches

You can use 12 (4-inch) square waffles instead of 6 (7-inch) round waffles. Add a splash of red pepper sauce over the top of these sandwiches for a wake-up surprise.

PREP 25 Minutes **TOTAL** 25 Minutes • *6 sandwiches*

½ **medium orange or yellow bell pepper, cut into 12 strips**	1 **tablespoon lemon or lime juice**
6 **slices prosciutto (about 3 oz)**	½ **teaspoon salt**
1 **medium avocado**	¼ **teaspoon pepper**
¼ **cup mayonnaise or salad dressing**	2 **tablespoons vegetable oil**
	6 **eggs**
	6 **Waffles (at left), cut in half and toasted**

1 Roll 2 pepper strips into each prosciutto slice; set aside. Cut avocado lengthwise in half; remove pit and peel. In medium bowl, mash avocado with fork. Stir in mayonnaise, lemon juice, salt and pepper. Set aside.

2 In 10-inch nonstick skillet, heat 1 tablespoon of the vegetable oil over medium-high heat. Break 1 egg into custard cup or small glass bowl; carefully slide into skillet. Repeat with 2 more eggs. Immediately reduce heat to medium-low. Cook 4 minutes, spooning oil over eggs, until film forms over top and whites and yolks are firm, not runny. Remove from skillet and keep warm. Repeat with remaining 1 tablespoon oil and 3 eggs.

Waffles

Sunny Breakfast Waffle-Wiches

Apricot-Stuffed French Toast

3 To assemble sandwiches, spread about 2 tablespoons of the avocado mixture on half of the waffle pieces, which will become the bottoms of the sandwiches; top with 1 pepper-prosciutto roll, 1 egg and remaining waffle half. Serve immediately.

1 Sandwich Calories 470; Total Fat 31g (Saturated Fat 7g, Trans Fat 0g); Cholesterol 230mg; Sodium 870mg; Total Carbohydrate 34g (Dietary Fiber 3g); Protein 15g **Carbohydrate Choices:** 2

KITCHEN SECRET: To toast waffles, place in large-slice toaster. Or heat oven to 350°F. Place ovenproof cooling rack on large rimmed baking sheet. Place waffles on rack. Bake 3 to 4 minutes or until toasted.

MAKE-AHEAD DIRECTIONS: Make avocado spread and pepper-prosciutto rolls up to 12 hours before serving. Store separately in airtight containers in refrigerator. Waffles can be made and toasted up to 2 hours before serving. Cook eggs to order and assemble sandwiches as eggs are finished cooking.

FAST • CALORIE SMART • VEGETARIAN

French Toast

PREP 25 Minutes **TOTAL** 25 Minutes • *8 slices*

3 eggs	8 slices firm-textured sandwich bread, Texas toast or 1-inch-thick French bread
¾ cup milk	
1 tablespoon granulated sugar	
¼ teaspoon vanilla	Powdered sugar, if desired
⅛ teaspoon salt	Real maple syrup or maple-flavored syrup, if desired

1 In medium bowl, beat eggs, milk, sugar, vanilla and salt with whisk until well mixed. Pour into shallow bowl.

2 Heat griddle or 12-inch skillet over medium-high heat or electric griddle to 375°F. (To test griddle, sprinkle with a few drops of water. If bubbles jump around, heat is just right.) Grease griddle with vegetable oil if necessary.

3 Dip one side of bread slice into egg mixture; turn slice over to coat other side.. Place on hot griddle. (If using a skillet, work in batches, coating and cooking half of the bread at a time.) Cook about 4 minutes on each side or until golden brown. Sprinkle with powdered sugar. Serve with syrup.

1 Slice Calories 230; Total Fat 3.5g (Saturated Fat 1g, Trans Fat 0g); Cholesterol 80mg; Sodium 490mg; Total Carbohydrate 39g (Dietary Fiber 1g); Protein 10g **Carbohydrate Choices:** 2½

LIGHTER DIRECTIONS: For 2 grams of fat and 95 calories per serving, substitute 1 whole egg and 2 egg whites for 3 eggs, use ⅔ cup fat-free (skim) milk and increase vanilla to ½ teaspoon.

OVEN FRENCH TOAST: Heat oven to 450°F. Generously butter 15x10x1-inch pan. Heat pan in oven 1 minute; remove from oven. Arrange dipped bread in hot pan. Drizzle any remaining egg mixture over bread. Bake 5 to 8 minutes or until bottoms are golden brown; turn bread. Bake 2 to 4 minutes longer or until golden brown.

APRICOT-STUFFED FRENCH TOAST: Increase bread slices to 12. Cut a horizontal slit in the side of each bread slice, cutting to but not through the other side. Beat 3 oz softened cream cheese, 3 tablespoons apricot preserves and ¼ teaspoon grated lemon zest with electric mixer, about 1 minute or until well mixed; spread about 2 teaspoons inside the slit of each bread slice. Place bread slices in 13x9-inch pan. Prepare egg mixture as directed in Step 1 above—except increase sugar to 2 tablespoons and vanilla to 1 teaspoon. Pour egg mixture over bread slices in pan; turn slices carefully to coat. Cover and refrigerate at least 30 minutes but no longer than 24 hours. Bake uncovered at 425°F 20 to 25 minutes or until golden brown. Top with 2 tablespoons softened butter and sprinkle with powdered sugar.

Banoffee French Toast

Nothing beats the sizzling sound of French toast on the griddle early on a Sunday morning. But you know us—we can never leave good enough alone. We took our go-to easy French toast recipe and gave it a banana-toffee twist. This decadent breakfast is so delish, it doesn't even need maple syrup.

PREP 25 Minutes **TOTAL** 25 Minutes •
4 servings (2 slices each)

1⅓ cups Sweetened Whipped Cream (page 639)	**TOPPINGS**
2 eggs	2 firm medium bananas, cut into ¼-inch slices (about 2 cups)
½ cup heavy whipping cream	½ cup caramel-flavored topping
1 tablespoon packed brown sugar	4 teaspoons shaved semisweet chocolate baking bar (about ¼ oz)
¼ teaspoon vanilla	
8 (1-inch-thick) slices French bread	

1 Cover and refrigerate sweetened whipped cream until ready to use.

2 Heat griddle or skillet over medium heat or electric griddle to 350°F. (To test griddle, sprinkle with a few drops of water. If bubbles jump around, heat is just right.) Brush griddle with vegetable oil or shortening if necessary. In medium bowl, beat eggs, whipping cream, brown sugar and vanilla with whisk until well mixed. Pour into shallow bowl.

3 Dip one side of bread slice into egg mixture; soak 5 to 10 seconds. Turn slice over and repeat soaking. Drain excess egg mixture back into bowl. Place dipped bread slices on hot griddle. Repeat with remaining bread slices and egg mixture. Cook about 1 to 2 minutes on each side or until golden brown.

4 Divide French toast among serving plates; top each with ⅓ cup sweetened whipped cream, about ½ cup sliced banana, 2 tablespoons caramel topping and 1 teaspoon shaved chocolate. Serve warm.

1 Serving Calories 680; Total Fat 32g (Saturated Fat 19g, Trans Fat 1g); Cholesterol 180mg; Sodium 580mg; Total Carbohydrate 82g (Dietary Fiber 3g); Protein 13g **Carbohydrate Choices:** 5 ½

Apple Pie–Zucchini Breakfast Cookies

PREP 25 Minutes **TOTAL** 1 Hour 30 Minutes • **20 cookies**

1 cup packed brown sugar	1 cup old-fashioned or quick-cooking oats
½ cup butter, softened	½ cup chopped pecans
1¼ cups shredded zucchini	½ cup chopped dried apple slices
½ cup sweetened applesauce	1 teaspoon baking soda
1 egg	1 teaspoon apple pie spice
1½ cups all-purpose flour	¾ teaspoon salt
1 cup whole wheat flour	Additional oats, if desired

1 Heat oven to 350°F. In large bowl, mix brown sugar and butter with spoon until smooth. Stir in zucchini, applesauce and egg until well blended. Stir in remaining ingredients except additional oats.

2 Drop dough by ¼ cupfuls about 2 inches apart onto large ungreased cookie sheet. Flatten slightly with damp fingers. Sprinkle tops of cookies with additional oats.

3 Bake 14 to 16 minutes or until edges and tops of cookies are set. Cool 5 minutes; remove from cookie sheet to cooling racks. Cool completely.

1 Cookie Calories 190; Total Fat 7g (Saturated Fat 3.5g, Trans Fat 0g); Cholesterol 20mg; Sodium 200mg; Total Carbohydrate 28g (Dietary Fiber 2g); Protein 3g **Carbohydrate Choices:** 2

Banoffee French Toast

Apple Pie–Zucchini Breakfast Cookies

Triple Berry Oats-Flax Muesli

1 In 2-cup container with tight-fitting cover, mix yogurt, almond milk and 2 teaspoons honey until blended. Stir in oats. Cover; refrigerate at least 8 hours but no longer than 3 days before eating.

2 To serve, top oatmeal with mango and pistachio nuts. Drizzle with additional honey.

1 Serving Calories 390; Total Fat 10g (Saturated Fat 3g, Trans Fat 0g); Cholesterol 20mg; Sodium 70mg; Total Carbohydrate 50g (Dietary Fiber 5g); Protein 24g **Carbohydrate Choices:** 3

TO RIPEN A MANGO: Place it in a paper bag at room temperature. Ripe mangoes can be refrigerated in a plastic bag for up to 3 days.

CALORIE SMART • VEGETARIAN

Triple Berry Oats-Flax Muesli

PREP 10 Minutes **TOTAL** 45 Minutes • *6 servings*

2¾ cups old-fashioned oats or rolled barley	1½ cups fat-free (skim) milk
½ cup sliced almonds	¼ cup ground flaxseed or flaxseed meal
2 containers (6 oz each) banana crème or French vanilla fat-free yogurt	½ cup fresh blueberries
	½ cup fresh raspberries
	½ cup sliced fresh strawberries

1 Heat oven to 350°F. In ungreased 15x10x1-inch pan, spread oats and almonds.

2 Bake 18 to 20 minutes, stirring occasionally, until light golden brown. Cool 15 minutes.

3 In large bowl, mix yogurt and milk until well blended. Stir in flaxseed and toasted oats and almonds. Top each serving with berries.

1 Serving Calories 290; Total Fat 8g (Saturated Fat 1g, Trans Fat 0g); Cholesterol 0mg; Sodium 55mg; Total Carbohydrate 42g (Dietary Fiber 7g); Protein 11g **Carbohydrate Choices:** 3

MAKE AHEAD • CALORIE SMART • GLUTEN FREE • VEGETARIAN

Mango and Pistachio Overnight Oats

See page 600 for how to cut a mango. For creamier oatmeal, stir in an additional 1 to 2 tablespoons almond milk before serving.

PREP 10 Minutes **TOTAL** 8 Hours 10 Minutes • *1 serving*

1 container (5.3 oz) plain yogurt (⅔ cup)	¼ cup chopped fresh mango
¼ cup unsweetened almond milk	1 tablespoon chopped shelled pistachio nuts
2 teaspoons honey	Additional honey, if desired
½ cup gluten-free old-fashioned oats	

MAKE AHEAD • CALORIE SMART • VEGETARIAN

Baked Pumpkin-Oatmeal Cups

This make-ahead breakfast is perfect when you're on the go. Serve it with maple syrup, Greek yogurt, fresh berries, sliced bananas or chopped pecans.

PREP 10 Minutes **TOTAL** 8 Hours 35 Minutes • *12 cups*

2 cups old-fashioned oats	⅓ cup pure maple syrup or packed brown sugar
1¾ cups unsweetened almond milk or milk	1½ teaspoons pumpkin pie spice
1 cup (from 15-oz can) pumpkin (not pumpkin pie filling)	1 teaspoon vanilla
	¼ teaspoon salt
	1 egg

1 Generously spray 12 regular-size muffin cups with cooking spray or line with paper baking cups.

2 In medium bowl, mix all ingredients except toppings with spoon until well mixed. Divide mixture evenly among muffin cups (cups will be full); cover loosely and refrigerate at least 8 hours but no longer than 12 hours.

3 Heat oven to 350°F.

4 Uncover pan and bake 20 to 25 minutes or until edges are lightly browned and tops are set. Cool 5 minutes; run knife around edges to loosen and remove from pan. Top with toppings.

1 Cup Calories 100; Total Fat 1.5g (Saturated Fat 0g, Trans Fat 0g); Cholesterol 15mg; Sodium 85mg; Total Carbohydrate 17g (Dietary Fiber 2g); Protein 2g **Carbohydrate Choices:** 1

MAKE-AHEAD DIRECTIONS: Baked oatmeal cups can be stored, loosely covered, in refrigerator up to 3 days. To reheat, remove paper liner from 1 oatmeal cup and place on microwavable plate or bowl and microwave on High power for 30 to 60 seconds or until heated through. For a traditional oatmeal consistency, stir in ¼ cup milk, breaking up oatmeal cup with a spoon.

INSTANT BAKED PUMPKIN-OATMEAL CUPS: Prepare as directed—except substitute quick-cooking oats for old-fashioned oats and let stand for 10 minutes before dividing among muffin cups. Do not refrigerate. Bake uncovered at 350°F for 20 to 25 minutes or until edges are lightly browned and tops are set.

5-INGREDIENT RECIPE

Chia Seeds

CHIA SEEDS

Vanilla Almond Milk

Maple Syrup

Almonds

Overnight Chia Seed Breakfast Pudding

Strawberries

MAKE AHEAD • GLUTEN FREE • VEGETARIAN

Overnight Chia Seed Breakfast Pudding

This quick and easy pudding would be a delicious treat for breakfast or dessert!

PREP 5 Minutes **TOTAL** 8 Hours 5 Minutes • *2 servings*

¼ cup chia seeds	½ cup chopped fresh strawberries
1 cup vanilla almond milk	2 teaspoons coarsely chopped unsalted roasted almonds
2 tablespoons plus 2 teaspoons pure maple or maple-flavored syrup	

1 In ½-pint (8-oz) jar, mix 2 tablespoons of the chia seeds, ½ cup almond milk and 1 tablespoon plus 1 teaspoon maple syrup; stir with fork until well mixed. Repeat using another ½-pint (8-oz) jar and remaining chia seeds, almond milk and syrup. Cover; refrigerate at least 8 hours or overnight.

2 Top each chia pudding with ¼ cup of the strawberries and 1 teaspoon of the almonds. Stir before serving.

1 Serving Calories 250; Total Fat 9g (Saturated Fat 1g, Trans Fat 0g); Cholesterol 0mg; Sodium 70mg; Total Carbohydrate 37g (Dietary Fiber 8g); Protein 4g **Carbohydrate Choices:** 2½

MAKE AHEAD • SLOW COOKER • VEGETARIAN

Peach-Raspberry Cinnamon Bagel Casserole

PREP 15 Minutes **TOTAL** 3 Hours 15 Minutes •
8 servings (about 1¼ cups each)

8½ cups (1-inch pieces) cinnamon-raisin bagels (about 6 bagels)	1 teaspoon vanilla
6 eggs	2 cups frozen sliced peaches
1½ cups half-and-half	1 cup frozen unsweetened raspberries
⅓ cup sugar	Powdered sugar and real maple syrup or maple-flavored syrup, if desired
1 teaspoon salt	
1 teaspoon almond extract	

1 Heat oven to 300°F. On large cookie sheet, spread bagel pieces. Bake about 20 minutes or until dry. Spray 3½- or 4-quart slow cooker with cooking spray.

2 Meanwhile, in large bowl, beat eggs, half-and-half, sugar, salt, almond extract and vanilla.

3 Fold in bagel pieces. Spoon half of bagel mixture (about 4 cups) into slow cooker. Top with half of each of the peaches and raspberries. Repeat layers.

4 Cover; cook 3 hours on Low heat setting or until temperature reaches 160°F and center is set. Sprinkle with powdered sugar and drizzle with maple syrup.

1 Serving Calories 420; Total Fat 11g (Saturated Fat 4.5g, Trans Fat 0g); Cholesterol 155mg; Sodium 690mg; Total Carbohydrate 65g (Dietary Fiber 4g); Protein 15g **Carbohydrate Choices:** 4

GLUTEN FREE

Cheese Grits

Coarsely ground dried corn kernels called hominy grits are a treasured tradition in many families. A bowl of steaming-hot grits, topped with a pat of butter, is a breakfast favorite. The cheese can be left out if you prefer.

PREP 20 Minutes **TOTAL** 1 Hour 10 Minutes • *8 servings*

2 cups milk	2 medium green onions, sliced (2 tablespoons)
2 cups water	2 eggs, slightly beaten
½ teaspoon salt	1 tablespoon butter, cut into small pieces
¼ teaspoon pepper	¼ teaspoon paprika
1 cup uncooked quick-cooking corn grits	
1½ cups shredded cheddar cheese (6 oz)	

1 Heat oven to 350°F. Spray 1½-quart casserole with cooking spray.

2 In 2-quart saucepan, heat milk, water, salt and pepper to boiling. Gradually add grits, stirring constantly; reduce heat. Simmer uncovered about 5 minutes, stirring frequently, until thickened. Stir in cheese and onions.

3 Stir 1 cup of the grits mixture into eggs, then stir mixture back into saucepan. Pour into casserole. Sprinkle with butter and paprika.

4 Bake uncovered 35 to 40 minutes or until set. Let stand 10 minutes before serving.

1 Serving Calories 220; Total Fat 11g (Saturated Fat 6g, Trans Fat 0g); Cholesterol 75mg; Sodium 340mg; Total Carbohydrate 20g (Dietary Fiber 1g); Protein 10g **Carbohydrate Choices:** 1

LIGHTER DIRECTIONS: For 1 gram of fat and 125 calories per serving, use fat-free (skim) milk and 1 cup shredded reduced-fat cheddar cheese; substitute ½ cup fat-free egg product for eggs. Omit butter.

BACON AND CHEESE GRITS: Stir in 4 slices cooked gluten-free bacon, crumbled, just before pouring into casserole. Bake as directed.

Salads & Salad Dressings

Salad Basics

What can go in a salad? It's safe to say: practically anything! From an array of greens and fresh fruit to cooked pasta and colorful vegetables—a salad can be soft or crunchy, cold or warm, with a delicious range of flavors and textures. It's the perfect way to get cheffy . . . or to use up what you have in your fridge. Here you'll find the perfect side salad to round out your meal, and main dish salads that stand alone as a meal. Or make your own salad creation with mixed greens and one of the simple-to-make dressings starting on page 147.

If you are planning to toss a mixed green salad, try mixing some of the newer greens available with one or two that are familiar. The variety of flavors, colors and textures make for an adventure in eating. From mild greens like mesclun, leaf or Bibb lettuce to bolder varieties like kale or radicchio, the choices are nearly endless, and each brings its own yummy personality to the bowl.

Selecting and Handling Greens

- Choose the freshest greens possible—there should be no bruising, discoloration or wilting.
- Keep greens chilled—store unwashed in the refrigerator, wrapped in a paper towel and placed in a plastic bag or tightly covered container for up to 5 days.
- Wash greens well just before using—rinse well in cold water, removing any dirt.
- Dry greens well—use a salad spinner or pat dry with paper towels.
- Trim greens—remove and discard stems and roots as necessary. Serve small leaves whole or cut up larger pieces.

About Greens

There are two categories of lettuce—mild and delicate flavored or assertive and slightly bitter. Within those categories, there are four types of lettuces:

- Crisp Head (iceberg lettuce)
- Butter Head (Bibb or Boston lettuce)
- Loose Leaf (oak leaf lettuce)
- Long Leaf (romaine lettuce)

MILD GREENS

Butterhead Lettuce (Bibb, Boston) Small, rounded heads of soft, tender, buttery leaves; delicate, mild flavor.

Crisphead Lettuce (Iceberg) Solid, compact heads with leaves ranging in color from medium green outer leaves to pale green inner ones; very crisp; mild flavor.

Long Leaf Lettuce (Romaine, Cos) Narrow, elongated dark green crispy leaves with tips sometimes tinged with red. The broad white center rib is especially crunchy.

Loose Leaf Lettuce (Green, Red, Oak) Tender, crisp leaves in loose heads; mildly flavored but stronger than iceberg lettuce.

Mâche (Lamb's Lettuce, Corn Salad) Spoon-shaped medium-to-dark green leaves with velvety texture; mild, subtly sweet and nutty.

Mesclun (Field or Wild Greens) A mixture of young, tender small greens often including arugula, chervil, chickweed, dandelion, frisée, mizuna and oak leaf lettuce.

Mixed Salad Greens (Prepackaged) These prewashed greens come in many varieties, some with dressing, croutons or cheese.

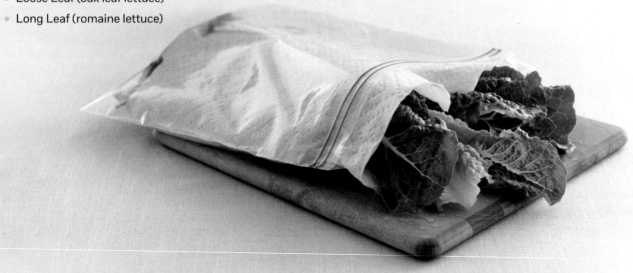

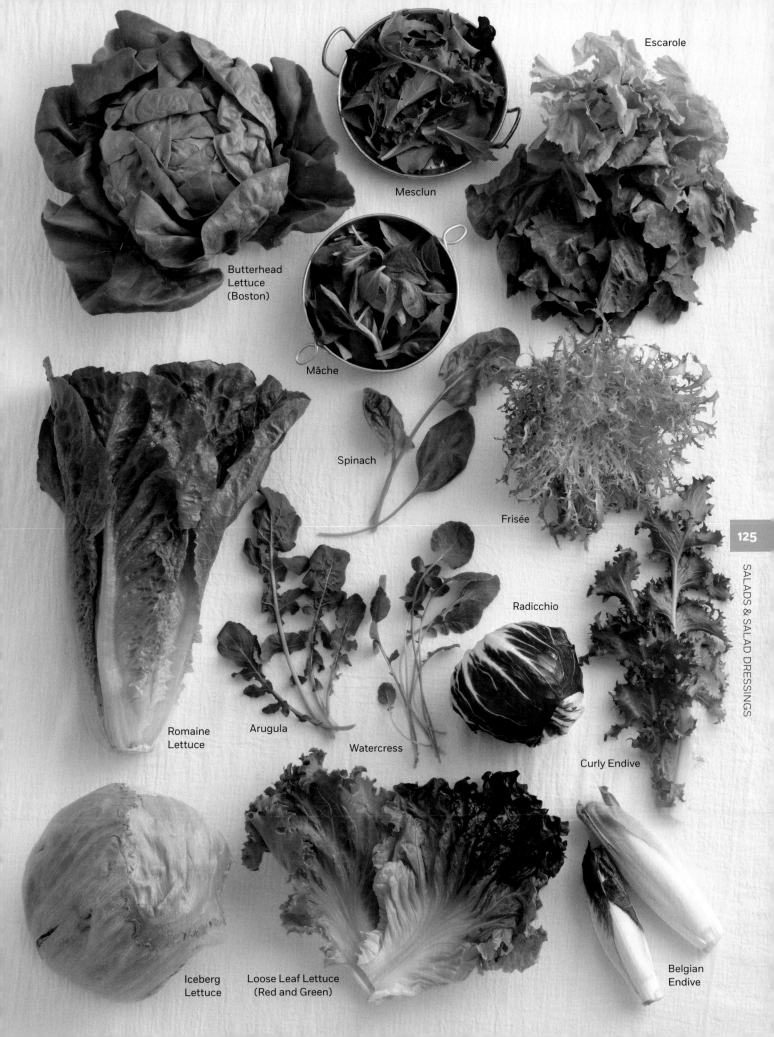

Mesclun

Escarole

Butterhead
Lettuce
(Boston)

Mâche

Spinach

Frisée

Radicchio

Romaine
Lettuce

Arugula

Watercress

Curly Endive

Iceberg
Lettuce

Loose Leaf Lettuce
(Red and Green)

Belgian
Endive

BOLD GREENS AND CABBAGE

Arugula (Rocket) Small, slender, dark green leaves similar to radish leaves; slightly bitter, peppery mustard flavor. Pick smaller leaves for milder flavor.

Belgian Endive (French) Narrow, cupped cream-colored leaves tinged with green or red; slightly bitter flavor.

Cabbage Comes in several distinctly flavored varieties. *Green* and *red* cabbage are most common; look for compact heads of waxy, tightly wrapped leaves. *Savoy cabbage* has crinkled leaves; *Chinese* (or *napa*) cabbage has long, crisp leaves. Newest to the scene, *Caraflex* (or *conehead*) *cabbage* has tender, mild-flavored leaves with a lettuce-like crunch.

Curly Endive Frilly, narrow, slightly prickly leaves; slightly bitter taste.

Escarole Broad, wavy, medium-green leaves; slightly bitter flavor but milder than Belgian or curly endive.

Frisée Slender, curly leaves ranging in color from yellow-white to yellow-green; slightly bitter flavor.

Greens (Beet, Chard, Collard, Dandelion, Mustard) All have a strong, sharp flavor. Young greens are milder and more tender for tossed salads; older greens are more bitter and should be cooked for best flavor.

Kale Firm, dark green leaves with frilly edges tinged with shades of blue and purple; mild cabbage taste. Pick young, small leaves for best flavor.

Radicchio Looks like a small, loose-leaf cabbage with smooth, tender leaves; slightly bitter flavor. The two most common radicchios in the United States are a ruby-red variety with broad white veins and one with leaves speckled in shades of pink, red and green.

Sorrel (Sour Grass) Resembles spinach, but with smaller leaves; sharp, lemony flavor.

Spinach Smooth, tapered, dark green leaves, sometimes with crumpled edges; slightly bitter flavor. Baby spinach leaves are smaller and milder in flavor than regular spinach leaves.

Watercress Small, crisp, dark green coin-size leaves; strong, peppery flavor.

DRYING FRESH GREENS

Salad Spinner Place washed leaves in basket of spinner; cover spinner and spin until lettuce is dry.

Towel Dry Place washed leaves on clean kitchen towel or in several layers of paper towels and pat dry.

Collard Greens

Dandelion Greens

Mustard Greens

Beet Greens

Chard

Caesar Salad

This classic salad is the perfect go-to recipe to accompany most any meal. It's not hard to whip up, but knowing how to make a great dressing and crisp croutons turns a ho-hum Caesar into a specialty salad that folks will ask you to make again and again.

PREP 15 Minutes **TOTAL** 15 Minutes •
6 servings (1¾ cups each)

1 clove garlic, cut in half	Freshly ground pepper to taste
8 anchovy fillets, cut up*	1 large or 2 small heads romaine lettuce, torn into bite-size pieces (10 cups)
⅓ cup olive oil	
3 tablespoons fresh lemon juice	
1 pasteurized egg yolk**	1 cup Garlic Croutons (at right)
1 teaspoon Worcestershire sauce	⅓ cup freshly grated Parmesan cheese
¼ teaspoon salt	
¼ teaspoon ground mustard	

1 Rub large salad bowl with cut clove of garlic for extra flavor, if desired. Chop garlic and place in bowl.

2 In salad bowl, using whisk, mix anchovies, oil, lemon juice, egg yolk, Worcestershire sauce, salt, mustard and pepper. Add lettuce; toss to coat. Sprinkle with croutons and cheese; toss. Serve immediately.

1 Serving Calories 210; Total Fat 17g (Saturated Fat 4.5g, Trans Fat 0g); Cholesterol 40mg; Sodium 430mg; Total Carbohydrate 7g (Dietary Fiber 2g); Protein 6g **Carbohydrate Choices:** ½

*2 teaspoons anchovy paste can be substituted for the anchovies. If you prefer, anchovies can be omitted.

**Use only pasteurized eggs in this recipe to prevent the risk of foodborne illness that can result from eating raw or undercooked eggs.

CHICKEN CAESAR SALAD: Broil or grill 6 boneless skinless chicken breasts (see pages 319 and 426); slice diagonally and arrange on salads. Serve chicken warm or chilled.

Caesar Salad

GRILLED CAESAR SALAD: Heat gas or charcoal grill. Make dressing as directed in small bowl instead of salad bowl; omit garlic. Do not tear romaine. Slice very thin discolored portion off end of stem, leaving stem intact. Remove any wilted or brown outer leaves. Rinse head without separating leaves; shake to dry. Carefully cut head lengthwise in half through stem. Brush each cut side with 1 tablespoon of the dressing. Grill cut side down 2 to 4 minutes over medium-high heat or until lightly charred. Before turning, brush each half of romaine with 1 tablespoon of the dressing. Use tongs to turn. Grill 2 to 4 minutes longer or until lightly charred. Place romaine on serving platter. Drizzle with desired amount of remaining dressing; sprinkle with cheese and croutons.

KALE CAESAR SALAD: Substitute baby kale leaves for romaine lettuce.

SHRIMP CAESAR SALAD: Broil or grill 1 lb deveined peeled large shrimp (see pages 376 and 442); arrange on salads. Serve shrimp warm or chilled.

Croutons

Homemade croutons taste so much better than purchased ones, and are super easy to make. We've suggested cutting the bread into ½-inch cubes, but by all means, if you love big croutons, cut them larger (they will take longer to get golden and crisp).

PREP 10 Minutes **TOTAL** 55 Minutes • **16 servings**

10 slices (½ inch thick) firm white or whole grain bread	½ cup butter, melted*

1 Heat oven to 300°F. Cut bread slices into ½-inch cubes. In ungreased 15×10×1-inch pan, spread bread cubes in single layer. Drizzle butter evenly over bread cubes; toss until coated.

2 Bake 30 to 35 minutes, stirring occasionally, until golden brown, dry and crisp. Cool completely. Store tightly covered at room temperature up to 2 days.

1 Serving Calories 90; Total Fat 6g (Saturated Fat 4g, Trans Fat 0g); Cholesterol 15mg; Sodium 150mg; Total Carbohydrate 8g (Dietary Fiber 0g); Protein 1g **Carbohydrate Choices:** ½

*Olive oil can be substituted for the melted butter. After drizzling bread cubes with oil, sprinkle evenly with ½ teaspoon coarse (kosher or sea) salt; toss until coated.

GARLIC CROUTONS: Add 3 cloves garlic, very finely chopped, or ¼ teaspoon garlic powder to butter before drizzling over bread cubes.

HERBED CROUTONS: Substitute olive oil for butter. Sprinkle cubes with 2 teaspoons Italian seasoning and ½ teaspoon salt; toss until coated.

PUMPERNICKEL OR RYE CROUTONS: Substitute pumpernickel or rye bread. Bake as directed or until pumpernickel cubes are dry and crisp, or rye cubes are light golden brown, dry and crisp.

Avocado-Caesar
Panzanella Salad

CALORIE SMART

Avocado-Caesar Panzanella Salad

Purchase hard-cooked eggs from the dairy section of the grocery store, or cook a few extra when making them for another recipe.

PREP 15 Minutes **TOTAL** 45 Minutes •
6 servings (1¼ cups each)

1 ripe avocado	1½ cups halved grape tomatoes or quartered cherry tomatoes
3 tablespoons Caesar dressing	
3 tablespoons water	½ cup chopped green onions (8 medium)
2 tablespoons cider vinegar	3 Hard-Cooked Eggs (page 102), chopped
4 cups torn romaine lettuce	¼ cup salted sunflower nuts
2 cups 1-inch cubes day-old French bread	

1 Cut avocado lengthwise in half; remove pit and peel.

2 In small bowl, mash half of the avocado with fork. Add dressing, water and vinegar; stir until smooth.

3 In large bowl, mix lettuce, bread cubes and avocado mixture; toss to coat. Chop remaining half of avocado; sprinkle over lettuce. Top with tomatoes, onions, eggs and nuts. Cover; refrigerate 30 minutes. Toss just before serving.

1 Serving Calories 200; Total Fat 13g (Saturated Fat 2.5g, Trans Fat 0g); Cholesterol 95mg; Sodium 210mg; Total Carbohydrate 14g (Dietary Fiber 4g); Protein 7g **Carbohydrate Choices:** 1

NUTTY PANZANELLA SALAD: Toss in your favorite nuts instead of the sunflower nuts. Dry-roasted peanuts, walnuts or pine nuts would all add flair to the salad.

CHICKEN OR SHRIMP PANZANELLA SALAD: Make a hearty main-dish salad by stirring in chopped cooked chicken or cooked shrimp before refrigerating the salad.

FAST • CALORIE SMART • VEGETARIAN

Greek Salad

PREP 20 Minutes **TOTAL** 20 Minutes •
8 servings (1¾ cups each)

SALAD

5 cups fresh baby spinach leaves	3 medium tomatoes, cut into wedges
1 head Boston lettuce, torn into bite-size pieces (4 cups)	1 medium cucumber, sliced
	LEMON DRESSING
1 cup crumbled feta cheese (4 oz)	¼ cup olive oil
24 pitted kalamata or Greek olives*	2 tablespoons fresh lemon juice
4 medium green onions, sliced (¼ cup)**	1½ teaspoons Dijon mustard
	½ teaspoon sugar
	¼ teaspoon salt
	⅛ teaspoon pepper

1 In large bowl, mix all salad ingredients.

2 In jar with tight-fitting lid, shake all dressing ingredients. Pour dressing over salad; toss until coated. Serve immediately.

1 Serving Calories 160; Total Fat 12g (Saturated Fat 3.5g, Trans Fat 0g); Cholesterol 15mg; Sodium 420mg; Total Carbohydrate 7g (Dietary Fiber 2g); Protein 4g **Carbohydrate Choices:** ½

*Extra-large pitted ripe olives can be substituted for the kalamata or Greek olives.

**Chopped red onion can be substituted for the green onions.

FAST • GLUTEN FREE

Italian Chopped Salad

PREP 25 Minutes **TOTAL** 25 Minutes • **4 servings**

SALAD

6 cups chopped romaine lettuce	1 can (15 to 19 oz) cannellini beans, drained, rinsed
1 cup chopped fresh basil leaves	BASIL VINAIGRETTE
1 cup chopped cooked chicken	⅓ cup olive oil
2 large tomatoes, chopped (2 cups)	¼ cup red wine vinegar
2 medium cucumbers, chopped (1½ cups)	2 tablespoons chopped fresh or 2 teaspoons dried basil leaves
1 package (3 oz) gluten-free Italian salami, chopped	1 teaspoon sugar
	¼ teaspoon salt

1 In large bowl, mix all salad ingredients.

2 In jar with tight-fitting lid, shake all dressing ingredients. Pour dressing over salad; toss until coated. Serve immediately.

1 Serving Calories 470; Total Fat 29g (Saturated Fat 6g, Trans Fat 0g); Cholesterol 55mg; Sodium 900mg; Total Carbohydrate 29g (Dietary Fiber 8g); Protein 24g **Carbohydrate Choices:** 2

Seven-Layer Salad

PREP 25 Minutes **TOTAL** 2 Hours 25 Minutes •
6 servings (1¼ cups each)

6 cups bite-size pieces mixed salad greens	1 cup frozen sweet peas, cooked, drained
2 medium stalks celery, thinly sliced (1 cup)	1½ cups mayonnaise or salad dressing (for homemade mayonnaise, see page 479)
1 cup thinly sliced radishes	
8 medium green onions, sliced (½ cup)	½ cup grated Parmesan cheese or shredded cheddar cheese (2 oz)
12 slices gluten-free bacon, crisply cooked, crumbled (¾ cup)	

1 In large glass bowl, layer salad greens, celery, radishes, onions, bacon and peas. Spread mayonnaise over peas, covering top completely all the way to edge of bowl. Sprinkle with cheese.

2 Cover and refrigerate at least 2 hours, but no longer than 12 hours, to blend flavors. Toss before serving, if desired.

1 Serving Calories 520; Total Fat 49g (Saturated Fat 10g, Trans Fat 0g); Cholesterol 45mg; Sodium 830mg; Total Carbohydrate 8g (Dietary Fiber 2g); Protein 11g **Carbohydrate Choices:** ½

LIGHTER DIRECTIONS: For 200 calories and 12 grams of fat per serving, substitute ½ cup reduced-fat mayonnaise and 1 cup plain fat-free yogurt for the 1½ cups mayonnaise. Reduce bacon to 6 slices and cheese to ¼ cup.

MAKE-AHEAD DIRECTIONS: Prepare dressing; cover and refrigerate up to 3 days before serving. Place all salad ingredients in bowl; cover and refrigerate up to several hours before serving. To serve, shake dressing; add to salad ingredients; toss.

Spinach-Bacon Salad with Hard-Cooked Eggs

A little bit sweet, a little bit salty—this classic salad is delicious. Look for bags of prewashed spinach to get this on the table faster.

PREP 30 Minutes **TOTAL** 30 Minutes •
6 servings (1½ cups each)

4 slices gluten-free bacon, cut into ½-inch pieces	½ teaspoon salt
	¼ teaspoon pepper
3 tablespoons vegetable oil	2 tablespoons white or cider vinegar
5 medium green onions, chopped (⅓ cup)	8 oz fresh spinach leaves (9 cups)
2 teaspoons sugar	2 Hard-Cooked Eggs (page 102), sliced

1 In 10-inch skillet, cook bacon over medium heat, stirring occasionally, until crisp. Remove bacon with slotted spoon; drain on paper towels. Drain all but 3 tablespoons bacon drippings from skillet (if less than 3 tablespoons remains, add enough vegetable oil to drippings to equal 3 tablespoons).

2 Add oil, onions, sugar, salt and pepper to drippings in skillet. Cook over medium heat 2 to 3 minutes, stirring occasionally, until onions are slightly softened. Stir in vinegar.

3 Place spinach in very large bowl. Pour warm dressing over spinach; toss until coated. Arrange egg slices on top. Crumble bacon; sprinkle on top. Serve immediately.

1 Serving Calories 130; Total Fat 11g (Saturated Fat 2.5g, Trans Fat 0g); Cholesterol 65mg; Sodium 340mg; Total Carbohydrate 4g (Dietary Fiber 1g); Protein 5g **Carbohydrate Choices:** 0

Seven-Layer Salad

Spinach-Bacon Salad with Hard-Cooked Eggs

USE IT UP
CLEVER SALAD TOPPERS

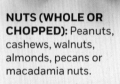

Spice up your salads with any of these topper ideas from your pantry. Use what you have on hand to create a new salad every time.

CHOW MEIN NOODLES

CRACKERS (COARSELY CRUSHED)

DAY-OLD BREAD: Make your own Croutons (page 127)

FRENCH-FRIED CRISPY ONIONS

NUTS (WHOLE OR CHOPPED): Peanuts, cashews, walnuts, almonds, pecans or macadamia nuts.

SHOESTRING POTATOES

SPICY NUTS: Add ⅛ teaspoon black pepper or ground red pepper with the sugar in Sugared Nuts (below).

SUGARED NUTS: Cook ¼ cup nuts with 4 teaspoons sugar over low heat in skillet, stirring constantly, until sugar is melted and nuts are coated. Cool; break apart.

TORTILLA CHIPS (coarsely crushed)

130

Market Corn Salad

PREP 30 Minutes **TOTAL** 1 Hour •
6 servings (about ¾ cup each)

ROASTED CORN

- 2 ears fresh sweet corn, husks removed, cleaned
- 1 tablespoon vegetable oil
- 1 teaspoon salt
- 1 teaspoon ground cumin
- ½ teaspoon garlic-pepper blend

SALAD

- 2 cups sliced red cabbage
- 1 cup chopped cucumber
- ¾ cup halved grape tomatoes
- ¼ cup sliced green onions
- 2 tablespoons chopped Italian parsley
- 1 medium avocado, pitted, peeled, coarsely chopped
- ¼ cup crumbled feta cheese (1 oz)

CUMIN VINAIGRETTE

- ¼ cup olive or vegetable oil
- 2 tablespoons white wine vinegar
- 1 tablespoon chopped Italian parsley
- 1 teaspoon organic sugar
- 1 teaspoon ground cumin
- ½ teaspoon garlic-pepper blend

1 Heat oven to 400°F. Line 15×10×1-inch pan with foil. Place corn on pan. In small bowl, mix remaining roasted corn ingredients; brush over corn.

2 Bake 20 to 25 minutes, turning after 15 minutes, until corn is tender. Let corn stand 5 to 10 minutes or until cool enough to handle. Cut kernels from ears of corn. Discard cobs.

3 In large bowl, mix all salad ingredients except feta. In jar with tight-fitting lid, shake all vinaigrette ingredients.

4 Add corn and vinaigrette to salad mixture; toss to coat. Serve immediately or cover and refrigerate up to 3 hours. Just before serving, sprinkle with feta cheese.

1 Serving Calories 220; Total Fat 17g (Saturated Fat 3g, Trans Fat 0g); Cholesterol 0mg; Sodium 530mg; Total Carbohydrate 15g (Dietary Fiber 4g); Protein 3g **Carbohydrate Choices:** 1

Apple-Walnut Salad with Cranberry Vinaigrette

You can keep the cut-up apples from browning by tossing them with a bit of orange juice.

PREP 20 Minutes **TOTAL** 20 Minutes • *8 servings*

CRANBERRY VINAIGRETTE

- ½ cup jellied cranberry sauce (from 14-oz can)
- ¼ cup olive oil
- 2 tablespoons sugar
- 1 tablespoon grated orange zest
- 2 tablespoons white vinegar
- 2 tablespoons fresh orange juice
- ¼ teaspoon salt

SALAD

- 2 medium apples (such as Gala or Braeburn), cut into bite-size pieces
- 3 medium stalks celery, sliced
- ¾ cup sweetened dried cranberries
- 8 Bibb lettuce leaves
- 6 oz Brie cheese, rind removed, cubed
- ½ cup chopped toasted walnuts (see page 28)

1 In blender or food processor, place vinaigrette ingredients. Cover; blend or process 15 to 20 seconds or until smooth. Pour into 2-cup measuring cup. Cover and refrigerate up to 2 days. Let stand at room temperature about 1 hour before serving.

2 In large bowl, mix apples, celery and cranberries. Place lettuce leaves on serving plates; top with apple mixture. Top each salad with cheese and walnuts. Serve with vinaigrette.

1 Serving Calories 280; Total Fat 16g (Saturated Fat 4g, Trans Fat 0g); Cholesterol 15mg; Sodium 170mg; Total Carbohydrate 31g (Dietary Fiber 3g); Protein 4g **Carbohydrate Choices:** 2

PEAR-WALNUT SALAD: Substitute cut-up ripe pears for the apples.

Market Corn Salad

Apple-Walnut Salad with Cranberry Vinaigrette

5-INGREDIENT RECIPE

Ranch Dressing

Peas and Cheese Salad

132

Red Onion

Cheddar Cheese

Bacon

Frozen Sweet Peas

5-INGREDIENT RECIPE

EASY • MAKE AHEAD

Peas and Cheese Salad

We liked the thicker consistency of the dressing and dip product, rather than regular ranch dressing, for this salad, as it clung to the peas nicely and provided the right amount of coverage.

PREP 15 Minutes **TOTAL** 1 Hour 15 Minutes •
6 servings (about ½ cup each)

2½ cups frozen sweet peas	½ cup shredded sharp cheddar cheese (2 oz)
6 slices bacon	⅓ cup chopped red onion
¾ cup refrigerated ranch dressing and dip	¼ teaspoon pepper, if desired

1 Cook peas as directed on package; drain and rinse in cold water. Cook bacon in microwave as directed on page 33; coarsely chop to make about ¾ cup.

2 In medium bowl, mix peas and ranch dip. Add bacon, cheese, onion and pepper; toss to mix. Cover; refrigerate 1 hour before serving.

1 Serving Calories 250; Total Fat 19g (Saturated Fat 5g, Trans Fat 0g); Cholesterol 25mg; Sodium 500mg; Total Carbohydrate 11g (Dietary Fiber 3g); Protein 8g **Carbohydrate Choices:** 1

FAST • CALORIE SMART • GLUTEN FREE • VEGETARIAN

Cherry-Walnut Kale Salad

Massaging kale means to rub the leaves with a bit of oil, lemon juice and salt. This makes the fibrous green more tender and palatable. Wear plastic gloves to do this if you wish; or instead, toss the leaves with oil, lemon juice and salt and refrigerate overnight. If you like, substitute baby kale for part of the kale. Add with the vinaigrette.

PREP 20 Minutes **TOTAL** 20 Minutes • **4 servings**

1 bunch (8 oz) fresh kale, ribs removed, leaves thinly sliced (6 cups)	1 tablespoon honey
3 tablespoons lemon juice	½ teaspoon pepper
3 teaspoons olive oil, divided	2 tablespoons dried tart cherries
½ teaspoon salt	2 tablespoons chopped toasted walnuts (see page 28), if desired
1 tablespoon white balsamic or white wine vinegar	2 tablespoons crumbled blue cheese

1 In large bowl, mix kale, lemon juice, 1 teaspoon of the oil and the salt. Massage kale with your hands 3 to 5 minutes or until it starts to wilt; set aside.

2 In small bowl, using whisk, beat vinegar, honey and pepper. Slowly pour in remaining 2 teaspoons oil while continuing to beat. Pour vinaigrette over kale mixture; toss to coat.

3 Top individual servings with cherries, walnuts and cheese.

1 Serving Calories 120; Total Fat 5g (Saturated Fat 1.5g, Trans Fat 0g); Cholesterol 0mg; Sodium 380mg; Total Carbohydrate 16g (Dietary Fiber 1g); Protein 3g **Carbohydrate Choices:** 1

Cherry-Walnut Kale Salad

Creamy Potato Salad

Creamy Potato Salad

This classic potato salad recipe is always a favorite for picnics and potlucks. Customize it by adding a variety of flavorful ingredients such as bacon, herbs, fresh veggies or capers.

PREP 20 Minutes **TOTAL** 5 Hours •
10 servings (¾ cup each)

6 medium unpeeled round red or Yukon Gold potatoes (2 lb)	1 tablespoon yellow mustard
1½ cups mayonnaise or salad dressing (for homemade mayonnaise, see page 479)	1 teaspoon salt
	¼ teaspoon pepper
	2 medium stalks celery, chopped (1 cup)
	1 medium onion, chopped (½ cup)
1 tablespoon white or cider vinegar	4 Hard-Cooked Eggs (page 102), chopped
	Paprika, if desired

1 In 3-quart saucepan, place potatoes and just enough water to cover potatoes. Cover and heat to boiling; reduce heat to low.

2 Cook 30 to 35 minutes or until tender; drain. Let stand until cool enough to handle. Peel potatoes; cut into cubes.

3 In large glass or plastic bowl, mix mayonnaise, vinegar, mustard, salt and pepper. Add potatoes, celery and onion; toss. Stir in eggs. Sprinkle with paprika. Cover and refrigerate at least 4 hours to chill and blend flavors.

1 Serving Calories 360; Total Fat 27g (Saturated Fat 4.5g, Trans Fat 0g); Cholesterol 90mg; Sodium 500mg; Total Carbohydrate 24g (Dietary Fiber 2g); Protein 5g **Carbohydrate Choices:** 1½

LIGHTER DIRECTIONS: For 210 calories and 13 grams of fat per serving, use reduced-fat mayonnaise and 2 eggs.

 **USE IT UP**
CELERY

If you purchase celery for a recipe or two and the rest goes forgotten in your refrigerator crisper drawer, try any of these delicious ways to use it up:

SALAD SAVVY: Chicken, egg or tuna salad will love the crunch that chopped or sliced celery adds.

BUMPS ON LOGS: For a fun snack, spread peanut or other nut butter in 3-to-4-inch pieces of celery; top with raisins, dried sweetened cranberries or pieces of freeze-dried strawberries.

STIR-FRIES: Add sliced celery with the other veggies in your favorite stir-fries. The flavor and crunch will get along with any other veggies, and the celery helps bulk up the dish.

SMOOTHIES: Add a stalk to a blender-full of smoothie ingredients. The bright flavor will add a fresh note to the other ingredients.

SOUPS AND STOCKS: Add crunch to soups or flavor to stocks. Don't forget the leaves!

Creamy Coleslaw

This is a delicious coleslaw to make for any occasion. For variety, you could substitute red cabbage for the green cabbage or add ¼ to ½ cup chopped red bell pepper.

PREP 15 Minutes **TOTAL** 1 Hour 15 Minutes •
8 servings (⅔ cup each)

½ cup mayonnaise or salad dressing (for homemade mayonnaise, see page 479)	½ teaspoon celery seed, if desired
	¼ teaspoon salt
	¼ teaspoon pepper
¼ cup sour cream	½ medium head green cabbage, thinly sliced or chopped (4 cups)
1 tablespoon sugar	
2 teaspoons fresh lemon juice	1 medium carrot, shredded (½ cup)
2 teaspoons Dijon mustard	1 small onion, finely chopped (⅓ cup)

1 In large glass or plastic bowl, mix all ingredients except cabbage, carrot and onion. Add cabbage, carrot and onion; toss until evenly coated.

2 Cover and refrigerate at least 1 hour to blend flavors. Stir before serving.

1 Serving Calories 140; Total Fat 12g (Saturated Fat 2.5g, Trans Fat 0g); Cholesterol 10mg; Sodium 210mg; Total Carbohydrate 7g (Dietary Fiber 1g); Protein 1g **Carbohydrate Choices:** ½

LIGHTER DIRECTIONS: For 85 calories and 6 grams of fat per serving, use reduced-fat mayonnaise and sour cream.

CREAMY PINEAPPLE COLESLAW: Add 1 can (8 oz) pineapple tidbits or chunks, drained, with the cabbage, carrot and onion.

HEIRLOOM ⟶ NEW TWIST

HEIRLOOM

GLUTEN FREE

Cobb Salad

The original Hollywood Brown Derby restaurant, where owner Robert H. Cobb created the Cobb salad, is gone but this hearty dish remains popular.

PREP 25 Minutes **TOTAL** 1 Hour 25 Minutes • *4 servings*

LEMON VINAIGRETTE

- ½ cup vegetable oil
- ¼ cup fresh lemon juice
- 1 tablespoon red wine vinegar
- 1 clove garlic, finely chopped
- 2 teaspoons sugar
- ½ teaspoon salt
- ½ teaspoon ground mustard
- ½ teaspoon gluten-free Worcestershire sauce
- ¼ teaspoon pepper

SALAD

- 1 medium head (about 1 lb) iceberg lettuce, shredded (6 cups)
- 2 cups chopped cooked chicken
- 3 Hard-Cooked Eggs (page 102), chopped
- 2 medium tomatoes, chopped (1½ cups)
- 1 medium avocado, pitted, peeled and chopped
- ¼ cup crumbled blue cheese (1 oz)
- 4 slices gluten-free bacon, crisply cooked, coarsely crumbled (¼ cup)

1 In jar with tight-fitting lid, shake all dressing ingredients. Refrigerate at least 1 hour to blend flavors.

2 Divide lettuce among 4 salad plates or shallow bowls. Arrange remaining salad ingredients in rows on lettuce. Serve with dressing.

1 Serving Calories 620; Total Fat 49g (Saturated Fat 11g, Trans Fat 0.5g); Cholesterol 215mg; Sodium 890mg; Total Carbohydrate 14g (Dietary Fiber 5g); Protein 31g **Carbohydrate Choices:** 1

Buffalo Chicken Cobb Salad

NEW TWIST

Buffalo Chicken Cobb Salad

PREP 25 Minutes **TOTAL** 55 Minutes •
4 servings (about 1¾ cups each)

- 2 cups chopped cooked chicken
- ¼ cup Buffalo wing sauce
- 10 cups bite-size pieces romaine lettuce
- 1 stalk celery, sliced (½ cup)
- ½ cup matchstick-sliced carrot (from 10-oz bag)
- 1 ripe medium avocado, pitted, peeled, chopped
- ½ cup black beans, drained (from 15-oz can)
- 3 Hard-Cooked Eggs, sliced (page 102)
- 1 cup crumbled blue cheese (4 oz)
- ¾ cup Spicy Buffalo Dressing (page 148)

  Pepper, if desired

1 In medium bowl, mix chicken and wing sauce until well coated. Refrigerate 30 minutes.

2 Divide lettuce among 4 salad plates or shallow bowls. Arrange chicken mixture and remaining ingredients except dressing in rows on lettuce. Serve with dressing. Sprinkle with pepper.

1 Serving Calories 650; Total Fat 49g (Saturated Fat 14g, Trans Fat 0g); Cholesterol 240mg; Sodium 1310mg; Total Carbohydrate 16g (Dietary Fiber 7g); Protein 35g **Carbohydrate Choices:** 1

Cobb Salad

Heirloom Tomato Caprese Salad

Heirloom Tomato Caprese Salad

Choose heirloom tomatoes in a variety of colors for a stunning presentation. If you want to splurge with ingredients, buy balsamic vinegar aged over 20 years. It has a syrupy consistency and a heavenly sweet and tangy flavor.

PREP 10 Minutes **TOTAL** 10 Minutes • *8 servings*

- 2 containers (8 oz each) bocconcini (small fresh mozzarella cheese balls), drained
- 4 medium to large heirloom tomatoes, cut into wedges or slices
- 2 tablespoons balsamic vinegar
- 1 tablespoon olive oil
  Coarse sea salt, flaked salt or colored salt, if desired
  Freshly ground pepper, if desired
- 6 large fresh basil leaves, thinly sliced

On serving platter, arrange cheese and tomatoes. Drizzle with vinegar and oil; sprinkle with salt and pepper. Sprinkle with basil. Serve immediately.

1 Serving Calories 170; Total Fat 12g (Saturated Fat 0g, Trans Fat 0g); Cholesterol 40mg; Sodium 170mg; Total Carbohydrate 5g (Dietary Fiber 0g); Protein 10g **Carbohydrate Choices:** ½

CUTTING FRESH BASIL

Basil leaves cut into thin strips is called "chiffonade." To cut, stack the leaves on top of each other, then roll up. Slice across the roll to form long shreds.

Fattoush Salad

This Middle Eastern salad is bursting with fresh flavors—it might just become a new favorite.

PREP 25 Minutes **TOTAL** 25 Minutes • *4 servings*

- ¾ cup fresh lemon juice
- ¼ cup olive oil
- ¼ teaspoon salt
- ½ teaspoon pepper
- 4 cloves garlic, finely chopped
- 1 cup chopped seeded English (hothouse) cucumber*
- 3 plum (Roma) tomatoes, diced (1¾ cups)
- ½ red bell pepper, diced (½ cup)
- 3 cups thinly sliced red cabbage
- ½ cup chopped fresh Italian (flat-leaf) parsley
- ¼ cup chopped fresh mint leaves
- 2 (6-inch) vegan pita (pocket) breads, toasted, torn into 1-inch pieces

1 In large bowl, using whisk, beat lemon juice, oil, salt, pepper and garlic. Add remaining ingredients except pita bread pieces; toss well to mix.

2 Spoon salad into shallow bowls or onto plates. Top with pita bread pieces.

1 Serving Calories 250; Total Fat 14g (Saturated Fat 2g, Trans Fat 0g); Cholesterol 0mg; Sodium 290mg; Total Carbohydrate 25g (Dietary Fiber 3g); Protein 4g **Carbohydrate Choices:** 1½

*Regular cucumber, peeled and seeded, can be substituted for the English cucumber.

Fattoush Salad

Cilantro-Lime Coleslaw

138

Moroccan Carrot Salad

Watermelon Cucumber Feta Salad

Cilantro-Lime Coleslaw

This recipe uses something that might go unused in your fridge—pickle juice! If you have sweet pickle juice and like a little sweeter salad, substitute it for the dill pickle juice.

PREP 20 Minutes TOTAL 20 Minutes •
8 servings (¾ cup each)

2 teaspoons grated lime zest	1 cup shredded carrot (1½ to 2 medium)
1 tablespoon lime juice	5 medium green onions, sliced (⅓ cup)
3 tablespoons dill pickle juice	¼ cup chopped fresh cilantro
3 tablespoons olive oil	2 tablespoons chopped fresh carrot greens or parsley
½ teaspoon salt	
6 cups finely chopped cabbage (green cabbage or mixture of green and red cabbage)	

1 In large bowl, mix lime zest, lime juice, pickle juice, oil and salt. Add remaining ingredients; toss to mix well.

2 Serve immediately, or cover and refrigerate up to 24 hours. Stir before serving.

1 Serving Calories 70; Total Fat 5g (Saturated Fat 0.5g, Trans Fat 0g); Cholesterol 0mg; Sodium 200mg; Total Carbohydrate 6g (Dietary Fiber 2g); Protein 1g **Carbohydrate Choices:** ½

Moroccan Carrot Salad

You can shred carrots using the coarse side of a box grater, the shredding attachment on your food processor or a mandoline. You'll need 7 to 8 medium carrots to get 5 cups.

PREP 15 Minutes TOTAL 2 Hours 15 Minutes • **5 servings**

DRESSING	SALAD
¼ cup orange juice	1 bag (10 oz) julienne (matchstick-cut) carrots (5 cups)
2 tablespoons olive oil	1 can (15 oz) chick peas (garbanzo beans), drained, rinsed
1 teaspoon grated orange zest	¼ cup golden raisins
1 teaspoon ground cumin	3 tablespoons salted roasted whole almonds, coarsely chopped
1 teaspoon paprika	¼ cup coarsely chopped fresh cilantro or parsley
¼ teaspoon salt	
⅛ to ¼ teaspoon ground red pepper (cayenne)	
⅛ teaspoon ground cinnamon	

1 In small bowl, using whisk, mix all dressing ingredients until blended; set aside.

2 In large bowl, mix carrots, chick peas and raisins; toss to combine. Add dressing; mix thoroughly. Cover and refrigerate at least 2 hours or overnight, stirring occasionally. Just before serving, sprinkle with almonds and cilantro.

1 Serving Calories 310; Total Fat 11g (Saturated Fat 1g, Trans Fat 0g); Cholesterol 0mg; Sodium 230mg; Total Carbohydrate 44g (Dietary Fiber 10g); Protein 10g **Carbohydrate Choices:** 3

FAST • CALORIE SMART • GLUTEN FREE • VEGETARIAN

Watermelon Cucumber Feta Salad

Salty feta and cool watermelon make a refreshing combination when paired with this easy vinaigrette. Add fresh blueberries or strawberries or pitted kalamata olives, if you like.

PREP 20 Minutes **TOTAL** 20 Minutes • *6 servings*

DRESSING
- 2 tablespoons red wine vinegar
- 2 tablespoons olive oil
- ¼ teaspoon salt
- ⅛ teaspoon pepper
- 2 tablespoons chopped fresh mint leaves

SALAD
- 6 cups 1-inch cubes seedless watermelon (from 5-lb watermelon)
- 1 cup sliced quartered cucumber
- ½ small red onion, cut into quarters and thinly sliced
- 1 cup crumbled feta cheese (4 oz)
- Additional mint leaves, if desired

1 In small bowl, using whisk, mix vinegar, olive oil, salt and pepper. Stir in mint.

2 In large bowl, mix watermelon, cucumber, onion and ¾ cup of the feta cheese.

3 Pour dressing over watermelon mixture; toss gently to combine. Sprinkle salad with remaining feta cheese. Garnish with mint.

1 Serving Calories 160; Total Fat 10g (Saturated Fat 4.5g, Trans Fat 0g); Cholesterol 20mg; Sodium 330mg; Total Carbohydrate 14g (Dietary Fiber 1g); Protein 4g **Carbohydrate Choices:** 1

MAKE-AHEAD DIRECTIONS: Cover and chill salad for no longer than 2 hours before serving. The watermelon keeps releasing its juices so the longer it stands, the more liquid will gather in your bowl.

EASY • FAST • CALORIE SMART • GLUTEN FREE • VEGETARIAN

Asparagus-Strawberry Salad

PREP 15 Minutes **TOTAL** 15 Minutes • *4 servings*

- 1 lb fresh asparagus spears, trimmed, cut into 1-inch pieces (2 cups)
- ¼ cup fresh lemon juice
- 2 tablespoons vegetable oil
- 2 tablespoons honey
- 2 cups sliced fresh strawberries

1 In 2-quart saucepan, heat 1 inch of water to boiling. Add asparagus. Return to boiling; boil uncovered 2 to 4 minutes or until crisp-tender. Remove asparagus from boiling water; immediately plunge into ice water until cold to stop cooking. Drain.

2 In jar with tight-fitting lid, shake lemon juice, oil and honey.

3 On salad plates or in bowls, arrange asparagus and strawberries; drizzle with dressing.

1 Serving Calories 150; Total Fat 7g (Saturated Fat 1g, Trans Fat 0g); Cholesterol 0mg; Sodium 0mg; Total Carbohydrate 19g (Dietary Fiber 3g); Protein 2g **Carbohydrate Choices:** 1

Asparagus-Strawberry Salad

Mexican Broccoli Slaw

PREP 20 Minutes **TOTAL** 20 Minutes • *6 servings*

SALAD

- 1½ cups broccoli slaw (from 9-oz bag)
- ½ cup black beans, rinsed and drained (from 15-oz can)
- ¼ cup frozen corn, cooked as directed on bag, cooled
- ¼ cup chopped green bell pepper
- ¼ cup chopped tomato
- 2 oz pepper Jack cheese, cut into ½-inch cubes (½ cup)
- 2 tablespoons chopped fresh cilantro

CHILE CUMIN VINAIGRETTE

- 2 tablespoons olive oil
- 1 tablespoon fresh lime juice
- 1 tablespoon cider vinegar
- ½ teaspoon organic sugar
- ¼ teaspoon ground cumin
- ¼ teaspoon chili powder
- ¼ teaspoon hot pepper sauce
- ⅛ teaspoon salt

1 In large bowl, mix all salad ingredients.

2 In jar with tight-fitting lid, shake all vinaigrette ingredients.

3 Pour vinaigrette over salad and toss until coated. Serve immediately.

1 Serving Calories 120; Total Fat 8g (Saturated Fat 2.5g, Trans Fat 0g); Cholesterol 10mg; Sodium 170mg; Total Carbohydrate 8g (Dietary Fiber 2g); Protein 4g **Carbohydrate Choices:** ½

MAKE AHEAD • CALORIE SMART • GLUTEN FREE • VEGETARIAN

Green and Yellow Bean Salad

Three-bean salad gets a vibrant take in this make-over of the classic—with two colors of fresh beans, cannellini beans, grape tomatoes and fresh basil. Garnish with shaved Parmesan cheese, if desired.

PREP 20 Minutes **TOTAL** 1 Hour 20 Minutes • *10 servings*

SALAD

- 8 oz fresh green beans, trimmed
- 8 oz fresh yellow wax beans, trimmed
- 1 cup grape tomatoes, cut in half
- 1 can (15 oz) cannellini beans, drained, rinsed
- ¼ cup lightly packed fresh basil leaves, torn

SHERRY VINAIGRETTE

- ¼ cup olive oil
- 2 tablespoons sherry vinegar
- ½ teaspoon salt
- ¼ teaspoon coarse ground black pepper

1 In 2-quart saucepan, place green and wax beans in 1 inch water. Heat to boiling; reduce heat. Simmer uncovered 8 to 10 minutes or until beans are crisp-tender. Rinse with cold water; drain.

2 In medium bowl, mix cooked beans, tomatoes, cannellini beans and basil.

3 In jar with tight-fitting lid, shake vinaigrette ingredients. Pour over salad; toss to coat. Refrigerate at least 1 hour to blend flavors. Stir before serving.

1 Serving Calories 110; Total Fat 6g (Saturated Fat 1g, Trans Fat 0g); Cholesterol 0mg; Sodium 220mg; Total Carbohydrate 12g (Dietary Fiber 3g); Protein 4g **Carbohydrate Choices:** 1

GLUTEN FREE • VEGETARIAN

Roasted Sweet Potato and Kale Salad

PREP 25 Minutes **TOTAL** 50 Minutes • *8 servings*

MAPLE-DIJON DRESSING

- ¼ cup olive oil
- 2 tablespoons cider vinegar
- 1 tablespoon pure maple syrup
- 2 teaspoons Dijon mustard
- 2 cloves garlic, finely chopped (1 teaspoon)
- ⅛ teaspoon salt
- ⅛ teaspoon coarse ground black pepper

SALAD

- 2 medium dark-orange sweet potatoes (about 1 lb), peeled, cut into 1-inch cubes
- 1 medium red onion, cut into ½-inch slices
- ½ teaspoon salt
- ¼ teaspoon coarse ground black pepper
- 1 tablespoon olive oil
- 1 package (5 oz) baby kale, stems removed (6 cups)
- 1 medium ripe pear, cut vertically into quarters, core removed, sliced lengthwise into ¼-inch slices
- ½ cup dried cherries
- ½ cup coarsely chopped toasted pecans (see page 28)
- ⅓ cup crumbled blue cheese

1 In jar with tight-fitting lid, shake all dressing ingredients. Refrigerate until serving time.

2 Heat oven to 450°F. Line 15×10×1-inch pan with parchment paper. In large bowl, mix sweet potatoes, onion, ½ teaspoon salt, ¼ teaspoon pepper and 1 tablespoon olive oil until well mixed. Spread evenly in pan.

3 Bake 20 to 25 minutes until potatoes are tender and golden around edges, stirring once. Cool 10 minutes.

4 In large serving bowl, mix kale with half of the dressing. Top salad with cooled sweet potato mixture, pear and cherries. Drizzle remaining dressing over salad. Sprinkle with pecans and blue cheese. Serve immediately.

1 Serving Calories 250; Total Fat 15g (Saturated Fat 2.5g, Trans Fat 0g); Cholesterol 0mg; Sodium 310mg; Total Carbohydrate 23g (Dietary Fiber 4g); Protein 3g **Carbohydrate Choices:** 1½

Mexican Broccoli Slaw

Green and Yellow Bean Salad

141

Roasted Sweet
Potato and Kale Salad

Brussels Sprouts Slaw with
Honey-Mustard Dressing

Brussels Sprouts Slaw with Honey-Mustard Dressing

To save some time, look for shredded or shaved sprouts in your grocery's produce section. Otherwise, the shredding attachment of a food processor makes quick work of these tiny cabbages.

PREP 30 Minutes **TOTAL** 8 Hours 30 Minutes • *8 servings*

DRESSING

- ¼ cup olive oil
- ¼ cup honey
- 2 tablespoons Dijon mustard
- 1 tablespoon lemon juice
- ¾ teaspoon salt
- ½ teaspoon pepper
- 3 cloves garlic, finely chopped

SLAW

- 4 cups shaved or shredded fresh Brussels sprouts (from a 9-oz bag)

- 1 medium Honeycrisp or Gala apple, cored, julienne (matchstick-cut; about 1½ cups)
- 4 green onions, chopped (¼ cup)
- ½ cup chopped cooked gluten-free bacon (about 8 slices)
- ¼ cup chopped toasted walnuts (see page 28)

1 In large bowl, mix all dressing ingredients. Stir in Brussels sprouts, apple and onions.

2 Cover and refrigerate at least 8 hours but no longer than 24 hours. Just before serving, top with bacon and walnuts.

1 Serving Calories 190; Total Fat 11g (Saturated Fat 2g, Trans Fat 0g); Cholesterol 0mg; Sodium 410mg; Total Carbohydrate 17g (Dietary Fiber 2g); Protein 4g **Carbohydrate Choices:** 1

Warm Brussels Sprouts Salad

PREP 15 Minutes **TOTAL** 35 Minutes •
8 servings (¾ cup each)

- 2 lb fresh Brussels sprouts, trimmed, quartered
- ¼ cup olive oil
- 1 teaspoon salt
- 2 tablespoons sesame oil
- ½ teaspoon pepper
- 1 shallot, finely chopped
- 2 cloves garlic, finely chopped
- ¼ cup gluten-free seasoned rice vinegar
- 2 tablespoons chopped fresh cilantro
- 2 tablespoons sliced green onions (2 medium)

1 Heat oven to 450°F. Spray 15×10×1-inch pan with cooking spray. In large bowl, toss Brussels sprouts, 2 tablespoons of the olive oil and ½ teaspoon of the salt until coated. Spread in single layer in pan.

2 Bake 10 to 15 minutes or just until sprouts are tender and lightly browned. Cool 5 minutes.

3 Meanwhile, in small bowl using whisk, mix sesame oil, the remaining ½ teaspoon salt, the pepper, shallot, garlic, vinegar and remaining 2 tablespoons olive oil until blended.

4 Spoon Brussels sprouts into serving dish; drizzle with dressing. Sprinkle with cilantro and onions. Serve warm.

1 Serving Calories 150; Total Fat 11g (Saturated Fat 1.5g, Trans Fat 0g); Cholesterol 0mg; Sodium 320mg; Total Carbohydrate 11g (Dietary Fiber 4g); Protein 4g **Carbohydrate Choices:** 1

Roasted Beet Salad

PREP 15 Minutes **TOTAL** 1 Hour 25 Minutes • *4 servings*

- 1½ lb small (1½- to 2-inch-diameter) beets
- 1 tablespoon olive or vegetable oil
- 4 cups bite-size pieces mixed salad greens
- 1 medium orange, peeled, sliced
- ½ cup walnut halves, toasted (see page 28), coarsely chopped
- ¼ cup crumbled chèvre (goat) cheese (1 oz)
- ½ cup Fresh Herb Vinaigrette (page 147)

1 Heat oven to 425°F. Remove greens from beets, leaving about ½ inch of stem. Wash beets well; leave whole with root ends attached. Place beets in ungreased 13×9-inch pan; drizzle with oil. Bake uncovered about 40 minutes or until tender.

2 Let beets cool until easy to handle, about 30 minutes. Remove the skins from beets under running water. Cut off root ends from beets; cut beets into ¼-inch slices.

3 On 4 salad plates, arrange salad greens. Top with beets, orange slices, walnuts and cheese. Serve with dressing.

1 Serving Calories 410; Total Fat 33g (Saturated Fat 5g, Trans Fat 0g); Cholesterol 5mg; Sodium 440mg; Total Carbohydrate 19g (Dietary Fiber 6g); Protein 7g **Carbohydrate Choices:** 1

MAKE AHEAD • CALORIE SMART • VEGETARIAN

Thai Pasta Salad

This salad can be made up to 4 hours before serving. Leave off the peanuts and sesame seed; cover and refrigerate until ready to serve. Top with the peanuts and sesame seed just before serving.

PREP 30 Minutes **TOTAL** 30 Minutes • *8 servings*

SALAD

- 8 oz linguine, broken in half
- 1½ cups shredded red cabbage (from 10-oz bag)
- 1 cup frozen peas (from 12-oz bag), cooked, cooled
- ½ cup sliced green onions (about 8)
- ⅓ cup chopped fresh cilantro leaves
- 1 medium orange bell pepper, thinly sliced (about 1 cup)
- ½ cup lightly salted roasted peanuts

- 1 teaspoon sesame seed, toasted (see page 28)

GINGER-PEANUT DRESSING

- ½ cup creamy peanut butter
- ¼ cup fresh lime juice
- ¼ cup vegetable oil
- 2 tablespoons honey
- 2 teaspoons soy sauce
- 2 teaspoons grated fresh gingerroot
- ½ teaspoon sesame oil
- ¼ teaspoon crushed red pepper flakes
- ¼ teaspoon garlic powder

1 Cook and drain linguine as directed on package. Rinse with cold water to cool; drain.

2 In large serving bowl, mix linguine and all remaining salad ingredients except peanuts and sesame seed.

3 In jar with tight-fitting lid, shake all dressing ingredients (dressing will be slightly thick). Pour over linguine mixture; toss until well coated. Top with peanuts and sesame seed. Serve immediately.

1 Serving Calories 400; Total Fat 21g (Saturated Fat 3.5g, Trans Fat 0g); Cholesterol 0mg; Sodium 190mg; Total Carbohydrate 40g (Dietary Fiber 4g); Protein 12g **Carbohydrate Choices:** 2½

EASY • CALORIE SMART • GLUTEN FREE

Cranberry-Orange Mold

Whether you need a side for a holiday meal or an easy, refreshing choice to bring to a potluck, this recipe will fill the bill.

PREP 10 Minutes **TOTAL** 4 Hours 10 Minutes • *8 servings*

- 1 can (11 oz) mandarin orange segments, drained, juice reserved
- 1 box (4-serving size) orange-flavored gelatin

- 1 can (14 oz) whole berry cranberry sauce
- Salad greens, if desired

1 Spray 4-cup mold with cooking spray. Add enough water to reserved mandarin orange juice to measure 1¼ cups. In 1-quart saucepan, heat juice mixture to boiling.

2 In medium bowl, pour boiling mixture over gelatin; stir until gelatin is dissolved. Stir in cranberry sauce until sauce is melted. Stir in orange segments. Pour into mold.

3 Refrigerate about 4 hours or until firm. Unmold; serve on salad greens.

1 Serving Calories 140; Total Fat 0g (Saturated Fat 0g, Trans Fat 0g); Cholesterol 0mg; Sodium 60mg; Total Carbohydrate 33g (Dietary Fiber 0g); Protein 1g **Carbohydrate Choices:** 2

Roasted Beet Salad

Cranberry-Orange Mold

Mediterranean Tuna Salad

PREP 20 Minutes **TOTAL** 1 Hour 20 Minutes •
4 servings (1½ cups each)

LEMON-THYME VINAIGRETTE

- ¼ cup olive oil
- 2 tablespoons plus 1½ teaspoons fresh lemon juice
- ¼ teaspoon gluten-free Worcestershire sauce
- 1 clove garlic, finely chopped
- 1 teaspoon sugar
- 1 teaspoon chopped fresh thyme leaves
- ¼ teaspoon ground mustard
- ¼ teaspoon salt
- ⅛ teaspoon pepper
- ½ teaspoon grated lemon zest

SALAD

- 1 can (15 oz) chick peas (garbanzo beans), drained, rinsed
- 1 cup sliced quartered cucumber, peeled if desired
- 1½ cups grape or cherry tomatoes, halved
- ½ cup kalamata olives, pitted, halved (from 6-oz jar)
- ½ cup chopped red onion
- ¼ teaspoon pepper
- 2 cans (5 oz each) albacore tuna, drained
- ½ cup crumbled feta cheese (2 oz)

1 In jar with tight-fitting lid, shake all dressing ingredients.

2 In large bowl, mix all salad ingredients except tuna and cheese. Add dressing; toss to coat. Stir in tuna and feta cheese. Cover; refrigerate at least 1 hour to blend flavors but no longer than 4 hours.

1 Serving Calories 390; Total Fat 22g (Saturated Fat 5g, Trans Fat 0g); Cholesterol 40mg; Sodium 830mg; Total Carbohydrate 24g (Dietary Fiber 6g); Protein 23g **Carbohydrate Choices:** 1½

144

Mediterranean Tuna Salad

Asian Salad with Wonton Crisps

This very pretty and fresh-tasting arranged salad would pair great with any grilled meat, chicken, fish or seafood.

PREP 30 Minutes **TOTAL** 30 Minutes • ***4 servings***

WONTON CRISPS

- 4 wonton wrappers (about 3¼-inch square), cut into ¼-inch strips

PEANUTTY SOY DRESSING

- ¼ cup vegetable oil
- 2 tablespoons lemon juice
- 4 teaspoons sugar
- 4 teaspoons soy sauce
- 2 teaspoons Dijon mustard
- ¼ cup chopped dry-roasted peanuts

SALAD

- 1 cup small fresh broccoli florets
- 1 cup fresh snow pea pods (4 oz), strings removed
- 4 cups bite-size pieces mixed salad greens
- ½ cup shredded red cabbage
- ½ cup shredded radishes, patted dry

1 Heat oven to 350°F. On ungreased cookie sheet, arrange wonton strips in single layer. Bake 5 to 6 minutes or until lightly browned.

2 Meanwhile, in jar with tight-fitting lid, shake all dressing ingredients. Set aside.

3 In 2-quart saucepan, heat 2 cups water to boiling. Add broccoli and pea pods; boil uncovered 1 to 2 minutes or just until bright green. Remove vegetables from boiling water; immediately place in ice water until cold. Drain well.

4 Divide salad greens among 4 plates. Top evenly with broccoli, pea pods, cabbage and radishes. Drizzle with dressing; top with wonton strips.

1 Serving Calories 270; Total Fat 19g (Saturated Fat 3g, Trans Fat 0g); Cholesterol 0mg; Sodium 500mg; Total Carbohydrate 18g (Dietary Fiber 4g); Protein 6g **Carbohydrate Choices:** 1

LEARN TO BLANCH

Why blanch? Placing fruits and vegetables in boiling water for a brief time can preserve color, texture and nutritional value. It's also a faster, easier way to remove the skin from some fruits or vegetables when you are using a lot of them, such as for canning. Once you realize how simple it is to blanch, it will be easy to see the many ways you can use this technique. Try blanching in Asian Salad with Wonton Crisps (left).

Blanching is most often done in boiling water on the stove-top. Although steaming is appropriate for a few vegetables, that method does take longer and is not as effective as boiling in water. Microwave blanching is not recommended.

The blanching process is easy if you follow these steps.

Prepare the vegetables or fruits just before blanching to prevent oxidation. Some vegetables can be blanched whole (string or wax beans) and some will be cut (carrots). Cut vegetables should be uniform in size. If you are blanching to remove skins (peaches, nectarines, tomatoes), wash just before blanching to remove any visible dirt.

1 Fill a large pot with water and bring it to a boil. Use 1 gallon of water per pound of vegetables (about 2 cups). Salt (1 teaspoon) can be added to help maintain color and flavor but is not necessary.

2 Place the vegetables or fruit in a wire basket or the basket insert from a vegetable blancher and immerse in the boiling water. Bring the water back to a boil. Boil most vegetables uncovered 2 to 4 minutes or until color brightens. The skin on tomatoes and peaches may start to wrinkle slightly or crack.

3 Remove the items from the boiling water and immediately plunge them into ice water to cool quickly and stop the cooking process.

4 Drain well when cooled. Use in recipes or freeze as desired. For tomatoes and peaches, use your fingers and a small knife to pull off the skins.

Blanching time will depend on the vegetable and its size. Watch carefully, as overblanching can cause loss of flavor and color.

Asian Salad with Wonton Crisps

Dressing Basics

Dressings are usually either a vinaigrette or creamy variety. *Vinaigrettes* are an emulsion of oil and vinegar, flavored with other ingredients such as herbs, spices, garlic and mustard. *Creamy dressings* usually start with a mayonnaise and/or sour cream or yogurt base before other savory ingredients are added for flavor. Dressings can be made ahead, which not only helps get dinner on the table faster, but improves the flavor since they get a chance to mingle before using.

About Oil

Oils range in flavor from earthy and nutty to neutral to fruity and mildly sweet. Recipes often call for a specific oil either designed to be neutral to carry other flavors or to complement the salad ingredients. Feel free to experiment with a different oil or combination of oils for a different dressing each time!

TYPE OF OIL	CHARACTERISTICS
VEGETABLE OILS	
Often generically labeled as vegetable oil; check label for oil source.	
Canola, Corn, Soybean, Sunflower	Delicate/neutral
Peanut	Mildly buttery
Safflower	Mildly nutty
OLIVE OILS	
Olive Oil, Light Olive Oil	Delicate/neutral; golden color and mild flavor
Extra-Virgin Olive Oil	Fruity olive flavor that is stronger than regular olive oil; golden to green or bright-green color
NUT OILS	
Highly flavorful; start with a small amount, adding more as needed.	
Almond	Nutty, mildly sweet
Avocado	Nutty, sharp
Hazelnut	Nutty, rich
Walnut	Mildly nutty
SESAME OIL	
Highly flavorful; start with a small amount, adding more as needed.	
Light Sesame Oil	Nutty; light color
Dark Sesame Oil (also called Asian)	Strong, toasted sesame seed flavor; amber color

About Vinegar

There are many kinds of vinegar on the market, and they all add a lively zing to salad dressings. Most recipes call for one type of vinegar, but you can try mixing and matching vinegars in your recipes to change up the flavor of your dressings.

TYPE OF VINEGAR	CHARACTERISTICS
Cider (fermented apple cider)	Mild apple flavor; golden brown
Balsamic (fermented juice from white grapes)	Rich, sweet; dark brown or white
Fruit (blueberries, raspberries or strawberries steeped in cider vinegar or white wine vinegar)	Mildly sweet; flavor and color of berry used
Herb (basil, chives, dill weed or tarragon steeped in white wine vinegar or cider vinegar)	Flavor of herb used
Rice (fermented rice)	Unseasoned and seasoned/flavored varieties; delicate, sweet flavor; pale gold color
White (distilled grain alcohol)	Strong, pungent flavor; clear
Wine (champagne, sherry, red or white wine)	Flavor and color of wine used

BASIC VINAIGRETTE

3 parts oil to 1 part vinegar. Use a wire whisk, immersion blender or covered jar to mix.

Fresh Herb Vinaigrette

PREP 10 Minutes **TOTAL** 10 Minutes • About ¾ cup dressing

½ cup olive or vegetable oil	1 tablespoon chopped fresh parsley
3 tablespoons red or white wine vinegar*	1 tablespoon finely chopped shallot or green onion
1 tablespoon chopped fresh herb leaves (basil, marjoram, oregano, rosemary, tarragon or thyme)	¾ teaspoon salt
	¼ teaspoon pepper

In jar with tight-fitting lid, shake all ingredients. Shake before serving. Store tightly covered in refrigerator up to 1 week.

1 Tablespoon Calories 80; Total Fat 9g (Saturated Fat 1g, Trans Fat 0g); Cholesterol 0mg; Sodium 150mg; Total Carbohydrate 0g (Dietary Fiber 0g); Protein 0g **Carbohydrate Choices:** 0

*Balsamic, cider, white, or plain or gluten-free seasoned rice vinegar can be substituted.

BLUE CHEESE HERB VINAIGRETTE: Stir in ⅓ cup crumbled blue cheese.

CREAMY FRESH HERB VINAIGRETTE: In small bowl combine all dressing ingredients and ⅓ cup mayonnaise. Beat with whisk until well blended. Stir before serving.

Dill Pickle Brine Dressing

Not only is this dressing tasty on fresh greens, but we also loved it tossed with coleslaw mix or served over sliced fresh tomatoes.

PREP 15 Minutes **TOTAL** 15 Minutes • 1¼ cups dressing

½ cup dill pickle juice	1 tablespoon finely chopped fresh dill weed
⅓ cup vegetable oil	
3 tablespoons finely chopped dill pickle	4 cloves garlic, finely chopped (2 teaspoons)
2 tablespoons stone-ground mustard	¼ teaspoon salt
1 tablespoon honey	⅛ teaspoon pepper
1 tablespoon finely chopped red onion	

In jar with tight-fitting lid, shake all ingredients. Store tightly covered in refrigerator up to 1 week. Shake before serving.

1 Tablespoon Calories 40; Total Fat 3.5g (Saturated Fat 0.5g, Trans Fat 0g); Cholesterol 0mg; Sodium 110mg; Total Carbohydrate 1g (Dietary Fiber 0g); Protein 0g **Carbohydrate Choices:** 0

Thousand Island Dressing

PREP 10 Minutes **TOTAL** 10 Minutes • 1 cup dressing

1 cup mayonnaise or salad dressing (for homemade mayonnaise, see page 479)	2 tablespoons chili sauce or ketchup
	1 tablespoon chopped fresh parsley
2 tablespoons chopped pimiento-stuffed green olives or sweet pickle relish	1 teaspoon finely chopped onion
	1 Hard-Cooked Egg (page 102), finely chopped
	½ teaspoon paprika

In small bowl, mix all ingredients. Store tightly covered in refrigerator up to 5 days. Stir before serving.

1 Tablespoon Calories 110; Total Fat 11g (Saturated Fat 2g, Trans Fat 0g); Cholesterol 30mg; Sodium 140mg; Total Carbohydrate 0g (Dietary Fiber 0g); Protein 1g **Carbohydrate Choices:** 0

LIGHTER DIRECTIONS: For 55 calories and 5 grams of fat per serving, use reduced-fat mayonnaise; substitute 2 hard-cooked egg whites for the hard-cooked whole egg.

RUSSIAN DRESSING: Omit olives, parsley and egg. Increase chili sauce to ¼ cup. Add 1 teaspoon prepared horseradish.

USE IT UP
PICKLE BRINE

When those yummy pickles are gone, don't throw away the brine! Use in these creative ways, so you won't lose out on all that flavor.

SALAD DRESSING: Make our Dill Pickle Brine Dressing (this page) with some of the juice. Use it on green salads, coleslaw or sliced tomatoes.

REFRIGERATOR PICKLED VEGGIES: Heat the pickle brine to boiling with bite-size pieces of fresh veggies such as carrots, green beans, cauliflower or cucumbers. Let cool. Store in a covered jar in the refrigerator for up to 2 weeks (use enough brine to cover the vegetables). The longer the veggies sit, the more they will take on the flavor of the juice. Serve as a condiment for sandwiches, burgers or on an appetizer board. Discard brine after making one batch of refrigerator pickles (do not reuse again).

BLOODY MARY SECRET: Add a splash of pickle brine to your bloody Mary, for a secret ingredient that makes your drinks legendary.

POTATO SALAD PUNCH: Add some pickle brine to the water you're cooking your potatoes in for potato salad, for a vinegary pop of flavor.

Italian Dressing

PREP 10 Minutes **TOTAL** 10 Minutes • 1¼ cups dressing

1 cup olive or vegetable oil	1 teaspoon organic sugar
¼ cup white or cider vinegar	1 teaspoon ground mustard
2 tablespoons finely chopped onion	½ teaspoon salt
1 tablespoon chopped fresh or 1 teaspoon dried basil leaves	½ teaspoon dried oregano leaves
	¼ teaspoon pepper
	2 cloves garlic, finely chopped

In jar with tight-fitting lid, shake all ingredients. Store tightly covered in refrigerator up to 1 week. Shake before serving.

1 Tablespoon Calories 100; Total Fat 11g (Saturated Fat 1.5g, Trans Fat 0g); Cholesterol 0mg; Sodium 60mg; Total Carbohydrate 0g (Dietary Fiber 0g); Protein 0g **Carbohydrate Choices:** 0

LIGHTER DIRECTIONS: For 50 calories and 5 grams of fat per serving, substitute ½ cup vegan apple juice for ½ cup of the oil.

CREAMY ITALIAN DRESSING: In small bowl, beat ½ cup Italian Dressing and ½ cup vegan mayonnaise or salad dressing with whisk until smooth.

Blue Cheese Dressing

PREP 10 Minutes **TOTAL** 3 Hours 10 Minutes • 1⅔ cups dressing

¾ cup crumbled blue or Gorgonzola cheese (3 oz)	½ cup mayonnaise or salad dressing
3 oz cream cheese, softened (from 8-oz package)	⅓ cup half-and-half
	1 teaspoon cider vinegar
	⅛ teaspoon pepper

1 Reserve ⅓ cup of the blue cheese. In small bowl, mix remaining blue cheese and the cream cheese until well blended. Stir in mayonnaise, half-and-half, vinegar and pepper until creamy. Stir in reserved ⅓ cup blue cheese.

2 Cover and refrigerate at least 3 hours to blend flavors. Stir before serving. Store tightly covered in refrigerator up to 5 days.

1 Tablespoon Calories 60; Total Fat 7g (Saturated Fat 2.5g, Trans Fat 0g); Cholesterol 10mg; Sodium 85mg; Total Carbohydrate 0g (Dietary Fiber 0g); Protein 1g **Carbohydrate Choices:** 0

LIGHTER DIRECTIONS: For 35 calories and 3 grams of fat per serving, reduce blue cheese to ½ cup. Substitute 4 oz (from 8-oz package) ⅓-less-fat cream cheese (Neufchâtel) for regular cream cheese and ¼ cup fat-free (skim) milk for half-and-half. Use reduced-fat mayonnaise.

Spicy Buffalo Dressing

PREP 10 Minutes **TOTAL** 2 Hours 10 Minutes • 1¼ cups dressing

1 cup mayonnaise or salad dressing	2 tablespoons whipping cream
3 tablespoons Buffalo wing sauce	½ teaspoon Worcestershire sauce
2 tablespoons sliced green onions	1 clove garlic, finely chopped

In small bowl, mix all ingredients. Cover and refrigerate at least 2 hours to blend flavors. Store tightly covered in refrigerator up to 5 days. Stir before serving.

3 Tablespoons Calories 240; Total Fat 26g (Saturated Fat 5g, Trans Fat 0g); Cholesterol 20mg; Sodium 390mg; Total Carbohydrate 0g (Dietary Fiber 0g); Protein 0g **Carbohydrate Choices:** 0

Creamy Avocado Dressing

PREP 10 Minutes **TOTAL** 10 Minutes • ¾ cup dressing

2 ripe medium avocados, pitted, peeled	3 tablespoons cider vinegar
½ cup oat or coconut milk	2 tablespoons olive oil
¼ cup coarsely chopped fresh parsley	1 teaspoon fresh lemon juice
¼ cup coarsely chopped onion	½ teaspoon salt
	¼ teaspoon pepper
	2 cloves garlic, peeled

In food processor bowl or blender container, combine all ingredients. Cover; process on high speed about 1 minute or until smooth, scraping down sides if necessary. Serve immediately or cover and refrigerate up to 2 days.

2 Tablespoons Calories 140; Total Fat 12g (Saturated Fat 1.5g, Trans Fat 0g); Cholesterol 0mg; Sodium 210mg; Total Carbohydrate 7g (Dietary Fiber 3g); Protein 1g **Carbohydrate Choices:** ½

Buttermilk Ranch Dressing

PREP 10 Minutes **TOTAL** 2 Hours 10 Minutes • 1¼ cups dressing

¾ cup mayonnaise or salad dressing	½ teaspoon dried minced onion
1 clove garlic, finely chopped	½ teaspoon salt
½ cup buttermilk	Dash freshly ground pepper
1 teaspoon parsley flakes	

In small bowl, mix all ingredients. Cover and refrigerate at least 2 hours to blend flavors. Stir before serving. Store tightly covered in refrigerator up to 5 days.

1 Tablespoon Calories 60; Total Fat 7g (Saturated Fat 1g, Trans Fat 0g); Cholesterol 0mg; Sodium 110mg; Total Carbohydrate 0g (Dietary Fiber 0g); Protein 0g **Carbohydrate Choices:** 0

LIGHTER DIRECTIONS: For 45 calories and 4 grams of fat per serving, use reduced-fat mayonnaise.

BUTTERMILK RANCH–PARMESAN DRESSING: Add ⅓ cup grated Parmesan cheese and ½ teaspoon paprika.

FAST • MAKE AHEAD • CALORIE SMART • GLUTEN FREE • VEGETARIAN

Chipotle-Avocado Dressing

Because of its thicker consistency, this dressing can also be used as a dip for veggies or chips.

PREP 10 Minutes TOTAL 10 Minutes • 1 cup dressing

1 ripe medium avocado, pitted, peeled	4 teaspoons lemon or lime juice
¼ cup vegetable oil	1½ teaspoons honey
3 tablespoons fresh cilantro leaves	¼ teaspoon salt
2 tablespoons water	⅛ teaspoon chipotle powder
2 teaspoons seeded and coarsely chopped fresh jalapeño chile	2 tablespoons chunky-style salsa

In food processor or blender container, place all ingredients except salsa. Cover and process on high speed until smooth, scraping down sides, if necessary. Using spoon, stir in salsa. Serve immediately or cover and refrigerate up to 2 days.

2 Tablespoons Calories 100; Total Fat 9g (Saturated Fat 1.5g, Trans Fat 0g); Cholesterol 0mg; Sodium 105mg; Total Carbohydrate 3g (Dietary Fiber 1g); Protein 0g **Carbohydrate Choices:** 0

FAST • CALORIE SMART • GLUTEN FREE • VEGETARIAN

Miso Dressing

Miso, also called bean paste, is a Japanese staple available in many flavors and colors. This salty fermented soybean paste can be found in the refrigerated section of the grocery store with other international foods, often near the tofu, and in Asian food markets.

PREP 5 Minutes TOTAL 5 Minutes • ¾ cup dressing

¼ cup unseasoned rice vinegar or cider vinegar	1 teaspoon grated gingerroot or ¼ teaspoon ground ginger
¼ cup vegetable oil	¼ teaspoon salt
¼ cup white or yellow gluten-free miso	1 clove garlic, finely chopped
1 teaspoon dark sesame oil	

In small bowl, using whisk, beat all ingredients until well blended. Store tightly covered in refrigerator up to 1 week. Stir before serving.

1 Tablespoon Calories 60; Total Fat 5g (Saturated Fat 1g, Trans Fat 0g); Cholesterol 0mg; Sodium 260mg; Total Carbohydrate 2g (Dietary Fiber 0g); Protein 0g **Carbohydrate Choices:** 0

HONEY MISO DRESSING: Beat in 1 tablespoon honey.

SRIRACHA MISO DRESSING: Beat in 2 to 3 teaspoons sriracha sauce.

149

Dill Pickle Brine Dressing

Chipotle-Avocado Dressing

Miso Dressing

Soups, Stews & Chilies

Soup, Stew & Chili Basics

The original one-pot meals, soups, stews and chilies are loved for their simple preparation and delicious ingredient combinations, whether made on the stove-top or in a slow cooker or multi cooker. Though similar in many respects, there are some differences between them:

- Soups are combinations of vegetables, noodles, or rice and often meat with a liquid base. Soups can be thick or thin, and can be served hot or cold. Chowders fall in the soup category even though they usually contain cream or milk and can be very thick.

- Stews are made by cooking ingredients slowly for a long period of time so that everything is very tender. Usually a thickener such as flour or cornstarch is used to thicken the liquid. Stews are often thicker than their soup cousins.

- Chilies are filled with variety but typically are stew-like soups made with chili powder, chiles, meat and—depending on what part of the country you are from—sometimes beans.

Storage

Refrigerate soups, stews and chilies covered in shallow containers so they cool rapidly.

To store in refrigerator, cover tightly and refrigerate for up to 3 days. Items made with fish or shellfish should be stored no longer than 24 hours.

To store in freezer, pour into freezer-safe food storage containers, leaving ½ to 1 inch at the top of the container for expansion. Resealable freezer plastic bags can work too, if freezer space is tight.

- Broth and tomato-based soups, stews and chilies freeze well.

- Recipes made with cream may separate after freezing so add the cream when reheating.

- Potatoes get mushy when frozen so add them when reheating.

Thaw frozen soups, stews and chilies overnight in the refrigerator.

Reheat broth or tomato-based soups, stews and chilies over medium heat until hot. Those made with cream can be reheated over low heat, stirring frequently. Do not boil as these mixtures may separate.

Soups and stews can thicken with storage. While reheating, add a little broth, water, or milk to thin them and return them to their original consistency.

TIPS FOR GREAT SOUPS, STEWS AND CHILIES

- Use the pan size specified in the recipe. If the pan is too small, the mixture may boil over. Or it may heat too slowly, resulting in overcooked ingredients.

- To ensure even cooking, cut vegetables so they are similar in size.

- Heat cream or cheese mixtures slowly. Boiling can cause the soup to separate or curdle.

- Rice and pasta absorb liquid, so if you are preparing your recipe ahead of time, cook them separately and add them just before serving, or see Storage (above) for reheating directions.

Roasted Chicken and Broth

PREP 25 Minutes **TOTAL** 2 Hours 15 Minutes •
About 4 cups broth and 4 cups cooked chicken

ROASTED CHICKEN AND VEGETABLES

- 1 cut-up whole chicken (3 to 3½ lb)
- 2 medium carrots or parsnips
- 2 medium stalks celery, cut up
- 1 medium onion, quartered

BROTH

- 1 teaspoon salt
- ½ teaspoon pepper
- 5 cups cold water

1 Heat oven to 400°F. In ungreased 15x10x1-inch pan, arrange all roasted chicken and vegetable ingredients. Roast 1 hour to 1 hour 15 minutes or until juice of chicken is clear when thickest piece is cut to bone, temperature reaches at least 165°F and pan juices are deep golden brown.

2 Cool slightly. Remove chicken from bones, reserving bones, skin, pan juices and any browned bits from bottom of pan. Cut chicken into ½-inch pieces; cover and refrigerate.

3 In 4-quart saucepan, place roasted vegetables, chicken bones, skin, pan juices and browned bits; add broth ingredients. Heat to boiling; skim foam from broth. Reduce heat to low. Cover and simmer about 30 minutes to develop flavors.

4 Carefully remove bones and skin from broth with slotted spoon. Strain broth through fine-mesh strainer; discard vegetables and parsley. Skim fat from broth. Use broth and chicken immediately, or cover and refrigerate broth and chicken in separate containers up to 4 days , or freeze up to 3 months.

¾ cup broth and ¾ cup cooked chicken Calories 160; Total Fat 7g (Saturated Fat 2g, Trans Fat 0g); Cholesterol 80mg; Sodium 530mg; Total Carbohydrate 0g (Dietary Fiber 0g); Protein 26g **Carbohydrate Choices:** 0

SKIMMING FAT

With Fat Separator: Pour or ladle warm broth into fat separator; let stand a few minutes for fat to rise to surface. Pour out broth carefully, stopping when you get to the layer of fat.

By Chilling: Refrigerate broth 6 to 8 hours or overnight, until fat hardens on surface. Carefully scoop fat from surface with spoon.

SLOW-COOKER CHICKEN BONE BROTH: Prepare roasted chicken as directed—except use 2 chickens. Do not roast vegetables with the chickens; omit broth ingredients. Remove meat from cooked chicken, reserving skin and bones; save chicken for another use. In 5- to 6-quart slow cooker, place bones, skin, 6 cups water, 2 tablespoons cider vinegar, ½ teaspoon pepper, the quartered onion, and the celery and carrots (peeled if desired), cut into 3-inch chunks. Add 6 cloves garlic and 4 sprigs each fresh thyme and Italian (flat-leaf) parsley. Cover; cook on Low heat setting 10 to 12 hours. With slotted spoon, remove bones and skin. Pour broth through fine-mesh strainer into shallow container to remove any food particles. Cover; refrigerate overnight. Skim fat and discard. Use broth immediately or refrigerate up to 4 days or freeze up to 3 months.

ROTISSERIE CHICKEN BONE BROTH: Follow variation above for bone broth, except use 2 deli rotisserie chickens (2 lb each) instead of cooking chicken in slow cooker. Remove meat from cooked chickens, reserving skin and bones. Save meat for another use. Continue as directed in bone broth variation.

Italian Chicken-Lentil Soup

PREP 15 Minutes **TOTAL** 5 Hours 30 Minutes • *6 servings*

- 4 medium carrots, sliced (2 cups)
- 1 medium zucchini, chopped (2 cups)
- 1 small onion, chopped (½ cup)
- 1 cup dried lentils (8 oz), sorted, rinsed
- 4½ cups gluten-free chicken broth (for homemade broth, see left)
- ½ teaspoon salt
- ¼ teaspoon pepper
- 1 lb boneless skinless chicken thighs, trimmed of excess fat
- 1 can (28 oz) diced tomatoes, undrained
- 1 cup sliced fresh mushrooms (3 oz)
- ¼ cup chopped fresh or 1 tablespoon dried basil leaves
- Shredded Parmesan cheese, if desired

1 Spray 5- to 6-quart slow cooker with cooking spray. In slow cooker, mix carrots, zucchini, onion, lentils, broth, salt and pepper; top with chicken. Cover; cook on Low heat setting 5 to 6 hours.

2 Remove chicken from slow cooker; place on cutting board or plate. Use two forks to pull chicken into shreds. Return chicken to slow cooker. Stir in tomatoes and mushrooms. Cover; cook about 15 minutes longer or until thoroughly heated. Sprinkle individual servings with basil. Serve with cheese.

1 Serving Calories 280; Total Fat 4g (Saturated Fat 1g, Trans Fat 0g); Cholesterol 30mg; Sodium 1200mg; Total Carbohydrate 35g (Dietary Fiber 10g); Protein 25g **Carbohydrate Choices:** 2

HEIRLOOM

CALORIE SMART

Chicken Noodle Soup

PREP 15 Minutes **TOTAL** 40 Minutes •
6 servings (1⅔ cups each)

Roasted Chicken and Broth (page 153)	1 medium onion, chopped (½ cup)
4 medium carrots, sliced (2 cups)	1 cup uncooked medium egg noodles (2 oz)
6 medium stalks celery, sliced (2 cups)	Chopped fresh parsley, if desired

1 Refrigerate cut-up cooked chicken. Add enough water to broth to measure 5 cups.

2 In 4-quart saucepan, heat broth, carrots, celery and onion to boiling; reduce heat. Cover and simmer about 15 minutes or until carrots are tender.

3 Stir in noodles and chicken. Heat to boiling; reduce heat to low. Simmer uncovered, stirring occasionally, 7 to 10 minutes or until noodles are tender. Sprinkle with parsley.

1 Serving Calories 240; Total Fat 8g (Saturated Fat 2g, Trans Fat 0g); Cholesterol 90mg; Sodium 990mg; Total Carbohydrate 14g (Dietary Fiber 3g); Protein 29g **Carbohydrate Choices:** 1

CHICKEN RICE SOUP: Substitute ½ cup uncooked regular long-grain white rice for noodles. Stir in rice with vegetables. Cover and simmer about 15 minutes or until rice is tender. Stir in chicken; heat until chicken is hot.

CONFETTI CHICKEN NOODLE SOUP: Add ½ cup each frozen sweet peas and frozen sweet corn with noodles and chicken in Step 3. Continue as directed.

QUICKER CHICKEN NOODLE SOUP: Make as directed—except substitute 3 cans (14 oz each) chicken broth and 2½ to 3 cups cut-up cooked chicken or turkey for broth and chicken.

HOMESTYLE CHICKEN NOODLE SOUP: Substitute 1½ cups frozen homestyle egg noodles (from 12-oz bag) for uncooked egg noodles. Add frozen noodles with vegetables in Step 2. Add chicken; heat through. Stir in parsley.

Red Curry Chicken Noodle Soup

Chicken Noodle Soup

Chicken-Gnocchi Soup

NEW TWIST

CALORIE SMART • GLUTEN FREE

Red Curry Chicken Noodle Soup

PREP 20 Minutes **TOTAL** 40 Minutes •
8 servings (1¼ cups each)

1 tablespoon vegetable oil	4 cups chopped cooked chicken
3 cloves garlic, finely chopped	1 can (13.66 oz) coconut milk (not cream of coconut)
1 tablespoon finely chopped gingerroot	4 oz rice stick noodles (from 6.5- or 8-oz package), broken into 2-inch pieces
3 tablespoons Thai red curry paste	
4 cups (32-oz carton) gluten-free chicken broth (for homemade broth, see page 153)	8 medium green onions, sliced (½ cup)
4 medium carrots, sliced (2 cups)	1 tablespoon thinly sliced fresh basil leaves
1 large yellow bell pepper, cut into strips (1½ cups)	1 tablespoon gluten-free fish sauce
	Additional basil leaves and lime wedges, if desired

1 In 5-quart Dutch oven or stockpot, heat oil over medium-low heat. Cook and stir garlic and gingerroot 30 seconds to 1 minute or until fragrant. Stir in curry paste.

2 Stir in chicken broth, carrots and bell pepper. Heat to boiling; reduce heat. Cover; simmer 12 to 15 minutes or until carrots are tender.

3 Stir in chicken, coconut milk, noodles, onions, basil and fish sauce. Heat to boiling; reduce heat. Simmer uncovered 3 to 5 minutes or until noodles are tender.

4 Spoon soup into bowls; garnish with basil leaves and serve with lime wedges.

1 Serving Calories 320; Total Fat 15g (Saturated Fat 9g, Trans Fat 0g); Cholesterol 60mg; Sodium 1170mg; Total Carbohydrate 22g (Dietary Fiber 2g); Protein 24g **Carbohydrate Choices:** 1½

FAST • CALORIE SMART

Chicken-Gnocchi Soup

PREP 30 Minutes **TOTAL** 30 Minutes •
7 servings (1⅓ cups each)

2 tablespoons olive oil	1 medium red bell pepper, chopped (about 1 cup)
1 small onion, chopped (about ½ cup)	1 dried bay leaf
2 medium carrots, diced (about 1 cup)	2 tablespoons chopped fresh Italian parsley
2 cloves garlic, finely chopped	2 teaspoons chopped fresh thyme leaves
4 cups (32-oz carton) chicken broth (for homemade broth, see page 153)	¼ teaspoon pepper
	¼ teaspoon salt
2 cups shredded cooked chicken	1 package (16 oz) dried gnocchi (not frozen or refrigerated)
2 cups frozen French-cut green beans (from 16-oz bag)	Shredded Parmesan cheese, if desired

1 In 4-quart saucepan, heat oil over medium heat. Add onion, carrots and garlic; cook 2 to 3 minutes, stirring occasionally, until crisp-tender.

2 Add chicken broth; heat to boiling. Stir in remaining ingredients except gnocchi and Parmesan cheese. Heat to boiling; reduce heat. Simmer uncovered 8 to 10 minutes, stirring occasionally. Add gnocchi; cook uncovered 3 to 4 minutes or until gnocchi are thoroughly heated. Remove bay leaf. Sprinkle with Parmesan cheese.

1 Serving Calories 260; Total Fat 9g (Saturated Fat 1.5g, Trans Fat 0g); Cholesterol 35mg; Sodium 840mg; Total Carbohydrate 31g (Dietary Fiber 2g); Protein 16g **Carbohydrate Choices:** 2

SHREDDING CHICKEN

Use one fork to hold the chicken in place and another to pull away a piece of chicken. Pieces will continue to break apart when added to dishes, so pull off shreds that are slightly larger than bite-size.

SOUP, STEWS & CHILIES

Chicken "Fridge Sweep" Chowder

White Chicken Chili

CALORIE SMART

Chicken "Fridge Sweep" Chowder

This chunky chowder is designed to use any leftover veggies, bacon, broth, chicken and on-hand pantry ingredients you have to make a tasty main dish in minutes. No fresh tomatoes? Substitute a 14.5-oz can fire-roasted tomatoes.

PREP 40 Minutes **TOTAL** 40 Minutes •
6 servings (1⅓ cups each)

- 6 slices bacon, cut into 1-inch pieces
- 1 small onion, chopped (½ cup)
- 2 cloves garlic, finely chopped
- 1 orange bell pepper, chopped
- 2 tablespoons all-purpose flour
- ½ teaspoon salt
- ¼ teaspoon pepper
- 1 cup whole milk
- 2 cups chicken broth (for homemade broth, see page 153)
- 1 can (14.75 oz) cream-style corn
- 2 cups chopped cooked broccoli
- 2 cups shredded or cubed cooked chicken
- 1 large tomato, chopped

1 In 4-quart saucepan, cook bacon over medium-high heat 5 to 8 minutes, stirring occasionally, until crisp. Drain on paper towels. Reserve 3 tablespoons drippings in saucepan.

2 Add onion, garlic and bell pepper to bacon drippings; cook 3 to 5 minutes, stirring occasionally, until onion is tender. Stir in flour, salt and pepper. Cook over medium heat, stirring constantly, until blended.

3 Gradually stir in milk. Heat to boiling; boil 1 minute, stirring constantly. Stir in broth, corn, broccoli, chicken and tomato. Cook about 5 minutes, stirring occasionally, until thoroughly heated. Top individual servings with bacon.

1 Serving Calories 260; Total Fat 8g (Saturated Fat 2.5g, Trans Fat 0g); Cholesterol 55mg; Sodium 890mg; Total Carbohydrate 24g (Dietary Fiber 3g); Protein 21g **Carbohydrate Choices:** 1½

SLOW COOKER • CALORIE SMART • GLUTEN FREE

White Chicken Chili

Top servings of this tasty chili with shredded cheese, tortilla chips, chopped green onions, diced tomatoes, chopped fresh cilantro, sliced avocado or sour cream.

PREP 20 Minutes **TOTAL** 45 Minutes •
6 servings (1⅓ cups each)

- 1 tablespoon vegetable oil
- 1 medium onion, chopped (1 cup)
- 2 cloves garlic, finely chopped
- 3 cups gluten-free chicken broth (for homemade broth, see page 153)
- 1 can (11 oz) white shoepeg or whole kernel sweet corn, drained
- 1 can (15.5 oz) great northern beans, drained, rinsed
- 1 can (15.5 oz) butter beans, drained, rinsed
- 2 tablespoons chopped fresh cilantro
- 2 tablespoons lime juice
- 1 teaspoon ground cumin
- ½ teaspoon dried oregano leaves
- ¼ teaspoon red pepper sauce
- ¼ teaspoon salt
- 2 cups chopped cooked chicken breast

1 In 4-quart saucepan, heat oil over medium heat. Add onion and garlic; cook 4 to 6 minutes, stirring occasionally, until onion is tender.

2 Stir in remaining ingredients except chicken. Heat to boiling; reduce heat to low. Simmer uncovered 20 minutes. Stir in chicken; simmer about 5 minutes or until hot.

1 Serving Calories 320; Total Fat 8g (Saturated Fat 2g, Trans Fat 0g); Cholesterol 40mg; Sodium 830mg; Total Carbohydrate 34g (Dietary Fiber 8g); Protein 27g **Carbohydrate Choices:** 2

SLOW-COOKER DIRECTIONS: Spray 4-quart slow cooker with cooking spray. Omit oil; substitute 2 lb skinless chicken breast, cut in half lengthwise then crosswise for 2 cups cooked chicken. In slow cooker, mix all ingredients except cilantro. Cover; cook on Low heat setting 6 to 7 hours or until chicken is no longer pink. Stir in cilantro during last 15 minutes of cooking.

Chicken and Wild Rice Soup

PREP 1 Hour 15 Minutes **TOTAL** 1 Hour 15 Minutes •
8 servings (about 1 cup each)

- 4 cups (32-oz carton) chicken broth (for homemade broth, see page 153)
- 1 cup uncooked wild rice
- ¾ teaspoon salt
- 2 tablespoons butter
- 1 large onion, finely chopped (2 cups)
- 1 medium carrot, peeled, chopped (½ cup)
- 1 stalk celery, diced (⅓ cup)
- ½ lb fresh mushrooms, chopped
- 2 tablespoons chopped fresh thyme
- ¼ cup all-purpose flour
- 2 cups water
- 2 cups chopped deli rotisserie chicken
- 1 cup heavy whipping cream
  Additional chopped fresh thyme, if desired

1 In 4-quart saucepan, heat broth, wild rice and ¼ teaspoon of the salt to boiling over high heat. Stir; cover and reduce heat. Simmer about 45 minutes, without lifting cover, until rice is tender but still firm.

2 Meanwhile, in 12-inch nonstick skillet, melt butter over medium-high heat. Add onion, carrot, celery and remaining ½ teaspoon salt; cook 5 to 7 minutes, stirring frequently, until vegetables begin to brown. Add mushrooms; cook 3 to 5 minutes or until mushrooms brown and soften. Add thyme and flour; cook 1 to 2 minutes, stirring constantly, until flour begins to brown and smells nutty. Add water; simmer 5 minutes, stirring frequently.

3 Stir vegetable mixture into wild rice. Stir in chicken and cream; heat to a simmer over high heat. Reduce heat; simmer 3 minutes to heat through and blend flavors. Serve soup topped with additional thyme.

1 Serving Calories 310; Total Fat 15g (Saturated Fat 8g, Trans Fat 0.5g); Cholesterol 70mg; Sodium 850mg; Total Carbohydrate 27g (Dietary Fiber 3g); Protein 16g **Carbohydrate Choices:** 2

Beef and Broth

PREP 30 Minutes **TOTAL** 3 Hours 45 Minutes •
6 cups broth and 1 cup cooked beef

- 2 lb beef shank crosscuts or soup bones
- 2 tablespoons vegetable oil, if desired
- 6 cups cold water
- 1 medium carrot, chopped (½ cup)
- 1 medium stalk celery with leaves, chopped (⅓ cup)
- 1 small onion, chopped (½ cup)
- 1 teaspoon salt
- ¼ teaspoon dried thyme leaves
- 5 black peppercorns
- 3 whole cloves
- 3 sprigs fresh parsley
- 1 dried bay leaf

1 Remove marrow from centers of bones. In 4-quart saucepan, melt marrow over medium heat until hot (for soup bones, heat oil until hot). Cook beef shanks in marrow or soup bones in oil until brown on both sides.

2 Add water; heat to boiling. Skim foam from broth. Stir in remaining ingredients; heat to boiling. Skim foam; reduce heat. Cover and simmer 3 hours.

3 Remove beef from broth with slotted spoon. Cool beef about 10 minutes or until cool enough to handle. Strain broth through fine-mesh strainer; discard vegetables and seasonings.

4 Remove beef from bones. Cut beef into ½-inch pieces. Skim fat from broth. Use broth and beef immediately, or cover and refrigerate broth and beef in separate containers up to 24 hours or freeze up to 6 months.

1 Cup Calories 120; Total Fat 3g (Saturated Fat 1g, Trans Fat 0g); Cholesterol 50mg; Sodium 440mg; Total Carbohydrate 2g (Dietary Fiber 0g); Protein 20g **Carbohydrate Choices:** 0

SLOW-COOKER DIRECTIONS: Decrease water to 5 cups. Increase salt to 1¼ teaspoons. Cook bones in 10-inch skillet. Spray 3½- to 6-quart slow cooker with cooking spray. In slow cooker, mix remaining ingredients; add beef. Cover; cook on Low heat setting 8 to 10 hours. Continue as directed in Step 3.

Chicken and Wild Rice Soup

STORING BROTH

Freeze broth in ice-cube trays. Once frozen, put broth cubes into freezer plastic bags and store in freezer.

Beef–Stuffed Pepper Soup

Beef—Stuffed Pepper Soup

Montreal steak grill seasoning can be found with the other spices in the grocery store. It is a salt-and-pepper mixture with other herbs and spices added.

PREP 25 Minutes **TOTAL** 2 Hours 45 Minutes •
8 servings (about 1⅓ cups each)

- 1 lb ground beef (at least 80% lean)
- 1 medium onion, finely chopped (1 cup)
- 1 medium carrot, cut in half lengthwise and thinly sliced (about ⅔ cup)
- 1 medium green bell pepper, coarsely chopped (about 1⅓ cups)
- 1 medium orange or yellow bell pepper, coarsely chopped (about 1⅓ cups)
- 1 can (14.5 oz) diced tomatoes, undrained
- 1 can (15 oz) tomato sauce
- 4 cups (32-oz carton) gluten-free chicken broth (for homemade broth, see page 153)
- 1 tablespoon gluten-free Montreal steak grill seasoning
- 1 teaspoon sugar
- ¾ cup uncooked instant white rice
- 1 cup shredded white cheddar cheese (4 oz)
- 2 tablespoons finely chopped fresh parsley

1 In 10-inch skillet, cook beef and onions over medium-high heat 7 to 9 minutes, stirring frequently, until beef is brown. Drain.

2 Spray 5-quart slow cooker with cooking spray. In slow cooker, mix beef mixture, carrot, bell peppers, tomatoes, tomato sauce, broth, grill seasoning and sugar; stir to combine. Cover; cook on High heat setting 2 hours to 2 hours 30 minutes or until vegetables are crisp-tender. Stir in rice. Cover and cook about 20 minutes longer or until rice tender. Top servings with cheese and parsley.

1 Serving Calories 280; Total Fat 11g (Saturated Fat 5g, Trans Fat 0g); Cholesterol 50mg; Sodium 1090mg; Total Carbohydrate 29g (Dietary Fiber 2g); Protein 16g **Carbohydrate Choices:** 2

Beef Pho

PREP 45 Minutes **TOTAL** 1 Hour 30 Minutes • **6 servings**

BEEF AND NOODLES

- 2 medium onions, cut in half
- 1 (5-inch) piece gingerroot, peeled, cut in half lengthwise
- 6 whole cloves
- 5 whole star anise
- 1 (3-inch) cinnamon stick
- 4 cups (32-oz carton) gluten-free beef broth (for homemade broth, see page 157)
- 1 lb beef sirloin steak, 1 inch thick
- 7 oz Thai stir-fry rice noodles (from 14-oz box)
- 1 cup water
- ¼ cup gluten-free fish sauce
- 2 tablespoons palm sugar or brown sugar

TOPPINGS, IF DESIRED

Sliced green onions
Sliced jalapeño chiles
Lime wedges
Thinly sliced Thai basil leaves
Cilantro leaves
Gluten-free hoisin sauce
Sriracha sauce

1 Set oven control to broil. Spray broiler pan rack with cooking spray. Place onion halves and gingerroot on rack in pan. Broil with tops 4 to 6 inches from heat 10 to 15 minutes or until onions begin to char. Turn; broil 10 to 15 minutes longer or until the other side of onions begins to char. Remove from oven; set aside.

2 Heat 4-quart saucepan over medium heat. Add cloves, star anise and cinnamon stick; cook over medium heat 2 to 3 minutes, stirring frequently, until toasted. Add 2 cups of the broth and the charred onions and gingerroot. Heat to boiling; reduce heat. Cover and simmer 30 minutes, stirring occasionally.

3 Meanwhile, cut beef in half crosswise. Place one half on plate and freeze until partially frozen, about 20 to 30 minutes (do not freeze solid). While beef is freezing, cut remaining beef into 1-inch cubes; cover and refrigerate. Cook noodles as directed on package; keep warm.

4 Strain simmered broth through fine-mesh strainer into heatproof bowl; discard spices, onions and gingerroot. Return broth to saucepan. Add remaining 2 cups broth, the water, fish sauce, sugar and cubed beef. Heat to boiling; reduce heat. Simmer 10 to 15 minutes or until beef is tender.

5 If noodles have become sticky, rinse with hot water; drain. To serve, divide noodles among individual bowls. Cut partially frozen beef into paper-thin slices; place on noodles in each bowl. Immediately pour hot soup and cubed beef over sliced beef and noodles. Add toppings.

1 Serving Calories 260; Total Fat 3.5g (Saturated Fat 1g, Trans Fat 0g); Cholesterol 50mg; Sodium 1690mg; Total Carbohydrate 33g (Dietary Fiber 1g); Protein 23g **Carbohydrate Choices:** 2

One-Pot Lasagna Soup

Garnish this soup with chopped fresh basil leaves, additional grated Parmesan cheese and crushed red pepper flakes, if desired.

PREP 15 Minutes **TOTAL** 35 Minutes •
6 servings (about 1½ cups each)

- 1 lb bulk spicy or mild Italian sausage
- 1 small onion, chopped (½ cup)
- 4 cups (32-oz carton) chicken broth (for homemade broth, see page 153)
- 2 cans (14.5 oz each) diced tomatoes with Italian herbs, undrained
- ¼ teaspoon pepper
- 6 oz lasagna noodles (from 16-oz box), broken into 1- to 2-inch pieces
- ½ cup grated Parmesan cheese
- 1½ cups whole-milk ricotta cheese
  Chopped fresh parsley, if desired

1 In 5- to 6-quart Dutch oven, cook sausage and onion over medium heat 8 to 10 minutes, stirring occasionally, until sausage is brown and onion is tender. Drain; return to Dutch oven.

2 Stir in broth, tomatoes, pepper and noodles. Heat to boiling; reduce heat. Cover and simmer about 10 minutes, stirring occasionally, until noodles are tender.

3 Serve soup with Parmesan and ricotta cheeses and sprinkle with parsley.

1 Serving Calories 490; Total Fat 26g (Saturated Fat 12g, Trans Fat 0g); Cholesterol 70mg; Sodium 1650mg; Total Carbohydrate 37g (Dietary Fiber 2g); Protein 27g **Carbohydrate Choices:** 2½

Beef Pho

One-Pot Lasagna Soup

MULTI COOKER • SLOW COOKER

Swedish Meatball Soup

PREP 15 Minutes **TOTAL** 3 Hours 10 Minutes •
6 servings (about 1⅓ cups each)

- 1 (16-oz bag) frozen cooked original flavor meatballs, thawed (for homemade meatballs, see page 63)
- 1 package (8 oz) white button mushrooms, sliced
- 1 small onion, chopped (½ cup)
- 4 cups (32-oz carton) beef broth
- 1 tablespoon Worcestershire sauce
- ½ teaspoon ground nutmeg
- ¼ teaspoon ground allspice
- ¼ teaspoon salt
- ¼ teaspoon pepper
- 6 oz uncooked medium egg noodles (about 3½ cups)
- 1½ cups heavy whipping cream
- Chopped fresh dill weed, if desired

1 In 5-quart slow cooker, mix meatballs, mushrooms, onion, broth, Worcestershire sauce, nutmeg, allspice, salt and pepper.

2 Cover; cook on High heat setting 2½ to 3 hours or until vegetables are tender. Stir in egg noodles until mixed well; cook covered on High heat setting 15 to 20 minutes, stirring halfway through cook time, until noodles are tender.

3 Stir in whipping cream; cook covered about 5 minutes or until heated through. Garnish with fresh dill weed before serving.

1 Serving Calories 680; Total Fat 42g (Saturated Fat 21g, Trans Fat 1.5g); Cholesterol 225mg; Sodium 1500mg; Total Carbohydrate 41g (Dietary Fiber 2g); Protein 34g **Carbohydrate Choices:** 3

MULTI COOKER • SLOW COOKER • CALORIE SMART • GLUTEN FREE

Family-Favorite Chili

PREP 20 Minutes **TOTAL** 6 Hours 35 Minutes •
8 servings (1½ cups each)

- 2 lb ground beef (at least 80% lean)
- 1 medium onion, chopped (1 cup)
- 2 cloves garlic, finely chopped
- 1 can (28 oz) diced tomatoes, undrained
- 1 can (15 oz) tomato sauce
- 2 tablespoons chili powder
- 1½ teaspoons ground cumin
- ½ teaspoon salt
- ½ teaspoon pepper
- 1 can (15 to 16 oz) kidney or pinto beans, drained, rinsed
- Shredded cheddar cheese, if desired

1 In 12-inch skillet, cook beef over medium heat 8 to 10 minutes, stirring occasionally, until thoroughly cooked; drain.

2 Spray 3½- to 6-quart slow cooker with cooking spray. In slow cooker, mix beef and remaining ingredients except beans and cheese. Cover; cook on Low heat setting 6 to 8 hours or on High heat setting 3 to 4 hours.

3 Stir in beans. If using Low heat setting, increase to High. Cover; cook 15 to 20 minutes longer or until slightly thickened. Sprinkle individual servings with cheese.

1 Serving Calories 290; Total Fat 14g (Saturated Fat 5g, Trans Fat 0.5g); Cholesterol 70mg; Sodium 710mg; Total Carbohydrate 17g (Dietary Fiber 5g); Protein 24g **Carbohydrate Choices:** 1

MULTI-COOKER DIRECTIONS: Use at least 90% lean ground beef. On 6-quart multi cooker, select SAUTE; adjust to normal. Place beef and onion in insert. Cook 9 to 11 minutes, stirring occasionally, until beef is browned. Select CANCEL. Add remaining ingredients except cheese. Secure lid; set pressure valve to SEALING. Select MANUAL; cook on high pressure 5 minutes. Select CANCEL. Set pressure valve to VENTING to quick-release pressure. Sprinkle individual servings with cheese.

FAMILY-FAVORITE CHILI WITH SMOKED SAUSAGE: Reduce ground beef to 1 lb. Add 1 lb gluten-free beef smoked sausage, cut into ½-inch slices, in Step 2. Serve with shredded smoked cheddar or smoked Gouda cheese.

FAMILY-FAVORITE TURKEY CHILI WITH BROWN RICE: Substitute ground turkey breast for ground beef; cook until no longer pink in Step 1. Proceed as directed. Serve chili over cooked brown rice. Serve with reduced-fat cheddar cheese.

CALORIE SMART • GLUTEN FREE

Vegetable Beef Soup

PREP 20 Minutes **TOTAL** 1 Hour 5 Minutes •
7 servings (1½ cups each)

- Beef and Broth (page 157)
- 1 ear fresh sweet corn or ½ cup frozen whole kernel corn
- 2 medium potatoes, cut into pieces (2 cups)
- 2 medium tomatoes, chopped (1½ cups)
- 2 medium carrots, thinly sliced (1 cup)
- 2 medium stalks celery, sliced (⅔ cup)
- 1 medium onion, chopped (1 cup)
- 1 cup 1-inch pieces fresh green beans or frozen cut green beans
- 1 cup shelled green peas or frozen sweet peas
- ¼ teaspoon pepper

1 In 4-quart saucepan, place beef and strained broth.

2 Cut kernels from ear of corn. Stir corn kernels and remaining ingredients into broth. Heat to boiling. Reduce heat; cover and simmer about 30 minutes or until vegetables are tender.

1 Serving Calories 240; Total Fat 9g (Saturated Fat 3.5g, Trans Fat 0g); Cholesterol 45mg; Sodium 640mg; Total Carbohydrate 19g (Dietary Fiber 4g); Protein 20g **Carbohydrate Choices:** 1

Swedish Meatball Soup

Family-Favorite Chili

Pancetta-Bean Soup

PREP 35 Minutes **TOTAL** 9 Hours 50 Minutes •
8 servings (about 1⅓ cups each)

1 cup dried navy or great northern beans	1½ teaspoons ground cumin
8 cups (two 32-oz cartons) gluten-free chicken broth (for homemade broth, see page 153)	1 teaspoon ground coriander
5 medium carrots, sliced (2½ cups)	½ teaspoon coarsely ground pepper
2 medium stalks celery, chopped (⅔ cup)	1 can (15 oz) chick peas (garbanzo beans), drained, rinsed
1 medium onion, chopped (1 cup)	2 (4 oz) packages pancetta, diced
1 tablespoon dried rosemary leaves, crushed	2 cups loosely packed baby kale leaves, coarsely chopped

1 Soak dried beans as directed on page 270, using quick-soak method.

2 In 5- to 6-quart slow cooker, mix all ingredients except chick peas, pancetta and kale. Cover; cook on Low heat setting 9 to 10 hours or until beans are tender.

3 Meanwhile, in 10-inch nonstick skillet, cook pancetta over medium-high heat, 5 to 6 minutes, stirring occasionally, until browned. Drain on paper towels.

4 Remove cover from slow cooker. Stir in chick peas, half the pancetta and the kale; cover. Cook on High heat setting about 15 to 20 minutes longer or until kale is wilted. Serve topped with remaining pancetta.

1 Serving Calories 280; Total Fat 11g (Saturated Fat 3.5g, Trans Fat 0g); Cholesterol 20mg; Sodium 1350mg; Total Carbohydrate 31g (Dietary Fiber 10g); Protein 12g **Carbohydrate Choices:** 2

MULTI-COOKER DIRECTIONS: In 6-quart multi-cooker insert, mix all ingredients except chick peas, pancetta and kale. Secure lid; set pressure valve to SEALING. Select MANUAL; cook on high pressure 20 minutes. Select CANCEL. Keep pressure valve in SEALING position to release pressure naturally for 20 minutes. Release any remaining pressure by moving valve to VENTING. Meanwhile, in 10-inch nonstick skillet, cook pancetta over medium-high heat, 5 to 6 minutes, stirring occasionally, until browned; drain on paper towels. Stir into soup mixture with chick peas, half of the pancetta and the kale; cover. Let stand covered 10 minutes or until kale is wilted. Serve as directed.

MAKE-AHEAD DIRECTIONS: Soak the dried beans the night before so they are ready to pop in the slow cooker in the morning.

Pork and Chicken Burgoo

A hearty stew, burgoo is a popular way to serve a crowd in America's southern states. It is often prepared communally; each family or guest brings an ingredient. The gathering centers around making and devouring it!

PREP 50 Minutes **TOTAL** 2 Hours 5 Minutes •
14 servings (1½ cups each)

2 tablespoons all-purpose flour	1 lb small red potatoes, cut into 1-inch pieces
2 teaspoons salt	1 large onion, cut into 1-inch pieces
1 teaspoon pepper	4 medium carrots, sliced (2 cups)
2 lb pork blade steak or pork shoulder, trimmed, cut into ¾-inch pieces	3 cups cauliflower florets
2 tablespoons vegetable oil	1 cup frozen whole kernel corn
1 package (20 oz) bone-in chicken thighs, skin removed	½ medium eggplant, cut into 1-inch pieces (2¾ cups)
6 cups water	1 can (15 oz) black-eyed peas, drained, rinsed
2 bay leaves	¼ cup chopped parsley
1 can (15 oz) fire-roasted diced tomatoes, undrained	
1 cup barbecue sauce	

1 In 1-gallon resealable food-storage plastic bag, combine flour, 1 teaspoon of the salt and ½ teaspoon of the pepper; add pork. Close bag; shake until pork is evenly coated.

2 In 8-quart stockpot, heat 1 tablespoon of the oil over medium-high heat. Add half of the pork; cook and stir 4 to 5 minutes, stirring occasionally, until pork is brown on all sides. Remove pork from stockpot to heatproof bowl. Repeat with remaining oil and pork. Return pork to stockpot.

3 Stir in chicken, water and bay leaves, scraping up browned bits from bottom of pan. Heat to boiling; reduce heat. Cover and simmer 45 minutes to 1 hour or until pork is tender. Place chicken thighs on plate; cool slightly. Remove bay leaves; discard.

4 Stir in tomatoes, barbecue sauce, potatoes, onion, carrots and the remaining salt and pepper. Heat to boiling; reduce heat. Cover and simmer 15 minutes. Stir in cauliflower, corn, eggplant and black-eyed peas. Heat to boiling; reduce heat. Cover and simmer 15 minutes longer or until vegetables are tender.

5 Meanwhile, using two forks, shred chicken from bones; discard bones. Stir chicken and parsley into soup; heat until hot.

1 Serving Calories 300; Total Fat 10g (Saturated Fat 3.5g, Trans Fat 0g); Cholesterol 60mg; Sodium 720mg; Total Carbohydrate 29g (Dietary Fiber 4g); Protein 22g **Carbohydrate Choices:** 2

Cheesy Potato-Bacon Soup

Look for bacon that is already cooked at the grocery store to save prep and clean-up time. Or pick up a package of microwave-ready bacon instead.

PREP 15 Minutes **TOTAL** 6 Hours 35 Minutes •
6 servings (1½ cups each)

- 1 bag (32 oz) frozen southern-style diced hash brown potatoes, thawed
- 1 small onion, chopped (½ cup)
- 1 medium stalk celery, diced (⅓ cup)
- 3½ cups chicken broth (for homemade broth, see page 153)
- 1 cup water
- 3 tablespoons all-purpose flour
- 1 cup half-and-half
- 2 cups shredded cheddar cheese (8 oz)
- 12 slices bacon, crisply cooked, crumbled
- 4 medium green onions, thinly sliced (¼ cup)

1 Spray 3½- to 4-quart slow cooker with cooking spray. In slow cooker, mix potatoes, chopped onion, celery, broth and water. Cover; cook on Low heat setting 6 to 8 hours.

2 In small bowl, mix flour and half-and-half; stir into potato mixture. Increase heat setting to High. Cover; cook 20 to 30 minutes or until mixture thickens.

3 Stir in cheese until melted; stir in half of the bacon. Sprinkle individual servings with remaining bacon and the green onions.

1 Serving Calories 440; Total Fat 25g (Saturated Fat 12g, Trans Fat 0.5g); Cholesterol 70mg; Sodium 800mg; Total Carbohydrate 33g (Dietary Fiber 4g); Protein 21g **Carbohydrate Choices:** 2

Pork and Chicken Burgoo

Cheesy Potato-Bacon Soup

163

Beef Stew

Look for beef stew meat, already trimmed and cut into 1/2- to 1-inch pieces, in the meat department.

PREP 15 Minutes **TOTAL** 3 Hours 45 Minutes • *8 servings*

- 1 lb beef stew meat, cut into ½-inch pieces
- 1 medium onion, cut into 8 wedges
- 1 bag (8 oz) ready-to-eat baby-cut carrots (about 30)
- 1 can (14.5 oz) diced tomatoes, undrained
- 1 can (10.5 oz) condensed beef broth
- 1 can (8 oz) tomato sauce
- ⅓ cup all-purpose flour
- 1 tablespoon Worcestershire sauce
- 1 teaspoon salt
- 1 teaspoon sugar
- 1 teaspoon dried marjoram leaves
- ¼ teaspoon pepper
- 12 small red potatoes (1½ lb), cut into quarters
- 2 cups sliced fresh mushrooms (about 5 oz) or 1 package (about 3.5 oz) fresh shiitake mushrooms, sliced

1 Heat oven to 325°F. In 4-quart ovenproof saucepan or casserole dish, mix all ingredients except potatoes and mushrooms. Cover and bake 2 hours, stirring once.

2 Stir in potatoes and mushrooms. Cover and bake 1 hour to 1 hour 30 minutes longer or until beef and vegetables are tender.

1 Serving Calories 230; Total Fat 6g (Saturated Fat 2.5g, Trans Fat 0g); Cholesterol 30mg; Sodium 820mg; Total Carbohydrate 28g (Dietary Fiber 4g); Protein 15g **Carbohydrate Choices:** 2

SLOW-COOKER DIRECTIONS: Chop onion (1 cup). Omit tomato sauce. Increase flour to ½ cup. Spray 3½- to 6-quart slow cooker with cooking spray. In slow cooker, mix all ingredients except beef. Add beef (do not stir). Cover; cook on Low heat setting 8 to 9 hours. Stir well before serving.

CHUNKY TOMATO-PEPPER BEEF STEW: Add 1 cup diced bell pepper (any color) with the onion; omit mushrooms. Substitute 1 additional can (14.5 oz) diced tomatoes for tomato sauce.

CONFETTI BEEF STEW: Omit potatoes. Bake 2 hours. Add 1 cup frozen cut green beans and 1 cup frozen whole kernel corn in Step 2.

Moroccan Lamb Stew

PREP 25 Minutes **TOTAL** 1 Hour 10 Minutes • *6 servings*

- 1 lb boneless lamb shoulder, trimmed of excess fat, cut into cubes
- 1½ cups chicken broth (for homemade broth, see page 153)
- 1 medium onion, chopped (1 cup)
- 3 cloves garlic, finely chopped
- 1 tablespoon all-purpose flour
- 1 cup dry red wine or chicken broth
- 1 cup dried apricots
- ¼ cup pitted dried plums
- ¼ cup raisins
- 1 teaspoon paprika
- 1 can (14.5 oz) whole peeled tomatoes, undrained
- ⅓ cup chopped fresh parsley
- 3 cups hot cooked couscous

1 Spray 4-quart saucepan with cooking spray; heat over medium-high heat. Add lamb; cook, stirring frequently, until brown. Remove lamb and set aside.

2 Add ½ cup of the broth to saucepan; heat to boiling. Stir in onion and garlic. Cook 3 minutes, stirring frequently. Stir in flour. Cook 1 minute, stirring constantly.

3 Stir in the lamb, remaining 1 cup broth, the wine, apricots, plums, raisins, paprika and tomatoes, breaking up tomatoes. Heat to boiling; reduce heat. Cover and simmer 45 minutes. Stir in parsley. Serve over couscous.

1 Serving Calories 350; Total Fat 6g (Saturated Fat 2g, Trans Fat 0g); Cholesterol 50mg; Sodium 480mg; Total Carbohydrate 49g (Dietary Fiber 5g); Protein 23g **Carbohydrate Choices:** 3

Beef Stew

Moroccan Lamb Stew

Pulled Pork Chili

Spicy Thai Pork Stew

SLOW COOKER • CALORIE SMART • GLUTEN FREE

Pulled Pork Chili

This recipe would be great served with hot cooked white rice, shredded cheddar cheese, sour cream, chopped fresh cilantro leaves, sliced green onions and lime wedges.

PREP 35 Minutes TOTAL 8 Hours 35 Minutes • *12 servings*

- 2 cans (15 oz each) red kidney beans, drained, rinsed
- 1 can (28 oz) fire-roasted diced tomatoes, undrained
- 2 cans (4.5 oz each) chopped green chiles
- 2 packages (1 oz each) gluten-free taco seasoning mix
- 3- to 4-lb boneless pork shoulder roast, trimmed

1 Spray 5-quart slow cooker with cooking spray. In slow cooker, mix beans, tomatoes, chiles and taco seasoning mix.

2 Trim excess fat from pork. Add to cooker and turn to coat. Cover and cook on Low heat setting 8 to 9 hours or until pork is fork-tender.

3 Place pork on cutting board; shred using two forks. Add shredded pork back to slow cooker; stir to mix. Cover and cook on Low heat setting 10 to 15 minutes or until hot.

1 Serving Calories 300; Total Fat 14g (Saturated Fat 4.5g, Trans Fat 0g); Cholesterol 70mg; Sodium 610mg; Total Carbohydrate 17g (Dietary Fiber 3g); Protein 27g **Carbohydrate Choices:** 1

Spicy Thai Pork Stew

PREP 30 Minutes TOTAL 1 Hour 40 Minutes •
6 servings (1 cup each)

- ⅓ cup all-purpose flour
- ½ teaspoon garlic-pepper blend
- 4 boneless pork loin chops (1½ lb), cut into 1-inch cubes
- 3 tablespoons vegetable oil
- 1 bottle (11.5 oz) peanut sauce
- 1 cup chicken broth (for homemade broth, see page 153)
- 1 teaspoon crushed red pepper flakes
- 2 cups cubed (1-inch) peeled butternut squash (about ¾ lb)
- 1 medium red bell pepper, cut into 1-inch pieces (1¼ cups)
- 4 oz fresh snow pea pods (1 cup), strings removed, cut diagonally in half

  Hot cooked white rice (page 224), if desired

  Chopped dry-roasted peanuts or fresh cilantro, if desired

1 In large resealable food-storage plastic bag, mix flour and garlic-pepper blend. Add pork; seal bag and shake until pork is evenly coated. In 5-to 6-quart Dutch oven or stockpot, heat oil over medium heat. Add pork; cook, stirring occasionally, until golden brown on all sides.

2 Stir in peanut sauce, broth and pepper flakes. Heat to boiling. Boil 1 minute, scraping browned bits from bottom of pan; reduce heat. Cover and simmer 30 minutes.

3 Add squash. Cover and simmer 30 minutes or until pork and squash are tender.

4 Stir in bell pepper and snow peas. Simmer uncovered 5 to 7 minutes or until bell pepper is crisp-tender. Serve over rice; garnish with peanuts or cilantro.

1 Serving Calories 480; Total Fat 30g (Saturated Fat 7g, Trans Fat 0g); Cholesterol 70mg; Sodium 350mg; Total Carbohydrate 19g (Dietary Fiber 3g); Protein 34g **Carbohydrate Choices:** 1

Rosemary

Pancetta
Bean Soup
(see page 162)

LEARN TO USE SLOW COOKERS AND MULTI COOKERS

Slow cookers and multi cookers can be a great help in getting homemade meals on the table. Slow cookers eliminate a lot of the hands-on prep and the need to watch what you're cooking, since usually everything gets tossed in at once and is left to simmer unattended all day. When time is short, multi cookers can come to the rescue, as the pressure cooker function of these appliances cooks food faster than other cooking methods. Look here for helpful information on cooking with these popular appliances. You'll find delicious recipes throughout this book that use a slow cooker or multi cooker.

Slow Cookers

SLOW-COOKER SUCCESS

Use these tips to ensure great results from your slow cooker:

- Spray the inside of the insert or cooker with cooking spray for easy cleanup.
- Slow cookers work most efficiently when two-thirds to three-fourths full.
- Always keep the slow cooker covered for the specified cooking time. Each time the lid is removed, heat escapes, adding 15 to 20 minutes to the cooking time. *Exception: large cuts of meat should be rotated halfway through cooking for best results.*
- Root vegetables take longer to cook than other vegetables, so cut them smaller and put them on the bottom of the cooker.
- Cover raw potatoes with liquid to prevent them from turning dark.

SLOW-COOKER SAFETY

Slow cookers heat up more slowly and cook at lower temperatures than other appliances. To keep food safe, follow these guidelines:

- Use meat or poultry that is completely thawed.
- Keep perishable foods refrigerated separately until you are ready to prepare the recipe and cook it.
- Do not place ingredients in the slow cooker ahead of time and refrigerate to cook later.
- Always cook and drain ground beef just before placing it in the cooker, not ahead of time.
- Brown poultry and meats just before placing them in the cooker, not ahead of time.
- Whole chickens can be cooked in a slow cooker if they are 4½ lb or smaller and are cooked in a 5- to 6-quart slow cooker, so they have enough room and can reach the proper temperature quickly enough.
- Follow recipes exactly for specific sizes when cutting ingredients and for layering so that the dish cooks properly.
- Place leftovers in shallow containers and refrigerate within 2 hours of cooking. Don't use the insert for storage.
- Always reheat food in your microwave or conventional oven or on the stove-top before placing it in the slow cooker to keep warm until serving. Don't use a slow cooker to heat up food.

Multi Cookers

Multi cookers are programmable cookers that have the functions and capabilities of several other kitchen tools including a pressure cooker, slow cooker, yogurt maker, steamer and warmer. They also have sautéing and searing capabilities. These features can vary by manufacturer and model.

MULTI-COOKER FUNCTIONS

PRESSURE COOKER The sealed chamber raises the pressure and temperature of the food rapidly to cook it quickly and make less-tender cuts of meat very tender.

SLOW COOKER See Slow Cookers (at left)

YOGURT MAKER Some models have a yogurt function that turns milk into yogurt.

STEAMER Steams vegetables without the need for a pan of boiling water and a steamer basket.

SAUTÉ AND SEAR Allows you to brown meat or partially cook foods quickly before using the slow cooker or pressure cooker functions, eliminating the need to cook in a pan for longer times.

- Be sure to always press CANCEL and then reprogram for the next step after sautéing. You cannot go directly from SAUTE to MANUAL or PRESSURE COOK.
- You can brown meat in the multi cooker using the SAUTE feature. To brown meat, depending on the cut you may need to do it in 2 or 3 batches. This way, the cooking juices have a chance to evaporate rather than steam the meat, if done all at once, which can discolor the finished dish.
- If small bits are left in the bottom of your multi cooker after sautéing, the sensor may notice them and indicate that the food is burning, when it isn't. Be sure to use the amount of liquid called for in the recipe, and stir up any bits from the bottom of the multi cooker after sautéing in it.
- The SAUTE feature can also be used after your food is cooked, to thicken the sauce or to cook noodles for the dish.

WARMER Some models allow you to keep cooked food warm until serving time.

(continued)

LEARN TO USE SLOW COOKERS AND MULTI COOKERS *continued*

GENERAL GUIDELINES

- Start with reputable kitchen-tested recipes to ensure you end up with great results. These appliances are not as forgiving as a slow cooker, since you must release the pressure before you can check for doneness; for food safety and safe handling, you shouldn't add extra time after releasing pressure.

- They're great for tough cuts such as brisket and shoulder, recipes where the meat will be shredded. Bone-in pork chops work better than boneless chops, and the fat in chicken thighs help them stay more moist and tender than leaner chicken breasts. Smaller cuts of meat work well in stews and chilies.

- Foods generally take about 13 to 15 minutes to get to the correct pressure before the programmed buttons start to cook and count down the indicated time. There is also time for the pressure to release once the cooking program is finished. This extra time is reflected in the "Total" time on our recipes.

- For some recipes, multi cookers can cut down on cooking time with other appliances. For others, the cooking time plus the time it takes to build up the proper pressure and then release it at the end can end up about the same as with other cooking methods.

- Multi-cooker recipes cannot be used interchangeably with stove-top pressure cookers, as multi cookers don't generate the same pressure.

- For best results, don't fill your multi-cooker insert past the indicator line (usually about ⅔ full for most recipes or half full for foods that expand, such as rice).

- At least 1 cup liquid is needed for the cooker to get to the correct pressure to cook.

RELEASING PRESSURE

Pressure inside the chamber needs to be released before the appliance can be safely opened. **NATURAL RELEASE** slowly releases the built-up pressure without your having to do anything. Because it's a slower release, this method is used when ingredients in the pot can benefit from residual additional cooking at a lower temperature, rather than on high heat. It's like letting microwaved foods stand before serving. The process can take up to 30 minutes, depending on the food. **MANUAL/QUICK RELEASE** releases pressure quickly to halt the cooking process.

- Multi cookers with pressure valves show visually when the steam has been released. For those that don't have pressure valves, pressure has been released when steam no longer comes out of the unit. Do not attempt to open the lid until the pressure has completely released.

- Meats may look dry when removed from the cooker, but will be moist when eaten if cooked properly. You can baste the cooked meat with a little of the cooking juices to remedy the dry appearance.

- Cooked under pressure, the texture of rice and pasta isn't quite the same as when cooked with other methods.

Tomato-Basil Soup

Fully ripe, juicy tomatoes provide the best flavor for this soup. If your tomatoes aren't completely ripe, you may need to increase the salt and sugar just a bit.

PREP 30 Minutes **TOTAL** 1 Hour • *4 servings*

2 tablespoons olive or vegetable oil	1 can (8 oz) tomato sauce
1 medium carrot, finely chopped (½ cup)	¼ cup thinly sliced fresh or 2 teaspoons dried basil leaves
1 small onion, finely chopped (½ cup)	½ teaspoon organic sugar
1 clove garlic, finely chopped	¼ teaspoon salt
6 large tomatoes, peeled, seeded and chopped (6 cups)*	Dash pepper

1 In 3-quart saucepan, heat oil over medium heat. Add carrot, onion and garlic; cook about 10 minutes, stirring occasionally, until tender but not browned.

2 Stir in tomatoes. Cook uncovered about 10 minutes, stirring occasionally, until thoroughly heated.

3 Stir in remaining ingredients. Cook uncovered about 10 minutes, stirring occasionally, until hot.

1 Serving Calories 160; Total Fat 8g (Saturated Fat 1g, Trans Fat 0g); Cholesterol 0mg; Sodium 440mg; Total Carbohydrate 19g (Dietary Fiber 5g); Protein 3g **Carbohydrate Choices:** 1

*3 cans (14.5 oz each) diced tomatoes, undrained, can be substituted for the fresh tomatoes. Omit salt; increase sugar to 1 teaspoon.

Vegetable Broth

Mild vegetables are preferred for a well-balanced neutral flavor. Broccoli, rutabaga, red cabbage or other strong-flavored vegetables would overpower the broth, and may give it a muddy, objectionable color.

PREP 20 Minutes **TOTAL** 1 Hour 30 Minutes • *8 cups broth*

8 cups cold water	½ cup fresh parsley sprigs
6 cups coarsely chopped mild vegetables (bell peppers, carrots, celery, leeks, mushrooms,* potatoes, spinach and/or zucchini)	2 tablespoons chopped fresh or 2 teaspoons dried basil leaves
	2 tablespoons chopped fresh or 2 teaspoons dried thyme leaves
1 small onion, coarsely chopped (½ cup)	1 teaspoon salt
4 cloves garlic, finely chopped	¼ teaspoon cracked black pepper
	2 dried bay leaves

1 In 4-quart saucepan, mix all ingredients. Heat to boiling; reduce heat. Cover and simmer 1 hour, stirring occasionally.

2 Cool about 10 minutes. Strain broth through fine-mesh strainer; discard vegetables and seasonings. Use broth immediately, or cover and refrigerate up to 24 hours or freeze up to 6 months. Stir before measuring.

1 Cup Calories 0; Total Fat 0g (Saturated Fat 0g, Trans Fat 0g); Cholesterol 0mg; Sodium 300mg; Total Carbohydrate 0g (Dietary Fiber 0g); Protein 0g **Carbohydrate Choices:** 0

*Some mushrooms have woody stems that cannot be eaten, but they can be used to flavor the broth.

Minestrone with Italian Sausage

PREP 45 Minutes **TOTAL** 45 Minutes •
7 servings (1½ cups each)

1 tablespoon olive or vegetable oil	5½ cups beef broth (for homemade broth, see page 157)
1 lb bulk sweet Italian pork sausage	1 can (14.5 oz) diced tomatoes, undrained
2 medium carrots, coarsely chopped (1 cup)	1 can (15.5 oz) great northern beans, drained, rinsed
1 small onion, chopped (½ cup)	1 cup uncooked small elbow macaroni (4 oz)
2 teaspoons dried basil leaves	1 medium zucchini, cut in half lengthwise, then cut into ¼-inch slices (1 cup)
2 teaspoons finely chopped garlic	1 cup frozen cut green beans

1 In 5- to 6-quart Dutch oven or stockpot, heat oil over medium-high heat. Add sausage, carrots, onion, basil and garlic; cook 5 to 7 minutes, stirring frequently, until sausage is no longer pink. Drain; return to Dutch oven.

2 Stir broth, tomatoes and great northern beans into sausage mixture. Heat to boiling; reduce heat to medium-low. Cover and cook 7 to 8 minutes, stirring occasionally.

3 Stir in macaroni, zucchini and green beans. Heat to boiling over medium-high heat. Cook 5 to 6 minutes, stirring occasionally, until vegetables are hot and macaroni is tender.

1 Serving Calories 300; Total Fat 12g (Saturated Fat 3.5g, Trans Fat 0g); Cholesterol 25mg; Sodium 1160mg; Total Carbohydrate 32g (Dietary Fiber 6g); Protein 16g **Carbohydrate Choices:** 2

MEATLESS MINESTRONE: Substitute 1 additional can (15.5 oz) great northern beans (or your favorite canned beans) for sausage, and vegetable broth for beef broth.

5-INGREDIENT RECIPE

Chicken Broth

Cumin

Spinach

Roasted Garlic Hummus

Broccoli Stir-Fry

Savory Hummus Soup

5-INGREDIENT RECIPE

FAST • CALORIE SMART

Savory Hummus Soup

PREP 20 Minutes **TOTAL** 20 Minutes •
4 servings (1⅓ cups each)

2½ cups chicken or vegetable broth (for homemade broth, see page 153 or 169)	1 teaspoon ground cumin
1 container (10 oz) roasted garlic hummus (about 1¼ cups)	¼ teaspoon salt
	¼ teaspoon pepper
	1 bag (14.4 oz) frozen broccoli stir-fry
	2½ cups loosely packed fresh baby spinach (from 5-oz bag)

1 In 3-quart saucepan, combine broth, hummus, cumin, salt and pepper. Heat to boiling; reduce heat to low.

2 Stir in broccoli stir-fry. Cook 10 to 12 minutes or until vegetables are crisp-tender. Stir in spinach; cook 1 to 2 minutes or until wilted.

1 Serving Calories 210; Total Fat 8g (Saturated Fat 1.5g, Trans Fat 0g); Cholesterol 0mg; Sodium 700mg; Total Carbohydrate 24g (Dietary Fiber 7g); Protein 11g **Carbohydrate Choices:** 1½

CALORIE SMART • GLUTEN FREE

Fish Broth

Celery leaves add great flavor to broth. Try adding chopped celery leaves along with the celery stalks called for in soup recipes.

PREP 20 Minutes **TOTAL** 1 Hour • **6 cups broth**

1½ lb fish bones and trimmings (no gills)	3 medium fresh mushrooms, chopped
4 cups cold water	1 tablespoon lemon juice
2 cups dry white wine or clam juice	1 teaspoon salt
1 large stalk celery with leaves, chopped	½ teaspoon dried thyme leaves
1 small onion, sliced	3 sprigs fresh parsley
	1 dried bay leaf

1 Rinse fish bones and trimmings with cold water; drain. In 4-quart saucepan, mix bones, trimmings, and remaining ingredients; heat to boiling. Skim foam from broth. Reduce heat, cover and simmer 30 minutes.

2 Cool about 10 minutes. Strain broth through fine-mesh strainer; discard skin, bones, vegetables and seasonings. Use broth immediately, or cover and refrigerate up to 24 hours or freeze up to 6 months.

1 Cup Calories 15; Total Fat 0g (Saturated Fat 0g, Trans Fat 0g); Cholesterol 0mg; Sodium 400mg; Total Carbohydrate 0g (Dietary Fiber 0g); Protein 0g **Carbohydrate Choices:** 0

EASY • FAST • CALORIE SMART

Oyster Stew

PREP 15 Minutes **TOTAL** 15 Minutes • **4 servings** (1 cup each)

¼ cup butter	½ cup half-and-half
1 pint shucked oysters, undrained, or fresh shucked oysters with their liquid	½ teaspoon salt
	Dash pepper
2 cups milk	Oyster crackers, if desired

1 In 1½-quart saucepan, melt butter over low heat. Stir in oysters. Cook 2 to 4 minutes, stirring occasionally, just until edges curl.

2 In 2-quart saucepan, heat milk and half-and-half over medium-low heat until hot. Stir in salt, pepper and oyster mixture; heat until hot. Serve with oyster crackers.

1 Serving Calories 290; Total Fat 20g (Saturated Fat 12g, Trans Fat 1g); Cholesterol 120mg; Sodium 600mg; Total Carbohydrate 12g (Dietary Fiber 0g); Protein 15g **Carbohydrate Choices:** 1

CALORIE SMART

New England Clam Chowder

One pint shucked fresh clams with their liquid can be substituted for the canned clams. Chop the clams and stir in with the potatoes in Step 2.

PREP 20 Minutes **TOTAL** 35 Minutes • **4 servings** (1¼ cups each)

4 slices bacon, cut into ½-inch pieces	2¾ cups milk or half-and-half
1 small onion, chopped (½ cup)	2 medium potatoes, peeled, diced (2 cups)
1 medium stalk celery, sliced (⅓ cup)	¼ teaspoon salt
2 cans (6½ oz each) minced or chopped clams, drained, ¼ cup liquid reserved	Dash pepper
	¼ cup all-purpose flour
	Chopped fresh parsley, if desired

1 In 3-quart saucepan, cook bacon, onion and celery over medium heat, stirring occasionally, until bacon is crisp and onion is tender. Drain; return to saucepan.

2 Stir in clams, reserved clam liquid, ¾ cup of the milk, the potatoes, salt and pepper. Heat to boiling; reduce heat. Cover and simmer about 15 minutes or until potatoes are tender.

3 In medium bowl, using whisk, mix remaining milk and the flour until smooth and blended. Stir into clam mixture. Heat to boiling, stirring frequently. Boil and stir 1 minute until thickened. Garnish with parsley.

1 Serving Calories 280; Total Fat 7g (Saturated Fat 3g, Trans Fat 0g); Cholesterol 45mg; Sodium 450mg; Total Carbohydrate 34g (Dietary Fiber 2g); Protein 20g **Carbohydrate Choices:** 2

USE IT UP

Don't throw away those unused veggies, peels and seeds! Here are some terrific ways to avoid tossing them into the trash.

UNUSED FRESH VEGGIES Add to casseroles, soups, stews or chilies; toss with salads; roast (see page 254) or grill (see page 444).

WILTED CARROTS OR ZUCCHINI Shred and add to muffin, quick bread, or pancake batter.

LEEK TOPS OR CELERY LEAVES Chop and add to stir-fries or add to soups, stews or casseroles before cooking.

VEGGIE PEELS, SEEDS OR ENDS Store in freezer-safe food storage container in freezer. Add with the water when making Vegetable Broth (page 169), the broth from Roasted Chicken and Broth (page 153), or Beef and Broth (page 157).

LEFTOVER FROZEN VEGGIES Microwave to reheat and add to scrambled eggs, quesadillas or macaroni and cheese, or add frozen to soups, stews or chilies during cooking.

Sweet Potato Chili

The secret to great-tasting chili is to make it ahead, cover and refrigerate so the flavors can blend. Reheat it just before serving.

PREP 45 Minutes **TOTAL** 45 Minutes •
6 servings (1½ cups each)

- 1 tablespoon vegetable oil
- 1 medium onion, chopped (1 cup)
- 2 cloves garlic, finely chopped
- 1 large poblano chile, seeded, chopped (about 1 cup)
- 1 large dark-orange sweet potato, peeled, cut into ½-inch cubes (about 2 cups)
- 2 tablespoons chili powder
- 2 teaspoons ground cumin
- 1 teaspoon dried oregano leaves
- ½ teaspoon smoked paprika
- ½ teaspoon salt
- ½ teaspoon pepper
- 1½ cups vegetable broth (for homemade broth, see page 169)
- 2 cans (14.5 oz each) fire-roasted diced tomatoes, undrained
- 1 can (15 oz) chick peas (garbanzo beans), drained, rinsed
- 1 can (15 oz) pinto beans, drained, rinsed
- 1 can (15.25 oz) whole kernel sweet corn, drained

  Avocado slices and chopped fresh cilantro, if desired

1 In 5- or 6-quart Dutch oven or stockpot, heat oil over medium-high heat. Add onion, garlic, chile and sweet potato; cook 3 to 5 minutes, stirring frequently, or until onion is tender.

2 Stir in remaining ingredients except avocado slices and cilantro. Heat to boiling; reduce heat. Cover; simmer 20 minutes or until sweet potato is tender, stirring occasionally. Serve topped with avocado slices and cilantro.

1 Serving Calories 270; Total Fat 5g (Saturated Fat 1g, Trans Fat 0g); Cholesterol 0mg; Sodium 990mg; Total Carbohydrate 46g (Dietary Fiber 10g); Protein 10g **Carbohydrate Choices:** 3

MULTI-COOKER DIRECTIONS: Select SAUTE; adjust to normal. Heat oil in 6-quart insert. Add onion, garlic, chile and sweet potato; cook 4 to 5 minutes, stirring frequently, until onion is tender. Select CANCEL. Add remaining ingredients except avocado and cilantro. Secure lid; set pressure valve to SEALING. Select MANUAL; cook on high pressure 3 minutes. Select CANCEL. Set pressure valve to VENTING to quick-release pressure. Serve with avocado slices and cilantro.

Manhattan Clam Chowder

Which chowder is which? Manhattan Clam Chowder is tomato-based, whereas New England Clam Chowder is cream based.

PREP 20 Minutes **TOTAL** 35 Minutes • **4 servings**

- ¼ cup chopped gluten-free bacon or salt pork
- 1 small onion, finely chopped (½ cup)
- 2 cans (6.5 oz each) minced or chopped clams, undrained*
- 2 medium potatoes, peeled, diced (2 cups)
- 1 stalk celery, chopped (⅓ cup)
- 1 cup water
- 1 can (14.5 oz) whole tomatoes, undrained
- 2 teaspoons chopped fresh parsley
- 1 teaspoon chopped fresh or ¼ teaspoon dried thyme leaves
- ¼ teaspoon salt
- ⅛ teaspoon pepper

1 In 2-quart saucepan, cook bacon and onion over medium heat 8 to 10 minutes, stirring occasionally, until bacon is crisp and onion is tender. Drain; return to saucepan.

2 Stir in clams, potatoes, celery and water. Heat to boiling; reduce heat. Cover and simmer about 15 minutes or until potatoes are tender.

3 Stir in remaining ingredients, breaking up tomatoes. Heat until hot, stirring occasionally.

1 Serving Calories 240; Total Fat 3.5g (Saturated Fat 1g, Trans Fat 0g); Cholesterol 50mg; Sodium 470mg; Total Carbohydrate 25g (Dietary Fiber 3g); Protein 26g **Carbohydrate Choices:** 1½

*1 pint shucked fresh clams with their liquid can be substituted for the canned clams. Chop the clams and stir in with the potatoes in Step 2.

SLOW-COOKER DIRECTIONS: In 10-inch skillet, cook bacon as directed in Step 1—except without onion. Spray 2- to 3½-quart slow cooker with cooking spray. In slow cooker, mix bacon, onion and remaining ingredients except clams and thyme. Cover; cook on Low heat setting 9 to 10 hours. Stir in undrained clams and thyme. Increase heat setting to High. Cover; cook 10 to 20 minutes or until hot.

Sweet Potato Chili

Lemony Lentil Soup

PREP 20 Minutes **TOTAL** 30 Minutes •
4 servings (1½ cups each)

- 1 tablespoon
vegetable oil
- 1 small onion, chopped
(½ cup)
- 1 medium stalk celery,
chopped (⅓ cup)
- 2 cloves garlic,
finely chopped
- 1 cup dried yellow
(golden) lentils or
yellow split peas*,
sorted, rinsed
- 4 cups (32-oz carton)
vegetable broth
(for homemade broth,
see page 169)
- 2 teaspoons chopped
fresh or ½ teaspoon
dried rosemary leaves
- ½ teaspoon salt
- ¼ teaspoon pepper
- 1 cup fresh or frozen
sweet peas
- 1 small carrot, peeled,
shredded (½ cup)
- 1 teaspoon grated
lemon zest
- ¼ cup fresh lemon juice
Fresh lemon slices
and fresh rosemary
sprigs, if desired

1 In 3-quart saucepan, heat oil over medium heat. Add onion, celery and garlic; cook 3 to 5 minutes, stirring occasionally, until onion is tender.

2 Stir in lentils, broth, chopped rosemary, salt and pepper. Heat to boiling; reduce heat. Cover; simmer 8 to 10 minutes or until lentils are just tender.

3 Stir in peas, carrot, lemon zest and juice. Cook an additional 3 to 5 minutes until peas are tender. Top each serving with fresh lemon slices and rosemary sprig.

1 Serving Calories 260; Total Fat 4.5g (Saturated Fat 0.5g, Trans Fat 0g); Cholesterol 0mg; Sodium 970mg; Total Carbohydrate 40g (Dietary Fiber 11g); Protein 15g **Carbohydrate Choices:** 2½

*For yellow split peas, in Step 2, cook 35 to 40 minutes, stirring occasionally.

Split Pea Soup

PREP 20 Minutes **TOTAL** 2 Hours 20 Minutes • *8 servings*

- 1 bag (16 oz) dried
green or yellow split
peas (2 cups), sorted,
rinsed
- 8 cups water
- ¼ teaspoon pepper
- 1 medium onion,
chopped (1 cup)
- 3 medium stalks celery,
finely chopped (1 cup)
- 1 ham bone or 2 lb ham
shanks or smoked
pork hocks
- 3 medium carrots, cut
into ¼-inch slices
(1½ cups)

1 In 4-quart saucepan, mix all ingredients except carrots. Heat to boiling; reduce heat. Cover and simmer 1 hour to 1 hour 30 minutes.

2 Remove ham bone; let stand until cool enough to handle. Remove ham from bone. Remove excess fat from ham; cut ham into ½-inch pieces.

3 Stir ham and carrots into soup. Heat to boiling; reduce heat. Cover and simmer about 30 minutes or until carrots are tender and soup is desired thickness. Top each serving with fresh lemon slices and rosemary.

1 Serving Calories 290; Total Fat 4g (Saturated Fat 1g, Trans Fat 0g); Cholesterol 45mg; Sodium 75mg; Total Carbohydrate 34g (Dietary Fiber 16g); Protein 29g **Carbohydrate Choices:** 2

SLOW-COOKER DIRECTIONS: Reduce water to 7 cups. Spray 4- to 6-quart slow cooker with cooking spray. In slow cooker, mix all ingredients. Cover; cook on Low heat setting 3 to 4 hours or until peas are tender. Remove ham bone and cut ham as directed in Step 2. Stir ham into soup.

Mexican Street Corn Chowder

PREP 45 Minutes **TOTAL** 45 Minutes •
6 servings (about 1½ cups each)

- 6 slices gluten-free
bacon, cut into
½-inch pieces
- 1 cup chopped red
onion (1 medium)
- 2 teaspoons
chili powder
- 1 teaspoon salt
- 1 teaspoon
ground cumin
- 2 cloves garlic,
finely chopped
- 3 cups gluten-free
chicken broth
(for homemade broth,
see page 153)
- 4 cups cubed peeled
(½-inch) russet or
Idaho baking potatoes
(about 1½ lb)
- 1 medium red bell
pepper, chopped
(about 1 cup)
- 1 jalapeño chile,
seeded,
finely chopped
- 1 bag (14.4 oz) frozen
corn (about 3 cups)
- 1 cup half-and-half
- ½ cup crumbled Cotija
or feta cheese (2 oz)
- 2 tablespoons chopped
fresh cilantro
Additional crumbled
Cotija cheese and
chili powder,
if desired

1 In 4-quart saucepan, cook bacon over medium-high heat until crisp. Using slotted spoon, remove bacon from pan to paper towel–lined plate. Reserve 2 tablespoons drippings in pan; discard remaining drippings.

2 Add onion, chili powder, salt, cumin and garlic to drippings in pan. Cook over medium heat 2 to 3 minutes, stirring frequently, or until onion is tender. Add broth and potatoes. Heat to boiling over high heat; reduce heat. Cover; simmer 8 to 10 minutes or until potatoes are almost tender.

3 Place 3 cups of the potato mixture in blender container. Cover; blend on high speed 10 to 15 seconds or until mixture is smooth. Return mixture to saucepan. Add bell pepper, jalapeño and corn.

4 Cook over medium heat 4 to 6 minutes or until corn is tender. Stir in half of the bacon, the half-and-half, cheese and cilantro. Heat over medium heat 1 to 2 minutes or until hot, but not boiling. Sprinkle with remaining bacon. Garnish with additional cheese and chili powder.

1 Serving Calories 330; Total Fat 13g (Saturated Fat 6g, Trans Fat 0g); Cholesterol 35mg; Sodium 930mg; Total Carbohydrate 39g (Dietary Fiber 4g); Protein 13g **Carbohydrate Choices:** 2½

CALORIE SMART • VEGETARIAN • VEGAN

Cauliflower Barley Mushroom Soup

PREP 45 Minutes TOTAL 45 Minutes •
6 servings (1⅓ cups each)

- 3 tablespoons olive oil
- 1 package (8 oz) sliced fresh mushrooms
- 2 leeks, cut in half lengthwise, rinsed and thinly sliced (about 2 cups)
- 2 cloves garlic, finely chopped
- 4 cups (32-oz carton) vegetable broth (for homemade broth, see page 169)
- 1 cup coarsely chopped cauliflower florets
- 1 cup diced carrots (2 medium)
- ½ cup uncooked quick-cooking barley
- 1 teaspoon dried Italian seasoning
- ½ teaspoon salt
- ¼ teaspoon pepper
- 3 cups loosely packed fresh baby spinach leaves
  Additional leek slices, if desired

1 In 3-quart saucepan, heat oil over medium heat. Add mushrooms, leeks and garlic; cook over medium heat, stirring frequently, about 5 minutes or until vegetables are tender. Place half of vegetable mixture in heatproof bowl; set aside. Place remaining vegetable mixture in blender container.

2 Add 2 cups of the broth to blender container. Cover; blend on high speed 15 to 30 seconds or until smooth. Return blended mixture to saucepan; add remaining 2 cups vegetable broth, the chopped cauliflower, carrots, barley, Italian seasoning, salt and pepper. Heat to boiling, stirring occasionally. Reduce heat; cover and simmer 10 to 12 minutes or until barley and vegetables are tender.

3 Stir in reserved vegetable mixture and spinach. Cook over medium heat 1 to 2 minutes or until hot and spinach is wilted. Garnish soup with additional leek slices.

1 Serving Calories 180; Total Fat 7g (Saturated Fat 1g, Trans Fat 0g); Cholesterol 0mg; Sodium 670mg; Total Carbohydrate 24g (Dietary Fiber 5g); Protein 4g **Carbohydrate Choices:** 1½

Lemony Lentil Soup

Mexican Street Corn Chowder

175

Cauliflower Barley Mushroom Soup

Butternut Squash Soup in progress
(see recipe on page 178)

LEARN TO PUREE

To puree is to mash or blend food until smooth, using a blender or food processor or by forcing the food through a sieve. Pureed soups are likely the most common foods made using this method. But you can also puree foods to feed a baby, and foods like sweet potatoes can be pureed to serve as part of a meal. Pureeing can be done with a blender, food processor or immersion blender; each of these appliances works a little differently. Try this technique with yummy Butternut Squash Soup, page 178.

- **Blender** This appliance will provide a smooth puree. Blend in small batches for the best results.
- **Food Processor** Because they tend to chop, not puree, food processors do not provide the smoothest mixture. The soup or vegetable mixture is often gritty with small bits of food left behind.
- **Immersion Blender** This tool will provide the smoothest puree with the least work. Immersion blenders are made to go right into a pan of hot soup or sauce, eliminating the need to puree the mixture in batches in a blender or food processor. To avoid damaging the motor, submerge the blender just to the top of the stem. Follow the manufacturer's directions before using or washing.

Tips for Great Results

- Food should be fully cooked before pureeing. If it is not, it is more difficult to get the puree really smooth. Food should be cooked to the eating stage—and not beyond that. If it is overcooked and mushy, the puree could lack flavor.

- Blend or process in batches, adding the food with a ladle. Having too much food in either appliance will make it difficult to create a smooth puree.

- Hot foods can release a lot of steam, so allow the soup to cool slightly before pureeing. Also, pureeing small amounts at a time allows for room in the appliance for the steam to expand. Trapped steam can push the lid off, so for safety, hold a kitchen towel on the top of the appliance. If the lid has a vent, leave it open to allow the steam to escape.

- If you have the option of more than one speed, start slow and increase the speed as you puree.

- After pureeing, strain the soup through a strainer back into the soup pot. The food pieces left behind can be re-pureed.

- For pureed baby food, cook the food in a small amount of water. Set the water aside and add small amounts of it while you process or blend the food, until you have the consistency you like. Foods such as avocado or watermelon do not need to be cooked.

SOUPS, STEWS & CHILIES

Butternut Squash Soup

178

Roasted Red Pepper
Soup with Mozzarella

Fresh Greens and Basil Soup

Butternut Squash Soup

This wonderfully rich, thick and flavorful soup became a staff favorite while being tested in our kitchens. Try it sprinkled with pumpkin seeds and chopped toasted walnuts.

PREP 30 Minutes **TOTAL** 45 Minutes • *6 servings*

2 tablespoons butter	½ teaspoon dried marjoram leaves
1 small onion, chopped (½ cup)	¼ teaspoon black pepper
1 (2-lb) butternut squash, peeled, seeded and cut into pieces*	⅛ teaspoon ground red pepper (cayenne)
2 cups gluten-free chicken broth (for homemade broth, see page 153)	1 package (8 oz) cream cheese, cut into cubes
	Additional gluten-free chicken broth or water, if desired

1 In 3-quart saucepan, melt butter over medium heat. Add onion; cook, stirring occasionally, until crisp-tender.

2 Add squash, 2 cups broth, the marjoram, black pepper and red pepper. Heat to boiling; reduce heat. Cover and simmer 12 to 15 minutes or until squash is tender.

3 In blender or food processor, place one-third each of the soup mixture and cream cheese. Cover and blend on high speed until smooth, scraping down side if needed. Repeat twice with remaining soup mixture and cream cheese. Return mixture to saucepan. Heat over medium heat, stirring with whisk, until blended and hot (do not boil). Add additional broth if thinner consistency is desired.

1 Serving Calories 260; Total Fat 18g (Saturated Fat 10g, Trans Fat 0.5g); Cholesterol 50mg; Sodium 270mg; Total Carbohydrate 18g (Dietary Fiber 4g); Protein 5g **Carbohydrate Choices:** 1

*Squash will be easier to peel if you microwave it first: Pierce whole squash with knife in several places to allow steam to escape. Place on microwavable paper towel; microwave on High 4 to 6 minutes or until squash is hot and peel is firm but easy to cut. Cool slightly before peeling.

SLOW-COOKER DIRECTIONS: In 10-inch skillet, melt butter over medium heat. Add onion; cook, stirring occasionally, until crisp-tender. Spray 3½- to 4-quart slow cooker with cooking spray. In slow cooker, mix onion and remaining ingredients except cream cheese and additional broth. Cover; cook on Low heat setting 6 to 8 hours. In blender or food processor, place one-third to one-half of the soup mixture at a time. Cover and blend on high speed until smooth. Return mixture to slow cooker. Stir in cream cheese with whisk. Cover; cook on Low heat setting about 30 minutes, stirring occasionally with whisk, until cheese is melted and soup is smooth.

Roasted Red Pepper Soup with Mozzarella

You can make your own vegetable broth (page 169) or chicken broth (page 153) and keep it in the freezer for recipes such as this one.

PREP 40 Minutes **TOTAL** 1 Hour 10 Minutes •
4 servings (about 1½ cups each)

- 4 red bell peppers
- 1 tablespoon olive oil
- 2 medium onions, chopped (2 cups)
- 3 cloves garlic, sliced
- 2 cups vegetable broth or reduced-sodium chicken broth (for homemade broth, see page 169 or 153)
- 1 cup water
- ¼ teaspoon cracked black pepper
- 1 cup loosely packed thinly sliced fresh basil leaves
- ½ yellow bell pepper, diced
- 8 bocconcini (small fresh mozzarella cheese balls), cut into quarters
- 4 slices crusty multigrain or whole wheat bread

1 Set oven control to broil. On rack in broiler pan, place red bell peppers. Broil with tops about 5 inches from heat, turning occasionally, until skin is blistered and evenly browned. Place roasted peppers in large heatproof bowl; cover with plastic wrap. Let stand 15 minutes.

2 Meanwhile, in 4-quart saucepan, heat oil over medium-low heat. Add onions and garlic; cook, stirring occasionally, 7 to 9 minutes or until onions begin to turn brown; remove from heat.

3 Remove skin, stems, seeds and membranes from roasted peppers. Cut peppers into strips. Stir bell pepper strips, broth, water and pepper into onion mixture. Heat to boiling; reduce heat. Simmer uncovered 10 minutes, stirring occasionally. Stir in ½ cup of the basil. Remove from heat; cool slightly.

4 In blender or food processor, ladle about one-third of the soup mixture. Cover and blend on high speed until smooth, stopping blender to scrape side if necessary. Pour into large heatproof bowl. Repeat two times more with remaining soup mixture.

5 Return soup to saucepan; heat through. Top individual servings with yellow bell pepper and mozzarella; sprinkle evenly with remaining ½ cup basil. Serve with bread.

1 Serving Calories 200; Total Fat 6g (Saturated Fat 1.5g, Trans Fat 0g); Cholesterol 0mg; Sodium 620mg; Total Carbohydrate 29g (Dietary Fiber 6g); Protein 7g **Carbohydrate Choices:** 2

Fresh Greens and Basil Soup

Serve this soup hot or cold.

PREP 35 Minutes **TOTAL** 40 Minutes •
6 servings (about 1 cup each)

- 2 tablespoons olive oil
- 3 medium stalks celery, sliced (1 cup)
- 1 medium onion, chopped (1 cup)
- 1 medium jalapeño chile, seeded, finely chopped
- ½ cup finely ground walnuts (1.5 oz)
- 3 cloves garlic, finely chopped
- 4 cups (32-oz carton) vegetable broth (for homemade broth, see page 169)
- 1 teaspoon ground turmeric
- ½ teaspoon salt
- ½ teaspoon pepper
- 1 package (10 oz) fresh spinach
- 2 tablespoons chopped fresh or 1 teaspoon dried basil
- ½ cup coconut cream (from 13.66-oz can; not cream of coconut)
- Additional coconut cream and chopped walnuts, if desired

1 In 5-quart Dutch oven or stockpot, heat oil over medium heat. Add celery, onion, jalapeño, ½ cup walnuts and garlic; cook, stirring constantly, 4 to 6 minutes or until walnuts are golden brown.

2 Stir in vegetable broth, turmeric, salt and pepper. Heat to boiling; reduce heat. Simmer uncovered 5 minutes or until vegetables are tender. Stir in spinach and basil. Cook, stirring to push down spinach, until spinach is wilted, about 2 minutes. Remove from heat.

3 In blender or food processor, ladle about one-third of the soup mixture. Cover; blend on high speed 30 seconds to 1 minute or until smooth. Pour into large heatproof bowl. Repeat two more times with remaining soup.

4 Return soup to Dutch oven; stir in ½ cup coconut cream. Cook until hot, stirring occasionally. Serve soup with additional coconut cream and chopped walnuts.

1 Serving Calories 200; Total Fat 16g (Saturated Fat 7g, Trans Fat 0g); Cholesterol 0mg; Sodium 690mg; Total Carbohydrate 9g (Dietary Fiber 3g); Protein 4g **Carbohydrate Choices:** ½

Pasta & Pizza

Pasta Basics

Pasta is so versatile, so easy to cook, so budget-friendly and ideal for any occasion, no wonder it's a popular choice for meals. Whether mixed in a comforting casserole, the star of a bowl or simply topped or tossed with a sensational sauce, the meal possibilities with purchased dried, fresh, frozen or alternative or homemade pasta are endless.

Purchasing and Storage

Dried Pasta Avoid broken pasta or pasta that looks cracked, as it might fall apart during cooking. Be sure to check expiration dates on packages, as pasta past its prime may be stale, moldy or have bugs in it and may break apart when cooked. Label, date and store tightly covered in a cool, dry place up to 1 year.

Fresh Pasta Avoid packages with moisture droplets or liquid inside. Pasta should be smooth and evenly colored, without broken or crumbly pieces. Look for sell-by dates on packages.

Refrigerate and use by package sell-by date. Store opened uncooked pasta in a tightly covered container in refrigerator up to 3 days.

Frozen Pasta Avoid packages that are frozen as a solid block and those with ice crystals or freezer burn (dry, white spots).

Freezing Fresh Pasta Freeze unopened fresh pasta in the original package up to 9 months. Leftover uncooked fresh pasta can be frozen in a tightly covered container up to 3 months.

Storing Cooked Pasta To prevent sticking during storage, toss cooked pasta with 1 to 2 teaspoons olive or vegetable oil after draining. Refrigerate tightly covered up to 5 days or freeze up to 2 months.

Pasta Yields

Plan on ½ to ¾ cup cooked pasta per side dish and 1 to 1½ cups per main dish serving.

To easily measure 4 oz (2 servings) of dried spaghetti, make a circle with your thumb and index finger about the size of a quarter and fill it with pasta.

TYPE OF PASTA	UNCOOKED	COOKED	SERVINGS
Short Pasta	6 to 7 oz	4 cups	4 to 6
Long Pasta	7 to 8 oz	4 cups	4 to 6
Egg Noodles	8 oz	4 to 5 cups	4 to 6

Cooking Pasta

- Use 1 quart (4 cups) water for every 4 oz of pasta. When the water is boiling vigorously, gradually add the pasta. Reduce the heat just a bit so that the pasta can boil gently, and stir frequently to prevent sticking.

- If desired for added flavor, add ½ teaspoon salt for every 8 oz of pasta. Add the salt just as the water comes to a boil.

- Follow package directions for the correct cook times. For baked recipes, slightly undercook pasta by a minute or two since it will continue to cook during baking.

- Taste pasta as it approaches doneness to determine when it is ready. *Cooked pasta* should be al dente, or tender but firm to the bite, without any raw flavor. *Overcooked pasta* is mushy, waterlogged and bland.

- Unless the recipe specifies, do not rinse pasta after draining; sauces will not cling well. Pasta is usually only rinsed for cold salads.

Herb Pasta, page 197

Alternative Pastas

Most of the pasta available today is made with wheat flour, but new alternative pastas are continually making their debuts in the fresh, frozen and shelf-stable sections of grocery stores. These pasta options can be gluten free, plant based, lower in carbs or higher in protein and/or fiber, depending on the variety. Their flavors and textures may not be exactly like traditional pasta, but they can be a terrific alternative, when you're looking for pasta with these attributes:

Almond Flour Pasta Grain free and gluten free.

Black Bean Pasta Plant based, typically higher in protein and fiber than traditional pasta. Black in color, with a mild flavor.

Brown Rice Pasta Gluten free and whole grain. Somewhat nutty flavor.

Buckwheat or Soba Noodles When made exclusively with buckwheat flour, this pasta is gluten free. The earthy, nutty flavored noodles can be served hot or cold, and are typically used in Asian-style recipes. Coarser texture than traditional pasta.

Legume Pasta Made from chick peas, edamame, yellow peas, lentils or mung beans.

Tofu Shirataki Made from tofu and Asian yam (konnyaku). Low in calories and carbs; gluten free. Slightly chewy and rubbery with little flavor.

Vegetable Pasta Made from cauliflower or spiralized veggies such as zucchini or sweet potato.

Spinach Fettuccine

Gnocchi

Mini Gnocchi

Cheese Ravioletti

Cellophane Noodles

Ditalini   Rigatoni

Ziti

Lasagnotte

Couscous

Couscous (Israeli)

Cheese Ravioli

Fusilli Bucati

Spinach Cheese Tortellini

Sausage Ravioli

Cheese Tortellini

Lasagna

Acini di Pepe

184

Long Ziti

Orzo

Mafalde

Vermicelli

Angel Hair

Spaghetti

Brown Rice Gluten-Free Spaghetti

Linguine

Elbow Macaroni

Gemelli

Tri-Color Rotini

Rotelle

Pappardelle

Radiatore

Campanelle

Fusilli Bucati

Trivelli

Angel Hair Nests

Tagliatelle

Wagon Wheels

Farfalle (Bow Ties)

Egg Bows

Mezze Penne

Penne

Garganelli

Orecchiette

Mostaccioli

Beet Rotini

Casarecci

Fine Egg Noodles

Conchiglioni

Gnocchi

Dumpling Egg Noodles

Torchio

Chiocciole

Manicotti

185

Extra Wide Egg Noodles

Lumache

Whole Wheat Gobbetti

Whole Wheat Penne

Whole Wheat Elbow Macaroni

Fettuccini

Bucatini

Tagliatelle

Rice Bran Pad Thai

Whole Wheat Linguine

Macaroni and Cheese

PREP 25 Minutes TOTAL 50 Minutes •
4 servings (1 cup each)

1 package (7 oz) elbow macaroni (2½ cups)	¼ teaspoon ground mustard
¼ cup butter	¼ teaspoon Worcestershire sauce
¼ cup all-purpose flour	2 cups milk or half-and-half
½ teaspoon salt	2 cups shredded sharp cheddar cheese (8 oz)
¼ teaspoon pepper	

Macaroni and Cheese

1 Heat oven to 350°F. Cook and drain macaroni as directed on package, using minimum cook time.

2 Meanwhile, in 3-quart saucepan, melt butter over low heat. Stir in flour, salt, pepper, mustard and Worcestershire sauce. Cook over low heat, stirring constantly, until mixture is smooth and bubbly; remove from heat.

3 Stir in milk until smooth. Heat to boiling, stirring constantly. Boil and stir 1 minute; remove from heat. Stir in cheese until melted. Gently stir macaroni into cheese sauce.

4 Pour into ungreased 2-quart casserole. Bake uncovered 20 to 25 minutes or until bubbly.

1 Serving Calories 610; Total Fat 34g (Saturated Fat 19g, Trans Fat 1g); Cholesterol 100mg; Sodium 980mg; Total Carbohydrate 51g (Dietary Fiber 3g); Protein 26g **Carbohydrate Choices:** 3½

LIGHTER DIRECTIONS: For 10 grams of fat and 390 calories per serving, reduce butter to 2 tablespoons. Use fat-free (skim) milk and 1½ cups reduced-fat cheddar cheese (6 oz).

STOVE-TOP MACARONI AND CHEESE: Cook and drain macaroni as directed on package. Continue as directed in Steps 2 and 3; omit Step 4.

BACON MACARONI AND CHEESE: Stir in ⅔ cup crumbled crisply cooked bacon with the macaroni in Step 3.

CARAMELIZED ONION MACARONI AND CHEESE: Stir in 1 cup Caramelized Onions (page 67) with macaroni in Step 3.

FIRE-ROASTED TOMATO MACARONI AND CHEESE: Stir in ½ teaspoon smoked paprika with flour in Step 2. Add 1 can (14.5 oz) fire-roasted diced tomatoes, drained, with macaroni in Step 3.

LOBSTER MACARONI AND CHEESE: Stir in ⅛ teaspoon each ground red pepper (cayenne) and ground nutmeg with flour in Step 2. Substitute ¾ cup each shredded fontina and Gruyère cheese for 1½ cups of the cheddar cheese. Stir in 2 cups cooked lobster pieces with macaroni in Step 3.

SOUTHWEST-STYLE MACARONI AND CHEESE: Omit ground mustard and Worcestershire sauce. Add 2 teaspoons ground ancho chile or chili powder, ½ teaspoon ground cumin and ¼ teaspoon garlic powder with flour in Step 2. Stir in 1 can (4.5 oz) diced green chiles, ¼ cup thinly sliced green onions, ¼ cup diced bell pepper (any color) and ¼ cup chopped fresh cilantro with macaroni in Step 3. Top with coarsely crushed corn chips before serving.

FAST

Fettuccine Alfredo

This is a perfect dinner for nights you're short on time or don't know what to make. It's our version of the famous dish created in the early 1890s or 1900s by restaurateur Alfredo di Lelio in Rome. The combination of whipping cream and Parmesan cheese is the secret to thickening the sauce.

PREP 25 Minutes TOTAL 25 Minutes •
4 servings (about 1 cup each)

8 oz uncooked fettuccine (from 16-oz package)	¾ cup grated Parmesan cheese
½ cup butter, cut into pieces	½ teaspoon salt
	Dash pepper
½ cup whipping cream	Chopped fresh parsley, if desired

1 Cook and drain fettuccine as directed on package.

2 Meanwhile, in 10-inch skillet, heat butter and whipping cream over medium heat, stirring frequently, until butter is melted and mixture starts to bubble. Reduce heat to low; simmer uncovered 6 minutes, stirring frequently, until slightly thickened. Remove from heat. Stir in cheese, salt and pepper.

3 In large bowl, toss fettuccine with sauce until well coated. Sprinkle with parsley.

1 Serving Calories 570; Total Fat 40g (Saturated Fat 21g, Trans Fat 2g); Cholesterol 155mg; Sodium 810mg; Total Carbohydrate 38g (Dietary Fiber 2g); Protein 15g **Carbohydrate Choices:** 2½

LIGHTER DIRECTIONS: For 17 grams of fat and 370 calories per serving, reduce butter to ¼ cup and Parmesan cheese to ½ cup; substitute evaporated milk for whipping cream.

CHICKEN FETTUCCINE ALFREDO: Stir in 1½ cups diced cooked chicken with cheese, salt and pepper.

Cacio e Pepe

Cacio e Pepe translates to "cheese and pepper" and is a very quick, simple, zesty pasta dish. And that is not a typo—the recipe really does have 2 teaspoons of pepper. For those a bit faint of heart, use half that amount.

PREP 25 Minutes **TOTAL** 25 Minutes •
6 servings (1 cup each)

1 tablespoon salt	1½ cups finely shredded Pecorino Romano cheese (6 oz)
1 package (16 oz) spaghetti	Chopped fresh parsley
¼ cup olive oil	Additional finely shredded Pecorino Romano cheese, if desired
2 teaspoons coarse ground black pepper	

1 In 8-quart Dutch oven or stockpot, heat 5 quarts water and salt to boiling. Add spaghetti. Cook as directed on package. Remove 1 cup of the cooking water; set aside. Drain spaghetti but do not rinse; set aside.

2 In Dutch oven, heat oil over medium heat. Add pepper. Cook 1 minute, stirring constantly. Add ¾ cup of the cooking water; heat until simmering. Add spaghetti; sprinkle with cheese. Toss with tongs until mixture clings to spaghetti. If mixture seems dry, add remaining ¼ cup reserved cooking water. (Pasta dish will not be saucy.)

3 Sprinkle with parsley and additional cheese.

1 Serving Calories 520; Total Fat 19g (Saturated Fat 6g, Trans Fat 0g); Cholesterol 30mg; Sodium 640mg; Total Carbohydrate 67g (Dietary Fiber 4g); Protein 21g **Carbohydrate Choices:** 4½

Udon Bowl with Veggies

Miso, also called bean paste, is a common ingredient used in Japanese cooking. It comes in a variety of flavors and colors, with lighter varieties adding a subtle flavor while darker varieties are frequently used in fuller-flavored dishes.

PREP 20 Minutes **TOTAL** 35 Minutes •
8 servings (about ¾ cup each)

1 package (10 oz) Japanese udon noodles	1 package (10 oz) frozen stir-fry blend vegetables
2 cartons (32 oz) unsalted chicken broth	¼ cup white miso
1 tablespoon low-sodium soy sauce	3 tablespoons water
12 green onions, cut diagonally in ½-inch pieces, white and green parts separated	¼ cup chopped Thai basil leaves or regular basil leaves (0.75-oz container)

1 Cook udon noodles as directed on package; drain and rinse well under cold water.

2 Meanwhile, in 4-quart saucepan, heat broth and soy sauce to boiling. Add green onion whites and stir-fry vegetables. Cook about 3 minutes or until vegetables are crisp-tender.

3 In small bowl, using whisk beat miso and water until blended; stir into vegetable mixture. Reduce heat to low; add cooked noodles. Simmer about 3 minutes or just until noodles are warm. To serve, divide noodles, vegetables and broth among individual bowls; top with remaining onions and basil leaves.

1 Serving Calories 180; Total Fat 1g (Saturated Fat 0g, Trans Fat 0g); Cholesterol 0mg; Sodium 520mg; Total Carbohydrate 32g (Dietary Fiber 4g); Protein 11g **Carbohydrate Choices:** 2

Cacio e Pepe

Udon Bowl with Veggies

Creamy Chick Pea and Brussels Sprouts Pasta

If you like, you can roast up to four bulbs of garlic in the foil packet, drizzling each bulb with 1 teaspoon olive oil. Use one bulb for this recipe. For the remaining garlic bulbs, squeeze garlic from the cloves and mash with a fork. Store in a covered container in the refrigerator up to 3 days or add enough olive oil to jar to cover garlic; store up to 2 weeks (drain before using and use the garlic-scented oil in savory recipe). Or freeze 1-teaspoon amounts of garlic on cooking parchment—lined plate; freeze. Transfer to freezer food-storage plastic bag; freeze up to 8 months and use in your favorite recipes.

PREP 1 Hour **TOTAL** 1 Hour • *6 servings* (1⅓ cups each)

ROASTED GARLIC
- 1 bulb garlic
- 1 teaspoon olive oil

ROASTED VEGETABLES
- ¾ lb Brussels sprouts, halved (about 2½ cups)
- 1 tablespoon olive oil
- ¼ teaspoon salt
- ⅛ teaspoon pepper
- 1 pint grape or cherry tomatoes, halved

PASTA AND SAUCE
- 1 cup vegetable broth (for homemade broth, see page 169)
- 1 tablespoon cornstarch

- 1 box (8 oz) cavatappi or penne pasta made from chick peas
- 1 tablespoon olive oil
- 1 medium onion, chopped (1 cup)
- 1 can (15 oz) chick peas (garbanzo beans), rinsed, drained
- 1 tablespoon fresh lemon juice
- 1 teaspoon Dijon mustard
- ¼ teaspoon salt
- ¼ teaspoon crushed red pepper flakes
- 2 tablespoons chopped Italian parsley

1 Heat oven to 425°F.

2 Carefully peel paperlike skin from garlic bulb, leaving just enough to hold cloves together. Cut ¼- to ½-inch slice from top of bulb to expose cloves. Place garlic bulb, cut side up, on 12-inch square of foil. Drizzle with 1 teaspoon oil. Wrap securely in foil. Place on 15x10x1-inch baking pan. Roast 15 minutes.

3 Meanwhile, in medium bowl, toss Brussels sprouts, oil, salt and pepper. Place in single layer on baking pan with garlic. Roast 8 minutes. Add tomatoes. Roast 5 minutes longer or until Brussels sprouts are tender.

4 Remove from oven; set Brussels sprouts and tomatoes aside. Unwrap foil; let garlic stand 5 to 10 minutes or until cool enough to handle. Squeeze garlic out of cloves into small bowl; mash with fork. Stir in vegetable broth and cornstarch; set aside.

5 Cook and drain pasta as directed on package; return to pan.

6 Meanwhile, in 10-inch skillet, heat oil over medium-high heat. Cook and stir onion in oil 3 to 4 minutes or until tender. Stir in roasted vegetables, vegetable broth mixture and remaining ingredients except pasta and parsley. Heat to boiling, stirring constantly, about 1 minute or until slightly thickened and bubbly.

7 Toss pasta lightly with sauce until well coated. Spoon into serving dish; sprinkle with parsley.

1 Serving Calories 340; Total Fat 10g (Saturated Fat 1.5g, Trans Fat 0g); Cholesterol 0mg; Sodium 440mg; Total Carbohydrate 49g (Dietary Fiber 12g); Protein 14g **Carbohydrate Choices:** 3

Spinach Lasagna Cups

Lasagna gets an updated look with these cute personal-size cups. Feel free to use whatever tomato pasta sauce you have on hand.

PREP 15 Minutes **TOTAL** 1 Hour 5 Minutes • *6 servings*

- 6 lasagna noodles, cooked and drained as directed on box, cut crosswise in half
- 1½ cups tomato pasta sauce
- 1 box (9 oz) frozen chopped spinach, cooked, drained, squeezed dry
- 1 container (15 oz) ricotta cheese

- 1 teaspoon dried oregano leaves
- ½ teaspoon garlic powder
- ¼ teaspoon salt
- 1 egg
- ½ cup shredded mozzarella cheese (2 oz)
- 2 tablespoons grated Parmesan cheese
- Additional tomato pasta sauce, warmed

1 Heat oven to 350°F. Spray 6 jumbo muffin cups with cooking spray.

2 Line each muffin cup with 2 lasagna noodle halves, crisscrossing over bottom of cup, coming up sides of cup. Spoon about 1 tablespoon pasta sauce over noodles in each cup.

3 In medium bowl, mix spinach, ricotta cheese, oregano, garlic powder, salt and egg. Place about ½ cup spinach mixture over sauce in each muffin cup; top each with about 3 tablespoons pasta sauce, 1½ tablespoons mozzarella cheese and 1 teaspoon Parmesan cheese. Cover with foil.

4 Bake 35 minutes. Uncover; bake about 5 minutes longer or until cheese is melted. Let stand in pan 10 minutes; remove from pan, and serve immediately. If desired, serve with additional pasta sauce.

1 Serving Calories 340; Total Fat 16g (Saturated Fat 8g, Trans Fat 0g); Cholesterol 75mg; Sodium 680mg; Total Carbohydrate 33g (Dietary Fiber 3g); Protein 17g **Carbohydrate Choices:** 2

Pumpkin Risotto

Risotto is actually a rice dish served like pasta and can typically be found on restaurant menus alongside pasta dishes. If you like, you can also serve this creamy recipe as a vegetarian main dish that will serve three people.

PREP 30 Minutes **TOTAL** 30 Minutes •
6 servings (½ cup each)

1 cup vegetable broth (from 32-oz carton; for homemade broth, see page 169)	½ cup dry white wine or vegetable broth
1 cup water	⅓ cup grated Parmesan cheese
1 tablespoon olive oil	¼ teaspoon freshly ground pepper
1 small onion, chopped (½ cup)	¼ cup chopped fresh parsley
1 cup uncooked Arborio or regular long-grain rice	⅛ teaspoon ground nutmeg
¾ cup canned pumpkin (not pumpkin pie mix)	Freshly shredded Parmesan cheese, if desired

1 In 1-quart saucepan, heat vegetable broth and water over medium-high heat just until simmering. Keep broth mixture at a simmer while preparing risotto.

2 Meanwhile, in 3-quart saucepan, heat oil over medium-high heat. Cook onion in oil 2 to 3 minutes, stirring frequently, until softened. Stir in rice; cook, stirring frequently, 5 to 8 minutes or until edges of kernels are translucent. Stir in pumpkin and wine.

3 Reduce heat to medium. Stir in 1 cup of the broth mixture. Cook uncovered, stirring frequently, about 5 minutes or until broth is absorbed. Stir in remaining broth mixture. Cook 10 to 15 minutes longer, stirring frequently, until rice is just tender and mixture is creamy. Stir in grated Parmesan cheese and pepper.

4 To serve, sprinkle parsley, nutmeg and shredded Parmesan over each serving.

1 Serving Calories 200; Total Fat 4.5g (Saturated Fat 1.5g, Trans Fat 0g); Cholesterol 0mg; Sodium 260mg; Total Carbohydrate 32g (Dietary Fiber 1g); Protein 5g **Carbohydrate Choices:** 2

Creamy Chick Pea and Brussels Sprouts Pasta

Spinach Lasagna Cups

189

Pumpkin Risotto

HEIRLOOM

MAKE AHEAD

Italian Sausage Lasagna

When cooking the lasagna noodles, cook them just until al dente. If the noodles are overcooked, they might fall apart when you are layering the lasagna. After cooking the noodles, place them in a bowl of cold water until you're ready to layer. This keeps them from sticking together.

PREP 1 Hour **TOTAL** 2 Hours • *8 servings*

- 1 lb bulk sweet or hot Italian pork sausage
- 1 small onion, chopped (½ cup)
- 1 clove garlic, finely chopped
- 3 tablespoons chopped fresh parsley
- 1 tablespoon chopped fresh or 1 teaspoon dried basil leaves
- 1 teaspoon sugar
- 1 can (15 oz) tomato sauce
- 1 can (14.5 oz) whole tomatoes, undrained
- 8 uncooked lasagna noodles
- 1 container (15 to 16 oz) ricotta cheese or small-curd cottage cheese
- ½ cup grated Parmesan cheese
- 1 tablespoon chopped fresh or 1½ teaspoons dried oregano leaves
- 2 cups shredded mozzarella cheese (8 oz)

1 In 10-inch skillet, cook sausage, onion and garlic over medium heat, stirring occasionally, 8 to 10 minutes or until sausage is no longer pink; drain.

2 Stir in 2 tablespoons of the parsley, the basil, sugar, tomato sauce and tomatoes, breaking up tomatoes. Heat to boiling, stirring occasionally; reduce heat. Simmer uncovered about 45 minutes or until slightly thickened.

3 Heat oven to 350°F. Cook and drain noodles as directed on package, using minimum cook time.

4 Meanwhile, in small bowl mix ricotta cheese, ¼ cup of the Parmesan cheese, the oregano and remaining 1 tablespoon parsley.

5 In ungreased 13x9-inch (3-quart) glass baking dish, spread half of the sausage mixture (about 2 cups). Top with 4 noodles. Spread half of the cheese mixture (about 1 cup) over noodles. Sprinkle with half of the mozzarella cheese. Repeat layers, ending with mozzarella. Sprinkle with remaining ¼ cup Parmesan cheese.

6 Spray foil with cooking spray; cover lasagna with foil, sprayed side down. Bake 30 minutes. Uncover; bake about 15 minutes longer or until hot and bubbly. Let stand 15 minutes before cutting 4 rows by 2 rows.

1 Serving Calories 430; Total Fat 23g (Saturated Fat 11g, Trans Fat 0g); Cholesterol 70mg; Sodium 1110mg; Total Carbohydrate 28g (Dietary Fiber 3g); Protein 28g **Carbohydrate Choices:** 2

MAKE-AHEAD DIRECTIONS: Spray foil with cooking spray; cover unbaked lasagna with foil, sprayed side down. Refrigerate no longer than 24 hours or freeze up to 2 months. Bake covered 45 minutes, then bake uncovered 15 to 20 minutes longer, or 35 to 45 minutes if frozen. Check to see that the center is hot by inserting table knife blade, removing it and quickly touching it. Bake a little longer if necessary until hot and bubbly.

EASY ITALIAN SAUSAGE LASAGNA: Substitute 4 cups (from two 24-oz jars) tomato pasta sauce with meat for the first 8 ingredients. Skip Steps 1 and 2.

GROUND BEEF LASAGNA: Prepare as directed—except substitute 1 lb ground beef (at least 80% lean) for the pork sausage.

ITALIAN TURKEY SAUSAGE LASAGNA: Prepare as directed—except substitute 1 lb sweet or hot Italian turkey sausage (casings removed) for the pork sausage.

Italian Sausage Lasagna

Jalapeño Tuna and Zucchini Lasagna

NEW TWIST

VEGETARIAN

Jalapeño Tuna and Zucchini Lasagna

Some vegetable peelers or a mandoline slicer works well to cut zucchini into ribbons if you can't get them thin enough with a knife.

PREP 25 Minutes **TOTAL** 1 Hour 20 Minutes • *6 servings*

2 **medium zucchini, cut lengthwise into ⅛-inch-thick slices**	½ **teaspoon sriracha sauce**
2 **teaspoons salt**	2 **cans (5 oz each) tuna in water, drained**
1 **package (8 oz) cream cheese, softened**	1 **jar (2 oz) diced pimientos, drained**
½ **cup mayonnaise**	½ **cup plain panko crispy bread crumbs**
¼ **cup sour cream**	2 **cups shredded pepper Jack cheese (8 oz)**
1½ **cups frozen roasted whole-kernel or frozen whole-kernel corn, thawed**	2 **tablespoons chopped fresh cilantro**
1 **medium jalapeño chile, seeded, finely chopped**	

1 Place zucchini on paper towel–lined cookie sheet. Sprinkle zucchini with 1 teaspoon of the salt; let stand 10 minutes. Turn zucchini over; sprinkle with remaining salt. Let stand 10 minutes. Rinse; pat dry with paper towels.

2 Meanwhile, in medium bowl mix cream cheese, mayonnaise and sour cream until well mixed. Gently stir in corn, jalapeño, sriracha sauce, tuna and pimientos.

3 Heat oven to 350°F. Spray 11x7-inch (2-quart) glass baking dish with cooking spray. Spread 1 cup of the tuna mixture in bottom of baking dish. Sprinkle with 2 tablespoons of the bread crumbs. Layer with half of the zucchini. Spread remaining tuna mixture over zucchini slices; top with 1 cup of the pepper Jack cheese. Sprinkle with 2 tablespoons of the bread crumbs. Arrange remaining zucchini over bread crumbs. Sprinkle with the remaining 1 cup pepper Jack cheese and the bread crumbs. Spray foil with cooking spray; cover baking dish tightly with foil, sprayed side down.

4 Bake 35 minutes. Remove foil; bake 10 to 15 minutes longer or until top is light golden brown. Let stand about 10 minutes before serving. Sprinkle with cilantro.

1 Serving Calories 560; Total Fat 43g (Saturated Fat 19g, Trans Fat 1g); Cholesterol 105mg; Sodium 1450mg; Total Carbohydrate 20g (Dietary Fiber 2g); Protein 24g **Carbohydrate Choices:** 1

Zucchini and Ground Beef Orzo Casserole

One-Pot Curry Chicken and Pasta

Parmesan Meatball Spaghetti Bake

Zucchini and Ground Beef Orzo Casserole

Ricotta is a fresh Italian cheese made from sheep, cow, goat or buffalo milk whey left over from the production of cheese. Traditional fresh ricotta is smoother than cottage cheese and tastes mildly sweet.

PREP 40 Minutes **TOTAL** 1 Hour 25 Minutes •
6 servings (about 1 cup each)

½ cup uncooked orzo pasta (3 oz)	1 can (14.5 oz) fire-roasted crushed tomatoes, undrained
2 teaspoons vegetable oil	1 cup shredded part-skim mozzarella cheese (4 oz)
1 lb zucchini squash, cut in half lengthwise, then cut crosswise in ⅛-inch slices	½ cup part-skim ricotta cheese
½ teaspoon dried Italian seasoning	¼ cup shredded Parmesan cheese (1 oz)
½ teaspoon salt	1 tablespoon finely chopped fresh basil leaves*
1 lb ground beef (at least 90% lean)	
1 small onion, chopped (½ cup)	½ teaspoon finely chopped fresh thyme leaves*
2 teaspoons finely chopped garlic	¼ teaspoon crushed red pepper flakes

1 Heat oven to 350°F. Spray 8-inch square (2-quart) glass baking dish with cooking spray. Cook and drain pasta as directed on package.

2 In 12-inch nonstick skillet, heat 1 teaspoon of the oil over medium heat. Cook zucchini, Italian seasoning and ¼ teaspoon of the salt in oil, stirring occasionally, 4 to 7 minutes or until zucchini has started to soften but is still crisp-tender. Transfer to large bowl; stir in pasta.

3 In same skillet, heat remaining 1 teaspoon oil over medium-high heat. Cook beef, onion, garlic and remaining ¼ teaspoon salt in oil, stirring frequently, 7 to 8 minutes or until no pink remains in beef; drain. Add to bowl with zucchini and pasta. Add tomatoes, ¾ cup of the mozzarella cheese, the ricotta cheese, Parmesan cheese, basil, thyme and pepper flakes; stir to mix. Spoon mixture into baking dish.

4 Bake 35 to 40 minutes or until bubbling on edges and completely heated through. Top with remaining ¼ cup mozzarella cheese; let stand 5 minutes.

1 Serving Calories 320; Total Fat 15g (Saturated Fat 7g, Trans Fat 0g); Cholesterol 70mg; Sodium 560mg; Total Carbohydrate 20g (Dietary Fiber 2g); Protein 26g **Carbohydrate Choices:** 1

*1½ teaspoons dried Italian seasoning can be substituted for the fresh basil and thyme.

One-Pot Curry Chicken and Pasta

PREP 50 Minutes **TOTAL** 50 Minutes •
6 servings (1⅓ cups each)

GREEN CURRY SAUCE

- 2½ cups chicken broth (from 32-oz carton; for homemade broth, see page 153)
- 2 tablespoons green Thai curry paste
- 2 tablespoons fish sauce or soy sauce
- 1 teaspoon packed brown sugar
- 1 teaspoon curry powder
- ½ teaspoon ground coriander
- ¼ teaspoon ground red pepper (cayenne)

CHICKEN AND PASTA

- 1 tablespoon olive oil
- 1 lb boneless skinless chicken breasts or thighs, cut into ¾-inch pieces
- 4 green onions, sliced (¼ cup)
- 2 cloves garlic, finely chopped
- 2 cups uncooked gemelli or cavatappi pasta (about 8 oz)
- 1½ cups sliced carrots
- 1 medium red bell pepper, sliced
- 2 cups broccoli florets
- ½ cup coconut milk (from 13.66-oz can; not cream of coconut)
- 2 tablespoons cornstarch
- ¼ cup chopped peanuts
- 2 tablespoons chopped fresh cilantro

1 In medium bowl, mix all sauce ingredients until blended.

2 In 5-quart Dutch oven, heat oil over medium-high heat. Cook chicken, onion and garlic in oil, stirring frequently, about 3 minutes, until chicken is white.

3 Add sauce; heat to boiling. Add pasta and carrots. Heat to boiling; reduce heat. Simmer uncovered, stirring occasionally and pushing pasta that rises above sauce back down, 8 to 10 minutes, or until pasta is almost tender. Add bell pepper and broccoli. Cook, stirring frequently, 2 minutes or until chicken is no longer pink in center and vegetables are crisp-tender.

4 In small bowl, mix coconut milk and cornstarch; add to Dutch oven. Cook until mixture is thickened and bubbly. Serve garnished with peanuts and cilantro.

1 Serving Calories 410; Total Fat 13g (Saturated Fat 5g, Trans Fat 0g); Cholesterol 45mg; Sodium 980mg; Total Carbohydrate 46g (Dietary Fiber 5g); Protein 27g **Carbohydrate Choices:** 3

Parmesan Meatball Spaghetti Bake

Cooking the spaghetti in chicken broth is an easy way to add extra flavor to this classic spaghetti and meatball bake.

PREP 45 Minutes **TOTAL** 1 Hour 20 Minutes • *8 servings*

PARMESAN MEATBALLS

- 1 lb ground beef (at least 80% lean)
- ⅓ cup finely chopped onion
- 1 clove garlic, finely chopped
- 1 egg, beaten
- ¼ cup shredded Parmesan cheese (1 oz)
- ½ teaspoon salt
- ½ cup Italian-style bread crumbs
- ¼ teaspoon pepper

SPAGHETTI AND SAUCE

- 12 oz spaghetti, broken in half (from 16-oz box)
- 1 carton (32 oz) chicken broth (4 cups; for homemade broth, see page 153)
- 1 can (28 oz) crushed tomatoes
- 1 cup basil tomato pasta sauce (from 24-oz jar)
- 2 tablespoons chopped fresh basil leaves
- ¼ teaspoon crushed red pepper flakes
- 1 package (8 oz) shredded Italian cheese blend (2 cups)

1 Heat oven to 350°F. Line 15x10x1-inch pan with foil. Spray 13x9-inch (3-quart) baking dish with cooking spray.

2 In large bowl, mix all meatball ingredients until blended. Shape mixture into 1½-inch meatballs (about 24). Place 1 inch apart on foil-lined pan.

3 Bake 18 to 23 minutes or until no longer pink in center.

4 Meanwhile, in 4- to 5-quart saucepan or Dutch oven, heat spaghetti and broth just to boiling over high heat. Reduce heat to medium. Cook 15 to 20 minutes, stirring frequently, until pasta is firm but tender and liquid is absorbed. Remove from heat; let stand 1 minute.

5 Toss meatballs, tomatoes, pasta sauce, 1 tablespoon of the basil and the pepper flakes with spaghetti until well mixed. Pour into baking dish and spread evenly. Sprinkle Italian cheese blend over pasta.

6 Bake 15 to 20 minutes or until bubbly and cheese is melted. Sprinkle with remaining basil. Cut into 4 rows by 2 rows.

1 Serving Calories 450; Total Fat 16g (Saturated Fat 8g, Trans Fat 0g); Cholesterol 85mg; Sodium 1350mg; Total Carbohydrate 48g (Dietary Fiber 3g); Protein 27g **Carbohydrate Choices:** 3

Mongolian-Style Beef and Noodles

Partially freezing the steak makes it easier to slice thinly.

PREP 20 Minutes **TOTAL** 1 Hour 30 Minutes • *4 servings*

¾ lb beef flank steak

⅓ cup gluten-free reduced-sodium soy sauce

3 tablespoons packed brown sugar

1 tablespoon grated gingerroot

2 teaspoons toasted sesame oil

½ teaspoon crushed red pepper flakes

2 cloves garlic, finely chopped

½ cup gluten-free reduced-sodium beef broth (from 32-oz carton; for homemade broth, see page 157)

1 tablespoon cornstarch

1 tablespoon water

2 tablespoons vegetable oil

10 oz uncooked stir-fry rice noodles (from 14-oz package)

1 cup julienne carrots (1½x¼x¼ inch)

3 green onions, cut diagonally into 1-inch pieces

3 green onions, thinly sliced (3 tablespoons)

1 Place flank steak in freezer 30 minutes.

2 Meanwhile, in small bowl, stir soy sauce, brown sugar, gingerroot, sesame oil, pepper flakes and garlic until sugar is dissolved. Place ¼ cup of the soy sauce mixture in medium bowl. Add broth, cornstarch and water to remaining soy sauce mixture; mix with whisk until blended. Set aside.

3 Cut beef against the grain into ⅛-inch slices; place in bowl with ¼ cup soy sauce mixture; toss to coat. Cover and refrigerate 45 minutes.

4 Prepare noodles and drain as directed on package.

5 Meanwhile, in 12-inch nonstick skillet, heat 1 tablespoon of the oil over medium-high heat. Spread half of the marinated beef in single layer in skillet; cook 1 minute on each side until browned. Transfer beef to plate. Repeat with remaining oil and beef.

6 Reduce heat to medium. In same skillet, add carrots. Cook and stir about 2 minutes or until carrots begin to soften. Add onion pieces. Cook 1 minute. Stir reserved soy sauce mixture; add to skillet. Cook, stirring frequently, 1 to 2 minutes or until sauce is thickened. Add beef and rice noodles. Toss to coat with sauce and heat through. Transfer to serving plate; garnish with sliced onions.

1 Serving Calories 570; Total Fat 16g (Saturated Fat 4g, Trans Fat 0g); Cholesterol 60mg; Sodium 1090mg; Total Carbohydrate 78g (Dietary Fiber 4g); Protein 29g **Carbohydrate Choices:** 5

Mongolian-Style Beef and Noodles

Pad Thai with Shrimp

GLUTEN FREE

Pad Thai with Shrimp

Pad Thai is Thailand's best-known noodle dish; you'll find it on almost all Thai restaurant menus in America. Look for the traditional ingredients in the international foods aisle.

PREP 35 Minutes **TOTAL** 40 Minutes •
4 servings (about 2 cups each)

8 oz stir-fry rice noodles (from 14-oz package)	3 cloves garlic, finely chopped
3 tablespoons fresh lime juice	1 medium shallot, finely chopped or ¼ cup finely chopped onion
3 tablespoons packed brown sugar	2 eggs, beaten
2 tablespoons fish sauce or gluten-free soy sauce	¾ lb frozen cooked deveined peeled medium shrimp (31 to 35 count), thawed
2 tablespoons gluten-free soy sauce	¼ cup finely chopped dry-roasted peanuts
1 tablespoon rice vinegar or white vinegar	3 cups fresh bean sprouts
¾ teaspoon ground red pepper (cayenne)	4 medium green onions, thinly sliced (¼ cup)
3 tablespoons vegetable oil	¼ cup firmly packed fresh cilantro leaves

1 Prepare noodles and drain as directed on package. Rinse with cold water; drain.

2 Meanwhile, in small bowl, stir lime juice, brown sugar, fish sauce, soy sauce, vinegar, red pepper and 1 tablespoon of the oil until well mixed; set aside.

3 In nonstick wok or 12-inch skillet, heat remaining 2 tablespoons oil over medium heat. Cook garlic and shallot in oil about 30 seconds, stirring constantly, until starting to brown. Add eggs. Cook about 2 minutes, stirring gently and constantly, until scrambled but still moist.

4 Stir in noodles and lime juice mixture. Increase heat to high. Cook about 1 minute, tossing constantly with 2 wooden spoons, until sauce begins to thicken. Add remaining ingredients except cilantro. Cook 2 to 3 minutes, tossing with 2 wooden spoons, until noodles are tender and bean sprouts are thoroughly cooked and no longer crisp.

5 Spoon pad Thai onto serving platter. Sprinkle with cilantro. Garnish with additional chopped peanuts and green onions, if desired.

1 Serving Calories 560; Total Fat 23g (Saturated Fat 4g, Trans Fat 0g); Cholesterol 240mg; Sodium 1310mg; Total Carbohydrate 59g (Dietary Fiber 4g); Protein 29g **Carbohydrate Choices:** 4

PAD THAI WITH CHICKEN: Substitute 2 cups chopped cooked chicken for the shrimp.

PAD THAI WITH PORK: Substitute 2 cups shredded cooked pork for the shrimp.

CALORIE SMART

One-Pot Penne Bolognese

Mirepoix refers to the combination of onions, celery and carrots used to season soups, stews and other dishes or as a bed on which to place meat for braising. The frozen product will slash prep time, but you can substitute ⅔ cup each finely chopped fresh onion, celery and carrot if you like.

PREP 45 Minutes **TOTAL** 45 Minutes •
8 servings (1⅓ cups each)

2 tablespoons olive oil	1 carton (32 oz) beef broth (4 cups; for homemade broth, see page 157)
1 bag (10 oz) frozen mirepoix (onions, celery and carrots)	2 teaspoons Italian seasoning
½ teaspoon salt	½ teaspoon crushed red pepper flakes
1 lb ground beef (at least 90% lean)	1 tablespoon balsamic vinegar, if desired
12 oz uncooked penne pasta (3¾ cups)	½ cup shredded Parmesan cheese (2 oz)
1 can (28 oz) fire-roasted crushed tomatoes, undrained	¼ cup thinly sliced fresh basil leaves

1 In 5-qt Dutch oven, heat oil over medium-high heat until hot. Add mirepoix; sprinkle with salt. Cook, stirring frequently, 5 to 8 minutes, until softened. Add beef. Cook, stirring frequently, 5 to 8 minutes, until browned.

2 Stir in pasta, tomatoes, broth, Italian seasoning and pepper flakes. Heat to boiling; reduce heat. Simmer uncovered, stirring occasionally, 16 to 20 minutes or until pasta is cooked to desired tenderness and sauce is thickened. Stir in balsamic vinegar. Top with Parmesan cheese and basil.

1 Serving Calories 380; Total Fat 11g (Saturated Fat 3.5g, Trans Fat 0g); Cholesterol 40mg; Sodium 860mg; Total Carbohydrate 47g (Dietary Fiber 3g); Protein 22g **Carbohydrate Choices:** 3

LEARN TO MAKE PASTA

Making homemade pasta is a fun and easy activity to do with others, whether it's with your kids, friends or even on a date night. A pasta machine makes the process go quickly, but the dough can be rolled by hand, too. Have fun with these techniques by trying Homemade Pasta (right) or any of the delicious variations.

The Italian word *pasta* translates to "paste" in English, a reference to the dough, which is a combination of flour, water and eggs. Pasta is generally made with durum wheat, which has a high gluten content well suited for the proper texture. The dough is pressed into sheets and cut into a variety of shapes, or extruded by machine, and cooked in boiling water. To make homemade ravioli, see Four-Cheese Homemade Ravioli, page 198.

Make a well in the center of the flour mixture. Add eggs, water and oil to well.

Roll one quarter of dough at a time into a rectangle $\frac{1}{16}$- to $\frac{1}{8}$-inch thick.

Loosely fold rectangle crosswise into thirds.

Cut pasta crosswise into 2-inch strips for lasagna, lengthwise into $\frac{1}{4}$-inch strips for fettuccine or $\frac{1}{8}$-inch strips for linguine.

TIPS FOR MAKING FRESH PASTA

- If rolling the dough by hand, do so on a large wooden board or laminated counter. Avoid cold surfaces like granite, metal or marble because the dough tends to stick.

- Pasta dough that is dry will be fragile, so handle carefully. Keep dough covered with plastic wrap until you're ready to roll and cut it. Once cut, let it dry as directed to prevent it from sticking together while cooked.

- Be sure the water is boiling before you add the pasta. Do not rinse pasta after cooking unless directed in the recipe. Drain carefully and toss with 1 to 2 teaspoons olive oil.

- Store uncooked fresh pasta, tightly wrapped, up to 2 days in the refrigerator or up to 1 month in the freezer.

Unfold strips and hang on pasta drying rack or arrange in single layer on lightly floured towels.

Homemade Pasta

You may need a little extra flour when rolling this dough on cold surfaces like granite, metal or marble because the dough tends to stick. Or use a large wooden board instead.

PREP 30 Minutes **TOTAL** 1 Hour 15 Minutes • *8 servings*

2 cups all-purpose flour	¼ cup water
½ teaspoon salt	1 tablespoon olive or vegetable oil
2 eggs	

1 In medium bowl, mix flour and salt. Make a well in center of mixture. Break eggs into well; add water and oil and mix thoroughly. If dough is too dry and crumbly, mix in water 1 teaspoon at a time until dough is easy to handle. If dough is too sticky, gradually add flour while kneading.

2 Gather dough into a ball. On lightly floured surface, knead 3 to 5 minutes or until firm and smooth. Cover with plastic wrap or foil; let stand 15 minutes.

3 Divide dough into 4 equal parts. On lightly floured surface, roll one quarter of dough at a time (keep remaining dough covered with damp towel) into rectangle 1/16 to 1/8 inch thick (if using hand-crank pasta machine pass dough through machine until 1/16 inch thick*). Loosely fold rectangle crosswise into thirds. Cut crosswise into 2-inch strips for lasagna, or lengthwise into ¼-inch strips for fettuccine or 1/8-inch strips for linguine. Unfold and gently shake out strips. Hang pasta on pasta drying rack or arrange in single layer on lightly floured towels; let stand 30 minutes or until dry.

4 In 6- to 8-quart Dutch oven or stockpot, heat 4 quarts water, salted if desired, to boiling; add pasta. Boil uncovered, stirring occasionally, 2 to 5 minutes, until firm but tender. Begin testing for doneness when pasta rises to surface of water; drain.

1 Serving Calories 150; Total Fat 3.5g (Saturated Fat 0.5g, Trans Fat 0g); Cholesterol 45mg; Sodium 160mg; Total Carbohydrate 24g (Dietary Fiber 1g); Protein 4g **Carbohydrate Choices:** 1½

*Our recipes were not developed for or tested in electric extrusion roller-cutter attachments for electric mixers or pasta machines. These machines generally have specific measuring devices for dry and liquid ingredients unique to each machine. We recommend following manufacturer's directions.

MAKE-AHEAD DIRECTIONS: Toss fresh pasta lightly with flour. Allow to stand until partially dry but still pliable; loosely coil fettuccine or linguine into rounds for easier storage. Store in sealed food storage container or plastic bags in refrigerator up to 3 days or in freezer up to 1 month. Cook as directed in Step 4, increasing cook time 1 to 2 minutes.

HERB PASTA: Add 1 tablespoon chopped fresh or 1 teaspoon dried crumbled herb leaves to flour mixture before adding eggs.

WHOLE WHEAT PASTA: Make as directed—except use 3 cups whole wheat or white whole wheat flour and 5 eggs, beaten. Omit water.

GLUTEN-FREE HOMEMADE PASTA: Prepare as directed—except substitute gluten-free all-purpose rice flour blend for the all-purpose flour; increase water to ⅓ cup. Knead on surface dusted with flour blend 3 to 5 minutes. Divide dough into 6 equal parts.** On surface lightly sprinkled with flour blend, roll one sixth of dough at a time. Keep remaining dough covered or it will dry out and crack.

**Gluten-free pasta dough is more fragile and can break more easily. We found working with smaller dough portions and keeping dough sheets to 12 inches or shorter worked best.

USING A PASTA MAKER

Pass dough through pasta machine until dough is 1/16- to 1/8-inch thick.

Pasta can be cut into several widths: 2 inches (lasagna), ¼ inch (fettuccine) or 1/8 inch (linguine).

Insert handle of pasta maker in hole for desired width; slowly pass dough through machine.

Arrange pasta in single layer on lightly floured towels.

Four-Cheese Homemade Ravioli

Homemade ravioli are easy and fun to make! Serve with your favorite sauce or one of ours (see right, page 201) or Basil Pesto (page 480). Or top with melted butter, shredded Parmesan and sliced fresh basil leaves.

PREP 1 Hour **TOTAL** 1 Hour 15 Minutes •
5 servings (4 ravioli each)

PASTA

1 batch Homemade Pasta (page 197)

FILLING

¾ cup ricotta cheese (from 15-oz container)

¼ cup shredded fontina cheese (1 oz)

¼ cup shredded Parmesan cheese (1 oz)

¼ cup shredded mozzarella cheese (1 oz)

Pasta sauce (any variety), if desired

1 Make pasta as directed through Step 2. Divide dough into 4 equal parts. On lightly floured surface, roll one quarter of dough at a time (keep remaining dough covered with damp towel) into rectangle ¹⁄₁₆ to ⅛ inch thick. If using hand-crank pasta machine or roller-cutter attachment for electric mixer, pass dough through machine until ¹⁄₁₆ inch thick*. Cut each dough piece into 14x4-inch rectangle. Cover with damp towel until ready to fill.

2 In medium bowl, mix all filling ingredients until blended. On one dough rectangle, place 10 mounds filling in 2 rows, about 1½ inches apart. (Use slightly less than 1 measuring tablespoon for each mound.) Moisten dough lightly with water around mounds; top with second rectangle of dough, lining up edges of sheets. Press gently around edges to seal. Cut between mounds, using pizza cutter, pastry wheel or knife, into 10 squares. Trim any uneven edges and reseal if needed. Repeat with remaining dough and filling.

3 In 6- to 8-quart Dutch oven or stockpot, heat 4 quarts water, salted if desired, to boiling; add ravioli. Boil uncovered about 7 to 10 minutes, stirring occasionally, until tender. (Ravioli will rise to the top during first few minutes.) Transfer ravioli with large slotted spoon to colander to drain; do not rinse. Do not dump pasta and water into colander to drain, or ravioli will break open. Serve with pasta sauce.

1 Serving Calories 340; Total Fat 13g (Saturated Fat 6g, Trans Fat 0g); Cholesterol 100mg; Sodium 480mg; Total Carbohydrate 41g (Dietary Fiber 1g); Protein 16g **Carbohydrate Choices:** 3

MAKING RAVIOLI

Trim dough into 4 rectangles.

Onto each of 2 dough rectangles, place 10 mounds filling in 2 rows.

Top with remaining dough rectangles. Press gently between mounds and dough edges to seal filling inside each ravioli.

Cut between mounds into squares, using a pizza cutter, pastry wheel or knife.

Four-Cheese Homemade Ravioli

Bolognese Sauce

Creamy Tomato-Vodka Sauce

BACON, CHIVE AND PARMESAN RAVIOLI: Make pasta as directed. Omit filling ingredients. In medium bowl, stir 1 container (8 oz) chives-and-onion cream cheese, 6 slices crumbled crisply cooked bacon, and ¼ cup grated Parmesan cheese until well mixed. Continue as directed.

SPICY SAUSAGE, SUN-DRIED TOMATO AND MOZZARELLA RAVIOLI: Make pasta as directed. Omit filling ingredients. In 8-inch skillet, cook ½ lb bulk spicy Italian pork sausage over medium heat, stirring occasionally, until no longer pink; drain. Place in medium bowl; cool 15 minutes. Add ¼ cup chopped drained sun-dried tomatoes in oil, ½ cup shredded mozzarella cheese (2 oz) and 1 beaten egg; mix well. Continue as directed.

*Our recipes were not developed for or tested in electric extrusion pasta machines. These machines generally have specific measuring devices for dry and liquid ingredients unique to each machine. We recommend following manufacturer's directions.

MAKE AHEAD • GLUTEN FREE

Bolognese Sauce

A staple of Northern Italy, bolognese sauce is a hearty, thick meat sauce with canned tomatoes, wine and milk or cream. Think of it as a meat sauce with tomato rather than a tomato sauce with meat. It's a hearty meal when served over pasta with shaved Parmesan cheese.

PREP 25 Minutes **TOTAL** 1 Hour 10 Minutes • *6 cups*

2 tablespoons olive or vegetable oil	¼ cup chopped pancetta or bacon
1 tablespoon butter	½ cup dry red wine, nonalcoholic red wine or gluten-free beef broth (for homemade broth, see page 157)
2 medium carrots, finely chopped (1 cup)	
1 medium stalk celery, finely chopped (½ cup)	
1 small onion, chopped (½ cup)	3 cans (28 oz each) whole tomatoes, drained, chopped
2 cloves garlic, finely chopped	1 teaspoon dried oregano leaves
1 lb ground beef (at least 80% lean)	½ teaspoon pepper
	½ cup milk or whipping cream

1 In 12-inch skillet, heat oil and butter over medium-high heat. Add carrots, celery, onion and garlic. Cook, stirring frequently, until vegetables are crisp-tender. Stir in beef and pancetta. Cook, stirring occasionally, 8 to 10 minutes or until no pink remains in beef.

2 Stir in wine. Heat to boiling; reduce heat to low. Simmer uncovered until wine has evaporated. Stir in tomatoes, oregano and pepper. Heat to boiling; reduce heat to low. Cover and simmer 45 minutes, stirring occasionally, or until thickened. Remove from heat; stir in milk.

3 Use sauce immediately. Or cool; cover and refrigerate up to 2 days or freeze up to 2 months.

½ Cup Calories 160; Total Fat 9g (Saturated Fat 3g, Trans Fat 0g); Cholesterol 30mg; Sodium 310mg; Total Carbohydrate 9g (Dietary Fiber 4g); Protein 9g **Carbohydrate Choices:** ½

FAST • CALORIE SMART • GLUTEN FREE • VEGETARIAN

Creamy Tomato-Vodka Sauce

The vodka in this sauce adds complexity and depth to the overall flavor, but it doesn't leave behind a vodka taste.

PREP 10 Minutes **TOTAL** 30 Minutes • *3 cups*

1 tablespoon olive or vegetable oil	½ cup vodka or gluten-free chicken broth (for homemade broth, see page 153)
1 small onion, chopped (½ cup)	
2 cloves garlic, finely chopped	1 teaspoon sugar
1 can (28 oz) crushed tomatoes with basil, undrained	¼ teaspoon coarse (kosher or sea) salt
	⅛ teaspoon pepper
	½ cup whipping cream

1 In 10-inch skillet, heat oil over medium heat. Cook onion and garlic in oil, stirring constantly, 3 to 4 minutes or until crisp-tender.

2 Stir in tomatoes, vodka, sugar, salt and pepper. Heat to boiling; reduce heat. Simmer uncovered 20 minutes, stirring occasionally, or until slightly thickened. Stir in whipping cream. Heat just until hot. Serve immediately.

½ Cup Calories 130; Total Fat 9g (Saturated Fat 4g, Trans Fat 0g); Cholesterol 20mg; Sodium 270mg; Total Carbohydrate 8g (Dietary Fiber 1g); Protein 2g **Carbohydrate Choices:** ½

PASTA & PIZZA

USE IT UP
PASTA SAUCE

If you find yourself with pasta sauce getting lonely in your refrigerator, here are some great ways to use it up before it gets moldy:

DIPPING SAUCE
Heat (and stir in fresh chopped herbs, if desired) to serve with French fries, potato nuggets or mozzarella sticks.

PIZZA TOAST Place sliced bread or roll halves on cookie sheet; broil on low, 6 inches from heat, 2 to 3 minutes or until toasted. If using bread, turn over and broil again until tops are toasted. Spread with pasta sauce; top with your favorite pizza toppings and shredded pizza cheese. Broil 2 to 3 minutes longer or until cheese is melted.

SLOPPY JOES Use in place of ketchup in Sloppy Joes (page 289), for more tomato flavor.

SOUPS, STEWS OR CHILI Use it in recipes calling for tomato products such as tomato sauce, tomato soup or tomatoes. Or add it with the tomato products for a richer tomato flavor.

TOMATO-LIME VINAIGRETTE Mix ½ cup pasta sauce, ¼ cup each olive oil and fresh lime juice, ¼ teaspoon pepper and 2 finely chopped garlic cloves. Serve over lettuce or vegetable salads, or toss with cooked quinoa or pasta, veggies and crumbled blue cheese.

Easy Pasta Sauce with Mushrooms

This easy-to-make homemade sauce could very likely become your go-to. Use 3 to 3½ cups of this homemade sauce for recipes that call for a 24- to 27-oz jar of tomato pasta sauce.

PREP 15 Minutes **TOTAL** 6 Hours 15 Minutes • *8 cups*

- 1 tablespoon olive oil
- 1 package (8 oz) sliced fresh mushrooms (3 cups)
- 2 medium onions, chopped (2 cups)
- 3 cloves garlic, finely chopped
- 2 cans (15 oz each) tomato sauce
- 1 can (28 oz) diced tomatoes, undrained
- 1 can (6 oz) tomato paste
- 2 tablespoons sugar
- 1 tablespoon dried basil leaves
- 1 teaspoon dried oregano leaves
- ½ teaspoon salt
- ½ teaspoon pepper
- ½ teaspoon crushed red pepper flakes

1 Spray 4- to 5-quart slow cooker with cooking spray. In 12-inch skillet, heat oil over medium heat. Add mushrooms, onions and garlic. Cook 4 to 5 minutes, stirring occasionally, until onions are tender.

2 Add vegetables and remaining ingredients to slow cooker; stir until mixed.

3 Cover and cook on Low heat setting 6 to 8 hours. Use sauce immediately, or cool and ladle into food storage or freezer-safe containers; cover and refrigerate up to 4 days or freeze up to 4 months. To thaw frozen spaghetti sauce, place container in refrigerator for about 8 hours.

½ Cup Calories 60; Total Fat 1g (Saturated Fat 0g, Trans Fat 0g); Cholesterol 0mg; Sodium 510mg; Total Carbohydrate 11g (Dietary Fiber 2g); Protein 2g **Carbohydrate Choices:** 1

SPAGHETTI SAUCE WITH MEAT: Stir 1 lb crumbled cooked lean ground beef into 3 cups Easy Spaghetti Sauce.

SPAGHETTI SAUCE WITH MEATBALLS: Add cooked meatballs to spaghetti sauce during the last 15 minutes of cooking time to heat thoroughly.

Tomato-Herb Pasta Sauce

Make a batch or two and freeze it in portion sizes that work for you. Use as is or toss in some pepperoni, cooked Italian sausage and mushrooms or olives. Use 3 to 3½ cups of this homemade sauce for recipes that call for a 24- to 27-oz jar of tomato pasta sauce.

PREP 15 Minutes **TOTAL** 1 Hour • *4 cups*

- 2 tablespoons olive or vegetable oil
- 1 medium onion, chopped (1 cup)
- ½ medium green bell pepper, chopped (½ cup)
- 2 cloves garlic, finely chopped
- 1 can (28 oz) whole tomatoes, undrained
- 2 cans (8 oz each) tomato sauce
- 2 tablespoons chopped fresh or 2 teaspoons dried basil leaves
- 1 tablespoon chopped fresh or 1 teaspoon dried oregano leaves
- ½ teaspoon salt
- ½ teaspoon fennel seed
- ¼ teaspoon pepper

1 In 3-quart saucepan, heat oil over medium heat. Cook onion, bell pepper and garlic in oil, stirring occasionally, 2 minutes, or until vegetables are softened.

2 Stir in remaining ingredients, breaking up tomatoes. Heat to boiling; reduce heat. Simmer uncovered 45 minutes, until slightly thickened.

3 Use sauce immediately. Or cool and transfer to food storage container, cover and refrigerate up to 2 weeks or freeze up to 1 year.

½ Cup Calories 90; Total Fat 3.5g (Saturated Fat 0g, Trans Fat 0g); Cholesterol 0mg; Sodium 670mg; Total Carbohydrate 11g (Dietary Fiber 2g); Protein 2g **Carbohydrate Choices:** 1

SLOW-COOKER DIRECTIONS: Use 1 small onion, chopped (½ cup), and 1 can (8 oz) tomato sauce. Substitute 1 can (28 oz) diced tomatoes, undrained, for the whole tomatoes. Spray 3½- to 6-quart slow cooker with cooking spray. In slow cooker, mix all ingredients. Cover; cook on Low heat setting 8 to 10 hours.

Easy Pasta Sauce with Mushrooms

Tomato-Herb Pasta Sauce

5-INGREDIENT RECIPE

Harissa Waffle Fries Pizza

Cheddar-Monterey Jack Cheese Blend

CLASSIC

Cilantro

Mild Harissa

Harissa

Waffle Fries

Mini Pepperoni

202

5-INGREDIENT RECIPE

EASY

Harissa Waffle Fries Pizza

This super-simple pizza is a dinner game changer. Or set out a platter of these as an appetizer that's sure to be the talk of your gathering!

PREP 15 Minutes TOTAL 45 Minutes • **4 servings**

- 1 package (20 to 24 oz) frozen plain or seasoned waffle fries
- ½ cup mini sliced pepperoni (from 5-oz package)
- 1 jar (10 oz) mild harissa (for homemade harissa, see page 457)
- 1 cup shredded cheddar−Monterey Jack cheese blend (4 oz)
- 2 tablespoons chopped fresh cilantro

1 Heat oven as directed on package. Arrange fries on 15x10x1-inch pan. Bake as directed on package.

2 Remove from oven. Top with pepperoni. Spoon harissa over pepperoni. Sprinkle with cheese. Bake 2 to 3 minutes or until cheese is melted. Sprinkle with cilantro. Serve immediately.

1 Serving Calories 430; Total Fat 30g (Saturated Fat 12g, Trans Fat 0g); Cholesterol 50mg; Sodium 1090mg; Total Carbohydrate 28g (Dietary Fiber 3g); Protein 11g **Carbohydrate Choices:** 2

Cheesy Turkish Pides

This is our take on the Istanbul street-food pide (pronounced PEA-day), which is a boat-shaped, savory pizza. The unique shape and ingredients are a nice change of pace from traditional pizza.

PREP 1 Hour 5 Minutes TOTAL 1 Hour 40 Minutes • **4 pides**

CRUST

- 1 batch Pizza Crust (page 204)

FILLING

- ½ lb ground beef (at least 85% lean)
- 1 cup lightly-packed chopped fresh baby spinach leaves
- ½ cup chopped red bell pepper
- ½ cup chopped tomato
- ¼ cup chopped onion
- 1 Anaheim or poblano chile, seeded, chopped
- 1 clove garlic, finely chopped
- 1½ teaspoons dried oregano leaves
- ½ teaspoon smoked paprika
- ½ teaspoon salt

CREAM CHEESE LAYER AND TOPPINGS

- 4 oz (half of 8-oz package) cream cheese, softened
- ½ cup crumbled feta cheese (2 oz)
- 1 teaspoon olive oil
- ¾ cup shredded mozzarella cheese (3 oz)
- Fresh baby spinach leaves, cut into thin strips, if desired

1 Prepare dough and let rest as directed in Step 1 of Pizza Crust recipe—except divide dough in half. Wrap one half in plastic wrap; refrigerate or freeze as directed in Pizza Crust recipe. Set aside remaining half.

2 Meanwhile, in 12-inch skillet, cook ground beef until browned. Add remaining filling ingredients. Cook over medium heat, about 3 minutes or until vegetables are softened. Remove from heat; place in colander to drain and cool for 15 minutes.

3 Meanwhile, heat oven to 400°F. In small bowl, mix cream cheese and feta cheese until blended.

4 Divide reserved dough into 4 equal pieces. Roll out each piece into an 11x4-inch oval shape. Gently spread one quarter of the cream cheese mixture down center of each oval, leaving 3 inches from each narrow end uncovered. Spoon meat mixture over cream cheese mixture.

5 Work with one pide at a time: starting at one of the narrow ends of dough, bring sides up and together; twist. Continue twisting slightly over the filling. Pinch and twist end into a point. Continue bringing dough up around sides of filling to make boat-like shape. Twist other narrow end of dough in the same fashion.

6 Onto large cookie sheet, carefully place pides; retwist pointed ends, if necessary. Brush dough with olive oil.

7 Bake 14 to 16 minutes until crust is golden brown. Remove from oven, sprinkle filling with mozzarella cheese. Bake 2 to 4 minutes longer or until cheese is melted. Garnish with spinach.

1 Pide Calories 520; Total Fat 30g (Saturated Fat 13g, Trans Fat 1g); Cholesterol 90mg; Sodium 1020mg; Total Carbohydrate 40g (Dietary Fiber 3g); Protein 24g **Carbohydrate Choices:** 2½

Cheesy Turkish Pides

203

Queso Taco Pockets

Queso Taco Pockets

You can wrap these tacos in foil and take them with you for an on-the-go meal, or serve them on a plate loaded with your favorite fresh toppings for a fun new way to enjoy taco night! Heat the remaining refried beans and top with shredded cheese as a delicious side dish.

PREP 30 Minutes **TOTAL** 1 Hour • **8 pockets**

½ lb ground beef (at least 90% lean)	4 oz prepared cheese product (from 16-oz loaf), cut into ½-inch cubes (about ¾ cup)
2 tablespoons taco seasoning mix (from 1-oz package; for homemade seasoning mix, see page 454)	1 box refrigerated pie crusts, softened as directed on box
2 tablespoons water	Diced tomatoes, shredded lettuce, shredded cheese, taco sauce or salsa, if desired
¾ cup refried beans (from 16-oz can)	

1 Heat oven to 400°F.

2 In 10-inch nonstick skillet, cook beef over medium-high heat 3 to 5 minutes, stirring frequently, until no longer pink; drain. Reduce heat to medium-low. Add taco seasoning mix and water; stir about 1 minute or until well mixed. Remove from heat; let stand 5 minutes. Stir in refried beans and cheese product cubes.

3 On surface sprinkled lightly with flour, roll each crust into 12-inch circle. Using 4-inch round cutter, cut each crust into 7 circles for a total of 14 circles. Reroll remaining dough scraps to cut 2 more circles for a total of 16. Discard any remaining scraps.

4 Top 8 of the circles each with about ¼ cup beef mixture, flattening mixture slightly and leaving at least ¼ inch around edges of circles. Moisten edges of dough with water; top with another dough circle, stretching dough slightly to fit. Press edges with fork to seal. Pierce top of each with fork to create vent.

5 Place pockets at least 1 inch apart on ungreased large cookie sheet. Bake 21 to 24 minutes or until golden brown. Serve warm with remaining ingredients.

1 Pocket Calories 200; Total Fat 12g (Saturated Fat 5g, Trans Fat 0g); Cholesterol 35mg; Sodium 530mg; Total Carbohydrate 16g (Dietary Fiber 1g); Protein 9g **Carbohydrate Choices:** 1

Pizza Crust

Homemade pizza crust is easy to make ahead, to have on hand for pizzas any time. Whether you make it with whole wheat, all-purpose or bread flour, this customizable crust can be made thick or thin to your liking.

PREP 20 Minutes **TOTAL** 1 Hour 35 Minutes •
2 pizza crusts (8 slices each)

2½ to 3 cups all-purpose, bread or whole wheat flour	1 cup very warm water (120°F to 130°F)
1 tablespoon sugar	3 tablespoons olive or vegetable oil
1 teaspoon salt	1 tablespoon cornmeal
1 package (2¼ teaspoons) regular active or fast-acting dry yeast	

1 In large bowl, mix 1 cup of the flour, the sugar, salt and yeast. Add warm water and oil. Beat with electric mixer on medium speed 2 minutes, scraping bowl frequently. Stir in enough remaining flour until dough is soft and leaves side of bowl. Place dough on lightly floured surface; knead 5 to 8 minutes or until dough is smooth and springy. Cover dough loosely with plastic wrap; let rest 30 minutes.

2 Place dough in greased bowl; cover with plastic wrap. Refrigerate up to 24 hours. Remove from refrigerator 1 hour before shaping crusts. Shape crusts and bake as directed below for thin or thick crusts.

3 **For Thin Crust Pizzas** Heat oven to 425°F. Grease 2 cookie sheets or 12-inch pizza pans with oil. Sprinkle with cornmeal. Divide dough in half. Pat each half into 12-inch round on cookie sheet using floured fingers. Partially bake 7 to 8 minutes or until crust just begins to brown; top as desired. Bake 8 to 10 minutes or until cheese is melted.

4 **For Thick Crust Pizzas** Move oven rack to lowest position. Heat oven to 375°F. Grease 2 (9-inch round or 8-inch square) pans with oil. Sprinkle with cornmeal. Divide dough in half. Pat each half in bottom of pan using floured fingers. Cover loosely with plastic wrap; let rise in warm place 30 to 45 minutes or until almost doubled in size. Remove plastic wrap. Partially bake 20 to 22 minutes or until crust just begins to brown; top as desired. Bake pizzas about 20 minutes or until cheese is melted.

5 Cut each pizza into 8 slices to serve.

1 Slice Calories 100; Total Fat 3g (Saturated Fat 0g, Trans Fat 0g); Cholesterol 0mg; Sodium 150mg; Total Carbohydrate 16g (Dietary Fiber 0g); Protein 2g **Carbohydrate Choices:** 1

Pizza Crust

MAKE-AHEAD DIRECTIONS: To Freeze Unbaked Dough After removing dough from refrigerator in Step 2, shape it into 2 balls. Wrap each ball tightly in plastic wrap and place in resealable plastic bag. **To Freeze Partially Baked Crusts** Partially bake as directed for thin or thick crusts. Wrap cooled crust as directed for unbaked dough. Freeze dough or partially baked crusts up to 2 months. **To Use Unbaked Dough** Remove from freezer and place in refrigerator until thawed, 4 to 6 hours. Shape and bake as directed in Step 3 for desired crust type. **To Use Partially Baked Crusts** Unwrap and place in pan. Top loosely with same plastic wrap and let stand at room temperature until thawed. Top and bake as directed.

CHEESE PIZZA: Partially bake 1 thin or thick crust as directed. Spread with ¾ cup pizza sauce. Sprinkle with 3 cups shredded pizza cheese, mozzarella cheese or Italian cheese blend. Bake as directed for crust type.

FRESH VEGETABLE AND BASIL PIZZA: Partially bake 1 thin or thick crust as directed. Spread with ¾ cup pizza sauce. Top with ½ large bell pepper (any color), thinly sliced, 1½ cups sliced fresh mushrooms, 2 tablespoons sliced fresh basil leaves and 1 cup shredded mozzarella cheese (4 oz). Bake as directed for crust type.

CHEESY BEEF PIZZA: Partially bake 1 thin or thick crust as directed. Spread 1 can (8 oz) pizza sauce over crust. In 8-inch skillet, cook ½ lb lean ground beef with ½ cup chopped onion, ½ teaspoon Italian seasoning and ⅛ teaspoon garlic powder until no pink remains in beef.

Drain; spoon over pizza sauce. Top with 2 cups each sliced fresh mushrooms and shredded mozzarella cheese. Bake as directed for crust type.

MEAT LOVER'S PIZZA: Make Cheesy Beef Pizza as directed—except use bulk regular or hot Italian pork sausage instead of ground beef and omit Italian seasoning and garlic powder. Top pizza with 1 cup diced or sliced pepperoni with the sausage.

SHAPING PIZZA DOUGH

Thin Crust Pat each half of dough into 12-inch round on cookie sheet or pizza pan greased with oil and sprinkled with cornmeal.

Thick Crust Pat each half of dough into bottom of round or square pan greased with oil and sprinkled with cornmeal. Cover and let rise until almost doubled in size.

Spinach-Feta Naan Pizzas

PREP 30 Minutes **TOTAL** 45 Minutes • *4 pizzas*

QUICK NAAN

- 2 teaspoons cornmeal
- 2 cups original all-purpose baking mix
- 1½ teaspoons finely chopped garlic
- ¼ cup warm water
- 1 tablespoon olive or vegetable oil
- 1 container (5.3 oz) plain Greek yogurt

SAUCE

- ¾ cup Alfredo pasta sauce (from 15-oz jar)

- ½ cup thawed frozen chopped spinach, drained, squeezed*
- 1½ teaspoons finely chopped garlic

PIZZA TOPPINGS

- 1 jar (7.5 oz) marinated artichokes, drained, coarsely chopped
- 1 small tomato, coarsely chopped (½ cup)
- ¼ cup crumbled feta cheese (1 oz)
- ½ cup finely shredded mozzarella cheese (2 oz)

1 Heat oven to 450°F. Spray 2 large cookie sheets with cooking spray. Sprinkle each pan evenly with 1 teaspoon cornmeal.

2 In medium bowl, stir baking mix and garlic until well mixed. Stir in water, oil and yogurt; mix until soft dough forms. On surface generously sprinkled with baking mix, knead 10 to 12 times or until dough is soft and not sticky. Cover and let stand 5 minutes.

3 Meanwhile, in small bowl, stir together sauce ingredients; set aside.

4 Divide dough into 4 pieces. Using rolling pin, roll each piece into 9x5-inch oval.

5 Heat 12-inch nonstick skillet over medium heat. Brush one side of each naan with water. Carefully place 1 naan in hot skillet, water side down. Brush top of naan with water. Cover; cook about 1 minute on each side or until golden. Remove naan to cookie sheet. Repeat with remaining naans, placing 2 naans on each cookie sheet.

6 Spread about ¼ cup sauce on each naan to within ½ inch from edge. Top naans evenly with artichokes and tomato. Sprinkle feta and mozzarella cheese on top of each pizza.

7 Bake 6 to 8 minutes or until cheese is melted. Serve hot.

1 Pizza Calories 600; Total Fat 37g (Saturated Fat 16g, Trans Fat 2g); Cholesterol 60mg; Sodium 1350mg; Total Carbohydrate 51g (Dietary Fiber 6g); Protein 16g **Carbohydrate Choices:** 3½

*To prevent the pizzas from getting soggy, place the squeezed spinach between paper towels and press to remove any remaining moisture.

MAKE-AHEAD DIRECTIONS: Prepare naan as directed in Steps 1, 2, 4 and 5; cool completely on cooling rack. Place in resealable freezer plastic bag or airtight container. Freeze up to 2 months. Thaw at room temperature while preparing sauce in Step 3. Continue with Step 6.

Spinach-Feta Naan Pizza

Chicken Sausage and
Mini Pepper Pizza

Chorizo-Manchego Flatbread

Ground chorizo is available in bulk 1-lb packages. Cook the whole package, use a quarter for this recipe, then freeze the remainder. Or use to fill omelets or stir into pasta or chili. This recipe will come together in minutes if you already have pizza dough and cooked chorizo.

PREP 20 Minutes **TOTAL** 35 Minutes •
5 servings (2 pieces each)

1 batch Pizza Crust (page 204)	¼ cup quartered pitted Spanish or Italian green olives
1 tablespoon olive oil	
1 clove garlic, finely chopped	¼ lb ground chorizo sausage, cooked, drained
4 oz Manchego cheese, shredded (1 cup)	1 cup shredded mozzarella cheese (4 oz)
½ cup sliced drained roasted red bell peppers (from a jar), patted dry	2 green onions, cut diagonally into thin slices
	2 tablespoons chopped fresh cilantro

1 Heat oven to 400°F. Spray large cookie sheet with cooking spray. Prepare dough and let rest as directed in Step 1 of Pizza Crust recipe. Divide dough into two pieces. Wrap one half in plastic wrap and freeze as directed in Make-Ahead Directions. Press remaining dough into 15x10-inch rectangle on cookie sheet.

2 In small bowl, mix olive oil and garlic. Brush dough with olive oil mixture. Bake 8 to 10 minutes or until light golden brown. Remove from oven.

3 Top partially baked crust with Manchego cheese, followed by roasted peppers, olives and chorizo. Sprinkle evenly with mozzarella cheese. Bake 7 to 11 minutes or until crust edges are golden brown and mozzarella cheese is melted. Top with green onions and cilantro. Cut flatbread 2 rows by 5 rows. Serve hot.

1 Serving Calories 400; Total Fat 24g (Saturated Fat 10g, Trans Fat 0g); Cholesterol 45mg; Sodium 980mg; Total Carbohydrate 29g (Dietary Fiber 2g); Protein 18g **Carbohydrate Choices:** 2

QUICK CHORIZO-MANCHEGO FLATBREAD: Prepare as directed—except substitute 1 can (11 oz) refrigerated thin pizza crust for the Pizza Crust. Unroll on cookie sheet and continue as directed.

Chicken Sausage and Mini Pepper Pizza

Miniature peppers are a hybrid sweet pepper known for their sweet taste and crisp texture. We loved the unique flavor of this pizza that came from these little cuties. It's a little different from regular bell peppers. You can find them in a trio of colors (orange, red and yellow) in 1-lb packages.

PREP 10 Minutes **TOTAL** 20 Minutes •
4 servings (2 slices each)

1 package (10 oz) prebaked thin pizza crust (12-inch)	3 miniature bell peppers (from 1-lb bag), cut into rings
½ cup salsa verde (from 16-oz jar)	1 tablespoon chopped fresh cilantro
1 pineapple-bacon or chicken & apple chicken sausage link, cut in half lengthwise if desired, thinly sliced (from 12-oz package)	1 cup shredded Colby-Monterey Jack cheese blend (4 oz)

1 Heat oven to 450°F. On ungreased cookie sheet or 14-inch pizza pan, place pizza crust. Spread salsa verde over crust to within ½ inch of edge.

2 Arrange chicken sausage slices and pepper rings over pizza crust; sprinkle with cilantro. Top with cheese.

3 Bake 9 to 11 minutes or until cheese is melted and pizza is thoroughly heated. To serve, cut into 8 wedges.

1 Serving Calories 380; Total Fat 17g (Saturated Fat 6g, Trans Fat 0g); Cholesterol 45mg; Sodium 940mg; Total Carbohydrate 42g (Dietary Fiber 3g); Protein 16g **Carbohydrate Choices:** 3

Roasted Root
Veggie Pizza with
Beer Bread Crust

Buffalo
Cauliflower
Pizza

Barbecue Cheeseburger
Pizza with
Cauliflower Crust

Roasted Root Veggie Pizza with Beer Bread Crust

The roasted sweet potatoes and beets make irresistible pizza toppings, but if you have about 1½ cups of leftover roasted veggies, feel free to use them instead! Heat the oven as directed in Step 1 and then dive into the recipe at Step 3, skipping the rest of Step 1 and all of Step 2.

PREP 30 Minutes **TOTAL** 1 Hour 20 Minutes • *6 slices*

VEGETABLES

- 1 medium sweet potato (about 0.75 lb)
- 4 medium beets, stems and greens attached
- 1 tablespoon olive oil

CRUST

- 2 cups all-purpose flour
- 1 tablespoon sugar
- 1 package (2¼ teaspoons) regular active dry yeast
- 1 teaspoon baking powder
- 1 teaspoon coarse (kosher or sea) salt
- ¾ cup lager beer, warmed to 105°F
- 1 tablespoon olive oil

TOPPINGS

- ¾ cup ricotta cheese
- 1½ cups shredded Gruyère cheese (6 oz)
- 1 tablespoon chopped fresh rosemary leaves

1 Heat oven to 425°F. Peel sweet potato; cut lengthwise into quarters, then crosswise into ½-inch slices Cut stems and greens from beets; set aside. Peel beets and cut into ¾- to 1-inch cubes. Chop enough greens to make ½ to 1 cup loosely packed; set aside for topping. Discard stems.

2 Spray 2 cookie sheets with cooking spray. Spread sweet potato pieces and beet cubes on cookie sheets in single layer; brush with 1 tablespoon oil. Roast 30 minutes or until tender when pierced with fork. Remove from oven and let cool.

3 Meanwhile, in medium bowl, mix 1 cup of the flour, the sugar, yeast, baking powder and salt. Stir in beer and oil until smooth. Stir in remaining 1 cup flour to make a soft dough. On lightly floured surface, knead dough until smooth and elastic, about 5 minutes. Cover; let rest 30 minutes.

4 Spray large cookie sheet with cooking spray. On cookie sheet, press dough evenly into 13-inch round, patting and using heel of hand to push dough out from center. Build up ½-inch rim around dough.

5 Spread ricotta cheese evenly over dough. Sprinkle with cheese, top evenly with roasted vegetables and sprinkle with rosemary.

6 Bake 15 to 18 minutes or until crust is golden and cheese is melted. Sprinkle with reserved beet greens; pat down lightly. Cut into 6 slices. Serve hot.

1 Slice Calories 410; Total Fat 17g (Saturated Fat 8g, Trans Fat 0g); Cholesterol 40mg; Sodium 760mg; Total Carbohydrate 46g (Dietary Fiber 4g); Protein 18g **Carbohydrate Choices:** 3

Buffalo Cauliflower Pizza

For maximum Buffalo flavor, take the extra time to thoroughly coat each cauliflower floret with sauce and crumbs.

PREP 20 Minutes **TOTAL** 50 Minutes • *4 slices*

BUFFALO CAULIFLOWER

- 2 cups bite-size fresh cauliflower florets
- ½ cup gluten-free Buffalo wing sauce (for homemade sauce, see page 456)
- ½ cup gluten-free plain panko crispy bread crumbs

CHICK PEA FLOUR PIZZA CRUST

- 1 cup chick pea (garbanzo) flour
- ¼ teaspoon salt
- 1 cup water
- 2 tablespoons olive oil

TOPPINGS

- ½ cup chunky blue cheese or ranch dressing
- 1 cup shredded mozzarella cheese (4 oz)
- ⅓ cup thinly sliced celery
- ⅓ cup crumbled blue cheese (1½ oz)

1 Heat oven to 425°F. Line 15x10x1-inch pan with cooking parchment paper; spray with cooking spray.

2 In medium bowl, mix cauliflower and wing sauce until completely coated. Add bread crumbs; toss to coat well. Spread in single layer in pan. Bake 18 to 20 minutes or until golden brown and cauliflower is tender when pierced with a fork.

3 Meanwhile, in medium bowl, mix chick pea flour and salt. Add water; mix with whisk until smooth. Let stand 10 minutes.

4 Add 1 tablespoon of the olive oil; mix until smooth. In 12-inch ovenproof nonstick skillet, heat remaining 1 tablespoon oil over medium-high heat. Pour batter into skillet. Cook about 5 to 6 minutes, until bottom is crisp and golden and top is set. Remove from heat. Spray top of crust with cooking spray. Place skillet with crust in oven; bake 5 minutes. Remove from oven (pan handle will be hot).

5 Spread crust with dressing to within ½ inch of edge. Sprinkle with half of the mozzarella cheese. Top evenly with cauliflower and celery. Sprinkle with remaining mozzarella cheese and blue cheese.

6 Bake 3 to 5 minutes or until cheese is melted and crust edge is golden brown. Remove pizza from pan to cooling rack. Gently slide pizza from pan to cutting board. Cut into 4 slices; serve immediately.

1 Slice Calories 520; Total Fat 37g (Saturated Fat 10g, Trans Fat 0g); Cholesterol 30mg; Sodium 1110mg; Total Carbohydrate 31g (Dietary Fiber 4g); Protein 17g **Carbohydrate Choices:** 2

Barbecue Cheeseburger Pizza with Cauliflower Crust

PREP 45 Minutes **TOTAL** 1 Hour • *6 servings* (2 pieces each)

CAULIFLOWER CRUST

- 2 packages (12 oz each) frozen riced cauliflower
- 2 eggs, slightly beaten
- 1 tablespoon cornmeal
- ¾ cup finely shredded cheddar cheese (3 oz)
- ½ teaspoon garlic salt

TOPPINGS

- ¾ lb ground beef (at least 80% lean)
- 1 medium onion, chopped (1 cup)
- ¼ teaspoon salt
- ¼ teaspoon pepper
- ½ cup barbecue sauce
- 6 slices (¾ oz each) cheddar cheese, cut in half diagonally
- 1 cup shredded lettuce
- 1 small tomato, chopped (½ cup)
- ⅓ cup hamburger dill pickle chips (from 24-oz jar)
- 2 tablespoons ketchup
- 1 tablespoon yellow mustard

1 Cook cauliflower as directed on package; drain. Carefully spoon cooked cauliflower onto 2 thicknesses of clean kitchen towels. Let cool 5 minutes. Gather towels around cauliflower and squeeze to remove additional liquid. Place cauliflower in medium bowl; cool 5 minutes longer.

2 Meanwhile, heat oven to 425F. Spray 15x10x1-inch pan with cooking spray; sprinkle evenly with cornmeal.

3 Stir eggs, shredded cheddar cheese and garlic salt into cauliflower. Pat mixture evenly in pan. Bake 14 to 18 minutes or until golden brown. Remove from oven.

4 Meanwhile, in 10-inch nonstick skillet, cook and stir ground beef and onion over medium-high heat 6 to 8 minutes or until beef is no longer pink; drain. Stir in salt and pepper.

5 Spread barbecue sauce over baked crust. Top with ground beef mixture and cheddar cheese slices. Bake 4 to 5 minutes or until cheese is melted. Run sharp knife around edges of pizza to loosen from pan. Top pizza with lettuce, tomatoes and pickles. Drizzle with ketchup and mustard. Cut into 6 rows by 2 rows.

1 Serving Calories 360; Total Fat 20g (Saturated Fat 10g, Trans Fat 0.5g); Cholesterol 130mg; Sodium 830mg; Total Carbohydrate 21g (Dietary Fiber 4g); Protein 22g **Carbohydrate Choices:** 1½

FRESH CAULIFLOWER CRUST: Cut 1 medium head cauliflower (about 2½ lb) into florets. In food processor, place half of florets. Cover and process, using quick on-and-off pulses, 10 to 15 times, or until consistency of coarse crumbs. In 3-quart microwavable bowl, place cauliflower. Process remaining florets; add to bowl. Cover bowl and microwave on High 6 to 7 minutes, stirring every 2 minutes, until tender. Spoon cauliflower onto towels as directed in Step 1. Continue as directed.

Whole Grains & Rice

Whole Grain Basics

Cultivated for centuries, grains are eaten by every culture in a variety of dishes. Whole grains are getting their day in the sun as we recognize them for their nutritional benefits. They are one of the least water- and energy-intensive foods to produce, and farmers are figuring out how to produce more with less energy consumption, soil loss and greenhouse gas emissions. Not only are whole grains budget friendly, they are high in fiber and generally low in fat.

What Is a Whole Grain?

It is the entire seed of a grass plant and contains all parts of the kernel, including the fiber-rich outer coating of bran, the energy-dense middle layer called the endosperm and the nutrient-packed germ. If any part of the grain is removed, it's not considered whole. Whole grains contain essential vitamins, minerals, antioxidants and phytonutrients, plus healthy fats. Whole grains include barley, quinoa and brown rice.

In contrast, a refined grain has been through the milling process, which removes the bran and germ. The process gives the grain a finer texture, but also removes important fiber and vitamins. Most refined grains are labeled "enriched," meaning some nutrients have been added back in after processing. Refined grains include white rice and white flour.

Storage

Because whole grains contain all parts of the kernel—the germ contains beneficial fat—they will not keep as long as refined grains and flours. Store whole grain flours in the refrigerator for up to 6 months or freeze for up to 1 year. Uncooked rice and grains can be stored, tightly covered, in a cool dry place.

Cooking Hints

Check Package Directions We provide some guidelines, but it is always good to do what is recommended by the manufacturer.

Simmer, Don't Boil Heat the water to a boil. Add the grain, cover the pan and reduce the heat. Water should be barely simmering so that the grain cooks slowly, giving it enough time to absorb liquid and soften.

Keep It Covered Simmer with the lid on and check occasionally to be sure the liquid is at a low simmer. If the liquid is almost gone before the grain is done, add a few additional tablespoons to the pot and continue cooking.

Make Ahead Cook grains to have on hand for quick meals. Cool them completely and store in the refrigerator up to 5 days or freeze in 2-cup quantities for up to 3 months. Thaw them quickly in the microwave or overnight in the refrigerator to add to soups, stews and salads.

FABULOUS FIBER

Whole grains naturally contain fiber in the outer coating of the grain kernel (the bran). But there are many other important nutrients and natural compounds found in whole grains that work together for health benefits.

TIMETABLE FOR COOKING COMMON GRAINS

Water or broth can be used for the liquid. Heat to boiling, reduce heat and simmer as directed below. Check product package for additional information.

TYPE OF GRAIN (1 CUP)	AMOUNT OF LIQUID IN CUPS	COOKING DIRECTIONS	YIELD IN CUPS
Barley, Hulled	3½	Simmer covered 40 minutes; drain if necessary. For softer barley, simmer up to an additional 40 minutes, stirring occasionally.	3
Barley, Pearled	8	Simmer covered 45 to 50 minutes; drain if necessary.	4
Barley, Quick Cooking	2	Simmer covered 10 to 12 minutes. Remove from heat; let stand 5 minutes.	3
Bulgur or Golden Bulgur	2	Simmer about 12 minutes; drain if necessary. Fluff with a fork.	2½
Cornmeal (Polenta)	4	Mix cornmeal with ¾ cup of the water to prevent clumping. Stir into remaining water with 1½ teaspoons salt. Cook over medium heat, 8 to 10 minutes, stirring constantly, until mixture thickens and boils; reduce heat. Simmer covered about 10 minutes, stirring occasionally until very thick. Stir in 1 tablespoon butter or olive oil.	4½
Oats, Steel	4	Heat water to boiling; add oats. Simmer uncovered 25 to 30 minutes.	1
Quinoa	2	Simmer covered 12 to 15 minutes.	3 to 4

Rye Berries

Gold Quinoa

213

Red Quinoa

Buckwheat

Bulgur

Pearled
Barley

Spelt

Wheat
Berries

Rolled Rye Flakes

Millet

Teff

Hulled Barley

Oat Groats

Coarse Ground
Cornmeal

Steel-Cut
Oats

Blue Cornmeal

Kamut®

Flaxseed

Kasha

Amaranth

MAKE AHEAD • SLOW COOKER • CALORIE SMART • VEGETARIAN

Overnight Spiced Peach Breakfast Wheat Berries

Wheat berries will soften but absorb liquid differently than other grains during cooking. Expect their cooked texture to be chewy, and flavor to be sweet and nutty.

PREP 10 Minutes **TOTAL** 10 Hours 20 Minutes •
6 servings (½ cup each)

1 cup uncooked wheat berries, rinsed, drained	3 tablespoons honey
½ teaspoon ground cinnamon	1 package (12 oz) frozen sliced peaches (3 cups), thawed, drained
½ teaspoon ground ginger	¼ cup chopped pecans, toasted (see page 28)
¼ teaspoon ground nutmeg	Additional honey and yogurt, if desired
⅛ teaspoon salt	
2 cups water	

1 Spray 3½- to 4-quart slow-cooker insert with cooking spray. In slow cooker, mix wheat berries, cinnamon, ginger, nutmeg, salt, water and 3 tablespoons honey.

2 Cover and cook on Low heat setting at least 10 hours but no longer than 12 hours, until wheat berries are tender but still chewy. Stir peaches into wheat berry mixture. Cover and cook an additional 10 minutes or until peaches are heated through. Top each serving with pecans and a drizzle of honey. Serve with yogurt. Spoon any remaining wheat berry mixture into food-safe container. Cover and refrigerate up to 5 days.

1 Serving Calories 200; Total Fat 4g (Saturated Fat 0g, Trans Fat 0g); Cholesterol 0mg; Sodium 55mg; Total Carbohydrate 36g (Dietary Fiber 5g); Protein 4g **Carbohydrate Choices:** 2½

MAKE-AHEAD DIRECTIONS: To reheat, place ½ cup wheat berry mixture in individual microwavable serving bowl; cover with waxed paper. Microwave on High 30 seconds, then stir.

FAST • CALORIE SMART • GLUTEN FREE • VEGETARIAN

Raspberry Amaranth Pancakes

If amaranth flour is not available, you can easily make your own in a blender using amaranth grain. Process 1⅓ cups amaranth grain with on-and-off pulses 1 to 2 minutes until the consistency of coarse flour, stirring halfway through pulsing.

PREP 20 Minutes **TOTAL** 20 Minutes • **16 pancakes**

2 eggs, beaten	1 teaspoon baking soda
1⅔ cup amaranth flour	½ teaspoon salt
1 cup milk or unsweetened almond milk	1 cup fresh raspberries, broken in small pieces if large
3 tablespoons butter or coconut oil, melted	Maple-flavored syrup or pure maple syrup, if desired
2 tablespoons sugar	Additional raspberries, if desired
1 tablespoon fresh lemon juice	

1 In medium bowl, using whisk, mix all ingredients except raspberries and syrup until blended. Fold in raspberries. Let stand 2 minutes.

2 Meanwhile, heat griddle or skillet over medium-low heat (300°F). Brush with vegetable oil.

3 For each pancake, pour slightly less than ¼ cup batter onto hot griddle, spreading slightly to 3½ to 4 inches. Cook 2 to 3 minutes or until bubbly on top and dry around edges. Turn; cook other side until golden brown. Serve pancakes with maple syrup and additional raspberries.

1 Pancake Calories 120; Total Fat 4.5g (Saturated Fat 2g, Trans Fat 0g); Cholesterol 30mg; Sodium 190mg; Total Carbohydrate 16g (Dietary Fiber 2g); Protein 3g **Carbohydrate Choices:** 1

Overnight Spiced Peach Breakfast Wheat Berries

Raspberry Amaranth Pancakes

Teff Energy Bars

Blueberry Breakfast Millet

GLUTEN FREE • VEGETARIAN • VEGAN

Teff Energy Bars

You can use almond, cashew or other nut butters instead of peanut butter if you prefer. Depending on which you use, the texture of the bars may vary slightly.

PREP 15 Minutes **TOTAL** 1 Hour 45 Minutes • *18 bars*

BARS

- ¾ cup peanut butter or other nut butter
- ⅔ cup agave nectar
- 2 teaspoons vanilla
- 1 cup pure old-fashioned oats
- ½ cup uncooked teff
- ½ cup hemp protein powder (from 16-oz container)
- ½ cup sweetened dried organic cherries or sweetened dried cranberries
- ½ cup roasted, salted hulled pumpkin seeds (pepitas)
- ¼ cup chia seeds

CHOCOLATE DRIZZLE

- ¼ cup vegan dark chocolate chips
- 1 teaspoon vegetable oil
- ¼ teaspoon coarse sea salt
  Additional dried cherries and pumpkin seeds, if desired

1 Heat oven to 350°F. Line 9-inch square pan with foil, leaving 2 inches overhanging; spray with cooking spray.

2 In large bowl, using spoon, mix peanut butter, agave nectar and vanilla until well blended; stir in remaining bar ingredients. Press mixture evenly in pan (mixture will be sticky).

3 Bake about 20 minutes or until top is set and firm, and edges begin to brown. Cool completely in pan on cooling rack, about 1 hour.

4 Lift foil from pan; place on cutting board. Fold back foil and cut bars into 6 rows by 3 rows. In small microwavable bowl, place chocolate chips and oil. Microwave uncovered on High about 40 seconds, stirring once, or until chips can be stirred smooth. Drizzle chocolate over bars; sprinkle with salt. Top with cherries and pumpkin seeds. Refrigerate 15 minutes or until chocolate is set.

1 Bar Calories 220; Total Fat 10g (Saturated Fat 2g, Trans Fat 0g); Cholesterol 0mg; Sodium 90mg; Total Carbohydrate 26g (Dietary Fiber 3g); Protein 6g **Carbohydrate Choices:** 2

FAST • CALORIE SMART • GLUTEN FREE • VEGETARIAN • VEGAN

Blueberry Breakfast Millet

Resembling mustard seed, whole millet has a chewy texture when cooked and a mild, nutty flavor similar to brown rice. Top with reduced-fat (lite) coconut milk, or if you are not following a vegan diet, top with fat-free half-and-half.

PREP 30 Minutes **TOTAL** 30 Minutes • *4 servings* (1 cup each)

- 3 cups water
- 1 cup uncooked millet
- ½ teaspoon salt
- ½ teaspoon ground cinnamon
- ¼ teaspoon ground nutmeg
- 1 cup frozen blueberries
- ¼ cup chopped walnuts
  Organic brown sugar, if desired

1 In 2-quart saucepan heat water, millet, salt, cinnamon and nutmeg to boiling; reduce heat. Cover and simmer 20 to 25 minutes, stirring occasionally, until millet is tender and most of water is absorbed. Remove from heat.

2 Stir in blueberries; cover and let stand about 3 minutes or until blueberries are warm and remaining water is absorbed.

3 To serve, spoon millet into 4 bowls. Top with walnuts. Serve with brown sugar.

1 Serving Calories 270; Total Fat 7g (Saturated Fat 1g, Trans Fat 0g); Cholesterol 0mg; Sodium 310mg; Total Carbohydrate 45g (Dietary Fiber 6g); Protein 7g **Carbohydrate Choices:** 3

Classic Tabbouleh

Whole Beet Tabbouleh

MAKE AHEAD • CALORIE SMART • VEGETARIAN • VEGAN

Classic Tabbouleh

This traditional Middle Eastern dish is always made with bulgur. It's served cold with a crisp bread.

PREP 10 Minutes **TOTAL** 1 Hour 40 Minutes •
6 servings (¾ cup each)

¾ cup uncooked bulgur	¼ cup olive oil or vegetable oil
1½ cups chopped fresh parsley	¼ cup fresh lemon juice
3 medium tomatoes, chopped (2¼ cups)	¾ teaspoon salt
5 medium green onions, thinly sliced (⅓ cup)	¼ teaspoon pepper
2 tablespoons chopped fresh or 2 teaspoons crushed dried mint leaves	Whole ripe olives, if desired

1 In small bowl, cover bulgur with water. Let stand 30 minutes. Drain; press out as much water as possible.

2 In medium glass or plastic bowl, combine bulgur, parsley, tomatoes, onions and mint; mix well.

3 In tightly covered container, shake oil, lemon juice, salt and pepper. Pour over bulgur mixture; toss until coated. Cover and refrigerate at least 1 hour. Garnish with olives.

1 Serving Calories 170; Total Fat 10g (Saturated Fat 1.5g, Trans Fat 0g); Cholesterol 0mg; Sodium 310mg; Total Carbohydrate 18g (Dietary Fiber 3g); Protein 3g **Carbohydrate Choices:** 1

CHICK PEA TABBOULEH: Add 1 can (15 to 16 oz) chick peas (garbanzo beans), drained and rinsed, and 1 cup chopped green bell pepper to the bulgur in Step 2.

MINTY TABBOULEH: Use ¾ cup each chopped fresh mint and parsley in place of the 1½ cups chopped fresh parsley. Omit the additional 2 tablespoons mint.

SOUTHWESTERN TABBOULEH: Substitute 1 cup chopped fresh cilantro for the parsley. Reduce lemon juice to 2 tablespoons; increase salt to 1 teaspoon. Add 2 teaspoons ground cumin with the salt and pepper in Step 3.

MAKE AHEAD • VEGETARIAN • VEGAN

Whole Beet Tabbouleh

Carrot greens work great in recipes, but the part in between the carrots and the leaves can be stringy and hard to chew, so it's best to compost or throw out that portion. Beet tops, however, are completely edible and one of the most vitamin-packed parts of this colorful root vegetable.

PREP 25 Minutes **TOTAL** 1 Hour 25 Minutes •
6 servings (1⅓ cups each)

2 cups boiling water	8 medium green onions, sliced (½ cup)
1 cup uncooked bulgur	1 teaspoon salt
3 medium fresh beets with tops	½ teaspoon pepper
4 small fresh carrots with tops	⅓ cup lemon juice
6 medium stalks celery with leaves, sliced (2½ cups)	¼ cup olive oil
	3 cloves garlic, finely chopped

1 In medium bowl, pour boiling water over bulgur. Let stand while preparing vegetables.

2 Chop beet tops and carrot greens. Peel beets; cut into julienne strips. Thinly slice carrots. In large bowl, toss beets and carrots with tops, celery, onions, salt and pepper.

3 Drain bulgur if necessary; stir into vegetable mixture.

4 In tightly covered container, shake lemon juice, oil and garlic. Add to bulgur mixture; mix well. Cover; refrigerate at least 1 hour or up to 3 days. Stir before serving.

1 Serving Calories 220; Total Fat 10g (Saturated Fat 1.5g, Trans Fat 0g); Cholesterol 0mg; Sodium 480mg; Total Carbohydrate 28g (Dietary Fiber 7g); Protein 4g **Carbohydrate Choices:** 2

FAST • GLUTEN FREE • VEGETARIAN

Strawberry-Avocado Quinoa Salad Bowl

PREP 20 Minutes **TOTAL** 30 Minutes • **8 servings**

- 1 cup uncooked quinoa
- 2 cups water
- 2 tablespoons fresh lime juice
- 2 tablespoons olive oil
- ½ teaspoon salt
- 2 cups chopped fresh strawberries (from a 16-oz container)

- 2 avocados, peeled, pitted, chopped
- 3 tablespoons chopped fresh basil leaves
- 1 package (4 oz) chèvre (goat) cheese, crumbled

1 Rinse quinoa well in mesh strainer. In 1-quart saucepan, mix quinoa and water. Heat to boiling; cover and simmer until liquid is absorbed, about 15 minutes. Spoon cooked quinoa into large heatproof bowl; cool 15 minutes

2 In small bowl, using whisk, beat lime juice, olive oil and salt. Drizzle quinoa with lime mixture; toss to combine. Arrange strawberries, avocados, basil and cheese on quinoa mixture.

1 Serving Calories 250; Total Fat 15g (Saturated Fat 5g, Trans Fat 0g); Cholesterol 15mg; Sodium 200mg; Total Carbohydrate 20g (Dietary Fiber 4g); Protein 8g **Carbohydrate Choices:** 1

MAKE-AHEAD DIRECTIONS: Make the quinoa mixture up to a day ahead. Add the strawberries, basil, avocado and cheese just before serving.

CALORIE SMART

Kibbeh Patties

Bulgur (partially processed whole wheat) is well known in Middle Eastern cooking, especially in tabbouleh and kibbeh. Kibbeh is claimed as the national dish by many Middle Eastern countries. It's often torpedo shaped and usually deep-fried, but we've streamlined the process to make delicious panfried patties. Try them as is, or serve in pita (pocket) bread or on a bun for a new burger flavor.

PREP 25 Minutes **TOTAL** 55 Minutes • **6 servings**

PATTIES

- ¾ cup uncooked bulgur
- 1 cup water
- 1 lb ground lamb
- 1 small onion, finely chopped (½ cup)
- ¼ cup finely chopped fresh mint leaves
- 1 teaspoon dried marjoram leaves
- ¾ teaspoon salt

- ½ teaspoon ground allspice
- ½ teaspoon ground cinnamon
- ¼ teaspoon ground red pepper (cayenne)
- 2 tablespoons olive oil

TOPPINGS, IF DESIRED

Tzatziki Dip (page 41) or Hummus (page 48)

Cucumber and tomato slices

1 In medium bowl, cover bulgur with water. Let stand 30 minutes. Drain; press out as much water as possible.

2 Add lamb, onion, mint, marjoram, salt, allspice, cinnamon, red pepper and 1 tablespoon of the oil to bulgur; mix just until blended. Divide mixture into 6 equal portions; shape into patties about ½ inch thick.

3 In 12-inch nonstick skillet, heat remaining 1 tablespoon oil over medium heat. Cook patties 9 to 12 minutes, turning once, until deep golden brown and instant-read meat thermometer inserted in center of patties reads 160°F. Serve with tzatziki dip or hummus, cucumber and tomato.

1 Serving Calories 260; Total Fat 15g (Saturated Fat 5g, Trans Fat 0g); Cholesterol 50mg; Sodium 340mg; Total Carbohydrate 16g (Dietary Fiber 4g); Protein 14g **Carbohydrate Choices:** 1

MAKING KIBBEH PATTIES

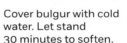

Cover bulgur with cold water. Let stand 30 minutes to soften.

Divide mixture into 6 equal portions; shape into ½-inch-thick patties.

Kibbeh Patties

Quinoa
Harvest Bowls

3 In large bowl, mix kale with remaining 1 tablespoon oil, ¼ teaspoon salt and ¼ teaspoon pepper; toss to thoroughly coat. Place on top of sweet potatoes; return pan to oven and bake 3 to 4 minutes or until kale is wilted.

4 In medium bowl, using whisk, beat all sauce ingredients.

5 Divide quinoa among 4 serving bowls. Top with sweet potatoes and kale, chick peas, avocado and pepitas. Serve with tahini-yogurt sauce and harissa on the side.

1 Serving Calories 530; Total Fat 26g (Saturated Fat 4g, Trans Fat 0g); Cholesterol 0mg; Sodium 950mg; Total Carbohydrate 57g (Dietary Fiber 11g); Protein 18g **Carbohydrate Choices:** 4

CALORIE SMART • GLUTEN FREE • VEGETARIAN

Quinoa Harvest Bowls

Harissa is a Middle Eastern condiment made with red bell peppers, used as an accompaniment to grain dishes, soups and stews. There are mild and spicy varieties. Tahini is a thick paste of ground sesame seed, often found in the aisle with the nut butters.

PREP 30 Minutes **TOTAL** 1 Hour • *4 servings*

BOWL BASE

- 2 medium sweet potatoes (about 1½ lb), peeled and cut into ½-inch cubes (5 cups)
- 2 tablespoons olive oil
- ¾ teaspoon salt
- ½ teaspoon pepper
- 1 cup uncooked white quinoa
- 2 cups (from 32-oz carton) vegetable broth (for homemade broth, see page 169)
- 1 large bunch kale, stemmed and torn into bite-size pieces (about 4 cups)

TAHINI-YOGURT SAUCE

- ¾ cup plain Greek yogurt
- ¼ cup water
- 3 tablespoons tahini
- 2 tablespoons lemon juice
- 1 tablespoon chopped fresh cilantro
- 1 clove garlic, finely chopped
- ¼ teaspoon salt

TOPPINGS

- 1 can (19 oz) chick peas (garbanzo beans), drained, rinsed
- 1 avocado, pitted, peeled and chopped
- ¼ cup roasted unsalted pumpkin seeds (pepitas)
  Harissa, if desired

1 Heat oven to 425°F. Spray 15x10x1-inch pan with cooking spray. Place sweet potatoes on pan. Add 1 tablespoon of the oil, ½ teaspoon of the salt and ¼ teaspoon of the pepper; toss to coat. Bake 20 to 25 minutes, stirring after 10 minutes, until just tender.

2 Meanwhile, rinse quinoa well in mesh strainer. In 2-quart saucepan, combine quinoa and broth. Heat to boiling; reduce heat to simmer. Cover; cook 18 to 23 minutes or until all of the broth is absorbed. Remove from heat; let stand about 5 minutes. Fluff with fork.

CALORIE SMART

Toasted Barley with Mixed Vegetables

PREP 20 Minutes **TOTAL** 1 Hour 20 Minutes • *6 servings*

- ½ cup uncooked hulled barley
- 1¾ cups (from 32-oz carton) chicken broth (for homemade broth, see page 153)
- 2 large onions, chopped (2 cups)
- 2 packages (8 oz each) sliced fresh mushrooms (6 cups)
- 4 medium carrots, cut into julienne strips (2 cups)
- 1 large red bell pepper, coarsely chopped (1½ cups)
- 2 tablespoons chopped fresh or 1 tablespoon dried dill weed
- ½ teaspoon pepper
- 4 medium green onions, chopped (¼ cup)

1 Spray 12-inch skillet with cooking spray; heat over medium heat. Add barley; cook 6 to 8 minutes, stirring frequently until barley begins to brown, then stirring constantly until golden brown. Reduce heat to low; stir in broth. Cover and simmer 40 minutes.

2 Stir in remaining ingredients except green onions. Heat to boiling over high heat; reduce heat to low. Cover and simmer 20 minutes longer or until vegetables are tender. Sprinkle with green onions.

1 Serving Calories 140; Total Fat 1g (Saturated Fat 0g, Trans Fat 0g); Cholesterol 0mg; Sodium 320mg; Total Carbohydrate 26g (Dietary Fiber 6g); Protein 6g **Carbohydrate Choices:** 2

TYPES OF BARLEY

Barley Grits Barley kernels cut into pieces

Hulled Barley Whole grain barley

Hulless Barley A whole grain variety grown to lose its hull during harvesting

Pearl Barley Polished to remove part or all of the outer bran layer along with hull. Not whole grain, but some of the bran may still be intact.

Quick-Cooking Barley Pearl barley that's been partially cooked, then dried

LEARN TO SIMMER

Do you wonder why simmer, when you could just boil food to get it done faster? Simmering is one of the most useful techniques in cooking. Poached eggs, soups, stews and sauces will be a cinch when you understand this method. Simmering is a way to cook ingredients gently and allow flavors to blend and become more concentrated.

Boiling creates lots of bubbles constantly and vigorously breaking on the surface, while simmering makes smaller bubbles, slowly rising and breaking just below the surface. A rolling boil causes ingredients to bump around a lot, often cooking the outside before the inside is done. For foods like cream sauces and custards, boiling at high heat can cause curdling, and in some instances food will burn at the bottom.

At a simmer, the food is jostled just enough to move it around and mix flavors while it cooks more evenly. Simmering also helps keep food from cooking too quickly,

helps prevent curdling and tenderizes food. It can be a little tricky because it requires careful regulation of the temperature—you may need to adjust the heat during the cooking process. Here are two ways to cook at a simmer.

- Heat liquid to boiling over medium-high or high heat; reduce the heat until the liquid reaches a simmer. This method is often used for soups, stews, and vegetables cooked in water, since it requires less attention.

- Gradually increase the heat of liquid until it reaches a simmer. Recipes in this category typically state "do not boil."

Greek Kamut®

Creamy Mushroom-Herb Grits

Wheat Berry Salad

Greek Kamut®

Kamut is a grain with a chewy texture and rich, buttery flavor. It does not absorb liquid like other grains. Soaking Kamut overnight helps it soften during cooking.

PREP 30 Minutes **TOTAL** 9 Hours 30 Minutes •
5 servings (⅔ cup each)

1 cup uncooked Kamut	⅓ cup kalamata olives, pitted, halved
1 tablespoon olive oil	¼ cup chopped Italian (flat-leaf) parsley
1 small onion, chopped (½ cup)	1 teaspoon lemon zest
3 cloves garlic, finely chopped	⅓ cup chopped cucumber
3 cups water	¼ cup quartered grape tomatoes
¾ teaspoon salt	Additional lemon zest and pepper, if desired
½ cup crumbled feta cheese (2 oz)	

1 In medium bowl, soak Kamut in enough water to cover for at least 8 hours at room temperature but no longer than 18 hours. Drain; discard water.

2 In 2-quart saucepan, heat oil over medium heat. Cook onion in oil 2 to 3 minutes, stirring frequently, until tender. Add garlic; cook and stir 30 seconds. Stir in water, salt and Kamut.

3 Heat to boiling; reduce heat. Simmer uncovered, stirring occasionally, about 1 hour or until Kamut is tender. (If Kamut is not tender, add a few tablespoons additional water and cook a few minutes longer.) Pour Kamut into strainer to drain. Cool 5 minutes; return Kamut mixture to pan.

4 Add cheese, olives, parsley and lemon zest to Kamut; stir well. Spoon into serving bowl; top with cucumber, tomatoes, additional lemon zest and pepper. Serve immediately.

1 Serving Calories 210; Total Fat 7g (Saturated Fat 2g, Trans Fat 0g); Cholesterol 10mg; Sodium 560mg; Total Carbohydrate 30g (Dietary Fiber 5g); Protein 7g **Carbohydrate Choices:** 2

Creamy Mushroom-Herb Grits

PREP 20 Minutes **TOTAL** 17 Hours 30 Minutes •
6 servings (1 cup each)

4 cups water	¼ teaspoon coarse ground black pepper
1 cup stone-ground yellow grits	1 package (4 oz) chèvre (goat) cheese, crumbled
1 package (8 oz) sliced mushrooms (2½ cups)	2 tablespoons chopped Italian (flat-leaf) parsley
1 large onion, thinly sliced (1 cup)	2 teaspoons chopped fresh thyme leaves
¼ cup butter, melted	
1 teaspoon salt	

1. In medium bowl or 1-quart food storage container, mix 1 cup of the water and grits; stir. Cover and refrigerate at least 8 hours but no longer than 18 hours.

2. Spray 4½- to 5-quart slow-cooker insert with cooking spray. Place mushrooms, onion, butter, salt and pepper in cooker; mix. Cover; cook on High heat setting 1 hour.

3. Stir grits and soaking liquid; spoon over vegetables in slow cooker, spreading evenly. Slowly pour remaining 3 cups water evenly over grits. Cover; cook on Low heat setting 5 to 6 hours or until grits are very tender.

4. Stir in goat cheese until well mixed. Stir in 1 tablespoon of the parsley and 1 teaspoon of the thyme. Top with remaining herbs. Serve warm.

1 Serving Calories 250; Total Fat 14g (Saturated Fat 9g, Trans Fat 0.5g); Cholesterol 35mg; Sodium 550mg; Total Carbohydrate 24g (Dietary Fiber 2g); Protein 7g **Carbohydrate Choices:** 1½

221

Cranberry-Almond Rye Berry Salad

MAKE AHEAD • VEGETARIAN

Wheat Berry Salad

PREP 15 Minutes TOTAL 2 Hours 45 Minutes • *5 servings*

WHEAT BERRIES
- ¾ cup uncooked wheat berries
- 3 cups water

CREAMY VINAIGRETTE DRESSING
- ⅓ cup vegetable oil
- 2 tablespoons mayonnaise or salad dressing (for homemade mayonnaise, see page 479)
- 2 tablespoons red wine vinegar
- ½ teaspoon salt
- ¼ teaspoon garlic powder
- ⅛ teaspoon pepper

SALAD
- 1 cup chopped fresh broccoli
- 1 cup chopped fresh cauliflower
- 1 cup grape or cherry tomatoes, cut in half
- ½ cup chopped green bell pepper
- 4 medium green onions, sliced (¼ cup)
- ½ cup crumbled feta cheese (2 oz)

1. In 3-quart saucepan, soak wheat berries in water 30 minutes. Heat to boiling over high heat. Reduce heat. Partially cover and simmer 55 to 60 minutes or until wheat berries are tender. Drain; rinse with cold water.

2. In small bowl, mix all dressing ingredients until well blended. In large serving bowl, mix wheat berries, salad ingredients and dressing. Cover; refrigerate at least 1 hour before serving.

1 Serving Calories 330; Total Fat 22g (Saturated Fat 5g, Trans Fat 0g); Cholesterol 15mg; Sodium 460mg; Total Carbohydrate 25g (Dietary Fiber 5g); Protein 7g **Carbohydrate Choices:** 1½

MAKE AHEAD • VEGETARIAN

Cranberry-Almond Rye Berry Salad

Rye berries can often be found in the self-serve bins in large supermarkets, in co-ops or natural-food stores or online. If you love grains, this chewy, flavorful side dish will soon become a new favorite—it sure disappeared fast in our test kitchens.

PREP 10 Minutes TOTAL 2 Hours 40 Minutes • *8 servings* (½ cup each)

RYE BERRIES
- 1 cup uncooked rye berries or wheat berries
- 4 cups water

DRESSING
- ¼ cup vegetable oil
- ¼ cup honey
- 2 tablespoons fresh lemon juice
- ½ teaspoon salt

SALAD
- 3 medium stalks celery, cut diagonally into slices (1 cup)
- ½ cup dried cranberries
- 4 medium green onions, sliced (¼ cup)
- ¼ cup chopped fresh parsley
- ½ cup slivered almonds, toasted (see page 28)

1. In 2-quart saucepan, soak rye berries in water 30 minutes. Heat to boiling; reduce heat. Partially cover and simmer 55 to 60 minutes or until tender. Drain; rinse with cold water.

2. In small bowl, using whisk, beat all dressing ingredients until blended. In medium bowl, toss rye berries, celery, cranberries, onions, parsley and dressing. Cover and refrigerate 1 hour to blend flavors. Stir in almonds just before serving.

1 Serving Calories 250; Total Fat 10g (Saturated Fat 1.5g, Trans Fat 0g); Cholesterol 0mg; Sodium 160mg; Total Carbohydrate 34g (Dietary Fiber 4g); Protein 4g **Carbohydrate Choices:** 2

MAKE AHEAD • VEGETARIAN • VEGAN

Fruit and Farro Salad

PREP 40 Minutes **TOTAL** 4 Hours •
6 servings (about ¾ cup each)

SALAD

2½	cups water
¾	cup uncooked farro
¼	teaspoon salt
3	medium stalks celery, sliced (1 cup)
1	cup halved red or green seedless grapes
¼	cup slivered almonds, toasted (see page 28)
3	medium green onions, sliced
2	medium oranges, peeled, sectioned and cut in half (about 1 cup)

ORANGE-MISO DRESSING

3	tablespoons olive oil
3	tablespoons white miso
2	tablespoons finely chopped organic crystallized ginger
2	tablespoons fresh orange juice
1	tablespoon rice vinegar
1	teaspoon Sriracha sauce
½	teaspoon salt

1 In 2-quart saucepan, mix water, farro and salt; heat to boiling. Reduce heat; cover and simmer 25 to 30 minutes or until farro is tender. Drain; cool in strainer until farro is almost room temperature, about 30 minutes.

2 Meanwhile in small bowl, using whisk, beat all dressing ingredients until well blended.

3 In medium bowl, mix farro, celery, grapes, almonds, onions and oranges; drizzle with dressing. Toss to coat. Cover and refrigerate to blend flavors, at least 3 hours but no longer than 2 days.

1 Serving Calories 250; Total Fat 10g (Saturated Fat 1.5g, Trans Fat 0g); Cholesterol 0mg; Sodium 660mg; Total Carbohydrate 34g (Dietary Fiber 6g); Protein 6g **Carbohydrate Choices:** 2

MAKE AHEAD • VEGETARIAN

Italian Farro Salad

Try this delicious and refreshing salad made with the ancient grain farro! It can be made up to 4 hours ahead of time.

PREP 25 Minutes **TOTAL** 1 Hour • *8 servings (1 cup each)*

FARRO

| 1½ | cups uncooked farro |
| 4 | cups water |

DRESSING

¼	cup red wine vinegar
2	tablespoons olive oil
½	cup chopped fresh basil leaves
½	teaspoon salt
½	teaspoon pepper
1	clove garlic, finely chopped

SALAD

1	can (14 oz) artichoke hearts, drained and quartered
1	pint grape tomatoes, halved lengthwise
¾	cup chopped red onion
½	cup mozzarella pearls or bocconcini (small fresh mozzarella cheese balls)

1 In large saucepan, mix farro ingredients and heat to boiling. Reduce heat; cover and simmer 25 to 30 minutes or until farro is tender. Drain and place in large heatproof bowl. Stirring occasionally, cool to almost room temperature, about 35 minutes.

2 Meanwhile, in small bowl, mix all dressing ingredients.

3 Add all salad ingredients to farro. Add dressing; toss to mix.

1 Serving Calories 230; Total Fat 6g (Saturated Fat 2g, Trans Fat 0g); Cholesterol 10mg; Sodium 320mg; Total Carbohydrate 33g (Dietary Fiber 6g); Protein 9g **Carbohydrate Choices:** 2

Mexican Chicken Pizza with Whole Grain Cornmeal Crust

PREP 20 Minutes **TOTAL** 50 Minutes • *6 servings*

CORNMEAL CRUST

1	to 1½ cups all-purpose flour
¾	cup whole grain yellow cornmeal
1	tablespoon sugar
½	teaspoon salt
1	package regular active dry yeast (2¼ teaspoons)
¾	cup very warm water (120°F to 130°F)
1	tablespoon olive oil
½	cup whole wheat flour
	Additional whole grain yellow cornmeal

TOPPINGS

2	cups shredded Mexican cheese blend (8 oz)
1½	cups shredded cooked chicken
1	can (14.5 oz) fire-roasted or plain diced tomatoes, drained
1	can (4 oz) chopped green chiles, drained
½	cup diced yellow bell pepper
2	medium green onions, sliced (2 tablespoons)
¼	cup chopped fresh cilantro

1 Heat oven to 450°F. In medium bowl, mix 1 cup of the all-purpose flour, ¾ cup cornmeal, sugar, salt and yeast. Stir in warm water and oil. Beat with electric mixer on low speed 30 seconds. Beat on medium speed 1 minute. Beat in whole wheat flour. Beat in just enough of the remaining ½ cup all-purpose flour until dough forms and leaves side of bowl.

2 Place dough on lightly floured surface. Knead dough about 5 minutes until smooth and elastic, sprinkling lightly with some of the remaining flour as needed if dough is sticky. Cover with clean dish towel; let rest 10 minutes.

3 Spray large cookie sheet with cooking spray; sprinkle with additional cornmeal. On cookie sheet, press dough into 14x10-inch rectangle. Prick with fork in several places to prevent the crust from puffing during baking. Bake 8 to 10 minutes or until edges are light golden brown.

4 Sprinkle 1 cup of the cheese over partially baked crust. Top with chicken, tomatoes, chiles, bell pepper and remaining 1 cup cheese. Bake 6 to 8 minutes or until cheese is melted and edges are golden brown. Sprinkle with onions and cilantro. Serve warm.

1 Serving Calories 460; Total Fat 18g (Saturated Fat 8g, Trans Fat 0.5g); Cholesterol 65mg; Sodium 630mg; Total Carbohydrate 48g (Dietary Fiber 4g); Protein 24g **Carbohydrate Choices:** 3

Fruit and Farro Salad

Italian Farro Salad

Mexican Chicken Pizza with
Whole Grain Cornmeal Crust

Rice Basics

Rice is a staple for almost half of the world's population. It is incredibly versatile and can add texture and bulk to dishes. White rice comes in many forms; it's available in long, medium, and short varieties. Converted rice is partially cooked, and takes a little less time to cook. When you are really in a hurry, instant rice is the fastest, cooking in about 5 minutes. Instant brown rice is also a great last-minute choice; it takes about 10 minutes to cook.

How to Cook Rice

Measure rice and water into saucepan. If desired, add ½ teaspoon salt and 1 tablespoon butter. Heat to boiling; reduce heat. Cover and simmer as directed for each type of rice.

Rice Varieties

Arborio Contains a high proportion of starch, which gives risotto its characteristic creamy texture.

Bamboo White rice infused with fresh bamboo juice, which imparts a pale jade color and a fragrance like jasmine tea. A very moist, sticky rice.

Basmati Long grains stay separate (not sticky) when cooked. Aromatic with a subtle flavor.

Brown White rice without the outer brown hull removed, so it's considered a whole grain. It contains more nutrients than white rice.

Jasmine Fragrant white rice with a subtle nutty flavor that differs from basmati. It is moist, soft and slightly sticky when cooked.

Organic Sweet Brown Sweeter and more sticky than regular brown rice, with the benefits of whole grain.

Red Russet-colored whole grain rice. It has a complex, nutty flavor and soft texture that pairs well with assertive flavors like duck, pork and wild mushrooms. Great steamed plain, or used in pilafs and risotto.

Sushi The right proportion of starches allows grains to stick together, to be shaped for sushi.

White Includes three main types, with different characteristics:

> **Long-grain** Grains stay separate and fluffy when cooked; good for side dishes.
>
> **Medium-grain** Plumper and shorter; good for paella or as a substitute for Arborio in risotto.
>
> **Short-grain** The shortest and most moist; good for puddings and molded salads.

Wild Not actually rice, but seeds from a semiaquatic grass, with benefits of whole grain. Somewhat chewy with a nutty flavor, wild rice is significantly higher in protein than regular white rice and is a good source of fiber.

TIMETABLE FOR COOKING RICE

Water or broth can be used for the liquid. Heat to boiling, reduce heat and simmer as directed below. Check product package for additional information.

TYPE OF RICE (1 CUP)	AMOUNT OF WATER IN CUPS	COOKING DIRECTIONS	YIELD IN CUPS
Basmati White	1½	Simmer 15 to 20 minutes.	3
Jasmine	1¾	Simmer 15 to 20 minutes.	3
Long-Grain White	2	Simmer 20 to 25 minutes.	3
Converted (Parboiled) White	2½	Simmer 20 minutes; let stand 5 minutes.	3 to 4
Instant (Precooked) White	1	Heat water to boiling. Stir in rice; cover and remove from heat. Let stand 5 minutes.	2
Long-Grain Brown (Regular and Basmati)	2¾	Simmer 45 to 50 minutes.	4
Instant (Precooked) Brown	1½	Simmer 10 minutes.	2
Wild Rice	2½	Simmer 40 to 50 minutes.	3

Sushi

Colusari Red

Organic Sweet Brown

Bamboo

Basmati

Jasmine

Arborio

White

Wild

Brown

5-INGREDIENT RECIPE

Cheesy Chicken, Broccoli and Rice

Chicken Thighs

Chicken Broth

Broccoli Florets

Cheddar Cheese

Long-Grain White Rice

5-INGREDIENT RECIPE

EASY • MULTI COOKER • CALORIE SMART • GLUTEN FREE

Cheesy Chicken, Broccoli and Rice

PREP 10 Minutes **TOTAL** 35 Minutes • *4 servings*

1½ cups (from 32-oz carton) gluten-free chicken broth (for homemade broth, see page 153)

1 cup uncooked long-grain white rice

½ teaspoon salt

¼ teaspoon pepper

1 package (20 oz) boneless skinless chicken thighs, cut into 1-inch pieces

1 package (10 oz) fresh broccoli florets (about 4 cups)

1 cup shredded sharp cheddar cheese (4 oz)

1 Spray 6-quart multi-cooker insert with cooking spray. Mix broth, rice, salt and pepper in insert. Stir in chicken and broccoli.

2 Secure lid; set pressure valve to SEALING. Select MANUAL/PRESSURE COOK; cook on high pressure 10 minutes. Select CANCEL. Set pressure valve to VENTING to quick-release pressure.

3 Once pressure has released (about 5 minutes), stir in cheese. Broccoli may start to fall apart while stirring.

1 Serving Calories 500; Total Fat 17g (Saturated Fat 7g, Trans Fat 0g); Cholesterol 165mg; Sodium 920mg; Total Carbohydrate 46g (Dietary Fiber 2g); Protein 42g **Carbohydrate Choices:** 3

CALORIE SMART • GLUTEN FREE

Spanish Rice

Rich, smoky fire-roasted tomatoes provide a unique flavor twist in this new version of a classic recipe. Serve it alongside gluten-free tacos or use as one of your taco fillings.

PREP 15 Minutes **TOTAL** 40 Minutes •
6 servings (⅔ cup each)

1 tablespoon olive oil

2 cloves garlic, finely chopped

1 small onion, chopped (½ cup)

½ medium green bell pepper, diced (½ cup)

1 cup uncooked regular long-grain rice

¼ teaspoon coarse (kosher or sea) salt

¼ teaspoon crushed red pepper flakes

1 can (14.5 oz) fire-roasted diced tomatoes, undrained

1¾ cups (from 32-oz carton) reduced-sodium gluten-free chicken broth (for homemade broth, see page 153)

1 In 3-quart saucepan, heat oil over medium heat. Cook garlic, onion and bell pepper in oil about 5 minutes, stirring constantly, until crisp-tender. Stir in rice, salt and pepper flakes.

2 Stir in tomatoes and broth. Heat to boiling. Reduce heat; cover and simmer 20 to 25 minutes or until rice is tender.

1 Serving Calories 170; Total Fat 2.5g (Saturated Fat 0g, Trans Fat 0g); Cholesterol 0mg; Sodium 360mg; Total Carbohydrate 33g (Dietary Fiber 1g); Protein 4g **Carbohydrate Choices:** 2

Spanish Rice

CALORIE SMART • VEGETARIAN

Wild Rice and Spinach Gratin

PREP 35 Minutes **TOTAL** 1 Hour 30 Minutes • *9 servings*

1 cup uncooked wild rice	2 cloves garlic, finely chopped
1 tablespoon butter	3 tablespoons all-purpose flour
⅔ cup plain panko crispy bread crumbs	2 cups fat-free (skim) milk
¾ cup shredded Gruyère cheese (3 oz)	½ teaspoon salt
4 green onions, thinly sliced (¼ cup)	¼ teaspoon pepper
1 medium onion, finely chopped (1 cup)	1 box (9 oz) frozen chopped spinach, thawed, squeezed to drain

1 In 1½-quart saucepan, cover wild rice with 2 inches water. Heat to boiling; reduce heat. Cover and simmer 40 to 50 minutes or until tender; drain and discard any remaining water.

2 Meanwhile, in small microwavable bowl, microwave butter uncovered on High about 25 seconds or until melted. Stir in bread crumbs, ½ cup of the cheese and the green onions. Heat oven to 350°F. Spray 13x9-inch (3-quart) glass baking dish with cooking spray.

3 Spray 1½-quart saucepan with cooking spray; heat over medium-high heat. Add chopped onion; cook and stir about 3 minutes or until almost tender. Add garlic; cook and stir about 30 seconds longer or until fragrant. Stir in flour. Cook and stir 1 minute (mixture will be dry). Using whisk, gradually stir in milk. Heat to boiling; cook and stir about 2 minutes or until thickened. Remove from heat. Stir in remaining ¼ cup cheese, the salt and pepper.

4 In medium bowl, mix hot wild rice, spinach (breaking up with fingers) and milk mixture. Spoon into baking dish. Sprinkle with bread crumb mixture.

5 Bake uncovered 30 to 35 minutes or until topping is golden brown.

1 Serving Calories 200; Total Fat 5g (Saturated Fat 2.5g, Trans Fat 0g); Cholesterol 15mg; Sodium 230mg; Total Carbohydrate 29g (Dietary Fiber 2g); Protein 9g **Carbohydrate Choices:** 2

MAKE AHEAD

Andouille Sausage, Squash and Wild Rice Casserole

Cooking 1 cup of wild rice makes about 4 cups cooked. If you like, use canned wild rice to shave time from making this casserole.

PREP 25 Minutes **TOTAL** 2 Hours 30 Minutes • *4 servings* (1½ cups each)

CASSEROLE

1 cup uncooked wild rice	¾ cup shredded Asiago cheese (3 oz)
2½ cups water	½ cup reduced-fat sour cream
2 cups cubed (½-inch) butternut squash (about 10 oz)	½ teaspoon garlic powder
1 link smoked andouille sausage (from 13.5-oz package), cut in half lengthwise, then crosswise into ¼-inch slices	½ teaspoon dried rubbed sage
	¼ teaspoon pepper
1 can (10¾ oz) condensed 98% fat-free cream of chicken soup with 30% less sodium	**TOPPING**
	2 teaspoons butter
	⅓ cup crushed oval buttery crackers (10 crackers)
	¼ cup shredded Asiago cheese (1 oz)
	1 green onion, chopped

1 In 2-quart saucepan, heat wild rice and water to boiling, stirring occasionally. Reduce heat to low; cover and cook 40 to 50 minutes or until tender. Drain and discard excess water.

2 Heat oven to 350°F. Spray 2-quart round or oval casserole with cooking spray. In large bowl, mix remaining casserole ingredients. Stir in wild rice; spoon into casserole.

3 In small microwavable bowl, microwave butter uncovered on High about 20 seconds or until melted. Stir in crushed crackers; sprinkle over wild rice mixture.

4 Bake uncovered about 1 hour 10 minutes or until squash is just tender when pierced with fork. (If topping browns too quickly, loosely cover casserole with foil.) Remove from oven. Sprinkle with ¼ cup cheese and the green onion. Let stand 10 minutes before serving.

1 Serving Calories 500; Total Fat 22g (Saturated Fat 12g, Trans Fat 0.5g); Cholesterol 70mg; Sodium 790mg; Total Carbohydrate 54g (Dietary Fiber 5g); Protein 20g **Carbohydrate Choices:** 3½

MAKE-AHEAD DIRECTIONS: Cook the wild rice a day ahead; cool, cover and refrigerate. Finish making the casserole the next day. Or prep the casserole the day ahead but do not bake; cover and refrigerate until you're ready to bake. Uncover and add the topping just before baking, adding a few extra minutes baking time, if necessary.

EASY • FAST • GLUTEN FREE

Rice Pilaf

Rice pilaf can be a new dish each time you make it just by using different add-ins. The secret to the flavor is browning the rice in butter until it is golden brown before adding the liquid.

PREP 10 Minutes **TOTAL** 30 Minutes • *4 servings*

- 2 tablespoons butter
- 1 small onion, chopped (½ cup)
- 1 cup uncooked regular long-grain white rice
- 2 cups (from 32-oz carton) gluten-free chicken broth (for homemade broth, see page 153)
- ¼ teaspoon salt

1 In 3-quart saucepan, melt butter over medium heat. Cook onion in butter about 3 minutes, stirring occasionally, until tender.

2 Stir in rice. Cook 5 minutes, stirring frequently, until rice is golden brown. Stir in broth and salt.

3 Heat to boiling, stirring once or twice; reduce heat to low. Cover and simmer 15 minutes (do not lift lid or stir). Remove from heat; let stand covered 5 minutes.

1 Serving Calories 260; Total Fat 7g (Saturated Fat 3g, Trans Fat 0g); Cholesterol 15mg; Sodium 700mg; Total Carbohydrate 42g (Dietary Fiber 0g); Protein 7g **Carbohydrate Choices:** 3

BROWN RICE PILAF: Substitute uncooked regular brown rice for the white rice. Make as directed—except in Step 3, increase simmer time to 45 to 50 minutes.

CASHEW PILAF: Stir ¼ cup coarsely chopped cashews and 2 tablespoons chopped fresh parsley into cooked rice pilaf.

CURRY PILAF: Stir in ½ cup diced dried fruit and raisin mixture, ¼ teaspoon ground allspice, ¼ teaspoon ground turmeric and ¼ teaspoon gluten-free curry powder with broth and salt in Step 2.

MUSHROOM PILAF: Cook 1 cup sliced fresh mushrooms or 1 can (4 oz) mushrooms pieces and stems, drained, with onion in Step 1.

ORANGE AND CRANBERRY PILAF: Add ½ teaspoon orange zest with broth and salt in Step 2. Stir ¼ cup sweetened dried cranberries into cooked rice pilaf.

PINE NUT AND GREEN ONION PILAF: Cook ½ cup sliced green onions (about 8 medium) and ¼ cup pine nuts with rice in Step 2.

PROSCIUTTO, PARMESAN AND PEA PILAF: Cook 3 oz gluten-free prosciutto, chopped, with rice in Step 2. Stir ¼ cup frozen sweet peas, thawed, and ¼ cup shredded Parmesan cheese into cooked rice pilaf.

CHERRY-PISTACHIO RICE PILAF: Substitute uncooked wild and whole grain brown rice blend for the white rice. Make as directed—except in Step 3, increase simmer time to 45 to 50 minutes. Stir ¼ cup each chopped dried cherries and chopped pistachio nuts into cooked rice pilaf.

Wild Rice and Spinach Gratin

Andouille Sausage, Squash and Wild Rice Casserole

Proscuitto, Parmesan and Pea Pilaf

HEIRLOOM

CALORIE SMART • GLUTEN FREE

Classic Risotto

PREP 35 Minutes **TOTAL** 35 Minutes • *4 servings*

2 tablespoons olive oil or vegetable oil

1 tablespoon butter

1 small onion, thinly sliced

1 tablespoon chopped fresh parsley

1 cup uncooked Arborio rice or regular long-grain white rice

½ cup dry white wine or gluten-free chicken broth

3 cups (from 32-oz carton) gluten-free chicken broth, warmed (for homemade broth, see page 153)

½ cup freshly grated Parmesan cheese (2 oz)

¼ teaspoon coarse ground black pepper

1 In 10-inch nonstick skillet or 3-quart saucepan, heat oil and butter over medium-high heat until butter is melted. Add onion and parsley; cook about 5 minutes, stirring frequently, until onion is tender.

2 Stir in rice. Cook, stirring occasionally, until edges of kernels are translucent. Stir in wine. Cook about 3 minutes, stirring constantly, until wine is absorbed.

3 Reduce heat to medium. Stir in 1 cup of the warm broth. Cook uncovered about 5 minutes, stirring frequently, until broth is absorbed. Repeat, adding another 1 cup of broth. Stir in remaining 1 cup broth. Cook about 8 minutes, stirring frequently, until rice is just tender and mixture is creamy. Stir in cheese and pepper.

1 Serving Calories 360; Total Fat 15g (Saturated Fat 5g, Trans Fat 0g); Cholesterol 15mg; Sodium 1020mg; Total Carbohydrate 43g (Dietary Fiber 0g); Protein 13g **Carbohydrate Choices:** 3

RISOTTO WITH PEAS: Just before serving, stir in 1 box (9 oz) frozen baby sweet peas, cooked and drained.

BUTTERNUT SQUASH RISOTTO: Stir in 1 cup mashed cooked butternut squash or sweet potato with the first cup of broth in Step 3. Continue as directed.

RISOTTO WITH SHRIMP: Stir in 8 oz cooked peeled medium shrimp during last 3 to 5 minutes of cooking.

COOKING RISOTTO

Stir rice with the onion and parsley, cooking until the edges of the rice are translucent.

Stir warm broth, 1 cup at a time, into the rice, stirring until each broth addition is absorbed.

Risotto with Peas

Barley and Roasted Butternut Squash Risotto

NEW TWIST

CALORIE SMART

Barley and Roasted Butternut Squash Risotto

This recipe uses pearl barley, which technically isn't a whole grain, but it's much healthier than other refined grains and it keeps the cooking time do-able. The chewy-tender barley paired with the other ingredients was a hit in our test kitchens.

PREP 55 Minutes **TOTAL** 55 Minutes •
4 servings (1½ cups each)

ROASTED BUTTERNUT SQUASH

- 2 cups ready-to-use cubed fresh butternut squash (from 16-oz package)
- 2 tablespoons olive oil
- ¼ teaspoon salt

BROTH MIXTURE

- 2 cups (from 32-oz carton) reduced-sodium chicken or vegetable broth (for homemade broth, see pages 153 or 169)
- 3 cups water
- 2 fresh thyme sprigs

RISOTTO

- 1 small onion, chopped (½ cup)
- 2 cloves garlic, finely chopped
- ½ cup dry white wine or chicken broth
- 2 dried bay leaves
- 1 cup uncooked medium pearl barley
- 4 cups lightly-packed baby arugula (about 3 oz)
- 1 tablespoon grated Parmesan cheese
- ¼ teaspoon coarse ground black pepper

1 Heat oven to 450°F. Spray 15x10x1-inch pan with cooking spray. Place squash in pan. Drizzle with 1 tablespoon of the oil; toss to coat. Sprinkle with salt; toss to coat. Spread in single layer in pan. Bake about 20 minutes, stirring after 10 minutes, until squash is tender when pierced with fork.

2 Meanwhile, in 1½-quart saucepan, heat broth, water and thyme over medium-high heat just to simmering. Keep broth mixture at a simmer while preparing risotto.

3 In 5-quart Dutch oven, heat remaining 1 tablespoon oil over medium-high heat. Cook onion and garlic in oil about 3 minutes or until onion starts to soften. Stir in wine and bay leaves; cook until wine is almost completely evaporated. Stir in barley. Cook and stir 3 to 4 minutes or until barley is toasted.

4 Stir in 1 cup hot broth mixture; reduce temperature to medium. Cook uncovered, stirring frequently, until broth is absorbed; repeat with 3 more cups broth, adding 1 cup at a time. Remove and discard thyme sprigs and stir in remaining 1 cup broth. Cook, stirring frequently, until almost all liquid is absorbed. Remove and discard bay leaves. Remove from heat; fold in roasted squash. Cover and let stand about 5 minutes or until barley is just tender and liquid is absorbed. Fold in arugula. Sprinkle with cheese and pepper. Serve immediately.

1 Serving Calories 310; Total Fat 8g (Saturated Fat 1.5g, Trans Fat 0g); Cholesterol 0mg; Sodium 480mg; Total Carbohydrate 50g (Dietary Fiber 10g); Protein 8g **Carbohydrate Choices:** 3

Vegetables, Beans & Legumes

Vegetable Basics

Nutritious, flavorful and colorful, versatile vegetables shouldn't just play a supporting role on the dinner plate. They are becoming the centerpiece of meals throughout the day. Browse any farmers' market or grocery store and you'll see the array of choices available. Many items in the grocery produce section make it super-convenient to put fresh produce on the table, with prepackaged, prewashed and proportioned options, as well as veggie choices that come in microwavable steam bags. No wonder people are eating more fresh veggies!

Health Benefits

Vegetables provide nutrients vital for general wellness. People who eat more vegetables as part of a healthy diet are likely to have a reduced risk of some chronic diseases, and protection against certain types of cancers.

All vegetables are cholesterol-free; all fresh veggies are also gluten free. Most vegetables are naturally low in fat and calories, which may be helpful if you wish to lower your caloric intake.

Vegetables are important sources of many nutrients, including potassium, dietary fiber, folic acid and vitamins A and C.

Dietary fiber from veggies as part of an overall healthy diet can help reduce blood cholesterol levels and may lower risk of heart disease.

To gain the most nutritional value from vegetables, choose a variety and plan for several servings each day. See the USDA guidelines at https://www.myplate.gov for more information.

Look for ways to work veggies into your dishes throughout the day, to increase the amount you eat. You'll find veggies in recipes such as Apple Pie–Zucchini Breakfast Cookies (page 118) and Sweet Potato Cupcakes with Cinnamon-Marshmallow Frosting (page 598)—and you won't even feel like you're eating vegetables! See the Veggie Forward chapter starting on page 384, as well as the index, for loads of recipes for every eating occasion throughout this book that contain veggies in so many delicious (and sometimes sneaky, for your kiddos) ways.

Buying Vegetables

Look for the freshest vegetables possible. Appearance is usually a great indicator, with good, bright color at the top of the list. Avoid any vegetable that looks withered or has soft spots. Leafy tops and vegetable greens should be crisp and fresh looking. Many vegetables are available grown with either traditional methods or organic methods. Organic vegetables are grown without synthetic fertilizers or pesticides. Look for organic produce at most larger grocery stores and specialty foods stores.

Ugly Produce

Ugly produce—sometimes known as "produce with personality"—doesn't necessarily equal bad produce. Imperfect vegetables (oddly shaped or with visible flaws other than those that show lack of freshness) can be just as good-quality, tasty and healthy as perfect ones. This category of veggies or fruit can be cheaper than their perfect counterparts, and buying them can cut down on food waste and make a dent in the estimated $15+ billion in edible produce that gets thrown out each year.

Storing Vegetables

Storing varies for vegetables, but in general, fresh vegetables should be used within a few days of purchase, as they do start to lose flavor, quality and nutritional value if stored too long. See the listings starting on page 237 for recommendations on storing vegetables.

Types of Vegetables

CHILES

Choose firm chiles; avoid if shriveled or with soft spots. Store fresh chiles in refrigerator drawer; store dried chiles in airtight container in cool, dark place. Transfer canned chiles, once opened, to covered container and refrigerate. Typically, the larger the chile, the milder the flavor.

Anaheim Long; bright green to red. Mild. Available fresh, canned. Frequently stuffed.

Chipotle Dried, smoked jalapeño. Smoky, sweet, with a hint of chocolate flavor. Dried, pickled and canned in adobo sauce.

Fresno Medium-size; yellow-green or red. Similar in flavor to jalapeño. Fresh.

Habanero Small, roundish; color ranges from light green to bright orange. Distinctively hot. Fresh and dried.

Jalapeño Fairly small; dark green or bright red when ripe. Hot to very hot. Fresh, pickled and canned.

Poblano Large. Dark green: flavor ranges from mild to zippy; reddish-brown: sweeter than green. Fresh and canned. **Ancho** is a dried poblano.

Serrano Medium-size. Very hot and green at first, ripening to red or orange. Fresh.

Thai Small; green to red. Very hot. Fresh and dried.

TOMATOES

Choose firm, unblemished tomatoes heavy for their size. Store at room temperature; refrigeration will cause flavor loss. Use within a few days.

Beefsteak Rich flavor, meaty texture. Good fresh or cooked.

Cherry Red or yellow, bite-size; great flavor. Use in salads, as garnish or cooked.

Heirloom Seeds are passed down through generations. Each variety has distinct attributes such as exceptional flavor or unusual coloring.

Plum (Roma) Great flavor; fleshy, making them great for sauces and salads as there is less juice than a round tomato.

- **Grape tomatoes** are baby plum tomatoes, frequently used interchangeably with cherry tomatoes.

ONIONS

The onion group are members of the lily family. Most grow as bulbs; asparagus grow as stalks.

Asparagus Green, white, or purple. Choose firm, bright-colored stalks with tight tips. Refrigerate in plastic bag up to 3 days.

Garlic Head has papery-coated sections called cloves. Choose fresh, firm heads with no green sprouts.

Leeks Long, straight, with white bulbs and pale to dark green leaves which resemble giant green onions. Look for crisp leaves, unblemished bulbs; avoid withered, yellow leaves. Milder than onions. Refrigerate in plastic bag up to 5 days. Cut lengthwise; wash thoroughly to remove dirt trapped between layers.

Onions Choose firm, blemish-free onions with thin skins and no sign of mold or sprouting. Store in well-ventilated area in pantry.

- **Green (Scallions)** Look for bright green, fresh tops and white bulb ends. Refrigerate in plastic bag up to 1 week.

- **Red, Yellow, White** Store whole in cool (45°F to 60°F), dry, dark place with good ventilation up to 2 months. Once cut, cover with plastic wrap and refrigerate up to 4 days.

- **Sweet** Very juicy; mild sugary taste without the "burn" associated with other onions. Varieties include Maui, Vidalia, Walla Walla. Refrigerate whole sweet onions in single layer up to 6 weeks.

Shallots Small; light red, papery skin. More like garlic than onions. Store in cool, dry place up to 2 weeks.

MUSHROOMS

Store unwashed, wrapped in paper towel in a plastic or paper bag. Refrigerate up to 4 days. For fresh, look for firm caps with good color and no soft spots or decay. Wash just before using.

Chanterelle Yellow-orange. Delicate, nutty flavor; chewy texture. Fresh and dried. Cook as side dish, or add to soups, sauces, stir-fries.

Dried (Various) More concentrated flavor than fresh. Store in cool, dry place up to 1 year. Rehydrate as directed on package or in recipe. When rehydrated, 1 oz dried = 4 oz fresh.

Morel Brown-gray; elongated caps with small, wavy indentations. Fresh, dried. Smoky, earthy, nutty flavor. Cook in butter.

Oyster Broad with a fan-shaped cap; white to gray or tan to dark-brown. Mild flavor with anise-like quality. Cook in butter or as a vegan seafood replacement for scallops.

Porcini Brown. Strong, earthy flavor; firm texture. Usually dried. Popular in French and Italian cooking.

Portabella Very large deep brown cap with dense, meaty texture. Grill for sandwiches, panfry, or slice for salads. **Cremini** is a young portabella.

Shiitake Meaty; strong flavored. Choose plump ones with edges that curl under.

White (Button): Mild, earthy flavor. Small to quite large (for stuffing). Choose firm caps with no sign of decay.

American Eggplant

Asian Eggplant

Heirloom Tomatoes

Yellow Pear Tomatoes

Beefsteak Tomatoes

Campari Tomatoes

Cherry Tomatoes

Plum (Roma) Tomatoes

Grape Tomatoes

Tomatillos

Sweet Bell Peppers

CABBAGES

Members of the cabbage family are known as cruciferous vegetables. Store unwashed in a plastic bag in the refrigerator for time given below.

Bok Choy Mild. Crunchy stalks, tender leaves. Use in salads, stir-fries, as side dish. Store up to 1 week.

Broccoli Florets and stalks are edible. Use raw in salads or cook. Florets should be tight and not flowering or yellow. Store up to 5 days.

Broccolini Cross between regular and Chinese broccoli. Mildly sweet, slightly peppery; crunchy. Refrigerate up to 10 days. Use raw in salads, crudités; cook crisp-tender as side dish. See broccoli for storage.

Brussels Sprouts Strong flavor similar to cabbage. Small sprouts will be milder than large ones. Look for compact heads. Cook for side dishes. Store up to 1 week.

Cabbage Light green or red. Choose cabbage with fresh, crisp, firmly packed leaves. Refrigerate, tightly wrapped, up to 1 week. **Savoy** cabbage leaves are crinkled; heads of **Napa** cabbage are football-shaped. Store up to 1 week.

Cauliflower Usually white. Mild. Florets should be firm and compact. Stems usually not eaten. Use raw in salads, or cook. Store up to 5 days.

Collard Greens: Leafy greens used raw in salads, wraps or sandwiches. Cooked in soups or stews or braised, boiled or panfried. Leaves can be difficult to clean, so separate leaves and rinse in a bowl of cold water to remove dirt and sand. Dry on paper towels. Store up to 1 week.

Kale Mild cabbage flavor; many varieties, colors. Store in coldest part of refrigerator up to 3 days; any longer, and flavor gets very strong. Remove and discard tough center stalk. Store up to 2 weeks.

Kohlrabi (Cabbage Turnip) Bulbs have mild broccoli-like flavor. Leaves have flavor similar to collard greens. Peel and use raw; add to soups, stews, stir-fries. Refrigerate leaves up to 4 days, bulbs up to 10 days.

ROOT VEGETABLES

Beets Colors range from red or purple to white to golden. Choose bright-colored, firm beets with smooth skins. Remove greens as soon as possible; store separately. Greens and roots should be cooked. Refrigerate in plastic bag up to 1 week.

Carrots and Parsnips Mild, sweet flavor. Choose those with no signs of decay or cracking. Carrots are available in orange, white, and rainbow colors. Refrigerate in plastic bag up to 2 weeks.

Cassava (Yuca) Bland, starchy; absorbs other flavors. Two types: sweet and bitter, which must be cooked before eating. Choose hard, evenly shaped cassava; avoid blemishes, cracks, mold, stickiness. Store in cool, dark place up to 3 days. Use as side dish or in soups.

Daikon is much larger with a fresh, sweet flavor. Moist, crunchy with white or black skin. Good in salads, stir-fries, kimchi.

Gingerroot Peppery, slightly sweet. Choose firm, smooth roots. Refrigerate fresh, unpeeled in plastic bag up to 3 weeks; freeze up to 6 months.

Jicama Looks like a turnip with rough brown skin. Sweet and crunchy. Peel; use raw in salads; stays crisp when cooked. Store in a plastic bag in the refrigerator up to 2 weeks.

Potatoes Store potatoes away from other vegetables as they can absorb flavors, keeping them in a cool (45°F to 60°F), dry, dark, well-ventilated place for time indicated for the varieties below. Potatoes that turn completely green should not be used, but any small spots can be trimmed off. Cut off and discard any sprouts before cooking.

- **All-Purpose Potatoes** *Purple:* Small with dense texture like russets. Most of the purple fades from skin during cooking. *Yellow (Yellow Finn, Yukon Gold):* Skin and flesh range from buttery yellow to golden. Mild butterlike flavor, which fades slightly during cooking. Store 1 month.

- **Baking/Frying Potatoes** Both *Russet* and *Idaho* have dry, light and fluffy interiors when cooked. Store 2 weeks.

- **Roasting/Boiling** *Fingerling, New* and *Red* have waxy, creamy-moist interiors that hold their shape in salads or when roasted or boiled. Store up to 2 weeks.

Radish Mild to peppery flavor. Great in salads, as snacks. Choose firm radishes with bright colors. Refrigerate any variety in plastic bag up to 1 week.

Sweet Potato Available in varieties ranging from pale skin with light yellow flesh to dark orange or red skin and flesh. Often called yams, but not related to true yams. Choose nicely shaped, smooth, firm sweet potatoes with even-colored skins. Store in cool (45°F to 60°F), dry, dark, well-ventilated place up to 2 weeks.

Turnip, Rutabaga, Celeriac (Celery Root) Good roasted, used in stews, baked dishes. Choose firm vegetables with no signs of decay or bruising. Refrigerate in plastic bag up to 2 weeks.

SQUASH

Two basic types: winter and summer. Winter squash have thick, hard rind and hard seeds. Choose squash heavy for their size, with no soft spots. Store whole in cool (45°F to 60°F), dry, dark place with good ventilation up to 2 months. Refrigerate cut and peeled in plastic wrap up to 5 days. Summer: Refrigerate in plastic bag up to 5 days.

Acorn Green rind; acorn-shaped. Bake halves with filling or remove rind, cut up and roast.

Butternut Large, cylindrical with skin color varying from yellow to tan. Orange-color flesh is sweet. Cook as for acorn squash.

(continued on page 245)

Yellow Onion

Red Onion

Sweet Onions

White Onion

Cipollini Onions

Shallots

Elephant Garlic

Garlic

Asparagus

Pearl Onions

White Asparagus

Green Onions (Scallions)

Leek

Savoy Cabbage

Red Cabbage

Broccoli Rabe (Rapini)

Kohlrabi

Green Cabbage

Brussels Sprouts

Broccoli

Kale

Cauliflower

Broccolini

Baby Bok Choy

Napa (Chinese) Cabbage

Bok Choy

Hubbard Squash

Kabocha Squash

Sweet Dumpling Squash

Buttercup Squash

Sugar Pie Pumpkin

Acorn Squash

Delicata Squash

Turban Squash

Carnival Squash

Zucchini

Pattypan Squash

Yellow Crookneck Squash

Butternut Squash

Spaghetti Squash

Jack Be Little Pumpkin

Yellow Summer Squash

Chayote Squash

Parsnips

Cassava (Yuca)

Rutabaga

Taro

Turnip

Carrots

Gingerroot

Beets

Sweet Potatoes

Celeriac

Radishes

Fennel

Daikon Radish

Shiitake

Dried Porcini

Portabella

Chanterelle

Enoki

White Button

Oyster

Morel

Cremini/ Brown

Mini Cucumbers

Cucumbers

Bi-color Corn

White Corn

Jerusalem Artichoke

Okra

English Cucumbers

Globe Artichokes

Celery

Carnival Cream, orange or green. Flavor similar to sweet potato or butternut squash. Bake or steam.

Delicata Pale yellow skin with green stripes. Sweet, buttered-corn flavor. Seed cavity is small; lots of edible flesh. Bake or steam.

Patty Pan Small, flying saucer–shaped summer squash with thin, smooth to slightly bumpy edible skin. Cut into halves or quarters; cook as for yellow summer squash.

Yellow Summer Thin, edible yellow skins; soft, edible seeds. Choose firm squash with shiny, unblemished skin. Bake, deep-fry, grill or steam.

Zucchini A variety of summer squash; can range from light green to dark green, sometimes mottled or somewhat striped. Creamy, white flesh is light and delicate in flavor. Choose tender small squash for more delicate flavor than very large squash. Cook as for summer squash.

OTHER VEGETABLES

Artichoke, Globe Available fresh, canned (hearts and bottoms) in various sizes: jumbo for stuffing and steaming, baby in marinated salads, panfried, roasted. Refrigerate in plastic bag up to 1 week.

Celery Crisp, mild, stringy stalks. Use raw in salads or cook.

Corn White, yellow, bi-colored. Choose bright green, tight-fitting husks, fresh-looking silk, plump, consistently sized kernels. Wrap unhusked in damp paper towels; refrigerate up to 2 days.

Cucumber Choose firm cucumbers with smooth skins; avoid shriveled or soft spots. May be peeled, or peel left on if tender; often seeded. Use raw in salads

- **English** Available year-round; peak is May to August. Virtually seedless. Refrigerate in plastic bag up to 10 days.

- **Mini** Similar to English, but shorter and thinner.

Fennel Mild licorice flavor. Bulbs and greens (fronds) can be eaten raw or cooked. Choose clean, firm bulbs with fresh-looking greens. Refrigerate in plastic bag up to 1 week.

Okra Available fresh year-round in the South, May to October in rest of United States; canned, frozen. Choose tender, unblemished, bright green pods less than 4 inches long. Refrigerate in plastic bag up to 3 days.

Sunchoke (Jerusalem Artichoke) Available year-round; season peaks October to March. Choose hard sunchokes with smooth skins and no soft spots. Peel and use raw in salads; boil, steam, fry. Refrigerate in a plastic bag up to 1 week.

Eggplant Choose firm, even-colored, unblemished eggplants heavy for their size. Caps and stems should be intact with no mold. Refrigerate in a plastic bag up to 5 days.

- **Asian (Chinese, Japanese, Thai)** Colors include purple, green, white or striated. Longer, smaller than common eggplant.

Sweet Peppers Choose shiny, bright-colored, unblemished peppers with firm sides. Refrigerate in a plastic bag up to 5 days.

- **Banana** Long, yellow; banana-shaped.

- **Bell** Round with 3 or 4 lobes; green, red, yellow, orange, purple, brown.

Tomatillos Pale green, with papery husk. Choose firm, unblemished fruit with tight-fitting husks. Store in a paper bag in refrigerator up to 1 month. Remove husks and wash tomatillos before using.

Fresh Vegetable Cooking Chart

Use the following chart for preparing and cooking vegetables. Wash all vegetables well just before use. Use fresh vegetables within a few days for the best results. Most vegetables are best if cooked until they are crisp-tender. Some vegetables, such as potatoes and squash, are best cooked until tender. For grilling directions, see page 444.

Bake Heat oven to 350°F. Place vegetables in oven as directed. Bake for amount of time in chart.

Boil In saucepan, heat 1 inch water to boiling, unless stated otherwise. Add vegetables. Return to boiling; reduce heat to low. Cook for amount of time in chart; drain.

Microwave See Microwave Cooking (page 33).

Roast See Learn to Roast Vegetables (page 254).

Sauté In skillet, cook in butter or oil over medium-high heat for amount of time in chart.

Steam In saucepan or skillet, place steamer basket in ½-inch water; water should not touch bottom of basket. Place vegetables in basket. Cover tightly and heat to boiling; reduce heat to low. Steam for amount of time in chart.

VEGETABLE (AMOUNT FOR 4 SERVINGS)	PREPARATION	CONVENTIONAL DIRECTIONS (UNTIL CRISP-TENDER)	MICROWAVE DIRECTIONS (UNTIL CRISP-TENDER)
Artichokes, Globe (4 medium)	Remove discolored leaves; trim stem even with base. Cut 1 inch off top. Snip tips off leaves. To prevent discoloration, dip in cold water mixed with small amount of lemon juice.	**Steam:** 20 to 30 minutes, adding 2 tablespoons lemon juice to water, until leaves pull out easily and bottom is tender when pierced with knife.	Place 1 or 2 artichokes in dish; add ¼ cup water. Microwave 5 to 7 minutes, until leaves pull out easily.
Asparagus (1½ lb)	Break off ends as far down as stalks snap easily. For spears, tie stalks in bundles with string, or hold together with band of foil. Or cut stalks and tips into 1-inch pieces.	**Boil:** 6 to 8 minutes, uncovered **Steam:** 6 to 8 minutes **Roast whole:** 10 to 15 minutes (do not tie in bundle)	Do not tie in bundle. Place in dish. Microwave 4 to 6 minutes.
Beans: Green, Purple Wax, Yellow Wax (1 lb)	Remove ends. Leave beans whole or cut into 1-inch pieces.	**Boil:** 6 to 8 minutes, uncovered **Steam:** 10 to 12 minutes **Roast whole:** 10 to 15 minutes	Place in dish. Microwave 8 to 10 minutes.
Beans, Lima (3 lb unshelled; 3 cups shelled)	To shell beans, remove thin outer edge of pod with sharp knife or scissors. Slip out beans.	**Boil:** 15 to 20 minutes, covered	Place in dish; add ½ cup water. Microwave on High 4 to 5 minutes or until boiling. Microwave on Medium-Low (30%) 20 to 25 minutes.
Beets (5 medium)	Leave whole with root end attached.	**Boil:** Add water to cover and 1 tablespoon vinegar. Boil covered 20 to 30 minutes. Peel if desired. **Steam:** 45 to 50 minutes. Peel if desired **Roast unpeeled:** 35 to 40 minutes	Place in dish. Microwave 12 to 16 minutes.
Broccoli (1½ lb)	Trim off large leaves; remove tough ends of stems. Cut as desired.	**Boil:** 4 to 6 minutes, uncovered **Steam:** 10 to 11 minutes **Roast:** 20 to 25 minutes	Place in dish. Microwave 6 to 8 minutes.
Brussels Sprouts (1 lb)	Remove discolored leaves; cut off stem end. Cut large sprouts in half.	**Boil:** 8 to 12 minutes, uncovered **Steam:** 8 to 12 minutes **Roast:** 20 to 25 minutes	Place in dish. Microwave 5 to 6 minutes.
Carrots (6 or 7 medium; 1 lb baby-cut)	Peel if desired; cut off ends. Leave carrots whole or cut as desired.	**Boil:** 7 to 10 minutes, covered **Steam:** 8 to 10 minutes **Roast:** 35 to 40 minutes	Place in dish. Microwave 5 to 9 minutes.

VEGETABLE (AMOUNT FOR 4 SERVINGS)	PREPARATION	CONVENTIONAL DIRECTIONS (UNTIL CRISP-TENDER)	MICROWAVE DIRECTIONS (UNTIL CRISP-TENDER)
Cauliflower (1 small head)	Remove outer leaves and stalk; cut off any discoloration. Leave whole or separate into florets.	**Boil:** 8 to 12 minutes, uncovered **Steam:** 8 to 12 minutes **Roast:** 20 to 25 minutes	Place in dish. Microwave 8 to 10 minutes.
Corn on the Cob (4 ears)	Husk ears and remove silk just before cooking.	**Boil:** Add water to cover and 1 tablespoon sugar. Boil 5 to 7 minutes, uncovered **Steam:** 5 to 7 minutes	Wrap ears in plastic wrap or place in dish. Microwave 3 to 4 minutes.
Eggplant (1 medium)	Cut off ends. Peel can be left on, or peel if desired. Cut as desired.	**Boil:** 5 to 8 minutes, covered **Steam:** 5 to 7 minutes **Sauté:** With 2 tablespoons butter, 5 to 10 minutes	Place in dish. Microwave 7 to 9 minutes.
Fennel (3 to 4 medium bulbs)	Remove feathery tops and tough or discolored outer ribs; trim base. Cut bulbs into quarters.	**Boil:** 8 to 11 minutes, covered **Steam:** 12 to 15 minutes **Roast:** 35 to 40 minutes	Place in dish. Microwave 4 to 5 minutes.
Greens: Beet, Chicory, Collards, Escarole, Kale, Mustard, Spinach, Swiss Chard, Turnip (1 lb)	Remove root ends and imperfect leaves.	**Steam:** 5 to 8 minutes **Sauté:** See Use It Up: Spinach (page 107) and Use It Up: Salad Greens (page 400).	*Beet, Chicory, Collards, Escarole, Turnip:* Place in dish. Microwave 8 to 10 minutes. *Kale, Mustard, Spinach, Swiss Chard:* Place in dish. Microwave 4 to 6 minutes.
Kohlrabi (4 medium)	Cut off root ends and tops. Cut as desired.	**Boil:** 15 to 20 minutes, covered **Steam:** 8 to 12 minutes	Place in dish. Microwave 3 to 5 minutes or until tender.
Leeks (6 medium)	Remove green tops to within 2 inches of white part. Peel outside layer of bulbs. Cut as desired.	**Boil:** 10 to 12 minutes, covered **Steam:** 10 to 12 minutes **Roast:** 10 to 15 minutes	Place in dish. Microwave 4 to 5 minutes.
Mushrooms (1 lb)	Trim off stem ends; do not peel. Leave whole or cut as desired.	**Sauté:** With 1 tablespoon butter, 4 to 6 minutes, stirring frequently **Roast:** 5 to 10 minutes	Place in dish; add 1 tablespoon butter. Microwave 3 to 4 minutes.
Okra (1 lb)	Remove stem ends. Leave whole or cut into slices.	**Boil:** 8 to 10 minutes, uncovered **Steam:** 6 to 8 minutes	Place in dish; add ¼ cup water. Microwave 5 to 6 minutes.
Onions: White, Yellow, Red (8 to 10 small)	Peel in cold water to prevent eyes from watering. Cut as desired; to sauté, cut into ¼-inch slices.	**Steam:** 15 to 20 minutes **Sauté:** With 2 tablespoons butter, 6 to 9 minutes **Roast:** 25 to 30 minutes	Place in dish; add ¼ cup water. Microwave 7 to 9 minutes.
Parsnips (6 to 8 medium)	Peel; cut off ends. Leave whole or cut as desired.	**Boil:** 9 to 15 minutes, covered **Steam:** 9 to 15 minutes **Roast:** 25 to 30 minutes	Place in dish. Microwave 5 to 6 minutes.
Peas, Snow or Sugar Snap (1 lb)	Snip off stem ends and strings.	**Boil:** 2 to 3 minutes, uncovered **Steam:** 3 to 5 minutes	Place in dish. Microwave 6 to 7 minutes.
Peas, Sweet (2 lb unshelled; 2 cups shelled)	Shell just before cooking.	**Boil:** 5 to 10 minutes, uncovered **Steam:** 8 to 10 minutes	Place in dish. Microwave 4 to 6 minutes.
Peppers, Bell (2 medium)	Remove stems, seeds and membranes. Leave whole to stuff and bake or cut as desired for other cooking methods.	**Steam:** 4 to 6 minutes **Sauté:** With 1 tablespoon butter, 3 to 5 minutes **Roast:** 20 to 25 minutes	Place in dish. Microwave 3 to 4 minutes.

VEGETABLE (AMOUNT FOR 4 SERVINGS)	PREPARATION	CONVENTIONAL DIRECTIONS (UNTIL CRISP-TENDER)	MICROWAVE DIRECTIONS (UNTIL CRISP-TENDER)
Potatoes: **Red, White, Yukon Gold** (6 medium); **Russet** (4 medium); **Fingerling or Small Red Potatoes** (10 to 12)	Leave whole or peel and cut as desired.	**Boil:** Add water to cover. Boil 15 to 20 minutes or until tender, uncovered. **Steam:** 15 to 20 minutes or until tender. **Bake:** 1 hour or until tender, uncovered **Roast:** 35 to 40 minutes or until tender	Pierce whole potatoes to allow steam to escape. Place on paper towel. 1 or 2 potatoes: Microwave 4 to 6 minutes or until tender, uncovered. Cover; let stand 5 minutes. 3 or 4 potatoes: Microwave 8 to 12 minutes or until tender, uncovered. Cover; let stand 5 minutes.
Rutabagas (2 medium)	Peel; cut as desired.	**Boil:** 20 to 25 minutes or until tender, covered **Steam:** 20 to 25 minutes or until tender **Roast:** 35 to 40 minutes or until tender	Place in dish; add ¼ cup water. Microwave 13 to 15 minutes or until tender.
Squash, Summer: Chayote, Yellow (Crookneck, Straightneck), Pattypan, Zucchini (1½ lb)	Remove stem and blossom ends, but do not peel. Cut as desired.	**Boil:** 5 to 10 minutes, uncovered **Steam:** 5 to 7 minutes **Sauté:** With 1 tablespoon olive oil, 5 to 10 minutes Roast: 15 to 20 minutes	Place in dish. Microwave 4 to 6 minutes.
Squash, Winter: Acorn, Buttercup, Butternut, Pumpkin, Spaghetti (2 lb)	Cook in halves or pieces with seeds removed.	**Boil:** Peeled and cut up: 10 to 15 minutes or until tender, covered **Steam:** 10 to 15 minutes or until tender **Bake:** Place squash halves cut side up in baking dish; bake 40 minutes or until tender, covered. **Roast bite-size pieces:** 20 to 25 minutes or until tender	*Whole squash except Spaghetti:* Pierce with knife in several places to allow steam to escape. Place on paper towel. Microwave uncovered 5 minutes or until squash feels warm to the touch. Cut in half; remove seeds. Arrange halves in dish. Microwave 5 to 8 minutes or until tender. *Whole Spaghetti Squash:* Pierce with knife in several places to allow steam to escape. Place on paper towel. Microwave uncovered 18 to 23 minutes or until tender. Cut in half; remove seeds and fibers.
Sunchokes (Jerusalem Artichokes) (1 lb)	Leave whole or cut as desired. To prevent discoloration, toss with cold water mixed with small amount of lemon juice.	**Boil:** 7 to 9 minutes, covered **Steam:** 15 to 20 minutes	Place in dish. Microwave 5 to 7 minutes.
Sweet Potatoes (4 medium)	Leave whole or peel and cut as desired.	**Boil:** Add water to cover. Boil 10 to 15 minutes or until tender, uncovered. **Steam:** 15 to 20 minutes or until tender **Bake:** 1 hour or until tender, uncovered **Roast:** 40 to 45 minutes or until tender	Pierce whole sweet potatoes to allow steam to escape. Place on paper towel. Microwave 9 to 11 minutes or until tender, uncovered. Cover; let stand 5 minutes.
Turnips (4 medium)	Cut off tops. Leave whole or cut as desired.	**Boil:** 20 to 25 minutes or until tender, covered **Steam:** 15 to 20 minutes or until tender **Roast:** 35 to 40 minutes or until tender	Place in dish. Microwave 6 to 8 minutes or until tender.

EASY • GLUTEN FREE • VEGETARIAN

Artichokes with Rosemary Butter

To eat a fresh artichoke, remove a leaf, dip it in the butter mixture and draw it between your teeth to scrape off the meaty part. Continue removing leaves until you see the center cone of light green leaves. Cut the leaves from the cone, then remove and discard the fuzzy choke to reveal the meaty heart in the center.

PREP 10 Minutes **TOTAL** 45 Minutes • *4 servings*

4 medium artichokes	1 teaspoon chopped fresh or ¼ teaspoon dried rosemary leaves, crushed
½ cup butter	
	1 teaspoon lemon juice

1 Remove any discolored leaves and the small leaves at base of artichokes. Trim stems even with base of artichokes. Cutting straight across, slice 1 inch off tops; discard tops. Cut off points of remaining leaves with scissors. Rinse artichokes with cold water.

2 Place steamer basket in ½ inch water in 4-quart Dutch oven (water should not touch bottom of basket). Place artichokes in basket. Cover tightly. Heat to boiling; reduce heat. Steam 20 to 25 minutes or until bottoms are tender when pierced with knife.

3 In small microwavable bowl, melt butter. Stir in rosemary and lemon juice. Divide butter among 4 small serving bowls. Pluck out artichoke leaves one at a time. Dip base of leaf into rosemary butter.

1 Serving Calories 280; Total Fat 23g (Saturated Fat 15g, Trans Fat 1g); Cholesterol 60mg; Sodium 300mg; Total Carbohydrate 14g (Dietary Fiber 12g); Protein 4g **Carbohydrate Choices:** 1

FAST • CALORIE SMART • GLUTEN FREE • VEGETARIAN • VEGAN

Roasted Lemony Asparagus

This easy recipe is a perfect side dish to pair with any grilled or roast dinner.

PREP 20 Minutes **TOTAL** 20 Minutes • *8 servings*

2 lb fresh asparagus spears	½ teaspoon salt
	½ teaspoon pepper
2 tablespoons olive oil	1 lemon, thinly sliced

1 Set oven control to broil. Snap off and discard tough ends of asparagus.

2 In large bowl, toss asparagus with oil, salt, pepper and lemon slices. Arrange asparagus in single layer in 18x13-inch half-sheet pan.

3 Broil with tops 3 inches from heat 5 to 10 minutes or until browned.

1 Serving Calories 50; Total Fat 3.5g (Saturated Fat 0.5g, Trans Fat 0g); Cholesterol 0mg; Sodium 150mg; Total Carbohydrate 5g (Dietary Fiber 3g); Protein 3g **Carbohydrate Choices:** 0

ROASTED GARLIC-LEMONY ASPARAGUS: Add thinly sliced garlic cloves with the asparagus to the olive oil mixture.

VEGETABLES, BEANS & LEGUMES

PREPARING ARTICHOKES

Remove small leaves at the base and any that are discolored.

Trim stem even with base of artichoke. Cut 1 inch from top of artichoke; discard top.

Using scissors, cut points from remaining leaves; rinse artichokes with cold water.

REMOVING TOUGH ENDS FROM ASPARAGUS

Remove tough ends of asparagus by snapping asparagus where they break easily.

Green Beans with
Glazed Shallots in Lemon-Dill Butter

Blue Cheese Pecan Green Beans

FAST • CALORIE SMART • GLUTEN FREE •
VEGETARIAN

Green Beans with Glazed Shallots in Lemon-Dill Butter

PREP 15 Minutes **TOTAL** 15 Minutes • *6 servings*

1 lb fresh green beans, trimmed	½ teaspoon sugar
2 tablespoons butter	1 teaspoon lemon juice
2 shallots, finely chopped	1 tablespoon chopped fresh dill weed
	¼ teaspoon salt

1 In 3-quart saucepan, place green beans in 1 inch water. Heat to boiling; reduce heat. Cook uncovered 6 to 8 minutes or until crisp-tender. Drain; return to saucepan.

2 Meanwhile, in 10-inch skillet, melt butter over medium heat. Cook shallots in butter 2 to 3 minutes, stirring occasionally, or until crisp-tender. Stir in sugar. Cook 2 to 3 minutes longer, stirring occasionally, or until shallots are glazed and brown. Stir in lemon juice, dill weed and salt.

3 Add shallot mixture to green beans; toss to coat.

1 Serving Calories 70; Total Fat 4g (Saturated Fat 2.5g, Trans Fat 0g); Cholesterol 10mg; Sodium 135mg; Total Carbohydrate 6g (Dietary Fiber 2g); Protein 1g **Carbohydrate Choices:** ½

EASY • CALORIE SMART • GLUTEN FREE •
VEGETARIAN

Blue Cheese Pecan Green Beans

The pungent blue cheese tang plays well with the flavor of the green beans. The longer this cheese is aged, the stronger the flavor will be. Look for it in pieces that you can crumble, or buy it already crumbled. You could also use Gorgonzola or Stilton cheese instead of regular blue cheese.

PREP 15 Minutes **TOTAL** 35 Minutes •
6 servings (½ cup each)

12 oz fresh green beans, trimmed	2 tablespoons butter*
½ cup pecan halves	3 oz blue cheese, crumbled (¾ cup)

1 In 2-quart saucepan, place beans in 1 inch water. Heat to boiling; reduce heat. Simmer uncovered 8 to 10 minutes or until beans are crisp-tender; drain. Place in serving bowl; cover to keep warm.

2 Meanwhile, in 1-quart saucepan, cook pecans over medium heat 5 to 7 minutes, stirring frequently until nuts begin to brown, then stirring constantly until nuts are golden brown and toasted. Place in small bowl; reserve.

3 In same 1-quart saucepan, heat butter over low heat about 6 minutes, stirring constantly, or until butter is golden brown. (Once the butter begins to brown, it browns very quickly and can burn, so use low heat and watch carefully.) Immediately remove from heat. Pour over beans; toss to coat. Sprinkle with cheese and reserved pecans.

1 Serving Calories 170; Total Fat 14g (Saturated Fat 6g, Trans Fat 0g); Cholesterol 20mg; Sodium 230mg; Total Carbohydrate 6g (Dietary Fiber 2g); Protein 5g **Carbohydrate Choices:** ½

* Do not use any margarine product for this recipe, as it won't brown correctly.

Roasted Beets

Beets are usually available year-round. If given a choice, pick small, young beets for the best flavor.

PREP 10 Minutes **TOTAL** 1 Hour 20 Minutes • *6 servings*

2 lb small beets (1½ to 2 inch)	2 tablespoons olive oil
½ teaspoon salt	2 tablespoons chopped fresh basil leaves
¼ teaspoon coarse ground black pepper	1 tablespoon balsamic vinegar

1 Heat oven to 425°F.

2 Cut off all but 2 inches of beet tops. Wash beets; leave whole with root ends attached. Place beets in ungreased 13x9-inch pan. Sprinkle with salt and pepper. Drizzle with oil.

PREPARING BEETS

Before cooking, cut off all but 2 inches of stems. Wash beets, leave whole with root ends attached.

After cooking, peel beets with paring knife under cold water, removing stems, skins and roots.

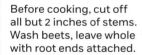
Roasted Beets

3 Roast uncovered about 40 minutes or until beets are tender. Let beets cool until easy to handle, about 30 minutes. Cut off root ends and tops; peel beets. Cut into ½-inch slices.

4 In medium bowl, toss beets, basil and vinegar. Serve warm or at room temperature.

1 Serving Calories 90; Total Fat 4.5g (Saturated Fat 0.5g, Trans Fat 0g); Cholesterol 0mg; Sodium 280mg; Total Carbohydrate 10g (Dietary Fiber 3g); Protein 1g **Carbohydrate Choices:** ½

251

Cheesy Ranch Broccoli Bake

Fresh broccoli meets a cheesy ranch sauce in this colorful side dish that'll have everyone going for seconds. If you like, you can use a 4-oz jar of diced pimientos, drained, in place of the red bell pepper. Add the pimientos to the cream cheese mixture along with the cheddar cheese.

PREP 20 Minutes **TOTAL** 50 Minutes • *10 servings*

10 cups small fresh broccoli florets (from two 12-oz bags)	1 package (1 oz) ranch dressing and seasoning mix
1 medium red bell pepper, chopped	2 cups shredded cheddar cheese (8 oz)
¼ cup water	15 buttery crackers, coarsely broken
1 container (8 oz) cream cheese spread, softened	1 tablespoon butter, melted
½ cup milk	

1 Heat oven to 350°F. Spray 12x8-inch (2-quart) baking dish with cooking spray.

2 In large (at least 4-quart) microwavable bowl, mix broccoli, bell pepper and water; cover with plastic wrap. Microwave on High 4 to 5 minutes, stirring after 2 minutes, until broccoli is bright green in color and hot; drain. Return broccoli and bell pepper to bowl.

3 In medium microwavable bowl, place cream cheese spread and milk. Microwave uncovered on High 1 minute. Use whisk to blend (mixture will have a few small lumps).

4 Stir dressing mix into cream cheese mixture; mix well. Add cheddar cheese; mix well. Pour cheese mixture over broccoli and bell pepper; toss to coat. Spread in baking dish.

5 In small bowl, toss crackers with melted butter. Sprinkle over broccoli.

6 Bake 25 to 30 minutes or until hot and bubbly.

1 Serving Calories 250; Total Fat 18g (Saturated Fat 10g, Trans Fat 0.5g); Cholesterol 50mg; Sodium 500mg; Total Carbohydrate 12g (Dietary Fiber 2g); Protein 10g **Carbohydrate Choices:** 1

EASY • AIR FRYER • CALORIE SMART • GLUTEN FREE

Roasted Balsamic-Bacon Brussels Sprouts

If you're dealing with oversized Brussels sprouts, cut them in quarters and check for doneness at the minimum cooking time.

PREP 15 Minutes **TOTAL** 45 Minutes •
4 servings (½ cup each)

- 1 lb medium Brussels sprouts, trimmed, cut in half (about 4 cups)
- 2 tablespoons olive oil
- ¼ teaspoon salt
- ¼ teaspoon pepper
- 1 tablespoon balsamic vinegar
- 2 tablespoons grated Parmesan cheese
- 2 slices gluten-free bacon, crisply cooked, chopped

1 Heat oven to 400°F. Spray 15x10x1-inch pan with cooking spray.

2 Spread Brussels sprouts in single layer in pan. Drizzle with oil, sprinkle with salt and pepper; toss to coat.

3 Roast uncovered 25 to 30 minutes, stirring twice, or until Brussels sprouts are tender and browned on edges.

4 Remove Brussels sprouts to medium bowl; toss with vinegar and cheese. Top with bacon.

1 Serving Calories 150; Total Fat 9g (Saturated Fat 2g, Trans Fat 0g); Cholesterol 5mg; Sodium 280mg; Total Carbohydrate 10g (Dietary Fiber 4g); Protein 6g **Carbohydrate Choices:** ½

AIR FRYER DIRECTIONS: Reduce oil to 1 tablespoon. Microwave Brussels sprouts in microwavable bowl on High 7 minutes, covered loosely with damp paper towel. Drain and pat dry. Toss with oil, salt and pepper. Spray basket of air fryer with cooking spray. Place sprouts in even layer in basket. Cook at 375°F for 12 to 14 minutes, shaking basket after 8 minutes or until sprouts are tender and browned. Continue as directed in Step 4.

FAST • CALORIE SMART • GLUTEN FREE • VEGETARIAN

Broccoli with Sweet Red Pepper and Garlic

PREP 20 Minutes **TOTAL** 20 Minutes •
4 servings (½ cup each)

- 1 tablespoon olive or vegetable oil
- 2 cloves garlic, finely chopped
- 2 cups broccoli florets
- 1 large red bell pepper, coarsely chopped (1 cup)
- 1 small onion, coarsely chopped (½ cup)
- 3 tablespoons water
- ¼ teaspoon salt
- 2 tablespoons shredded Parmesan cheese

1 In 12-inch nonstick skillet, heat oil over medium-high heat. Add garlic. Cook about 1 minute or until fragrant. Immediately add broccoli, bell pepper, onion and water. Cook 4 to 6 minutes, stirring constantly, or until broccoli is crisp-tender and onions begin to brown. Stir in salt.

2 Place in serving dish; top with cheese.

1 Serving Calories 80; Total Fat 4.5g (Saturated Fat 1g, Trans Fat 0g); Cholesterol 0mg; Sodium 210mg; Total Carbohydrate 8g (Dietary Fiber 2g); Protein 3g **Carbohydrate Choices:** ½

FAST • CALORIE SMART • GLUTEN FREE

Cranberry-Pistachio Brussels Sprouts

PREP 25 Minutes **TOTAL** 25 Minutes • *6 servings*

- 2 slices thick-sliced gluten-free bacon
- 1 lb Brussels sprouts, trimmed, cut in half (about 4 cups)
- ¼ cup gluten-free chicken broth (for homemade broth, see page 153)
- ⅓ cup sweetened dried cranberries
- ¼ cup salted roasted pistachio nuts
- 1 tablespoon honey
- ¼ teaspoon cracked black pepper

Roasted Balsamic-Bacon Brussels Sprouts

Cranberry-Pistachio Brussels Sprouts

Cumin-Chili Roasted Carrots

Spicy Cabbage Stir-Fry

1 In 10-inch skillet, cook bacon over medium-high heat until crisp. Drain on paper towels. Crumble bacon; set aside. Reserve 1 tablespoon drippings in skillet.

2 Cook Brussels sprouts in bacon drippings over medium heat 3 to 4 minutes, stirring frequently, until they just begin to brown. Add broth; reduce heat to medium-low. Cover and cook 5 to 6 minutes longer or until broth has evaporated and Brussels sprouts are tender.

3 Add bacon and remaining ingredients; toss to coat.

1 Serving Calories 110; Total Fat 4.5g (Saturated Fat 1g, Trans Fat 0g); Cholesterol 0mg; Sodium 170mg; Total Carbohydrate 14g (Dietary Fiber 2g); Protein 4g **Carbohydrate Choices:** 1

EASY • CALORIE SMART • GLUTEN FREE • VEGETARIAN

Cumin-Chili Roasted Carrots

PREP 10 Minutes **TOTAL** 35 Minutes • **6 servings**

- 1 bag (2 lb) fresh carrots, cut lengthwise into ½-inch-wide strips and crosswise in half
- 2 tablespoons vegetable oil
- 1 tablespoon honey or real maple syrup
- 2 teaspoons ground cumin
- 2 teaspoons chili powder
- 1 teaspoon salt

1 Heat oven to 425°F. Line 15x10x1-inch pan with foil; spray foil with cooking spray.

2 In large bowl, place carrots. Drizzle with oil and honey; toss to coat. Sprinkle with cumin, chili powder and salt; toss to coat. Spread carrots in single layer in pan.

3 Roast 20 to 25 minutes, turning once, or until tender.

1 Serving Calories 130; Total Fat 5g (Saturated Fat 1g, Trans Fat 0g); Cholesterol 0mg; Sodium 510mg; Total Carbohydrate 18g (Dietary Fiber 4g); Protein 1g **Carbohydrate Choices:** 1

CUMIN-CHILI ROASTED CARROTS AND PARSNIPS: Substitute 1 lb peeled parsnips for 1 lb carrots.

FAST • CALORIE SMART • GLUTEN FREE • VEGETARIAN • VEGAN

Spicy Cabbage Stir-Fry

PREP 25 Minutes **TOTAL** 25 Minutes •
4 servings (about ⅔ cup each)

SAUCE
- 1 tablespoon gluten-free soy sauce
- 2 teaspoons rice vinegar
- 1 teaspoon toasted sesame oil
- ½ teaspoon packed organic brown sugar
- ¼ teaspoon mustard seed

VEGETABLES
- 1 tablespoon vegetable oil
- 1 medium carrot, cut into julienne pieces (1½ x ¼ x ¼ inch)
- 3 cups shredded green cabbage
- 1½ cups shredded red cabbage (from 10-oz package)
- 2 teaspoons finely chopped gingerroot
- 1 clove garlic, finely chopped
- ½ medium red jalapeño chile, seeded, thinly sliced
- 2 teaspoons chopped fresh cilantro

1 In small bowl, mix sauce ingredients.

2 In wok or 12-inch nonstick skillet, heat oil over medium-high heat. Add carrots; cook and stir 1 minute. Add cabbages, gingerroot, garlic and jalapeño. Cook 4 to 5 minutes, stirring frequently, or until cabbage is just tender.

3 Stir in sauce. Reduce heat to medium-low. Simmer uncovered 1 to 2 minutes, stirring occasionally to coat vegetables in sauce. Sprinkle with cilantro.

1 Serving Calories 80; Total Fat 5g (Saturated Fat 0.5g, Trans Fat 0g); Cholesterol 0mg; Sodium 250mg; Total Carbohydrate 8g (Dietary Fiber 2g); Protein 1g **Carbohydrate Choices:** ½

LEARN TO ROAST VEGETABLES

Roasting is a healthful, easy way to cook vegetables. Roasting is a dry-heat cooking technique that is easy to master. Dry heat simply means that no liquid is added so it is only the heat of the oven that cooks the food, rather than moisture added to the food. Foods that are roasted are cooked uncovered. Baking is also a dry-heat cooking method; the primary difference between roasting and baking is based on the food being cooked and the temperature used to cook it. To roast vegetables, the oven temperature is higher than for baking so that veggies get a browned, slightly caramelized exterior with a moist interior.

Many vegetables benefit from roasting, as the caramelization that takes place brings out the natural sweetness of the vegetables. If just enough oil is used to coat the veggies, it will help the browning process without adding a lot of extra fat and calories. Start with just a teaspoon or two, adding more if needed to coat. For a slightly crispy exterior with a crisp-tender or tender interior results, roast at a high enough temperature and don't crowd the pan. We can't say it enough—this is a very tasty way to enjoy veggies! Use the tips and chart below as a guide when roasting veggies.

Tips for Roasting Vegetables

- Roast vegetables at 425°F unless recipe specifies a different temperature.

- Cut vegetables into similar size pieces so that they cook evenly.

- Use a large enough pan so that the vegetables can be in a single layer without crowding.

- For easy cleanup, line the pan with heavy-duty foil or cooking parchment paper before adding the vegetables.

- Place the vegetables on pan; drizzle with a little olive or vegetable oil; toss to coat. Or if adding additional vegetables to ones already roasting, toss the ones you will be adding with a little oil in a bowl before adding them to the pan.

- Spread vegetables in a single layer. Do not crowd the pan, or the vegetables will steam and turn soft without browned edges or slightly crisp exteriors instead of roast.

- Roast vegetables for the minimum time, turning the vegetables halfway through cooking. Roast until desired doneness.

- Individual recipes will provide specific directions. But in general, cook until crisp-tender. Winter squash, potatoes and sweet potatoes should be cooked until tender.

TIMETABLE FOR ROASTING VEGETABLES

ROASTING TIME UNTIL CRISP-TENDER	VEGETABLE PIECES (BITE-SIZE PIECES, FLORETS OR SLICES) *vegetable can be left whole
10 to 15 Minutes	Asparagus*
	Beans* (green, purple wax, yellow wax)
	Leeks
15 to 20 Minutes	Squash, Summer (chayote, yellow crookneck and straightneck, pattypan, zucchini)
20 to 25 Minutes	Bell Peppers
	Broccoli
	Brussels Sprouts (cut in half)
	Cauliflower
	Mushrooms*
	Parsnips
Roast squash until tender	Squash, Winter (acorn, buttercup, butternut, pumpkin)
25 to 30 Minutes	Onions
30 to 35 Minutes, until tender	Potatoes
	Sweet Potatoes
35 to 40 Minutes	Beets, Carrots, Fennel

CUTTING BUTTERNUT SQUASH

Cut 1 inch from top and bottom of squash; peel off skin with vegetable peeler down to darker orange flesh.

Cut squash in half lengthwise. Use spoon to scoop out and discard seeds and membranes. Cut into pieces.

Roasting Vegetables That Cook in Different Amounts of Time

Vegetables cook at different rates, depending on their makeup and water content. If you're not following a specific recipe, check the chart for roasting times of the vegetables you want to roast together. If they require different cooking times, start roasting the ones that take the longest and add the faster-cooking vegetables later.

Here's an example for roasting carrots and zucchini.

VEGETABLE		ROASTING TIME
Carrots		35 minutes (minimum time on chart)
Zucchini	–	15 minutes (minimum time on chart)
Time to roast carrots before adding zucchini:	=	**20 minutes**
Roast zucchini with carrots	+	15 minutes (minimum time on chart for zucchini)
Add up to 5 minutes longer for desired doneness	+	Until crisp-tender
Total time vegetables roast		**Carrots:** 35 to 40 minutes (20 + 15 = 35 minutes + up to 5 minutes longer)
		Zucchini: 15 to 20 minutes (15 minutes + up to 5 minutes longer)

CALORIE SMART • GLUTEN FREE • VEGETARIAN • VEGAN

Roasted Vegetables

Pick packaged baby-cut carrots that are all about the same size so they cook evenly and are done at the same time. If you have regular carrots on hand, simply cut them into about 2x½-inch sticks.

PREP 15 Minutes **TOTAL** 40 Minutes • *10 servings*

- 3 tablespoons olive or vegetable oil
- ½ teaspoon salt
- ⅛ teaspoon pepper
- 1 clove garlic, finely chopped
- 1 cup ready-to-eat baby-cut carrots
- 6 small red potatoes, cut in quarters
- 2 small onions, cut into ½-inch wedges
- 1 medium red bell pepper, cut into 1-inch pieces
- 1 medium zucchini, cut in half lengthwise, then cut crosswise into 1-inch slices
- 1 cup grape or cherry tomatoes

1 Heat oven to 450°F.

2 In small bowl, stir oil, salt, pepper and garlic until well mixed. In ungreased 15x10x1-inch pan, toss carrots, potatoes, onions, bell pepper and zucchini with oil mixture until coated.

3 Roast uncovered 20 minutes, stirring once. Stir in tomatoes. Roast about 5 minutes longer or until vegetables are tender and starting to brown.

1 Serving Calories 140; Total Fat 4.5g (Saturated Fat 0.5g, Trans Fat 0g); Cholesterol 0mg; Sodium 140mg; Total Carbohydrate 22g (Dietary Fiber 3g); Protein 2g **Carbohydrate Choices:** 1½

Roasted Vegetables

Roasted Vegetables with Turmeric-Tahini Sauce

Creamy Cauliflower Mash

CALORIE SMART • GLUTEN FREE • VEGETARIAN

Roasted Vegetables with Turmeric-Tahini Sauce

PREP 20 Minutes TOTAL 50 Minutes • *8 servings*

VEGETABLES

- 1 lb fresh carrots, cut lengthwise in half (or in quarters, if large)
- 1 medium yellow squash, cut lengthwise into eighths
- 1 medium zucchini, cut lengthwise into sixths
- 1 tablespoon olive oil
- ½ teaspoon salt
- 1 large red bell pepper, cut into ¼-inch strips

TURMERIC-TAHINI SAUCE

- 2 tablespoons tahini
- 2 tablespoons water
- 1 tablespoon honey
- 1 tablespoon fresh lemon juice
- ¼ teaspoon ground turmeric
- ⅛ teaspoon salt

TOPPINGS

- 2 tablespoons chopped roasted, salted cashews
- 2 tablespoons chopped fresh cilantro

1 Heat oven to 425°F. Spray 18x13-inch half-sheet pan with cooking spray.

2 In pan, place carrots, squash and zucchini. Drizzle with olive oil and sprinkle with ½ teaspoon salt; turn to coat. Roast uncovered 20 minutes. Add bell pepper to pan; turn to coat. Roast 17 to 20 minutes longer or until vegetables are tender and edges are browned.

3 Meanwhile, in small bowl, mix sauce ingredients until blended.

4 Transfer vegetables to serving platter. Drizzle with sauce; top with cashews and cilantro.

1 Serving Calories 100; Total Fat 5g (Saturated Fat 1g, Trans Fat 0g); Cholesterol 0mg; Sodium 240mg; Total Carbohydrate 12g (Dietary Fiber 3g); Protein 2g **Carbohydrate Choices:** 1

CALORIE SMART • GLUTEN FREE • VEGETARIAN

Creamy Cauliflower Mash

Once you try this deliciously creamy mashed cauliflower, you'll wonder why you ever bothered with potatoes. To save time, measure the cauliflower from 3 (10-oz) bags of cauliflower florets instead of cutting up heads of cauliflower. Either way, expect a few lumps, as cauliflower won't get quite as smooth as mashed potatoes.

PREP 40 Minutes TOTAL 40 Minutes • *4 servings* (1 cup each)

- ¼ cup butter
- 7 to 8 cups fresh cauliflower florets (from 2 medium heads)
- ½ teaspoon salt
- ¼ teaspoon pepper
- 1 cup water
- ⅔ cup plain Greek yogurt
- Chopped parsley, if desired
- Coarsely ground pepper, if desired

1 In 5-quart Dutch oven, heat butter over medium-high heat. Add cauliflower, salt and ¼ teaspoon pepper. Cook 8 to 10 minutes, stirring occasionally, or until tops of florets are soft.

2 Add water. Heat to boiling; reduce heat. Simmer uncovered, 10 to 12 minutes longer, stirring occasionally, or until cauliflower stems are very tender. Remove from heat.

3 Stir in yogurt with potato masher or electric mixer on medium speed 1 to 2 minutes or until creamy and smooth. Sprinkle with parsley and coarsely ground pepper.

1 Serving Calories 190; Total Fat 13g (Saturated Fat 8g, Trans Fat 0g); Cholesterol 35mg; Sodium 450mg; Total Carbohydrate 10g (Dietary Fiber 4g); Protein 8g **Carbohydrate Choices:** ½

USE IT UP
VEGETABLE TOPS

Fresh greens from the tops of vegetables typically get chopped off and tossed away—but rather than throwing them out, put them to use! They can be used as garnishes or added to recipes to increase flavor, color and nutritional value in what you serve, while cutting down on food waste.

BEET TOPS FOR PIZZA TOPPING Roasted Root Veggie Pizza with Beer Bread Crust (page 208) uses both the beets and beet tops. Use beet tops on other pizzas instead of spinach or arugula or simply add to your favorite topping combos. Chop ½ to 1 cup of beet greens and sprinkle over hot baked pizza. Press lightly into toppings.

SALSA VERDE WITH CARROT TOPS Prepare Salsa Verde (page 479), substituting carrot tops for half or all of the parsley. Garnish with chopped bell pepper and carrot tops.

CITRUS–WHOLE FENNEL SALAD Mix bite-size pieces of romaine, avocado, fennel bulb, peeled clementine segments (or drained canned mandarin oranges), red onion, thin slices of fennel stem (sliced on the diagonal) and chopped fennel fronds with Lemon Vinaigrette Dressing (page 135). Garnish with shaved Parmesan cheese and toasted walnuts.

WILTED RADISH LEAVES Cook 1 clove garlic, finely chopped, in 1 tablespoon olive oil in large skillet over medium heat 1 minute. Add 1 bunch radish leaves, washed and coarsely chopped, 1 to 2 tablespoons water and ¼ teaspoon crushed red pepper flakes, if desired. Cover and cook on low heat until wilted. Drizzle with 1 teaspoon fresh lemon juice; season with salt and pepper. Toss with sliced radishes, if desired.

CELERY LEAF LOVE Chop up the leaves of celery and add when making your favorite potato or egg salad, soups or stews. Or use instead of parsley for a garnish.

258

Roasted Cauliflower
with Asiago Cheese

Roasted Cauliflower with Asiago Cheese

Sprinkle with additional red pepper flakes for a pop of color and heat.

PREP 10 Minutes **TOTAL** 40 Minutes • *6 servings*

2 tablespoons olive oil	1 medium head cauliflower (2 lb), separated into florets
½ teaspoon orange zest	
½ teaspoon salt	1 cup shredded Asiago cheese (4 oz)
¼ teaspoon pepper	

1 Heat oven to 450°F.

2 In large bowl, mix oil, orange zest, salt and pepper. Add cauliflower; toss until evenly coated. Spread in ungreased 15x10x1-inch pan.

3 Roast uncovered 20 to 25 minutes; stir. Sprinkle with cheese. Roast 1 to 2 minutes longer or until cheese is melted.

1 Serving Calories 150; Total Fat 12g (Saturated Fat 5g, Trans Fat 0g); Cholesterol 20mg; Sodium 430mg; Total Carbohydrate 5g (Dietary Fiber 1g); Protein 6g **Carbohydrate Choices:** ½

Lemon-Ricotta Cauliflower Casserole

Lemon-Ricotta Cauliflower Casserole

Sprinkle with additional red pepper flakes, for a pop of color and heat.

PREP 20 Minutes **TOTAL** 45 Minutes •
4 servings (1 cup each)

1 cup whole milk ricotta cheese (from 16-oz container)	1 clove garlic, finely chopped
⅓ cup plus 2 tablespoons grated Parmesan cheese	1 package (12 oz) riced fresh cauliflower (3 cups)
½ cup milk	4 cups lightly packed fresh baby spinach leaves (from 10-oz container), coarsely chopped
2 teaspoons lemon zest	
2 tablespoons fresh lemon juice	
½ teaspoon salt	⅓ cup plain panko crispy bread crumbs
⅛ teaspoon crushed red pepper flakes	1 tablespoon butter, melted
	¼ teaspoon pepper

1 Heat oven to 350°F.

2 In medium bowl, mix ricotta cheese, ⅓ cup of the Parmesan cheese and the milk until well blended. Stir in 1½ teaspoons of the lemon zest, the lemon juice, salt, pepper flakes and garlic; set aside.

Grilled Mexican-Style
Street Corn

3 In large microwavable bowl, place cauliflower. Cover with plastic wrap. Microwave on High 3 minutes or until tender. Stir in spinach. Stir in ricotta mixture.

4 Spoon cauliflower mixture into 1½-quart casserole. In small bowl, mix bread crumbs, remaining 2 tablespoons Parmesan cheese, the butter, remaining ½ teaspoon lemon zest and the pepper until well mixed; sprinkle over ricotta mixture.

5 Bake uncovered 20 to 25 minutes or until mixture is heated through and bread crumbs are golden brown.

1 Serving Calories 260; Total Fat 14g (Saturated Fat 8g, Trans Fat 0g); Cholesterol 50mg; Sodium 620mg; Total Carbohydrate 19g (Dietary Fiber 2g); Protein 14g **Carbohydrate Choices:** 1

FAST

Grilled Mexican-Style Street Corn

Known as elote in Mexico, this street food typically is grilled with the husks pulled down for a handle and served with flavorful toppings such as chili powder, lime juice, mayonnaise or sour cream. Our husked-corn version can be done on the grill or in the microwave.

PREP 20 Minutes **TOTAL** 20 Minutes • *4 servings*

4 ears fresh sweet corn, husks and silk removed	1 teaspoon taco seasoning mix (from 1-oz package; for homemade seasoning, see page 454)
¼ cup mayonnaise (for homemade mayonnaise, see page 479)	¼ cup crumbled Mexican cheese (such as Cotija)
	Chopped fresh cilantro, if desired

1 Heat gas or charcoal grill to medium-high for direct heat (page 421). Carefully brush vegetable oil on grill rack.

2 Place corn on grill; cover grill. Cook 8 to 10 minutes, turning occasionally, until lightly browned on all sides.

3 Brush corn with mayonnaise; sprinkle with taco seasoning, cheese and cilantro. Serve hot.

1 Serving Calories 240; Total Fat 14g (Saturated Fat 3g, Trans Fat 0g); Cholesterol 10mg; Sodium 250mg; Total Carbohydrate 23g (Dietary Fiber 2g); Protein 6g **Carbohydrate Choices:** 1½

MICROWAVE DIRECTIONS: Prepare as directed—except do not grill corn. Place corn on microwavable dish; cover with plastic wrap. Microwave on High 5 to 7 minutes or until tender. Proceed with Step 3.

CALORIE SMART • GLUTEN FREE

Spicy Collard Greens with Bacon

Collard greens are a form of cabbage, but instead of forming a head, they stay in a loose-leaf form. They're an excellent source of vitamins A and C as well as calcium and iron.

PREP 25 Minutes **TOTAL** 1 Hour 30 Minutes • *4 servings*

2 lb collard greens, ribs and stems removed, leaves coarsely chopped (about 8 cups)	1 jalapeño chile, seeded, finely chopped
	½ teaspoon dried thyme leaves
6 slices gluten-free bacon, chopped	½ teaspoon seasoned salt
1 small onion, chopped (½ cup)	½ teaspoon pepper

1 In 4-quart Dutch oven or saucepan, heat 6 cups water to boiling. Add collard greens; return to boiling. Cook 30 minutes.

2 Meanwhile, in 12-inch skillet, cook bacon over medium-high heat, stirring occasionally, until crisp. Drain on paper towels; set aside. Reserve 1 tablespoon drippings in skillet.

3 Heat bacon drippings over medium heat. Add remaining ingredients; cook about 5 minutes, stirring frequently, or until onion is tender. Drain collard greens. Stir greens and bacon into skillet. Reduce heat to low; cover. Cook about 15 minutes, stirring occasionally, until greens are very tender.

1 Serving Calories 160; Total Fat 6g (Saturated Fat 1.5g, Trans Fat 0g); Cholesterol 10mg; Sodium 410mg; Total Carbohydrate 16g (Dietary Fiber 9g); Protein 11g **Carbohydrate Choices:** 1

COLLARD GREENS WITH BLACK-EYED PEAS: During last 5 minutes of cooking, stir in 1 can (15 to 16 oz) black-eyed peas, rinsed, drained.

PREPARING COLLARD GREENS

Remove thick ribs from centers of collard leaves by holding leaf with hand and stripping away rib with other hand.

Layer several leaves in a stack; roll up and cut into ½- to 1-inch-thick slices. Coarsely chop slices.

260

BETTY CROCKER COOKBOOK

HEIRLOOM

EASY • FAST • CALORIE SMART • GLUTEN FREE • VEGETARIAN

Mashed Potatoes

PREP 10 Minutes **TOTAL** 30 Minutes • *6 servings*

- 6 medium round red or white potatoes or Yukon Gold potatoes, or 4 russet potatoes (2 lb), peeled if desired, cut into 2-inch pieces
- ⅓ to ½ cup milk, warmed
- ¼ cup butter, softened
- ½ teaspoon salt
  Dash pepper
  Chopped fresh parsley or chives, if desired

1 In 2½-quart saucepan, place potatoes and enough water just to cover potatoes. Heat to boiling; reduce heat. Cover; simmer 20 to 30 minutes or until potatoes are tender when pierced with fork. Drain; return potatoes to pan. Shake pan with potatoes over low heat to dry potatoes (this will help the mashed potatoes be fluffier).

2 Mash potatoes in pan with potato masher until no lumps remain. Add milk in small amounts, stirring after each addition (amount of milk needed to make potatoes smooth and fluffy depends on type of potatoes used).

3 Add butter, salt and pepper. Stir vigorously until potatoes are light and fluffy and desired consistency. If desired, dot with small pieces of butter or sprinkle with chopped fresh parsley.

1 Serving Calories 200; Total Fat 8g (Saturated Fat 5g, Trans Fat 0g); Cholesterol 20mg; Sodium 270mg; Total Carbohydrate 29g (Dietary Fiber 2g); Protein 3g **Carbohydrate Choices:** 2

LIGHTER DIRECTIONS: For 4 grams of fat and 145 calories per serving, use fat-free (skim) milk and reduce butter to 2 tablespoons.

BUTTERMILK MASHED POTATOES: Substitute buttermilk for the milk.

CHEESY MASHED POTATOES: Stir in 1 cup (4 oz) shredded cheese (Asiago, cheddar, Monterey Jack or Parmesan) or crumbled cheese (blue or Gorgonzola) with the butter, salt and pepper in Step 3.

CHIPOTLE-CHEDDAR MASHED POTATOES: Stir in 1 cup (4 oz) shredded cheddar cheese and 1 or 2 chipotle chiles in adobo sauce (from 7-oz can), finely chopped, with the butter, salt and pepper in Step 3.

GARLIC MASHED POTATOES: Cook 6 peeled garlic cloves with the potatoes. Mash garlic with potatoes.

HERBED MASHED POTATOES: Stir in 2 tablespoons chopped fresh chives and ½ teaspoon each chopped fresh thyme leaves and rosemary leaves with the butter, salt and pepper in Step 3.

HORSERADISH MASHED POTATOES: Add 2 tablespoons prepared mild or hot horseradish with the butter, salt and pepper in Step 3.

Mashed Potatoes

Cheesy Herb and Bacon Mashed Potatoes

NEW TWIST

Cheesy Herb and Bacon Mashed Potatoes

PREP 15 Minutes TOTAL 55 Minutes • *6 servings*

- 6 medium round red or white potatoes or Yukon Gold potatoes, or 4 medium russet potatoes (2 lb), peeled if desired, cut into 2-inch pieces
- 1 package (5.2 oz) soft garlic-and-herbs cheese
- ¼ teaspoon salt
- ¼ teaspoon pepper
- ¼ to ⅓ cup half-and-half, warmed
- 1½ cups shredded cheddar cheese (6 oz)
- 2 tablespoons chopped fresh parsley
- 6 slices bacon, crisply cooked, crumbled (½ cup)

1 In 2½-quart saucepan, place potatoes and enough water just to cover potatoes. Heat to boiling; reduce heat. Cover; simmer 15 to 20 minutes or until potatoes are tender when pierced with fork. Drain; return potatoes to pan. Shake pan with potatoes over low heat to dry potatoes (this will help mashed potatoes be fluffier).

2 Meanwhile, heat oven to 350°F. Spray 1½-quart casserole with cooking spray.

3 Mash potatoes in pan with potato masher until no lumps remain. Stir in garlic-and-herbs cheese, salt and pepper. Add half-and-half in small amounts, stirring after each addition (amount of half-and half needed to make potatoes smooth and fluffy depends on type of potatoes used). Stir in ¾ cup of the cheddar cheese and 1 tablespoon of the parsley. Spread in casserole. Sprinkle with remaining cheddar cheese and bacon.

4 Bake uncovered 15 to 20 minutes or until potatoes are hot and cheese is melted on top. Sprinkle with remaining parsley.

1 Serving Calories 420; Total Fat 22g (Saturated Fat 12g, Trans Fat 0.5g); Cholesterol 65mg; Sodium 550mg; Total Carbohydrate 40gc (Dietary Fiber 4g); Protein 15g **Carbohydrate Choices:** 2½

KEEPING HERBS FRESH

Keep leafy herbs such as parsley or cilantro fresh by storing the bunch in a glass of water in the refrigerator, covered loosely with a plastic bag.

Cheesy Au Gratin Potatoes

Rosemary-Garlic Hasselback Potatoes

VEGETARIAN

Cheesy Au Gratin Potatoes

Not only does using unpeeled potatoes save you time, but you get more nutrition as well. Much of a potato's fiber and vitamins are found in or directly under the peel.

PREP 15 Minutes **TOTAL** 1 Hour 35 Minutes •
6 servings (about ½ cup each)

6	medium round red or white potatoes or Yukon Gold potatoes, or 4 medium russet potatoes (2 lb)	1	teaspoon salt
¼	cup butter	¼	teaspoon pepper
1	small onion, chopped (½ cup)	2	cups milk
1	tablespoon all-purpose flour	2	cups shredded sharp cheddar cheese (8 oz)
		¼	cup dry bread crumbs (any flavor)
			Paprika

1 Heat oven to 375°F.

2 Scrub potatoes but do not peel. Cut into ⅛-inch slices, to measure about 4 cups.

3 In 2-quart saucepan, heat butter over medium heat until melted. Cook onion in butter about 2 minutes, stirring occasionally, or until tender. Stir in flour, salt and pepper. Cook, stirring constantly, or until bubbly; remove from heat.

4 Gradually stir in milk and heat to boiling, stirring constantly; boil and stir 1 minute. Stir in 1½ cups of the cheese until melted. Spread potatoes in ungreased 1½-quart casserole. Pour cheese sauce over potatoes.

5 Bake uncovered 1 hour. In small bowl, mix remaining cheese and the bread crumbs; sprinkle over potatoes. Sprinkle with paprika. Bake uncovered 15 to 20 minutes longer or until top is brown and bubbly.

1 Serving Calories 450; Total Fat 22g (Saturated Fat 13g, Trans Fat 1g); Cholesterol 65mg; Sodium 780mg; Total Carbohydrate 46g (Dietary Fiber 5g); Protein 15g **Carbohydrate Choices:** 3

GLUTEN FREE • VEGETARIAN

Rosemary-Garlic Hasselback Potatoes

For best results, try to use potatoes that are of equal size and shape. When stacking the potato slices, it is not necessary to make the stacks precise. The slight unevenness of the stacks is what gives this potato dish its impressive presentation. If you have a mandoline, use it to slice the potatoes quickly.

PREP 35 Minutes **TOTAL** 2 Hours • **9 servings**

3	tablespoons butter, melted	3½	lb Yukon Gold potatoes, peeled and cut crosswise into ⅛-inch slices (about 8 medium potatoes)
2	tablespoons olive oil		
1	tablespoon chopped fresh rosemary leaves	⅓	cup grated Parmesan cheese
1½	teaspoons kosher or sea salt		Fresh rosemary sprigs, if desired
½	teaspoon pepper		
4	cloves garlic, finely chopped		

1 Heat oven to 375°F.

2 In large bowl, stir together butter, oil, chopped rosemary, salt, pepper and garlic. Add potato slices to butter mixture; toss to thoroughly coat slices.

3 Pick up potatoes by the handful, and place slices one on top of another, forming a small stack. Place potato stack on its side in ungreased 8-inch square (2-quart) baking dish. Continue making small stacks with remaining potatoes and arranging them side-by-side in dish to form 3 rows of tightly packed stacked slices. Scrape bowl for any remaining butter mixture and spread mixture over potatoes.

4 Bake 1 hour. Sprinkle with Parmesan cheese. Bake 15 to 20 minutes longer or until potatoes are tender and golden brown on top. Let stand 10 minutes before serving. Garnish with fresh rosemary sprigs.

1 Serving Calories 220; Total Fat 8g (Saturated Fat 3.5g, Trans Fat 0g); Cholesterol 15mg; Sodium 490mg; Total Carbohydrate 31g (Dietary Fiber 2g); Protein 4g **Carbohydrate Choices:** 2

GLUTEN FREE • VEGETARIAN

Sheet-Pan Hash Browns

Our sheet pan version of hash browns makes it easy to have evenly browned and crispy potatoes, without all the babysitting of the pan that's required when they're made stove-top.

PREP 10 Minutes **TOTAL** 40 Minutes • *6 servings*

- 1 package (20 oz) refrigerated shredded hash browns
- ½ cup pepper Jack cheese, shredded (2 oz; from 8-oz block)
- ½ cup shredded cheddar cheese (2 oz)
- 1 tablespoon chopped fresh chives
- 1 tablespoon vegetable oil
- ¼ teaspoon seasoned salt
- ⅛ teaspoon pepper
- 2 tablespoons ranch dressing
  Additional chopped fresh chives, if desired

1 Heat oven to 425°F. Line cookie sheet with cooking parchment paper. Spray with cooking spray.

2 In large bowl, stir together all ingredients except dressing and additional chives. Spread mixture on cookie sheet in 10-inch square.

3 Bake 30 to 35 minutes or until potatoes are golden brown. Drizzle hash browns with ranch dressing; sprinkle with additional chives. Serve immediately.

1 Serving Calories 260; Total Fat 11g (Saturated Fat 4.5g, Trans Fat 0g); Cholesterol 20mg; Sodium 230mg; Total Carbohydrate 33g (Dietary Fiber 3g); Protein 7g **Carbohydrate Choices:** 2

EXTRA-CHEESY HASH BROWNS: Sprinkle the baked hash browns with an additional ¼ cup shredded cheddar cheese; bake 1 to 2 minutes longer or until cheese is melted before topping with the ranch dressing and chives.

AIR FRYER • GLUTEN FREE • VEGETARIAN

Loaded Taco Fries

Shaking is essential to crispy fries. When food touches in the air fryer basket, it cannot crisp fully, so it must be shaken or turned often.

PREP 35 Minutes **TOTAL** 35 Minutes • *8 servings*

SEASONED SOUR CREAM
- ⅓ cup sour cream
- 1 teaspoon original gluten-free taco seasoning mix (from 1-oz package; for homemade seasoning, see page 454)

TACO FRIES
- 2 tablespoons vegetable oil
- 1 tablespoon original gluten-free taco seasoning mix (from 1-oz package; for homemade seasoning, see page 454)
- 16 oz (4 cups) frozen French-fried potatoes (from 32-oz bag)
- 1 cup shredded Colby–Monterey Jack cheese blend (4 oz)
- ½ medium avocado, pitted, peeled and diced (½ cup)
- ¼ cup diced tomato
- 2 green onions, sliced (2 tablespoons)
- 2 tablespoons chopped fresh cilantro

1 In small bowl, mix seasoned sour cream ingredients. Cover and refrigerate until ready to serve.

2 In large bowl, mix oil and 1 tablespoon taco seasoning mix. Add potatoes; toss to coat. Pour mixture into air fryer basket; set to 400°F. Cook 22 to 26 minutes or until crispy, shaking basket every 5 minutes.

3 Transfer potatoes to microwavable serving plate. Top with cheese. Microwave uncovered on High 30 to 90 seconds or until cheese melts. Top with avocado, tomato, green onions and cilantro. Serve with seasoned sour cream.

1 Serving Calories 220; Total Fat 14g (Saturated Fat 5g, Trans Fat 0g); Cholesterol 20mg; Sodium 170mg; Total Carbohydrate 17g (Dietary Fiber 2g); Protein 5g **Carbohydrate Choices:** 1

Sheet-Pan Hash Browns

Loaded Taco Fries

VEGETARIAN

Sheet-Pan Roasted Veggies with Gnocchi

PREP 25 Minutes **TOTAL** 45 Minutes • *8 servings*

- 3 tablespoons butter, melted
- 1 tablespoon chopped fresh or 1 teaspoon dried rosemary leaves
- ¾ teaspoon salt
- ¼ teaspoon pepper
- ½ butternut squash (3½ lb), peeled, seeded, cut into ½-inch pieces (4 cups)
- ½ small red onion, sliced into thin wedges (1 cup)
- ⅓ cup unblanched whole almonds, coarsely chopped
- 1 package (16 oz) refrigerated potato gnocchi
- 2 cups fresh broccoli florets (from 12-oz bag)
- ¼ cup finely shredded Parmesan or Asiago cheese (1 oz)

1 Heat oven to 450°F. Line 18x13-inch half-sheet pan with cooking parchment paper or spray with cooking spray.

2 In small bowl, mix butter, rosemary, salt and pepper. In large bowl, toss squash, onion, almonds and half of the butter mixture until evenly coated. Spread in pan in single layer. Bake 10 minutes or until squash is almost tender; stir. Push squash mixture onto one half of pan.

3 In same large bowl, place gnocchi and broccoli. Stir in remaining butter mixture. Spread in a single layer in other half of pan.

4 Bake 10 minutes longer, stirring once, or until squash is tender. Sprinkle with cheese.

1 Serving Calories 210; Total Fat 12g (Saturated Fat 6g, Trans Fat 0g); Cholesterol 25mg; Sodium 340mg; Total Carbohydrate 19g (Dietary Fiber 4g); Protein 5g **Carbohydrate Choices:** 1

Sheet-Pan Roasted Veggies with Gnocchi

CALORIE SMART • GLUTEN FREE • VEGETARIAN

Creamy Mashed Sweet Potatoes with Maple Syrup

If the marshmallows do not melt completely, cover the bowl with plastic wrap and microwave on High 1 minute. Stir and serve.

PREP 5 Minutes **TOTAL** 55 Minutes • *10 servings*

- 2 to 2½ lb dark-orange sweet potatoes
- 1 cup miniature vegan marshmallows
- ¼ cup pure maple syrup
- ¼ cup heavy whipping cream
- 2 tablespoons butter, softened
- 3 tablespoons chopped pecans, toasted, if desired

1 Peel and cut sweet potatoes in large pieces. In 5-quart saucepan, place sweet potatoes and just enough water to cover them. Heat to boiling; reduce heat. Cover; simmer 25 to 30 minutes, or until tender when pierced with a fork. Drain. Place in large bowl. Cover with foil; let stand 5 minutes.

2 Mash sweet potatoes with potato masher until no lumps remain. Immediately stir in marshmallows, maple syrup, cream and butter until marshmallows are melted. Sprinkle with pecans. Serve immediately.

1 Serving Calories 160; Total Fat 4.5g (Saturated Fat 3g, Trans Fat 0g); Cholesterol 15mg; Sodium 75mg; Total Carbohydrate 28g (Dietary Fiber 2g); Protein 1g **Carbohydrate Choices:** 2

EASY • CALORIE SMART • GLUTEN FREE • VEGETARIAN

Roasted Sweet Potato Wedges

PREP 15 Minutes **TOTAL** 45 Minutes • *6 servings*

- 3 small sweet potatoes (1 lb), peeled, cut into 2-inch wedges
- 1 tablespoon olive oil
- 2 teaspoons chopped fresh thyme leaves
- ½ teaspoon kosher (coarse) salt
- ¼ teaspoon freshly ground black pepper
- ⅛ teaspoon ground red pepper (cayenne)
- ¼ cup shredded Parmesan cheese (1 oz)

1 Heat oven to 450°F.

2 Place sweet potato wedges on ungreased cookie sheet. Drizzle with oil. Sprinkle with thyme, salt, black pepper and red pepper; toss to coat.

3 Roast 30 minutes, turning after 20 minutes, until lightly browned and tender. Sprinkle with cheese.

1 Serving Calories 100; Total Fat 3g (Saturated Fat 1g, Trans Fat 0g); Cholesterol 0mg; Sodium 260mg; Total Carbohydrate 15g (Dietary Fiber 2g); Protein 2g **Carbohydrate Choices:** 1

Peas and Corn with Thyme

This easy way to prepare familiar veggies will surely be a favorite with kids and adults alike. If you have regular bacon on hand, you can use that instead of the precooked bacon: Cook 3 slices about 3 to 4 minutes per side, or until crisp. Drain thoroughly on paper towels; chop.

PREP 10 Minutes **TOTAL** 10 Minutes •
5 servings (½ cup each)

2 slices packaged precooked gluten-free bacon	1 box (9 oz) frozen baby sweet peas
1 box (9 oz) frozen corn	¼ teaspoon dried thyme leaves

1 Heat bacon as directed on package; chop. Set aside.

2 Cook corn and peas as directed on boxes; place in heatproof serving bowl. Stir in thyme; sprinkle with bacon.

1 Serving Calories 90; Total Fat 2.5g (Saturated Fat 1g, Trans Fat 0g); Cholesterol 0mg; Sodium 250mg; Total Carbohydrate 13g (Dietary Fiber 3g); Protein 4g **Carbohydrate Choices:** 1

EASY • CALORIE SMART • GLUTEN FREE • VEGETARIAN

Maple-Ginger Squash

PREP 10 Minutes **TOTAL** 55 Minutes • *4 servings*

1 large acorn squash (2 lb)	2 teaspoons butter, melted
¼ teaspoon salt	1 teaspoon finely chopped gingerroot or ¼ teaspoon ground ginger
2 tablespoons maple-flavored syrup	

1 Heat oven to 400°F.

2 Cut squash lengthwise into quarters; remove seeds and fibers. In ungreased 13x9-inch (3-quart) glass baking dish, place squash, cut sides up. Sprinkle with salt. In small bowl, mix remaining ingredients; drizzle over squash.

3 Bake uncovered about 45 minutes or until tender.

1 Serving Calories 150; Total Fat 2g (Saturated Fat 1.5g, Trans Fat 0g); Cholesterol 5mg; Sodium 170mg; Total Carbohydrate 30g (Dietary Fiber 7g); Protein 1g **Carbohydrate Choices:** 2

265

Creamy Mashed Sweet Potatoes with Maple Syrup

Roasted Sweet Potato Wedges

Peas and Corn with Thyme

5-INGREDIENT RECIPE

Savory Stuffed Summer Squash

Panko Crispy Bread Crumbs

Cilantro

Pico de Gallo

Cheddar Cheese

Yellow Summer Squash

Spiral Summer Squash

5-INGREDIENT RECIPE

CALORIE SMART • VEGETARIAN

Savory Stuffed Summer Squash

PREP 20 Minutes **TOTAL** 45 Minutes •
4 servings (½ squash each)

2 medium yellow summer squash, cut in half lengthwise	½ cup pico de gallo (from 12-oz container; for homemade pico de gallo, see page 47)
¼ teaspoon salt	
⅓ cup finely shredded cheddar cheese (about 1½ oz)	2 tablespoons chopped fresh cilantro
⅓ cup plain panko crispy bread crumbs	⅛ teaspoon pepper

1 Heat oven to 375°F. Spray 8-inch square (2-quart) baking dish with cooking spray.

2 Scoop pulp with spoon from each squash half, leaving ½-inch shell. Sprinkle inside of squash shells with salt. Coarsely chop pulp; set aside. In small bowl, mix cheese and bread crumbs; set aside.

3 In 10-inch skillet, add squash pulp, pico de gallo and 1 tablespoon of the cilantro. Cook uncovered over medium heat, 3 to 4 minutes, stirring frequently, or until squash is tender. Drain; return to skillet. Stir in ½ cup of the bread crumb mixture and the pepper. Spoon filling into squash shells.

4 Bake uncovered 20 minutes or until squash shell is almost tender. Remove dish from oven. Top squash with remaining bread crumb mixture. Bake about 5 minutes longer or until crumbs are light brown and squash shell is tender. Sprinkle with remaining cilantro.

1 Serving Calories 200; Total Fat 4.5g (Saturated Fat 2g, Trans Fat 0g); Cholesterol 10mg; Sodium 380mg; Total Carbohydrate 31g (Dietary Fiber 1g); Protein 7g **Carbohydrate Choices:** 2

MAKING SPIRAL SUMMER SQUASH

Create veggie noodles by running vegetable through spiralizer.

Place veggie spirals in pan; toss with oil and salt.

SPIRALIZED VEGETABLES

Spiralized vegetables are a fun way to eat more veggies. Use them in place of noodles if you're looking to cut down on carbs, calories or gluten. Spiralized veggies can be found in larger grocery stores fresh and/or frozen, or you can make your own. Beets, butternut squash, carrots, sweet potatoes, potatoes, yellow summer squash and zucchini are some of the vegetables that spiralize well.

Spiralizers can range from very inexpensive handheld or countertop models to pricey attachments for your stand mixer. Fresh, firm, straight, even-sized vegetables work the best to push through the gadget. While they won't be the same shape or thickness, you can make long, thin noodles without a spiralizer by pulling a vegetable peeler lengthwise along softer vegetables like zucchini and yellow squash to make long, thin strips. Cook time may be a few minutes shorter.

EASY • FAST • CALORIE SMART • GLUTEN FREE • VEGETARIAN

Spiral Summer Squash

If you love gadgets, try a vegetable spiralizer! Straight, even vegetables work best when using spiralizers. If you don't have a spiralizer, use a vegetable peeler. Pull the peeler down the sides of the squash, making long strips. Baking time may be shorter.

PREP 10 Minutes **TOTAL** 20 Minutes • *4 servings*

1 (6-inch) zucchini	Freshly ground pepper, chopped parsley and grated Parmesan cheese, if desired
1 (6-inch-long) yellow summer squash	
2 teaspoons olive oil	
¼ teaspoon salt	

1 Heat oven to 400°F. Line 15x10x1-inch pan with foil.

2 Cut off ends of zucchini and squash. Cut each with spiralizer according to manufacturer's directions. Place in pan. Drizzle with oil; sprinkle with salt. Toss to coat. Spread squash in single layer.

3 Bake 8 to 10 minutes or just until tender. Sprinkle with pepper.

1 Serving Calories 40; Total Fat 2.5g (Saturated Fat 0g, Trans Fat 0g); Cholesterol 0mg; Sodium 150mg; Total Carbohydrate 3g (Dietary Fiber 1g); Protein 1g **Carbohydrate Choices:** 0

Grilled Zucchini with Tomatoes and Basil

Zucchini Parmesan

FAST • CALORIE SMART • GLUTEN FREE • VEGETARIAN • VEGAN

Grilled Zucchini with Tomatoes and Basil

PREP 15 Minutes **TOTAL** 15 Minutes • *8 servings* (1 cup each)

- 2 lb zucchini (about 5 medium), trimmed, cut in half lengthwise
  Cooking spray
- ½ teaspoon lemon zest
- 1½ tablespoons lemon juice
- 2 tablespoons extra-virgin olive oil
- ¼ teaspoon salt

- ¼ teaspoon Dijon mustard
- ⅛ teaspoon freshly ground pepper
- 2 cups grape tomatoes, cut in half lengthwise
- ½ cup thinly sliced red onion
- ½ cup lightly packed fresh basil leaves, torn
- 12 pitted kalamata olives

1 Heat gas or charcoal grill to medium-high heat for direct heat (page 421).

2 Spray zucchini with cooking spray. Place zucchini on grill. Cover grill; cook 8 minutes, turning once, just until tender. Remove from grill; cool slightly. Cut zucchini into ½-inch-thick slices.

3 In large bowl, beat lemon zest, lemon juice, olive oil, salt, mustard and pepper with whisk. Add zucchini, tomatoes, onion, basil and olives; toss to coat.

1 Serving Calories 80; Total Fat 5.5g (Saturated Fat 1g, Trans Fat 0g); Cholesterol 0mg; Sodium 180mg; Total Carbohydrate 6.5g (Dietary Fiber 1.5g); Protein 2g **Carbohydrate Choices:** ½

VEGETARIAN

Zucchini Parmesan

PREP 35 Minutes **TOTAL** 55 Minutes •
4 servings (about 1 cup each)

- ½ cup plain panko crispy bread crumbs
- ½ cup grated Parmesan cheese
- 1 lb medium zucchini squash, cut crosswise into ¼-inch slices
- 2 tablespoons all-purpose flour
- ½ teaspoon salt
- 1 egg, slightly beaten

- 1 cup vegetable oil
- 1¼ cups tomato basil pasta sauce (from 26-oz jar)
- 1 cup shredded mozzarella cheese (4 oz)
- 2 tablespoons thinly sliced fresh basil leaves

1 Heat oven to 375°F. Spray 2-quart baking dish with cooking spray.

2 In shallow dish or pie plate, mix bread crumbs and ¼ cup of the Parmesan cheese; set aside. In medium bowl, mix zucchini, flour and salt; stir in egg. Working in batches, dip coated zucchini in bread crumb mixture, pressing to coat on both sides. Place on cookie sheet in single layer.

3 In 12-inch skillet, heat oil over medium-high heat. Working in batches, cook zucchini 3 to 4 minutes, turning once, or until evenly golden and crispy. (Reduce heat to medium if zucchini is browning too quickly.) Transfer to cooling rack. Repeat with remaining zucchini.

4 Spoon ¾ cup of the pasta sauce into baking dish. Top with ½ cup of the mozzarella cheese. Carefully place half of zucchini in single layer on top of cheese. Top with remaining ½ cup mozzarella cheese, remaining half of zucchini, remaining ½ cup of pasta sauce and remaining ¼ cup Parmesan cheese.

5 Bake 15 to 18 minutes or until bubbling around edges and cheese is melted. Top with basil.

1 Serving Calories 360; Total Fat 21g (Saturated Fat 7g, Trans Fat 0g); Cholesterol 75mg; Sodium 920mg; Total Carbohydrate 24g (Dietary Fiber 2g); Protein 18g **Carbohydrate Choices:** 1½

Bean & Legume Basics

A staple used around the world, the family of legumes (which includes beans, lentils, peas, soybeans and peanuts) is an inexpensive source of protein, fiber, vitamins and other nutrients. The members of this family, also known as pulses, are the basis of many meatless and veggie-forward dishes, and are encouraged as part of a healthy diet in the USDA Dietary Guidelines. (See also the Veggie Forward chapter, starting on page 384.) Plants in the legume family have stems with pods that split open to reveal seeds; the edible seeds are referred to as pulses. Look for common varieties of pulses in grocery stores; for less-common varieties, look in natural-food stores, food co-ops and online.

Available dried, canned and frozen, beans and other legumes are extremely versatile; with their mild flavor, they pair well with countless seasonings. Beans may be round, oval or kidney shaped; lentils are flat, round disks. Bean varieties include: black, black-eyed peas, butter, canary, cannellini, cranberry, fava, great northern, light and dark red kidney, lima, mung, navy, pinto, pink and red, as well as whole and split peas, soybeans and edamame (immature green soybeans). Lentils may be black (Beluga), brown, green (Puy), red or yellow.

Cooking Dried Beans and Lentils

Before cooking dried beans or lentils, sort through them to remove any shriveled or damaged ones. Rinse and drain well. It's important to soak most dried beans before cooking so they are easier to digest and to make them soft and plump, so they cook evenly; black-eyed peas, lentils and split peas don't require soaking. Because beans rehydrate to triple their dry size when cooked, choose a pot that's big enough to allow them room to expand. Choose one of these two methods for soaking beans.

Quick-Soak Method Place dried beans in a large saucepan and add enough water to cover. Heat to boiling; boil 2 minutes. Remove from heat; cover and let stand for at least 1 hour. Drain, then cook in fresh cold water.

Long-Soak Method Place dried beans in a large saucepan or bowl and add enough water to cover. Let stand 8 to 24 hours. Drain, then cook in fresh cold water.

Place drained soaked beans or rinsed lentils in a 3-quart saucepan and add fresh cold water to cover. Heat to boiling; boil uncovered for 2 minutes. Reduce heat to low. Cover and simmer (do not boil or beans will burst), stirring occasionally, for time indicated in cooking chart (right), or until tender. Skim any foam that rises to the top of the pan. Since beans soak up water, they may get dry before they are tender; if this happens, add water ¼ cup at a time and continue to cook. Season after cooking.

TIMETABLE FOR COOKING DRIED BEANS AND LENTILS

LEGUME TYPE (1 CUP DRY = 2 TO 3 CUPS COOKED)	COOKING TIME
Lentils (do not soak)	5 to 45 minutes, depending on variety; split or whole
Adzuki, Great Northern	45 to 60
Baby Lima Beans	1 hour
Black Beans, Cannellini Beans, Chick Peas (Garbanzo Beans), Kidney Beans (light or dark red), Large Lima Beans, Pinto Beans	1 to 1½ hours

BEAN YIELDS

15½-oz can beans = about 2 cups beans (drained)

1 lb (2 cups) dried beans = 5 to 6 cups cooked beans

3 (15½-oz) cans = 1 lb dried beans, cooked

TESTING BEAN DONENESS

If you test just one bean when cooking dried beans, you might be tempted to think that they are all tender. Choose about six beans from various locations in the cooking vessel to pierce with a fork. If they all aren't tender, cook them a bit longer, until all beans tested are tender.

Fresh Legumes

Legumes are seed pods that split along both sides when ripe. Choose bright, smooth, fresh, crisp pods. Refrigerate in plastic bag up to 4 days.

Edamame (Fresh Soybeans) Often sold in their fuzzy green pods or frozen. Serve as snack; add to rice, salads, scrambled eggs; mash into guacamole.

Long Beans (Asparagus Bean, Chinese Long Bean, Yard-Long Bean) Same family as black-eyed peas. Milder, less sweet than green beans. Usually cut in half or smaller pieces, then sautéed or stir-fried. Mushy if overcooked.

Mung Bean Sprouts Tender; great for salads or stir-fries. Refrigerate in plastic bag up to 3 days.

Pea Shoots The best leaves and tendrils from pea plants. Choose young, tender shoots with top leaves. Remove coarse stems. Use raw in salads; steam as a side dish with lemon or sprinkled with ginger and sugar. Use within 2 days.

Peas (English, Sugar Snap, Snow) English peas must be removed from pods before cooking; sugar snaps and snow peas can be eaten in the pod. All can be eaten raw or cooked; great in salads or side dishes.

Skillet Mushrooms and Chick Peas with Burrata

Farmers' Market Breakfast Hash

CALORIE SMART • GLUTEN FREE

Skillet Mushrooms and Chick Peas with Burrata

Burrata is stretched mozzarella cheese curd filled with more bits of mozzarella and cream. When cut, the soft, creamy center oozes out, for a delightful eating experience. Balls of various sizes come packed in water. For this delicious main or side dish recipe, feel free to substitute one larger 7- to 8-oz ball or 4 smaller 2-oz balls. If using the large ball, quarter the cheese and place it rounded side down in the mushroom mixture.

PREP 40 Minutes **TOTAL** 40 Minutes •
4 servings (about 1 cup each)

- 2 oz diced pancetta (from 4-oz package)
- 1 lb fresh mushrooms such as cremini, oyster, shiitake, cut in half or quartered if large (6 cups)
- ½ cup thinly sliced red onion (from 1 medium)
- 1 package (5 oz) baby arugula leaves
- 1 can (15 oz) chick peas (garbanzo beans), rinsed, drained
- 2 cloves garlic, finely chopped
- 3 teaspoons chopped fresh thyme leaves
- 1 container (8 oz) fresh burrata cheese (2 balls), drained and cut in half
- ¼ teaspoon crushed red pepper flakes, if desired

1 Spray 12-inch skillet with cooking spray. Heat over medium heat. Add pancetta. Cook 7 to 9 minutes, stirring frequently, or until browned. Using slotted spoon, transfer to paper towel–lined plate.

2 Add mushrooms and onion to skillet. Cook over medium-high heat 9 to 11 minutes, stirring frequently, or until mushrooms and onion begin to soften and brown. Add half of the arugula; stir until slightly wilted. Add remaining arugula, the chick peas, garlic and 2 teaspoons of the thyme. Cook 2 to 4 minutes, stirring occasionally, or until arugula is wilted. Remove from heat.

3 Top with burrata, pancetta, the remaining 1 teaspoon thyme and the pepper flakes. Serve immediately.

1 Serving Calories 380; Total Fat 21g (Saturated Fat 11g, Trans Fat 0g); Cholesterol 60mg; Sodium 790mg; Total Carbohydrate 24g (Dietary Fiber 6g); Protein 23g **Carbohydrate Choices:** 1½

FAST • CALORIE SMART • GLUTEN FREE

Farmers' Market Breakfast Hash

For an extra-hearty breakfast, top each serving of this veggie-rich hash with a fried egg (page 101) or poached egg (page 102).

PREP 30 Minutes **TOTAL** 30 Minutes •
6 servings (1 cup each)

- 1 tablespoon vegetable oil
- ¾ lb small Yukon Gold or red potatoes (from 1.5-lb bag), quartered
- ¾ teaspoon salt
- 1 package (8 oz) sliced fresh mushrooms (about 3 cups)
- ½ lb fresh asparagus spears, tough ends removed, cut into 1½-inch pieces
- 1 medium red bell pepper, cut into 1-inch pieces
- 4 thin slices red onion, cut in half
- 3 links (3 oz each) gluten-free smoked chicken and apple sausage (from 12-oz package), cut in half lengthwise, then crosswise in ½-inch slices
- 3 tablespoons coarse-grained mustard
- 1 tablespoon honey
- ¼ teaspoon pepper
- 3 cups lightly packed fresh baby spinach leaves (from 5-oz bag), coarsely chopped

1 In 12-inch nonstick skillet, heat oil over medium high heat. Add potatoes; sprinkle with ¼ teaspoon of the salt. Cook uncovered 8 to 10 minutes, stirring frequently, or until potatoes are golden brown.

2 Add mushrooms, asparagus, bell pepper, onion and sausage to skillet. Cook uncovered 5 to 7 minutes, stirring frequently, or until potatoes and vegetables are tender.

3 In small bowl, mix mustard, honey, the remaining ½ teaspoon salt and the pepper until blended. Stir spinach into vegetables and sausage; cook until spinach just begins to soften. Stir in mustard mixture until everything is coated.

1 Serving Calories 220; Total Fat 8g (Saturated Fat 2g, Trans Fat 0g); Cholesterol 20mg; Sodium 770mg; Total Carbohydrate 26g (Dietary Fiber 4g); Protein 11g **Carbohydrate Choices:** 2

FAST • MAKE AHEAD • GLUTEN FREE •
VEGETARIAN • VEGAN

Moroccan-Style Chick Peas with Raisins

PREP 25 Minutes **TOTAL** 25 Minutes •
8 servings (about ⅔ cup each)

- 2 tablespoons peanut or vegetable oil
- 1 large onion, sliced
- 1 small onion, chopped (½ cup)
- 2 cloves garlic, finely chopped
- 2 cups (½-inch pieces) seeded peeled acorn or butternut squash (from a 1-lb squash)
- ½ cup organic raisins
- 2 cups vegetable broth (from 32-oz carton; for homemade broth, see page 169)
- 2 teaspoons ground turmeric
- 2 teaspoons ground cinnamon
- 1 teaspoon ground ginger
- 2 cans (15 oz each) chick peas (garbanzo beans), rinsed, drained
  Hot cooked rice (page 224) or gluten-free couscous, if desired

1 In 4-quart saucepan, heat oil over medium heat. Add sliced onion, chopped onion and garlic. Cook about 7 minutes, stirring occasionally, or until onions are tender. Stir in remaining ingredients except chick peas and rice.

2 Heat to boiling; reduce heat. Cover; simmer about 8 minutes, stirring occasionally, until squash is tender.

3 Stir in chick peas; cook until chick peas are heated through. Serve over rice.

1 Serving Calories 220; Total Fat 6g (Saturated Fat 1g, Trans Fat 0g); Cholesterol 0mg; Sodium 410mg; Total Carbohydrate 35g (Dietary Fiber 8g); Protein 6g **Carbohydrate Choices: 2**

MAKE-AHEAD DIRECTIONS: Prepare as directed in Step 1. Remove from heat; cool completely. Spoon into freezer-safe food storage container; seal tightly. Freeze up to 3 months. Thaw in refrigerator overnight. Transfer mixture to 4-quart saucepan. Continue as directed in Step 2.

EASY • SLOW COOKER • GLUTEN FREE

Homemade Baked Beans

PREP 15 Minutes **TOTAL** 8 Hours 30 Minutes •
10 servings (½ cup each)

- 1 bag (16 oz) dried navy beans (2 cups), sorted, rinsed
- 13 cups water
- ½ cup packed brown sugar
- ¼ cup molasses
- 1 teaspoon salt
- 6 slices gluten-free bacon, crisply cooked, crumbled
- 1 small onion, chopped (½ cup)

1 Heat oven to 350°F.

2 In 4-quart ovenproof Dutch oven, heat beans and 10 cups of the water to boiling. Cook uncovered 2 minutes. Stir in brown sugar, molasses, salt, bacon and onion. Cover; bake 4 hours, stirring occasionally.

3 Stir in remaining 3 cups water. Bake uncovered 2 hours to 2 hours 15 minutes longer, stirring occasionally, or until beans are tender and of desired consistency.

1 Serving Calories 240; Total Fat 2.5g (Saturated Fat 0.5g, Trans Fat 0g); Cholesterol 0mg; Sodium 340mg; Total Carbohydrate 45g (Dietary Fiber 11g); Protein 10g **Carbohydrate Choices: 3**

SLOW-COOKER DIRECTIONS: Spray 3½- to 6-quart slow cooker with cooking spray. In slow cooker, place beans and 5 cups water. Cover; cook on High heat setting 2 hours. Turn off heat; let stand 8 to 24 hours. Stir in brown sugar, molasses, salt, bacon and onion. Cover; cook on Low heat setting 10 to 12 hours or until beans are very tender and most of liquid is absorbed.

Moroccan-Style Chick Peas with Raisins

Homemade Baked Beans

Black Beans and Kale with Feta Cheese

Spicy Papaya Black Beans

CALORIE SMART • GLUTEN FREE • VEGETARIAN

Black Beans and Kale with Feta Cheese

A squeeze of fresh lemon over this dish really brightens the flavors.

PREP 35 Minutes TOTAL 35 Minutes •
4 servings (about 2 cups each)

1 teaspoon olive oil	1 can (15 oz) black beans, rinsed, drained
1 medium onion, thinly sliced	1 teaspoon fresh thyme leaves
2 tablespoons water	2 cups hot cooked brown rice (page 224)
1 bunch (8 oz) kale, ribs removed, leaves thinly sliced (6 cups)	½ cup crumbled gluten-free reduced-fat feta cheese, crumbled (2 oz)
⅛ teaspoon salt	

1 In 10-inch nonstick skillet, heat oil over medium heat. Add onion; cook about 5 minutes or until tender. Reduce heat to low; cook about 5 minutes longer or until light brown and very soft. Add water. Heat to boiling; reduce heat. Simmer uncovered about 2 minutes or until water has evaporated.

2 Increase heat to medium-high; add kale and salt. Cook about 5 minutes, stirring frequently, or until kale wilts. Add black beans and thyme. Cook 3 to 5 minutes, stirring occasionally, or until heated through. Serve over rice; top with cheese.

1 Serving Calories 310; Total Fat 4.5g (Saturated Fat 1.5g, Trans Fat 0g); Cholesterol 5mg; Sodium 280mg; Total Carbohydrate 52g (Dietary Fiber 12g); Protein 14g **Carbohydrate Choices:** 3½

GLUTEN FREE • VEGETARIAN • VEGAN

Spicy Papaya Black Beans

PREP 15 Minutes TOTAL 3 Hours •
5 servings (about 2 cups each)

4½ cups water	1 small red onion, finely chopped (½ cup)
1½ cups dried black beans (10 oz), sorted, rinsed	½ cup fresh orange juice
2 teaspoons vegetable oil	¼ cup lime juice
1 medium papaya or mango, seeds removed, peeled and diced (about 1½ cups)	2 tablespoons chopped fresh cilantro
	½ teaspoon ground red pepper (cayenne)
1 medium red bell pepper, finely chopped (1 cup)	2 cloves garlic, finely chopped
	5 cups hot cooked rice (page 224)

1 Soak beans by one of the methods on page 270; drain.

2 In 2-quart saucepan, heat water and beans to boiling. Boil uncovered 2 minutes; reduce heat. Cover; simmer about 45 minutes, stirring occasionally, until beans are tender. Drain.

3 In 10-inch skillet, heat oil over medium heat. Add remaining ingredients except rice. Cook about 5 minutes, stirring occasionally, or until bell pepper is crisp-tender. Stir in beans. Cook about 5 minutes, stirring occasionally, or until hot. Serve over rice.

1 Serving Calories 460; Total Fat 3.5g (Saturated Fat 0.5g, Trans Fat 0g); Cholesterol 0mg; Sodium 10mg; Total Carbohydrate 91g (Dietary Fiber 14g); Protein 17g **Carbohydrate Choices:** 6

QUICK CARIBBEAN-STYLE BLACK BEANS:
Prepare as directed—except substitute 2 cans (15 oz each) black beans, rinsed and drained, for the dried beans. Omit water and Steps 1 and 2.

Black Cumin

Mangosteen

Fenugreek Seed

Ground Fenugreek

Dried Fenugreek

Bishop Weed (Ajowain)

Karhi Leaves

Nigella Seed

Cumin Seed

Jaggery

Paneer

Gingerroot

Banana Leaf

Okra

Ground Turmeric

Turmeric

Tamarind Pod

Black Cardamom

White Cardamom

Cardamom Pods

Cardamom Seed

Ground Cardamom

Coconut

Green Mangos

Garam Masala

Flaked Coconut

Red Lentils

Pappadam

Ghee

Green Lentils

Black Lentils

Thai Chiles

Yogurt

Mint

GLOBAL FLAVORS

India

Loved throughout the world for their fragrant aromas and alluring flavors, Indian-inspired dishes have gained popularity because of their variety of ingredients and creative flavor combinations.

GHEE Clarified butter (slowly melted to separate milk solids from the golden fat) that's been further simmered until all the moisture has evaporated and the milk solids begin to brown, giving it a caramel-like, nutty flavor and aroma. Used for frying and sautéing and as an ingredient.

JAGGERY A distinctively flavored coarse, dark sugar. Many forms are available; the more common are a soft form that is spread on breads and sweets, and a solid form that is typically crushed and used on cereal and for making candy.

LENTILS A staple in most Indian kitchens, these high-protein pulses are commonly used in place of meat. Many dishes, from flatbreads to noodles to stews, are made with lentils—dal, a spicy stewed dish, is one of the most popular.

MANGOSTEEN Similar in size and form to tangerines. The sweet-tart flavor and soft, creamy-colored fruit are juicy and refreshing. The purple-brown skin is hard.

PANEER (PANIR) Fresh cheese made from cow's or buffalo's milk curdled with lemon or lime juice, and traditionally pressed. Similar to firm tofu in texture.

PAPPADAM (POPPADUM) Tortilla-like breads made with lentil flour. In northern India, they may be flavored with red or black pepper, garlic or other seasonings; southern Indians prefer an unflavored variety. When deep fried, they puff up to double their size; grilling pappadams gives them a smoky flavor.

SPICES

CARDAMOM, an aromatic member of the ginger family, can be purchased in the pod or ground. The warm, spicy-sweet flavor is used in stews and curries—a little goes a long way.

CUMIN, the dried fruit of a plant from the parsley family, is available both as seeds and ground.

BISHOP WEED (AJOWAIN) is available ground and as whole seeds. Its astringent, thyme-like flavor is commonly used in curries, chutneys, breads and legumes.

FENUGREEK seeds can be purchased whole or ground. The aromatic leaves are more commonly available dried than fresh. Faintly similar in flavor to maple syrup, typically used in curry powders, spice blends and tea.

GARAM MASALA is a blend of dry-roasted, ground spices; there are many varieties. Used to add warmth to a dish, it is added toward the end of cooking or sprinkled over a dish before serving.

NIGELLA SEEDS, with a peppery-nutty-oniony flavor, are used to season vegetables, legumes and bread.

TAMARIND is a sweet-sour fruit with pulp surrounding inedible seeds in a pod. When dried, it becomes very sour. Used like lemon juice in full-flavored chutneys and curried dishes, and to make a syrup to flavor soft drinks and Worcestershire sauce. Available in jars of concentrated pulp, canned paste, dried whole pods and bricks of pulp and seeds.

TURMERIC imparts its characteristic deep yellow-orange and slightly bitter flavor to many dishes.

CALORIE SMART

Indian-Inspired Lentils and Rice

Dal (or dahl) is a dish often made with lentils, and is sometimes spicy. In India, "dal" also refers to the many varieties of pulses that include beans, peas and lentils.

PREP 25 Minutes **TOTAL** 55 Minutes •
6 servings (about 1⅓ cups each)

8 medium green onions, chopped (½ cup)	1 teaspoon ground turmeric
1 tablespoon finely chopped gingerroot	½ teaspoon salt
⅛ teaspoon crushed red pepper flakes	1 large tomato, chopped (1 cup)
2 cloves garlic, finely chopped	¼ cup shredded coconut
5¼ cups vegetable broth (from two 32-oz containers; for homemade broth, see page 169)	2 tablespoons chopped fresh or 2 teaspoons dried mint leaves
	3 cups hot cooked rice (page 224)
1½ cups dried lentils (12 oz), sorted, rinsed	1½ cups plain fat-free yogurt

1 Spray 3-quart saucepan with cooking spray. Add onions, gingerroot, pepper flakes and garlic; cook over medium heat 3 to 5 minutes, stirring occasionally, until onions are tender.

2 Stir in 5 cups of the broth, the lentils, turmeric and salt. Heat to boiling; reduce heat and simmer covered 25 to 30 minutes, adding remaining ¼ cup broth if needed, until lentils are tender.

3 Stir in tomato, coconut and mint. Serve over rice; top with yogurt.

1 Serving Calories 330; Total Fat 2g (Saturated Fat 1.5g, Trans Fat 0g); Cholesterol 0mg; Sodium 1050mg; Total Carbohydrate 61g (Dietary Fiber 9g); Protein 17g **Carbohydrate Choices:** 4

Beef, Pork & Lamb

Beef, Pork & Lamb Basics

Knowing which cut of meat is the right one for your recipe or cooking method can be daunting. Look here for information on a variety of beef, pork and lamb cuts, detailed cooking directions and tasty recipes, to turn out delicious, tender results every time.

Tips for Purchasing

- Choose packages without any tears, holes or leaks. There should be little or no liquid in the bottom of the tray.

- Packages should be cold and feel firm. Avoid packages that are stacked too high in the meat case, as they may not have been kept cold enough.

- Check the sell-by date carefully and use or freeze within two days of the date.

- Choose meat that has good color. Any that is gray or off-color should not be purchased.

- Place packages of meat in plastic bags so that juices from meat will not contaminate other food in your grocery cart.

- Refrigerate meat as soon as you get home from shopping. For longer commutes from the grocery store or on hot days, place meat in a small cooler with ice packs.

Servings per Pound

The number of servings per pound varies depending on the type of meat and the amount of bone and fat present.

TYPE OF MEAT	SERVINGS PER POUND
Boneless Cuts (ground, boneless chops, loin, tenderloin)	3 to 4
Bone-In Cuts (rib roasts, pot roasts, country-style ribs)	2 to 3
Very Bony Cuts (back ribs, spareribs, short ribs, shanks)	1 to 1½

What's on the Label?

Organic Certified organic beef will have an official label on the package. It means that the cattle never received any antibiotics or growth-promoting hormones and that they were raised in living conditions that are custom to their natural behaviors, such as grazing on pasture and being fed 100% organic feed and forage.

Grass-Fed vs. Grain-Fed Cattle spend most of their lives eating grass and forage in pastures. **Grass-Fed** cattle then may be "finished" on a diet of forage, hay or silage at the feed yard and may receive supplements to gain weight rapidly and to treat, prevent or control disease. **Grain-fed** cattle are "finished" on a balanced diet of grain and local feed ingredients such as cull potatoes or sugar beets as well as hay and forage at the feed yard. Similarly, they may receive supplements to treat, prevent or control disease. Most beef, pork and lamb are grain-fed, but grass-fed meats are becoming more popular.

All Natural vs. Naturally Raised If a meat package is labeled **all natural**, it means that it doesn't contain any artificial ingredients or added color, or is minimally processed. But the cattle may or may not have been fed organic feed. **Naturally raised** refers to cattle that have never received any growth hormones or antibiotics.

Storing Meat

- Store uncooked meat in the coldest part of the refrigerator, away from cooked and ready-to-eat foods.

- Place uncooked meat on a tray or plate in the refrigerator to catch any drips of meat juices.

- Refrigerate uncooked meat for no longer than two days or freeze for up three months.

- For freezer storage, label with the name of the cut and the date.

- Thaw frozen meat on a tray or plate in the refrigerator.

- Do not refreeze meat that has been thawed, as texture and flavor can change.

HANDLING RAW MEAT

To avoid any cross-contamination when preparing raw meat for cooking, follow the tips in Don't Cross-Contaminate, page 30. Cooking meat to the recommended doneness destroys bacteria that may be present.

Thawing Meat

Thaw meat in a dish or baking pan with sides, or in a resealable food-storage plastic bag in the refrigerator to catch any drips during thawing. Don't thaw meat on the countertop because the outside of the meat (where bacteria can thrive) will get too warm before the center is thawed.

AMOUNT OF FROZEN MEAT	THAWING TIME IN THE REFRIGERATOR
Large Roast (4 lb or larger)	4 to 7 hours per pound
Small Roast (under 4 lb)	3 to 5 hours per pound
Steak or Chops (1-inch thick)	12 to 14 hours total
Ground Meat or Meat Cubes (1- to 1½-lb package)	24 hours total
Ground Beef Patties (½- to ¾-inch thick)	12 hours total

CUTTING RAW MEAT

Cutting raw meat into cubes, thin slices or strips is easy if the meat is frozen until firm but not solidly frozen, about 30 to 60 minutes, depending on the size of the piece. Cutting slices against the grain will help ensure they will be tender when cooked.

FAST • CALORIE SMART

Sheet-Pan Fajitas

PREP 30 Minutes TOTAL 30 Minutes • *6 servings*

- 2 tablespoons chili powder
- 2 teaspoons ground cumin
- 2 teaspoons salt
- ½ teaspoon garlic powder
- 1 medium red onion, halved, cut into ¼-inch slices
- 2 medium red or yellow bell peppers, cut into ¼-inch strips
- ¼ cup vegetable oil
- 1 beef flank steak (about 1.3 lb)
- 6 (6-inch) soft flour tortillas (from 8.2 oz package)
  Lime wedges, sour cream, salsa, guacamole, chopped fresh cilantro, if desired

1 Spray 18x13x1-inch half-sheet pan with cooking spray. In small bowl, mix chili powder, cumin, salt and garlic powder. In large bowl, mix onion, bell peppers, 2 tablespoons of the vegetable oil and 1 tablespoon of the chili powder mixture until evenly coated. Spoon vegetable mixture into pan in single layer, leaving room for steak.

2 In same large bowl, mix remaining 2 tablespoons oil and remaining chili powder mixture. Add steak; rub mixture into steak. Place steak in pan with vegetables.

3 Broil with top 4 to 6 inches from heat 9 to 11 minutes, stirring vegetables and turning steak once. Cook until steak is medium-rare to medium (145°F to 160°F). Remove steak to cutting board. Cover with foil; let stand 5 minutes. Stir vegetables and return to oven 2 to 6 minutes longer or until vegetables are blackened in spots.

4 Cut steak across grain into thin slices. Serve with vegetables in tortillas with remaining ingredients.

1 Serving Calories 320; Total Fat 16g (Saturated Fat 4g, Trans Fat 0g); Cholesterol 65mg; Sodium 1080mg; Total Carbohydrate 17g (Dietary Fiber 2g); Protein 27g **Carbohydrate Choices:** 1

EASY • CALORIE SMART • GLUTEN FREE

Korean Barbecue Beef

Bulgogi, or marinated beef, is one of the most popular dishes in Korea with its distinctive sweet-salty flavor. If you're adventurous, add a side of kimchi (page 466), a super-spicy cabbage condiment you can make ahead and have on hand or find in many supermarkets.

PREP 10 Minutes TOTAL 40 Minutes • *4 servings*

- 1 lb boneless beef top loin or sirloin steak
- ¼ cup gluten-free soy sauce
- 3 tablespoons sugar
- 2 tablespoons sesame or vegetable oil
- ¼ teaspoon pepper
- 3 medium green onions, finely chopped (3 tablespoons)
- 2 cloves garlic, chopped
  Hot cooked rice (page 224), if desired
  Sliced green onions, if desired

1 Cut beef diagonally across grain into ⅛-inch slices (beef is easier to cut if partially frozen). In medium glass or plastic bowl, mix remaining ingredients except rice and sliced green onions. Add beef; stir until well coated. Cover; refrigerate 30 minutes.

2 Drain beef; discard marinade. Heat 10-inch skillet over medium heat. Add beef; cook 2 to 3 minutes, stirring frequently, until brown. Serve with rice. Garnish with sliced green onions.

1 Serving Calories 280; Total Fat 11g (Saturated Fat 2.5g, Trans Fat 0g); Cholesterol 80mg; Sodium 940mg; Total Carbohydrate 12g (Dietary Fiber 0g); Protein 33g **Carbohydrate Choices:** 1

Sheet-Pan Fajitas

Korean Barbecue Beef

Brandy-Herb Pan Steaks

PREP 25 Minutes TOTAL 25 Minutes • *4 servings*

- 1 teaspoon cracked or coarse ground black pepper
- ¾ teaspoon chopped fresh or ¼ teaspoon dried basil leaves
- ¾ teaspoon chopped fresh or ¼ teaspoon dried rosemary leaves
- ½ teaspoon coarse (kosher or sea) salt
- 4 boneless beef tenderloin steaks, 1-inch thick (1 to 1½ lb)
- 1 tablespoon butter
- 1 cup gluten-free beef broth (for homemade broth, see page 157)
- 2 tablespoons brandy or additional beef broth
   Additional chopped fresh basil leaves, if desired

1 In small bowl, mix pepper, basil, rosemary and salt. Rub mixture into both sides of each steak.

2 In 12-inch skillet, melt butter over medium heat. Add steaks; cook 6 to 8 minutes, turning once, until medium-rare to medium (145°F to 160°F). Remove steaks from skillet; cover with foil to keep warm.

3 Add broth and brandy to skillet. Heat to boiling, stirring to loosen browned bits from bottom of skillet; reduce heat. Simmer uncovered 3 to 4 minutes or until slightly thickened. Serve with steaks; sprinkle with additional basil leaves.

1 Serving Calories 200; Total Fat 5g (Saturated Fat 2g, Trans Fat 0g); Cholesterol 90mg; Sodium 110mg; Total Carbohydrate 0g (Dietary Fiber 0g); Protein 37g **Carbohydrate Choices:** 0

MUSHROOM BRANDY-HERB PAN STEAKS: After removing steaks from skillet, add 1 teaspoon additional butter and 1 cup sliced fresh mushrooms. Cook 2 to 3 minutes, stirring frequently, until tender. Leave mushrooms in skillet and make sauce as directed in Step 3.

MAKING A PAN SAUCE

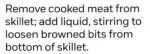

Remove cooked meat from skillet; add liquid, stirring to loosen browned bits from bottom of skillet.

Simmer uncovered until mixture is slightly thickened.

283

Brandy-Herb Pan Steaks

CUTTING-EDGE BEEF CUTS

These newer, lesser-known cuts of beef bring some innovation to your dinner table. Look for them at your grocery stores or butcher shop.

HOW TO COOK	CHARACTERISTICS	BEST COOKING METHODS
Flat-Iron Steak	Extremely tender, well marbled, flavorful	Grilling, smoking, broiling, skillet or stir-fry dishes
Denver Steak	Extremely tender, good marbling and flavor	Grill or broil (over high heat), skillet or stir-fry dishes
Chuck Flap (Edge Roast)	Rich flavor, fine texture	Grill or broil (thinly sliced across the grain), stove-top or slow-cooker pot roasts (whole)
Sirloin Bavette (Flap)	Boneless with hearty texture; great marinated for fajitas	Grill or broil or for skillet dishes
Shoulder Petite Tender	Juicy and tender; smaller and more affordable than tenderloin	Grill or broil

Herb and Garlic-Crusted Beef Rib Roast

CARVING A BEEF RIB ROAST

With roast on cutting board, carefully cut bone portion away from meat.

Turn roast bone side down. Cut slices evenly and toward bone side of roast.

EASY • CALORIE SMART • GLUTEN FREE

Herb and Garlic—Crusted Beef Rib Roast

When buying the roast, it may also be called beef rib roast, standing rib roast or prime rib roast, depending on where you live.

PREP 10 Minutes **TOTAL** 3 Hours • *8 servings*

1 (4- to 6-lb) beef rib roast, small end	1 teaspoon coarse (kosher or sea) salt
2 teaspoons dried basil leaves	1 teaspoon garlic powder
2 teaspoons dried thyme leaves	¼ teaspoon coarse ground black pepper

1 Heat oven to 350°F. Line shallow roasting pan with foil. Place rib roast, fat side up, in pan.

2 In small bowl, mix remaining ingredients; press mixture onto all surfaces of roast. Insert ovenproof meat thermometer so tip is in thickest part of roast and does not rest in fat or touch bone.

3 For medium-rare, roast uncovered 1 hour 45 minutes to 2 hours 15 minutes or until thermometer reads 135°F. Remove from oven and cover loosely with foil; let stand 15 to 20 minutes until thermometer reads 145°F. For medium, roast 2 hours 15 minutes to 2 hours 45 minutes or until thermometer reads 150°F. Cover loosely with foil; let stand 15 to 20 minutes or until thermometer reads 160°F.

4 Remove roast from pan to cutting board; cut into slices. Serve with pan drippings, if desired.

1 Serving Calories 250; Total Fat 16g (Saturated Fat 6g, Trans Fat 0.5g); Cholesterol 80mg; Sodium 200mg; Total Carbohydrate 0g (Dietary Fiber 0g); Protein 27g **Carbohydrate Choices:** 0

BEEF RIB ROAST WITH OVEN-BROWNED POTATOES: About 1 hour 30 minutes before roast is done, prepare and boil 8 medium potatoes as directed on page 248. For decorative potatoes, make crosswise cuts almost through whole potatoes to make thin slices, and reduce boiling time to 10 minutes. Place potatoes in beef drippings in pan, turning to coat completely, or brush potatoes with melted butter and place on rack with roast. Continue cooking about 1 hour 15 minutes, turning potatoes once, until golden brown. Season with salt and pepper, if desired.

Pancetta-Wrapped Beef Tenderloin

PREP 25 Minutes **TOTAL** 1 Hour 20 Minutes • *10 servings*

1 (5 to 6 lb) beef tenderloin, trimmed of fat

2 teaspoons kosher (coarse or sea) salt

1 teaspoon coarse ground black pepper

3 tablespoons olive oil

3 cloves garlic, finely chopped

2 tablespoons chopped fresh rosemary leaves

About 16 very thin slices gluten-free pancetta (from two 2-oz packages)

1 Heat oven to 425°F. Place rack in shallow roasting pan. Sprinkle tenderloin with salt and pepper. In 12-inch skillet, heat 2 tablespoons of the oil over medium-high heat. Add tenderloin; cook 10 minutes, turning once, until browned. Place tenderloin on rack; cool 5 minutes.

2 Sprinkle tenderloin with garlic and rosemary. Cover top of tenderloin with pancetta slices, overlapping pieces slightly and allowing pieces to drape over sides. Tie tenderloin with kitchen string, securing at 1½-inch intervals. Brush with remaining 1 tablespoon oil.

3 Insert ovenproof meat thermometer in thickest part of tenderloin. For medium-rare, roast uncovered 35 to 40 minutes or until thermometer reaches 140°F. For medium, roast uncovered 45 to 50 minutes or until thermometer reads 155°F. Remove from oven and cover loosely with foil; let stand 10 minutes for temperature to rise to 145°F for medium-rare or 160°F for medium. Remove string before slicing.

1 Serving Calories 380); Total Fat 20g (Saturated Fat 7g, Trans Fat 0.5g); Cholesterol 145mg; Sodium 630mg; Total Carbohydrate 0g (Dietary Fiber 0g); Protein 49g **Carbohydrate Choices:** 0

TYING A WHOLE BEEF TENDERLOIN

To make tenderloin same thickness, turn small end of beef under about 6 inches.

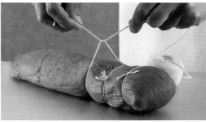

Tie beef with kitchen string at about 1½-inch intervals.

Cut string from cooked beef with kitchen scissors and remove before carving.

Pancetta-Wrapped Beef Tenderloin

Beef Stroganoff

PREP 25 Minutes **TOTAL** 50 Minutes • *6 servings*

1½ lb beef tenderloin
or boneless top
loin steak

2 tablespoons butter

1½ cups beef broth
(for homemade broth,
see page 157)

2 tablespoons ketchup

1 teaspoon salt

1 clove garlic,
finely chopped

1 package (8 oz) sliced
fresh mushrooms
(about 3 cups)

1 small onion, chopped
(½ cup)

¼ cup all-purpose flour

1 cup sour cream or
plain yogurt

Hot cooked noodles
(page 182) or rice
(page 224), if desired

Chopped fresh
parsley, if desired

1 Partially freeze beef, if desired, for easier cutting.
Cut beef across grain into 1½x½-inch strips.
In 12-inch skillet, melt butter over medium-high heat.
Add beef; cook, stirring occasionally, until brown.

2 Reserve ⅓ cup of the broth. Stir remaining broth, the
ketchup, salt and garlic into beef. Heat to boiling; reduce
heat. Cover and simmer about 10 minutes or until beef
is tender.

3 Stir in mushrooms and onion. Heat to boiling; reduce
heat. Cover and simmer about 5 minutes longer or until
onion is tender.

4 In tightly covered container, shake reserved ⅓ cup
broth and the flour until mixed; gradually stir into beef
mixture. Heat to boiling, stirring constantly. Boil and
stir 1 minute; reduce heat to low. Stir in sour cream; heat
just until heated through. Serve over noodles. Sprinkle
with parsley.

1 Serving Calories 320; Total Fat 19g (Saturated Fat 9g, Trans Fat 1g);
Cholesterol 105mg; Sodium 630mg; Total Carbohydrate 10g
(Dietary Fiber 0g); Protein 28g **Carbohydrate Choices:** ½

SLOW-COOKER DIRECTIONS: Substitute boneless
beef bottom round steak for tenderloin or top loin steak;
cut and cook in butter as directed in Step 1. Reserve
⅓ cup of the broth. Spray 3½- to 4-quart slow cooker
with cooking spray. In slow cooker, mix beef, remaining
broth, the ketchup, salt, garlic, mushrooms and onion.
Cover; cook on Low heat setting 8 to 9 hours or until beef
is tender. In tightly covered container, shake reserved
⅓ cup broth and the flour until mixed; stir into beef
mixture. Increase heat setting to High. Cover; cook 15 to
20 minutes or until thickened. Stir in sour cream; heat
until hot.

GROUND BEEF STROGANOFF: Substitute 1 lb ground
beef (at least 80% lean) for tenderloin; omit butter. In
12-inch skillet, cook beef over medium heat, stirring
occasionally, until thoroughly cooked. Drain; return to
skillet. Continue as directed.

Smothered Beef Brisket

PREP 40 Minutes **TOTAL** 8 Hours 40 Minutes • *6 servings*

3 tablespoons
vegetable oil

4 medium shallots,
thinly sliced (about
2 cups)

1 package (8 oz)
baby portabella
mushrooms,
thickly sliced

2 teaspoons finely
chopped garlic

1 fresh beef brisket
(2¼ lb; not
corned beef)

½ teaspoon salt

¼ teaspoon pepper

½ cup plus
2 tablespoons
gluten-free beef broth
(for homemade broth,
see page 157)

5 teaspoons gluten-free
Worcestershire sauce

1 tablespoon gluten-
free soy sauce

2 tablespoons
cornstarch

¼ cup whipping cream

Chopped Italian (flat-
leaf) parsley, if desired

Mashed Potatoes
(page 260), if desired

1 Spray 5- to 6-quart slow cooker with cooking spray.
In 12-inch nonstick skillet, heat 2 tablespoons of the
oil over medium-high heat. Add shallots; cook 3 to
4 minutes, stirring frequently, until shallots start to
brown. Add mushrooms; cook 3 to 4 minutes, stirring
frequently, until mushrooms are tender. Stir in garlic;
cook 30 to 60 seconds or until fragrant. Remove from
skillet to small bowl.

2 Rub brisket with remaining 1 tablespoon oil; sprinkle
with salt and pepper. Heat same skillet over medium-
high heat. Add brisket; cook 1 to 2 minutes on each side,
until browned. Place fat side up in slow cooker; top with
shallot mixture.

3 In small bowl, mix ½ cup broth, the Worcestershire
sauce and soy sauce. Pour into slow cooker around
brisket. Cover; cook on Low heat setting 8 to 9 hours
or until brisket is very tender. Remove brisket to cutting
board; cover with foil to keep warm. With slotted spoon,
place shallots and mushrooms in small bowl.

4 Skim fat from cooking juices. Strain juices using
fine-mesh sieve into heatproof bowl. Pour 1½ cups of the
juices into 1½-quart saucepan. Discard any remaining
juices. In small bowl, using whisk, mix remaining
2 tablespoons beef broth and the cornstarch; beat into
juices in saucepan. Simmer over medium heat 2 to
3 minutes, stirring constantly, until slightly thickened.
Remove from heat; stir in whipping cream.

5 With a sharp knife, cut brisket across grain into
½-inch-thick slices by pressing down through meat.
Arrange sliced brisket on serving platter, using large
flat spatula or fish turner. Top brisket with shallots and
mushrooms; drizzle with sauce before serving. Garnish
with chopped parsley. Serve with mashed potatoes.

1 Serving Calories 400; Total Fat 21g (Saturated Fat 7g, Trans Fat 0.5g);
Cholesterol 120mg; Sodium 560mg; Total Carbohydrate 15g
(Dietary Fiber 2g); Protein 39g **Carbohydrate Choices:** 1

Beef Stroganoff

MAKE AHEAD • SLOW COOKER • CALORIE SMART • GLUTEN FREE

Korean Beef Short Ribs

A fat separator works well to remove the fat from the sauce. Or, using the make-ahead directions will solidify the fat, making it easy to scoop up and remove. Cooked rice is an excellent side dish to soak up the delicious sauce from the short ribs.

PREP 25 Minutes TOTAL 8 Hours • *6 servings*

KAHLBI SAUCE

- ½ cup soy sauce
- ¼ cup honey
- 3 tablespoons rice vinegar
- 1 tablespoon toasted sesame oil
- 1 tablespoon finely chopped gingerroot
- 1 teaspoon pepper
- ½ teaspoon crushed red pepper flakes
- 1 medium onion, coarsely chopped (1 cup)
- 3 cloves garlic, peeled

SHORT RIBS

- 4 lb bone-in beef short ribs
- 2 tablespoons cornstarch
- 4 medium green onions, sliced (¼ cup)
- 1 tablespoon sesame seed
  Cooked rice, if desired

1 In food processor or blender container, place all sauce ingredients. Cover; process 30 seconds or until well blended; set aside.

2 Place short ribs in to 4- to 5-quart slow cooker. Pour sauce over short ribs. Cover and cook on Low heat setting 7 hours 30 minutes to 8 hours 30 minutes or until short ribs are very tender.

3 Remove short ribs from slow cooker; place in large heatproof bowl. Cover with foil to keep warm. Strain sauce into 2-quart saucepan. Discard strained solids and excess fat.

4 In small bowl, stir cornstarch into 2 tablespoons water. Stir into sauce. Heat over high heat, stirring constantly, 2 to 3 minutes, until thickened; remove from heat. Pour sauce over short ribs in bowl, stirring gently to coat short ribs in sauce and rice.

5 Place short ribs on platter; top with green onions and sesame seed. Serve with remaining sauce and rice.

1 Serving Calories 340; Total Fat 20g (Saturated Fat 7g, Trans Fat 0.5g); Cholesterol 80mg; Sodium 1210mg; Total Carbohydrate 19g (Dietary Fiber 1g); Protein 23g **Carbohydrate Choices:** 1

MAKE-AHEAD DIRECTIONS: Prepare short ribs up to 1 day before serving through Step 3. Cover and refrigerate ribs separately from sauce. To reheat, skim any additional fat from sauce. Thicken with cornstarch as directed in Step 4. Place short ribs in 5-quart Dutch oven; stir in sauce. Bake covered at 350°F 30 minutes or until hot.

Smothered Beef Brisket

Korean Beef Short Ribs

Beer-Braised Short Rib Dinner

Beef Gyros

Beer-Braised Short Rib Dinner

PREP 15 Minutes TOTAL 8 Hours 15 Minutes • *4 servings*

- 4 bone-in beef short ribs (about 3¼ lb), cut crosswise in half
- 2 tablespoons applewood rub for meat
- 1 can (6 oz) tomato paste
- 1 bottle (12 oz) regular or nonalcoholic pale ale
- 6 medium carrots
- 1 medium leek, cut in half, rinsed, finely chopped
- 3 cloves garlic, finely chopped
- 1 teaspoon salt
- ¼ teaspoon pepper
- 3 medium Yukon Gold potatoes (about 1¼ lb), cut lengthwise into sixths

    Chopped fresh parsley, if desired

1 Line 15x10x1-inch pan with heavy-duty foil; spray foil with cooking spray. Rub short ribs on all sides with applewood rub. Place short ribs in pan.

2 In medium bowl, using whisk, stir tomato paste and beer until smooth. Finely chop 1 of the carrots. Stir chopped carrot, the leek, garlic, salt and pepper into tomato mixture. Pour over short ribs; turn to coat. Cover pan tightly with heavy-duty foil. Refrigerate at least 6 hours or up to 24 hours to marinate, turning short ribs occasionally.

3 Heat oven to 400°F. Cut remaining 5 carrots into 2-inch pieces. Uncover pan and place carrot pieces in pan with short ribs, turning in marinade to coat. Arrange short ribs fat side up. Bake uncovered 1 hour.

4 Reduce oven temperature to 350°F. Turn short ribs on side; add potatoes to pan, turning in pan juices to coat. Bake 45 to 60 minutes longer, occasionally turning. (Add a little water to pan if pan is almost dry.) Sprinkle with parsley. Serve short ribs and carrots with slotted spoon. Sprinkle with parsley.

1 Serving Calories 510; Total Fat 20g (Saturated Fat 8g, Trans Fat 1g); Cholesterol 95mg; Sodium 1010mg; Total Carbohydrate 48g (Dietary Fiber 7g); Protein 31g **Carbohydrate Choices:** 3

SLOW COOKER • MULTI COOKER

Beef Gyros

To easily slice the beef, partially freeze it first and cut it across the grain.

PREP 25 Minutes TOTAL 4 Hours 25 Minutes • *6 servings*

- 2 lb boneless beef chuck roast, trimmed of fat, thinly sliced
- 1 cup beef broth (for homemade broth, see page 157)
- 2 teaspoons Greek seasoning
- 1 teaspoon salt
- ½ teaspoon pepper
- 2 slices lemon
- 8 (6-inch) pita (pocket) breads
- 1 cup Tzatziki Dip (for homemade, see page 41)
- 1 cup loosely packed spinach leaves
- ¾ cup diced tomato
- ⅓ cup chopped red onion

1 Stir beef, beef broth, Greek seasoning, salt, pepper and lemon slices in slow cooker.

2 Cover; cook on Low heat setting 4 to 5 hours, until beef is tender. Stir halfway through cooking, to break up beef and ensure it is covered in liquid.

3 Drain beef; discard cooking liquid and lemon slices. To serve, divide beef on top of pitas; top with tzatziki dip, spinach, tomato and onion.

1 Serving Calories 450; Total Fat 17g (Saturated Fat 7g, Trans Fat 0.5g); Cholesterol 85mg; Sodium 920mg; Total Carbohydrate 37g (Dietary Fiber 2g); Protein 37g **Carbohydrate Choices:** 2½

MULTI-COOKER DIRECTIONS: Spray 6-quart multi-cooker insert with cooking spray. In insert, mix beef, broth, Greek seasoning, salt, pepper and lemon slices. Secure lid; set pressure valve to SEALING. Select MANUAL; cook on high pressure 30 minutes. Select CANCEL. Keep pressure valve in SEALING position to release pressure naturally. Discard cooking liquid and lemon slices; serve as directed.

Sheet-Pan Carne Asada

If your broiler only covers the center of your oven, start the steak in the center of the pan, then thoroughly stir vegetables and position them in the center while the steak rests to ensure all elements get plenty of time directly under the flames.

PREP 15 Minutes **TOTAL** 35 Minutes • *6 servings*

- ¼ cup vegetable oil
- 1½ teaspoons ground cumin
- 1½ teaspoons ground coriander
- ¾ teaspoon salt
- 2 ears fresh sweet corn, cut into thirds, or 6 pieces frozen corn-on-the-cob, thawed (from 12-count package)
- 1 medium red bell pepper, cut in thin strips
- 1 medium yellow bell pepper, cut in thin strips
- 1 medium yellow onion, thinly sliced
- 1 package (1 oz) taco seasoning mix or ¼ cup Salt-Free Taco Seasoning Mix (page 454)
- ¼ teaspoon ground red pepper (cayenne)
- 1 beef flank steak (about 1.3 lb)

1 Set oven control to broil. Spray 18x13x1-inch half-sheet pan with cooking spray. In large bowl, mix 2 tablespoons of the vegetable oil, the cumin, coriander and salt. Add corn, bell peppers and onion; toss to coat. Spoon into pan.

2 In same large bowl, mix remaining 2 tablespoons oil, the taco seasoning mix and red pepper. Add steak; rub mixture into steak. Place in pan with vegetables.

3 Broil 8 to 10 minutes, turning steak and stirring vegetables once, until instant-read thermometer inserted in thickest part of steak reads 135°F (for medium-rare). Remove steak to cutting board. Cover with foil; let stand at least 5 minutes.

4 Meanwhile, stir vegetables in pan; return to oven. Broil 4 to 6 minutes longer or until vegetables are blackened in spots. Thinly slice steak against the grain. Serve steak with vegetables.

1 Serving Calories 290; Total Fat 14g (Saturated Fat 3g, Trans Fat 0g); Cholesterol 65mg; Sodium 650mg; Total Carbohydrate 15g (Dietary Fiber 2g); Protein 26g **Carbohydrate Choices:** 1

Sloppy Joes

PREP 30 Minutes **TOTAL** 30 Minutes • *6 sandwiches*

- 1 lb ground beef (at least 80% lean)
- 1 small onion, chopped (½ cup)
- 1 medium stalk celery, chopped (⅓ cup)
- 1 cup ketchup
- 1 tablespoon Worcestershire sauce
- 1 teaspoon ground mustard
- ⅛ teaspoon pepper
- 6 burger buns, split

1 In 10-inch skillet, cook beef, onion and celery over medium heat 8 to 10 minutes, stirring occasionally, until beef is thoroughly cooked. Drain; return mixture to skillet.

2 Stir in ketchup, Worcestershire sauce, mustard and pepper. Heat to boiling; reduce heat. Simmer uncovered 10 to 15 minutes, stirring occasionally, until hot and bubbly. Spoon into buns.

1 Sandwich Calories 320; Total Fat 11g (Saturated Fat 4g, Trans Fat 1.5g); Cholesterol 50mg; Sodium 630mg; Total Carbohydrate 35g (Dietary Fiber 1g); Protein 18g **Carbohydrate Choices:** 2

LIGHTER DIRECTIONS: For 3 grams of fat and 235 calories per serving, substitute ground turkey breast for ground beef; spray skillet with cooking spray before heating.

SLOPPY JOE–POTATO NUGGET CASSEROLE: Heat oven to 350°F. Spray 13x9-inch (3-quart) glass baking dish with cooking spray. Increase onion to 1 cup; substitute 1 can (15 oz) tomato sauce and 2 tablespoons brown sugar for ketchup. Substitute 1 tablespoon yellow mustard for ground mustard. Cook beef mixture as directed. Place half of a 32-oz bag frozen potato nuggets in single layer in baking dish. Pour beef mixture over nuggets. Top with 1 cup shredded cheddar cheese, then the remaining potato nuggets. Top with another 1 cup shredded cheddar cheese. Bake 45 to 55 minutes or until casserole is bubbly and potatoes are lightly browned. Top wwith ¼ cup chopped dill pickles.

WHAT ARE WAGYU AND KOBE BEEF?

Wagyu refers to Japanese beef cattle that have been bred to produce very well-marbled meat, which translates into very tender, flavorful meat when cooked. **Kobe** beef is Wagyu that comes only from the Kobe region of Japan. It's the most expensive beef in the world. It's incredibly tender with a very rich flavor because the cattle produce well-marbled meat. Beer and massages are given to the cattle to help distribute the fat and make it more consistent. It causes the meat to have a pinker color, rather than the bright red color we associate with beef in the United States.

GLOBAL FLAVORS

South America

The diverse cuisines of South America are as different as the countries and regions found there. Influences from Africa and European countries have created a mash-up of indigenous ingredients paired with external cuisines. Try Sheet-Pan Carne Asada, page 289, for a South American–inspired dish.

CARNE SECA

Brazilian salted dried beef, similar to beef jerky.

DRIED SHRIMP/PRAWNS

Popular in Brazilian cooking and also in other parts of South America, dried shrimp have a strong, fishy taste. Used in small amounts to add flavor to stews, spicy sauces and other dishes; reconstituted whole, chopped or ground. The liquid used to soak them may also be added for flavor.

MATÉ

The leaves and young twigs of the maté tree, dried, shredded and aged in cedar containers before being sold to make the popular tea-like, energy-boosting drink.

PALM OIL

Distinctively flavored reddish-orange oil, integral to Brazilian cooking. Also known as dende oil, it's extracted from the fruit of the African palm. It's not to be confused with palm kernel oil, which is used to make margarine and cosmetics.

PLANTAINS

Large, firm cooking bananas, usually cooked when green and used like potatoes in vegetable side dishes. When green, they have a mild, squash-like flavor; when allowed to ripen and turn yellow, the flavor becomes slightly sweet, with a soft, spongy texture when cooked.

SEASONINGS

Annatto is a derivative of achiote seed used to add color and flavor to Latin American dishes. Ají amarillo paste is made from ají amarillo hot pepper, a Peruvian staple made almost daily for use in most recipes. Black mint paste (huacatay) is made from the pungent herb, adding a unique flavor to Peruvian meals.

YERBA MATÉ

A tea-like drink made by steeping the dried, aged leaves and young twigs of the maté tree in hot water. South Americans have been sipping this energy-boosting earthy, herbal beverage for centuries, but its popularity is now spreading globally. Bottled varieties (frequently sweetened) and the dried "tea" are available in Latin markets.

YUCA/YUCA ROOT

Essential tuber in South American cuisine. Also called cassava or manioc. Sold with a waxy coating to protect its skin from bruising, yuca is traditionally boiled, roasted or fried in thin chips. It can be ground into flour or tapioca to thicken dishes.

Plantains

Palm Oil

Sugar Cane

Yellow Hot Pepper
(Ají Amarillo)

Avocados

Yerba
Maté

Annatto Seeds

291

Aloe

Sorrel

Pine
Nuts

Yellow Hot
Pepper Paste
(Ají Amarillo)

Queso Fresco

Carne Seca

Dried Prawns

Dried Black
Beans

Manioc Flour

Tapioca Flour

Dried Red
Corn

Black Mint Paste
(Huacatay)

Yuca Root

Dried White Corn

Limes

Dried Yellow
Hot Pepper
(Ají Mirasol)

Dried Panca Pepper
(Ají Panca)

Meat Loaf

Cover and refrigerate any leftover meat loaf for up to 2 days. Use the slices for delicious sandwiches!

PREP 20 Minutes **TOTAL** 1 Hour 40 Minutes • *6 servings*

1½ lb ground beef (at least 80% lean)
1 cup milk
1 tablespoon Worcestershire sauce
1 teaspoon chopped fresh or ¼ teaspoon dried sage leaves
½ teaspoon salt
½ teaspoon ground mustard
¼ teaspoon pepper

1 clove garlic, finely chopped, or ⅛ teaspoon garlic powder
1 egg
3 slices bread, torn into small pieces*
⅓ cup finely chopped onion
½ cup ketchup, chili sauce or barbecue sauce

1 Heat oven to 350°F. In large bowl, mix all ingredients except ketchup. Spread mixture in ungreased 8x4- or 9x5-inch loaf pan, or shape into 9x5-inch loaf in ungreased 13x9-inch pan. Spread ketchup over top.

2 Insert ovenproof meat thermometer so tip is in center of loaf. Bake uncovered 1 hour to 1 hour 15 minutes or until beef is no longer pink in center and thermometer reads 160°F; drain. Let stand 5 minutes; remove meat loaf from pan. Cut into slices.

1 Serving Calories 290; Total Fat 15g (Saturated Fat 6g, Trans Fat 0.5g); Cholesterol 105mg; Sodium 570mg; Total Carbohydrate 16g (Dietary Fiber 0g); Protein 23g **Carbohydrate Choices:** 1

*½ cup dry bread crumbs or ¾ cup quick-cooking oats can be substituted for the bread.

LIGHTER DIRECTIONS: For 7 grams of fat and 240 calories per serving, substitute ground turkey breast for ground beef and ¼ cup fat-free egg product for egg. Use fat-free (skim) milk. Bake as directed, until turkey is no longer pink in center and thermometer reads at least 165°F.

MINI MEAT LOAVES: Spray 12 regular-size muffin cups with cooking spray. Divide beef mixture evenly among cups (cups will be very full). Brush tops with about ¼ cup ketchup. Place muffin pan on cookie sheet. Bake about 30 minutes or until loaves are no longer pink in center and thermometer reads 160°F when inserted in center of loaves in middle of muffin pan (outer loaves will be done sooner). Immediately remove from cups.

GREEK MEAT LOAF: Substitute 1½ teaspoons dried oregano leaves for sage leaves. Omit ketchup, chili sauce or barbecue sauce. Stir in 2 cups chopped fresh baby spinach leaves and ½ cup crumbled feta cheese into the beef mixture before baking. Bake in 9x5-inch loaf pan.

MEXICAN MEAT LOAF: Omit sage. Substitute ⅔ cup milk and ⅓ cup salsa for 1 cup milk. Stir in ½ cup shredded Colby-Monterey Jack cheese blend (2 oz) and 1 can (4.5 oz) chopped green chiles, drained, in Step 1. Substitute ⅔ cup salsa for ketchup.

HORSERADISH MEAT LOAF: Omit sage. Stir in 1 to 2 tablespoons cream-style prepared horseradish in Step 1.

Greek Meat Loaf Sandwiches

This is a delicious use for leftover Greek Meat Loaf! Simply warm the slices before making into sandwiches.

PREP 25 Minutes **TOTAL** 25 Minutes • *4 sandwiches*

8 slices white sandwich bread
¼ cup mayonnaise
8 slices Havarti cheese (from 7-oz package)
¼ cup crumbled feta cheese (1 oz)
4 slices Greek Meat Loaf, ¾ inch thick, warmed (at left)

½ cup roasted red bell pepper, cut into 1-inch-wide strips
16 thin slices cucumber or zucchini
4 thin slices red onion, separated
½ cup loosely packed fresh baby spinach leaves

1 Spread one side of 4 slices of bread with about 1 teaspoon mayonnaise each. Place bread slices, mayonnaise side down, on griddle or in 12-inch skillet. Top each with 1 slice Havarti cheese; sprinkle with 1 tablespoon crumbled feta cheese. Top each with slice of meat loaf. Divide pepper strips, cucumber slices, red onion slices and baby spinach leaves among sandwiches. Top each with another slice of cheese and remaining bread slices. Spread tops of sandwiches with remaining mayonnaise.

2 Cook uncovered over medium-low heat 3 to 4 minutes or until bottoms are golden brown. Carefully turn; cook 2 to 3 minutes longer until bottoms are golden brown and cheese is melted. Cut sandwiches in half before serving.

1 Sandwich Calories 760; Total Fat 47g (Saturated Fat 21g, Trans Fat 1.5g); Cholesterol 175mg; Sodium 1320mg; Total Carbohydrate 43g (Dietary Fiber 3g); Protein 41g **Carbohydrate Choice:** 3

Meat Loaf

Bacon Cheeseburger–Potato
Nugget Bake

Beef-Mushroom Smash Burgers

Bacon Cheeseburger–Potato Nugget Bake

For a truly loaded dish, offer more sour cream that you've mixed with a little red pepper sauce to spoon onto each serving.

PREP 20 Minutes **TOTAL** 1 Hour 10 Minutes • **8 servings**

- 1 lb ground beef (at least 80% lean)
- 1 medium onion, chopped (1 cup)
- 2 teaspoons Montreal steak grill seasoning
- 1 can (10.5 oz) condensed cream of onion or cream of mushroom soup

- ½ cup sour cream
- 1 bag (32 oz) frozen potato nuggets
- 4 slices bacon, cooked, coarsely chopped
- 2 cups shredded cheddar cheese (8 oz)
- 4 medium green onions, chopped (¼ cup)

1 Heat oven to 350°F. Spray 13x9-inch (3-quart) glass baking dish with cooking spray. In 10-inch nonstick skillet, cook beef and onion over medium-high heat 7 to 9 minutes, stirring frequently, until brown. Drain; return mixture to skillet.

2 Stir in grill seasoning, soup and sour cream; stir to mix completely.

3 Place half of the frozen potato nuggets in single layer in baking dish. Spoon beef mixture on top. Top with half of the bacon, 1 cup of the cheddar cheese, the remaining frozen potatoes and remaining 1 cup cheese.

4 Bake 40 minutes. Top with remaining bacon. Bake 5 to 10 minutes or until casserole edges are bubbly and potatoes are lightly browned. Sprinkle with green onions.

1 Serving Calories 520; Total Fat 33g (Saturated Fat 13g, Trans Fat 0.5g); Cholesterol 75mg; Sodium 1280mg; Total Carbohydrate 34g (Dietary Fiber 3g); Protein 21g **Carbohydrate Choices:** 2

BACON TURKEY BURGER–POTATO NUGGET BAKE: Substitute ground turkey for ground beef.

CALORIE SMART

Beef-Mushroom Smash Burgers

PREP 25 Minutes **TOTAL** 45 Minutes • **4 burgers**

SPICY MAYONNAISE
- ¼ cup mayonnaise
- 2 teaspoons Sriracha sauce
- 1 teaspoon Asian chili garlic sauce (sambal oelek)
- ½ teaspoon lemon juice

BURGERS
- 1 package (8 oz) sliced baby portabella mushrooms

- 1 small onion, peeled, quartered
- 1 tablespoon plus 2 teaspoons vegetable oil
- ½ lb ground beef (at least 80% lean)
- ¼ teaspoon salt
- ¼ teaspoon pepper
  Baby arugula or baby spinach, if desired
- 4 burger buns
  Coarsely ground pepper, if desired

1 In small bowl, mix mayonnaise ingredients. Cover; refrigerate until serving time.

2 In food processor, pulse mushrooms and onion until finely chopped. In 12-inch nonstick skillet, heat 1 tablespoon of the oil over medium-high heat. Add mushroom and onion mixture; cook, stirring occasionally, 4 to 6 minutes or until most of the liquid is gone. Spoon into medium heatproof bowl; cool 10 minutes.

3 Add ground beef, salt and pepper to cooked mushroom mixture; mix well. Press mixture evenly into 4 patties, about ½-inch thick.

4 In same skillet, heat remaining 2 teaspoons oil over medium-high heat until hot. Place patties in pan; press down with spatula until they are each ¼-inch thick. Cook 4 minutes; carefully turn and cook 2 to 4 minutes longer, until no longer pink in center and crust forms around edges. Place patties on bun bottoms; spread with mayonnaise. Top with arugula, coarsely ground pepper and bun tops.

1 Burger Calories 390; Total Fat 24g (Saturated Fat 5g, Trans Fat 0g); Cholesterol 40mg; Sodium 560mg; Total Carbohydrate 27g (Dietary Fiber 1g); Protein 16g **Carbohydrate Choices:** 2

HEIRLOOM

SLOW COOKER

Pot Roast

Spreading a layer of horseradish all over the outside of the meat is the secret to making this pot roast. Contrary to what you might think, the horseradish doesn't add a hot or spicy flavor. Instead, it mellows during cooking, leaving behind a delicious flavor.

PREP 30 Minutes **TOTAL** 4 Hours • *8 servings*

2 tablespoons vegetable oil	8 small potatoes, cut in half
1 boneless beef chuck, arm, shoulder or blade pot roast (4 lb)*	8 medium carrots or parsnips, peeled, cut into quarters
1 teaspoon salt	8 small whole onions, peeled
1 teaspoon pepper	½ cup cold water
1 jar (8 oz) prepared white horseradish	¼ cup all-purpose flour
1 cup water	Chopped fresh parsley, if desired

1 In 4-quart saucepan, heat oil over medium-high heat until hot. Add roast; cook until brown on all sides. Reduce heat to low.

2 Sprinkle roast with salt and pepper. Spread horseradish over all sides of roast. Add 1 cup water to saucepan. Heat to boiling; reduce heat. Cover; simmer 2 hours 30 minutes.

3 Add potatoes, carrots and onions to saucepan. Cover; simmer about 1 hour longer or until roast and vegetables are tender. Remove roast and vegetables to warm platter; cover with foil to keep warm.

4 Skim excess fat from liquid in saucepan. Add enough water to liquid to measure 2 cups. In tightly covered container, shake ½ cup cold water and the flour; gradually stir into liquid in saucepan. Heat to boiling, stirring constantly. Boil and stir 1 minute. Serve gravy with roast and vegetables. Sprinkle with parsley.

1 Serving Calories 590; Total Fat 24g (Saturated Fat 9g, Trans Fat 1g); Cholesterol 145mg; Sodium 560mg; Total Carbohydrate 47g (Dietary Fiber 7g); Protein 46g **Carbohydrate Choices:** 3

*A 3-lb beef bottom round, rolled rump, tip or chuck eye roast can be used; reduce salt to ¾ teaspoon.

SLOW-COOKER DIRECTIONS: In 12-inch skillet, heat oil over medium-high heat until hot. Add roast; cook until brown on all sides. Spray 4- to 6-quart slow cooker with cooking spray. In slow cooker, place potatoes, carrots and onions. Place roast on vegetables. In small bowl, mix horseradish, salt and pepper; spread evenly over roast. Add 1 cup water. Cover; cook on Low heat setting 8 to 10 hours or until roast and vegetables are tender. Continue as directed in Step 4.

BARBECUE POT ROAST: Reduce pepper to ½ teaspoon. Omit horseradish and water. Make Smoky Barbecue Sauce (page 440). After browning roast in Step 1, pour barbecue sauce over beef. Omit ½ cup cold water and the flour. Continue as directed in Step 4.

CONFETTI POT ROAST: Omit horseradish and potatoes. Sprinkle beef with ½ teaspoon Italian seasoning. Add ½ lb fresh green beans, trimmed, and 1 cup whole kernel frozen corn with the carrots in Step 3. Continue as directed. Serve with mashed potatoes.

Pot Roast

NEW TWIST

MULTI COOKER • CALORIE SMART • GLUTEN FREE

Pho-Style Pot Roast Dinner

Cutting the roast into four pieces before cooking allows the meat to cook until very tender in the time everything else gets done. For a more robust flavor, add 2 whole star anise with the lemongrass. Star anise adds the sweet and spicy licorice-like flavor used in Vietnamese cuisine to flavor pho. It can be found either in the spice aisle, in the produce section or where other Asian ingredients are located.

PREP 25 Minutes TOTAL 1 Hour 35 Minutes • **6 servings**

- 1 tablespoon vegetable oil
- 1 boneless beef chuck roast (2 lb), cut into 4 pieces
- ½ teaspoon salt
- ¼ teaspoon pepper
- 2 cups gluten-free beef broth (for homemade broth, see page 157)
- 1 cup water
- ¼ cup rice vinegar
- 3 tablespoons gluten-free fish sauce (from 6.76-oz bottle)
- 1 tablespoon grated fresh gingerroot
- 2 cloves garlic, finely chopped

- 1½ teaspoons gluten-free five-spice powder
- 3 (3-inch) pieces lemongrass stalk, crushed slightly with meat mallet to break outer layers
- 2 large sweet potatoes (1½ lb), peeled, cut into 1-inch pieces (4 cups)
- 7 oz uncooked rice noodles (from 14-oz package)
- 1 small red bell pepper, cut into very thin strips or 1 fresh red Thai chile, sliced
- 6 lime slices, cut in half
- 6 sprigs fresh Thai basil, if desired

1 In 6-quart Dutch oven or stockpot, heat oil over medium heat. Add roast pieces; sprinkle with salt and pepper. Cook 4 to 6 minutes, turning once, until browned. Add broth, water, vinegar, fish sauce, gingerroot, garlic, five-spice powder and lemongrass; reduce heat. Cover and simmer 30 minutes.

2 Add sweet potatoes. Cover and simmer 30 minutes or until roast and sweet potatoes are tender. Using slotted spoon, place beef and sweet potatoes in heatproof bowl; cover with foil to keep warm. Remove lemongrass.

3 Heat liquid in Dutch oven to boiling. Stir noodles into liquid; cover and remove from heat. Let stand 10 minutes or until noodles are soft yet firm.

4 To serve, remove roast to cutting board. Cut into bite-size pieces. Using tongs, place about ½ cup of the noodles into each of six individual serving bowls. Top each with roast pieces and sweet potatoes. Pour ⅓ cup broth over roast and potatoes. Top with bell pepper strips and lime slices. Garnish with basil.

Pho-Style Pot Roast Dinner

1 Serving Calories 460; Total Fat 19g (Saturated Fat 7g, Trans Fat 0.5g); Cholesterol 80mg; Sodium 1240mg; Total Carbohydrate 40g (Dietary Fiber 3g); Protein 32g **Carbohydrate Choices:** 2½

MULTI-COOKER DIRECTIONS: Decrease broth to 1½ cups and water to ¾ cup. Spray 6-quart multi-cooker insert with cooking spray. Select SAUTE; adjust to normal. Heat oil in insert. Sprinkle roast pieces with salt and pepper. Cook half of roast 2 to 3 minutes on first side until browned; turn. Cook 2 to 3 minutes on second side or until browned; remove to heatproof plate. Repeat with remaining roast pieces. Select CANCEL. Return all roast pieces to insert. Add broth, water, vinegar, fish sauce, gingerroot, garlic, five-spice powder and lemongrass to roast in insert; stir to mix. Place sweet potatoes on top of roast. Secure lid; set pressure valve to SEALING. Select MANUAL/PRESSURE COOK; cook on high pressure 45 minutes. Select CANCEL. Set pressure valve to VENTING to quick-release pressure. Once all pressure has been released (about 5 minutes), remove roast and sweet potatoes with slotted spoon; cover with foil to keep warm. Select SAUTE. Heat liquid in insert to boiling. Stir noodles into liquid mixture. Select CANCEL. Cover; let stand 10 minutes or until noodles are soft yet firm. Discard lemongrass. To serve, place beef on cutting board. Using two forks, break roast into bite-size pieces. Continue as directed in Step 4.

5-INGREDIENT RECIPE

Ground Beef

Black Beans

Pico de Gallo

Pepper Jack Cheese

Stacked Beef Enchilada Bake

Corn Tortillas

PROGRESSO
BLACK BEANS

296

5-INGREDIENT RECIPE

GLUTEN FREE

Stacked Beef Enchilada Bake

PREP 20 Minutes **TOTAL** 50 Minutes • *6 servings*

1 lb ground beef (at least 80% lean)	9 (6-inch) soft corn tortillas
1 can (15 oz) black beans, drained, rinsed	3 cups shredded cheddar cheese (12 oz)
2 cups pico de gallo, drained	

1 Heat oven to 350°F. Spray 8-inch square (2-quart) glass baking dish with cooking spray.

2 In 10-inch skillet, cook beef over medium heat 8 to 10 minutes, stirring occasionally, until beef is thoroughly cooked. Drain; return to skillet. Stir in black beans and 1 cup of the pico de gallo; heat through.

3 Place 3 corn tortillas on bottom of dish, tearing and overlapping as needed to cover bottom. Spoon half of beef mixture over tortillas. Sprinkle 1 cup of the cheese over beef mixture; repeat layers, ending with 3 tortillas. Top with remaining 1 cup pico de gallo and 1 cup cheese.

4 Cover with foil. Bake about 20 minutes; uncover and bake about 10 minutes longer until mixture is hot.

1 Serving Calories 510; Total Fat 28g (Saturated Fat 15g, Trans Fat 1g); Cholesterol 100mg; Sodium 840mg; Total Carbohydrate 32g (Dietary Fiber 7g); Protein 32g **Carbohydrate Choices:** 2

SLOW COOKER

French Dip Sandwiches

PREP 10 Minutes **TOTAL** 7 Hours 10 Minutes • *10 sandwiches*

1 boneless beef chuck roast (3 lb)	1 clove garlic, finely chopped
1½ cups water	1 dried bay leaf
⅓ cup soy sauce	3 or 4 black peppercorns
1 teaspoon dried rosemary leaves	2 loaves (1 lb each) French bread
1 teaspoon dried thyme leaves	

1 Spray 3½- to 4-quart slow cooker with cooking spray. Place roast in slow cooker (if roast comes in netting or is tied, do not remove). In medium bowl, mix remaining ingredients except bread; pour over roast.

2 Cover; cook on Low heat setting 7 to 8 hours. Skim fat from surface of juices; discard bay leaf and peppercorns. Remove roast from slow cooker; place on cutting board (remove netting or strings). Cut roast into thin slices.

3 Cut loaf horizontally in half; cut loaf crosswise into 5 pieces, about 4 inches long. Fill bread with beef. Serve cooking juices in small bowls for dipping.

1 Sandwich Calories 480; Total Fat 16g (Saturated Fat 6g, Trans Fat 0.5g); Cholesterol 75mg; Sodium 1070mg; Total Carbohydrate 48g (Dietary Fiber 2g); Protein 35g **Carbohydrate Choices:** 3

SLOW COOKER

Barbecue Beef Sandwiches

PREP 15 Minutes **TOTAL** 7 Hours 35 Minutes •
12 sandwiches

1 boneless beef chuck roast (3 lb), trimmed of fat	1 tablespoon Dijon mustard
1 cup barbecue sauce	2 teaspoons packed brown sugar
½ cup apricot or peach preserves	1 small onion, sliced
⅓ cup chopped green bell pepper	12 kaiser rolls or burger buns, split

1 Spray 4- to 5-quart slow cooker with cooking spray. Cut beef into 4 pieces; place in slow cooker. In medium bowl, mix remaining ingredients except rolls; pour over beef. Cover; cook on Low heat setting 7 to 8 hours or until beef is tender.

2 Remove beef from slow cooker to cutting board; cut into thin slices. Return beef to slow cooker. Cover; cook 20 to 30 minutes longer or until hot. Spoon beef mixture into buns with slotted spoon. If desired, serve juices in small bowls for dipping.

1 Sandwich Calories 440; Total Fat 14g (Saturated Fat 5g, Trans Fat 1g); Cholesterol 60mg; Sodium 620mg; Total Carbohydrate 50g (Dietary Fiber 2g); Protein 27g **Carbohydrate Choices:** 3

French Dip Sandwiches

Barbecue Beef Sandwiches

Smothered Beef Burritos

PREP 30 Minutes **TOTAL** 1 Hour 5 Minutes • *8 burritos*

- 1 tablespoon vegetable oil
- 1 lb ground beef (at least 80% lean)
- 1 small onion chopped (½ cup)
- 1 package (1 oz) taco seasoning mix or ¼ cup Salt-Free Taco Seasoning Mix (page 454)
- ½ cup water
- 1 package (11 oz) flour tortillas for burritos (8 tortillas; 8 inch)
- 1 cup refried beans (from 16-oz can)
- 1½ cups cooked rice (page 224)
- 2 cups shredded Mexican cheese blend (8 oz)
- 1 can (10 oz) enchilada sauce
- Chopped fresh cilantro leaves, if desired
- Lime wedges, if desired

1 Heat oven to 350°F. In 12-inch ovenproof skillet, heat oil over medium-high heat. Add beef and onion; cook 5 to 7 minutes, stirring frequently, until thoroughly cooked. Drain; return mixture to skillet.

2 Stir taco seasoning mix and water into beef mixture. Cook over medium heat 2 to 3 minutes or until thickened, stirring occasionally. Spoon mixture into medium heatproof bowl. Carefully wipe out skillet with paper towel. Spray skillet with cooking spray.

3 Place tortillas on work surface. Spoon refried beans, rice and beef mixture in center of each tortilla in 4-inch-long strip. Top with 1 cup of the cheese. Fold one edge of each tortilla over length of filling, tucking filling in slightly. Then fold two short edges over. Roll filled tortilla over toward remaining unfolded edge. Place seam side down in skillet. Bake uncovered 25 minutes.

4 Drizzle burritos with enchilada sauce; sprinkle with remaining 1 cup cheese. Bake 8 to 10 minutes longer or until cheese is melted and burritos are heated through. Serve with cilantro and lime wedges.

1 Burrito Calories 430; Total Fat 21g (Saturated Fat 9g, Trans Fat 1.5g); Cholesterol 60mg; Sodium 1070mg; Total Carbohydrate 38g (Dietary Fiber 2g); Protein 22g **Carbohydrate Choices:** 2½

Cuban Picadillo Tacos

PREP 35 Minutes **TOTAL** 35 Minutes • *5 servings* (2 tacos each)

PICADILLO

- ½ lb ground beef (at least 80% lean)
- ½ lb ground pork
- 1 medium zucchini, chopped (1 cup)
- 1 medium onion, chopped (1 cup)
- ½ cup chopped red bell pepper
- 2 tablespoons tomato paste
- 2 tablespoons balsamic vinegar
- 2 cloves garlic, finely chopped
- 1 teaspoon ground cumin
- 1 teaspoon dried oregano leaves
- ½ teaspoon ground cinnamon
- ½ teaspoon salt
- ¼ teaspoon pepper
- 1 can (14.5 oz) diced tomatoes, undrained
- ½ cup raisins
- ½ cup sliced pimiento stuffed olives

TACOS

- 10 (6-inch) flour tortillas, heated as directed on package
- 1 cup cubed fresh mango
- 1 cup crumbled Cotija or feta cheese
- ¼ chopped fresh cilantro

1 In 12-inch nonstick skillet, cook beef, pork, zucchini, onion and bell pepper over medium-high heat 8 to 10 minutes, stirring occasionally, until beef and pork are thoroughly cooked. Drain; return mixture to skillet.

2 Stir in tomato paste, vinegar, garlic, cumin, oregano, cinnamon, salt and pepper. Cook 1 minute. Add tomatoes, raisins and olives. Heat to boiling; reduce heat. Simmer 5 minutes, stirring occasionally.

3 Spoon about ⅔ cup picadillo filling down center of each tortilla. Top each with mango, cheese and cilantro.

1 Serving Calories 590; Total Fat 28g (Saturated Fat 11g, Trans Fat 0.5g); Cholesterol 85mg; Sodium 1440mg; Total Carbohydrate 56g (Dietary Fiber 7g); Protein 30g **Carbohydrate Choices:** 4

Smothered Beef Burritos

Cuban Picadillo Tacos

Stuffed Cuban Pork Tenderloin

CALORIE SMART • GLUTEN FREE

Stuffed Cuban Pork Tenderloin

Lining the pan with cooking parchment paper will cut down on mess and make cleanup easier. Pork tenderloins are sometimes sold in packages of two. If so, freeze the second for another use.

PREP 30 Minutes TOTAL 1 Hour 5 Minutes • *6 servings*

1 pork tenderloin (1¼ lb), trimmed of fat	3 deli slices ham (about ¼ lb)
1 tablespoon yellow mustard	1 tablespoon vegetable oil
6 thin slices Swiss cheese (½ oz each)	½ teaspoon salt
⅓ cup dill pickle relish	½ teaspoon pepper

1 Heat oven to 350°F. Line 15x10x1-inch pan with cooking parchment paper. Insert knife one-third of way up from bottom of tenderloin along one long side and cut horizontally, stopping ½ inch before edge. Open up tenderloin; lay it flat on cutting board. Keep knife parallel to cutting board, level with first cut (about one-third of way up from bottom) and start from the center to cut through thicker portion of tenderloin horizontally, stopping about ½ inch before edge. Open up this flap.

2 Press down flaps of tenderloin so it lies flat. Cover with plastic wrap; pound with flat side of meat mallet until ½-inch thick. Spread mustard down center of tenderloin. Top with cheese slices, pickle relish and ham slices, folding to fit if necessary. Tightly roll up tenderloin lengthwise; tie tightly with twine. Brush tenderloin with oil; sprinkle with salt and pepper.

3 Heat 12-inch nonstick skillet over medium-high heat. Add pork; cook, turning once, 5 to 6 minutes or until browned on all sides. Remove from skillet to parchment-lined pan. Insert ovenproof meat thermometer into pork. Roast 28 to 32 minutes or until thermometer reads 145°F. Remove from oven. Cover with foil; let stand 3 minutes.

4 Remove strings from pork; cut into ½-inch slices. Serve with extra mustard, if desired.

1 Serving Calories 230; Total Fat 12g (Saturated Fat 4.5g, Trans Fat 0g); Cholesterol 80mg; Sodium 740mg; Total Carbohydrate 2g (Dietary Fiber 0g); Protein 29g **Carbohydrate Choices:** 0

Katsu Sando

This homey Japanese sandwich is a cinch to put together for quick meals when you have the shokupan already made. Juicy pork cutlets are panfried with a crispy coating and sandwiched between pillow-soft slices of shokupan (milk bread) with shredded cabbage and an Asian sauce.

PREP 25 Minutes **TOTAL** 25 Minutes • *4 sandwiches*

KATSU SAUCE

- ½ cup ketchup
- 3 tablespoons Worcestershire sauce
- 2 tablespoons soy sauce
- 2 teaspoons Dijon mustard
- 2 teaspoons packed brown sugar
- 1½ teaspoons ground ginger
- ½ teaspoon garlic powder

PORK CHOPS

- 4 boneless pork loin chops (3 to 4 oz each; about ½-inch thick)

- 2 eggs
- ¼ cup all-purpose flour
- 1 teaspoon chopped fresh thyme leaves
- ½ teaspoon salt
- ¼ teaspoon pepper
- 1¼ cups crispy panko bread crumbs
- 3 tablespoons vegetable oil
- 8 slices Shokupan (page 526) or sandwich bread, toasted, if desired
- 8 teaspoons coarse ground mustard
- 2¾ cups coleslaw mix (from 16-oz bag)

1 In small bowl, using whisk, stir all sauce ingredients until well mixed; set aside.

2 Between pieces of plastic wrap or waxed paper, place each pork chop. Gently pound pork chops with flat side of meat mallet or rolling pin to about ¼-inch thickness.

3 In small shallow bowl, beat eggs. In another small shallow bowl, stir flour, thyme, salt and pepper until well mixed. In a third shallow bowl, place panko bread crumbs.

Dip 1 pork chop in flour mixture to coat completely; shake off excess flour. Dip in egg on both sides; drain excess egg back into bowl. Place pork chop in panko bread crumbs. Turn; press into crumbs so they stick. Repeat dipping in egg and panko bread crumbs, to coat twice. Set aside on cooling rack. Repeat with remaining pork chops.

4 In 12-inch nonstick skillet, heat oil over medium heat. Add pork chops. Cook 4 to 6 minutes, turning once, until no longer pink in center. Remove from skillet; place on plate and cover with foil to keep warm.

5 Spread one side of each of 4 bread slices with 2 teaspoons mustard. Top with pork chop. Drizzle 2 teaspoons sauce over each pork chop. Top each pork chop with about ⅓ cup coleslaw blend. Spread one side of remaining 4 bread slices with 1 tablespoon sauce; place sauce side down on pork chops. Cut sandwiches in half; serve immediately, with remaining sauce.

1 Sandwich Calories 860; Total Fat 31g (Saturated Fat 10g, Trans Fat 0g); Cholesterol 200mg; Sodium 1960mg; Total Carbohydrate 107g (Dietary Fiber 4g); Protein 37g **Carbohydrate Choices:** 7

Smothered Skillet Pork Chops with Apples and Onions

PREP 40 Minutes **TOTAL** 40 Minutes • *4 servings*

- 4 boneless pork loin chops, 1-inch thick (about 1½ lb), trimmed of fat
- 1 teaspoon salt
- ¼ teaspoon pepper
- 4 tablespoons butter
- 1 cup thinly sliced onion

- 4 teaspoons chopped fresh thyme leaves
- 1 large Honeycrisp, Braeburn or Fuji apple, cut into ¼-inch slices (about 2 cups)
- 1 cup gluten-free chicken broth (for homemade broth, see page 153)

1 Rub pork chops with salt and pepper. In 12-inch nonstick skillet, heat 2 tablespoons of the butter over medium-high heat until melted. Add pork chops; cook 3 to 4 minutes or until browned on bottom. Turn pork; reduce heat to medium. Cook 4 to 6 minutes longer or until pork is no longer pink in center. Remove from skillet to plate; cover with foil to keep warm.

2 In same skillet, melt remaining 2 tablespoons butter over medium heat. Add onion and 3 teaspoons of the thyme; cook 5 to 6 minutes, stirring occasionally, until onions are tender and begin to brown.

3 Add apple; cook 1 to 2 minutes. Add chicken broth; simmer uncovered 6 to 7 minutes, stirring occasionally, until apples are crisp-tender and sauce is reduced. Serve onion mixture over pork. Garnish with remaining 1 teaspoon thyme.

1 Serving Calories 380; Total Fat 19g (Saturated Fat 10g, Trans Fat 0g); Cholesterol 135mg; Sodium 980mg; Total Carbohydrate 12g (Dietary Fiber 2g); Protein 40g **Carbohydrate Choices:** 1

Katsu Sando

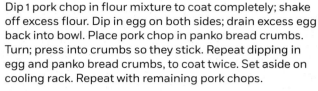

Retail Pork Cuts

Here are many of the pork cuts available at the market. They will have different names in different regions of the country, but this should help you identify what you are purchasing.

Diagram: **1** Shoulder Butt **2** Loin **3** Picnic Shoulder **4** Side **5** Leg

Pork Center Rib Roast (bone-in)

Pork Center Cut Rib Chop (bone-in)

Pork Loin Boneless Rolled Roast (double)

Pork Sirloin Chop (bone-in)

Pork Crown Roast (bone-in)

Pork Loin Chop (bone-in)

Pork Tenderloin

Pork Loin Center Cut Boneless Roast and Chops

Pork Spareribs

Pork Loin Back Ribs

Pork Blade Steak (bone-in)

Pork Blade Roast (bone-in)

Pork Ham (bone-in/shank half)

Pork Center-Cut Ham Steak

Pork Loin Country-Style Ribs

Pork Smoked Picnic

LEARN TO SEAR AND PANFRY

Searing and panfrying—terms that refer to cooking in a skillet but with subtle differences in the technique and results.

Searing is all about building flavor and caramelizing the outside of foods by cooking quickly over a fairly high heat. Meats are the foods most often seared. Sear with a small amount of oil so that the meat has direct contact with the pan. This is best accomplished in a stainless-steel or cast-iron skillet. Once meat is seared, then it is often finished in another way—braising, roasting or simmering. See also Deglazing the Pan, right.

Panfrying is different from searing in that you are cooking in a larger amount of oil—the hot oil helps to brown food first, and then the food continues to cook in the oil in the pan until it's completely done. Panfrying requires less oil than deep-frying, sometimes just a very thin layer, so there is not as much spatter. Often, panfried foods are coated with flour or other ingredients before cooking. Meats, vegetables and even tofu are candidates for this technique. Any skillet with sloping sides can be used for panfrying. Panfried Pork Chops with Cider Sauce (right) use both the sear and panfrying techniques.

Panfried Pork Chops
with Cider Sauce

Guidelines for Searing or Panfrying Meats

CHOOSE THE CORRECT PAN

SEAR Stainless-steel or cast-iron skillets are the best pans for searing. These pans can be heated to a high enough heat to brown the outside of meat evenly and quickly. Do not use nonstick pans for searing—the lower heat required for these pans is not high enough for searing.

PANFRY Use any skillet that has high, sloping sides—nonstick, stainless-steel or cast-iron skillets can all be used for this technique.

PREPARING THE MEAT AND PAN

TO SEAR This technique can be done with small cubes of meat or chops, or larger cuts of meat before roasting. Add a small amount of oil to the skillet and swirl it around to cover the bottom—1 teaspoon to 1 tablespoon is usually enough. Heat pan over medium-high heat. Sprinkle the meat with salt and pepper just before placing it in the pan.

TO PANFRY Coat with seasonings, flour, or crumbs just before cooking. Use about ¼ inch oil in the pan.

HEATING THE SKILLET

Use medium-high heat to start for both techniques. The skillet should be hot when the meat is added.

ADDING THE MEAT

TO SEAR Add the meat slowly to the pan—it should sizzle as you add it. The meat will stick to the bottom of the pan as you add it; that is okay. It is the contact with the bottom of the pan that helps to provide the desired browning. Let the meat sizzle and cook uncovered a couple of minutes, lowering the heat slightly if it seems to be burning. Do not add any liquid. When the meat is seared and browned, it will start to come loose from the bottom of the pan. As it loosens, turn the meat over. Cook the other side until it is also browned. Continue with the recipe as directed.

TO PANFRY Allow food to brown before turning; ideally, turn only one time. Continue cooking the food uncovered as directed in the recipe.

Panfried Pork Chops with Cider Sauce

PREP 25 Minutes **TOTAL** 25 Minutes • *4 servings*

4 boneless pork loin chops, ½- to ¾-inch thick (1 lb), trimmed of fat	⅛ teaspoon garlic powder
¼ teaspoon gluten-free seasoned salt	⅛ teaspoon pepper
¼ teaspoon dried thyme leaves	1 tablespoon vegetable oil
	½ cup apple cider
	¼ cup brandy or additional apple cider
	1 tablespoon butter

1 Sprinkle both sides of pork chops with seasoned salt, thyme, garlic powder and pepper. In 12-inch skillet, heat oil over medium-high heat. Add pork; cook about 5 minutes or until bottoms are browned.

2 Turn pork chops; reduce heat to medium-low. Cook uncovered 5 to 10 minutes longer or until pork is no longer pink in center. Remove from skillet to plate; cover with foil to keep warm.

3 Add cider and brandy to skillet. Heat to boiling, stirring to loosen browned bits from bottom of skillet; reduce heat to low. Add butter; simmer 1 to 3 minutes, stirring frequently, until sauce is slightly thickened. Serve sauce over pork.

1 Serving Calories 250; Total Fat 15g (Saturated Fat 5g, Trans Fat 0g); Cholesterol 75mg; Sodium 150mg; Total Carbohydrate 4g (Dietary Fiber 0g); Protein 24g **Carbohydrate Choices:** 0

BONE-IN PORK CHOPS WITH CIDER SAUCE: Substitute 4 bone-in pork loin chops, ½-inch thick, for boneless chops. Cook about 5 minutes on each side or until browned. Reduce heat to low. Cover and cook about 10 minutes longer or until pork is no longer pink in center. Continue with Step 3.

PORK CHOPS WITH MUSTARD-CHIVE CREAM SAUCE: Omit cider, brandy and butter. Prepare recipe as directed through Step 2. Add ¼ cup dry sherry to skillet. Heat to boiling, stirring to loosen browned bits from bottom of skillet. Stir in ½ cup whipping cream, 1 tablespoon country-style Dijon mustard, 2 teaspoons

chopped fresh chives, ⅛ teaspoon salt and ⅛ teaspoon pepper. Simmer 3 minutes, stirring frequently, until slightly thickened. Serve sauce over chops.

SPICY SOUTHWESTERN PORK CHOPS: Omit all ingredients except pork chops. In small bowl, mix 1 teaspoon chili powder, 1 teaspoon finely crushed dried chipotle chile, ½ teaspoon ground cumin, ¼ teaspoon salt, ¼ teaspoon ground red pepper (cayenne), ¼ teaspoon garlic powder and ⅛ teaspoon black pepper. Rub on both sides of pork. Cook as directed in Step 2. (Pork will get very dark from the spice coating.)

Herbed Pork Loin Roast

PREP 10 Minutes **TOTAL** 1 Hour 15 Minutes • *6 servings*

1 boneless pork loin roast (1½ lb), trimmed of fat	2 tablespoons chopped fresh oregano leaves
½ teaspoon olive oil	4½ teaspoons chopped fresh chives
3 tablespoons chopped fresh sage leaves	½ teaspoon salt
2 tablespoons chopped fresh parsley	½ teaspoon freshly ground pepper

1 Heat oven to 375°F. Spray shallow roasting pan or broiler pan with cooking spray. Rub pork roast with oil. In small bowl, mix remaining ingredients. Rub mixture over roast.

2 Place roast on rack in pan. Insert ovenproof meat thermometer so tip is in thickest part of roast and does not rest in fat.

3 Roast uncovered 1 hour or until thermometer reads 145°F. Remove from rack to cutting board. Cover loosely with foil; let stand at least 3 minutes before slicing.

1 Serving Calories 130; Total Fat 6g (Saturated Fat 2g, Trans Fat 0g); Cholesterol 0mg; Sodium 250mg; Total Carbohydrate 0g (Dietary Fiber 0g); Protein 18g **Carbohydrate Choices:** 0

DEGLAZING THE PAN

After searing or panfrying meat, a brown glaze will be left in the bottom of the pan. Remove the meat from the pan and add about 1 cup broth, water or wine. Heat to boiling, scraping up the glaze from the bottom of the pan. The flavorful mixture can be added to a stew or roast, or simply reduced and used as a delicious drizzle for the meat. At the end of cooking, stir in a pat of butter until melted to add flavor and slightly thicken the sauce.

Herbed Pork Loin Roast

USE IT UP
PULLED PORK

Having a batch of pulled pork on hand is a clever way to have several creative meals practically already on the table.

BUFFALO PORK SLIDERS
Toss pulled pork with Buffalo wing sauce; heat. Place in slider buns spread with ranch dressing; top with blue cheese and spinach leaves.

PORK SPAGHETTI
Add pulled pork to spaghetti sauce; heat through. Top hot cooked spaghetti with sauce and sprinkle with Parmesan cheese.

BARBECUE OMELET
Toss pulled pork with barbecue sauce; heat through. Spoon onto one half of omelet; top with shredded cheese and sliced green onions. Fold other half of omelet over filling.

PORK-CHUTNEY EMPANADAS
Toss pulled pork with chutney, chopped red onion and jalapeño. Use as the filling for Empanadas (page 59).

PORK TACOS
Heat pulled pork; spoon into taco shells. Top with your favorite taco toppings.

CALORIE SMART • GLUTEN FREE

Oven-Roasted Pulled Pork

This flavorful, tender pulled pork can be used for sandwiches (try topping with coleslaw!), tacos, burritos, quesadillas, salads or soup.

PREP 10 Minutes **TOTAL** 5 Hours 20 Minutes • *10 servings*

- 1 boneless pork shoulder blade roast (4 lb)
- ¼ cup packed brown sugar
- 2 teaspoons salt
- 1 teaspoon garlic powder
- 1 teaspoon onion powder
- 1 teaspoon paprika
- 1 teaspoon smoked paprika
- 1 teaspoon pepper

1 Heat oven to 325°F. In 13x9-inch (3-quart) glass baking dish, place pork, fat side up (if roast has netting, do not remove). In small bowl, mix remaining ingredients. Sprinkle mixture over all pork surfaces; rub and press into meat.

2 Cover with foil. Roast 4 hours to 4 hours 30 minutes or until very tender. Place pork on cutting board. Remove excess fat from top of roast and discard. Cover roast loosely with foil; let stand 30 minutes or until cool enough to handle. Using two forks, pull pork apart into bite-size pieces; discard any fat or gristle.

3 Pour pan drippings into fat separator or skim fat from drippings. Pour pan drippings into small bowl, leaving fat in separator.

4 To use immediately, add enough pan drippings to moisten pork, if desired. Cover and microwave on High until hot. Or to make ahead, add pan drippings to keep pork moist; cover and refrigerate 3 to 4 days or freeze up to 3 months.

1 Serving Calories 270; Total Fat 15g (Saturated Fat 5g, Trans Fat 0g); Cholesterol 80mg; Sodium 520mg; Total Carbohydrate 6g (Dietary Fiber 0g); Protein 27g **Carbohydrate Choices:** ½

FAST • CALORIE SMART

Garlic Pork Marsala

PREP 30 Minutes **TOTAL** 30 Minutes • *4 servings*

- 1 pork tenderloin (about 1 lb)
- ¼ cup finely chopped fresh parsley
- 1 tablespoon finely chopped fresh sage leaves or 1 teaspoon dried sage leaves, crushed
- 1 tablespoon garlic-pepper blend
- ½ teaspoon salt
- 4 cloves garlic, finely chopped
- 2 tablespoons olive oil
- 1 package (8 oz) sliced fresh baby portabella mushrooms
- ½ cup sweet or dry Marsala wine, or chicken broth
- 2 teaspoons cornstarch
  Mashed Potatoes (page 260), if desired
  Chopped fresh sage or parsley, if desired

1 Cut pork into ½-inch slices. In small bowl, stir chopped parsley and sage, garlic-pepper, salt, garlic and 1 tablespoon of the olive oil; reserve 1 tablespoon of the mixture. Rub remaining parsley mixture over both sides of pork slices.

2 In 12-inch nonstick skillet, heat remaining 1 tablespoon olive oil over medium-high heat. Add pork; cook 5 to 7 minutes, turning once, until no longer pink in center. Remove pork from skillet to heatproof platter; cover with foil to keep warm.

3 Add mushrooms and reserved parsley mixture to skillet. Reduce heat to medium; cook 2 to 3 minutes, stirring frequently, until mushrooms are almost tender.

4 In small bowl, combine wine and cornstarch until smooth. Add to skillet; cook about 1 minute, stirring frequently, until mixture thickens. Return pork and juices to pan; cook 1 to 2 minutes or until thoroughly heated. Serve with potatoes. Sprinkle with sage.

1 Serving Calories 250; Total Fat 12g (Saturated Fat 2.5g, Trans Fat 0g); Cholesterol 70mg; Sodium 680mg; Total Carbohydrate 5g (Dietary Fiber 0g); Protein 27g **Carbohydrate Choices:** ½

Garlic Pork Marsala

Spicy Barbecue
Pork Loin Ribs

Italian Grilled Cheese Sandwiches

Spicy Barbecue Pork Loin Ribs

PREP 15 Minutes **TOTAL** 2 Hours 45 Minutes • *6 servings*

RIBS

4½	lb pork back ribs
½	teaspoon salt
¼	teaspoon pepper

SPICY BARBECUE SAUCE

⅓	cup butter
2	tablespoons white or cider vinegar
2	tablespoons water

1	teaspoon sugar
½	teaspoon garlic powder
½	teaspoon onion powder
½	teaspoon black pepper
	Dash ground red pepper (cayenne)

1 Heat oven to 325°F. With knife or kitchen scissors, cut ribs into six serving pieces. Place ribs, meat side up, on rack in roasting pan or 13x9-inch pan. Sprinkle with salt and ¼ teaspoon pepper. Cover and bake 1 hour 45 minutes.

2 In 1-quart saucepan, heat sauce ingredients over medium heat, stirring frequently, until butter is melted.

3 Brush some of the sauce over ribs. Bake uncovered 30 minutes, brushing frequently with sauce. Bake 15 minutes longer or until meat is tender and no longer pink next to bones. Heat remaining sauce to boiling; serve with ribs.

1 Serving Calories 520; Total Fat 40g (Saturated Fat 18g, Trans Fat 0.5g); Cholesterol 165mg; Sodium 380mg; Total Carbohydrate 1g (Dietary Fiber 0g); Protein 37g **Carbohydrate Choices:** 0

SLOW-COOKER DIRECTIONS: Spray 5- to 6-quart slow cooker with cooking spray. Cut ribs into 2- or 3-rib portions; place in slow cooker. Sprinkle with ½ teaspoon salt and ¼ teaspoon pepper. Pour ½ cup water into slow cooker. Cover; cook on Low heat setting 8 to 9 hours. Remove ribs. Drain and discard liquid from slow cooker. Make sauce as directed in Step 2; pour into bowl. Dip rib sections in sauce to coat. Return ribs to slow cooker. Pour remaining sauce over ribs. Cover; cook 1 hour.

BEEF SHORT RIBS: Substitute bone-in beef short ribs for pork ribs. Heat oven to 350°F. Place short ribs in 13x9-inch pan. Prepare sauce as in Step 2; pour sauce over short ribs. Cover and bake about 2 hours 30 minutes or until meat is tender.

COUNTRY-STYLE PORK RIBS: Substitute 3 lb country-style pork loin ribs for back ribs. Heat oven to 350°F. Place ribs in 13x9-inch pan. Cover and bake about 2 hours; drain. Prepare sauce as in Step 2; pour sauce over ribs. Bake uncovered 30 minutes longer or until meat is tender.

PORK SPARERIBS: Substitute pork spareribs for back ribs. Heat oven to 325°F. Cut ribs into 6 serving pieces. Place ribs, meat side up, on rack in roasting pan or 13x9-inch pan. Cover and bake 1 hour 15 minutes. Prepare sauce as in Step 2; brush ribs with sauce. Bake uncovered 30 minutes, brushing frequently with sauce. Bake about 15 minutes longer or until meat is tender and no longer pink next to bones.

MOLASSES-MUSTARD BARBECUE SAUCE: Omit sauce ingredients. In small bowl, mix ½ cup molasses and ⅓ cup Dijon mustard; stir in ⅓ cup cider vinegar or white vinegar. Use in Step 3.

SWEET-SAVORY BARBECUE SAUCE: Omit sauce ingredients. In 1-quart saucepan, mix 1 cup chili sauce, ¾ cup grape jelly, 1 tablespoon plus 1½ teaspoons dry red wine or gluten-free beef broth and 1 teaspoon Dijon mustard. Heat over medium heat, stirring occasionally, until jelly is melted. Use in Step 3.

Italian Grilled Cheese Sandwiches

PREP 20 Minutes **TOTAL** 20 Minutes • *4 sandwiches*

¼	cup basil pesto (for homemade pesto, see page 480)
8	slices Italian bread
12	slices provolone cheese (8 oz)
½	cup roasted red bell pepper strips, drained, patted dry
4	thin 4-inch-diameter slices salami (about 2 oz)

1	cup loosely packed arugula or spinach leaves
2	oz thinly sliced prosciutto (from 2- to 3-oz package)
4	thin slices red onion
8	teaspoons olive oil
	Additional pesto, if desired

1 Spread pesto on one side of each slice of bread. On each of 4 bread slices, divide remaining ingredients except olive oil over pesto, layering slices of cheese on bottom, middle and top. Top each with remaining bread slices, pesto side down.

2 Brush about 1 teaspoon of the olive oil over each top slice of bread.

3 Place sandwiches, olive oil side down, on griddle or in 12-inch skillet. Brush remaining olive oil over top slices of bread. Cook uncovered over medium-low heat about 4 minutes or until bottoms are golden brown, pressing lightly with pancake turner during cooking. Turn; cook 2 to 3 minutes longer or until bottoms are golden brown and cheese is melted. Serve with additional pesto.

1 Sandwich Calories 720; Total Fat 39g (Saturated Fat 15g, Trans Fat 0.5g); Cholesterol 65mg; Sodium 1860mg; Total Carbohydrate 60g (Dietary Fiber 2g); Protein 32g **Carbohydrate Choices:** 4

SLOW COOKER • CALORIE SMART • GLUTEN FREE

Glazed Baked Ham

PREP 10 Minutes **TOTAL** 1 Hour 50 Minutes • *10 servings*

- 1 (6-lb) fully cooked gluten-free bone-in smoked ham
- 1 cup packed brown sugar
- 1 tablespoon cornstarch
- ¼ teaspoon salt
- 1 can (8 oz) crushed pineapple, undrained
- 2 tablespoons lemon juice
- 1 tablespoon yellow or Dijon mustard

1 Heat oven to 325°F. Place ham on rack in shallow roasting pan. Insert ovenproof meat thermometer so tip is in center of thickest part of ham and does not touch bone or rest in fat. Bake uncovered 1 hour 30 minutes.

2 Meanwhile, in 1-quart saucepan, mix brown sugar, cornstarch and salt. Stir in pineapple, lemon juice and mustard. Cook and stir over medium heat until mixture thickens and boils; boil and stir 1 minute. Brush glaze over ham during last 45 minutes of baking.

3 When thermometer reads at least 140°F, remove ham from oven. Cover loosely with foil; let stand 10 to 15 minutes before slicing.

1 Serving Calories 390; Total Fat 14g (Saturated Fat 5g, Trans Fat 0g); Cholesterol 110mg; Sodium 170mg; Total Carbohydrate 26g (Dietary Fiber 0g); Protein 39g **Carbohydrate Choices:** 2

SLOW-COOKER DIRECTIONS: Spray 6- to 7-quart oval slow cooker with cooking spray. Place 6½- to 8½-lb fully cooked bone-in spiral-cut half-ham in slow cooker, cuts facing up. Decrease brown sugar to ½ cup. Omit cornstarch, salt and pineapple; increase Dijon mustard to ¼ cup. Mix all ingredients with ¼ cup orange juice in small bowl (do not cook); pour over ham and between slices. Cover and cook on Low heat setting 4 to 6 hours or until instant-read thermometer inserted in center of ham, without touching bone, reads at least 140°F. Serve ham with cooking liquid.

HAM WITH BROWN SUGAR–ORANGE GLAZE: Omit all ingredients except ham. Bake ham as directed in Step 1. In small bowl, mix ½ cup packed brown sugar, 2 tablespoons orange juice and ½ teaspoon ground mustard. Brush glaze over ham during last 45 minutes of baking.

ALL ABOUT HAMS

Hams come from cured pork leg meat, no matter what type of ham you choose. Curing gives ham its distinctive sweet-smoky and salty flavor. Hams are usually either wet or dry cured.

Wet-Cured Hams These hams have been processed with a brine of water, salt, sugar and spices, which keeps the meat moist and tender. Most grocery store hams, including spiral-cut hams, are wet cured.

Dry-Cured Hams These hams are rubbed with salt, sugar and spices and then aged anywhere from several weeks to more than a year. Also known as *country hams*, they are often named for the city where they are processed. Because of their slightly salty flavor, follow package directions for how to use.

CARVING HAM

Place ham on carving board or platter, fat side up, bone facing you. Cut in half next to bone. Place boneless side of ham fat side up; cut slices. Cut slices from bone-in portion, cutting away from bone.

Glazed Baked Ham

Balsamic Braised Lamb Shanks

The classic long, slow method of braising in a flavorful marinade is perfect for making lamb shanks fall-off-the-bone tender.

PREP 20 Minutes **TOTAL** 11 Hours 20 Minutes •
6 servings

LAMB SHANKS

- 1 tablespoon olive oil
- 6 lamb shanks (12 to 16 oz each)

MARINADE

- 1 cup balsamic vinegar
- 1 cup gluten-free beef broth (for homemade broth, see page 157)
- ¼ cup gluten-free soy sauce
- ¼ cup olive oil
- ¼ cup packed brown sugar
- 2 teaspoons ground mustard
- ½ teaspoon coarse ground black pepper
- ¼ cup chili sauce
  Chopped fresh parsley, if desired

1 In 12-inch nonstick skillet, heat 1 tablespoon oil over medium-high heat. Add lamb shanks; cook about 8 to 10 minutes, turning frequently, or until brown on all sides (brown in batches if necessary). Remove from heat and let cool for 10 minutes.

2 In large shallow glass or plastic dish or 2-gallon resealable food-storage plastic bag, mix all marinade ingredients except chili sauce and parsley. Add lamb shanks. Cover dish or seal bag; refrigerate at least 8 hours but no longer than 24 hours, turning occasionally.

3 In 8-quart Dutch oven or stockpot, place lamb shanks and marinade. Heat to boiling; reduce heat. Cover and simmer 2 hours 30 minutes to 3 hours, turning lamb shanks once, until very tender. Remove lamb to heatproof serving platter; cover with foil. Keep warm in 225°F oven.

4 Pour pan juices into fat separator, or skim fat from juices. Return juices to Dutch oven, leaving fat in separator. Stir in chili sauce. Heat to boiling; reduce heat to medium. Cook until reduced by half, about 20 to 30 minutes. Serve lamb shanks with sauce; sprinkle with parsley.

1 Serving Calories 440; Total Fat 17g (Saturated Fat 6g, Trans Fat 0.5g); Cholesterol 165mg; Sodium 950mg; Total Carbohydrate 19g (Dietary Fiber 1g); Protein 53g **Carbohydrate Choices:** 1

Greek Lamb Chops

PREP 35 Minutes **TOTAL** 35 Minutes • *4 servings*

- 4 lamb sirloin chops or 8 lamb loin or rib chops (1½ lb)
- 1 teaspoon dried oregano leaves
- ¼ teaspoon salt
- ¼ teaspoon pepper
- 1 tablespoon finely chopped garlic
- 1 tablespoon olive or vegetable oil
- ½ cup gluten-free chicken broth (for homemade broth, see page 153)
- 1 tablespoon lemon juice
- 1 tablespoon butter
- ¼ cup sliced pitted kalamata or ripe olives
- 2 tablespoons chopped fresh parsley
- 2 tablespoons crumbled feta cheese

1 Sprinkle both sides of lamb chops with oregano, salt and pepper. Press garlic into chops. In 12-inch skillet, heat oil over medium-high heat. Add chops; cook 4 to minutes, turning once, or until brown.

2 Add broth to skillet; reduce heat to medium-low. Cover and cook 8 to 10 minutes, turning chops once, until tender. Remove chops from skillet; cover with foil to keep warm.

3 Heat cooking juices to boiling; boil 1 to 2 minutes or until slightly reduced. Stir in lemon juice and butter. Cook and stir just until slightly thickened. Stir in olives and parsley. Spoon sauce over lamb chops. Top with cheese.

1 Serving Calories 250; Total Fat 16g (Saturated Fat 6g, Trans Fat 0g); Cholesterol 85mg; Sodium 390mg; Total Carbohydrate 2g (Dietary Fiber 0g); Protein 23g **Carbohydrate Choices:** 0

Balsamic Braised Lamb Shanks

Retail Lamb Cuts

These cuts of lamb show what is available at grocery stores. For specific cuts, ask a butcher to provide it for you, because lamb is not as readily available as pork or beef.

Diagram: **1** Shoulder **2** Rib **3** Loin and Sirloin **4** Leg and Hind Shank **5** Breast and Foreshank

Lamb Stew Meat

Lamb Boneless Shoulder Roast

Lamb Loin Roast (bone-in)

Lamb Loin Chops

Lamb Foreshank

Lamb Arm Chop (bone-in)

Lamb Blade Chop (bone-in)

Lamb Loin Roast (boneless)

Lamb Spareribs

Lamb Sirloin Chop (bone-in)

Lamb Leg Sirloin (half of leg bone-in)

Lamb Rib Roast (bone-in)

Lamb Leg Roast (bone-in sirloin half of leg)

Lamb Leg Roast (boned and tied)

Lamb Frenched Chops

Lamb Rib Chops (bone-in)

310

Herb and Garlic Roast Leg of Lamb

Venison with Cranberry-Wine Sauce

PREP 35 Minutes **TOTAL** 2 Hours 35 Minutes • *4 servings*

4 venison tenderloin steaks, about 1 inch thick (1¼ lb)	1 tablespoon olive or vegetable oil
½ cup dry red wine or nonalcoholic red wine	½ cup gluten-free beef broth (for homemade broth, see page 157)
1 tablespoon Dijon mustard	½ cup dried cranberries
¼ teaspoon salt	2 tablespoons currant or apple jelly
¼ teaspoon coarse ground black pepper	1 tablespoon butter
	2 medium green onions, sliced (2 tablespoons)

1 Place venison in resealable food-storage plastic bag or shallow glass or plastic dish. In small bowl, mix wine and mustard. Pour over venison; turn to coat. Seal bag or cover dish; refrigerate at least 2 hours but no longer than 4 hours to marinate, turning venison occasionally.

2 Remove venison from marinade; reserve marinade. Pat venison dry with paper towels; sprinkle with salt and pepper. In 12-inch nonstick skillet, heat oil over medium-high heat. Add venison; cook about 4 minutes, turning once, or until brown.

3 Add broth to skillet; reduce heat to low. Cover and cook about 10 minutes, turning venison once, until venison is tender and desired doneness. (Don't overcook or venison will become tough.)

4 Remove venison from skillet; cover with foil to keep warm. Pour reserved marinade into skillet. Heat to boiling, scraping up any browned bits from bottom of skillet. Reduce heat to medium; cook about 5 minutes until mixture is slightly reduced. Stir in cranberries, jelly, butter and onions. Cook 1 to 2 minutes, stirring occasionally, until butter is melted and mixture is hot. Serve sauce with venison.

1 Serving Calories 320; Total Fat 10g (Saturated Fat 3.5g, Trans Fat 0g); Cholesterol 125mg; Sodium 440mg; Total Carbohydrate 20g (Dietary Fiber 1g); Protein 32g **Carbohydrate Choices:** 1

Herb and Garlic Roast Leg of Lamb

PREP 10 Minutes **TOTAL** 2 Hours 45 Minutes • *10 servings*

1 boneless leg of lamb (5 to 6 lb)	1 tablespoon chopped fresh or 1 teaspoon dried thyme leaves, crushed
¼ cup finely chopped fresh parsley	2 teaspoons kosher (coarse) salt
1 tablespoon chopped fresh or 1 teaspoon dried rosemary leaves, crushed	½ teaspoon pepper
	2 cloves garlic, finely chopped
	3 tablespoons olive or vegetable oil

1 Heat oven to 325°F. Place lamb on rack in shallow roasting pan (if lamb comes in netting or is tied, do not remove).

2 In small bowl, stir remaining ingredients until well mixed. Spread mixture over entire surface of lamb. Insert ovenproof meat thermometer so tip is in thickest part of lamb and does not rest in fat.

3 For medium-rare, roast uncovered 2 hours 5 minutes to 2 hours 15 minutes or until thermometer reads 140°F. (For medium, roast until thermometer reads 155°F.) Cover lamb in pan loosely with foil; let stand 15 to 20 minutes or until thermometer reads 145°F (or 160°F for medium). Remove lamb to cutting board. Remove netting or string before slicing. Serve lamb with pan juices, if desired.

1 Serving Calories 370; Total Fat 19g (Saturated Fat 6g, Trans Fat 0.5g); Cholesterol 155mg; Sodium 340mg; Total Carbohydrate 0g (Dietary Fiber 0g); Protein 47g **Carbohydrate Choices:** 0

TIMETABLE FOR PANFRYING MEAT

CUT OF MEAT	THICKNESS IN INCHES	APPROXIMATE COOKING TIME IN MINUTES	FINAL DONENESS TEMPERATURE
BEEF			
Steak: Rib-Eye	¾	9 to 11	145°F medium-rare
	1	12 to 15	160°F medium
Steak: Porterhouse/T-Bone	¾	10 to 13	145°F medium-rare
	1	14 to 17	160°F medium
Steak: Strip (boneless)	¾	8 to 11	145°F medium-rare
	1	12 to 15	160°F medium
Steak: Flat Iron	8 oz each	11 to 14	145°F medium-rare
			160°F medium
Steak: Tenderloin	½	3 to 5	145°F medium-rare
Use medium-high heat if over ½-inch thick	¾	7 to 10	160°F medium
	1	10 to 13	
Steak: Top Sirloin (boneless)	¾	12 to 15	145°F medium-rare
	1	15 to 17	160°F medium
Ground Patties (4-inch diameter)	½	10 to 12	160°F medium
	¾	14 to 16	160°F medium
VEAL			
Chop: Loin or Rib	¾	10 to 14	145°F medium-rare
Use medium-high heat Let stand 3 minutes			
Cutlet	⅛	3 to 4	145°F medium-rare
Use medium-high heat Let stand 3 minutes	¼	5 to 6	
Ground Patties	½	9 to 12	160°F medium
Use medium-high heat			
PORK*			
Chop: Loin or Rib (bone-in or boneless)	¾ to 1	8 to 16	145°F medium-rare 160°F medium
Let stand 3 minutes			
Tenderloin Medallions	¼ to ½	4 to 8	145°F medium-rare
Let stand 3 minutes			160°F medium
Ground Patties	½	8 to 11	160°F
Ham Steak, Cooked	½	6	140°F
LAMB			
Chop: Loin or Rib	1 to 1¼	9 to 11	145°F medium-rare
Let stand 3 minutes			
Ground Patties	½	9 to 12	160°F

*The USDA recommends pork be cooked to 145°F (medium-rare) to 160°F (well), followed by 3 minutes standing time. Cooked to 145°F (with 3 minutes standing time), pork may appear pink but is safe to eat.

BETTY CROCKER COOKBOOK

Chicken & Turkey

Chicken & Turkey Basics

From simple, throw-together weeknight meals to company-worthy whole chickens or the star-of-the-table holiday bird, poultry's versatility is undeniable. There are so many options for chicken and turkey products, and they pair well with just about any flavor combination and cooking method. Here are some useful guidelines for buying and storing poultry.

Buying Chicken and Turkey

- Look for tightly wrapped packages without tears, holes or leaks, and with little or no liquid.

- Check for a fresh odor; if it does not smell right, don't buy it.

- Choose cold packages and stay away from those stacked above the meat case as they might not be cold enough.

- Do not purchase any packages if the sell-by or use-by date has already passed.

- Whole birds and cut-up pieces should be plump and meaty with smooth, moist-looking skin and no traces of feathers.

- Can be purchased fresh or frozen. Do not purchase refrigerated pre-stuffed turkey. Only purchase frozen turkey (pre-stuffed, uncooked or cooked whole poultry) if it displays the USDA or state mark of inspection, to be sure it has been processed under controlled conditions.

- Boneless, skinless products should look plump and moist.

- Chicken skin color can vary from yellow to white and does not indicate quality. Turkey skin should be cream colored.

- Cut ends of bones should be pink to red in color.

- Place packages in plastic bags so juices don't drip and contaminate other foods.

- Place all poultry in the refrigerator as soon as you get home. If you're shopping on a hot day or are more than 30 minutes from home, place poultry in an ice-packed cooler.

Storing Chicken and Turkey

- Poultry packaged in clear, sealed plastic wrap on a plastic tray does not need to be repackaged.

- Poultry wrapped in butcher paper should be repackaged in plastic wrap, foil or resealable freezer plastic bags.

- Store poultry in the meat compartment or coldest part of the refrigerator, or freeze as soon as possible.

- Cook or freeze poultry within 2 days of the sell-by date.

- If poultry was purchased frozen or was frozen at home, keep it in the refrigerator after thawing for no longer than 2 days.

Thawing Chicken and Turkey

- Thaw poultry completely before cooking.

- Thaw poultry in the refrigerator, not at room temperature.

- Remove giblets as soon as possible during thawing, then wrap and refrigerate.

- There should be no ice crystals in thawed poultry. Meat will be soft and joints will be flexible when fully thawed.

- Do not thaw a commercially prepared frozen stuffed turkey before cooking; cook from a frozen state.

TIMETABLE FOR ROASTING POULTRY

Roasting times are general guidelines. Also check turkey labels for timing recommendations.

Begin checking turkey doneness about 1 hour before end of recommended roasting time. For purchased frozen pre-stuffed turkeys, follow package directions instead of this timetable.

TYPE OF POULTRY	WEIGHT IN POUNDS	OVEN TEMPERATURE	ROASTING TIME IN HOURS
CHICKEN			
Whole Chicken (Not Stuffed*)	3 to 3½	375°F	1¾ to 2
TURKEY			
Whole Turkey (Not Stuffed*)	8 to 12	325°F	2¾ to 3
	12 to 14	325°F	3 to 3¾
	14 to 18	325°F	3¾ to 4¼
	18 to 20	325°F	4¼ to 4½
	20 to 24	325°F	4½ to 5
Whole Turkey Breast (Bone-In)	4 to 6	325°F	1½ to 2¼
	6 to 8	325°F	2¼ to 3¼
GAME			
Whole Duck Domestic or Wild		375°F	20 minutes per pound
		350°F	18 to 20 minutes per pound
Whole Goose	7 to 9	325°F	2¼ to 3¾
	9 to 11	325°F	3¾ to 4½
	11 to 13	325°F	4½ to 5½
Whole Pheasant	2 to 3	350°F	1 to 1½
Whole Rock Cornish Hen	1½ to 2	350°F	1¼ to 1½

*For optimal food safety and even doneness, the USDA recommends cooking stuffing separately. However, if you choose to stuff poultry or game birds, it is necessary to use an accurate food thermometer to make sure the center of the stuffing reaches a safe minimum temperature of 165°F. Cooking home-stuffed poultry or game birds is riskier than cooking those that are not stuffed. Even if the poultry or game bird itself has reached the safe minimum internal temperature of 165°F, the stuffing may not have reached the same temperature. Bacteria can survive in stuffing that has not reached 165°F, possibly resulting in foodborne illness. Do not stuff poultry or game birds that will be grilled, smoked, fried, microwaved or prepared in a slow cooker, because the stuffing will never get hot enough in the center.

TIMETABLE FOR BROILING POULTRY

Cook poultry right from refrigerator. Set oven control to broil. Check owner's manual for whether oven door should be partially opened or closed while broiling. Place poultry on rack in broiler pan. Broil for the time listed, turning once, until thermometer reaches at least 165°F or until juice is clear when centers of thickest pieces are cut.

CUT OF POULTRY	WEIGHT IN POUNDS	BROILING TIME
CHICKEN		
Cut-Up	3 to 3½	Skin side down 30 minutes; turn. Broil 15 to 25 minutes longer (7 to 9 inches from heat)
Bone-In Split Breasts	2½ to 3	25 to 35 minutes (7 to 9 inches from heat)
Boneless Skinless Breasts	1¼	15 to 20 minutes (4 to 6 inches from heat)
Wings	2 to 2½	10 minutes (5 to 7 inches from heat)
TURKEY		
Tenderloins	1 to 1½	8 to 12 minutes (4 to 6 inches from heat)
Breast Slices	1 to 1½	7 minutes (4 to 6 inches from heat)

COOKED POULTRY YIELDS

Here's a handy chart to know if you'll have enough poultry for your recipe.

TYPE OF POULTRY	WEIGHT IN POUNDS	YIELD OF CHOPPED, CUBED OR SHREDDED COOKED POULTRY IN CUPS
CHICKEN		
Whole Chicken	3 to 3½	2½ to 3
Bone-In Split Breasts	1½	2
Boneless Skinless Breasts	1½	3
Legs (Thighs and Drumsticks)	1½	1¾
Deli-Cooked Rotisserie Chicken	2 lb	4
	3 lb	6
TURKEY		
Whole Turkey	6 to 8	7 to 10
Bone-In Breast	3 to 9	5 to 13
Tenderloins	1½	3

Jalapeño Popper Chicken

PREP 25 Minutes **TOTAL** 1 Hour 5 Minutes • *4 servings*

CHICKEN

- 6 oz cream cheese, softened (from 8-oz package)
- ½ cup finely shredded sharp cheddar cheese (2 oz)
- 2 teaspoons chopped fresh cilantro
- ½ teaspoon salt
- ½ teaspoon pepper
- 4 (6 to 8 oz) boneless skinless chicken breasts
- 1 large red or green jalapeño chile, seeded if desired, cut crosswise into 8 slices

TOPPING

- ½ cup plain panko crispy bread crumbs
- ¼ cup finely shredded sharp cheddar cheese (1 oz)
- 2 tablespoons butter, melted
- 1 tablespoon chopped fresh cilantro
- 4 slices bacon, crisply cooked, coarsely crumbled

  Additional jalapeño slices and chopped cilantro if desired

1 Heat oven to 400°F. Spray 13×9-inch baking dish with cooking spray.

2 In medium bowl, stir cream cheese, cheddar cheese, cilantro, ¼ teaspoon of the salt and ¼ teaspoon of the pepper until mixed; set aside.

3 Cut pocket in each chicken breast by making a horizontal slit along one long side, being careful to not cut through to opposite side. Stuff each pocket with about ¼ cup of the cream cheese mixture; top mixture with 2 jalapeño slices. Press edges of chicken over filling. Sprinkle chicken breasts with remaining ¼ teaspoon salt and ¼ teaspoon pepper.

4 In small bowl, stir together all topping ingredients except additional jalapeño slices. Sprinkle bread crumb mixture evenly over chicken breasts.

5 Bake uncovered 30 to 35 minutes or until juice of chicken is clear when center of thickest part of chicken is cut (at least 165°F). Garnish with jalapeño slices and chopped cilantro. Cool 5 minutes before serving.

1 Serving Calories 580; Total Fat 36g (Saturated Fat 19g, Trans Fat 1g); Cholesterol 195mg; Sodium 870mg; Total Carbohydrate 14g (Dietary Fiber 0g); Protein 50g **Carbohydrate Choices:** 1

CALORIE SMART • GLUTEN FREE

Chicken with Lemon-Artichoke Cauliflower

As with many frozen vegetables, there may be clumps of frozen cauliflower in the package. Be sure to break up any clumps with your hand or microwave as directed on package before adding to skillet.

PREP 15 Minutes **TOTAL** 35 Minutes •
4 servings (1 thigh and ¾ cup cauliflower mixture)

- 2 teaspoons lemon-pepper seasoning
- 2 cloves garlic, finely chopped
- ½ teaspoon salt
- 4 bone-in chicken thighs, skin removed (about 1½ lb)
- 1 tablespoon olive oil
- 1 bag (10 oz) frozen riced cauliflower (about 2 cups)
- 1 jar (12 oz) marinated quartered artichoke hearts, drained
- ¾ cup coarsely chopped roasted red pepper (from 12-oz jar)
- ¼ cup finely chopped fresh cilantro

1 In small bowl, mix lemon-pepper, garlic and salt; reserve and set aside 1½ teaspoons. Rub remaining lemon-pepper mixture on all sides of chicken thighs.

2 In 12-inch skillet, heat olive oil over medium-high heat. Cook chicken about 10 minutes, turning chicken once, until browned on both sides.

Jalapeño Popper Chicken

Chicken with Lemon-Artichoke Cauliflower

Chicken with
Tomatoes and Spinach

Skillet Chicken Thighs
with Bacon and Spinach

3 Meanwhile, in medium bowl, combine cauliflower, artichokes, roasted pepper, 3 tablespoons of the cilantro and reserved 1½ teaspoons lemon-pepper mixture.

4 Add cauliflower mixture to skillet; reduce heat to medium. Cook uncovered 8 to 12 minutes, turning chicken and stirring vegetable mixture frequently, until juice of chicken is clear when thickest part is cut (at least 165°F) and vegetables are tender. Sprinkle with remaining 1 tablespoon cilantro.

1 Serving Calories 250; Total Fat 9g (Saturated Fat 2g, Trans Fat 0g); Cholesterol 110mg; Sodium 1120mg; Total Carbohydrate 13g (Dietary Fiber 5g); Protein 27g **Carbohydrate Choices:** 1

CALORIE SMART • GLUTEN FREE

Chicken with Tomatoes and Spinach

PREP 10 Minutes **TOTAL** 40 Minutes • *4 servings*

1 tablespoon olive or vegetable oil	½ teaspoon gluten-free seasoned salt
4 boneless skinless chicken breasts (about 1¼ lb)	¼ teaspoon pepper
	¼ cup dry white wine or water
1 clove garlic, finely chopped	2 medium plum (Roma) tomatoes, sliced
½ teaspoon dried oregano leaves	1 bag (6 oz) fresh baby spinach leaves

1 In 12-inch nonstick skillet, heat oil over medium heat. Sprinkle chicken with garlic, oregano, seasoned salt and pepper. Add chicken to skillet; cook uncovered 15 to 20 minutes, turning once, until juice of chicken is clear when center of thickest part is cut (at least 165°F).

2 Stir in wine. Arrange tomato slices on chicken. Cover and cook 2 to 3 minutes or until tomatoes are thoroughly heated.

3 Add spinach to skillet. Cover and cook 2 to 3 minutes longer or until spinach is wilted.

1 Serving Calories 230; Total Fat 8g (Saturated Fat 2g, Trans Fat 0g); Cholesterol 90mg; Sodium 270mg; Total Carbohydrate 3g (Dietary Fiber 1g); Protein 33g **Carbohydrate Choices:** 0

CALORIE SMART • GLUTEN FREE

Skillet Chicken Thighs with Bacon and Spinach

PREP 40 Minutes **TOTAL** 40 Minutes • *4 servings*

8 boneless skinless chicken thighs (about 1½ lb)	½ cup gluten-free store-bought or homemade chicken broth (for homemade broth, see page 153)
3 slices gluten-free bacon, chopped	
2 large carrots, chopped (1½ cups)	1 bag (8 oz) fresh baby spinach leaves
2 small onions, sliced	½ teaspoon salt
3 cloves garlic, finely chopped	¼ teaspoon pepper
	1 tablespoon chopped fresh or ½ teaspoon dried sage leaves
	1 tablespoon grated lemon zest

1 In 12-inch skillet, cook chicken and bacon over medium-high heat 5 minutes, turning chicken once. Stir in carrots, onions, garlic and broth. Cook uncovered 15 to 20 minutes, turning chicken and stirring frequently, until juice of chicken is clear when thickest part is cut (at least 165°F) and vegetables are tender.

2 Remove from heat. Add spinach, salt and pepper; stir about 3 minutes or until spinach is wilted. Stir in sage and lemon zest.

1 Serving Calories 350; Total Fat 16g (Saturated Fat 5g, Trans Fat 0g); Cholesterol 110mg; Sodium 720mg; Total Carbohydrate 11g (Dietary Fiber 3g); Protein 40g **Carbohydrate Choices:** 1

Chicken with Pan-Roasted Cauliflower and Orzo

Chicken Sausage Philly Cheesesteaks

Moroccan Chicken Skillet

Chicken with Pan-Roasted Cauliflower and Orzo

PREP 25 Minutes **TOTAL** 25 Minutes • *4 servings*

- 1 tablespoon olive oil
- 2 cups bite-size fresh cauliflower florets
- 1½ cups chicken broth (for homemade broth, see page 153)
- 1¼ lb boneless skinless chicken thighs, cut into bite-size pieces
- 1 cup uncooked orzo or rosamarina pasta (6 oz)
- ¼ cup thinly sliced green onions (4 medium)
- 1 can (14.5 oz) diced tomatoes with basil, garlic and oregano, drained
- 2 cups packed arugula or fresh baby spinach leaves
- ½ cup shredded Parmesan cheese (2 oz)

1 In 12-inch nonstick skillet, heat oil over medium heat. Cook cauliflower in oil about 5 minutes, stirring occasionally, until lightly browned.

2 Add broth, chicken, pasta, onions and tomatoes. Heat to boiling; reduce heat. Cover and simmer 8 to 10 minutes, stirring occasionally, until chicken is no longer pink in center and pasta is tender.

3 Remove from heat. Stir in arugula; cover and let stand about 1 minute or until arugula is partially wilted. Sprinkle with cheese before serving.

1 Serving (1½ Cups) Calories 380; Total Fat 14g (Saturated Fat 5g, Trans Fat 0g); Cholesterol 55mg; Sodium 780mg; Total Carbohydrate 35g (Dietary Fiber 3g); Protein 28g **Carbohydrate Choices:** 2

Chicken Sausage Philly Cheesesteaks

An easy way to eat these hearty sandwiches is to wrap each of them food-truck style, in waxed or cooking parchment paper.

PREP 30 Minutes **TOTAL** 35 Minutes • *4 sandwiches*

- 4 hoagie buns, partially sliced, leaving one side attached
- ¼ cup mayonnaise
- 1 clove garlic, finely chopped
- 4 slices (¾ oz each) provolone cheese, cut in half
- 1 tablespoon vegetable oil
- 1 medium onion, thinly sliced
- 1 medium green bell pepper, cut into ¼-inch strips
- 1 medium red bell pepper, cut into ¼-inch strips
- 1 teaspoon Montreal steak grill seasoning
- 1 package (12 oz) cooked chicken apple sausages, cut diagonally into ¼-inch slices

1 Heat oven to 350°F. Line cookie sheet with foil. Place hoagie buns, cut side up, on cookie sheet. Press each bun at cut to open into V-shape, making sure buns stay attached on one side.

2   In small bowl, mix mayonnaise and garlic; spread on cut sides of buns. Bake 7 to 10 minutes or until lightly toasted. Place ½ slice of cheese in center of each bun.

3   Meanwhile, in 12-inch nonstick skillet, heat oil over medium-high heat. Add onion, bell peppers and steak seasoning. Cook 5 minutes, stirring frequently. Add sausage; cook about 5 minutes, stirring occasionally, until sausage is lightly browned.

4   Divide sausage mixture evenly among buns. Top each sandwich with another ½ slice of cheese.

5   Bake about 3 minutes or just until cheese is melted.

1 Sandwich Calories 670; Total Fat 34g (Saturated Fat 9g, Trans Fat 0g); Cholesterol 70mg; Sodium 1490mg; Total Carbohydrate 62g (Dietary Fiber 3g); Protein 31g **Carbohydrate Choices:** 4

FAST • CALORIE SMART

Moroccan Chicken Skillet

PREP 20 Minutes   **TOTAL** 30 Minutes   •   *4 servings*
(1 chicken breast and 1 cup couscous)

2 tablespoons olive oil	1½ cups store-bought or homemade chicken broth (for homemade broth, see page 153)
1 teaspoon ground coriander	
1 teaspoon ground cumin	1 cup Israeli (pearl) couscous
¾ teaspoon salt	2 tablespoons butter
¼ teaspoon ground cinnamon	1 medium red onion, cut into 8 wedges
¼ teaspoon crushed red pepper flakes	1 medium zucchini, cut lengthwise into quarters and crosswise into 1-inch slices
4 boneless skinless chicken breasts (about 1½ lb)	Prepared harissa (to make your own, see page 457), if desired

1   In small bowl, mix 1 tablespoon of the olive oil, the coriander, cumin, ½ teaspoon of the salt, the cinnamon and pepper flakes; brush mixture over both sides of chicken.

2   In 12-inch nonstick skillet, heat remaining 1 tablespoon oil over medium heat. Add chicken; cook 4 minutes on each side or until brown. Remove chicken to a serving plate; cover with foil to keep warm.

3   Add chicken broth, couscous, butter, remaining ¼ teaspoon salt, the onion and zucchini to skillet; stir. Heat to boiling; reduce heat. Add chicken to skillet. Cover and simmer 8 to 10 minutes or until couscous is tender and juice of chicken is clear when thickest part is cut (at least 165°F). Serve with harissa.

1 Serving Calories 510; Total Fat 19g (Saturated Fat 6g, Trans Fat 0g); Cholesterol 125mg; Sodium 940mg; Total Carbohydrate 39g (Dietary Fiber 3g); Protein 45g **Carbohydrate Choices:** 2½

Cheesy Chicken and Sweet Potato Casserole

MAKE AHEAD

Cheesy Chicken and Sweet Potato Casserole

PREP 25 Minutes   **TOTAL** 2 Hours 30 Minutes   •   *6 servings*

3 lb sweet potatoes	8 oz Gruyère or Swiss cheese, shredded (2 cups)
⅓ cup butter	
¼ cup all-purpose flour	3 cups fresh kale, coarsely chopped
1 teaspoon salt	
¼ teaspoon pepper	2 cups shredded cooked chicken
3 cups half-and-half	

1   Heat oven to 350°F. Spray 13×9-inch (3-quart) glass baking dish with cooking spray.

2   Pierce sweet potatoes with fork; place on cookie sheet. Bake 50 to 60 minutes or until potatoes can be easily pierced with a knife. Cool 20 minutes. Peel potatoes; cut each into ¼-inch slices.

3   Meanwhile, in 2-quart saucepan, melt butter over medium heat. Stir in flour, salt and pepper using wire whisk. Cook until smooth and bubbly, stirring frequently. Gradually stir in half-and-half. Cook 5 to 7 minutes, stirring frequently, until slightly thickened. Stir in 1 cup of the cheese.

4   In large bowl, toss potatoes, half-and-half mixture, kale and chicken until well coated. Spoon into baking dish. Sprinkle with remaining 1 cup cheese.

5   Bake 25 to 30 minutes or until thoroughly heated and cheese is melted. Let stand 15 minutes before serving.

1 Serving Calories 670; Total Fat 41g (Saturated Fat 24g, Trans Fat 1.5g); Cholesterol 155mg; Sodium 1070mg; Total Carbohydrate 43g (Dietary Fiber 5g); Protein 31g **Carbohydrate Choices:** 3

MAKE-AHEAD DIRECTIONS: Bake sweet potatoes the day before preparing this casserole and refrigerate overnight. Continue as directed in Step 3.

CHEESY SWEET POTATO CASSEROLE: Omit chicken.

5-INGREDIENT RECIPE

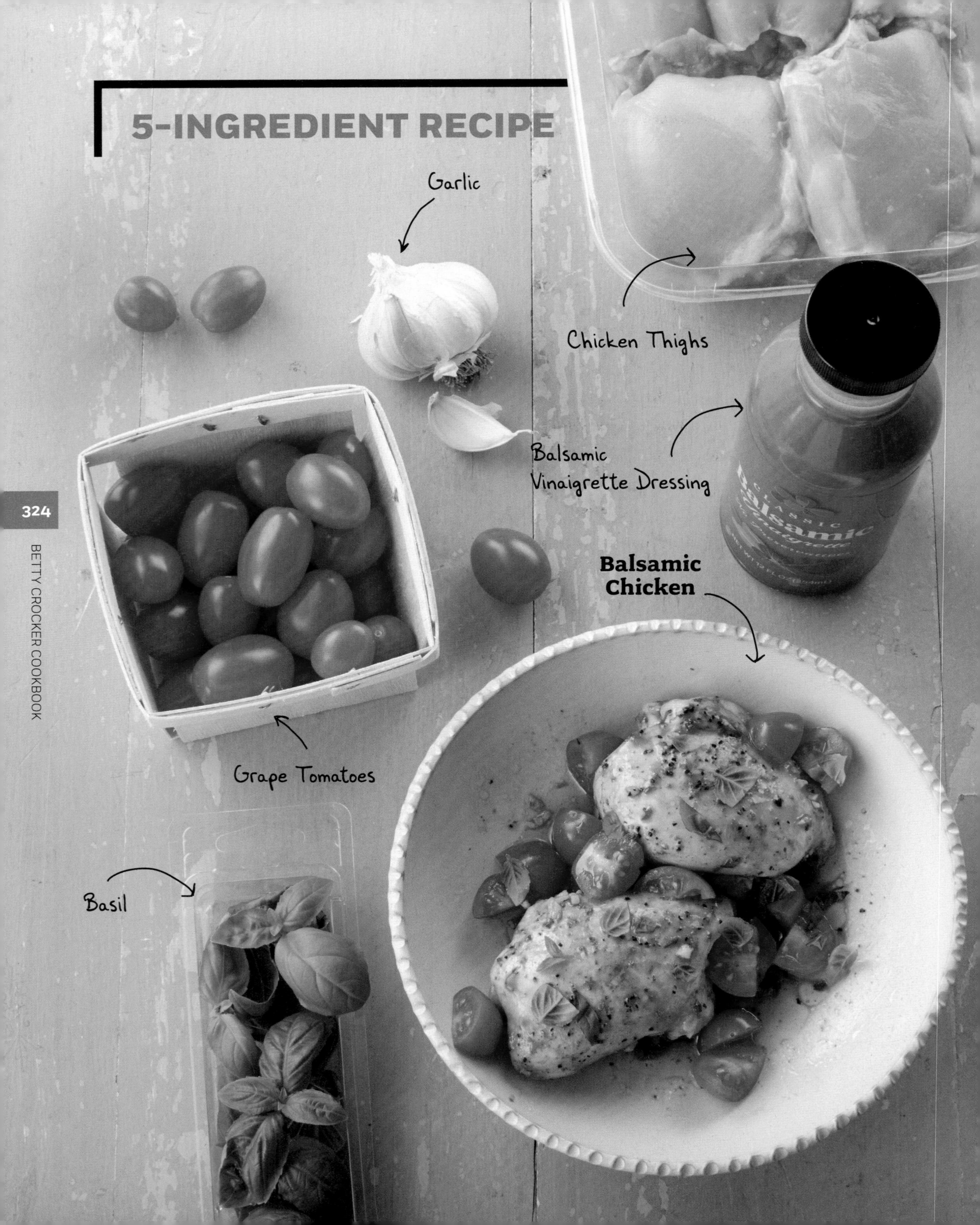
Garlic
Chicken Thighs
Balsamic
Vinaigrette Dressing
Balsamic Chicken
Grape Tomatoes
Basil

5-INGREDIENT RECIPE

EASY • SLOW COOKER • CALORIE SMART • GLUTEN FREE

Balsamic Chicken

PREP 15 Minutes **TOTAL** 4 Hours 15 Minutes • *6 servings*

2½ lb boneless skinless chicken thighs (about 12)

1¼ cups balsamic vinaigrette dressing

1 teaspoon chopped fresh garlic

½ cup grape tomatoes, quartered

¼ cup fresh basil leaves, coarsely chopped

1 Spray 3½- to 4-quart slow cooker with cooking spray. Place chicken thighs in slow cooker, layering if necessary. Top with ½ cup of the dressing, and sprinkle with garlic; refrigerate remaining dressing for later.

2 Cover; cook on Low heat setting 4 to 4½ hours or until juice of chicken is clear when thickest part is cut (at least 165°F).

3 Remove chicken to rimmed serving dish, and discard cooking liquid. to serve, drizzle remaining ¾ cup dressing over chicken; top with tomatoes and basil.

1 Serving Calories 340; Total Fat 18g (Saturated Fat 4g, Trans Fat 0g); Cholesterol 180mg; Sodium 670mg; Total Carbohydrate 4g (Dietary Fiber 0g); Protein 39g **Carbohydrate Choices:** 0

SLOW COOKER • CALORIE SMART

Chicken and Barley Risotto with Edamame

PREP 15 Minutes **TOTAL** 4 Hours 40 Minutes •

9 servings (about 1 cup each)

1¼ lb boneless skinless chicken breasts, cut into ¾-inch cubes

3 medium onions, chopped (1½ cups)

1¼ cups uncooked pearl barley (not quick-cooking)

½ cup shredded carrot

½ teaspoon salt

½ teaspoon dried thyme leaves

2 cloves garlic, finely chopped

1 carton (32 oz) chicken broth (4 cups; for homemade broth, see page 153)

1 cup frozen shelled edamame (from 10-oz bag), thawed

½ cup shredded Parmesan cheese (2 oz)

1 Spray 4- to 5-quart slow cooker with cooking spray. In slow cooker, mix chicken, onions, barley, carrot, salt, thyme, garlic and 3 cups of the broth.

2 Cover; cook on Low heat setting 4 to 5 hours.

3 In 2-cup microwavable measuring cup, microwave remaining 1 cup broth uncovered on High 2 to 3 minutes or until boiling. Stir boiling broth and edamame into chicken mixture.

4 Increase heat setting to High. Cover; cook 25 to 30 minutes or until edamame are tender. Stir in cheese.

1 Serving Calories 250; Total Fat 6g (Saturated Fat 2g, Trans Fat 0g); Cholesterol 45mg; Sodium 690mg; Total Carbohydrate 27g (Dietary Fiber 6g); Protein 23g **Carbohydrate Choices:** 2

VEGETARIAN BARLEY RISOTTO WITH EDAMAME: Omit chicken and use vegetable broth instead of chicken broth.

Chicken and Barley Risotto with Edamame

Chicken and Dumplings

PREP 20 Minutes **TOTAL** 1 Hour 10 Minutes • *6 servings*

BROTH

- ½ cup all-purpose flour
- 5 cups chicken broth (for homemade broth, see page 153)
- 1 cup frozen sweet peas
- 2 medium carrots, thinly sliced (1 cup)
- 1 large onion, chopped (1 cup)
- ¼ cup chopped fresh parsley or 1 tablespoon parsley flakes
- ⅛ teaspoon pepper

- 3 cups cubed cooked chicken

DUMPLINGS

- 1½ cups all-purpose flour
- 1 tablespoon chopped fresh parsley or parsley flakes
- 2 teaspoons baking powder
- ¼ teaspoon salt
- 3 tablespoons cold butter or shortening
- ¾ cup milk

1 In 4-quart saucepan, add ½ flour. Gradually whisk in 1 cup of the broth until smooth. Gradually stir in remaining broth. Add vegetables, parsley and pepper; heat to boiling. Reduce heat to low. Stir in chicken. Cook uncovered about 20 minutes or until carrots are tender.

2 In medium bowl, mix dumpling ingredients except butter and milk. Cut in butter, using pastry blender or fork, until mixture looks like fine crumbs. Stir in milk. Drop dough by heaping tablespoonfuls onto hot chicken mixture. Cook uncovered over low heat 10 minutes. Cover; cook 10 minutes longer or until dumplings are completely cooked in center.

1 Serving Calories 400; Total Fat 14g (Saturated Fat 6g, Trans Fat 0g); Cholesterol 110mg; Sodium 1190mg; Total Carbohydrate 42g (Dietary Fiber 3g); Protein 26g **Carbohydrate Choices:** 3

Turkey Sausage and Pepper Skillet

Feel free to use any color of bell peppers you desire or have on hand. A rainbow of colors makes for a beautiful presentation and tastes great!

PREP 40 Minutes **TOTAL** 50 Minutes • *4 servings (about 1½ cups each)*

- 2 teaspoons olive oil
- 1 lb gluten-free Italian turkey sausage links, cut into 1-inch slices
- 1½ cups sliced onions
- 2 medium red, yellow or green bell peppers, cut into strips (about 2 cups)

- 2 teaspoons finely chopped garlic
- ½ teaspoon Italian seasoning
- 1 can (14.5 oz) fire-roasted crushed tomatoes, undrained
- ¼ cup thinly sliced fresh basil

- ½ cup grated Parmesan cheese

1 In 12-inch nonstick skillet, heat oil over medium-high heat. Add sausage; cook 8 to 10 minutes or until no longer pink and completely cooked (at least 165°F). Using slotted spoon, transfer to plate, and keep warm.

2 Reduce heat to medium; add onions and peppers to drippings. Cook 8 to 10 minutes, stirring occasionally, until tender. Stir in garlic and seasoning; cook 30 to 60 seconds or until garlic is fragrant.

3 Stir in tomatoes and sausage; heat to simmering, stirring occasionally. Reduce heat; cook uncovered 8 to 10 minutes or until completely heated through.

4 Garnish with fresh basil and Parmesan cheese.

1 Serving Calories 290; Total Fat 14g (Saturated Fat 5g, Trans Fat 0g); Cholesterol 85mg; Sodium 770mg; Total Carbohydrate 15g (Dietary Fiber 2g); Protein 25g **Carbohydrate Choices:** 1

Rosemary Chicken and Potato Sheet-Pan Dinner

If you have fresh thyme on hand, you can substitute it for the rosemary in this easy dinner. Garnish with lemon slices or shredded Parmesan cheese, if you wish.

PREP 20 Minutes **TOTAL** 1 Hour 5 Minutes • *6 servings*

- ¼ cup olive oil
- 2 tablespoons chopped fresh rosemary leaves
- 1 teaspoon salt
- ½ teaspoon pepper
- 1 lb baby red potatoes, quartered

- 6 boneless skinless chicken thighs (about 1½ lb)
- 1 bunch asparagus (about 1 lb), cut into 2-inch pieces

1 Heat oven to 425°F. Spray 18×13-inch half-sheet pan with cooking spray.

2 In large bowl, mix 2 tablespoons of the olive oil, 1 tablespoon of the rosemary, ½ teaspoon of the salt and ¼ teaspoon of the pepper. Add potatoes; toss to coat. Place potatoes skin side down in single layer on pan. Roast 23 to 25 minutes or until tender when pierced with a fork. Remove from oven; stir.

3 In same large bowl, mix remaining 2 tablespoons olive oil, 1 tablespoon rosemary leaves, ½ teaspoon salt and ¼ teaspoon pepper. Add chicken and asparagus; toss to coat. Arrange in single layer on pan along with potatoes.

4 Roast 16 to 20 minutes longer or until juice of chicken is clear when center of thickest part is cut (at least 165°F) and potatoes are browned.

1 Serving Calories 300; Total Fat 14g (Saturated Fat 3g, Trans Fat 0g); Cholesterol 110mg; Sodium 490mg; Total Carbohydrate 16g (Dietary Fiber 3g); Protein 26g **Carbohydrate Choices:** 1

Indian Chicken Skewers with Roasted Veggies

This perfectly seasoned chicken recipe is inspired by tandoori-style chicken recipes, which typically are cooked in a clay oven. Marinating the chicken in whole milk Greek yogurt protects the chicken from drying out when cooked.

PREP 40 Minutes **TOTAL** 1 Hour 10 Minutes •
4 servings (1 skewer, about ¾ cup veggies and ¼ cup yogurt)

- 3 cups 1-inch cauliflower florets (about ½ head cauliflower)
- 1 medium red onion, cut into wedges
- 1 green bell pepper, cut into 1-inch pieces
- 1 orange bell pepper, cut into 1-inch pieces
- 2 tablespoons vegetable oil
- 2½ teaspoons garam masala
- ¾ teaspoon salt
- 1⅓ cups plain whole milk Greek yogurt
- 1 tablespoon fresh lemon juice
- 3 cloves garlic, finely chopped
- 2 tablespoons chopped fresh cilantro
- 1½ teaspoons smoked paprika
- 1½ lb boneless skinless chicken breasts, cut into ½-inch-wide strips

1 Heat oven to 450°F. Spray 15×10×1-inch pan with cooking spray or line with foil.

2 In large bowl, stir cauliflower, onion, bell peppers and vegetable oil until vegetables are coated in oil. Sprinkle with 1 teaspoon of the garam masala and ¼ teaspoon of the salt, stirring until vegetables are evenly coated. Arrange vegetables in single layer on pan. Roast 10 minutes; remove from oven. Reduce oven temperature to 425°F. Drain any liquid from pan; move vegetables to one side of pan.

3 Meanwhile, in small bowl, stir yogurt, lemon juice, garlic, and remaining 1½ teaspoons garam masala until well blended. In large bowl, place ⅓ cup of the yogurt mixture. Stir cilantro into remaining yogurt mixture; cover and refrigerate.

4 Stir paprika and remaining ½ teaspoon salt into yogurt mixture in large bowl. Add chicken; stir until well coated. On each of 4 (10- to 12-inch) metal skewers, thread chicken strips. Place skewers on empty side of sheet pan. (Spread vegetables, if possible, up to but not touching skewers.)

5 Roast 25 to 30 minutes, turning skewers and stirring vegetables once, until chicken is no longer pink in center.

6 Serve yogurt sauce with chicken and vegetables.

1 Serving Calories 400; Total Fat 16g (Saturated Fat 5g, Trans Fat 0g); Cholesterol 120mg; Sodium 600mg; Total Carbohydrate 14g (Dietary Fiber 3g); Protein 48g **Carbohydrate Choices:** 1

Turkey Sausage and Pepper Skillet

Rosemary Chicken and Potato Sheet-Pan Dinner

327

Indian Chicken Skewers with Roasted Veggies

Herb-Roasted Chicken and Vegetables

PREP 20 Minutes **TOTAL** 2 Hours 5 Minutes • *6 servings*

¼ cup olive or vegetable oil	1 lemon
2 tablespoons chopped fresh or 1 teaspoon dried thyme leaves	1 whole chicken (4 to 5 lb)
2 tablespoons chopped fresh or 1 teaspoon dried marjoram leaves	6 small red potatoes, cut in half
½ teaspoon salt	1 cup ready-to-eat baby-cut carrots
¼ teaspoon coarse ground black pepper	8 oz fresh green beans, trimmed

1 Heat oven to 375°F. In small bowl, mix oil, thyme, marjoram, salt and pepper. Grate 1 teaspoon zest from lemon; stir zest into oil mixture. Cut lemon into quarters; place in cavity of chicken.

2 Fold wings across back of chicken so tips are touching. Skewer or tie legs together. Place chicken, breast side up, on rack in shallow roasting pan or 13×9-inch pan fitted with rack. Brush some of the oil mixture on chicken. Insert ovenproof meat thermometer so tip is in thickest part of thigh and does not touch bone.

3 Roast uncovered 45 minutes. Arrange potatoes, carrots and green beans around chicken; brush remaining oil mixture on chicken and vegetables. Roast uncovered 30 to 45 minutes longer or until thermometer reads at least 165°F, legs move easily when lifted or twisted and vegetables are tender. Cover loosely with foil; let stand 15 to 20 minutes.

4 Remove lemon and discard. Place chicken on platter; arrange vegetables around chicken. Serve with pan drippings.

1 Serving Calories 540; Total Fat 27g (Saturated Fat 6g, Trans Fat 0.5g); Cholesterol 115mg; Sodium 340mg; Total Carbohydrate 34g (Dietary Fiber 5g); Protein 40g **Carbohydrate Choices:** 2

ROSEMARY-HONEY ROASTED CHICKEN AND VEGETABLES: Omit all ingredients except chicken. Place chicken on rack in roasting pan as directed in Step 2. Arrange 1½ lb buttercup or acorn squash, seeded, cut into ½-inch rings or slices, then cut in half crosswise, and 2 medium onions, cut into 1-inch wedges, around chicken. In small bowl, mix ½ cup melted butter, ¼ cup lemon juice, 2 tablespoons honey, 2 teaspoons dried rosemary, crushed, and 1 clove garlic, finely chopped. Brush half of mixture on chicken and vegetables. Insert thermometer as directed. Roast uncovered 1 hour. Brush chicken and vegetables with remaining butter mixture. Cover loosely with foil. Roast 45 to 55 minutes longer. Continue as directed.

GARLIC BUTTER HERB-ROASTED CHICKEN AND VEGETABLES: Omit oil and lemon. Make Garlic Butter (see page 496) but do not chill. Starting at leg end of chicken, gently separate skin (do not peel back) from chicken breast using fingers, being careful not to tear or puncture skin. Rub ¼ cup of the garlic butter under skin to cover entire chicken breast; gently replace skin. Melt remaining garlic butter; stir in thyme, marjoram, salt and pepper. Continue as directed, brushing melted garlic butter on chicken and vegetables after roasting 45 minutes.

PREPARING CHICKEN FOR ROASTING

Cut lemon into quarters; place in cavity of chicken

Skewer or tie legs together.

Brush some of the oil mixture on chicken.

Insert ovenproof meat thermometer so tip is in thickest part of thigh but does not touch bone.

Herb-Roasted Chicken and Vegetables

Honey-Garlic Chicken with Noodles

Korean Fried Chicken

SLOW COOKER • CALORIE SMART • GLUTEN FREE

Honey-Garlic Chicken with Noodles

PREP 20 Minutes **TOTAL** 3 Hours 50 Minutes •
6 servings (1⅓ cups)

- 1 can (14.5 oz) gluten-free chicken broth
- ¼ cup honey
- 2 tablespoons fresh lemon juice
- 12 cloves garlic, finely chopped (2 tablespoons)
- 1 tablespoon finely chopped gingerroot
- 1 tablespoon toasted sesame oil
- ¼ teaspoon crushed red pepper flakes
- 1½ lb boneless skinless chicken breasts, cut into 1-inch pieces
- 3 cups broccoli florets (1-inch pieces)
- 1 red bell pepper, cut in thin strips
- 1 package (8.8 oz) thin rice stick noodles
  Garnishes, if desired
  Gluten-free soy sauce, coarsely chopped cilantro leaves and sesame seed

1 Spray 4- to 5-quart slow cooker with cooking spray.

2 In slow cooker, stir chicken broth, honey, lemon juice, garlic, gingerroot, sesame oil and pepper flakes. Stir in chicken.

3 Cover; cook on Low heat setting 3 hours. Stir broccoli and bell pepper into chicken mixture. Cover; cook on High heat setting 30 minutes or until vegetables are crisp-tender.

4 Break up noodles slightly; stir into chicken and vegetables. Cook, uncovered, 5 minutes longer, stirring occasionally, until noodles are tender. Top individual servings with garnishes just before serving.

1 Serving Calories 400; Total Fat 7g (Saturated Fat 1.5g, Trans Fat 0g); Cholesterol 70mg; Sodium 360mg; Total Carbohydrate 54g (Dietary Fiber 3g); Protein 30g **Carbohydrate Choices:** 3½

GLUTEN FREE

Korean Fried Chicken

Gochujang is a spicy Korean condiment. This dark red paste is usually made from red chiles, glutinous rice, fermented soybeans, salt and sometimes a sweetener such as sugar.

PREP 1 Hour 20 Minutes **TOTAL** 1 Hour 20 Minutes •
6 servings (5 pieces each)

SAUCE
- ¼ cup gluten-free gochujang (Korean chile pepper paste)
- ¼ cup honey
- 1 tablespoon gluten-free soy sauce
- 1 tablespoon unseasoned rice vinegar
- 1 tablespoon toasted sesame oil

CHICKEN
  Vegetable oil
- ½ cup cornstarch
- ½ teaspoon salt
- ½ teaspoon ground ginger
- ½ teaspoon pepper
- 1 package (3 lb) chicken wingettes and drummettes, patted dry
  Cilantro leaves, if desired

1 Heat oven to 350°F. In small bowl, mix all sauce ingredients until well blended and smooth; set aside.

2 In deep fryer or 4-quart saucepan, heat 3 to 4 inches oil to 350°F. In 1-gallon resealable food-storage plastic bag, mix cornstarch, salt, ginger and pepper. Add chicken; seal bag and toss until chicken is completely coated.

3 Fry 4 to 6 pieces of chicken at a time in oil 6 minutes; drain on paper towels. Fry the same pieces again about 4 to 6 minutes longer or until golden brown and juice of chicken is clear when thickest part is cut to bone (at least 165°F). Drain on paper towels. Repeat with remaining chicken. (To keep first batches hot, place chicken in single layer in 15×10×1-inch pan in oven.)

4 Pour sauce over chicken; toss until evenly coated. Garnish with cilantro leaves. Serve hot.

1 Serving Calories 420; Total Fat 20g (Saturated Fat 4.5g, Trans Fat 0g); Cholesterol 150mg; Sodium 760mg; Total Carbohydrate 28g (Dietary Fiber 0g); Protein 30g **Carbohydrate Choices:** 2

Oven-Fried Chicken

EASY • CALORIE SMART
Skillet-Fried Chicken

PREP 10 Minutes **TOTAL** 40 Minutes • *6 servings*

½ cup all-purpose flour	1 cut-up whole chicken (3 to 3½ lb)
1 tablespoon paprika	Vegetable oil
1½ teaspoons salt	
½ teaspoon pepper	

1 In shallow dish, mix flour, paprika, salt and pepper. Coat chicken with flour mixture.

2 In 12-inch nonstick skillet, heat ¼ inch oil over medium-high heat. Add chicken, skin side down; cook about 10 minutes or until light brown on all sides.

3 Reduce heat to low. Turn chicken skin side up. Cook uncovered about 20 minutes, without turning, until juice of chicken is clear when thickest piece is cut to bone (at least 165°F).

1 Serving Calories 340; Total Fat 22g (Saturated Fat 5g, Trans Fat 0g); Cholesterol 85mg; Sodium 670mg; Total Carbohydrate 9g (Dietary Fiber 0g); Protein 28g **Carbohydrate Choices:** ½

LIGHTER DIRECTIONS: For 250 calories and 11 grams of fat per serving, remove skin from chicken before cooking. Use 2 tablespoons oil in Step 2.

BUTTERMILK FRIED CHICKEN: Increase flour to 1 cup. Dip chicken in 1 cup buttermilk before coating with flour mixture.

CUTTING UP A WHOLE CHICKEN

Cut off each leg by cutting between thigh and body through meat between tail and hip joint, cutting as closely as possible to backbone. Bend leg back until hip joint pops out as shown.

Separate thigh and drumstick by cutting about ⅛ inch from the fat line toward the drumstick as shown. (A thin white fat line runs crosswise at joint between drumstick and thigh.)

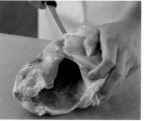

Remove each wing from body, cutting into wing joint with sharp knife, rolling knife to let the blade follow through at the curve of joint as shown.

Separate back from breast by holding body, neck end down, and cutting downward along each side of backbone

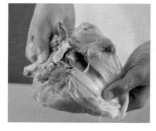

Bend breast halves back to pop out the keel bone. Remove keel bone as shown in Boning Chicken Breasts on page 333.

CALORIE SMART
Oven-Fried Chicken

PREP 10 Minutes **TOTAL** 1 Hour • *6 servings*

¼ cup butter	½ teaspoon garlic powder
½ cup all-purpose flour	¼ teaspoon pepper
1 teaspoon seasoned salt	1 cut-up whole chicken (3 to 3½ lb)
1 teaspoon paprika	

1 Heat oven to 425°F. In 13×9-inch pan, melt butter in oven. In shallow dish, mix flour, seasoned salt, paprika, garlic powder and pepper. Coat chicken with flour mixture. Place chicken, skin side down, in pan.

2 Bake uncovered 30 minutes. Turn chicken skin side up; bake about 20 minutes longer or until juice of chicken is clear when thickest piece is cut to bone (at least 165°F).

1 Serving Calories 340; Total Fat 21g (Saturated Fat 9g, Trans Fat 1g); Cholesterol 105mg; Sodium 370mg; Total Carbohydrate 9g (Dietary Fiber 0g); Protein 28g **Carbohydrate Choices:** ½

LIGHTER DIRECTIONS: For 240 calories and 11 grams of fat per serving, remove skin from chicken before cooking. Do not melt butter in pan; spray pan with cooking spray. Reduce butter to 2 tablespoons; drizzle melted butter over chicken after turning in Step 2.

CRUNCHY OVEN-FRIED CHICKEN: Remove skin from chicken, if desired. Substitute 1 cup corn flake crumbs or panko crispy bread crumbs for the ½ cup flour. Dip chicken into ¼ cup melted butter before coating with crumb mixture.

OVEN-FRIED CHICKEN FINGERS: Substitute 1½ lb boneless skinless chicken breasts, cut crosswise into 1½-inch strips, for the cut-up whole chicken. Reduce butter to 2 tablespoons. After coating chicken with flour mixture in Step 1, toss with melted butter in pan. Bake uncovered 15 minutes. Turn strips; bake 10 to 15 minutes longer or until no longer pink in center.

CARVING A WHOLE CHICKEN

Place chicken breast up, on cutting board. Remove ties or skewers.

While holding drumstick, cut through joint between thigh and body. Separate drumstick and thigh by cutting through connecting joint.

Remove wing from body by cutting through wing joint.

Just to right of breastbone, cut down through meat to remove, slice breast meat.

SWEET POTATO CHIP–COATED CHICKEN TENDERS: Omit seasoned salt, paprika, garlic powder and pepper. Season chicken with ¼ teaspoon salt. In shallow dish, mix 1 egg with 2 tablespoons porter-style beer. Place crushed contents of 1 bag (4.5 oz) sweet potato chips in another small dish. Dip chicken in flour, then egg mixture and then the chips; place on pan. Bake at 375°F 12 to 15 minutes, turning once or until chicken is no longer pink in center (at least 165°F). Serve with ½ cup barbecue sauce mixed with 3 additional tablespoons of beer and 1 teaspoon Sriracha sauce.

SLOW COOKER • CALORIE SMART • GLUTEN FREE

Rotisserie Spiced Chicken

PREP 10 Minutes   **TOTAL** 4 Hours 10 Minutes   •   *4 servings*

SPICE RUB

- 2 teaspoons paprika
- 1 teaspoon garlic salt
- 1 teaspoon onion powder
- 1 teaspoon sugar
- 1 teaspoon chili powder
- ½ teaspoon dried thyme leaves, crushed
- ½ teaspoon dried marjoram leaves, crushed
- ½ teaspoon pepper

CHICKEN

- 1 whole chicken (3½ to 4½ lb)

1 Spray 5- to 6-quart oval slow cooker with cooking spray. In small bowl, mix spice rub ingredients until well blended.

2 Rub spice mixture on all sides of chicken. Do not tie legs. Place chicken in slow cooker, making sure it fits loosely (leave at least 1 inch of space around chicken).

3 Cover; cook on Low heat setting 4 to 5 hours or until instant-read thermometer inserted in thickest part of inside thigh muscle and not touching bone reads at least 165°F and legs move easily when lifted or twisted. Do not remove lid before 4 hours.

1 Serving Calories 270; Total Fat 11g (Saturated Fat 3g, Trans Fat 0g); Cholesterol 125mg; Sodium 370mg; Total Carbohydrate 3g (Dietary Fiber 1g); Protein 40g **Carbohydrate Choices:** 0

Rotisserie Spiced Chicken

LEARN TO BRAISE

Why braise? The long, slow cook time helps develop rich flavor and tenderizes the meat. It's a great way to use cheaper, less-tender cuts of meat, but this technique can be used any time you want to have rich, deep flavor.

Braising starts with browning meat or poultry in a small amount of oil, then cooking it slowly in a small amount of liquid in a tightly covered pan—either on the stove-top or in the oven. Most braising is accomplished with broth or water, but other liquids can be added to the mix for flavor and color, such as wine or beer (the long slow cooking mellows the alcohol but the flavor lingers), apple cider, tomatoes (or tomato sauce) or a splash of balsamic vinegar.

For the best flavor, cook braised dishes the day before you want to serve them, and refrigerate the food overnight so the flavors can develop more fully. Spoon off any congealed fat from the top; reheat slowly and serve. Try Chicken Tagine (right) for a great braised recipe.

Braising Tips

1 Use a pot or skillet with a tight cover. Dutch ovens or enameled pots are good choices, as are stainless-steel skillets with lids. If you are braising in the oven, the pot should be oven-safe.

2 Season meat or poultry on all sides. Brown or sear (see Learn to Sear and Panfry, page 302) meat in a small amount of oil. Remove meat from pan and place on a plate.

3 Add liquid to pan to deglaze (¾ to 1 cup). Cook and stir, scraping browned bits from bottom of pan.

4 Return meat or poultry to pan with any accumulated liquid. There should be just enough liquid to come one-fourth to two-thirds of the way up sides of meat.

5 Often other ingredients will be added such as potatoes, carrots, other vegetables. For the best results, add these ingredients about 45 minutes before dish is done to prevent overcooking.

6 Cover and cook on stove-top or in oven for the time indicated in the recipe.

Chicken Tagine

BRAISING VS. STEWING

Braising is typically used for larger cuts of meat, with less liquid. Stewing is typically used for smaller, uniform pieces of meat with enough liquid to submerge them in. Both methods work for tenderizing less-tender cuts.

Chicken Tagine

PREP 30 Minutes **TOTAL** 1 Hour • *6 servings*

- 1 tablespoon olive or vegetable oil
- 1 cut-up whole chicken (3 to 3½ lb)
- 1 medium onion, sliced
- 2 cloves garlic, finely chopped
- ¼ cup chopped fresh cilantro
- 1 teaspoon ground cumin
- 1 teaspoon ground turmeric
- 1 teaspoon ground ginger
- 1 teaspoon salt
- 1 cinnamon stick (2-inch)

- 1 cup chicken broth (for homemade broth, see page 153)
- 1 can (14.5 oz) diced tomatoes, undrained
- 1 cup pitted dried plums, cut into bite-size pieces
- ½ cup pitted green olives
- 1 small lemon, cut into quarters
- Additional chopped fresh cilantro, if desired
- Hot cooked couscous or rice (page 224), if desired

1 In 4-quart saucepan, heat oil over medium-high heat. Add chicken skin side down, onion and garlic. Cook uncovered 6 to 10 minutes, turning chicken occasionally, until chicken is brown on all sides.

2 Reduce heat to medium. Sprinkle cilantro, cumin, turmeric, ginger and salt over chicken. Add cinnamon stick; pour broth and tomatoes over chicken. Turn chicken several times to coat evenly. Add dried plums, olives and lemon, pressing into liquid around chicken. Heat to boiling; reduce heat. Cover and simmer about 30 minutes or until juice of chicken is clear when thickest piece is cut to bone (at least 165°F).

3 Place chicken on platter; cover to keep warm. Increase heat to high; boil sauce uncovered about 5 minutes, stirring occasionally, until thickened. Pour sauce over chicken. Garnish with additional cilantro. Serve with couscous.

1 Serving Calories 420; Total Fat 15g (Saturated Fat 4g, Trans Fat 0g); Cholesterol 130mg; Sodium 740mg; Total Carbohydrate 25g (Dietary Fiber 4g); Protein 45g **Carbohydrate Choices:** 1½

Chicken Marsala

PREP 25 Minutes **TOTAL** 35 Minutes • *4 servings*

- 4 boneless skinless chicken breasts (about 1¼ lb)
- ½ cup all-purpose flour
- ¼ teaspoon salt
- ¼ teaspoon pepper
- 2 tablespoons olive or vegetable oil
- 1 cup sliced fresh mushrooms (3 oz)

- ¼ cup chopped fresh parsley or 1 tablespoon parsley flakes
- 2 cloves garlic, finely chopped
- ½ cup Marsala wine or store-bought or homemade chicken broth (for homemade broth, see page 153)
- Hot cooked pasta (page 182), if desired

1 Between pieces of plastic wrap or waxed paper, place each chicken breast; gently pound with flat side of meat mallet or rolling pin until about ¼-inch thick. In shallow dish, mix flour, salt and pepper. Coat chicken with flour mixture.

2 In 10-inch skillet, heat oil over medium-high heat. Cook mushrooms, parsley and garlic in oil 5 minutes, stirring frequently. Add chicken to skillet. Cook about 8 minutes, turning once, until brown.

3 Stir in wine. Cook 8 to 10 minutes longer or until chicken is no longer pink in center. Serve chicken and sauce with pasta.

1 Serving Calories 330; Total Fat 12g (Saturated Fat 2.5g, Trans Fat 0g); Cholesterol 100mg; Sodium 240mg; Total Carbohydrate 14g (Dietary Fiber 1g); Protein 39g **Carbohydrate Choices:** 1

BONING CHICKEN BREASTS

Loosen keel bone and white cartilage by running tip of index finger around both sides. Pull out bone in one or two pieces.

Insert tip of knife under long rib bones. Using steady, even pressure, gradually trim meat away from bones. Cut through shoulder joint to remove entire rib cage. Repeat on other side.

Slip knife under white tendons on either side of breast; loosen and pull out tendons (grasp end of tendons with paper towel if tendons are slippery.) Remove skin if desired. Cut breast lengthwise in half.

Chicken Marsala

Spicy Chicken in Peanut Sauce

SLOW COOKER • GLUTEN FREE

Spicy Chicken in Peanut Sauce

Pass small bowls of dry-roasted peanuts and chopped fresh cilantro to sprinkle over the chicken and serve with wedges of warm gluten-free pita bread.

PREP 15 Minutes **TOTAL** 7 Hours 15 Minutes • *4 servings*

- 1 tablespoon olive or vegetable oil
- 8 large bone-in chicken thighs (about 3 lb), skin removed
- 1 large onion, chopped (1 cup)
- 2 cans (14.5 oz each) diced tomatoes with green chiles, undrained
- 1 can (14.5 oz) crushed fire-roasted or regular diced tomatoes, undrained
- 2 tablespoons honey
- 1½ teaspoons ground cumin
- 1 teaspoon ground cinnamon
- ⅓ cup creamy peanut butter
- 2 cups hot cooked couscous or jasmine or basmati rice (page 224)

1 In 12-inch nonstick skillet, heat oil over medium-high heat. Cook chicken in oil about 4 minutes, turning once, until brown.

2 Spray 4- to 5-quart slow cooker with cooking spray. In slow cooker, mix onion, diced and crushed tomatoes, honey, cumin and cinnamon. Add chicken; spoon tomato mixture over chicken. Cover; cook on Low heat setting 7 to 8 hours.

3 Stir peanut butter into mixture in slow cooker until melted and well blended. Serve chicken and sauce over couscous.

1 Serving Calories 740; Total Fat 33g (Saturated Fat 8g, Trans Fat 0.5g); Cholesterol 140mg; Sodium 1180mg; Total Carbohydrate 52g (Dietary Fiber 8g); Protein 60g **Carbohydrate Choices:** 3½

CALORIE SMART • GLUTEN FREE

Chicken Adobo

PREP 30 Minutes **TOTAL** 4 Hours 50 Minutes • *4 servings*

MARINADE
- ½ cup cider vinegar
- ½ cup gluten-free soy sauce
- ¼ cup packed brown sugar
- 1 teaspoon black peppercorns
- ⅛ teaspoon crushed red pepper flakes
- 4 cloves garlic, crushed
- 3 bay leaves

CHICKEN
- 4 chicken thighs
- 4 chicken drumsticks

  Hot cooked rice (page 224), if desired

  Green onions, cut diagonally into slices, if desired

1 In shallow glass or plastic dish or resealable food-storage plastic bag, mix all marinade ingredients. Add chicken. Cover dish or seal bag; refrigerate at least 4 hours but no longer than 24 hours, turning chicken occasionally.

2 Heat 12-inch nonstick skillet over medium-high heat. Remove chicken from marinade; reserve marinade. Place chicken, skin side down, in skillet. Cook 6 to 8 minutes, turning once, until deep golden brown. Pour marinade over chicken; heat to boiling. Cover and simmer 20 minutes, turning once, until juice of chicken is clear when thickest part is cut to bone (at least 165°F). Remove chicken to plate; cover to keep warm.

3 Heat marinade to boiling; reduce heat to medium. Cook about 5 to 7 minutes or until reduced by half or to desired consistency. Pour into fat separator, or skim fat from marinade. Serve chicken and marinade with rice; sprinkle with green onions.

1 Serving Calories 280; Total Fat 8g (Saturated Fat 2g, Trans Fat 0g); Cholesterol 155mg; Sodium 1880mg; Total Carbohydrate 17g (Dietary Fiber 0g); Protein 36g **Carbohydrate Choices:** 1

USE IT UP
COOKED CHICKEN

Use leftover bite-size pieces of cooked chicken to make these easy dishes.

CHICKEN TACOS Heat chicken with salsa; spoon into tortillas; sprinkle with shredded cheese for a quick snack or dinner.

BUFFALO PIZZA Top your favorite crust with ranch dressing; top with chicken tossed with Buffalo wing sauce, thinly sliced red onion and celery and blue cheese crumbles. Sprinkle shredded mozzarella cheese over all; bake as directed.

QUICK CHICKEN SALAD Toss chicken with seedless grape halves, chopped apples, onion, celery and pecans and enough mayonnaise to coat. Toss with 1 teaspoon prepared yellow mustard and garlic salt to taste.

CHICKEN-CHILE QUESADILLAS Place tortillas in nonstick skillet; top with chicken, canned chopped green chiles, drained, and shredded Monterey Jack cheese. Top with another tortilla; cook over medium-low heat, turning once, until golden brown on both sides and cheese is melted. Cut into wedges to serve.

Rosemary

Basil

Oregano

Thyme

Orange

Kefalotiri

Olive Oil

Parmigiano
Reggiano

Garlic

Sun-Dried
Tomatoes

Manouri

Kasseri

Roasted Red
Bell Peppers

Mixed Mediterranean
Olives

Tomato
Paste

Honeycomb

Marcona
Almonds

Dukka

Chorizo

Greek
Yogurt

Prosciutto

Anchovies

Caraway
Seeds

Capers   Caperberries

Feta

Feta with Herbs

Saffron

Phyllo (Filo)

Smoked Paprika   Paprika   Anise Seed

Lemon

GLOBAL FLAVORS

Chicken with Romesco Sauce (right) will give you the taste of the Mediterranean in the Spanish dish.

Mediterranean

Simple ingredients used in uncomplicated ways bring out the flavors of Mediterranean cooking.

ANCHOVIES
Tiny salt-cured fish fillets canned in oil, used in small amounts to intensify and add depth of flavor to sauces, pasta and other dishes. **Anchovy paste,** available in tubes in the condiment aisle of most larger grocery stores, is a convenient way to keep this ingredient on hand for occasional use.

CAPERS
Sun-dried and pickled or salt-cured small flower buds from a bush native to the Mediterranean, used to add a pungent bite to dishes. **Caperberries** are larger buds from the same plant, with a less-intense flavor.

CHORIZO
Spicy paprika gives Spanish cured chorizo its signature color and smoky flavor. When fried, adds flavor to stews and other dishes. Sliced and served as tapas.

GREEK CHEESE
The main protein source of the Mediterranean diet, it's eaten all day long. **Kefalotiri,** one of the most popular hard cheeses, has a sharp, salty flavor, somewhat similar to Gruyère or Pecorino Romano. **Manouri** is typically an unsalted soft white cheese, somewhat like cream cheese.

HONEY
Greeks make and use a lot of honey in both sweet and savory dishes. Honey varies greatly in flavor, depending on where it's made. Both the comb and the honey in it are edible.

MARCONA ALMONDS
Spanish almonds long loved for being more tender, sweet and delicate than California almonds. Traditionally used in tapas and turrón—a Spanish nougat candy.

PHYLLO (FILO)
Tissue-thin sheets of pastry used in Greek savory and sweet dishes, most commonly baklava and spanakopita. Look for it near other frozen doughs.

SEASONINGS
Dukka Egyptian spice blend sprinkled over meats or vegetables or made into a dip. Typically contains hazelnuts or chick peas ground together with toasted nuts, sesame seed, coriander and cumin. **Saffron** Stigmas from the purple crocus that are hand-picked and dried; available in threads or powdered. Very expensive; a little goes a long way to add color, aroma and flavor to dishes. **Urfa Biber** Sun-dried Turkish chiles containing chocolate and wine flavors, typically ground with a bit of salt. Adds heat, saltiness and acidity to dishes.

MAKE AHEAD • CALORIE SMART

Chicken with Romesco Sauce

PREP 25 Minutes **TOTAL** 45 Minutes • *6 servings*

ROMESCO SAUCE
- ½ cup slivered almonds
- 1 slice firm crusty white bread (about 5×5×½-inch)
- 1 medium tomato, cut in half, seeded
- 2 cloves garlic, peeled
- 1 jar (12 oz) roasted red bell peppers, rinsed, drained and patted dry
- ¼ cup olive oil
- 1 tablespoon sherry vinegar
- ½ teaspoon salt
- ¼ teaspoon smoked paprika

CHICKEN
- 2 tablespoons olive oil
- 6 boneless skinless chicken breasts (about 1¾ lb)
- 1 teaspoon garlic salt
  Chopped fresh parsley, if desired

1 Heat oven to 400°F. In 15×10×1-inch pan, place almonds, bread, tomato and garlic in single layer. Bake 5 to 6 minutes or until almonds and bread are lightly toasted. Break bread into bite-size pieces.

2 In food processor, place almonds, bread, tomato and garlic. Cover and process, using quick on-and-off motions, until coarsely chopped. Add remaining romesco sauce ingredients. Cover and process, using quick on-and-off motions, until almost smooth. Transfer sauce to small bowl; set aside. Sauce will thicken as it stands.

3 In 12-inch nonstick skillet, heat oil over medium heat. Sprinkle both sides of chicken with garlic salt; add to skillet. Cook 15 to 20 minutes, turning once, until juice of chicken is clear when center of thickest piece is cut (at least 165°F). Serve chicken with sauce. Sprinkle with parsley.

1 Serving Calories 400; Total Fat 23g (Saturated Fat 4g, Trans Fat 0g); Cholesterol 105mg; Sodium 630mg; Total Carbohydrate 8g (Dietary Fiber 1g); Protein 39g **Carbohydrate Choices:** ½

MAKE-AHEAD DIRECTIONS: Prepare Romesco Sauce up to 1 day ahead; cover and refrigerate. Let stand at room temperature 30 minutes before serving.

Chicken with Romesco Sauce

Thai-Style Coconut Chicken

PREP 35 Minutes **TOTAL** 35 Minutes • *4 servings*

1 tablespoon vegetable oil	1 cup fresh sugar snap peas
1 lb boneless skinless chicken breasts, cut into bite-size pieces	1 teaspoon packed brown sugar
¼ cup finely chopped fresh cilantro	1 tablespoon gluten-free soy sauce
1 teaspoon grated lime zest	½ teaspoon salt
1 teaspoon grated gingerroot	1 medium green bell pepper, cut into 1-inch pieces
2 serrano chiles or 1 jalapeño chile, seeded, finely chopped	1 medium tomato, seeded, chopped (¾ cup)
1 clove garlic, finely chopped	1 tablespoon chopped fresh basil leaves
1 can (14 oz) coconut milk (not cream of coconut)	Hot cooked jasmine rice (page 224), if desired

1 In nonstick wok or 12-inch skillet, heat oil over medium-high heat. Add chicken; cook 2 to 3 minutes, stirring constantly, until chicken is no longer pink in center. Add cilantro, lime zest, gingerroot, chilies and garlic; cook and stir 1 minute.

2 Pour coconut milk over chicken. Stir in sugar snap peas, brown sugar, soy sauce, salt and bell pepper. Heat to boiling; reduce heat. Simmer uncovered 3 to 5 minutes, stirring occasionally, until vegetables are crisp-tender. Stir in tomato.

3 Spoon into shallow serving bowls; top with basil. Serve with rice.

1 Serving Calories 380; Total Fat 25g (Saturated Fat 17g, Trans Fat 0g); Cholesterol 70mg; Sodium 590mg; Total Carbohydrate 10g (Dietary Fiber 2g); Protein 28g **Carbohydrate Choices:** ½

Chicken Cacciatore

PREP 35 Minutes **TOTAL** 1 Hour 15 Minutes • *6 servings*

1 cut-up whole chicken (3 to 3½ lb)	1½ teaspoons chopped fresh or ½ teaspoon dried oregano leaves
½ cup all-purpose flour	
¼ cup vegetable oil	1 teaspoon chopped fresh or ¼ teaspoon dried basil leaves
2 medium onions	
1 medium green bell pepper	½ teaspoon salt
1 can (14.5 oz) diced tomatoes, undrained	2 cloves garlic, finely chopped
1 can (8 oz) tomato sauce	Hot cooked pasta (page 182), if desired
1 cup sliced fresh mushrooms (3 oz)	Grated Parmesan cheese, if desired

1 Coat chicken with flour. In 12-inch skillet, heat oil over medium-high heat. Cook chicken in oil 15 to 20 minutes or until brown on all sides; drain off fat.

2 Cut onions and bell pepper in half; remove seeds from pepper. Cut each half crosswise into quarters. Add onions, bell pepper and remaining ingredients except pasta and cheese to skillet with chicken; stir.

3 Heat to boiling; reduce heat. Cover and simmer 30 to 40 minutes or until juice of chicken is clear when thickest piece is cut to bone (at least 165°F). Serve over pasta with cheese.

1 Serving Calories 400; Total Fat 23g (Saturated Fat 5g, Trans Fat 0g); Cholesterol 85mg; Sodium 540mg; Total Carbohydrate 17g (Dietary Fiber 3g); Protein 30g **Carbohydrate Choices:** 1

SLOW-COOKER DIRECTIONS: Remove skin from chicken. Reduce flour to ⅓ cup and oil to 2 tablespoons; omit tomato sauce. Substitute 1 jar (4.5 oz) sliced mushrooms, drained, for the fresh mushrooms. Brown chicken as directed. Cut onions and bell pepper as directed. Spray 3½- to 6-quart slow cooker with cooking spray. In slow cooker, place half of chicken. Mix onions, bell pepper and remaining ingredients except pasta and cheese; spoon half of mixture over chicken. Add remaining chicken; top with remaining vegetable mixture. Cover; cook on Low heat setting 4 to 6 hours. Serve over pasta with cheese.

Thai-Style Coconut Chicken

Chicken Bratwurst One-Pot Casserole

Chicken Korma

CALORIE SMART

Chicken Bratwurst One-Pot Casserole

PREP 35 Minutes TOTAL 45 Minutes •
6 servings (about 1⅔ cups)

- 1 tablespoon olive oil
- 1 package (12 oz) fully-cooked chicken bratwurst or chicken sausages, cut into ½-inch slices
- 3 cups store-bought or homemade chicken broth (for homemade broth, see page 153)
- 2½ cups (8 oz) uncooked penne pasta (from 16-oz box)
- ⅓ cup coarsely chopped drained sun-dried tomatoes in oil (from 12-oz jar)
- 2 medium red bell peppers, cut into strips (about 2 cups)
- 1 can (14 oz) quartered artichoke hearts, drained
- ¼ teaspoon salt
- ¼ to ½ teaspoon crushed red pepper flakes, if desired
- 4 cloves garlic, chopped
- ⅓ cup whipping cream
- ⅓ cup grated Parmesan cheese
- 2 teaspoons grated lemon zest
- ½ cup chopped fresh basil leaves

1 In 5- or 6-qt Dutch oven, heat oil over medium-high heat. Add sausages; cook 4 to 5 minutes, stirring occasionally, until browned; transfer to plate and keep warm. Stir in chicken broth, pasta, tomatoes, bell peppers, artichokes, salt, pepper flakes and garlic. Heat to boiling.

2 Reduce heat; simmer uncovered 11 to 13 minutes, stirring occasionally, until pasta is tender and most of the liquid has been absorbed. Stir in sausages and remaining ingredients except basil, cook 2 to 3 minutes longer or until heated through.

3 Let stand 10 minutes; toss with basil. Serve immediately.

1 Serving Calories 420; Total Fat 18g (Saturated Fat 7g, Trans Fat 0g); Cholesterol 55mg; Sodium 1160mg; Total Carbohydrate 45g (Dietary Fiber 6g); Protein 21g **Carbohydrate Choices:** 3

CALORIE SMART • GLUTEN FREE

Chicken Korma

No fenugreek? Watercress leaves or fresh parsley can be substituted, but the flavor will be milder.

PREP 20 Minutes TOTAL 1 Hour 30 Minutes • **4 servings**

- 1 lb boneless skinless chicken breasts, cut crosswise into ½-inch strips
- ¼ cup whipping cream
- 2 tablespoons finely chopped gingerroot
- 5 cloves garlic, finely chopped
- 1 tablespoon finely chopped fresh cilantro
- ¾ teaspoon ground coriander seed
- ¼ teaspoon ground cumin
- ½ teaspoon salt
- ¼ teaspoon ground red pepper (cayenne)
- 2 tablespoons Clarified Butter (page 498) or butter
- ½ cup tomato sauce
- ¼ cup finely chopped fresh or 2 tablespoons crumbled dried fenugreek leaves (methi)
- Hot cooked rice (page 224), if desired

1 In medium bowl, mix all ingredients except clarified butter, tomato sauce, fenugreek and rice. Cover and refrigerate at least 1 hour but no longer than 24 hours.

2 In 10-inch skillet, heat clarified butter over medium heat. Add chicken mixture and tomato sauce. Cook about 5 minutes, stirring frequently, until chicken is partially cooked.

3 Stir in fenugreek; reduce heat. Cover and simmer about 10 minutes or until chicken is no longer pink in center. Serve with rice.

1 Serving Calories 270; Total Fat 15g (Saturated Fat 8g, Trans Fat 0g); Cholesterol 100mg; Sodium 570mg; Total Carbohydrate 7g (Dietary Fiber 2g); Protein 28g **Carbohydrate Choices:** ½

HEIRLOOM

Individual Chicken Pot Pies

PREP 40 Minutes **TOTAL** 1 Hour 15 Minutes • *6 servings*

- ⅓ cup butter
- ⅓ cup all-purpose flour
- ⅓ cup chopped onion
- ½ teaspoon salt
- ¼ teaspoon pepper
- 1¾ cups chicken broth (for homemade broth, see page 153)
- ⅔ cup milk
- 3 cups cut-up cooked chicken or turkey
- 2 cups frozen peas and carrots
- Pie Pastry for Two-Crust Pie (page 607)

1 Lightly spray 6 (10-oz) ramekins or custard cups with cooking spray.

2 In 2-quart saucepan, melt butter over medium heat. Stir in flour, onion, salt and pepper. Cook and stir until mixture is bubbly, about 2 to 3 minutes. Stir in broth and milk. Heat to boiling; cook, stirring constantly, for 3 to 5 minutes or until thickened. Boil and stir 1 minute longer. Stir in chicken and peas and carrots; remove from heat.

3 Heat oven to 425°F. Prepare pastry as directed in Steps 1 and 2 of Two-Crust Pastry. Using floured rolling pin, roll one round of pastry on lightly floured surface into 16-inch circle. Using a ramekin or custard cup as a guide, cut dough with a sharp knife at least 1 inch around the dish (about 5½ inches in diameter) to make three pastry circles, rerolling pasty if necessary. Repeat to make 6 pastry rounds. Place ramekins on 15×10×1-inch baking pan. Evenly divide chicken mixture among dishes. Top each ramekin or custard cup with a pastry circle, gently pressing overhang down over the edge of the ramekin. Make a slit in the top of each circle.

4 Bake 30 to 35 minutes or until golden brown.

1 Serving Calories 680; Total Fat 42g (Saturated Fat 15g, Trans Fat 1g); Cholesterol 90mg; Sodium 1100mg; Total Carbohydrate 46g (Dietary Fiber 3g); Protein 29g **Carbohydrate Choices:** 3

FAMILY-SIZE POT PIE: Prepare as directed—except roll two-thirds of pastry into 13-inch square. Ease into ungreased 9-inch square (2-quart) glass baking dish. Pour chicken mixture into pastry-lined dish. Roll remaining pastry into 11-inch square. Cut out designs with 1-inch cookie cutter. Place square over chicken mixture. Arrange cutouts on pastry. Turn edges of pastry under and flute. Bake about 35 minutes or until golden brown.

PORTABELLA CHICKEN POT PIES: Add 1½ cups sliced fresh baby portabella mushrooms to the flour mixture before cooking in Step 2. Continue as directed.

TUNA POT PIES: Substitute 1 can (12 oz) tuna in water, drained, for the chicken.

COLORFUL CHICKEN AND VEGGIE POT PIES: Prepare recipe as directed—except substitute 1 cup chopped bell pepper (any color) for 1 cup of the peas and carrots. Add ½ teaspoon dried thyme leaves with the vegetables.

PUFF PASTRY–TOPPED POT PIES: Omit pie pastry. Cut six 6-inch squares puff pastry from two thawed puff pastry sheets; place over chicken mixture in ramekins. Brush tops with 2 teaspoons melted butter; sprinkle with ½ teaspoon chopped fresh parsley. Bake at 400°F 30 to 35 minutes.

Individual Chicken Pot Pies

Chicken-Broccoli
Biscuit Pot Pies

NEW TWIST

AIR FRYER

Chicken-Broccoli Biscuit Pot Pies

PREP 30 Minutes   **TOTAL** 55 Minutes   •   *4 servings*

½ batch Drop Baking Powder Biscuits (page 518)	1 cup milk
1½ cups shredded cheddar cheese (6 oz)	1 tablespoon all-purpose flour
1 jar (2 oz) chopped pimentos, drained	4 oz cream cheese, cut into small pieces, softened (from 8-oz pkg)
2 cups coarsely chopped broccoli florets	½ teaspoon salt
1 tablespoon water	¼ teaspoon pepper
	2 cups cubed cooked chicken

1 Heat oven to 425°F. Lightly spray 4 (8-oz) individual baking dishes (ramekins) with cooking spray. Place dishes on foil-lined 15×10×1-inch pan.

2 Make Drop Baking Powder Biscuits as directed, using half the ingredients—except gently fold in ½ cup of the cheddar cheese and the pimentos into the dough; set aside.

3 In medium microwavable bowl, place broccoli and water. Cover with plastic wrap. Microwave on High 3 minutes. Let stand covered 2 minutes; drain.

4 In small bowl, mix ¼ cup of the milk and the flour with whisk until blended. In 3-quart saucepan, heat cream cheese and remaining ¾ cup milk over medium heat, stirring until cheese is melted. Stir in flour mixture, salt and pepper with whisk. Cook, stirring constantly, until boiling; boil and stir 1 minute. Remove from heat. Stir in broccoli, chicken and remaining 1 cup cheddar cheese.

5 Spoon hot chicken-broccoli mixture evenly into ramekins. Top with large spoonfuls of biscuit mixture and spread evenly over chicken-broccoli mixture.

6 Bake 15 to 18 minutes or until biscuits are golden brown. Cool 5 minutes before serving.

1 Serving Calories 700; Total Fat 44g (Saturated Fat 19g, Trans Fat 1g); Cholesterol 140mg; Sodium 1250mg; Total Carbohydrate 38g (Dietary Fiber 2g); Protein 38g **Carbohydrate Choices:** 2½

AIR FRYER DIRECTIONS: Using 4-quart-size air fryer, bake at 350°F for 12 to 14 minutes or until golden brown. Cool 5 minutes before serving.

Skillet Chicken Nachos

PREP 20 Minutes **TOTAL** 20 Minutes • *6 servings*

- 1 tablespoon olive or vegetable oil
- 1¼ lb boneless skinless chicken breasts, cut into ¼-inch pieces
- 1 medium red bell pepper, chopped (1 cup)
- 1 can (15 oz) black beans, drained, rinsed
- 1 can (8 oz) tomato sauce
- 1 can (7 oz) whole kernel sweet corn, drained
- 1 package (1 oz) gluten-free taco seasoning mix or ¼ cup Salt-Free Taco Seasoning Mix (page 454)
- 2 cups shredded Mexican cheese blend (8 oz)
- 6 oz gluten-free tortilla chips (about 42 chips)
- ¼ cup chopped fresh cilantro

1 In 12-inch nonstick skillet, heat oil over medium-high heat. Cook chicken in oil 3 to 5 minutes, stirring occasionally, until no longer pink in center.

2 Stir in bell pepper, beans, tomato sauce, corn, taco seasoning and 1 cup of the cheese. Reduce heat to medium; cook 3 to 5 minutes, stirring occasionally, until thoroughly heated and cheese is melted.

3 Divide tortilla chips among 6 plates. Spoon chicken mixture evenly over chips. Sprinkle with remaining 1 cup cheese and the cilantro.

1 Serving Calories 520; Total Fat 24g (Saturated Fat 9g, Trans Fat 0g); Cholesterol 95mg; Sodium 1320mg; Total Carbohydrate 38g (Dietary Fiber 5g); Protein 36g **Carbohydrate Choices:** 2½

Tuscan Chicken and White Beans

PREP 15 Minutes **TOTAL** 30 Minutes • *4 servings*

- ⅓ cup Italian dressing
- 4 boneless skinless chicken breasts (about 1¼ lb)
- ¼ cup water
- 2 medium carrots, sliced (1 cup)
- 2 medium stalks celery, sliced (1 cup)
- ¼ cup coarsely chopped drained sun-dried tomatoes in oil
- 1 teaspoon dried rosemary leaves, crushed
- 1 can (19 oz) cannellini beans, drained, rinsed

1 In 12-inch skillet, heat dressing over medium-high heat. Add chicken; cook 4 to 6 minutes, turning once, until lightly browned.

2 Reduce heat to medium-low. Add water, carrots, celery, tomatoes and rosemary. Cover and simmer about 10 minutes or until carrots are crisp-tender and juice of chicken is clear when center of thickest piece is cut (at least 165°F).

3 Stir in beans. Cover and cook 5 minutes or until beans are thoroughly heated.

1 Serving Calories 410; Total Fat 11g (Saturated Fat 2.5g, Trans Fat 0g); Cholesterol 100mg; Sodium 630mg; Total Carbohydrate 31g (Dietary Fiber 7g); Protein 47g **Carbohydrate Choices:** 2

Skillet Chicken Nachos

Chicken Salad Sandwiches

EASY • FAST

Chicken Salad Sandwiches

PREP 10 Minutes TOTAL 10 Minutes • *4 sandwiches*

1½ cups chopped cooked chicken or turkey	½ cup mayonnaise or salad dressing
1 medium stalk celery, chopped (½ cup)	¼ teaspoon salt
	¼ teaspoon pepper
1 small onion, finely chopped (⅓ cup)	8 slices bread

In medium bowl, mix all ingredients except bread. Spread mixture on 4 of the bread slices. Top with remaining bread.

1 Sandwich Calories 460; Total Fat 28g (Saturated Fat 5g, Trans Fat 0g); Cholesterol 55mg; Sodium 820mg; Total Carbohydrate 30g (Dietary Fiber 3g); Protein 21g **Carbohydrate Choices: 2**

LIGHTER DIRECTIONS: for 260 calories and 6 grams of fat per serving, use fat-free mayonnaise.

EGG SALAD SANDWICHES: Substitute 6 Hard-Cooked Eggs (page 102), chopped, for the chicken.

HAM SALAD SANDWICHES: Substitute 1½ cups chopped cooked ham for the chicken. Omit salt and pepper. Stir in 1 teaspoon yellow mustard.

TUNA SALAD SANDWICHES: Substitute 2 cans (5 oz each) tuna in water, drained, for the chicken. Reduce onion to ¼ cup. Add 1 teaspoon fresh lemon juice with the mayonnaise.

CALORIE SMART • GLUTEN FREE

Creamy Turkey Kielbasa and Potatoes

PREP 30 Minutes TOTAL 45 Minutes •
6 servings (about 1⅓ cups)

1 lb small Yukon Gold potatoes, cut in half (from 1½-lb bag)	2 garlic cloves, finely chopped
	½ cup whipping cream
1 tablespoon vegetable oil	1 tablespoon honey
1 package (13 or 14 oz) gluten-free turkey kielbasa, cut into ½-inch slices	2 teaspoons country-style Dijon mustard
	1 teaspoon gluten-free Worcestershire sauce
3 cups fresh broccoli florets (from 12-oz bag)	½ teaspoon salt
	¼ teaspoon pepper
1 cup thinly sliced red onion (1 medium)	2 teaspoons chopped fresh thyme or 1 teaspoon dried thyme leaves
1 medium bell pepper, thinly sliced	

1 In 6-quart Dutch oven, heat 1 inch water to a boil; add potatoes. Cover; heat to boiling. Reduce heat and simmer 12 to 14 minutes or until potatoes are tender but firm. Drain potatoes and set aside.

2 In same Dutch oven, heat oil over medium-high heat. Add kielbasa, broccoli, onion, bell pepper and garlic; cook uncovered 2 to 3 minutes, stirring occasionally. Reduce heat to medium, cover and cook 2 to 3 minutes, stirring occasionally, until sausage is golden brown and broccoli is crisp-tender. Add potatoes and all remaining ingredients except thyme. Cook uncovered over medium heat 2 to 3 minutes or until thoroughly heated. Toss with thyme.

1 Serving Calories 280; Total Fat 15g (Saturated Fat 7g, Trans Fat 0g); Cholesterol 55mg; Sodium 940mg; Total Carbohydrate 23g (Dietary Fiber 3g); Protein 13g **Carbohydrate Choices: 1½**

Turkey Meatball "Pot Roast"

SLOW COOKER • CALORIE SMART

Turkey Meatball "Pot Roast"

PREP 25 Minutes TOTAL 4 Hours 35 Minutes • **6 servings** (about 1½ cups)

2 tablespoons butter, melted	2 medium onions, peeled, cut in quarters
1 tablespoon Worcestershire sauce	2 cups chicken broth (for homemade broth, see page 153)
1 tablespoon tomato paste	Turkey Meatballs (at right)
½ teaspoon salt	2 tablespoons cornstarch
½ teaspoon dried thyme leaves	2 tablespoons cold water
½ teaspoon crushed dried rosemary leaves	Chopped parsley, if desired
6 medium carrots	
6 medium red potatoes, cut in half (about 1½ lb)	

1 In 5- or 6-quart slow cooker, mix melted butter, Worcestershire sauce, tomato paste, salt, thyme and rosemary. Peel carrots and cut into 2½-inch pieces, cutting in half lengthwise if carrots are large. Add carrots, potatoes and onions to slow cooker; toss to coat. Stir in broth.

2 Prepare meatballs as directed in Steps 3 and 4 (right). Place meatballs on vegetable mixture in slow cooker.

3 Cover; cook on Low heat setting 4 to 5 hours or until meatballs are thoroughly cooked and no longer pink in center and vegetables are crisp-tender.

4 In small bowl, mix cornstarch and water until smooth. Stir into juices in slow cooker; cover. Increase to High heat setting and cook 10 to 15 minutes or until bubbly and slightly thickened. Sprinkle with parsley.

1 Serving Calories 470; Total Fat 16g (Saturated Fat 6g, Trans Fat 0g); Cholesterol 105mg; Sodium 850mg; Total Carbohydrate 57g (Dietary Fiber 6g); Protein 23g **Carbohydrate Choices:** 4

Asian-Glazed Turkey Meatballs and Veggie Rice

Panko bread crumbs are crispier than traditional bread crumbs. We've used a Japanese-brand panko for these meatballs as the smaller pieces help hold the meatballs together nicely. Look for them in the aisle with ethnic ingredients.

PREP 40 Minutes TOTAL 45 Minutes •
4 servings (4 meatballs and ½ cup rice)

VEGGIE RICE

1 cup uncooked brown or white rice	1 tablespoon Montreal chicken or 1½ teaspoons Montreal steak grill seasoning
2 cups water	
½ cup finely chopped fresh Italian (flat-leaf) parsley	1 egg
½ cup matchstick carrots (from 10-oz bag)	**ASIAN GLAZE**

TURKEY MEATBALLS

1 lb ground turkey	½ cup soy sauce
½ cup plain Japanese panko crispy bread crumbs	¼ cup packed brown sugar
¼ cup grated Parmesan cheese	¼ cup hoisin sauce (from 9.4-oz jar)
2 tablespoons finely chopped fresh Italian (flat-leaf) parsley	¼ cup sweet Thai chile sauce
	2 teaspoons finely chopped peeled gingerroot (about 1-inch piece)
	Additional chopped fresh Italian (flat-leaf) parsley, if desired

1 Heat oven to 400°F.

2 Cook rice in water as directed on package—except add parsley and carrots during last 5 minutes of cooking. Remove from heat; set aside.

3 Meanwhile, in large bowl, place meatball ingredients; mix well. Shape mixture into 16 (1¾-inch) balls; place in foil-lined 13×9-inch pan or on rack in broiler pan, about 1 inch apart.

4 Bake meatballs 22 minutes.

5 Meanwhile, in 1-quart saucepan, stir together glaze ingredients except additional parsley. Heat to boiling over medium heat; reduce heat. Cook and stir 2 to 3 minutes or until glaze thickens; set aside.

6 Brush glaze over baked meatballs, coating meatballs twice. Bake 3 minutes or until thoroughly cooked and no longer pink in center. Serve remaining glaze with meatballs and rice. Top with parsley.

1 Serving Calories 610; Total Fat 15g (Saturated Fat 4.5g, Trans Fat 0g); Cholesterol 140mg; Sodium 2970mg; Total Carbohydrate 83g (Dietary Fiber 3g); Protein 36g **Carbohydrate Choices:** 5½

Artichoke-and-Spinach-Stuffed Turkey Tenderloin

Packages of whole mushrooms have a wide variety of sizes in them. Before mixing the vegetables, cut large mushrooms in half or quarters for more even cooking and easier eating.

PREP 30 Minutes **TOTAL** 1 Hour 20 Minutes • *6 servings*

TURKEY

- 1 cup Hot Artichoke-Spinach Dip (page 50) or ¾ cup purchased spinach-artichoke dip
- ¾ cup plain panko crispy bread crumbs
- ½ cup grated Parmesan cheese
- 2 tablespoons olive oil
- 1 teaspoon Italian seasoning
- 2 cloves garlic, finely chopped
- 1 package (1½ lb) turkey tenderloins (2 tenderloins)

VEGETABLE MIXTURE

- 2 packages (8 oz each) white mushrooms
- 1 medium red bell pepper, cut into strips
- 1 tablespoon olive oil
- 1 teaspoon Italian seasoning
- ¾ teaspoon salt

1 Heat oven to 375°F. Line 15×10×1-inch pan with foil, with foil hanging slightly over the edge. Cut another 18x15-inch piece of heavy-duty foil; grab center of foil at short edges to to create a 1-inch ridge. Place in the pan with the 1-inch ridge in the center of the pan and the remaining foil covering the edges.

2 Make Hot Artichoke-Spinach Dip as directed, but do not spoon into casserole or bake; set aside.

3 In medium bowl, stir together panko, Parmesan cheese, olive oil, Italian seasoning and garlic. Spoon one-third of mixture onto one long side of pan in 12-inch length.

4 Pat tenderloins dry with paper towel. Place each tenderloin between 2 sheets of plastic wrap or waxed paper; pound with flat side of meat mallet or rolling pin until ⅜-inch thick. Remove plastic wrap over top. Place the 2 flattened tenderloins together, pressing pieces together with fingers where the pieces meet, to form 12x8-inch rectangle. Spread dip to within ½ inch of edges. Starting at one long edge, roll up. Remove plastic wrap. Tie tenderloin with kitchen string at about 1½-inch intervals.

5 Place tenderloin on crumb mixture in pan. Press tenderloin into crumb mixture so it adheres to bottom of tenderloin. Pat remaining crumb mixture evenly over tenderloin.

6 In large bowl, stir together vegetable mixture. Spoon onto other side of pan.

7 Roast 40 to 50 minutes, stirring vegetables halfway through roasting, until instant-read thermometer inserted in thickest part of tenderloin reads 165°F. Let stand 5 minutes; cut string from turkey with kitchen scissors and discard. Slice turkey and serve with vegetables.

1 Serving Calories 430; Total Fat 23g (Saturated Fat 5g, Trans Fat 0g); Cholesterol 85mg; Sodium 770mg; Total Carbohydrate 19g (Dietary Fiber 3g); Protein 37g **Carbohydrate Choices:** 1

PREPARING STUFFED TURKEY TENDERLOIN

Create a 1-inch ridge in foil down length of pan to prevent veggie juices from softening the crumb-topped tenderloin.

Using fingers, press two tenderloins together to form one large rectangle.

Starting on long edge, roll up stuffed tenderloin using the plastic wrap to help push the tenderloin over into a roll.

Artichoke-and-Spinach Stuffed Turkey Tenderloin

TIMETABLE FOR THAWING POULTRY

To keep poultry safe to eat, never thaw it at room temperature. Cook poultry within 2 days of being thawed.

Refrigerator Thawing: Place poultry in a pan with sides or in resealable food-storage plastic bag to catch drips. Allow about 24 hours for every 4 to 5 lb.

Cold-Water Thawing: Submerge packaged poultry in cold water, changing water every 30 minutes. Allow 30 minutes per pound.

TYPE OF POULTRY	WEIGHT IN POUNDS	REFRIGERATOR THAWING TIME (DAYS)	COLD-WATER THAWING TIME (HOURS)
Chicken, Whole	3 to 4	1 to 2	2 to 2½
Turkey, Whole (Not Stuffed)	8 to 12	2 to 2½	4 to 6
	12 to 16	2½ to 4	6 to 8
	16 to 20	4 to 5	8 to 10
	20 to 24	5 to 6	10 to 12
Cut-Up Pieces	Up to 4	½ up to 3	1½ up to 3

CALORIE SMART • GLUTEN FREE

Roast Turkey

PREP 20 Minutes **TOTAL** 3 Hours 35 Minutes •
12 to 15 servings

- 1 whole turkey (12 to 15 lb), thawed if frozen*
- 3 tablespoons butter, melted, or vegetable oil

1 Heat oven to 325°F. Discard giblets and neck or reserve for another use.

2 If desired, fold and tuck wings under turkey so tips are touching to prevent burning. If turkey doesn't have ovenproof plastic leg band holding legs together, tuck legs under band of skin at tail (if present), or tie legs together with kitchen string, then tie to tail if desired. Place turkey, breast side up, on rack in large roasting pan. Brush butter over turkey. Insert ovenproof meat thermometer so tip is in thickest part of thigh but does not touch bone. (Do not add water or cover turkey.)

3 Roast uncovered 3 hours to 3 hours 45 minutes. After roasting about 2 hours, remove leg band, cut band of skin or remove string holding legs to allow the inside of the thighs to cook thoroughly and evenly. Place tent of foil loosely over turkey to prevent excessive browning.

4 Turkey is done when thermometer reads at least 165°F** at right and legs move easily when lifted or twisted. Place turkey on warm platter; cover with foil to keep warm. Reserve drippings if making Pan Gravy (at right). Let turkey stand 15 to 20 minutes for easiest carving.

1 Serving Calories 320; Total Fat 15g (Saturated Fat 5g, Trans Fat 0g); Cholesterol 150mg; Sodium 160mg; Total Carbohydrate 0g (Dietary Fiber 0g); Protein 46g **Carbohydrate Choices:** 0

*For optimal food safety and even doneness, the USDA recommends cooking stuffing separately. However, if you choose to stuff poultry or game birds, it's necessary to use an accurate food thermometer to make sure the center of the stuffing reaches a safe minimum temperature of 165°F. Cooking home-stuffed poultry or game birds is riskier than cooking those that are not stuffed. Even if the poultry or game bird itself has reached the safe minimum internal temperature of 165°F, the stuffing may not have reached same temperature. Bacteria can survive in stuffing that has not reached 165°F, possibly resulting in foodborne illness. Do not stuff poultry or game birds that will be grilled, smoked, fried, microwaved or prepared in a slow cooker, because the stuffing will never get hot enough in the center to be safe.

**165°F is the minimum temperature to safely cook turkey, but you may prefer roasting to 170°F for the most velvety, tender texture while still maintaining moistness.

BRINED WHOLE TURKEY: in large stainless-steel stockpot, mix 2 gallons cold water and 2 cups kosher (coarse) salt until salt is dissolved. Add turkey (brine should cover bird). Cover and refrigerate 8 to 12 hours. Remove turkey from brine; thoroughly rinse under cool water, gently rubbing inside and outside of turkey to release salt. Pat dry inside and out with paper towels. Follow directions in Step 2 to prepare turkey for roasting. In medium bowl, toss 1 medium onion, quartered; 1 carrot, coarsely chopped; 1 stalk celery, coarsely chopped; 1 teaspoon dried thyme leaves and 1 tablespoon of the melted butter. Spoon into turkey cavity. Place turkey in roasting pan and insert thermometer as directed in Step 2. Brush all sides of turkey with remaining melted butter. Roast turkey as directed. Remove turkey from oven. Remove vegetables from cavity and discard.

EASY • FAST • CALORIE SMART

Pan Gravy

Feel free to double the recipe, if you'd like 2 cups of gravy. If you didn't end up with enough drippings to really flavor the gravy, add the browning sauce.

PREP 10 Minutes **TOTAL** 10 Minutes • 1 cup gravy

- Drippings from roast turkey or other cooked meat
- 2 tablespoons all-purpose flour
- 1 cup liquid (turkey or meat juices, broth, water)
- Few drops browning sauce, if desired
- Salt and pepper to taste

1 After removing turkey from roasting pan, pour drippings (turkey juices and fat) into fat separator or glass measuring cup, leaving browned bits in pan. The fat will rise to the top. With spoon, return 2 tablespoons of the fat to the pan. Pour or spoon off and discard any remaining fat; reserve remaining drippings.

2 Stir flour into fat in roasting pan. Cook over low heat, stirring constantly and scraping up browned bits, until mixture is smooth and bubbly. Remove from heat.

Roast Turkey

3 Gradually stir in reserved drippings plus enough broth or water to equal 1 cup. Heat to boiling, stirring constantly. Boil and stir 1 minute. Stir in browning sauce if darker color is desired. Stir in salt and pepper.

1 Tablespoon Calories 20; Total Fat 1.5g (Saturated Fat 0.5g, Trans Fat 0g); Cholesterol 0mg; Sodium 65mg; Total Carbohydrate 0g (Dietary Fiber 0g); Protein 0g **Carbohydrate Choices:** 0

PAN CREAM GRAVY: Substitute half-and-half or whole milk for the liquid.

THIN GRAVY: Reduce fat from meat drippings and flour to 1 tablespoon each.

Bread Stuffing

PREP 15 Minutes **TOTAL** 55 Minutes • *10 servings* (½ cup)

¾ cup butter	1½ teaspoons chopped fresh or ½ teaspoon dried thyme leaves
2 large stalks celery (with leaves), chopped (1½ cups)	
1 large onion, chopped (1 cup)	1½ teaspoons chopped fresh or ½ teaspoon dried sage leaves or ¼ teaspoon ground sage
9 cups soft bread cubes (about 15 slices bread)	1 teaspoon salt
	¼ teaspoon pepper

1 Heat oven to 350°F. Spray 13×9-inch (3-quart) glass baking dish with cooking spray.

2 In 4-quart saucepan, melt butter over medium-high heat. Cook celery and onion in butter 4 to 6 minutes, stirring occasionally, until tender. Add remaining ingredients; stir gently to mix well. Spoon into baking dish.

3 Cover with foil; bake 25 minutes. Remove foil; bake 10 to 15 minutes longer or until center is hot and edges are beginning to brown.

1 Serving Calories 220; Total Fat 15g (Saturated Fat 9g, Trans Fat 0.5g); Cholesterol 35mg; Sodium 510mg; Total Carbohydrate 17g (Dietary Fiber 1g); Protein 3g **Carbohydrate Choices:** 1

LIGHTER DIRECTIONS: For 135 calories and 6 grams of fat per serving, reduce butter to ¼ cup, and add ½ cup chicken broth when cooking the celery and onion.

CORNBREAD STUFFING: Substitute cornbread cubes for the soft bread cubes. For Cornbread-Sausage Stuffing, omit salt; add ½ lb cooked crumbled bulk pork or chorizo sausage (see Sausage Stuffing, below) and 1 cup chopped toasted pecans with the remaining stuffing ingredients.

GIBLET STUFFING: Place giblets (but not liver) and neck from turkey or chicken in 2-quart saucepan. Add enough water to cover; season with salt and pepper. Simmer uncovered over low heat 1 to 2 hours or until tender; drain. Remove meat from neck and finely chop with giblets; add with the remaining stuffing ingredients.

OYSTER STUFFING: Add 2 cans (8 oz each) whole oysters, drained and chopped, with the remaining stuffing ingredients.

SAUSAGE STUFFING: Omit salt. In 10-inch skillet, cook 1 lb bulk pork sausage or fresh chorizo sausage over medium heat, stirring occasionally, until no longer pink; drain, reserving drippings. Substitute drippings for part of the butter. Add cooked sausage with the remaining stuffing ingredients.

WILD RICE STUFFING: in ungreased 2-quart casserole, mix 3 cups cooked wild rice, ¼ cup melted butter, 1 cup orange juice, 1 medium apple, peeled and cut into chunks, 1 cup dry bread crumbs and ½ cup each raisins and chopped walnuts. Cover and bake at 325°F for 55 to 60 minutes or until apple is tender.

Turkey Breast with Gravy

MULTI COOKER

Turkey Breast with Gravy

See Learn to Use Slow Cookers and Multi Cookers (page 167) for great success with recipes like this one.

PREP 20 Minutes **TOTAL** 1 Hour 5 Minutes • *4 servings*

- 2 tablespoons butter
- 1 teaspoon garlic salt
- ½ teaspoon dried thyme leaves
- ¼ teaspoon dried sage leaves
- 1 bone-in skin-on turkey breast half (2.5 lb), thawed if frozen
- 1 cup reduced-sodium chicken broth (from 32-oz carton)
- 3 tablespoons cornstarch
- 3 tablespoons water

1 On 6-quart multi cooker, select SAUTE; adjust to normal. Melt butter in insert. In small bowl, mix garlic salt, thyme and sage. Rub turkey breast all over with spice mixture, and place in insert, skin side down; cook 12 to 14 minutes or until browned. Using tongs, transfer to plate. Select CANCEL.

2 Carefully place rack in insert. Add broth. Place turkey, skin side up, on rack. Secure lid; set pressure valve to SEALING. Select MANUAL; cook on high pressure 22 minutes. Select CANCEL. Keep pressure valve in SEALING position to release pressure naturally. Internal temperature in thickest part of breast should be at least 165°F using instant-read thermometer.*

3 When cool enough to handle, carefully transfer turkey to cutting board, and remove rack.

4 Select SAUTE, and adjust to normal; heat liquid to simmering. In small bowl, beat cornstarch and water with whisk; stir into liquid and cook 1 to 2 minutes, stirring constantly, until thickened.

5 Carve turkey; serve with gravy.

1 Serving Calories 430; Total Fat 20g (Saturated Fat 8g, Trans Fat 0.5g); Cholesterol 165mg; Sodium 530mg; Total Carbohydrate 6g (Dietary Fiber 0g); Protein 54g **Carbohydrate Choices:** ½

*We tested with a 2.5-lb turkey breast. Larger turkey breasts will require a longer cooking time. If turkey is not done, select MANUAL, and cook on high pressure 4 to 6 minutes longer. Select CANCEL. Set pressure valve to VENTING to quick-release pressure. Internal temperature in thickest part of breast (and not touching bone) should be at least 165°F using instant-read thermometer.

DRY-BRINED ROASTED TURKEY BREAST WITH GRAVY: Omit all ingredients except butter, turkey and broth; increase broth to 2 cups. Spray 15×10×1-inch pan with cooking spray. Place turkey breast, skin side up, on rack in pan. Rub turkey with a mixture of 1 tablespoon chopped fresh thyme leaves, 3 cloves garlic, chopped, 2 teaspoons coarse (kosher or sea) salt and 1 teaspoon pepper. Cover with plastic wrap; refrigerate 2 hours. Remove plastic wrap; refrigerate uncovered at least 1 hour longer but no longer than 12 hours. Heat oven to 350°F. In 12-inch skillet, melt 2 tablespoons butter over medium heat. Cook turkey breast skin side down 1 to 3 minutes or until browned; turn and cook 30 to 60 seconds longer or until browned. Remove from heat. Reserve skillet and drippings. Place turkey skin side up on rack in small roasting pan. Roast uncovered 55 minutes to 1 hour 20 minutes or until instant-read thermometer inserted in thickest part of breast reads at least 165°F. Place turkey on warm platter; cover with foil. Let stand 15 minutes before carving. Meanwhile, add 2 tablespoons butter to drippings in skillet; melt over medium-high heat. Add 1 cup chopped onion and ½ cup each chopped carrot and celery; cook 6 to 8 minutes or until softened. Stir in ¼ cup flour; cook 1 to 2 minutes longer or until thickened. Stir in broth; heat to boiling, stirring frequently. Boil and stir 2 to 4 minutes or until thickened. Strain; season with salt and pepper to taste; serve with turkey.

SLOW COOKER • CALORIE SMART

Herbed Turkey and Wild Rice Casserole

PREP 25 Minutes **TOTAL** 6 Hours 55 Minutes • *6 servings*

- 6 slices bacon, cut into ½-inch pieces
- 1 lb turkey breast tenderloins, cut into ¾-inch pieces
- 1 medium onion, chopped (½ cup)
- 1 medium carrot, sliced (½ cup)
- 1 medium stalk celery, sliced (½ cup)
- 3½ cups chicken broth (for homemade broth, see page 153)
- 1 can (10¾ oz) condensed cream of chicken soup
- ¼ teaspoon dried marjoram leaves
- ⅛ teaspoon pepper
- 1¼ cups uncooked wild rice, rinsed, drained

1 In 10-inch skillet, cook bacon over medium heat, stirring occasionally, until crisp. Stir in turkey. Cook 3 to 5 minutes, stirring occasionally, until turkey is brown. Stir in onion, carrot and celery. Cook 2 minutes, stirring occasionally; drain.

2 Spray 3½- to 6-quart slow cooker with cooking spray. In slow cooker, beat 1¾ cups of the broth and the soup with whisk until smooth. Stir in remaining 1¾ cups broth, the marjoram and pepper. Stir in turkey mixture and wild rice.

3 Cover; cook on High heat setting 30 minutes. Reduce heat setting to Low. Cook 6 to 7 hours or until rice is tender and liquid is absorbed.

1 Serving Calories 350; Total Fat 9g (Saturated Fat 3g, Trans Fat 0g); Cholesterol 50mg; Sodium 750mg; Total Carbohydrate 36g (Dietary Fiber 3g); Protein 29g **Carbohydrate Choices:** 2½

MAKE AHEAD • CALORIE SMART

Roasted Brined Duck with Cranberry-Chipotle Glaze

For a simple, attractive garnish, arrange fresh sage leaves and whole crab apples around the duck on the platter.

PREP 25 Minutes   **TOTAL** 15 Hours 20 Minutes   •   *4 servings*

BRINE

- 6 cups cold water
- 2 cups cider vinegar
- 3 tablespoons dried sage leaves
- 1 tablespoon whole peppercorns
- 1 bulb garlic, cloves separated, peeled and smashed
- 1 cup boiling water
- ¾ cup coarse (kosher or sea) salt
- ¾ cup packed brown sugar

DUCK

- 1 whole duckling (4 to 6 lb), thawed if frozen

GLAZE

- 1 can (14 oz) jellied cranberry sauce
- ¼ cup cider vinegar
- 3 or 4 chipotle chiles in adobo sauce (from 7-oz can), finely chopped

1 Place 2-gallon resealable food-storage plastic bag in stockpot or very large bowl. Add cold water, vinegar, sage, peppercorns and garlic to bag.

2 In medium bowl, stir together 1 cup boiling water, the salt and brown sugar until dissolved. Pour into vinegar mixture.

3 Remove excess fat from body cavity and neck of duck. Rinse inside and out under cool running water. With large, sharp fork, prick skin all over at an angle, being careful not to pierce meat. Carefully place duck in brine, making sure entire duck is submerged in brine (weight down with a plate, if necessary). Cover; refrigerate at least 12 but not longer than 24 hours.

4 Heat oven to 350°F. Remove duck from brine; discard brine. Rinse duck inside and out and pat dry. Place duck breast side up on rack in large roasting pan. Tie legs with kitchen string. Insert ovenproof meat thermometer so tip is in thickest part of inside thigh and does not touch bone.

5 Roast 1 hour 40 minutes. Carefully remove duck from pan; pour drippings and cooking juices from pan into large heatproof bowl or container. Discard or save for another use. Return duck to rack in roasting pan.

6 In medium bowl, stir together all glaze ingredients; reserve half of glaze for serving. Brush about ¼ cup of the remaining glaze over duck.

7 Roast 45 minutes to 1 hour longer, brushing with glaze every 10 minutes, until thermometer reads 165°F. Place duck on warm serving platter. Cover; let stand 15 minutes for easiest carving. Heat reserved glaze until warm; serve with duck.

1 Serving Calories 350; Total Fat 5g (Saturated Fat 1.5g, Trans Fat 0g); Cholesterol 125mg; Sodium 2530mg; Total Carbohydrate 45g (Dietary Fiber 2g); Protein 31g **Carbohydrate Choices:** 3

Roasted Brined Duck with Cranberry-Chipotle Glaze

 **USE IT UP**
DUCK FAT

Preparing a duck? Don't throw out the rendered (cooked) fat after roasting the bird.

Allow the fat to cool slightly; strain through a fine mesh strainer lined with cheesecloth into a resealable container. Store covered up to 3 months in the refrigerator or 6 months in the freezer. Try these ways to use it up while adding flavor and texture.

POTATOES Toss potatoes with a little duck fat before roasting potatoes or oven-frying French fries. Or stir into mashed potatoes.

BROWNING MEAT Brown pork chops, chicken breasts or shrimp in a little duck fat for beautiful evenly browned and flavorful results.

WHOLE CHICKEN OR TURKEY Rub a little duck fat under and over the skin and in the cavity for a photo-worthy golden-brown and crispy-crusted bird.

ROASTED VEGGIES Use a little duck fat to toss with your veggies before roasting them, to get a nice caramelized crust and rich flavor.

Roast Goose with Apple Stuffing

PREP 30 Minutes TOTAL 4 Hours 20 Minutes • **8 servings**

1 whole goose (8 to 10 lb), thawed if frozen
¼ cup butter
2 medium stalks celery (with leaves), chopped (1 cup)
1 medium onion, chopped (½ cup)
6 cups soft bread crumbs (about 9 slices bread)
3 medium unpeeled tart apples, chopped (3 cups)
1½ teaspoons chopped fresh sage leaves or ½ teaspoon rubbed sage or ground sage
¾ teaspoon chopped fresh or ¼ teaspoon dried thyme leaves
½ teaspoon salt
¼ teaspoon pepper
Pan Gravy (page 346), if desired

1 Heat oven to 350°F. Discard giblets and neck or reserve for another use. Remove excess fat from goose.

2 Place goose, breast side up, on rack in shallow roasting pan. Fasten neck skin to back of goose with skewer. Fold wings across back of goose so tips are touching. Pierce skin all over with fork so fat can drain. Insert ovenproof meat thermometer so tip is in thickest part of inside thigh and does not touch bone. (Do not add water or cover goose.)

3 Roast uncovered 3 hours to 3 hours 30 minutes (if necessary, place tent of foil loosely over goose during last hour to prevent excessive browning), removing excess fat from pan occasionally.

4 Meanwhile, spray 2-quart casserole with cooking spray. In 3-quart saucepan, melt butter over medium-high heat. Add celery and onion and cook about 5 minutes, stirring occasionally, until tender; remove from heat. Stir in remaining ingredients except gravy. Spoon into casserole. Cover with foil and refrigerate until baking time.

5 Bake stuffing, covered, alongside goose after goose has roasted 2 hours 15 minutes, removing foil from stuffing during last 10 minutes of baking, until center is hot and edges are beginning to brown. Goose is done when thermometer reads at least 165°F and legs move easily when lifted or twisted. Reserve drippings if making Pan Gravy (page 346) or save for another use. (Geese will release a substantial amount of fat). Let stand 15 to 20 minutes for easiest carving.

1 Serving Calories 760; Total Fat 49g (Saturated Fat 17g, Trans Fat 1g); Cholesterol 190mg; Sodium 490mg; Total Carbohydrate 27g (Dietary Fiber 3g); Protein 51g **Carbohydrate Choices:** 2

Orange-Roasted Pheasants

It may seem like you are cooking a lot when you cook a couple of pheasants, but there is not much meat to the amount of bone. With two pheasants, you'll have four nice servings.

PREP 20 Minutes TOTAL 1 Hour 35 Minutes • **4 servings**

½ cup butter, softened
2 tablespoons honey
2 teaspoons grated orange zest
1 teaspoon salt
¼ teaspoon pepper
4 medium green onions, sliced (¼ cup)
2 pheasants (2½ to 3 lb each), thawed if frozen
½ cup orange-flavored liqueur or orange juice
1 cup gluten-free chicken broth (for homemade broth, see page 153)

1 Heat oven to 350°F. In small bowl, stir butter, honey, orange zest, salt, pepper and onions until well mixed.

2 Place pheasants breast side up in shallow roasting pan. Starting at the back opening, gently separate skin from breast of each pheasant, using fingers. Spread butter mixture under skin. Secure skin to flesh with toothpick if necessary. Insert ovenproof meat thermometer so tip is in thickest part of inside thigh and does not touch bone.

3 Roast uncovered about 50 to 60 minutes or until thermometer reads at least 165°F and legs move easily when lifted or twisted. Remove pheasants to warm platter; cover loosely with foil.

4 Pour liqueur and broth into roasting pan, scraping up browned bits from pan. Pour mixture into 1-quart saucepan. Heat to boiling, stirring occasionally; boil about 15 minutes, stirring occasionally, until liquid is reduced to 1 cup. Serve sauce with pheasants.

1 Serving Calories 1090; Total Fat 65g (Saturated Fat 28g, Trans Fat 1.5g); Cholesterol 365mg; Sodium 1010mg; Total Carbohydrate 13g (Dietary Fiber 0g); Protein 112g **Carbohydrate Choices:** 1

Orange-Roasted Pheasants

Fish & Shellfish

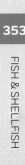

Fish Basics

Fish is delicious, naturally rich in high-quality protein, yet generally low in fat, saturated fat and cholesterol. Plus, many fish contain good amounts of omega-3 fatty acids that we hear so much about. It can be fixed many ways—yet for many, preparing it at home can be daunting. Let us show you how to select delicious fish, and easy ways to prepare it. Check out our guide for the information you need about buying, storing and cooking fish.

The USDA requires that all fish labels must state its harvesting method and country of origin. The way fish are farmed can affect ocean health. For more information go to www.seafoodwatch.org/ocean-issues/fishing-and-farming-methods.

Buying Fish
(FRESH OR FROZEN FILLETS, STEAKS OR WHOLE FISH)

- Flesh should be shiny and firm, and spring back when touched. Avoid fish with dark edges or brown or yellowish discoloration.
- Contents of the package should smell fresh and mild, not "fishy" or like ammonia.
- Be sure to buy and use the fish by the sell-by date.
- For whole fish, eyes should be bright, clear and just slightly bulging. Only a few fish, such as walleye, have naturally cloudy eyes.
- Gills should be bright pink to red, and scales should be bright and shiny.
- Frozen fish should be tightly wrapped and not have any freezer burn (dry or dark spots).

Storing Fish

- Keep fresh or thawed fish in the original packaging in the coldest part of your refrigerator. Use within 2 days.
- For longer storage, fish packaged in clear plastic wrap on a tray can be frozen as it is. Other fish should be tightly wrapped in a resealable plastic freezer bag or foil. Freeze for up to 6 months. Thaw overnight in the refrigerator.

Cooking Fish

Fish is naturally delicate and tender, and overcooking makes it dry. Use the "10-minute" rule for moist, flaky fish. Here is how to do it.

- Measure the fish at its thickest point. If it will be stuffed or rolled, measure it before stuffing or rolling.
- Fish fillets will often have skin on one side. Cook the fish skin side down. The skin helps hold the fish together and is easy to remove after cooking.
- Cook 10 minutes per inch of thickness. Turn over halfway through cooking time only if specified. Fillets less than ½-inch thick generally need no turning. Cook frozen fish (not thawed) 20 minutes per inch. Add 5 minutes to the total cooking time if the fish is cooked in foil or in a sauce.
- Cook just until the fish flakes easily with a fork. Insert the tines of a fork gently into the thickest part of the fish and twist slightly. The flesh should begin to separate along the natural lines.

Mercury in Fish

Nearly all fish contain traces of mercury. For most people, the risk of consuming mercury by eating fish is not a concern. But the FDA recommends limiting mercury in the diets of women who may become pregnant or are pregnant and breastfeeding, and of young children. For more information go to www.fda.gov/food/consumers/advice-about-eating-fish

MOST COMMON LOW-MERCURY FISH

- Shrimp
- Canned light tuna (substitute in recipes calling for albacore or white tuna)
- Salmon
- Pollock
- Catfish

FISH WITH HIGH MERCURY LEVELS

- Shark
- Swordfish
- King mackerel
- Tilefish

CHOOSING FISH BY FLAVOR AND TEXTURE

Fish can be categorized by flavor and texture, making it easy to substitute one fish for another within a category.

MILD FLAVOR	MEDIUM FLAVOR	FULL FLAVOR
DELICATE TO MEDIUM TEXTURE		
Alaskan Pollock	Atlantic Salmon	Herring/Sardines
Barramundi	Branzino	Smelt
Flounder	Chinook Salmon	
Sole	Walleye	
	Whitefish	
MEDIUM-FIRM TEXTURE		
Butterfish/Sablefish	Catfish	Bluefish
Cod	Char	Mackerel
Haddock	Coho Salmon	Salmon (Alaskan, Sockeye)
Lingcod	Drum	Shad
Snapper/Red Snapper	Hake/Whiting	Wahoo/Ono
Tilapia	Lake Perch	
Tilefish	Mahi Mahi	
	Porgy/Scup	
	Rainbow Trout	
	Redfish	
	Rockfish/Ocean Perch	
	Sea Bass	
FIRM TEXTURE		
Grouper	Shark	Marlin
Halibut	Tuna (Albacore, Skipjack, Yellowfin/Ahi)	Swordfish
Monkfish		Tuna (Bluefin, Bonito)
Pompano		
Striped Bass		
Sturgeon		

SEAFOOD SUSTAINABILITY

Many consumers, restaurants and chefs are trying to use sustainable seafood. To maintain sustainability, the population of a fish species is managed to provide for today's needs without damaging the ability of the species to reproduce. Purchasing fish managed under a U.S. fishery management plan considers the social and economic outcomes for fishing communities; prevents overfishing; rebuilds depleted stocks; minimizes bycatch and interactions with protected species; and identifies and conserves essential habitat. For more information, go to www.fishwatch.gov.

FISH POUNDS PER SERVING

The number of pounds per serving varies depending on the form of fish.

TYPE OF FISH	POUNDS PER SERVING
Fillets or Steaks	⅓ to ½
Pan-Dressed (often scaled, with internal organs, head, tail and fins removed)	½
Drawn (whole, with head and tail; only internal organs removed)	½ to ¾
Whole (completely intact, nothing removed)	¾ to 1

THE BEST COOKING METHODS FOR FISH

Instead of shopping for a specific fish, scan the seafood counter for what's freshest and on sale. If you're not preparing a specific recipe, you can decide what to buy based on the cooking method you wish to use or the type of fish that appeals to you most that day. Look to this chart to match the fish to the best cooking methods and you're on your way to cooking fish successfully!

COOKING METHODS	FISH TYPE
Panfrying	Delicate to medium-textured fish such as flounder, halibut, salmon or sole (with skin on); medium-firm fish such as char, perch or snapper
Oven-Frying	Medium-firm, mild-flavored fish such as cod or haddock
Broiling	Fillets or steaks of firm-textured fish such as shark or swordfish. Thin or delicate-textured fish should not be turned or it can fall apart.
Grilling	Fillets or steaks of medium-firm texture; steaks or whole medium-firm-textured fish such as mahi mahi, redfish or ono.
Baking	Delicate or medium-firm fillets or steaks, such as tilapia, rockfish or red snapper. (Any skin on fish can be removed either before or after cooking.)
Steaming (packets made with cooking parchment or foil)	Skinless fillets or steaks of any texture fish; our favorites include flounder, grouper or tuna
Roasting	Whole fish or large fillets or steaks, such as snapper, trout or sea bass
Deep-Frying	Mild-flavored delicate or medium-firm-textured fillets such as cod, halibut or catfish (without skin)

Tuna Melt–Tot Bake

Tuna Tortellini Skillet

CALORIE SMART

Tuna Melt–Tot Bake

PREP 20 min **TOTAL** 50 min • *6 servings* (about 1 cup each)

2	tablespoons butter
2	tablespoons all-purpose flour
¼	teaspoon salt
⅛	teaspoon pepper
1½	cups milk
1¼	cups shredded sharp Cheddar cheese (5 oz)
1½	cups halved grape tomatoes

2	stalks celery, chopped (about ⅔ cup)
4	medium green onions, sliced (¼ cup)
1	can (12 oz) albacore tuna in water, drained
½	package (28 oz) frozen miniature potato nuggets (about 3½ cups)
	Chopped fresh parsley, if desired

1 Heat oven to 350°F. Spray 11×7-inch (2-quart) glass baking dish with cooking spray.

2 In 3-quart saucepan, melt butter over low heat. Stir in flour, salt and pepper. Cook over low heat, stirring constantly, until mixture is smooth and bubbly. Using whisk, gradually stir in milk. Heat to boiling, stirring constantly. Boil and stir 1 minute. Stir in 1 cup of the cheese until melted. Stir in tomatoes, celery, green onions and tuna until mixed.

3 Pour tuna mixture into baking dish; top evenly with potato nuggets.

4 Bake 20 to 25 minutes or until potato nuggets are golden brown. Sprinkle with remaining ¼ cup cheese; bake about 2 minutes longer or until cheese is melted. Let stand 5 minutes. Garnish with parsley.

1 Serving Calories 380; Total Fat 21g (Saturated Fat 9g, Trans Fat 3g); Cholesterol 60mg; Sodium 830mg; Total Carbohydrate 27g (Dietary Fiber 2g); Protein 22g **Carbohydrate Choices:** 2

CHICKEN MELT–TOT BAKE: Substitute 1¼ cups chopped cooked chicken for the tuna.

FAST

Tuna Tortellini Skillet

PREP 30 min **TOTAL** 30 min • *4 servings* (about 1¼ cups each)

5	tablespoons butter
2	packages (9 oz each) refrigerated cheese tortellini
1	teaspoon Italian seasoning
2	cups chicken broth
4	oz cream cheese (from 8-oz package), cubed, softened

4	cups lightly packed fresh baby spinach leaves
1	can (12 oz) albacore tuna in water, drained, broken into chunks
1	cup halved grape or cherry tomatoes
⅓	cup shredded Parmesan cheese

1 In 12-inch nonstick skillet, melt butter over medium-high heat. Add tortellini and Italian seasoning; cook 3 minutes, stirring frequently, until tortellini are light golden brown.

2 Stir in broth. Reduce heat; simmer uncovered 4 to 5 minutes, stirring frequently, until tortellini are tender. Stir in cream cheese until melted.

3 Add spinach, half at a time, gently folding into tortellini mixture. Stir in tuna and tomatoes; cook just until heated through. Sprinkle with Parmesan cheese.

1 Serving Calories 590; Total Fat 36g (Saturated Fat 21g, Trans Fat 1g); Cholesterol 220mg; Sodium 1790mg; Total Carbohydrate 32g (Dietary Fiber 2g); Protein 34g **Carbohydrate Choices:** 2

TUNA GNOCCHI SKILLET: Substitute 1 package (16 oz) potato gnocchi for the tortellini. Cook gnocchi in butter 5 to 6 minutes. Reduce chicken broth to 1½ cups.

Tuna Pot Pie Stuffed Peppers

PREP 25 min **TOTAL** 1 Hour 15 min • *4 servings*

4	large (any color) bell peppers	6	medium green onions, thinly sliced (⅓ cup)
1	can (10½ oz) condensed cream of chicken soup	1¼	cups shredded cheddar cheese (5 oz)
½	teaspoon Italian seasoning	½	sheet frozen puff pastry, thawed (from 17.3-oz package)
¼	teaspoon salt	2	tablespoons butter, melted
¼	teaspoon pepper		Chopped Italian (flat-leaf) parsley, if desired
1	can (12 oz) albacore tuna in water, drained		
2	cups frozen mixed vegetables		

1 Heat oven to 425°F. Line 15×10×1-inch pan with cooking parchment paper. Cut each bell pepper in half lengthwise. Remove seeds and membranes; place peppers, cut side up, in pan.

2 In large bowl, combine soup, Italian seasoning, salt and pepper; mix well. Stir in tuna, vegetables, green onions and 1 cup of the cheese. Divide mixture evenly between peppers (peppers will be full). Spray one side of foil with cooking spray; cover pan tightly with foil, sprayed side down.

3 Bake covered 30 minutes. Remove foil. Cut puff pastry sheet into 2 equal rectangles; cut each rectangle diagonally into 4 triangles. Place 1 puff pastry triangle on top of each pepper; brush melted butter over top of pastry.

4 Bake uncovered 15 to 18 minutes or until pastry is golden brown and peppers are fork-tender. Sprinkle remaining ¼ cup cheese on top of pastry. Bake 1 to 2 minutes longer or until cheese is melted. Let stand 5 minutes. Sprinkle with parsley.

1 Serving Calories 260; Total Fat 16g (Saturated Fat 6g, Trans Fat 2.5g); Cholesterol 30mg; Sodium 390mg; Total Carbohydrate 16g (Dietary Fiber 2g); Protein 12g **Carbohydrate Choices:** 1

CHICKEN POT PIE STUFFED PEPPERS: Substitute 1 cup chopped cooked chicken or 1 can (12 oz) chicken for the tuna.

Tuna Pot Pie Stuffed Peppers

Albacore Tuna

ALBACORE
TUNA
WHITE CHUNK

ALBACORE
TUNA
WHITE CHUNK

**Tuna-Stuffed
Avocados**

Cucumber

Pico De Gallo

Mango

Avocados

ALL NATURAL · TRADITIONAL
Pico de Gallo
MILD

NET WT 12 OZ (340g)

5-INGREDIENT RECIPE

EASY • FAST • CALORIE SMART • GLUTEN FREE

Tuna-Stuffed Avocados

PREP 15 min TOTAL 15 min • *4 servings*

- 2 cans (5 oz each) albacore tuna in water, drained
- 1 cup chopped cucumber
- 1 cup pico de gallo
- ½ cup chopped fresh or refrigerated mango
- ½ teaspoon salt
- 4 medium ripe avocados, halved, pitted

1 In medium bowl, mix all ingredients except avocados.

2 Cut very thin slice from bottom of each avocado half to prevent tipping.

3 Place 2 avocado halves on each serving plate; spoon about ½ cup of the tuna mixture into center of each avocado half. Serve immediately.

1 Serving Calories 350; Total Fat 23g (Saturated Fat 3.5g, Trans Fat 0g); Cholesterol 25mg; Sodium 750mg; Total Carbohydrate 18g (Dietary Fiber 10g); Protein 18g **Carbohydrate Choices:** 1

EASY • FAST • CALORIE SMART

Panfried Fish

PREP 20 min TOTAL 20 min • *6 servings*

- 1½ lb perch, red snapper or other medium-firm fish fillets (½- to ¾-inch thick), skin removed
- ¾ teaspoon salt
- ¼ teaspoon pepper
- 1 egg
- 1 tablespoon water
- ⅔ cup all-purpose flour, cornmeal or unseasoned dry bread crumbs
- Vegetable oil or shortening

1 Cut fish into 6 serving pieces. Sprinkle both sides of fish with salt and pepper. In small bowl, using whisk, beat egg and water until blended. Place flour in shallow dish. Dip fish into egg; coat with flour.

2 In 12-inch skillet, heat about ⅛-inch oil over medium heat. Fry fish in oil 6 to 8 minutes, turning once, until fish flakes easily with fork and is brown on both sides. (Tail sections may cook more quickly) Remove with slotted spatula; drain on paper towels.

1 Serving Calories 240; Total Fat 11g (Saturated Fat 2g, Trans Fat 0g); Cholesterol 130mg; Sodium 370mg; Total Carbohydrate 11g (Dietary Fiber 0g); Protein 24g **Carbohydrate Choices:** 1

BROWNED BUTTER PANFRIED FISH: Omit oil. In skillet, heat ¼ cup butter over medium heat 3 to 4 minutes, stirring constantly, until light brown. Coat fish as directed in Step 1; cook in butter as directed in Step 2.

GARLIC BUTTER PANFRIED FISH: Omit salt. Substitute crushed garlic butter–flavored croutons for the flour. (Place croutons in resealable food-storage plastic bag and crush with rolling pin.) Continue as directed.

PARMESAN, HERB AND LEMON PANFRIED FISH: Omit salt and pepper. Substitute ⅓ cup Italian-style panko crispy bread crumbs for the ⅔ cup flour. In shallow dish, mix bread crumbs, ⅓ cup grated Parmesan cheese and 1 teaspoon grated lemon peel. Continue as directed.

PANFRYING FISH

Dip fish in egg.

Coat both sides of fish with flour.

Fry fish in oil, turning once.

Fish is done when golden brown on both sides and flakes easily with a fork.

Basmati Rice

Sugar Snap Peas

Green Onion

Thai Coconut Curry Sauce

YELLOW
THAI
Coconut
Curry
SAUCE
MEDIUM
NET WT 16OZ (454g)

Fish Fillets

**Coconut
Curry Sole**

Lemon-Garlic Halibut

5-INGREDIENT RECIPE

Coconut Curry Sole

PREP 10 min **TOTAL** 15 min • *4 servings*

1 jar (16 oz) gluten-free yellow Thai coconut curry sauce	8 oz fresh sugar snap peas, cut in half lengthwise
¾ teaspoon salt, if desired	2 cups cooked basmati or jasmine rice (page 224)
1½ lb sole, flounder or Alaskan pollock fillets (about ¼-inch thick)	1 medium green onion, sliced, if desired

1 In 12-inch skillet, mix sauce and salt. Cover; heat to boiling. Add fish and peas to sauce. Reduce heat. Cover; simmer 5 to 7 minutes or until fish easily flakes with fork.

2 Spoon rice into shallow serving bowls. Top with fish, peas and sauce. Sprinkle with green onion.

1 Serving Calories 410; Total Fat 18g (Saturated Fat 10g, Trans Fat 0g); Cholesterol 90mg; Sodium 620mg; Total Carbohydrate 32g (Dietary Fiber 3g); Protein 31g **Carbohydrate Choices:** 2

Lemon-Garlic Halibut

Be sure to grate your lemon for the peel you'll need before you cut it open to squeeze the juice!

PREP 20 min **TOTAL** 20 min • *4 servings*

½ cup butter, melted	2 tablespoons olive oil
6 cloves garlic, finely chopped	⅓ cup fresh lemon juice
½ cup all-purpose flour	2 tablespoons water
1 teaspoon ground coriander	1 teaspoon dried oregano leaves
¾ teaspoon salt	1 cup halved grape or cherry tomatoes
¼ teaspoon coarsely ground pepper	⅓ cup chopped Italian (flat-leaf) parsley
¼ teaspoon ground red pepper (cayenne)	1 teaspoon grated lemon zest
4 (6 oz) halibut fillets, skin removed, patted dry (about 1-inch thick)	

1 In shallow dish, mix melted butter and 1 teaspoon of the garlic. In another shallow dish, mix flour, coriander, salt, pepper and red pepper. Dip fish into melted butter, then coat with flour mixture (reserve remaining butter and flour mixtures).

2 In 12-inch skillet, heat oil over medium heat until hot. Add fish; cook 3 to 6 minutes, turning once, until browned on both sides. Remove fish from skillet; place on plate. Add remaining garlic, the lemon juice, water, oregano and

reserved butter mixture to skillet, scraping any brown bits from bottom of pan. Using whisk, beat in 2 tablespoons of the remaining flour mixture until bubbly.

3 Return fish to skillet. Reduce heat to medium-low. Cover and cook 3 to 4 minutes or just until fish flakes easily with fork. Add tomatoes. Cover and remove from heat; let stand 2 minutes. Top with parsley and lemon peel. Serve immediately.

1 Serving Calories 490; Total Fat 32g (Saturated Fat 16g, Trans Fat 1g); Cholesterol 140mg; Sodium 740mg; Total Carbohydrate 17g (Dietary Fiber 1g); Protein 32g **Carbohydrate Choices:** 1

REMOVING FILLETS FROM COOKED FISH

Remove any fatty, gelatinous portion from belly of fish with spoon.

Cut off head and tail using a sharp knife.

Gently slice along backbone, using a table knife loosening top fillet.

Open fish flat: pull back bone from fish, staring at head end.

Roasted Tilapia and Vegetables

PREP 15 min **TOTAL** 40 min • *4 servings*

8 oz fresh asparagus spears	2 tablespoons olive oil
2 small zucchini, cut in half lengthwise, then cut into ½-inch pieces	2 teaspoons gluten-free Montreal steak grill seasoning
1 medium bell pepper, cut into ½-inch strips	4 tilapia fillets (about 1½ lb)
1 large onion, cut into ½-inch wedges, separated	1 tablespoon butter, melted
	½ teaspoon paprika

1 Heat oven to 450°F. Snap off tough ends of asparagus; cut each spear crosswise in half. In large bowl, mix asparagus, zucchini, bell pepper, onion and oil. Sprinkle with 1 teaspoon of the grill seasoning; toss to coat. Spread vegetables in ungreased 15×10×1-inch pan. Roast 5 minutes on lowest oven rack.

2 Meanwhile, spray 13×9-inch (3-quart) glass baking dish with cooking spray. Pat fish dry with paper towels. Brush fish with butter; sprinkle with paprika and remaining 1 teaspoon grill seasoning. Place fish in baking dish.

3 Place baking dish on middle oven rack in oven. Roast fish and vegetables uncovered 17 to 18 minutes or until fish flakes easily with fork and vegetables are tender.

1 Serving Calories 310; Total Fat 14g (Saturated Fat 4g, Trans Fat 0g); Cholesterol 85mg; Sodium 470mg; Total Carbohydrate 9g (Dietary Fiber 3g); Protein 37g **Carbohydrate Choices:** ½

Tilapia with Lemony Veggies

PREP 25 min **TOTAL** 40 min • *2 servings*

1 large unpeeled potato, cut into ½-inch pieces	2 tablespoons butter, melted
2 teaspoons olive oil	2 tilapia fillets (5 to 6 oz each)
¼ teaspoon salt	1 medium zucchini, cut into ½-inch slices
2 tablespoons all-purpose flour	2 teaspoons chopped fresh thyme leaves
1 egg	2 teaspoons grated lemon peel
¾ cup plain panko crispy bread crumbs	
¾ teaspoon seasoned salt	

1 Heat oven to 425°F. Spray 15×10×1-inch pan with cooking spray. In medium bowl, toss potato, oil and salt to coat. Spread potato on one half of pan. Bake 15 to 20 minutes or until potato is tender.

2 Meanwhile, place flour on plate. In shallow dish, beat egg with fork. In another shallow dish, mix bread crumbs, seasoned salt and butter. Coat fillets with flour, then dip into egg. Coat well with bread crumb mixture.

3 Remove pan from oven. Toss zucchini with potato. Place fillets on other half of pan.

4 Bake 10 to 12 minutes or until fish flakes easily with fork and vegetables are tender. Sprinkle fish with thyme. Sprinkle vegetables with lemon peel; toss.

1 Serving Calories 660; Total Fat 23g (Saturated Fat 10g, Trans Fat 0.5g); Cholesterol 210mg; Sodium 1360mg; Total Carbohydrate 71g (Dietary Fiber 6g); Protein 41g **Carbohydrate Choices:** 5

Thai Tilapia Cakes with Peanut Sauce

PREP 30 min **TOTAL** 30 min • *4 servings*

PEANUT SAUCE

¼ cup creamy peanut butter	¼ cup chopped dry-roasted salted peanuts
¼ cup water	2 tablespoons chopped fresh cilantro
1 tablespoon fresh lime juice	1 teaspoon Sriracha sauce
1 teaspoon Sriracha sauce	½ teaspoon salt

TILAPIA CAKES

1 lb tilapia, cod or haddock fillets, cut into chunks	2 medium green onions, thinly sliced (2 tablespoons)
¼ cup plain panko crispy bread crumbs	1 egg
	1 tablespoon vegetable oil
	Toppings, if desired: chopped cilantro, chopped peanuts

1 In small bowl, using whisk, mix ingredients for peanut sauce until smooth. Spoon 2 tablespoons of the sauce into food processor. Set remaining sauce aside.

2 Place all tilapia cake ingredients except oil and toppings in food processor with sauce. Cover and process, using quick on-and-off motions, until fish is coarsely chopped. Shape into 4 patties (½-inch thick).

3 In 12-inch nonstick skillet, heat oil over medium heat. Cook patties in oil 5 minutes or until golden brown; turn. Cook 4 to 5 minutes longer or until golden brown. Serve with remaining sauce and toppings.

1 Serving Calories 360; Total Fat 20g (Saturated Fat 4g, Trans Fat 0g); Cholesterol 95mg; Sodium 550mg; Total Carbohydrate 12g (Dietary Fiber 2g); Protein 31g **Carbohydrate Choices:** 1

THAI TILAPIA BURGERS: Split 4 burger buns in half. On bottom half of buns, place a lettuce leaf, tilapia cake, some peanut sauce and a ring of fresh or canned pineapple. Sprinkle with toppings; cover with tops of buns.

Roasted Tilapia and Vegetables

Tilapia with Lemony Veggies

Thai Tilapia Cakes
with Peanut Sauce and
Thai Tilapia Burgers

Crunchy Panko Fish Nuggets with Lemon-Dill Sauce

To make cleanup easier, line the pan with regular or nonstick foil before baking.

PREP 15 min **TOTAL** 35 min • *4 servings*

LEMON-DILL SAUCE

- ¼ cup mayonnaise
- 2 tablespoons plain yogurt
- 1 teaspoon chopped fresh or ¼ teaspoon dried dill weed
- 1 teaspoon grated lemon peel
- 2 teaspoons fresh lemon juice

FISH NUGGETS

- 3 tablespoons all-purpose flour
- 1 teaspoon garlic salt
- 1 teaspoon paprika
- 1 egg
- 2 tablespoons water
- ½ teaspoon red pepper sauce
- 1¼ cups plain panko crispy bread crumbs
- 3 tablespoons butter, melted
- 1 lb cod fillets (½-inch thick), cut into 1½-inch pieces

1 Heat oven to 425°F. Spray 15×10×1-inch pan with cooking spray.

2 In small bowl, mix all sauce ingredients until blended. Cover; refrigerate until serving time.

3 In shallow dish, mix flour, garlic salt and paprika. In another shallow dish, using whisk, beat egg, water and pepper sauce. In third shallow dish, mix bread crumbs and butter. Coat fish with flour mixture; dip into egg mixture. Coat with crumb mixture, pressing crumbs into fish. Place coated fish in pan.

4 Bake 15 to 20 minutes or until fish flakes easily with fork. Serve with sauce.

1 Serving Calories 430; Total Fat 23g (Saturated Fat 8g, Trans Fat 0g); Cholesterol 125mg; Sodium 570mg; Total Carbohydrate 31g (Dietary Fiber 0g); Protein 27g **Carbohydrate Choices:** 2

Fresh Flounder Rolls

PREP 35 min **TOTAL** 35 min • *12 sandwiches*

FISH AND BUNS

- 2 lb fresh flounder, halibut or cod fillets, skin removed
- ½ cup milk
- 1 egg
- 1 cup plain panko crispy bread crumbs
- 1 teaspoon salt
- 2 tablespoons vegetable oil
- 2 tablespoons butter, melted
- 12 hot dog buns, split
  Lemon slices, if desired
  Fresh dill weed sprigs, if desired

CUCUMBER SAUCE

- 1 container (6 oz) plain Greek yogurt
- 3 tablespoons mayonnaise
- 1 medium cucumber, peeled, seeded and coarsely grated
- 3 tablespoons chopped fresh dill weed
- 1 tablespoon chopped green onion (1 medium)
- 1 tablespoon lemon juice
- ½ teaspoon salt

1 Cut fish into 12 serving pieces. In pie plate, mix milk and egg. In another pie plate, mix bread crumbs and salt. Dip fish into milk mixture; roll in bread crumbs to coat. Shake off excess crumbs.

2 In 12-inch skillet, heat oil over medium-high heat. Cook fish in oil 10 to 12 minutes, turning once, until fish flakes easily with fork.

3 Meanwhile, in small bowl, mix all sauce ingredients.

4 Heat 10-inch skillet over medium heat. Brush melted butter on cut sides of buns. Place buns, cut sides down, in skillet; cook about 3 minutes or until toasted. Serve fish on buns with sauce. Garnish with lemon and dill sprigs.

1 Sandwich Calories 280; Total Fat 11g (Saturated Fat 3g, Trans Fat 0g); Cholesterol 55mg; Sodium 630mg; Total Carbohydrate 30g (Dietary Fiber 1g); Protein 15g **Carbohydrate Choices:** 2

Crunchy Panko Fish Nuggets with Lemon-Dill Sauce

Fresh Flounder Rolls

USE IT UP
COOKED
FISH FILLETS

FISH MELTS: Mix ¾ cup flaked cooked fish, ¼ cup mayonnaise, 2 tablespoons chopped onion and 1 teaspoon dried dill weed. Spread on 4 slices bread. Top each with 2 slices plum (Roma) tomato and 1 slice American cheese. Place on cookie sheet and broil on high, with tops 7 inches from heat, 2 to 4 minutes or until sandwiches are hot and cheese is melted.

CRISPY POTATO-FISH CAKES: Mix 2 cups refrigerated mashed potatoes (from 24-oz package), 1 cup flaked cooked fish, 1 beaten egg and 2 sliced green onions. Drop by ⅓-cupfuls onto plate with 1 cup finely crushed rippled potato chips; roll to coat. Shape into 3-inch patties. Panfry in 12-inch nonstick skillet in ¼ cup vegetable oil 2 to 3 minutes on each side or until golden brown.

YUMMY BOWLS: Add cooked fish to a bowl with your favorite hot cooked grains (page 212), chopped fresh or cooked veggies and dressing or sauce.

ADD TO SOUP: Stir bite-size pieces of fish into your favorite heated soup.

ADD TO SALAD: Top Caesar Salad (page 127) or other salad with bite-size pieces of fish.

365

HEIRLOOM

EASY • FAST • CALORIE SMART

Beer Batter–Fried Fish

PREP 25 min **TOTAL** 25 min • *4 servings*

- 1 lb walleye, sole or other delicate- to medium-textured fish fillets (about ½-inch thick), skin removed
- 1 cup plus 3 to 4 tablespoons all-purpose flour
- ½ cup regular or nonalcoholic beer
- 1 egg
- ½ teaspoon salt
  Vegetable oil for frying
  Tartar Sauce (page 484), if desired

1 Cut fish into 8 serving pieces. Lightly coat fish with 3 to 4 tablespoons flour. In medium bowl, mix 1 cup flour, the beer, egg and salt with wooden spoon until smooth. (If batter is too thick, stir in additional beer, 1 tablespoon at a time, until desired consistency.)

2 In deep fryer or 4-quart saucepan, heat 1½ inches oil to 350°F. Dip fish into batter, letting excess drip into bowl. Fry fish in oil, in batches, about 4 minutes, turning once, until golden brown (tail sections may cook more quickly). Remove with slotted spoon; drain on paper towels. Serve hot with tartar sauce.

1 Serving Calories 390; Total Fat 17g (Saturated Fat 3g, Trans Fat 0g); Cholesterol 115mg; Sodium 410mg; Total Carbohydrate 30g (Dietary Fiber 1g); Protein 27g **Carbohydrate Choices:** 2

NEW TWIST

AIR FRYER • CALORIE SMART

Oven-Fried Beer Batter Fish Tacos with Orange Slaw

PREP 40 min **TOTAL** 40 min • *4 tacos*

ORANGE SLAW
- 1 orange
- 1 cup thinly sliced green cabbage
- ⅓ cup thinly sliced red onion
- 3 tablespoons finely chopped seeded jalapeño
- 2 tablespoons chopped fresh cilantro
- 1 tablespoon vegetable oil
- ⅛ teaspoon salt
- ⅛ teaspoon pepper

AVOCADO CREAM
- ½ cup guacamole
- 3 tablespoons sour cream

FISH
- ¼ cup regular or nonalcoholic beer
- 1 egg white
- ½ cup all-purpose flour
- 1 teaspoon mesquite seasoning
- ½ teaspoon chili powder
- ½ teaspoon ground cumin
- ½ teaspoon salt
- 1 lb cod or other medium-firm white fish fillets (about ½-inch thick), skin removed, cut into 8 serving pieces
- 4 (8-inch) flour tortillas, heated as directed on package

1 Grate orange to get 2 teaspoons grated peel; place peel in medium bowl. Using paring knife, cut orange into sections. Remove remaining peel and white membrane. Chop orange; place in bowl with any juice. Add remaining slaw ingredients; toss to coat. Cover and refrigerate until you are ready to assemble tacos.

2 In small bowl, mix guacamole and sour cream. Cover and refrigerate until you are ready to assemble tacos.

3 Heat oven to 400°F. Line cookie sheet with foil; spray with cooking spray. In small bowl, using whisk, mix beer and egg white until frothy. In shallow dish, mix remaining fish ingredients except fish and tortillas.

4 Dip each fish piece into flour mixture to coat both sides, then dip into beer mixture, allowing excess to drip off. Coat again with flour mixture; place on cookie sheet. Spray fish with just enough cooking spray to barely moisten flour coating.

5 Bake 6 minutes. Carefully turn fish; bake an additional 2 to 3 minutes or until fish flakes easily with fork.

6 Spread each warm tortilla with about 3 tablespoons avocado mixture. Place 2 pieces fish on half of each tortilla. Top each with about ½ cup of the slaw; fold tortillas over filling. Serve immediately.

1 Taco Calories 410; Total Fat 13g (Saturated Fat 3.5g, Trans Fat 0g); Cholesterol 55mg; Sodium 1030mg; Total Carbohydrate 46g (Dietary Fiber 5g); Protein 28g **Carbohydrate Choices:** 3

AIR-FRIED BEER BATTER FISH (2 SERVINGS):
Prepare half recipe each of Orange Slaw and Avocado Cream, using half of the ingredients. Use ½ lb fish and cut into 4 pieces. Prepare beer mixture and flour mixture as directed in the recipe. Spray air fryer screen with cooking spray. Place coated fish pieces on screen. Spray fish with cooking spray to moisten flour coating. Set air fryer to 375°F; cook 5 minutes. Turn fish over; cook an additional 1 to 2 minutes or until fish flakes easily with fork.

Beer Batter–Fried Fish

Oven-Fried Beer Batter Fish Tacos with Orange Slaw

LEARN TO BROIL

Broiling is cooking foods a short distance from a direct heat source, in a gas or electric oven. The broiler is located either in the oven or sometimes in a compartment under the oven. Some think of broiling as a cousin to grilling since the surfaces of food become well-browned with this method, creating a wonderful caramelized flavor while quickly cooking the food. There's also minimal clean-up, making it a favorite for hectic-night suppers.

Use the distance between the top of the food and the broiler element that's recommended in the recipe you are using or refer to the oven manufacturer's recommendations. Always watch food carefully while broiling to prevent burning. Buttery Broiled Fish Steaks (right) is a great recipe to try for this method.

Broiling Tips

1 Preheat the broiler 5 to 10 minutes before cooking.

2 For easy cleanup, line both parts of the broiler pan with foil and poke holes through the top foil layer to let the juices drain.

3 Place the food in the center of the pan.

4 Place the pan under the broiler at the distance indicated in the recipe (see above).

5 With some ovens, you will leave the oven door open slightly while broiling. This helps to keep steam from forming in the oven—too much steam and the food will not have a crisp crust. But check the oven manufacturer's guidelines to be sure this is recommended.

6 Remove the pan from the oven to turn the food as indicated in the recipe directions.

7 Follow recipe times carefully. If food is not quite cooked, you can place it under the broiler for a bit longer.

Best Foods for Broiling

- **Beef and Pork** Meats less than 1½ inches thick, such as steaks and chops, are good candidates for broiling. Use tender cuts or marinate for tenderness. Ground-meat patties and sausages are also great under the broiler.

- **Chicken and Turkey** Most pieces work well under the broiler. Chicken quarters, legs and bone-in or boneless breasts are ideal, as are turkey cutlets and tenderloins. Try to broil the same thickness or size of pieces for even cooking.

- **Fish and Shellfish** Fillets and steaks are ideal to cook under the broiler. They cook quickly and evenly. Shrimp and scallops also perform well under the broiler.

- **Vegetables** Many vegetables are great under the broiler. Good candidates include asparagus spears, bell pepper halves or strips and onion wedges.

- **Fruits** Many fruits can be broiled, such as peach or nectarine halves, grapefruit halves, pineapple slices and bananas.

Lemon and Parmesan–
Crusted Salmon

Buttery Broiled Fish Steaks

PREP 20 min **TOTAL** 20 min • *4 servings*

4 salmon, tuna, halibut or other medium-firm to firm fish steaks, about ¾-inch thick (6 oz each) Salt and pepper	2 tablespoons butter, melted Lemon wedges, if desired

1 Set oven control to broil. Sprinkle both sides of fish with salt and pepper. Place fish on rack in broiler pan. Brush with 1 tablespoon of the butter.

2 Broil with tops about 4 inches from heat 5 minutes. Carefully turn fish; brush with remaining 1 tablespoon butter. Broil 4 to 6 minutes longer or until fish flakes easily with fork. Serve with lemon wedges.

1 Serving Calories 360; Total Fat 25g (Saturated Fat 7g, Trans Fat 0g); Cholesterol 110mg; Sodium 290mg; Total Carbohydrate 0g (Dietary Fiber 0g); Protein 34g **Carbohydrate Choices:** 0

BROILED FISH FILLETS: Substitute 1 lb fish fillets, cut into 4 serving pieces, for the fish steaks. Broil with tops about 4 inches from heat 5 to 6 minutes or until fish flakes easily with fork (do not turn).

Lemon and Parmesan– Crusted Salmon

PREP 10 min **TOTAL** 35 min • *4 servings*

1 salmon fillet (1¼ lb)	¼ cup grated Parmesan cheese
2 tablespoons butter, melted	2 medium green onions, thinly sliced (2 tablespoons)
¼ teaspoon salt	2 teaspoons grated lemon peel
¾ cup crumbs from medium- to firm-textured bread (about 1 slice bread)*	¼ teaspoon dried thyme leaves

1 Heat oven to 375°F. Spray 13×9-inch pan with cooking spray. Pat salmon dry with paper towels. Place salmon, skin side down, in pan. Brush with 1 tablespoon of the butter. Sprinkle with salt.

2 In small bowl, mix bread crumbs, cheese, onions, lemon peel and thyme. Stir in remaining 1 tablespoon butter. Press bread crumb mixture evenly on salmon.

3 Bake uncovered 15 to 25 minutes or until fish flakes easily with fork. Cut into 4 serving pieces. Serve immediately.

1 Serving Calories 380; Total Fat 22g (Saturated Fat 8g, Trans Fat 0g); Cholesterol 90mg; Sodium 490mg; Total Carbohydrate 16g (Dietary Fiber 1g); Protein 29g **Carbohydrate Choices:** 1

*Soft-textured bread is not recommended because it's too moist and won't create a crisp crumb topping.

5 TOPPINGS
for Fish

1 Quick-Pickled Onions
(page 51)

2 Romesco Sauce (page 337)

3 Mango-Avocado Salsa
Mix in a medium bowl: ¾ cup chopped fresh mango, ½ cup each chopped red onion and avocado, ¼ cup chopped fresh cilantro, 1 medium seeded and chopped jalapeño, 1 tablespoon fresh lime juice, ¼ teaspoon salt.

4 Tzatziki Dip (page 41)

5 Gremolata
Process in food processor until finely chopped: ¼ cup fresh Italian (flat-leaf) parsley and 2 cloves garlic. Transfer to small bowl; stir in 2 teaspoons lemon zest.

Miso-Glazed Salmon Sheet-Pan Dinner

PREP 20 min **TOTAL** 50 min • *4 servings*

RICE

- 1 cup instant rice
- 1 cup water
- 1 medium green onion, chopped (1 tablespoon)
- 1 tablespoon butter, melted

MISO GLAZE

- ⅓ cup gluten-free white miso paste (from 14-oz container)
- 2 tablespoons honey
- 3 tablespoons water
- 1 tablespoon reduced-sodium gluten-free soy sauce
- 1 tablespoon olive oil
- 2 teaspoons gluten-free gochujang paste (from 11.5-oz bottle)
- 2 teaspoons finely chopped fresh gingerroot

FISH AND VEGETABLES

- 1 (1 lb) salmon fillet
- 12 oz baby bok choy, cut lengthwise into quarters
- 2 cups fresh broccoli florets (12 oz)
- 1 cup baby carrots, cut in half lengthwise
- Toppings, if desired: sliced green onion, coarse ground pepper

Miso-Glazed Salmon Sheet-Pan Dinner

1   Heat oven to 425°F. Line 15×10×1-inch pan with heavy-duty foil; spray with cooking spray.

2   In medium bowl, stir rice, water and green onion; let stand 10 minutes or until most of liquid is absorbed. Stir in melted butter.

3   Meanwhile, in small bowl, using whisk, mix miso paste, honey, 1 tablespoon of the water, soy sauce, olive oil, gochujang paste and ginger until well blended. Set aside.

4   Cut 1 (16×12-inch) sheet heavy-duty foil; spray with cooking spray. Spoon rice in center of foil. Bring up 2 sides of foil so edges meet. Seal edges, making ½-inch fold; fold again, allowing for heat circulation and expansion. Fold other sides to seal. Place foil packet on one side of pan.

5   Place salmon on other half of pan; brush with 2 tablespoons of the miso mixture. Stir remaining 2 tablespoons water into remaining miso mixture. Arrange vegetables around salmon; drizzle with miso mixture.

6   Bake 25 to 28 minutes or until salmon flakes easily with fork and vegetables are crisp-tender. Gently stir vegetables to distribute sauce. Serve immediately. Sprinkle salmon with coarse pepper and sliced green onion.

1 Serving Calories 500; Total Fat 21g (Saturated Fat 5g, Trans Fat 0g); Cholesterol 70mg; Sodium 1250mg; Total Carbohydrate 47g (Dietary Fiber 5g); Protein 30g **Carbohydrate Choices:** 3

LEARN WITH BETTY SALMON DONENESS

Ideal Doneness Salmon flesh is opaque pink and flakes easily with a fork.

Underdone Salmon is translucent and does not flake easily with a fork.

Overdone Salmon is dry and tough.

Mediterranean Breaded Salmon with Vegetables

PREP 25 min TOTAL 1 Hour 15 min • *4 servings*

VEGETABLES

- 1 box (9 oz) frozen baby lima beans
- 1 medium unpeeled eggplant, cut lengthwise into quarters, then crosswise into 1-inch pieces
- 2 tablespoons olive oil
- ¼ teaspoon salt
- ⅛ teaspoon pepper
- 1 cup fresh baby spinach leaves, loosely packed
- ½ cup roasted red bell peppers (from a jar), drained, cut into thin strips

SALMON

- 1 salmon fillet (1¼ lb)
- 1 teaspoon olive oil
- ⅛ teaspoon salt
- ⅛ teaspoon pepper

TOPPING

- 1 cup plain panko crispy bread crumbs
- 2 tablespoons grated lemon peel
- 1 teaspoon dried oregano leaves
- 1 clove garlic, finely chopped
- 1 tablespoon olive oil

1 Heat oven to 375°F. Line 15×10×1-inch pan with heavy-duty foil; spray foil with cooking spray.

2 If lima beans are frozen, microwave on High about 1 minute or just until beans break apart. Place beans and eggplant in pan; drizzle with 2 tablespoons oil. Sprinkle with ¼ teaspoon salt and ⅛ teaspoon pepper; toss. Spread in single layer on pan. Bake 15 minutes.

3 Pat salmon dry with paper towels. Remove pan from oven. Push vegetables to sides of pan; place salmon, skin side down, in center. Brush salmon with 1 teaspoon oil; sprinkle with ⅛ teaspoon salt and ⅛ teaspoon pepper. Arrange vegetables in single layer around salmon.

4 In small bowl, mix all topping ingredients. Press half of topping (about ½ cup) evenly on salmon. Sprinkle remaining topping over vegetables.

5 Bake 20 to 30 minutes or until fish flakes easily with fork and vegetables are crisp-tender. (If topping browns too quickly, cover loosely with foil.)

6 Spoon beans and eggplant into large heatproof bowl; cover salmon with foil. Add spinach and roasted peppers to bowl with beans and eggplant; toss. Cover; let stand 2 to 3 minutes or until spinach is slightly wilted. Cut salmon into 4 serving pieces; carefully lift fish from skin with pancake turner to serving plate. Serve salmon with vegetables.

1 Serving Calories 500; Total Fat 24g (Saturated Fat 4g, Trans Fat 0g); Cholesterol 80mg; Sodium 510mg; Total Carbohydrate 33g (Dietary Fiber 9g); Protein 38g **Carbohydrate Choices:** 2

CALORIE SMART • GLUTEN FREE

Lemon and Herb Salmon Packets

PREP 15 min TOTAL 35 min • *2 servings*

- 1¼ cups reduced-sodium gluten-free chicken broth
- 1 cup uncooked instant brown rice
- ½ cup julienne carrots (from 10-oz bag)
- 1 salmon fillet (½ to ¾ lb), cut into 2 serving pieces
- ½ teaspoon gluten-free lemon-pepper seasoning
- 2 tablespoons chopped fresh chives
- 2 lemon slices (¼ inch thick)

1 Heat oven to 450°F. In 1-quart saucepan, heat broth to boiling over high heat. Stir in rice; reduce heat to low. Cover and simmer 5 minutes or until most of broth is absorbed. Stir in carrots.

2 Meanwhile, cut 2 (18×12-inch) sheets of heavy-duty foil; spray foil with cooking spray. Place salmon piece on center of each sheet. Sprinkle with lemon-pepper seasoning; top with chives. Arrange lemon slices over fish.

3 Spoon rice mixture around salmon. Bring up 2 sides of foil so edges meet. Seal edges, making tight ½-inch fold; fold again, allowing space for heat circulation and expansion. Fold other sides to seal. Place packets in ungreased 15×10×1-inch pan.

4 Bake 16 to 20 minutes or until fish flakes easily with fork. Place packets on plates. Cut large X across top of each packet; carefully fold back foil to allow steam to escape.

1 Serving Calories 380; Total Fat 8g (Saturated Fat 2g, Trans Fat 0g); Cholesterol 75mg; Sodium 540mg; Total Carbohydrate 47g (Dietary Fiber 3g); Protein 31g **Carbohydrate Choices:** 3

Mediterranean Breaded Salmon with Vegetables

LEARN TO
MAKE FOIL OR PARCHMENT PACKETS

Hands down, cooking in packets is one of the easiest ways to get dinner on the table quickly and easily. One of the biggest benefits is the easy cleanup—no pots to clean!

You can cook a whole meal or part of a meal in a tightly sealed packet in the oven or on the grill (do not cook parchment packets on the grill; they could catch fire). Packets can be made ahead, if you like, and refrigerated until ready to cook, but they may need to add a little extra cooking time. Lemon and Herb Salmon Packets (left) is a delicious recipe using this method.

How to Make Fuss-Free Packets

Use heavy-duty foil for the most secure packets, or cooking parchment paper.

1. Cut foil or parchment pieces so that you can easily wrap contents tightly with a good fold at top and sides. Refer to recipe you are using for specific size pieces needed.

2. Spray foil or parchment with cooking spray if not using nonstick foil.

3. Use minimal liquid in packets, if called for—no more than 2 to 3 tablespoons.

4. Use foods that have similar cook times.

5. Use boneless meats such as meat patties, boneless pork chops or chicken breasts, fish fillets or steaks.

6. Place food on center of foil or parchment, usually with meat pieces first, topped with other foods.

7. To seal each packet, bring up sides of foil or parchment over contents so edges meet.
   Foil: Seal edges, making tight ½-inch fold; fold again, allowing a little space for heat circulation and expansion. Fold other sides to seal.
   Parchment: Starting on one side, fold edge over tightly 3 or 4 times, rotating and making small triangle-like folds to other side; leave a little space for heat circulation and expansion. Fold packet edge under.

8. Place packets in shallow baking pan with sides. Bake as directed in recipe.

9. Remove from oven carefully. Cut large X across top of each packet; carefully fold back foil or parchment.

373

Lemon and Herb
Salmon Packets

Shellfish Basics

Because shellfish are a rich source of protein, have many vitamins and minerals *and* taste delicious, their popularity is no surprise. Shellfish are grouped into two main categories: crustaceans and mollusks. Crustaceans have long bodies with soft, jointed shells, and include crab, crayfish, lobsters and shrimp. Mollusks have soft bodies with no spinal column, covered by a shell, and include abalone, clams, mussels, octopus, oysters, scallops and squid (calamari). For more information about shellfish handling, safety and nutrition, visit the FDA's website at www.fda.gov/food/resources-you-food/seafood.

Buying and Using Shellfish

Most supermarkets carry both fresh and frozen shellfish. Here are some tips when buying shellfish:

- **Clams, Mussels and Oysters (in the shell)**
  Clam varieties include hard shell (cherrystone and littleneck) and soft shell (razor and steamers). Clams, mussels and oysters in shells should be purchased alive. Look for tightly closed shells that are not cracked, chipped or broken. They should have a very mild aroma. Shells may open naturally but will close if lightly tapped, indicating they are still alive. If shells do not close, throw them out.

- **Shucked Clams, Mussels and Oysters (no shells)**
  These shellfish should be plump and surrounded by a clear, slightly milky or light gray liquid. They should have a mild aroma.

- **Scallops** Varieties include sea scallops (1½ to 2 inches wide) and tiny bay scallops (½ inch wide). Scallops should look moist and have a mild sweet aroma. They should not be standing in liquid or stored directly on ice. These shellfish are creamy white and may have a light orange, light tan or pink tint.

- **Crabs and Lobsters** Live crabs and lobsters will show some leg movement and lobsters will curl their tails under when picked up. These shellfish must be cooked live or killed immediately before cooking; throw out any that are dead. Crabmeat is available fresh, and both crab and lobster meat are available canned and frozen.

- **Shrimp** Varieties include uncooked ("green") with heads on; uncooked in the shell without heads; uncooked, peeled and deveined; cooked, in the shell; or cooked, peeled and deveined. Shrimp should have a clean sea aroma. If they have an ammonia smell, they are spoiled and should be discarded.

- **Squid (Calamari)** Color of squid ranges from cream with reddish-brown spots to light pink. Buy fresh squid that's whole with clear eyes and a fresh sea aroma. Cleaned squid is also available in juices; the meat should be firm.

Storing Shellfish

- **Live Crabs (hard shell and soft shell), Lobsters**
  Store on a tray with sides; cover with a clean, damp cloth. Refrigerate until ready to cook. Cook the same day they're purchased.

- **Raw Scallops, Shrimp, Squid, Shucked Shellfish**
  Store in a leak-proof bag or plastic container with a lid. Cook within 2 days.

- **Live Clams, Mussels, Oysters** Store in a container covered with a clean, damp cloth (an airtight container with lid or a plastic bag will cause suffocation). Shells may open during refrigeration. Tap shells—they will close if alive; if not, throw them out. Cook within 2 days.

IMITATION SEAFOOD PRODUCTS

Imitation seafood products shaped into pieces to resemble crab or lobster are usually made from pollock; they are less expensive than shellfish but similar in taste and texture to the real thing. Because some of these products (often labeled surimi) contain a shellfish extract, check labels carefully if you have a seafood allergy.

Lobster

Snow Crab

King
Crab

Crayfish

Tiger Shrimp

Brown Shrimp

Salad Shrimp

Laughing Bird Shrimp

Soft-Shell Crab

Hard-Shell
Blue Crab

Cherrystone
Clams

375

Sea Scallops

Countneck
Clams

Littleneck
Clams

Lantern Bay Scallops

Squid (Calamari)

Manila Clams

Blue Point Oysters

Prince-Edward Island (P.E.I.) Mussels

HOW MUCH DO I NEED?

The amount of shellfish you need per person depends on the type you're preparing.

TYPE OF SHELLFISH	AMOUNT PER SERVING
CLAMS, MUSSELS OR OYSTERS	
In shell	3 large hard-shell clams
	6 small hard-shell clams
	18 soft-shell clams
	18 mussels
	6 oysters
Shucked	¼ lb
Crab (hard shell) or Lobster	1 ¼ lb live or ¼ lb cooked meat
Crab (soft shell)	¼ lb
SHRIMP	
With head, unpeeled	1 lb
Without head, unpeeled	½ lb
Without head, peeled	¼ lb
SQUID	
Whole	½ lb
Cleaned	¼ lb

UNDERSTANDING SHRIMP COUNT

Fresh and frozen shrimp are sold by descriptive size names like *jumbo* or *large,* as well as by "count" or number per pound. The larger the shrimp, the lower the count. Sizes and counts vary throughout the United States.

COMMON SHRIMP SIZE MARKET NAME	COUNT (APPROXIMATE NUMBER PER POUND)
Colossal	Under 10
Jumbo	11 to 15
Extra Large	16 to 20
Large	21 to 30
Medium	31 to 35
Small	36 to 45
Miniature or Tiny	About 100

Successfully Cooking Shellfish

Cooked shellfish should be moist and slightly chewy; overcooking makes it tough and rubbery. Follow these guidelines to determine when shellfish is done.

Crabs and Lobsters turn bright red.

Scallops turn milky white or opaque and get firm.

Raw Shrimp turn pink and get firm.

Live Clams, Oysters and Mussels open their shells.

Shucked Clams, Oysters and Mussels get plump and opaque; oyster edges start to curl.

TIMETABLE FOR COOKING SHELLFISH

Shellfish can be cooked in a variety of ways. Keep in mind that cooking time varies depending on the method of preparation.

To Cook in a Skillet (Panfry) Heat about 1 tablespoon oil over medium-high heat. Cook shellfish as directed below.

To Boil Heat water to boiling in large saucepan. Add shellfish and cook as directed below.

To Broil Place shellfish on broiler rack. Broil 7 to 9 inches from heat as directed below.

TYPE OF SHELLFISH	AMOUNT IN POUNDS	METHOD AND COOK TIME
Clams or Oysters (in shell)	4	**Boil or steam** 5 to 7 minutes
Mussels (in shell)	2	**Boil or steam** 5 to 7 minutes
Scallops (bay or sea)	1	**Panfry** 3 to 6 minutes
	1	**Boil** 2 to 3 minutes
		Broil 3 to 5 minutes
Shrimp (in shell)	1	**Boil** 4 to 6 minutes
Shrimp (peeled and deveined)	1	**Panfry** 3 to 6 minutes
		Boil 2 to 3 minutes
		Broil 3 to 5 minutes
Squid	1	**Panfry** 2 to 3 minutes

Reheating Cooked Crab Legs

Most crab legs available for purchase are already cooked. Follow these steps to reheat them before serving.

1. Cut 2 lb crab legs to fit an 8-inch microwavable dish.
2. Cover with plastic wrap, folding one edge or corner back about ¼ inch to vent steam.
3. Microwave on Medium-High (70%) 5 to 6 minutes, rotating the dish once if the microwave has no turntable, or until hot.
4. Let stand 5 minutes before serving.

SOFT-SHELL CRABS

Soft-shell crabs are the same species as Atlantic hard-shell blue crabs, except soft-shell crabs have been caught immediately after they shed their old hard shells. They stay soft for only a couple of hours before their shells harden again.

Low Country Shrimp Foil Packets

PREP 25 min **TOTAL** 40 min • *4 servings*

- 1 lb small red potatoes, halved
- 4 pieces frozen mini corn on the cob, thawed, cut crosswise in half
- 2 teaspoons vegetable oil
- 2 teaspoons gluten-free seafood seasoning
- 1 lb uncooked extra-large shrimp, thawed if frozen, peeled, deveined
- 12 oz cooked gluten-free andouille sausage, sliced
- 1 lemon, cut into 8 wedges
- ¼ cup chopped fresh parsley leaves

1 Heat oven to 375°F. Cut 4 (18×12-inch) sheets heavy-duty foil. Spray with cooking spray.

2 Place potatoes in microwavable bowl. Microwave uncovered on High 5 to 6 minutes or until potatoes are just tender. Add corn to potatoes; drizzle with 1 teaspoon of the oil, sprinkle with 1 teaspoon of the seasoning and mix until evenly coated.

3 Place shrimp in medium bowl; toss with remaining 1 teaspoon oil and 1 teaspoon seasoning; mix until evenly coated.

4 Place equal amount of sausage on center of each sheet of foil. Dividing evenly, arrange potato and corn mixture around sausage. Divide shrimp evenly over sausage. Squeeze 1 wedge of lemon over each pack.

5 Bring up 2 sides of foil so edges meet. Seal edges, making tight ½-inch fold; fold again, allowing space for heat circulation and expansion. Fold other sides to seal. Place packs on cookie sheet.

6 Bake 23 to 25 minutes or until shrimp are pink and sausage is heated through (open packet to check for doneness). Cut large X across top of each pack. Carefully fold back foil; sprinkle with parsley; top with remaining lemon wedges.

1 Serving Calories 540; Total Fat 26g (Saturated Fat 8g, Trans Fat 0g); Cholesterol 230mg; Sodium 1120mg; Total Carbohydrate 35g (Dietary Fiber 4g); Protein 40g **Carbohydrate Choices:** 2

SHRIMP WITH FRESH CORN: Two ears of fresh sweet corn can be substituted for the frozen corn in this recipe. Cut each ear into 4 pieces.

GRILL DIRECTIONS: Heat gas or charcoal grill to medium. Place packets on grill over heat. Cover grill; cook 6 minutes. Rotate packets ½ turn; cook 5 to 7 minutes longer or until shrimp turn pink and sausage is heated through (open packet to check for doneness). Remove packets from grill.

Low Country Shrimp Foil Packets

Deep-Fried Shrimp

Watch the temperature of the oil carefully during frying. If it starts to smoke, turn down heat and wait a few minutes before putting in the next batch of shrimp.

PREP 40 min **TOTAL** 40 min • ***4 servings***

½ cup all-purpose flour	1 lb uncooked medium shrimp, thawed if frozen, peeled (with tail shells left on), deveined
1 teaspoon salt	
½ teaspoon pepper	
2 eggs	
¾ cup dry bread crumbs	Vegetable oil for frying

1 In shallow dish, mix flour, salt and pepper. In another shallow dish, using whisk, beat eggs slightly. In third shallow dish, place bread crumbs. Pat shrimp dry with paper towels. Coat shrimp with flour mixture; dip into egg, then coat with bread crumbs.

2 In deep fryer or 4-quart saucepan, heat 2 to 3 inches oil to 350°F. Fry 4 or 5 shrimp at a time in oil about 1 minute, turning once, until golden brown. Drain on paper towels.

1 Serving Calories 340; Total Fat 13g (Saturated Fat 2.5g, Trans Fat 0g); Cholesterol 250mg; Sodium 860mg; Total Carbohydrate 27g (Dietary Fiber 1g); Protein 27g **Carbohydrate Choices:** 2

DEEP-FRIED OYSTERS OR CLAMS: Substitute ¾ lb shucked oysters or clams, drained, for the shrimp.

DEEP-FRIED SEA SCALLOPS: Substitute ¾ lb sea scallops, drained, for the shrimp. Fry 3 to 4 minutes or until golden brown on outside and white and opaque inside. Bay scallops, which are smaller, will cook more quickly.

SHUCKING FRESH OYSTERS

Grasp cleaned oyster in a towel, flat side up and hinged side out. Slip oyster knife into the hinge. Carefully run knife around oyster to other side of hinge, using twisting motion, until top shell pops open.

Slip knife behind muscle attached to both shells to spread apart and separate. Remove top shell, being careful not to spill oyster juice into bottom shell.

Slip knife between shell and oyster meat in bottom shell to loosen from shell while keeping meat intact.

Deep-Fried Shrimp

DEVEINING SHRIMP

Using a small pointed knife, make a shallow cut along the center back of shrimp and wash out the vein.

Restaurant-Style Coconut Shrimp

Restaurant-Style Coconut Shrimp

When frying, use a thermometer to ensure oil is at the proper temperature. If the oil is too hot, the shrimp will brown too quickly. If the oil is not hot enough, the shrimp will absorb oil and have a greasy flavor.

PREP 35 min TOTAL 35 min • *4 servings*

SAUCE

- 2 containers (5 oz each) French-style coconut yogurt
- 4 teaspoons (from 8-oz can) crushed pineapple
- 2 teaspoons frozen concentrated piña colada mix, thawed

SHRIMP

- 1 cup sweetened shredded coconut
- 1 cup plain panko crispy bread crumbs
- ½ cup frozen concentrated piña colada mix, thawed
- ½ cup cornstarch
- ½ teaspoon salt
- 1 lb uncooked extra-large shrimp, thawed if frozen, peeled, deveined and butterflied (see Butterflying Shrimp, at right)
  Vegetable oil for frying

1 In small bowl, mix all sauce ingredients. Cover; refrigerate until serving time.

2 In shallow dish, mix coconut and bread crumbs. Spoon the ½ cup piña colada mix into small bowl. In another small bowl, mix cornstarch and salt. Working with 2 to 3 shrimp at a time, coat shrimp with cornstarch mixture; dip into piña colada mix. Coat with bread crumb mixture, coating completely and pressing lightly.

3 In deep fryer or 4-quart saucepan, heat about 2 inches oil to 350°F. Add shrimp to hot oil; cook 2 to 3 minutes or until golden brown. Carefully transfer to paper towel–lined plate to drain. Serve immediately with sauce.

1 Serving Calories 840; Total Fat 39g (Saturated Fat 17g, Trans Fat 0g); Cholesterol 170mg; Sodium 570mg; Total Carbohydrate 95g (Dietary Fiber 1g); Protein 26g **Carbohydrate Choices:** 6

BUTTERFLYING SHRIMP

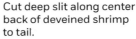

Cut deep slit along center back of deveined shrimp to tail.

Use thumbs to open and flatten shrimp.

Jambalaya

SLOW COOKER • CALORIE SMART • GLUTEN FREE

Jambalaya

PREP 25 min **TOTAL** 8 Hours 25 min • *8 servings*

1 large onion, chopped (1 cup)	1 tablespoon parsley flakes
1 medium green bell pepper, chopped (1 cup)	½ teaspoon dried thyme leaves
2 medium stalks celery, chopped (1 cup)	½ teaspoon salt
3 cloves garlic, finely chopped	¼ teaspoon pepper
1 can (28 oz) diced tomatoes, undrained	¼ teaspoon red pepper sauce
2 cups chopped gluten-free cooked smoked sausage	¾ lb uncooked medium shrimp, thawed if frozen, peeled, deveined
	4 cups hot cooked rice (page 224)

1 Spray 3½- to 6-quart slow cooker with cooking spray. In slow cooker, mix all ingredients except shrimp and rice.

2 Cover; cook on Low heat setting 7 to 8 hours (or High heat setting 3 to 4 hours) or until vegetables are tender. Stir in shrimp. Cover; cook about 1 hour longer or until shrimp are pink. Serve jambalaya with rice.

1 Serving Calories 280; Total Fat 10g (Saturated Fat 3.5g, Trans Fat 0g); Cholesterol 90mg; Sodium 960mg; Total Carbohydrate 30g (Dietary Fiber 2g); Protein 17g **Carbohydrate Choices:** 2

FAST • CALORIE SMART

Pan-Seared Parmesan Scallops

PREP 20 min **TOTAL** 20 min • *4 servings*

16 large sea scallops (about 1½ lb)	1 tablespoon butter
½ cup grated Parmesan cheese	Coarse ground black pepper
1 tablespoon olive or vegetable oil	Chopped fresh chives or parsley

1 Pat scallops dry with paper towels. Place cheese in shallow dish or resealable food-storage plastic bag. Add scallops to dish or bag; toss to coat with cheese. Discard any remaining cheese.

2 In 12-inch nonstick skillet, heat oil and butter over medium-high heat. Add half of the scallops to skillet; cook 3 to 6 minutes, turning once, until golden brown on outside and white and opaque inside. Repeat with remaining scallops. Sprinkle with pepper and chives.

1 Serving Calories 170; Total Fat 11g (Saturated Fat 4.5g, Trans Fat 0g); Cholesterol 50mg; Sodium 410mg; Total Carbohydrate 0g (Dietary Fiber 0g); Protein 19g **Carbohydrate Choices:** 0

PAN-SEARED ASIAGO SCALLOPS: Substitute Asiago cheese for the Parmesan.

SEARING SCALLOPS

Cook scallops without moving until they release from bottom of pan and bottoms are golden brown. Turn; cook until bottoms are golden brown.

Steamed Clams

PREP 20 min TOTAL 50 min • *4 servings*

- 4 lb cherrystone, littleneck or steamer clams in shells
- 6 cups water
- ⅓ cup white vinegar
- ½ cup water, chicken broth or white wine
- Melted butter or Clarified Butter (page 498), if desired

1 Discard any broken-shell or open (dead) clams that do not close when tapped. Place remaining clams in large container. Cover with 6 cups water and the vinegar. Let stand 30 minutes; drain. Scrub clams in cold water.

2 In steamer,* heat ½ cup water to boiling. Add clams to boiling water. Cover; steam 5 to 8 minutes or until clam shells open at least 1 inch. Remove clams as they open. Discard any unopened clams. Serve hot clams in shells with butter.

1 Serving Calories 70; Total Fat 1g (Saturated Fat 0g, Trans Fat 0g); Cholesterol 25mg; Sodium 60mg; Total Carbohydrate 3g (Dietary Fiber 0g); Protein 13g **Carbohydrate Choices:** 0

*If steamer is not available, place clams in 6-quart Dutch oven. Add 1 inch boiling water; cover tightly.

OPENING RAW CLAMS

Hold clam firmly with small, thick towel, hinged side out. Insert oyster knife or blunt-tipped knife between shell halves.

Working over a bowl or plate, gently twist knife to crack open the shell and release juices. Angle blade, scraping and twisting along top shell to cut muscle attached to top shell; open shells.

Gently slide knife between shell and clam meat, cutting away meat from shell. Remove any shell fragments.

Pan-Seared Parmesan Scallops

Smoky Tomato-Herb Mussels

CLEANING MUSSELS

Swish or agitate the water with hands to help remove sand from mussels.

CALORIE SMART

Smoky Tomato-Herb Mussels

PREP 45 min TOTAL 45 min • *4 servings*

- 2 lb fresh mussels in shells
- 2 tablespoons olive oil
- 1 large onion, chopped (1 cup)
- 4 cloves garlic, finely chopped
- 2 pints grape or cherry tomatoes, halved
- 2 teaspoons smoked paprika
- ½ teaspoon salt
- ¼ teaspoon pepper

- 1 cup dry white wine or vegetable broth
- ⅓ cup sliced stuffed Manzanilla or pitted ripe olives (from 5.75-oz jar)
- ½ cup coarsely chopped Italian (flat-leaf) parsley
- 1 lemon, thinly sliced
- 3 cups hot cooked farro or brown rice (pages 222, 224)

1 To clean mussels, discard any broken-shell or open (dead) mussels. Scrub remaining mussels in cold water, removing any barnacles with a dull paring knife. If there are beards, remove them by tugging them away from shells. Place mussels in large container. Cover with cool water. Agitate water with hand; drain off and discard water. Repeat several times until water runs clear; drain.

2 In 5- to 6-quart Dutch oven, heat oil over medium heat. Cook and stir onion and garlic in oil 2 to 3 minutes or until onion is softened. Stir in tomatoes, paprika, salt and pepper; cook 4 minutes, stirring occasionally, until tomatoes are softened.

3 Stir in wine, olives, half the parsley, the lemon slices and mussels. Cover; heat to boiling. Reduce heat. Cover; cook 6 to 9 minutes or until mussel shells have opened. Discard any unopened mussels.

4 Spoon farro and mussel mixture into 4 large soup bowls. Top with remaining parsley.

1 Serving Calories 350; Total Fat 11g (Saturated Fat 1.5g, Trans Fat 0g); Cholesterol 20mg; Sodium 860mg; Total Carbohydrate 45g (Dietary Fiber 9g); Protein 15g **Carbohydrate Choices:** 3

CHECKING MUSSEL FRESHNESS (DETERMINING SPOILED MUSSELS)

After cooking mussels, discard those that did not open; they are spoiled.

Boiled Lobsters

PREP 20 min TOTAL 35 min • *2 servings*

2 to 4 quarts water	Melted butter or
2 live lobsters	Clarified Butter
(about 1 lb each)	(page 498), if desired
	Lemon wedges,
	if desired

1 Fill 5- to 6-quart Dutch oven or stockpot one-third full with water. Heat to boiling. Plunge lobsters headfirst into water. Cover and return to boiling. Reduce heat to low. Simmer 10 to 12 minutes or until lobsters turn bright red; drain.

2 To remove meat, follow directions below. Serve with butter and lemon wedges. Serve green tomalley (liver) and coral roe (only in females) if desired.

1 Serving Calories 100; Total Fat 1g (Saturated Fat 0g, Trans Fat 0g); Cholesterol 170mg; Sodium 570mg; Total Carbohydrate 0g (Dietary Fiber 0g); Protein 22g **Carbohydrate Choices:** 0

Boiled Hard-Shell Blue Crabs

PREP 20 min TOTAL 1 Hour • *4 servings*

4 quarts water	Melted butter or
16 live hard-shell	Clarified Butter
blue crabs	(page 498), if desired
	Cocktail sauce,
	if desired

1 In 5- to 6-quart Dutch oven or stockpot, heat water to boiling. Drop 4 crabs at a time into water. Cover and return to boiling. Reduce heat. Simmer 10 minutes; drain. Repeat with remaining crabs.

2 To remove meat, follow directions below. Serve with butter and cocktail sauce.

1 Serving Calories 80; Total Fat 1g (Saturated Fat 0g, Trans Fat 0g); Cholesterol 100mg; Sodium 410mg; Total Carbohydrate 0g (Dietary Fiber 0g); Protein 18g **Carbohydrate Choices:** 0

REMOVING COOKED LOBSTER MEAT

Separate tail from body by breaking shell in half where tail and body meet.

Cut away membrane on tail to expose meat. Discard vein that runs through tail and sac near head of lobster.

Twist large claws away from body of lobster. Use nutcracker to break open claws. Remove meat from claws, tail and body.

REMOVING COOKED CRABMEAT

With crab on its back, use thumbs to pry up tail flap; twist off and discard. Turn right side up; pry up top shell, pulling it away from body, and discard.

Using small knife or fingers, cut the gray-white gills from both sides of crab. Discard gills and internal organs. Twist off claws and legs; use seafood cracker to crack shells at joints.

Remove meat with seafood pick or cocktail fork. Break body in half; remove remaining meat.

Veggie Forward

Veggie-Forward Basics

What exactly is "veggie forward"? It's smart, balanced food choices that flip the emphasis of what's on your plate. Traditionally, animal protein, such as chicken, beef or pork, is the star of the dinner plate, with vegetables and other side dishes having supporting roles. Veggie-forward eating gives the biggest plate real estate to veggies and whole grains with protein, which may or may not include a smaller amount of animal-based protein.

Veggie-forward eating was created to change habits that have led to problems with our health, the environment and food system sustainability. What started as a solution to those problems has led to more flavorful meals, with amazing creativity for both visual and eating enjoyment! "Veggie-forward" doesn't have to mean vegan or vegetarian. It's simply an approach to cooking and eating that encourages more plants in your meals.

How to Get Started Eating Plant-Forward Meals

Eating veggie-forward (also known as plant-forward) meals doesn't mean removing all animal protein from your diet. The goal is to let plants take up more of your plate. Here are some ways to eat more plants:

Meatless Mondays Start by having one dinner a week that doesn't include meat, poultry or seafood.

Plant Dedication Use smaller portions of dairy, meat, eggs and poultry to add nutrients and flavor, and make half your plate veggies, even when you have a traditional main dish such as a burger, by serving it in a whole-grain bun and topping the burger with veggies. Serve the burger with a salad or more nutrient-dense roasted veggies rather than fries.

Mix and Match Meals Choose a combination of meals throughout the week: some that are animal protein–based, some that combine mostly plants with less animal protein and some that are entirely plant-based.

Clever Choices Craving pizza? Choose veggie pizza rather than one loaded with meat. Want a burger? Try Kimchi Veggie Beef Burgers with Sesame Slaw (page 411), which swap out half of the meat for veggies, or a meatless burger such as the Zucchini Corn Bean Burgers (page 388).

Add Color The most colorful—and the most nutritious—foods tend to be plant-based. Include at least three colors of foods with every meal.

Choose Combo Dishes Many cuisines from around the world are naturally veggie-forward, as their dishes tend to contain very little (if any) animal protein. Look for Asian, Indian, Mediterranean and Latin American dishes, just to name a few. You'll see a wide variety of recipes in this chapter, as well as other chapters in this book, that are plant-based, so your taste buds will never get bored!

Sneaky Sauces Plant-based sauces such as Hummus (page 48), Guacamole (page 50), Salsa (page 479) and Basil Pesto (page 480) are delicious ways to increase the amount of plants you consume upping the amounts of plants on your plate, even when you eat a traditional animal-protein main dish!

PLANT-BASED FOODS

A shift to plant-based foods is sweeping the nation, as more and more people discover the benefits to making veggie-forward meals a priority. More plant-based products keep showing up on grocery shelves and on restaurant menus.

There are many brands available made with plant-based protein; here's a look at the most common choices. While the taste and texture of the products might not be exactly like the traditional meat versions, some have come very close. If one doesn't suit your taste buds, try another, as they can be very different from one another. When paired with other ingredients, you may not be able to tell the difference!

Chick'n Nuggets, Patties and Tenders Use in place of these chicken products.

Ground or Shreds Use in recipes calling for ground beef, chicken or turkey.

Meatballs Use in recipes calling for meatballs.

Patties Use in place of beef or turkey burger patties.

Sausages Include bratwurst, breakfast sausage, chorizo crumbles, hot dogs, Italian sausage and flavored sausages such as apple and sage. Use in place of the traditional meat products.

What Plants Are Good Choices?

Focus on whole grains, beans and other legumes, vegetables, fruits, nuts, seeds and healthy oils including olive, avocado and flaxseed. Plenty of these foods, including mushrooms, jackfruit and soy foods such as tofu, can take the place of meat. Many vegetables are also good forms of protein, such as asparagus, broccoli, collard greens, peppers, spinach and sweet potatoes, in addition to beans.

Health Benefits

The key is eating high-quality, nutrient-dense plant-based foods. There are many health benefits to eating this way, as the ingredients are packed with essential nutrients that promote good health. Plant-forward dishes also tend to have significantly high levels of fiber, which has a lot of health benefits.

Budget Friendliness

Veggie-forward meals tend to be less expensive than animal-based meals. Unprocessed or minimally processed whole plant foods cost less than items from the meat department for protein and other nutrients. Dried or canned beans, whole grains, fresh and frozen fruits, and frozen vegetables are some of the most affordable foods to purchase when on a budget, in terms of nutritional value.

Environmental Benefits

Plants require significantly less water and resources to grow, produce and distribute than livestock. Locally grown foods are better for the environment, as they don't require large amounts of fossil fuels to be transported across the country or world. Regeneratively grown foods also encourage environmental health, as they can be grown in a way that promotes cleaner air and improved soil by harnessing the sun's energy, water and carbon dioxide in the air to grow. As the plants grow, they add nutrients to the soil and release oxygen back into the air.

Veggie Nuggets with Barbecue-Hummus Dipping Sauce

CALORIE SMART • VEGETARIAN

Veggie Nuggets with Barbecue-Hummus Dipping Sauce

PREP 25 Minutes **TOTAL** 1 Hour 30 Minutes •
4 servings (5 nuggets and 2 tablespoons sauce each)

VEGGIE NUGGETS

- 1⅔ cups water
- ⅔ cup yellow split peas, sorted, rinsed
- 3 cups fresh cauliflower florets, cooked (page 247), drained
- ½ teaspoon salt
- ¼ teaspoon garlic-pepper blend
- ¼ cup plain or Italian-style bread crumbs
- 2 tablespoons water
- ½ cup cooked fresh or frozen sweet peas, drained

HUMMUS DIPPING SAUCE

- ¼ cup hummus (from 10-oz container)
- ¼ cup Carolina or regular barbecue sauce

1 In 2-quart saucepan, mix water and split peas. Heat to boiling; reduce heat. Cover; simmer 35 to 40 minutes or until split peas are soft but not mushy. Drain.

2 Heat oven to 425°F. Line 15x10x1-inch pan with cooking parchment paper or heavy-duty foil; spray with cooking spray.

3 In food processor, place split peas, cauliflower, salt and garlic pepper. Cover; process with 10 to 15 on-and-off pulses or until finely chopped. Add bread crumbs and water. Cover; process with a few pulses just until mixture just holds together. Stir in peas.

4 For each nugget, shape about 2 tablespoons pea mixture into 2x1-inch oval. Place 1 inch apart on pan. Spray nuggets with cooking spray.

5 Bake 17 to 22 minutes, turning once, until light golden brown.

6 Meanwhile, in small bowl, mix hummus and barbecue sauce until blended. Serve with warm nuggets.

1 Serving Calories 220; Total Fat 2.5g (Saturated Fat 0g, Trans Fat 0g); Cholesterol 0mg; Sodium 640mg; Total Carbohydrate 39g (Dietary Fiber 12g); Protein 11g **Carbohydrate Choices:** 2½

Zucchini Corn Bean Burgers

PREP 30 Minutes **TOTAL** 30 Minutes • *4 burgers*

- 1 can (15 oz) great northern beans, rinsed, drained
- 1 cup shredded zucchini, squeezed dry with paper towels
- ½ cup canned or frozen (thawed) whole kernel corn, drained
- ¼ cup finely chopped red onion
- ¼ cup finely chopped red bell pepper
- 2 teaspoons dried oregano leaves
- ½ teaspoon salt
- ½ teaspoon pepper
- ¾ cup plain panko crispy bread crumbs
- 1 egg, beaten
- 1 tablespoon vegetable oil
- 8 slices (¾ oz each) provolone cheese
- 4 whole wheat burger buns
- ¼ cup mayonnaise
- 1 cup lightly-packed fresh arugula leaves (from 5-oz container)
- 4 slices tomato (from 1 medium)

1 In medium bowl, place beans; mash with potato masher or fork until partially mashed. Add zucchini, corn, red onion, bell pepper, oregano, salt and pepper; mix well. Add bread crumbs and egg; mix well. Shape mixture into 4 patties, each about 3½ inches in diameter.

2 In 12-inch nonstick skillet, heat oil over medium heat. Cook patties uncovered in oil 10 to 12 minutes, turning at least once, until browned on each side and instant-read thermometer inserted in center of patties reaches 160°F.

3 Spread bottom halves of buns with mayonnaise. Top each with bean patty, 2 slices cheese, arugula leaves and 1 slice tomato. Cover with bun tops.

1 Burger Calories 620; Total Fat 29g (Saturated Fat 10g, Trans Fat 0g); Cholesterol 80mg; Sodium 1200mg; Total Carbohydrate 59g (Dietary Fiber 9g); Protein 28g **Carbohydrate Choices:** 4

Zucchini Corn Bean Burgers

Easy Sweet Potato Enchiladas

If your family likes enchiladas, this recipe is a great way to introduce a vegetarian version to your weekday lineup. Look for red-skinned sweet potatoes (sometimes mislabeled as "yams")— they have sweet, flavorful orange flesh, which is what you want for the filling. Serve the enchiladas with lime wedges to squeeze over them if you like.

PREP 30 Minutes **TOTAL** 1 Hour 10 Minutes •
5 servings (2 enchiladas each)

- 1 lb sweet potatoes, peeled and cut into ½-inch cubes (about 2½ cups)
- 2 tablespoons vegetable oil
- ¼ teaspoon salt
- ⅛ teaspoon pepper
- 1 small onion, chopped (½ cup)
- 2 cloves garlic, finely chopped
- 1 teaspoon chili powder
- 3 cups lightly-packed fresh baby spinach leaves (from 5-oz bag)
- 1 can (15 oz) chick peas (garbanzo beans), rinsed, drained
- 2 cups shredded Mexican cheese blend (8 oz)
- 1 package (8.2 oz) 6-inch flour tortillas for soft tacos and fajitas
- 2 cans (10 oz each) mild red enchilada sauce
- Fresh chopped cilantro and crema Mexicana, if desired

1 Heat oven to 400°F. Spray 13x9-inch (3-quart) baking dish with cooking spray.

2 Place sweet potatoes on 15x10-inch pan. Drizzle 1 tablespoon of the oil over sweet potatoes; sprinkle with salt and pepper. Toss to coat; spread in single layer. Bake 18 to 23 minutes or until sweet potatoes are tender and lightly browned.

3 Meanwhile, in 10-inch nonstick skillet, heat remaining 1 tablespoon oil over medium heat. Add onion. Cook 4 to 5 minutes, stirring frequently, or until onion is tender. Add garlic. Cook 30 to 60 seconds, stirring frequently, or until softened. Stir in chili powder and spinach. Cook 30 to 60 seconds or until spinach is wilted.

4 In medium heatproof bowl, place spinach mixture. Stir in chick peas and roasted sweet potatoes. Let stand 5 minutes. Stir in 1 cup of the cheese.

5 Place tortillas on work surface. Spread heaping ⅓ cup vegetable mixture down center of each tortilla. Wrap tortillas around filling; place seam side down in baking dish. Top enchiladas with enchilada sauce and remaining cheese.

6 Bake 15 to 20 minutes or until hot and cheese is melted. Let stand 5 minutes before serving. Top with cilantro; drizzle with crema Mexicana.

1 Serving Calories 550; Total Fat 25g (Saturated Fat 11g, Trans Fat 0g); Cholesterol 50mg; Sodium 1380mg; Total Carbohydrate 63g (Dietary Fiber 7g); Protein 18g **Carbohydrate Choices:** 4

Red Lentil Buffalo Sloppy Joes

White Cheddar, Bean and Sausage "Mac and Cheese"

Red Lentil Buffalo Sloppy Joes

If you like a more traditional sloppy joe taste, use tomato sauce. If you prefer a barbecue twang, use ketchup and omit the brown sugar.

PREP 30 Minutes **TOTAL** 30 Minutes • *6 sloppy joes*

- 1 cup water
- ½ cup red lentils, sorted, rinsed
- 1 small onion, chopped (½ cup)
- 1 medium carrot, chopped (½ cup)
- 2 stalks celery, sliced (1 cup)
- 2 cloves garlic, finely chopped
- ¼ cup tomato sauce or ketchup
- ¼ cup Buffalo wing sauce
- 1 tablespoon packed brown sugar
- 1 teaspoon smoked paprika
- 6 burger buns, split
- ⅓ cup crumbled blue cheese (about 1½ oz)

1 In 2-quart saucepan, heat water to boiling over high heat. Stir in lentils, onion, carrot, ⅔ cup of the celery and the garlic. Heat to boiling; reduce heat. Simmer uncovered 5 to 8 minutes, stirring occasionally, just until lentils are tender. Drain; return to saucepan.

2 Stir in tomato sauce, Buffalo wing sauce, brown sugar and paprika. Cook over medium heat, stirring frequently, 1 to 2 minutes or until hot. On bun bottoms, spoon about ⅓ cup lentil mixture. Top each with about 1 tablespoon cheese and 1 tablespoon of remaining celery; cover with bun tops.

1 Sloppy Joe Calories 230; Total Fat 5g (Saturated Fat 2g, Trans Fat 0g); Cholesterol 5mg; Sodium 500mg; Total Carbohydrate 36g (Dietary Fiber 4g); Protein 10g **Carbohydrate Choices:** 2½

White Cheddar, Bean and Sausage "Mac and Cheese"

Sprinkle servings with crushed red pepper flakes, if you like a little heat.

PREP 30 Minutes **TOTAL** 30 Minutes •
4 servings (1¼ cups each)

- ½ lb sweet Italian sausage links
- 2 tablespoons butter
- 1 clove garlic, finely chopped
- 2 tablespoons all-purpose flour
- ½ teaspoon Italian seasoning
- ½ teaspoon salt
- ¼ teaspoon pepper
- ⅛ teaspoon crushed red pepper flakes
- 2 cups milk
- 2 cans (15 oz each) cannellini beans, rinsed, drained
- ¼ cup finely chopped drained sun-dried tomatoes in oil (from 7-oz jar)
- 1½ cups shredded white cheddar cheese (6 oz; from 1-lb block)
- ¼ cup grated Parmesan cheese
- 1½ cups lightly-packed fresh arugula leaves (from 5-oz container)

1 Pierce sausages with knife. In 10-inch nonstick skillet, cook sausages uncovered over medium heat 17 to 19 minutes, turning occasionally, until browned and instant-read meat thermometer inserted in center of sausages reads 165°F. Remove from pan; let stand 5 minutes. Cut sausages in half lengthwise, then crosswise in ½-inch slices.

2 In 4-quart saucepan, heat butter over medium heat until melted. Stir in garlic. Cook 30 seconds or until tender. Stir in flour, Italian seasoning, salt, pepper and pepper flakes. Cook and stir 1 minute or until mixture is bubbly.

3 Gradually stir in milk. Heat over medium heat, stirring constantly, until boiling; boil and stir 1 minute. Stir in sausage, beans and sun-dried tomatoes. Heat to boiling; stir in cheeses until melted. Remove from heat. Gently stir in arugula. Serve immediately.

1 Serving Calories 660; Total Fat 38g (Saturated Fat 18g, Trans Fat 1g); Cholesterol 105mg; Sodium 1120mg; Total Carbohydrate 45g (Dietary Fiber 8g); Protein 36g **Carbohydrate Choices:** 3

Roasted Vegetable Macaroni and Cheese

If you have the time, shred the cheeses from a block for the best flavor and creamiest cheesy sauce. On rushed nights, use packaged shredded Colby and cheddar cheeses.

PREP 30 Minutes **TOTAL** 1 Hour • *6 servings* (1¼ cups each)

ROASTED VEGETABLES

- 2 cups small fresh broccoli florets
- 2 medium carrots, peeled, cut into ½-inch pieces (about 1 cup)
- 1 tablespoon olive oil
- ¼ teaspoon salt
- ⅛ teaspoon pepper

MACARONI AND CHEESE

- 2¼ cups uncooked cavatappi pasta (6 oz)
- ¼ cup butter

- 3 tablespoons all-purpose flour
- ½ teaspoon salt
- ¼ teaspoon pepper
- 2 cups milk
- 1 cup shredded cheddar cheese (4 oz)
- 1 cup shredded Colby cheese (4 oz)

TOPPING

- 1 cup plain panko crispy bread crumbs
- 3 tablespoons butter, melted

1 Place oven rack in middle position; heat oven to 400°F. Spray 8-inch square (2-quart) baking dish with cooking spray; set aside. Spray 15x10x1-inch pan with cooking spray.

2 In medium bowl, add all roasted vegetable ingredients; mix well. Spread in pan in single layer. Bake 10 minutes; stir. Continue baking 8 to 12 minutes longer or until vegetables are lightly brown and just tender.

3 Meanwhile, cook and drain pasta as directed on package. While pasta is cooking, melt ¼ cup of the butter in 3-quart saucepan over medium-low heat. Stir in flour, ½ teaspoon of the salt and ¼ of the teaspoon pepper.

Cook over medium-low heat, stirring constantly, until mixture is smooth and bubbly; remove from heat. Stir in milk. Increase heat to medium-high. Heat to boiling, stirring constantly. Boil and stir 1 minute. Stir in cheeses. Cook, stirring constantly, until cheeses are melted; remove from heat.

4 Gently stir pasta into cheese sauce. Stir in roasted vegetables; pour mixture into baking dish. In small bowl, mix bread crumbs and 3 tablespoons melted butter until well mixed. Sprinkle over pasta mixture.

5 Bake 20 to 25 minutes or until bubbly and topping is golden brown. Let stand 5 minutes before serving.

1 Serving Calories 560; Total Fat 31g (Saturated Fat 17g, Trans Fat 1g); Cholesterol 80mg; Sodium 740mg; Total Carbohydrate 49g (Dietary Fiber 3g); Protein 19g **Carbohydrate Choices:** 3

Jackfruit "Pulled Pork" Sandwiches

Jackfruit is the world's largest fruit, weighing up to 100 lb. When green, the fruit is used more like a vegetable, and is a great substitute for meat. It can be found fresh, dried and canned. This is a terrific way to use up leftover Cilantro-Lime Coleslaw (page 138)!

PREP 15 Minutes **TOTAL** 15 Minutes • *4 sandwiches*

- 2 teaspoons olive oil
- 1½ teaspoons Cowboy Coffee Rub (page 424)
- 1 can (14 oz) young green jackfruit in water, drained

- ½ cup barbecue sauce
- 4 kaiser rolls or burger buns, split
- 1 cup Cilantro-Lime Coleslaw (page 138), drained

Roasted Vegetable Macaroni and Cheese

Jackfruit "Pulled Pork" Sandwiches

Chick Pea and Tomato Curry

1 In 10-inch nonstick skillet, heat oil over medium-high heat; stir in rub. Add jackfruit. Cook 3 to 5 minutes, stirring occasionally with heat-resistant spatula, or until jackfruit begins to brown on edges.

2 Stir in barbecue sauce; reduce heat to medium-low. Cook uncovered, 5 to 8 minutes, stirring frequently and breaking up with spatula, until mixture is hot.

3 On bun bottoms, spoon jackfruit and coleslaw. Cover with bun tops.

1 Sandwich Calories 340; Total Fat 7g (Saturated Fat 1g, Trans Fat 0.5g); Cholesterol 0mg; Sodium 830mg; Total Carbohydrate 63g (Dietary Fiber 3g); Protein 6g **Carbohydrate Choices:** 4

FAST • CALORIE SMART • GLUTEN FREE • VEGETARIAN

Chick Pea and Tomato Curry

PREP 30 Minutes **TOTAL** 30 Minutes •
6 servings (1 cup each)

1 tablespoon olive or vegetable oil	2 cans (14.5 oz each) fire-roasted diced tomatoes, undrained
1 small onion, chopped (½ cup)	½ cup chopped fresh cilantro
3 cloves garlic, finely chopped	1 tablespoon fresh lemon juice
1 tablespoon finely chopped gingerroot	½ teaspoon coarse (kosher or sea) salt
1 tablespoon gluten-free curry powder	Hot cooked rice (page 224), if desired
2 cans (15 oz each) chick peas (garbanzo beans), rinsed, drained	Plain yogurt, if desired
	Cilantro sprigs, if desired
	Lemon wedges, if desired

1 In 3-quart saucepan, heat oil over medium heat. Cook onion, garlic, gingerroot and curry powder in oil about 2 minutes, stirring frequently, or until onion is tender.

2 Stir in chick peas and tomatoes. Heat to boiling; reduce heat. Simmer uncovered 15 minutes, stirring occasionally.

3 Stir in cilantro, lemon juice and salt. Serve over rice; top individual servings with yogurt and cilantro sprigs. Serve with lemon wedges.

1 Serving Calories 190; Total Fat 5g (Saturated Fat 0.5g, Trans Fat 0g); Cholesterol 0mg; Sodium 590mg; Total Carbohydrate 29g (Dietary Fiber 7g); Protein 7g **Carbohydrate Choices:** 2

FAST • CALORIE SMART • GLUTEN FREE

Zoodle-Turkey Chili Mac

PREP 30 Minutes **TOTAL** 30 Minutes •
8 servings (1 cup each)

2 teaspoons vegetable oil or olive oil	1 teaspoon salt
1 lb ground turkey (at least 93% lean)	1 can (19 oz) red kidney beans, rinsed, drained
1 medium onion, chopped (1 cup)	1 can (14.5 oz) fire-roasted crushed tomatoes, undrained
2 cloves garlic, chopped	4 cups fresh zucchini spirals
1 package (1 oz) gluten-free taco seasoning mix (for homemade seasoning, see page 454)	1 cup frozen whole kernel sweet corn
	1 cup shredded cheddar cheese (4 oz)
1 tablespoon chili powder	

1 In 12-inch nonstick skillet, heat oil over medium-high heat. Add turkey and onions. Cook 5 to 7 minutes, stirring frequently, or until turkey is no longer pink. Add garlic. Cook about 1 minute or until fragrant.

2 Stir in taco seasoning, chili powder, salt, beans and tomatoes; heat to boiling; reduce heat. Cook uncovered 3 to 4 minutes, stirring occasionally, or until heated through and bubbling on edges.

3 Stir in zucchini and corn. Cook 4 to 5 minutes, stirring occasionally, or until corn is heated through and zucchini is tender. Top with cheese. Serve immediately.

1 Serving Calories 280; Total Fat 12g (Saturated Fat 4.5g, Trans Fat 0g); Cholesterol 55mg; Sodium 860mg; Total Carbohydrate 24g (Dietary Fiber 5g); Protein 20g **Carbohydrate Choices:** 1½

Black Bean Chili with Cilantro

Creamy Tuscan-Inspired Gnocchi Skillet

CALORIE SMART • GLUTEN FREE

Black Bean Chili with Cilantro

PREP 30 Minutes **TOTAL** 1 Hour 30 Minutes •
5 servings (1⅓ cups each)

- ¼ cup dry sherry or gluten-free chicken broth (for homemade broth, see page 153)
- 1 tablespoon olive oil
- 2 medium onions, chopped (2 cups)
- 1 medium stalk celery, chopped (½ cup)
- 1 small carrot, chopped (½ cup)
- ½ cup chopped red bell pepper
- 3 cans (15 oz each) black beans, rinsed, drained
- 2 cups gluten-free chicken broth (for homemade broth, see page 153)
- 1 large tomato, chopped (1 cup)
- 6 cloves garlic, finely chopped
- 2 tablespoons honey
- 2 tablespoons tomato paste
- 4 teaspoons chili powder, or to taste
- 1 teaspoon ground cumin
- ½ teaspoon dried oregano leaves
- ¼ cup chopped fresh cilantro
  Salt and pepper to taste

  GARNISHES, IF DESIRED
  Additional chopped onion
  Shredded Monterey Jack cheese
  Plain Greek yogurt or sour cream

1 In 4- to 5-quart Dutch oven, heat sherry and oil over medium heat; add onions. Cook uncovered about 3 minutes, stirring occasionally, or until softened. Add celery, carrot and bell pepper. Cook 5 minutes, stirring frequently.

2 Stir in remaining ingredients except garnishes. Heat to boiling; reduce heat. Cover; simmer 45 to 60 minutes or until chili is desired thickness. Garnish individual servings with onion, cheese and a dollop of yogurt.

1 Serving Calories 410; Total Fat 4.5g (Saturated Fat 0.5g, Trans Fat 0g); Cholesterol 0mg; Sodium 450mg; Total Carbohydrate 71g (Dietary Fiber 23g); Protein 19g **Carbohydrate Choices:** 5

FAST • VEGETARIAN

Creamy Tuscan-Inspired Gnocchi Skillet

"Gnocchi" is the Italian word for dumplings. In the US, gnocchi are generally potato dumplings made with flour and sometimes egg and cheese. Packaged gnocchi are typically available at large grocery stores and can be found in the freezer section or fresh in the dried pasta section. Since packaged gnocchi tend to stick together, break them apart before cooking for even cooking and best results. The soft, chewy texture of cooked gnocchi is both comforting and fun to eat.

PREP 30 Minutes **TOTAL** 30 Minutes •
6 servings (about 1 cup each)

- 6 tablespoons butter
- ½ cup plain panko crispy bread crumbs
- 1 clove garlic, finely chopped
- 2 packages (16 oz each) gnocchi
- 1 tablespoon Italian seasoning
- ¼ teaspoon crushed red pepper flakes
- 2 cups vegetable broth (from 32-oz carton; for homemade broth, see page 169)
- 4 oz cream cheese (from 8-oz package), softened, cut into cubes
- 4 cups lightly-packed fresh baby spinach leaves (from 10-oz container)
- 1 cup quartered cherry tomatoes
- ½ cup shredded Parmesan cheese (2 oz)

1 In 12-inch skillet, melt 1 tablespoon of the butter over medium heat. Add bread crumbs and garlic. Cook 1 to 3 minutes, stirring constantly, or until toasted. Pour into small bowl and set aside; clean out skillet.

2 In same skillet, heat remaining 5 tablespoons butter over medium-high heat until melted. Add gnocchi, Italian seasoning and pepper flakes. Cook 13 to 15 minutes, stirring frequently, or until golden brown.

3 Add broth to skillet. Heat to boiling; reduce heat. Simmer 4 to 6 minutes, stirring frequently, or until slightly thickened. Stir in cream cheese until melted. Stir in spinach, a handful at a time, until wilted. Remove from heat; stir in tomatoes. Top with bread crumbs and Parmesan.

1 Serving Calories 560; Total Fat 22g (Saturated Fat 13g, Trans Fat 0.5g); Cholesterol 55mg; Sodium 450mg; Total Carbohydrate 73g (Dietary Fiber 4g); Protein 16g **Carbohydrate Choices:** 5

CALORIE SMART

One-Pot Mexican-Inspired Burrito Bowl

We start with dried beans because they cost about one-third of what canned beans cost, and the texture holds up better to the long cooking time without breaking apart.

PREP 20 Minutes **TOTAL** 3 Hours 20 Minutes •
8 servings (1¼ cups each)

1 cup dried black beans (8 oz), sorted, rinsed	½ teaspoon crushed red pepper flakes
1 tablespoon vegetable oil	½ teaspoon paprika
1 medium onion, chopped (1 cup)	1 cup uncooked brown rice
3 cloves garlic, finely chopped	¾ cup dried brown lentils (6 oz), sorted, rinsed
5 cups vegetable broth or chicken broth (for homemade broth, see pages 169 or 153)	1 can (4.5 oz) chopped green chiles
	1 can (28 oz) petite diced tomatoes, undrained
1 tablespoon chili powder	¼ cup chopped fresh cilantro
1½ teaspoons ground cumin	Chopped avocado, if desired
1 teaspoon salt	Shredded cheddar cheese, if desired

1 Soak black beans by one of the methods on page 270.

2 In 5-quart Dutch oven, heat oil over medium heat. Add onion and garlic. Cook 2 to 3 minutes, stirring frequently, until onion is soft. Add drained black beans, broth, chili powder, cumin, salt, pepper flakes and paprika. Heat to boiling; reduce heat. Cover; simmer 45 minutes.

3 Add rice, lentils and green chiles. Heat to boiling; reduce heat. Cover; simmer about 45 minutes, stirring occasionally, or until rice is tender and lentils are almost tender.

4 Stir in tomatoes. Cover; cook 10 to 15 minutes, stirring occasionally, or until lentils are tender and mixture is hot. Sprinkle with cilantro. Serve with avocado and cheese.

1 Serving Calories 310; Total Fat 3.5g (Saturated Fat 0.5g, Trans Fat 0g); Cholesterol 0mg; Sodium 930mg; Total Carbohydrate 55g (Dietary Fiber 11g); Protein 14g **Carbohydrate Choices:** 3½

MEXICAN-INSPIRED LENTIL BURRITOS: Prepare as directed—except cover and refrigerate cooked mixture overnight. For each burrito, spoon about ½ cup onto (8-inch) flour tortilla. Sprinkle with cilantro and shredded cheddar cheese. Tuck in ends and roll up. Place seam side down on microwavable dinner plate. Microwave uncovered about 1 minute on High or until heated through. Top with additional shredded cheese, sour cream and salsa.

ONE-POT ITALIAN-INSPIRED RED LENTIL, RICE AND BEANS BOWL: Prepare as directed—except substitute 1 cup dried great northern beans for the black beans and red lentils for the brown lentils. Omit chili powder, cumin and paprika. Add 2 teaspoons dried rosemary and 1 teaspoon dried oregano. Omit green chiles and cilantro. Stir in 3 cups chopped spinach or kale. Substitute grated Parmesan cheese and chopped tomato for avocado and cheddar cheese, if desired.

ONE-POT MEXICAN-INSPIRED CHICKEN BURRITO BOWL: Prepare as directed—except add 2 cups cut-up cooked chicken with the tomatoes.

ONE-POT MEXICAN-INSPIRED SAUSAGE BURRITO BOWL: Prepare as directed—except add ¾ lb cooked smoked sausage, quartered lengthwise and sliced, with the lentils.

SPEEDY ONE-POT MEXICAN-INSPIRED BURRITO BOWL: Prepare recipe as directed—except omit Step 1 and substitute 2 cans (15 oz each) black beans, rinsed and drained, for the dried black beans. Reduce broth to 4 cups. Add canned black beans with tomatoes.

One-Pot Mexican-Inspired Burrito Bowl

393

5-INGREDIENT RECIPE

Goat Cheese with Herbs

Cherry Tomato Medley

Oregano Leaves

Tomato–Goat Cheese French Bread Pizza

French Bread

Olive Oil-and-Vinegar Dressing

394

5-INGREDIENT RECIPE

1 Serving Calories 550; Total Fat 21g (Saturated Fat 13g, Trans Fat 0.5g); Cholesterol 45mg; Sodium 1140mg; Total Carbohydrate 63g (Dietary Fiber 3g); Protein 25g **Carbohydrate Choices:** 4

EASY • FAST • VEGETARIAN

Tomato—Goat Cheese French Bread Pizza

If you like, sprinkle the pizza with additional fresh oregano leaves.

PREP 15 Minutes **TOTAL** 30 Minutes •
4 servings (2 pieces each)

- 2 logs (4 oz each) goat cheese with herbs, softened
- 1 loaf (1 lb) French bread
- 2 tablespoons olive oil-and-vinegar dressing (from 16-oz bottle)
- 1 tablespoon chopped fresh oregano leaves
- ¼ teaspoon salt
- ⅛ teaspoon pepper
- 1 container (1 pint) cherry tomato medley, quartered

1 Crumble half of one cheese log into small bowl. Cover and refrigerate. Let remaining cheese stand at room temperature to soften.

2 Heat oven to 425°F. Line large cookie sheet with foil. Cut bread in half crosswise, then in half lengthwise.

3 Place bread on cookie sheet, cut sides up. Bake about 5 minutes or until lightly toasted around edges. Spread softened cheese on toasted bread.

4 In medium bowl, toss 1 tablespoon of the dressing, the oregano, salt, pepper and tomatoes until well mixed. Using slotted spoon, spoon tomato mixture over toasted bread. Top with crumbled goat cheese. Drizzle with remaining 1 tablespoon dressing.

5 Bake 7 to 10 minutes or until cheese crumbles are soft and bread is golden brown. To serve, cut each bread section in half crosswise.

CALORIE SMART • GLUTEN FREE • VEGETARIAN

Veggie Hash and Eggs

PREP 30 Minutes **TOTAL** 40 Minutes •
4 servings (1 egg and about 1¼ cups vegetables each)

- 2 tablespoons olive oil
- 1 medium sweet potato (about 10 oz), peeled, cut into ½-inch pieces (about 2 cups)
- 2 teaspoons chopped fresh or ½ teaspoon dried thyme leaves
- ½ teaspoon salt
- ⅛ teaspoon pepper
- 2 cloves garlic, finely chopped
- 3 cups broccoli slaw (from 12-oz package)
- 1 medium bell pepper (any color), chopped (1 cup)
- ½ cup quartered grape or cherry tomatoes
- 4 eggs
  Additional fresh or dried thyme leaves, if desired

1 Heat oven to 400°F.

2 In 10-inch ovenproof nonstick or cast-iron skillet, heat oil over medium-high heat. Add sweet potatoes; sprinkle with 2 teaspoons chopped thyme, salt, pepper and garlic. Cook 4 to 6 minutes, stirring frequently, or until sweet potatoes are crisp-tender. Gently stir in broccoli slaw, bell pepper and tomatoes until well mixed; remove from heat.

3 Spread vegetable mixture evenly in skillet. Make 4 (3-inch-wide) indentations in mixture with bottom of custard cup. One at a time, break eggs into custard cup and carefully slide egg into an indentation. Bake uncovered 10 to 12 minutes or until whites and yolks are firm, not runny, and vegetables are tender. Sprinkle with additional thyme leaves.

1 Serving Calories 210; Total Fat 12g (Saturated Fat 2.5g, Trans Fat 0g); Cholesterol 185mg; Sodium 400mg; Total Carbohydrate 15g (Dietary Fiber 4g); Protein 9g **Carbohydrate Choices:** 1

Veggie Hash and Eggs

Sweet Potato—Cauliflower Curry

Couscous would also be equally as good as rice with this curry.

PREP 30 Minutes **TOTAL** 1 Hour •
6 servings (about 1⅓ cups curry and ½ cup rice each)

CURRY

- 2 tablespoons vegetable oil
- 1 medium onion, chopped (1 cup)
- 2 cloves garlic, finely chopped
- 2 medium dark-orange sweet potatoes, peeled, cut into 1-inch cubes (4 cups)
- 4 cups fresh cauliflower florets
- 1 tablespoon finely chopped gingerroot
- 4 teaspoons curry powder
- ½ teaspoon salt
- ¼ teaspoon pepper
- 1 can (13.5 oz) coconut milk (not cream of coconut)
- 1 cup vegetable broth (for homemade broth, see page 169)
- 2 teaspoons cornstarch
- 2 tablespoons cold water

TOPPINGS

- 1½ cups hot cooked white or brown rice (page 224)
- ⅓ cup sliced almonds, toasted (page 28)
- 5 green onions, sliced (about ⅓ cup)
- ⅓ cup chopped fresh cilantro

1 In 5-quart Dutch oven or stockpot, heat oil over medium-high heat. Cook onion in oil 5 minutes, stirring frequently, or until tender. Add garlic. Cook 1 minute. Stir in remaining curry ingredients except cornstarch and water. Reduce heat to low. Cover; cook 30 minutes or until vegetables are tender.

2 Uncover; increase heat to medium-high. In small bowl, blend cornstarch and water until smooth paste forms. Stir cornstarch mixture into curry. Cook uncovered 5 to 10 minutes, stirring frequently, or until thickened and bubbly.

3 Serve curry in individual deep bowls. Top each serving with ¼ cup rice. Sprinkle evenly with almonds, green onions and cilantro.

1 Serving Calories 400; Total Fat 23g (Saturated Fat 13g, Trans Fat 0g); Cholesterol 0mg; Sodium 440mg; Total Carbohydrate 40g (Dietary Fiber 7g); Protein 7g **Carbohydrate Choices:** 2½

Indian-Style Stew

In India, curry powder is traditionally ground every day. It's a blend of many spices including cardamom, chiles, cinnamon, saffron and turmeric, and can vary widely by the cook and region. Different curry powder products can vary as well, so experiment with a variety of blends until you find your favorite.

PREP 30 Minutes **TOTAL** 1 Hour 15 Minutes •
6 servings (1 cup stew and ½ cup rice each)

STEW

- 2 tablespoons butter
- 2 medium onions, chopped (2 cups)
- 2 tablespoons gluten-free curry powder
- 2 teaspoons garam masala
- ½ teaspoon salt
- 2 teaspoons grated gingerroot
- 2 cloves garlic, chopped
- 1 cup chopped peeled carrots
- 1 cup chopped peeled potatoes
- 1 cup gluten-free vegetable broth (for homemade broth, see page 169)
- 1 can (28 oz) fire-roasted diced tomatoes, undrained
- 1 can (19 oz) chick peas (garbanzo beans), rinsed, drained
- 1 cup canned light coconut milk (from 14-oz can; not cream of coconut)

SERVING SUGGESTIONS

- 3 cups hot cooked basmati, jasmine, white or brown rice (page 224)

  Fresh cilantro leaves, if desired
- 2 green onions, sliced, if desired (2 tablespoons)
- 6 tablespoons plain yogurt, if desired

1 In 5-quart Dutch oven, heat butter over medium-high heat until melted. Add onions. Cook about 3 minutes, stirring frequently, or until softened. Add curry powder, garam masala and salt. Cook uncovered 3 to 5 minutes, stirring frequently, or until fragrant and brown. Add gingerroot and garlic. Cook and stir 1 minute. Add carrots and potatoes. Cook and stir 2 minutes. Add broth. Heat to boiling; reduce heat. Simmer uncovered about 5 minutes or until potatoes and carrots are softened. Stir in tomatoes, chick peas and coconut milk.

2 Heat to boiling; reduce heat. Simmer uncovered 30 to 45 minutes, stirring occasionally, or until carrots and potatoes are tender and liquid is slightly reduced. Remove from heat; cool slightly. Serve over rice, and top with remaining ingredients.

1 Serving Calories 360; Total Fat 8g (Saturated Fat 4.5g, Trans Fat 0g); Cholesterol 10mg; Sodium 780mg; Total Carbohydrate 61g (Dietary Fiber 8g); Protein 10g **Carbohydrate Choices:** 4

Stuffed Spaghetti Squash with Sausage and Spinach

PREP 40 Minutes **TOTAL** 2 Hours 5 Minutes • *6 servings*

- 1 large (4½ lb) spaghetti squash, cut in half lengthwise, seeded
- 2 tablespoons olive oil
- 1 lb bulk sweet Italian pork sausage
- 1 medium onion, chopped (1 cup)
- 3 cloves garlic, finely chopped
- 2 tablespoons all-purpose flour
- ¾ teaspoon salt
- ½ teaspoon pepper
- ½ teaspoon crushed red pepper flakes
- ¼ teaspoon ground nutmeg
- 1 bag (5 oz) fresh baby spinach leaves
- 1 cup heavy whipping cream
- 1½ cups shredded mozzarella cheese (6 oz)
- ¾ cup grated Parmesan cheese
- ½ cup plain panko crispy bread crumbs
- Chopped fresh parsley, if desired

1 Heat oven to 400°F. Line 15x10x1-inch pan with cooking parchment paper; spray with cooking spray. Place both squash halves cut side down on pan.

2 Bake 45 to 50 minutes or until tender.

3 In 12-inch nonstick skillet, heat 1 tablespoon of the oil over medium-high heat. Cook sausage, onion and garlic in oil 5 to 7 minutes, stirring occasionally, or until sausage is no longer pink. Reduce heat to medium; stir in flour, salt, pepper, pepper flakes and nutmeg. Cook and stir 1 minute. Gradually add spinach. Cook 1 to 2 minutes, stirring constantly, or just until spinach is wilted. Stir in whipping cream; heat to boiling. Cook 1 to 2 minutes, stirring constantly, or just until thickened. Remove from heat; stir in mozzarella and ½ cup of the Parmesan cheese until melted.

4 When squash is cool enough to handle, use fork to remove squash strands from shells into skillet with sausage mixture, leaving shells intact. Mix squash strands into sausage mixture; spoon filling evenly between both squash shell halves.

5 Arrange squash halves on same baking pan. Bake 35 to 40 minutes or until bubbly around edges and heated through. Let stand 10 minutes.

6 Meanwhile, in 8-inch skillet, heat remaining 1 tablespoon oil over medium heat. Stir in bread crumbs to coat. Cook about 3 minutes, stirring constantly, or until lightly browned. Transfer to small bowl; mix in remaining ¼ cup Parmesan cheese. Sprinkle bread crumb mixture over squash halves; sprinkle with parsley. Serve immediately.

1 Serving Calories 640; Total Fat 42g (Saturated Fat 19g, Trans Fat 1g); Cholesterol 105mg; Sodium 1220mg; Total Carbohydrate 38g (Dietary Fiber 5g); Protein 26g **Carbohydrate Choices:** 2½

Sweet Potato–Cauliflower Curry

Indian-Style Stew

Stuffed Spaghetti Squash with Sausage and Spinach

HEIRLOOM

SLOW COOKER • CALORIE SMART

Pizza-Stuffed Peppers

Here's an easy way to remove the cooked bell peppers from the slow cooker without spilling the filling: Lift one pepper at a time, scooping it up with a large slotted spoon in one hand and holding it lightly with tongs in the other hand to support the pepper—do not squeeze the tongs.

PREP 20 Minutes **TOTAL** 4 Hours 30 Minutes • *6 servings*

4½ cups water	½ cup diced pepperoni (about 2½ oz)
½ cup uncooked orzo or rosamarina pasta	1 can (15 oz) pizza sauce
6 small bell peppers (about 5 oz each)	1½ cups shredded pizza cheese blend (6 oz)
1¼ cups ground turkey at least 93% lean (10 oz ground)	½ cup water

1 In 2-quart saucepan, heat 4 cups of the water to boiling. Add pasta and cook 3 minutes; drain. Rinse pasta with cold water to cool; drain well.

2 Meanwhile, cut thin slice from stem end of each bell pepper; set tops aside. Remove seeds and membranes from peppers. If necessary, cut thin slice from bottom of peppers so peppers stand up straight.

3 In 10-inch nonstick skillet, cook turkey and pepperoni over medium-high heat 4 to 6 minutes, stirring occasionally, or until turkey is no longer pink. (Drain if any liquid remains in skillet; return turkey mixture to skillet.) Stir in pizza sauce, 1 cup of the cheese and the cooked pasta. Divide turkey filling among peppers.

4 Spray 5- to 6-quart slow cooker with cooking spray. In 1-cup glass measuring cup in microwave, heat remaining ½ cup water to boiling. Pour into slow cooker. Stand peppers upright in cooker; replace pepper tops. Cover; cook on Low heat setting 4 to 5 hours.

5 Remove pepper tops; reserve. Top peppers with remaining ½ cup cheese. Cover; cook 5 to 10 minutes longer or until cheese is melted. Top with pepper tops.

1 Serving Calories 330; Total Fat 18g (Saturated Fat 8g, Trans Fat 0g); Cholesterol 70mg; Sodium 670mg; Total Carbohydrate 21g (Dietary Fiber 3g); Protein 22g **Carbohydrate Choices:** 1½

Pizza-Stuffed Peppers

Veggie-Stuffed Peppers

MAKE AHEAD • GLUTEN FREE

Veggie-Stuffed Peppers

Not only does the brown rice in this recipe add a bit of texture and whole grain goodness to these peppers, but it absorbs excess moisture from the vegetables, so the filling isn't watery.

PREP 40 Minutes **TOTAL** 1 Hour 30 Minutes • *4 peppers*

- 4 large bell peppers (about 8 oz each)
- ¼ cup uncooked instant brown rice
- 2 cups sliced fresh mushrooms
- 1 small onion, chopped (½ cup)
- 2 cloves garlic, finely chopped
- 2 tablespoons olive oil
- 1 bag (5 oz) fresh baby spinach leaves
- ½ cup gluten-free all-purpose baking mix
- ½ cup milk
- ½ teaspoon salt
- ⅛ teaspoon pepper
- 2 eggs
- 1 cup shredded Asiago cheese (4 oz)

1 Heat oven to 375°F.

2 Cut thin slice from stem end of each bell pepper and set aside; discard stems. Remove seeds and membranes from peppers. If necessary, cut thin slice from bottom of pepper so pepper stands up straight.

3 In 8-inch microwavable baking dish, place peppers. Add ¼ cup water; cover with plastic wrap. Microwave on High 3 minutes. Drain peppers; wipe out baking dish. Return peppers to baking dish. Spoon 1 tablespoon of the brown rice into bottom of each pepper.

4 Meanwhile, chop pepper tops and any thin slices from bottoms.

5 In 12-inch skillet, cook chopped bell pepper, mushrooms, onion and garlic in olive oil over medium heat 8 to 10 minutes, stirring occasionally, or until vegetables are tender. Stir in spinach. Cook 2 to 3 minutes, stirring constantly, or until spinach wilts and moisture evaporates.

6 In medium bowl, stir baking mix, milk, salt, pepper and eggs until blended. Stir in vegetable mixture and cheese. Divide vegetable mixture among peppers.

7 Bake 40 to 50 minutes or until knife inserted in center comes out clean. Let stand 5 minutes before serving.

1 Pepper Calories 420; Total Fat 22g (Saturated Fat 9g, Trans Fat 0g); Cholesterol 125mg; Sodium 850mg; Total Carbohydrate 39g (Dietary Fiber 5g); Protein 17g **Carbohydrate Choices:** 2½

MAKE-AHEAD DIRECTIONS: Cool baked peppers; cover plastic wrap and refrigerate up to 3 days. To reheat one pepper, place pepper on a microwavable plate; cover loosely with plastic wrap. Microwave on Medium (50%) 2 minutes 30 seconds to 3 minutes 30 seconds or until hot. Let stand 30 seconds before serving.

Roasted Butternut Squash with Farro

CALORIE SMART • VEGETARIAN • VEGAN

Roasted Butternut Squash with Farro

PREP 25 Minutes **TOTAL** 55 Minutes • *6 servings* (1 cup each)

SQUASH AND VEGETABLES

- ½ medium butternut squash, peeled, seeded, cut into ¾-inch pieces (3 cups)
- ½ medium onion, cut into ¼-inch slices (½ cup)
- ½ lb medium Brussels sprouts, trimmed and quartered lengthwise (2 cups)
- 1 (8 oz) package sliced fresh mushrooms (about 3 cups)
- 1 tablespoon olive oil
- ½ teaspoon dried sage leaves
- ½ teaspoon salt
- ¼ teaspoon pepper
- ¼ cup vegan sweetened dried cranberries

FARRO

- 1½ cups vegetable broth or water (for homemade broth, see page 169)
- ½ cup uncooked farro
- ¼ teaspoon salt

1 Heat oven to 425°F. Move 2 oven racks to upper and lower thirds of oven. Spray two 15x10x1-inch pans with cooking spray.

2 In large bowl, toss all squash and vegetables ingredients together except cranberries. Divide evenly between pans and spread in single layer. Bake 20 to 30 minutes, stirring once and rotating pans between racks, or until vegetables are tender and golden brown.

3 Meanwhile, in 1-quart saucepan, heat farro ingredients to boiling. Reduce heat. Cover; simmer 20 to 25 minutes or until farro is tender. Drain.

4 In large serving bowl, toss farro with vegetables and cranberries.

1 Serving Calories 170; Total Fat 3g (Saturated Fat 0g, Trans Fat 0g); Cholesterol 0mg; Sodium 470mg; Total Carbohydrate 30g (Dietary Fiber 6g); Protein 5g **Carbohydrate Choices:** 2

USE IT UP
SALAD GREENS

Before your greens get a chance to wilt in the refrigerator, or you just can't eat another salad, try one of these ways to use up those greens, boosting the nutritional content of the food you add them to.

BERRY DELICIOUS SMOOTHIES Fill blender about ⅓ full of water. Add 2 or 3 large handfuls of greens mixes, such as power greens, spring mix or mesclun, or spinach or baby kale leaves to blender. Top with 1 cup frozen berries, 1 tablespoon each flax seed, honey and fresh lemon juice. Cover and blend on high speed until greens are very finely chopped. (Add a few tablespoons additional water, if mixture won't blend.) Taste; add additional berries or honey, if desired.

GRILLED GREENS Trim tops from romaine or radicchio heads. Cut lengthwise into halves or quarters. Drizzle with olive oil; sprinkle with salt and pepper. Grill over medium direct heat, turning once, until slightly softened. Drizzle romaine with vinaigrette; sprinkle with grated Parmesan.

Top cut sides of radicchio with a soft cheese such as soft garlic-and-herbs cheese or burrata: drizzle with balsamic vinegar.

SPINACH, BABY KALE OR ARUGULA PESTO Follow directions for Spinach Pesto (page 480). If using baby kale or arugula, simply swap for the spinach.

EGGS WITH GREENS AND HAM Stir coarsely chopped spinach, baby kale leaves or arugula into scrambled eggs when they first hit the pan along with crisply cooked and crumbled prosciutto or bacon.

SOUP SAVVY Stir chopped kale or spinach into soup a few minutes before serving.

400

Sweet Potato–Black Bean Lasagna

Immediately rinsing cooked broccoli in cold water stops the cooking process so that when the lasagna is baked, the broccoli will still have its bright-green color.

PREP 30 Minutes **TOTAL** 1 Hour 25 Minutes • *6 servings*

2 large dark-orange sweet potatoes (about 2 lb)	6 oven-ready lasagna noodles
1½ cups coarsely chopped fresh broccoli	1 teaspoon garlic salt
	½ teaspoon pepper
1 tablespoon water	1 (15 oz) can black beans, rinsed, drained
2¼ cups roasted garlic Alfredo pasta sauce	1 medium red bell pepper, coarsely chopped (about ¾ cup)
1 clove garlic, finely chopped	
¼ cup chopped fresh basil leaves	2 cups finely shredded Italian cheese blend (8 oz)

1   Heat oven to 350°F. Spray 11x7-inch (2-quart) baking dish with cooking spray.

2   Pierce sweet potatoes with fork. Place on paper towel in microwave oven. Microwave on High 9 to 11 minutes or until slightly soft to the touch. Cool 15 minutes. Peel sweet potatoes; cut lengthwise into ¼-inch slices.

3   Meanwhile, in 1-quart microwavable bowl, place broccoli and water; cover loosely with plastic wrap. Microwave on High 2 minutes or until crisp-tender. Immediately rinse with cold water and drain. Set aside.

4   In medium bowl, mix Alfredo pasta sauce, garlic and 3 tablespoons of the basil.

5   Place 3 noodles in bottom of baking dish (trim to fit, if necessary); spread ½ cup of the Alfredo pasta sauce mixture evenly over noodles. Layer half of the sweet potatoes over sauce, sprinkle with ½ teaspoon of the garlic salt and ¼ teaspoon of the pepper. Top sweet potatoes with broccoli, beans and ½ cup of the bell pepper; sprinkle with 1 cup of the cheese. Top with remaining noodles, ¾ cup of the Alfredo pasta sauce, remaining sweet potatoes, remaining ½ teaspoon garlic salt and remaining ¼ teaspoon pepper. Spoon remaining sauce evenly over sweet potatoes. Sprinkle with remaining bell pepper and cheese. Spray sheet of foil with cooking spray. Cover baking dish tightly with foil, sprayed side down.

6   Bake covered 40 to 45 minutes or until hot and cheese is melted. Remove foil; sprinkle with remaining basil. Let stand 15 minutes before serving.

1 Serving Calories 710; Total Fat 38g (Saturated Fat 23g, Trans Fat 1g); Cholesterol 120mg; Sodium 1080mg; Total Carbohydrate 67g (Dietary Fiber 11g); Protein 23g **Carbohydrate Choices:** 4½

Sweet Potato–Black Bean Lasagna

Artichoke-Spinach Lasagna

PREP 25 Minutes TOTAL 1 Hour 35 Minutes • *8 servings*

1 small onion, chopped (½ cup)	1 box (9 oz) frozen chopped spinach, thawed, squeezed to drain
4 cloves garlic, finely chopped	
1¾ cups vegetable broth (for homemade broth, see page 169)	1 jar (15 to 16 oz) Alfredo pasta sauce
	9 uncooked regular lasagna noodles
1 tablespoon chopped fresh or 1 teaspoon dried rosemary leaves	3 cups shredded mozzarella cheese (12 oz)
1 can (14 oz) artichoke hearts, drained, coarsely chopped	1 package (4 oz) crumbled herb-and-garlic feta cheese (1 cup)

1   Heat oven to 350°F. Spray 13x9-inch (3-quart) baking dish with cooking spray.

2   Spray 12-inch skillet with cooking spray. Heat over medium-high heat; add onion and garlic. Cook about 3 minutes, stirring occasionally, or until onion is crisp-tender. Stir in broth and rosemary. Heat to boiling. Stir in artichokes and spinach; reduce heat. Cover; simmer 5 minutes. Stir in pasta sauce.

3   Spread one-fourth of the artichoke mixture in baking dish; top with 3 noodles. Sprinkle with ¾ cup of the mozzarella. Repeat layers twice. Spread with remaining artichoke mixture; top with remaining ¾ cup mozzarella. Sprinkle with feta.

4   Cover; bake 40 minutes. Uncover; bake about 15 minutes longer or until bubbly and noodles are tender. Let stand 10 to 15 minutes before cutting.

1 Serving Calories 520; Total Fat 31g (Saturated Fat 19g, Trans Fat 1g); Cholesterol 95mg; Sodium 960mg; Total Carbohydrate 35g (Dietary Fiber 7g); Protein 24g **Carbohydrate Choices:** 2

MEDITERRANEAN-STYLE LASAGNA: Stir in ½ cup chopped pitted kalamata, Greek or ripe olives with the Alfredo pasta sauce.

Quinoa Taco Salad

Serrano chiles are fresh green chiles that are smaller in diameter than jalapeños. Although serrano chiles are spicier than jalapeños, they offer a consistent spice level, making them a great choice for recipes. When handling chiles, be sure to wear clean food-safe plastic or rubber gloves to protect your hands, and be careful not to touch your face or eyes because oils in the seeds and membranes can cause burns. Always wash your hands thoroughly after handling them, to remove any oils.

PREP 30 Minutes **TOTAL** 50 Minutes •
4 servings (about 1¼ cups each)

- 1 tablespoon vegetable oil
- 1 medium serrano chile, seeded, finely chopped (about 2 teaspoons)
- 2 cloves garlic, finely chopped
- 1 cup white quinoa, rinsed, drained well
- 1 package (1 oz) gluten-free original taco seasoning mix (for homemade seasoning, see page 454)
- 1½ cups gluten-free chicken broth (for homemade broth, see page 153)
- 1 can (15 oz) black beans, rinsed, drained
- 4 teaspoons fresh lime juice
- ½ teaspoon honey
- ¼ teaspoon salt
- 2 tablespoons olive oil
- ¾ cup diced tomato
- 1 medium avocado, pitted, peeled and diced
- ¼ cup chopped red onion
- 2 tablespoons chopped fresh cilantro

1 In 2-quart saucepan, heat vegetable oil over medium heat. Cook serrano and garlic in oil 2 to 3 minutes, stirring frequently, or until softened and fragrant. Add quinoa and taco seasoning. Cook 1 minute, stirring constantly. Stir in broth. Heat to boiling; reduce heat. Cover; simmer 18 to 20 minutes or until liquid has been absorbed. Transfer to serving bowl; stir in beans. Let stand 15 minutes.

2 Meanwhile, in small bowl, beat lime juice, honey and salt with whisk. Slowly beat in olive oil; set aside.

3 Top quinoa mixture with tomato, avocado and red onion. Drizzle with dressing; sprinkle with cilantro.

1 Serving Calories 430; Total Fat 19g (Saturated Fat 2.5g, Trans Fat 0g); Cholesterol 0mg; Sodium 1240mg; Total Carbohydrate 54g (Dietary Fiber 11g); Protein 13g **Carbohydrate Choices:** 3½

MAKE-AHEAD DIRECTIONS: Prepare as directed through Step 2. Cover quinoa and dressing separately and refrigerate up to 3 days. Just before serving, continue with Step 3.

Veggie Lover's Overnight Breakfast Casserole

Don't want to wait? You can bake this veggie-packed casserole right away, rather than refrigerating it until morning. Bake at 350°F 30 to 35 minutes or until a knife inserted in center comes out clean. Garnish with sliced fresh basil leaves for even more flavor if you like.

PREP 30 Minutes **TOTAL** 9 Hours 25 Minutes • ***8 servings***

- 3 cups finely shredded Italian cheese blend (12 oz)
- 3 tablespoons butter
- 2 cups coarsely chopped fresh broccoli
- 1 cup sliced fresh mushrooms
- 1 clove garlic, finely chopped
- 3 cups fresh baby spinach leaves (from 5-oz bag), chopped
- ½ cup chopped red bell pepper
- 4 green onions, chopped (¼ cup)
- 8 eggs
- 1¾ cups half-and-half
- ¼ cup all-purpose flour
- ½ teaspoon Italian seasoning
- ½ teaspoon salt
- ¼ teaspoon pepper
  Sliced fresh basil leaves, if desired

1 Spray 13x9-inch (3-quart) baking dish with cooking spray. Sprinkle 2 cups of the cheese evenly in bottom of baking dish.

402

Quinoa Taco Salad

Veggie Lover"s Overnight Breakfast Casserole

2 In 12-inch nonstick skillet, heat butter over medium heat until melted. Add broccoli, mushrooms and garlic. Cook 3 to 4 minutes, stirring occasionally, or until broccoli is crisp-tender. Cool 5 minutes. Stir in spinach, bell pepper and green onions until well mixed. Spoon evenly onto cheese. Sprinkle with remaining 1 cup cheese. Set aside.

3 In large bowl, beat eggs, half-and-half, flour, Italian seasoning, salt and pepper until well blended. Pour egg mixture evenly over cheese and vegetable mixture in baking dish. Cover; refrigerate 8 hours or overnight.

4 Heat oven to 350°F. Uncover baking dish. Bake 33 to 38 minutes or until knife inserted in center comes out clean. Let stand 10 minutes before serving. Garnish with fresh basil.

1 Serving Calories 350; Total Fat 26g (Saturated Fat 15g, Trans Fat 0.5g); Cholesterol 255mg; Sodium 590mg; Total Carbohydrate 11g (Dietary Fiber 1g); Protein 19g **Carbohydrate Choices:** 1

Eggplant Parmigiana

CALORIE SMART • VEGETARIAN

Eggplant Parmigiana

PREP 25 Minutes **TOTAL** 50 Minutes • *6 servings*

- 1 egg
- 2 tablespoons water
- 2/3 cup seasoned dry bread crumbs
- 1/3 cup grated Parmesan cheese
- 2 small unpeeled eggplants (about 1 lb each), cut crosswise into 1/4-inch slices
- 1/4 cup olive or vegetable oil
- 2 cups meatless tomato pasta sauce (from 24- to 27-oz jar; for homemade sauce, see page 201)
- 2 cups shredded mozzarella cheese (8 oz)

1 Heat oven to 350°F. In shallow dish, beat egg and water. In another shallow dish, mix bread crumbs and Parmesan. Dip eggplant in egg mixture, then coat with crumb mixture.

2 In 12-inch nonstick skillet, heat 2 tablespoons of the oil over medium heat. Cook half of the eggplant in oil about 5 minutes, turning once, until light golden brown. Drain on paper towels. Repeat with remaining 2 tablespoons oil and remaining eggplant, adding additional oil if necessary.

3 In ungreased 11x7-inch (2-quart) baking dish, place half of the eggplant, overlapping slices slightly. Spoon half of the pasta sauce over eggplant. Sprinkle with 1 cup of the mozzarella. Repeat with remaining eggplant, pasta sauce and mozzarella.

4 Bake uncovered about 25 minutes or until sauce is bubbly, cheese is light brown and eggplant is still slightly firm but can be easily pierced with fork.

1 Serving Calories 360; Total Fat 22g (Saturated Fat 7g, Trans Fat 0g); Cholesterol 60mg; Sodium 690mg; Total Carbohydrate 24g (Dietary Fiber 7g); Protein 16g **Carbohydrate Choices:** 1½

EGGPLANT-OLIVE PARMIGIANA: Prepare as directed—except stir ½ cup sliced pitted imported Italian black olives into pasta sauce before spooning over eggplant in Step 3.

EGGPLANT-RAVIOLI PARMIGIANA: Cook 1 bag (25 oz) frozen cheese-filled ravioli as directed on package; drain and keep warm. Prepare eggplant as directed—except arrange half of cooked ravioli over eggplant in Step 3. Spoon half of pasta sauce over ravioli. Sprinkle with 1 cup of the mozzarella cheese. Repeat with remaining eggplant, ravioli, sauce and cheese. Bake as directed.

PREPARING EGGPLANT PARMIGIANA

Dip eggplant slices in egg mixture; coat with crumb mixture.

Cook half of the eggplant at a time, turning once, until light golden brown.

Place half of the eggplant in dish, overlapping slightly.

Moroccan-Inspired
Sheet-Pan Veggie Dinner

Yummy Rice Bowls
with Kimchi Vinaigrette

404

Bell Peppers and
Burrata over Quinoa

Moroccan-Inspired Sheet-Pan Veggie Dinner

Ras el hanout is a Moroccan spice blend that's warm and pungent but not hot. Shop owners each stir up their own blend, which may include up to 50 ingredients. Moroccans love it because it provides a nice seasoning blend of many ingredients while only having to measure one! Store it in a covered small jar with your other spices up to 3 months. Use as a meat rub and in marinades, soups and stews; mix with softened butter to brush on fish or with melted butter to season popcorn.

PREP 25 Minutes **TOTAL** 50 Minutes •
4 servings (1 cup each)

RAS EL HANOUT

- 1 teaspoon salt
- 1 teaspoon ground coriander
- 1 teaspoon ground turmeric
- 1 teaspoon ground cardamom
- ½ teaspoon ground cloves
- ¼ teaspoon ground nutmeg
- ½ teaspoon ground cinnamon
- ½ teaspoon pepper
- ¼ teaspoon ground allspice
- ¼ teaspoon ground ginger
- ¼ teaspoon ground cumin
- ¼ teaspoon paprika

VEGETABLES

- ¾ teaspoon salt
- ½ teaspoon pepper
- 3 tablespoons olive oil
- 2 cups bite-size fresh cauliflower florets (from 10-oz bag)
- 4 medium carrots, cut into ¾-inch pieces
- 1 large red bell pepper, chopped (about 1 cup)
- 1 small red onion, cut in wedges (about ½ cup)
- 1 can (15 oz) chick peas (garbanzo beans), rinsed, drained

TOPPINGS

- ¼ cup halved pitted green olives (from 6-oz jar)
- ½ cup crumbled feta cheese
- 1 red jalapeño chile, seeded if desired, thinly sliced (about 2 tablespoons)
- 2 tablespoons chopped fresh cilantro
  Lemon wedges, if desired

1 Heat oven to 425°F. Spray 18x13-inch half-sheet pan with cooking spray.

2 In small bowl, mix all ras el hanout ingredients. Measure 1 teaspoon into large bowl; reserve remaining ras el hanout for garnish, if desired, and for other uses.

3 Add ¾ teaspoon salt, ½ teaspoon pepper and the oil to bowl with ras el hanout; mix well. Add cauliflower, carrots, bell pepper and onion to bowl; toss until evenly coated. Spread vegetable mixture in single layer on pan. Roast uncovered 20 minutes.

4 Stir chick peas into vegetables in pan. Roast uncovered 8 to 12 minutes longer or until vegetables are tender. Transfer vegetable mixture to serving bowl;

top with olives, cheese, jalapeño and cilantro. Sprinkle with additional seasoning. Serve with lemon wedges.

1 Serving Calories 330; Total Fat 18g (Saturated Fat 4.5g, Trans Fat 0g); Cholesterol 15mg; Sodium 1580mg; Total Carbohydrate 31g (Dietary Fiber 9g); Protein 10g **Carbohydrate Choices:** 2

MOROCCAN-INSPIRED SHEET-PAN VEGGIE DINNER WITH CHICKEN: Prepare as directed—except in Step 3, after spreading vegetables on pan, in same bowl used for vegetables add additional ½ teaspoon ras el hanout, ½ teaspoon salt and 1 tablespoon olive oil; mix well. Add 2 (8 oz each) boneless skinless chicken breasts; turn to coat. Push some of the vegetables aside to make room on pan for chicken in single layer. Continue as directed in Steps 3 and 4 until juice of chicken is clear when center of thickest part is cut and instant-read meat thermometer in center reads at least 165°F.

FAST

Yummy Rice Bowls with Kimchi Vinaigrette

This tasty kimchi vinaigrette is made with some of the kimchi pickling juice from the jar. It adds a flavorful punch in other dishes, too, like when drizzled over cooked eggs or stirred into sauces and soups.

PREP 30 Minutes TOTAL 30 Minutes • **4 servings**

KIMCHI VINAIGRETTE

- 3 tablespoons kimchi pickling juice (from 24-oz jar)
- 1 tablespoon soy sauce
- 1 tablespoon lime juice
- 1 tablespoon toasted sesame oil
- 1 tablespoon gochujang (Korean chile paste)
- 1 teaspoon finely chopped fresh gingerroot
- 1 teaspoon honey
- ¼ cup vegetable oil

BOWLS

- 4 cups chopped romaine lettuce
- 2 cups shredded cooked chicken
- 4 cups warm cooked short-grain brown rice (page 224)

- 1 medium carrot, shredded (1 cup)
- 1 medium red bell pepper, cut into thin strips
- ¼ cup thinly sliced radishes
- 1 cup thinly sliced kimchi, drained and patted dry (for homemade kimchi, see page 466)
  Gochujang Mayonnaise (page 456)
- 2 green onions, cut diagonally into thin slices
- ¼ cup chopped fresh cilantro
  Cubed avocado, if desired

1 In medium bowl, beat all vinaigrette ingredients except vegetable oil using whisk. Slowly beat in vegetable oil. Measure ⅓ cup of the vinaigrette in measuring cup; set aside.

2 Add romaine to remaining vinaigrette in bowl; toss to coat. Divide romaine among 4 bowls. Add reserved ⅓ cup vinaigrette and chicken to same bowl; toss to coat.

3 Divide rice among 4 bowls of romaine. Top with chicken mixture, carrots, bell pepper, radishes and kimchi. Drizzle with gochujang mayonnaise. Sprinkle with green onions, cilantro and avocado.

1 Serving Calories 800; Total Fat 47g (Saturated Fat 8g, Trans Fat 0.5g); Cholesterol 70mg; Sodium 1850mg; Total Carbohydrate 67g (Dietary Fiber 6g); Protein 28g **Carbohydrate Choices:** 4½

CALORIE SMART • GLUTEN FREE • VEGETARIAN

Bell Peppers and Burrata over Quinoa

Burrata cheese is a cow's milk cheese with a soft exterior and creamy interior. It is sold in various sizes of round balls and is usually packed in water. For this recipe, use larger balls of burrata, if possible, so that each person gets some of the creamy, cheesy goodness when you spoon the cheese over the quinoa and veggies.

PREP 30 Minutes TOTAL 40 Minutes •
6 servings (about 1 cup quinoa, vegetables and cheese each)

SAVORY THYME QUINOA

- 2 cups water
- 1 cup uncooked quinoa, rinsed, well drained
- ½ teaspoon salt
- ½ teaspoon dried thyme leaves
- 2 cloves garlic, finely chopped

PEPPERS AND BURRATA

- 1 bag (1 lb) mini bell peppers, halved lengthwise, seeded

- 2 cups lightly-packed fresh baby arugula or baby spinach leaves
- 1 container (8 oz) fresh burrata cheese (2 balls), drained
- 1 tablespoon olive oil
- ¼ teaspoon salt
- ¼ teaspoon coarse ground black pepper
- 3 tablespoons sliced kalamata olives (from a 6.7-oz jar)
- 2 tablespoons chopped fresh chives

1 Heat oven to 450°F.

2 In 2-quart saucepan, mix all quinoa ingredients. Heat to boiling; reduce heat. Cover; simmer 15 minutes or until quinoa is tender.

3 Meanwhile, line 15x10x1-inch pan with cooking parchment paper or foil. Place bell peppers in single layer on pan. Roast 12 to 17 minutes or until tender and slightly charred. Stir in arugula until slightly wilted.

4 Spoon quinoa into heatproof shallow serving bowl. Arrange pepper mixture over quinoa. Dollop large spoonfuls of cheese evenly onto peppers and quinoa. Drizzle with olive oil; sprinkle with salt and pepper. Top with olives and chives. Serve warm or at room temperature.

1 Serving Calories 270; Total Fat 14g (Saturated Fat 7g, Trans Fat 0g); Cholesterol 35mg; Sodium 600mg; Total Carbohydrate 24g (Dietary Fiber 3g); Protein 13g **Carbohydrate Choices:** 1½

Soy Foods

Soy foods are made from soybeans, which are legumes. High-protein plant powerhouses, soy-based foods can replace meat and poultry protein sources, helping to reduce the amount of saturated fat and dietary cholesterol in your diet. Here are a few of the most popular soy-based foods: Try Tofu Stir-Fry with Black Bean Sauce (page 409).

Edamame

Immature soybeans that are either sold whole in the pods or shelled. The pods are inedible, but the soybeans can be cooked in them before the pods are removed. Great for snacking, salads, casseroles, soups and stir-fries.

Miso

Fermented bean paste; a basic flavoring in Japanese cooking. There are many different colors and flavors, ranging from sweet to salty. Use lighter versions in mild soups or sauces, darker versions in highly flavored dishes. Found in Japanese markets and natural food stores. Refrigerate in airtight container up to 1 year.

Soymilk

Available refrigerated or unrefrigerated in aseptic cartons and as soymilk powder. Varieties include regular and light versions in plain, chocolate and vanilla. Once opened, refrigerate all soymilk; use within 5 days. Store soymilk powder in refrigerator or freezer.

Soy Protein Powder

Dissolves easily, so it can be added easily to shakes or smoothies or stirred into hot cereal for added nutrition

Soy Yogurt

Dairy free; some brands are vegan. Available flavors include plain, vanilla and fruit flavors.

Soybean Oil

Clean taste. Low in saturated fat, high in omega-3 fatty acids. Many cooking oils sold as "vegetable oil" are made from soybeans, but not all. Read ingredient list to be sure.

Tamari

Similar to but thicker than soy sauce; unique, mellow flavor. Often made without wheat, making it a great gluten-free substitute for soy sauce

Tempeh

Fermented cooked soybeans formed into dense, chewy cakes with nutty, yeasty flavor; use as a meat substitute. Holds shape when cooked, so it's great for veggie burgers; when crumbled, great in casseroles. Available fresh and frozen. Refrigerate fresh up to 2 weeks; freeze up to 3 months.

Tofu

Soybeans are soaked, cooked and ground, then mixed with a curdling ingredient. The resulting curds are pressed into cakes. Firmness depends on the amount of whey liquid extracted. Tofu is very mild in flavor and can take on flavors of the other ingredients it is cooked with. Three main types available: **Extra-Firm or Firm Tofu:** Highest in protein, fat and calcium; solid dense form that holds its shape. Use in casseroles, stews, soups, sandwiches, salads, stir-fries and grilling. **Soft Tofu:** Soft texture; doesn't hold its shape. Best used in dips, dressings, desserts, sauces, smoothies and spreads. **Silken Tofu:** Creamy, smooth, custard-like texture. Use in dips, dressings, desserts, sauces, smoothies and spreads. See also Learn to Prepare Tofu, page 408.

Soy Milk

Chocolate Soy Milk

Soybean Oil

Soy Sauce

Tamari

Soy Yogurt

Soy Mayonnaise

Soy Cheeses

Chocolate Tofu Pudding

Edamame (Pods and Shelled)

Flax Tempeh

Tempeh

Vegetable Tempeh

Silken Tofu

Firm Tofu

Red Miso

White Miso

Chocolate Soy Pudding

Soy Ice Cream (Strawberry)

Textured Soy Protein

Textured Soy Crumbles

Brown Miso

Soy Flour

Baked Tofu Italian

Soynut Butter

Baked Tofu Teriyaki

Soy Nuts

407

LEARN TO PREPARE TOFU

Tofu is made from soybeans processed into a solid cake. Sometimes referred to as bean curd, this versatile food absorbs flavors easily and can be used as a healthful source of protein in meals. Tofu is readily available in grocery stores—look for it refrigerated in the produce section, as it needs to be kept cold. Cooking tofu is not difficult, but there are some tips that will help make the process easy and result in great-tasting tofu recipes. Tofu Stir-Fry with Black Bean Sauce (right) is a great recipe to try tofu.

Tofu Storage

Tofu is perishable, so check the sell-by date on the package. If unopened, it will keep in the refrigerator up to 5 days. Once opened, use within 2 days. Store covered with water; change the water daily. Tofu can be frozen for up to 5 months. Freeze in original container or wrap tightly in plastic wrap. Frozen tofu will have a coarser texture than fresh tofu, as the water trapped inside it expands. Once thawed, it can be used as for fresh tofu.

Preparation Tips

- For use in most cooking, extra-firm and firm tofu will be the best types.

- Most tofu is packaged in water and is like a sponge, so it needs to be drained well before cooking. For extra-firm or firm tofu, on a plate or shallow bowl, press the tofu between layers of paper towels or kitchen towels; top with a weight such as a heavy skillet or another plate. Let it stand for at least 1 hour.

- Determine how to cut the tofu according to what you are making or what the recipe specifies. Cubes work well in stir-fries, soups and stews; cut into larger pieces or slices for frying, baking and grilling.

- To add flavor, place the tofu pieces in a container and pour a marinade over them. Cover and place in the refrigerator at least 1 hour or overnight to marinate.

- Tofu can also be frozen in a marinade. When ready to cook, just thaw in the refrigerator and cook as desired. Tofu becomes a bit firmer after freezing.

To Fry Tofu

For firm tofu with dry, firm texture and crispy edges:

1 Heat 1 tablespoon vegetable or olive oil in nonstick skillet over medium heat.

2 If marinated, drain tofu and blot dry. If not marinated, season both sides of tofu with salt and pepper or other desired seasonings.

3 Cook tofu 4 to 5 minutes, turning once, until light golden brown on both sides.

To Bake Tofu

For tofu with a very dry texture:

1 Heat oven to 350°F. Lightly spray shallow baking pan with cooking spray or grease lightly with vegetable shortening.

2 If marinated, drain tofu and blot dry. If not marinated, season both sides of tofu with salt and pepper or other desired seasonings. Place tofu in baking pan.

3 Bake 30 to 35 minutes, or until thoroughly heated and slightly golden brown.

PREPARING FIRM OR EXTRA-FIRM TOFU

Press tofu between layers of paper towels; top with weight, such as a heavy skillet or plate, to remove excess moisture.

Stir Fry Cook and stir 4 to 5 minutes or until light golden brown on all sides.

Bake Place tofu on pan; season. Bake until thoroughly heated and slightly golden brown.

Tofu Stir-Fry with Black Bean Sauce

Black bean sauce is robust in flavor, thin and salty. It is made from fermented black beans, garlic and often star anise. Look for it with other international ingredients in larger grocery stores and Asian markets.

PREP 25 Minutes **TOTAL** 25 Minutes •
5 servings (1 cup tofu and 1 cup rice each)

- 1 tablespoon olive oil
- 1 medium onion, thinly sliced (1 cup)
- 4 cups chopped fresh broccoli (from large head)
- 1 medium red bell pepper, cut vertically into ½-inch slices, then cut crosswise in half (1 cup)
- ⅓ cup gluten-free black bean garlic sauce (from 7-oz jar)
- 2 tablespoons gluten-free soy sauce

- 1 tablespoon chili garlic sauce (from 8-oz jar)
- 1 package (12 to 14 oz) firm lite tofu, drained, cut into ¾-inch cubes
- ⅓ cup chopped fresh cilantro
- 5 cups hot cooked brown basmati rice (page 224)
- ¼ cup gluten-free honey-roasted or regular sunflower nuts

1 In wok or 12-inch skillet, heat oil over medium-high heat. Cook onion in oil about 2 minutes, stirring occasionally, or until crisp-tender. Add broccoli and bell pepper. Cook and stir about 2 minutes or until almost crisp-tender.

2 In small bowl, mix black bean sauce, soy sauce and chili garlic sauce. Stir into vegetable mixture; add tofu. Cook and stir 2 to 3 minutes or until thoroughly heated. Stir in cilantro. Serve over rice. Sprinkle with nuts.

1 Serving Calories 380; Total Fat 10g (Saturated Fat 1.5g, Trans Fat 0g); Cholesterol 0mg; Sodium 830mg; Total Carbohydrate 58g (Dietary Fiber 7g); Protein 14g **Carbohydrate Choices:** 4

Tofu Stir-Fry with Black Bean Sauce

409

Tempeh Stir-Fry with Yogurt Peanut Sauce

Tempeh (also spelled tempe, and pronounced TEHM-pay) is a fermented, high-protein soybean cake with a chewy texture and slightly nutty flavor. If you can't find it in your supermarket (sometimes it's sold in the freezer case with other vegetarian foods), check a co-op or natural foods store.

PREP 40 Minutes **TOTAL** 40 Minutes •
4 servings (about 1¼ cups stir-fry and ½ cup rice each)

¼ cup creamy peanut butter	4 medium carrots, cut into 2x¼x¼-inch strips (2 cups)
¼ cup vanilla low-fat yogurt	12 oz fresh green beans, trimmed, cut in half crosswise (2 cups)
3 tablespoons gluten-free teriyaki marinade (from 12-oz bottle)	¼ cup water
1 tablespoon honey	1 medium red bell pepper, cut into thin bite-size strips (1 cup)
2 tablespoons vegetable oil	
1 package (8 oz) gluten-free tempeh, cut into 2x¼x¼-inch strips	2 cups hot cooked white or brown rice (page 224)
1 medium onion, cut into thin wedges	¼ cup chopped fresh cilantro

1 In small bowl, beat peanut butter, yogurt, teriyaki marinade and honey with whisk until smooth; set aside.

2 In wok or 12-inch skillet, heat 1 tablespoon of the oil over medium heat. Cook tempeh in oil 5 to 6 minutes, turning frequently, or until light golden brown. Remove tempeh to plate or bowl; cover to keep warm.

3 In same skillet, heat remaining 1 tablespoon oil over medium heat. Cook onion in oil 1 minute, stirring occasionally. Stir in carrots, green beans and water. Cover; cook 5 minutes. Stir in bell pepper. Cook 2 to 3 minutes, stirring occasionally, or until vegetables are crisp-tender.

4 Stir in tempeh and reserved peanut butter mixture until well mixed. Cook 1 to 2 minutes, stirring occasionally, until hot. Serve over rice. Sprinkle with cilantro.

1 Serving Calories 510; Total Fat 22g (Saturated Fat 4.5g, Trans Fat 0g); Cholesterol 0mg; Sodium 650mg; Total Carbohydrate 55g (Dietary Fiber 8g); Protein 21g **Carbohydrate Choices:** 3½

TEMPEH STIR-FRY WITH NOODLES: Substitute 8 oz gluten-free angel hair (capellini) pasta, cooked and drained, for the rice. Sprinkle each serving with chopped peanuts.

One-Pot Miso Chicken Udon

Patting the chicken dry before adding it to the hot Dutch oven not only helps it brown nicely, but will help it release more easily from the bottom of the pan.

PREP 45 Minutes **TOTAL** 45 Minutes •
6 servings (1⅓ cups each)

4 tablespoons butter	1 carton (32 oz) reduced-sodium chicken broth (4 cups; for homemade broth, see page 153)
1 package (20 oz) boneless skinless chicken thighs, cut into 1-inch cubes	
8 oz shiitake mushrooms, stems removed, thinly sliced	1 cup coarsely shredded carrots
1 medium red bell pepper, cut into thin strips	2 tablespoons white miso
	2 tablespoons reduced-sodium soy sauce
6 green onions, cut diagonally into thin slices, whites and greens separated	1 package (10 oz) uncooked Japanese udon noodles
2 cloves garlic, finely chopped	4 cups lightly-packed fresh baby spinach leaves (from 10-oz container)
1 teaspoon finely chopped gingerroot	2 teaspoons rice vinegar

1 In 5-quart Dutch oven, heat 2 tablespoons of the butter over medium-high heat until melted. Add chicken. Cook 5 to 7 minutes, without stirring, or until browned on bottom. Cook 2 to 4 minutes longer, stirring frequently, until chicken is no longer pink in center. Using slotted spoon, transfer to medium bowl; set aside.

2 Add remaining 2 tablespoons butter to Dutch oven; stir in mushrooms, bell pepper and green onion whites. Cook over medium-high heat 5 to 7 minutes, stirring frequently, or until softened. Stir in garlic and gingerroot; cook 30 seconds longer.

3 Stir in broth, carrots, miso and soy sauce. Heat to boiling over high heat. Stir in chicken and noodles. Heat to boiling; reduce heat. Simmer uncovered 11 to 13 minutes, stirring frequently, or until noodles are cooked through and sauce is thickened. Stir in spinach until wilted; stir in vinegar. Top with green onion greens.

1 Serving Calories 400; Total Fat 14g (Saturated Fat 6g, Trans Fat 0g); Cholesterol 110mg; Sodium 1040mg; Total Carbohydrate 43g (Dietary Fiber 4g); Protein 28g **Carbohydrate Choices:** 3

Kimchi Veggie-Beef Burgers with Sesame Slaw

The mushrooms and carrot can be shredded with a hand grater; if you have a food processor, use the shredding blade to make it extra easy.

PREP 1 Hour **TOTAL** 1 Hour • *4 burgers*

BURGERS

- 4 teaspoons vegetable oil
- 1 package (8 oz) fresh baby portabella mushrooms, shredded
- 1 medium carrot, shredded (1 cup)
- ½ lb ground beef (at least 93% lean)
- ⅓ cup drained kimchi, chopped (for homemade kimchi, see page 466)
- 2 green onions, chopped (2 tablespoons)
- 1 tablespoon soy sauce
- 2 teaspoons sesame oil
- 1 teaspoon grated gingerroot
- 1 egg white

SESAME SLAW

- 2 teaspoons rice vinegar
- 1 teaspoon soy sauce
- ½ teaspoon sugar
- ½ teaspoon sesame oil
- 1 cup coleslaw mix (from 14- to 16-oz bag)
- 3 thin slices red onion, cut into 1-inch strips
- 2 tablespoons chopped fresh cilantro leaves

BUNS AND TOPPINGS

- 4 sesame seed burger buns, split
- ¼ cup Sriracha mayonnaise

1 In 12-inch nonstick skillet, heat 2 teaspoons of the vegetable oil over medium-high heat. Cook mushrooms and carrot uncovered 3 to 5 minutes, stirring frequently, or until softened. Spoon into fine-mesh strainer. With back of spoon, gently press excess liquid from vegetable mixture; discard liquid. In medium bowl, place vegetables; let stand 10 minutes.

2 Add remaining burger ingredients except remaining 2 teaspoons vegetable oil; mix well. Shape into 4 patties, each about 3½ inches in diameter.

3 Wipe skillet with paper towel. Heat remaining 2 teaspoons vegetable oil over medium heat. Cook patties 10 to 12 minutes, gently turning twice, until instant-read meat thermometer inserted in center of the patties reads 165°F.

4 Meanwhile, in small bowl, mix rice vinegar, 1 teaspoon soy sauce, sugar and ½ teaspoon sesame oil. Add remaining slaw ingredients; toss to coat.

5 On bun bottoms, place patties. Drizzle with Sriracha mayonnaise. Top each patty with ¼ of the slaw mixture; cover with bun tops.

1 Burger Calories 400; Total Fat 24g (Saturated Fat 4.5g, Trans Fat 0g); Cholesterol 40mg; Sodium 670mg; Total Carbohydrate 29g (Dietary Fiber 3g); Protein 18g **Carbohydrate Choices:** 2

Tempeh Stir-Fry with Yogurt Peanut Sauce

411

One-Pot Miso Chicken Udon

Kimchi Veggie-Beef Burgers with Sesame Slaw

Sweet Potato Noodle— Chicken Lo Mein

PREP 45 Minutes **TOTAL** 45 Minutes • *4 servings*

4 teaspoons vegetable oil	¼ cup matchstick carrots (from 10-oz bag)
1 lb boneless skinless chicken breasts, cut in ¾-inch pieces	2 teaspoons finely chopped gingerroot
1½ teaspoons toasted sesame oil	2 cloves garlic, finely chopped
¼ teaspoon salt	3 tablespoons gluten-free soy sauce
4 cups fresh sweet potato spirals (1 lb)	1 teaspoon packed brown sugar
1 medium red bell pepper, thinly sliced	⅛ teaspoon crushed red pepper flakes
4 green onions, chopped (¼ cup)	1 teaspoon sesame seed
½ cup snow pea pods, diagonally cut in half	

1 In 12-inch nonstick skillet, heat 2 teaspoons of the vegetable oil over medium-high heat. Coat chicken with ½ teaspoon of the sesame oil and the salt; add to skillet. Cook 6 to 8 minutes, stirring occasionally, or until chicken is no longer pink in center. Transfer to plate using slotted spoon.

2 In same skillet, add remaining 2 teaspoons vegetable oil; heat over medium heat. Add sweet potatoes, bell pepper and green onions. Cover; cook 6 to 7 minutes, stirring occasionally, or until vegetables are crisp-tender. Add snow peas, carrots and chicken. Cover; cook 2 minutes. Push chicken and vegetables to edge of skillet; add gingerroot and garlic in center of skillet. Cook 1 to 2 minutes, stirring frequently, or until softened. Stir in soy sauce, brown sugar, remaining teaspoon sesame oil and the pepper flakes. Cook 1 to 2 minutes, stirring frequently, or until heated through. Garnish with sesame seed.

1 Serving Calories 350; Total Fat 11g (Saturated Fat 2g, Trans Fat 0g); Cholesterol 70mg; Sodium 950mg; Total Carbohydrate 33g (Dietary Fiber 5g); Protein 29g **Carbohydrate Choices:** 2

Taco Zucchini Noodle and Beef Skillet

To prevent this dish from being watery, squeeze excess water from the zucchini spirals: place them in a clean kitchen towel and roll up the towel while pressing on it to do the trick.

PREP 25 Minutes **TOTAL** 25 Minutes • *6 servings*

1 lb ground beef (at least 90% lean)	1 package (1 oz) original taco seasoning mix (for homemade seasoning, see page 454)
1 medium onion, chopped	¼ teaspoon salt
1 clove garlic, finely chopped	¼ teaspoon crushed red pepper flakes
1 tablespoon vegetable oil	1½ cups shredded cheddar cheese (6 oz)
6 cups fresh zucchini spirals, squeezed dry (1 lb)	1 tablespoon coarsely chopped fresh cilantro
1 can (14.5 oz) fire-roasted diced tomatoes, drained	

1 In 12-inch nonstick skillet, cook beef, onions and garlic uncovered over medium-high heat 5 to 7 minutes, stirring occasionally, or until no pink remains in beef. Remove to medium bowl; cover to keep warm. Wipe out skillet.

2 Add oil to skillet and heat over medium heat. Cook zucchini in oil uncovered 2 minutes, turning frequently with tongs. Add beef mixture and remaining ingredients except cheese and cilantro; stir to completely coat noodles. Cook uncovered 1 to 2 minutes, stirring occasionally, or until heated through. Stir in 1 cup of the cheese. Top with remaining ½ cup cheese and the cilantro. Serve immediately.

1 Serving Calories 310; Total Fat 18g (Saturated Fat 8g, Trans Fat 0g); Cholesterol 75mg; Sodium 720mg; Total Carbohydrate 12g (Dietary Fiber 2g); Protein 23g **Carbohydrate Choices:** 1

Sweet Potato Noodle–Chicken Lo Mein

Taco Zucchini Noodle and Beef Skillet

Pork Carnitas Rice Bowls

Pork Carnitas Rice Bowls

We used a hot serrano chile in the mango salsa, but if you would like milder heat, you can use a jalapeño chile or leave the chile out altogether.

PREP 1 Hour **TOTAL** 4 Hours 20 Minutes • *8 bowls*

PORK CARNITAS

- 1 teaspoon ground cumin
- ½ teaspoon coarse (kosher or sea) salt
- ½ teaspoon chili powder
- 1 boneless pork shoulder (2 lb), trimmed of fat, cut in 4 pieces
- 1 medium onion, chopped (1 cup)
- 3 cloves garlic, finely chopped
- ⅓ cup water
- 1 tablespoon fresh lime juice

MANGO SALSA

- 1 large ripe mango, seed removed, peeled and chopped (about 1½ cups)
- 1 small red onion, chopped (½ cup)
- ¼ cup chopped fresh cilantro
- 1 medium serrano chile, seeded, finely chopped
- 1 tablespoon fresh lime juice
- ¼ teaspoon salt

CILANTRO RICE

- 3 cups water
- 2 cups uncooked regular long-grain white rice
- ¾ teaspoon salt
- ¼ cup finely chopped fresh cilantro
- 2 tablespoons fresh lime juice
- 1 tablespoon olive oil

BOWLS

- 1 can (15 oz) black beans, rinsed, drained
- 1 cup thinly sliced radishes
- 2 medium avocados, pitted, peeled and chopped
  Lime wedges

1 Spray 4- or 5-quart slow cooker insert with cooking spray. In slow cooker, mix all pork carnitas ingredients except lime juice. Cover; cook on High heat setting 4 to 5 hours, or Low heat setting 7 to 8 hours or until pork is very tender. Skim fat from cooking liquid; reserve ¼ cup. Transfer pork to cutting board; shred with two forks. Return to slow cooker; stir in 1 tablespoon lime juice.

2 Meanwhile, in medium bowl, stir together mango salsa ingredients. Cover; refrigerate until ready to serve.

3 About 30 minutes before serving, in 3-quart saucepan, heat water, rice and ¾ teaspoon salt to boiling over medium-high heat; reduce heat to low. Cover; cook 15 to 18 minutes or until water is absorbed and rice is tender.

4 In small bowl, stir together ¼ cup cilantro, 2 tablespoons lime juice and olive oil. Stir into cooked rice; fluff with fork.

5 In medium microwavable bowl, place black beans. Add reserved ¼ cup cooking liquid; cover with plastic wrap. Microwave on High 1 to 2 minutes or until hot.

6 Divide cilantro rice among 8 serving bowls; top with pork, mango salsa, beans, radishes and avocado. Serve with lime wedges.

1 Bowl Calories 570; Total Fat 21g (Saturated Fat 6g, Trans Fat 0g); Cholesterol 70mg; Sodium 870mg; Total Carbohydrate 63g (Dietary Fiber 6g); Protein 31g **Carbohydrate Choices:** 4

Skillet Chicken and Riced Cauliflower

Resist the urge to move the chicken after adding it to the oil. To get nice browning, you have to let it cook without moving for a few minutes.

PREP 35 Minutes **TOTAL** 35 Minutes •
4 servings (1¾ cups each)

- ¼ cup olive oil
- 1 package (16 oz) boneless skinless chicken breasts, cut into 1-inch pieces
- 1 teaspoon salt
- ½ teaspoon dried oregano leaves
- ¼ teaspoon crushed red pepper flakes
- 1 bag (12 oz) frozen riced cauliflower
- 1 small red onion, chopped (½ cup)
- 1 medium red bell pepper, seeded and chopped
- 2 cloves garlic, finely chopped
- 1 cup halved cherry tomatoes
- ¼ cup halved pitted kalamata olives
- 4 oz feta cheese, crumbled (1 cup)
- 2 tablespoons finely chopped fresh Italian (flat-leaf) parsley

1 In 12-inch skillet, heat oil over medium-high heat. Add chicken in single layer; sprinkle with salt, oregano and pepper flakes. Cook without stirring 4 minutes.

2 Stir in frozen cauliflower. Cover; cook over medium heat 7 minutes, stirring frequently. Stir in onion, bell pepper and garlic. Cook uncovered 5 to 7 minutes, stirring occasionally, or until chicken is no longer pink in center and vegetables are tender. Stir in tomatoes and olives. Top with cheese and parsley. Serve immediately.

1 Serving Calories 400; Total Fat 24g (Saturated Fat 7g, Trans Fat 0g); Cholesterol 95mg; Sodium 1000mg; Total Carbohydrate 12g (Dietary Fiber 3g); Protein 32g **Carbohydrate Choices:** 1

CHICKEN AND RICED CAULIFLOWER SALAD:

Prepare as directed—except cool cooked mixture in skillet 20 minutes. Spoon into food storage container. Cover and refrigerate at least 2 hours or until chilled. Serve cold. Use within 3 to 4 days.

Easy Pork Stir-Fry

Cook the pork undisturbed long enough and it will release easily from the bottom of the pan without sticking. If you like, serve this stir-fry with hot cooked rice.

PREP 35 Minutes **TOTAL** 35 Minutes • *4 servings*

- ¾ cup gluten-free chicken broth (for homemade broth, see page 153)
- 2 tablespoons cornstarch
- 2 tablespoons gluten-free soy sauce
- 1 tablespoon rice vinegar
- 1 tablespoon packed brown sugar
- 2 tablespoons vegetable oil
- 1 lb pork tenderloin, cut crosswise into ½-inch-thick slices, then lengthwise in thirds
- 1 tablespoon chile garlic sauce (from 8-oz jar)
- 1 teaspoon finely chopped gingerroot
- 1 cup thinly sliced shiitake mushroom caps
- 1 cup thinly sliced bok choy
- 1 cup shredded red cabbage
- 1 teaspoon sesame seed, toasted (see page 28)

SERVING SUGGESTIONS, IF DESIRED

Hot cooked white rice (page 224)
Lime wedges
Sliced green onions
Fresh cilantro sprigs

1   In medium bowl, mix broth, cornstarch, soy sauce, vinegar and brown sugar until smooth; set aside.

2   In 12-inch nonstick skillet or wok, heat 1 tablespoon of the oil over medium-high heat. Swirl pan to coat sides with oil; add pork in a single layer. Cook 6 to 8 minutes, turning once after about 3 minutes, or until tender. Add chile garlic sauce and gingerroot; cook 30 to 60 seconds, stirring frequently, or until softened. Remove pork mixture to plate or bowl; cover and keep warm.

3   Wipe out skillet. Add remaining 1 tablespoon oil to skillet; heat over medium-high heat. Add mushrooms and bok choy. Cook 5 to 7 minutes, stirring frequently, or until mushrooms are tender and browned. Add red cabbage. Cook 30 to 60 seconds longer or until softened.

4   Return pork mixture to skillet. Stir broth mixture; add to pork and vegetables in skillet. Heat to boiling. Cook and stir 1 to 2 minutes or until sauce is thickened. Stir in sesame seed. Serve with rice, lime wedges, green onions and cilantro.

1 Serving Calories 270; Total Fat 13g (Saturated Fat 3g, Trans Fat 0g); Cholesterol 70mg; Sodium 720mg; Total Carbohydrate 11g (Dietary Fiber 1g); Protein 27g **Carbohydrate Choices:** 1

Sheet-Pan Kielbasa, Leek and Potato Dinner

Leeks can trap dirt in between their layers as they grow, so make sure to rinse and drain them thoroughly.

PREP 25 Minutes **TOTAL** 50 Minutes •
4 servings (2¼ cups each, with 3 tablespoons sauce)

- ¼ cup butter, melted
- 1 teaspoon salt
- 1½ lb Yukon Gold potatoes, cut into 1-inch pieces
- 1 package (14 oz) gluten-free kielbasa sausage, cut into 1-inch slices
- 4 cups fresh broccoli or cauliflower florets (12-oz bag)
- 2 small leeks, white and light green parts, thinly sliced, rinsed and drained (about 2 cups)
- 1 cup Gruyère cheese, shredded (4 oz)
- 2 tablespoons finely chopped parsley
- ¾ cup gluten-free sour cream
- 1 tablespoon whole-grain Dijon mustard

1   Heat oven to 425°F. Spray 15x10x1-inch pan with cooking spray.

2   In large bowl, mix 2 tablespoons of the butter and ½ teaspoon of the salt. Add potatoes; toss to coat. Place potatoes in single layer on pan. Roast 18 to 20 minutes or until tender when pierced with knife. Remove from oven; stir.

3   Add kielbasa to potatoes in pan. In same large bowl, mix 1 tablespoon of the melted butter, the broccoli and ¼ teaspoon of the salt; add to pan. In same large bowl, mix remaining 1 tablespoon melted butter, the leeks and remaining ¼ teaspoon salt. Sprinkle leeks over potatoes and kielbasa.

4   Roast 18 to 20 minutes or until leeks are tender, potatoes are browned and kielbasa is heated through. Stir to mix. Sprinkle with cheese. Roast about 2 minutes longer or until cheese is melted. Sprinkle with parsley.

5   Meanwhile, in small bowl, mix sour cream and mustard. Serve kielbasa mixture with sour cream mixture.

1 Serving Calories 720; Total Fat 57g (Saturated Fat 27g, Trans Fat 2g); Cholesterol 145mg; Sodium 1950mg; Total Carbohydrate 27g (Dietary Fiber 4g); Protein 25g **Carbohydrate Choices:** 2

Indian-Inspired Spiced Salmon Dinner

Garam masala is a flavor-packed blend of up to 12 ground dry-roasted spices. It originated in India and usually contains black pepper, cinnamon, cloves, coriander, cumin, cardamon, dried chiles, fennel, mace and nutmeg. Find it with the other spices in your grocery store.

PREP 20 Minutes **TOTAL** 1 Hour • *4 servings*

- ⅓ cup vegetable oil
- 1 tablespoon garam masala
- 2 teaspoons grated gingerroot
- 1 teaspoon kosher (coarse) salt
- 1 teaspoon paprika
- ¼ teaspoon crushed red pepper flakes
- 3 cloves garlic, finely chopped
- ½ head cauliflower, cut into 1-inch florets (2½ cups)
- 1½ cups ready-to-eat baby-cut carrots, cut in half lengthwise
- ½ large red onion, cut into 1-inch wedges
- 1 can (15.5 oz) chick peas (garbanzo beans), rinsed, drained
- 4 skin-on salmon fillets (4 oz each)
- 2 tablespoons chopped fresh cilantro

1 Heat oven to 425°F. Spray 18x13-inch half-sheet pan with cooking spray. In small bowl, mix oil, garam masala, gingerroot, salt, paprika, pepper flakes and garlic with whisk.

2 In large resealable food-storage plastic bag, place cauliflower, carrots, red onion and chick peas. Add 3 tablespoons of the oil mixture to vegetables in bag. Seal bag; rotate to coat vegetables. Remove vegetables from bag and place them in single layer on sheet pan.

3 Roast uncovered 20 minutes. Place salmon, skin side down, on sheet pan with vegetables. Brush remaining oil mixture over salmon fillets.

4 Roast 15 to 18 minutes longer or until salmon flakes easily and vegetables are tender. Sprinkle with cilantro.

1 Serving Calories 500; Total Fat 29g (Saturated Fat 5g, Trans Fat 0g); Cholesterol 65mg; Sodium 840mg; Total Carbohydrate 27g (Dietary Fiber 8g); Protein 32g **Carbohydrate Choices:** 2

Sheet-Pan Kielbasa, Leek and Potato Dinner

Indian-Inspired Spiced Salmon Dinner

415

Chorizo, White Bean and Kale Pot Pie

Loaded Tuna Wraps

Chorizo, White Bean and Kale Pot Pie

In a hurry? Use shredded carrots in bags or from the salad bar of your favorite grocery store to cut down on the prep time.

PREP 30 Minutes TOTAL 1 Hour 15 Minutes • *6 servings*

¾ lb bulk chorizo sausage	¼ teaspoon pepper
2 teaspoons vegetable oil	1 cup finely chopped fresh kale leaves
1 medium carrot, shredded (1 cup)	2 cans (15 oz each) cannellini beans, rinsed, drained
1 small onion, chopped (½ cup)	1 bag (24 oz) refrigerated mashed potatoes
2 cloves garlic, finely chopped	3 tablespoons grated Parmesan cheese
¼ cup all-purpose flour	1 teaspoon Italian seasoning
1 cup water	
½ cup Alfredo pasta sauce (from 15- to 16-oz jar)	

1 Heat oven to 375°F. Spray 9- or 10-inch deep-dish glass pie plate or shallow 1½-quart casserole with cooking spray.

2 In 12-inch nonstick skillet, cook sausage over medium-high heat, breaking up with spoon, until brown. Transfer sausage from skillet to paper towels to drain. Wipe skillet clean with paper towel. In same skillet, heat oil over medium heat. Add carrot and onion. Cook uncovered about 3 minutes, stirring frequently, or until softened. Add garlic; cook and stir 30 seconds longer.

3 Sprinkle flour over vegetable mixture in skillet; stir in until moistened. Stir in water, Alfredo pasta sauce and pepper. Cook over medium-high heat, stirring occasionally, until mixture boils and thickens. Stir in kale; remove from heat. Cover; let stand 3 minutes or until kale is softened. Stir in beans and cooked sausage. Pour into pie plate.

4 Heat potatoes as directed on bag; stir until smooth. Spoon evenly over bean mixture. In small cup or bowl, stir together cheese and Italian seasoning. Sprinkle over potatoes; swirl lightly into potatoes with back of spoon while spreading potatoes evenly over filling.

5 Bake 30 to 35 minutes or until filling is hot and bubbly and potatoes just begin to brown. Let stand 5 to 10 minutes before serving.

1 Serving Calories 590; Total Fat 31g (Saturated Fat 13g, Trans Fat 0g); Cholesterol 75mg; Sodium 1250mg; Total Carbohydrate 50g (Dietary Fiber 9g); Protein 28g **Carbohydrate Choices:** 3

CALORIE SMART

Loaded Tuna Wraps

PREP 15 Minutes TOTAL 15 Minutes • *2 wraps*

2 (9- or 10-inch) flour tortillas	2 thin slices red onion, separated into rings
¼ cup red pepper hummus (from 10-oz container)	1 can (5 oz) albacore tuna in water, drained, flaked
1 jar (6 to 7 oz) marinated artichoke hearts, drained, coarsely chopped	½ cup lightly-packed baby arugula leaves (from 5-oz container)
½ teaspoon dried dillweed	½ medium yellow bell pepper, cut into thin strips
6 thin slices tomato	2 tablespoons capers, drained, if desired

1 Heat tortillas as directed on package to soften. Spread center of each tortilla with 2 tablespoons hummus, leaving 2-inch border around edge.

2 In small bowl, mix artichokes and dillweed. On each tortilla, layer half of the tomato slices, red onion rings, tuna, artichoke mixture, arugula, bell pepper strips and capers evenly over hummus.

3 Fold bottom edges of tortillas over filling. Fold in sides of tortillas to enclose filling; roll up. Serve immediately.

1 Wrap Calories 280; Total Fat 7g (Saturated Fat 1.5g, Trans Fat 0g); Cholesterol 25mg; Sodium 530mg; Total Carbohydrate 31g (Dietary Fiber 7g); Protein 22g **Carbohydrate Choices:** 2

BETTY CROCKER COOKBOOK

Japanese-Inspired Smoked Salmon Rice Bowls

This veggie-loaded rice bowl packs the flavors of a sushi feast into an easy homemade meal. Make it your own by adding pickled ginger, shredded daikon radish, wasabi and/or strips of nori. Not a fan of salmon? Swap ½ lb fresh or frozen (thawed) medium shrimp, cooked, peeled and deveined, for the salmon.

PREP 30 Minutes **TOTAL** 1 Hour 10 Minutes • *4 servings*

STICKY RICE
- 1¼ cups sushi rice
- 1¾ cups water

EDAMAME
- 1 bag (12 oz) frozen shelled edamame (green soybeans)
- 2 tablespoons water
- 1 tablespoon toasted sesame oil
- ¼ teaspoon salt

RICE BOWL TOPPINGS
- 2 cups matchstick-cut carrots (from 10-oz bag) or shredded carrots
- 1 large red bell pepper, diced (about 1 cup)
- 1 medium avocado, pitted, peeled and sliced
- ¼ cup julienne-cut cucumber (1½x¼x¼ inch)
- 1 package (8 oz) thinly-sliced smoked salmon
- ½ cup Yum Yum Sauce (page 485)
- 2 green onions, diagonally thinly sliced (2 tablespoons)

1 In medium bowl, place rice and enough cold water to cover the rice. Let stand 30 minutes; drain.

2 Spray 2-quart saucepan with cooking spray; add rice and the 1¾ cups water. Heat to boiling; reduce heat. Simmer covered 15 to 20 minutes or until water is absorbed. Remove from heat; let stand covered 10 minutes.

3 Meanwhile, in medium microwavable bowl, place edamame and 2 tablespoons water; cover with plastic wrap. Microwave on High 3 to 5 minutes or until steaming; drain. Stir in sesame oil and salt.

4 Divide rice among 4 serving bowls. Top with edamame, carrots, bell pepper, avocado, cucumber and salmon. Drizzle with Yum Yum Sauce. Sprinkle with green onions.

1 Serving Calories 570; Total Fat 33g (Saturated Fat 6g, Trans Fat 0g); Cholesterol 30mg; Sodium 780mg; Total Carbohydrate 45g (Dietary Fiber 11g); Protein 24g **Carbohydrate Choices:** 3

Japanese-Inspired Smoked Salmon Rice Bowls

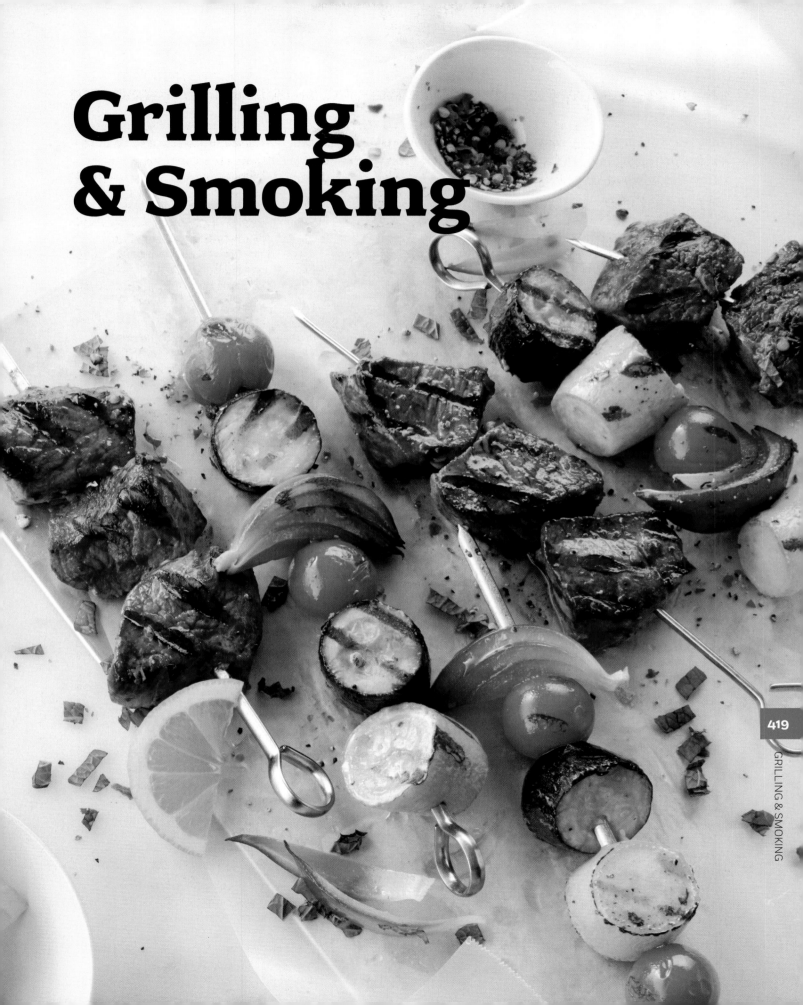

Grilling & Smoking

Grilling Basics

Grilling is a healthful, easy cooking method that also gets high marks for quick cleanup! Beef, poultry, pork and seafood are elevated to star status since grilling gives them smoky flavor and charred edges. And grilling vegetables brings out their sweetness. Here's everything you need to know to become a grill master.

Types of Grills

For **outside grilling**, choose between gas, charcoal and electric grills. For **indoor grilling**, you can use a countertop open electric grill, or a grill pan on your stove-top. The type of grill you choose will depend on your personal needs, space and preferences. No matter which type you choose, follow the manufacturer's directions for best results.

Gas An advantage to using a gas grill is that it heats up in 5 to 10 minutes, making it possible to grill on the spur of the moment. It can be more costly than a charcoal grill, but cleanup is quick and easy. It requires a tank of propane gas as fuel. When the tank is empty, bring it to a nearby gas station or grocery store that sells filled tanks for an exchange.

Charcoal Grilling with charcoal gives foods the iconic flavor and aroma some people prefer. However, it can take close to half an hour for coals to get hot—so you need to plan ahead when making your meals. Charcoal grills can be a cost-friendly option.

Electric Outdoor electric grills are perfect for people living in an apartment or condominium where live fire gas and charcoal grills are prohibited on small decks and balconies. Like gas grills, they are quick to heat and easy to clean. For indoors, choose a countertop electric open grill. While the flavor on these electric grills won't be the same as food grilled outside, the convenience of being able to grill without stepping outside could make this an appealing option. And you can still make grill marks on your food!

Grill Pans Used on your stove-top, grill pans can't replicate the flavor of cooking over an outdoor grill, but they can still cook meats and veggies with crusty, charred edges and grill marks. Because these pans aren't exactly the same as cooking on an outdoor grill, the cooking times will be different. Use the doneness cues from grilling recipes as a guide when cooking on a grill pan, rather than the stated cooking time. Many come with presses for panini and grilled cheese sandwiches, possibly giving you more reasons to choose this option.

All About Coals

STARTING BRIQUETTES

- **Pyramid Style** Place briquettes in firebox, arranging them in a mound like a pyramid. Squirt charcoal lighter fluid over the top and sides of the mound; light following the lighter fluid directions. NEVER USE GASOLINE OR KEROSENE TO START A FIRE. Briquette pyramids can also be lit with electric starters, fire starter gels or paraffin starters. Or look for instant-lighting briquettes that don't require lighter fluid.

- **Charcoal Chimney Starter** An easy-to-use cylindrical canister with a large handle that lights coals quickly and evenly with newspaper rather than lighter fluid. Follow manufacturer's directions for filling the chimney and lighting the newspaper and coals in it. When the coals are ready, carefully turn them out onto the bottom of the firebox, remove the chimney and spread out the hot coals.

WHEN ARE COALS READY?

After lighting briquettes with either method, leave them until they are glowing red (10 to 20 minutes) and mostly covered in gray ash. (After dark, you'll know the coals are ready when they have an even red glow.) Spread coals into a single layer for grilling.

Determine the temperature of the coals by holding the palm of your hand above the grill rack and timing how long you can comfortably keep it there:

2 seconds = high heat
3 seconds = medium-high heat
4 seconds = medium heat
5 seconds = low heat

GRILLING SAUSAGE AND BRATWURST

Uncooked Sausage and Bratwurst: Heat grill to medium-low for direct heat. Place links on grill. Cover grill; cook 15 to 20 minutes, turning occasionally, until no longer pink in center. If flare-ups occur, see page 422.

Uncooked sausage and bratwurst can also be cooked in cider, beer or water and then browned on the grill, adding flavor and cutting down on flare-ups. For 4 bratwurst, heat 1½ cups cider, beer or water to boiling in 2-quart saucepan. Add links; reduce heat. Cover and simmer 15 minutes. Drain meat (discard cooking liquid); grill over medium direct heat 6 minutes, turning once, until brown.

Fully Cooked Sausage and Bratwurst: Heat grill to medium-low for direct heat. Place links on grill. Cover grill; cook 7 to 10 minutes, turning frequently, until golden brown and heated through.

Direct and Indirect Heat

For best results, follow the grill manufacturer's directions for both methods. The directions in the recipe will tell you which way to heat your grill.

DIRECT-HEAT GRILLING

Best for foods that cook in 25 minutes or less: burgers, chicken pieces, chops, steaks

Gas, electric or charcoal grills Heat grill or coals to the temperature directed in recipe. Cook food on the grill rack directly over the heat.

INDIRECT-HEAT GRILLING

Best for foods that take longer than 25 minutes: ribs, whole chickens and turkeys, roasts.

Gas or Electric Grills Heat one or more burners to the temperature directed in the recipe, leaving one or more burners off. Cook food on the grill rack over the burners that are off. *For two-burner grills*, heat one burner; place food on unheated side. *For one-burner grill*, place food on grill rack over low heat.

Charcoal Grills Move hot white coals to the edge of the firebox, leaving the area in the middle free of coals. Place the empty drip pan (or with water added, if directed in recipe) in the open area. Grill food on the grill rack over the drip pan.

Oiling the Grill Rack

If you're grilling lean or plain meat (not marinated) or other foods, or if your marinade doesn't contain much oil, brush the hot grill rack with oil a few minutes before cooking to prevent food from sticking. Use a neutral-flavored oil such as vegetable oil; do not use olive oil. Moisten a paper towel or clean kitchen rag with a little oil; to prevent flare-ups, do not saturate towel. Use long-handled tongs to carefully brush oil on the grill rack area where the food will be cooked; it isn't necessary to oil the entire grill rack.

Controlling the Heat

Wind and ambient temperature can affect grill temperature and cooking time. Below are ways to adjust the grill temperature if your food is cooking too quickly or too slowly. As an alternative, you can also consider moving your food to hotter or cooler parts of the grill to get the right heat under it.

Gas or Electric Grill If the heat is too high, use a lower burner setting. If heat is too low, use a higher setting.

Charcoal Grill If coals are too hot, spread them out more or close the air vents halfway. If too cool, move coals closer together, knock off the ashes by tapping them with long-handled tongs or open the air vents.

SETTING UP GRILL FOR DIRECT HEAT

For gas or electric grill, heat all burners on high for 10 to 15 minutes, then reduce heat to desired temperature.

For charcoal grill, evenly spread hot white coals evenly over firebox. Grill when coals are desired temperature.

SETTING UP GRILL FOR INDIRECT HEAT

For gas or electric grill, heat all burners on high for 10 to 15 minutes. Turn off center burner. Reduce heat on remaining burners to desired temperature.

For charcoal grill, move hot white coals to edge of firebox, leaving empty area in center. Place drip pan in open area. Grill over center when coals are desired temperature.

Preventing and Taming Flare-Ups

Fats and sugary sauces dripping through the grill rack can cause flare-ups that may burn the food and cause a fire hazard. Use these tricks to prevent flare-ups.

- Trim excess fat from meats.
- Keep the bottom of the grill uncovered so that the grease can drain easily into the drip pan.
- Keep the grill bottom and drip pan clean and debris free.
- Brush sugary or tomato-based sauces on food only during the last 10 to 15 minutes to prevent them from burning.
- Clean off residue from grill rack after each use. For a gas grill, turn the heat setting to high for 10 to 15 minutes with the grill cover closed to burn off residue from grill rack and lava rock or ceramic briquettes (in gas grills). Scrape residue off the grill rack with a brass bristle brush while it is still warm, or crumple a large sheet of foil and hold it with long-handled tongs to scrape.

WHEN A FLARE-UP HAPPENS

- Move food to a different area of the grill rack; cover the grill to extinguish flames.
- For a charcoal grill, spread the coals farther apart, or move the food and spritz the flames with water from a spray bottle. When the flames are extinguished, move the food back to the desired area on the grill rack.
- For gas or electric grill, turn off all burners. NEVER USE WATER TO EXTINGUISH FLAMES ON A GAS OR ELECTRIC GRILL. When flames are gone, light the grill again.

Food Safety When Grilling

- If you've brushed raw meat or poultry with a marinade or sauce, wash the brush with hot, soapy water before using it on cooked meat.
- Use a clean plate to place the grilled food on, not the same plate that carried the raw food to the grill.
- To prevent contamination, set aside some of the marinade or sauce for serving before you brush any of it on raw meat. If the marinade has been brushed on raw meat and the brush then dipped again into the marinade, it's best to discard the marinade.

Citrus Marinade

PREP 5 Minutes TOTAL 5 Minutes • *About ½ cup marinade*

1 tablespoon chopped fresh or 1 teaspoon dried basil leaves	2 tablespoons olive or vegetable oil
3 tablespoons orange juice	½ teaspoon salt
2 tablespoons lemon juice	¼ teaspoon pepper
	2 cloves garlic, finely chopped

1 In shallow glass or plastic bowl or resealable food-storage plastic bag, mix all ingredients.

2 Add 1 lb boneless or 2 to 3 lb bone-in chicken, turkey, beef or pork; 1 to 2 lb fish or seafood; about 14 oz cubed tofu; or up to 4 cups cut-up fresh vegetables. Turn to coat food with marinade. Cover bowl or seal bag. Let tofu marinate at room temperature, or fish, seafood or vegetables in the refrigerator, no longer than 30 minutes; refrigerate beef, pork or poultry at least 1 hour but no longer than 24 hours. Turn food occasionally.

3 Remove poultry, meat, fish or seafood, tofu or vegetables from marinade. Cook as desired, brushing occasionally with marinade while cooking. Discard remaining marinade.

1 Tablespoon Calories 35; Total Fat 3.5g (Saturated Fat 0g, Trans Fat 0g); Cholesterol 0mg; Sodium 150mg; Total Carbohydrate 1g (Dietary Fiber 0g); Protein 0g **Carbohydrate Choices:** 0

Herbed Garlic Pepper Rub

PREP 5 Minutes TOTAL 5 Minutes •
4 servings (about 1 teaspoon each)

1½ teaspoons dried oregano leaves	½ teaspoon onion powder
1 teaspoon garlic pepper	½ teaspoon chili powder
½ teaspoon salt	⅛ teaspoon ground red pepper (cayenne)

1 Mix all ingredients.

2 Rub on both sides of 1 lb boneless or 2 to 3 lb bone-in chicken, turkey, beef or pork; 1 to 2 lb fish or seafood; about 14 oz cubed tofu; or up to 4 cups cut-up fresh vegetables. Let stand 15 minutes.

3 Cook as desired.

1 Serving Calories 5; Total Fat 0g (Saturated Fat 0g, Trans Fat 0g); Cholesterol 0mg; Sodium 300mg; Total Carbohydrate 1g (Dietary Fiber 0g); Protein 0g **Carbohydrate Choices:** 0

Buffalo Beer-Can Chicken

PREP 15 Minutes **TOTAL** 1 Hour 50 Minutes • *4 servings*

- 1 whole chicken (3½ to 4 lb)
- 2 tablespoons cold butter, cut into small slices
- 3 green onions, thinly sliced, white and green parts separated
- 2 tablespoons vegetable oil

- 1 tablespoon Montreal chicken grill seasoning
- 1 can (12 oz) beer
- ¼ cup Buffalo wing sauce (for homemade sauce, see page 456)
- Additional Buffalo wing sauce, ranch dressing and crumbled blue cheese, if desired

Buffalo Beer-Can Chicken

1 Heat gas or charcoal grill for indirect cooking (see page 421). For two-burner gas grill, heat one burner to medium; for one-burner gas grill, heat to low. For charcoal grill, move medium coals to edge of firebox and place drip pan in center.

2 Remove and discard neck and giblets from chicken cavity. Pat chicken dry with paper towels. Carefully loosen skin over breast. Place butter and green onion whites evenly under skin of breast, without removing skin.

3 In small bowl, mix vegetable oil and grill seasoning. Rub all over outside of chicken. Open beer can; with can opener, make several other openings in top. Measure out ⅔ cup beer; reserve for another use. Carefully place chicken cavity over partially-filled beer can until chicken is balanced on can.

4 Place chicken with can on grill rack, making sure chicken stays balanced (on two-burner gas grill, place on unheated side; on one-burner gas grill, place in center of grill; for charcoal grill, place over drip pan). Cover grill; cook 1 hour to 1 hour 15 minutes or until legs move easily when twisted or lifted and thermometer inserted in thickest part of thigh reads at least 165°F. Brush chicken all over with ¼ cup sauce. Cover grill; cook 5 to 8 minutes longer or until skin of chicken is crisp.

5 With tongs and flat metal spatula, carefully remove chicken and can from grill; place clean cutting board or serving platter. Let chicken stand 5 to 10 minutes. Twist can to remove from chicken; discard can. Serve carved chicken with green onion greens and additional Buffalo wing sauce.

1 Serving Calories 540; Total Fat 38g (Saturated Fat 12g, Trans Fat 1g); Cholesterol 165mg; Sodium 560mg; Total Carbohydrate 1g (Dietary Fiber 0g); Protein 47g **Carbohydrate Choices:** 0

BAKED BUFFALO BEER-CAN CHICKEN: Place oven rack in lowest position and heat oven to 375°F. Prepare as directed through Step 4—except place chicken on can in shallow baking pan. Bake 1 hour to 1 hour 15 minutes or until legs move easily when twisted or lifted and instant-read meat thermometer inserted in thickest part of thigh (not touching bone) reads at least 165°F. Brush chicken all over with ¼ cup Buffalo wing sauce. Bake 5 to 8 minutes longer or until skin of chicken is crisp. Continue as directed in Step 5, removing chicken and can from pan on oven rack.

MAKING BEER-CAN CHICKEN

Sprinkle seasoning inside cavity of chicken and rub all over on the outside.

Carefully place chicken cavity over partially-filled beer can.

Using tongs and flat metal spatula, carefully lift grilled chicken from pan, holding metal spatula under beer can for support.

Cowboy Coffee–Rubbed Chicken

If you like, substitute 2 tablespoons used coffee grounds (after making coffee) instead of the expresso powder. Process the rub in a small food processor, using about 5 on-and-off pulses to make it smooth before rubbing on the chicken. Use this versatile rub to season 1½ lb boneless or 3 to 3½ lb bone-in chicken, beef or pork before cooking with your favorite method. For even more Buffalo chicken–themed fun, serve with carrot and celery sticks.

PREP 15 Minutes **TOTAL** 3 Hours • *6 servings*

COWBOY COFFEE RUB

- 1½ teaspoons instant espresso powder
- 1½ teaspoons dried oregano leaves
- ¾ teaspoon salt
- ½ teaspoon paprika
- ¼ teaspoon ground red pepper (cayenne)
- ⅛ teaspoon dried thyme leaves

ADDITIONAL ITEMS FOR GRILLING

- 1 cut-up whole chicken (3 to 3½ lb)
  Up to 2 cups wood chips or shreds or 2 to 3 cups wood chunks (hickory, apple or cherry)
- 1 tablespoon white wine vinegar

1 In small bowl, mix all rub ingredients. In 13x9-inch baking dish, place chicken. Mix rub with vinegar; spoon evenly over chicken. Rub well into chicken, coating all sides. Cover with plastic wrap; refrigerate at least 1 hour but no longer than 2 hours.

2 Meanwhile, cover wood with water; soak at least 30 minutes. If using charcoal grill, place drip pan directly under center of grill rack and arrange coals around edge of firebox.

3 Heat gas or charcoal grill to medium for indirect heat (see page 421). Drain wood. Add wood to grill according to instructions in Infusing Food with Smoke on a Grill, page 446.

4 Carefully brush grill rack with vegetable oil (see Oiling the Grill Rack, page 421). Place chicken skin side up on grill. Close grill; cook 35 to 45 minutes or until juice of chicken is clear when thickest pieces are cut to bone (at least 165°F. Smaller pieces of chicken will cook faster than larger pieces. To avoid overcooking, remove chicken pieces from grill when done; cover and keep warm while larger pieces continue to cook.)

1 Serving Calories 230; Total Fat 13g (Saturated Fat 4g, Trans Fat 0g); Cholesterol 85mg; Sodium 380mg; Total Carbohydrate 0g (Dietary Fiber 0g); Protein 27g **Carbohydrate Choices:** 0

10-Minute Chicken Tacos

10-Minute Chicken Tacos

PREP 10 Minutes **TOTAL** 10 Minutes •
4 servings (2 tacos each)

TACOS

- 1¼ lb chicken breast tenders (not breaded)
- 1 package (1 oz) original taco seasoning mix (for homemade seasoning, see page 454)
- 1 package (6.7 oz) soft (flour) tortilla bowls or 1 package (4.7 oz) taco shells that stand on their own
- ¾ cup medium chunky salsa (from 24-oz jar; for homemade salsa, see page 479)

TOPPINGS, IF DESIRED

Diced avocado
Shredded cheese
Lime wedges

1 Heat gas or charcoal grill to medium for direct heat (see page 421).

2 In large resealable food-storage plastic bag, place chicken tenders. Sprinkle with taco seasoning mix; seal bag, and shake to coat chicken. Remove chicken from bag and place chicken on grill rack. Cover grill; cook chicken about 2 minutes on each side or until chicken is no longer pink in center.

3 Heat tortillas in microwave as directed on package. Cut chicken into 1-inch pieces; divide among tortillas. Top with salsa and desired toppings.

1 Serving Calories 360; Total Fat 10g (Saturated Fat 4g, Trans Fat 0g); Cholesterol 90mg; Sodium 1240mg; Total Carbohydrate 33g (Dietary Fiber 2g); Protein 36g **Carbohydrate Choices:** 2

Lemon Chicken and Zucchini Foil Packets

See Making Foil Packets for the Grill, at right, for more information. Zucchini and yellow squash tend to give up a lot of liquid when cooked. Don't let any of these delicious juices go unused—serve the packet contents over a side of cooked rice or quinoa.

PREP 20 Minutes **TOTAL** 50 Minutes • *4 servings*

1 lb zucchini or yellow summer squash (about 3 medium)	4 (6 to 7 oz each) boneless skinless chicken breasts
1 tablespoon chopped fresh thyme leaves	2 teaspoons lemon-pepper seasoning
1 teaspoon lemon zest	8 lemon slices
1 teaspoon salt	¼ cup butter
	Shredded Parmesan cheese, if desired

1 Heat gas or charcoal grill to medium for direct heat (see page 421). Cut 4 (18x12-inch) sheets heavy-duty foil. Spray foil with cooking spray.

2 Cut zucchini in half lengthwise, then crosswise into 1½-inch slices. In small bowl, add zucchini, thyme leaves, lemon zest and salt; toss to mix. Place 1 chicken breast on center of each sheet of foil; season with lemon-pepper. Spoon one quarter of zucchini mixture evenly around each chicken breast. Top each chicken breast with 2 lemon slices and 1 tablespoon butter.

3 Bring up 2 sides of foil so edges meet. Seal edges, making tight ½-inch fold; fold again, allowing space for heat circulation and expansion. Fold in ends to seal.

4 Place packets on grill. Cover grill; cook 10 minutes. Rotate packets a half-turn. Cook 9 to 10 minutes longer or until juice of chicken is clear when center of thickest part is cut at least 165°F. Remove packets from grill. Carefully fold back foil, and garnish with Parmesan cheese.

1 Serving Calories 340; Total Fat 18g (Saturated Fat 9g, Trans Fat 0.5g); Cholesterol 135mg; Sodium 960mg; Total Carbohydrate 6g (Dietary Fiber 2g); Protein 40g **Carbohydrate Choices:** ½

BAKED LEMON CHICKEN AND ZUCCHINI FOIL PACKETS: Prepare as directed through Step 3. Place packets on cookie sheet. Bake at 375°F 29 to 33 minutes or until juice of chicken is clear when center of thickest part is cut (instant-read meat thermometer reads 165°F). Carefully fold back foil, and garnish with Parmesan cheese.

MAKING FOIL PACKETS FOR THE GRILL

Fold edges of packets twice to prevent leakage, leaving room in packets for heat circulation and expansion.

Lemon Chicken and Zucchini Foil Packets

HEIRLOOM

CALORIE SMART • GLUTEN FREE

Make it a picnic by serving Grilled Corn on the Cob with Herb Butter (page 444) with the chicken.

Easy Barbecue Chicken

PREP 50 Minutes **TOTAL** 50 Minutes • *6 servings*

BARBECUE SAUCE

- 1 small onion, finely chopped (½ cup)
- 1 cup ketchup or 1 can (8 oz) tomato sauce
- ½ cup hot water
- ⅓ cup lemon juice
- 1 tablespoon gluten-free Worcestershire sauce
- 2 teaspoons paprika
- 1 teaspoon sugar
- 1 teaspoon salt
- ½ teaspoon pepper

CHICKEN

- 1 teaspoon salt
- 1 teaspoon paprika
- ¼ teaspoon pepper
- 1 cut-up whole chicken (3 to 3½ lb)

1 Heat gas or charcoal grill to medium for direct heat (see page 421).

2 In 1-quart saucepan, stir together all sauce ingredients. Heat over medium heat until boiling, stirring occasionally. Remove from heat.

3 In small bowl, mix 1 teaspoon salt, 1 teaspoon paprika and ¼ teaspoon pepper. Sprinkle mixture over both sides of chicken.

4 Carefully brush grill rack with vegetable oil (see page 421). Place chicken skin side up on grill. Cover grill; cook 15 minutes. Turn chicken; brush with barbecue sauce. Cover grill; cook 20 to 25 minutes longer, turning and brushing with sauce, until juice of chicken is clear when thickest part is cut (at least 165°F).

1 Serving Calories 380; Total Fat 13g (Saturated Fat 3.5g, Trans Fat 0g); Cholesterol 155mg; Sodium 1410mg; Total Carbohydrate 14g (Dietary Fiber 1g); Protein 51g **Carbohydrate Choices:** 1

GRILLED BARBECUE CHICKEN BREASTS: Substitute 6 bone-in chicken breasts for the cut-up whole chicken. Prepare as directed—except cook seasoned chicken breasts 10 minutes. Turn chicken; brush with barbecue sauce. Cover grill; cook 10 to 15 minutes longer, or until juice of chicken is clear when thickest part is cut (at least 165°F).

Easy Barbecue Chicken

Huli Huli Chicken and Mango Bowls

NEW TWIST

CALORIE SMART • GLUTEN FREE

Huli Huli Chicken with Mango

PREP 1 Hour **TOTAL** 1 Hour • *4 servings*

HULI HULI MARINADE AND SAUCE
- ⅓ cup packed brown sugar
- ¼ cup ketchup
- ¼ cup reduced-sodium gluten-free soy sauce
- ¼ cup sherry or apple juice
- 1 teaspoon finely chopped gingerroot
- 1 clove garlic, finely chopped

MANGO AND CHICKEN
- 2 ripe medium mangos, seed removed, peeled and cut lengthwise into planks (about 2x¼ inch)
- 2 (8 oz each) boneless skinless chicken breasts
- 4 teaspoons vegetable oil
- 4 green onions, thinly sliced (¼ cup)

1 In small bowl, mix all huli huli marinade and sauce ingredients. For sauce, pour ½ cup of the mixture into a 2-cup or larger microwave-safe bowl. Microwave uncovered on High 3 to 4 minutes, stirring once, until sauce thickens slightly (it will continue to thicken while it stands); reserve sauce for serving. Set remaining huli huli mixture aside for marinade.

2 Heat gas or charcoal grill to medium for direct heat (see page 421).

3 In medium bowl, place mango planks. Add 2 teaspoons of the vegetable oil; toss to coat.

4 Place mango on grill. Cover grill; cook 3 minutes. Brush slices with marinade; turn. Brush with marinade. Cook 3 to 4 minutes longer or until grill marks appear. Transfer to serving platter; cover to keep warm.

5 In same bowl, place chicken breasts. Add remaining 2 teaspoons vegetable oil to chicken; toss to coat. Place chicken on grill. Cover grill; cook 10 minutes. Brush chicken with some of the remaining marinade. Turn chicken; brush with additional marinade. Discard any remaining marinade. Cook 10 to 12 minutes longer or until juice of chicken is clear when center of thickest part is cut (at least 165°F).

6 Transfer chicken to cutting board. Cover loosely with foil; let stand 5 minutes or until cool enough to handle. Thinly slice chicken; arrange on top of mango. Drizzle with sauce; sprinkle with green onions. Serve immediately.

1 Serving Calories 400; Total Fat 9g (Saturated Fat 2g, Trans Fat 0g); Cholesterol 70mg; Sodium 780mg; Total Carbohydrate 50g (Dietary Fiber 3g); Protein 29g **Carbohydrate Choices:** 3

HULI HULI CHICKEN AND MANGO BOWLS: Prepare as directed—except do not arrange mango and chicken on platter. In medium bowl, mix 1 tablespoon olive oil and 1 teaspoon fresh lime juice. Add 4 cups lightly packed fresh baby spinach leaves; toss to coat. In another medium bowl, stir ¼ cup chopped fresh cilantro into 4 cups hot cooked brown rice. Cut 1 large red bell pepper into strips; cut strips crosswise in half. Divide rice among 4 serving bowls. Top with spinach, sliced chicken, mango and bell pepper strips. Drizzle with sauce; top with green onion.

Persian-Style Chicken Kabobs

Cardamom (KAR-duh-muhm), a member of the ginger family, has a pungent, warm, slightly lemony-sweet and spicy flavor. It's often used in Scandinavian, South Asian and Middle Eastern cooking in both sweet and savory dishes, depending on the area.

PREP 25 Minutes **TOTAL** 35 Minutes • *4 servings*

8 (8-inch) bamboo skewers

HONEY YOGURT

½ cup plain fat-free yogurt

1 tablespoon honey

KABOBS

3 tablespoons lime juice

1 tablespoon olive oil

1 teaspoon salt

1 teaspoon ground cardamom

1 teaspoon ground cinnamon

1 teaspoon ground cumin

½ teaspoon ground ginger

¼ teaspoon ground cloves

1 lb boneless skinless chicken breasts, cut into 1-inch pieces

½ medium red onion, cut into 1-inch pieces

2 cups hot cooked brown rice (page 224)

10 fresh mint leaves, chopped

1 Soak skewers in water 20 minutes. Heat gas or charcoal grill to medium-high for direct heat (see page 421).

2 In a small bowl, beat yogurt and honey with whisk. Cover and refrigerate.

3 In large bowl, beat half of the lime juice, the oil, salt, cardamom, cinnamon, cumin, ginger and cloves with whisk. Add chicken; toss to coat. Drain skewers. On each skewer, alternately thread chicken and onion, starting and ending with chicken. (There should be 5 or 6 pieces of chicken on each skewer.)

4 Brush grill rack with vegetable oil (see Oiling the Grill Rack, page 421). Place kabobs on grill. Cover grill; cook 3 to 4 minutes on each side or until chicken is no longer pink in center. On each of 4 serving plates, place ½ cup rice and 2 kabobs. Drizzle with remaining lime juice and honey yogurt. Top with chopped mint.

1 Serving Calories 340; Total Fat 8g (Saturated Fat 2g, Trans Fat 0g); Cholesterol 70mg; Sodium 680mg; Total Carbohydrate 36g (Dietary Fiber 2g); Protein 30g **Carbohydrate Choices:** 2½

Peach and Bourbon–Marinated Turkey Tenderloins

Serve on a bed of arugula, topped with the peach sauce (right) for even more peachy-bourbon goodness.

PREP 55 Minutes **TOTAL** 8 Hours 55 Minutes • *6 servings*

4 firm, ripe medium peaches, halved and pitted

2 tablespoons fresh thyme leaves

¼ cup bourbon whiskey

1 teaspoon garlic salt

¼ teaspoon pepper

2 (¾ lb each) unseasoned turkey tenderloins

Fresh thyme sprigs, if desired

1 Heat gas or charcoal grill to medium for direct heat (see page 421). Carefully rush grill rack with vegetable oil (see page 421).

2 Place peaches on grill. Cover grill; cook 4 to 5 minutes or until grill marks appear on bottom of peaches. Turn peaches. Grill 4 to 5 minutes longer, or until peaches are tender. Remove peaches to small plate; remove peel from peaches if desired. Turn off grill.

3 In mini chopper or blender, place 2 of the peach halves and remaining ingredients except turkey and thyme sprigs. Cover; process until smooth. Cover and refrigerate remaining peach halves.

4 In large resealable food-storage plastic bag or shallow glass or plastic dish, place turkey. Pour peach mixture over turkey; turn to coat. Cover and refrigerate at least 8 hours but no longer than 24 hours, turning occasionally.

5 Heat gas or charcoal grill to medium for direct heat (see page 421). Carefully brush grill rack with vegetable oil.

6 Remove turkey from marinade. Discard marinade. Place turkey on grill. Cover grill; cook 25 to 30 minutes, turning occasionally, or until juice of turkey is clear when center of thickest part is cut (at least 165°F).

7 During last 5 minutes of grilling, spray 12-inch square of foil with cooking spray. Place on grill sprayed side up; place reserved peaches on foil to warm.

8 Remove turkey and peaches from grill to cutting board; cover with foil to keep warm. Let turkey stand at least 3 minutes before slicing. Cut each peach half into 4 slices. Serve turkey with peach slices. Garnish with thyme sprigs.

1 Serving Calories 170; Total Fat 2g (Saturated Fat 0.5g, Trans Fat 0g); Cholesterol 70mg; Sodium 250mg; Total Carbohydrate 10g (Dietary Fiber 1g); Protein 27g **Carbohydrate Choices:** ½

PEACH SAUCE: Grill an extra peach (cut in half) in Step 2. In mini food chopper or blender, process the 2 extra grilled peach halves, 1 tablespoon bourbon whiskey, ¼ teaspoon fresh thyme leaves and ¼ teaspoon salt until smooth. Spoon mixture into small microwavable bowl. Microwave on High 30 seconds or until boiling. Cover and refrigerate separately from remaining peaches in Step 3. Remove from refrigerator while grilling turkey. Serve at room temperature with turkey and peaches.

PEACH AND BOURBON–MARINATED PORK TENDERLOINS: Prepare as directed—except substitute 2 (¾ lb each) unseasoned pork tenderloins for the turkey tenderloins. Grill 15 to 20 minutes or until instant-read meat thermometer inserted in center reads at least 145°F.

Persian-Style Chicken Kabobs

FAST • CALORIE SMART

Turkey–Goat Cheese Juicy Lucys

PREP 30 Minutes **TOTAL** 30 Minutes • *4 burgers*

JUICY LUCYS

- 1 lb ground turkey (at least 93% lean)
- ¾ cup finely chopped loosely packed fresh spinach (from 8-oz bag)
- ¼ cup chopped drained roasted red bell peppers (from 12-oz jar)
- ½ teaspoon Italian seasoning
- ½ teaspoon salt
- ¼ teaspoon pepper
- 1 log (4 oz) goat cheese with herbs, cut into 4 pieces

BUNS AND TOPPINGS

- 4 whole wheat burger buns, split
  Additional fresh spinach leaves, if desired
- ¼ cup tzatziki dip (for homemade tzatziki, see page 41)

1 Heat gas or charcoal grill to medium for direct heat (see page 421).

2 In medium bowl, mix all juicy lucy ingredients except goat cheese. On large plastic cutting board, shape mixture into 8 patties, each about 4 inches in diameter (patties will be thin). With fingers, press each slice of goat cheese to about 3 inches in diameter. Place 1 goat cheese slice onto center of each of 4 patties. Top with remaining patties; press edges together firmly to seal.

3 Carefully brush grill rack with vegetable oil (see Oiling the Grill Rack, page 421). Place patties on grill. Cover grill; cook 12 to 17 minutes, turning after 6 minutes, until instant-read meat thermometer inserted near center of patties reads at least 165°F (avoid inserting in cheese). Spread cut sides of bun bottoms with tzatziki; top with spinach leaves and burgers. Cover burgers with bun tops.

1 Burger Calories 400; Total Fat 20g (Saturated Fat 9g, Trans Fat 0g); Cholesterol 110mg; Sodium 810mg; Total Carbohydrate 20g (Dietary Fiber 3g); Protein 34g **Carbohydrate Choices:** 1

Peach and Bourbon–Marinated Turkey Tenderloins with Peach Sauce

429

Turkey–Goat Cheese Juicy Lucys

5-INGREDIENT RECIPE

Salt-Free Bloody Mary Rim Mix

Turkey Kofta-Style Sandwiches

Ground Turkey

Baby Spinach

Mini Naan Breads

Greek Yogurt

430

5-INGREDIENT RECIPE

FAST • CALORIE SMART

Turkey Kofta-Style Sandwiches

Love dishes highly seasoned? Sprinkle a little extra rim mix over the sandwiches before you sink your teeth into them.

PREP 30 Minutes **TOTAL** 30 Minutes • *4 sandwiches*

½ cup plain Greek yogurt	2 cups lightly packed fresh baby spinach leaves (from 5-oz package)
3 teaspoons Salt-Free Bloody Mary Rim Mix (page 455)	1 lb ground turkey (at least 85% lean)
½ teaspoon plus ⅛ teaspoon salt	4 mini naan breads (about 4x6-inch ovals; from 7.05-oz package)

1 Heat gas or charcoal grill to medium-high for direct heat (see page 421).

2 In small bowl, mix yogurt, ½ teaspoon of the rim mix and ⅛ teaspoon salt. Cover; refrigerate until ready to serve.

3 Chop 1 cup of the spinach leaves. In medium bowl, mix chopped spinach, ground turkey, remaining 2½ teaspoons rim mix and remaining ½ teaspoon salt until well mixed. Shape mixture into 12 meatballs. On each of 4 (10- to 12- inch) metal skewers, thread 3 meatballs, leaving about ¼-inch space between meatballs.

4 Carefully brush grill rack with vegetable oil (see Oiling the Grill Rack, page 421). Place skewers on grill. Cover grill; cook 10 to 12 minutes, turning once, or until instant-read meat thermometer inserted near center of meatballs (not touching skewer) reads at least 165°F. Remove from grill; cover to keep warm.

5 Spray both sides of naan breads with cooking spray. Grill 1 to 2 minutes, turning once, or until lightly toasted.

6 To serve, top each naan bread with ¼ cup of remaining spinach leaves, 2 tablespoons yogurt sauce and a skewer of kofta. To eat, fold naan around the meatballs; slide skewer out from meatballs.

1 Sandwich Calories 380; Total Fat 20g (Saturated Fat 7g, Trans Fat 0g); Cholesterol 105mg; Sodium 620mg; Total Carbohydrate 22g (Dietary Fiber 1g); Protein 28g **Carbohydrate Choices:** 1½

CALORIE SMART • GLUTEN FREE

Turkey Breast with Chili-Cumin Rub

Whole turkey breasts grill beautifully. Because they're available in different sizes, adjust the grilling time as needed, using the instant-read meat thermometer to determine when it's done.

PREP 10 Minutes **TOTAL** 2 Hours 50 Minutes • *8 servings*

CHILI-CUMIN RUB

2 tablespoons packed brown sugar	½ teaspoon ground ginger
2 teaspoons paprika	½ teaspoon gluten-free garlic-pepper blend
1 teaspoon chili powder	
1 teaspoon ground cumin	**TURKEY**
½ teaspoon salt	1 bone-in whole turkey breast (5 to 6 lb), thawed if frozen
½ teaspoon ground mustard	2 tablespoons cold butter, cut into small slices

1 In small bowl, mix rub ingredients.

2 Loosen skin on turkey breast in 4 or 5 places. Place butter randomly under skin of turkey. Sprinkle rub mixture over entire outside of turkey; rub with fingers.

3 For gas grill, place drip pan under grill rack where the burner won't be turned on. Heat gas or charcoal grill to medium for indirect heat (see page 421). For charcoal grill, move coals to edge of firebox, place drip pan in center of area without coals and fill with ½ inch water. Place turkey skin side up on grill rack over drip pan.

4 Cover grill; cook 30 minutes. Turn turkey. Cover grill; cook 1 hour 30 minutes to 2 hours longer or until instant-read meat thermometer inserted in thickest part of breast (not touching bone) reads at least 165°F. Remove turkey to cutting board; cover with foil. Let stand 10 minutes before slicing.

1 Serving Calories 390; Total Fat 18g (Saturated Fat 6g, Trans Fat 0g); Cholesterol 155mg; Sodium 330mg; Total Carbohydrate 4g (Dietary Fiber 0g); Protein 54g **Carbohydrate Choices:** 0

Bacon Burgers with Beer Caramelized Onions

Sweet onions have less bite than regular yellow, white or red onions. Look for any of these varieties, depending on the season, in your grocery store: Maui, Vidalia, Walla Walla, Oso Sweet or Rio Sweet. Use whatever variety is available in recipes calling for sweet onions.

PREP 1 Hour 15 Minutes **TOTAL** 1 Hour 15 Minutes • **4 burgers**

8 slices bacon, crisply cooked, drippings reserved	¼ teaspoon pepper
2 large sweet onions (about 1½ lb), thinly sliced	4 slices (about ¾ oz each) cheddar or American cheese
1 bottle (12 oz) pilsner-style beer	4 kaiser rolls or crusty rolls, split
1½ lb ground beef (at least 80% lean)	8 leaves red leaf lettuce or red romaine lettuce
½ teaspoon salt	4 slices tomato

1 In 10-inch skillet, heat 1 tablespoon bacon drippings over medium-high heat. Add onions; cook about 15 minutes, stirring frequently, until softened.

2 Reserve ½ cup of the beer. Stir remaining beer into onions. Heat to boiling; reduce heat. Simmer uncovered about 30 minutes, stirring occasionally, or until onions are golden and liquid has evaporated. Cool 10 minutes. Meanwhile, coarsely chop 4 slices of the cooked bacon; set aside.

3 Heat gas or charcoal grill to medium for direct heat (see page 421).

4 Coarsely chop half of the onion mixture. In medium bowl, stir chopped onion mixture and bacon into beef. Add salt and pepper. Shape beef mixture into 4 large patties, thinner at center and thicker at edge (for even cooking).

5 Place patties on grill. Cover grill; cook 11 to 13 minutes, turning once, until instant-read meat thermometer inserted in center of patties reads 160°F. After turning, brush burgers with reserved ½ cup beer, then top burgers with cheese. Cover grill; cook about 1 minute longer or until cheese is melted.

6 On roll bottoms, place burgers. Top with lettuce leaves, tomato slice, and remaining caramelized onions. Cut remaining 4 slices bacon in half; crisscross 2 pieces on top of onions on each burger. Cover with tops of rolls.

1 Burger Calories 620; Total Fat 35g (Saturated Fat 14g, Trans Fat 2g); Cholesterol 145mg; Sodium 1090mg; Total Carbohydrate 30g (Dietary Fiber 2g); Protein 46g **Carbohydrate Choices:** 2

Korean Barbecue–Style Burgers

Look for kimchi in jars in the refrigerated section of your grocery store or Asian markets.

PREP 45 Minutes **TOTAL** 45 Minutes • **4 burgers**

KIMCHI MAYONNAISE

⅓ cup mayonnaise (for homemade mayonnaise, see page 479)	⅓ cup Korean-style barbecue sauce (from 15-oz bottle)
¼ cup chopped drained kimchi (for homemade kimchi, see page 466)	2 tablespoons sesame seed
	2 tablespoons toasted sesame oil

BURGERS

1½ lb ground beef (at least 80% lean)	½ cup shredded cabbage
6 green onions, sliced (6 tablespoons)	4 Fried Eggs, Sunny Side Up (page 101)
	4 brioche burger buns, split (from 7-oz package)
	Crushed red pepper flakes, if desired

1 In small bowl, mix mayonnaise and kimchi. Cover and refrigerate until ready to serve.

2 Heat gas or charcoal grill to medium for direct heat (see page 421).

432

Bacon Burgers with Beer Caramelized Onions

Korean Barbecue–Style Burgers

3 In medium bowl, mix beef, green onions, 2 tablespoons of the barbecue sauce, the sesame seed and sesame oil. Shape mixture into 4 patties, about ¾ inch thick.

4 Carefully brush grill rack with vegetable oil (see Oiling the Grill Rack, page 421). Place patties on grill. Cover grill; cook 11 to 13 minutes, turning once, until instant-read meat thermometer inserted in center of burgers reads 160°F. If desired, place bun halves cut-sides down on grill until toasted, about 1 minute. Spread remaining barbecue sauce on burgers.

5 On cut sides of each bun, spread 1 tablespoon kimchi mayonnaise. On bun bottoms, place cabbage and burgers. Place fried eggs on burgers; sprinkle with red pepper flakes and cover with bun tops.

1 Burger Calories 930; Total Fat 61g (Saturated Fat 17g, Trans Fat 2g); Cholesterol 365mg; Sodium 720mg; Total Carbohydrate 51g (Dietary Fiber 3g); Protein 45g **Carbohydrate Choices:** 3½

Chile and Cheese–Stuffed Burgers

FAST

Chile and Cheese–Stuffed Burgers

Monterey Jack is a great cheese to use for its meltability. However, feel free to substitute your favorite cheese, such as cheddar or pepper Jack. Add a slice of cheddar cheese to these burgers for an over-the-top burger joint experience.

PREP 30 Minutes **TOTAL** 30 Minutes • *6 burgers*

BURGERS

- 1 can (4.5 oz) chopped green chiles
- 2 lb ground beef (at least 80% lean)
- 1 package (1 oz) taco seasoning mix (for homemade seasoning, see page 454)
- ½ cup shredded Monterey Jack cheese (2 oz)
- 6 burger buns

TOPPINGS, IF DESIRED

- 1 medium avocado, pitted, peeled and mashed
  Salsa (for homemade salsa, see page 479)

1 Heat gas or charcoal grill to medium for direct heat (see page 421). Reserve 1 tablespoon of the green chiles.

2 In medium bowl, add beef, taco seasoning mix and remaining green chiles; mix well. Divide into 6 portions. In small bowl, mix cheese and reserved green chiles. Divide into 6 portions.

3 Starting with 1 portion of beef, remove a small chunk from portion. Carefully wrap around 1 cheese portion. Wrap remaining portion of beef around wrapped ball of cheese, and flatten slightly into a patty. Repeat to form 6 patties.

4 Place patties on grill. Cover grill; cook 14 to 16 minutes, turning once, until burgers are slightly firm when pressed in center and instant-read meat thermometer inserted in burger (not in cheese) reads 160°F. On bun bottoms, place burgers; top with toppings. Cover with bun tops.

1 Burger Calories 440; Total Fat 23g (Saturated Fat 9g, Trans Fat 1.5g); Cholesterol 105mg; Sodium 800mg; Total Carbohydrate 27g (Dietary Fiber 1g); Protein 33g **Carbohydrate Choices:** 2

LEARN WITH BETTY HAMBURGERS

Ideal Hamburger: The center of this hamburger has reached a safe 160°F, evidenced by light brown color (no pink) inside.

Undercooked Hamburger: The center of this hamburger is below 160°F, evidenced by pink color inside.

Overcooked Hamburger: The center of this hamburger is above 160°F, the center is dark brown and the burger is hard and dry.

♻ USE IT UP
HAMBURGER AND HOT DOG BUNS

No matter how hard you try, it always seems that you end up with extra buns when dinner is done. Try one of these delicious ideas with your extras, so they don't go to waste!

PARMESAN-GARLIC TOAST Mix ¼ cup softened butter and ¼ teaspoon garlic powder; spread on the cut sides of 2 buns. Place on cookie sheet buttered side up. Sprinkle with grated Parmesan and chopped parsley. Broil 6 inches from heat 2 to 3 minutes or until light golden brown. Serve with spaghetti.

MINI PIZZAS Place buns, cut side up, on cookie sheet. Broil 6 inches from heat 1 to 2 minutes or until very lightly toasted. Spread with pizza sauce, top with your favorite pizza toppings and shredded cheese. Broil until cheese is melted and edge of buns is golden brown.

EASY POT PIES Pour ready-to-eat canned rich & hearty chicken pot pie style with dumplings soup into 2 (10- to 12-oz) ramekins. Stir in additional bite-size pieces of cooked chicken and vegetables. Cover and microwave on High 1 to 2 minutes or until hot and bubbly. Meanwhile, toast hamburger bun tops (use the bottoms for another use). Brush tops of buns with melted butter; sprinkle with chopped fresh parsley leaves and grated Parmesan cheese. Place cut side down on hot soup.

PANZANELLA SALAD Heat grill pan over medium-high heat. Cut 3 buns into 1½-inch pieces; toss with ¼ cup melted butter, ¼ teaspoon each coarsely ground pepper and garlic salt. Spread in single layer on grill pan. Cook, turning every 2 to 3 minutes, or until toasted on all sides. Cool. Toss with salad greens, vinaigrette, cut-up cooked chicken or shrimp and your other favorite salad ingredients.

434

Mediterranean Beef
and Veggie Kabobs

Mediterranean Beef and Veggie Kabobs

Turn these kabobs into a hearty meal by serving them on top of hot cooked gluten-free orzo or rice, with hummus and harissa (see pages 48, 457) on the side. For added interest and flavor, sprinkle with additional herbs, such as cilantro or parsley, with the mint.

PREP 45 Minutes **TOTAL** 1 Hour 15 Minutes •
4 servings (3 kabobs each)

LEMON MARINADE

- ⅓ cup fresh lemon juice
- 2 tablespoons vegetable oil
- ½ teaspoon salt
- ¼ teaspoon pepper
- 4 cloves garlic, finely chopped

BEEF AND VEGETABLES

- 1 lb boneless beef rib eye steak, cut into 1½-inch pieces

- 1 pint (2 cups) cherry tomatoes
- 1 (8-inch) yellow summer squash, cut crosswise into 8 pieces
- 1 (8-inch) zucchini, cut crosswise into 8 pieces
- 1 medium red onion, cut into 8 wedges
- 2 tablespoons chopped fresh mint leaves

1 In small bowl, mix marinade ingredients with whisk until well blended. Divide marinade between 2 large resealable food-storage plastic bags. Add beef to one bag; add tomatoes, squashes and onion to second bag. Seal bags; shake each to coat meat and vegetables. Place each bag in a shallow dish. Refrigerate, turning bags occasionally, to marinate at least 30 minutes but no longer than 3 hours.

2 Heat gas or charcoal grill to medium for direct heat (see page 421).

3 Remove vegetables from marinade; reserve vegetable marinade. On each of 8 (10- to 12-inch) metal skewers, alternate threading vegetables on each skewer, leaving about ¼-inch space between pieces. Remove beef from marinade; discard remaining beef marinade. On each of 4 (10- to 12-inch) metal skewers, thread beef, leaving about ¼-inch space between pieces.

4 Carefully brush grill rack with vegetable oil (see Oiling the Grill Rack, page 421). Place kabobs on grill. Cover grill; cook kabobs 5 minutes. Turn kabobs; brush vegetables and beef with reserved vegetable marinade. Discard any remaining marinade. Grill kabobs 5 to 7 minutes longer, or until beef is cooked to desired doneness (instant-read meat thermometer reads 145°F for medium-rare) and yellow squash is crisp-tender.

5 Place kabobs on platter or serving plates; sprinkle with mint.

1 Serving Calories 310; Total Fat 15g (Saturated Fat 4g, Trans Fat 0g); Cholesterol 80mg; Sodium 340mg; Total Carbohydrate 12g (Dietary Fiber 2g); Protein 30g **Carbohydrate Choices:** 1

LEARN TO GRILL A SPECTACULAR STEAK

Many would argue that not much tastes better than a delicious and tender steak grilled properly, with a charred, crusty exterior and juicy interior. And knowing how to grill up a good steak is definitely a good recipe to keep in your repertoire. Use these tips to help you become a steak grill master. Try out these techniques by making Easy Blue Cheese–Topped Steaks (right).

- Choose a steak based on your preference for tenderness, your budget and/or what's on sale (see Great Steaks for Grilling, right). Very tender steaks are more expensive and have more fat marbling—which, in turn, makes them very flavorful. You could almost cut them with a butter knife! Tender steaks with less marbling are more economical. These steaks are still flavorful and tender but not butter-knife tender.

- Trim and discard nearly all the fat around the perimeter of the steak.

- Season the steak and let it sit at room temperature 15 to 30 minutes. While salt does draw out some moisture from the exterior of the steaks, it helps the meat retain moisture on the interiors, for a juicy, tender and flavorful result.

- Heat the grill as directed on page 421 before cooking the steaks. You don't need to oil the grate unless the recipe directs you to do so.

- Grill the steak as directed in the recipe until it lifts easily from the grill rack. Turn the steak only once during cooking.

- Grilling time is based on medium doneness of 160°F. For medium-rare, cook steaks to 145°F; for well-done, cook to 170°F.

- Use an instant-read meat thermometer inserted in the thickest part of the steak (not touching bone) to measure the temperature.

- Let the steak rest 3 to 5 minutes before serving, to allow the juices to spread throughout the steak and to soften the fibers.

GREAT STEAKS FOR GRILLING

VERY TENDER STEAKS	TENDER STEAKS
Filet Mignon	Flank Steak
New York Strip	Flat-Iron Steak
Porterhouse	Hanger Steak
Rib Eye	Skirt Steak
T-Bone	Top Sirloin

Making Grill Marks

Everyone loves the look of steaks with grill marks. They also add flavor because of the Maillard reaction (similar to caramelization) that takes place when the meat hits the hot grill rack.

TO MAKE GRILL MARKS: Place steaks on hot grill. Cover, grill steak at least 2 minutes without moving it, until dark sear marks are visible on the bottom. Turn steak and continue grilling as directed.

TO MAKE CROSSHATCH MARKS: Make grill marks on bottom. Before turning steak, rotate it 45 degrees and place on another hot area of grill. Grill 2 minutes longer or until the crosshatch marks appear on bottom. Turn steak, continue grilling until desired doneness. (Actual cooking time might be a few minutes less than recipe indicates.)

LEARN WITH BETTY BEEF STEAK DONENESS

Medium-Rare (145°F): Steak is very pink in center and slightly brown toward exterior.

Medium (160°F): Steak is light pink in center and brown toward exterior.

Well-Done (170°F): Steak is uniformly brown throughout inside and dark brown on exterior.

Easy Blue Cheese—Topped Steaks

PREP 10 Minutes **TOTAL** 55 Minutes • *4 servings*

¼ cup balsamic vinegar	2 beef rib eye steaks (about 1 inch thick; 8 to 10 oz each)
1 tablespoon honey	
2 teaspoons gluten-free Worcestershire sauce	2 green onions, finely chopped (2 tablespoons)
1 teaspoon salt	
½ teaspoon cracked black pepper	½ cup crumbled blue cheese (2 oz), if desired
6 cloves garlic, finely chopped	

1 In small bowl, stir balsamic vinegar, honey, Worcestershire sauce, salt, pepper and garlic with wire whisk until blended. Place steaks in 1-gallon resealable food-storage plastic bag. Pour marinade over steaks; seal. Shake bag to coat steaks. Let stand at room temperature 30 minutes to marinate.

2 Meanwhile, heat gas or charcoal grill to medium for direct heat (see page 421).

3 Carefully brush grill with vegetable oil (see Oiling the Grill Rack, page 421). Remove steaks from marinade; discard marinade. Place steaks on grill. Cover grill; cook 10 to 15 minutes, turning once, for medium doneness (160°F). Remove steaks to heatproof platter; let stand 5 minutes. Sprinkle with blue cheese and green onions.

1 Serving Calories 220; Total Fat 8g (Saturated Fat 3g, Trans Fat 0g); Cholesterol 80mg; Sodium 660mg; Total Carbohydrate 10g (Dietary Fiber 0g); Protein 28g **Carbohydrate Choices:** ½

BLACK AND BLUE STEAKS WITH BALSAMIC SAUCE: Prepare as directed—except after removing steaks from marinade, do not discard marinade. Sprinkle both sides of steaks with additional 1½ teaspoons cracked pepper; press pepper lightly into steak. While steak is grilling, spray 10-inch skillet with cooking spray; heat pan over medium heat. Cook 2 chopped shallots in pan 1 to 2 minutes or until softened. Stir in reserved marinade. Heat to boiling; boil 1 to 2 minutes or until mixture has reduced by half. To serve, omit green onions. Drizzle reduced marinade mixture over steaks. Top steaks with blue cheese.

STEAKS WITH CARAMELIZED ONIONS: Prepare Caramelized Onions (page 67); keep warm. Prepare steaks as directed—except omit green onions and blue cheese. Serve steaks with caramelized onions.

STEAKS WITH STEAK SAUCE: Prepare as directed— except after removing steaks from marinade, do not discard marinade In 8-inch nonstick pan, melt 2 tablespoons butter. With whisk, stir in reserved marinade and 1 tablespoon Dijon mustard. Heat to boiling; cook 3 to 4 minutes, stirring frequently, until slightly thickened. Serve with steak.

GARLICKY GRILLED STEAKS: Prepare as directed— except add 2 or 3 finely chopped garlic cloves with the balsamic vinegar.

Easy Blue Cheese—Topped Steaks

PREPARING STEAKS FOR THE GRILL

Trim most of the fat from the perimeter of steak to cut down on flare-ups while grilling.

Rub seasonings on steaks. Let steak stand at room temperature 15 to 30 minutes for best flavor and texture when grilled.

Garlic-Lime Flank Steak Fajitas

Flank steak varies in thickness, so for best doneness results, select a steak that is an even thickness throughout.

PREP 40 Minutes **TOTAL** 40 Minutes • *6 servings*

FAJITAS

- 1 beef flank steak (about 1⅓ lb), trimmed of fat
- 1 package (1 oz) original taco seasoning mix (for homemade seasoning, see page 454)
- 1 tablespoon packed brown sugar
- 3 cloves garlic, finely chopped
- ¼ teaspoon ground red pepper (cayenne)
- ¼ cup lime juice
- 2 large red or yellow bell peppers, cut into ¼-inch strips (about 3 cups)
- 1 medium onion, sliced (1 cup)
- 1 tablespoon vegetable oil
- 1 teaspoon ground cumin
- 1 teaspoon ground coriander
- ½ teaspoon salt
- 6 (8-inch) flour tortillas for burritos (from 11.5-oz package), heated as directed on package

TOPPINGS, IF DESIRED

Chopped fresh cilantro leaves

Sliced green onions

Sliced avocado

Sour cream

1 Place beef in 1-gallon resealable food-storage plastic bag. In small bowl, mix taco seasoning, brown sugar, garlic, red pepper and lime juice. Pour mixture over beef. Seal bag; place in shallow dish. Refrigerate 8 to 10 hours, turning bag occasionally.

2 In medium bowl, mix bell peppers, onion, oil, cumin, coriander and salt; set aside.

3 Heat gas or charcoal grill to medium-high for direct heat (see page 421).

4 Spray 12- to 13-inch grill basket with cooking spray; place on grill to heat. Remove beef from marinade and place in grill basket; discard any remaining marinade.

5 Cook 10 to 20 minutes, turning once, until instant-read meat thermometer inserted in thickest part of steak reads 135°F (for medium). Transfer steak to cutting board; tent with foil and let stand 5 minutes.

6 Meanwhile, spray same grill basket with cooking spray. Cook pepper and onion mixture 5 to 7 minutes, stirring occasionally, or until vegetables are crisp-tender and edges begin to char.

7 Cut steak across grain into thin slices. To serve, place beef and vegetables down center of warmed tortillas. Top with toppings.

1 Serving Calories 330; Total Fat 10g (Saturated Fat 3g, Trans Fat 1g); Cholesterol 65mg; Sodium 900mg; Total Carbohydrate 32g (Dietary Fiber 2g); Protein 28g **Carbohydrate Choices:** 2

SLICING FLANK STEAK

Using sharp knife, cut steak across the grain, at a slight angle, into thin slices.

Garlic-Lime Flank Steak Fajitas

438

Bourbon-Tangy Mustard Barbecue Pork Chops with Veggies

PREP 35 Minutes **TOTAL** 35 Minutes • *4 servings*

- ⅓ cup Dijon mustard
- ¼ cup packed brown sugar
- ¼ cup bourbon or other whiskey
- 2 tablespoons molasses
- 2 tablespoons cider vinegar
- 1 teaspoon red pepper sauce
- 1 large sweet onion, cut into ¼-inch-thick slices
- 2 medium tomatoes, cut in half
- 4 (½-inch-thick) bone-in pork loin or rib chops (1 lb), trimmed of fat
- Chopped fresh Italian (flat-leaf) parsley, if desired

1 Heat gas or charcoal grill to medium for direct heat (see page 421)

2 Meanwhile, in 1-quart saucepan, stir mustard, brown sugar, whiskey, molasses, vinegar and pepper sauce with whisk. Cook over medium-low heat 10 minutes, stirring occasionally, until slightly thickened. Remove from heat. Pour ¼ cup of the sauce into small bowl.

Bourbon-Tangy Mustard Barbecue Pork Chops with Veggies

Inside-Out Cuban-Inspired Pork Tenderloin Roll

3 Carefully brush grill rack with vegetable oil (see page 421). Generously brush cut sides of onion slices and tomato halves with 2 tablespoons of sauce in bowl. Generously brush pork chops with half of the remaining sauce in pan. Place pork chops, onions and tomatoes, cut side down, on grill. Brush tops of onions and tomatoes with remaining sauce in bowl. Brush tops of pork chops with remaining sauce in pan. Discard any remaining sauce in pan.

4 Cover grill; cook 5 to 7 minutes, turning pork chops and onions once (do not turn tomatoes), or until instant-read thermometer inserted in center (not touching bone) reads 145°F, onions are crisp-tender and tomatoes are tender. Sprinkle with parsley.

1 Serving Calories 270; Total Fat 8g (Saturated Fat 2.5g, Trans Fat 0g); Cholesterol 50mg; Sodium 570mg; Total Carbohydrate 29g (Dietary Fiber 2g); Protein 19g **Carbohydrate Choices:** 2

GLUTEN FREE

Inside-Out Cuban-Inspired Pork Tenderloin Roll

We've taken the classic flavors of a Cuban sandwich and literally rolled them all together in this delightful new way to prepare pork tenderloin for dinner.

PREP 30 Minutes **TOTAL** 1 Hour 5 Minutes • *4 servings*

SWEET MUSTARD SAUCE AND GLAZE
- ¼ cup butter
- ¼ cup packed brown sugar
- ¼ cup yellow mustard
- 1 tablespoon chili powder

PORK TENDERLOIN
- 1¼ lb pork tenderloin

- 3 thin slices Swiss cheese
- 3 thin slices gluten-free Black Forest ham
- ½ cup dill pickle slices
- 2 cloves garlic, finely chopped
- 1 tablespoon vegetable oil
- ½ teaspoon salt
- ½ teaspoon pepper

1 Heat gas or charcoal grill to medium for direct heat (see page 421). Soak 4 (10-inch) pieces of kitchen twine in water 10 minutes to prevent burning.

2 Meanwhile, in 2-quart saucepan, melt butter over low heat. Stir in brown sugar, mustard and chili powder. Cook 2 to 3 minutes, stirring frequently, or until boiling. Pour ¼ cup of the sauce into small bowl; reserve. Leave remaining sauce in pan for basting pork.

3 Insert knife one-third of way up from bottom of tenderloin along one long side and cut horizontally, stopping ½ inch before edge. Open up flap. Keeping knife parallel to cutting board, cut through thicker portion of tenderloin about ½ inch from bottom of tenderloin, keeping knife level with first cut and stopping about ½ inch before edge. Open up this flap. Press sides of tenderloin down so it lies flat. Cover with plastic wrap; pound with flat side of meat mallet to ½ inch thick.

4 Remove plastic wrap. Place cheese down center of tenderloin; top with ham. Arrange pickles on top of ham. Sprinkle garlic evenly over filling. Tightly roll up tenderloin, starting from long edge. Tie tenderloin tightly with twine.

5 Brush tenderloin with oil, then rub with salt and pepper. Place seam side up on grill. Cover grill; cook 15 minutes. Turn pork; brush with remaining glaze in pan. Cover grill; cook 10 to 15 minutes longer or until instant-read meat thermometer inserted in center of tenderloin reads at least 145°F.

6 Transfer to cutting board; cover with foil and let stand 5 minutes. Cut and discard twine. Cut tenderloin into slices with serrated knife. Serve with the reserved sauce.

1 Serving Calories 510; Total Fat 30g (Saturated Fat 14g, Trans Fat 0.5g); Cholesterol 150mg; Sodium 1180mg; Total Carbohydrate 18g (Dietary Fiber 1g); Protein 43g **Carbohydrate Choices:** 1

REMOVING SILVERSKIN FROM PORK TENDERLOIN

Slide long, narrow knife under silverskin. Hold silverskin tightly with one hand and pull while cutting it away from meat with knife.

Pork Ribs with Smoky Barbecue Sauce

PREP 30 Minutes **TOTAL** 1 Hour 40 Minutes • *4 servings*

RIBS

- 2 racks (2 lb each) pork back ribs (not cut into serving pieces), silverskin removed (see below)
- 1 tablespoon vegetable oil
- 4 teaspoons chopped fresh or 1½ teaspoons dried thyme leaves

SMOKY BARBECUE SAUCE

- ½ cup ketchup
- ¼ cup water
- 3 tablespoons packed brown sugar
- 2 tablespoons white vinegar
- 2 teaspoons celery seed
- ¼ teaspoon liquid smoke
- ¼ teaspoon red pepper sauce

1 Brush meaty side of ribs with oil; sprinkle with thyme. Heat gas or charcoal grill to medium for indirect heat (see page 421).

2 Place ribs meat side up on grill. Cover grill; cook 1 hour to 1 hour 10 minutes or until meat is tender.

3 Meanwhile, in 1-quart saucepan, mix sauce ingredients. Heat to boiling; reduce heat. Simmer uncovered, 15 minutes, stirring occasionally, or until slightly thickened. Reserve ½ cup; set aside.

REMOVING SILVERSKIN FROM PORK RIBS

Slide long, narrow knife under silverskin at one end; lift and loosen until you can grab it with a paper towel. Pull it off in one piece, if possible.

4 Brush remaining sauce over pork 2 or 3 times and turn pork once during last 15 minutes of grilling. Cut ribs into 4 serving pieces. Serve with reserved sauce.

1 Serving Calories 960; Total Fat 70g (Saturated Fat 25g, Trans Fat 0g); Cholesterol 265mg; Sodium 550mg; Total Carbohydrate 18g (Dietary Fiber 0g); Protein 64g **Carbohydrate Choices:** 1

PORK RIBS WITH CHERRY COLA BARBECUE SAUCE: Prepare as directed—except omit thyme. After rubbing ribs with oil in Step 1, rub with ½ teaspoon each seasoned salt, gluten-free garlic-pepper blend and ¼ teaspoon ground ginger. In Step 3, substitute ¾ cup cherry cola, ¼ cup barbecue sauce, 2 tablespoons cherry preserves, ¼ teaspoon ground mustard and 1 teaspoon Buffalo-style hot sauce (or other hot sauce) for all barbecue sauce ingredients. Continue as directed in Step 4.

SLOW-COOKER PORK RIBS WITH SMOKY BARBECUE SAUCE: Spray 5- to 6-quart slow cooker with cooking spray. Cut ribs into 4 serving pieces. Omit oil and thyme. Place ribs in slow cooker. Pour ½ cup apple juice over ribs. Cover; cook on Low heat setting 6 hours or just until tender. Prepare sauce as directed in Step 3. Heat gas or charcoal grill to medium for direct heat. Place ribs on grill meat side up. Continue as directed in Step 4.

Southwestern-Seasoned Pork Chops

PREP 5 Minutes **TOTAL** 45 Minutes • *4 servings*

- 1 tablespoon chili powder
- 1 tablespoon vegetable oil
- 1 teaspoon ground cumin
- ¼ teaspoon salt
- ¼ teaspoon ground red pepper (cayenne)

- 1 large clove garlic, finely chopped
- 8 (½-inch-thick) pork loin or rib chops (2¼ lb)
- 4 cups hot steamed broccoli
- 4 teaspoons butter, melted

Pork Ribs with Smoky Barbecue Sauce

Southwestern-Seasoned Pork Chops

1 In small bowl, stir together chili powder, oil, cumin, salt, red pepper and garlic. Spread mixture evenly on both sides of pork. Place in dish. Cover and refrigerate at least 30 minutes but no longer than 24 hours.

2 Heat gas or charcoal grill to medium for direct heat (see page 421).

3 Place pork chops on grill. Cover grill; cook 10 to 12 minutes, turning frequently, until instant-read meat thermometer inserted in center (not touching bone) reads at least 145°F.

4 Divide pork chops among 4 serving plates. Divide broccoli among plates; drizzle with butter.

1 Serving Calories 430; Total Fat 22g (Saturated Fat 8g, Trans Fat 0g); Cholesterol 125mg; Sodium 280mg; Total Carbohydrate 11g (Dietary Fiber 6g); Protein 46g **Carbohydrate Choices:** 1

FAST • CALORIE SMART • GLUTEN FREE

Rosemary Lamb Chops

French-cut lamb chops are small and very tender. If these chops are not available, the recipe can also be made with lamb loin or sirloin chops. Both of these cuts are a little meatier, so allow 1 or 2 chops per serving.

PREP 20 Minutes **TOTAL** 20 Minutes •
2 servings (3 chops each)

1 tablespoon country-style Dijon mustard	½ teaspoon salt
1 tablespoon chopped fresh rosemary leaves	¼ teaspoon coarse ground black pepper
2 teaspoons honey	6 French-cut lamb chops (1 to 1¼ inches thick)
1 clove garlic, finely chopped	

1 Heat gas or charcoal grill to medium for direct heat (see page 421).

2 Meanwhile, in small bowl, mix all ingredients except lamb. Spread mixture on one side of each lamb chop.

3 Place lamb coated side up on grill. Cover grill; cook 12 to 15 minutes, turning once or twice, or until desired doneness (145°F rare to 160°F medium).

1 Serving Calories 390; Total Fat 21g (Saturated Fat 7g, Trans Fat 1g); Cholesterol 135mg; Sodium 900mg; Total Carbohydrate 7g (Dietary Fiber 0g); Protein 41g **Carbohydrate Choices:** ½

FAST • CALORIE SMART • GLUTEN FREE

Buttery Fish

PREP 20 Minutes **TOTAL** 20 Minutes • ***4 servings***

1½ lb fish steaks or 1 lb fish fillets (halibut, lake trout, mahi mahi, marlin, red snapper, salmon, swordfish or tuna; each about ¾ inch thick)	2 tablespoons butter, melted
	1 teaspoon salt
	¼ teaspoon pepper
	1 lemon, cut into 4 wedges

1 Heat gas or charcoal grill to medium for direct heat (see page 421).

2 Cut fish into 4 serving pieces, if necessary. Brush fish with 1 tablespoon of the butter; sprinkle with salt and pepper.

3 Carefully brush grill with vegetable oil (see Oiling the Grill Rack, page 421). Place fish on grill (if fish fillets have skin, place skin side down). Cover grill; cook 10 to 14 minutes, brushing fish 2 or 3 times with remaining 1 tablespoon butter, or until fish flakes easily with fork. Serve with lemon.

1 Serving Calories 200; Total Fat 8g (Saturated Fat 4g, Trans Fat 0g); Cholesterol 95mg; Sodium 740mg; Total Carbohydrate 1g (Dietary Fiber 0g); Protein 30g **Carbohydrate Choices:** 0

HERBED GRILLED FISH: Sprinkle fish with 1 teaspoon Italian seasoning with the salt and pepper. Substitute olive oil for butter.

HONEY-DIJON GRILLED FISH: Mix 2 tablespoons each honey and Dijon mustard. Brush mixture on fish before grilling. Omit butter and salt.

REMOVING SKIN FROM COOKED FISH

Small fish with skin on both sides: Grab skin from tail end with tongs or fingers and gently peel off. Turn fish and repeat on other side.

Large pieces with skin on one side: Insert pancake turner between fish and skin and slide off skin.

Rosemary Lamb Chops

Salmon and Pineapple with Maple-Soy Sauce

PREP 30 Minutes **TOTAL** 1 Hour • *4 servings*

- ½ cup pure maple syrup
- ¼ cup gluten-free reduced-sodium soy sauce
- 2 tablespoons lime juice
- ½ medium pineapple, rind removed, cored, cut into 1-inch spears
- 4 (4-oz) skin-on salmon fillets
- 1 teaspoon olive oil
- ⅛ teaspoon salt
- 2 cups hot cooked brown rice (page 224)

1 In 1-quart saucepan, heat maple syrup and soy sauce to boiling over medium heat. Reduce heat. Simmer 10 to 15 minutes or until reduced by half. Remove from heat; stir in lime juice. Cover to keep warm; set aside.

2 Heat gas or charcoal grill to medium for direct heat (see page 421).

3 Carefully brush grill with vegetable oil (see Oiling the Grill Rack, page 421). Place pineapple on grill. Cook 2 to 4 minutes on each side, or until grill marks form and pineapple turns easily. Transfer to cutting board; cover with foil tent to keep warm.

4 Rub flesh side of salmon with olive oil and salt. Place salmon skin side down on grill. Cover grill; cook 10 to 12 minutes or until salmon flakes easily with fork. Lift salmon from skin with spatula to platter; discard skin.

5 Cut pineapple into 1-inch chunks. Divide rice among 4 plates; top with salmon and pineapple. Serve with maple-soy sauce.

1 Serving Calories 470; Total Fat 11g (Saturated Fat 2.5g, Trans Fat 0g); Cholesterol 65mg; Sodium 840mg; Total Carbohydrate 66g (Dietary Fiber 4g); Protein 29g **Carbohydrate Choices:** 4½

GRILL PAN DIRECTIONS: Prepare as directed—except spray grill pan with cooking spray. Heat grill pan over medium heat. Cook pineapple 2 to 4 minutes on each side, until grill marks form and pineapple lifts easily from grill pan. Cook salmon skin side up in grill pan 5 minutes; reduce heat to low; turn and cook 5 to 8 minutes longer or until salmon flakes easily with fork.

Shrimp with Lemon-Basil Tartar Sauce

Enjoy this wonderful grilled shrimp served with basil tartar sauce—a seafood dinner ready in 20 minutes.

PREP 10 Minutes **TOTAL** 20 Minutes • *4 servings*

- 2 tablespoons butter, melted
- 1 tablespoon lemon juice
- ¼ teaspoon garlic powder
- ¾ teaspoon lemon-pepper seasoning
- 1½ lb uncooked peeled, deveined large shrimp, thawed if frozen, tails removed
- ½ cup mayonnaise or salad dressing (for homemade mayonnaise, see page 479)
- 2 tablespoons chopped drained roasted red bell pepper (from 12-oz jar)
- 2 tablespoons chopped fresh basil leaves
- ½ teaspoon lemon zest

1 Heat closed medium-size contact grill for 5 to 10 minutes.

2 In large bowl, mix butter, lemon juice, garlic powder and ½ teaspoon of the lemon-pepper seasoning. Add shrimp; toss to coat.

3 Place shrimp on grill. Close grill; cook 4 to 6 minutes or until shrimp are pink.

4 Meanwhile, in small bowl, mix mayonnaise, roasted pepper, basil, lemon zest and remaining ¼ teaspoon lemon-pepper seasoning. Serve with shrimp.

1 Serving Calories 370; Total Fat 27g (Saturated Fat 7g, Trans Fat 0g); Cholesterol 260mg; Sodium 480mg; Total Carbohydrate 1g (Dietary Fiber 0g); Protein 30g **Carbohydrate Choices:** 0

Salmon and Pineapple with Maple-Soy Sauce

Shrimp with Lemon-Basil Tartar Sauce

Adobo Fish Tacos

Adobo Fish Tacos

PREP 30 Minutes **TOTAL** 30 Minutes •
4 servings (2 tacos each)

2 tablespoons lime juice

2 tablespoons adobo sauce (from 7-oz can chipotle chiles)

1 lb fresh or frozen (thawed) cod, haddock or other medium-firm fish fillets (about 1 inch thick), cut into 4 pieces

8 taco shells (any variety)

1 cup shredded red cabbage (from 10-oz bag)

1 medium ripe avocado, pitted, peeled and chopped

½ cup crumbled Cotija (white Mexican) cheese (2 oz)

Fish Taco Sauce, if desired (page 483)

Fresh cilantro leaves, if desired

1 Heat gas or charcoal grill to medium for direct heat (see page 421).

2 In small bowl, stir together lime juice and adobo sauce. Reserve 2 tablespoons of mixture; set aside. Brush remaining mixture over fish; let stand at room temperature 15 minutes to marinate.

3 Carefully brush grill rack with vegetable oil (see Oiling the Grill Rack, page 421). Place fish on the grill. Cover grill; cook 5 to 8 minutes, or until fish flakes easily with a fork, brushing with reserved adobo mixture the last minute of cooking. (Fish cooks quickly, especially the thinner tail sections; be careful not to overcook.)

4 Divide fish among taco shells, breaking up as necessary to fit shells. Top with cabbage, avocado and cheese. Top tacos with taco sauce and cilantro.

1 Serving Calories 340; Total Fat 17g (Saturated Fat 5g, Trans Fat 0g); Cholesterol 65mg; Sodium 430mg; Total Carbohydrate 22g (Dietary Fiber 4g); Protein 26g **Carbohydrate Choices:** 1½

SKILLET DIRECTIONS: Prepare fish as directed above—except in Step 3, heat 10-inch nonstick skillet over medium heat. Cook fish uncovered in skillet 8 to 10 minutes or until fish flakes easily with fork, turning once and brushing with reserved adobo mixture the last minute of cooking.

CHIPOTLE CHILES

Chipotle chiles add a lot of flavor to Mexican-inspired dishes, but typically only the chiles are used, not the sauce that clings to them. In Adobo Fish Tacos, we call for the sauce only in the marinade for the fish. Spoon any leftover chiles and sauce onto a piece of plastic wrap and roll up in a log, about the size of a stick of butter. Keep in the freezer for recipes calling for chipotle chiles; when frozen and then thawed, the chiles will soften, and you can use both chiles and sauce in recipes calling for chiles. From the frozen log, simply cut a slice about the size of a pat of butter to equal 1 chile or 1 tablespoon sauce.

Grilling Fresh Vegetables

Toss vegetables (except corn) with a little olive or vegetable oil (1 to 2 tablespoons per pound); sprinkle with salt and pepper. Heat grill to medium for direct heat and grill in grill basket (see Using a Grill Basket, page 445) for time indicated.

VEGETABLE	FORM	GRILL TIME (MINUTES)
Asparagus	Whole spears	8 to 10
Bell Peppers	Cut into ½-inch-wide strips	10 to 15
Broccoli	Bite-size florets	15 to 20
Carrots	Whole baby cut	20 to 25
Cauliflower	Bite-size florets	10 to 15
Corn on the Cob	Whole, husked and wrapped in foil	12 to 18
Grape or Cherry Tomatoes	Whole	5 to 10
Green Beans	Whole	10 to 15
Mushrooms, White or Baby Portabella	Whole, stems removed	8 to 10
Onions	½-inch slices or wedges	10 to 15
Potatoes, Russet or Idaho	Cut lengthwise into quarters	20 to 30
Potatoes, Small Red	Cut into quarters	10 to 15
Zucchini	Cut lengthwise in half	10 to 15

FAST • GLUTEN FREE • VEGETARIAN • VEGAN

Herbed Red Potatoes

PREP 25 Minutes **TOTAL** 25 Minutes • *4 servings*

- 2 tablespoons olive or vegetable oil
- 1 tablespoon chopped fresh parsley leaves or ½ teaspoon dried parsley flakes
- 1 tablespoon chopped fresh or ½ teaspoon dried rosemary leaves, crumbled
- ½ teaspoon lemon-pepper seasoning
- ¼ teaspoon salt
- 8 small red potatoes, cut into quarters

1 Heat gas or charcoal grill to medium for direct heat (see page 421).

2 In large bowl, mix all ingredients except potatoes. Add potatoes; toss to coat. Place potatoes in grill basket.

3 Place grill basket on grill. Cover grill; cook 10 to 15 minutes, shaking basket or stirring potatoes occasionally, or until tender.

1 Serving Calories 330; Total Fat 7g (Saturated Fat 1g, Trans Fat 0g); Cholesterol 0mg; Sodium 220mg; Total Carbohydrate 59g (Dietary Fiber 6g); Protein 7g **Carbohydrate Choices:** 4

FAST • GLUTEN FREE • VEGETARIAN

Grilled Corn on the Cob with Herb Butter

Husks may appear charred even though the corn inside is not. Use oven mitts or pot holders to hold corn and remove husks before placing corn on serving platter or individual plates. Or you can fully husk the corn and place each ear on a 12-inch square of heavy-duty foil. Spread with herb butter. Wrap foil around corn, sealing edges and allowing space for heat circulation and expansion.

PREP 25 Minutes **TOTAL** 25 Minutes • *4 servings*

- ¼ cup butter, softened
- 2 tablespoons chopped fresh chives
- 1 tablespoon chopped fresh basil leaves
- 1 tablespoon chopped fresh oregano leaves
- 4 medium ears fresh sweet corn with husks

1 In small bowl, mix butter, chives, basil and oregano.

2 Heat gas or charcoal grill to medium for direct heat (see page 421). Remove all but innermost husks from corn. Fold back inner husks and remove corn silk. Brush corn with herb butter. Rewrap inner husks around corn. Place corn on grill. Cover grill; cook 10 to 15 minutes, turning occasionally, or until corn is tender and husks are slightly brown.

1 Serving Calories 230; Total Fat 13g (Saturated Fat 8g, Trans Fat 0g); Cholesterol 30mg; Sodium 100mg; Total Carbohydrate 25g (Dietary Fiber 4g); Protein 3g **Carbohydrate Choices:** 1½

CILANTRO-GARLIC GRILLED CORN ON THE COB: Omit herbs. Mix 2 finely chopped garlic cloves and 1 tablespoon chopped fresh cilantro with the butter.

BUFFALO GRILLED CORN ON THE COB: Omit herbs. Mix 2 teaspoons red pepper sauce and 2 teaspoons finely chopped green onion into butter. Sprinkle cooked corn with crumbled blue cheese.

PARMESAN-PEPPER GRILLED CORN ON THE COB: Omit herbs. Stir ¼ teaspoon pepper into butter. Sprinkle cooked corn with grated Parmesan cheese.

Herbed Red Potatoes

Herbed
Zucchini
and
Tomatoes

Garlicky Summer Vegetables

FAST • CALORIE SMART • GLUTEN FREE •
VEGETARIAN

Herbed Zucchini and Tomatoes

Sprinkle any leftover fresh herbs you have on hand or growing in your garden as a pretty garnish for this simple side dish.

PREP 20 Minutes TOTAL 20 Minutes • *4 servings*

3 tablespoons olive oil	2 teaspoons chopped fresh thyme leaves
⅛ teaspoon ground cumin	1 teaspoon finely chopped fresh rosemary leaves
4 small zucchini (1½ lb), cut in half lengthwise	¼ teaspoon kosher (coarse) salt
4 medium plum (Roma) tomatoes, cut in half lengthwise, seeded	

1 Heat gas or charcoal grill to medium-high for direct heat (see page 421).

2 In large bowl, mix olive oil and cumin. Add zucchini and tomatoes; sprinkle with thyme, rosemary and salt. Toss gently to coat.

3 Place vegetables cut side up on grill. Cover grill; cook 5 minutes. Turn vegetables; cook 5 minutes longer or until crisp-tender.

1 Serving Calories 130; Total Fat 11g (Saturated Fat 1.5g, Trans Fat 0g); Cholesterol 0mg; Sodium 160mg; Total Carbohydrate 6g (Dietary Fiber 2g); Protein 2g **Carbohydrate Choices:** ½

CHEESY GRILLED ZUCCHINI AND TOMATOES: After grilling, sprinkle ¼ cup grated Parmesan cheese over vegetables.

ITALIAN-INSPIRED GRILLED ZUCCHINI AND TOMATOES: Omit cumin, thyme and rosemary. Drizzle zucchini and tomatoes with olive oil; sprinkle with 2 finely chopped medium garlic cloves. Grill as directed. Sprinkle with 1 tablespoon sliced fresh basil leaves and drizzle with 2 teaspoons balsamic vinegar.

GLUTEN FREE • VEGETARIAN • VEGAN

Garlicky Summer Vegetables

PREP 20 Minutes TOTAL 40 Minutes • *4 servings*

¼ cup olive oil	1 medium yellow summer squash, cut into ¼-inch slices
½ teaspoon salt	
½ teaspoon pepper	1 medium red onion, cut into ½-inch slices
1 small eggplant (about ¾ lb), cut into ¼-inch slices	1 large yellow or red bell pepper, cut into quarters
1 lb fresh asparagus spears, trimmed	4 cloves garlic, thinly sliced

1 Heat gas or charcoal grill to medium for direct heat (see page 421).

2 In small bowl, mix olive oil, salt and pepper. Brush vegetables with olive oil mixture; toss with garlic slices. Place vegetables in grill basket.

3 Place basket on grill. Cover grill; cook 15 to 20 minutes, stirring occasionally, or until vegetables are crisp-tender. Serve warm.

1 Serving Calories 210; Total Fat 14g (Saturated Fat 2g, Trans Fat 0g); Cholesterol 0mg; Sodium 300mg; Total Carbohydrate 17g (Dietary Fiber 6g); Protein 4g **Carbohydrate Choices:** 1

USING A GRILL BASKET

A grill basket, also known as a grill wok, lets foods like veggies (which might fall through the spaces in the grill rack) cook and get caramelized, crusty edges because the steam can escape through the holes in the basket. Spray the basket with cooking spray over the sink for easy cleanup. Place food that's been tossed with a little olive or vegetable oil in basket; place basket directly on grill. Shake using a pot holder or stir food in basket for even cooking.

Smoking Basics

To traditionalists, smoking is the original, the only barbecue. Smoking is an unfussy form of outdoor cooking that uses low heat and hardwoods to impart smoky flavor to meat, poultry, fish and vegetables. If you don't own a smoker, you can impart smoked flavor on your grill.

Types of Smokers

Smokers come in a variety of shapes and sizes. Regardless of their style, all smokers contain a firebox, water pan and grill racks. The most common smokers are charcoal water smokers and electric water smokers. When choosing a smoker, its cost and fuel source will be important factors to consider, as different types will require more or less time tending the fire and watching the temperature of the foods you are smoking. Be realistic about how much time you want to tend to these tasks, to help you find the best smoker for you.

To smoke, the food is placed on a grill rack high above or next to the heat. A pan of water or other liquid (beer, fruit juice, wine, soda) rests between the heat source and the food. Water-soaked aromatic wood chunks, chips or shreds are burned. Food is cooked very slowly in the dense fog created from the damp wood chips, infusing it with the characteristic flavor, moistness and tenderness smoked foods are known for. Foods best for smoking include ribs, beef brisket, roasts, poultry and fish. Follow the smoker manufacturer's directions for best results.

Safety Tips for Smoking

Follow the manufacturer's directions for specific safety tips for your smoker, and use these basic tips to ensure successful results.

- Always position the smoker on a level, heatproof, sturdy surface. Keep the smoker away from buildings and from where people will frequently walk by, since the smoky aromas can last for hours.

- Smoke only completely thawed meats, poultry, fish or seafood. The heat inside the cooker is too low to thaw and cook the food safely.

- It's best to smoke foods when the outside temperature is 65°F or higher and there is little or no wind. Below 55°F, the smoker and the food will not get hot enough to cook properly and may require an additional 2 to 3 hours of cooking.

- To avoid burns, use long tongs and barbecue mitts when doing anything inside the hot smoker.

- It's important to monitor the temperature inside the smoker and of the meat. To ensure that the smoker stays between 225°F and 300°F throughout the cooking process, use an oven thermometer.

- Smoked meat can have a reddish appearance inside, even when fully cooked, so it's important to gauge the temperature of the food to know that it's cooked properly. A digital oven probe thermometer can stay in the food in the smoker and will sound an alarm when the food reaches the correct temperature. This prevents you from having to open the smoker to check the meat's temperature. If using an ovenproof thermometer, you'll have to open the smoker to check it, which can let heat out and increase the cook time. See Thermometers (page 21) for more information.

Wood Chips

Look for wood chips, shreds or chunks for smoking near the grill supplies at home improvement, hardware and discount stores. Experiment with different chips to add different flavors to your smoked foods.

Infusing Food with Smoke on a Grill

If you don't own a smoker, you can use your grill to add smoky flavor to meat while grilling. (Use grill recipes, rather than smoker recipes, for your food to cook properly); here's how. Start with up to 2 cups wood chips or shreds or 2 to 3 cups wood chunks. Experiment with how much smokiness you like. Start with a small amount of wood and add more next time if you want more smoke flavor. (But remember that too much smokiness can cause foods to taste bitter.) Whichever grill and form of wood you use, soak the wood for at least 30 minutes, then drain well.

Using a Charcoal Grill: Prepare grill for indirect-heat grilling (see page 421). For recipes that require more than 45 minutes cooking time, fill the pan with liquid. The water will add moistness to the food while cooking and helps maintain the grill temperature.

Add the damp wood to the hot coals. Cover the grill; let the wood get hot enough that it gives off smoke before you place food to smoke on the grill rack, over the drip pan.

Hickory
Mesquite
Apple
Cedar

Using a Gas Grill: Prepare grill for direct-heat or indirect-heat grilling (see page 421) as directed in recipe. Place the damp wood on a piece of heavy-duty foil; seal tightly to form a pouch. Poke 6 to 8 slits in the pouch with a sharp knife. Place the pouch on the hot grill rack. (Or follow the manufacturer's directions for adding wood chips.) Cover the grill; let the pouch get hot enough for the wood to start smoking, about 10 minutes. Add food to the grill rack, leaving the pouch on the grill during cooking.

GLUTEN FREE

Hot and Spicy Ribs

PREP 15 Minutes TOTAL 5 Hours 15 Minutes • *6 servings*

RIBS	HOT AND SPICY RUB
4 cups hickory wood chips	1 tablespoon garlic powder
5 lb pork spareribs (not cut into serving pieces), silverskin removed (see page 440)	1 tablespoon paprika
	2 teaspoons ground red pepper (cayenne)
Gluten-free barbecue sauce, if desired	2 teaspoons dried thyme leaves, crushed
	1 teaspoon salt
	1 teaspoon pepper

1 In large bowl, cover wood chips with water; soak 30 minutes. Drain. Prepare and heat smoker using wood chips and adding water to water pan following manufacturer's directions.

2 In small bowl, mix rub ingredients. Cut rack of ribs in half to fit on smoker rack if necessary. Rub spice mixture into pork.

3 Place pork on rack in smoker. Cover smoker; cook 4 hours 30 minutes to 5 hours, maintaining temperature inside smoker following manufacturer's directions, or until meat is very tender and can be pulled away from bones in center of pork rack when one side of rib rack is lifted with tongs. If smoke stops, add additional wood to smoker following manufacturer's directions. Cut ribs into serving pieces; serve with barbecue sauce.

1 Serving Calories 770; Total Fat 59g (Saturated Fat 22g, Trans Fat 0g); Cholesterol 235mg; Sodium 580mg; Total Carbohydrate 3g (Dietary Fiber 1g); Protein 57g **Carbohydrate Choices:** 0

CALORIE SMART • GLUTEN FREE

Smoky Beef Brisket

PREP 10 Minutes TOTAL 5 Hours 50 Minutes • *12 servings*

2	cups hickory wood chips	2 teaspoons garlic powder	
BRISKET RUB		1 teaspoon ground mustard	
1	tablespoon coarse sea salt	1 teaspoon smoked paprika	
1	tablespoon coarse ground black pepper	1 teaspoon chili powder	
1	tablespoon packed brown sugar	**BRISKET**	
2	teaspoons onion powder	1 piece (3 lb) fresh beef brisket (not corned beef)	

1 In large bowl, cover wood chips with water; soak 30 minutes. Drain.

2 Prepare and heat smoker using wood chips and adding water to pan following manufacturer's directions.

3 In small bowl, mix all brisket rub ingredients. Rub mixture onto all surfaces of beef.

4 Carefully brush smoker rack with vegetable oil (see Oiling the Grill Rack, page 421). Place beef on rack in smoker. Cover smoker; cook about 4 to 5 hours, maintaining temperature following manufacturer's directions, or until the beef is very tender. If smoke stops, add additional wood chips following manufacturer's directions. Remove beef from smoker to cutting board or plate; cover and let stand 10 minutes. Cut beef across grain into thin slices.

1 Serving Calories 170; Total Fat 7g (Saturated Fat 2.5g, Trans Fat 0g); Cholesterol 70mg; Sodium 1210mg; Total Carbohydrate 2g (Dietary Fiber 0g); Protein 24g **Carbohydrate Choices:** 0

OVEN-BAKED BEEF BRISKET: Prepare beef as directed for cooking—except omit wood chips. Heat oven to 325°F. Place beef in 4-quart ovenproof Dutch oven or 3-quart casserole. Cover and bake 3 hours, turning beef halfway through baking, or until tender. Let stand 10 minutes before slicing.

447

Hot and Spicy Ribs

Smoky Beef Brisket

Do It Yourself

Preserving Food Basics

DIY has come full circle when you talk about food. Past generations put up their own pickles, jellies and jams, and canned vegetables because they had to. Today, the make-it-yourself movement in the kitchen has become "because we *want* to." While there are many choices to choose from in our grocery stores, people are opting to make their own versions of preserved foods for many reasons. Whether it's a way to avoid chemical preservatives, to control seasoning and salt levels, to take advantage of fresh, locally grown produce at its peak or to make foods to share as gifts from your kitchen—nothing beats homemade.

Preserving your own food is rewarding, and can be an economical way to stock your pantry and refrigerator. Preserving food keeps it longer, so that you can enjoy it later. You can preserve foods by freezing, drying, canning or fermenting. The method you choose will depend on what you are trying to preserve and the result you wish to achieve.

Freezing Foods

Freezing is a terrific way to preserve in-season produce. When it's frozen at the peak of freshness, much of the nutrient value is left, making it a great way to have fresh-tasting, nutritious produce all year long. It's a clever way to take advantage of a bountiful harvest and low prices. Fruits and vegetables can each be stored in clean food-storage freezer containers with lids or resealable freezer plastic bags. Look for reusable bags in discount stores and online. Produce will freeze faster, be easier to store and keep longer if stored in containers that aren't too large; slow freezing allows ice crystals to form on the food, causing freezer burn. Most fruits and vegetables can be frozen up to 1 year.

VEGETABLES

To freeze most vegetables successfully, you'll want to blanch them first. Blanching stops the enzyme actions that cause loss of flavor, color and texture. It also slows the loss of vitamins, brightens the color and softens vegetables for easier packing in freezer containers.

To blanch, heat 1 gallon of water per pound of cleaned vegetables to boiling. Add the vegetables and let the water return to boiling. Boil vegetables according to

the chart (below). After boiling, immediately remove vegetables from the water with a strainer with a handle or slotted spoon and plunge them into a bowl of ice-cold water to stop the cooking process and cool them quickly.

VEGETABLE BLANCHING TIME

VEGETABLE	BLANCHING TIME
Green peas, turnips or parsnips (cubed)	2 minutes
Asparagus (medium stalks), broccoli or cauliflower florets, Brussels sprouts (small), bell pepper halves, green or wax beans, okra	3 minutes
Asparagus (thick stalks), Brussels sprouts (large), carrots (baby), edamame pods, corn on the cob (small to medium ears)*	5 minutes

*Cut corn kernels from cobs after boiling and cooling.

FRUITS

To freeze fruits, sort, wash and drain carefully. Prepare fruits as you would serve them, removing stems, coring, peeling and slicing as needed. Frozen fruit will be softer after freezing.

Small whole fruits such as berries and cherries can be frozen individually on a small tray, and then placed in resealable freezer plastic bags for use in smoothies, salads and desserts. Some fruits, such as apples, peaches, nectarines and pears, might need acid added to keep their color during freezing. Look for ascorbic acid products, to help fruits maintain their color, near the canning supplies. Be sure to follow the package directions carefully. Citric acid or lemon juice can be used instead: Dissolve ¼ teaspoon in 1 quart of cold water. Place the prepared fruit in the mixture for 1 to 2 minutes. Drain; freeze in resealable freezer plastic bags or pack in freezer-safe food storage containers with sugar, water or fruit juice as directed in individual recipes.

Home Canning

Home canning isn't difficult, but it's important to do it correctly so the food you preserve is safe from microorganisms that could cause spoilage or health hazards. To destroy spoilage organisms such as mold, yeast and bacteria, food must be processed long enough and at a high enough temperature. The amount of acidity of the food determines which canning method to use.

Pressure Canning Use for low-acid foods such as meat, poultry and vegetables. Most pressure canners today have removable racks, an automatic vent/cover lock, a vent pipe (steam vent) and a safety fuse. Pressure canners are not the same as a pressure cooker or multicooker. Do not attempt to process foods in a pressure cooker. It's important to know your canner is working properly. Follow both the canner manual instructions and the recipe accurately to be sure you are cooking and cooling your food properly to preserve it safely for eating later.

Water Bath Canning Use for all acidic foods such as fruits, tomatoes with added acid, jams, jellies and pickled vegetables. A boiling water canner consists of a large pot with a lid and a rack to hold canning jars. The open kettle method of canning, which doesn't use the lid, isn't recommended, as it can't get the jars to temperatures hot enough to kill harmful microorganisms.

PREPARING JARS AND LIDS FOR CANNING

Check jars for chips or cracks and metal bands for dents or rust Inspect the jars and metal bands; discard or repurpose any with imperfections. Lids should never be reused: always can using new lids.

Wash jars, bands and lids Always clean jars just before filling, no matter whether they are brand new or have been used many times and stored. Wash in dishwasher or with hot, soapy water; rinse well. Dry lids and metal band thoroughly with clean kitchen towel. Let stand at room temperature while sterilizing jars.

Keep jars warm until ready to fill, by leaving them in a closed dishwasher after the rinse cycle, placing them in your canner as the water is heating or placing them in another pan of hot water that will keep the jars both clean and warm. Remove jars from water and drain just before filling.

Sterilize jars if necessary Jars need to be sterile to kill any organisms that could contaminate the food being processed in them, so nothing has a chance to grow while the food is stored. *No sterilizing is needed* if the processing time of your recipe is 10 minutes or more, or if you are using a pressure canner. *Sterilizing is needed* if processing time of your recipe is less than 10 minutes. (See next page for instructions.)

Water Bath Canner

Pressure Canner/Cooker

Canning Jars, Lids and Bands

Canning Funnel

Jar Lifter

Jar Wrench

Canning Rack

Magnetic Jar Lifter

Tongs

STERILIZING JARS

Place the cleaned jars right side up on the rack in the canner; fill jars and canner with water to 1 inch above the tops of the jars. Heat water to boiling; let boil 10 minutes at elevations less than 1,000 feet above sea level. Add an additional minute for each additional 1,000 feet of elevation. To fill the jars, remove one at a time, emptying the water back into the canner, so the water can be reused for processing the jars. Fill and cap the jar; return it to the canner. Process for the time required in your recipe.

WHEN IN DOUBT, THROW IT OUT

If any of these signs are present in your canned jars, do not eat the food. Discard the food in such a way that children or pets won't accidentally eat it either.

- Lid is loose and no longer vacuum sealed, or lid swells.
- Gas bubbles are present inside the jar.
- Liquid spurts out when the container is opened.
- Mold, cloudiness, yeast growth or fermentation is present.
- Jar is leaking.
- Unpleasant odor is present when jar is opened.

Drying Herbs and Fruit

HERBS

Drying herbs in the peak of growing season is a way to save money and enjoy their flavors throughout the year. Pick herbs in the morning, after the dew has dried, for the best flavor. Dry them until the leaves are crisp enough that they crumble in your hands. Store dried herbs as whole leaves in small containers with tight-fitting lids in a cool, dry place. For the best flavor, crumble the leaves only when you are ready to use them. Dried herbs are stronger in flavor than fresh, so use about one-third the amount of the fresh herb called for; if recipe calls for 1 tablespoon of a fresh herb, substitute 1 teaspoon dried.

Sturdy Herbs (rosemary, sage, thyme, summer savory and parsley) Keep the herb leaves on the stems for easy drying. Bundle the stems; secure the bottoms with a rubber band. Hang and let dry indoors for best color and flavor. Remove leaves from stems and discard stems.

Tender Herbs (basil, oregano, tarragon, lemon balm and mint) These herbs have a high moisture content and will mold if not dried quickly. Prepare as directed above for sturdy herbs, except put small bunches inside clean paper bags; secure stems and bag with rubber band. Cut holes in bag sides to allow air to circulate. (The bags will catch any leaves or seeds that fall.) Hang in place where there are air currents so the herbs can dry quickly. In humid areas, dry mint and bay leaves only (remove from stems) on paper towel–lined trays or sheet pans in single layer, with no leaves touching one another. Cover with another layer of paper towels. To dry a large quantity, stack layers of leaves in this manner with paper towels between the layers.

FRUIT

Dried fruit makes a delicious, portable snack you can enjoy anywhere. Good choices for drying include apples, pears, peaches, plums, apricots, strawberries and blueberries. You can dry fruit in your oven if you can set it to 135°F and in 5°F increments up to 145°F. Keep the door open a few inches to allow moisture to escape. Use a convection oven, if you have one, since it blows hot air over the fruits, helping to dry them more quickly.

Peel the fruit, if desired. (If the peels are left on, they may take longer to dry than the flesh, and discolor and become tough when dried.) Remove cores, stems and seeds. Cut fruit in same-thickness slices or same-size pieces to ensure even drying. Some fruit, such as apples and peaches, need to be soaked in a mixture of equal parts of lemon juice and water for 10 minutes before drying to prevent browning.

Place fruit in single layer on sheet pans, with no pieces touching. Start drying the fruit at 145°F in the oven for about an hour; there will still be moisture on the surface. Reduce the oven temperature to 135°F or 140°F and continue until the fruit is pliable and no moisture forms when pressed between your fingers. (If dried at too high a temperature, the outer surface will harden, preventing moisture from being released from inside the fruit.) Fruit will shrink as it dries.

Fermenting Vegetables

Fermentation, also called lacto-fermentation, is the decomposition of food by healthy bacteria and enzymes. Lactic-acid producing bacteria convert sugars naturally present in vegetables into lactic acid in an oxygen-free environment. This inhibits bad bacteria and acts as a preservative, giving the vegetables a distinctively tangy flavor.

Fermenting is not the same as canning, and is not used for long-term preservation. It's also different from pickling: Fermented foods are preserved by adding bacteria that convert sugars into acids, while pickled foods are preserved by a high-acid brine, such as vinegar.

Until a few generations ago, fermenting was a common practice for food preservation. Both home cooks and chefs are again getting interested in fermenting their own vegetables. Why? Fermented vegetables take on new flavors, adding interest—they are usually more tart in flavor than their raw versions. They are also easier to digest than raw, and help you digest other foods in the digestive track, similar to yogurt made with live cultures. (See Learn to Ferment Hot Sauce, page 458.)

Just about any raw vegetable can be safely fermented at home, if done properly. Properly fermented and stored vegetables may actually be safer to eat than raw vegetables because the fermentation process hunts down and kills harmful bacteria that may be present in the raw vegetables.

While there's no veggie you can't ferment, green tomatoes, green beans, cucumbers, cabbage, daikon radishes, parsnips and okra the best choices for fermenting, because the end result will be flavorful. Some veggies, due to their makeup, end up with an undesirable flavor. Kale is an example, as its high chlorophyll content gives the fermented version a flavor most wouldn't enjoy.

GIFTABLE JARS

Decorating jars as gifts makes them as cute to give as they'll be delicious to devour!

- Add a decorative ribbon or string with a tag with the recipe name on it.

- Add fabric on top of the lids before securing the band and/or fabric and a ribbon over the tops. For a quilted appearance, place a piece of batting the size of the lid under the fabric first. (See page 471.)

- Add a label with the recipe to use the jar contents to the top of the jar.

- Use a glue gun to attach faux foliage or plastic snow globes (the size of the jar lids) to the tops of the jars.

EASY • FAST • MAKE AHEAD • CALORIE SMART • GLUTEN FREE • VEGETARIAN

Everything Bagel Seasoning

Everything bagel seasoning is popping up all over the place, but you don't make an extra trip to the store to buy a jar, you can easily make it yourself at home with just five ingredients. If you like, black sesame seed may be substituted for some of the regular sesame seed. Use it to season everything from scrambled eggs to cooked veggies.

PREP 5 Minutes **TOTAL** 5 Minutes • *About ½ cup*

- 3 tablespoons sesame seed*
- 2 tablespoons dried minced onion
- 2 tablespoons dried minced garlic
- 1 tablespoon kosher salt
- 1 tablespoon poppy seed*

In small container with tight fitting lid, stir all ingredients until well mixed; cover. Store in cool, dry place for up to 6 months. Stir or shake well before each use.

½ Teaspoon Calories 5; Total Fat 0g (Saturated Fat 0g, Trans Fat 0g); Cholesterol 0mg; Sodium 65mg; Total Carbohydrate 0g (Dietary Fiber 0g); Protein 0g **Carbohydrate Choices:** 0

*Sesame seed and poppy seed can go rancid after time. Be sure to buy fresh when you need them, or store them in the freezer to keep them fresh until needed.

FAST • MAKE AHEAD • CALORIE SMART • GLUTEN FREE • VEGETARIAN • VEGAN

Salt-Free Taco Seasoning Mix

Use this homemade taco seasoning in any recipe calling for the store-bought version. The beauty of this mix is you can add your own salt to taste. A quarter-cup of this mix is equal to a 1-oz package of purchased taco seasoning mix.

PREP 5 Minutes **TOTAL** 5 Minutes • *½ cup*

- 2 tablespoons chili powder
- 1 tablespoon onion powder
- 5 teaspoons ground cumin
- 5 teaspoons paprika
- 2½ teaspoons garlic powder
- ⅛ to ¼ teaspoon ground red pepper (cayenne)

In small container with tight-fitting lid, stir all ingredients until well mixed; cover. Store in cool, dry place up to 6 months. Stir or shake well before each use.

1 Teaspoon Calories 10; Total Fat 0g (Saturated Fat 0g, Trans Fat 0g); Cholesterol 0mg; Sodium 10mg; Total Carbohydrate 1g (Dietary Fiber 0g); Protein 0g **Carbohydrate Choices:** 0

SMOKY SALT-FREE TACO SEASONING MIX: Substitute 2 teaspoons smoked paprika for 2 teaspoons of the regular paprika.

Fajita Seasoning and Quick Skillet Fajitas

FAST • MAKE AHEAD • CALORIE SMART

Fajita Seasoning

If you don't have a mini food processor, place the toasted ancho chile in a resealable freezer plastic bag and use a potato masher, rolling pin or meat mallet to crush the chile until finely broken up.

PREP 20 Minutes **TOTAL** 20 Minutes • *⅓ cup*

- 1 dried medium ancho chile
- 1 tablespoon chili powder
- 1¼ teaspoons salt
- 1 teaspoon ground cumin
- 1 teaspoon dried oregano leaves
- ½ teaspoon garlic powder
- ½ teaspoon cornstarch
- ¼ teaspoon crushed red pepper flakes, if desired

1 Cut ancho chile in half lengthwise; empty seeds into small bowl. Remove and discard stem. Cut each chile half crosswise into two pieces.

2 In 8-inch skillet, cook chile pieces over medium heat, pressing with spatula to make contact with pan and turning occasionally, 5 to 7 minutes or until chile is dark brown in spots. Remove from skillet. Cool at least 5 minutes.

3 In mini food processor, place chile. Cover and process until pieces are finely chopped. Add chile to bowl with seeds. Add remaining ingredients; stir until well mixed. Place seasoning mix into small jar. Cover and store in cool, dry place up to 3 months. Stir or shake well before each use.

2½ Teaspoons Calories 15; Total Fat 0g (Saturated Fat 0g, Trans Fat 0g); Cholesterol 0mg; Sodium 500mg; Total Carbohydrate 3g (Dietary Fiber 1g); Protein 0g **Carbohydrate Choices:** 0

QUICK SKILLET FAJITAS: In medium bowl or 1-gallon resealable food-storage plastic bag, toss 1 lb thin strips boneless sirloin steak or boneless skinless chicken breast with half of the fajita seasoning. In another bowl or 1-gallon resealable food-storage plastic bag, toss 2 bell peppers (any color), cut into thin strips, and 1 sliced medium onion with remaining fajita seasoning. Heat 1 tablespoon vegetable oil in 10-inch nonstick skillet over medium-high heat. Cook meat in oil, stirring occasionally, 4 to 5 minutes or until no longer pink. Remove from skillet; keep warm. Wipe skillet with paper towel. Heat 1 tablespoon vegetable oil in same skillet over medium-high heat. Cook pepper mixture, stirring occasionally, 5 minutes or until crisp-tender. Stir in meat; heat through. Serve in warmed tortillas, topped with sour cream, your favorite shredded cheese and cilantro.

CHOOSING FOOD STORAGE CONTAINERS

When making your own foods, it's important to choose the right containers so the food will be delicious when you are ready to enjoy it. Follow these general guidelines, or see individual recipes for specific requirements:

Freezer Jams/Chutney Choose freezer-safe plastic food storage containers or glass preserving jars without curves under the neck of the jars. Be sure to choose a size that will leave enough room for the food to expand.

Fruit Butter Choose wide-mouth glass preserving jars or plastic food storage containers with tight-fitting lids.

Home-Canned Jelly Choose glass preserving jars (regular or wide mouth) with lids and bands.

Pickles Choose glass preserving jars (regular or wide mouth) with lids and bands. For whole pickles, choose wide-mouth jars.

Pickled Vegetables Choose nonreactive glass or plastic food storage covered containers.

Vinegar Choose glass bottles with a narrow neck and screw top, cork or two-piece canning lid. Sterilize bottles before using. (See page 451.)

Dried Vegetables Choose containers with tight-fitting lids.

Seasoning Mixes/Dried Herbs Choose small containers with tight-fitting lids.

Dessert/Beverage Mixes Choose food-safe glass jars with screw-on lids to show off the layers, or plastic containers with tight-fitting lids.

EASY • FAST • MAKE AHEAD • GLUTEN FREE • VEGETARIAN • VEGAN

Bloody Mary Rim Salt Mix

Wake up your Classic Bloody Mary Cocktails (page 94) with this spicy mix on the glasses. Or use with other beverages such as gluten-free beer or gin and tonics for a zippy flavor twist. If you don't want salt, try our flavorful salt-free variation.

PREP 10 Minutes **TOTAL** 10 Minutes • *About 3 tablespoons*

DRY MIX
- 1 tablespoon gluten-free seafood seasoning (from 6-oz container)
- 2 teaspoons kosher salt
- 1 teaspoon dried minced garlic
- 1 teaspoon smoked paprika
- ½ teaspoon celery salt
- ¼ teaspoon pepper

GARNISH
- 1 lemon

1 In small bowl, stir together all ingredients except lemon.

2 Just before serving, spread some of the salt mix on a small, shallow plate. Coat the rim of each glass with mix. (See Rimming the Edge of Glass, page 92.) Add desired drink to glasses. Cut lemon in half lengthwise; cut each half into 4 wedges. Make a small cut in center of each wedge. Lightly dip edge of lemon wedge in mix. Garnish each drink with lemon wedge.

3 Store any remaining salt mix in tightly covered container up to 3 months.

¾ Teaspoon Calories 0; Total Fat 0g (Saturated Fat 0g, Trans Fat 0g); Cholesterol 0mg; Sodium 390mg; Total Carbohydrate 0g (Dietary Fiber 0g); Protein 0g **Carbohydrate Choices:** 0

SALT-FREE BLOODY MARY RIM MIX: In small bowl, stir together 1 tablespoon smoked paprika, 2 teaspoons dried minced garlic, 2 teaspoons celery seed, 1 teaspoon onion powder, ¼ teaspoon black pepper and ⅛ teaspoon ground red pepper (cayenne).

Bloody Mary Rim Salt Mix

FAST • MAKE AHEAD • CALORIE SMART •
GLUTEN FREE • VEGETARIAN • VEGAN

Salt-Free Herb Mix

*This super-versatile salt-free seasoning is great
to sprinkle on meats, poultry, fish and vegetables.
Or toss hot cooked pasta with olive oil or melted butter
and some of this blend, then sprinkle with shredded
cheese.*

PREP 5 Minutes **TOTAL** 5 Minutes • *¼ cup*

1 tablespoon onion powder	1 teaspoon dried thyme leaves
1 tablespoon garlic powder	1 teaspoon dried marjoram leaves
1 tablespoon parsley flakes	1 teaspoon coarse ground black pepper
1 teaspoon dried basil leaves	

In small container with tight-fitting lid, stir all ingredients
until well mixed; cover. Store in cool, dry place up to
6 months. Stir or shake well before each use.

1 Teaspoon Calories 5; Total Fat 0g (Saturated Fat 0g, Trans Fat 0g);
Cholesterol 0mg; Sodium 0mg; Total Carbohydrate 1g (Dietary Fiber 0g);
Protein 0g **Carbohydrate Choices:** 0

Gochujang Mayonnaise

FAST • MAKE AHEAD • CALORIE SMART •
GLUTEN FREE • VEGETARIAN

Buffalo Wing Sauce

*Both regular and smoked paprika are used in this
recipe to achieve a full-flavored, traditional Buffalo
wing sauce flavor. The butter will harden when the
sauce is refrigerated. Before using, place sauce in a
small microwavable bowl and microwave on High
20 to 40 seconds until melted, then whisk until
smooth.*

PREP 5 Minutes **TOTAL** 5 Minutes • *1¼ cups*

⅔ cup cider vinegar	½ teaspoon smoked paprika
2 tablespoons chili powder	½ teaspoon salt
1 tablespoon garlic powder	½ cup butter, melted
1 teaspoon paprika	1 teaspoon Worcestershire sauce
1 teaspoon ground red pepper (cayenne)	

In small bowl, stir all ingredients except butter and
Worcestershire sauce with whisk until blended.
Add butter and Worcestershire sauce; whisk until
blended. Use immediately. Or transfer to glass jar, cover
and refrigerate up to 1 month.

1 Tablespoon Calories 50; Total Fat 5g (Saturated Fat 3g, Trans Fat 0g);
Cholesterol 10mg; Sodium 125mg; Total Carbohydrate 1g (Dietary Fiber 0g);
Protein 0g **Carbohydrate Choices:** 0

EASY • FAST • MAKE AHEAD • CALORIE SMART •
GLUTEN FREE • VEGETARIAN

Gochujang Mayonnaise

*More than just spicy, this ready-for-anything
condiment is made with gochujang (Korean chile
pepper paste), giving it a deep, rich flavor like no other.
Use it as a dipping sauce for fries or potato, tortilla
or corn chips, drizzle it over a salad, spread it on a
sandwich . . . and be prepared to make more, as this
yummy condiment will get used up quickly!*

PREP 5 Minutes **TOTAL** 5 Minutes • *About ⅔ cup*

½ cup mayonnaise (for homemade mayonnaise, see page 479)	1 tablespoon gochujang paste or sauce
	1 tablespoon lime juice

In small bowl, beat all ingredients with whisk until well
mixed. Cover and refrigerate; store up to 4 days.

1 Tablespoon Calories 70; Total Fat 8g (Saturated Fat 1g, Trans Fat 0g);
Cholesterol 0mg; Sodium 105mg; Total Carbohydrate 1g (Dietary Fiber 0g);
Protein 0g **Carbohydrate Choices:** 0

MAKE AHEAD • CALORIE SMART

Harissa

Harissa is a hot Tunisian chile paste made with dried chiles, garlic, coriander, cumin and a bit of caraway. It has a few steps, but it's easy to make. It's a delicious change of pace from salsa, whether served on eggs or tacos, or spread on meats before grilling. Use it in our Harissa Waffle Fries Pizza (page 203), or over cream cheese to serve as a spread with crackers.

PREP 35 Minutes **TOTAL** 1 Hour 45 Minutes • **1¾ cups**

1 large red bell pepper	1¼ teaspoons cumin seed
½ teaspoon olive oil	½ teaspoon caraway seed
2 oz dried ancho or pasilla chiles*	2 tablespoons olive oil
2 oz dried guajillo or New Mexican chiles*	2 cloves garlic, peeled
1¼ teaspoons coriander seed	1½ teaspoons salt
	1 teaspoon mint flakes

1 Heat oven to 400°F. Line glass pie plate with foil. Place bell pepper in pie plate; brush with ½ teaspoon oil. Roast 30 to 40 minutes, turning every 10 minutes, until pepper is charred and dark brown in spots and slightly collapsed.

2 Meanwhile, place ancho and guajillo chiles in large bowl. Cover with boiling water. Place plate or bowl over chiles, weighted if necessary to keep chiles submerged. Let stand 30 minutes to soften completely. Drain. Remove stems.

3 Remove bell pepper from oven. Wrap bell pepper in foil; let stand 15 minutes to steam and allow skin to loosen. Unwrap; remove stem. Cut bell pepper and chiles open; place skin side down on cutting board. Scrape off seeds with spoon; discard seeds. Turn bell pepper over; peel off skin, scraping off with edge of knife if necessary. Place roasted pepper and chiles in food processor.

4 Heat 8-inch skillet over medium-high heat. Add coriander, cumin and caraway seed; toast 2 to 3 minutes, stirring constantly, until coriander seed turns golden brown and mixture becomes fragrant.** Place toasted spices in spice grinder. Grind until mixture looks like finely ground pepper. Add to food processor along with 2 tablespoons oil, the garlic, salt and mint. Cover and process until smooth, scraping side of bowl if necessary. Store covered in refrigerator up to 1 week or freeze up to 3 months.

1 Teaspoon Calories 10; Total Fat 0.5g (Saturated Fat 0g, Trans Fat 0g); Cholesterol 0mg; Sodium 45mg; Total Carbohydrate 0g (Dietary Fiber 0g); Protein 0g **Carbohydrate Choices:** 0

*If you can't find the dried chiles in your area, check online sources.

**We found that toasting the spices adds depth of flavor and more complexity to the paste, but this step can be left out if desired.

MAKING HARISSA

Cover dried chiles with water. Place plate over chiles to keep them submerged.

Place toasted spices in spice grinder. Grind until mixture looks like finely ground pepper.

FAST • MAKE AHEAD • CALORIE SMART • GLUTEN FREE • VEGETARIAN • VEGAN

Homemade Enchilada Sauce

Use this flavorful sauce in your favorite Mexican-style recipes calling for prepared enchilada sauce.

PREP 10 Minutes **TOTAL** 25 Minutes • **2 cups**

2 teaspoons vegetable oil	1 can (15 oz) tomato sauce
1 cup chopped onion	¾ teaspoon dried oregano
¼ cup chopped Anaheim or poblano chiles	¾ teaspoon ground cumin
2 cloves garlic, finely chopped	½ teaspoon salt
	¼ teaspoon pepper

1 Heat oil in 3-quart saucepan over medium heat. Cook onion, chiles and garlic in oil about 5 minutes, stirring occasionally, until tender. Stir in remaining ingredients.

2 Heat to boiling. Reduce heat to low; simmer, uncovered, 15 minutes.

3 Cool 30 minutes or until room temperature. If not using immediately, transfer to a covered glass jar; cover. Refrigerate up to 1 month.

⅓ Cup Calories 50; Total Fat 2g (Saturated Fat 0g, Trans Fat 0g); Cholesterol 0mg; Sodium 530mg; Total Carbohydrate 7g (Dietary Fiber 1g); Protein 1g **Carbohydrate Choices:** ½

LEARN TO FERMENT HOT SAUCE

The popularity of hot sauces has exploded as people find more ways to enjoy them. Hot sauces come in two varieties: fresh and fermented. A fresh hot sauce is made by combining mashed chiles and sometimes other ingredients with vinegar. Fresh sauces tend to be less complex in flavor, but hotter. Fermented hot sauces tend to have more complex flavor profiles and taste less hot, as fermentation can mellow the spiciness.

Creating a Flavorful Hot Sauce

To make fermented hot sauce, submerge chiles in salt brine; seal with an airtight lid and hold at room temperature for at least 7 days. Which chiles you use, in what combination, will directly impact the flavor and spiciness of your sauce, as chiles range in flavor, heat and spice level. **Green chiles** tend to be more bitter and have a slightly grassier flavor compared with **red, yellow and orange chiles**, which tend to be sweeter and fruitier. See page 237 for more information about chile types.

Tips for Fermenting

- **Use clean jars and fresh vegetables** Make sure jars are clean and dry, and vegetables are very fresh (not starting to decay), for proper bacteria to form.

- **Use filtered water** Water from the tap may contain too much chlorine, which can slow or prevent fermentation. Any source of filtered water is fine—home filtration systems in your refrigerator, on the tap or in a pitcher; or you can purchase bottled filtered water.

Fermented Hot Sauce

- **Remove chile pith and seeds** Cut away pith (white membranes) and seeds from chiles, as they can impart a bitter flavor to the hot sauce.
- **Measure salt carefully** Too much salt can slow the fermentation process. Use the amount of salt and water given in the recipe.
- **Leave air space** Don't overpack the jar; leave at least a 1-inch air space at the top of the jar.
- **Keep vegetables submerged in brine** Weigh the vegetables down with a clean small glass preserving jar, or purchase a fermentation weight (available online) for proper fermentation.
- **Ferment at the proper room temperature** If the room is too cool or too warm, the fermentation process may not work as it should, which could affect the flavor of the sauce or cause improper fermentation (see below).
- **Keep the jar lid on, but loosen it daily** This allows the carbon dioxide gas created during fermentation to escape. Or purchase fermentation air-lock lids, which allow carbon dioxide to escape while preventing outside air from entering.
- **A white film may appear** on the surface of the brine, if the other tips above aren't followed. It is harmless but could affect the flavor of the sauce, so scrape it off as soon as it appears; immediately re-cover the jar to continue the fermentation process.
- **Fermentation time** Seven days is the minimum time for the hot sauce to ferment properly, but you can continue to let it ferment up to 10 days. The longer it ferments, the more complex the flavor and the milder the heat of the sauce. Even after the chiles are drained and pureed, the flavor will continue to develop and become richer and deeper.
- **Adjust the sauce consistency** If you like your sauce thicker, don't add additional brine in Step 4. If you want your sauce thinner, add more of the remaining brine.

COMMON SIGNS OF IMPROPER FERMENTATION

If any of these conditions occurs, do not eat; discard the sauce in such a way that children or pets won't accidentally eat it later:

- Rotten smell
- Mold growth (raised surface and fuzzy appearance) that is green, blue, black or orange
- Overly slimy vegetables
- Rancid flavor

Is It Fermenting Properly?

After a few days of fermenting, the **brine will have turned cloudy** and when you tap on the jar, **bubbles will rise to the surface**. These are signs of a safe and successful ferment. Some brines will be cloudier than others. Over time, the cloudiness may settle to the bottom of the jar as the vegetables dull and change color slightly.

MAKE AHEAD • CALORIE SMART • GLUTEN FREE • VEGETARIAN

Fermented Hot Sauce

Depending on the chiles you choose, the sauce can range from mild to very spicy. See page 237 for chile descriptions.

PREP 25 Minutes TOTAL 10 Days 30 Minutes • *2 cups*

1¼ cups filtered water	1 dried ancho or chipotle chile
2 teaspoons noniodized kosher salt	6 oz red Fresno chiles, seeded, cut into 1½-inch strips
1 wide-mouth 32-oz glass preserving jar with lid and band	1 (½-inch-thick) slice yellow onion
½ lb mixture of poblano, serrano and jalapeño chiles, seeded, cut into 1½-inch strips	1 small (4-oz) glass preserving jar
3 cloves garlic, crushed	2 tablespoons honey
	1 tablespoon cider vinegar

1 In 1-quart saucepan, heat water and salt over medium heat just until salt dissolves. Set aside to cool to lukewarm.

2 In bottom of 32-oz jar, place poblano, serrano and jalapeño chile strips; press lightly to compact. Top with garlic and ancho chile. Top with Fresno chile strips; press lightly. Pour salt water over mixture.

3 Place onion slice on top of mixture. Place 4 oz glass preserving jar (without lid or band), open top up, on onion slice. Press small jar down to submerge onion under the brine and keep chiles and onion submerged during fermentation. Cover 32-oz jar with lid and band. Let stand at room temperature (70°F to 75°F) for 7 to 10 days. Loosen band and lid daily just enough to release gas but do not remove lid.

4 After end of fermentation period, remove small jar; pour contents of jar through strainer over bowl to catch brine. In food processor or blender, place vegetables. Cover and process 1 to 2 minutes or until pureed. Add honey, vinegar and ½ cup of the brine; cover and process until smooth. Stir in additional brine until sauce is desired consistency; discard any remaining brine. Store in covered jar in refrigerator up to 1 month. Shake well before each use.

1 Teaspoon Calories 0; Total Fat 0g (Saturated Fat 0g, Trans Fat 0g); Cholesterol 0mg; Sodium 10mg; Total Carbohydrate 0g (Dietary Fiber 0g); Protein 0g **Carbohydrate Choices:** 0

MAKE AHEAD • CALORIE SMART • GLUTEN FREE •
VEGETARIAN • VEGAN

Triple Berry Pomegranate Freezer Jam

PREP 10 Minutes **TOTAL** 24 Hours 20 Minutes • *6 half-pints*

2 cups strawberries,
   stems removed,
   cut in half
2 cups raspberries
1 cup blueberries
4¼ cups organic sugar
¾ cup organic
   pomegranate juice
   (from 8-oz bottle)

1 package (1¾ oz)
   powdered fruit pectin
6 (8-oz) clean
   preserving jars with
   bands and lids or
   freezer-safe food
   storage containers

1 In large bowl, mash berries with potato masher
to make 2½ cups crushed berries. Or process in food
processor until slightly chunky, not pureed. Add sugar;
mix well. Let stand at room temperature 10 minutes,
stirring occasionally.

2 In 1-quart saucepan, mix juice and pectin until pectin
is dissolved. Heat, stirring constantly, to a full rolling
boil that cannot be stirred down. Boil hard 1 minute,
continuing to stir. Pour hot pectin mixture over berry
mixture; stir constantly until sugar is completely
dissolved, about 3 minutes.

3 Immediately pour mixture into jars, leaving ½-inch
headspace; cover. Let stand at room temperature about
24 hours or until set.

4 Store in freezer up to 12 months or in refrigerator
up to 3 weeks. Thaw frozen jam in refrigerator and stir
before serving.

1 Tablespoon Calories 40; Total Fat 0g (Saturated Fat 0g, Trans Fat 0g);
Cholesterol 0mg; Sodium 0mg; Total Carbohydrate 10g (Dietary Fiber 0g);
Protein 0g **Carbohydrate Choices:** ½

CREATIVE USES FOR JAM

Jam isn't just arm candy for breakfast toast—try one of
these surprising ways to use it!

Fruity Vinaigrette Mix ⅓ cup vinegar (any variety),
⅓ cup jam, ¼ cup olive or vegetable oil, ¼ teaspoon
salt and ⅛ teaspoon pepper with whisk until blended.

Jazzed-Up Yogurt Top plain yogurt with a spoonful
of jam and roasted pumpkin seeds or nuts for a quick
breakfast or snack.

Meat Glaze Brush on chicken, turkey, pork or beef
during roasting, baking, or grilling for a flavorful glaze.
Brush on during the last 15 to 20 minutes of cooking to
prevent burning.

Quick Spread Spoon over a block of softened cream
cheese to serve with crackers as a quick appetizer
or snack.

Zesty BBQ Sauce Heat 1 cup barbecue sauce in a small
saucepan over medium-low heat, stirring occasionally.
Stir in 3 to 4 tablespoons jam until melted.

DISSOLVING PECTIN TO MAKE JAM

Mix water and pectin in
saucepan until pectin is
dissolved. Heat to boiling,
stirring constantly.

Pour hot pectin mixture
over fruit mixture; stir
constantly until sugar is
completely dissolved.

Triple Berry Pomegranate Freezer Jam

Strawberry Freezer Jam

RASPBERRY FREEZER JAM: Substitute 3 pints (6 cups) raspberries, crushed (3 cups when crushed) for the strawberries. Increase sugar to 5¼ cups.

STRAWBERRY-BALSAMIC FREEZER JAM: Make as directed—except reduce water to ¼ cup and add ½ cup balsamic vinegar with the hot pectin mixture in Step 2.

MAKE AHEAD • CALORIE SMART • GLUTEN FREE • VEGETARIAN

Peach-Jalapeño Jam

PREP 1 Hour 10 Minutes **TOTAL** 25 Hours 55 Minutes • *6 half-pints*

- 6 (8-oz) glass preserving jars with lids and bands (see Preparing Jars and Lids for Canning, page 451)
- 4 cups finely chopped peeled peaches (about 3 lb)
- ¼ cup fresh lemon juice
- ½ teaspoon butter
- 1 package (1¾ oz) powdered fruit pectin
- 3 cups organic sugar*
- ⅓ cup finely diced seeded jalapeño chiles (about 2 medium)

1 Fill boiling water canner half full with water; heat until water is simmering. Wash jars and keep them warm as directed in Preparing Jars and Lids for Canning, page 451.

2 In 4-quart saucepan, mix peaches, lemon juice, butter (which helps reduce foaming) and pectin, stirring until pectin is dissolved. Heat to boiling over medium heat, stirring frequently; remove from heat. Stir in sugar all at once; mix well. Stir in chiles. Heat, stirring constantly, until mixture comes to a full rolling boil that covers the entire surface, not just the edges of the pan. Boil and stir 1 minute; remove from heat.

3 Quickly skim off any foam. Immediately ladle or pour jam into jars, leaving ¼- to ½-inch headspace. Wipe rims and threads of jars. Place flat lids on jars and screw bands on tightly to seal. Place jars on elevated rack in canner; lower rack into canner. To process jam safely, water must cover jars by 1 to 2 inches; add additional boiling water if necessary. Cover. Heat to boiling; boil 10 minutes. Turn off heat. Remove canner lid. Let jars stand in canner 5 minutes.

4 Carefully remove jars with canning jar lifter or heavy-duty tongs; place jars upright on dry towel. Cool jars completely. After 24 hours, check seal on cooled jars by pressing middle of lids with finger. If the lids spring back, jars are not sealed and must be reprocessed or stored in the refrigerator. Store completely sealed, unopened jars in a cool, dry place up to 1 year. Once opened, store in refrigerator up to 3 weeks.

1 Tablespoon Calories 30; Total Fat 0g (Saturated Fat 0g, Trans Fat 0g); Cholesterol 0mg; Sodium 0mg; Total Carbohydrate 7g (Dietary Fiber 0g); Protein 0g **Carbohydrate Choices:** ½

*This recipe was tested with regular white granulated sugar. Do not reduce the sugar or use sugar substitutes, or the jam will not set properly. Organic cane or coarse-grain sugars were not tested and may give different results.

EASY • MAKE AHEAD • CALORIE SMART • GLUTEN FREE • VEGETARIAN • VEGAN

Strawberry Freezer Jam

Freezer jams have become very popular not only because of their fresh, just-picked flavor, but also because they are easy to make. Strawberry Freezer Jam is a favorite for us; it was first printed in the 1995 edition of this cookbook.

PREP 10 Minutes **TOTAL** 24 Hours 20 Minutes • *5 half-pints*

- 1 quart (4 cups) strawberries, stems and leaves removed, cut in half
- 4 cups organic sugar
- ¾ cup water
- 1 package (1¾ oz) powdered fruit pectin
- 5 (8-oz) preserving jars with bands and lids or freezer-safe food storage containers

1 In large bowl, mash strawberries with potato masher to make 2 cups crushed strawberries. Or process in food processor until slightly chunky, not pureed. Add sugar; mix well. Let stand at room temperature 10 minutes, stirring occasionally.

2 In 1-quart saucepan, mix water and pectin until pectin is dissolved. Heat, stirring constantly, to a full rolling boil that cannot be stirred down. Boil hard 1 minute, continuing to stir. Pour hot pectin mixture over strawberry mixture; stir constantly until sugar is completely dissolved, about 3 minutes.

3 Immediately pour mixture into jars, leaving ½-inch headspace; cover. Let stand at room temperature 24 hours or until set.

4 Store in freezer up to 12 months or in refrigerator up to 3 weeks. Thaw frozen jam in refrigerator and stir before serving.

1 Tablespoon Calories 45; Total Fat 0g (Saturated Fat 0g, Trans Fat 0g); Cholesterol 0mg; Sodium 0mg; Total Carbohydrate 11g (Dietary Fiber 0g); Protein 0g **Carbohydrate Choices:** 1

BLUEBERRY FREEZER JAM: Substitute 2 pints (4 cups) blueberries, crushed (2½ cups when crushed) for the strawberries. Reduce sugar to 3 cups. Add 1 teaspoon lemon or orange zest, if desired. Reduce water to ½ cup.

LEARN TO CAN HOMEMADE JAM

Making homemade jam isn't difficult, but it does require close attention to directions from trusted recipes so that the end results are safe to store and eat. Food canning techniques have changed over the years, so it is best to be up-to-date with the latest techniques and recipes, rather than following Grandma's famous jam recipe, for example. If done incorrectly, you can put your family and friends at risk of potentially ingesting very dangerous bacteria in the food you processed. Follow the general guidelines on page 451 and specific directions on recipes. Try Peach-Jalapeño Jam (page 461).

How to "Put Up" Jam Successfully

- **Use proper canning techniques** See page 451, for more information.

- **Skim foam from jam mixture** Foam forms while jam cooks; skim and discard it for the best-looking jam, and also so it won't affect headspace.

- **Don't overfill jars** The proper amount of headspace is necessary to ensure no mold grows, so fill jars only as much as recipe states.

- **Wipe rims and threads** Wipe off any jam which might be on the rim or threads of the jar, to prevent spoilage during storage.

- **Cover with new lids** New lids have fresh seals that are necessary for proper processing to get a vacuum seal. Do not reuse lids.

- **Screw on bands securely** Bands can be reused. Tighten enough to secure lid well but do not overtighten. Bands may loosen during processing but can be retightened after the processed jam has cooled.

- **Place jars on rack in canner** Do not put jars directly on the bottom of the canner. Jars need water boiling all around them to be properly processed, and could potentially break if they sit directly on the bottom of the pan.

- **Have enough water in the canner** There should be enough water to cover the jars by 1 inch above the tops. Add additional boiling water if necessary.

- **Cover and boil for the full time given** Follow directions exactly: be sure the water is fully boiling and the canner is covered. Process jars the full time called for in the recipe, to kill organisms that could grow in the food and/or on the jar during storage.

- **Remove and cool jars carefully** Jars can slip and break if not taken out of the boiling water with a large canning or heavy-duty tongs. To prevent jars from cracking, let them cool on a towel rather than directly on a cold countertop.

- **Check the seals after 24 hours** Press on the center of each lid with finger. If the lid springs back, it didn't seal properly. Reprocess any jars that didn't seal well, or refrigerate and use within 1 month. Tighten any bands that have loosened.

- **Store jars properly** Properly sealed, unopened jars can be stored in a cool, dry place up to 1 year. Once jars are opened, they should be stored in the refrigerator and used within 1 month.

JELLY, JAM OR PRESERVES?

Jelly is the clear, bright condiment made with fruit juice, sugar and possibly pectin to help it gel. It will hold its shape when turned out of its container.

Jam uses crushed or chopped fruits and is usually more fluid than jelly.

Conserves are jams made with a mix of fruit and/or nuts.

Preserves are like jam, but usually with intact pieces of fruit.

Marmalade is preserves made from citrus fruit and peel.

CANNING JAM

Add sugar and pectin to fruit and heat it to a full rolling boil.

Quickly ladle hot jam into sterilized jars.

After processing, carefully remove jars from water bath.

Check seals after 24 hours by pressing on the tops to see if they spring back.

Easy Refrigerator Pickles

MAKE AHEAD • CALORIE SMART • GLUTEN FREE • VEGETARIAN • VEGAN

Garlic Dill Pickles

PREP 1 Hour 20 Minutes TOTAL 1 Week 2 Hours • *4 quarts*

- 4 (32-oz) glass preserving jars with lids and bands, prepared (see page 451)
- 24 to 30 (3-inch) unwaxed pickling cucumbers (about 7 pints or 8 lb total)
- 12 to 16 sprigs fresh dill weed
- 12 cloves garlic, peeled
- 4 (½-inch-thick) slices onion
- 4 teaspoons mustard seed
- 4 cups water
- 2 cups cider or white vinegar
- 2 tablespoons pickling or canning salt*

1 Fill boiling water canner half full with water; heat until water is simmering. Wash jars and lids as directed in Preparing Jars and Lids for Canning (page 451).

2 Wash cucumbers; cut off stem and blossom ends. Pack cucumbers loosely in jars. To each jar, add 3 or 4 dill weed sprigs, 3 garlic cloves, 1 onion slice and 1 teaspoon mustard seed. In large stainless-steel saucepan, heat water, vinegar and salt to boiling. Pour into jars, leaving ½-inch headspace.

3 Drain flat lids well. Wipe rims and threads of jars. Place flat lids on jars and screw bands on tightly to seal. Place jars on elevated rack in canner; lower rack into canner. To process pickles safely, water must cover jars by 1 to 2 inches; add additional boiling water if necessary. Cover. Heat to boiling; boil 10 minutes. Carefully remove jars with canning jar lifter or heavy-duty tongs and place upright on towel. Cool completely.

4 After 24 hours, check seal on cooled jars by pressing middle of lids with finger. If lid springs back, jar is not sealed and must be stored in refrigerator. Store completely sealed, unopened jars in a cool, dry place at least 1 week to blend flavors before serving but no longer than 1 year. Once opened, store in refrigerator up to 3 weeks.

1 Pickle Calories 5; Total Fat 0g (Saturated Fat 0g, Trans Fat 0g); Cholesterol 0mg; Sodium 220mg; Total Carbohydrate 1g (Dietary Fiber 0g); Protein 0g **Carbohydrate Choices:** 0

*Pickling or canning salt, available in most grocery stores, is preferred for making pickles. Table salt can cause the brine to become cloudy and darken the pickles.

MAKE AHEAD • CALORIE SMART • GLUTEN FREE • VEGETARIAN • VEGAN

Easy Refrigerator Pickles

When choosing cucumbers for pickles, pick out the smaller ones, and pickle them soon after buying or harvesting, for the best flavor.

PREP 10 Minutes TOTAL 24 Hours 10 Minutes • *6 cups*

- 6 cups thinly sliced unpeeled unwaxed cucumbers (about 2 lb)
- 2 small onions, sliced
- 1 medium carrot, thinly sliced (½ cup)
- 1¾ cups organic sugar
- 1 cup white or cider vinegar
- 2 tablespoons salt
- 1 tablespoon chopped fresh or 1 teaspoon dried dill weed

1 In 2½- or 3-quart glass container, layer cucumbers, onions and carrot.

2 In medium bowl, stir remaining ingredients until sugar is dissolved; pour over vegetables. Cover and refrigerate at least 24 hours before serving, to blend flavors. Store covered in refrigerator up to 2 weeks.

¼ Cup Calories 70; Total Fat 0g (Saturated Fat 0g, Trans Fat 0g); Cholesterol 0mg; Sodium 590mg; Total Carbohydrate 16g (Dietary Fiber 0g); Protein 0g **Carbohydrate Choices:** 1

EASY BELL PEPPER–GARLIC REFRIGERATOR PICKLES: Cut ½ medium red bell pepper into thin strips; layer with cucumbers, onions and carrot in container. Add 1 clove garlic, peeled, with remaining ingredients.

PACKING CUCUMBERS

Wash cucumbers; cut off stem and blossom ends.

Pack cucumbers loosely in jars before adding dill, onion and mustard seed.

Jalapeño-Garlic
Pickled Green Beans

Spicy Pickled Vegetables

MAKE AHEAD • CALORIE SMART • GLUTEN FREE • VEGETARIAN • VEGAN

Jalapeño-Garlic Pickled Green Beans

Green beans will lose their bright green color during the cooking and pickling process, so using half yellow wax beans and half green beans gives a beautiful balance of color.

PREP 30 Minutes **TOTAL** 24 Hours 30 Minutes • *4 pints*

2 lb fresh green beans, trimmed	4 (16-oz) glass preserving jars with lids and bands (see Preparing Jars and Lids for Canning, page 451)
2¾ cups white vinegar	
1½ cups water	
¼ cup organic sugar	
1 teaspoon canning and pickling salt	12 (¼-inch) slices red or green jalapeño chiles
	8 whole peeled cloves garlic

1 Cut beans into 4-inch lengths to fit into jars. In 4-quart stainless-steel saucepan, heat vinegar, water, sugar and salt to boiling. Add beans, pushing them into liquid; heat to boiling. Boil 1 minute. Place strainer over large glass bowl. Drain beans in strainer over bowl, reserving liquid.

2 Pack beans upright into preserving jars. To each jar, add 3 chile slices and 2 garlic cloves. Pour hot liquid into jars, leaving ½-inch headspace. Make sure all beans are submerged in liquid. Place flat lids on jars and screw bands on tightly to seal. Let stand at room temperature to cool completely. Refrigerate at least 24 hours before serving; store up to 3 months. Flavor will intensify the longer the beans are refrigerated. Or to process for canning, see Garlic Dill Pickles, page 463.

¼ Cup Calories 15; Total Fat 0g (Saturated Fat 0g, Trans Fat 0g); Cholesterol 0mg; Sodium 30mg; Total Carbohydrate 2g (Dietary Fiber 0g); Protein 0g **Carbohydrate Choices:** 0

LEMON-DILL PICKLED GREEN BEANS: Make as directed—except omit jalapeño and garlic. To each jar, add 2 (3x⅛-inch) strips lemon peel and 4 sprigs fresh dill weed. Continue as directed.

MAKE AHEAD • CALORIE SMART • GLUTEN FREE • VEGETARIAN • VEGAN

Spicy Pickled Vegetables

PREP 15 Minutes **TOTAL** 24 Hours 15 Minutes • *2 quarts*

3 cups vegan white wine vinegar	1 medium head cauliflower (1½ lb), separated into small florets (6 cups)
1½ cups organic sugar	
2 cloves garlic, finely chopped	
2 (32-oz) clean glass preserving jars with lids and bands or glass food storage containers with lids	½ lb fresh green beans, trimmed
	2 medium carrots, cut into 3x¼x¼-inch pieces (1½ cups)
	2 jalapeño chiles, cut lengthwise into quarters, seeded

1 In 1½-quart stainless-steel saucepan, heat vinegar, sugar and garlic over medium heat just until mixture begins to simmer and sugar is dissolved. Remove from heat; cool 5 minutes.

2 Meanwhile, in jars, layer cauliflower, beans, carrots and chiles, dividing evenly between jars. Pour vinegar mixture over vegetables, dividing evenly between jars. Cover and refrigerate at least 24 hours before serving, but no longer than 2 weeks.

¼ Cup Calories 70; Total Fat 0g (Saturated Fat 0g, Trans Fat 0g); Cholesterol 0mg; Sodium 15mg; Total Carbohydrate 16g (Dietary Fiber 1g); Protein 1g **Carbohydrate Choices:** 1

MAKE AHEAD • CALORIE SMART • GLUTEN FREE • VEGETARIAN

Pickled Beets

Classic pickled beets get a bit of an update with less sugar in the brine. They are still sweetly delicious. Try them on a salad with toasted walnuts and crumbles of creamy Gorgonzola or blue cheese.

PREP 1 Hour 10 Minutes **TOTAL** 25 Hours 10 Minutes • *4 pints*

3	lb small to medium beets (1½ to 2½ inch)	2	(3-inch) cinnamon sticks
1¼	cups cider vinegar	4	(16-oz) glass preserving jars with lids and bands (see Preparing Jars and Lids for Canning, page 451)
¾	cup water		
¾	cup organic sugar		
½	teaspoon whole cloves		
½	teaspoon salt		

1 Cut off all but 2 inches of beet tops; leave beets whole with root ends attached. Wash beets. Place in 4-quart saucepan. Add water to cover. Heat to boiling; boil uncovered, 20 to 30 minutes or just until beets are tender. Check smaller beets for doneness first. Drain beets and let cool until easy to handle, about 30 minutes. Peel beets; cut off root ends and tops. Cut beets into wedges, 1½-inch chunks or ¼-inch slices.

2 In 3-quart stainless-steel saucepan, heat vinegar, water, sugar, cloves, salt and cinnamon sticks to boiling. Reduce heat; simmer 5 minutes. Add beets. Heat to boiling; remove from heat. Discard cinnamon sticks.

3 Spoon hot beets and liquid into preserving jars, leaving ½-inch headspace. Place flat lids on jars and screw bands on tightly to seal. Let stand at room temperature to cool completely. Refrigerate at least 24 hours before serving; store up to 3 months. Flavor will intensify the longer they are refrigerated. Or to process for canning, see Garlic Dill Pickles, page 463.

¼ Cup Calories 25; Total Fat 0g (Saturated Fat 0g, Trans Fat 0g); Cholesterol 0mg; Sodium 45mg; Total Carbohydrate 5g (Dietary Fiber 1g); Protein 0g **Carbohydrate Choices:** ½

MAKE AHEAD • CALORIE SMART • GLUTEN FREE • VEGETARIAN • VEGAN

Pickled Peppers

There's no lengthy canning process required to pickle these peppers . . . just the microwave and refrigerator. A jar of this tangy condiment would make a great gift from the kitchen.

PREP 30 Minutes **TOTAL** 7 Days 30 Minutes • *1 quart*

2	cups water	1	yellow bell pepper, seeded, cut lengthwise into 6 pieces
1	cup white vinegar		
1	tablespoon organic sugar	1	green bell pepper, seeded, cut lengthwise into 6 pieces
1	tablespoon salt		
1	(32-oz) wide-mouth glass preserving jar with lid (see Preparing Jars and Lids for Canning, page 451)	1	small onion, sliced, separated into rings
		2	cloves garlic, cut in half
1	red bell pepper, seeded, cut lengthwise into 6 pieces	1	sprig fresh tarragon or ¼ teaspoon dried tarragon leaves

1 In 2-quart microwavable bowl, mix water, vinegar, sugar and salt. Microwave uncovered on High 8 to 14 minutes or until mixture boils. Stir to dissolve sugar.

2 In jar, pack all remaining ingredients. Pour hot vinegar mixture over vegetables; cover with tight-fitting lid. Refrigerate at least 7 days before serving to blend flavors. Store opened jar in refrigerator up to 3 weeks.

¼ Cup Calories 10; Total Fat 0g (Saturated Fat 0g, Trans Fat 0g); Cholesterol 0mg; Sodium 440mg; Total Carbohydrate 3g (Dietary Fiber 0g); Protein 0g **Carbohydrate Choices:** 0

Pickled Beets

Pickled Peppers

MAKE AHEAD • CALORIE SMART • GLUTEN FREE

Kimchi

Kimchi is a spicy-hot fermented condiment that is served at almost every Korean meal. Try it on a sandwich, on hot dogs, pizza, eggs, in fried rice, in spring rolls, in soups . . . just to name a few uses!

PREP 20 Minutes TOTAL 5 Days • *3 cups*

- 1 large head napa cabbage (2 lb)
- ¼ cup noniodized coarse (kosher or sea) salt*
- 1 tablespoon crushed red pepper flakes
- 1 teaspoon finely chopped gingerroot
- 1 teaspoon organic sugar
- 4 cloves garlic, finely chopped
- 2 tablespoons fish sauce or water
- 1 small daikon radish (about 8 oz), peeled, cut into 2x¼-inch strips (2¼ cups)
- 2 medium carrots, cut into 2x¼-inch strips (1 cup)
- 4 medium green onions, cut into ¼-inch slices
- 1 (1-gallon) clean food storage glass container or plastic food storage container with tight-fitting lid

1 Cut cabbage lengthwise into quarters; remove core. Cut quarters crosswise into 1-inch strips. Place cabbage in large bowl. Sprinkle with salt; gently rub salt into cabbage until cabbage just starts to soften. Cover cabbage with water. Place plate on top and weight with something heavy so cabbage remains submerged. Let stand 1 hour.

2 Drain cabbage in large colander; rinse thoroughly to remove salt. Drain (cabbage leaves will still be wet). Rinse and dry bowl used for soaking cabbage. Working in batches, lift cabbage above bowl and squeeze cabbage over bowl to catch juices. Place cabbage in bowl with juices.

3 Add radish, carrots and onions to cabbage. In small bowl, mix pepper flakes, gingerroot, sugar, garlic and fish sauce until sugar is dissolved. Add to vegetable mixture; toss to coat, making sure vegetable mixture is thoroughly coated (gloved hands may work more easily).

4 Spoon vegetable mixture into container, leaving 1-inch headspace. Press vegetable mixture into container with back of spoon, allowing liquid to rise to top. Cover and let stand at room temperature 3 to 5 days to ferment and develop flavor. You may see bubbles develop inside container. Check daily to make sure vegetable mixture is submerged in juices. If not, push vegetable mixture down with back of spoon and re-cover container.

5 Kimchi can be tasted during this period; if you like the level of fermentation, place container in refrigerator. Store kimchi tightly covered in refrigerator up to 3 months.

1 Tablespoon Calories 5; Total Fat 0g (Saturated Fat 0g, Trans Fat 0g); Cholesterol 0mg; Sodium 220mg; Total Carbohydrate 1g (Dietary Fiber 0g); Protein 0g **Carbohydrate Choices:** 0

*Iodized salt can interfere with fermentation; noniodized salt is readily available.

MAKE AHEAD • CALORIE SMART • GLUTEN FREE • VEGETARIAN • VEGAN

Golden Syrup

Golden syrup is a staple in the British Isles; it can be purchased at some grocery stores carrying English ingredients. Enjoy this light and flavorful syrup drizzled over pancakes, waffles, biscuits or scones.

PREP 1 Hour 25 Minutes TOTAL 1 Hour 25 Minutes • *2 cups*

- 2½ cups organic sugar
- ¼ cup cold water
- 1¼ cups boiling water
- 1 slice lemon

1 In heavy 2-quart saucepan, place ½ cup of the sugar and the cold water. Heat uncovered over medium-low heat 18 to 20 minutes, swirling pan occasionally, or until caramel colored.

2 Carefully stir in the 1¼ cups boiling water (mixture will sputter), the remaining 2 cups sugar and the lemon slice with whisk. Cook uncovered over low heat, stirring occasionally, 30 minutes or until sugar and caramel dissolve and mixture is thick and syrupy. Remove lemon slice.

3 Cool at least 30 minutes. Serve immediately or cover and refrigerate up to 1 week.

2 Tablespoons Calories 130; Total Fat 0g (Saturated Fat 0g, Trans Fat 0g); Cholesterol 0mg; Sodium 0mg; Total Carbohydrate 31g (Dietary Fiber 0g); Protein 0g **Carbohydrate Choices:** 2

MAKING KIMCHI

Keep cabbage submerged in the brine by placing a plate with something heavy on it on top of cabbage.

Use a spoon to press kimchi ingredients into container with tight-fitting lid, leaving 1-inch headspace.

HEIRLOOM AND *NEW TWIST*

HEIRLOOM

EASY • MAKE AHEAD • CALORIE SMART •
GLUTEN FREE • VEGETARIAN • VEGAN

Herb Vinegar

Flavored vinegars can add distinctive taste to your favorite recipes. Making them yourself not only gives satisfaction, but also can be less costly than buying them.

PREP 5 Minutes **TOTAL** 10 Days • **2 cups**

½ cup firmly packed fresh herb leaves (basil, chives, dill weed, mint, oregano, rosemary or tarragon)	2 cups vegan white wine vinegar or white vinegar
	1 sprig herb used above, if desired

1 In tightly covered glass jar or bottle, place herb leaves; cover with vinegar. Let stand in cool, dry place 10 days.

2 Strain vinegar; discard herbs. Place fresh herb sprig in jar to identify flavor. Store covered at room temperature up to 6 months.

1 Tablespoon Calories 0; Total Fat 0g (Saturated Fat 0g, Trans Fat 0g); Cholesterol 0mg; Sodium 0mg; Total Carbohydrate 0g (Dietary Fiber 0g); Protein 0g **Carbohydrate Choices:** 0

BERRY VINEGAR: Substitute 2 cups fresh berries, crushed, for herb leaves.

GARLIC VINEGAR: Substitute 6 cloves garlic, peeled and cut in half, for herb leaves.

LEMON VINEGAR: Substitute peel from 2 well-scrubbed lemons for herb leaves.

NEW TWIST

EASY • MAKE AHEAD • CALORIE SMART •
GLUTEN FREE • VEGETARIAN • VEGAN

Orange-Jalapeño Vinegar

This super-simple vinegar is a delightful combination to give as a gift or to use to make the unique vinaigrette below. Look for small bottles of pomegranate juice in the produce section, near other refrigerated juices.

PREP 10 Minutes **TOTAL** 10 Days 10 Minutes • **1¼ cups**

4 medium oranges, well scrubbed and dried	1½ cups vegan white wine vinegar
1 jalapeño chile, thinly sliced	

1 Using vegetable peeler, peel oranges into long strips, being careful not to remove the white pith of the oranges. In 16-oz glass jar, place orange peel and chile slices. Pour vinegar into jar. Cover tightly and let stand in cool dark place 7 to 10 days.

2 Strain vinegar; discard orange peel and chile slices. Store covered at room temperature up to 6 months.

1 Tablespoon Calories 15; Total Fat 0g (Saturated Fat 0g, Trans Fat 0g); Cholesterol 0mg; Sodium 0mg; Total Carbohydrate 3g (Dietary Fiber 0g); Protein 0g **Carbohydrate Choices:** 0

POMEGRANATE-ORANGE VINAIGRETTE: In 1-quart saucepan, heat ½ cup pomegranate juice to boiling over high heat. Boil uncovered 3 to 5 minutes or until reduced by half. Let cool 5 minutes. In tightly-covered jar, shake reduced juice, ¼ cup vegetable oil, ¼ cup Orange-Jalapeño Vinegar (above) and ¼ teaspoon salt. Store tightly covered in refrigerator up to 1 week. Shake before serving.

Orange-Jalapeño Vinegar

Apple Butter

EASY • MAKE AHEAD • CALORIE SMART •
GLUTEN FREE • VEGETARIAN • VEGAN

Oven-Dried Tomatoes

Plum tomatoes work best for drying because they are thick-fleshed with few seeds. Regular tomatoes can be used but may take longer to dry.

PREP 10 Minutes **TOTAL** 12 Hours 10 Minutes • *24 tomatoes*

24 plum (Roma) tomatoes

1 Heat oven to 200°F. Rinse tomatoes under cold water and remove stems; drain on paper towels. Cut each tomato in half lengthwise. Using small spoon, scoop out and discard seeds.

2 Place tomato halves, cut side down, in single layer on broiler rack over broiler pan. Place larger halves on outer edges of rack for even drying.

3 Dry in oven 6 to 12 hours, turning once after 4 hours, or until tomatoes are shriveled, dry to the touch and very chewy in texture. Edges may be crisp, but tomatoes should not be crisp in center; they should be somewhat pliable. Check after 6 hours and remove any smaller tomatoes that have dried enough. Tomatoes will be dark red and some pieces may have brown or dark spots.

4 Remove from oven and cool completely. Store in tightly covered container in cool, dark place, up to 6 months. To rehydrate, place tomatoes in small bowl. Cover with hot or boiling water. Let stand 15 to 30 minutes or until softened; drain before using.

2 Tomatoes Calories 20; Total Fat 0g (Saturated Fat 0g, Trans Fat 0g); Cholesterol 0mg; Sodium 5mg; Total Carbohydrate 4g (Dietary Fiber 1g); Protein 1g **Carbohydrate Choices:** 0

DRYING TOMATOES

Cut each tomato in half lengthwise, remove seeds with small spoon.

Place tomato halves cut side down on broiler rack.

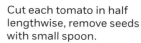

Oven-Dried Tomatoes

SLOW COOKER • MAKE AHEAD • CALORIE SMART •
GLUTEN FREE • VEGETARIAN • VEGAN

Apple Butter

PREP 20 Minutes **TOTAL** 4 Hours 20 Minutes • *4 cups*

12 medium Granny Smith or other cooking apples (4 lb), peeled, cut into quarters, cored	1 teaspoon ground allspice
	1 teaspoon ground nutmeg
1½ cups packed organic brown sugar	½ teaspoon ground cloves
	1¼ cups apple juice
1 tablespoon ground cinnamon	1 tablespoon lemon juice

1 In 4-quart saucepan, mix all ingredients. Heat to boiling, stirring occasionally; reduce heat. Cover and simmer, stirring occasionally, 1 hour.

2 Mash apples with potato masher or large fork. Simmer uncovered about 1 hour longer, stirring occasionally, until mixture is very thick. Cool about 2 hours.

3 Spoon into glass or plastic food storage containers. Cover and store in refrigerator up to 3 weeks.

1 Tablespoon Calories 40; Total Fat 0g (Saturated Fat 0g, Trans Fat 0g); Cholesterol 0mg; Sodium 0mg; Total Carbohydrate 9g (Dietary Fiber 0g); Protein 0g **Carbohydrate Choices:** ½

SLOW-COOKER DIRECTIONS: Reduce apple juice to ½ cup. Spray 5- to 6-quart slow cooker with cooking spray. In slow cooker, mix all ingredients. Cover; cook on Low heat setting 8 to 10 hours or until apples are very tender. Mash apples with potato masher or large fork. Cook uncovered 1 to 2 hours longer, stirring occasionally, until very thick. Cool about 2 hours.

EASY • MAKE AHEAD • CALORIE SMART

Raspberry-Lemon Infused Vodka

PREP 15 Minutes **TOTAL** 7 Days 15 Minutes •
four 8-oz bottles

3 packages (6 oz each) fresh raspberries (about 4 cups)	1 bottle (750 ml) 80 proof vodka
2 lemons, well scrubbed	4 (8-oz) bottles with lids

1 Place raspberries in strainer; gently wash. Remove and discard any dead leaves or moldy berries. Pat dry raspberries dry with clean kitchen towel.

2 In 1½- to 2-quart jar with tight fitting lid, place raspberries. Using vegetable peeler, peel lemons into long strips, being careful not to remove white pith of lemon; add to jar. (Wrap peeled lemons in plastic wrap; refrigerate for another use.) Pour vodka into jar. Press any raspberries or peel not covered by vodka under vodka to submerge. Cover jar tightly and let stand in cool, dark place 4 to 7 days, until desired raspberry flavor is reached.

3 Strain vodka through fine-mesh strainer into pitcher to remove raspberries and lemon peel. Gently press solids against strainer with flat-bottomed measuring cup to get all of the juice. Divide vodka evenly among bottles. (If making Adult Chocolate-Raspberry Milk Shakes, reserve raspberries. Otherwise, discard raspberries.) Store covered at room temperature up to 3 months.

3 Tablespoons Calories 100; Total Fat 0g (Saturated Fat 0g, Trans Fat 0g); Cholesterol 0mg; Sodium 0mg; Total Carbohydrate 0g (Dietary Fiber 0g); Protein 0g **Carbohydrate Choices:** 0

ADULT CHOCOLATE-RASPBERRY MILK SHAKE:
For each serving, in blender container, place ¾ cup milk, ½ cup of the strained vodka-soaked raspberries, ¼ cup chocolate-flavor syrup and 3 scoops ice cream. Cover; blend on medium speed 15 to 30 seconds or until blended.

HARD LEMONADE OR TEA: For each serving, in ice-filled glass, stir ¾ cup lemonade or iced tea and 3 tablespoons infused vodka.

HARD SELTZER: For each serving, in ice-filled glass, stir ¾ cup sparkling water and 3 tablespoons infused vodka; stir in 1 to 2 tablespoons simple syrup (page 95), if desired.

EASY • MAKE AHEAD • CALORIE SMART • GLUTEN FREE • VEGETARIAN • VEGAN

Carrot Baby Food

Making baby food at home is easy and puts you in charge of what goes in it! This recipe can easily be doubled or tripled to meet your needs.

PREP 10 Minutes **TOTAL** 50 Minutes • *4 servings*

4 medium carrots, cut into 1-inch chunks

1 In 2-quart saucepan, heat 1 inch of water to boiling. Add carrots; heat to boiling. Reduce heat. Simmer uncovered 7 to 10 minutes or until carrots are tender. Drain.

2 Place carrots in food processor or blender. Cover and process until smooth, adding water as needed for desired consistency. Spoon puree into ice cube trays or freezer-safe jars. Cover and freeze. If using ice cube trays, remove frozen cubes from trays and transfer to resealable freezer plastic bag. Freeze up 3 months.

3 To serve, thaw in the refrigerator several hours. Or place cube in small microwavable bowl; microwave uncovered on 30% power, stirring every few seconds, about 20 seconds or just until thawed and barely warm. Check temperature of baby's food before serving. Discard any uneaten portions.

1 Serving Calories 20; Total Fat 0g (Saturated Fat 0g, Trans Fat 0g); Cholesterol 0mg; Sodium 30mg; Total Carbohydrate 5g (Dietary Fiber 1g); Protein 0g **Carbohydrate Choices:** ½

SWEET PEA BABY FOOD: Cook 1 bag (12 oz) frozen sweet peas as directed on bag; drain. Cool 5 minutes. Continue as directed in Step 2.

Raspberry-Lemon Infused Vodka

Carrot Baby Food

USE IT UP
CITRUS PEELS

The colors and scent of citrus can add a fresh aroma or a pop of color to a variety of foods. Next time you eat or juice citrus fruits including grapefruit, clementines, oranges and lemons, try saving the peel for one of these uses. If possible, peel the citrus fruit with a vegetable peeler or paring knife (or use a channel knife for extra-long pieces of peel) before using the citrus, as it will be easier to peel when the fruit is whole.

CANDIED PEEL

Cut the peel of 2 oranges or lemons or 1 grapefruit into thin strips. Mix ¾ cup sugar, ½ cup water and peel in small saucepan. Heat to boiling; reduce heat. Cover and simmer 15 minutes; drain. Spread peel on cookie sheet lined with cooking parchment paper or waxed paper; cool 10 minutes. Place 3 tablespoons sugar on small plate; roll peel in sugar until well coated. Return to cookie sheet; let dry overnight. Store in airtight container up to 2 weeks at room temperature or up to 3 months in refrigerator. Use as a garnish for pies, cake or frozen desserts, add to cookie trays as an edible garnish/candy, or package in pretty clear bags to give as gifts.

CITRUS CURLS OR PICKS

To garnish to cocktails: Trim peels with paring knife to even sides. Wrap peel around a chopstick or wooden spoon handle to create a twist. Or skewer pieces of peel on cocktail picks, creating fun shapes or twists.

FLAVOR ENHANCER

Add a citrus peel piece to a glass of water, lemonade or iced tea, or hot tea or apple cider, to add flavor and interest. Twist the peel over the beverage before adding it, so the aromatic oils from the peel add even more flavor to your drink.

INFUSED OIL OR LIQUOR

Add fresh flavor to plain liquor (see Raspberry–Lemon Infused Vodka, page 469) or depth to olive or vegetable oil for salad dressings. Place peel in jar; add liquor or oil to cover peel. Cover jar and let stand in a cool, dark place, up to 1 week. Strain liquor or oil into clean bottle. Refrigerate liquor up to 1 month or store oil in cool, dark place up to 6 months.

QUICK ZEST FOR RECIPES

Zest the peel. Spread out zest on a paper towel–lined cookie sheet and let dry for about an hour, rubbing zest between fingers occasionally to separate pieces. Transfer dried zest to small freezer-safe food storage container with lid or small resealable freezer plastic bag. Store in freezer to use in recipes calling for zest.

EASY • MAKE AHEAD • CALORIE SMART • GLUTEN FREE • VEGETARIAN

Greek Yogurt

Greek yogurt is concentrated yogurt with a silky, smooth texture. Do not start with yogurt that contains gelatin. The gelatin prevents the liquid from draining from the yogurt.

PREP 5 Minutes **TOTAL** 7 Hours 5 Minutes • *2 cups*

> 2 cups regular or
> fat-free plain yogurt
> (from 32-oz container)

1 Line medium colander with cheesecloth. Place colander in bowl. Spoon or pour yogurt into lined colander; let drain 1 hour.

2 Loosely cover colander and bowl. Refrigerate 6 to 8 hours or until texture of yogurt is smooth and silky. Transfer yogurt from cheesecloth to medium bowl; cover. Discard whey (liquid) in bowl. Store yogurt covered in refrigerator up to 3 days.

¼ Cup Calories 35; Total Fat 0g (Saturated Fat 0g, Trans Fat 0g); Cholesterol 0mg; Sodium 45mg; Total Carbohydrate 5g (Dietary Fiber 0g); Protein 3g **Carbohydrate Choices:** ½

BACON-RANCH GREEK YOGURT DIP: In a medium bowl, stir together 1 cup Greek Yogurt, ⅓ cup shredded cheddar cheese, 2 tablespoons crumbled crisply cooked gluten-free bacon, 2 tablespoons chopped green onion (1 onion) and 2 tablespoons ranch dressing (to make your own Buttermilk Ranch Dressing, see page 148). Cover and refrigerate 2 hours to blend flavors. Sprinkle with additional crumbled bacon and green onion, if desired. Recipe can be doubled to use all of the yogurt, if desired.

CARDAMOM-SCENTED YOGURT: Make yogurt as directed in recipe. Stir ¼ teaspoon saffron threads into 1 tablespoon hot milk. Let stand 1 to 2 minutes or until milk is a rich golden yellow-orange color. Stir milk mixture, ¼ cup chopped unsalted pistachio nuts, ⅛ teaspoon ground nutmeg and ⅛ teaspoon ground cardamom into yogurt. Cover and refrigerate about 2 hours or until chilled.

Silky Chocolate-Caramel Sauce

EASY • FAST • MAKE AHEAD • GLUTEN FREE • VEGETARIAN

Silky Chocolate-Caramel Sauce

A pretty jar of this homemade dessert topping is a simply sweet gift. All you need are 4 ingredients and 10 minutes! Purchase whipping cream with the furthest-out "use by" date as possible, as this is as long as the sauce can be refrigerated. A very versatile sauce, it's delicious on cheesecake, ice cream—topped brownies or simple vanilla ice cream.

PREP 10 Minutes **TOTAL** 10 Minutes • *2 cups*

> ¾ cup packed
> brown sugar
> ⅔ cup whipping cream
>
> ½ cup plus
> 2 tablespoons butter,
> cut into pieces
> 4 oz semisweet baking
> chocolate, chopped

1 In 2-quart saucepan, cook brown sugar, whipping cream and butter over medium heat 2 to 3 minutes, stirring constantly, until mixture comes to a full boil.

2 Add chocolate; cook and stir about 2 minutes longer until chocolate is melted and sauce is smooth. Serve warm, or cover and refrigerate until serving time. To reheat, place desired amount in small microwavable bowl; cover with plastic wrap. Microwave on Medium (50%) in 30-second intervals, stirring after each interval, until warm.

2 Tablespoons Calories 180; Total Fat 14g (Saturated Fat 9g, Trans Fat 0g); Cholesterol 30mg; Sodium 65mg; Total Carbohydrate 12g (Dietary Fiber 1g); Protein 1g **Carbohydrate Choices:** 1

STRAINING YOGURT

Spoon or pour yogurt into cheesecloth-lined colander.

Drain yogurt until yogurt is smooth and silky.

5-INGREDIENT RECIPE

Sesame Sticks

SESAME STICKS

Candy-Coated Milk Chocolate Baking Bits

Kitchen Sink Cookie Mix

Chocolate Chip Cookie Mix

Pistachio Nuts

Betty Crocker™
Chocolate Chip
COOKIE MIX

☑ NO colors
☑ NO artificial flavors
☑ NO preservatives

Caramel Bits

Caramel

5-INGREDIENT RECIPE

EASY • MAKE AHEAD

Kitchen Sink Cookie Mix

*What a delicious treat to give and receive! Attach a
fabric circle under the lid, tie a ribbon around the
top of the jar and attach a card with instructions for
making the cookies.*

PREP 10 Minutes **TOTAL** 45 Minutes • *1 jar* (16 cookies)

1 (32-oz) jar with lid

KITCHEN SINK COOKIE MIX

1 pouch (17.5 oz)
chocolate chip
cookie mix

⅓ cup caramel bits
(from 11-oz bag)

⅓ cup pistachio nuts

⅓ cup miniature
candy-coated milk
chocolate baking bits

⅓ cup sesame sticks

TO COMPLETE COOKIES

½ cup butter, melted,
cooled

1 egg, slightly beaten

1 In jar, pour cookie mix; tap jar on counter to pack mix
into jar. Layer with caramel bits, pistachios, candy bits
and sesame sticks; cover.

2 To make cookies, heat oven to 375°F. Line two
cookie sheets with cooking parchment paper or silicone
baking mats.

3 In large bowl, stir contents of jar, butter and egg until
dough forms. Onto each cookie sheet, drop dough in
8 mounds by ¼-cupfuls, about 3 inches apart, pressing to
reform mounds if necessary.

4 Bake one cookie sheet 10 to 12 minutes or until edges
are light golden brown. Cool 5 minutes; remove cookies
from cookie sheet to cooling rack. Repeat with second
cookie sheet.

1 Cookie Calories 250; Total Fat 12g (Saturated Fat 7g, Trans Fat 0g);
Cholesterol 30mg; Sodium 230mg; Total Carbohydrate 31g (Dietary Fiber 1g);
Protein 2g **Carbohydrate Choices:** 2

**EASY • MAKE AHEAD • CALORIE SMART •
GLUTEN FREE • VEGETARIAN • VEGAN**

Cranberry-Orange Relish

PREP 10 Minutes **TOTAL** 24 Hours 10 Minutes • *2½ cups*

1 bag (12 oz) fresh or
frozen cranberries
(3 cups)

1 seedless orange,
well scrubbed

1 cup organic sugar

1 Wash cranberries; remove any stems and discard
any blemished berries. Cut orange into 1-inch pieces.
(The peel adds a tangy orange flavor; it won't make the
relish bitter tasting.)

2 Place sugar in medium bowl. In food processor, place
half of the cranberries and orange pieces. Cover and
process about 15 seconds, using short on-and-off pulses,
until evenly chopped. Stir cranberry mixture into sugar.
Repeat with remaining cranberries and orange pieces.

3 Cover and refrigerate at least 24 hours to blend flavors
before serving, but no longer than 1 week.

2 Tablespoons Calories 50; Total Fat 0g (Saturated Fat 0g, Trans Fat 0g);
Cholesterol 0mg; Sodium 0mg; Total Carbohydrate 13g (Dietary Fiber 0g);
Protein 0g **Carbohydrate Choices:** 1

CRANBERRY-ORANGE-GINGER RELISH:
Stir 1 tablespoon finely chopped organic crystallized
ginger into sugar in Step 2.

Cranberry-Orange Relish

MAKING CRANBERRY-ORANGE RELISH

Place half of cranberries
and orange pieces in
food processor.

Process using short on-
and-off pulses until evenly
chopped; mix with sugar.

EASY • MAKE AHEAD • CALORIE SMART •
GLUTEN FREE • VEGETARIAN

Kefir

Plain, unflavored kefir tastes like a cross between buttermilk and sour cream, with the benefit of containing probiotics just like yogurt and strains of beneficial yeasts.

PREP 10 Minutes **TOTAL** 32 Hours 10 Minutes • **4 cups**

4 cups whole milk*	1 envelope (5 grams) freeze-dried kefir starter (from 1-oz box)

1 In 3-quart saucepan, heat milk just to boiling, stirring frequently to avoid scorching. Pour into large bowl. Cool milk at room temperature until it reaches 73°F to 77°F, about 45 to 60 minutes.

2 Remove 1 cup cooled milk to small bowl; add kefir starter. Mix thoroughly with whisk. Add milk with kefir starter back to milk in large bowl; mix thoroughly with whisk. Cover with plastic wrap and let stand at room temperature 24 hours or until kefir has thickened.

3 Cover and refrigerate 8 hours to stop fermentation process. Pour into glass bottles or jars; cover with tight-fitting lids. Shake or stir before using to liquefy. Store covered in refrigerator up to 2 weeks.

1 Cup Calories 150; Total Fat 8g (Saturated Fat 4.5g, Trans Fat 0g); Cholesterol 25mg; Sodium 125mg; Total Carbohydrate 13g (Dietary Fiber 0g); Protein 7g **Carbohydrate Choices:** 1

*For food safety, make sure to use pasteurized milk for this recipe. Nondairy milk alternatives such as almond, cashew, coconut, hemp, rice and soy may not work with kefir starter products. Please check product packages and websites for information.

BLUEBERRY KEFIR: In blender, place ½ cup fresh blueberries, 1 cup kefir and 1 to 2 tablespoons honey or agave nectar. Cover and blend on high speed about 30 seconds or until smooth.

MANGO KEFIR: In blender, place 1 cup cubed fresh mango, 1 cup kefir and 1 to 2 tablespoons agave nectar or honey. Cover and blend on high speed about 30 seconds or until smooth.

STRAWBERRY-BANANA KEFIR: In blender, place ½ cup sliced fresh strawberries, ½ cup sliced ripe banana, 1 cup kefir and 2 to 3 tablespoons agave nectar or honey. Cover and blend on high speed about 30 seconds or until smooth.

STRAWBERRY KEFIR: In blender, place 1 cup sliced fresh strawberries, 1 cup kefir and 4 to 5 tablespoons agave nectar or honey. Cover and blend on high speed about 30 seconds or until smooth.

MAKE AHEAD • SLOW COOKER • CALORIE SMART

Bean and Barley Chili Mix

The seeds of chiles, such as in the dried ancho chile used here, contain some heat. You can leave them out of the mix or add a few or all, depending on how spicy you want the chili to be.

PREP 20 Minutes **TOTAL** 2 Hours 15 Minutes • **4 jars** (6 servings; 1⅓ cups each)

CHILI MIX

- ¼ cup chili powder
- 4 teaspoons dried minced garlic or 1 teaspoon garlic powder
- 4 teaspoons ground cumin
- 4 teaspoons smoked paprika
- 4 teaspoons dried oregano leaves
- 1 tablespoon salt
- 1 teaspoon ground red pepper (cayenne)
- ½ cup chicken or vegetable bouillon powder
- 4 teaspoons baking soda

- 4 (16-oz) jars with lids or food-safe plastic containers
- 2 cups dried red kidney beans
- 2 cups hulled barley
- ¾ cup parsley flakes
- ¼ cup chopped ancho chile
- 2 cups dried great northern beans

TO COMPLETE CHILI (PER JAR)

- 8 cups water
- 1 can (14.5 oz) diced tomatoes with green chiles, undrained
  Shredded cheese, coarsely crushed tortilla chips, chopped tomatoes, sour cream, if desired

1 In small bowl, stir together chili powder, garlic, cumin, paprika, oregano, salt and red pepper. In another small bowl, stir together chicken bouillon powder and baking soda.

2 In each jar, layer about 2 tablespoons of the bouillon mixture, ½ cup of the kidney beans, ½ cup of the barley, 3 tablespoons of the parsley, about 2 tablespoons of the chili powder mixture, 1 tablespoon of the chile and ½ cup of the great northern beans. Cover and store up to 1 month.

3 To make chili, in 4-quart saucepan, stir contents of 1 jar and water. Heat to boiling; reduce heat. Cover and simmer about 1 hour and 45 minutes or until beans are tender. Stir in tomatoes. Top individual servings with desired toppings.

1 Serving Calories 200; Total Fat 1g (Saturated Fat 0g, Trans Fat 0g); Cholesterol 0mg; Sodium 1530mg; Total Carbohydrate 37g (Dietary Fiber 9g); Protein 10g **Carbohydrate Choices:** 2½

SLOW-COOKER BEAN AND BARLEY CHILI: In 5-quart slow cooker, stir contents of 1 jar and 6½ cups water. Cook on High heat setting 4 to 5 hours or Low heat setting 6½ to 7½ hours or until beans are tender.

MAKE AHEAD • VEGETARIAN

Elf Chow

This eye-catching sweet-and-salty snack mix would make a great hostess gift. Package it in holiday food-safe tins or decorative bags and tie with ribbon.

PREP 20 Minutes TOTAL 4 Hours 50 Minutes • *18 cups*

- 12 cups popped unsalted popcorn
- 2 cups roasted whole almonds
- 2 cups small pretzel twists
- 1 cup red and green candy-coated chocolate candies
- 1 cup packed brown sugar
- ¾ cup butter
- ½ cup light corn syrup
- 1 teaspoon baking soda
- ½ teaspoon salt
- ½ teaspoon vanilla
- ¾ cup dark chocolate chips
- ½ cup white vanilla baking chips
- ½ teaspoon vegetable oil
- ½ cup crushed hard peppermint candies

1 Heat oven to 250°F. Lightly spray large roasting pan with cooking spray. In roasting pan, mix popcorn, almonds, pretzels and chocolate candies; set aside.

2 In 2-quart saucepan, heat brown sugar, butter and corn syrup to boiling over medium heat. Boil 8 to 10 minutes, stirring occasionally. Remove from heat; stir in baking soda, salt and vanilla until well mixed. Pour over popcorn mixture; toss until coated.

3 Bake 1 hour, stirring every 15 minutes. Immediately spread on waxed paper or cooking parchment paper. Cool 30 minutes.

4 In small microwavable bowl, microwave chocolate chips and ¼ teaspoon of the oil on High 30 to 60 seconds, stirring every 15 seconds, until melted and smooth. Drizzle over popcorn mixture.

5 In another small microwavable bowl, microwave white baking chips and remaining ¼ teaspoon oil on High 30 to 40 seconds, stirring every 15 seconds, until melted and smooth. Drizzle over popcorn mixture. Sprinkle with peppermint candies. Let stand 3 to 4 hours or until chocolate is set. Store in airtight container at room temperature up to 4 days.

1 Cup Calories 450; Total Fat 25g (Saturated Fat 10g, Trans Fat 0g); Cholesterol 25mg; Sodium 270mg; Total Carbohydrate 50g (Dietary Fiber 3g); Protein 5g **Carbohydrate Choices:** 3

Kefir

Bean and Barley Chili Mix

Elf Chow

Sauce Basics

Sauces are the equivalent of the perfect accessory: They transform a meal from ordinary to extraordinary. We'll show you how easy it is to masterfully create delicious sauces worthy of putting you in the "great cook" category!

Thickening Sauces

Sauces can be thickened in different ways, depending on what they are used for and the ingredients used. Here are the four classic thickening methods.

Roux: A mixture of flour and fat (usually butter) is cooked over low to medium heat until smooth and bubbly, cooking to remove the floury taste before liquid is added. Some recipes call for cooking the roux until it turns golden to deep brown, which adds color and flavor. See White Sauce: Roux, page 483.

Cornstarch: Often stirred into cold water or other liquid to thoroughly blend it before being added to a hot mixture. Sauces thickened with cornstarch become clear and almost shiny. See Ginger-Garlic Stir-Fry Sauce, page 488.

Emulsion: An egg-based sauce cooked over low heat. If the temperature is too hot, the mixture will overcook and curdle. These sauces must be cooked thoroughly to kill any potential salmonella bacteria. See Hollandaise Sauce, page 495.

Reduction: A liquid such as broth, wine or a gravy is boiled or simmered to evaporate some of the water in it until the volume is decreased and the sauce thickens, which concentrates the flavor. To speed this process, use a skillet (which has a large surface area) instead of a saucepan. See Peppery Red Wine Sauce, page 495.

Tips for Ideal Sauces

It's easy to make an ultra-smooth lump-free sauce if you follow these tips. Take your time—if you rush it, the sauce could curdle or separate. If it doesn't turn out the way you wanted, look below for our special kitchen secrets on how to fix a sauce.

MAKING SAUCE

- Gather all the ingredients before beginning to give full attention to cooking the sauce.
- Use the heat specified in the recipe.
- Use a whisk to mix sauces, and stir constantly to avoid lumps.
- Finish savory sauces with a pat of butter to enhance the flavor and give the sauce a velvety texture. Season with salt and pepper to taste before serving.

FIXING SAUCE PROBLEMS

- **Lumpy Sauce:** Strain through a fine-mesh strainer, pushing the liquid through the strainer with the back of a spoon. Discard what is left in the strainer.
- **Sauce Too Thin:** For a gravy or other sauce that was thickened with flour, mix ¼ cup cold water with 1 to 2 tablespoons all-purpose flour with a spoon or mini whisk until smooth. Stir into the boiling gravy. Cook and stir with a whisk a few minutes until thickened and the floury taste is gone. Repeat if an even thicker sauce is desired. Or stir a little plain-flavored instant mashed potato flakes or cake flour into the hot sauce until the desired consistency. (The sauce will continue to thicken as it cools.)
- **Curdled Egg-Based Sauce:** Strain out the lumps and try whisking the sauce into another gently heated egg yolk in a clean bowl.
- **Curdled Cream Sauce:** Reduce additional cream down to ⅓ its original volume by boiling in a pan; slowly stir into hot, curdled sauce a tablespoon at a time.

MAKE AHEAD • CALORIE SMART • GLUTEN FREE • VEGETARIAN • VEGAN

Salsa

This amazing classic salsa is full of tomato flavor. From a dip for tortilla chips to topping your favorite Mexican dishes, this fresh condiment will be a hit no matter what you serve it with.

PREP 15 Minutes **TOTAL** 1 Hour 15 Minutes • *3½ cups*

3 large tomatoes, seeded, chopped (3 cups)	2 tablespoons chopped fresh cilantro
½ cup chopped green bell pepper	2 to 3 tablespoons lime juice
8 medium green onions, sliced (½ cup)	1 tablespoon finely chopped seeded jalapeño chiles
3 cloves garlic, finely chopped	½ teaspoon salt

In medium glass or plastic bowl, mix all ingredients. Cover and refrigerate at least 1 hour to blend flavors. Store covered in refrigerator up to 1 week.

¼ Cup Calories 15; Total Fat 0g (Saturated Fat 0g, Trans Fat 0g); Cholesterol 0mg; Sodium 90mg; Total Carbohydrate 3g (Dietary Fiber 0g); Protein 0g **Carbohydrate Choices:** 0

BLACK BEAN SALSA: Stir in 1 can (15 oz) black beans, drained and rinsed. Makes about 5 cups.

MANGO-PEPPER SALSA: Omit tomatoes, substitute 1 red bell pepper for the green pepper, reduce green onions to 1 tablespoon. Add 1 cup peeled, pitted and diced mango. Makes 2½ cups.

EASY • FAST • CALORIE SMART • VEGETARIAN • VEGAN

Salsa Verde

This tasty alternative to classic salsa is made with tomatillos (tohm-ah-TEE-ohs), which are from the same family as tomatoes. Tomatillos have a thick skin with a papery covering and a firm texture. They are green, with a flavor that hints of lemon and apples.

PREP 15 Minutes **TOTAL** 15 Minutes • *1¼ cups*

½ lb tomatillos, husks removed, rinsed and cut in half*	¼ cup chopped red onion
2 canned pickled serrano chiles, rinsed and seeded, or 1 fresh serrano chile, seeded	¼ cup chopped fresh cilantro or parsley
	¼ teaspoon salt
	Tortilla chips, if desired

In blender or food processor, place all ingredients except tortilla chips. Cover and blend until well blended. Use immediately, or transfer to food storage container; cover and refrigerate up to 1 week. Serve with tortilla chips.

¼ Cup Calories 20; Total Fat 0g (Saturated Fat 0g, Trans Fat 0g); Cholesterol 0mg; Sodium 120mg; Total Carbohydrate 4g (Dietary Fiber 1g); Protein 0g **Carbohydrate Choices:** 0

*Small green tomatoes can be substituted for the tomatillos.

EASY • FAST • CALORIE SMART • GLUTEN FREE • VEGETARIAN

Mayonnaise

Homemade mayonnaise is deceptively easy to make and deliciously lush. You may never go back to store-bought again. Use it in any recipe calling for mayonnaise or as a sandwich condiment.

PREP 10 Minutes **TOTAL** 10 Minutes • *1¾ cups*

1¼ cups vegetable oil	1 tablespoon Dijon mustard
2 tablespoons fresh lemon juice	¼ teaspoon salt
	1 pasteurized egg*

1 In blender, place ¼ cup of the oil, the lemon juice, mustard, salt and egg. Cover and blend until smooth.

2 Leave cover on blender but remove center cap. With blender running on medium-high speed, slowly add remaining 1 cup oil in thin stream through opening in cover. Scrape down sides of container as needed. Store in tightly covered container in refrigerator up to 5 days.

1 Tablespoon Calories 90; Total Fat 10g (Saturated Fat 1.5g, Trans Fat 0g); Cholesterol 10mg; Sodium 35mg; Total Carbohydrate 0g (Dietary Fiber 0g); Protein 0g **Carbohydrate Choices:** 0

*Pasteurized eggs are uncooked eggs that have been heat-treated to kill bacteria that can cause food-borne illness and gastrointestinal distress. Because the egg in this recipe is not cooked, be sure to use a pasteurized egg. Look for them in the dairy case at large supermarkets.

CURRIED MAYONNAISE: Add ½ to 1 teaspoon gluten-free curry powder to egg mixture before blending in Step 1.

GARLIC MAYONNAISE: Stir 1 clove garlic, finely chopped, into prepared mayonnaise.

HERBED MAYONNAISE: Stir 1 tablespoon chopped fresh basil, chervil, chives, cilantro, marjoram, oregano or parsley into mayonnaise. If using dried herbs, use only 1 teaspoon.

Salsa Verde

EASY • MAKE AHEAD • CALORIE SMART •
GLUTEN FREE

Aioli

Aioli is a garlicky mayonnaise-like spread that is delicious on fish, chicken, meat and vegetables. The size of garlic cloves matters here; to make sure the sauce isn't overly garlicky, you should use about 1 teaspoon of the garlic-salt paste.

PREP 15 Minutes **TOTAL** 1 Hour 15 Minutes • *About ⅓ cup*

2 medium cloves garlic	½ teaspoon Dijon mustard
¼ teaspoon salt	
1 pasteurized egg yolk*	⅓ cup olive oil
1½ teaspoons lemon juice	⅛ teaspoon pepper

1 On cutting board, chop garlic. Sprinkle with salt; mash garlic and salt with fork to form a paste.

2 In small bowl, mix egg yolk, lemon juice and mustard with whisk. Slowly mix oil into yolk mixture, a few drops at a time, until all oil is mixed in and mixture is smooth. (If mixture separates, stop adding oil and whisk until mixture comes together, then continue to add oil.)

3 Stir in garlic paste and pepper. Cover and refrigerate 1 hour to blend flavors. Store covered in refrigerator up to 3 days.

1 Tablespoon Calories 120; Total Fat 13g (Saturated Fat 2g, Trans Fat 0g); Cholesterol 30mg; Sodium 110mg; Total Carbohydrate 0g (Dietary Fiber 0g); Protein 0g **Carbohydrate Choices:** 0

*Pasteurized eggs yolks have been heat-treated to kill bacteria that can cause food-borne illness and gastrointestinal distress.

JALAPEÑO-LIME AIOLI: Prepare as directed—except mash 1 to 1½ teaspoons finely chopped seeded jalapeño chile with the garlic and salt. Substitute lime juice for the lemon juice and add ¼ teaspoon lime zest to the prepared aioli.

VEGAN AIOLI: Omit egg yolk. Place 2 tablespoons liquid from chick peas (aquafaba), ¼ teaspoon ground turmeric and remaining ingredients in 1-cup liquid measuring cup. Blend with immersion blender 20 to 30 seconds or until thick and smooth.

MAKING PESTO

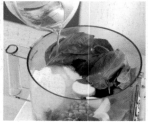

Place all ingredients in food processor blender container.

Cover and process, stopping occasionally to scrape down sides.

EASY • FAST • MAKE AHEAD • CALORIE SMART •
GLUTEN FREE • VEGETARIAN

Basil Pesto

Versatile pesto can be tossed with hot pasta or hot cooked vegetables, or used as a sandwich condiment or spread for crostini or crackers, or to top soup.

PREP 10 Minutes **TOTAL** 10 Minutes • *1¼ cups*

2 cups firmly packed fresh basil leaves	¼ cup pine nuts, toasted if desired (see page 28)
¾ cup grated Parmesan cheese	3 cloves garlic, peeled
½ cup olive or vegetable oil	

In blender or food processor, place all ingredients. Cover and blend on medium speed, stopping occasionally to scrape down sides with rubber spatula, about 3 minutes or until smooth. Use immediately, or transfer to food storage container; cover and refrigerate up to 5 days or freeze up to 1 month (color will darken as it stands).

1 Tablespoon Calories 80; Total Fat 8g (Saturated Fat 1.5g, Trans Fat 0g); Cholesterol 0mg; Sodium 70mg; Total Carbohydrate 0g (Dietary Fiber 0g); Protein 2g **Carbohydrate Choices:** 0

BASIL, ROASTED RED PEPPER AND WALNUT PESTO: Use food processor. Reduce basil to 1 cup and oil to ⅓ cup. Add ½ cup drained roasted red or yellow bell peppers (from a jar). Substitute walnuts for the pine nuts.

CILANTRO PESTO: Substitute 1½ cups firmly packed fresh cilantro and ½ cup firmly packed fresh parsley for the basil.

SPINACH PESTO: Substitute 2 cups firmly packed fresh spinach leaves for the basil.

SUN-DRIED TOMATO PESTO: Use food processor. Omit basil. Reduce oil to ⅓ cup. Add ½ cup sun-dried tomatoes in oil, undrained.

Basil Pesto

USE IT UP
PESTO

BREAKFAST EGGS Drizzle over breakfast eggs and sprinkle with red pepper flakes and pepper.

SALAD TOPPER Drizzle a little over sliced tomatoes and fresh mozzarella slices for simple and delicious salad.

SANDWICH CONDIMENT Use instead of mayonnaise in deli meat sandwiches, or spread it on the cheese sides of bread when making grilled cheese.

SENSATIONAL SIDES Upgrade your side dishes by tossing in a little into hot cooked mashed potatoes, rice or vegetables. Garnish with grated Parmesan cheese and pepper.

SIMPLE SNACK Toss a little with leftover cooked pasta before reheating for a hearty snack.

FAST • MAKE AHEAD • CALORIE SMART • GLUTEN FREE • VEGETARIAN

Broccoli-Walnut Pesto

Pesto doesn't have to be "herb-centric." In fact, vegetable-based pestos are varied, come in beautiful hues and are absolutely delicious! We love pesto stirred into hummus for a colorful dip or as a super-fast appetizer when spread on crostini.

PREP 15 Minutes **TOTAL** 15 Minutes • *1½ cups*

2 cups small fresh broccoli florets	½ cup olive oil or vegetable oil
½ cup lightly packed fresh basil leaves	⅓ cup shredded Parmesan cheese
½ cup chopped walnuts, toasted (see page 28)	¼ teaspoon salt
	¼ teaspoon pepper
	1 clove garlic, peeled

1 In 2-quart saucepan, heat 2 cups water to boiling. Add broccoli; boil uncovered 1 to 2 minutes or just until bright green. Remove broccoli from boiling water; immediately place in ice water until cold. Drain well.

2 In food processor, place broccoli and remaining ingredients. Cover and process until smooth, stopping occasionally to scrape down sides with rubber spatula.

MAKE-AHEAD PESTO CUBES

Freeze pesto in ice cube trays. Once frozen, move cubes to a resealable freezer plastic bag. Store in freezer up to 6 months. Thaw before using.

Broccoli-Walnut Pesto and Beet-Dill Pesto

3 Use pesto immediately or transfer to food storage container, press and smooth plastic wrap directly on surface of pesto, cover and refrigerate up to 3 days or freeze up to 1 month.

2 Tablespoons Calories 130; Total Fat 13g (Saturated Fat 2g, Trans Fat 0g); Cholesterol 0mg; Sodium 105mg; Total Carbohydrate 2g (Dietary Fiber 0g); Protein 2g **Carbohydrate Choices:** 0

BEET-DILL PESTO: Substitute 1 oz fresh red beets (cooked as directed in Roasted Beets, page 251), cooled and peeled, or 1 can (15 oz) whole beets, well drained, for the broccoli. Substitute 3 tablespoons fresh dill weed for the basil and reduce oil to 2 tablespoons. Continue as directed in Step 2.

BRUSSELS SPROUTS–CASHEW PESTO: Substitute 2 cups halved fresh Brussels sprouts for the broccoli and boil 3 minutes. Omit basil, substitute ½ cup cashew halves and pieces (not toasted) for the walnuts and add 2 tablespoons water.

ROASTED CARROT–ALMOND PESTO: Omit broccoli and basil. Substitute slivered almonds for the walnuts. Heat oven to 350°F. Spray 15x10x1-inch pan with cooking spray. Spread 1 bag (12 oz) ready-to-eat baby-cut carrots in pan. Drizzle with 1 tablespoon of the oil; toss to coat. Bake uncovered 35 to 45 minutes, stirring occasionally, until tender. Cool completely. Continue as directed in Step 2. Add 1 to 2 tablespoons water if necessary.

FAST • MAKE AHEAD • CALORIE SMART • GLUTEN FREE

French Fry Dipping Sauce

Use what you have on hand to customize this versatile sauce, which is perfect for French fries, veggie sticks, tots or other favorite dippers. Try barbecue sauce instead of ketchup or Dijon mustard instead of yellow. Or add a splash of soy sauce, Worcestershire sauce or Sriracha sauce for a flavor twist.

PREP 10 Minutes **TOTAL** 10 Minutes • *1 cup*

½ cup mayonnaise (for homemade mayonnaise, see page 479)	1 tablespoon sweet pickle juice
¼ cup ketchup	1 tablespoon yellow mustard
2 medium green onion, finely chopped (2 tablespoons) or 2 tablespoons finely chopped chives	½ teaspoon paprika or smoked paprika
	¼ teaspoon salt
	¼ teaspoon garlic powder
	Sliced green onion or chives, if desired

In small bowl, mix all ingredients except sliced onion until well blended. Serve immediately or cover and refrigerate until serving. Sprinkle with sliced onion. Store covered in refrigerator up to 5 days.

2 Tablespoons Calories 110; Total Fat 10g (Saturated Fat 1.5g, Trans Fat 0g); Cholesterol 5mg; Sodium 260mg; Total Carbohydrate 3g (Dietary Fiber 0g); Protein 0g **Carbohydrate Choices:** 0

Fish Taco Sauce

White Sauce

Also known as béchamel sauce, white sauce is the base for many creamy recipes from sauces to soups. If you're not partial to canned cream soups, this is a great alternative as a base sauce. Check out the variations to make it thicker or thinner, and to customize the flavor.

PREP 10 Minutes **TOTAL** 10 Minutes • *1 cup*

2 tablespoons butter	¼ teaspoon salt
2 tablespoons all-purpose flour	⅛ teaspoon pepper
	1 cup milk

1 In 1½-quart saucepan, melt butter over low heat. Using whisk, stir in flour, salt and pepper. Cook and stir over medium heat until mixture is smooth and bubbly, about 1 minute; remove from heat.

2 Gradually stir in milk. Heat to boiling, stirring constantly; boil and stir 1 minute. Serve immediately.

1 Tablespoon Calories 25; Total Fat 1.5g (Saturated Fat 1g, Trans Fat 0g); Cholesterol 5mg; Sodium 55mg; Total Carbohydrate 1g (Dietary Fiber 0g); Protein 0g **Carbohydrate Choices:** 0

THICK WHITE SAUCE: Increase butter and flour to ¼ cup each.

THIN WHITE SAUCE: Reduce butter and flour to 1 tablespoon each.

CHEESE SAUCE: Stir in ¼ teaspoon ground mustard with the flour. After boiling and stirring sauce 1 minute, stir in ½ cup shredded cheddar cheese (2 oz) until melted. Serve with eggs and vegetables. Makes about 1⅓ cups.

CREAMY MUSHROOM SAUCE: Cook ½ cup chopped fresh mushrooms in butter about 3 minutes, stirring occasionally, until golden brown, before stirring in flour, salt and pepper.

CURRY SAUCE: Stir in ½ teaspoon curry powder with the flour. Serve with chicken, lamb or shrimp.

DILL SAUCE: Stir in 1 teaspoon chopped fresh or ½ teaspoon dried dill weed and dash ground nutmeg with the flour. Serve with fish.

MUSTARD SAUCE: Reduce butter and flour to 1 tablespoon each. After boiling and stirring sauce 1 minute, stir in 3 tablespoons Dijon mustard. Serve with beef, veal, ham or vegetables.

ROUX (TO THICKEN SOUP, GUMBO OR GRAVY): To thicken soup or gumbo, prepare as directed in Step 1. Omit milk, add liquid for soup or gumbo. Cook as directed in Step 2.

To thicken gravy, cook and stir flour mixture longer in Step 1 to develop rich brown color and deeper flavor. Omit milk, add desired liquid for gravy. Cook as directed in Step 2.

Fish Taco Sauce

Not only is this sauce great on tacos, it's delicious as a dip for fish sticks or Cheesy Jalapeño-Cauliflower Tots (page 55).

PREP 10 Minutes **TOTAL** 2 Hours 10 Minutes • *1 cup*

½ cup sour cream	1 tablespoon finely chopped fresh cilantro leaves
⅓ cup mayonnaise (for homemade mayonnaise, see page 479)	½ teaspoon dried oregano leaves
1 tablespoon fresh lime juice	½ teaspoon ground cumin
1 tablespoon adobo sauce (from 7-oz can chipotle peppers in adobo sauce)	¼ teaspoon salt
	1 clove garlic, finely chopped

In small bowl, mix all ingredients until well blended. Cover and refrigerate at least 2 hours to blend flavors. Store covered in refrigerator up to 1 week.

1 Tablespoon Calories 45; Total Fat 5g (Saturated Fat 1.5g, Trans Fat 0g); Cholesterol 5mg; Sodium 75mg; Total Carbohydrate 0g (Dietary Fiber 0g); Protein 0g **Carbohydrate Choices:** 0

PREPARING ROUX

Cook flour and butter until smooth and bubbly. Cook an additional minute to remove floury taste before stirring in liquid.

HEIRLOOM

EASY • MAKE AHEAD • CALORIE SMART • GLUTEN FREE

Tartar Sauce

Tartar sauce is a favorite to serve with most any type of fish or seafood. If you make it with salad dressing, it will be sweeter.

PREP 5 Minutes **TOTAL** 1 Hour 5 Minutes • *1 cup*

- 1 cup mayonnaise or spreadable salad dressing (for homemade mayonnaise, see page 479)
- 2 tablespoons pickle relish or finely chopped dill pickles
- 1 tablespoon chopped fresh parsley
- 2 teaspoons diced pimientos, drained
- 1 teaspoon grated onion

In small bowl, mix all ingredients. Cover and refrigerate about 1 hour or until chilled. Store covered in refrigerator up to 5 days.

1 Tablespoon Calories 100; Total Fat 11g (Saturated Fat 1.5g, Trans Fat 0g); Cholesterol 10mg; Sodium 95mg; Total Carbohydrate 0g (Dietary Fiber 0g); Protein 0g **Carbohydrate Choices:** 0

LIGHTER DIRECTIONS: For 5 grams of fat and 50 calories per serving, use reduced-fat mayonnaise.

DILL TARTAR SAUCE: Stir in 1 tablespoon chopped fresh or 1 teaspoon dried dill weed.

NEW TWIST

MAKE AHEAD • CALORIE SMART • GLUTEN FREE

Chipotle-Lemon Tartar Sauce

This flavorful spread is great with fish or crab cakes, or as a sandwich spread.

PREP 10 Minutes **TOTAL** 1 Hour 10 Minutes • *1¼ cups*

- 1 cup mayonnaise or spreadable salad dressing (for homemade mayonnaise, see page 479)
- 2 tablespoons sweet pickle relish
- 2 tablespoons chopped fresh cilantro
- 1 tablespoon fresh lemon juice
- 2 to 3 teaspoons finely chopped chipotle peppers in adobo sauce (from 7-oz can)
- 2 medium green onions, sliced (2 tablespoons)

In small bowl, mix all ingredients until well blended. Cover and refrigerate about 1 hour or until chilled. Store covered in refrigerator up to 5 days.

2 Tablespoons Calories 160; Total Fat 17g (Saturated Fat 2.5g, Trans Fat 0g); Cholesterol 10mg; Sodium 170mg; Total Carbohydrate 2g (Dietary Fiber 0g); Protein 0g **Carbohydrate Choices:** 0

Tartar Sauce

Chipotle-Lemon Tartar Sauce

FAST • CALORIE SMART • GLUTEN FREE

Yum Yum Sauce

This delicious dipping sauce works great for fried shrimp, chicken tenders, fish and beef. And it's also a great sauce for drizzling over rice bowls or fried egg sandwiches.

PREP 5 Minutes **TOTAL** 5 Minutes • *½ cup*

- ⅓ cup mayonnaise (for homemade mayonnaise, see page 479)
- 1 tablespoon butter, melted
- 1 tablespoon chili garlic sauce
- 1 tablespoon unseasoned rice vinegar
- 1 tablespoon packed brown sugar
- 1 teaspoon smoked paprika
- 1 teaspoon toasted sesame oil, if desired

In small bowl, mix all ingredients. Cover and refrigerate until ready to serve.

1 Tablespoon Calories 90 ; Total Fat 8g (Saturated Fat 2g, Trans Fat 0g); Cholesterol 10mg; Sodium 75mg; Total Carbohydrate 3g (Dietary Fiber 0g); Protein 0g **Carbohydrate Choices:** 0

FAST • CALORIE SMART • GLUTEN FREE • VEGETARIAN

Cauliflower Alfredo Sauce

This delicious sauce is great on pasta or drizzled over hot cooked vegetables.

PREP 30 Minutes **TOTAL** 30 Minutes • *1½ cups*

- 2 tablespoons butter
- 1½ cups coarsely chopped fresh cauliflower florets
- 2 cloves garlic, finely chopped
- ¾ cup milk
- ⅛ teaspoon salt
- 2 oz (from 8-oz package) cream cheese, cubed small, softened
- ½ cup grated Parmesan cheese (2 oz)

1 In 2-quart saucepan, heat butter over medium heat until melted. Add cauliflower and garlic; cook, stirring constantly, about 1 minute or until garlic is fragrant. Add milk and salt. Heat to boiling; reduce heat. Cover and simmer 5 to 7 minutes or until cauliflower is very tender. Remove from heat; uncover and cool 5 minutes.

2 In blender, ladle cauliflower mixture. Cover; blend on high speed, stopping occasionally and scraping down sides with rubber spatula, about 2 minutes or until completely smooth. Add cheeses; cover and blend 15 to 30 seconds or until smooth. Serve immediately.

¼ Cup Calories 130; Total Fat 10g (Saturated Fat 6g, Trans Fat 0g); Cholesterol 30mg; Sodium 240mg; Total Carbohydrate 4g (Dietary Fiber 0g); Protein 5g **Carbohydrate Choices:** 0

FAST • CALORIE SMART

Creamy Mushroom-Herb Sauce

This delicious creamy mushroom sauce is made with almond milk, but you can substitute regular milk if you prefer. Serve it with meatloaf, burgers, chicken or potatoes; sprinkle with fresh thyme leaves, if you like.

PREP 20 Minutes **TOTAL** 20 Minutes • *1¼ cups*

- 1 tablespoon all-purpose flour
- ¼ teaspoon salt
- ¼ teaspoon dried thyme leaves
- ⅛ teaspoon dried rosemary leaves, crushed
- Pinch of black pepper, if desired
- Pinch of ground red pepper (cayenne), if desired
- 1 tablespoon plus 1½ teaspoons olive oil
- ½ package (8 oz) baby portabella mushrooms, thinly sliced
- 2 tablespoons finely chopped onion
- 1 clove garlic, finely chopped
- ⅔ cup chicken broth (for homemade broth, see page 153)
- ¼ cup unsweetened almond milk

1 In small bowl, mix flour, salt, thyme, rosemary, black pepper and red pepper; set aside.

2 In 8-inch skillet, heat olive oil over medium heat until hot. Add mushrooms, onion and garlic. Cook, stirring occasionally, 5 to 6 minutes or until mushrooms start to brown. Sprinkle with flour mixture; stir until well mixed.

3 Gradually stir in broth; heat to boiling. Boil and stir 1 to 2 minutes or until thickened. Stir in almond milk; cook until heated through.

¼ Cup Calories 60; Total Fat 4.5g (Saturated Fat 0.5g, Trans Fat 0g); Cholesterol 0mg; Sodium 250mg; Total Carbohydrate 3g (Dietary Fiber 0g); Protein 1g **Carbohydrate Choices:** 0

Creamy Mushroom-Herb Sauce

LEARN TO STIR-FRY

Stir-fry dinners are a delicious way to add veggies to your plate while customizing the dish each time, depending on what you add. They're a great way to use up veggies and chicken or meat you have on hand.

Stir-Fry Tips

- Use a wok or 12-inch skillet to stir-fry. Woks are preferred, as the sloped sides allow you to control the cooking of the various ingredients in your dish because you can push an ingredient up the side of the pan to slow the cooking and keep it warm while other ingredients in the bottom of the pan cook quickly. Skillets or Dutch ovens are great substitutes if you don't have a wok. Simply remove any food that you don't want to overcook to a heatproof bowl and keep warm until you're ready to add it back to the pan.

- Have all meat and veggies cut up and prepped before starting to stir-fry, as the cooking itself will go very quickly. Place ingredients in bowls near your stove-top to add them quickly and easily when cooking.

- Use vegetable or peanut oil for cooking as they have a high smoke point, meaning that unlike other oils, such as olive or canola, they won't burn at high temperatures.

Stir-Fry Essentials

Use these ingredients for a great-tasting, successful stir-fry dish.

- **Cooking sauce** if desired, fresh (see Ginger-Garlic Stir-Fry Sauce, page 488) or prepared

- Finely chopped **garlic** (1 or 2 cloves if your sauce doesn't have it or you want extra flavor)

- Finely chopped or grated fresh **gingerroot** (1 teaspoon if your sauce doesn't have it or you want extra flavor)

- 5 to 6 cups bite-size pieces fresh or frozen **veggies**

- 1 lb uncooked **beef, chicken, pork or shrimp**, or **tofu**, in bite-size pieces

- **Nuts** such as peanuts, cashews or almonds, if desired

- **Cooked rice or Asian noodles**, if desired

Stir-Fry Steps

1 If making your own sauce (such as Ginger-Garlic Stir-Fry Sauce, page 488), prepare and set it aside.

2 **If adding garlic and gingerroot to stir-fry (see above),** in pan, heat 1 tablespoon oil over medium-high heat until hot.

3 Stir-fry garlic and gingerroot 1 to 2 minutes or until fragrant.

4 Add vegetables to wok; stir-fry until crisp-tender.

If using hard veggies such as fresh broccoli or carrots, stir-fry these first for 2 minutes; then add a few ice cubes (about ¼ cup) to create steam. Cover and cook 2 to 3 minutes. Add remaining vegetables; stir-fry uncovered until all veggies are crisp-tender.

If using frozen veggies, prevent sauce from getting watery by draining any water from cooked frozen vegetables before continuing as they may release a lot of water during cooking.

5 Push veggies up side of wok or remove to heatproof bowl; cover with foil and keep warm.

6 Add another tablespoon of oil to pan; heat until hot. Add meat to pan; stir-fry until desired doneness is reached.

7 Add sauce to pan; stir in veggies if they had been removed. Cook 1 to 2 minutes or until meat and veggies are evenly coated and sauce is thickened.

8 Top with nuts. Serve with rice.

DONENESS INDICATORS WHEN STIR-FRYING MEAT

PROTEIN USED IN STIR-FRY	COOK UNTIL
BEEF OR PORK	
Uncooked bite-size pieces beef sirloin or flank steak, or boneless pork chops or tenderloin	Slightly pink to no pink in center
CHICKEN	
Uncooked bite-size pieces boneless breast or thighs	No longer pink in center
SHRIMP	
Deveined, shells removed, tails on or off	Shrimp are pink
TOFU (FIRM)	
Pressed between paper towels to remove moisture	Golden brown on all sides

FAST • CALORIE SMART • GLUTEN FREE

Ginger-Garlic Stir-Fry Sauce

Let this be your go-to sauce for stir-fries of any kind.

PREP 10 Minutes **TOTAL** 10 Minutes • *⅔ cup*

- 2 teaspoons vegetable oil
- 1 tablespoon finely chopped gingerroot
- 1 tablespoon plus 1 teaspoon finely chopped garlic (8 cloves)
- ⅓ cup gluten-free reduced-sodium chicken broth (for homemade chicken broth, page 153)
- 3 tablespoons gluten-free reduced-sodium soy sauce
- 2 tablespoons rice vinegar
- 1 tablespoon hoisin sauce
- 2 teaspoons cornstarch
- ¼ teaspoon crushed red pepper flakes, if desired

1 In wok or 12-inch skillet that will be used for stir-frying, heat oil over medium heat until hot; add ginger and garlic. Cook and stir 2 to 3 minutes or until tender. Remove from heat. In small bowl, mix remaining ingredients and garlic and ginger mixture until well blended.

2 Continue with Step 2 in Stir-Fry steps in Learn to Stir-Fry, page 486.

About 2 Tablespoons Calories 35; Total Fat 2g (Saturated Fat 0g, Trans Fat 0g); Cholesterol 0mg; Sodium 410mg; Total Carbohydrate 4g (Dietary Fiber 0g); Protein 1g **Carbohydrate Choices:** 0

EASY • FAST • MAKE AHEAD • CALORIE SMART • GLUTEN FREE • VEGETARIAN • VEGAN

Easy Tomato Pizza Sauce

Fresh sauce is the secret to the best homemade pizza. You can also use it as a dip for breadsticks or cheesy bread.

PREP 10 Minutes **TOTAL** 10 Minutes • *3 cups*

- 1 can (28 oz) whole tomatoes, drained
- 1 can (6 oz) tomato paste
- 1 tablespoon olive oil
- 1 teaspoon dried oregano leaves
- ½ teaspoon salt
- ¼ teaspoon pepper
- 2 cloves garlic, finely chopped

In blender or food processor, place all ingredients. Cover; blend until smooth, stopping occasionally to scrape down sides with rubber spatula. Use immediately or transfer to food storage container; cover and refrigerate up to 1 week.

1 Tablespoon Calories 20; Total Fat 0.5g (Saturated Fat 0g, Trans Fat 0g); Cholesterol 0mg; Sodium 160mg; Total Carbohydrate 3g (Dietary Fiber 0g); Protein 0g **Carbohydrate Choices:** 0

MAKE-AHEAD DIRECTIONS: Freeze ½- or 1-cup portions in freezer-safe food storage containers. Thaw overnight in refrigerator or transfer to a microwavable bowl. Cover and microwave on Medium-Low (30%) until sauce can be stirred smooth.

BASIL TOMATO PIZZA SAUCE: Add about 6 fresh basil leaves before blending.

FAST • MAKE AHEAD • CALORIE SMART

Parmesan White Pizza Sauce

For a change from red pizza sauce, try this creamy chicken broth–based version. Or fold some into hot cooked riced cauliflower—yum!

PREP 15 Minutes **TOTAL** 15 Minutes • *1 cup*

- 1 tablespoon butter
- 1 small onion, chopped (½ cup)
- 1 clove garlic, finely chopped
- 1 tablespoon all-purpose flour
- ½ cup chicken broth (for homemade broth, see page 153)
- ⅓ cup milk or half-and-half
- 1 teaspoon dried basil leaves
- ¼ cup grated Parmesan cheese (1 oz)

1 In 1-quart saucepan, melt butter over medium heat. Cook onion and garlic in butter about 5 minutes, stirring occasionally, until soft. Stir in flour until blended.

2 Gradually stir in broth, milk and basil. Cook about 3 minutes, stirring constantly, until thickened. Remove from heat; stir in cheese until melted. Use immediately or transfer to food storage container; cover and refrigerate up to 1 week.

1 Tablespoon Calories 40; Total Fat 2.5g (Saturated Fat 1.5g, Trans Fat 0g); Cholesterol 5mg; Sodium 125mg; Total Carbohydrate 3g (Dietary Fiber 0g); Protein 2g **Carbohydrate Choices:** 0

MAKE AHEAD • CALORIE SMART • GLUTEN FREE • VEGETARIAN • VEGAN

Red Curry Paste

This Thai condiment tastes great in curries made with coconut milk, and can be used to add flavor and heat to everything from marinades and dips to sauces and stews. It's a great use for cilantro stems, as they give the strongest cilantro flavor but typically go to waste. For the most flavor, select the tender, bright green portions.

PREP 50 Minutes **TOTAL** 50 Minutes • *½ cup*

- 10 dried chiles de arbol chiles
  Boiling water
- 4 fresh red Fresno or serrano chiles
- ½ cup coarsely chopped shallots (about 3 medium)
- ¼ cup coarsely chopped garlic (about 20 cloves)
- 2 tablespoons chopped fresh cilantro stems
- 1 tablespoon finely chopped gingerroot
- 1 tablespoon ground coriander
- 2 teaspoons finely chopped lemongrass (see page 490)
- 1 teaspoon ground cumin
- ½ teaspoon salt
- 1 strip (1½ x ½ inch) fresh lime peel
- 4 to 6 teaspoons water

1 Soak dried chiles in boiling water 30 minutes (place plate on top and weight with can to keep chiles submerged). Cut tops off fresh chiles, cut in half lengthwise and remove seeds; coarsely chop.

2 Drain soaked chiles; discard soaking water. Place all ingredients except water in small food processor or blender. Cover and process until finely chopped. Add just enough water until a paste forms, stopping food processor and scraping down sides with rubber spatula as needed. Use immediately or store in tightly covered jar in refrigerator up to 6 months.

1 Tablespoon Calories 25; Total Fat 0g (Saturated Fat 0g, Trans Fat 0g); Cholesterol 0mg; Sodium 150mg; Total Carbohydrate 4g (Dietary Fiber 1g); Protein 0g **Carbohydrate Choices:** 0

489

Easy Tomato Pizza Sauce

MAKE AHEAD • CALORIE SMART • GLUTEN FREE • VEGETARIAN • VEGAN

Roasted Roma Tomato Sauce

This is a great recipe to make when you have a bumper crop of tomatoes from your garden or the farmers' market. Delicious with pasta or as a pizza sauce.

PREP 25 Minutes **TOTAL** 2 Hours 10 Minutes • *8 cups*

24 plum (Roma) tomatoes, stem end trimmed off, halved lengthwise	½ teaspoon crushed red pepper flakes
¼ cup olive oil	2 large onions, thickly sliced (¾ inch), not separated into rings
1 tablespoon salt	2 bulbs garlic, root end sliced off

1 Heat oven to 425°F. Line 2 cookie sheets with sides with foil; spray foil with cooking spray.

2 In large bowl, toss tomatoes, oil, salt and pepper flakes. Place tomatoes, cut sides up, in single layer on 1 cookie sheet, tightly packed in rows. Place onions on second cookie sheet. Press cut side of garlic into oil mixture remaining in bowl; place on cookie sheet with onions. Scrape remaining oil mixture from bowl onto onions.

3 Roast 55 minutes to 1 hour 15 minutes or until tomatoes are charred on edges and onions are browned.

4 Squeeze garlic pulp from skins into blender; discard skins. Working in batches, add tomatoes, onions and pan juices to blender and then cover. Blend until smooth, starting on low speed and working up to high speed, and stopping occasionally to scrape down sides with rubber spatula, blend 30 to 60 seconds or until smooth. Use immediately or freeze as directed below.

¼ Cup Calories 40; Total Fat 2g (Saturated Fat 0g, Trans Fat 0g); Cholesterol 0mg; Sodium 230mg; Total Carbohydrate 5g (Dietary Fiber 0g); Protein 1g **Carbohydrate Choices:** ½

MAKE-AHEAD DIRECTIONS: Transfer to large glass or stainless steel bowl. Cover loosely with plastic wrap; refrigerate about 30 minutes or until lukewarm. Spoon 1-cup portions into freezer containers or 1-quart resealable freezer plastic bags; seal tightly. Freeze up to 3 months. Thaw overnight in refrigerator or in microwave on Medium (50%) 3 to 5 minutes or until completely thawed, then use immediately.

Red Curry Paste

Roasted Roma Tomato Sauce

GLOBAL FLAVORS

Asia

The ingredients of Asian cuisines encompass a large diversity of tastes and regional specialties. Here is a sampling of some of the most commonly used ingredients. Try Beef Pho (page 158), which combines several Asian ingredients into an easy yet delicious dinner.

CONDIMENTS

Chile bean paste or sauce (known as **gochujang** in Korea), a popular condiment in Sichuanese, Hunanese and Korean cooking, contains fermented soy beans, dried chiles, garlic and seasonings. **Other bean sauces and pastes,** ranging in thickness, are intensely flavored mixtures used to perk up the flavor of many dishes. **Sriracha,** similar in consistency to ketchup (and used as frequently in Southeast Asian cuisine as ketchup is used in the US) is a spicy sauce of red chiles, vinegar, garlic and salt. **Sambal oelek** is a thick, chunky puree of chiles, vinegar and salt from Indonesia, served with rice and as an all-purpose spicy condiment.

NOODLES

Noodles can be made from wheat, rice, potato or buckwheat flour, cornstarch, and bean, yam or soybean starch. Popular Chinese noodles include **cellophane** (made from mung bean starch), **egg noodles** (usually wheat) and **rice noodles.** Japan's most popular noodles include **harusame** (cellophane noodles made with rice, potato, sweet potato or mung bean starch), **ramen** (wheat-flour egg noodles) and **soba** noodles (made with buckwheat flour). Korea has many kinds of noodles—some are like buckwheat soba noodles but chewier, others are made from sweet potato starch or wheat, corn or rice flour. Many dried noodles are available in supermarkets; both fresh and dried noodles can be found in Asian markets. Noodles can be served hot or cold and cooked in a variety of ways, including stir-frying and steaming.

SEASONINGS

Native to Asia, **star anise** is the pod from a small evergreen tree. Slightly more bitter than anise, it's commonly used in tea and as a spice. **Furkake** is a dried seasoning blend sprinkled over rice, vegetables or fish. Ingredients vary from region to region. **Lemongrass** is an integral flavoring in Thai and Vietnamese cooking; it is available both fresh and dried. Thai chiles, popular in many South Asian dishes, are small, very spicy chiles that don't lose their flavor when cooked. They can range in color from green to red when ripe.

DRIED SEAFOOD

With a strong fishy taste, small amounts of dried anchovies, shrimp, and bonito (tuna) are commonly used to flavor a variety of Asian dishes. They may need to be reconstituted in warm water to be used; many dishes then use the water they were soaked in for additional flavor.

EDIBLE SEAWEED

An important component of Asian cuisine, belonging to the algae family. Different varieties are used for different dishes. Deep green **wakame** is used fresh or dried as a vegetable in soups and simmered dishes. **Kombu** (kelp) is edible brown seaweed used with bonito to make Japanese soup stock. **Nori** is seaweed dried into sheets to make sushi.

KIMCHI

Korean pickled and fermented vegetables, sometimes made spicy with chiles. Served at nearly every Korean meal, kimchi can vary widely depending on the produce in season.

MIRIN

Rice wine made from glutinous rice. An essential Japanese staple, used to add sweetness and flavor to a variety of dishes.

MISO

Fermented soybean paste used in a wide variety of Japanese recipes including soups, sauces, marinades, dips, dressings and as a condiment. Available in a wide variety of types and colors with different flavors for different dishes.

SAKE

Often called "rice wine"; however, it is brewed like beer, from rice, water and koji (a type of mold). It comes in a wide variety of types used both for drinking and in Japanese sauces and marinades.

SESAME OIL

An excellent choice for frying, sesame oil is made from sesame seed; available in both light and dark varieties. Light has a light, nutty flavor and is used for salad dressings and a variety of dishes. Dark has a stronger flavor and fragrance, so it is used sparingly as an accent in Asian dishes.

TOFU

(also known as bean curd or soybean curd)

Made from ground cooked soybeans, the curds are pressed in a similar way that cheese is made. Its bland, slightly nutty flavor can absorb other flavors in a dish. It's used as a plant-based source of protein in many Asian dishes.

Light
Sesame Oil

Black Sesame Oil

Rice
Vinegar

Mirin

Sake

Dried Kelp

491

Sesame
Seeds

Black
Sesame
Seeds

Soy Sauce

Fish Sauce

Wakame
Seaweed

Brown
Miso

Limes

Mung Beans

Red Miso

White Miso

Coconut Milk

Roasted
Seaweed

Dried
Anchovy

Dried Shrimp

Dried Bonito
Shavings

Korean
Noodles

Kimchi

Vietnamese
Noodles

Hot Sauces

Chinese
Chives

Thai Chiles

Korean Melon

Chrysanthemum
Greens

Parwal (Pointed Gourd)

Gingerroot

Lemongrass

Star Anise

Red Bean Paste

Black Bean Paste

Fermented Bean Curd

Whole Cloves

Ground Cloves

Galangal

5-INGREDIENT RECIPE

492

Rice Vinegar

White Miso

Brown Sugar

Butter

Green Onion–Miso Butter Sauce

Green Onions

WHITE **MISO**
LIGHT SOYBEAN PASTE
GLUTEN FREE
NET WT. 5.64 OZ (160g)

5-INGREDIENT RECIPE

Green Onion—Miso Butter Sauce

This is sure to be the best friend of fish, chicken, steaks and even veggies!

PREP 20 Minutes **TOTAL** 20 Minutes • *About ½ cup*

- 2 tablespoons butter, cut into pieces
- 6 medium green onions, finely chopped, white and green parts separated
- 1 tablespoon packed brown sugar
- 1 tablespoon gluten-free white miso
- ¼ cup unseasoned rice vinegar

1 In 1-quart saucepan, heat butter over medium heat until melted. Add white parts of onions to saucepan. Cook, stirring frequently, 2 to 3 minutes or until onions are soft. Reduce heat to low.

2 Stir in brown sugar and miso until well mixed. Remove from heat; stir in vinegar. Heat to boiling; reduce heat. Simmer, stirring occasionally, 3 to 5 minutes or until thickened. Stir in green parts of onions.

2 Tablespoons Calories 80; Total Fat 6g (Saturated Fat 3.5g, Trans Fat 0g); Cholesterol 15mg; Sodium 210mg; Total Carbohydrate 6g (Dietary Fiber 0g); Protein 1g **Carbohydrate Choices:** ½

Bourbon Steak Sauce

Whether this is served with steaks or burgers, or even as a dipping sauce for grilled cheese sandwiches, you'll want to lick up every drop! Top with pepper, if you like.

PREP 10 Minutes **TOTAL** 20 Minutes • *1 cup*

- 2 tablespoons butter
- ½ cup finely chopped shallots (about 2 large)
- ¼ teaspoon coarse ground black pepper
- 1 tablespoon all-purpose flour
- ¼ cup bourbon
- 1 cup (from 32-oz carton) beef broth (for homemade, see page 157)
- 2 teaspoons Dijon mustard

1 In 1½-quart saucepan, heat butter over medium heat until melted. Stir in shallots and pepper. Cook, stirring frequently, 5 to 6 minutes or until shallots are soft and golden brown. Stir flour into shallot mixture. Cook, stirring frequently, 1 minute, until bubbly.

2 Remove from heat; stir in bourbon. Heat to boiling; cook, stirring constantly, for 15 seconds.

3 Stir in beef broth and mustard; heat to boiling. Boil, stirring occasionally, 2 to 3 minutes or until sauce is thickened.

¼ Cup Calories 90; Total Fat 6g (Saturated Fat 3.5g, Trans Fat 0g); Cholesterol 15mg; Sodium 330mg; Total Carbohydrate 5g (Dietary Fiber 0g); Protein 1g **Carbohydrate Choices:** ½

Bourbon Steak Sauce

White Wine–Garlic Sauce

Serve this velvety-smooth sauce over pasta, chicken, pork or vegetables.

PREP 15 Minutes **TOTAL** 35 Minutes • *1 cup*

- ¼ cup olive oil
- 4 cloves garlic, finely chopped
- 2 cups dry white wine (such as chardonnay or sauvignon blanc) or nonalcoholic white wine
- ¼ cup white wine vinegar
- ½ cup whipping cream
- ¼ cup chopped fresh parsley
- ½ teaspoon salt
- ½ teaspoon pepper

1 In 10-inch skillet, heat oil over medium-high heat. Add garlic; cook 1 minute, stirring constantly. Add wine and vinegar; heat to boiling over high heat. Reduce heat.

Simmer until mixture coats back of metal spoon, 10 to 12 minutes.

2 Stir in cream; simmer, stirring constantly, until mixture coats back of metal spoon and is slightly reduced, 3 to 4 minutes longer. Remove from heat. Stir in parsley, salt and pepper.

¼ Cup Calories 260; Total Fat 25g (Saturated Fat 9g, Trans Fat 0g); Cholesterol 40mg; Sodium 310mg; Total Carbohydrate 3g (Dietary Fiber 0g); Protein 1g **Carbohydrate Choices:** 0

DEGLAZING

Capture the delicious bits from the bottom of the pan to make a flavorful sauce!

Loosen any burnt bits and excess fat from pan.

Add liquid; heat to boiling and stir constantly to loosen stuck bits.

White Wine–Garlic Sauce

 USE IT UP
WINE

CHILLED BERRY SOUP Mix 2 tablespoons plus 1½ teaspoons each sugar and cornstarch in small saucepan. Stir in 1¼ cups red wine and 1 cup water. Boil and stir 1 minute; remove from heat. Stir in 1½ cups cranberry juice cocktail. Chill. Stir in 1½ cups cut-up fresh berries.

GRAVY Substitute dry white wine for up to half the liquid when making chicken or turkey gravy. Or use up to half red wine when making beef gravy.

SANGRIA SALAD DRESSING Mix ¼ cup each white wine and vegetable oil with 2 tablespoons each honey and orange juice. Drizzle over jicama and citrus for a fresh salad.

WINE CUBES Freeze leftover wine in ice cube trays; remove and store in freezer in resealable freezer plastic bags. Use white wine or rosé cubes to keep glasses of the same wines chilled on a hot day, or use red wine cubes to add to soups or stews.

WINE SPRITZER Serve leftover white or rosé wine in tall glasses with ice cubes, sparkling water, and bite-size pieces of fresh fruit.

MAKING A WINE SAUCE

Cook until mixture coats back of spoon.

Beat in butter, 1 tablespoon at a time.

Peppery Red Wine Sauce

This full-flavored sauce would be delicious over burgers, steak or lamb. If you've cooked your meat in a skillet, make the sauce in the same pan, using the deglazing tips.

PREP 15 Minutes **TOTAL** 35 Minutes • *1 cup*

- 6 tablespoons butter
- ½ cup finely chopped shallots (about 2 large or 3 medium)
- 1 cup dry red wine (such as merlot or zinfandel) or nonalcoholic red wine
- 1 cup beef broth (for homemade broth, see page 157)
- 1 tablespoon balsamic vinegar
- 2 teaspoons Dijon mustard
- 1 teaspoon coarse ground black pepper

1 In 8-inch skillet, melt 2 tablespoons of the butter over medium-high heat. Add shallots; cook 1 minute, stirring frequently. Add wine; heat to boiling over high heat. Reduce heat to medium-high; cook until mixture coats back of metal spoon, 10 to 12 minutes.

2 Stir in broth. Heat to boiling. Reduce heat to medium-high; cook 8 to 10 minutes longer, stirring constantly, until mixture coats back of metal spoon and is slightly reduced.

3 With whisk, beat in remaining 4 tablespoons butter, 1 tablespoon at a time. Reduce heat to low. Beat in vinegar, mustard and pepper.

¼ Cup Calories 200; Total Fat 17g (Saturated Fat 11g, Trans Fat 0.5g); Cholesterol 45mg; Sodium 330mg; Total Carbohydrate 5g (Dietary Fiber 1g); Protein 2g **Carbohydrate Choices:** ½

Hollandaise Sauce

Here's the classic hollandaise—lusciously rich, lemony and smooth, and perfect over vegetables, eggs, fish and seafood.

PREP 10 Minutes **TOTAL** 10 Minutes • *¾ cup*

- 3 egg yolks
- 1 tablespoon fresh lemon juice
- ½ cup cold butter, cut into pieces*

1 In 1½-quart saucepan, vigorously stir egg yolks and lemon juice with whisk. Add ¼ cup of the butter. Heat over very low heat, stirring constantly with whisk, until butter is melted.

2 Add remaining ¼ cup butter. Continue stirring vigorously until butter is melted and sauce is thickened. (Be sure butter melts slowly so eggs have time to cook and thicken sauce without curdling.) If the sauce curdles (begins to separate), add about 1 tablespoon boiling water and beat vigorously with whisk until smooth. Serve immediately.

1 Tablespoon Calories 80; Total Fat 9g (Saturated Fat 4.5g, Trans Fat 0g); Cholesterol 75mg; Sodium 55mg; Total Carbohydrate 0g (Dietary Fiber 0g); Protein 0g **Carbohydrate Choices:** 0

*Do not use margarine or vegetable oil spread.

BÉARNAISE SAUCE: Stir in 1 tablespoon dry white wine with the lemon juice. After sauce thickens, stir in 1 tablespoon finely chopped onion, 1½ teaspoons chopped fresh or ½ teaspoon dried tarragon leaves and 1½ teaspoons chopped fresh or ¼ teaspoon dried chervil leaves.

LEARN WITH BETTY HOLLANDAISE SAUCE

Ideal Sauce: This sauce is just the right consistency, smooth without lumps.

Undercooked Sauce: This sauce is too thin because it wasn't cooked long enough.

Overcooked Sauce: This sauce is curdled because it was cooked too long or over too high heat.

Flavored Butters and Cream Cheese Spreads

Plain butter and cream cheese can be turned into flavorful spreads that will enhance the foods you spread them on, making them even more delicious and fun to eat. With just a few ingredients plus what you have on hand, you can change the flavor to suit your food and your cravings.

Flavored Butters

Mix ½ cup softened butter, flavorings or seasonings and additional ingredients in a small bowl with an electric mixer on medium speed about 1 minute or until light and fluffy. Store covered in the refrigerator up to 1 week.

SWEET BUTTERS
Spread sweet butters on quick breads such as banana or zucchini bread, muffins, bagels or popovers.

Add flavorings and additional ingredients to ½ cup softened butter	+ FLAVORINGS	+ ADDITIONAL INGREDIENTS
Almond	½ teaspoon almond extract	1 tablespoon finely chopped almonds, sliced, slivered, whole skin on
Apricot-Curry	1 teaspoon curry powder	2 tablespoons finely chopped dried apricots 1½ teaspoons honey
Chocolate-Hazelnut		2 tablespoons hazelnut spread with cocoa 1 tablespoon finely chopped toasted hazelnuts 1 tablespoon miniature semisweet chocolate chips
Honey		½ cup honey
Maple		½ cup pure maple or maple-flavored syrup
Orange	1 teaspoon orange zest	1 tablespoon orange juice
Pecan		¼ cup chopped pecans 2 tablespoons packed brown sugar
Raspberry-Jalapeño	⅛ to ¼ teaspoon ground red pepper (cayenne)	1½ teaspoons finely chopped seeded jalapeño chile 1 teaspoon cider vinegar ¼ cup fresh raspberries, mashed

SAVORY BUTTERS
Use savory butters on top of cooked fish, chicken, burgers or steak, tossed with hot, cooked vegetables or slathered on plain or savory breads.

Add liquid and dry ingredients to ½ cup softened butter	+ SEASONINGS	+ ADDITIONAL INGREDIENTS
Garlic	¼ to ½ teaspoon garlic powder or 1 to 2 cloves garlic, finely chopped	
Herb	2 tablespoons chopped fresh or 2 teaspoons dried herb leaves (basil, chives, oregano, savory, tarragon or thyme)	1 clove garlic, finely chopped 2 tablespoons finely chopped red onion
Italian Parmesan	½ teaspoon Italian seasoning	2 tablespoons grated Parmesan cheese
Lemon-Pepper	⅛ to ¼ teaspoon pepper	2 tablespoons lemon zest

Cream Cheese Spreads

Mix 8-oz package softened cream cheese and ¼ cup milk or other liquid ingredients in small bowl with whisk until smooth and creamy. Stir in dry ingredients with spoon. Store covered in refrigerator up to 1 week.

Spread on bagels or hot cooked vegetables, use as a sandwich condiment or whisk a few tablespoons into beaten eggs for a tasty omelet.

Add liquid and dry ingredients to an 8-oz pkg softened cream cheese	+ LIQUID INGREDIENTS	+ DRY INGREDIENTS
Bacon Chive Cheddar	¼ cup milk	½ cup shredded cheddar cheese, ¼ cup crumbled crisply cooked bacon, 2 tablespoons chopped fresh chives
Honey-Walnut	¼ cup honey or maple syrup (omit milk)	½ cup finely chopped walnuts, toasted if desired (see page 28)
Maple-Cinnamon	¼ cup maple-flavored or pure maple syrup (omit milk)	½ teaspoon ground cinnamon
Olive-Walnut	¼ cup milk	½ cup finely chopped walnuts, toasted if desired (see page 28), ¼ to ½ cup finely chopped kalamata or pimiento-stuffed green olives
Peanut Butter–Honey	2 tablespoons honey ¼ cup milk	¼ to ½ cup peanut butter

Cream Cheese Spreads

Herbed Butter Sauce

HERBED BROWNED BUTTER SAUCE: In 1-quart saucepan, heat butter over medium heat just until light brown. Watch carefully because butter can brown and then burn quickly. Continue as directed.

FAST • GLUTEN FREE • VEGETARIAN

Clarified Butter

Clarifying butter removes the milk solids and evaporates the water in it to give it a nutty flavor, increase its smoking point and extend its storage life. It won't burn at high temperatures, so it can be used for sautéing and stir-frying. Many seafood restaurants serve it hot with lobster and crab. It's a staple in Indian cuisine, where it's known as ghee. It's also great brushed over warm Naan (page 534) or pita bread, or drizzled over hot cooked basmati rice.

PREP 20 Minutes **TOTAL** 30 Minutes • ¾ *cup*

    1 lb (2 cups) unsalted
       butter, cut into
       1-inch pieces

1 In 1-quart saucepan, melt butter over low heat. Continue simmering over low heat 15 to 20 minutes, occasionally skimming off milk solids that rise to surface, until butter is clear and deep yellow in color. Do not stir (some of the milk solids will turn brown and sink to bottom of pan).

2 Remove from heat. Cool 5 to 10 minutes; do not stir. Gently pour clarified butter into airtight container, leaving milk solids in saucepan. Discard milk solids. Store covered in refrigerator up to 4 weeks.

1 Tablespoon Calories 280; Total Fat 31g (Saturated Fat 19g, Trans Fat 1g); Cholesterol 80mg; Sodium 0mg; Total Carbohydrate 0g (Dietary Fiber 0g); Protein 0g **Carbohydrate Choices:** 0

EASY • FAST • CALORIE SMART

Herbed Butter Sauce

Sometimes simple is best, as with this easy butter sauce speckled with herbs. It's sensational drizzled over fish, seafood, poultry or vegetables, or tossed with pasta.

PREP 5 Minutes **TOTAL** 5 Minutes • ½ *cup*

    ½ cup butter, cut   2 teaspoons fresh
       into pieces*   lemon juice
    2 tablespoons chopped
       fresh or 2 teaspoons
       dried herb leaves
       (basil, chives,
       oregano, savory,
       tarragon or thyme)

In 1-quart saucepan or 8-inch skillet, heat butter over medium heat until melted. Stir in herbs and lemon juice. Use immediately.

1 Tablespoon Calories 100; Total Fat 12g (Saturated Fat 7g, Trans Fat 0g); Cholesterol 30mg; Sodium 100mg; Total Carbohydrate 0g (Dietary Fiber 0g); Protein 0g **Carbohydrate Choices:** 0

*Do not use margarine or vegetable oil spread.

CLARIFYING BUTTER

Simmer butter over low heat, occasionally skimming off milk solids that rise to surface.

Continue cooking until butter is clear and deep yellow in color.

Carefully pour warm butter into airtight container, leaving any milk solids in saucepan.

Seasoning Basics

Much of what makes a dish great is the flavor. Seasonings are added in the right combination, at the right level and at the right time. With a little practice, you can learn what seasonings enhance your dishes and create your own signature flavor combinations.

When to Season

Seasoning can be done at the beginning of making a dish, while working on parts of a recipe and also once the dish is finished.

- Meat dishes have better flavor if the meat is seasoned before it is cooked and then the entire dish is seasoned at the end, so that both the meat and other ingredients have a lot of flavor.

- Salt causes moisture to be drawn out of foods. Add it before cooking if you are going to cook an ingredient that you want to soften, such as onions. If you want a food to be crisper, salt after cooking.

- Spices and herbs should be used to enhance the natural flavors in a dish, not disguise it. Many spices and herbs go well with a dish and with each other, but too much won't make it better. Avoid using too many at one time.

- Whole spices and bay leaves release their flavors over time, so they can be added before cooking. But be sure to remove bay leaves before serving.

- Ground spices and herbs release their flavors easily, so it's better to add them towards the end of long-cooking dishes.

- For uncooked foods like salad dressings, sauces such as salsa and salads like pasta salads, add the spices and herbs with the other ingredients and then allow enough time for the flavors to blend before eating.

- Taste foods at their serving temperature to accurately determine if the level of seasoning is good or not. Also, keep in mind that flavors can build in your mouth, so what can seem like too little seasoning when a small spoonful is eaten could actually be very flavorful when an entire serving is eaten.

How Much to Add?

Everyone has a different idea of what tastes good. Some are more sensitive to salt levels, others to the spiciness or heat of a dish. In general, less is more, particularly if you are serving people you know will be sensitive. It's easier to add more when the dish is served than it is to correct a dish that has too much. You can place salt, pepper and hot sauce on the table for folks to add more if necessary.

Our recipes are tasted by several people with a wide range of taste preferences. You'll find the seasoning levels to be in the average category in terms of salt level

Seasoned Brine

and spiciness, unless otherwise indicated by the title. Sometimes we call for an ingredient with a range of amount—typically done where the hotness of a dish can be varied.

Herbs Fresh herbs are less potent than dried. In general, use ⅓ the amount of dried herbs for what is called for fresh. See fresh herbs (page 500) and dried seasonings (page 501).

Crushed Red Pepper Flakes When adding red pepper flakes to a dish, keep in mind that the heat can intensify over time as the flavor is released. What seems to be a mildly spicy dish when first seasoned might actually be spicier when served.

EASY • CALORIE SMART

Seasoned Brine

Brining is a great way to impart flavor to meat or poultry and also is a surefire way to ensure it will cook up incredibly tender and juicy. You may find that brined meat and poultry takes a little less time to roast than unbrined.

PREP 5 Minutes TOTAL 24 Hours 5 Minutes • *4 cups*

4 cups water	2 cloves garlic, finely chopped
½ cup packed brown sugar	1 teaspoon cracked black pepper*
2 tablespoons salt	

1 In medium bowl, mix all ingredients until brown sugar and salt are dissolved.

2 Place up to 5 lb meat or poultry in 2-gallon resealable freezer plastic bag. Add brine; seal bag. Place in pan with sides. Refrigerate 24 hours, turning occasionally.

3 Remove meat or poultry from brine; discard brine. Grill or cook as desired.

1 Tablespoon Calories 5; Total Fat 0g (Saturated Fat 0g, Trans Fat 0g); Cholesterol 0mg; Sodium 220mg; Total Carbohydrate 2g (Dietary Fiber 0g); Protein 0g **Carbohydrate Choices:** 0

*If you can't find cracked pepper, use whole peppercorns. To crack peppercorns, place in small resealable food-storage plastic bag. Seal bag; pound with meat mallet or rolling pin just to crack open. Or use a mortar and pestle.

Thyme

Lemon Thyme

Cilantro

Dill Weed

Sage

Parsley

Mint

Rosemary

Purple Sage

Italian (Flat-Leaf) Parsley

Oregano

Bay Leaves

Chives

Basil

Lemongrass

Tarragon

Marjoram

Sesame Seed

Allspice

Black
Sesame Seed

Cumin

Anise Seed

Cardamom

Mace

Dill Seed

Minced Garlic

Ginger

Turmeric

Nutmeg

Dill Weed

Celery Seed

Cinnamon

Cloves

Coriander

Paprika

Mustard Seed

Caraway Seed

Saffron

Poppy Seed

Fennel Seed

LEARN TO MARINATE POULTRY, MEAT OR FISH

Marinating is a great way to add flavor and tenderness to the main attraction on your plate. Follow these easy tips and choose a recipe that fits your craving. You'll love the results!

Marinade Success

- Marinades usually contain a mixture of oil, acid and seasonings. Oil helps the meat retain moisture while the acid breaks down meat fibers to make the food more tender. The seasonings infuse the food with a lot of flavor.

- Use glass, stainless-steel or food-grade plastic containers or resealable food-storage plastic bags to mix and marinate in. They won't react with acidic ingredients like wine, lemon juice or vinegar.

- Use ½ cup marinade for each 1 lb of meat, poultry, or fish.

- Place meat in marinade; turn to coat. Cover container or seal bag and marinate as directed.

- Marinate all foods except fish in the refrigerator up to 24 hours—any longer and food can become mushy. Marinate fish only 15 to 30 minutes.

- Remove meat from marinade; reserve or discard marinade (see below).

- Cook meat with desired cooking method, brushing occasionally with marinade. (Refer to respective chapters for cooking methods.)

- The reserved marinade can be served with meat as a sauce, if it's boiled first to destroy any bacteria that may be present from being in contact with raw meat. Heat marinade in a 1-quart saucepan to a rolling boil, stirring occasionally; boil and stir 1 minute. Or discard any remaining marinade; do not reuse uncooked.

MARINADE	USE WITH	INGREDIENTS
Citrus	Chicken, Pork or Turkey 1 lb boneless or 1 to 2 lb bone-in Fish or Seafood 1 lb fish fillets or uncooked, peeled and deveined shrimp or scallops	1 tablespoon chopped fresh or 1 teaspoon dried basil leaves 3 tablespoons orange juice 2 tablespoons lemon juice 2 tablespoons olive or vegetable oil ½ teaspoon salt ¼ teaspoon pepper 2 cloves garlic, finely chopped
Cowboy	Beef or Pork 1 lb boneless or 1 to 2 lb bone-in	2 tablespoons packed brown sugar 1 tablespoon melted butter 2 tablespoons olive or vegetable oil 2 tablespoons honey 2 tablespoons soy sauce 2 cloves garlic, finely chopped
Fajita	Beef, Chicken or Pork 1 lb boneless or 2 to 3 lb bone-in	¼ cup vegetable oil ¼ cup red wine vinegar 1 teaspoon sugar 1 teaspoon dried oregano leaves 1 teaspoon chili powder ½ teaspoon garlic powder ½ teaspoon salt ¼ teaspoon pepper
Lemon-Herb	Beef, Chicken, Pork or Turkey 1½ to 2 lb boneless or 2½ to 3½ lb bone-in	⅓ cup vegetable oil 1 teaspoon lemon zest 2 tablespoons fresh lemon juice 1 tablespoon dry vermouth, dry white wine or beef broth 1 teaspoon chopped fresh or ¼ teaspoon dried sage leaves 1 teaspoon chopped fresh or ¼ teaspoon dried oregano leaves ½ teaspoon salt ¼ teaspoon coarse black ground pepper
Maple-Bourbon	Beef, Chicken, Pork or Turkey 1 to 2 lb boneless or 1½ to 2½ lb bone-in	¼ cup maple-flavored syrup ¼ cup bourbon or apple juice 1 tablespoon vegetable oil ½ teaspoon salt
Teriyaki	Beef, Chicken or Pork 1 lb boneless or 2 to 3 lb bone-in	¼ cup water 3 tablespoons soy sauce 1 tablespoon fresh lemon juice 1 tablespoon vegetable oil
Tequila-Lime	Chicken Pork or Turkey 1 to 1½ lb boneless or 2 to 3 lb bone-in Fish or Seafood 1 to 1½ lb fish fillets or uncooked, peeled and deveined shrimp or scallops	2 teaspoons lime zest ¼ cup fresh lime juice ¼ cup olive or vegetable oil 2 tablespoons chopped fresh cilantro ½ teaspoon sugar ½ teaspoon salt 1 small jalapeño chile, seeded, finely chopped 1 clove garlic, finely chopped

Breads

Quick Bread Basics

What is a quick bread? Breads that use baking powder or baking soda as the leavening to make them rise are called quick breads. Unlike yeast breads that require rising time, quick breads usually can be baked as soon as they are mixed. Muffins, scones and biscuits are a few common types of quick breads you can easily make no matter what your skill level.

Selecting Pans

Use only the pan size indicated in the recipe.

For golden-brown color and tender crusts, use shiny pans and cookie sheets that reflect the heat, rather than pans with dark finishes. If using dark or nonstick pans, reduce oven temperature by 25°F. These pans absorb heat more easily than shiny pans, causing baked goods to brown more quickly.

Insulated pans often require slightly longer baking times and result in baked goods that may be less brown.

Prepping Ingredients

- Check expiration dates on leavening packages for freshness. Old product may inhibit quick breads from rising properly.
- Chop, mash or shred fruits (except small berries) or vegetables or nuts so they are ready to be added to the batter.
- Measure flour by spooning it into a dry measuring cup and leveling off with the straight edge of a knife or metal spatula.
- Use liquid measuring cups to measure liquids by filling and placing on the counter to read amount accurately.
- In recipes calling for butter, it's best to use real butter. If you use margarine, be sure the product has at least 65% fat. Don't use reduced-fat butter or whipped butter or margarine.

Tips for Ideal Quick Breads

- Mix batters for quick breads with a spoon or rubber scraper, not an electric mixer, and just until the dry ingredients are moistened. Overmixing can make quick breads tough and have peaked tops.
- To prevent gummy, soggy or heavy loaves, don't use more fruit or vegetables than called for in the recipe.
- Grease only the bottom of loaf or muffin pans unless otherwise specified. This prevents a lip and hard, dry edge from forming.
- Allow at least 2 inches of space around pans in oven for good heat circulation.
- Quick bread loaves normally form cracks on top, due to the leavening action.
- Cool loaves completely, about 2 hours, to prevent crumbling when slicing.
- Flavor improves and slicing is easier if loaves have been refrigerated for 24 hours.
- Cut loaves with serrated knife, using a light sawing motion.
- Wrap completely cooled loaves tightly in plastic wrap or foil and refrigerate up to 1 week. To freeze, place tightly wrapped loaves in resealable freezer plastic bags and freeze up to 3 months.

LEARN WITH BETTY MUFFINS

Overmixed Muffins: Overmixing causes muffins to have peaks on top and tunnels inside.

Ideal Muffins: This muffin has a nicely rounded top and even grain inside.

Blueberry Muffins

Whether you buy blueberries specifically for this recipe or you have blueberries that need using up, you'll love this easy recipe with homemade flavor.

PREP 10 Minutes **TOTAL** 40 Minutes • *12 muffins*

¾ cup milk	½ teaspoon salt
¼ cup vegetable oil or melted butter	1 cup fresh, canned (drained) or frozen (do not thaw) blueberries
1 egg	2 tablespoons coarse sugar or additional granulated sugar, if desired
2 cups all-purpose flour	
½ cup granulated sugar	
2 teaspoons baking powder	

1 Heat oven to 400°F. Grease bottoms only of 12 regular-size muffin cups with shortening or cooking spray, or place paper baking cup in each muffin cup.

2 In large bowl, beat milk, oil and egg with fork or whisk until well mixed. Stir in flour, granulated sugar, baking powder and salt all at once just until flour is moistened (batter will be lumpy). Fold in blueberries. Divide batter evenly among muffin cups; sprinkle each with ½ teaspoon coarse sugar.

3 Bake 20 to 25 minutes or until golden brown and toothpick inserted in center comes out clean. If baked in greased pan, let stand about 5 minutes in pan, then remove from pan to cooling rack; if baked in paper baking cups, immediately remove from pan to cooling rack. Serve warm if desired.

1 Muffin Calories 170; Total Fat 6g (Saturated Fat 1g, Trans Fat 0g); Cholesterol 15mg; Sodium 190mg; Total Carbohydrate 27g (Dietary Fiber 1g); Protein 3g **Carbohydrate Choices:** 2

STREUSEL-TOPPED BLUEBERRY MUFFINS: Omit coarse sugar. Make batter as directed; divide evenly among muffin cups. In medium bowl, mix ¼ cup all-purpose flour, ¼ cup packed brown sugar and ¼ teaspoon ground cinnamon. Cut in 2 tablespoons cold butter using pastry blender or fork until crumbly. Sprinkle about 1 tablespoon streusel over batter in each muffin cup. Bake as directed.

APPLE-CINNAMON MUFFINS: Omit blueberries. Stir in 1 cup chopped peeled apple (about 1 medium) and ½ teaspoon ground cinnamon with flour. Bake 25 to 30 minutes.

BANANA MUFFINS: Omit blueberries. Reduce milk to ⅓ cup. Beat in 1 cup mashed very ripe bananas (2 medium) with milk. Use packed brown sugar instead of granulated sugar in muffins.

CHOCOLATE CHIP MUFFINS: Omit blueberries. Fold 1 cup miniature semisweet chocolate chips into batter.

CRANBERRY-ORANGE MUFFINS: Omit blueberries. Beat in 1 tablespoon orange zest with the milk. Fold 1 cup coarsely chopped sweetened dried cranberries into batter.

PREPARING MUFFINS

Stir in dry ingredients all at once, just until flour is moistened.

Divide batter evenly among muffin cups using spoons or cookie scoop.

Blueberry Muffins

508

Glazed Lemon-Crumb Muffins

PREP 30 Minutes **TOTAL** 1 Hour 35 Minutes • *24 muffins*

TOPPING

- 1¼ cups all-purpose flour
- 1 cup granulated sugar
- ⅛ teaspoon salt
- ½ cup butter, melted

MUFFINS

- 4 cups all-purpose flour
- 2 teaspoons baking soda
- 1 teaspoon salt
- 4 eggs
- 2 cups granulated sugar
- 1 cup vegetable oil
- 2 cups sour cream
- 1 tablespoon lemon zest
- 2 tablespoons fresh lemon juice
- 1 teaspoon lemon extract
- 1 teaspoon vanilla

GLAZE

- ¾ cup powdered sugar
- 5 teaspoons fresh lemon juice

1 Heat oven to 375°F. Place paper baking cup in each of 24 regular-size muffin cups or 12 jumbo muffin cups. In small bowl, mix all topping ingredients with fork until crumbly; set aside.

2 In large bowl, mix 4 cups flour, the baking soda and 1 teaspoon salt. In another large bowl, beat eggs with electric mixer on medium speed about 2 minutes or until frothy. Add 2 cups granulated sugar and oil; beat until creamy. Add sour cream, lemon zest, 2 tablespoons lemon juice, the lemon extract and vanilla; mix well. Stir in flour mixture just until blended. Divide batter evenly among muffin cups. Sprinkle topping evenly over batter in each muffin cup.

3 Bake regular-size muffins 20 to 22 minutes, jumbo muffins 22 to 28 minutes or until toothpick inserted in center comes out clean. Cool 5 minutes; remove from pan to cooling rack. Cool 30 minutes.

4 In small bowl, mix glaze ingredients until well blended. Drizzle over muffins.

1 Muffin Calories 380; Total Fat 18g (Saturated Fat 6g, Trans Fat 0g); Cholesterol 55mg; Sodium 260mg; Total Carbohydrate 51g (Dietary Fiber 1g); Protein 4g **Carbohydrate Choices:** 3½

Gingersnap Streusel– Pumpkin Muffins

PREP 20 Minutes **TOTAL** 45 Minutes • *12 muffins*

MUFFINS

- 1½ cups all-purpose flour
- 1 cup packed brown sugar
- 1 teaspoon baking soda
- 1 teaspoon pumpkin pie spice
- ¼ teaspoon salt
- 1 cup canned pumpkin (not pumpkin pie mix)
- ½ cup buttermilk
- 2 tablespoons vegetable oil
- 1 egg

STREUSEL

- ¾ cup crushed gingersnap cookies (about 13 cookies; for homemade gingersnaps, see page 549)
- 3 tablespoons all-purpose flour
- 3 tablespoons packed brown sugar
- 3 tablespoons butter, softened
  Sliced almonds, if desired

1 Heat oven to 350°F. Place paper baking cup in each of 12 regular-size muffin cups; spray baking cups with cooking spray.

2 In large bowl, mix 1½ cups flour, 1 cup brown sugar, the baking soda, pumpkin pie spice and salt. Stir in pumpkin, buttermilk, oil and egg all at once just until moistened. Divide batter evenly among muffin cups.

3 In small bowl, stir gingersnap crumbs, 3 tablespoons flour, 3 tablespoons brown sugar and the butter with fork until crumbly. Sprinkle evenly over batter in each cup.

4 Bake 24 minutes or until toothpick inserted in center comes out clean. Remove muffins from pan to cooling rack. Sprinkle with sliced almonds. Serve warm.

1 Muffin Calories 250; Total Fat 7g (Saturated Fat 2.5g, Trans Fat 0g); Cholesterol 25mg; Sodium 250mg; Total Carbohydrate 43g (Dietary Fiber 1g); Protein 3g **Carbohydrate Choices:** 3

Glazed Lemon-Crumb Muffins

Gingersnap Streusel–Pumpkin Muffins

Banana Bread

Oat and Almond Pumpkin Bread

Banana Bread

Although the true origin of banana bread is not known, this enduring favorite has been around since at least the 1930s. Our version of banana bread has appeared in all editions of the Betty Crocker Cookbook. It's a great way to use those bananas that are turning brown and soft.

PREP 15 Minutes **TOTAL** 3 Hours 40 Minutes •
2 loaves (12 slices each)

1¼	cups sugar	1	teaspoon vanilla
½	cup butter, softened	2½	cups all-purpose flour
2	eggs	1	teaspoon baking soda
1½	cups mashed very ripe bananas (3 medium)	1	teaspoon salt
½	cup buttermilk	1	cup chopped nuts, if desired

1 Heat oven to 350°F. Grease bottoms only of two 8x4- or 9x5-inch loaf pans with shortening or cooking spray.

2 In large bowl, stir sugar and butter until well mixed. Stir in eggs until well mixed. Stir in bananas, buttermilk and vanilla; beat with spoon until smooth. Stir in flour, baking soda and salt just until moistened. Stir in nuts. Divide batter evenly between pans.

3 Bake 8-inch loaves about 1 hour, 9-inch loaves about 1 hour 15 minutes, or until toothpick inserted in center comes out clean. Cool 10 minutes in pans on cooling rack.

4 Loosen sides of loaves from pans; remove from pans and place top side up on cooling rack. Cool completely, about 2 hours, before slicing. Wrap tightly and store at room temperature up to 4 days or refrigerate up to 10 days.

1 Slice Calories 150; Total Fat 4.5g (Saturated Fat 2.5g, Trans Fat 0g); Cholesterol 30mg; Sodium 190mg; Total Carbohydrate 24g (Dietary Fiber 0g); Protein 2g **Carbohydrate Choices:** 1½

BLUEBERRY-BANANA BREAD: Omit nuts. Stir 1 cup fresh or frozen (do not thaw) blueberries into batter.

Oat and Almond Pumpkin Bread

PREP 15 Minutes **TOTAL** 2 Hours 15 Minutes •
1 loaf (16 slices)

3	eggs	2	teaspoons pumpkin pie spice
¾	cup almond butter	1	teaspoon salt
¾	cup canned pumpkin (from 15-oz can; not pumpkin pie filling)	2	tablespoons sliced almonds
½	cup honey	2	tablespoons pure quick-cooking or old-fashioned oats
1	cup pure oat flour		
2½	teaspoons gluten-free baking powder		

1 Heat oven to 375°F. Grease bottom only of 8x4- or 9x5-inch loaf pan with shortening or cooking spray. In medium bowl, beat eggs with electric mixer on medium speed 2 minutes or until light and foamy. Beat in almond butter, pumpkin and honey until blended; beat 1 minute longer.

2 Add oat flour, baking powder, pumpkin pie spice and salt; beat on low speed until blended. Spread in pan. Sprinkle with almonds and oats, pressing lightly into batter.

3 Bake 40 to 50 minutes or until toothpick inserted in center comes out clean. Cool in pan 10 minutes. Loosen sides of loaf from pan; carefully remove from pan and place top side up on cooling rack. Cool completely, about 1 hour, before slicing. Wrap tightly and store at room temperature 4 days or refrigerate up to 10 days.

1 Slice Calories 170; Total Fat 8g (Saturated Fat 1g, Trans Fat 0g); Cholesterol 35mg; Sodium 260mg; Total Carbohydrate 18g (Dietary Fiber 2g); Protein 5g **Carbohydrate Choices:** 1

HEIRLOOM

CALORIE SMART • VEGETARIAN

Zucchini Bread

You don't need to peel the zucchini if it is very fresh and green. Older, larger zucchini may require peeling before shredding. The peel adds little green flecks to the bread.

PREP 20 Minutes **TOTAL** 3 Hours 50 Minutes •
2 loaves (12 slices each)

510

BETTY CROCKER COOKBOOK

3 cups shredded zucchini (2 to 3 medium)	1 teaspoon salt
1⅔ cups sugar	1 teaspoon ground cinnamon
⅔ cup vegetable oil	½ teaspoon baking powder
2 teaspoons vanilla	½ teaspoon ground cloves
4 eggs	½ cup chopped nuts
3 cups all-purpose or whole wheat flour	½ cup raisins, if desired
2 teaspoons baking soda	

1 Heat oven to 350°F. Grease bottoms only of two 8x4- or 9x5-inch loaf pans with shortening or cooking spray.

2 In large bowl, stir zucchini, sugar, oil, vanilla and eggs until well mixed. Stir in flour, baking soda, salt, cinnamon, baking powder and cloves just until moistened. Stir in nuts and raisins. Divide batter evenly between pans.

3 Bake 8-inch loaves 50 to 60 minutes, 9-inch loaves 1 hour 10 minutes to 1 hour 20 minutes, or until toothpick inserted in center comes out clean. Cool 10 minutes in pans on cooling rack.

4 Loosen sides of loaves from pans; remove from pans and place top side up on cooling rack. Cool completely, about 2 hours, before slicing. Wrap tightly and store at room temperature up to 4 days or refrigerate up to 10 days.

1 Slice Calories 200; Total Fat 9g (Saturated Fat 1.5g, Trans Fat 0g); Cholesterol 35mg; Sodium 230mg; Total Carbohydrate 27g (Dietary Fiber 1g); Protein 3g **Carbohydrate Choices:** 2

CRANBERRY BREAD: Omit zucchini, cinnamon, cloves and raisins. Add ½ cup milk and 2 teaspoons orange zest with the oil. Stir 3 cups fresh or frozen (thawed and drained) cranberries into batter. Bake 1 hour to 1 hour 10 minutes.

ORANGE ZUCCHINI BREAD: Stir in 2 teaspoons orange zest with flour mixture. When loaf is cooled, drizzle with Orange Glaze (page 603). Let stand until set.

PUMPKIN BREAD: Substitute 1 can (15 oz) pumpkin (not pumpkin pie mix) for the zucchini.

Zucchini Bread

Chocolate-Hazelnut Zucchini Bread

CALORIE SMART • VEGETARIAN

Chocolate-Hazelnut Zucchini Bread

Top slices of this decadent bread with peanut butter or another nut butter for an over-the-top satisfying snack.

PREP 20 Minutes **TOTAL** 3 Hours 5 Minutes •
1 loaf (16 slices)

⅓ cup hazelnuts, chopped	¾ cup buttermilk
1⅓ cups all-purpose flour	⅓ cup butter, melted
⅔ cup packed brown sugar	1 egg
⅓ cup unsweetened baking cocoa	1 teaspoon vanilla
¾ teaspoon baking soda	1½ cups coarsely shredded zucchini (about 1 medium)
½ teaspoon salt	1 cup semisweet chocolate chips

1 Heat oven to 350°F. Grease bottom only of 8x4- or 9x5-inch loaf pan with shortening or cooking spray. Reserve 2 tablespoons hazelnuts; set aside. Finely chop remaining hazelnuts.

2 In large bowl, mix flour, brown sugar, cocoa, baking soda and salt until well blended. In small bowl, using whisk, beat buttermilk, butter, egg and vanilla until blended. Pour buttermilk mixture into flour mixture; stir just until moistened. Stir in zucchini, ¾ cup of the chocolate chips and the finely chopped hazelnuts. Spoon batter into pan, spreading evenly (batter will be thick). Sprinkle remaining ¼ cup chocolate chips and the reserved chopped hazelnuts over batter.

3 Bake 8-inch loaf 65 to 75 minutes, 9-inch loaf 55 to 65 minutes, or until toothpick inserted in center comes out clean. Cool 15 minutes in pan on cooling rack.

4 Loosen sides of loaf from pan; carefully remove from pan and place top side up on cooling rack. Cool about 1½ hours or until completely cooled before slicing. Wrap tightly and store at room temperature up to 4 days or refrigerate up to 10 days.

1 Slice Calories 200; Total Fat 9g (Saturated Fat 5g, Trans Fat 0g); Cholesterol 25mg; Sodium 180mg; Total Carbohydrate 26g (Dietary Fiber 2g); Protein 3g **Carbohydrate Choices:** 2

VEGETARIAN

Cranberry–Sweet Potato Bread

PREP 25 Minutes **TOTAL** 3 Hours 35 Minutes •
2 loaves (12 slices each)

2⅓ cups sugar	1½ teaspoons salt
⅔ cup water	1 teaspoon ground cinnamon
⅔ cup vegetable oil	½ teaspoon baking powder
1 teaspoon vanilla	½ teaspoon ground nutmeg
2 cups mashed cooked dark-orange sweet potatoes (about 1¼ lb)*	1 cup sweetened dried cranberries
4 eggs	1 cup chopped pecans, if desired
3⅓ cups all-purpose flour	
2 teaspoons baking soda	

1 Heat oven to 350°F. Grease two 8x4- or 9x5-inch loaf pans with shortening or cooking spray; lightly flour.

2 In large bowl, mix sugar, water, oil, vanilla, sweet potatoes and eggs until well blended. In medium bowl, mix flour, baking soda, salt, cinnamon, baking powder and nutmeg. Add to sweet potato mixture; stir just until dry ingredients are moistened. Stir in cranberries and pecans. Divide batter evenly between pans.

3 Bake 8-inch loaves about 1 hour, 9-inch loaves about 1 hour 10 minutes, or until toothpick inserted in center comes out clean. Cool 15 minutes in pans on cooling rack.

4 Loosen sides of loaves from pans; remove from pans and place top side up on cooling rack. Cool completely, about 2 hours, before slicing. Wrap tightly and store at room temperature up to 4 days or refrigerate up to 10 days.

1 Slice Calories 240; Total Fat 7g (Saturated Fat 1.5g, Trans Fat 0g); Cholesterol 35mg; Sodium 280mg; Total Carbohydrate 41g (Dietary Fiber 1g); Protein 3g **Carbohydrate Choices:** 3

*1 can (23 oz) sweet potatoes in syrup, drained and mashed, can be substituted for the cooked sweet potatoes.

Cranberry–Sweet Potato Bread

Oatmeal Streusel Bread

PREP 25 Minutes **TOTAL** 3 Hours 30 Minutes •
1 loaf (12 slices)

STREUSEL
- ¼ cup packed brown sugar
- ¼ cup chopped walnuts, toasted (see page 28)
- 2 teaspoons ground cinnamon

BREAD
- 1 cup all-purpose flour
- ½ cup whole wheat flour
- ½ cup old-fashioned oats
- 2 tablespoons ground flaxseed or flaxseed meal
- 1 teaspoon baking powder
- ½ teaspoon salt
- ¼ teaspoon baking soda
- ¾ cup packed brown sugar
- ⅔ cup vegetable oil
- 2 eggs
- ¼ cup sour cream
- 2 teaspoons vanilla
- ½ cup milk

ICING
- ¾ to 1 cup powdered sugar
- 1 tablespoon milk
- 2 teaspoons light corn syrup

1 Heat oven to 350°F. Spray bottom only of 9x5-inch loaf pan with cooking spray. In small bowl, stir streusel ingredients until mixed; set aside.

2 In medium bowl, using whisk, stir all-purpose flour, whole wheat flour, oats, flaxseed, baking powder, salt and baking soda until blended.

3 In large bowl, beat ¾ cup brown sugar and the oil with electric mixer on medium speed 1 minute or until blended. Add eggs, one at a time, beating well after each addition. Beat in sour cream and vanilla. Add flour mixture alternately with ½ cup milk, beating on low speed after each addition until smooth.

4 Spoon ⅓ of batter (about 1 cup) into pan; sprinkle with half of streusel (about ⅓ cup). Top with half of remaining batter (about 1 cup), spreading gently. Sprinkle with remaining streusel. Top with remaining batter. Gently run knife through batter to swirl.

5 Bake 50 to 55 minutes or until toothpick inserted in center comes out clean. Cool on cooling rack 10 minutes. Loosen sides of loaf from pan; remove from pan and place top side up on cooling rack. Cool completely, about 2 hours.

6 In small bowl, using whisk, beat icing ingredients, adding enough of the powdered sugar for desired drizzling consistency. Drizzle icing over bread. Let stand until set. Wrap tightly and store at room temperature up to 4 days or refrigerate up to 10 days.

1 Slice Calories 320; Total Fat 16g (Saturated Fat 2g, Trans Fat 0g); Cholesterol 40mg; Sodium 190mg; Total Carbohydrate 40g (Dietary Fiber 1g); Protein 4g **Carbohydrate Choices:** 2½

Mango-Almond Coffee Cake

Frozen mangoes or refrigerated mango slices in light syrup can be substituted for the fresh mango. Do not thaw frozen mangoes; drain refrigerated mangoes, pat dry with a paper towel and chop as directed to avoid wet spots in the cake from too much moisture.

PREP 20 Minutes **TOTAL** 1 Hour 20 Minutes • *9 servings*

STREUSEL
- ⅓ cup all-purpose flour
- ⅓ cup packed dark brown sugar
- ⅓ cup old-fashioned oats
- ⅓ cup chopped slivered almonds
- 1 teaspoon ground cinnamon
- ¼ cup cold butter, cut into small pieces

CAKE
- 1 cup all-purpose flour
- ½ cup granulated sugar
- 1 teaspoon baking powder
- ½ teaspoon salt
- 1 teaspoon ground cinnamon
- ¼ cup cold butter, cut into small pieces
- ½ cup milk
- ½ teaspoon almond extract
- 1 egg, slightly beaten
- ¾ cup chopped (¼- to ½-inch pieces) peeled ripe mango (from 1 medium)

1 Heat oven to 350°F. Grease bottom and sides of 8-inch square pan with shortening or spray with cooking spray. In small bowl, mix all streusel ingredients with pastry blender or fork until crumbly; set aside.

2 In large bowl, combine 1 cup flour, the granulated sugar, baking powder, salt and 1 teaspoon cinnamon; mix well. Cut in ¼ cup butter using pastry blender or fork until mixture is crumbly. Stir in milk, almond extract and egg until flour is moistened.

3 Spread half of the batter (about ¾ cup) in pan, forming thin layer. Top with half of mango; sprinkle with half of streusel. Drizzle remaining batter evenly over streusel. Carefully spread batter to completely cover streusel. Sprinkle with remaining mango and streusel.

4 Bake 40 to 45 minutes or until center is set when jiggled and toothpick inserted in moist spot near center comes out clean. Cool 15 minutes. Serve warm or cool.

1 Serving Calories 300; Total Fat 13g (Saturated Fat 7g, Trans Fat 0g); Cholesterol 50mg; Sodium 290mg; Total Carbohydrate 39g (Dietary Fiber 2g); Protein 4g **Carbohydrate Choices:** 2½

Oatmeal
Streusel Bread

513

VEGETARIAN

Sour Cream Coffee Cake

PREP 30 Minutes **TOTAL** 2 Hours • *16 servings*

BROWN SUGAR FILLING

- ½ cup packed brown sugar
- ½ cup finely chopped nuts
- 1½ teaspoons ground cinnamon

COFFEE CAKE

- 3 cups all-purpose or whole wheat flour
- 1½ teaspoons baking powder
- 1½ teaspoons baking soda
- ¾ teaspoon salt
- 1½ cups granulated sugar
- ¾ cup butter, softened
- 1½ teaspoons vanilla
- 3 eggs
- 1½ cups sour cream

GLAZE

- ½ cup powdered sugar
- ¼ teaspoon vanilla
- 2 to 3 teaspoons milk

1 Heat oven to 350°F. Grease bottom, side and tube of 10-inch angel food (tube) cake pan or 12-cup fluted tube cake pan, or bottoms and sides of two 9x5-inch loaf pans with shortening or cooking spray.

2 In small bowl, stir filling ingredients until well mixed; set aside. In large bowl, stir flour, baking powder, baking soda and salt until well mixed; set aside.

3 In another large bowl, beat granulated sugar, butter, 1½ teaspoons vanilla and the eggs with electric mixer on medium speed 2 minutes, scraping bowl occasionally. Alternately add flour mixture and sour cream, beating on low speed until blended.

4 For angel food or fluted tube cake pan, spread ⅓ of batter (about 2 cups) in pan, then sprinkle with ⅓ of filling; repeat twice. For loaf pans, spread ¼ of batter (about 1½ cups) in each pan, then sprinkle each with ¼ of filling; repeat once.

5 Bake angel food or fluted tube cake pan about 1 hour, loaf pans about 45 minutes, or until toothpick inserted near center comes out clean. Cool 10 minutes; remove cake from pan to cooling rack, top side up. Cool 20 minutes.

6 In small bowl, stir glaze ingredients until smooth and thin enough to drizzle. Drizzle glaze over coffee cake. Serve warm if desired.

1 Serving Calories 360; Total Fat 16g (Saturated Fat 8g, Trans Fat 0.5g); Cholesterol 70mg; Sodium 360mg; Total Carbohydrate 49g (Dietary Fiber 1g); Protein 4g **Carbohydrate Choices:** 3

Mango-Almond Coffee Cake

Sour Cream Coffee Cake

Lemon Curd–Filled Brunch Cake

Cornbread

VEGETARIAN

Lemon Curd–Filled Brunch Cake

A classic lemon curd is the filling in this buttery-rich dense yellow cake. To save time, you can substitute a 10-oz jar of purchased lemon curd.

PREP 30 Minutes **TOTAL** 2 Hours 45 Minutes • *12 servings*

LEMON CURD
- ¼ cup granulated sugar
- 2 tablespoons cornstarch
- ¾ cup cold water
- 3 egg yolks
- 1 tablespoon lemon zest
- 3 tablespoons lemon juice

CAKE
- 1 cup butter, softened
- 1 cup granulated sugar
- 5 eggs
- 1¾ cups all-purpose flour
- 2 teaspoons lemon zest
- 1½ teaspoons baking powder
- 1 teaspoon vanilla
- ⅓ cup slivered almonds, toasted (see page 28)
- ½ teaspoon powdered sugar, if desired

1 In 1-quart saucepan, mix ¼ cup granulated sugar and the cornstarch. Using whisk, stir in water and egg yolks until well mixed and no lumps remain. Heat to boiling over medium heat, stirring constantly, until mixture begins to thicken. Cook and stir 1 minute; remove from heat. Stir in 1 tablespoon lemon zest and the lemon juice. Refrigerate uncovered 20 minutes, stirring once, until room temperature.

2 Heat oven to 350°F. Grease bottom and side of 9-inch springform pan with shortening; lightly flour.

3 In large bowl, beat butter and 1 cup granulated sugar with electric mixer on medium speed about 1 minute or until smooth. Beat in eggs, one at a time, just until blended, then continue beating on medium speed 2 minutes, scraping bowl once. On low speed, beat in flour, 2 teaspoons lemon zest, the baking powder and vanilla about 30 seconds or just until blended.

4 Spread half of batter (about 2 cups) in bottom of pan. Spoon lemon curd evenly onto batter, spreading to ½ inch of edge. Drop remaining batter by tablespoonfuls around edge of curd and pan; spread batter evenly toward center to cover curd. Sprinkle almonds over top.

5 Bake 45 to 55 minutes or until center is set, cake is firm to touch and top is golden brown. Cool in pan on cooling rack at least 1 hour (center will sink slightly). Run thin knife around side of cake; remove side of pan. Sprinkle with powdered sugar before serving. Store covered in refrigerator.

1 Serving Calories 360; Total Fat 20g (Saturated Fat 11g, Trans Fat 0.5g); Cholesterol 165mg; Sodium 210mg; Total Carbohydrate 38g (Dietary Fiber 1g); Protein 6g **Carbohydrate Choices:** 2½

CALORIE SMART

Cornbread

PREP 10 Minutes **TOTAL** 35 Minutes • *12 servings*

- 1 cup milk
- ¼ cup butter, melted
- 1 egg
- 1¼ cups yellow, white or blue cornmeal
- 1 cup all-purpose flour
- ½ cup sugar
- 1 tablespoon baking powder
- ½ teaspoon salt

1 Heat oven to 400°F. Grease bottom and side of 9-inch round pan, 8-inch square pan or 8-inch cast-iron skillet with shortening or cooking spray.

2 In large bowl, using whisk, beat milk, butter and egg. Stir in remaining ingredients all at once just until flour is moistened (batter will be lumpy). Pour into pan.

3 Bake 20 to 25 minutes or until golden brown and toothpick inserted in center comes out clean. Serve warm if desired.

1 Serving Calories 180; Total Fat 5g (Saturated Fat 3g, Trans Fat 0g); Cholesterol 25mg; Sodium 270mg; Total Carbohydrate 31g (Dietary Fiber 1g); Protein 3g **Carbohydrate Choices:** 2

CORN MUFFINS: Grease bottoms only of 12 regular-size muffin cups with shortening or cooking spray. Divide batter evenly among muffin cups. Bake as directed.

BACON–BROWN SUGAR CORNBREAD: Substitute brown sugar for the sugar and add ½ cup crumbled crisply cooked bacon (about 8 slices) with the cornmeal.

CHEESY JALAPEÑO CORNBREAD: Add ½ cup chopped pickled jalapeño chiles and 1 cup shredded pepper Jack cheese (4 oz) with the cornmeal.

Scones

PREP 15 Minutes **TOTAL** 35 Minutes • *8 scones*

1¾ cups all-purpose flour	½ teaspoon vanilla
3 tablespoons granulated sugar	4 to 6 tablespoons whipping cream
2½ teaspoons baking powder	Additional whipping cream
½ teaspoon salt	Coarse sugar or additional granulated sugar
⅓ cup cold butter, cut into 8 pieces	
1 egg, beaten	

1 Heat oven to 400°F. In large bowl, mix flour, 3 tablespoons granulated sugar, the baking powder and salt. Cut in butter using pastry blender or fork until mixture looks like fine crumbs. Stir in egg, vanilla and 4 tablespoons of the whipping cream. Stir in additional whipping cream, 1 tablespoon at a time, until dough leaves side of bowl.

2 Place dough on lightly floured surface; gently roll in flour to coat. Knead lightly 10 times. On ungreased cookie sheet, roll or pat dough into 8-inch round. Cut into 8 wedges with sharp knife or pizza cutter that has been dipped in flour, but do not separate wedges. Brush with additional whipping cream; sprinkle with coarse sugar.

3 Bake 14 to 16 minutes or until light golden brown. Immediately remove from cookie sheet; carefully separate wedges. Serve warm.

1 Scone Calories 230; Total Fat 11g (Saturated Fat 7g, Trans Fat 0g); Cholesterol 55mg; Sodium 370mg; Total Carbohydrate 28g (Dietary Fiber 0g); Protein 4g **Carbohydrate Choices:** 2

CHOCOLATE CHIP SCONES: Stir in ½ cup miniature semisweet chocolate chips with the egg.

CHERRY–CHOCOLATE CHIP SCONES: Stir in ½ cup each chopped dried cherries and miniature semisweet chocolate chips with egg, vanilla and whipping cream.

LEMON–BLUEBERRY SCONES: Stir in ½ cup dried blueberries and 2 teaspoons lemon zest with egg, vanilla and whipping cream.

RASPBERRY–WHITE CHOCOLATE SCONES: Substitute almond extract for the vanilla; increase whipping cream to ½ cup. Stir in ¾ cup frozen unsweetened raspberries (do not thaw) and ⅔ cup white vanilla baking chips with egg, almond extract and whipping cream. Omit kneading in Step 2. On ungreased cookie sheet, pat dough into 8-inch round. Continue as directed—except bake 18 to 23 minutes. Raspberries will color dough a little bit.

ORANGE–CRANBERRY SCONES: Stir in ½ cup sweetened dried cranberries and 2 teaspoons orange zest with egg, vanilla and whipping cream.

MAKING SCONES

Roll or pat dough into round on ungreased cookie sheet.

Cut into 8 wedges with sharp knife or pizza cutter dipped in flour; do not separate.

Cherry-Chocolate Chip Scones

Cake Doughnuts

Don't forget to also cook the holes—no one can resist bite-size treats.

PREP 45 Minutes **TOTAL** 45 Minutes • **24 doughnuts**

Vegetable oil
3⅓ cups all-purpose flour
1 cup granulated sugar
¾ cup milk
1 tablespoon baking powder
½ teaspoon salt
½ teaspoon ground cinnamon
¼ teaspoon ground nutmeg
2 tablespoons shortening
2 eggs
Additional granulated sugar or powdered sugar, if desired

1 In deep fryer or 3-quart saucepan, heat 3 to 4 inches oil to 375°F. Line two 15x10-inch pans with sides with a few layers of paper towels.

2 In large bowl, beat 1½ cups of the flour and the remaining ingredients except additional sugar with electric mixer on low speed 30 seconds, scraping bowl constantly. Beat on medium speed 2 minutes, scraping bowl occasionally. Stir in remaining flour.

3 On generously floured surface, roll dough lightly to coat. Gently roll to ⅜-inch thickness. Cut dough with floured 2½-inch doughnut cutter, rerolling and cutting scraps as needed to get 24 doughnuts.

4 Slide doughnuts into hot oil a few at a time, using wide spatula. Turn doughnuts as they rise to the surface. Fry 2 to 3 minutes until golden brown on both sides. Remove from oil with long fork through center hole; do not prick doughnuts. Drain on paper towels. Repeat with remaining doughnuts and holes (remove holes from oil with slotted spoon), letting oil return to 375°F before adding next batch. Roll in powdered or granulated sugar while warm.

1 Doughnut Calories 200; Total Fat 11g (Saturated Fat 2g, Trans Fat 0g); Cholesterol 15mg; Sodium 120mg; Total Carbohydrate 22g (Dietary Fiber 0g); Protein 2g **Carbohydrate Choices:** 1½

GLAZED DOUGHNUTS: Glaze cooled doughnuts with Doughnut Glaze (below) or Chocolate or Vanilla Glaze (pages 602, 603). Sprinkle with candy sprinkles, if desired.

BUTTERMILK DOUGHNUTS: Substitute buttermilk for milk, reduce baking powder to 2 teaspoons and add 1 teaspoon baking soda.

APPLESAUCE DOUGHNUTS: Reduce sugar to ¾ cup. Add 1 cup applesauce. Increase cinnamon to 1 teaspoon; omit nutmeg. Cover and refrigerate about 1 hour or until dough stiffens. Divide dough in half; roll half of the dough; cut doughnuts. Repeat with remaining dough. Sprinkle hot doughnuts with cinnamon-sugar, if desired.

CINNAMON-SUGAR DOUGHNUTS: Roll cooked doughnuts in cinnamon-sugar.

DOUGHNUT GLAZE

If you're a glazed doughnut lover, then you'll love spreading this glaze on your doughnuts rather than rolling them in sugar.

4½ cups powdered sugar (from a 2-lb bag)
6 tablespoons milk
¼ cup light corn syrup
Gel icing food color (not liquid food color)

1 Mix all ingredients except gel food color in a large bowl. Stir in food color to desired shade.

2 Place cooling rack on large cookie sheet; place doughnuts on rack. Spoon and spread glaze over doughnuts. Let stand at least 30 minutes or until glaze is set.

STRIPED DOUGHNUTS: Prepare another batch of Doughnut Glaze. Divide the glaze into separate bowls and tint each with a different gel icing color. Place glazes into separate small resealable food-storage bags. Cut tiny corner of each bag. Working with one or two doughnuts at a time, pipe stripes of colored glazes over glazed doughnuts.

Cake Doughnuts and Glazed Doughnuts

Snickerdoodle Mini Doughnuts

Popovers

VEGETARIAN

Snickerdoodle Mini Doughnuts

Refrigerating the dough makes it easier to roll, but extra flour is still needed to keep the dough from sticking to the work surface and rolling pin. Shake off any excess flour before placing the dough rounds on the cookie sheet.

PREP 45 Minutes **TOTAL** 1 Hour 45 Minutes •
26 mini doughnuts

DOUGHNUTS
- ⅓ cup sugar
- ¼ cup butter, melted
- 2 eggs
- ⅓ cup milk
- 3 tablespoons sour cream
- 1 teaspoon vanilla
- 2 cups all-purpose flour
- 1½ teaspoons ground cinnamon
- 1 teaspoon cream of tartar
- 1 teaspoon baking powder

TOPPING
- ¾ cup sugar
- 1 tablespoon ground cinnamon
- 6 tablespoons butter, melted

1 In medium bowl, mix ⅓ cup sugar, ¼ cup melted butter and eggs until smooth. Using whisk, stir in milk, sour cream and vanilla. Stir in flour, 1½ teaspoons cinnamon, cream of tartar and baking powder just until moistened.

2 Grease medium bowl with shortening. Place dough in bowl, turning to grease all sides. Cover bowl with plastic wrap; refrigerate 1 hour.

3 Heat oven to 450°F. Line 2 cookie sheets with cooking parchment paper. Place dough on generously floured work surface. Roll dough in flour to coat. With floured rolling pin, roll dough to ½-inch thickness. Cut dough with floured 1¾-inch round cookie cutter. Place dough rounds on cookie sheets about 1 inch apart. Cut out centers using floured ¾-inch round cookie cutter. Reroll scraps to cut additional doughnuts.

4 Bake 8 to 10 minutes or just until edges are light golden brown. Immediately remove from cookie sheet to cooling rack. Cool 3 minutes.

5 In small bowl, stir ¾ cup sugar and 1 tablespoon cinnamon until mixed. Place melted butter in another small bowl. Quickly dip both sides of each warm doughnut into butter; let excess drip off. Using spoon, roll each doughnut in cinnamon-sugar mixture to coat. Return doughnuts to cooling rack. Serve warm.

1 Mini Doughnut Calories 120; Total Fat 5g (Saturated Fat 3g, Trans Fat 0g); Cholesterol 30mg; Sodium 60mg; Total Carbohydrate 17g (Dietary Fiber 1g); Protein 1g **Carbohydrate Choices:** 1

EASY • CALORIE SMART

Popovers

Popovers get their name because they pop up high out of their baking cups in the oven. Serve them hot with plain butter, or try one of the sweet or savory butters on page 496.

PREP 10 Minutes **TOTAL** 45 Minutes • **6 popovers**

- 2 eggs
- 1 cup all-purpose flour
- 1 cup milk
- ½ teaspoon salt
- Sweet or Savory Flavored Butter (page 496), if desired

1 Heat oven to 450°F. Generously grease 6-cup popover pan with shortening. Heat popover pan in oven 5 minutes.

2 Meanwhile, in medium bowl, beat eggs slightly with fork or whisk. Beat in remaining ingredients just until smooth (do not overbeat or popovers may not puff as high). Fill cups about half full.

3 Bake 20 minutes. Reduce oven temperature to 325°F. Bake 10 to 15 minutes longer or until deep golden brown. Immediately remove from cups. Serve hot with flavored butter.

1 Popover Calories 120; Total Fat 3g (Saturated Fat 1g, Trans Fat 0g); Cholesterol 65mg; Sodium 240mg; Total Carbohydrate 18g (Dietary Fiber 0g); Protein 5g **Carbohydrate Choices:** 1

YORKSHIRE PUDDING: Heat oven to 350°F. Place ¼ cup vegetable oil or drippings from meat roasting pan in 9-inch square pan; place pan in oven and heat until hot. Increase oven temperature to 450°F. Prepare popover batter; carefully pour into hot oil. Bake 18 to 23 minutes or until puffy and golden brown (pudding will puff during baking but will deflate shortly after being removed from oven). Cut pudding into squares; serve immediately.

3 Bake 10 to 12 minutes or until golden brown. Immediately remove from cookie sheet to cooling rack. Serve warm.

1 Biscuit Calories 160; Total Fat 9g (Saturated Fat 2.5g, Trans Fat 0g); Cholesterol 0mg; Sodium 330mg; Total Carbohydrate 18g (Dietary Fiber 0g); Protein 2g **Carbohydrate Choices:** 1

DROP BISCUITS: Increase milk to 1 cup. Grease cookie sheet with shortening. Drop dough into 12 mounds, using serving tablespoon, about 2 inches apart onto cookie sheet.

GARLIC-CHEESE BISCUITS: Add ½ cup shredded cheddar cheese (2 oz) with milk. Mix 2 tablespoons melted butter and ⅛ teaspoon garlic powder; brush over warm biscuits.

BUTTERMILK BISCUITS: Reduce baking powder to 2 teaspoons; add ¼ teaspoon baking soda with the sugar. Substitute buttermilk for the milk. (If buttermilk is thick, use slightly more than ¾ cup.)

HAM 'N EGG BISCUIT SANDWICHES: Make biscuits as directed—except use 3-inch cutter (you will get 6 biscuits). Split biscuits in half while still warm. Spread with mayonnaise and mustard if desired. On each biscuit bottom, place 1 slice American cheese, 1 fried or poached egg and 1 slice deli ham; cover with biscuit tops. Serve immediately.

FAST • EASY • CALORIE SMART

Baking Powder Biscuits

PREP 10 Minutes **TOTAL** 25 Minutes • *12 biscuits*

2 cups all-purpose or whole wheat flour	1 teaspoon salt
1 tablespoon sugar	½ cup shortening or cold butter, cut into 8 pieces
1 tablespoon baking powder	¾ cup milk

1 Heat oven to 450°F. In medium bowl, mix flour, sugar, baking powder and salt. Cut in shortening using pastry blender or fork until mixture looks like fine crumbs. Stir in milk until dough leaves side of bowl (dough will be soft and sticky).

2 Place dough on lightly floured work surface. Knead lightly 10 times. Roll or pat until ½ inch thick. Cut with floured 2- to 2¼-inch biscuit cutter. On ungreased cookie sheet, place biscuits about 1 inch apart for crusty sides, touching for soft sides.

MAKING BAKING POWDER BISCUITS

Cut shortening into flour mixture until it looks like fine crumbs.

LEARN WITH BETTY BISCUITS

Ideal Biscuit: Light golden brown with high, straight sides. It will be tender and light.

Underleavened Biscuit: Too little leavening or it was out of date, and dough was mixed too much. It will be tough and not flaky.

Overleavened Biscuit: Overbaked or the oven was too hot. It will be hard and crumbly.

Yeast Bread Basics

Nothing says "Welcome Home" like the aroma of yeast bread baking in the oven. Making yeast breads is a lot easier than you would think when you know all the tips and tricks. And with our kitchen-tested recipes, you can turn out beautiful, delicious breads every time!

Yeast Bread Ingredients

Flour: All-purpose and bread flour both have enough gluten-forming protein to develop the gluten necessary to provide the structure for yeast bread recipes. (See Learn to Knead Yeast Dough, page 522.)

Whole wheat flour has a high level of protein but won't make the same lofty loaves that all-purpose or bread flour can because the shards of bran in the flour tear the strands of gluten, inhibiting its development and impeding the bread structure. Rye flour doesn't have enough gluten-forming protein to be used on its own—it is used in combination with all-purpose or bread flour so it develops enough gluten to make desirable loaves.

Yeast: Proper yeast growth is necessary for dough to rise the way it should, and yeast is temperature sensitive. If the liquid in the dough recipe is too hot, it can kill the yeast; if liquid is too cool, it can prevent growth. Always check the package expiration date before use, as expired yeast may not allow bread to rise properly.

Dry yeast is the most commonly available form; it comes in **active dry yeast** and **fast-acting dry yeast** varieties, which may shorten rising times. Be sure to use the type of yeast called for in the recipe, as not all yeasts work well in all dough preparation methods. **Bread machine yeast,** a type of fast-acting yeast, can also be used in traditional baking methods.

Liquid: Water gives bread a crisp crust, while milk results in a softer crust plus adds nutrients to the bread. Use an instant-read thermometer to accurately determine the liquid's temperature before adding it. If the liquid was heated in the microwave, stir it before taking the temperature, as microwaves don't heat evenly. Heat liquid to within the range of temperatures given in your recipe for the best results.

Sweetener: Sugar, honey and molasses feed the yeast to help it grow, add flavor, and help brown the crust. Don't use artificial sweeteners because they won't feed the yeast.

Salt: Salt adds flavor, provides structure to dough by strengthening the gluten and keeps yeast growth in check. Never omit salt if specified in recipe.

Fat: Butter, shortening and vegetable and olive oil make bread tender and moist, and add flavor.

Eggs: Eggs add richness, color and structure.

Storing and Serving Yeast Breads

- See Refrigerator and Freezer Storage Chart, page 36.
- If breads are frozen, frost or glaze only after they have been thawed.
- Store soft-crust breads and rolls in resealable food-storage plastic bags or airtight containers in a cool, dry place up to 7 days.
- Store unsliced crisp-crust breads unwrapped at room temperature up to 3 days. Once sliced, place in a closed paper bag or tightly wrapped in foil and use within 1 day, or freeze.
- To freeze, wrap loaves or roll tightly in plastic wrap. Place in resealable freezer plastic bags. Freeze up to 3 months.
- To reheat frozen loaves or rolls, remove plastic bag and plastic wrap. Wrap in foil and bake at 350°F, 10 to 15 minutes for rolls or 15 to 20 minutes for loaves. For a crisper crust, unwrap during the last 5 minutes.

Making Bread with a Bread Machine

Using a bread machine is a quick and easy way to mix, raise and bake fresh, homemade bread anytime.

BREAD MACHINE TIPS

Follow these tips for bread machine techniques.

- Follow the directions in your manual for the order ingredients should be placed in your bread machine.
- Carefully measure the ingredients, using dry measuring cups for flour and sugar, liquid measuring cups for liquids; use measuring spoons, not serving spoons.
- Use bread machine yeast. It has a fine granulation that disperses more evenly during the mixing and kneading cycles.
- Don't open the machine during the rising or baking cycles, as it can cause the dough to collapse. If you need to check the progress of your dough, only check during mixing or kneading cycles.
- When using the delay cycle, be sure the yeast does not come in contact with liquid. Don't use the delay cycle with recipes using eggs, fresh dairy products (except butter), honey, meats or fresh fruits or vegetables, because bacteria can grow during this cycle.
- Keep the area around the bread machine open for good ventilation.

BREAD MACHINE RECIPES

Measure carefully, placing all ingredients in bread machine pan in the order recommended by the manufacturer.

INGREDIENT	CLASSIC WHITE BREAD (1½-LB LOAF; 12 SLICES) AMOUNT	HONEY–WHOLE WHEAT BREAD (1½-LB LOAF; 12 SLICES) AMOUNT	DINNER ROLLS (15 ROLLS) AMOUNT
Water	1 cup + 2 tablespoons	1 cup + 2 tablespoons	1 cup
Butter	2 tablespoons	2 tablespoons	2 tablespoons
Honey	—	3 tablespoons	—
Eggs	—	—	1
Bread Flour	3 cups	1½ cups	3¼ cups
Whole Wheat Flour	—	1½ cups	—
Instant Nonfat Dry Milk	3 tablespoons	—	—
Sugar	2 tablespoons	—	¼ cup
Salt	1½ teaspoons	1 teaspoon	1 teaspoon
Bread Machine Yeast	2 teaspoons	1½ teaspoons	1 tablespoon
DIRECTIONS			
	Select Basic/White cycle. **Use** Medium or Light crust color. Remove baked bread from pan; cool on cooling rack.	**Select** Whole Wheat or Basic/White cycle. **Use** Medium or Light crust color. Do not use Delay cycle. Remove baked bread from pan; cool on cooling rack.	**Select** Dough/Manual cycle. Do not use Delay cycle. Remove dough from pan using lightly floured hands. Cover and let rest 10 minutes on lightly floured work surface. Grease large cookie sheet with shortening. **Divide** dough into 15 equal pieces. Shape each piece into a ball. Place 2 inches apart on cookie sheet. Cover and let rise in warm place 30 to 40 minute or until doubled in size. **Bake** at 375°F 12 to 15 minutes or until golden brown. Brush tops with melted butter. Serve warm or cool on cooling rack.

MAKING BREAD DOUGH

After first addition of flour, dough will be very soft and fall off rubber spatula in "sheets."

To knead, fold dough toward you, then push away from you with short rocking motion. Rotate dough a quarter turn; repeat. Dough will feel springy and smooth when properly kneaded.

Let dough rise until doubled in size. Press a fingertip about ½ inch into dough; if indentation remains, dough has risen enough.

Gently push fist into dough to deflate.

Classic White Bread

PREP 35 Minutes **TOTAL** 3 Hours • *2 loaves* (16 slices each)

6 to 7 cups all-purpose or bread flour	2 packages (¼ oz each) regular active or fast-acting dry yeast (4½ teaspoons)
3 tablespoons sugar	
1 tablespoon salt	2¼ cups very warm water (120°F to 130°F)
2 tablespoons vegetable shortening or softened butter	2 tablespoons butter, melted, if desired

1 In large bowl, stir 3½ cups of the flour, the sugar, salt, shortening and yeast until well mixed. Add warm water. Beat with electric mixer on low speed 1 minute, scraping bowl frequently. Beat on medium speed 1 minute, scraping bowl frequently. Stir in enough remaining flour, 1 cup at a time, to make dough easy to handle.

2 Place dough on lightly floured work surface. Knead about 10 minutes or until dough is smooth and springy. Grease large bowl with shortening. Place dough in bowl, turning dough to grease all sides. Cover bowl loosely with plastic wrap and let rise in warm place 40 to 60 minutes or until dough has doubled in size. Dough is ready if indentation remains when touched.

3 Grease bottoms and sides of two 8x4- or 9x5-inch loaf pans with shortening or cooking spray. Gently push fist into dough to deflate. Divide dough in half. On lightly floured work surface, flatten each half with hands or rolling pin into 18x9-inch rectangle. Roll dough up tightly, beginning at 9-inch side. Press with thumbs to seal after each turn. Pinch edge of dough into roll to seal. Pinch each end of roll to seal. Fold ends under loaf. Place loaves seam side down in pans. Brush loaves using 1 tablespoon of the melted butter. Cover loosely with plastic wrap and let rise in warm place 35 to 50 minutes or until loaves have doubled in size.

4 Move oven rack to low position so that tops of pans will be in center of oven. Heat oven to 425°F. Bake 25 to 30 minutes or until loaves are deep golden brown and sound hollow when tapped. Remove from pans to cooling rack. Brush loaves with remaining 1 tablespoon melted butter. Cool completely.

1 Slice Calories 100; Total Fat 1g (Saturated Fat 0g, Trans Fat 0g); Cholesterol 0mg; Sodium 220mg; Total Carbohydrate 19g (Dietary Fiber 0g); Protein 2g **Carbohydrate Choices:** 1

Classic White Bread

521

SHAPING TRADITIONAL BREAD LOAVES

Flatten dough with hands or rolling pin into 18x9-inch rectangle.

Tightly roll up dough toward you, beginning at 9-inch side. Pinch edges of dough into roll.

MAKING FREE-FORM LOAVES

Shape dough into smooth ball by stretching surface of dough around bottom on all four sides; pinch at bottom to seal.

Place on cookie sheet; carefully slash top of dough a few times with serrated knife.

LEARN TO KNEAD YEAST DOUGH

Properly kneading yeast dough helps the dough rise and produces bread with a finer grain and better texture. When flour is mixed with liquid, gluten strands form. Kneading makes the gluten stronger and more elastic, allowing the dough to stretch, expand and hold its shape as it rises and then bakes.

Dough recipes usually give a range of how much flour to add. This is because conditions can change, particularly the moisture content of the flour, due to weather and/or storage conditions and the humidity level in the air when you're making bread. Don't worry if you don't use all the flour called for. Use just enough so that the dough isn't sticky, and knead the dough until it's smooth and elastic so it will rise and bake well. The range of flour given includes what you will use to make the dough and to knead it.

For the best volume and texture of yeast breads, use these tips.

- Start by adding the minimum amount of flour. If dough is still sticky, add more (about ¼ to ½ cup at a time).

- Keep any remaining flour you didn't use from the maximum amount called for in the recipe in a measuring cup on the work surface.

- Sprinkle the work surface lightly with some of the flour. Dust your hands with a little of the flour.

- Place the dough on the work surface. Press the dough into an oval; fold it toward you in half.

- Using the floured lower palm and heel of your hand, press down lightly on the dough, pressing it away from you.

- Give the dough a quarter turn; repeat pressing motions.

- Repeat, sprinkling a little additional flour on the work surface or dough as needed if the dough is sticky, until it is smooth and elastic.

- If your hands become sticky, sprinkle a little of the flour on them, rubbing them together to remove stickiness.

- Check for proper kneading by pressing a floured fingertip lightly into the top of the dough. If the dough springs back to its original shape, it has been kneaded long enough.

LEARN WITH BETTY YEAST BREAD

Ideal Yeast Bread:
This loaf is high, evenly shaped and golden brown, with an even texture.

Underrisen Yeast Bread:
This loaf did not rise because the water was too hot, the yeast was out of date or the dough was not kneaded enough.

Flat, Sunken Yeast Bread:
This loaf was kneaded too much and contained too much flour.

Honey—Whole Wheat Bread

PREP 35 Minutes **TOTAL** 3 Hours 10 Minutes •
2 loaves (16 slices each)

- 3 cups whole wheat flour
- ⅓ cup honey or pure maple syrup
- ¼ cup vegetable shortening or softened butter
- 3 teaspoons salt

- 2 packages (¼ oz each) regular active or fast-acting dry yeast (4½ teaspoons)
- 2¼ cups very warm water (120°F to 130°F)
- 3 to 4 cups all-purpose or bread flour
- 2 tablespoons butter, melted, if desired

1 In large bowl, beat whole wheat flour, honey, shortening, salt and yeast with electric mixer on low speed until well mixed. Add warm water. Beat on low speed 1 minute, scraping bowl frequently. Beat on medium speed 1 minute, scraping bowl frequently. Stir in enough all-purpose flour, 1 cup at a time, to make dough easy to handle.

2 Place dough on lightly floured work surface. Knead about 10 minutes or until dough is smooth and springy. Grease large bowl with shortening. Place dough in bowl, turning dough to grease all sides. Cover bowl loosely with plastic wrap and let rise in warm place 40 to 60 minutes or until dough has doubled in size. Dough is ready if indentation remains when touched.

3 Gently push fist into dough to deflate. Divide dough in half. On lightly floured work surface, flatten each half with hands or rolling pin into 18x9-inch rectangle. Roll dough up tightly, beginning at 9-inch side. Press with thumbs to seal after each turn. Pinch edge of dough into roll to seal. Pinch each end of roll to seal. Fold ends under loaf.

4 Grease bottoms and sides of two 8x4- or 9x5-inch loaf pans with shortening or cooking spray. Place loaves seam sides down in pans. Brush loaves using 1 tablespoon of the melted butter. Cover loosely with plastic wrap and let rise in warm place 35 to 50 minutes or until loaves have doubled in size.

5 Move oven rack to low position so that tops of pans will be in center of oven. Heat oven to 375°F. Uncover loaves. Bake 40 to 45 minutes or until loaves are deep golden brown and sound hollow when tapped. Remove from pans to cooling rack. Brush loaves using remaining 1 tablespoon melted butter. Cool completely.

1 Slice Calories 110; Total Fat 2g (Saturated Fat 0g, Trans Fat 0g); Cholesterol 0mg; Sodium 220mg; Total Carbohydrate 20g (Dietary Fiber 1g); Protein 3g **Carbohydrate Choices:** 1

SUNFLOWER-HERB WHOLE WHEAT BREAD: Add 1 tablespoon dried basil leaves and 2 teaspoons dried thyme leaves with salt. Stir in 1 cup unsalted sunflower nuts with all-purpose flour.

Honey—Whole Wheat Bread

French Bread

CALORIE SMART • VEGETARIAN

French Bread

The traditional flavor and texture of French bread are developed by making a sponge and refrigerating the loaves before baking. A sponge is a bread-dough mixture made with yeast, water and some of the flour. Spraying the loaves with cool water and adding a water pan to the oven help to make a crisp crust. Crispy French bread is best the day you bake it.

PREP 25 Minutes TOTAL 8 Hours • *2 loaves* (16 slices each)

1½ cups all-purpose flour	1 teaspoon salt
1 package (¼ oz) regular active dry yeast (2¼ teaspoons)	Additional 1⅓ to 1⅔ cups all-purpose flour or bread flour
1 cup very warm water (120°F to 130°F)	

1 In large bowl, mix 1½ cups all-purpose flour and the yeast. Add warm water. Beat with whisk or electric mixer on low speed 1 minute, scraping bowl frequently, until batter is very smooth. Cover tightly with plastic wrap and let stand about 1 hour or until bubbly.

2 Stir in salt and enough of the additional flour, ½ cup at a time, until a soft dough forms. Place dough on lightly floured work surface. Knead 5 to 10 minutes or until dough is smooth and springy (dough will be soft). Grease large bowl with shortening. Place dough in bowl, turning dough to grease all sides. Cover bowl loosely with plastic wrap and let rise in warm place 1 hour to 1 hour 15 minutes or until dough has doubled in size. Dough is ready if indentation remains when touched.

3 Grease uninsulated cookie sheet with shortening or cooking spray. Place dough on lightly floured work surface, forming it into an oval-shaped mound. Sprinkle top of dough with flour. With a straight-edged knife, press straight down on dough lengthwise to divide it into 2 equal parts (the parts will be elongated in shape). Gently shape each part into a narrow loaf about 16 inches long, stretching the top of the loaf slightly to make it smooth. Place loaves, smooth sides up, about 4 inches apart on cookie sheet.

4 Cover loaves loosely, but airtight, with plastic wrap. (Loaves will expand slightly in the refrigerator.) Refrigerate at least 4 hours but no longer than 24 hours. (This step can be omitted, but refrigerating develops the flavor and texture of the bread.)

MAKING FRENCH BREAD

Cover batter in bowl tightly with plastic wrap; let stand 1 hour or until bubbly.

Add flour ½ cup at a time, until soft dough forms. Knead 5 to 10 minutes.

Press straight down on oval-shaped dough with straight knife to divide into two equal parts.

With serrated knife, carefully cut ¼-inch-deep slashes diagonally across tops of loaves at 2-inch intervals.

5 Uncover loaves and spray with cool water; let rise in warm place about 1 hour or until refrigerated loaves have come to room temperature.

6 Move bottom oven rack to lowest position. Place 8- or 9-inch square metal pan on bottom oven rack; add hot water to pan until about ½ inch from the top. Heat oven to 450°F.

7 With serrated knife, carefully cut ¼-inch-deep slashes diagonally across tops of loaves at 2-inch intervals. Spray loaves with cool water. Place cookie sheet on middle oven rack. Spray loaves again.

8 Bake 18 to 20 minutes or until loaves are deep golden brown with crisp crust, and sound hollow when tapped. Remove from cookie sheet to cooling rack; cool.

1 Slice Calories 40; Total Fat 0g (Saturated Fat 0g, Trans Fat 0g); Cholesterol 0mg; Sodium 75mg; Total Carbohydrate 9g (Dietary Fiber 0g); Protein 1g **Carbohydrate Choices:** ½

CHEESY HERBED FRENCH BREAD: Stir in ¼ cup grated Parmesan cheese and 1 teaspoon dried basil leaves with the flour in Step 2.

GARLIC BREAD: Heat oven to 400°F. In small bowl, mix ⅓ cup softened butter and ¼ teaspoon garlic powder. Slice 1 loaf baked French bread into 1-inch slices. Spread each slice with butter mixture; reassemble loaf. Wrap in foil. Bake 10 to 15 minutes or until hot.

CALORIE SMART • VEGETARIAN

Artisan Asiago Bread

This large flour-dusted loaf looks and tastes like it came from a bakery. When you slice it, you'll find pockets of cheese scattered throughout.

PREP 25 Minutes **TOTAL** 4 Hours 15 Minutes •
1 loaf (24 slices)

3½ to 3¾ cups bread flour	2 tablespoons olive or vegetable oil
1 teaspoon sugar	2 teaspoons dried rosemary or thyme leaves, if desired
1 package (¼ oz) regular active or fast-acting dry yeast (2¼ teaspoons)	1 teaspoon salt
1¼ cups very warm water (120°F to 130°F)	1¼ cups diced Asiago cheese (about 5 oz)*

1 In large bowl, mix 1½ cups of the flour, the sugar and yeast. Add warm water. Beat with wooden spoon or electric mixer on low speed 1 minute, scraping bowl frequently. Cover tightly with plastic wrap and let stand about 1 hour or until bubbly.

2 Stir in oil, rosemary and salt. Stir in enough remaining flour ½ cup at a time until a soft, smooth dough forms. Let stand 15 minutes.

3 Place dough on lightly floured work surface. Knead 5 to 10 minutes or until dough is smooth and springy. Knead in 1 cup of the cheese. Grease large bowl with shortening. Place dough in bowl, turning dough to grease all sides. Cover bowl tightly with plastic wrap and let rise in warm place 45 to 60 minutes or until dough has doubled in size. Dough is ready if indentation remains when touched.

4 Lightly grease uninsulated cookie sheet with shortening or cooking spray. Place dough on lightly floured work surface. Gently shape into football-shaped loaf about 12 inches long by stretching sides of dough downward to make a smooth top. Place loaf smooth side up on cookie sheet. Coat loaf generously with flour. Cover loosely with plastic wrap and let rise in warm place 45 to 60 minutes or until loaf has almost doubled in size.

5 Move bottom rack to lowest position. Place 8- or 9-inch square metal pan on bottom oven rack; add hot water to pan until about ½ inch from the top. Heat oven to 450°F. Spray loaf with cool water; sprinkle with flour. With serrated knife, carefully cut ½-inch-deep slash lengthwise down center of top of loaf. Sprinkle remaining ¼ cup cheese into slash. Place cookie sheet on middle oven rack.

6 Bake 10 minutes. Reduce oven temperature to 400°F. Bake 20 to 25 minutes longer or until loaf is deep golden and sounds hollow when tapped. Remove from cookie sheet to cooling rack; cool.

1 Slice Calories 110; Total Fat 4g (Saturated Fat 2g, Trans Fat 0g); Cholesterol 5mg; Sodium 170mg; Total Carbohydrate 15g (Dietary Fiber 0g); Protein 4g **Carbohydrate Choices:** 1

*Swiss or another firm cheese can be substituted for the Asiago.

MAKING ARTISAN ASIAGO BREAD

Mix batter 1 minute, scraping bowl frequently.

Gently shape dough into football-shaped loaf.

Spray loaf with cool water; sprinkle with flour.

Carefully cut ½-inch-deep slash down center of top of loaf.

CALORIE SMART

Shokupan

This Japanese milk bread is slightly sweet and reminiscent of Hawaiian bread. It's great for toast, French toast and sandwiches such as Katsu Sando (page 300).

PREP 20 Minutes **TOTAL** 2 Hours 45 Minutes •
1 loaf (12 slices)

3 to 4 cups all-purpose or bread flour	1 teaspoon salt
¼ cup sugar	½ cup whole milk
1 package (¼ oz) regular active dry yeast (2¼ teaspoons)	¼ cup water
	¼ cup butter, softened
	1 egg

1 In large bowl, stir 1 cup of the flour, the sugar, yeast and salt until well mixed. In 1-quart saucepan, heat milk, water and butter over medium-low heat, stirring occasionally until very warm (120°F to 130°F).

2 Add warm milk mixture and egg to flour mixture. Beat with electric mixer on low speed until moistened. Beat on medium speed 2 minutes, scraping the bowl frequently. Stir in enough remaining flour, ¼ cup at a time, to make dough easy to handle.

3 Place dough on lightly floured work surface. Knead 6 to 8 minutes or until dough is smooth and springy. Spray large bowl with cooking spray. Place dough in bowl, turning dough to grease all sides. Cover bowl loosely with plastic wrap and let rise 1 hour or until dough has doubled in size. Dough is ready if indentation remains when touched.

4 Grease bottom and sides of 9x5-inch loaf pan with shortening or spray with cooking spray. Gently push fist into dough to deflate. On lightly floured work surface, roll dough with rolling pin into 18x9-inch rectangle. Roll dough up tightly, beginning with 9-inch side. Press thumbs to seal dough after each turn. Pinch edge of dough to seal. Pinch ends of roll to seal. Fold ends under dough; pinch to seal. Place seam side down in pan. Cover loosely with plastic wrap sprayed with cooking spray. Let rise about 30 minutes or until 1 inch from top of pan.

5 Heat oven to 375°F. Cover pan with heavy-duty foil. Place in oven; cover pan with 15x10x1-inch pan with sides and heavy ovenproof bowl or skillet in center of pan for weight. Bake 25 minutes; if dough has risen above top of pan, press pan down onto loaf to flatten. Carefully remove hot bowl and pan.

BAKING SHOKUPAN

Cover top of loaf pan with foil and weighted pan to prevent dough from rising above pan. Remove weighted pan halfway through baking.

6 Bake, still covered with foil, 25 to 30 minutes longer or until loaf is deep golden brown and sounds hollow when tapped. Uncover loaf and remove from pan to cooling rack. Cool completely, about 1 hour.

1 Slice Calories 180; Total Fat 5g (Saturated Fat 3g, Trans Fat 0g); Cholesterol 25mg; Sodium 240mg; Total Carbohydrate 29g (Dietary Fiber 1g); Protein 4g **Carbohydrate Choices:** 2

VEGETARIAN

Dried Cherry and Walnut Bread

PREP 25 Minutes **TOTAL** 3 Hours 30 Minutes •
1 loaf (16 slices)

3¼ to 3¾ cups bread flour	1 cup coarsely chopped walnuts
2 tablespoons sugar	1 cup dried cherries
1 package (¼ oz) fast-acting dry yeast (2¼ teaspoons)	1 tablespoon orange zest
1¼ cups very warm water (120°F to 130°F)	1 teaspoon salt
	1 tablespoon cornmeal
2 tablespoons vegetable oil	1 teaspoon milk

1 In large bowl, mix 1½ cups of the flour, the sugar and yeast. Add warm water and oil. Beat with electric mixer on low speed 1 minute, scraping bowl frequently. Beat on medium speed 1 minute, scraping bowl frequently. Stir in 1¾ cups flour, the walnuts, cherries, orange zest and salt with wooden spoon until dough pulls away from side of bowl and forms a sticky ball.

2 Place dough on lightly floured work surface. Knead 2 to 3 minutes or until dough is smooth and springy, using enough of the remaining ½ cup flour as necessary to form into smooth ball. Grease large bowl with oil. Place dough in bowl, turning to grease all sides. Cover bowl

Dried Cherry and Walnut Bread

loosely with plastic wrap and let rise in warm place 1 hour or until dough has doubled in size.

3 Lightly grease large cookie sheet with shortening or cooking spray; sprinkle with cornmeal. Gently push fist into dough to deflate. Place dough on lightly floured work surface. Gently shape into smooth ball by stretching surface of dough around to bottom on all sides; pinch bottom to seal. Place on cookie sheet. Cover dough loosely with plastic wrap sprayed with cooking spray and let rise in warm place 30 to 40 minutes or until loaf has doubled in size.

4 Heat oven to 350°F. Brush top of loaf with milk. With serrated knife, cut three ¼-inch-deep slashes across top of loaf. Bake 35 to 40 minutes or until loaf is deep golden brown and sounds hollow when tapped. Cool completely on cooling rack, about 1 hour, before slicing.

1 Slice Calories 210; Total Fat 7g (Saturated Fat 1g, Trans Fat 0g); Cholesterol 0mg; Sodium 150mg; Total Carbohydrate 32g (Dietary Fiber 2g); Protein 5g **Carbohydrate Choices:** 2

Sourdough Bread

527

CALORIE SMART • VEGETARIAN

Sourdough Bread

PREP 30 Minutes **TOTAL** 11 Hours 45 Minutes •
2 loaves (16 slices each)

1 cup Sourdough Starter (at right)	2 cups warm water (105°F to 115°F)
6¼ to 6¾ cups all-purpose or bread flour	3 tablespoons sugar
	1 teaspoon salt
	3 tablespoons vegetable oil

1 In 3-quart glass bowl, mix sourdough starter, 2½ cups of the flour and the warm water with wooden spoon until smooth. Cover and let stand in warm, draft-free place 8 hours.

2 Add 3¾ cups of remaining flour, the sugar, salt and oil to mixture in bowl. Stir with wooden spoon until dough is smooth and flour is completely absorbed. (Dough should be just firm enough to gather into ball. If necessary, add up to ½ cup of remaining flour gradually, stirring until all flour is absorbed.)

3 On heavily floured work surface, knead dough about 10 minutes or until smooth and springy. Grease large bowl with shortening. Place dough in bowl, turning to grease all sides. Cover and let rise in warm place about 1 hour 30 minutes or until dough has doubled in size. Dough is ready if indentation remains when touched.

4 Grease large cookie sheet with shortening. Gently push fist into dough several times to remove air bubbles. Divide dough in half. Shape each half into round, slightly flat loaf. Do not tear dough by pulling. Place loaves on opposite corners on cookie sheet. With sharp serrated knife, make three ¼-inch-deep slashes in top of each loaf. Cover and let rise about 45 minutes or until loaves have doubled in size.

5 Heat oven to 375°F. Brush loaves with cold water. Place cookie sheet on middle oven rack. Bake 35 to 45 minutes, brushing occasionally with water, until golden brown and loaves sound hollow when tapped. Remove from cookie sheet to cooling rack. Cool completely, about 1 hour.

1 Slice Calories 110; Total Fat 1.5g (Saturated Fat 0g, Trans Fat 0g); Cholesterol 0mg; Sodium 75mg; Total Carbohydrate 21g (Dietary Fiber 0g); Protein 3g **Carbohydrate Choices:** 1½

SOURDOUGH STARTER

1 teaspoon regular active dry yeast	¾ cup milk
¼ cup warm water (105°F to 115°F)	1 cup all-purpose flour

1 In 3-quart glass bowl, dissolve yeast in warm water. Stir in milk. Gradually stir in flour; beat until smooth. Cover with clean dish towel or cheesecloth; let stand in warm, draft-free place (80°F to 85°F) about 24 hours or until starter begins to ferment (bubbles will appear on surface of starter). If starter has not begun fermentation after 24 hours, discard and begin again. If fermentation has begun, stir well; cover tightly with plastic wrap and return to warm, draft-free place. Let starter stand 2 to 3 days or until foamy.

2 When starter has become foamy, stir well; pour into 1-quart crock or glass jar with tight-fitting cover. Store in refrigerator. Starter is ready to use when clear liquid has risen to top. Stir before using. Use 1 cup starter in Sourdough Bread recipe. To remaining starter, add ¾ cup milk and ¾ cup flour. Store covered at room temperature about 12 hours or until bubbles appear; refrigerate.

3 Use starter regularly, every week or so. If volume of breads you bake begins to decrease, dissolve 1 teaspoon active dry yeast in ¼ cup warm water. Stir in ½ cup milk, ¾ cup flour and the remaining starter. Store at room temperature about 12 hours or until bubbles appear; refrigerate.

Rich Egg Bread

PREP 30 Minutes **TOTAL** 3 Hours 5 Minutes •
1 loaf (16 slices)

3 to 3¼ cups all-purpose or bread flour	1 cup very warm water (120°F to 130°F)
¼ cup sugar	2 tablespoons vegetable oil
1½ teaspoons salt	1 egg
1 package (¼ oz) regular active or fast-acting dry yeast (2¼ teaspoons)	Melted butter, if desired

1 In large bowl, mix 1½ cups of the flour, the sugar, salt and yeast. Add warm water and oil. Beat with electric mixer on low speed 1 minute, scraping bowl frequently. Beat on medium speed 1 minute, scraping bowl frequently. Add egg; beat until smooth. Stir in enough remaining flour, ¼ cup at a time, to make dough easy to handle.

2 Place dough on lightly floured work surface. Knead about 10 minutes or until dough is smooth and springy. Grease large bowl with shortening. Place dough in bowl, turning dough to grease all sides. Cover bowl loosely with plastic wrap and let rise in warm place about 1 hour or until dough has doubled in size. Dough is ready if indentation remains when touched. (At this point, dough can be refrigerated up to 24 hours.)

3 Grease bottom and sides of 9x5- or 8x4-inch loaf pan with shortening or cooking spray. Gently push fist into dough to deflate. On lightly floured work surface, flatten dough with hands or rolling pin into 18x9-inch rectangle. Roll up tightly, beginning at 9-inch side. Pinch edge of dough into roll to seal. Pinch each end of roll to seal. Fold ends under loaf. Place loaf seam side down in pan. Cover loosely with plastic wrap lightly sprayed with cooking spray and let rise in warm place about 1 hour or until loaf has doubled in size.

4 Move oven rack to low position so that top of pan will be in center of oven. Heat oven to 375°F. Bake 30 to 35 minutes or until loaf is deep golden brown and sounds hollow when tapped. Remove from pan to cooling rack. Brush loaf with melted butter. Cool completely.

1 Slice Calories 120; Total Fat 2.5g (Saturated Fat 0g, Trans Fat 0g); Cholesterol 10mg; Sodium 230mg; Total Carbohydrate 21g (Dietary Fiber 0g); Protein 3g **Carbohydrate Choices:** 1½

CHALLAH BRAID: Make dough as directed. Lightly grease cookie sheet with shortening or cooking spray. After pushing fist into dough, divide into 3 equal parts. Roll each part into 14-inch rope. Place ropes close together on cookie sheet. Braid ropes gently and loosely, starting in middle; do not stretch. Pinch ends; tuck ends under braid securely. Brush with vegetable oil. Cover loosely with plastic wrap and let rise in warm place 40 to 50 minutes or until loaf has doubled in size. Heat oven to 375°F. In small bowl, beat 1 egg yolk and 2 tablespoons water; brush over braid. Sprinkle with poppy seed. Bake 25 to 30 minutes or until golden brown.

CINNAMON SWIRL RAISIN BREAD: Knead ½ cup raisins into dough after deflating in Step 3. Before rolling up dough, brush with 2 teaspoons softened butter. Mix ¼ cup sugar with 1½ teaspoons ground cinnamon; sprinkle over dough.

BRAIDING CHALLAH

Braid ropes gently and loosely, starting at middle; do not stretch.

Challah Braid

Chocolate-Orange Babka

PREP 1 Hour 5 Minutes **TOTAL** 13 Hours 40 Minutes •
1 loaf (12 slices)

FILLING

- 7 tablespoons butter
- ¾ cup sugar
- 3 oz bittersweet chocolate (from 4-oz package), coarsely chopped
- 5 tablespoons unsweetened baking cocoa
- 1 tablespoon orange zest

DOUGH

- 1 package (¼ oz) regular active dry yeast (2¼ teaspoons)
- ½ cup very warm milk (120°F to 130°F)
- 1 teaspoon sugar
- 2 to 2½ cups all-purpose flour
- 6 tablespoons butter, chopped, softened
- 1 egg

SYRUP

- ¼ cup sugar
- ¼ cup fresh orange juice
- 1 tablespoon orange zest

1 In 1-quart saucepan, heat 7 tablespoons butter over medium heat, stirring frequently, until melted. Stir in ¾ cup sugar. Cook, stirring constantly, about 3 minutes or until sugar is nearly dissolved. Remove from heat. Add chocolate to sugar mixture; stir until chocolate is melted. Cool 1 minute. Stir in cocoa and 1 tablespoon orange zest until blended. Cool 30 to 40 minutes or until room temperature. Cover; store at room temperature until ready to assemble loaf.

2 Meanwhile, in large bowl, mix yeast, warm milk, 1 teaspoon sugar and ⅓ cup of the flour until smooth. Let stand 10 to 15 minutes or until bubbles appear on surface.

3 Using spoon, stir 6 tablespoons softened butter and egg into milk mixture. Stir in 1⅔ cups of the flour until dough forms. Turn dough onto well-floured work surface. Knead 10 minutes, adding just enough of remaining flour until dough is soft, smooth and elastic (pieces of butter will gradually work into dough during kneading process). Grease same bowl with shortening or spray with cooking spray; place dough back into greased bowl. Cover bowl with plastic wrap sprayed with cooking spray. Refrigerate at least 8 hours, but no longer than 18 hours.

4 Spray 9x5-inch loaf pan with cooking spray; line with cooking parchment paper. Spray parchment paper with cooking spray.

5 On lightly floured work surface, roll dough to 20x12-inch rectangle. Spread reserved filling evenly over dough to edges. Roll dough up, starting with long side; pinch seam to seal. Place seam side down on work surface. Using sharp knife, slice dough lengthwise to within ½ inch from one end. Twist dough strips together by placing one strip over the other, keeping cut surfaces facing up; pinch ends together to seal. Fold twisted dough roll loosely in half, keeping cut surfaces facing up. Twist dough halves together. Place in loaf pan. Cover dough with plastic wrap sprayed with cooking spray. Let rise in warm place about 2 hours or until babka has doubled in size.

6 Meanwhile, heat oven to 375°F. In 1-quart saucepan, mix syrup ingredients. Heat to boiling, stirring constantly; boil 2 minutes or until light caramel in color. Remove from heat; cool at room temperature while bread bakes.

7 Bake loaf 30 to 35 minutes or until deep golden brown. Drizzle syrup evenly over top of hot loaf. Place pan on cooling rack. Cool in pan about 2 hours or until completely cooled. Remove from pan before slicing.

1 Slice Calories 350; Total Fat 17g (Saturated Fat 11g, Trans Fat 0.5g); Cholesterol 50mg; Sodium 110mg; Total Carbohydrate 42g (Dietary Fiber 3g); Protein 5g **Carbohydrate Choices:** 3

BRAIDING BABKA

Twist dough strips together by placing one strip over the other, keeping cut surfaces facing up.

Fold twisted dough roll in half, keeping cut surfaces facing up; twist dough halves together.

Chocolate-Orange Babka

Caramel Sticky Rolls

PREP 40 Minutes **TOTAL** 3 Hours 20 Minutes • *15 rolls*

ROLLS

- 3½ to 4 cups all-purpose or bread flour
- ⅓ cup granulated sugar
- 1 teaspoon salt
- 2 packages (¼ oz each) regular active or fast-acting dry yeast (4½ teaspoons)
- 1 cup very warm milk (120°F to 130°F)
- ¼ cup butter, softened
- 1 egg

CARAMEL TOPPING

- 1 cup packed brown sugar
- ½ cup butter, softened
- ¼ cup light corn syrup
- 1 cup pecan halves, if desired

FILLING

- ½ cup chopped pecans or raisins, if desired
- ¼ cup granulated sugar or packed brown sugar
- 1 teaspoon ground cinnamon
- 2 tablespoons butter, softened

1 In large bowl, mix 2 cups of the flour, ⅓ cup granulated sugar, the salt and yeast. Add warm milk, ¼ cup butter and the egg. Beat with electric mixer on low speed 1 minute, scraping bowl frequently. Beat on medium speed 1 minute, scraping bowl frequently. Stir in enough remaining flour, ½ cup at a time, to make dough easy to handle.

2 Place dough on lightly floured work surface. Knead about 5 minutes or until dough is smooth and springy. Grease large bowl with shortening. Place dough in bowl, turning dough to grease all sides. Cover bowl loosely with plastic wrap and let rise in warm place about 1 hour 30 minutes or until dough has doubled in size. Dough is ready if indentation remains when touched.

3 In 2-quart saucepan, heat brown sugar and ½ cup butter to boiling, stirring constantly; remove from heat. Stir in corn syrup. Pour into 13x9-inch pan. Sprinkle with pecan halves.

4 In small bowl, mix filling ingredients except 2 tablespoons butter; set aside.

5 Gently push fist into dough to deflate. On lightly floured work surface, flatten dough with hands or rolling pin into 15x10-inch rectangle. Spread with 2 tablespoons butter; sprinkle with filling. Roll rectangle up tightly, beginning at long side. Pinch edge of dough into roll to seal. With fingers, shape roll until evenly round. With dental floss or serrated knife, cut roll into 15 (1-inch) slices.

6 Place slices slightly apart in pan, cut sides down. Cover loosely with plastic wrap and let rise in warm place about 30 minutes or until rolls have doubled in size.

MAKING CARAMEL STICKY ROLLS

Sprinkle pecans over caramel topping in pan.

Roll dough up tightly, beginning at 15-inch side.

Using dental floss or a serrated knife, cut into slices.

Place slices slightly apart in pan, cut sides down.

Caramel Sticky Rolls

7 Heat oven to 350°F. Uncover rolls. Bake 30 to 35 minutes or until golden brown. Let stand 2 to 3 minutes. Place heatproof platter upside down over pan; carefully turn platter and pan over together. Let stand 1 minute so caramel can drizzle over rolls; remove pan. Serve warm.

1 Roll Calories 320; Total Fat 12g (Saturated Fat 7g, Trans Fat 0g); Cholesterol 40mg; Sodium 260mg; Total Carbohydrate 50g (Dietary Fiber 1g); Protein 4g **Carbohydrate Choices:** 3

LIGHTER DIRECTIONS: For 4 grams of fat and 255 calories per serving, make recipe as directed—except omit caramel topping and pecan halves. Line pan with foil; spray foil with cooking spray. Drizzle 1 cup caramel ice cream topping (from 12.5-oz jar) over foil (heat topping slightly if it is stiff). Continue as directed—except omit chopped pecans from filling.

MAKE-AHEAD DIRECTIONS: After placing slices in pan, cover tightly with plastic wrap or foil; refrigerate 4 to 24 hours. About 2 hours before baking, remove from refrigerator; remove plastic wrap or foil and cover loosely with plastic wrap. Let rise in warm place until rolls have doubled in size. If some rising has occurred in the refrigerator, rising time may be less than 2 hours. Bake and serve as directed.

CINNAMON ROLLS: Omit caramel topping and chopped pecans in filling. Grease bottom and sides of 13x9-inch pan with shortening or cooking spray. Place dough slices in pan. Let rise and bake as directed in Steps 6 and 7—except do not turn pan upside down. Remove rolls from pan to cooling rack. Cool 10 minutes. Drizzle rolls with Vanilla Glaze (page 602) if desired. Serve warm or cooled.

VEGETARIAN

Mallorca Breads

Mallorcas are sweet Puerto Rican rolls typically served warm so that you can sink your teeth into their buttery fluffiness.

PREP 40 Minutes **TOTAL** 2 Hours 40 Minutes • *12 rolls*

¾ cup milk	1 package (¼ oz) regular active or fast-acting dry yeast (2¼ teaspoons)
¾ cup water	
½ cup butter, softened	
5 to 6 cups all-purpose or bread flour	4 egg yolks
½ cup granulated sugar	¼ cup butter, melted
1½ teaspoons salt	2 tablespoons powdered sugar

1 In 2-quart saucepan, heat milk, water and ½ cup butter over medium-low heat to 120°F to 130°F (butter may not melt). Remove from heat; cover to keep warm.

2 Meanwhile, in large bowl, mix 2½ cups of the flour, the granulated sugar, salt and yeast; add warm milk mixture and egg yolks. Beat with electric mixer on low speed 1 minute, scraping bowl frequently. Beat on medium speed 1 minute, scraping bowl frequently. Stir in enough remaining flour, ¼ cup at a time, to make dough easy to handle.

531

Coconut-Chocolate Chip Mallorcas

3 Place dough on lightly floured work surface. Knead about 5 minutes or until dough is smooth and elastic. Grease large bowl with shortening. Place dough in bowl, turning dough to grease all sides. Cover bowl loosely with plastic wrap and let rise in warm place about 1 hour or until dough has doubled in size. Dough is ready if indentation remains when touched.

4 Line 2 large cookie sheets with cooking parchment paper. Gently push fist into dough to deflate. Roll dough into 15x12-inch rectangle. Brush dough with 2 tablespoons of the melted butter. Cut dough into twelve 1-inch-wide strips with sharp knife or pizza cutter. Roll each strip into a spiral, tucking end under dough slightly. Place on cookie sheet. Cover loosely with plastic wrap; let rise in warm place about 30 minutes or until rolls have doubled in size.

5 Heat oven to 350°F. Uncover rolls. Brush with remaining 2 tablespoons melted butter. Bake 17 to 22 minutes or until light brown. Remove from cookie sheet to cooling rack; cool 5 minutes. Sprinkle powdered sugar over hot rolls. Serve warm.

1 Roll Calories 360; Total Fat 14g (Saturated Fat 8g, Trans Fat 0g); Cholesterol 90mg; Sodium 400mg; Total Carbohydrate 51g (Dietary Fiber 2g); Protein 7g **Carbohydrate Choices:** 3½

COCONUT–CHOCOLATE CHIP MALLORCAS: Prepare as directed—except in Step 4, after brushing dough with butter, sprinkle with 1 cup sweetened flaked coconut and ¼ cup miniature chocolate chips. Cut and coil as directed. Sprinkle baked rolls with powdered sugar.

No-Knead Oatmeal-Molasses Bread

No-Knead Everything Bagel Bread

BETTY CROCKER COOKBOOK

CALORIE SMART • VEGETARIAN

No-Knead Oatmeal-Molasses Bread

Cut this delicious bread into wedges to serve with soup or chili.

PREP 15 Minutes **TOTAL** 2 Hours 35 Minutes •
1 loaf (16 slices)

BREAD

1	cup very warm water (120°F to 130°F)
½	cup old-fashioned or quick-cooking oats
¼	cup light molasses
3	tablespoons shortening
1	egg
2¾	cups all-purpose flour
1	teaspoon salt
1	package (¼ oz) regular active or fast-acting dry yeast (2¼ teaspoons)

TOPPINGS

1	tablespoon old-fashioned or quick-cooking oats
½	teaspoon coarse (kosher or sea) salt

1 Grease 1½-quart round casserole with shortening or cooking spray. In large bowl, mix water, ½ cup oats, molasses, shortening and egg until well blended. In medium bowl, mix flour, salt and yeast; add to bowl with oats mixture. Beat with electric mixer, on medium speed, 2 minutes, scraping bowl frequently.

2 Spread batter evenly in casserole (batter will be sticky; smooth and pat into shape with floured hands). Sprinkle with 1 tablespoon oats and coarse salt, pressing in slightly. Cover loosely with plastic wrap. Let rise at room temperature 1 hour 30 minutes or until batter has doubled in size.

3 Heat oven to 375°F. Bake 30 to 35 minutes or until golden brown and loaf sounds hollow when tapped. (If loaf browns too quickly, cover loosely with foil during last 15 minutes of baking.) Cool casserole on cooling rack 5 minutes. Remove bread from casserole; place with rounded side up on cooling rack. Serve warm or cool.

1 Slice Calories 130; Total Fat 3g (Saturated Fat 1g, Trans Fat 0g); Cholesterol 10mg; Sodium 230mg; Total Carbohydrate 23g (Dietary Fiber 1g); Protein 3g **Carbohydrate Choices:** 1½

CALORIE SMART

No-Knead Everything Bagel Bread

PREP 15 Minutes **TOTAL** 2 Hours 55 Minutes •
1 loaf (12 slices)

3¼	to 3½ cups all-purpose flour
2	tablespoons sugar
1	teaspoon salt
1	package (¼ oz) regular active dry yeast (2¼ teaspoons)
1¼	cups very warm water (120°F to 130°F)
1	egg white, beaten
1	tablespoon everything bagel seasoning (for homemade seasoning, see page 454)
	Any flavor cream cheese spread (for homemade spreads, see page 497), if desired

1 In large bowl, mix 1½ cups of the flour, the sugar, salt and yeast. Add warm water; beat on medium speed with electric mixer until well mixed. Beat on high speed 2 minutes, scraping bowl occasionally. Stir in enough remaining flour until dough is stiff and leaves side of bowl.

2 Line cookie sheet with cooking parchment paper. Lightly flour work surface. Turn out dough onto work surface; roll dough in flour and shape into a ball; pinch seam to seal. Place loaf seam side down on cookie sheet. Cover with plastic wrap sprayed with cooking spray; let rise in warm place 45 to 60 minutes or until loaf has doubled in size.

3 Heat oven to 375°F. Brush with egg white; sprinkle with bagel seasoning. With serrated knife, carefully cut several ½-inch-deep slashes in top of dough. Bake 35 to 40 minutes, or until golden brown and loaf sounds hollow when tapped. Place loaf on cooling rack. Cool at least 30 minutes before slicing. Serve warm or cool with cream cheese spread.

1 Slice Calories 130; Total Fat 0g (Saturated Fat 0g, Trans Fat 0g); Cholesterol 0mg; Sodium 280mg; Total Carbohydrate 28g (Dietary Fiber 1g); Protein 4g **Carbohydrate Choices:** 2

RED PEPPER–FETA NO-KNEAD BREAD: Prepare as directed—except reduce water by 2 tablespoons. In Step 2, before turning out dough onto work surface, stir in ½ cup crumbled feta cheese and ½ cup diced jarred roasted red bell pepper, patted dry. In Step 3, omit bagel seasoning.

Dinner Rolls

PREP 30 Minutes **TOTAL** 2 Hours 15 Minutes • *15 rolls*

3½ to 3¾ cups all-purpose or bread flour	½ cup very warm water (120°F to 130°F)
¼ cup sugar	½ cup very warm milk (120°F to 130°F)
¼ cup butter, softened	1 egg
1 teaspoon salt	Melted butter, if desired
1 package (¼ oz) regular active or fast-acting dry yeast (2¼ teaspoons)	

1 In large bowl, stir 2 cups of the flour, the sugar, ¼ cup butter, the salt and yeast until well mixed. Add warm water, warm milk and egg. Beat with electric mixer on low speed 1 minute, scraping bowl frequently. Beat on medium speed 1 minute, scraping bowl frequently. Stir in enough remaining flour, ¼ cup at a time, to make dough easy to handle.

2 Place dough on lightly floured work surface. Knead about 5 minutes or until dough is smooth and springy. Grease large bowl with shortening. Place dough in bowl, turning dough to grease all sides. Cover bowl loosely with plastic wrap and let rise in warm place about 1 hour or until dough has doubled in size. Dough is ready if indentation remains when touched.

3 Grease bottom and sides of 13x9-inch pan with shortening or cooking spray. Gently push fist into dough to deflate. Divide dough into 15 equal pieces. Shape each piece into a ball; place in pan. Brush with melted butter. Cover loosely with plastic wrap and let rise in warm place about 30 minutes or until rolls have doubled in size.

4 Heat oven to 375°F. Uncover rolls. Bake 12 to 15 minutes or until golden brown. Serve warm if desired.

1 Roll Calories 160; Total Fat 4g (Saturated Fat 2g, Trans Fat 0g); Cholesterol 20mg; Sodium 190mg; Total Carbohydrate 26g (Dietary Fiber 1g); Protein 4g **Carbohydrate Choices:** 2

MAKE-AHEAD DIRECTIONS: After placing rolls in pan, cover tightly with foil and refrigerate 4 to 24 hours. About 2 hours before baking, remove from refrigerator; remove foil and cover loosely with plastic wrap. Let rise in warm place until rolls have doubled in size. If some rising has occurred in the refrigerator, rising time may be less than 2 hours. Bake as directed.

CLOVERLEAF ROLLS: Grease 12 regular-size muffin cups with shortening or cooking spray. Make dough as directed—except after pushing fist into dough, divide dough into 72 equal pieces. (To divide, cut dough in half, then continue cutting pieces in halves or thirds until there are 72 pieces.) Shape each piece into a ball. Place 3 balls in each muffin cup. Brush with melted butter. Cover loosely with plastic wrap and let rise in warm place about 30 minutes or until rolls have doubled in size. Bake as directed. Repeat with remaining dough. Makes 24 rolls.

CRESCENT ROLLS: Grease cookie sheet with shortening or cooking spray. Make dough as directed—except after pushing fist into dough, cut dough in half. Roll each half into 12-inch round on floured work surface. Spread with softened butter. Cut each round into 16 wedges. Roll up each wedge, beginning at rounded edge. Place rolls, with points underneath, on cookie sheet and curve slightly. Brush with melted butter. Cover loosely with plastic wrap and let rise in warm place about 30 minutes or until rolls have doubled in size. Bake as directed. Makes 32 rolls.

Dinner Rolls

MAKING DINNER ROLLS

Place dough balls slightly apart in pan so they have room to double in size.

MAKING CLOVERLEAF ROLLS

Place 3 dough balls next to each other in each muffin cup.

MAKING CRESCENT ROLLS

Cut dough circles into wedges. Roll up each wedge, beginning at rounded edge.

Easy Naan

VEGETARIAN

Easy Naan

Easy to make and very versatile, naan bread can be used in many ways! On its own, it makes a great accompaniment to soups, stews, curry or stir-fries. Or it can be the base for delicious appetizers, flatbreads and so much more. You can also purchase it in several sizes near the deli of larger grocery stores or big box stores.

PREP 20 Minutes **TOTAL** 1 Hour 20 Minutes •
4 breads (½ bread per serving)

3 cups all-purpose flour	½ cup plain yogurt
1 tablespoon sugar	About ½ to ¾ cup water
1 teaspoon salt	
½ cup milk	1 tablespoon butter, melted*
2 tablespoons vegetable oil	

1 In large bowl, mix flour, sugar and salt. Stir in milk, oil and yogurt. Stir in water, 2 tablespoons at a time, until dough forms. The dough should not be sticky or dry.

2 Knead dough in bowl or on lightly floured work surface 2 to 3 minutes or until dough becomes smooth and elastic. Brush dough lightly with some of the melted butter and cover with plastic wrap; set aside 30 minutes. (At this point, dough can be covered and refrigerated up to 24 hours. When ready to roll, let dough stand at room temperature 30 minutes so it becomes soft and easy to handle.)

3 Heat oven to 450°F. Place pizza stone on middle rack in oven to heat. Divide dough into 4 equal pieces. Shape each into a ball; brush each lightly with some of the butter.

4 Roll one piece of dough into 8-inch round or teardrop shape, about ¼ inch thick, on lightly floured work surface, taking care not to tear dough. Repeat with remaining dough.

5 Place one piece of dough on hot pizza stone. Bake 3 to 4 minutes or until brown spots form and bubbles start to appear on surface. Turn; bake 7 to 8 minutes longer. Remove bread with spatula; brush lightly with butter. Wrap bread in foil to keep warm while baking remaining dough. Cut breads in half to serve.

1 Serving Calories 230; Total Fat 6g (Saturated Fat 2g, Trans Fat 0g); Cholesterol 5mg; Sodium 330mg; Total Carbohydrate 39g (Dietary Fiber 1g); Protein 6g **Carbohydrate Choices:** 2½

*Clarified butter (page 498) can be substituted for the melted butter.

MAKING NAAN

Roll 1 piece of dough at a time into circle or teardrop shape about ¼-inch thick.

Bake dough on hot pizza stone until brown spots or bubbles begin to appear on surface. Turn; bake other side.

USE IT UP
NAAN

CAPRESE SANDWICH SLIDERS Spread mini naan dipper with pesto, top with sliced tomatoes, fresh mozzarella and basil leaves, top with another mini naan dipper. Secure with toothpicks.

CINNAMON-SUGAR FRENCH TOAST Prepare French Toast (page 117) using naan halves for the bread. Immediately after cooking, sprinkle with cinnamon-sugar. Serve with maple syrup or preserves.

DIP DIPPER Cut naan into wedges or strips; serve with hummus, veggie dips or salsa.

MEDITERRANEAN FLATBREAD Drizzle warm naan with vinaigrette. Top with chopped marinated artichoke hearts, pitted kalamata olives, red onion slivers, pear tomato halves and feta cheese; drizzle with more vinaigrette.

SOUP OR STEW SERVE-WITH Mix 1 tablespoon melted butter with 1½ teaspoons each chopped fresh parsley and grated Parmesan cheese and ¼ teaspoon garlic powder; brush over naan. Serve with your favorite soup or stew.

535

5-INGREDIENT RECIPE

All-Purpose Baking Mix

Garlic and Herb Butter Spread

Garlic & Herb BUTTER SPREAD
NET WT 8 OZ. 227g

536

ORIGINAL Bisquick PANCAKE & BAKING MIX

No colors No artificial flavors

NET WT 20 OZ (1 LB 4 OZ) 567g

Quick Sour Cream Dinner Rolls

Fast-Acting INSTANT YEAST
1/4 OZ (7g)

Fast-Acting Dry Yeast

ALL NATURAL SOUR CREAM
NET WT 8 OZ. 227g

Sour Cream

Sugar

Seasame-Garlic Cloud "Bread"

5-INGREDIENT RECIPE

CALORIE SMART

Quick Sour Cream Dinner Rolls

PREP 30 Minutes TOTAL 1 Hour 15 Minutes • *12 rolls*

- 1 cup sour cream
- 1 tablespoon sugar
- 1 package (¼ oz) fast-acting dry yeast (2¼ teaspoons)
- 2½ to 3 cups original all-purpose baking mix
- 2 tablespoons garlic and herb butter spread

1 In large microwavable bowl, microwave sour cream on High about 1 minute, stirring after 30 seconds, or until instant-read thermometer inserted in sour cream reads 110°F to 115°F. Stir in sugar and yeast until well blended.

2 Add 2½ cups of the baking mix to sour cream mixture; stir until dough pulls away from side of bowl, adding additional baking mix if needed until dough forms a sticky ball. Place dough on work surface sprinkled lightly with baking mix. Knead 5 minutes or until dough is smooth and elastic.

3 Spray bottom and sides of 8- or 9-inch square pan with cooking spray. Divide dough into 12 equal pieces. Shape each piece into a ball; place in pan. Cover loosely with plastic wrap; let rise in warm place about 30 minutes or until rolls have almost doubled in size.

4 Heat oven to 350°F. Uncover rolls. Bake 15 to 20 minutes or until golden brown. Spread tops of warm rolls with garlic and herb butter spread. Serve warm.

1 Roll Calories 160; Total Fat 9g (Saturated Fat 3.5g, Trans Fat 1g); Cholesterol 15mg; Sodium 330mg; Total Carbohydrate 19g (Dietary Fiber 0g); Protein 2g **Carbohydrate Choices:** 1

DINNER ROLL TOPPERS

Brush any unbaked rolls with melted butter (about 1 tablespoon for each 12 rolls); sprinkle with one of the following before baking.

GARLIC–PARMESAN Mix 2 tablespoons grated Parmesan cheese and ¼ teaspoon garlic powder.

PANKO–GREEN ONION Mix 2 tablespoons each plain crispy panko bread crumbs and finely chopped green onion greens.

ROSEMARY–SEA SALT Mix 2 tablespoons coarsely chopped fresh rosemary leaves and 1 teaspoon coarse sea salt.

TWO-SEED Mix 2 tablespoons each sesame seed and poppy seed.

CALORIE SMART • GLUTEN FREE

Sesame-Garlic Cloud "Bread"

PREP 15 Minutes TOTAL 1 Hour • *6 cloud breads*

- 1 tablespoon toasted sesame seed
- 1 tablespoon grated Parmesan cheese
- 1 medium green onion, sliced
- 2 cloves garlic, finely chopped
- 3 eggs, separated
- ¼ cup plain Greek yogurt
- ¼ teaspoon salt
- ¼ teaspoon gluten-free baking powder

1 Heat oven to 300°F. Line cookie sheet with cooking parchment paper. In small bowl, mix sesame seed, cheese, onion and garlic until well blended. Reserve 2 tablespoons; set aside.

2 In medium bowl, mix egg yolks, yogurt, salt, and remaining sesame seed mixture until well blended.

3 In another medium bowl, beat egg whites and baking powder with electric mixer on high speed 1 to 2 minutes or just until stiff peaks form. Fold ⅓ of the egg whites into the egg yolk mixture until no streaks remain. Repeat twice with remaining egg whites.

4 On cookie sheet, drop mixture by spoonfuls into 6 mounds, 4 inches apart. Spread each mound into 3½-inch round with back of spoon, leaving at least 1 inch between rounds; smooth rounds. Sprinkle each round with 1 teaspoon of reserved sesame seed mixture.

5 Bake about 35 minutes or until deep golden brown. Immediately remove from parchment and pan to cooling rack. Cool completely, about 10 minutes. Use as bread for sandwiches or top a single bread with jam or cream cheese.

1 Cloud Bread Calories 60; Total Fat 4g (Saturated Fat 1.5g, Trans Fat 0g); Cholesterol 95mg; Sodium 170mg; Total Carbohydrate 2g (Dietary Fiber 0g); Protein 4g **Carbohydrate Choices:** 0

HONEY LEMON POPPY SEED CLOUD "BREAD": Prepare as directed—except omit sesame seed, green onion, Parmesan cheese and garlic. Stir in 1 tablespoon honey, 1 tablespoon poppy seed and 1 tablespoon lemon zest into egg yolks and yogurt. Prepare as directed—except sprinkle breads with additional poppy seed before baking.

Garlic-Herb Roadhouse Rolls

PREP 30 Minutes **TOTAL** 2 Hours 30 Minutes • *12 rolls*

ROLLS

3½ to 4 cups all-purpose flour
1 package (¼ oz) regular active or fast-acting dry yeast (2¼ teaspoons)
¼ cup sugar
1 teaspoon salt
2 teaspoons chopped fresh basil leaves
1 teaspoon chopped fresh thyme leaves
½ teaspoon chopped fresh rosemary leaves
¼ teaspoon garlic powder
1 cup milk
¼ cup water
3 tablespoons butter
2 tablespoons honey
1 egg
1 tablespoon butter, melted

GARLIC-HERB BUTTER

½ cup butter, softened
½ teaspoon chopped fresh basil leaves
½ teaspoon chopped fresh thyme leaves
¼ teaspoon chopped fresh rosemary leaves
¼ teaspoon garlic powder

1 In large bowl, mix 1½ cups of the flour, the yeast, sugar, salt, 2 teaspoons basil, 1 teaspoon thyme, ½ teaspoon rosemary and ¼ teaspoon garlic powder. In 1-quart saucepan, heat milk, water, 3 tablespoons butter and the honey over medium heat until very warm (120°F to 130°F). Pour over flour mixture. Add egg; beat with electric mixer on low speed 1 minute, scraping bowl frequently. Add enough of the remaining 2 to 2½ cups flour, about ½ cup at a time, beating on medium speed 5 minutes, until dough is smooth. (Dough will be slightly sticky.)

2 Grease large bowl with shortening or cooking spray. Place dough in bowl, turning dough to grease all sides. Cover loosely with plastic wrap and clean dish towel; let rise in warm place 1 hour or until doubled in size.

3 Line 2 cookie sheets with cooking parchment paper. Gently push fist into dough to deflate. On floured work surface, roll dough into 12x9-inch rectangle, about ½-inch thick. Using floured pizza cutter, cut dough into 12 (3-inch) squares. On cookie sheets, place dough squares 2 inches apart. Cover loosely with plastic wrap; let rise in warm place 30 to 40 minutes or until rolls have doubled in size.

4 Heat oven to 350°F. Uncover rolls; bake 15 to 20 minutes or until golden brown. Brush with melted butter. Remove from cookie sheets to cooling rack.

5 In small bowl, beat all garlic-herb butter ingredients with electric mixer until well blended. Serve with warm rolls.

1 Roll Calories 280; Total Fat 13g (Saturated Fat 8g, Trans Fat 0g); Cholesterol 50mg; Sodium 300mg; Total Carbohydrate 36g (Dietary Fiber 1g); Protein 5g **Carbohydrate Choices:** 2½

MAKE-AHEAD DIRECTIONS: Make these rolls up to 3 months in advance. For that just-baked aroma and texture, store cooled baked rolls in freezer in resealable freezer plastic bags. To reheat, remove rolls from bag; wrap in foil. Bake at 350°F for 15 to 20 minutes or until warm.

Garlic-Herb Roadhouse Rolls and Jalapeño Hawaiian Rolls

Jalapeño Hawaiian Rolls

PREP 35 Minutes **TOTAL** 2 Hours 25 Minutes • *24 rolls*

3½ to 4½ cups all-purpose flour

⅓ cup pineapple juice

¼ cup packed brown sugar

1 teaspoon salt

1 package (¼ oz) regular active or fast-acting dry yeast (2¼ teaspoons)

½ cup milk

¼ cup butter

2 tablespoons water

1 egg

1 cup shredded cheddar or pepper Jack cheese (4 oz)

½ cup chopped red bell pepper

2 tablespoons chopped seeded jalapeño chiles (about 2 medium)

1 tablespoon butter, melted

1 tablespoon pineapple juice

1 In large bowl, stir 2 cups of the flour, ⅓ cup pineapple juice, the brown sugar, salt and yeast with spoon until well mixed. In 1-quart saucepan, heat milk, ¼ cup butter and the water over medium heat, stirring frequently, until very warm (120°F to 130°F). Add milk mixture and egg to flour mixture. Beat with electric mixer on low speed 1 minute, scraping bowl frequently, until flour mixture is moistened. Beat on medium speed 1 minute. Stir in cheese, bell pepper, chiles and enough of remaining 1½ to 2½ cups flour, about ½ cup at a time, until dough is smooth, leaves side of bowl and is easy to handle (dough may be slightly sticky).

2 On lightly floured work surface, knead dough about 5 minutes until smooth and elastic (sprinkle work surface with more flour if dough starts to stick). Grease large bowl with shortening or cooking spray. Place dough in bowl, turning dough to grease all sides. Cover loosely with plastic wrap and clean dish towel; let rise in warm place about 1 hour or until doubled in size.

3 Spray 24 regular-size muffin cups with cooking spray. Gently punch fist into dough to deflate. Divide dough into 24 pieces. Using floured fingers, shape each piece into a ball, pulling edges under and pinching to seal. Place balls, pinched-sides down, in muffin cups. Cover loosely; let rise in warm place about 30 minutes or until rolls have doubled in size.

4 Heat oven to 375°F. Uncover rolls; bake 15 to 18 minutes or until golden brown. Remove from pan to cooling rack.

5 In small bowl, mix melted butter and 1 tablespoon pineapple juice. Brush over tops of rolls. Serve warm or cool.

1 Roll Calories 120; Total Fat 4.5g (Saturated Fat 2.5g, Trans Fat 0g); Cholesterol 20mg; Sodium 150mg; Total Carbohydrate 17g (Dietary Fiber 0g); Protein 3g **Carbohydrate Choices:** 1

MAKE-AHEAD DIRECTIONS: Cool rolls completely after baking and place in a resealable freezer plastic bag. Seal bag and freeze up to 3 months. To reheat, remove frozen rolls from bag; wrap in foil. Bake at 350°F for 15 to 20 minutes or until warm.

CREATIVE USES FOR JALAPEÑO HAWAIIAN ROLLS

A flavorful buddy to just about any meal—but don't stop there! Try one of these other tasty ways of using these delicious rolls:

- **Breakfast Sandwiches** Fill roll halves with scrambled eggs, cooked breakfast sausage and cheese.

- **Chili Toppers** Place on top of bowls of piping hot chili, just before serving.

- **Snacking Sliders** Fill with your favorite deli meat and cheese; wrap in foil and bake at 350°F about 15 minutes or until heated through.

- **Spicy Chicken Sandwiches** Fill roll halves with chipotle mayo, your favorite heated chicken nuggets and sliced pepper Jack cheese.

BETTY CROCKER COOKBOOK

Cookies, Bars & Candies

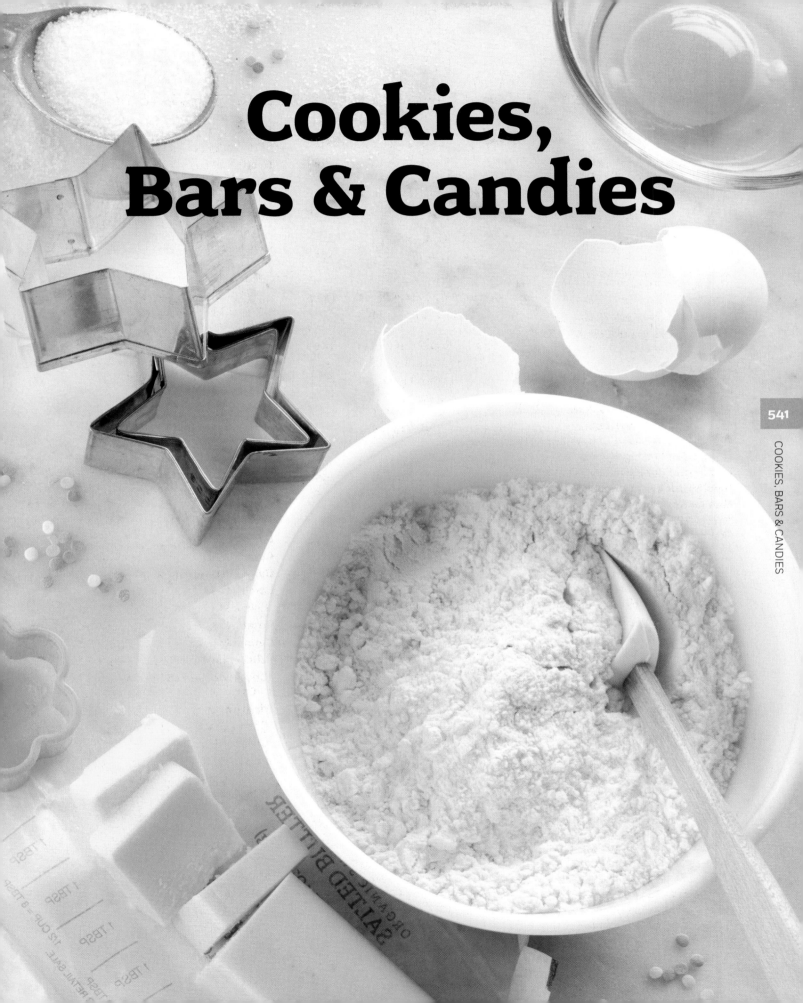

Cookie & Bar Basics

Freshly baked homemade cookies are simply irresistible ... seriously, who can say no to one of these sweet treats? Cookies are easy to make and a great place for beginner bakers to start. No matter what your baking experience, knowing all the secrets to perfectly baked cookies will up your baking game.

Cookie Sheets

- Choose cookie sheets that are at least 2 inches smaller than the inside of your oven to allow heat to circulate.

- Cookie sheets may be open on one to three sides. Jelly roll pans (15x10x1 inch) have four sides; if used for cookies, the cookies may not brown as evenly.

- Owning at least two cookie sheets is helpful. When one batch is baking, you can prepare the second batch for the oven.

SUCCESSFUL BAKING ON ANY TYPE OF COOKIE SHEET

SHINY ALUMINUM The best cookie sheets are shiny aluminum with a smooth surface. They reflect heat, letting cookies bake evenly and brown properly. The recipes in this book were tested using shiny aluminum cookie sheets.

NONSTICK AND DARK SURFACE Cookies baked on these cookie sheets may be smaller in diameter and more rounded. The tops and especially the bottoms will be more browned, and the bottoms will be hard. Check cookies at the minimum bake time and then add time as necessary, to avoid overbrowning and burning. Follow manufacturer's directions; some recommend reducing the oven temperature by 25°F.

INSULATED These cookie sheets help prevent cookies from becoming too dark on the bottom. Cookies baked on these sheets may take longer to bake; the bottoms will be light colored, and the cookies may not brown as much overall. Cookies may be difficult to remove from these cookie sheets because the bottoms of the cookies are more tender.

Choosing Pans for Bars

- Use the exact size of pan called for in the recipe when baking bars. Bars made in pans that are too big become hard and overcooked, and those made in pans that are too small can be doughy and raw in the center and hard at the edges.

- Shiny metal pans are recommended for baking bars. They reflect heat and prevent the bottom from getting too brown and hard. Follow the same guidelines as for nonstick and dark-surface cookie sheets (at left).

GREASING COOKIE SHEETS AND PANS FOR BARS

- Line baking pans for bars with foil for super-easy cleanup and ease in cutting. Turn pan upside down; smooth a piece of foil that's larger than the pan over the bottom and sides of pan; then remove foil.

- Flip the pan over and gently fit the shaped foil into the pan. When the bars are cool, lift them out of the pan using the edges of the foil as handles. Peel back the foil and cut bars as directed.

- Grease pans only when a recipe calls for it. Grease cookie sheets with vegetable shortening or cooking spray. Unless the recipe directs, do not use butter, margarine or oil because the area between the cookies can burn during baking.

- Don't grease nonstick cookie sheets, as the cookies can spread too much.

- As an alternative to greasing, line cookie sheets with parchment paper or reusable silicone baking mats.

Choosing the Right Ingredients

FLOUR All-purpose flour is recommended for cookies and bars. **Whole wheat flour** can also be used; if the recipe doesn't specifically call for it, only substitute it for one-third to one-half the amount of all-purpose flour, to keep the cookies from becoming too dry. **White whole wheat flour** is also available. It has the same nutritional benefits as whole wheat flour but with a lighter color and milder flavor than regular whole wheat. Experiment with substituting some or all white whole wheat flour for all-purpose flour in your cookie and bar recipes. For more information on flour and how to measure it correctly, see Measuring Correctly, page 25.

SWEETENERS In addition to adding sweetness, sugar helps browning and adds tenderness to baked goods.

LEAVENINGS Cookies and bars usually call for baking powder or baking soda, which are not interchangeable. For more information, see Baking Ingredients, page 9.

FATS AND OILS Fats add tenderness and flavor to cookies and bars, but they are not all equal. For best results, use butter; use shortening only if the recipe calls for it. If you choose to use margarine, use only products with at least 65% fat. Any other spreads or reduced-fat products contain more water, resulting in cookies that are soft, tough and puffy.

TO SOFTEN BUTTER Soften it at room temperature in 30 to 40 minutes. Or to soften it in the microwave, see Microwave Cooking and Heating chart, page 33. If the butter is too soft or at all melted, the dough will be too soft, causing the cookies to spread too much. See Learn with Betty, below.

EGGS Added for richness, moisture and structure to cookies and bars. All the recipes in this book were tested with large eggs. Egg products, made of egg whites, can be substituted for whole eggs, but the cookies and bars may be dry.

LIQUIDS Water, fruit juice, cream or milk tend to make cookies crisper by causing them to spread more. Add only as much liquid as the recipe calls for.

OATS Quick-cooking and old-fashioned oats are interchangeable unless a recipe calls for a specific type. Instant oatmeal products are not the same as quick-cooking oats and should not be used for baking.

NUTS, PEANUTS AND TOFFEE BITS When a recipe calls for nuts, feel free to substitute any variety of nut or peanuts. Nuts and milk chocolate toffee bits can easily become rancid, giving them an unpleasant, strong flavor that can ruin the taste of cookies. Always taste them before using. See page 37 for nut storage information. Store toffee bits in the refrigerator or freezer up to 6 months.

BAKE A TEST COOKIE

Before baking an entire sheet of cookies and not liking the results, bake just one cookie as directed in the recipe to see how it performs. Before baking the entire batch, make the needed adjustments to the remaining dough: **If the cookie is too flat**, add 1 to 2 tablespoons of flour to the dough, or refrigerate the dough 1 to 2 hours before baking. **If the cookie is too round or hard**, add 1 to 2 tablespoons milk to the dough.

Mixing

You can use a spoon or an electric mixer when mixing cookie or bar dough for most recipes in this book. The sugars, fats and liquids are usually beaten together first until well mixed. Flour and other ingredients are almost always stirred in by hand to avoid overmixing the dough, which can result in tough cookies.

LEARN WITH BETTY SOFTENING BUTTER

Ideal Softened Butter
Soft but not melted, still holding its shape; retains an indent when touched. It is ideal for baked goods calling for softened butter.

Overly Softened Butter
Too soft, with some melting; leaves a hole when touched. Cookie doughs made with this butter will be too soft, causing the baked cookies to be flat.

Insufficiently Softened Butter Not soft enough; does not retain an indent when touched. Hard to mix into cookie dough evenly, causing dough to be too stiff and the baked cookies to be too round and hard, with holes inside.

Tips for Perfect Cookies and Bars

- Use completely cooled cookie sheets, as cookies will spread too much if dough is placed on a warm or hot cookie sheet.

- Make cookies all the same size so they bake evenly. (See Cookie Scoop Sizes, below.)

- Bake cookies and bars in the middle of the oven. For even baking, bake one sheet at a time. If you do bake two sheets at one time, position oven racks as close to the middle of the oven as possible and rotate the position of the sheets halfway through baking.

- Wherever possible, Betty Crocker recipes give a doneness cue as well as time to determine when you're done cooking or baking. Set your timer for the minimum bake time on the cookie or bar recipe. When the timer rings, check for the doneness cue on the recipe (such as "until set" or "until golden brown"). If the doneness cue hasn't happened yet, then bake the cookies a minute or two longer or until the doneness cue happens.

- Cool cookies as directed. Use a flat, thin metal spatula to remove cookies from the baking sheet to a cooling rack.

- Cool bars and brownies in the pan on a cooling rack.

- Use a plastic knife to cut brownies and soft, sticky bars such as Lemon Bars (page 566) for the nicest edges, as well as to prevent pans from getting scratched by a metal knife.

Cookie Scoop Sizes

To get your cookies looking like they came from a bakery (all the same size and a uniform shape), you can use cookie scoops. They cut down on the time it takes to measure the dough and also ensure you get the yield indicated on the recipe, whether they are dropped onto the cookie sheet or the dough is then formed into balls before baking.

Scoops come in various sizes, and are referred to by number: the larger the number, the smaller the scoop. Scoops can vary by manufacturer, so measure the volume by first filling it with water and then measuring the water, to see how much the scoop holds.

AMOUNT OF COOKIE DOUGH	SCOOP SIZE	DOUGH BALL SIZE
¼ cup	16	
Rounded tablespoon	50	1¼ inch
Level tablespoon	70	1 inch
Rounded teaspoon	100	¾ inch

REMOVING STUCK COOKIES

If cookies are difficult to remove from the cookie sheet because they were left to cool too long, put the cookie sheet with the cookies back in the oven for 1 to 2 minutes. They should then come off easily.

Storing Cookies and Bars

- **Crisp cookies** Store at room temperature in loosely covered containers.

- **Chewy and soft cookies** Store at room temperature in resealable food-storage plastic bags or tightly covered containers.

- **Frosted or decorated cookies** Let set or harden before storing; store by placing cookies between layers of parchment or waxed paper, plastic wrap or foil.

- Store only one type of cookie in a container to keep the texture and flavor intact. If different types of cookies are stored in the same container, they can transfer moisture to one another, making crisp cookies soft; they can also pick up flavors from one another.

- **Bars** Most bars can be stored in pan, tightly covered, which is particularly helpful for frosted bars that should be stored in a single layer. But follow specific recipe directions, as some may need to be stored loosely covered or refrigerated.

- For general directions on freezing and thawing cookies and bars, see the Refrigerator and Freezer Food Storage Chart, page 36. Do not freeze meringue, or custard- or cream-filled cookies.

BAKING COCOA

When a recipe calls for cocoa, it means unsweetened baking cocoa, not hot chocolate products, which are sweetened and contain additional ingredients. Three types of baking cocoa are available:

Regular (nonalkalized) is the most commonly available, and used in most recipes calling for cocoa.

Dutch or **European (alkalized)** goes through a process called Dutching to neutralize the natural acids found in cocoa, resulting in a darker color and a more mellow chocolate flavor. Regular cocoa can be substituted for Dutch, but don't substitute Dutch in recipes calling for regular cocoa, because the leavening in the recipe may not work well with it, affecting rising.

Dark is a blend of regular and Dutch cocoas. It can be substituted for regular baking cocoa in recipes, but the baked goods will have a darker color and more intense flavor; depending on the amount of Dutch cocoa the dark cocoa contains, the baked goods may be lower in volume.

Iced Oatmeal-Raisin Cookies

Chocolate Crinkles

CALORIE SMART • VEGETARIAN

Oatmeal-Raisin Cookies

Quick-cooking and old-fashioned rolled oats are interchangeable unless a recipe calls for a specific type. Instant oatmeal products contain sugar and other added ingredients, and should not be used for baking.

PREP 15 Minutes **TOTAL** 50 Minutes • *3 dozen cookies*

⅔ cup granulated sugar	1 teaspoon ground cinnamon
⅔ cup packed brown sugar	½ teaspoon baking powder
½ cup butter, softened	½ teaspoon salt
½ cup vegetable shortening	3 cups quick-cooking or old-fashioned oats
1 teaspoon vanilla	1⅓ cups all-purpose flour
2 eggs	1 cup raisins
1 teaspoon baking soda	½ cup chopped nuts, if desired

1 Heat oven to 375°F.

2 In large bowl, beat granulated sugar, brown sugar, butter, shortening, vanilla and eggs with electric mixer on medium speed, or mix with spoon, until well blended. Beat or stir in baking soda, cinnamon, baking powder and salt. Stir in oats, flour, raisins and nuts.

3 Onto each of two ungreased cookie sheets, form 12 dough mounds by dropping dough by rounded tablespoonfuls, about 2 inches apart.

4 Bake one cookie sheet 9 to 11 minutes or until light brown. Immediately remove cookies from cookie sheet to cooling rack. Repeat with second cookie sheet.

5 Onto completely cooled cookie sheet, prepare remaining dough as directed in Step 3. Bake cookies as directed in Step 4.

1 Cookie Calories 140; Total Fat 6g (Saturated Fat 2.5g, Trans Fat 0g); Cholesterol 15mg; Sodium 100mg; Total Carbohydrate 19g (Dietary Fiber 1g); Protein 2g **Carbohydrate Choices:** 1

OATMEAL–CHOCOLATE CHIP COOKIES: Substitute 1 cup semisweet chocolate chips for the raisins.

ICED OATMEAL-RAISIN COOKIES: In medium bowl, beat 2 cups powdered sugar, 3 tablespoons melted butter, 2 tablespoons milk and ½ teaspoon vanilla until smooth and spreadable. Spread frosting on cooled cookies. Let stand about 30 minutes or until frosting is set. Store in airtight container.

CALORIE SMART • VEGETARIAN

Chocolate Crinkles

PREP 45 Minutes **TOTAL** 5 Hours • *3 dozen cookies*

2 cups granulated sugar	4 eggs
½ cup vegetable oil	2 cups all-purpose flour
2 teaspoons vanilla	2 teaspoons baking powder
4 oz unsweetened baking chocolate, melted, cooled	½ teaspoon salt
	¾ cup powdered sugar

1 In large bowl, stir granulated sugar, oil, vanilla and chocolate until well blended. Stir in eggs, one at a time, until well mixed. Stir in flour, baking powder and salt. Cover and refrigerate at least 3 hours.

2 Heat oven to 350°F. Grease two cookie sheets with vegetable shortening or cooking spray, or line with cooking parchment paper or silicone baking mat.

3 In small bowl, place powdered sugar. Drop dough by rounded tablespoonfuls into powdered sugar; roll around to coat. Shape into balls. Onto cookie sheets, place 12 balls about 2 inches apart.

4 Bake one cookie sheet 11 to 13 minutes or until almost no indent remains when touched in center. Immediately remove cookies from cookie sheet to cooling racks. Repeat with second cookie sheet.

5 Onto completely cooled cookie sheets, prepare and place remaining dough as directed in Step 3. Bake cookies as directed in Step 4.

1 Cookie Calories 140; Total Fat 5g (Saturated Fat 1.5g, Trans Fat 0g); Cholesterol 20mg; Sodium 70mg; Total Carbohydrate 20g (Dietary Fiber 0g); Protein 2g **Carbohydrate Choices:** 1

HEIRLOOM AND → NEW TWIST

HEIRLOOM

MAKE AHEAD • CALORIE SMART • VEGETARIAN

Favorite Chocolate Chip Cookies

This all-time favorite recipe makes a lot of cookies . . . but once you try them, you'll know why—they won't last long! You can store baked and cooled cookies in resealable freezer plastic bags for up to 2 months, taking out the number of cookies you want at a time. Or if you love freshly baked cookies, see the directions below for freezing the dough.

PREP 20 Minutes **TOTAL** 1 Hour 40 Minutes •

About 6 dozen cookies

1½ cups butter, softened	2 teaspoons baking soda
1¼ cups granulated sugar	½ teaspoon salt
1¼ cups packed brown sugar	1 bag (24 oz) semisweet chocolate chips (4 cups)
1 tablespoon vanilla	
2 eggs	
4 cups all-purpose flour	

1 Heat oven to 350°F.

2 In large bowl, beat butter, granulated sugar, brown sugar, vanilla and eggs with electric mixer on medium speed, or with spoon, until light and fluffy. Stir in flour, baking soda and salt. (Dough will be stiff.) Stir in chocolate chips.

3 Onto each of two ungreased cookie sheets, form 12 dough mounds by dropping dough by rounded tablespoonfuls, about 2 inches apart; flatten slightly

4 Bake one cookie sheet 11 to 13 minutes or until light brown; centers will be soft. Cool 1 to 2 minutes; remove from cookie sheet to cooling rack. Repeat with second cookie sheet.

5 Onto completely cooled cookie sheets, prepare remaining dough as directed in Step 3. Bake cookies as directed in Step 4.

Favorite Chocolate Chip Cookies

1 Cookie Calories 140; Total Fat 7g (Saturated Fat 4g, Trans Fat 0g); Cholesterol 15mg; Sodium 85mg; Total Carbohydrate 18g (Dietary Fiber 0g); Protein 1g **Carbohydrate Choices:** 1

PEANUT BUTTER CHOCOLATE CHIP COOKIES:
Make as directed—except substitute 2 cups of candy-coated peanut butter milk chocolate candies or peanut butter baking chips for 2 cups of the chocolate chips.

MAKE-AHEAD DIRECTIONS: Line cookie sheets with cooking parchment paper. Shape dough as directed in Step 2 on parchment-lined cookie sheets. Freeze uncovered 1 hour or until firm. Place frozen cookie dough balls in resealable freezer plastic bags; seal bag. Freeze up to 3 months. When ready to bake, bake as directed.

LEARN WITH BETTY MAKING CHOCOLATE CHIP COOKIES

Ideal Cookie Slightly rounded on top and evenly golden brown.

Flat Cookie Butter was too soft or partially melted, too little flour was used or cookie sheet was hot when dough was placed on it.

Round or Hard Cookie Butter wasn't soft, too much flour was used and/or cookie was overbaked.

CALORIE SMART • VEGETARIAN

Samoa-Style Chocolate Chip Shortbread Cookies

PREP 50 Minutes **TOTAL** 3 Hours 40 Minutes •
3 dozen cookies

1 cup butter, softened	1 bag (11 oz) caramel bits
½ cup packed brown sugar	¼ cup whipping cream
1 egg yolk	2 cups coconut, toasted (see page 28)
1 teaspoon vanilla	⅔ cup 60% cacao bittersweet chocolate chips (from 10-oz bag)
2¼ cups all-purpose flour	
¼ teaspoon salt	
½ cup miniature semisweet chocolate chips	

1 Heat oven to 350°F.

2 In large bowl, beat butter, brown sugar, egg yolk and vanilla with electric mixer at medium speed until light and fluffy. Add flour and salt; mix on low speed until soft dough forms. Add semisweet chocolate chips; mix on low speed until mixed.

3 Shape dough into 1¼-inch balls. Onto each of two ungreased cookie sheets, place 12 balls about 3 inches apart. Flatten balls to ½-inch thickness.

4 Bake one cookie sheet 10 to 12 minutes or until edges just begin to brown. Cool 5 minutes; remove from cookie sheet to cooling rack. Repeat with second cookie sheet.

5 Onto completely cooled cookie sheet, place remaining balls as directed in Step 3. Bake cookies as directed in Step 4. Cool cookies completely, about 10 minutes.

6 In medium microwavable bowl, mix caramel bits and whipping cream. Microwave uncovered on High 1 to 2 minutes, stirring every 30 seconds, or until mixture can be stirred smooth. Fold in coconut. Spoon and spread about 1 tablespoon of coconut mixture on top of each cookie. (If caramel mixture becomes too stiff, microwave uncovered on High 15 to 30 seconds.)

7 In small microwavable bowl, place bittersweet chocolate chips. Microwave uncovered on High about 1 minute, stirring every 30 seconds, or until chips can be stirred smooth. Slide piece of cooking parchment paper under cooling rack with cookies. Dip fork in chocolate; drizzle over cookies. Let stand until chocolate is set, about 2 hours. Store in tightly covered container with cooking parchment or waxed paper between layers at room temperature.

1 Cookie Calories 190; Total Fat 10g (Saturated Fat 7g, Trans Fat 0g); Cholesterol 20mg; Sodium 95mg; Total Carbohydrate 22g (Dietary Fiber 0g); Protein 1g **Carbohydrate Choices:** 1½

Samoa-Style Chocolate Chip Shortbread Cookies

Peanut Butter Cookies

PREP 20 Minutes **TOTAL** 55 Minutes • *2½ dozen cookies*

½ cup granulated sugar	1¼ cups all-purpose flour
½ cup packed brown sugar	¾ teaspoon baking soda
½ cup creamy or crunchy peanut butter	½ teaspoon baking powder
½ cup butter, softened	¼ teaspoon salt
1 egg	Additional granulated sugar

1 Heat oven to 375°F.

2 In large bowl, beat ½ cup granulated sugar, the brown sugar, peanut butter, butter and egg with electric mixer on medium speed, or mix with spoon, until well blended. Stir in flour, baking soda, baking powder and salt.

MAKING PEANUT BUTTER COOKIES

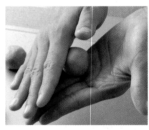 

Shape dough into balls by rolling between hands; place on cookie sheet.

Flatten balls in crisscross pattern with fork dipped in sugar.

Peanut Butter Cookies

3 Shape dough into 1¼-inch balls. Onto each of two ungreased cookie sheets, place 12 balls about 3 inches apart. Flatten in crisscross pattern with fork dipped in additional granulated sugar.

4 Bake one cookie sheet 9 to 10 minutes or until light brown. Cool 5 minutes; remove from cookie sheet to cooling rack. Repeat with second cookie sheet.

5 Onto completely cooled cookie sheet, shape, place and flatten remaining dough as directed in Step 3. Bake cookies as directed in Step 4.

1 Cookie Calories 110; Total Fat 6g (Saturated Fat 1.5g, Trans Fat 0g); Cholesterol 10mg; Sodium 95mg; Total Carbohydrate 13g (Dietary Fiber 0g); Protein 2g **Carbohydrate Choices:** 1

RICH PEANUT BUTTER CHIP COOKIES: Omit ½ cup granulated sugar; increase brown sugar to 1 cup. After stirring in flour, baking soda, baking powder and salt, stir in 1 cup peanut butter chips. Shape dough into balls as directed. Dip tops of balls into granulated sugar, but do not flatten. Bake as directed.

CALORIE SMART • GLUTEN FREE • VEGETARIAN

Espresso Turtle Thumbprint Cookies

PREP 50 Minutes **TOTAL** 1 Hour 40 Minutes • *2 dozen cookies*

½ cup sugar	½ teaspoon salt
½ cup butter, softened	¾ cup pecans, very finely chopped
1 egg	¾ cup caramel bits (from 11 oz bag)
1 teaspoon vanilla	
2¼ cups almond flour	1 tablespoon plus 1½ teaspoons whipping cream
3 tablespoons unsweetened baking cocoa	
2 teaspoons instant espresso powder	⅓ cup semisweet chocolate chips

1 Heat oven to 350°F.

2 In large bowl, beat sugar and butter with electric mixer on medium speed, or mix with spoon, until well blended. Add egg and vanilla; mix well. Add almond flour, cocoa, espresso powder and salt; mix until soft dough forms.

3 In shallow bowl, place pecans. Shape dough into 1¼-inch balls (dough will be sticky). Roll each ball in pecans until evenly coated. Onto each of two ungreased cookie sheets, place 12 balls about 2 inches apart. Press thumb into center of each cookie to make indent, but do not press all the way to the cookie sheet.

4 Bake one cookie sheet 11 to 12 minutes or until cookies are set when touched. Gently remake indents with end of wooden spoon handle. Cool 5 minutes; remove from cookie sheet to cooling rack. Repeat with second cookie sheet. Cool cookies completely, about 10 minutes.

5 In small microwavable bowl, place caramel bits and whipping cream. Microwave uncovered on High about 1 minute, stirring after 30 seconds, or until mixture can be stirred smooth. Fill each indent with about ½ teaspoon caramel mixture.

6 In another small microwavable bowl, place chocolate chips. Microwave uncovered on High about 1 minute, stirring after 30 seconds, or until chips can be stirred smooth. Place in small resealable food-storage plastic bag; seal bag. With scissors, snip one tiny corner off bag. Squeeze bag to drizzle chocolate over cookies. Refrigerate cookies about 15 minutes or until drizzle is set. Store in tightly covered container with cooking parchment or waxed paper between layers at room temperature.

1 Cookie Calories 190; Total Fat 14g (Saturated Fat 4.5g, Trans Fat 0g); Cholesterol 20mg; Sodium 100mg; Total Carbohydrate 14g (Dietary Fiber 2g); Protein 3g **Carbohydrate Choices:** 1

CALORIE SMART • VEGETARIAN

Gingersnaps

PREP 20 Minutes **TOTAL** 1 Hour 20 Minutes •

4 dozen cookies

1	cup packed brown sugar	1	teaspoon ground cinnamon
¾	cup vegetable shortening	1	teaspoon ground ginger
¼	cup molasses	½	teaspoon ground cloves
1	egg	¼	teaspoon salt
2¼	cups all-purpose flour		Granulated sugar
2	teaspoons baking soda		

1 Heat oven to 375°F. Lightly grease two cookie sheets with vegetable shortening or cooking spray, or line with cooking parchment paper or silicone baking mats.

2 In large bowl, beat brown sugar, shortening, molasses and egg with electric mixer on medium speed, or mix with spoon, until well blended. Stir in remaining ingredients except granulated sugar.

3 Shape dough by rounded teaspoonfuls into 1-inch balls. Dip tops into granulated sugar. Onto each cookie sheet, place 12 balls, sugared side up, about 3 inches apart.

4 Bake one cookie sheet 10 to 12 minutes or just until set. Immediately remove from cookie sheet to cooling rack. Repeat with second cookie sheet.

5 Onto completely cooled cookie sheets, prepare and place remaining dough as directed in Step 3. Bake cookies as directed in Step 4.

1 Cookie Calories 80; Total Fat 3.5g (Saturated Fat 1g, Trans Fat 0.5g); Cholesterol 0mg; Sodium 70mg; Total Carbohydrate 11g (Dietary Fiber 0g); Protein 0g **Carbohydrate Choices:** 1

549

Espresso Turtle Thumbprint Cookies

Gingersnaps

Almond Butter Blossoms

Soft No-Roll Sugar Cookies

CALORIE SMART • VEGETARIAN

Almond Butter Blossoms

We like to use chopped whole almonds with skin on to give an attractive look to the cookies. Almonds can be chopped by hand if you prefer a coarser look, or you can use a food processor if you prefer a more finely chopped look.

PREP 35 Minutes **TOTAL** 3 Hours 25 Minutes •
5 dozen cookies

½ cup creamy almond butter	½ teaspoon baking powder
½ cup butter, softened	¼ teaspoon salt
½ cup granulated sugar	2 egg whites
½ cup packed brown sugar	1½ cups whole almonds, chopped
1 egg	60 milk chocolate candy drops, unwrapped (from 10.8-oz bag)
1½ cups all-purpose flour	
¾ teaspoon baking soda	

1 Heat oven to 375°F.

2 In large bowl, beat almond butter, butter, granulated sugar, brown sugar and 1 egg with electric mixer on medium speed, or mix with spoon, until well blended. Stir in flour, baking soda, baking powder and salt.

3 Shape dough into 1-inch balls. In small bowl, beat 2 egg whites lightly with fork. Place chopped almonds in another small bowl. Dip each ball into egg white, then roll in almonds. Onto each of two ungreased cookie sheets, place 12 balls about 2 inches apart.

4 Bake one cookie sheet 8 to 10 minutes or until edges are light golden brown. Cool 1 minute, then press 1 milk chocolate candy in center of each cookie. Remove from cookie sheet to cooling rack. Repeat with second cookie sheet.

5 Onto completely cooled cookie sheets continue placing and baking balls as directed in Steps 3 and 4 until all balls are baked. Cool completely, about 2 hours or until chocolate candy is set.

1 Cookie Calories 100; Total Fat 6g (Saturated Fat 2g, Trans Fat 0g); Cholesterol 10mg; Sodium 55mg; Total Carbohydrate 10g (Dietary Fiber 1g); Protein 2g **Carbohydrate Choices:** ½

CALORIE SMART • VEGETARIAN

Soft No-Roll Sugar Cookies

PREP 25 Minutes **TOTAL** 3 Hours 25 Minutes •
3½ dozen cookies

1½ cups granulated sugar	4¼ cups all-purpose or white whole wheat flour
1 cup powdered sugar	
1 cup butter, softened	1 teaspoon baking soda
¾ cup vegetable oil	1 teaspoon cream of tartar
2 tablespoons milk	½ teaspoon salt
1 tablespoon vanilla	
2 eggs	

1 In large bowl, beat 1 cup of the granulated sugar, the powdered sugar, butter, oil, milk, vanilla and eggs with electric mixer on medium speed, or mix with spoon, until well blended. Stir in flour, baking soda, cream of tartar and salt. Cover and refrigerate about 2 hours or until firm.

2 Heat oven to 350°F.

3 Shape dough into 1½-inch balls. In small bowl, place remaining ½ cup granulated sugar. Roll balls in sugar. Onto each of two ungreased cookie sheets, place 12 balls about 3 inches apart. Press bottom of drinking glass on each ball until about ¼ inch thick. Sprinkle each cookie with a little additional granulated sugar.

4 Bake one cookie sheet 13 to 15 minutes or until cookies are set and edges just begin to turn brown. Immediately remove cookies from cookie sheet to cooling rack. Repeat with second cookie sheet.

5 Onto completely cooled cookie sheets, prepare and place remaining dough as directed in Step 3. Bake cookies as directed in Step 4.

1 Cookie Calories 160; Total Fat 9g (Saturated Fat 3g, Trans Fat 0g); Cholesterol 20mg; Sodium 90mg; Total Carbohydrate 20g (Dietary Fiber 0g); Protein 2g **Carbohydrate Choices:** 1

CHOCOLATE CHIP, CHERRY AND PISTACHIO SOFT NO-ROLL SUGAR COOKIES: Stir 1 cup semisweet chocolate chips, ½ cup dried cherries and ½ cup pistachio nuts into dough before refrigerating.

GLAZED SOFT NO-ROLL SUGAR COOKIES: After cooling, drizzle cookies with Chocolate Glaze (page 603). Let stand until set.

Ginger, Walnut and White Chocolate Chip Cookies

Crystallized ginger comes in different packages and shapes. It can be found in jars in the spice aisle, in packages in the produce section or sometimes in bulk bins.

PREP 10 Minutes **TOTAL** 25 Minutes • *1 dozen cookies*

6 tablespoons butter, softened	¼ teaspoon salt
¼ cup granulated sugar	4 tablespoons finely chopped crystalized ginger
¼ cup packed brown sugar	3 tablespoons white vanilla baking chips
¼ teaspoon vanilla	
1 egg white	3 tablespoons chopped walnuts
1 cup all-purpose flour	
¼ teaspoon baking soda	

1 Heat oven to 350°F.

2 In medium bowl, beat butter, granulated sugar and brown sugar with spoon until creamy. Stir in vanilla and egg white until well mixed. Stir in flour, baking soda and salt. Stir in 3 tablespoons of the crystallized ginger, the white vanilla chips and walnuts.

3 Onto ungreased large cookie sheet, drop dough by rounded tablespoonfuls about 2 inches apart. Flatten slightly; sprinkle with remaining ginger.

4 Bake 10 to 13 minutes or until edges are set and lightly browned. Cool 2 minutes; remove from cookie sheet to wire rack.

1 Cookie Calories 170; Total Fat 8g (Saturated Fat 4.5g, Trans Fat 0g); Cholesterol 30mg; Sodium 135mg; Total Carbohydrate 21g (Dietary Fiber 0g); Protein 2g **Carbohydrate Choices:** 1½

Brown Sugar Crackle Cookies

Coarse sparkling sugar adds extra sparkle to cookies; it can be found in the cake decorating section at most grocery stores.

PREP 25 Minutes **TOTAL** 2 Hours • *About 5½ dozen cookies*

2 cups packed brown sugar	3 cups all-purpose flour
1 cup butter, softened	½ teaspoon baking soda
2 eggs	½ teaspoon salt
1 tablespoon vanilla	¾ cup coarse white sparkling sugar

1 Heat oven to 350°F.

2 In large bowl, beat brown sugar and butter with electric mixer on medium speed about 1 minute or until fluffy; scrape side of bowl. Beat in eggs, one at a time, just until smooth. Beat in vanilla. On low speed, gradually beat in flour, baking soda and salt until well blended.

3 Shape dough into 1½-inch balls; roll in sparkling sugar. Onto each of two ungreased cookie sheets, place 12 balls about 2 inches apart.

4 Bake one cookie sheet 10 to 13 minutes or until edges are light golden brown. Cool 2 minutes; remove from cookie sheet to cooling rack. Repeat with second cookie sheet.

5 Onto completely cooled cookie sheets, place remaining dough as directed in Step 3. Bake and cool cookies as directed in Step 4. Cool completely, about 15 minutes.

1 Cookie Calories 100; Total Fat 3.5g (Saturated Fat 2g, Trans Fat 0g); Cholesterol 15mg; Sodium 65mg; Total Carbohydrate 16g (Dietary Fiber 0g); Protein 1g **Carbohydrate Choices:** 1

Ginger, Walnut and White Chocolate Chip Cookies

Brown Sugar Crackle Cookies

Lemon Birthday Cake Cookies

When purchasing ingredients for this recipe, you may need 5 lemons, depending on the size of each, to get enough zest for the cookies and frosting.

PREP 30 Minutes **TOTAL** 1 Hour 15 Minutes •
2 dozen cookies

LEMON BIRTHDAY COOKIES

- ¾ cup granulated sugar
- ½ cup sour cream
- ½ cup butter, softened
- 1 egg
- 1 tablespoon lemon zest
- 2¼ cups all-purpose flour
- ½ teaspoon baking powder
- ½ teaspoon baking soda
- ½ teaspoon salt
- ¼ cup multicolored candy sprinkles

LEMON FROSTING

- 2 cups powdered sugar
- ½ cup butter, softened
- 2 tablespoons fresh lemon juice
- 2 teaspoons lemon zest
- ⅛ teaspoon salt
- 2 tablespoons multicolored candy sprinkles

1 Heat oven to 350°F.

2 In large bowl, beat granulated sugar, sour cream and butter with mixer on medium speed until well blended. Add egg and 1 tablespoon lemon zest; continue beating until well blended. Add remaining cookie ingredients except sprinkles; mix until soft dough forms. Stir in ¼ cup sprinkles.

3 Shape dough into 1½-inch balls (dough will be soft). Onto each of two ungreased cookie sheets, place 12 balls about 2 inches apart. Flatten balls to ½-inch thickness.

4 Bake one cookie sheet 10 to 12 minutes or until set. Cool 5 minutes; remove from cookie sheet to cooling rack. Repeat with second cookie sheet. Cool cookies completely, about 15 minutes.

5 In medium bowl, beat frosting ingredients except sprinkles until smooth. Spread each cookie with scant 1 tablespoon frosting. Sprinkle cookies with sprinkles.

Let frosted cookies stand until the frosting is set. Store in a single layer in loosely covered containers at room temperature.

1 Cookie Calories 210; Total Fat 10g (Saturated Fat 5g, Trans Fat 0g); Cholesterol 30mg; Sodium 160mg; Total Carbohydrate 28g (Dietary Fiber 0g); Protein 1g **Carbohydrate Choices:** 2

Snickerdoodles

This favorite whimsically named cookie originated in New England in the 1800s. It's traditionally rolled in cinnamon-sugar before baking.

PREP 20 Minutes **TOTAL** 1 Hour 10 Minutes • *4 dozen cookies*

- 1¾ cups sugar
- ½ cup butter, softened
- ½ cup vegetable shortening
- 2 eggs
- 2¾ cups all-purpose flour
- 2 teaspoons cream of tartar
- 1 teaspoon baking soda
- ¼ teaspoon salt
- 1 tablespoon ground cinnamon

1 Heat oven to 400°F.

2 In large bowl, beat 1½ cups of the sugar, the butter, shortening and eggs with electric mixer on medium speed, or mix with spoon, until well blended. Stir in flour, cream of tartar, baking soda and salt.

3 Shape dough into 1¼-inch balls. In small bowl, mix remaining ¼ cup sugar and the cinnamon. Roll balls in cinnamon-sugar. Onto each of two ungreased cookie sheets, place 12 balls about 2 inches apart.

4 Bake one cookie sheet 8 to 10 minutes or just until set. Immediately remove cookies from cookie sheet to cooling rack. Repeat with second cookie sheet.

5 Onto completely cooled cookie sheets, prepare and place remaining dough as directed in Step 3. Bake cookies as directed in Step 4.

1 Cookie Calories 90; Total Fat 4.5g (Saturated Fat 1.5g, Trans Fat 0g); Cholesterol 15mg; Sodium 55mg; Total Carbohydrate 13g (Dietary Fiber 0g); Protein 1g **Carbohydrate Choices:** 1

Lemon Birthday Cake Cookies

Snickerdoodles

Refrigerator Cookies 3 Ways

This base recipe can be made into any of the three varieties below, so be sure to pick the one you'd like to make before you head to the store for the ingredients. For nicely shaped cookies, rotate the logs in the refrigerator every 30 minutes so the dough doesn't have a chance to settle and flatten on any one side.

PREP 20 Minutes **TOTAL** 3 Hours • *About 4½ dozen cookies*

1 cup butter, softened	1 egg
1 cup granulated sugar	2½ cups all-purpose flour
½ cup packed brown sugar	1½ teaspoons baking powder
1 teaspoon vanilla	½ teaspoon salt

1 Choose specific flavor of cookie to make at right. In large bowl, beat butter, granulated sugar, brown sugar, vanilla and egg with electric mixer on medium speed until well blended. Stir in remaining ingredients, as well as specific ingredients called for in chosen recipe at right.

2 Shape dough into 2 (8-inch long) round, rectangular or triangular logs. Wrap logs tightly in plastic wrap and refrigerate at least 2 hours or until firm, or up to 1 week.

3 Heat oven to 375°F.

4 Unwrap dough; trim and discard ends of dough. With sharp knife, cut into ¼-inch slices. Onto each of two ungreased cookie sheets, place slices about 2 inches apart.

5 Bake one cookie sheet 8 to 10 minutes or until edges are light golden brown. Cool 2 minutes; remove from cookie sheet to cooling rack. Repeat with second cookie sheet.

6 Onto completely cooled cookie sheets, prepare and place remaining dough as directed in Step 4. Bake cookies as directed in Step 5. Continue as directed in chosen recipe.

1 Cookie Calories 140; Total Fat 8g (Saturated Fat 4g, Trans Fat 0g); Cholesterol 10mg; Sodium 65mg; Total Carbohydrate 16g (Dietary Fiber 0g); Protein 1g **Carbohydrate Choices:** 1

Refrigerator Cookies 3 Ways

GINGER-ORANGE COOKIES: Stir in 3 tablespoons chopped crystallized ginger and 1 tablespoon orange zest with the dry ingredients. In small microwavable bowl, microwave ⅓ cup dark chocolate chips uncovered on High 30 seconds to 1 minute, stirring once, or until chips can be stirred smooth. Spoon melted chocolate into small resealable food-storage plastic bag; seal bag. Cut off tiny corner of bag; squeeze bag to drizzle onto cooled cookies; allow to set about 15 minutes.

PIÑA COLADA COOKIES: Stir in ½ cup toasted coconut, ⅓ cup finely chopped sweetened dried mango and ⅓ cup finely chopped sweetened dried pineapple with the dry ingredients.

TOFFEE-PECAN COOKIES: Stir in ½ cup finely chopped toasted pecans and ½ cup toffee bits with the dry ingredients. In small microwavable bowl, microwave 2 cups semisweet chocolate chips and 2 teaspoons vegetable shortening uncovered on High 1 to 2 minutes, stirring once, or until mixture can be stirred smooth. Dip half of each cooled cookie into melted chocolate, shaking off excess. Place on waxed paper. Sprinkle cookies with ½ cup finely chopped toasted pecans; allow to set.

MAKING REFRIGERATOR COOKIES

Shape dough on plastic wrap into round, rectangular or triangular logs.

Wrap and refrigerate, turning logs occasionally to hold shape.

Unwrap one log at a time; cut into ¼-inch slices.

LEARN TO MAKE CUTOUT COOKIES

Cutout cookies may be traditional for the holidays, but with so many cookie cutter shapes available, you can make them for any occasion! It's a perfect way to spend time with family and/or friends, baking and decorating together. Start with our favorite bakery-style Sugar Cookies recipe (right). With these tips and tricks, your cookies can taste and look amazing.

Tips for Pretty Cutout Cookies

1 Refrigerating the cookie dough eliminates; work with half of the dough at a time.

2 Sprinkle work surface and rolling pin lightly with flour to help prevent dough from sticking. Dip cookie cutters in flour and tap to remove excess before cutting cookies.

3 Roll dough to an even thickness so that cookies will bake evenly.

4 Cool cookies completely before frosting.

5 Let glaze dry completely before storing cookies.

Decorating Before You Bake

You can decorate cookies before they bake so the decorations become part of the cookies:

- **SPRINKLE WITH SUGAR** Sprinkle unbaked cookies on cookie sheet with coarse clear or colored sugar. (See Making Colored Sugar, page 555.) To keep the sugar off the cookie sheet where it can burn and on top of the cookies, place the cookie cutter used to cut the cookie back over it on the cookie sheet before sprinkling.

- **MAKE AN EGG YOLK PAINT** See Paintbrush Sugar Cookies, page 555, for making a "paint" from egg yolk to brush on the unbaked cookies before baking.

- **PIPE ON DECORATIONS** Mix ½ cup softened butter, ½ cup all-purpose flour and 1 tablespoon milk in a small bowl until well mixed. Divide mixture in half; tint each half with 4 drops liquid food color. Place the mixture in decorating bags fitted with small writing tips. Pipe onto unbaked sugar cookies before baking.

Tips for Decorating Baked Cookies

- Place cookies on cooling rack over 15x10x1-inch pan or piece of cooking parchment paper or waxed paper, to catch drips for easy cleanup. Spread cookies with Vanilla Glaze (page 602) or Chocolate Glaze (page 603).

- While glaze is wet, sprinkle with finely chopped nuts, colored sugar, candy sprinkles or tiny candies.

- Drop dots of a colored glaze onto glazed cookies while wet; pull through the dots with toothpick to make designs.

- Pipe designs onto cookies using colored glaze in decorating bag fitted with a small writing tip, in small resealable food-storage plastic bags (cut a tiny corner off one end) or in food-safe plastic squeeze bottles.

- Let glaze dry completely before storing cookies.

ROLLING AND CUTTING COOKIE DOUGH

On lightly floured surface, roll refrigerated dough disk into flattened round without cracks.

Using a ruler or sticks as guide, roll dough ¼ inch thick.

Use cookie cutters dipped in flour to cut desired shapes.

USING A DECORATING BAG

Insert tip inside pastry bag. (Cut end of disposable bag, if necessary, so tip will stick out end of bag.)

Attach coupler to tip on outside of bag. Pull open bag down over hand; fill no more than halfway with frosting.

Unfold bag; twist empty portion above frosting together. Squeeze bag with even pressure, twisting as needed to evenly pipe frosting.

Sugar Cookies

PREP 1 Hour **TOTAL** 3 Hours • *5 dozen cookies*

1½	cups powdered sugar
1	cup butter, softened
1	teaspoon vanilla
½	teaspoon almond extract
1	egg
2½	cups all-purpose flour
1	teaspoon baking soda
1	teaspoon cream of tartar
	Granulated sugar, colored sugar (below) or Vanilla Glaze (page 602)

1 In large bowl, beat powdered sugar, butter, vanilla, almond extract and egg with electric mixer on medium speed, or mix with spoon, until well blended. Stir in flour, baking soda and cream of tartar. Divide dough in half; shape each half into disk. Wrap with plastic wrap. Refrigerate at least 2 hours.

2 Heat oven to 375°F. Lightly grease two cookie sheets with vegetable shortening or cooking spray, or line with cooking parchment paper or silicone baking mats.

3 Roll one dough disk on lightly floured surface until ¼ inch thick. Cut with floured 2-inch cookie cutters. Reroll scraps to cut additional cookies. Sprinkle with granulated sugar. Onto cookie sheets, place cutouts about 1 inch apart.

4 Bake one cookie sheet 7 to 8 minutes or until edges are light brown. Remove cookies from cookie sheet to cooling rack. Repeat with second cookie sheet.

5 Onto completely cooled cookie sheets, roll, cut, sprinkle and place remaining dough as directed in Step 3. Bake and cool as directed in Step 4.

1 Cookie Calories 60; Total Fat 3g (Saturated Fat 1.5g, Trans Fat 0g); Cholesterol 10mg; Sodium 45mg; Total Carbohydrate 8g (Dietary Fiber 0g); Protein 0g **Carbohydrate Choices:** ½

PAINTBRUSH SUGAR COOKIES: Omit granulated sugar. Cut rolled dough into desired shapes with cookie cutters. (Cut no more than 12 cookies at a time to prevent dough from drying out.) Mix 1 egg yolk and ¼ teaspoon water. Divide mixture among several custard cups. Tint each with different food color to make bright colors. (If paint thickens while standing, stir in a few drops water.) Paint designs on cookies with small new paintbrushes. Bake as directed.

MAKING COLORED SUGAR

Colored sugars can dress up plain cookies without much work. Many colors are available at bakery supply stores or here's how you can make your own:

Place ½ cup granulated sugar in resealable food-storage plastic bag. Add liquid food color, by drops, to the sugar, for the tint you like. Seal bag. Squeeze and rub sugar in bag until evenly colored. Homemade colored sugar might clump; if it does, just break apart until clumps are gone.

DECORATING COOKIES

Colored Sugar Sprinkle cookies with colored sugar or decors before baking, or immediately after frosting so sugar will stick.

Painting Make Paintbrush Sugar Cookies (left), painting cookies with clean brush before baking.

Frosting Frost cookies with glaze or frosting; top with nuts, colored sugar or candy sprinkles. Or top frosted cookies with dots of colored glaze or gel food color; drag a toothpick through the dots to create designs.

Nuts Finely chopped nuts can be sprinkled on the cookies before baking; press lightly. Or, sprinkle over frosted cookies before the frosting sets.

Sugar Cookies

Shortbread Cookies

CALORIE SMART • VEGETARIAN

Shortbread Cookies

PREP 40 Minutes **TOTAL** 40 Minutes • *2 dozen cookies*

¾ cup butter, softened	2 cups all-purpose flour
5 tablespoons sugar	

1 Heat oven to 350°F.

2 In large bowl, stir butter and 4 tablespoons of the sugar until well mixed. Stir in flour. (If dough is crumbly, mix in 1 to 2 tablespoons more softened butter.)

3 Roll dough on lightly floured surface until ½ inch thick. Cut with floured 1½-inch cookie cutter. Onto each of two ungreased cookie sheets, place cutouts ½ inch apart. Sprinkle evenly with remaining 1 tablespoon sugar.

4 Bake one cookie sheet 15 to 20 minutes or just until set. Immediately remove cookies from cookie sheet to cooling rack. Repeat with second cookie sheet.

1 Cookie Calories 100; Total Fat 6g (Saturated Fat 3g, Trans Fat 0g); Cholesterol 15mg; Sodium 40mg; Total Carbohydrate 10g (Dietary Fiber 0g); Protein 1g **Carbohydrate Choices:** ½

CHERRY SHORTBREAD COOKIES: Stir in ½ cup chopped dried cherries, cranberries or blueberries with the flour.

DIPPING COOKIES IN CHOCOLATE

Microwave chocolate chips and oil, stirring every 30 seconds, or until mixture can be stirred smooth.

Dip cookies; wipe excess on edge of bowl. Place on waxed paper to set.

CHOCOLATE-DIPPED SHORTBREAD COOKIES: Make and bake cookies as directed; cool completely. In small microwavable bowl, microwave 1 cup chocolate chips and 1 teaspoon vegetable oil on High 30 to 60 seconds or until mixture can be stirred smooth. Dip cookies in chocolate; wipe excess on edge of bowl. Place on waxed paper to set.

GINGER SHORTBREAD COOKIES: Stir in 3 tablespoons chopped crystallized ginger with the flour.

SHORTBREAD COOKIE WEDGES: Make dough as directed. On ungreased cookie sheet, pat dough into 8-inch round. Sprinkle with 1 tablespoon sugar. Bake 20 to 24 minutes or until set. Cool 10 minutes on cookie sheet on cooling rack. Using sharp knife, cut into 24 wedges.

SHORTBREAD NUT COOKIES: Stir in ½ cup finely chopped hazelnuts (filberts), macadamia nuts, pecans, pistachio nuts or slivered almonds, toasted if desired, with the flour.

TOFFEE SHORTBREAD COOKIES: Stir in ½ cup toffee bits with the flour.

WHOLE WHEAT SHORTBREAD COOKIES: Substitute 1¼ cups whole wheat flour for the all-purpose flour. Continue as directed.

LEARN WITH BETTY MELTING CHOCOLATE

Ideally Melted This chocolate is smooth and creamy.

Seized: This chocolate was melted over too high a heat or for too long or came in contact with a small amount of liquid, making it firm and granular.

Correcting Seized Chocolate: Whisk in vegetable oil or melted butter or vegetable shortening. Heat over very low heat, if necessary, stirring constantly.

Gingerbread Cookies

To tint the Decorator's Frosting, use paste food color, which can be found at craft stores. You would have to use too much liquid food color to get a vivid color, and the frosting might separate and look curdled. Gel food color can be used but may not be as intense as you'd like for decorating.

PREP 1 Hour 40 Minutes **TOTAL** 3 Hours 30 Minutes • *5 dozen cookies*

COOKIES

- ½ cup packed brown sugar
- ½ cup butter, softened
- ½ cup molasses
- ⅓ cup cold water
- 3½ cups all-purpose flour
- 2 teaspoons baking soda
- 2 teaspoons ground ginger
- ½ teaspoon ground allspice
- ½ teaspoon ground cinnamon
- ¼ teaspoon ground cloves
- ¼ teaspoon salt

DECORATOR'S FROSTING

- 2 cups powdered sugar
- 2 tablespoons water or milk
- ½ teaspoon vanilla
- Paste food color, if desired
- Colored sugar (see page 555) and small candies, if desired

1 In large bowl, beat brown sugar, butter, molasses and water with electric mixer on medium speed, or mix with spoon, until well blended. Stir in remaining cookie ingredients until mixed. Cover and refrigerate at least 2 hours.

2 Heat oven to 350°F. Grease two cookie sheets with vegetable shortening or cooking spray, or line with cooking parchment paper or silicone baking mats.

3 Divide dough in half. Roll one half on lightly floured surface until ¼ inch thick. Cut with floured 2½-inch gingerbread boy or girl cookie cutter. Onto cookie sheets, place cutouts about 2 inches apart. After cutting as many cookies as possible, lightly press scraps of dough together; reroll dough and cut additional cookies.

4 Bake one cookie sheet 10 to 12 minutes or until no indent remains when cookie is touched in center. Immediately remove from cookie sheet to cooling rack. Repeat with second cookie sheet.

5 Onto completely cooled cookie sheets, repeat Steps 3 and 4 with remaining dough. Cool cookies completely before frosting, about 30 minutes.

6 Meanwhile, in medium bowl, mix powdered sugar, water and vanilla with spoon until smooth and spreadable. Stir in food color one drop at a time until frosting is desired color. Cover and set aside.

7 When you are ready to decorate, spoon frosting into small resealable food-storage plastic bag. Seal bag; push frosting down toward one corner. Cut off tiny corner of bag. Squeeze bag to pipe frosting onto cookies and make desired designs. Or spread frosting over cookies with small metal spatula. Decorate with colored sugar(s) and candies.

1 Cookie Calories 60; Total Fat 1.5g (Saturated Fat 1g, Trans Fat 0g); Cholesterol 0mg; Sodium 65mg; Total Carbohydrate 10g (Dietary Fiber 0g); Protein 0g **Carbohydrate Choices:** ½

Gingerbread Cookies

Spritz Cookies

Seed-Packed
Power Bites

Spritz Cookies

PREP 25 Minutes **TOTAL** 55 Minutes • *5 dozen cookies*

1 cup butter, softened*	Red or green food color, if desired
½ cup sugar	Granulated or sparkling sugar, colored sugar (see page 555) or multicolored candy sprinkles, if desired
2¼ cups all-purpose flour	
1 egg	
1 teaspoon almond extract or vanilla	
½ teaspoon salt	

1 Heat oven to 400°F.

2 In large bowl, beat butter and the ½ cup sugar with electric mixer on medium speed, or mix with spoon, until well blended. Stir in remaining ingredients except additional sugar.

3 Working in batches, place dough in cookie press. Onto each of two ungreased cookie sheets, form desired shapes, about 1 inch apart. Sprinkle with sugar.

4 Bake one cookie sheet 6 to 9 minutes or until cookies are set but not brown. Immediately remove cookies from cookie sheet to cooling rack. Repeat with second cookie sheet.

5 Onto completely cooled cookie sheets, press and sprinkle remaining dough as directed in Step 3. Bake cookies as directed in Step 4.

1 Cookie Calories 50; Total Fat 3g (Saturated Fat 1.5g, Trans Fat 0g); Cholesterol 10mg; Sodium 40mg; Total Carbohydrate 5g (Dietary Fiber 0g); Protein 0g **Carbohydrate Choices:** ½

MAKING SPRITZ COOKIES

Insert desired design disk into cookie press. Place dough in barrel of press; attach pressing mechanism. Squeeze dough through press onto cookie sheet.

CHOCOLATE SPRITZ COOKIES: Stir 2 oz unsweetened baking chocolate, melted and cooled, into butter-sugar mixture.

*Do not use margarine or vegetable oil spreads, as the cookies won't hold their shape.

Seed-Packed Power Bites

Toasted sesame seed can be purchased in the international ingredient section of the grocery store. To toast at home, sprinkle sesame seed in ungreased heavy skillet. Cook over medium-low heat 5 to 7 minutes, stirring frequently until browning begins, then stirring constantly until golden brown. Remove immediately from heat. Spread on heatproof plate to cool before using.

PREP 20 Minutes **TOTAL** 1 Hour 20 Minutes • *About 24 bites*

¼ cup toasted sesame seed	¼ cup whole flaxseed (any variety)
3 tablespoons poppy seed	¼ cup miniature semisweet chocolate chips
¼ cup quick-cooking oats	¼ cup almond or peanut butter
¼ cup sweetened dried cranberries or raisins	2 tablespoons honey

1 On small plate, stir together 2 tablespoons of the sesame seed and 2 teaspoons of the poppy seed; set aside.

2 In food processor, place remaining ingredients. Cover; process using quick on-and-off pulses until fruit is finely chopped and mixture holds together.

3 Shape dough into 1-inch balls. Roll in sesame-poppy seed mixture; if dough sticks to hands, wet hands or spray with cooking spray. Place in food storage container. Cover and refrigerate until firm, about 30 minutes. Serve cold or at room temperature.

1 Bite Calories 70; Total Fat 4g (Saturated Fat 0.5g, Trans Fat 0g); Cholesterol 0mg; Sodium 10mg; Total Carbohydrate 6g (Dietary Fiber 1g); Protein 1g **Carbohydrate Choices:** ½

Killer Candy Bar Brownies

PREP 35 Minutes **TOTAL** 3 Hours 15 Minutes • *24 brownies*

BROWNIES

- ⅔ cup butter
- 5 oz unsweetened baking chocolate, chopped (from two 4-oz boxes)
- 1¾ cups granulated sugar
- 3 eggs
- 2 teaspoons vanilla
- 1 cup all-purpose flour
- ¾ cup mini peanut butter cups (from 8-oz bag)
- 20 chewy caramels in milk chocolate, unwrapped (from a 10.6-oz bag)

PEANUT BUTTER FROSTING

- ½ cup butter, softened
- ½ cup creamy peanut butter
- 1 teaspoon vanilla
- 2½ cups powdered sugar
- 2 to 3 tablespoons milk
- ¼ cup candy-coated chocolate candies (from 10.7-oz bag)

1 Heat oven to 350° F. Spray 9-inch square pan with cooking spray.

2 In 1-quart saucepan, melt butter and chocolate over low heat, stirring constantly until melted. Remove from heat; cool 5 minutes.

3 Meanwhile, in medium bowl, beat granulated sugar, eggs and 2 teaspoons vanilla with electric mixer on high speed 5 minutes. Beat in chocolate mixture on low speed, scraping bowl occasionally. Beat in flour just until well blended, scraping bowl occasionally. Stir in peanut butter cups until well mixed; spread evenly in greased pan. Sprinkle with chocolate covered caramels, slightly pressing into batter.

4 Bake 35 to 40 minutes or until toothpick inserted 1 inch from edge of pan comes out almost clean. Cool completely in pan on cooling rack, about 2 hours.

5 In medium bowl, beat butter, peanut butter and 1 teaspoon vanilla with electric mixer on high 1 to 2 minutes or until creamy, scraping bowl occasionally. Add powdered sugar, 1 cup at a time, until well blended. Beat in milk, 1 tablespoon at a time, until spreading consistency. Spread evenly onto brownies. Sprinkle with candy-coated chocolate candies. Cut into 4 rows by 6 rows. Store pan covered in refrigerator.

1 Brownie Calories 360; Total Fat 19g (Saturated Fat 10g, Trans Fat 0g); Cholesterol 50mg; Sodium 130mg; Total Carbohydrate 42g (Dietary Fiber 1g); Protein 4g **Carbohydrate Choices:** 3

BROWNIES FOR A CROWD: Prepare as directed—except spray 13x9-inch pan with cooking spray. Double brownie ingredients and make brownies as directed above. Bake 50 to 55 minutes. Cool and frost as directed, doubling frosting ingredients.

CANDY BROWNIE ICE CREAM SQUARES: Prepare as directed—except omit frosting. Spread cooled brownies with ½ gallon softened ice cream. Drizzle with chocolate or caramel topping; sprinkle with desired candy. Cover and freeze 1 to 2 hours or until firm. Cut into squares.

COCONUT–PEANUT BUTTER CANDY BROWNIES: Prepare as directed—except reduce vanilla to 1½ teaspoons. Add ½ teaspoon coconut extract with vanilla. Omit candy-coated chocolate candies. Immediately after frosting brownies, sprinkle with ½ cup coconut.

PEANUT BUTTER OVERLOAD BROWNIES: Substitute ⅓ cup crunchy peanut butter for ⅓ cup of the butter in the brownies.

WHITE CHIP–ALMOND BROWNIES: Prepare as directed—except decrease vanilla to 1 teaspoon and add ½ teaspoon almond extract. Substitute ½ cup white vanilla baking chips for the peanut butter cups and ½ cup chopped almonds for the chewy caramels in milk chocolate; stir into batter before spreading in pan. Omit frosting. Dust cooled brownies with powdered sugar.

DETERMINING BROWNIE DONENESS

Brownies will start to pull away from sides of pan when done.

Killer Candy Bar Brownies

5-INGREDIENT RECIPE

Coconut Pecan Frosting

Butter

Egg

Gooey Chocolate-Coconut-Pecan Bars

Miniature Chocolate Chips

Oatmeal Chocolate Chip Cookie Mix

5-INGREDIENT RECIPE

EASY · VEGETARIAN

Gooey Chocolate-Coconut-Pecan Bars

PREP 15 Minutes **TOTAL** 1 Hour 55 Minutes · *16 bars*

1 pouch (17.5 oz) oatmeal chocolate chip cookie mix	½ cup butter, softened
	1 egg
½ cup coconut pecan creamy ready-to-spread frosting (from 15.5-oz container)	¼ cup miniature chocolate chips

1 Heat oven to 350°F. Spray 9-inch square pan with cooking spray.

2 In small bowl, place ¼ cup of the dry cookie mix. Add frosting; mix well and set aside.

3 In large bowl, beat remaining cookie mix, butter and egg with electric mixer on medium speed until mixed. Reserve ½ cup dough; set aside. Press remaining dough evenly in pan. (Dough will be sticky.)

4 Bake 18 to 20 minutes or until golden brown. Remove from oven. Drop reserved cookie dough by spoonfuls in random pattern over top of bars. Repeat with frosting mixture. Bake about 20 minutes longer or until top is golden brown. Immediately sprinkle with chocolate chips. Cool completely, about 1 hour.

5 For bars, cut into 4 rows by 4 rows. Store in tightly covered container at room temperature.

1 Bar Calories 220; Total Fat 10g (Saturated Fat 5g, Trans Fat 0g); Cholesterol 25mg; Sodium 180mg; Total Carbohydrate 31g (Dietary Fiber 1g); Protein 1g **Carbohydrate Choices:** 2

VEGETARIAN

Chocolate Brownies

If you like chewy, fudgy chocolate brownies, this is your recipe. We really like the walnuts in the recipe, but you could use pecans or cashews instead, or make the brownies without nuts.

PREP 20 Minutes **TOTAL** 3 Hours 10 Minutes · *16 brownies*

⅔ cup butter	1 cup all-purpose flour
5 oz unsweetened baking chocolate, chopped	½ cup chopped walnuts, toasted if desired (page 28)
1¾ cups sugar	½ batch Creamy Chocolate Frosting or Mocha Frosting (page 601), if desired
2 teaspoons vanilla	
3 eggs	

1 Heat oven to 350°F. Grease bottom and sides of 9-inch square pan with vegetable shortening.

2 In 1-quart saucepan, melt butter and chocolate over low heat, stirring constantly. Cool 5 minutes.

3 In medium bowl, beat sugar, vanilla and eggs with electric mixer on high speed 5 minutes until blended. Beat in chocolate mixture on low speed, scraping bowl occasionally. Beat in flour just until blended, scraping bowl occasionally. Stir in walnuts. Spread batter in pan.

4 Bake 40 to 45 minutes or just until brownies begin to pull away from sides of pan. Cool completely in pan on cooling rack, about 2 hours. Spread frosting over brownies. Cut into 4 rows by 4 rows.

1 Brownie Calories 310; Total Fat 18g (Saturated Fat 8g, Trans Fat 0g); Cholesterol 60mg; Sodium 65mg; Total Carbohydrate 31g (Dietary Fiber 2g); Protein 4g **Carbohydrate Choices:** 2

CHOCOLATE BROWNIE PIE: Grease bottom and side of 10-inch glass pie plate with vegetable shortening. Spread batter in pie plate. Bake 35 to 40 minutes or until center is set. Cool completely on cooling rack. Cut into wedges. Omit frosting. Serve with ice cream and Hot Fudge Sauce (page 661), if desired. Makes 12 servings.

CHOCOLATE-PEANUT BUTTER BROWNIES: Substitute ⅓ cup crunchy peanut butter for ⅓ cup of the butter. Omit walnuts. Before baking, arrange 16 miniature chocolate-covered peanut butter cup candies, unwrapped, on top of batter. Press into batter so tops of cups are even with top of batter. Continue as directed in Step 4.

DOUBLE CHOCOLATE BROWNIES: Stir in ½ cup semisweet or dark chocolate chips after adding flour.

MINT-TOPPED ESPRESSO BROWNIES: Stir 2 teaspoons instant espresso powder, coffee granules or crystals with the butter. Immediately after baking, arrange 20 unwrapped thin rectangular chocolate mint candies (from 4.67-oz pkg) over brownies. Let stand 5 minutes or until mints are softened. Using knife or spatula, spread mints gently, swirling slightly. Cool brownies until chocolate starts to set; cut into bars. Cool completely.

Chocolate-Peanut Butter Brownies

Blondies with Brown Sugar Frosting

Pumpkin-Cherry Bars

Grinch Pistachio Cookie Bars

Blondies with Brown Sugar Frosting

PREP 25 Minutes TOTAL 1 Hour 50 Minutes • *36 brownies*

BLONDIES	BROWN SUGAR FROSTING
1 cup granulated sugar	⅓ cup butter*
½ cup packed brown sugar	⅔ cup packed brown sugar
½ cup butter, softened	3 tablespoons milk
1 teaspoon vanilla	2 cups powdered sugar
2 eggs	½ teaspoon vanilla
1½ cups all-purpose flour	½ cup chopped pecans, toasted if desired (page 28)
1 teaspoon baking powder	
½ teaspoon salt	

1 Heat oven to 350°F.

2 In large bowl, beat granulated sugar, ½ cup brown sugar, ½ cup butter, 1 teaspoon vanilla and the eggs with electric mixer on medium speed, or mix with spoon, until light and fluffy. Stir in flour, baking powder and salt. In ungreased 13x9-inch pan, spread batter evenly.

3 Bake 20 to 23 minutes or until golden brown and toothpick inserted in center comes out clean. Cool completely in pan on cooling rack, about 1 hour.

4 In 2-quart saucepan, melt ⅓ cup butter over low heat. Stir in ⅔ cup brown sugar; cook over low heat 2 minutes, stirring constantly. Stir in milk; cook until mixture comes to a rolling boil. Remove from heat. Gradually stir in powdered sugar and vanilla, mixing well with spoon after each addition, until smooth and spreadable. If necessary, add more milk, a few drops at a time. Spread frosting over brownies. Immediately sprinkle with pecans. Cut into 6 rows by 6 rows.

1 Brownie Calories 150; Total Fat 6g (Saturated Fat 2.5g, Trans Fat 0g); Cholesterol 25mg; Sodium 80mg; Total Carbohydrate 23g (Dietary Fiber 0g); Protein 1g **Carbohydrate Choices:** 1½

*Do not use margarine or vegetable oil spreads in the frosting as it won't set up correctly when cooked.

Pumpkin-Cherry Bars

PREP 40 Minutes **TOTAL** 2 Hours 30 Minutes • *36 bars*

CRUST

- 1½ cups quick-cooking oats
- ½ cup packed brown sugar
- ¼ cup all-purpose flour
- ¼ teaspoon salt
- ½ cup butter, melted

FILLING

- 1 cup granulated sugar
- 1 cup pumpkin puree (from 15-oz can; not pumpkin pie mix)
- ½ cup vegetable oil
- 3 eggs
- 1½ cups all-purpose flour
- 2 tablespoons chopped fresh rosemary leaves
- 2 teaspoons pumpkin pie spice
- 1 teaspoon baking powder
- ¼ teaspoon salt
- ½ cup chopped dried cherries
- ½ cup chopped pecans

LEMON-SPICE FROSTING

- ⅓ cup butter, softened
- 3 cups powdered sugar
- 1 teaspoon lemon zest
- 1 teaspoon lemon juice
- ¾ teaspoon pumpkin pie spice
- 2 tablespoons milk

1 Heat oven to 350°F. Spray 13x9-inch pan with cooking spray or grease with vegetable shortening.

2 In large bowl, mix crust ingredients with spoon until well mixed. Press evenly into bottom of pan. Bake 9 to 11 minutes or until crust is light golden brown. Remove from oven.

3 Meanwhile, in large bowl, beat sugar, pumpkin, oil and eggs with whisk or spoon until smooth. Stir in flour, rosemary, 2 teaspoons pumpkin pie spice, the baking powder and salt. Stir in cherries and pecans.

4 Spread pumpkin layer evenly over crust.

5 Bake 25 to 30 minutes or until set. Cool completely in pan on cooling rack, about 1½ hours.

6 In medium bowl, beat frosting ingredients except milk with electric mixer on low speed until blended. Gradually beat in enough milk, 1 teaspoon at a time, until frosting is smooth and spreadable. Spread frosting over bars. Cut into 6 rows by 6 rows. Store bars in pan, tightly covered, in refrigerator.

1 Bar Calories 200; Total Fat 9g (Saturated Fat 3.5g, Trans Fat 0g); Cholesterol 25mg; Sodium 90mg; Total Carbohydrate 28g (Dietary Fiber 1g); Protein 2g **Carbohydrate Choices:** 2

PRESSING CRUST IN PAN

Using fingertips, press crust in pan; build up ½-inch edges.

Grinch Pistachio Cookie Bars

Candy décor hearts can be found by the cake and cookie decorating supplies in craft stores, grocery stores and discount stores, or you can purchase them online. For the fun "special effects" in the frosting, use neon green gel food color. As the gel color is swirled through the frosting several shades of green color will appear.

PREP 20 Minutes **TOTAL** 1 Hour 45 Minutes • *24 bars*

BARS

- 1 cup butter, softened
- ½ cup granulated sugar
- 2 boxes (4-serving size) instant pistachio pudding and pie filling mix (not sugar-free)
- 2 eggs
- 1 teaspoon vanilla
- 2 cups all-purpose flour
- 1 teaspoon baking powder

FROSTING

- 4 cups powdered sugar
- 1 cup butter, softened
- 1 teaspoon vanilla
- ½ teaspoon almond extract
- 3 to 4 teaspoons milk
- 12 drops neon green gel food color
- 24 red candy décor hearts

1 Heat oven to 350°F. Spray 13x9-inch pan with cooking spray.

2 In large bowl, stir 1 cup butter, the granulated sugar and dry pudding mix with spoon until blended. Add eggs and 1 teaspoon vanilla; mix until smooth. Stir in flour and baking powder. Press dough into bottom of pan.

3 Bake 25 to 27 minutes or until edges are lightly brown. Cool completely in pan on cooling rack, about 1 hour.

4 In large bowl, beat powdered sugar and 1 cup butter with electric mixer until smooth. Add 1 teaspoon vanilla and the almond extract. Add milk, 1 teaspoon at a time, until desired spreading consistency. Spread over bars. Place drops of food color evenly over frosting. Using a small metal spatula, swirl food color to create marbled appearance. Decorate with candy decor hearts. Cut into 6 rows by 4 rows.

1 Bar Calories 320; Total Fat 16g (Saturated Fat 10g, Trans Fat 0.5g); Cholesterol 55mg; Sodium 260mg; Total Carbohydrate 41g (Dietary Fiber 0g); Protein 1g **Carbohydrate Choices:** 3

GRINCH VANILLA COOKIE BARS: Substitute vanilla or French vanilla instant pudding and pie filling mix for the pistachio pudding and pie filling mix. If desired, add 1 drop each green and yellow liquid food color with the pudding mix.

USE IT UP
EGGS

Versatile, easy to prepare and inexpensive, eggs are a great choice for any time of day. When you find yourself with a lot of eggs in your fridge, try one of these tasty ways to use them up so they don't go to waste.

Whole Eggs

BREAKFAST EGG BAKES OR STRATA Whether for breakfast or for dinner, these hearty, heart-warming dishes can use up your eggs on hand. Try Overnight Everything Bagel Breakfast Casserole (page 103) or Ham and Cheddar Strata (page 104).

CURRIED EGG SALAD AND AVOCADO SANDWICHES Mix 6 chopped hard-cooked eggs (page 102), ½ cup mayonnaise, ¼ cup shredded carrot, 2 tablespoons chopped green onion, ¼ teaspoon each salt and curry powder. Top 4 slices of bread or bun bottoms with lettuce leaves, egg salad and avocado. Top with 4 more slices of bread or bun tops.

CAKE OR CHEESECAKE It's dessert time! Cakes and cheesecakes can use a lot of eggs. Try Mocha Streusel Espresso Cake (page 595) or New York Cheesecake (page 644).

SCRAMBLED EGG TORTILLA WRAPS Cut tortillas from edge to center. Spoon a little scrambled eggs, shredded Colby–Monterey Jack cheese blend, baby spinach leaves and sliced tomatoes over each quarter of the tortilla; fold up into quarters. Bake on cookie sheet at 350°F 10 minutes or until hot.

DEVILED EGG BREAKFAST PIZZA Bake prepared 10-oz pizza crust as directed on package; cool. Mix ½ cup mayonnaise or salad dressing, 1 tablespoon chopped chives, 2 teaspoons prepared mustard and ⅛ teaspoon pepper; spread over pizza crust. Top with sliced hard-cooked eggs, crumbled crisply cooked bacon, sliced pimiento-stuffed green olives and additional chopped chives.

Leftover Egg Whites or Yolks

If you have yolks or whites left over, use them up in any of these recipes:

EGG YOLKS	EGG WHITES
See page 593.	Angel Food Cake, page 593
	German Chocolate Cake, page 580
	White Cupcakes, page 599

Banana-Toffee Bars

Apple-Pecan Crumble Bars

VEGETARIAN

Banana-Toffee Bars

Perfect for a weeknight dessert or a potluck, these bars go heavy on the decadence with a pecan crust, banana filling and toffee topping.

PREP 15 Minutes **TOTAL** 2 Hours • *16 bars*

CRUST

- 6 tablespoons butter, softened
- ⅓ cup packed brown sugar
- ¾ cup all-purpose flour
- ¼ teaspoon salt
- ⅓ cup finely chopped pecans

FILLING

- 1 can (13.4 oz) dulce de leche (caramelized sweetened condensed milk)
- 2 ripe medium bananas, sliced

TOPPING

- ½ cup whipping cream
- 2 tablespoons powdered sugar
- 1 teaspoon vanilla
- ½ cup toffee bits

1 Heat oven to 350°F. Generously grease 8-inch square pan with vegetable shortening. In medium bowl, beat butter and brown sugar with electric mixer on medium speed 1 minute or until light and fluffy. On low speed, beat in flour and salt just until moistened. Stir in pecans. Press mixture into bottom of pan.

2 Bake 10 to 12 minutes or until golden around edges. Cool completely in pan on cooling rack, about 30 minutes.

3 Spread about half of the dulce de leche over cooled crust. Top with banana slices. Spread remaining dulce de leche over bananas.

4 In chilled small bowl, beat whipping cream, powdered sugar and vanilla with electric mixer on high speed until stiff peaks form. Spread whipped cream over top of dulce de leche; sprinkle with toffee bits. Refrigerate about 1 hour or until firm. Cut into 4 rows by 4 rows. Store bars in pan, tightly covered, in refrigerator.

1 Bar Calories 252; Total Fat 13g (Saturated Fat 7g, Trans Fat 0g); Cholesterol 0mg; Sodium 153mg; Total Carbohydrate 31g (Dietary Fiber 1g); Protein 3g **Carbohydrate Choices:** 2

VEGETARIAN • VEGAN

Apple-Pecan Crumble Bars

Obsessed is an understatement—we're borderline nuts over this apple-pecan bar that rivals the classic apple crisp, with the flavors of fall.

PREP 30 Minutes **TOTAL** 3 Hours 15 Minutes • *16 bars*

CRUST AND TOPPING

- 3 cups old-fashioned oats
- 2 cups all-purpose flour
- 1 cup packed organic brown sugar
- ¾ teaspoon ground cinnamon
- ½ teaspoon baking powder
- ½ teaspoon salt
- 1 cup vegan vegetable oil spread stick, softened
- 1 cup chopped pecans or walnuts

FILLING

- 5 cups coarsely chopped peeled Granny Smith apples (about 4 medium)
- ¾ cup organic granulated sugar
- 3 tablespoons all-purpose flour
- ¾ teaspoon ground cinnamon
- ¼ teaspoon salt

1 Heat oven to 375°F. Line 13x9-inch pan with foil, leaving 2-inch overhang on two opposite sides of pan for easy removal. Spray foil with vegan cooking spray.

2 In large bowl, mix oats, 2 cups flour, the brown sugar, ¾ teaspoon cinnamon, the baking powder, ½ teaspoon salt and the vegan vegetable oil spread stick with pastry blender or fork until crumbly. Transfer 1½ cups of the mixture to another medium bowl; stir in pecans. Press remaining oatmeal mixture into bottom of pan. Bake 10 minutes. Remove from oven.

3 Meanwhile, in medium bowl, mix filling ingredients. Spoon over hot crust. Sprinkle reserved oatmeal-pecan mixture on top.

4 Bake 38 to 43 minutes or until top is golden brown and apples are tender when pierced with knife.

5 Cool completely in pan on cooling rack, about 2 hours. Carefully remove from pan using foil overhangs; transfer to cutting board. Using serrated knife, cut into 4 rows by 4 rows.

1 Bar Calories 380; Total Fat 17g (Saturated Fat 4g, Trans Fat 0g); Cholesterol 0mg; Sodium 250mg; Total Carbohydrate 52g (Dietary Fiber 3g); Protein 4g **Carbohydrate Choices:** 3½

Caramel-Rum Eggnog Cups

Eggnog typically is only "in season" at grocery stores during the holidays. You can purchase it when it is available and freeze to have on hand for recipes such as this one, or make your own Eggnog (page 96) any time of the year!

PREP 35 Minutes **TOTAL** 55 Minutes • *2 dozen cookie cups*

FILLING
- ½ cup white vanilla baking chips
- ¼ cup dairy eggnog (do not use canned; for homemade eggnog, see page 96)

COOKIES
- ½ cup butter, softened
- ⅔ cup packed brown sugar
- 1 egg
- 1¼ cups all-purpose flour
- ¼ cup unsweetened baking cocoa
- ½ teaspoon baking soda
- ¼ teaspoon ground nutmeg

TOPPING
- 2 tablespoons salted caramel or caramel topping (from 15 oz jar)
- 1 or 2 drops rum extract
  Coarse kosher or sea salt, if desired

1 Heat oven to 350°F. Spray 24 mini muffin cups with cooking spray.

2 In small bowl, place vanilla baking chips. In 1-quart saucepan, heat eggnog just until hot; pour over baking chips. Let stand 3 to 5 minutes. Stir until chips are melted and smooth.

3 In medium bowl, beat butter, brown sugar and egg with electric mixer on medium speed until well mixed. Beat in remaining cookie ingredients until well mixed. Shape dough by rounded tablespoonfuls into 1¼-inch balls. (If dough is too sticky to handle, dust fingers with a little all-purpose flour.) Press 1 ball into bottom and up side of each muffin cup.

4 Bake 9 to 11 minutes or until set. Using the handle end of wooden spoon or rounded back of measuring teaspoon, make indent in center of each cookie cup. Cool completely in pan on cooling racks, about

15 minutes. Remove cookie cups from muffin cups to cooling rack. Cool completely, about 15 minutes.

5 Fill each cookie with 1 teaspoon filling. In small bowl, mix salted caramel topping and rum extract; drizzle over cups. Sprinkle with salt. Refrigerate cups in a single layer in a tightly-covered container.

1 Cookie Cup Calories 110; Total Fat 5g (Saturated Fat 3.5g, Trans Fat 0g); Cholesterol 20mg; Sodium 80mg; Total Carbohydrate 15g (Dietary Fiber 0g); Protein 1g **Carbohydrate Choices:** 1

Lemon Bars

PREP 10 Minutes **TOTAL** 2 Hours • *25 bars*

- 1 cup all-purpose flour
- ½ cup butter, softened
- ¼ cup powdered sugar
- 2 eggs
- 1 cup granulated sugar
- 2 teaspoons lemon zest
- 2 tablespoons lemon juice
- ½ teaspoon baking powder
- ¼ teaspoon salt
  Additional powdered sugar

1 Heat oven to 350°F.

2 In medium bowl, mix flour, butter and ¼ cup powdered sugar with spoon until well mixed. Press into ungreased 8- or 9-inch square pan, building up ½-inch edges. Bake crust 20 minutes; remove from oven.

3 In medium bowl, beat remaining ingredients except additional powdered sugar with electric mixer on high speed about 3 minutes or until light and fluffy. Pour over hot crust.

4 Bake 25 to 30 minutes or until no indent remains when touched lightly in center. Cool completely in pan on cooling rack, about 1 hour. Sprinkle with powdered sugar. Cut into 5 rows by 5 rows.

1 Bar Calories 100; Total Fat 4g (Saturated Fat 2g, Trans Fat 0g); Cholesterol 25mg; Sodium 65mg; Total Carbohydrate 14g (Dietary Fiber 0g); Protein 1g **Carbohydrate Choices:** 1

LEMON-COCONUT BARS: Stir ½ cup flaked coconut into egg mixture in Step 3.

Caramel-Rum Eggnog Cups

Lemon Bars

Candy Basics

Making candy is a fun way to fill your serving tray with holiday favorites, or to create yummy gifts or sweet treats to share any time. It's easy and rewarding if you have the right tools and the tips below.

Selecting and Preparing Pans

- Use the exact size saucepan called for in the recipe, or else cooking time and candy texture may be affected.

- Use the size metal pan or glass dish called for in the recipe so the candy will have the right thickness, set up properly and have the desired texture.

- Grease the pan with butter or line it with foil so the candy will be removed easily. See Greasing Cookie Sheets and Pans for Bars (page 542) for how to line a pan with foil.

Mixing, Cooking and Cooling

- A cool, dry day is best for making candy. Some candies, like pralines, won't set up properly on a humid day.

- For best results, use butter. If you use margarine, it needs to be at least 65% fat. Do not use vegetable oil spreads or reduced-calorie, reduced-fat or tub products.

- If directed, be sure to butter the side of the saucepan to prevent crystals from forming while the candy mixture cooks. Crystals can result in a grainy candy.

- Don't double a candy recipe. Increasing the amount of ingredients changes the cooking time, so the resulting candy may not set up properly. Make two batches instead.

- Unless otherwise directed, do not stir the candy mixture while it's cooling. Stirring during cooling can cause the mixture to crystallize, again resulting in a grainy candy. Follow the recipe exactly, stirring only when indicated.

- Candy mixtures, the pans used to cook them and candy thermometers usually get very hot. Use hot pads or mitts to touch utensils and be careful not to splash any hot candy mixture on your skin.

USING A CANDY THERMOMETER

Here are a few things to know when using a candy thermometer:

Check the Accuracy Always check the accuracy of your candy thermometer before making candy. Place the thermometer in a pan of water and heat the water to boiling. The thermometer should read 212°F. If it doesn't, note how much higher or lower the temperature reads than 212°F and make that adjustment to the temperature needed in the recipe you are making.

Read a Thermometer at Eye Level To get an accurate reading, the candy thermometer should stand upright in the candy mixture. The bulb or tip of the thermometer shouldn't rest on the bottom of the pan. Read the thermometer at eye level. And watch the temperature closely—after 200°F, it goes up very quickly.

Use a Cold-Water Test If you don't have a candy thermometer, use the cold-water test, in which a small amount of candy mixture is dropped into a cupful of very cold water. (See Testing Candy Temperatures, page 569.)

Cooking at High Elevation At elevations above sea level, the boiling point decreases, causing quicker water evaporation during cooking. In order to achieve the proper sugar-water concentration to make the desired candy consistency, for every 1,000 feet above sea level, the temperature candy should be cooked should be reduced by 2°F. See https://foodsmartcolorado.colostate.edu/recipes/cooking-and-baking/candy-making-at-high-altitude/ for more information about making candy at high elevations.

MAKING CARAMELS

Lift caramels with foil from pan; peel foil from caramels to cut into squares.

Potato Chip Toffee Bark

EASY • MAKE AHEAD • CALORIE SMART • GLUTEN FREE • VEGETARIAN

Potato Chip Toffee Bark

PREP 15 Minutes **TOTAL** 1 Hour 25 Minutes • *24 pieces*

5 cups rippled potato chips (from 8-oz bag)	1 cup dark chocolate chips
¾ cup butter	¼ cup toffee bits
¾ cup packed brown sugar	

1 Heat oven to 400°F. Line 13x9-inch pan with foil; spray with cooking spray.

2 Coarsely crush 1 cup of the potato chips; set aside. Spread remaining chips in pan.

3 In 1½-quart saucepan, heat butter and brown sugar over medium-high heat, stirring frequently, until sugar is dissolved and mixture begins to boil. Boil, stirring frequently, 4 to 5 minutes or until candy thermometer reaches 246°F.

4 Remove from heat; pour evenly over potato chips.

5 Bake 5 minutes or until mixture is bubbling over entire surface. Remove from oven; immediately sprinkle chocolate chips over mixture. Let stand about 2 minutes or until chocolate chips begin to melt. Carefully spread chocolate evenly over brown sugar layer; sprinkle with reserved potato chips and toffee bits.

6 Cool completely, about 1 hour. Refrigerate 15 minutes or until chocolate is set. Cut or break into 24 (2-inch) pieces. Refrigerate in covered container up to 1 week.

1 Piece Calories 170; Total Fat 11g (Saturated Fat 6g, Trans Fat 0g); Cholesterol 15mg; Sodium 95mg; Total Carbohydrate 16g (Dietary Fiber 1g); Protein 0g **Carbohydrate Choices:** 1

MAKE AHEAD • CALORIE SMART • VEGETARIAN

Caramels

Cut little rectangles of waxed paper ahead of time, so you're ready to wrap when it's time. Here's another hint: Cutting the caramels with a kitchen scissors is quicker and easier than using a knife.

PREP 40 Minutes **TOTAL** 2 Hours 40 Minutes • *64 candies*

2 cups sugar	½ cup butter, cut into pieces
2 cups whipping cream	
¾ cup dark corn syrup	¼ teaspoon salt

1 Line 8- or 9-inch square pan with heavy-duty foil, leaving 1 inch of foil hanging over two opposite sides of pan; grease foil with butter.

2 In 4-quart saucepan, heat all ingredients to boiling over medium heat, stirring constantly. Boil uncovered about 35 minutes, stirring frequently, until candy thermometer reaches 240°F. Immediately spread in pan. Cool completely, about 2 hours.

3 Using foil, lift caramels out of pan; place on cutting board. Peel foil from caramels. Cut into 8 rows by 8 rows. Wrap candies individually in waxed paper or plastic wrap. Store in tightly covered container at room temperature up to 2 weeks.

1 Candy Calories 70; Total Fat 4g (Saturated Fat 2.5g, Trans Fat 0g); Cholesterol 10mg; Sodium 25mg; Total Carbohydrate 10g (Dietary Fiber 0g); Protein 0g **Carbohydrate Choices:** ½

CHOCOLATE CARAMELS: Melt 2 oz unsweetened baking chocolate, chopped, with the sugar mixture.

CHOCOLATE-TOPPED SEA SALT CARAMELS: After spreading caramel mixture into pan in Step 2, refrigerate about 1 hour or until completely cooled. In small microwavable bowl, microwave ½ cup semisweet chocolate chips and ½ teaspoon vegetable oil on High 30 to 45 seconds, stirring every 10 seconds, until chocolate is melted. Using spatula, spread chocolate evenly over caramel layer. Sprinkle with 1 teaspoon coarse sea salt. Refrigerate about 30 minutes or until chocolate is set. Continue as directed in Step 3.

Caramels

Triple Chocolate Fudge

MAKE AHEAD • CALORIE SMART • VEGETARIAN

Triple Chocolate Fudge

PREP 30 Minutes TOTAL 2 Hours • *120 candies*

4½ cups sugar

½ cup butter

1 can (12 oz) evaporated milk

4½ cups vegan miniature marshmallows (from 10-oz bag)

1 bag (12 oz) semisweet chocolate chips (2 cups)

12 oz sweet baking chocolate, chopped

2 oz unsweetened baking chocolate, chopped

1 cup chopped walnuts or pecans

2 teaspoons vanilla

¼ teaspoon almond extract

Colored sugar (see page 555), if desired

1 Line 15x10x1-inch pan with foil, extending foil over sides of pan; grease foil with vegetable shortening or butter.

2 In 5- to 6-quart saucepan, cook sugar, butter and milk over medium heat, stirring constantly, until sugar is dissolved. Heat to full boil, stirring constantly. Boil uncovered over medium heat without stirring 5 minutes or until candy thermometer reaches 234°F.

3 Remove from heat. Add marshmallows; stir until melted. Add chocolate chips and baking chocolates, stirring constantly until all chocolate is melted and mixture is smooth. Stir in walnuts, vanilla and almond extract. Quickly spread mixture in pan. Cool 1 hour. Sprinkle with colored sugar. Cool completely, about 30 minutes.

4 Remove fudge from pan by lifting foil; remove foil from sides of fudge. With long knife, cut fudge into 12 rows by 10 rows. Store in airtight container with waxed paper between layers in a cool, dark place up to 2 weeks or in the refrigerator up to 3 weeks.

1 Candy Calories 90; Total Fat 3.5g (Saturated Fat 2g, Trans Fat 0g); Cholesterol 0mg; Sodium 10mg; Total Carbohydrate 13g (Dietary Fiber 0g); Protein 0g **Carbohydrate Choices:** 1

CHERRY-PISTACHIO FUDGE: Omit nuts and colored sugar. Stir in 1½ cups sweetened dried cherries and ½ cup chopped pistachio nuts in Step 3. After spreading fudge in pan, sprinkle top with ½ cup chopped pistachio nuts; press gently into fudge.

TESTING CANDY TEMPERATURES

Using a candy thermometer is recommended, but if you don't own one, use these guides for testing candy temperatures:

Thread stage (230°F to 235°F) Fine, thin 2-inch thread falls off spoon when removed from hot mixture.

Soft-ball stage (235°F to 240°F) Mixture dropped into very cold water forms a soft ball that flattens between fingers.

Firm-ball stage (242°F to 248°F) Mixture dropped into very cold water forms a firm ball that holds its shape until pressed.

Hard-ball stage (250°F to 265°F) Mixture dropped into very cold water forms a hard ball that holds its shape but is still pliable.

Soft-crack stage (270°F to 290°F) Mixture dropped into very cold water separates into hard but pliable threads.

Hard-crack stage (300°F to 310°F) Mixture dropped into very cold water separates into hard, brittle threads that break easily.

COCONUT FUDGE: Substitute 1 cup coconut for the colored sugar; press lightly into fudge.

PEANUT BUTTER CANDY FUDGE: Omit almond extract and nuts. Stir in 1 cup candy-coated peanut butter pieces and 1 cup chopped peanuts.

TRIPLE CHOCOLATE AND CANDY FUDGE: Omit nuts. Stir in 1½ cups miniature candy-coated chocolate chips in Step 3.

Pralines

Pronounced prah-LEEN or PRAY-leen, this confection originated in Louisiana, where brown sugar and pecans are abundant. These are best made on a day when the humidity is low.

PREP 25 Minutes **TOTAL** 1 Hour 15 Minutes • *36 candies*

1½ cups granulated sugar	⅛ teaspoon salt
1½ cups packed light brown sugar	2 tablespoons butter
1 cup half-and-half	1 teaspoon vanilla
2 tablespoons light corn syrup	1¾ cups pecan halves

1 Check the accuracy of your candy thermometer before starting (see Using a Candy Thermometer, page 567). Place 18-inch long piece of waxed paper on heatproof work surface.

2 In 3-quart saucepan, mix granulated sugar, brown sugar, half-and-half, corn syrup and salt. Heat to boiling, stirring constantly. Reduce heat to medium. Cook uncovered about 6 minutes, without stirring, until candy thermometer reaches 236°F; remove from heat. Drop butter into hot mixture (do not stir in). Cool uncovered 10 minutes without stirring.

3 Add vanilla and pecans. Beat with spoon about 2 minutes or until mixture is thickened and just begins to lose its gloss. On waxed paper, quickly drop mixture by heaping tablespoonfuls, dividing pecans equally; spread slightly. Let stand uncovered 30 minutes or until candies are firm.

4 Wrap candies individually in waxed paper or plastic wrap. Store in tightly covered container at room temperature up to 2 weeks.

1 Candy Calories 120; Total Fat 5g (Saturated Fat 1g, Trans Fat 0g); Cholesterol 0mg; Sodium 20mg; Total Carbohydrate 19g (Dietary Fiber 0g); Protein 0g **Carbohydrate Choices:** 1

Creme-Filled Caramel Triangles

PREP 1 Hour 40 Minutes **TOTAL** 3 Hours 5 Minutes • *96 candies*

1 batch Caramels (page 568)	2 teaspoons light corn syrup
1 cup powdered sugar	½ teaspoons vanilla
⅓ cup coconut oil	

1 Line 15x10x1-inch pan with heavy duty foil, leaving 1 inch of foil hanging over two opposite sides of pan; grease foil with butter.

2 Prepare caramels as directed through Step 2—except cool about 1 hour, to room temperature. Refrigerate uncovered 30 minutes or until firm.

3 In small bowl, beat remaining ingredients with electric mixer on medium speed until blended; set aside.

4 Lift caramels from pan and turn upside down onto large work surface. Peel foil from caramels. Cut crosswise in half. Place one half of caramel on cutting board; spread filling evenly over caramel. Top with remaining half of the caramel, pressing it lightly into filling. Cut candies into 6 rows by 8 rows. Cut each piece diagonally in half to form two triangles. (If caramel becomes too soft to cut easily, refrigerate 15 minutes.)

5 Wrap pieces individually in waxed paper or plastic wrap. Refrigerate in tightly covered container. Let candies stand at room temperature to soften, about 15 minutes, before serving.

1 Candy Calories 60; Total Fat 3.5g (Saturated Fat 2g, Trans Fat 0g); Cholesterol 10mg; Sodium 15mg; Total Carbohydrate 8g (Dietary Fiber 0g); Protein 0g **Carbohydrate Choices:** ½

Pralines

Creme-Filled Caramel Triangles

Peanut Brittle

MAKE AHEAD • CALORIE SMART • VEGETARIAN

Peanut Brittle

PREP 55 Minutes **TOTAL** 1 Hour 55 Minutes • *72 candies*

1½ teaspoons baking soda	1 cup light corn syrup
1 teaspoon water	3 tablespoons butter, cut into pieces
1 teaspoon vanilla	1 lb unsalted raw Spanish peanuts (3 cups)
1½ cups sugar	
1 cup water	

1 Check the accuracy of your candy thermometer before starting (see Using a Candy Thermometer, page 567). Heat oven to 200°F. Grease two 15x10x1-inch pans with butter; keep warm in oven. (Keeping the pans warm allows the candy to be spread ¼ inch thick without it setting up.) Grease long metal spatula with butter; set aside.

2 In small bowl, mix baking soda, 1 teaspoon water and the vanilla; set aside. In 3-quart saucepan, mix sugar, 1 cup water and the corn syrup. Cook over medium heat about 25 minutes, stirring occasionally, until candy thermometer reaches 240°F.

3 Stir in butter and peanuts. Cook over medium heat about 13 minutes longer, stirring constantly, until candy thermometer reaches 300°F. (Watch carefully so mixture does not burn.) Immediately remove from heat. Quickly stir in baking soda mixture until light and foamy.

4 Pour half of the mixture into each pan and quickly spread with buttered heatproof spatula to about ¼ inch thick. Cool completely, at least 1 hour. Break into pieces about 2½ x 1½ inches. Store in tightly covered container at room temperature up to 2 weeks.

1 Candy Calories 70; Total Fat 3.5g (Saturated Fat 0.5g, Trans Fat 0g); Cholesterol 0mg; Sodium 35mg; Total Carbohydrate 9g (Dietary Fiber 0g); Protein 2g **Carbohydrate Choices:** ½

MICROWAVE DIRECTIONS: Prepare pans and spatula as directed in Step 1. Omit all water. In 8-cup microwavable measuring cup, mix sugar, corn syrup and peanuts. Microwave uncovered on High 10 to 12 minutes, stirring every 5 minutes, until peanuts are light brown. Stir in vanilla and butter. Microwave uncovered on High 4 to 6 minutes or until microwave candy thermometer reaches 300°F. Quickly stir in baking soda until mixture is light and foamy. Continue as directed in Step 4.

ALMOND OR CASHEW BRITTLE: Substitute unsalted almonds or cashews for the peanuts.

Marshmallows

PREP 55 Minutes **TOTAL** 9 Hours • *77 marshmallows*

⅓ cup powdered sugar	1 cup corn syrup
2½ tablespoons unflavored gelatin	½ cup water
½ cup cold water	¼ teaspoon salt
1½ cups granulated sugar	

1 Check the accuracy of your candy thermometer before starting (see Using a Candy Thermometer, page 567). Generously grease bottom and sides of 11x7-inch (2-quart) glass baking dish with butter; sprinkle with 1 tablespoon of the powdered sugar. In bowl of stand mixer, sprinkle gelatin over ½ cup cold water to soften. Place bowl on mixer stand and attach whip attachment.

2 In 2-quart saucepan, heat granulated sugar, corn syrup, ½ cup water and the salt over medium heat, stirring constantly, until sugar is dissolved. Heat to boiling; cook uncovered about 25 minutes, without stirring, until candy thermometer reaches 240°F.

3 Remove from heat. Slowly pour syrup down side of bowl into softened gelatin while beating on low speed. When all syrup is added, increase speed to high; beat 6 to 8 minutes or until mixture is white and has almost tripled in volume. Pour into baking dish, patting lightly with wet hands. Let stand uncovered at least 8 hours or overnight.

4 Sprinkle cutting board with about 1 tablespoon of the powdered sugar. In small bowl, place remaining powdered sugar. Loosen sides of marshmallow from dish with sharp knife greased with butter; gently lift in one piece onto cutting board. Using sharp knife greased with butter, cut into 11 rows by 7 rows. Dip bottom and sides of each marshmallow into bowl of powdered sugar. Store in tightly covered container at room temperature up to 3 weeks.

1 Marshmallow Calories 35; Total Fat 0g (Saturated Fat 0g, Trans Fat 0g); Cholesterol 0mg; Sodium 10mg; Total Carbohydrate 8g (Dietary Fiber 0g); Protein 0g **Carbohydrate Choices:** ½

COCOA MARSHMALLOWS: In small bowl, mix ¼ cup powdered sugar and 1 tablespoon unsweetened baking cocoa. Sprinkle 1 tablespoon of the mixture in greased baking dish; set remaining powdered sugar mixture aside. In Step 3, after increasing mixer speed to high, gradually add ¼ cup unsweetened baking cocoa and 1 teaspoon vanilla; beat 6 to 8 minutes or until mixture is light brown in color and has almost tripled in volume. Continue as directed. In Step 4, use remaining powdered sugar mixture to sprinkle on cutting board and dip the marshmallows.

PEPPERMINT MARSHMALLOWS: In Step 3, after beating mixture 6 to 8 minutes, add 1 teaspoon peppermint extract; beat 1 minute longer. Pour into baking dish, patting lightly with wet hands. Drop 8 to 10 drops red food color randomly onto top of marshmallow mixture. Pull table knife through food color to create swirl pattern over top. Continue as directed.

MAKING MARSHMALLOWS

Beat syrup-gelatin mixture until it's almost tripled in volume; beat in peppermint extract.

Drop food color randomly onto marshmallow mixture; pull table knife through to swirl.

Peppermint Marshmallows

Cakes & Cupcakes

Cake Basics

With our foolproof kitchen-tested recipes, you'll be sweetly surprised at just how easy it is to make a delicious cake from scratch. Once you take a bite of a tender, moist, delicious scratch cake, you'll quickly see what makes them so special. Straight from the Betty Crocker Kitchens, you'll find all the tips and techniques you need to become a "Betty," too!

Tips for Perfect Cakes

More than cooking, baking requires accuracy for success.

- Heat the oven to the correct temperature. Invest in an oven thermometer to be sure your oven is at the correct temperature.

- Be sure to measure ingredients accurately, using the right measuring equipment for the ingredient being measured. (See Measuring Correctly, page 25.) Add ingredients in the order they are called for.

- Use butter for best results and flavor. If you choose to substitute margarine, use one with at least 65% fat. Do not use reduced-fat butter or whipped products.

- For testing, we used handheld mixers. If you have a stand mixer, follow the manufacturer's directions for speed settings.

- Don't judge cake doneness just by the time given. Bake for the minimum amount of time listed and check for doneness using the doneness indicator given in the recipe (usually the toothpick test or by touching the cake lightly with a finger). Bake longer if needed.

- Follow directions for cake cooling and pan removal. If a cake is left in the pan too long and sticks, try reheating it in the oven for 1 minute.

- Cool cakes on cooling racks to allow for air circulation.

PICKING CAKE PANS

- Use the pan size called for in the recipe. If the size isn't printed on the bottom of the pan, measure the length and width from inside edge to inside edge. Too small a pan may cause batter to overflow; too large a pan may result in a flatter cake.

- Shiny pans reflect heat, baking cakes that are tender and light. Dark pans or pans with nonstick coating absorb heat faster, causing cakes to brown too quickly.

- Unless otherwise specified, fill cake pans half-full with batter.

Storing Cakes

- Cool cakes completely before frosting or wrapping and storing.

- Refrigerate any cake that contains dairy products in the filling or frosting.

- Store layer or tube cakes on a plate under a cake cover or inverted mixing bowl.

- Serve cake with fluffy frosting as soon as possible as the cake will tend to absorb the frosting. Store under a cake cover but slip a knife under the edge so is isn't airtight.

- See Refrigerator and Freezer Food Storage Chart, page 36, for information on wrapping, refrigerating, freezing and thawing cakes.

REMOVING CAKES FROM PANS

Place wire rack upside down over loosened cake. Invert cake carefully onto rack; remove pan.

Invert cake and rack onto another rack and flip cake right side up. Remove first rack.

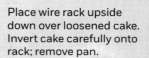

About Butter Cakes

Sometimes called shortening cakes, these are tender, fine-crumb cakes made with butter or shortening, and rely on baking powder or soda for their leavening.

- Avoid overmixing batter, which can cause tunnels or a sunken center.
- Bake cakes on the center oven rack, arranging pans so that there is at least 1 inch of space between them and the sides of the oven.
- If not all pans will fit on one rack, refrigerate one pan of batter until the others are baked and then bake remaining layer separately.
- Grease pans with shortening, not oil, butter or margarine. Use cooking spray or baking spray with flour if the recipe calls for it.
- To remove the cake from the pan, insert a knife between cake and pan, then slide it around the edge to loosen the cake. Place a wire rack upside down over the cake. Invert carefully so the cake is on the rack, then remove the pan. Invert onto another rack to flip the cake right side up.
- Cut cake with thin, sharp knife in gentle sawing motion.

About Foam Cakes

Angel food, sponge and chiffon cakes are types of foam cakes, which depend on beaten egg whites for their light and airy texture.

Angel food cakes contain no added leavening, fat or egg yolks. They have a high proportion of beaten egg whites to flour.

FOOLPROOF FOAM CAKES

The best foam cakes are high, golden brown with cracks in the surface, soft, moist and delicate. If your foam cake didn't turn out well, look here to see what when wrong:

Low and compact—underbeaten, overmixed or overfolded batter, incorrect cooling or underbaking

Coarse and not tender—underbeaten egg whites or underfolded batter

---

Sponge cakes use both egg whites and yolks and sometimes a little leavening, but do not contain other added fat.

Chiffon cakes are a cross between foam and butter cakes, made with some leavening, vegetable oil or shortening and egg yolks, as well as beaten egg whites.

- Use a clean, dry bowl and beaters to beat egg whites so they will whip properly. Even a speck of fat from egg yolk can keep them from whipping up.
- Do not grease and flour pans unless directed in a recipe. During baking, the batter needs to cling to and climb up the sides of the pans.

LEARN WITH BETTY FOAM CAKES

Ideal Cake: This cake is high and golden brown, with feathery, light texture.

Underrisen Cake: This cake is compact because of underbeaten or very overbeaten egg whites, overfolded batter or underbaking.

Overbaked Cake: This cake is too brown and crumbly from batter not being properly folded or underbeaten egg whites and overbaking.

Chocolate Layer Cake

Homemade chocolate cake layered with frosting is impressive but certainly not hard to achieve. To make great cakes, just remember that baking is more precise than cooking. You need to use the right pans, measure ingredients accurately and follow directions carefully.

PREP 20 Minutes **TOTAL** 2 Hours 5 Minutes • *12 servings*

2¼ cups all-purpose flour or 2½ cups cake flour	1¼ cups water
1⅔ cups sugar	¾ cup butter, softened
⅔ cup unsweetened baking cocoa	2 eggs
1¼ teaspoons baking soda	1 teaspoon vanilla
1 teaspoon salt	Fudge Frosting (page 602) or Fluffy White Frosting (page 600), if desired
¼ teaspoon baking powder	

1 Heat oven to 350°F. Grease bottoms and sides of 2 (9-inch) or 3 (8-inch) round cake pans with shortening; lightly flour.

2 In large bowl, beat all ingredients except frosting with electric mixer on low speed 30 seconds, scraping bowl constantly. Beat on high speed 3 minutes, scraping bowl occasionally. Pour batter into pans.

3 Bake 30 to 35 minutes or until toothpick inserted in center comes out clean. Cool in pans 10 minutes. Remove from pans to cooling racks; cool completely, about 1 hour.

4 Fill and frost layers with frosting.

1 Serving Calories 330; Total Fat 13g (Saturated Fat 8g, Trans Fat 0g); Cholesterol 60mg; Sodium 440mg; Total Carbohydrate 49g (Dietary Fiber 2g); Protein 4g **Carbohydrate Choices:** 3

CHOCOLATE SHEET CAKE: Grease bottom and sides of 13x9-inch pan with shortening; lightly flour. Make batter as directed; pour into pan. Bake 40 to 45 minutes or until toothpick inserted in center comes out clean. Cool completely in pan on cooling rack. Frost top of cake with frosting.

TURTLE LAYER CAKE: Substitute Caramel Frosting (page 602) for Fudge Frosting. After frosting first layer, press ½ cup coarsely chopped pecans gently into frosting on top of cake before topping with second layer. Sprinkle top of frosted cake with additional ½ cup coarsely chopped pecans; press lightly into frosting.

Chocolate-Hazelnut Party Cake

We've taken our beloved chocolate layer cake batter and added a few changes to it to turn it into this stunning beauty. We love this cake for both its irresistible flavor and its spectacular presentation, which even beginners can do!

PREP 55 Minutes **TOTAL** 4 Hours 35 Minutes • *12 servings*

HAZELNUT CAKE

Chocolate Layer Cake (at left)	2 teaspoons vanilla
1½ cups sugar	5 to 7 tablespoons milk
¼ cup butter, softened	½ batch Chocolate Ganache (page 603)
¼ cup hazelnut spread with cocoa	
½ cup chopped hazelnuts	

TOPPINGS

HAZELNUT FROSTING

4¾ cups powdered sugar	¼ cup finely chopped hazelnuts
½ cup hazelnut spread with cocoa	4 chocolate-covered hazelnut candies, if desired, halved
¼ cup butter, softened	4 to 6 hazelnut crème–filled tubular-shaped wafer cookies

1 Heat oven to 350°F. Grease bottoms and sides of 2 (8- or 9-inch) round cake pans with shortening or spray with cooking spray; line bottom of each pan with cooking parchment paper. Prepare Chocolate Layer Cake batter as directed—except reduce sugar to 1½ cups and butter to ¼ cup. Add ¼ cup hazelnut spread with butter. Mix as directed; stir ½ cup chopped hazelnuts into batter. Bake 25 to 30 minutes or until toothpick inserted in center comes out clean. Cool in pans 10 minutes. Remove from pans to cooling racks; cool completely, about 1 hour.

2 Meanwhile, in large bowl, mix all frosting ingredients, using 5 tablespoons of the milk, with electric mixer on low speed until blended. If necessary, beat in additional milk, 1 tablespoon at a time, until frosting is smooth and spreadable.

3 To assemble, place one cake layer top side up on plate. Spread with ½ cup of the frosting. Top with another layer top side down; spread with ½ cup of the frosting. Top with remaining cake layer, top side up. Spread remaining frosting on side and top of cake.

4 Prepare Chocolate Ganache as directed—except use half of the ingredients and let stand only 2 to 3 minutes in Step 2. Spread over the top of cake and allow ganache to drip down the sides. Let stand 2 to 3 minutes; sprinkle ¼ cup finely chopped hazelnuts around top edge of cake. Decorate with remaining toppings. Refrigerate at least 2 hours but no longer than 24 hours before serving.

1 Serving Calories 690; Total Fat 24g (Saturated Fat 9g, Trans Fat 0g); Cholesterol 60mg; Sodium 430mg; Total Carbohydrate 111g (Dietary Fiber 4g); Protein 7g **Carbohydrate Choices:** 7½

Chocolate Layer Cake

FLOURING PAN

Place 1 to 2 tablespoons flour in greased pan. Rotate pan until all sides and bottom are coated; tap pan and shake out excess flour.

SCRAPING BOWL

Beat cake ingredients on low speed. Scrape the bowl constantly while mixing on low speed and occasionally while beating on high speed.

Chocolate-Hazelnut Party Cake

German Chocolate Cake

VEGETARIAN

German Chocolate Cake

Samuel German, an employee of the Baker's Chocolate Company, developed a sweet chocolate in 1852. Over a hundred years later, in 1957, a reader of a Dallas newspaper submitted her recipe for this now-famous three-tiered cake with coconut-pecan frosting. Sales of sweet chocolate soared, and the rest is delicious history!

PREP 30 Minutes TOTAL 2 Hours 20 Minutes • *12 servings*

CAKE

- 4 oz sweet baking chocolate, chopped
- ½ cup water
- 2¼ cups all-purpose flour or 2½ cups cake flour
- 1 teaspoon baking soda
- 1 teaspoon salt
- 2 cups granulated sugar
- 1 cup butter, softened
- 4 whole eggs, separated
- 1 teaspoon vanilla
- 1 cup buttermilk

COCONUT-PECAN FROSTING

- 1 cup granulated sugar or packed brown sugar
- ½ cup butter, cut into pieces
- 1 cup evaporated milk or half-and-half
- 1 teaspoon vanilla
- 3 egg yolks
- 1⅓ cups flaked coconut
- 1 cup chopped pecans, toasted if desired (page 28)

1 Heat oven to 350°F. Grease bottoms and sides of 3 (8- or 9-inch) round cake pans with shortening. Line pan bottoms with waxed paper or cooking parchment paper; grease paper.

2 In 1-quart saucepan, heat chocolate and water over low heat, stirring frequently, until chocolate is completely melted; cool.

3 In medium bowl, mix flour, baking soda and salt; set aside. In another medium bowl, beat 2 cups granulated sugar and 1 cup butter with electric mixer on high speed until light and fluffy. Beat in 4 egg yolks, one at a time. Beat in chocolate mixture and vanilla on low speed. Add flour mixture alternately with buttermilk, beating on low speed after each addition just until smooth.

4 Wash and dry mixer beaters. In small bowl, beat 4 egg whites on high speed until stiff; fold into batter. Pour into pans. If all pans won't fit in oven at one time, refrigerate batter in third pan and bake separately.

5 Bake 8-inch pans 35 to 40 minutes or 9-inch pans 30 to 35 minutes, or until toothpick inserted in center comes out clean. Cool in pans 10 minutes. Remove from pans to cooling racks; remove waxed paper. Cool completely, about 1 hour.

6 Meanwhile, in 2-quart saucepan, stir together 1 cup granulated sugar, ½ cup butter, the milk, 1 teaspoon vanilla and 3 egg yolks until well mixed. Cook over medium heat about 12 minutes, stirring frequently, until thickened and bubbly. Stir in coconut and pecans. Cool about 30 minutes, beating occasionally with spoon, until spreadable.

7 Spread frosting between layers and on top of cake, leaving side of cake unfrosted. Store covered in refrigerator.

1 Serving Calories 670; Total Fat 33g (Saturated Fat 21g, Trans Fat 1g); Cholesterol 175mg; Sodium 600mg; Total Carbohydrate 82g (Dietary Fiber 2g); Protein 8g **Carbohydrate Choices:** 5½

Starlight Yellow Cake

This recipe originally appeared in our first cookbook, in 1950. It's been lovingly tweaked over the years for the best flavor and texture.

PREP 20 Minutes **TOTAL** 2 Hours 10 Minutes • *12 servings*

2¼ cups all-purpose flour
1½ cups sugar
3½ teaspoons baking powder
1 teaspoon salt
1¼ cups milk
½ cup butter, softened

1 teaspoon vanilla
3 eggs
Creamy Chocolate Frosting (page 601) or Peanut Butter Frosting (page 601), if desired

1 Heat oven to 350°F. Grease bottoms and sides of 2 (9-inch) round cake pans, 3 (8-inch) round cake pans or 13x9-inch pan with shortening; lightly flour.

2 In large bowl, beat all ingredients except frosting with electric mixer on low speed 30 seconds, scraping bowl constantly. Beat on high speed 3 minutes, scraping bowl occasionally. Pour batter into pan(s).

3 Bake 9-inch pans 25 to 30 minutes, 8-inch pans 30 to 35 minutes or 13x9-inch pan 35 to 40 minutes, or until toothpick inserted in center comes out clean or cake springs back when touched lightly in center. Cool rounds in pans 10 minutes; remove from pans to cooling racks. Cool 13x9-inch cake in pan on cooling rack. Cool completely, about 1 hour.

4 Fill and frost round layers or frost top of 13x9-inch cake with frosting.

1 Serving Calories 290; Total Fat 10g (Saturated Fat 6g, Trans Fat 0g); Cholesterol 70mg; Sodium 430mg; Total Carbohydrate 45g (Dietary Fiber 0g); Protein 5g **Carbohydrate Choices:** 3

STARLIGHT CHERRY CAKE: Stir in ½ cup dried cherries after beating batter in Step 2. Frost with Cherry-Nut Frosting (page 600).

STARLIGHT PEANUT BUTTER CAKE: Substitute peanut butter for butter. Frost with Fudge Frosting (page 602).

TESTING CAKE FOR DONENESS

Insert wooden cake tester or toothpick into center of cake.

When you remove cake tester, it should be clean, maybe with a few dry crumbs on it. If there is wet batter, the cake is not done.

Starlight Yellow Cake

581

LEARN WITH BETTY BUTTER CAKES

Ideal Cake: This cake is high and golden brown, with a slightly rounded top. The texture is soft, velvety and tender.

Underrisen Cake: This cake did not rise and is pale in color because of too much liquid or fat, not enough leavening or pan was too large.

Overbaked Cake: This cake is too brown and sunk in the middle because of too much leavening, too much liquid or too long in the oven.

Citrus-Gingerbread Cake

Whole-Grain Banana-Almond Cake

SLOW COOKER • CALORIE SMART • VEGETARIAN

Citrus-Gingerbread Cake

Crumpling the cooking parchment paper, then smoothing it out again, before placing it inside the slow-cooker insert makes it easier to fit. Sprinkle the citrus slices lightly with coarse sugar after removing the insert from the slow cooker, for a little sparkle and crunch.

PREP 20 Minutes **TOTAL** 4 Hours 30 Minutes • *12 servings*

1⅓ cups all-purpose flour	¼ teaspoon salt
¾ cup packed brown sugar	½ cup milk
1¼ teaspoons baking powder	¼ cup butter, melted
¾ teaspoon ginger	⅓ cup molasses
½ teaspoon ground cinnamon	1 egg
¼ teaspoon nutmeg	½ cup chopped pitted dates
	6 thin slices each orange and lemon

1 Line bottom and sides of 4-quart slow-cooker insert with one piece of cooking parchment paper; trim edges at top if needed; spray with cooking spray.

2 In medium bowl, mix flour, brown sugar, baking powder, ginger, cinnamon, nutmeg and salt until well blended. Mix in milk, butter, molasses and egg with whisk until well blended. Stir in dates. Spread batter evenly in slow-cooker insert. Place orange and lemon slices around top edge of batter, overlapping if needed, and tucking edges of slices down along side of slow-cooker insert.

3 Place folded clean dish towel under cover of cooker. Cook on Low heat setting 3 hours to 3 hours 30 minutes or until toothpick inserted in center comes out clean, carefully rotating slow-cooker insert 180 degrees (leaving cover on) every 45 minutes. Uncover; remove insert from slow cooker to cooling rack. Cool 10 minutes.

4 Using parchment paper, carefully lift cake out of slow-cooker insert and place on cooling rack. Cool 30 minutes. Slide cake off of parchment paper. Serve warm.

1 Serving Calories 200; Total Fat 4.5g (Saturated Fat 2.5g, Trans Fat 0g); Cholesterol 25mg; Sodium 150mg; Total Carbohydrate 38g (Dietary Fiber 1g); Protein 2g **Carbohydrate Choices:** 2½

VEGETARIAN

Whole Grain Banana-Almond Cake

Look for bananas that are about 8 inches long so they fit nicely in the pan.

PREP 15 Minutes **TOTAL** 45 Minutes • *9 servings*

⅔ cup sliced almonds	½ cup packed brown sugar
⅓ cup old-fashioned or quick-cooking oats	⅓ cup vegetable oil
⅓ cup all-purpose flour	1 teaspoon vanilla
⅓ cup whole wheat flour	1 egg
1 teaspoon baking soda	2 medium bananas, cut lengthwise in half
1 teaspoon apple pie or pumpkin pie spice	Maple-flavored or pure maple syrup, if desired
¼ teaspoon salt	
⅔ cup buttermilk	

1 Heat oven to 350° F. Grease 8- or 9-inch square pan with shortening or spray with cooking spray.

2 In food processor, place ⅓ cup of the almonds. Cover and process until coarsely ground. Add oats; process until very finely ground. Transfer to medium bowl; stir in all-purpose flour, wheat flour, baking soda, pie spice and salt.

3 In large bowl, mix buttermilk, brown sugar, oil, vanilla and egg with whisk until blended. Stir in flour mixture until well blended. Pour into pan. Place banana halves, cut side up, over batter; sprinkle with remaining almonds.

4 Bake 25 to 30 minutes or until toothpick inserted in center comes out clean. Serve warm or cool, drizzled with maple syrup.

1 Serving Calories 250; Total Fat 13g (Saturated Fat 2g, Trans Fat 0g); Cholesterol 20mg; Sodium 240mg; Total Carbohydrate 29g (Dietary Fiber 2g); Protein 4g **Carbohydrate Choices:** 2

Coconut Cake

PREP 50 Minutes TOTAL 2 Hours 20 Minutes • *16 servings*

CAKE

2¾	cups all-purpose flour
2	teaspoons baking powder
1	teaspoon salt
1	cup butter, softened
2	cups sugar
4	whole eggs
1½	teaspoons vanilla
1½	teaspoons almond extract
1	cup milk

BOILED FROSTING

1½ cups sugar

½ cup water
4 egg whites
½ teaspoon cream of tartar
⅛ teaspoon salt
6 large marshmallows, cut into small pieces

FILLING

2 tablespoons sugar
¼ cup reduced-fat (lite) coconut milk (from 14-oz can; not cream of coconut)
2 to 3 cups flaked coconut

1 Heat oven to 350°F. Grease 3 (9-inch) round cake pans with shortening; lightly flour. In medium bowl, mix flour, baking powder and 1 teaspoon salt; set aside.

2 In large bowl, beat butter with electric mixer on medium speed 30 seconds. Gradually add 2 cups sugar, ¼ cup at a time, beating well after each addition. Beat 2 minutes longer. Add whole eggs, one at a time, beating well after each addition. Beat in vanilla and almond extract. Add flour mixture alternately with milk, beating on low speed just until blended. Pour batter into pans.

3 Bake 18 to 20 minutes or until toothpick inserted in center comes out clean. Cool in pans 10 minutes. Remove from pans to cooling racks; cool completely, about 1 hour.

4 Meanwhile, in 2-quart saucepan, mix 1½ cups sugar and the water. Cook over medium heat, stirring constantly, until mixture is clear. Cook, without stirring, to 240°F on candy thermometer, about 10 minutes. Meanwhile, in large bowl, beat egg whites with electric mixer on low speed until foamy. Add cream of tartar and ⅛ teaspoon salt; beat on medium speed until soft peaks form. Increase speed to high; pour hot syrup down side of bowl into egg white mixture. Add marshmallows, a few pieces at a time, beating until stiff peaks form and frosting is thick enough to spread. Set aside.

5 In small microwavable bowl, microwave 2 tablespoons sugar and the coconut milk on High 1 minute; stir until sugar is dissolved. Place one cake layer, bottom side up, on serving plate; brush with half of the coconut milk mixture to within ½ inch of edge. Frost with 1 cup of the frosting; sprinkle with ½ cup of the coconut. Top with second cake layer, bottom side up; brush with remaining coconut milk mixture. Frost with 1 cup frosting; sprinkle with ½ cup coconut. Top with remaining cake layer, top side up. Spread remaining frosting on top and side of cake; sprinkle with remaining coconut.

1 Serving Calories 460; Total Fat 17g (Saturated Fat 11g, Trans Fat 0g); Cholesterol 80mg; Sodium 400mg; Total Carbohydrate 70g (Dietary Fiber 1g); Protein 5g **Carbohydrate Choices:** 4½

VEGETARIAN

Pumpkin–Cream Cheese Streusel Cake

PREP 25 Minutes TOTAL 2 Hours 35 Minutes • *12 servings*

STREUSEL

½ cup all-purpose flour
½ cup packed brown sugar
1 tablespoon chopped crystallized ginger
¼ teaspoon ground cinnamon
4 oz (half of 8-oz package) cream cheese, cut into cubes
⅓ cup coarsely chopped pecans

CAKE

1 cup pumpkin (from 15-oz can; not pumpkin pie mix)

½ cup vegetable oil
2 eggs
1¼ cups all-purpose flour
1 cup packed brown sugar
2 tablespoons chopped crystallized ginger
1½ teaspoons grated orange zest
1 teaspoon baking powder
1 teaspoon pumpkin pie spice
½ teaspoon baking soda
¼ teaspoon salt
¼ teaspoon ground cinnamon

1 Heat oven to 350°F. Grease bottom and sides of 9-inch square pan with shortening or spray with cooking spray.

2 In medium bowl, mix all streusel ingredients except cream cheese and pecans. Cut in cream cheese, using pastry blender or fork, until mixture is crumbly; stir in pecans. Set aside.

3 In large bowl, mix pumpkin, oil and eggs with whisk. Stir in remaining cake ingredients with spoon until all ingredients are moist. Spread half the batter into the pan; top with half of streusel mixture. Carefully spread remaining batter over streusel in pan; top with remaining streusel.

4 Bake 35 to 40 minutes or until toothpick inserted in the center comes out clean. Cool completely in pan, about 1 hour 30 minutes. Cut into 4 rows by 3 rows. Cover and refrigerate any remaining cake.

1 Serving Calories 360; Total Fat 16g (Saturated Fat 4g, Trans Fat 0g); Cholesterol 40mg; Sodium 190mg; Total Carbohydrate 50g (Dietary Fiber 1g); Protein 4g **Carbohydrate Choices:** 3

Coconut Cake

Silver White Cake

PREP 20 Minutes **TOTAL** 2 Hours 15 Minutes • *12 servings*

2¼ cups all-purpose flour	1 teaspoon vanilla or almond extract
1⅔ cups sugar	
⅔ cup shortening	5 egg whites
3½ teaspoons baking powder	Fluffy White Frosting (page 600) or Creamy Chocolate Frosting (page 601), if desired
1 teaspoon salt	
1¼ cups milk	

1 Heat oven to 350°F. Grease 2 (9-inch) round cake pans, 3 (8-inch) round cake pans or 13x9-inch pan with shortening; lightly flour.

2 In large bowl, beat all ingredients except egg whites and frosting with electric mixer on low speed 30 seconds, scraping bowl constantly. Beat on high speed 2 minutes, scraping bowl occasionally. Beat in egg whites on high speed 2 minutes, scraping bowl occasionally. Pour batter into pan(s).

3 Bake 9-inch rounds 30 to 35 minutes, 8-inch rounds 23 to 28 minutes or 13x9-inch pan 40 to 45 minutes, or until toothpick inserted in center comes out clean or cake springs back when touched lightly in center. Cool rounds in pans 10 minutes; remove from pans to cooling racks. Cool 13x9-inch cake in pan on cooling rack. Cool completely, about 1 hour.

MARBLING BATTER

Drop chocolate batter by tablespoonfuls randomly over white batter. Cut through batters with knife.

Cookies 'n Creme Cake

4 Fill and frost round layers or frost top of 13x9-inch cake with frosting.

1 Serving Calories 320; Total Fat 12g (Saturated Fat 3g, Trans Fat 0g); Cholesterol 0mg; Sodium 370mg; Total Carbohydrate 47g (Dietary Fiber 0g); Protein 4g **Carbohydrate Choices:** 3

CHOCOLATE CHIP CAKE: Fold ½ cup miniature or finely chopped regular semisweet chocolate chips into batter after beating in egg whites.

COOKIES 'N CREME CAKE: Stir 1 cup crushed creme-filled chocolate sandwich cookies into batter after beating in egg whites. Bake and cool as directed. Frost with Fluffy White Frosting; garnish with whole or coarsely crushed creme-filled chocolate sandwich cookies.

MARBLE CAKE: Reserve 1¾ cups of the batter. Pour remaining batter into pan(s). Stir 3 tablespoons unsweetened baking cocoa and ⅛ teaspoon baking soda into reserved batter. Drop chocolate batter by tablespoonfuls randomly onto white batter. Cut through batters with knife for marbled design. Bake as directed.

STRAWBERRY CAKE: Use 9-inch round cake pans and Fluffy White Frosting. After frosting first layer, top with 1 cup sliced fresh strawberries. Continue as directed. Garnish cake with whole or sliced strawberries.

Carrot Cake

PREP 20 Minutes **TOTAL** 1 Hour 5 Minutes • *12 servings*

1½ cups granulated sugar	½ teaspoon salt
1 cup vegetable oil	3 cups shredded carrots (5 medium)
3 eggs	
2 cups all-purpose flour	1 cup coarsely chopped walnuts
2 teaspoons ground cinnamon	Cream Cheese Frosting (page 601), if desired
1 teaspoon baking soda	
1 teaspoon vanilla	

1 Heat oven to 350°F. Grease bottom and sides of one 13x9-inch pan or two (8- or 9-inch) round pans with shortening; lightly flour.

2 In large bowl, beat granulated sugar, oil and eggs with electric mixer on low speed about 30 seconds or until blended. Add flour, cinnamon, baking soda, 1 teaspoon vanilla and the salt; beat on low speed 1 minute. Stir in carrots and nuts. Pour into pan(s).

3 Bake 40 to 45 minutes, round pans 30 to 35 minutes, or until toothpick inserted in center comes out clean. Cool 13x9-inch cake completely in pan on cooling rack. Cool rounds in pans 10 minutes; remove from pans to cooling racks. Cool completely, about 1 hour.

4 Frost top of 13x9-inch cake or fill and frost round layers with frosting. Store covered in refrigerator.

1 Serving Calories 440; Total Fat 26g (Saturated Fat 4g, Trans Fat 0g); Cholesterol 45mg; Sodium 240mg; Total Carbohydrate 45g (Dietary Fiber 2g); Protein 5g **Carbohydrate Choices:** 3

APPLE CAKE: Substitute 5 cups chopped peeled tart apples (5 medium) for the carrots.

ZUCCHINI CAKE: Substitute 5 cups shredded zucchini (3 to 4 medium) for the carrots.

Carrot Cake

VEGETARIAN

Mango-Strawberry Crumb Cake

PREP 30 Minutes **TOTAL** 2 Hours • *9 servings*

STREUSEL
- ¾ cup all-purpose flour
- ¼ cup packed brown sugar
- ¼ cup granulated sugar
- 1 teaspoon ground cinnamon
- ½ teaspoon ground cardamom
- ½ cup cold butter, cubed
- ¼ cup sliced almonds

CAKE
- 1½ cups all-purpose flour
- ¾ teaspoon baking powder
- ¾ teaspoon baking soda
- ¼ teaspoon salt
- ¾ cup granulated sugar
- ⅓ cup butter, softened
- 1 teaspoon vanilla
- 2 eggs
- ½ cup sour cream
- ¾ cup chopped fresh mango, patted dry
- ½ cup chopped fresh strawberries, patted dry

1 Heat oven to 350°F. Grease bottom and sides of 9-inch square pan with shortening or spray with cooking spray.

2 In small bowl, mix all streusel ingredients except butter and almonds. Cut in butter, using pastry blender or fork, until mixture is crumbly; stir in almonds. Set aside.

3 In medium bowl, mix flour, baking powder, baking soda and salt; set aside. In another medium bowl, beat granulated sugar, butter, vanilla and eggs with electric mixer on medium speed 2 minutes, scraping bowl occasionally. Add flour mixture alternately with sour cream, beating on low speed after each addition just until mixed. Gently stir mango and strawberries into batter. Spread batter evenly in pan; sprinkle evenly with streusel.

4 Bake 40 to 45 minutes or until toothpick inserted near center comes out clean. Cool in pan on cooling rack 45 minutes. Cut into 3 rows by 3 rows; serve warm.

1 Serving Calories 450; Total Fat 22g (Saturated Fat 13g, Trans Fat 1g); Cholesterol 95mg; Sodium 370mg; Total Carbohydrate 57g (Dietary Fiber 2g); Protein 6g **Carbohydrate Choices:** 4

Mango-Strawberry Crumb Cake

USE IT UP
POUND CAKE

CHOCOLATE-DIPPED SLICES Dip wedges in Chocolate Ganache (page 603). Let stand a minute or two; decorate with sprinkles, chopped or sliced nuts, cereal or chopped freeze-dried fruit.

FRUITY KABOBS Alternate cubes of pound cake on skewers with bite-size pieces of fresh fruit. Serve with chocolate glaze or melted peanut butter as a dip.

GLAZED PARTY BITES Cut shapes from slices of pound cake with 1- or 2-inch cutters. Dip in Vanilla Glaze (page 602); top with sprinkles.

GRILLED POUND CAKE AND PEACHES Brush slices of pound cake lightly with softened butter. Grill 1 to 2 minutes per side. Top with sliced peaches, whipped cream and raspberry sauce or syrup.

POUND CAKE FRENCH TOAST Substitute slices of pound cake for bread in French Toast (page 117).

Pound Cake

In 1895, Sperry Flour Company (a firm that later joined General Mills) produced a recipe booklet called Easy Cooking for Little Cooks. Included in this booklet was a recipe for pound cake, given its name because the primary ingredients were one pound each of butter, sugar and flour. This recipe has been a favorite ever since.

PREP 15 Minutes **TOTAL** 3 Hours 55 Minutes • *24 servings*

3 cups all-purpose flour	1 teaspoon vanilla or almond extract
1 teaspoon baking powder	5 eggs
¼ teaspoon salt	1 cup milk or evaporated milk
2½ cups granulated sugar	Powdered sugar, if desired
1 cup butter, softened	

1 Heat oven to 350°F. Generously grease bottom, side and tube of 10-inch angel food (tube) cake pan or 12-cup fluted tube cake pan, or bottoms and sides of 2 (9x5-inch) loaf pans with shortening; lightly flour.

2 In medium bowl, mix flour, baking powder and salt; set aside. In large bowl, beat granulated sugar, butter, vanilla and eggs with electric mixer on low speed 30 seconds, scraping bowl constantly. Beat on high speed 5 minutes, scraping bowl occasionally. Add flour mixture alternately with milk, beating on low speed just until smooth after each addition. Pour batter into pan(s).

3 Bake angel food or fluted tube cake pan 1 hour 10 minutes to 1 hour 20 minutes or loaf pans 55 to 60 minutes, or until toothpick inserted in center comes out clean. Cool in pan(s) 20 minutes. Remove from pan(s) to cooling rack; cool completely, about 2 hours. Sprinkle with powdered sugar.

1 Serving Calories 230; Total Fat 9g (Saturated Fat 5g, Trans Fat 0g); Cholesterol 60mg; Sodium 125mg; Total Carbohydrate 33g (Dietary Fiber 0g); Protein 3g **Carbohydrate Choices:** 2

LEMON–POPPY SEED POUND CAKE: Substitute 1 teaspoon lemon extract for vanilla. Fold 1 tablespoon grated lemon zest and ¼ cup poppy seed into batter. Drizzle with Lemon Glaze (page 603), if desired.

ORANGE-COCONUT POUND CAKE: Fold 1⅓ cups coconut and 2 tablespoons grated orange zest into batter. Drizzle with Orange Glaze (page 603), if desired.

TOASTED ALMOND POUND CAKE: Substitute almond extract for vanilla. Fold 1½ cups slivered almonds, toasted (page 28), into batter. Drizzle with Chocolate Glaze (page 603) or Vanilla Glaze (page 602) if desired.

RASPBERRY-TOPPED POUND CAKE: Make Raspberry Sauce (page 660). Spoon sauce over slices of pound cake. Top with Sweetened Whipped Cream (page 639).

Italian Orange-Almond Loaf Cake

Allow orange zest to dry on a plate while preparing the cake. Rub the dry zest between your fingers once or twice to break it apart.

PREP 25 Minutes **TOTAL** 2 Hours 20 Minutes • *10 servings*

2 cups all-purpose flour plus 1 teaspoon	1½ teaspoons baking powder
½ cup dark chocolate chips	½ teaspoon vanilla
1 cup granulated sugar	¼ teaspoon salt
3 eggs	⅓ cup finely chopped slivered almonds, toasted (page 28)
2 tablespoons grated orange zest	2 teaspoons powdered sugar
1 cup ricotta cheese	

1 Heat oven to 350°F. Grease bottom and sides of 9x5-inch loaf pan with shortening; lightly flour.

2 In small bowl, stir 1 teaspoon flour with chocolate chips; set aside.

3 In large bowl, beat granulated sugar and eggs with electric mixer on medium speed 1 to 2 minutes or until creamy. Reserve 1½ teaspoons orange zest; spread on cooking parchment paper or waxed paper to dry. Add remaining ingredients except chocolate chips, almonds and powdered sugar to egg mixture. Beat on medium speed, 1 to 2 minutes, scraping bowl occasionally until well mixed. Stir in chocolate chips and almonds until well mixed. Spread batter evenly in pan.

4 Bake 48 to 52 minutes or until toothpick inserted in center comes out clean. Cool in pan 15 minutes. Remove from pan to cooling rack; cool completely, about 2 hours.

5 Sprinkle cake with powdered sugar and reserved 1½ teaspoons orange zest.

1 Serving Calories 300; Total Fat 9g (Saturated Fat 4g, Trans Fat 0g); Cholesterol 70mg; Sodium 180mg; Total Carbohydrate 48g (Dietary Fiber 2g); Protein 7g **Carbohydrate Choices:** 3

Italian Orange–Almond Loaf Cake

HEIRLOOM and NEW TWIST

HEIRLOOM

CALORIE SMART • VEGETARIAN

Jelly Roll

If you tried to roll a regular layer cake, it would crack. This special kind of cake, called a sponge cake, is soft and flexible so it can be rolled up.

PREP 30 Minutes **TOTAL** 1 Hour 15 Minutes • *10 servings*

3 eggs	1 teaspoon baking powder
1 cup granulated sugar	¼ teaspoon salt
⅓ cup water	Powdered sugar
1 teaspoon vanilla	About ⅔ cup jelly or jam
¾ cup all-purpose flour	

1 Heat oven to 375°F. Line 15x10x1-inch pan with waxed paper, foil or cooking parchment paper; generously grease paper or foil with shortening.

2 In medium bowl, beat eggs with electric mixer on high speed about 5 minutes or until very thick and lemon colored. Gradually beat in granulated sugar. Beat in water and vanilla on low speed. Gradually add flour, baking powder and salt, beating on low speed just until smooth. Pour batter into pan, spreading to corners.

3 Bake 12 to 15 minutes or until toothpick inserted in center comes out clean. Immediately loosen cake from sides of pan and turn upside down onto clean dish towel generously sprinkled with powdered sugar. Carefully remove pan, then paper. Trim off edges of cake if stiff. While cake is hot, carefully roll cake and towel from narrow end. Cool on cooling rack at least 30 minutes.

4 Unroll cake and remove towel. Beat jelly slightly with fork to soften; spread over cake. Roll up cake again; place seam side down on serving plate. Sprinkle with powdered sugar.

1 Serving Calories 200; Total Fat 1.5g (Saturated Fat 0.5g, Trans Fat 0g); Cholesterol 65mg; Sodium 135mg; Total Carbohydrate 42g (Dietary Fiber 0g); Protein 3g **Carbohydrate Choices:** 3

MAKING A JELLY ROLL

Pour batter into 15x10x1-inch pan, spreading batter to the corners.

While cake is hot, carefully roll up with towel from narrow end.

Unroll cake; spread with jelly. Reroll cake without towel.

Jelly Roll

CHOCOLATE CAKE ROLL: Increase eggs to 4. Beat in ¼ cup unsweetened baking cocoa with the flour. If desired, fill cake with ice cream instead of jelly or jam. Unroll cake; spread with jelly. Reroll cake without towel. In Step 4, spread 1 to 1½ pints (2 to 3 cups) slightly softened ice cream over cake; roll up cake. Wrap in plastic wrap. Freeze about 4 hours or until firm.

LEMON CURD JELLY ROLL: Make cake as directed—except add 2 teaspoons grated lemon zest with the flour. Omit jelly. In Step 4, spread cake with ⅔ cup Lemon Curd (page 514) or purchased lemon curd; roll up cake. Store covered in refrigerator.

WHIPPED CREAM JELLY ROLL: Make cake as directed—except substitute ½ teaspoon almond extract for vanilla. In small bowl, beat ½ cup whipping cream, 2 teaspoons powdered sugar and ¼ teaspoon almond extract with electric mixer until stiff peaks form. In Step 4, spread over cake; roll up cake. Store covered in refrigerator.

VEGETARIAN

NEW TWIST

Pumpkin-Marshmallow Cream Cake Roll

To easily slice this cake roll, slide a piece of thin string or dental floss under the cake and wrap it around the cake. Gently cross the string at the top of the cake to cut through the roll.

PREP 25 Minutes **TOTAL** 1 Hour 45 Minutes • *12 servings*

Pumpkin-Marshmallow Cream Cake Roll

PUMPKIN CAKE ROLL

- 3 eggs
- 1 cup granulated sugar
- ⅔ cup pumpkin (from 15-oz can; not pumpkin pie mix)
- 1 teaspoon pumpkin pie spice
- 1 teaspoon vanilla
- 1 cup all-purpose flour
- 1 teaspoon baking powder
- ¼ teaspoon salt
- ⅓ cup powdered sugar

MARSHMALLOW CREAM FILLING

- 2 cups plus 1 tablespoon powdered sugar
- ¼ cup butter, softened
- 1 jar (7 oz) marshmallow creme
- 1 teaspoon vanilla
- 1 to 2 teaspoons milk
- ½ cup salted caramel topping
  Fresh mint leaves, if desired

1 Heat oven to 375°F. Line 15x10x1-inch pan with waxed paper, foil or cooking parchment paper. Spray paper or foil with cooking spray.

2 In medium bowl, beat eggs with electric mixer on high speed about 5 minutes or until very thick and lemon colored. Gradually beat in granulated sugar. Beat in pumpkin, pumpkin pie spice and 1 teaspoon vanilla on low speed until blended. Gradually add flour, baking powder and salt, beating on low speed, just until smooth. Pour batter into pan, spreading to corners.

3 Bake 10 to 13 minutes or until toothpick inserted in center comes out clean.

4 Meanwhile, sprinkle clean dish towel generously with ⅓ cup powdered sugar. Immediately loosen cake from sides of pan and turn upside down onto towel. Carefully remove pan, then paper. Trim off edges of cake if stiff. While cake is hot, carefully roll cake and towel from narrow end. Cool on cooling rack at least 1 hour or until completely cooled.

5 In medium bowl, beat 2 cups of the powdered sugar, the butter, marshmallow creme and 1 teaspoon vanilla with electric mixer on low speed until blended. Beat in 1 teaspoon milk until filling is thick and fluffy. Beat in up to 1 teaspoon additional milk, if necessary.

6 Unroll cake and remove towel. Spread filling over cake. Roll up cake again; place seam side down on serving plate. Sprinkle with the remaining 1 tablespoon powdered sugar.

7 To serve, cut into 12 slices. Drizzle about 2 teaspoons salted caramel topping onto each plate; place slice over caramel. Garnish with mint leaves.

1 Serving Calories 360; Total Fat 6g (Saturated Fat 3.5g, Trans Fat 0g); Cholesterol 60mg; Sodium 190mg; Total Carbohydrate 72g (Dietary Fiber 0g); Protein 3g **Carbohydrate Choices:** 5

5-INGREDIENT RECIPE

Frosting with Sprinkles

Cake Doughnut Holes

Triple Chocolate Fudge Cake Mix

Eggs

590

Vegetable Oil

Doughnut Chocolate Cake

5-INGREDIENT RECIPE
Doughnut Chocolate Cake

PREP 20 Minutes **TOTAL** 2 Hours 10 Minutes • *16 servings*

- 1 box (15.25 oz) Betty Crocker Super Moist ™ triple chocolate fudge cake mix with pudding
- 1¼ cups water
- ½ cup vegetable oil
- 3 eggs
- 16 cake doughnut holes (any flavor)
- 1 container chocolate or vanilla creamy ready-to-spread frosting with sprinkles

1 Heat oven to 350°F. Generously grease and lightly flour 12-cup fluted tube cake pan or spray with baking spray with flour.

2 In large bowl, mix cake mix, water, oil and eggs with electric mixer for 2 minutes on medium speed. Evenly space 8 of the doughnut holes in bottom of pan. Slowly pour batter into pan; place 4 of the remaining doughnut holes in batter between other doughnut holes, pushing holes downs gently into batter with spoon (doughnut holes on bottom of pan may move toward top).

3 Bake 40 to 45 minutes or until top springs back when touched lightly in center. Cool in pan 10 minutes. Turn pan upside down onto cooling rack; remove pan. Cool completely, about 1 hour.

4 Cut remaining 4 doughnut holes in half; set aside. Spoon frosting into small microwavable bowl. Microwave 15 to 20 seconds or until softened; stir until frosting is thin enough to be poured. Reserve 2 tablespoons frosting; set aside. Pour remaining frosting over the cake; top with doughnut halves. Drizzle reserved frosting over doughnut halves; top with sprinkles.

1 Serving Calories 350; Total Fat 17g (Saturated Fat 5g, Trans Fat 0.5g); Cholesterol 40mg; Sodium 340mg; Total Carbohydrate 47g (Dietary Fiber 0g); Protein 3g **Carbohydrate Choices:** 3

VEGETARIAN
Spiced Apple Cake with Maple Glaze

PREP 30 Minutes **TOTAL** 2 Hours 35 Minutes • *16 servings*

CAKE

- 3 cups chopped peeled apples (3 medium)
- 3 cups all-purpose flour
- 1 teaspoon baking powder
- ½ teaspoon baking soda
- ½ teaspoon salt
- 2 teaspoons ground cinnamon
- ½ teaspoon ground nutmeg
- ¼ teaspoon ground cloves
- 2 cups packed brown sugar
- 1 cup vegetable oil
- 4 eggs
- 1 teaspoon vanilla

GLAZE

- 1½ cups powdered sugar
- 3 to 4 tablespoons whipping cream
- ¼ teaspoon maple flavor

1 Heat oven to 350°F. Generously grease 12-cup fluted tube cake pan with shortening; lightly flour.

2 In medium bowl, toss apples with 2 tablespoons of the flour; set aside. In another medium bowl, mix baking powder, baking soda, salt, cinnamon, nutmeg, cloves and remaining flour. In large bowl, beat brown sugar, oil, eggs and vanilla with electric mixer on medium speed until well mixed. On low speed, beat in flour mixture just until blended. Stir in apples. Spoon batter into pan.

3 Bake 55 minutes or until toothpick inserted in center of cake comes out clean. Cool in pan 10 minutes; remove from pan to cooling rack. Cool completely, about 1 hour.

4 In medium bowl, mix glaze ingredients until smooth. Drizzle glaze over top of cake.

1 Serving Calories 400; Total Fat 16g (Saturated Fat 3g, Trans Fat 0g); Cholesterol 50mg; Sodium 170mg; Total Carbohydrate 60g (Dietary Fiber 1g); Protein 4g **Carbohydrate Choices:** 4

Spiced Apple Cake with Maple Glaze

LEARN TO BEAT, WHIP & FOLD

When baking, you'll run into these techniques often. They can be used for other dishes as well. Each technique is used for a specific purpose.

BEAT

Stirring in a rapid, circular motion; can be done with a spoon, rubber spatula or electric mixer. A hundred strokes by hand equals approximately 1 minute with a mixer. Beating ingredients is done to incorporate air into the mixture, to help lighten the texture of baked goods. If you are beating ingredients by hand and they don't seem to be combining easily, try a whisk—the loops of a whisk can break up ingredients to mix them together quickly.

WHIP

Beating ingredients (such as egg whites or cream) with a whisk or mixer to incorporate a lot of air, making them light and fluffy with loads of volume. Egg whites are beaten this way in foam cakes to give them structure, instead of the leavening ingredients used in butter cakes, which produce gas to create structure. Cream of tartar is commonly added to egg whites while whipping to improve stability and increase volume.

FOLD

Gently blending a light, whipped mixture (such as egg whites) with a heavier mixture (such as remaining cake ingredients) using a rubber spatula, so that the combined batter is also light and fluffy. The resulting baked goods, such as cake, will have a light and fluffy texture. See Making Angel Food Cake (at right).

MAKING ANGEL FOOD CAKE

Beat egg whites and cream of tartar until foamy.

Sprinkle flour mixture, ¼ cup at a time, over egg white mixture; fold in.

Cut through batter in pan with metal spatula to break air pockets.

Angel Food Cake

PREP 20 Minutes **TOTAL** 3 Hours 25 Minutes • *12 servings*

1½ cups egg whites (about 12)	½ teaspoon almond extract
1½ cups sugar	¼ teaspoon salt
1 cup cake flour	Chocolate Glaze (page 603) or Vanilla Glaze (page 602), if desired
1½ teaspoons cream of tartar	
1½ teaspoons vanilla	

1 Let egg whites stand at room temperature for 30 minutes. (Room temperature egg whites will have more volume when beaten than cold egg whites.) Move oven rack to lowest position. Heat oven to 375°F.

2 In medium bowl, mix ¾ cup of the sugar and the flour; set aside. In large, clean, dry bowl, beat egg whites and cream of tartar with electric mixer on medium speed until foamy. Beat in remaining ¾ cup sugar, 2 tablespoons at a time, on high speed, adding vanilla, almond extract and salt with the last addition of sugar. Continue beating until stiff and glossy. Do not underbeat.

3 Sprinkle flour mixture, ¼ cup at a time, over egg white mixture, folding in with rubber spatula, just until flour mixture disappears. Spoon and spread batter into ungreased 10-inch angel food (tube) cake pan. Cut gently through batter with metal spatula or knife to break air pockets.

4 Bake 30 to 35 minutes or until cracks feel dry and top springs back when touched lightly. Immediately turn pan upside down onto heatproof bottle or funnel. Let hang about 2 hours or until cake is completely cool.

5 Loosen side of cake with knife or long metal spatula; remove cake from pan. Drizzle glaze over top of cake, allowing some of glaze to drip down side.

1 Serving Calories 160; Total Fat 0g (Saturated Fat 0g, Trans Fat 0g); Cholesterol 0mg; Sodium 100mg; Total Carbohydrate 34g (Dietary Fiber 0g); Protein 4g **Carbohydrate Choices:** 2

ANGEL FOOD CUPCAKES: Place paper baking cup in each of 24 regular-size muffin cups. Spoon ⅓ cup batter into each cup. Bake 17 to 23 minutes or until cracks in cupcakes feel dry and tops spring back when touched lightly. Cool 10 minutes; remove from pans to cooling racks. Cool completely. Glaze if desired or serve with whipped cream and fresh fruit.

CHOCOLATE-CHERRY ANGEL FOOD CAKE: Stir 2 oz semisweet baking chocolate, grated, into sugar and flour in Step 2. Continue as directed. Gently fold ⅓ cup chopped very well–drained maraschino cherries into batter in Step 3.

Angel Food Cake

CHOCOLATE CONFETTI ANGEL FOOD CAKE: Stir 2 oz semisweet baking chocolate, grated, into sugar and flour in Step 2.

CHERRY ANGEL FOOD CAKE: Gently fold ⅓ cup chopped very well–drained maraschino cherries into batter in Step 3.

ESPRESSO ANGEL FOOD CAKE: Stir 2 tablespoons instant espresso coffee powder or granules into sugar and flour in Step 2.

⟳ USE IT UP
EGG YOLKS

Making angel food cake can use a lot of egg whites. Here are some delicious ways to use up the egg yolks from them:

RECIPES USING EGG YOLKS:

- Chocolate Mousse (page 646)
- Cold Brew Coffee Pie (page 626)
- Crème Brûlée (page 650)
- English Trifle (page 645)
- Hollandaise Sauce (page 495)
- Lemon Curd (page 514)
- Mallorca Breads (page 531)
- New York Cheesecake (page 644)
- Tiramisu (page 648)
- Vanilla Ice Cream (page 656)
- Vanilla Pudding (page 652)

Sour Cream Spice Cake

PREP 30 Minutes **TOTAL** 2 Hours 25 Minutes • *16 servings*

CAKE

- 2¼ cups all-purpose flour
- 1½ cups packed brown sugar
- 1 cup raisins, chopped
- 1 cup sour cream
- ½ cup chopped walnuts
- ¼ cup butter, softened
- ¼ cup shortening
- ½ cup water
- 2 teaspoons ground cinnamon
- 1¼ teaspoons baking soda
- 1 teaspoon baking powder
- ¾ teaspoon ground cloves
- ½ teaspoon salt
- ½ teaspoon ground nutmeg
- 2 eggs

BROWNED BUTTER CREAM FROSTING

- ⅓ cup butter*
- 3 cups powdered sugar
- 1½ teaspoons vanilla
- 1 to 2 tablespoons milk
  Walnut halves, broken, if desired

1 Heat oven to 350°F. Grease bottom and sides of 13x9-inch pan or 2 (8- or 9-inch) round cake pans with shortening; lightly flour.

2 In large bowl, beat all cake ingredients with electric mixer on low speed 30 seconds, scraping bowl constantly. Beat on high speed 3 minutes, scraping bowl occasionally. Pour batter into pan(s).

3 Bake 13x9-inch pan 40 to 45 minutes or round pans 30 to 35 minutes, or until toothpick inserted in center comes out clean. Cool 13x9-inch cake in pan on cooling rack. Cool rounds in pans 10 minutes; remove from pans to cooling racks. Cool completely, about 1 hour.

4 Meanwhile, in 1-quart saucepan, heat ⅓ cup butter over medium heat just until light brown, stirring constantly. Watch carefully because butter can brown and then burn quickly. Remove from heat; cool. In medium bowl, mix powdered sugar and browned butter until well blended. Add vanilla and milk; beat until frosting is smooth and spreadable. Frost top of 13x9-inch cake or fill and frost round layers with frosting. Garnish with walnut halves.

1 Serving Calories 420; Total Fat 16g (Saturated Fat 7g, Trans Fat 0g); Cholesterol 50mg; Sodium 290mg; Total Carbohydrate 65g (Dietary Fiber 1g); Protein 4g **Carbohydrate Choices:** 4

*Do not use margarine or vegetable oil spreads in the frosting.

Caramel Snickerdoodle Cake

PREP 20 Minutes **TOTAL** 2 Hours 40 Minutes • *16 servings*

- 2 tablespoons sugar
- 2 teaspoons ground cinnamon
- 2½ cups all-purpose flour
- 1¾ cups sugar
- 2 teaspoons baking soda
- 1 teaspoon salt
- 1 can (5 oz) evaporated milk
- 1 cup sour cream
- ½ cup butter, melted
- 1 teaspoon vanilla
- 2 eggs, beaten
- 10 caramels, unwrapped

1 Heat oven to 350°F. Grease 12-cup fluted tube cake pan with shortening. In small bowl, mix 2 tablespoons sugar and 1 teaspoon of the cinnamon. Sprinkle mixture over inside of pan, turning to evenly coat. Shake out any excess.

2 In large bowl, mix flour, 1¾ cups sugar, the baking soda, salt and remaining 1 teaspoon cinnamon. Reserve 1 tablespoon of the milk for topping. Add remaining milk, the sour cream, butter, vanilla and eggs to dry ingredients; stir until well blended. Pour batter into pan.

3 Bake 40 to 50 minutes or until toothpick inserted in center comes out clean. Cool in pan 30 minutes; remove from pan to cooling rack. Cool completely, about 1 hour.

4 In small microwavable bowl, microwave caramels with reserved milk, uncovered, on High 1 to 2 minutes, stirring every 30 seconds, until caramels are melted and mixture is smooth. Drizzle over top of cake.

1 Serving Calories 340; Total Fat 11g (Saturated Fat 6g, Trans Fat 0g); Cholesterol 50mg; Sodium 420mg; Total Carbohydrate 54g (Dietary Fiber 0g); Protein 4g **Carbohydrate Choices:** 3½

LEARN WITH BETTY BROWNED BUTTER

Ideal browned butter: This butter is golden brown.

Underbrowned butter: This butter is not browned enough.

Overbrowned butter: This butter is scorched and too brown.

Mocha Streusel Espresso Cake

PREP 30 Minutes **TOTAL** 4 Hours 30 Minutes • *16 servings*

STREUSEL

- 2 tablespoons all-purpose flour
- 2 tablespoons packed brown sugar
- 1 tablespoon instant espresso coffee powder or granules
- 1 tablespoon cold butter
- ½ cup miniature semisweet chocolate chips
- ¼ cup chopped pecans

CAKE

- 3 cups all-purpose flour
- 1 teaspoon baking powder
- ¼ teaspoon salt
- 1 cup milk
- ¼ cup instant espresso coffee powder or granules
- 2½ cups granulated sugar
- 1 cup butter, softened
- 1 teaspoon vanilla
- 5 eggs

GLAZE

- ⅔ cup miniature semisweet chocolate chips
- 3 tablespoons whipping cream
- 2 teaspoons instant espresso coffee powder or granules

1 Heat oven to 325°F. Grease 12-cup fluted tube cake pan with shortening; lightly flour.

2 In small bowl, mix 2 tablespoons flour, the brown sugar and 1 tablespoon espresso powder. Cut in 1 tablespoon butter, using pastry blender or fork, until crumbly. Stir in ½ cup chocolate chips and the pecans; set aside.

3 In medium bowl, mix 3 cups flour, the baking powder and salt; set aside. In 1-cup glass measuring cup, stir milk and ¼ cup espresso powder; set aside.

4 In large bowl, beat granulated sugar, 1 cup butter, the vanilla and eggs with electric mixer on low speed 30 seconds. Beat on high speed 5 minutes, scraping bowl occasionally. Add flour mixture alternately with milk mixture, beating on low speed just until smooth after each addition. Spread 3 cups of the batter into pan. Sprinkle streusel over batter. Carefully spread remaining batter over streusel.

5 Bake 1 hour 30 minutes to 1 hour 40 minutes or until toothpick inserted in center comes out clean and crack at the center top of cake no longer looks moist. Cool in pan 20 minutes. Remove from pan to cooling rack; cool completely, about 2 hours.

6 In small microwavable bowl, mix glaze ingredients. Microwave uncovered on High 30 seconds; stir until smooth. Spoon over top of cake, allowing glaze to drip down side of cake.

1 Serving Calories 450; Total Fat 20g (Saturated Fat 11g, Trans Fat 0.5g); Cholesterol 95mg; Sodium 210mg; Total Carbohydrate 61g (Dietary Fiber 2g); Protein 6g **Carbohydrate Choices:** 4

Sour Cream Spice Cake

Caramel Snickerdoodle Cake

Mocha Streusel Espresso Cake

Cupcake & Frosting Basics

Cupcakes

If you're ever unsure what to bring to a gathering, you can't go wrong with cupcakes! Frosted cupcakes are always a smile maker. Mix and match from our cupcake and frosting recipes. If you like heavily frosted, bakery-style cupcakes, consider doubling the frosting recipe you choose.

MINI CUPCAKES

Love 'em little? Use any of our recipes, following these guidelines:

- Place mini paper baking cups in each of 24 mini muffin cups.
- Make batter as directed in desired cupcake recipe; fill each mini muffin cup about two-thirds full. (Cover and refrigerate remaining batter until ready to bake.)
- Bake 12 to 16 minutes or until toothpick inserted in center comes out clean.
- Cool in pan 5 minutes; remove cupcakes from pans to cooling racks to cool completely.
- Cool pans completely before repeating Step 1.
- Repeat twice with remaining batter.
- Frost with desired frosting. Makes 72 mini cupcakes.

Frosting Tools of the Trade

Frosting a cake is a little like adding jewelry when getting dressed. The bling is what brings the outfit together! Look here for easy tips to make your frosted cakes and cupcakes social-media worthy.

It's easy to frost beautiful cakes when you have the right tools. Here are our favorites:

- Small flat and offset spatula for spreading frosting
- Cooking parchment or waxed paper
- Spoons to dollop or swirl
- Piping Equipment
  - Decorating bags (Disposable bags are the most convenient; however, reusable bags are available—simply wash out and dry to reuse them.)
  - Couplers for attaching the piping tips to the bag
  - Piping tips come in a variety of sizes or sets. Most commonly used tips: drop or dot, leaf, petal, star, grass and one or two writing tips
  - Resealable plastic bags are used in place of pastry bags. Fill one with frosting in one bottom corner. Snip off a tiny corner and "pipe" simple lines.

- Food colors made from gel, paste or liquid. Paste colors will make the most vivid colors, with gel food color being the next best choice.
- Assorted colored sugars, edible glitter or pearls
- Assorted candy sprinkles in a variety of colors and shapes

HOW MUCH FROSTING DO I NEED?

Use this handy chart to determine how much frosting you'll need for the size of your cake or cupcakes you wish to frost. For a cake that's frosted bakery-style (heavy on frosting), you may need additional frosting.

CAKE SIZE	FROSTING AMOUNT NEEDED
13x9 (single layer)	2 cups
8- or 9-inch square (single layer)	1 cup
2-layer cake	2½—3 cups
24 cupcakes	About 1¾ cups

FROSTING A LAYER CAKE

Brush any loose crumbs from cooled cake layer. Place 4 strips of waxed paper around edge of plate. Place layer, rounded side down, on plate.

Spread ⅓ to ½ cup frosting over top of first layer to within about ¼ inch of edge.

Place second cake layer, rounded side up, on frosted first layer. Coat side of cake with a very thin layer of frosting to seal in crumbs.

Frost side of cake in swirls, making a rim about ¼ inch high above top of cake. Spread remaining frosting on top, just to the built-up rim. Carefully remove waxed paper strips.

Chocolate, Yellow and White Cupcakes
with Creamy Chocolate Frosting

Yellow Cupcakes

Customize these every time by adding chocolate chips or your favorite chopped nuts!

PREP 15 Minutes **TOTAL** 1 Hour 15 Minutes • *24 cupcakes*

2⅓ cups all-purpose flour	1 teaspoon vanilla
2½ teaspoons baking powder	⅔ cup milk
½ teaspoon salt	Creamy Vanilla Frosting (page 601), Vodka Buttercream Frosting (page 602) or Peanut Butter Frosting (page 601), if desired
1 cup butter or margarine, softened	
1¼ cups sugar	
3 eggs	

1 Heat oven to 350°F. Place paper baking cup in each of 24 regular-size muffin cups.

2 In medium bowl, mix flour, baking powder and salt; set aside. In large bowl, beat butter with electric mixer on medium speed 30 seconds. Gradually add sugar, about ¼ cup at a time, beating well after each addition and scraping bowl occasionally. Beat 2 minutes longer. Add eggs, one at a time, beating well after each addition. Beat in vanilla. On low speed, alternately add flour mixture, about one-third of mixture at a time, and milk, about half at a time, beating just until blended.

3 Divide batter evenly among muffin cups, filling each with about 3 tablespoons batter or until two-thirds full.

4 Bake 20 to 25 minutes or until golden brown and toothpick inserted in center of cupcake comes out clean. Cool in pans 5 minutes. Remove cupcakes from pans; place on cooling racks to cool. Frost with frosting.

1 Cupcake Calories 170; Total Fat 9g (Saturated Fat 5g, Trans Fat 0g); Cholesterol 45mg; Sodium 190mg; Total Carbohydrate 20g (Dietary Fiber 0g); Protein 2g **Carbohydrate Choices:** 1

Chocolate Cupcakes

PREP 20 Minutes **TOTAL** 1 Hour 15 Minutes • *24 cupcakes*

2 cups all-purpose flour	¾ cup shortening
1¼ teaspoons baking soda	1½ cups sugar
1 teaspoon salt	2 eggs
¼ teaspoon baking powder	1 teaspoon vanilla
1 cup hot water	Creamy Chocolate Frosting (page 601) or Chocolate Martini Buttercream Frosting (page 602), if desired
⅔ cup unsweetened baking cocoa	

1 Heat oven to 350°F. Place paper baking cup in each of 24 regular-size muffin cups.

2 In medium bowl, mix flour, baking soda, salt and baking powder; set aside. In small bowl, mix hot water and cocoa until dissolved; set aside.

3 In large bowl, beat shortening with electric mixer on medium speed 30 seconds. Gradually add sugar about ¼ cup at a time, beating well after each addition and scraping bowl occasionally. Beat 2 minutes longer. Add eggs, one at a time, beating well after each addition. Beat in vanilla. On low speed, alternately add flour mixture, about one-third of mixture at a time, and cocoa mixture, about half at a time, beating just until blended.

4 Divide batter evenly among muffin cups, filling each about two-thirds full.

5 Bake 20 to 25 minutes or until toothpick inserted in center of cupcake comes out clean. Cool in pans 5 minutes. Remove cupcakes from pans; place on cooling racks to cool. Frost with frosting.

1 Cupcake Calories 160; Total Fat 7g (Saturated Fat 2g, Trans Fat 1g); Cholesterol 20mg; Sodium 180mg; Total Carbohydrate 22g (Dietary Fiber 1g); Protein 2g **Carbohydrate Choices:** 1½

CLEVER WAYS TO TOP CUPCAKES

You don't have to be a pastry chef to decorate cupcakes! Try one of these fun and simple toppers pressed into frosted cupcakes:

Candy Toppers Use small candies, fun-size candy bars or suckers.

Cookie-Kissed Use a small cookie or two.

Decadent Cupcakes Drizzle frosting with chocolate or caramel syrup just before serving.

Ice Cream Cakes Place mini drumstick or other ice cream novelty on cupcakes just before serving.

Pyramid Cakes Top regular-size frosted cupcake with mini frosted cupcake.

Cookie Butter
Mug Cakes

Sweet Potato Cupcakes with
Cinnamon-Marshmallow Frosting

FAST • VEGETARIAN

Cookie Butter Mug Cakes

For a delicious crunch, top these easy cakes with gingersnap or other crisp cookie such as shortbread or chocolate sandwich cookie. Or drizzle a little warmed cookie butter over the cakes before serving.

PREP 10 Minutes **TOTAL** 15 Minutes • *2 mug cakes*

MUG CAKES
- ¾ cup Scratch Mug Cake Mix (below)
- ¼ cup milk
- 2 tablespoons cookie butter spread
- ½ teaspoon vanilla
- 1 egg

- ¼ cup chopped gingersnap cookies (about 4 cookies)

TOPPING
- ¾ cup thawed frozen whipped topping
- 1½ tablespoons cookie butter spread (from 14.1-oz jar)

1 Spray two microwavable mugs (10 oz or larger) with cooking spray.

2 In medium bowl, mix all mug cake ingredients except cookies with spoon until well blended. Stir in cookies. Divide batter between mugs.

3 Microwave both cups uncovered on High 1½ to 2 minutes or until toothpick inserted in center comes out clean. Cool 5 minutes.

4 Meanwhile, in small bowl, mix topping ingredients with spoon until well blended. Top each cake with topping.

SCRATCH MUG CAKE MIX

Whip up and store this simple mix to have on hand whenever you want a little mug cake sweet treat! Use it for Cookie Butter Mug Cakes (above) and Mango-Mojito Mug Cakes (page 600). *Makes 2 cups*

- 1⅓ cups all-purpose flour
- ¾ cup sugar
- 1¼ teaspoons baking powder
- ¼ teaspoon salt

In medium bowl, mix all ingredients. Use immediately or store in a tightly-covered container in a cool, dark location up to 1 month or in a freezer-safe covered container up to 3 months.

---

1 Mug Cake Calories 570; Total Fat 20g (Saturated Fat 8g, Trans Fat 0g); Cholesterol 95mg; Sodium 410mg; Total Carbohydrate 87g (Dietary Fiber 2g); Protein 10g **Carbohydrate Choices:** 6

VEGETARIAN

Sweet Potato Cupcakes with Cinnamon-Marshmallow Frosting

If you start with 2 large sweet potatoes, you can shred enough from one to measure 1/2 cup, then cook the remainder (see page 264) to get 1 cup cooked mashed sweet potatoes.

PREP 45 Minutes **TOTAL** 1 Hour 40 Minutes • *24 cupcakes*

SWEET POTATO CUPCAKES
- 2⅓ cups all-purpose flour
- 2½ teaspoons baking powder
- 1½ teaspoons ground cinnamon
- ½ teaspoon salt
- ½ teaspoon ground ginger
- ¼ teaspoon ground nutmeg
- 1 cup butter, softened
- ¾ cup granulated sugar
- ½ cup packed brown sugar
- 3 eggs
- 1 cup mashed cooked dark-orange sweet potato (see page 264)

- 1 teaspoon vanilla
- ½ cup milk
- ½ cup shredded peeled uncooked dark-orange sweet potato, if desired

CINNAMON-MARSHMALLOW FROSTING
- 1 jar (7 oz) marshmallow creme
- 1 cup butter, softened
- ½ teaspoon vanilla
- 1 to 2 tablespoons milk
- 2¼ cups powdered sugar
- ½ teaspoon ground cinnamon plus additional for garnish, if desired

1 Heat oven to 350°F. Place paper baking cup in or spray with cooking spray each of 24 regular-size muffin cups.

2 In medium bowl, mix flour, baking powder, salt, 1½ teaspoons cinnamon, ginger and nutmeg; set aside. In large bowl, beat 1 cup butter with electric mixer on medium speed 30 seconds. Add granulated sugar and brown sugar, about ¼ cup at a time, beating after each addition and scraping the bowl occasionally. Beat 2 minutes longer. Add eggs, one at a time, beating well after each addition. Beat in mashed sweet potato and 1 teaspoon vanilla. Alternately add flour mixture and milk, beating on low speed after each addition just until mixed. Stir in shredded sweet potato. Divide batter evenly among muffin cups, filling each about two-thirds full.

3 Bake 20 to 25 minutes or until golden brown and toothpick inserted in center of cupcake comes out clean. Cool 5 minutes; remove cupcakes from pans to cooling racks. Cool completely, about 30 minutes.

4 Meanwhile, in large bowl, beat marshmallow creme, 1 cup butter, ½ teaspoon vanilla and 1 tablespoon of the milk with electric mixer on medium speed until blended. Beat in powdered sugar and ½ teaspoon cinnamon until fluffy. If necessary, beat in more milk, a few drops at a time, until thin enough to spread. Spread or pipe frosting onto cupcakes. Sprinkle with additional cinnamon.

1 Cupcake Calories 320; Total Fat 16g (Saturated Fat 10g, Trans Fat 0.5g); Cholesterol 65mg; Sodium 240mg; Total Carbohydrate 41g (Dietary Fiber 1g); Protein 2g **Carbohydrate Choices: 3**

VEGETARIAN

Lemon Meringue Cupcakes

PREP 1 Hour **TOTAL** 2 Hours • *24 cupcakes*

CUPCAKES

2⅓ cups all-purpose flour	⅔ cup milk
2½ teaspoons baking powder	1 jar (10 to 12 oz) lemon curd (for homemade lemon curd, see page 514)
½ teaspoon salt	
1 cup butter, softened	**MERINGUE**
1¼ cups sugar	4 egg whites
3 whole eggs	¼ teaspoon cream of tartar
2 tablespoons grated lemon zest	1½ teaspoons vanilla
1 teaspoon vanilla	⅔ cup sugar

1 Heat oven to 350°F. Place paper baking cup in each of 24 regular-size muffin cups; spray paper cups with baking spray with flour.

2 In medium bowl, mix flour, baking powder and salt; set aside. In large bowl, beat butter with electric mixer on medium speed 30 seconds. Gradually add 1¼ cups sugar, about ¼ cup at a time, beating well after each addition. Beat 2 minutes longer. Add eggs, one at a time, beating well after each addition. Beat in lemon zest and 1 teaspoon vanilla. Alternately add flour mixture and milk, beating on low speed just until blended. Divide batter evenly among muffin cups, filling each about two-thirds full.

3 Bake 20 to 25 minutes or until toothpick inserted in center comes out clean. Cool 5 minutes; remove from pans to cooling racks. Cool completely, about 30 minutes.

4 By slowly spinning end of round handle of wooden spoon back and forth, make deep, ¾-inch-wide indentation in center of top of each cupcake, not quite to bottom. (Wiggle end of handle in cupcake to make opening large enough.) Spoon lemon curd into small resealable food-storage plastic bag; seal bag. Cut ⅜-inch tip off one bottom corner of bag. Insert tip of bag into opening in each cupcake; squeeze bag to fill opening.

5 Heat oven to 450°F. In medium bowl, beat egg whites, cream of tartar and 1½ teaspoons vanilla with electric mixer on high speed until soft peaks form. Gradually add ⅔ cup sugar, 1 tablespoon at a time, beating until stiff peaks form and mixture is glossy. Frost cupcakes with meringue; place on cookie sheet. Bake 2 to 3 minutes or until lightly browned.

1 Cupcake Calories 230; Total Fat 9g (Saturated Fat 6g, Trans Fat 0g); Cholesterol 60mg; Sodium 210mg; Total Carbohydrate 34g (Dietary Fiber 0g); Protein 3g **Carbohydrate Choices: 2**

CALORIE SMART • VEGETARIAN

White Cupcakes

PREP 15 Minutes **TOTAL** 1 Hour 15 Minutes • *24 cupcakes*

2¾ cups all-purpose flour	2½ teaspoons vanilla or almond extract
3 teaspoons baking powder	1¼ cups milk
½ teaspoon salt	Creamy Vanilla Frosting (page 601) or Fudge Frosting (page 602), if desired
¾ cup shortening or butter	
1⅔ cups sugar	
5 egg whites	

1 Heat oven to 350°F. Place paper baking cup in each of 24 regular-size muffin cups.

2 In medium bowl, mix flour, baking powder and salt; set aside. In large bowl, beat shortening with electric mixer on medium speed 30 seconds. Gradually add sugar, about ⅓ cup at a time, beating well after each addition and scraping bowl occasionally. Beat 2 minutes longer. Add egg whites, one at a time, beating well after each addition. Beat in vanilla. On low speed, alternately add flour mixture, about one-third of mixture at a time, and milk, about half at a time, beating just until blended.

3 Divide batter evenly among muffin cups, filling each about two-thirds full.

4 Bake 18 to 20 minutes or until toothpick inserted in center of cupcake comes out clean. Cool in pans 5 minutes. Remove cupcakes from pans; place on cooling racks to cool. Frost with frosting.

1 Cupcake Calories 180; Total Fat 7g (Saturated Fat 2g, Trans Fat 1g); Cholesterol 0mg; Sodium 125mg; Total Carbohydrate 26g (Dietary Fiber 0g); Protein 2g **Carbohydrate Choices: 2**

Lemon Meringue Cupcakes

Mango-Mojito Mug Cakes

If fresh mango isn't available, use drained refrigerated mango instead. Add a fresh mint leaf or two, if you want an easy garnish.

PREP 10 Minutes **TOTAL** 20 Minutes • *2 mug cakes*

1 cup chopped mango (about 1 large)	2 tablespoons butter, melted
1½ teaspoons fresh lime juice	1 egg
1½ teaspoons rum extract	¾ cup Scratch Mug Cake Mix (page 598)
1 teaspoon chopped fresh mint	Whipped topping or pressurized whipped cream, if desired

1 Spray two microwavable mugs (10 oz or larger) with cooking spray.

2 In small food processor or blender container, combine mango, lime juice, rum extract and mint. Cover and process until about 1 minute or until smooth. Reserve 1 tablespoon mango mixture. In small bowl, beat butter, egg and remaining mango mixture with whisk. Stir in mug cake mix until blended.

CUTTING A MANGO

Stand mango upright on cutting board. Using paring knife, cut away flesh from seed; repeat on other side. Turn center piece ¼ turn and cut away remaining flesh along both sides of seed.

Mango-Mojito Mug Cakes

3 Divide batter between mugs. Microwave uncovered on High 2½ to 3½ minutes or until toothpick inserted in center comes out clean and cake pulls away from the sides of the mugs. Cool 5 minutes.

4 Top with whipped topping; drizzle with remaining mango mixture.

1 Mug Cake Calories 440; Total Fat 15g (Saturated Fat 8g, Trans Fat 0g); Cholesterol 125mg; Sodium 350mg; Total Carbohydrate 66g (Dietary Fiber 2g); Protein 7g **Carbohydrate Choices:** 4½

Fluffy White Frosting

This frosting got its name because its large white peaks hold up long after it's beaten. It's sometimes called White Mountain Frosting.

PREP 25 Minutes **TOTAL** 55 Minutes • *3 cups*

2 egg whites	2 tablespoons water
½ cup sugar	1 teaspoon vanilla
¼ cup light corn syrup	

1 Let egg whites stand at room temperature for 30 minutes. (Room temperature egg whites will have more volume when beaten than cold egg whites.) In medium heatproof bowl, beat egg whites with electric mixer on high speed just until stiff peaks form.

2 In 1-quart saucepan, stir sugar, corn syrup and water until well mixed. Cover and heat to rolling boil over medium heat. Uncover and boil 4 to 8 minutes, without stirring, until candy thermometer reads 242°F or small amount of hot syrup dropped into cup of very cold water forms a firm ball that holds its shape until pressed (see Testing Candy Temperatures, page 569). For accurate temperature reading, tilt saucepan slightly so syrup is deep enough for thermometer.

3 Pour hot syrup very slowly in thin stream down side of bowl into egg whites, beating constantly on medium speed. Add vanilla. Beat on high speed about 10 minutes or until stiff peaks form.

4 Frost 13x9-inch cake, two 8- or 9-inch square cakes, 36 cupcakes or fill and frost two-layer 8- or 9-inch cake. Leftover frosting can be tightly covered and refrigerated up to 2 days; do not freeze. Let stand 30 minutes at room temperature to soften; do not stir.

3 Tablespoons Calories 45; Total Fat 0g (Saturated Fat 0g, Trans Fat 0g); Cholesterol 0mg; Sodium 10mg; Total Carbohydrate 10g (Dietary Fiber 0g); Protein 0g **Carbohydrate Choices:** ½

BUTTERSCOTCH FROSTING: Substitute packed brown sugar for granulated sugar. Reduce vanilla to ½ teaspoon.

PEPPERMINT FROSTING: Stir ⅓ cup coarsely crushed hard peppermint candies or ½ teaspoon peppermint extract into finished frosting.

CHERRY-NUT FROSTING: Stir in ¼ cup chopped candied cherries, ¼ cup chopped nuts and, if desired, 6 to 8 drops red food color into finished frosting.

Creamy Chocolate Frosting

PREP 10 Minutes **TOTAL** 10 Minutes • *About 2 cups*

⅓ cup butter, softened	3 cups powdered sugar
3 oz unsweetened baking chocolate, melted, cooled at least 5 minutes	2 teaspoons vanilla
	3 to 4 tablespoons milk

1 In large bowl, beat butter and chocolate with electric mixer on low speed until blended. Gradually beat in powdered sugar until blended.

2 Gradually beat in vanilla and just enough milk to make frosting smooth and spreadable. If frosting is too thick, beat in more milk, a few drops at a time. If frosting becomes too thin, beat in a small amount of powdered sugar.

3 Frost 13x9-inch cake, two 8- or 9-inch square cakes or 24 cupcakes.* Leftover frosting can be tightly covered and refrigerated up to 5 days or frozen up to 1 month. Let stand 30 minutes at room temperature to soften; stir before using.

3 Tablespoons Calories 250; Total Fat 10g (Saturated Fat 6g, Trans Fat 0g); Cholesterol 15mg; Sodium 50mg; Total Carbohydrate 37g (Dietary Fiber 1g); Protein 1g **Carbohydrate Choices:** 2½

*To fill and frost an 8- or 9-inch two- or three-layer cake, use ½ cup butter, 4 oz chocolate, 4½ cups powdered sugar, 1 tablespoon vanilla and about ¼ cup milk.

CREAMY COCOA FROSTING: Substitute ⅓ cup unsweetened baking cocoa for chocolate.

MOCHA FROSTING: Add 2½ teaspoons instant coffee granules or crystals with powdered sugar.

WHITE CHOCOLATE FROSTING: Substitute 2 oz white chocolate baking squares or bars, melted and cooled at least 5 minutes, for chocolate. (Do not use white vanilla baking chips, because they will add a grainy texture.)

Creamy Vanilla Frosting

PREP 10 Minutes **TOTAL** 10 Minutes • *About 1¾ cups*

3 cups powdered sugar	1½ teaspoons vanilla
⅓ cup butter, softened	1 to 2 tablespoons milk

1 In large bowl, mix powdered sugar and butter with spoon or electric mixer on low speed until blended. Stir in vanilla and 1 tablespoon of the milk.

2 Gradually beat in just enough remaining milk to make frosting smooth and spreadable. If frosting is too thick, beat in more milk, a few drops at a time. If frosting becomes too thin, beat in a small amount of powdered sugar.

3 Frost 13x9-inch cake, two 8-or 9-inch square cakes or 24 cupcakes.* Leftover frosting can be tightly covered and refrigerated up to 5 days or frozen up to 1 month.

Let stand 30 minutes at room temperature to soften; stir before using.

3 Tablespoons Calories 220; Total Fat 7g (Saturated Fat 4.5g, Trans Fat 0g); Cholesterol 20mg; Sodium 55mg; Total Carbohydrate 40g (Dietary Fiber 0g); Protein 0g **Carbohydrate Choices:** 2½

*To fill and frost a two- or three-layer 8- or 9-inch cake, use 4½ cups powdered sugar, ½ cup butter, 2 teaspoons vanilla and about 3 tablespoons milk.

BROWNED BUTTER FROSTING: In 1-quart saucepan, heat ⅓ cup butter (do not use margarine or vegetable oil spreads) over medium heat just until light brown, stirring constantly. Watch carefully because butter can brown and then burn quickly. Cool. Substitute browned butter for softened butter.

LEMON FROSTING: Omit vanilla. Substitute lemon juice for milk. Stir in 1 teaspoon grated lemon zest.

MAPLE-NUT FROSTING: Omit vanilla. Substitute 1 to 2 tablespoons real maple or maple-flavored syrup for milk. Stir in ¼ cup finely chopped nuts.

ORANGE FROSTING: Omit vanilla. Substitute orange juice for milk. Stir in 1 teaspoon grated orange zest.

PEANUT BUTTER FROSTING: Substitute creamy peanut butter for butter. Increase milk to about ¼ cup, adding more if necessary, a few drops at a time.

Cream Cheese Frosting

This is the perfect frosting for gluten-free carrot cake, spice cake or applesauce cake. Be sure to refrigerate the frosted cake, since cream cheese is perishable.

PREP 10 Minutes **TOTAL** 10 Minutes • *About 2½ cups*

1 package (8 oz) cream cheese, softened	2 to 3 teaspoons milk
¼ cup butter, softened	1 teaspoon vanilla
	4 cups powdered sugar

1 In large bowl, beat cream cheese, butter, milk and vanilla with electric mixer on low speed until smooth.

2 Gradually beat in powdered sugar, 1 cup at a time, on low speed until frosting is smooth and spreadable.

3 Frost 13x9-inch cake, two 8-or 9-inch square cakes, 30 cupcakes or fill and frost two-layer 8- or 9-inch cake. Leftover frosting can be tightly covered and refrigerated up to 5 days or frozen up to 1 month. Let stand 30 minutes at room temperature to soften; stir before using.

3 Tablespoons Calories 240; Total Fat 10g (Saturated Fat 6g, Trans Fat 0g); Cholesterol 25mg; Sodium 85mg; Total Carbohydrate 38g (Dietary Fiber 0g); Protein 1g **Carbohydrate Choices:** 2½

CHOCOLATE CREAM CHEESE FROSTING: Add 2 oz unsweetened baking chocolate, melted and cooled 10 minutes, with butter.

CINNAMON CREAM CHEESE FROSTING: Stir in ½ teaspoon ground cinnamon with vanilla.

Vodka and Chocolate Martini
Buttercream Frosting

3 Frost 13x9-inch cake, two 8- or 9-inch square cakes, 24 cupcakes or fill and frost two-layer 8- or 9-inch cake. Leftover frosting can be tightly covered and refrigerated up to 5 days or frozen up to 1 month. Let stand 30 minutes at room temperature to soften; stir before using.

3 Tablespoons Calories 260; Total Fat 9g (Saturated Fat 6g, Trans Fat 0g); Cholesterol 25mg; Sodium 80mg; Total Carbohydrate 44g (Dietary Fiber 0g); Protein 0g **Carbohydrate Choices:** 3

SALTY CARAMEL FROSTING: Sprinkle ½ teaspoon kosher (coarse) salt over frosted gluten-free cupcakes or cake.

EASY • FAST • VEGETARIAN

Vodka Buttercream Frosting

PREP 10 Minutes **TOTAL** 10 Minutes • *2 cups*

½ cup butter, softened	4 to 5 tablespoons vanilla-flavored or plain vodka
4 cups powdered sugar	

1 In large bowl, beat butter, powdered sugar and 4 tablespoons of the vodka with electric mixer on low speed until blended. Add additional vodka 1 teaspoon at a time, beating on low speed, until frosting is smooth and spreadable.

2 Frosts 13x9-inch cake, two 8-or 9-inch square cakes or 24 cupcakes. Frosting is best served the same day it is prepared.

2 Tablespoons Calories 180; Total Fat 6g (Saturated Fat 3.5g, Trans Fat 0g); Cholesterol 15mg; Sodium 45mg; Total Carbohydrate 30g (Dietary Fiber 0g); Protein 0g **Carbohydrate Choices:** 2

CHOCOLATE MARTINI BUTTERCREAM FROSTING: Add 2 tablespoons unsweetened baking cocoa with powdered sugar. Reduce vodka to 3 tablespoons. Add 2 tablespoons chocolate liqueur with vodka, adding additional 1 teaspoon chocolate liqueur at a time, beating on low speed, until smooth and spreadable.

EASY • GLUTEN FREE • VEGETARIAN

Caramel Frosting

For a richer frosting, use whole milk or half-and-half.

PREP 10 Minutes **TOTAL** 40 Minutes • *About 2 cups*

½ cup butter	¼ cup milk
1 cup packed brown sugar	2 cups powdered sugar

1 In 2-quart saucepan, melt butter over medium heat. Stir in brown sugar. Heat to boiling, stirring constantly; reduce heat to low. Boil and stir 2 minutes. Stir in milk. Heat to boiling; remove from heat. Cool to lukewarm, about 30 minutes.

2 Gradually stir in powdered sugar. Place saucepan of frosting in bowl of cold water. Beat with spoon until frosting is smooth and spreadable. If frosting becomes too stiff, stir in additional milk, 1 teaspoon at a time, or heat over low heat, stirring constantly.

GLUTEN FREE • VEGETARIAN

Fudge Frosting

PREP 10 Minutes **TOTAL** 55 Minutes • *About 3½ cups*

2 cups granulated sugar	¼ cup light corn syrup
1 cup unsweetened baking cocoa	¼ teaspoon salt
1 cup milk	2 teaspoons vanilla
½ cup butter, cut into pieces	2½ to 3 cups powdered sugar

1 In 3-quart saucepan, mix granulated sugar and cocoa. Stir in milk, butter, corn syrup and salt. Heat to boiling over medium-high heat, stirring frequently. Boil 3 minutes, stirring occasionally to prevent mixture from bubbling over. Remove from heat. Cool at least 45 minutes.

2 Beat in vanilla and enough powdered sugar for spreading consistency.

3 Frost two 13x9-inch cakes, two 8- or 9-inch square cakes, 48 cupcakes or fill and frost two- or three-layer 8- or 9-inch cake. Leftover frosting can be tightly covered and refrigerated up to 5 days or frozen up to 1 month. Let stand 30 minutes at room temperature to soften; stir before using.

3 Tablespoons Calories 240; Total Fat 6g (Saturated Fat 3.5g, Trans Fat 0g); Cholesterol 15mg; Sodium 80mg; Total Carbohydrate 45g (Dietary Fiber 1g); Protein 1g **Carbohydrate Choices:** 3

EASY • FAST • CALORIE SMART • GLUTEN FREE • VEGETARIAN

Vanilla Glaze

PREP 5 Minutes **TOTAL** 5 Minutes • *1 cup*

⅓ cup butter	2 to 4 tablespoons hot water
2 cups powdered sugar	
1½ teaspoons vanilla	

1 In 1½-quart saucepan, melt butter over low heat; remove from heat. Stir in powdered sugar and vanilla.

2 Stir in hot water, 1 tablespoon at a time, until glaze is smooth and has the consistency of thick syrup.

3 Glaze 12-cup fluted tube cake, 10-inch angel food or chiffon cake or top of 8- or 9-inch layer cake or 24 cupcakes.

4 Teaspoons Calories 130; Total Fat 5g (Saturated Fat 3g, Trans Fat 0g); Cholesterol 15mg; Sodium 35mg; Total Carbohydrate 20g (Dietary Fiber 0g); Protein 0g **Carbohydrate Choices:** 1

BROWNED BUTTER GLAZE: Brown butter as directed in Browned Butter Frosting (page 601). Continue as directed.

LEMON GLAZE: Stir 1 teaspoon grated lemon zest into melted butter. Omit vanilla. Substitute lemon juice, heated, for hot water.

ORANGE GLAZE: Stir 1 teaspoon grated orange zest into melted butter. Omit vanilla. Substitute orange juice, heated, for hot water.

EASY • FAST • CALORIE SMART • GLUTEN FREE • VEGETARIAN

Chocolate Glaze

The corn syrup in this glaze not only adds sweetness but also gives it a glossy sheen.

PREP 5 Minutes **TOTAL** 15 Minutes • *1 cup*

1 cup semisweet chocolate chips	¼ cup light corn syrup
¼ cup butter	2 to 4 teaspoons hot water

1 In 1-quart saucepan, heat chocolate chips, butter and corn syrup over low heat, stirring frequently, until chocolate chips are melted. Cool about 10 minutes.

2 Stir in hot water, 1 teaspoon at a time, until glaze is smooth and has the consistency of thick syrup.

3 Glaze 12-cup fluted tube cake, 10-inch angel food or chiffon cake or top of 8- or 9-inch layer cake or 24 cupcakes.

4 Teaspoons Calories 130; Total Fat 8g (Saturated Fat 5g, Trans Fat 0g); Cholesterol 10mg; Sodium 40mg; Total Carbohydrate 14g (Dietary Fiber 0g); Protein 0g **Carbohydrate Choices:** 1

DARK CHOCOLATE GLAZE: Substitute dark chocolate chips for semisweet chips.

MILK CHOCOLATE GLAZE: Substitute milk chocolate chips for semisweet chips.

MINT CHOCOLATE GLAZE: Substitute mint-flavored chocolate chips for semisweet chips.

WHITE CHOCOLATE GLAZE: Substitute white vanilla baking chips for semisweet chocolate chips.

EASY • FAST • CALORIE SMART • GLUTEN FREE • VEGETARIAN

Chocolate Ganache

Ganache is a very rich chocolate glaze that hardens when it cools. If you glaze the cake on a cooling rack with waxed paper underneath the rack, the extra glaze will fall onto the paper, making it a breeze to clean up.

PREP 5 Minutes **TOTAL** 10 Minutes • *About 1¼ cups*

⅔ cup whipping cream	6 oz semisweet baking chocolate, chopped

1 In 1-quart saucepan, heat whipping cream over low heat until hot but not boiling; remove from heat.

2 Stir in chocolate until melted. Let stand about 5 minutes. Ganache is ready to use when it mounds slightly when dropped from a spoon. It will become firmer the longer it cools.

3 Glaze 13x9-inch cake or 24 cupcakes. For two-layer 8- or 9-inch cake, pour ganache carefully onto top center of cake; spread with large spatula so it flows evenly over top and down side to cover side of cake. Leftover ganache can be tightly covered and refrigerated up to 5 days; do not freeze. Let stand 30 minutes at room temperature to soften; stir before using. (If kitchen isn't warm enough to soften ganache, microwave on High for 10-second intervals, until ganache can be stirred to spreading consistency.)

2 Tablespoons Calories 150; Total Fat 11g (Saturated Fat 7g, Trans Fat 0g); Cholesterol 20mg; Sodium 5mg; Total Carbohydrate 11g (Dietary Fiber 1g); Protein 1g **Carbohydrate Choices:** 1

BITTERSWEET CHOCOLATE GANACHE: Substitute bittersweet chocolate for semisweet chocolate.

MAKING & DRIZZLING GLAZE

Glaze should be consistency of thick syrup.

With spoon, drizzle glaze over top of cake.

USING GANACHE

Ganache is ready to use when it is fairly thick and mounds slightly when dropped from a spoon.

Pour ganache carefully onto center of cake; spread to cover top and down side of cake.

Pies & Tarts

Pie Basics

What makes a pie stand out from the crowd? It's the crust. When you bite into a really flaky, tender crust, you immediately know that the pie is special. When you know how to work with pie pastry, it's not hard to turn out a beautiful pie. We'll show you all the tricks and tips you need to become a legendary pie maker.

Picking Pie Pans

The best pans to use for making pies are actually heat-resistant glass pie plates. The next-best alternative would be a dull aluminum pie pan. Shiny or disposable pie pans reflect the heat and prevent crusts from browning. Dark pans absorb heat, causing overbrowning. Nonstick pans can cause a filled crust that isn't well anchored to the edge of the pan or an unfilled pie crust to shrink excessively. Use the size pie plate or pan called for in the recipe. Since pastry is high in fat, there is no need to grease the pie plate.

Freezing Pie Pastry

You can make pastry ahead and freeze it to have on hand for when you are ready to make a pie. Better yet, freeze the pastry in a freezer-to-oven glass pie plate so you are even closer to homemade pie. Unbaked and baked pie pastry (without filling) can be frozen up to 2 months.

- For rounds of pastry dough, prepare through Step 2 of Pie Pastry (page 607). Wrap tightly in plastic wrap and freeze. Thaw in refrigerator before rolling and filling.
- For unbaked pastry crust in a pie plate, wrap tightly in foil or place in a resealable freezer plastic bag. Fill crust and bake while frozen so that the crust won't be soggy.
- For baked pastry crust in a pie plate, wrap tightly (when completely cooled) in foil or place in a resealable freezer plastic bag. Thaw before using.

Freezing Filled Pies

See Refrigerator and Freezer Food Storage Chart, page 36, for freezing pies.

- Completely cool baked pies before freezing.
- Do not freeze cream, custard and meringue-topped pies. The filling and the meringue will break down and become watery.
- Fruit pies can be frozen baked or unbaked. Pecan and pumpkin pies need to be baked before freezing.
- Freeze pies with room around them so that the pastry edge won't get broken or misshapen during freezing. Once they are frozen, other items can touch up against the pies.
- Thaw unbaked frozen pies in the refrigerator before baking.

Baking Methods for Pie Crust

For many pies, such as apple or pecan pie, the filling is added to the unbaked pastry so that the crust and filling bake together at the same time. For other pies, such as pumpkin or banana cream pie, the crust is either partially or completely baked before the filling is added. This method is used to prevent the crust from becoming soggy from liquid fillings or when the filling doesn't need to be baked.

Pie Pastry

This pastry recipe is perfect for making any pie or tart. You can bake the pastry before filling for a variety of cooked or fresh fillings, or fill and then bake. Individual recipes will indicate which method to use and how to bake. Make your pies extra special with our pastry edge treatments (see page 609) or a lattice crust (see page 619).

PREP 20 Minutes **TOTAL** 20 Minutes • *8 servings*

ONE-CRUST PIE

- 1 cup plus 1 tablespoon all-purpose flour
- ½ teaspoon salt
- ⅓ cup cold shortening
- 3 to 5 tablespoons ice-cold water

TWO-CRUST PIE

- 2 cups plus 2 tablespoons all-purpose flour
- 1 teaspoon salt
- ⅔ cup cold shortening
- 6 to 8 tablespoons ice-cold water

1 In medium bowl, mix flour and salt. Cut in shortening, using pastry blender, potato masher or fork, until mixture forms coarse crumbs the size of small peas. Sprinkle with water, 1 tablespoon at a time, tossing with fork until all flour is moistened and pastry almost leaves side of bowl.

2 Gather pastry into a ball. For one-crust pie pastry, shape dough into flattened round on lightly floured surface. For two-crust pie pastry, divide dough in half and flatten into 2 rounds on lightly floured surface.

3 Using floured rolling pin, roll pastry on lightly floured surface (or pastry board with floured pastry cloth) into round 2 inches larger than upside-down 9-inch glass pie plate or 3 inches larger than 10- or 11-inch tart pan. Fold pastry into fourths and place in pie plate or tart pan, or roll pastry loosely around rolling pin and transfer to pie plate or tart pan. Unfold or unroll pastry and ease into plate or pan, pressing firmly against bottom and side and being careful not to stretch pastry, which will cause it to shrink when baked.

4 For one-crust pie, trim overhanging edge of pastry 1 inch from rim of pie plate. Fold edge under to form standing rim; flute edges (see Decorating with Pastry Edge Treatments or Decorative Cutouts, pages 608, 609). For tart, trim overhanging edge of pastry even with top of tart pan. Fill and bake as directed in pie or tart recipe.

5 For two-crust pie, roll out second pastry round. Fold into fourths and place over filling, or roll loosely around rolling pin and place over filling. Unfold or unroll pastry over filling. Cut slits in pastry so steam can escape.

6 Trim overhanging edge of top pastry 1 inch from rim of plate. Fold edge of top crust under bottom crust, forming a stand-up rim of pastry that is even thickness on edge of pie plate, pressing on rim to seal; flute edges (see Decorating with Pastry Edge Treatments or Decorative Cutouts, pages 608, 609). Bake as directed in pie recipe.

1 Serving One-Crust Pie Pastry Calories 140; Total Fat 9g (Saturated Fat 2g, Trans Fat 0g); Cholesterol 0mg; Sodium 150mg; Total Carbohydrate 13g (Dietary Fiber 0g); Protein 1g **Carbohydrate Choices:** 1

BUTTER CRUST: Substitute cold butter, cut into ½-inch pieces, for half of the shortening. In Step 2, wrap rounds in plastic wrap and refrigerate 1 hour before continuing with Step 3.

TIPS FOR FLAKY PIE PASTRY

- Use ice-cold water when making pastry by adding an ice cube or two to the water.

- Use shortening for the most tender, ultra-flaky crusts with a neutral flavor that lets the filling flavors shine. If using butter, use a combination of shortening and butter; see Butter Crust (above).

- Use a pastry blender or potato masher to make quick work of mixing the shortening and flour. Finish mixing with a fork, if necessary, to get crumbs that are pea size. Alternately, a fork can be used for all the mixing, but it will take longer to do.

- Overworking the pastry dough will make it tough—handle it as little as possible.

- See Making Pastry (below) for how to easily roll and move the pastry to the pie plate.

MAKING PASTRY

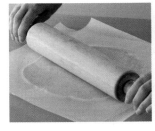

Sprinkle work surface with a few drops of water to anchor bottom sheet of waxed paper. Roll pastry round between 2 sheets of waxed paper.

Flip rolled pastry over with both sheets of waxed paper. Carefully remove top sheet.

Flip pastry over so remaining sheet of waxed paper is on top; center pastry over pie plate. Remove waxed paper.

Gently ease pastry into pie plate. Trim overhanging pastry to 1 inch.

Partially Baked One-Crust Pie

Use this when a recipe calls for a partially baked crust to prevent the bottom crust from becoming soggy, such as Pumpkin Pie (page 623).

1 Heat oven to 425°F. Prepare Pie Pastry for One-Crust Pie (page 607). Carefully cover pastry in plate with double thickness of foil, gently pressing foil to bottom and side of pastry. Let foil extend over edge to prevent excessive browning.

2 Bake 10 minutes; carefully remove foil and bake 2 to 4 minutes longer or until pastry just begins to brown and has become set. If crust bubbles, gently push bubbles down with back of spoon while hot.

3 Fill and bake as directed in pie or tart recipe, changing oven temperature if necessary.

Baked One-Crust Pie

Use this for pies or tarts that call for a baked pastry before filling is added, such as Lemon Meringue Pie (page 622).

1 Heat oven to 450°F. Prepare Pie Pastry for One-Crust Pie (page 607), except for pie, trim overhanging edge of pastry 1 inch from rim of pie plate. For tart, trim overhanging edge of pastry even with top of tart pan. Prick bottom and side of pastry thoroughly with fork to prevent puffing.

2 Bake 8 to 10 minutes or until light golden brown: cool on cooling rack.

3 Fill cooled crust as directed in pie or tart recipe.

Baked Tart Shells and Individual Pie Crusts

1 Prepare Pie Pastry for One-Crust Pie (page 607), except roll pastry into 13-inch round. Cut into 8 (4½-inch) rounds, rerolling pastry scraps if necessary.

2 Heat oven to 450°F. Fit rounds over backs of regular-size muffin cups or 6-oz custard cups, making pleats so pastry will fit snugly against the cups. If using individual pie pans or tart pans, cut pastry rounds 1 inch larger than the pans when upside down, then flip pans right side up and fit pastry into pans. Prick pastry thoroughly with fork to prevent puffing. Place on cookie sheet.

3 Bake 8 to 10 minutes or until light golden brown; cool before removing from cups. Fill each shell with ⅓ to ½ cup of your favorite filling, pudding, fresh fruit or ice cream.

DECORATIVE CUTOUTS

For an extra-pretty pie, make decorative cutouts on the top of a two-crust pie. Use a small cookie cutter or paring knife and cut shapes from the top crust before placing it on the filling. Once top crust is on filling, attach cutouts on top of crust with a little cold water. Sprinkle with coarse sugar, if desired.

PARTIALLY BAKING A ONE-CRUST PIE

To prevent pastry from puffing up and over-browning while baking, cover pastry loosely with double thickness of aluminum foil.

Easy Buttermilk Pastry

This pastry is a dream to work with because it's extra easy to roll and handle, and the baked crust is very flaky.

PREP 15 Minutes **TOTAL** 15 Minutes •
2 (9-inch) crusts (8 servings each)

2 cups all-purpose flour	1 cup cold shortening
1 teaspoon salt	⅓ cup buttermilk
1 teaspoon sugar	

1 In medium bowl, mix flour, salt and sugar. Cut in shortening, using pastry blender, potato masher or fork, until mixture forms coarse crumbs the size of small peas.

2 Mix in buttermilk with fork until all flour is moistened and pastry leaves side of bowl. Divide in half; shape each half into a ball. If making one-crust pie, wrap second ball of pastry and freeze for later use.

3 Roll pastry as directed in Step 3 of Pie Pastry (page 607). Fill and bake as directed in pie recipe. Or to bake before filling is added, see Baked One-Crust Pie (page 608).

1 Serving Calories 170; Total Fat 13g (Saturated Fat 3.5g, Trans Fat 0g); Cholesterol 0mg; Sodium 150mg; Total Carbohydrate 12g (Dietary Fiber 0g); Protein 1g **Carbohydrate Choices:** 1

Rich Pie Pastry

PREP 20 Minutes **TOTAL** 1 Hour • **8 servings**

1½ cups all-purpose flour	1 egg yolk
2 tablespoons sugar	4 to 6 tablespoons cold water
¼ teaspoon salt	
½ cup cold butter, cut into pieces	

1 In medium bowl, mix flour, sugar and salt. Cut in butter using pastry blender, potato masher or fork until mixture forms coarse crumbs the size of small peas. In small bowl, stir egg yolk and 4 tablespoons water with fork until blended. Add to flour mixture, tossing with fork until dough forms. Add 1 to 2 tablespoons water, if necessary, to form dough. Gather pastry into ball; flatten ball to ½-inch thickness. Wrap in plastic wrap; refrigerate 30 minutes.

2 Roll pastry as directed in Step 3 of Pie Pastry for One-Crust Pie (page 607). Fill and bake as directed in pie recipe. Or to bake before filling is added, heat oven to 425°F. Prick bottom and side of pastry thoroughly with fork. Bake 10 to 13 minutes or until light brown. Cool on cooling rack.

1 Serving Calories 210; Total Fat 12g (Saturated Fat 8g, Trans Fat 0g); Cholesterol 55mg; Sodium 170mg; Total Carbohydrate 21g (Dietary Fiber 0g); Protein 3g **Carbohydrate Choices:** 1½

DECORATING WITH PASTRY EDGE TREATMENTS

While it's important to seal the top and bottom pastry together to keep the filling from escaping, it doesn't have to be ugly! Seal edge as directed for Pie Pastry (page 607), Step 6. Then make it attractive with one of these eye-catching treatments.

Scalloped Edge Place thumb and index finger about 1 inch apart on outside of raised edge. With other index finger, push pastry toward outside, continuing around edge and repeating motion, to form scalloped edge.

Rope or Pinched Edge Place side of thumb on pastry rim at an angle. Pinch pastry by pressing knuckle of index finger down into pastry toward thumb. Continue around edge, repeating motion, to form rope edge.

Fork or Herringbone Edge Dip fork tines in flour; press fork diagonally onto edge without pressing through pastry. Rotate tines 90 degrees and press again next to first set of marks. Continue around edge of pastry, rotating tines back and forth.

Press-in-the-Pan Oil Pastry

No rolling is needed for this crust! Use it for pies that have only a bottom crust. Try it for Pumpkin Pie (page 623), as well as for pie crusts that are baked before being filled.

PREP 10 Minutes **TOTAL** 10 Minutes •
1 (9-inch) crust (8 servings)

1⅓ cups all-purpose flour	2 tablespoons ice-cold water
½ teaspoon salt	
⅓ cup vegetable oil	

1 In medium bowl, stir flour, salt and oil until all flour is moistened. Sprinkle with cold water, 1 tablespoon at a time, tossing with fork until all water is absorbed. Gather pastry into a ball. Press firmly and evenly against bottom and up side of 9-inch glass pie plate; flute (see Decorating with Pastry Edge Treatments, page 609).

2 Fill and bake as directed in pie recipe. Or to bake before filling is added, heat oven to 450°F. Prick bottom and side of pastry thoroughly with fork. Bake 10 to 12 minutes or until light brown; cool on cooling rack.

1 Serving Calories 160; Total Fat 9g (Saturated Fat 1.5g, Trans Fat 0g); Cholesterol 0mg; Sodium 150mg; Total Carbohydrate 16g (Dietary Fiber 0g); Protein 2g **Carbohydrate Choices:** 1

Graham Cracker Crust

PREP 10 Minutes **TOTAL** 10 Minutes • 1 (9-inch) crust (**8 servings**)

1½ cups finely crushed regular or cinnamon graham crackers (24 squares)	⅓ cup butter, melted
	3 tablespoons sugar

1 In medium bowl, stir all ingredients until well mixed. Reserve 3 tablespoons crumb mixture for garnishing top of pie before serving, if desired. Press remaining mixture firmly and evenly against bottom and side of 9-inch glass pie plate.

2 Fill and bake as directed in pie recipe. Or to bake before filling is added, heat oven to 350°F. Bake about 10 minutes or until light brown; cool on cooling rack.

1 Serving Calories 160; Total Fat 9g (Saturated Fat 5g, Trans Fat 0g); Cholesterol 20mg; Sodium 140mg; Total Carbohydrate 17g (Dietary Fiber 0g); Protein 1g **Carbohydrate Choices:** 1

COOKIE CRUMB CRUST: Substitute 1½ cups finely crushed chocolate wafer cookies (24 cookies), vanilla wafer cookies (35 cookies) or gingersnaps (30 cookies) for the graham crackers. Reduce butter to ¼ cup; omit sugar.

Press-in-the-Pan Tart Pastry

PREP 10 Minutes **TOTAL** 10 Minutes •
1 (10- or 11-inch) crust (8 servings)

1¼ cups all-purpose flour	2 tablespoons packed brown sugar
½ cup butter, softened	
	1 egg

1 In medium bowl, stir all ingredients until soft dough forms. Using lightly floured fingers, press firmly and evenly against bottom and side of ungreased 9-, 10- or 11-inch tart pan with removable bottom.

2 Fill and bake as directed in tart recipe. Or to bake before filling is added, heat oven to 450°F. Bake 8 to 10 minutes or until light brown; cool on cooling rack.

1 Serving Calories 200; Total Fat 12g (Saturated Fat 8g, Trans Fat 0g); Cholesterol 55mg; Sodium 100mg; Total Carbohydrate 18g (Dietary Fiber 0g); Protein 3g **Carbohydrate Choices:** 1

Easy Nut Crust

PREP 10 Minutes **TOTAL** 10 Minutes • 1 (9-inch) crust (**8 servings**)

1 cup all-purpose flour	¼ cup finely chopped nuts
½ cup butter, softened	

1 In medium bowl, mix all ingredients until soft dough forms. Using lightly floured fingers, press firmly and evenly against bottom and side of 9-inch glass pie plate.

2 Fill and bake as directed in pie recipe. Or to bake before filling is added, heat oven to 450°F. Bake 7 to 8 minutes or until light brown; cool on cooling rack.

1 Serving Calories 190; Total Fat 14g (Saturated Fat 8g, Trans Fat 0g); Cholesterol 30mg; Sodium 80mg; Total Carbohydrate 12g (Dietary Fiber 0g); Protein 2g **Carbohydrate Choices:** 1

MAKING GRAHAM CRACKER CRUST

Mix crumbs with butter until evenly mixed and mixture is crumbly.

Press crumb mixture firmly against side and bottom of pie plates

USE IT UP
GRAHAM CRACKER CRUMBS

Crushed too many crackers for your pie crust, or find a lot of crumbs in the bottom of the box? Try one of these delicious ways to save them from the trash.

S'MORE BANANAS
Roll or dip bananas in melted chocolate; roll in graham cracker crumbs to coat. Drizzle with marshmallow creme (heat in microwave 15 seconds or until drizzling consistency).

LAYERED POPS
Sprinkle between layers of fruit pie filling or yogurt when making frozen pops.

MALT MAGIC
Top malts with whipped cream, graham cracker crumbs and a maraschino cherry.

SMOOTHIE SECRET
Add to your favorite fruit smoothie while blending the ingredients in a blender, to add body, sweetness and flavor.

ICE CREAM STRATA PIE
Sprinkle a thin layer of graham cracker crumbs with other ingredients, such as mini chips, nuts or ice cream toppings, over softened ice cream, as you spoon it into pie shell. Freeze until firm. Sprinkle with additional graham cracker crumbs, if desired.

VEGETARIAN

HEIRLOOM

Classic Apple Pie

Once you've had homemade apple pie, nothing else will ever compare. What sets it apart is a tender, flaky crust that can only be achieved when made by hand.

PREP 30 Minutes **TOTAL** 3 Hours 20 Minutes • *8 servings*

Pie Pastry for Two-Crust Pie (page 607)
½ cup sugar
¼ cup all-purpose flour
¾ teaspoon ground cinnamon
¼ teaspoon ground nutmeg

Dash salt
6 cups thinly sliced (⅛-inch-thick) peeled tart apples (6 medium)
2 tablespoons cold butter, if desired
2 teaspoons water
1 tablespoon sugar

1 Heat oven to 425°F. Make pastry; place bottom pastry in 9-inch glass pie plate.

2 In large bowl, mix ½ cup sugar, the flour, cinnamon, nutmeg and salt. Stir in apples. Spoon into pastry-lined pie plate. Cut butter into small pieces; sprinkle over apples. Cover with top pastry; cut slits in pastry. Seal and flute (see Decorating with Pastry Edge Treatments or Decorative Cutouts, pages 608, 609).

3 Brush top crust with water; sprinkle with 1 tablespoon sugar. Cover crust edge with 2- to 3-inch strips of foil or pie crust shield ring to prevent excessive browning.

4 Bake 40 to 50 minutes or until crust is golden brown and juice begins to bubble through slits in crust. Remove foil or shield during last 15 minutes of baking. Cool on cooling rack at least 2 hours.

1 Serving Calories 390; Total Fat 18g (Saturated Fat 4.5g, Trans Fat 0g); Cholesterol 0mg; Sodium 320mg; Total Carbohydrate 53g (Dietary Fiber 2g); Protein 4g **Carbohydrate Choices:** 3½

FRENCH APPLE PIE: Heat oven to 400°F. Make Pie Pastry for One-Crust Pie (page 607) and place in 9-inch glass pie plate. Spoon apple mixture into pastry-lined pie plate. Omit butter, water and 1 tablespoon sugar. In small bowl, mix 1 cup all-purpose flour and ½ cup packed brown sugar. Cut in ½ cup cold butter with fork until crumbly. Sprinkle over apple mixture. Bake 35 to 40 minutes or until golden brown. Cover top with foil during last 10 to 15 minutes of baking, if necessary, to prevent excessive browning. Serve warm.

CLASSIC PEACH PIE: Prepare Classic Apple Pie as directed, except use ⅔ cup sugar and ⅓ cup flour. Decrease cinnamon to ¼ teaspoon and omit nutmeg. Substitute sliced peeled fresh peaches (6 to 8) for the sliced apples. Stir in 1 teaspoon lemon juice with the peaches. Decrease butter to 1 tablespoon. Bake pie about 45 minutes.

MAKING CLASSIC APPLE PIE

Spoon apple mixture nto pastry. Cut butter into small pieces; sprinkle over apples.

Cover pastry edge with 2- to 3-inch-wide strip of foil to prevent excess browning.

Cool baked pie on cooling rack at least 2 hours.

Classic Apple Pie

NEW TWIST

Blushing Apple Rose Pies

PREP 45 Minutes **TOTAL** 1 Hour 50 Minutes • *6 pies*

- 1 large apple, cored, halved and cut crosswise into ⅛-inch slices
- 2 teaspoons fresh lemon juice
- 12 teaspoons strawberry jam
- 2 oz cream cheese, softened (from 8-oz package)
- ¼ teaspoon ground cinnamon
  Pie Pastry for One-Crust Pie (page 607)
- 3 tablespoons finely chopped pecans
- ½ teaspoon clear sparkling sugar

1 Heat oven to 350°F. Spray 6 regular-size muffin cups with cooking spray. In large bowl, mix apple slices, lemon juice and 2 teaspoons of the strawberry jam; microwave on High 1 to 2 minutes or until softened; drain. Cool 5 minutes.

2 Meanwhile, in small bowl, mix cream cheese, 1 teaspoon of the strawberry jam and the cinnamon until smooth and creamy; spoon into 1-quart resealable food-storage plastic bag. Cut tiny corner from bag; set aside.

3 In medium bowl, make pastry as directed, except add pecans with the flour. Gather dough into a ball. On lightly floured surface, shape into flattened oval. Roll pastry into 12×12-inch square; cut into 6 (12×2-inch) strips; do not separate. Spread strips evenly with 6 teaspoons of the jam.

4 Separate pastry strips; pipe cream cheese mixture lengthwise down center of each strip. For each pie, place about 5 or 6 apples slices, skin side up, overlapping slightly on long side of pastry strip, just above cream cheese, making sure that about ¼ inch of the apple slice hangs over edge of strip. (Apples will cover top half of strip.) Fold bottom half of pastry over apple slices, covering bottom half of apple slices. Starting with short end of pastry, carefully roll up jelly-roll fashion, holding apples in place with one hand while rolling with the other hand. Place pastry side down in muffin cups. Repeat with remaining pastry and apple slices.

5 In small bowl, microwave remaining 3 teaspoons jam on High 15 to 20 seconds or until melted; drizzle over apples.

6 Bake 40 to 45 minutes or until crust is light golden brown. Immediately, sprinkle with sugar. Cool 10 minutes. Remove from pan to cooling rack. Serve warm if desired.

1 Pie Calories 300; Total Fat 17g (Saturated Fat 5g, Trans Fat 0g); Cholesterol 10mg; Sodium 230mg; Total Carbohydrate 33g (Dietary Fiber 2g); Protein 3g **Carbohydrate Choices:** 2

MAKING APPLE ROSE PIES

Overlap softened apple slices slightly, just above cream cheese, with ¼-inch of slices overhanging pastry strip.

Fold pastry over apple slices, covering cut sides of slices.

Carefully roll up strip, holding apples in place with one hand as you roll with the other. Place roll in muffin cup.

Blushing Apple Rose Pies

613

Red, White & Blue Slab Pie

Strawberry glaze can be found in the produce section of your grocery store.

PREP 30 Minutes **TOTAL** 2 Hours 10 Minutes • *15 servings*

Pie Pastry for Two-Crust and One-Crust Pie (page 607)*

- 4 tablespoons sugar, divided
- 2 packages (8 oz each) cream cheese, softened
- 2 containers (6 oz each) lemon yogurt

Grated zest and juice of 1 lemon (1 teaspoon zest and 3 tablespoons juice)

- 6 cups assorted berries (sliced strawberries, blueberries, raspberries, blackberries)
- 1 cup strawberry glaze (from 13.5-oz container)

1 Heat oven to 450°F. Stack 2 of the pastry rounds on lightly floured surface. Roll to 17×12-inch rectangle. Fit crust into ungreased 15×10×1-inch pan, pressing into corners. Fold crust even with edges of pan. Prick crust several times with fork.

2 Bake 10 to 12 minutes or until golden brown. Cool completely, about 30 minutes.

3 Meanwhile, on lightly floured surface, roll remaining pastry round to 12-inch circle. Cut stars using 1-, 1½- and 2-inch cookie cutters. Place 1 inch apart on large ungreased cookie sheet. Brush with water; sprinkle with 1 tablespoon of the sugar.

4 Bake 5 to 7 minutes or until golden brown. Cool 1 minute on cookie sheet. Remove to cooling rack. Cool completely, about 15 minutes.

5 Meanwhile, in medium bowl, beat remaining 3 tablespoons sugar, the cream cheese, yogurt, lemon zest and lemon juice with electric mixer on high speed until smooth and creamy. Spread evenly in crust-lined pan. Refrigerate about 30 minutes or until chilled.

6 In large bowl, gently mix berries and glaze until well blended. Spoon berry mixture evenly on top of cream cheese–topped pie crust. Place pie crust stars on top of berry mixture.

1 Serving Calories 340; Total Fat 20g (Saturated Fat 9g, Trans Fat 0g); Cholesterol 30mg; Sodium 290mg; Total Carbohydrate 34g (Dietary Fiber 2g); Protein 5g **Carbohydrate Choices:** 2

*You can substitute 3 refrigerated pie crusts (from 2 boxes), softened as directed on box, for the Pie Pastry for Two-Crust and One-Crust Pie.

Rhubarb Crunch Pie

If you don't have fresh rhubarb, two bags (16 oz each) frozen cut rhubarb, thawed and drained, can be used instead.

PREP 25 Minutes **TOTAL** 4 Hours 45 Minutes • *8 servings*

- 5 cups sliced fresh rhubarb
- 1¼ cups sugar
- 3 tablespoons quick-cooking tapioca
- 1 to 2 teaspoons grated orange zest

Pie Pastry for One-Crust Pie (page 607)*

- ½ cup all-purpose flour
- ½ cup sugar
- 6 tablespoons cold butter

1 In large bowl, mix rhubarb, ¾ cup of the sugar, the tapioca and orange zest; let stand 15 minutes.

2 Meanwhile, heat oven to 400°F. Place pastry in 9-inch glass pie plate; flute edges.

3 To make topping, in small bowl, mix flour and remaining ½ cup sugar. Cut in butter, using pastry blender or fork until mixture is crumbly.

4 Spoon rhubarb mixture into pastry-lined pie plate; sprinkle with topping. Cover crust edge with 2- to 3-inch strips of foil or pie crust shield ring to prevent excessive browning. Place cookie sheet on rack below pie in case of spillover.

MAKING SLAB PIE

Stack pastry rounds on top of each other on lightly floured surface. Roll into rectangle.

Fit crust into pan, pressing into corners. Fold extra pastry crust under, even with edges of pan; seal edges.

Red, White & Blue Slab Pie

5 Bake 15 minutes. Reduce oven temperature to 375°F. Bake 30 minutes longer. Remove foil; bake 15 to 20 minutes longer or until browned and bubbly. Cool 3 hours before serving.

1 Serving Calories 400; Total Fat 18g (Saturated Fat 8g, Trans Fat 0g); Cholesterol 25mg; Sodium 220mg; Total Carbohydrate 57g (Dietary Fiber 2g); Protein 3g **Carbohydrate Choices:** 4

*You can substitute 1 refrigerated pie crust, softened as directed on box, for Pie Pastry for One-Crust Pie.

VEGETARIAN

Raspberry-Almond Pie

PREP 50 Minutes   **TOTAL** 4 Hours 45 Minutes   •   *8 servings*

Pie Pastry for Two-Crust Pie (page 607)

½ cup whole blanched almonds

2 tablespoons butter

1¼ cups granulated sugar

2 teaspoons all-purpose flour

2 eggs

½ teaspoon almond extract

5 tablespoons cornstarch

1 tablespoon grated orange zest

5 cups fresh or frozen (thawed) raspberries

1 tablespoon whipping cream

2 tablespoons coarse sugar or sanding sugar

1 Heat oven to 400°F. Place bottom pastry round in 9-inch glass pie plate; flute edges. On lightly floured surface, roll second pastry to 13-inch round. With 1½-inch star cookie cutter, cut out 45 stars; set aside.

2 Place almonds in food processor. Cover and process until finely chopped. Add butter, ¼ cup of the granulated sugar and the flour; process until blended. Add 1 of the eggs and the almond extract; process until blended. Spread mixture evenly in pastry-lined pie plate.

3 In large bowl, mix remaining 1 cup granulated sugar, the cornstarch and orange zest. Add raspberries; toss gently. Spoon berry mixture evenly over almond layer. Arrange pastry stars on top of filling (with tips touching), covering entire surface. In small bowl, beat the remaining egg and the whipping cream. Brush mixture over stars and edge of crust; sprinkle with coarse sugar.

4 Place cookie sheet on rack below pie in case of spillover. Bake 10 minutes. Cover crust edge with 2- to 3-inch strips of foil or pie crust shield ring to prevent excessive browning. Bake 40 to 45 minutes longer or until crust is golden brown and juices are bubbly. (If crust becomes too brown, cover entire crust with foil.) Cool on cooling rack at least 3 hours.

1 Serving Calories 580; Total Fat 28g (Saturated Fat 7g, Trans Fat 0g); Cholesterol 55mg; Sodium 340mg; Total Carbohydrate 76g (Dietary Fiber 7g); Protein 8g **Carbohydrate Choices:** 5

Blueberry Hand Pies

VEGETARIAN

Blueberry Hand Pies

If you like, drizzle these little pies with a quick glaze: Mix 1 cup powdered sugar with about a tablespoon milk, just until desired consistency. Drizzle over cooled pies. Let stand 1 hour for glaze to dry.

PREP 35 Minutes   **TOTAL** 1 Hour   •   *8 pies*

CRUST

Pie Pastry for Two-Crust Pie (page 607)

FILLING

1½ cups fresh or frozen (thawed and drained) blueberries

½ cup granulated sugar

2 tablespoons cornstarch

¼ teaspoon ground cinnamon

TOPPING

1 egg, beaten

2 teaspoons white decorator sugar crystals or granulated sugar

1 Heat oven to 375°F. Line large cookie sheet with cooking parchment paper. Make pastry as directed, rolling into 2 (11-inch) rounds. With 4-inch round cutter, cut 8 rounds from each crust, rerolling scraps if necessary.

2 In medium bowl, mix filling ingredients. Spoon filling evenly in center of 8 pastry rounds to within ¼ inch of edge. Brush edge of pastry with water. Place remaining pastry rounds on top, stretching dough gently to fit if necessary; press edge firmly with fork to seal. Cut slit in top pastry.

3 Place pies on cookie sheet. Brush egg over tops of pies; sprinkle with sugar.

4 Bake 22 to 25 minutes or until light golden brown. Remove from cookie sheet to cooling rack; cool at least 30 minutes.

1 Pie Calories 380; Total Fat 20g (Saturated Fat 5g, Trans Fat 0g); Cholesterol 25mg; Sodium 300mg; Total Carbohydrate 45g (Dietary Fiber 2g); Protein 4g **Carbohydrate Choices:** 3

5-INGREDIENT RECIPE

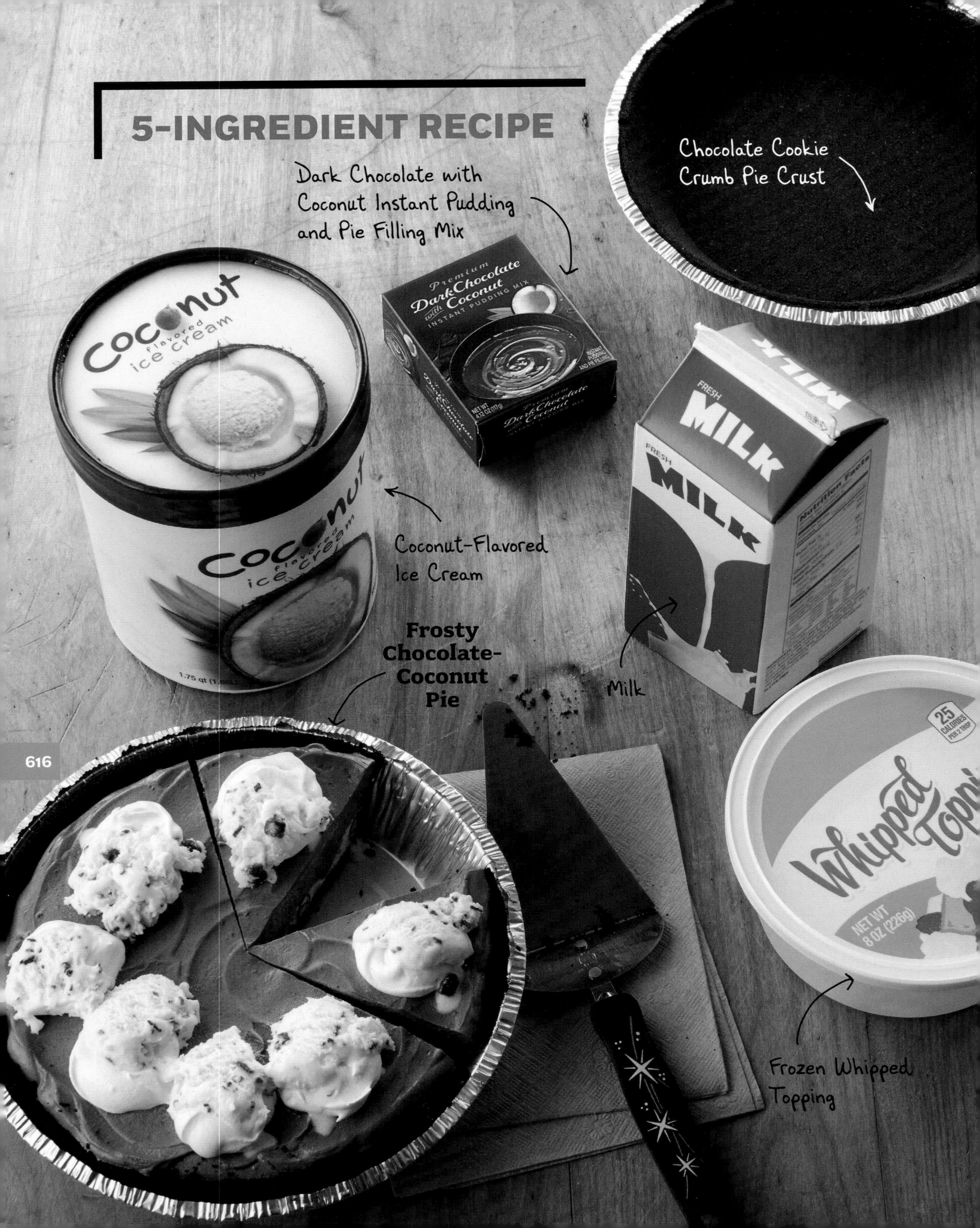

Dark Chocolate with
Coconut Instant Pudding
and Pie Filling Mix

Chocolate Cookie
Crumb Pie Crust

Coconut-Flavored
Ice Cream

**Frosty
Chocolate-
Coconut
Pie**

Milk

Frozen Whipped
Topping

5-INGREDIENT RECIPE

EASY • MAKE AHEAD

Frosty Chocolate-Coconut Pie

If you can't find the chocolate-coconut pudding mix, you can substitute a box of chocolate instant pudding mix and ½ teaspoon coconut extract. If you're not a coconut fan, you can use just the chocolate pudding mix and your favorite non-coconut ice cream.

PREP 15 Minutes   TOTAL 8 Hours 20 Minutes • **8 servings**

- 2 cups any coconut-flavored ice cream or gelato
- 1 box (4.12 oz) dark chocolate with coconut instant pudding and pie filling mix
- 1½ cups milk
- 1½ cups frozen whipped topping, thawed
- 1 package (6 oz) chocolate cookie crumb pie crust or 1 recipe Chocolate Cookie Crumb Crust (page 610)

1 Let ice cream stand at room temperature while preparing pudding.

2 In medium bowl, using whisk, beat pudding mix and milk for 2 minutes, until mixture is thickened. Stir in 1 cup of the whipped topping. Carefully spoon 1 cup of the softened ice cream into crust (return remaining ice cream to freezer); top with pudding. Cover with plastic cover from pie crust; freeze 8 hours or overnight.

3 Remove pie from freezer 5 minutes before slicing. Just before serving, garnish each slice with 1 tablespoon whipped topping. Scoop remaining ice cream into 8 scoops on top of pie.

1 Serving Calories 290; Total Fat 13g (Saturated Fat 6g, Trans Fat 0g); Cholesterol 20mg; Sodium 370mg; Total Carbohydrate 40g (Dietary Fiber 1g); Protein 4g **Carbohydrate Choices:** 2½

VEGETARIAN

Peach-Ricotta Crostata

PREP 40 Minutes   TOTAL 2 Hours 15 Minutes •
8 servings

Rich Pie Pastry (page 609)

RICOTTA FILLING
- 1 cup ricotta cheese
- ¼ cup sugar
- 1 teaspoon vanilla

PEACH FILLING
- ½ cup sugar
- 2 tablespoons all-purpose flour
- 1 tablespoon finely chopped crystallized ginger
- 1 teaspoon ground cinnamon
- ¼ teaspoon ground nutmeg
- 4 cups sliced peeled peaches (6 medium)

TOPPINGS, IF DESIRED
- 1 tablespoon coarse sugar
- 1 tablespoon shredded fresh basil leaves

1 Make pastry as directed in recipe.

2 While pastry is chilling, in medium bowl, mix ricotta filling ingredients until well blended. In large bowl, mix all peach filling ingredients except peaches; stir in peaches until well coated.

3 Heat oven to 425°F. On lightly floured surface, roll pastry into 14-inch round. Place on ungreased large cookie sheet (line with parchment, if desired, for easy transfer to serving tray). Spread ricotta filling to within 3 inches of edge of pastry. Spoon peaches over ricotta. Fold edge of pastry up and over fruit mixture, pleating crust lightly as necessary. Brush edge of pastry with water; sprinkle with coarse sugar.

4 Bake 30 to 40 minutes or until crust is golden brown and fruit is tender. Cool on cooling rack at least 1 hour. Just before serving, sprinkle basil over fruit.

1 Serving Calories 380; Total Fat 16g (Saturated Fat 10g, Trans Fat 0.5g); Cholesterol 70mg; Sodium 200mg; Total Carbohydrate 52g (Dietary Fiber 2g); Protein 6g **Carbohydrate Choices:** 3½

Peach-Ricotta Crostata

Cherry Pie

MAKE AHEAD
White and Dark Chocolate Raspberry Tart

This elegant tart can be a year-round favorite—just leave out the fresh raspberries when unavailable. For a pretty garnish, make white chocolate curls, using another white chocolate baking bar and a vegetable peeler.

PREP 1 Hour **TOTAL** 4 Hours 50 Minutes • *10 servings*

Pie Pastry for One-Crust Pie (page 607) or Press-in-the-Pan Tart Pastry (page 610)

2 tablespoons orange juice

1 teaspoon unflavored gelatin

1½ cups heavy whipping cream

6 oz white chocolate baking bars, finely chopped (from two 4-oz packages)

1 bag (12 oz) frozen raspberries, thawed, drained, juice reserved

1 tablespoon cornstarch

1 tablespoon sugar

1 cup fresh raspberries, if desired

2 oz semisweet baking chocolate, cut into pieces

2 tablespoons butter

1 Heat oven to 450°F. Place pastry in 10-inch tart pan with removable bottom or 10-inch springform pan, pressing 1 inch up side of pan. Bake as directed for Baked One-Crust Pie (page 608). Cool completely.

2 Pour orange juice into 2-quart saucepan. Sprinkle gelatin over juice; let stand 5 minutes to soften. Stir in ¾ cup of the whipping cream; heat over low heat, stirring frequently, until gelatin is dissolved. Stir in white chocolate until melted and smooth. Transfer to medium bowl; refrigerate about 30 minutes, stirring occasionally, until cool but not set.

3 In blender or food processor, place thawed raspberries and reserved juice. Cover and blend until pureed. Set strainer over 2-cup measuring cup. Press puree through strainer with back of spoon to remove seeds. If necessary, add water to raspberry puree to measure ½ cup. In 1-quart saucepan, mix cornstarch and 1 tablespoon sugar. Gradually add raspberry puree. Cook and stir over low heat until thickened. Fold in fresh raspberries. Spread into cooled baked crust. Refrigerate 15 minutes.

4 Meanwhile, in chilled small, deep bowl, beat remaining ¾ cup whipping cream with electric mixer on high speed until stiff peaks form. Fold whipped cream into white chocolate mixture. Spoon and spread over raspberry layer. Refrigerate 1 hour or until filling is set.

5 In 1-quart saucepan, heat semisweet chocolate and butter over low heat, stirring frequently, until melted. Carefully pour and spread over white chocolate layer. Refrigerate at least 2 hours or until set. Remove from refrigerator about 30 minutes before serving to soften chocolate layers. Remove tart from side of pan (if using springform pan, remove side of pan). Cover and refrigerate any remaining tart up to 2 days.

1 Serving Calories 390; Total Fat 27g (Saturated Fat 16g, Trans Fat 0g); Cholesterol 50mg; Sodium 135mg; Total Carbohydrate 33g (Dietary Fiber 2g); Protein 3g **Carbohydrate Choices:** 2

VEGETARIAN
Cherry Pie

Sour cherries—also called pie cherries, tart cherries or tart red cherries—make wonderful pies. Take advantage of their short season by making a homemade pie. If fresh aren't available, use our variation below, which uses bags of frozen sweet cherries.

PREP 30 Minutes **TOTAL** 3 Hours 15 Minutes • *8 servings*

Pie Pastry for Two-Crust Pie (page 607) or Easy Buttermilk Pastry (page 609)

1⅓ cups sugar

½ cup all-purpose flour

6 cups fresh sour cherries, pitted

2 tablespoons cold butter, if desired

1 Heat oven to 425°F. Place bottom pastry in 9-inch glass pie plate.

2 In large bowl, mix sugar and flour. Stir in cherries. Spoon into pastry-lined pie plate. Cut butter into small pieces; sprinkle over cherries.

3 Make classic lattice top (see page 619) or cover with top pastry and cut slits in pastry. Seal and flute (see Decorating with Pastry Edge Treatments, page 609). Cover edge with 2- to 3-inch strips of foil or pie crust shield ring to prevent excessive browning.

4 Bake 35 to 45 minutes or until crust is golden brown and juice begins to bubble through slits in crust. Remove foil or shield during last 15 minutes of baking. Cool on cooling rack at least 2 hours.

1 Serving Calories 500; Total Fat 18g (Saturated Fat 4.5g, Trans Fat 0g); Cholesterol 0mg; Sodium 300mg; Total Carbohydrate 79g (Dietary Fiber 3g); Protein 5g **Carbohydrate Choices:** 5

QUICK SWEET CHERRY PIE: Decrease sugar to ⅔ cup and substitute 2 bags (16 oz each) frozen pitted dark sweet cherries, thawed, for the fresh sour cherries.

LEARN TO MAKE A LATTICE CRUST

A lattice top crust is a gorgeous way to decorate a two-crust pie, allowing the filling to show through, for an easy "wow." Make Two-Crust Pastry, page 607, except trim overhanging edge of bottom crust 1 inch from rim of plate. Place filling in crust. After rolling pastry for top crust, cut into ½- to 1-inch wide strips using a pastry wheel or pizza cutter with a straight edge, such as a ruler, to even strips. You can use this technique when making Cherry Pie (left) or any two-crust pie.

Easy Lattice Top

Place half of the strips an equal distance apart on filling, using shorter strips toward the edge of the pie.
Place remaining strips an equal distance apart crosswise over the first strips. Trim strips evenly with edge of overhanging bottom crust. Fold edge up, forming high stand-up rim; flute as desired. (See page 609 for pastry edge treatments.)

Classic Lattice Top

Place half of the strips an equal distance apart on filling, using shorter strips toward the edge of pie.
Weave remaining strips over and under first strips.
Trim strips evenly with edge of overhanging bottom crust.
Fold edge up, forming high stand-up rim; flute as desired. (See page 609 for pastry edge treatments.)

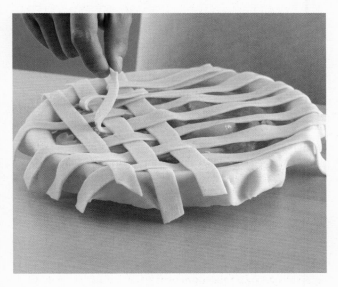

Giant Raspberry Toaster Tart

Adding the freeze-dried raspberries to the sprinkles on top will add an extra burst of raspberry flavor. Look for bags of them in the dried fruit section of your grocery store.

PREP 35 Minutes   **TOTAL** 1 Hour 25 Minutes   •   **8 servings**

FILLING AND CRUST

- 1½ cups fresh raspberries
- ¼ cup granulated sugar
- 2 tablespoons cornstarch
- 1 tablespoon water
- ¼ teaspoon almond extract
  Easy Buttermilk Pastry (page 609)
- 1 egg, beaten

GLAZE

- 1 cup powdered sugar
- 5 teaspoons milk
- ¼ teaspoon almond extract

GARNISH

- 2 teaspoons multicolored sprinkles
  Coarsely crushed freeze-dried raspberries, if desired

1 In 2-quart saucepan, mix raspberries, granulated sugar, cornstarch and water. Heat to boiling over medium heat, stirring constantly; boil 1 minute. Remove from heat; stir in ¼ teaspoon almond extract. Pour into heatproof bowl. Cover with plastic wrap; refrigerate until completely chilled, about 30 minutes.

2 Heat oven to 400°F. Line large cookie sheet with cooking parchment paper. Make pastry as directed. On lightly floured surface, roll 1 dough round to 12×8-inch rectangle; gently fold into thirds. Unfold onto cookie sheet. Spread raspberry filling on pastry to within ½ inch of edge. Brush edge with beaten egg.

3 On lightly floured surface, roll remaining dough round to 12×8-inch rectangle; gently fold into thirds. Center over raspberry filling; unfold pastry. Press edges together; seal with fork. Cut several small slits in top crusts. Brush top with remaining beaten egg.

4 Bake 25 to 28 minutes or until crust is golden brown. Place cookie sheet on cooling rack; cool 5 minutes.

5 In small bowl, mix powdered sugar, milk and ¼ teaspoon almond extract. Drizzle over tart. Top with sprinkles and freeze-dried raspberries. Cut tart into two rows by two rows, forming 4 rectangles; cut each rectangle in half diagonally to get 8 triangles.

1 Serving Calories 470; Total Fat 27g (Saturated Fat 7g, Trans Fat 0g); Cholesterol 25mg; Sodium 320mg; Total Carbohydrate 52g (Dietary Fiber 2g); Protein 5g **Carbohydrate Choices:** 3½

VEGETARIAN

Mixed Berry Crumble Tart

PREP 30 Minutes   **TOTAL** 1 Hour 15 Minutes   •   **8 servings**

- Pie Pastry for One-Crust Pie (page 607)
- 1½ cups sliced fresh strawberries
- 1½ cups fresh blueberries
- 1 cup fresh raspberries
- ⅔ cup sugar
- 2 tablespoons cornstarch
- ¾ cup all-purpose flour
- ½ cup sugar
- 1 teaspoon grated orange zest
- ⅓ cup butter, melted

1 Heat oven to 425°F. Make pastry as directed, except roll into 13-inch round. Place pastry in 10- or 11-inch tart pan with removable bottom; press against bottom and side of pan. Trim overhanging edge of pastry even with top of pan.

2 In large bowl, gently toss all berries with ⅔ cup sugar and the cornstarch. Spoon into pastry-lined pan.

3 In small bowl, stir flour, ½ cup sugar, the orange zest and butter with fork until crumbly. Sprinkle evenly over berries.

4 Bake 35 to 45 minutes or until fruit bubbles in center. Remove tart from side of pan. Serve warm.

1 Serving Calories 410; Total Fat 17g (Saturated Fat 7g, Trans Fat 0g); Cholesterol 20mg; Sodium 210mg; Total Carbohydrate 61g (Dietary Fiber 3g); Protein 3g **Carbohydrate Choices:** 4

620

Giant Raspberry Toaster Tart

Mixed Berry Crumble Tart

Strawberry-Lemon
Cheesecake Tart

Salted Cashew–
Bittersweet
Chocolate Tart

MAKE AHEAD • VEGETARIAN

Strawberry-Lemon Cheesecake Tart

PREP 30 Minutes **TOTAL** 5 Hours 15 Minutes • *8 servings*

Graham Cracker Crust (page 610)
2 packages (8 oz each) cream cheese, softened
¾ cup sugar
½ cup sour cream
2 teaspoons grated lemon zest
2 tablespoons fresh lemon juice

1 egg
4 cups sliced fresh strawberries
1 tablespoon chia seeds, if desired
⅓ cup sugar
Additional grated lemon zest or strips of lemon peel, if desired

1 Heat oven to 300°F. Make crust as directed in 10-inch round tart pan with removable bottom.

2 In medium bowl, beat cream cheese and ¾ cup sugar with electric mixer on medium speed 1 minute or until light and fluffy. Beat in sour cream, lemon zest, lemon juice and egg just until blended. Fold in 2 cups of the strawberries and the chia seeds. Spread over crust. Place tart on baking sheet.

3 Bake 45 to 60 minutes or until cheesecake is set at least 2 inches from edge of pan, but center of cheesecake still jiggles slightly when moved. Turn oven off; open oven door at least 4 inches. Let cheesecake remain in oven 30 minutes. Cool on cooling rack 30 minutes. Remove tart from side of pan. Refrigerate at least 4 hours but no longer than 8 hours.

4 Meanwhile, in medium bowl, mix remaining 2 cups sliced strawberries and ⅓ cup sugar. Let stand about 1 hour.

5 To serve, slice cheesecake into wedges; top with strawberries and lemon zest.

1 Serving Calories 540; Total Fat 33g (Saturated Fat 18g, Trans Fat 1g); Cholesterol 110mg; Sodium 330mg; Total Carbohydrate 55g (Dietary Fiber 2g); Protein 6g **Carbohydrate Choices:** 3½

MAKE AHEAD • VEGETARIAN

Salted Cashew—Bittersweet Chocolate Tart

PREP 25 Minutes **TOTAL** 2 Hours 40 Minutes • *16 servings*

Pie Pastry for One-Crust Pie (page 607) or Press-in-the Pan Tart Pastry (page 610)
1¼ cups whipping cream
12 oz bittersweet baking chocolate, chopped*
½ cup salted roasted cashew halves and pieces, coarsely chopped

1 can (13.4 oz) dulce de leche (caramelized sweetened condensed milk)
2 tablespoons salted roasted cashew halves and pieces
¼ teaspoon coarse (kosher or sea) salt

1 Heat oven to 450°F. Place pastry in 9-inch tart pan with removable bottom. Bake as directed for Baked One-Crust Pie (page 608), except do not prick crust. Cool completely.

2 Meanwhile, in 2-quart saucepan, heat whipping cream over medium-high heat just to boiling. Remove from heat; stir in chocolate with whisk until smooth. Stir in ½ cup chopped cashews. Pour into cooled baked crust. Refrigerate 2 hours or until firm.

3 Spread dulce de leche over chocolate layer. Sprinkle 2 tablespoons cashews and the salt evenly over top. Remove tart from side of pan. For easier cutting, use a thin, sharp knife, wiping it clean with paper towels and running it under hot water between cutting slices. Store any remaining tarts up to 3 days covered in refrigerator.

1 Serving Calories 370; Total Fat 26g (Saturated Fat 14g, Trans Fat 0g); Cholesterol 30mg; Sodium 150mg; Total Carbohydrate 28g (Dietary Fiber 4g); Protein 6g **Carbohydrate Choices:** 2

*Semisweet baking chocolate can be substituted for the bittersweet chocolate.

Chocolate-Hazelnut Gingerbread Cookie Tarts

PREP 45 Minutes   **TOTAL** 3 Hours 15 Minutes   •
12 cookie tarts

Gingersnaps (page 549)

¾ cup hazelnut spread with cocoa

½ cup dark chocolate chips

½ cup whipping cream

Powdered sugar, pomegranate seeds, fresh rosemary sprigs and blackberries, if desired

1 Heat oven to 350°F. Grease 12 regular-size muffin cups with shortening or spray with cooking spray. Make gingersnap dough as directed. For each tart, shape 2 tablespoons dough into a ball; roll in granulated sugar. Place in muffin cup, press dough in bottom and up side of cup. Reserve remaining dough.

2 Bake 9 to 11 minutes or until set. Remove from oven. Using end of wooden spoon, carefully press into center of each baked cookie to make 2-inch-wide, ¾-inch-deep indentation. Cool 10 minutes. With knife or metal spatula, carefully loosen edge. Remove from pan to cooling rack. Cool completely, about 30 minutes.

3 Line cookie sheet with cooking parchment paper. On lightly floured surface, roll ¼ cup of the reserved dough to ¼-inch thickness. Cut 12 miniatures with floured 1¼-inch miniature cookie cutters. Place 1 inch apart on cookie sheet. Bake 3 to 4 minutes or until set. Remove from cookie sheet to cooling rack. Cool completely. (Use remaining dough to make cookies as directed in Gingersnaps recipe.)

4 Meanwhile, in medium microwavable bowl, mix hazelnut spread, chocolate chips and whipping cream; microwave on High 40 to 50 seconds, stirring every 15 seconds, until mixture can be stirred smooth; set aside.

5 Spoon about 1½ tablespoons chocolate mixture into each cookie cup. Place cups on serving tray. Refrigerate uncovered about 2 hours or until chilled. Garnish with miniature cookies (one per tart), powdered sugar, pomegranate seeds, rosemary and blackberries just before serving. Store tarts tightly covered in refrigerator no longer than 24 hours. Let stand 15 minutes before serving.

1 Cookie Tart Calories 480; Total Fat 25g (Saturated Fat 8g, Trans Fat 0g); Cholesterol 25mg; Sodium 280mg; Total Carbohydrate 60g (Dietary Fiber 2g); Protein 4g **Carbohydrate Choices:** 4

Lemon Meringue Pie

When you separate the eggs, be sure to save the egg whites to make the meringue. To speed up the beating, let the egg whites warm up to room temperature (about 30 minutes).

PREP 50 Minutes   **TOTAL** 3 Hours 5 Minutes   •   *8 servings*

Pie Pastry for One-Crust Pie (page 607), Easy Buttermilk Pastry (page 609) or Press-in-the-Pan Oil Pastry (page 610)

Meringue for 9-inch Pie (at right)

3 egg yolks (reserve whites for meringue)

1½ cups sugar

⅓ cup plus 1 tablespoon cornstarch

1½ cups water

3 tablespoons butter

2 teaspoons grated lemon zest

½ cup lemon juice

2 drops yellow food color, if desired

1 Heat oven to 450°F. Place pastry in 9-inch glass pie plate; flute edges. Bake as directed for Baked One-Crust Pie (page 608). Cool completely.

2 Make sugar mixture for meringue (recipe at right). While sugar mixture is cooling, in small bowl, beat egg yolks with fork; set aside. In 2-quart saucepan, mix sugar and cornstarch. Gradually stir in water. Cook and stir over medium heat until mixture boils and thickens. Boil and stir 1 minute.

Chocolate-Hazelnut Gingerbread Cookie Tarts

Lemon Meringue Pie

Pumpkin Pie

3 Immediately stir about half of the hot mixture gradually into egg yolks, then stir back into hot mixture in saucepan. Boil and stir 2 minutes or until very thick. (Do not boil less than 2 minutes or filling may stay too soft or become runny.) Remove from heat. Stir in butter, lemon zest, lemon juice and food color. Press plastic wrap on surface of filling to prevent tough layer from forming on top.

4 Heat oven to 350°F. Finish making meringue. Pour hot lemon filling into cooled baked crust. Spoon meringue onto hot lemon filling; spread over filling, carefully sealing meringue to edge of crust to prevent shrinking or weeping.

5 Bake 12 to 15 minutes or until meringue is light brown. Cool away from drafts 2 hours. Serve immediately or loosely cover and refrigerate until serving time. This pie is best served the day it is made. Store any remaining pie up to 1 day covered in refrigerator.

1 Serving Calories 440; Total Fat 15g (Saturated Fat 6g, Trans Fat 0g); Cholesterol 80mg; Sodium 250mg; Total Carbohydrate 71g (Dietary Fiber 0g); Protein 4g **Carbohydrate Choices:** 5

MERINGUE FOR 9-INCH PIE: In 1-quart saucepan, mix ½ cup sugar and 4 teaspoons cornstarch. Stir in ½ cup cold water. Cook and stir over medium heat until mixture thickens and boils; boil and stir 1 minute. Remove from heat. Cool completely while making filling for pie recipe. (To cool more quickly, place in freezer about 10 minutes.) In large bowl, beat 4 egg whites and ⅛ teaspoon salt with electric mixer on high speed just until soft peaks begin to form. Very gradually, beat in sugar mixture until stiff peaks form.

SPREADING MERINGUE OVER FILLING

Spread meringue evenly over hot filling, sealing to edge of crust to help keep meringue from shrinking.

VEGETARIAN

Pumpkin Pie

Be sure to use canned pumpkin, not pumpkin pie mix, in this recipe. The mix has sugar and spices already in it, so if you have purchased the pumpkin pie mix, follow the directions on that label. Or if you like, use 1½ cups cooked fresh pumpkin.

PREP 30 Minutes **TOTAL** 3 Hours 45 Minutes • *8 servings*

Pie Pastry for One-Crust Pie (page 607) or Press-in-the-Pan Oil Pastry (page 610)
2 eggs
½ cup sugar
1 teaspoon ground cinnamon
½ teaspoon salt
½ teaspoon ground ginger
⅛ teaspoon ground cloves
1 can (15 oz) pumpkin (not pumpkin pie mix)
1 can (12 oz) evaporated milk
Sweetened Whipped Cream (page 639), if desired

1 Heat oven to 425°F. Place pastry in 9-inch glass pie plate; flute edge. Line pastry with foil and bake as directed in Partially Baked One-Crust Pie, Steps 1 and 2 (page 608).

2 In medium bowl, using whisk, beat eggs slightly. Beat in remaining ingredients except Whipped Cream.

3 Pour filling into hot crust. (To prevent spilling, place pie plate on oven rack before adding filling.) Cover edge with 2- to 3-inch strips of foil or pie crust shield ring to prevent excessive browning.

4 Bake 15 minutes. Reduce oven temperature to 350°F. Bake about 45 minutes longer or until knife inserted in center comes out clean. Remove foil or shield during last 15 minutes of baking. Cool on cooling rack 1 hour; refrigerate uncovered until completely chilled. Store loosely covered in refrigerator. Serve with Whipped Cream.

1 Serving Calories 270; Total Fat 11g (Saturated Fat 3g, Trans Fat 0g); Cholesterol 45mg; Sodium 360mg; Total Carbohydrate 37g (Dietary Fiber 2g); Protein 6g **Carbohydrate Choices:** 2½

PRALINE PUMPKIN PIE: Make pie as directed, except decrease second bake time to 35 minutes. Mix ⅓ cup packed brown sugar, ⅓ cup chopped pecans and 1 tablespoon softened butter. Sprinkle over pie. Bake about 10 minutes longer or until knife inserted in center comes out clean.

Banana Cream Pie

PREP 30 Minutes **TOTAL** 2 Hours 30 Minutes • *8 servings*

Pie Pastry for One-Crust Pie (page 607), Easy Buttermilk Pastry (page 609) or Press-in-the-Pan Oil Pastry (page 610)

4 egg yolks

⅔ cup sugar

¼ cup cornstarch

½ teaspoon salt

3 cups milk

2 tablespoons butter, softened

2 teaspoons vanilla

2 large ripe but firm bananas

1 cup Sweetened Whipped Cream (page 639)

1 Heat oven to 450°F. Place pastry in 9-inch glass pie plate; flute edge. Bake as directed for Baked One-Crust Pie (page 608). Cool completely.

2 Meanwhile, in medium bowl, beat egg yolks with fork; set aside. In 2-quart saucepan, mix sugar, cornstarch and salt. Gradually stir in milk. Cook over medium heat, stirring constantly, until mixture boils and thickens. Boil and stir 1 minute. Immediately stir about half of the hot mixture gradually into egg yolks, then stir back into hot mixture in saucepan. Boil and stir 1 minute. Remove from heat. Stir in butter and vanilla; cool filling slightly.

3 Slice bananas into cooled baked crust; pour warm filling over bananas. Press plastic wrap on surface of filling to prevent tough layer from forming on top. Refrigerate at least 2 hours or until set. Remove plastic wrap. Top with Whipped Cream. Serve immediately or loosely cover and refrigerate until serving time. Store any remaining pie up to 1 day covered in refrigerator.

1 Serving Calories 400; Total Fat 20g (Saturated Fat 9g, Trans Fat 0g); Cholesterol 120mg; Sodium 370mg; Total Carbohydrate 47g (Dietary Fiber 1g); Protein 6g **Carbohydrate Choices:** 3

CHOCOLATE-BANANA CREAM PIE: Make Chocolate Cream Pie filling (below). Cool slightly. Slice 2 large ripe but firm bananas into cooled baked crust; pour warm filling over bananas. Continue as directed.

CHOCOLATE CREAM PIE: Increase sugar to 1½ cups and cornstarch to ⅓ cup; omit butter and bananas. Stir in 2 oz unsweetened baking chocolate, chopped, after stirring in milk.

COCONUT CREAM PIE: Increase cornstarch to ⅓ cup. Substitute 1 can (14 oz) coconut milk (not cream of coconut) and enough milk to equal 3 cups for the milk. Stir in ¾ cup toasted coconut with the butter. Omit bananas. Refrigerate pie 3 hours or until set. Top with Whipped Cream; sprinkle with ¼ cup toasted coconut.

Pecan Pie

Pecan Pie

PREP 20 Minutes **TOTAL** 1 Hour 10 Minutes • *8 servings*

Pie Pastry for One-Crust Pie (page 607), Easy Buttermilk Pastry (page 609) or Press-in-the-Pan Oil Pastry (page 610)

⅔ cup sugar*

⅓ cup butter, melted

1 cup light or dark corn syrup

3 eggs

1 cup pecan halves or broken pecans

1 Heat oven to 375°F. Place pastry in 9-inch glass pie plate; flute edge.

2 In medium bowl, using whisk, beat sugar, butter, corn syrup and eggs until well blended. Stir in pecans. Pour into pastry-lined pie plate.

3 Bake 40 to 50 minutes or until center is set. Serve warm or at room temperature. Store any remaining pie covered in refrigerator.

1 Serving Calories 520; Total Fat 27g (Saturated Fat 8g, Trans Fat 0g); Cholesterol 90mg; Sodium 260mg; Total Carbohydrate 64g (Dietary Fiber 1g); Protein 5g **Carbohydrate Choices:** 4

*⅓ cup packed light or dark brown sugar can be used for half of the sugar.

KENTUCKY PECAN PIE: Add 2 tablespoons bourbon or 1 teaspoon brandy extract or vanilla with the corn syrup. Stir in 1 cup semisweet chocolate chips with the pecans.

Bourbon-Chocolate-Pecan Mini Pies

PREP 45 Minutes **TOTAL** 1 Hour 40 Minutes • *12 pies*

CRUST

- 1⅓ cups all-purpose flour
- ¼ cup unsweetened baking cocoa
- 2 tablespoons granulated sugar
- ¾ teaspoon salt
- ½ cup shortening
- ¼ cup ice-cold water

FILLING

- ¾ cup whole pecan halves, toasted (page 28)
- 4 oz bittersweet baking chocolate, coarsely chopped
- 1 egg
- ¼ cup packed dark brown sugar
- 2 tablespoons butter, melted
- 2 tablespoons light or dark corn syrup
- 2 tablespoons real maple syrup
- 1 tablespoon bourbon
- ½ teaspoon vanilla

TOPPING

- ¾ cup whipping cream
- 2 tablespoons granulated sugar or powdered sugar
- 2 tablespoons shaved bittersweet chocolate

1 Heat oven to 375°F. In medium bowl, mix flour, cocoa, 2 tablespoons granulated sugar and the salt. Cut in shortening using pastry blender, potato masher or fork until mixture is crumbly and resembles small peas. Sprinkle with water, 1 tablespoon at a time, tossing with fork until dry ingredients are moistened and dough almost leaves side of bowl. Gather dough into a ball.

2 Divide dough into 12 pieces. Place 1 piece in each of 12 ungreased regular-size muffin cups, pressing dough in bottom and up side of cups. Sprinkle pecan halves and chopped chocolate into crust-lined cups.

3 In medium bowl, using whisk, beat egg, brown sugar, melted butter, corn syrup, maple syrup, bourbon and vanilla. Spoon mixture evenly over pecans and chocolate, about 4 teaspoons per cup.

4 Bake 20 to 25 minutes or until filling is golden brown and slightly puffed in center. Cool 30 minutes; remove from pan to cooling rack.

5 In chilled small, deep bowl, beat whipping cream and 2 tablespoons sugar with electric mixer on high speed until soft peaks form. Spoon about 2 tablespoons whipped cream onto each pie. Sprinkle with shaved chocolate. Serve immediately. Store any remaining pies loosely covered in refrigerator.

1 Pie Calories 370; Total Fat 26g (Saturated Fat 10g, Trans Fat 0g); Cholesterol 35mg; Sodium 180mg; Total Carbohydrate 30g (Dietary Fiber 3g); Protein 4g **Carbohydrate Choices:** 2

MAKE-AHEAD DIRECTIONS: Tightly wrap cooled baked pies; freeze up to 1 month (do not prepare Topping). Thaw at room temperature. For warm pies, reheat in oven. Prepare Topping just before serving.

Classic French Silk Pie

Use only pasteurized eggs in this recipe to prevent the risk of foodborne illness that can result from eating raw eggs.

PREP 30 Minutes **TOTAL** 4 Hours 30 Minutes • *10 servings*

- Pie Pastry for One-Crust Pie (page 607) or Easy Buttermilk Pastry (page 609)
- 1 cup butter, softened
- 1½ cups sugar
- 1 tablespoon vanilla
- 3 oz unsweetened baking chocolate, melted, cooled
- 5 pasteurized eggs
- 1½ cups Sweetened Whipped Cream (page 639)
- Chocolate Curls (page 632), if desired

1 Heat oven to 450°F. Place pastry in 9-inch glass pie plate; flute edge. Bake as directed for Baked One-Crust Pie (page 608). Cool completely.

2 In medium bowl, beat butter with electric mixer on medium speed until creamy. Gradually beat in sugar until light and fluffy and sugar begins to dissolve, 3 to 5 minutes. Beat in vanilla and chocolate. Add eggs, one at a time, beating well on high speed after each addition. Beat until light and fluffy and sugar is completely dissolved, about 3 minutes. Pour into cooled baked crust. Refrigerate until set, at least 4 hours

3 Spread with Whipped Cream. Garnish with Chocolate Curls. Serve immediately or cover and refrigerate up to 5 days.

1 Serving Calories 550; Total Fat 38g (Saturated Fat 20g, Trans Fat 1g); Cholesterol 160mg; Sodium 300mg; Total Carbohydrate 45g (Dietary Fiber 2g); Protein 6g **Carbohydrate Choices:** 3

MOCHA FRENCH SILK PIE: Beat in 1½ teaspoons instant coffee granules or crystals with the baking chocolate.

Classic French Silk Pie

Roasted Sweet Potato Pie

Cold Brew Coffee Pie

Roasted Sweet Potato Pie

PREP 30 Minutes **TOTAL** 6 Hours 20 Minutes • *8 servings*

1½ lb dark-orange sweet potatoes (about 2 medium-large)
Pie Pastry for One-Crust Pie (page 607)
½ cup butter, softened
½ cup packed brown sugar
½ cup granulated sugar
½ cup whipping cream

2 tablespoons bourbon or 1 teaspoon bourbon extract, brandy extract or vanilla
½ teaspoon ground cinnamon
½ teaspoon ground nutmeg
¼ teaspoon salt
2 eggs

1 Heat oven to 400°F. Line cookie sheet with foil. Pierce sweet potatoes with fork; place on cookie sheet. Roast 1 hour or until tender. Cut potatoes in half. Scoop out pulp into medium bowl; discard skins. Reduce oven temperature to 350°F.

2 Place pastry in 9½-inch glass deep-dish pie plate; flute edge. Beat sweet potato pulp with electric mixer on medium speed until creamy. Add remaining ingredients; beat 1 minute or until well blended. Pour filling into pastry-lined pie plate.

3 Bake 45 to 50 minutes or until knife inserted near center comes out clean. Cover edge with 2- to 3-inch strips of foil or pie crust shield ring during last 15 minutes of baking if necessary to prevent excessive browning. Cool completely on cooling rack, about 4 hours. Store any remaining pie up to 3 days covered in refrigerator.

1 Serving Calories 440; Total Fat 24g (Saturated Fat 14g, Trans Fat 0.5g); Cholesterol 100mg; Sodium 360mg; Total Carbohydrate 51g (Dietary Fiber 2g); Protein 3g **Carbohydrate Choices:** 3½

ROASTED SWEET POTATO MERINGUE PIE: While pie is baking, make Meringue for 9-inch Pie (page 623). Remove baked pie from oven; spread meringue over hot filling, carefully sealing meringue to edge of crust to prevent shrinking or weeping. Bake 12 to 15 minutes or until meringue is light brown. Cool as directed.

Cold Brew Coffee Pie

Coffee shops and some grocery stores will let you grind your own beans, if you don't have your own coffee grinder at home. Select a coarse grind for this recipe, as it makes it easier to strain and less bitter.

PREP 55 Minutes **TOTAL** 16 Hours 55 Minutes • *8 servings*

FILLING

1⅓ cups coarsely ground regular or decaffeinated coffee beans (4 oz)
4 cups milk
4 egg yolks
⅔ cup sugar
¼ cup cornstarch
¼ teaspoon salt
1½ teaspoons vanilla

COOKIE CRUST

2 cups finely crushed creme-filled chocolate sandwich cookies (about 20 cookies)
3 tablespoons butter, melted

TOPPING

2 cups whipping cream
2 tablespoons sugar
1½ teaspoons vanilla
Additional fine crumbs from creme-filled chocolate sandwich cookies, if desired

1 In medium bowl or large jar, place coffee. Add milk and gently stir; cover. Let stand in refrigerator at least 12 hours, but no longer than 18 hours. Pour coffee and grounds through a fine-mesh strainer into pitcher (do not stir). Discard solids.

2 In medium bowl, beat egg yolks with fork. In 2-quart saucepan, mix ⅔ cup sugar, cornstarch and salt, Gradually stir in milk mixture. Cook over medium heat, stirring constantly, until mixture boils and thickens. Boil and stir 1 minute. Immediately stir about half of the hot mixture gradually into egg yolks; then stir back into hot mixture in pan. Boil and stir 1 minute; remove from heat. Stir in 1½ teaspoons vanilla; cool 15 minutes.

3 Reserve ½ cup crushed cookies; set aside. In medium bowl, mix remaining cookies and melted butter. Press mixture in bottom and up side of 9-inch glass pie plate. Pour filling into crust. Refrigerate at least 2 hours.

4 Sprinkle reserved cookies over filling. To make whipped cream, in chilled medium, deep bowl, beat whipping cream, 2 tablespoons sugar and 1½ teaspoons vanilla with electric mixer on low speed until mixture begins to thicken. Gradually increase speed to high until soft peaks form. Spread whipped cream over the cookie crumbs. Chill at least 3 hours. Garnish with additional cookie crumbs. Cover and refrigerate any remaining pie no longer than 24 hours.

1 Serving Calories 540; Total Fat 33g (Saturated Fat 18g, Trans Fat 1g); Cholesterol 180mg; Sodium 300mg; Total Carbohydrate 51g (Dietary Fiber 1g); Protein 8g **Carbohydrate Choices:** 3½

BANANA COLD BREW COFFEE PIE: Prepare as directed, except place a layer of thinly sliced bananas over the cookie crust before adding the filling and another layer over the cookie crumbs before adding the whipped cream. Top pie with additional banana slices just before serving.

TOASTED COCONUT–COFFEE PIE: Prepare as directed, except fold ⅓ cup toasted flaked coconut into the topping before spreading on pie. Sprinkle top of pie with additional toasted coconut along with cookie crumbs.

COLD BREW COFFEE S'MORE SQUARES: Prepare as directed, except omit crushed cookies and butter. Arrange 9 graham cracker squares in bottom of 9-inch square dish or pan; place another layer of crackers on top. Spoon coffee mixture on top; chill for 2 hours. Spread ¼ cup chocolate syrup over filling. Arrange another two layers of graham crackers on top. Reduce whipping cream to 1 cup and omit sugar and vanilla. Whip cream until soft peaks form; beat in 1 cup marshmallow creme until soft peaks form. Spread over graham crackers. Chill 3 hours. Drizzle with chocolate syrup.

COLD BREW COFFEE PARFAITS: Prepare as directed, except use 8 parfait glasses. Omit butter. Cool coffee mixture as directed; refrigerate in medium bowl 1 to 2 hours or until cool. Layer coffee mixture, whipped cream and crushed cookies in glasses; repeat layers. Chill at least 2 hours or until set.

MAKE AHEAD • VEGETARIAN

Key Lime Pie

This pie won the gold standard test when tested blind against other top Key lime pie recipes.

PREP 15 Minutes **TOTAL** 2 Hours 50 Minutes • *8 servings*

Graham Cracker Crust (page 610)

4 egg yolks

2 cans (14 oz each) sweetened condensed milk (not evaporated)

¾ cup bottled or fresh Key lime juice or regular lime juice

1 or 2 drops green food color, if desired

1½ cups Sweetened Whipped Cream (page 639)

1 Heat oven to 375°F. Make crust as directed but do not bake.

2 In medium bowl, beat egg yolks, condensed milk, lime juice and food color with electric mixer on medium speed about 1 minute or until well blended. Pour into unbaked crust.

3 Bake 14 to 16 minutes or until center is set. Cool on cooling rack 15 minutes. Cover and refrigerate until chilled, at least 2 hours. Spread with Whipped Cream. Cover and refrigerate any remaining pie up to 3 days.

1 Serving Calories 590; Total Fat 27g (Saturated Fat 16g, Trans Fat 1g); Cholesterol 170mg; Sodium 280mg; Total Carbohydrate 75g (Dietary Fiber 0g); Protein 11g **Carbohydrate Choices:** 5

Key Lime Pie

Drumstick Ice Cream Pie

Peanut Butter Candy Pie

Drumstick Ice Cream Pie

PREP 45 Minutes **TOTAL** 3 Hours 55 Minutes • *8 servings*

1 box (5 oz) sugar-style ice cream cones with pointed ends
½ cup butter
2 tablespoons semisweet chocolate chips
1 container (1.5-quart) vanilla ice cream

14 mini drumstick ice cream cones (from 20-count box)
1 cup chopped salted peanuts
½ cup hot fudge topping or Hot Fudge Sauce (page 661)
¼ cup finely chopped salted peanuts

1 In food processor, place ice cream cones; process until finely crushed. Place in medium bowl. In small microwavable bowl, heat butter and chocolate chips on High about 1 minute, stirring after 30 seconds, until mixture can be stirred smooth. Pour over crushed cones; mix well. Press in bottom and up side of ungreased 9-inch pie plate. Freeze 10 minutes. Remove ice cream from freezer to soften while crust is chilling.

2 Coarsely chop 6 of the mini drumsticks (keep remaining drumsticks in freezer) to equal 1 cup; set aside. In medium bowl, place softened ice cream; fold in chopped drumsticks and 1 cup chopped peanuts. Spoon one-third of ice cream mixture into crust.

3 Spoon 3 tablespoons of the hot fudge over ice cream in crust. Repeat with another third of the ice cream and 3 tablespoons hot fudge. Spoon remaining ice cream on top, mounding in center.

4 Place remaining 2 tablespoons hot fudge in small microwavable bowl. Microwave on High about 10 seconds or just until drizzling consistency. Drizzle around edge of pie. Top with ¼ cup finely chopped peanuts. Place remaining drumsticks on top of pie, arranging on their sides in a spoke fashion.

5 Freeze uncovered 45 minutes; cover loosely and freeze at least 4 hours or until firm, but no longer than 5 days. To serve, let stand at room temperature about 15 minutes before cutting; cut between drumsticks.

1 Serving Calories 700; Total Fat 43g (Saturated Fat 21g, Trans Fat 1g); Cholesterol 80mg; Sodium 410mg; Total Carbohydrate 67g (Dietary Fiber 4g); Protein 12g **Carbohydrate Choices:** 4½

Peanut Butter Candy Pie

Slightly warming hot fudge in microwave will make it easier to spread in bottom of pie crust.

PREP 30 Minutes **TOTAL** 3 Hours 55 Minutes • *8 servings*

Pie Pastry for One-Crust Pie (page 607)*
2½ cups whipping cream
8 oz cream cheese, softened
½ cup creamy peanut butter
¼ cup sugar

6 packages (1.5 oz each) peanut butter candy cups, chopped (about 1½ cups)
½ cup plus 1 tablespoon hot fudge topping or Hot Fudge Sauce (page 661)

1 Heat oven to 450°F. Place pastry in 9-inch glass pie plate; flute edge. Bake as directed for Baked One-Crust Pie (page 608). Cool completely, about 30 minutes.

2 Meanwhile, in large chilled bowl, beat whipping cream with electric mixer on high speed just until soft peaks form. Reserve 1 cup of the whipped cream for topping; refrigerate.

3 In large bowl, beat cream cheese, peanut butter and sugar with electric mixer on medium speed until smooth. Gently fold remaining whipped cream into cream cheese mixture. Fold in 1 cup of the chopped peanut butter cups. Refrigerate until ready to assemble pie.

4 In small microwavable bowl, microwave ½ cup of the hot fudge uncovered on High 10 to 20 seconds or until spreadable. Carefully spread hot fudge onto bottom of cooled crust. Spread cream cheese mixture evenly onto fudge layer.

5 Spoon reserved 1 cup whipped cream on top of cream cheese mixture, spreading evenly. Sprinkle with remaining ½ cup chopped peanut butter cups. In same small microwavable bowl, microwave remaining 1 tablespoon hot fudge uncovered on High 5 to 10 seconds or until thin enough to drizzle. Drizzle on top of pie. Refrigerate 3 hours before serving. Store any remaining pie covered in refrigerator up to 2 days.

1 Serving Calories 800; Total Fat 59g (Saturated Fat 28g, Trans Fat 1g); Cholesterol 120mg; Sodium 510mg; Total Carbohydrate 56g (Dietary Fiber 2g); Protein 11g **Carbohydrate Choices:** 4

*You can substitute 1 refrigerated pie crust, softened as directed on box, for Pie Pastry for One-Crust Pie.

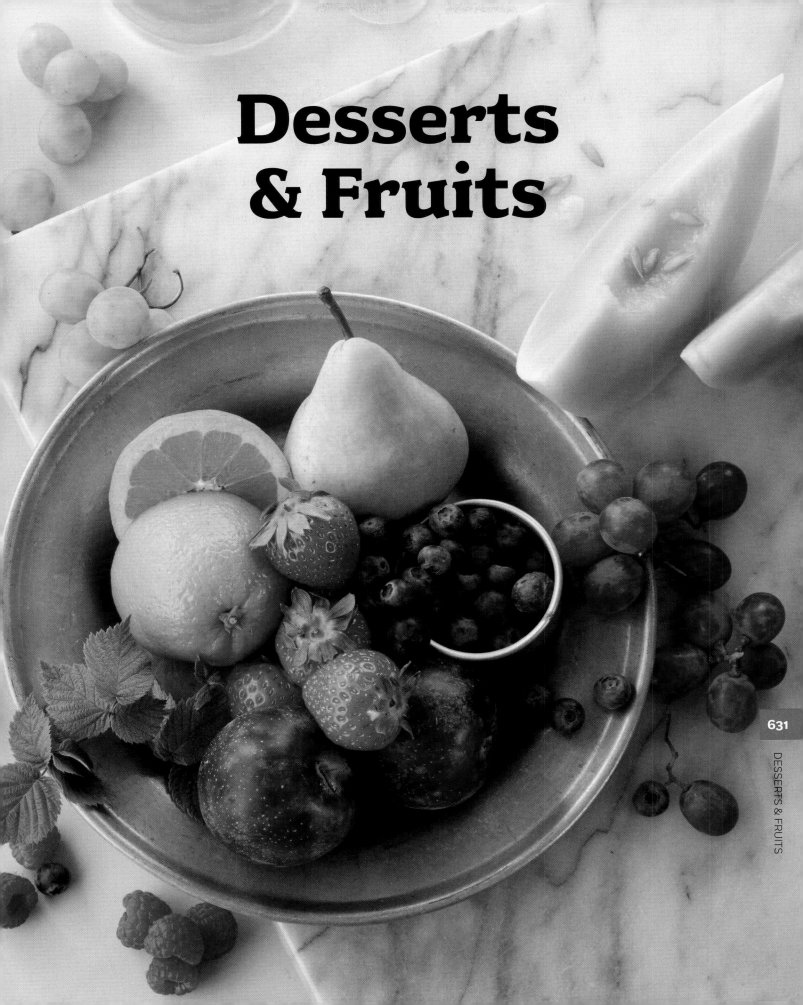

Desserts & Fruits

Dessert & Fruit Basics

Fruit is a terrific, portable snack food—sweet, juicy and delicious—and a natural energy booster that's loaded with nutrients. It's also a quick choice for appetizer boards, paired with cheese and nuts, or a lighter option if you're looking for dessert. Look here for how to buy and store fresh fruit so it will be at the peak of ripeness when you are ready to enjoy or use it in dessert recipes.

Buying and Storing Fresh Fruit

- Purchase fruit that is bright in color, heavy for its size (indicating juiciness) and firm to the touch for the variety.

- Fresh fruit should not show any sign of decay or have soft spots. For berries, check for mold that can occur in closed containers.

- To ripen fruits after purchase, place them in a paper bag (plastic bags can cause mold) at room temperature 1 to 2 days.

- The produce experts at your market are good resources to help you if you're unsure about what the ripeness of the fruit you are purchasing should be.

FRUITS TO CHOOSE RIPE (WILL NOT RIPEN AFTER PURCHASE)	FRUITS THAT CAN BE CHOSEN UNRIPE (WILL RIPEN AFTER PURCHASE)
Apples, Berries, Cherries, Grapefruit, Oranges, Pineapples, Tangerines, Watermelon	Apricots, Bananas, Cantaloupe, Kiwifruit, Nectarines, Peaches, Pears, Plums

SAVE FRUIT TO USE LATER

Berries and citrus fruits can be easily frozen if you can't use them soon enough before they'll decay. Wash berries (remove green tops from strawberries) and wash and slice citrus fruit. Place fruit in a single layer on a cooking parchment paper–lined cookie sheet. Freeze uncovered until frozen, 1 to 2 hours. Move frozen fruit to a resealable freezer plastic bag. Keep frozen for quick smoothies, to add to sparkling water or other drinks or to make fruit sauces (see recipes starting on page 660.)

Dessert Garnishes

Here are some easy ways to make your desserts stand out from the crowd.

Fruit Top dessert with fresh berries or sliced fruit and Sweetened Whipped Cream (page 639), or spoonful of fruit sauce (recipes start on page 660).

Chocolate-Covered Confections Dip dried apricots, fresh strawberries, cherries with stems, pretzels, marshmallows or whole nuts three-fourths of the way into melted chocolate; shake or gently wipe off excess. Immediately sprinkle or roll in candy décor or sprinkles, finely chopped nuts or shredded coconut. Place on cookie sheet lined with waxed paper. Refrigerate 10 minutes to set; chill until serving.

Chocolate Curls Pull a swivel vegetable peeler or thin sharp knife across a room-temperature bar of milk chocolate (or semisweet for smaller curls), using long, thin strokes. Lift the curls with a toothpick to prevent them from breaking. Or make chocolate shavings by using shorter strokes.

Chocolate Drizzle or Filigree Place melted chocolate in a resealable plastic bag; cut off tiny corner of the bag. Drizzle over dessert. Or pipe designs (such as stars, trees, letters, numbers or random patterns) onto a cookie sheet lined with waxed paper. (Print out or draw designs on paper and place underneath the waxed paper to trace with chocolate.) Refrigerate until the chocolate is set. Gently remove the designs from the paper; chill. Garnish desserts with filigree just before serving.

MELTING CHOCOLATE

In 1-quart saucepan, heat 1 cup semisweet or dark chocolate chips with 1 teaspoon shortening over low heat, stirring constantly until melted; remove from heat.

Berries

Choose firm, plump berries; avoid moldy, mushy or soft spots. Remove any moldy or damaged berries before refrigerating, unwashed. Very perishable; use within a few days. Available year-round but best when in season locally for superior flavor.

Blackberries: Largest wild berry. Best used immediately but can be refrigerated up to 2 days.

Blueberries: Juicy and sweet; range from tiny wild blueberries to large cultivated ones.

Cranberries: Available fresh September to December (bags can be frozen up to 1 year to use in cooked cranberry recipes); avoid shriveled, discolored ones. Also available dried or frozen. Fresh berries are very tart. Dried berries are usually sweetened; use like raisins in baked goods.

Gooseberries: Varieties include green, white, yellow or red with smooth or fuzzy skins. Limited season (March to June) depending on region; also canned. Great in jams, jellies, desserts.

Raspberries: The most intensely flavored berry. Red variety available year-round; yellow from June to September; black from mid-June to mid-August.

Red Currants: Related to gooseberries. Available June to August in red, black, white. Black typically used for preserves, syrups, liqueurs. Use red or white as snacks or for preserves.

Strawberries: Choose berries that are all red and brightly colored, with bright green tops. Great in salads, desserts and snacks.

Raspberries

Golden Raspberries

Blackberries

Cranberries

Red Currants

Blueberries

Strawberries

Cape Gooseberries

No-Bake Cookie and Berry Dessert

PREP 40 Minutes **TOTAL** 6 Hours 55 Minute • *16 servings*

2 cups crushed creme-filled chocolate sandwich cookies (about 23 cookies)

¼ cup butter, melted

12 oz cream cheese, softened (from two 8-oz pkgs)

¾ cup powdered sugar

1 cup heavy whipping cream

1 tablespoon vanilla

1 cup coarsely chopped creme-filled chocolate sandwich cookies (about 10 cookies)

2½ cups fresh berries (blueberries, raspberries, blackberries, strawberries)

8 creme-filled chocolate sandwich cookies, cut in half

1 In medium bowl, mix crushed cookies and butter. Press into 9-inch square pan; refrigerate uncovered 15 minutes.

2 Meanwhile, in large bowl, beat cream cheese and powdered sugar with electric mixer on medium speed until smooth, scraping sides of bowl as needed. Add cream and vanilla; beat on low speed until mixed. Beat 1 to 2 minutes on high speed or until mixture is thickened.

3 Spread 1 cup of the cream mixture over cookie crust. Sprinkle coarsely chopped cookies over cream layer. Top with 1½ cups of the berries (refrigerate remaining berries until ready to serve.) Spread remaining cream mixture over berry layer. Cover and refrigerate at least 6 hours but no longer than 48 hours.

4 When ready to serve, cut into 4 rows by 4 rows. Top each piece with some of the remaining berries and a cookie half. Cover and refrigerate any remaining dessert.

1 Serving Calories 340; Total Fat 22g (Saturated Fat 11g, Trans Fat 0.5g); Cholesterol 45mg; Sodium 210mg; Total Carbohydrate 32g (Dietary Fiber 1g); Protein 3g **Carbohydrate Choices:** 2

Apple Crisp

PREP 20 Minutes **TOTAL** 1 Hour • *6 servings*

6 medium tart cooking apples (Granny Smith or Rome), peeled, sliced (about 6 cups)

¾ cup packed brown sugar

½ cup all-purpose flour

½ cup quick-cooking or old-fashioned oats

1 teaspoon ground cinnamon

½ teaspoon ground nutmeg

⅓ cup cold butter

Cream or ice cream, if desired

1 Heat oven to 375°F. Spray bottom and sides of 8-inch square (2-quart) glass baking dish with cooking spray.

2 Spread apples in baking dish. In medium bowl, mix brown sugar, flour, oats, cinnamon and nutmeg. Cut in butter, using pastry blender or fork, until mixture is crumbly. Sprinkle evenly over apples.

3 Bake 35 to 40 minutes or until topping is golden brown and apples are tender when pierced with fork. Serve warm with cream.

1 Serving Calories 350; Total Fat 11g (Saturated Fat 7g, Trans Fat 0g); Cholesterol 25mg; Sodium 90mg; Total Carbohydrate 60g (Dietary Fiber 3g); Protein 2g **Carbohydrate Choices:** 4

BLUEBERRY CRISP: Substitute 6 cups fresh or frozen (thawed and drained) blueberries for the apples.

CARAMEL APPLE CRISP: Toss apples with ½ cup butterscotch caramel topping before spreading in pan.

RHUBARB CRISP: Substitute 6 cups chopped fresh or frozen (thawed and drained) rhubarb for the apples. Sprinkle ½ cup granulated sugar over rhubarb; stir to combine. Continue as directed in Step 2.

634

No-Bake Cookie and Berry Dessert

Apple Crisp

Layered Berry-Ganache
Summer Pudding

Layered Berry-Ganache Summer Pudding

Depending on the bread used, the slices may not soak up all of the fruit juice. If extra juice remains, drizzle it on the dessert plates before placing the pudding pieces on the plates.

PREP 50 Minutes **TOTAL** 12 Hours 50 Minutes • *16 servings*

½ batch Chocolate Ganache (page 603)	1 bag (16 oz) frozen whole strawberries, thawed, juice reserved
2 cups fresh blackberries	30 slices day-old soft Italian bread (from two 1-lb 4-oz loaves)
1 cup sugar	
1¾ cups water	Garnishes, if desired
2 cups fresh raspberries	Sweetened Whipped Cream (page 639)
	Fresh blackberries and raspberries

1 Line 8-inch square baking pan with foil, leaving 2 inches of foil overhanging on all sides of pan.

2 Make Chocolate Ganache as directed, using half of all the ingredients; set aside.

3 In 2-quart saucepan, heat blackberries, ⅓ cup of the sugar and ¾ cup of the water over medium heat until boiling, stirring occasionally and mashing berries with spoon or potato masher. Remove from heat; strain juice through fine-mesh strainer into shallow bowl. Set blackberry juice aside; discard remaining pulp and seeds.

4 In same 2-quart saucepan, heat raspberries, ⅓ cup of the sugar and ½ cup of the water over medium heat to boiling, stirring occasionally and mashing berries with spoon or potato masher. Remove from heat; strain juice through fine-mesh strainer into another shallow bowl. Add ¼ cup of the blackberry juice to the raspberry juice. Set raspberry juice aside; discard pulp and seeds.

5 In same 2-quart saucepan, heat strawberries and reserved juice from bag, remaining ⅓ cup sugar and remaining ½ cup water over medium heat to boiling, stirring occasionally and mashing berries with spoon or potato masher. Remove from heat; strain juice through fine-mesh strainer into another shallow bowl. Set strawberry juice aside; discard pulp and seeds.

6 Remove crusts from bread; cut 6 slices of the bread in half. Soak 4 whole slices and 2 of the half slices in the blackberry juice. Arrange slices in bottom of pan to form a flat layer. Repeat with 4 more whole slices and 2 half-slices of bread and remaining blackberry juice, placing in pan to form a second flat layer. Spread half of the ganache evenly over the top.

7 Repeat using the raspberry juice and more bread slices, as directed for the blackberry layers, to form two raspberry-soaked bread layers in pan; spread remaining ganache over the top.

8 Repeat using the strawberry juice and remaining bread slices as directed for the blackberry layers, to form two strawberry-soaked bread layers (layers will be above the top edge of the pan). Cover with plastic wrap. Place pan on 15×10×1-inch pan. Place another 8-inch pan on top of the plastic wrap. Place heavy cans in pan to weight down top pan. Refrigerate 12 hours or overnight.

9 To serve, remove cans, top pan and plastic wrap from top of pudding. Using foil, lift pudding out of pan. Pull back foil on sides; trim edges if necessary to keep pudding even. Cut into 4 squares, using serrated knife dipped in water. Cut each square diagonally in each direction to form 4 triangles. Place onto a serving plate. Garnish with whipped cream and berries. Cover and refrigerate any remaining pudding up to 2 days.

1 Serving Calories 220; Total Fat 4.5g (Saturated Fat 2.5g, Trans Fat 0g); Cholesterol 5mg; Sodium 240mg; Total Carbohydrate 40g (Dietary Fiber 3g); Protein 4g **Carbohydrate Choices:** 2½

USE IT UP
FRESH BERRIES

Don't let those berries go to waste! Here are some terrific ways to enjoy them. Use whole if small berries, or chop or slice if larger.

BERRY PANCAKES: Stir berries into pancake batter before cooking.

BERRY GOOD SMOOTHIES: Add berries to the blender with the other ingredients before blending.

FRUITY SALAD: Toss lettuce greens, berries, sliced almonds and crumbled blue cheese. Serve with balsamic vinaigrette.

FESTIVE SLAW: Fold berries into your favorite coleslaw just before serving.

SWEET TREAT: Fold berries into whipped cream or frozen whipped topping (thawed). Eat immediately, or freeze in small cups with sticks for a frozen snack.

Colorado Peaches

Peaches

Pluots

Black Plums

Nectarines

Prune Plums

Red Plums

Sweet Cherries

Stone Fruits

Choose plump stone fruits, free of bruises, soft or shriveled spots and not excessively hard. Avoid any greening (in lighter-colored fruit.) Refrigerate 3 to 5 days.

Cherries: **Sweet cherries** are available fresh (choose firm—not hard—cherries), dried, frozen. Stemmed cherries last longer. Eat out of hand or cooked. **Sour cherries,** also known as tart cherries, are smaller and typically too tart to eat fresh. They are, however, delicious in main dishes, jams, jellies and pies. Fresh sour cherries have a very short harvesting season and are typically found only at the farmers' markets and roadside stands. Dried, frozen and canned tart cherries are available year-round.

Nectarines: Sweeter, richer, firmer flesh than peaches. Available mid-spring to late September; peak season is July to August. Choose fragrant fruit that give to gentle pressure.

Peaches: Fuzzy-skinned varieties range from lightly shaded pink or creamy white to red-shaded yellow. Flesh ranges from pink-tinged white to yellow-gold. U.S. varieties available May to October in most regions; imports available during off-season. Choose intensely aromatic fruit that gives to gentle pressure.

Plums: Japanese varieties are larger, rounder; juicy; soft flesh; good for eating. European varieties (including prune plums or sugar plums) are smaller, less juicy; firmer flesh; good for baking and drying. Plumcots and Pluots are varieties of plums crossed with apricots.

5-INGREDIENT RECIPE

Easy Cherry Crisp

Old-Fashioned Oats

Brown Sugar

Cherry Pie Filling

Cinnamon Cereal

Butter

5-INGREDIENT RECIPE

EASY

Easy Cherry Crisp

A scoop of vanilla ice cream or whipped topping makes this easy dessert irresistible!

PREP 10 Minutes **TOTAL** 40 Minutes • *4 servings*

- 1 can (21 oz) more-fruit cherry pie filling
- 2 cups crispy sweetened whole wheat and rice cinnamon cereal, coarsely crushed
- ¾ cup old-fashioned oats
- ⅓ cup packed brown sugar
- ¼ cup butter, melted

1 Heat oven to 375°F. Spray bottom and sides of 8-inch square (2-quart) glass baking dish with cooking spray. Spoon pie filling into baking dish.

2 In medium bowl, mix remaining ingredients until evenly coated; spoon evenly over pie filling.

3 Bake 25 to 30 minutes or until topping is golden brown and filling is bubbly. Serve warm.

1 Serving Calories 490; Total Fat 15g (Saturated Fat 8g, Trans Fat 0g); Cholesterol 30mg; Sodium 220mg; Total Carbohydrate 85g (Dietary Fiber 5g); Protein 4g **Carbohydrate Choices:** 5½

VEGETARIAN

Strawberry Shortcakes

PREP 15 Minutes **TOTAL** 1 Hour 5 Minutes • *6 servings*

- 1 quart (4 cups) fresh strawberries, sliced
- 1 cup sugar
- 2 cups all-purpose flour
- 1 tablespoon baking powder
- ½ teaspoon salt
- ½ cup cold butter
- ⅔ cup milk
- 1 egg, slightly beaten
  Sweetened Whipped Cream (right), if desired

1 In large bowl, stir strawberries and ½ cup of the sugar until well mixed. Let stand about 1 hour so juice forms.

2 Heat oven to 375°F. Grease bottom and side of 8- or 9-inch round cake pan with shortening; lightly flour.

3 In medium bowl, mix flour, remaining ½ cup sugar, the baking powder and salt. Cut in butter, using pastry blender or fork, until mixture looks like coarse crumbs. Stir in milk and egg just until blended. Spoon and spread batter in pan.

Strawberry Shortcakes

4 Bake 30 to 35 minutes or until toothpick inserted in center comes out clean. Cool 10 minutes.

5 Place cooling rack upside down over pan; turn rack and pan over and remove pan. Carefully invert shortcake onto serving plate. Cut shortcake into 6 wedges. If desired, split each wedge horizontally in half. Fill and top with strawberries and whipped cream.

1 Serving Calories 490; Total Fat 18g (Saturated Fat 10g, Trans Fat 0.5g); Cholesterol 75mg; Sodium 590mg; Total Carbohydrate 76g (Dietary Fiber 3g); Protein 7g **Carbohydrate Choices:** 5

DROP SHORTCAKES: Heat oven to 425°F. Make dough as directed. Onto ungreased cookie sheet, drop dough in 6 mounds about 2 inches apart. Bake 12 to 14 minutes or until golden brown.

SWEETENED WHIPPED CREAM

An MVP for Strawberry Shortcake or English Trifle, sweetened whipped cream is also the perfect touch on a piece of pie, cut-up fresh fruit or even a coffee drink. This handy chart (below) will help you know how much of each ingredient you'll need to make the amount of whipped cream you need.

Chill the bowl and beaters in the freezer or refrigerator 10 to 20 minutes. In chilled bowl, beat whipping cream, sugar and vanilla with electric mixer on low speed until mixture begins to thicken. Gradually increase speed to high and beat just until soft peaks form. For stiffer whipped cream, beat just until stiff peaks form: do not overbeat or mixture will curdle.

2 Tablespoons Calories 60; Total Fat 5g (Saturated Fat 3.5g, Trans Fat 0g); Cholesterol 15mg; Sodium 0mg; Total Carbohydrate 1g (Dietary Fiber 0g); Protein 0g **Carbohydrate Choices:** 0

SWEETENED WHIPPED CREAM

YIELD OF WHIPPED CREAM	BOWL SIZE	HEAVY WHIPPING CREAM	POWDERED OR GRANULATED SUGAR	VANILLA
1 cup	Medium	½ cup	1 tablespoon	½ teaspoon
2 cups	Medium	1 cup	2 tablespoons	1 teaspoon
6 cups	Large	3 cups	¼ cup plus 2 tablespoons	1 tablespoon

Skillet Peach-Almond Buckle

A nonstick ovenproof 10-inch skillet can be used in place of the cast-iron skillet. With the nonstick skillet, no pan preparation before baking is necessary.

PREP 20 Minutes **TOTAL** 1 Hour 5 Minutes • **8 servings**

CAKE

- ½ cup packed brown sugar
- ½ cup butter, softened
- 1⅓ cups all-purpose flour
- 1¼ teaspoons baking powder
- ¼ teaspoon salt
- ⅓ cup buttermilk
- 1 egg
- 1½ cups sliced peaches, peeled if desired (about 2 medium)

STREUSEL TOPPING

- 3 tablespoons all-purpose flour
- 3 tablespoons packed brown sugar
- ¼ teaspoon ground nutmeg
- ¼ cup cold butter
- 2 tablespoons sliced almonds
  Ice cream, if desired

1 Heat oven to 350°F. Spray 10-inch cast-iron skillet with cooking spray.

2 In large bowl, beat ½ cup of the brown sugar and ½ cup butter with electric mixer on medium speed until well mixed. Add remaining cake ingredients except peaches; beat about 1 minute or until well mixed (batter will be thick). Spread batter evenly into skillet. Arrange peach slices on top of batter.

3 In small bowl, mix Streusel Topping ingredients except butter and almonds. With pastry blender or 2 forks, cut butter into flour mixture until crumbly. Stir in almonds. Sprinkle evenly over peaches.

4 Bake 36 to 38 minutes or until golden brown and toothpick inserted in center comes out clean. Cool 5 minutes before serving. Serve warm with ice cream.

1 Serving Calories 340; Total Fat 19g (Saturated Fat 11g, Trans Fat 0.5g); Cholesterol 70mg; Sodium 310mg; Total Carbohydrate 38g (Dietary Fiber 1g); Protein 4g **Carbohydrate Choices:** 2½

EASY • SLOW COOKER • GLUTEN FREE •
VEGETARIAN • VEGAN

Caramel-Maple Pears

PREP 5 Minutes **TOTAL** 2 Hours 35 Minutes • **6 servings**

- 6 yellow- or red-skinned pears, cored from bottom leaving stems attached
- 1 cup vegan caramel ice cream topping
- ⅓ cup real maple syrup
  Grated lemon zest, if desired

1 Spray 5- to 6-quart slow cooker with cooking spray. Place pears upright in cooker. (If all pears do not fit in bottom of cooker, place remaining pears suspended between 2 others in cooker.)

2 In small bowl, mix ice cream topping and syrup; pour over pears.

3 Cover; cook on High heat setting 2 hours 30 minutes to 3 hours 30 minutes.

4 Remove pears from cooker; place upright on serving plate or in individual dessert dishes. Spoon about ¼ cup topping mixture over each pear; sprinkle with lemon zest.

1 Serving Calories 310; Total Fat 0g (Saturated Fat 0g, Trans Fat 0g); Cholesterol 0mg; Sodium 190mg; Total Carbohydrate 76g (Dietary Fiber 6g); Protein 1g **Carbohydrate Choices:** 5

Peach Cobbler

No fresh peaches? Four cups frozen sliced peaches (from two 16-oz bags), thawed and drained, can be substituted for the fresh ones.

PREP 25 Minutes **TOTAL** 55 Minutes • **6 servings**

PEACH MIXTURE

- ½ cup sugar
- 1 tablespoon cornstarch
- ¼ teaspoon ground cinnamon
- 4 cups sliced peeled fresh peaches (6 medium)
- 1 teaspoon lemon juice

TOPPING

- 1 cup all-purpose flour
- 1 tablespoon sugar
- 1½ teaspoons baking powder
- ½ teaspoon salt
- 3 tablespoons cold butter
- ½ cup milk
- 2 tablespoons sugar, if desired
  Cream, if desired

1 Heat oven to 400°F. In 2-quart saucepan, mix ½ cup sugar, the cornstarch and cinnamon. Stir in peaches and lemon juice. Cook over medium-high heat 4 to 5 minutes, stirring constantly, until mixture thickens and boils. Boil and stir 1 minute. Pour into ungreased 2-quart casserole; keep peach mixture hot in oven.

2 In medium bowl, mix flour, 1 tablespoon sugar, the baking powder and salt. Cut in butter, using pastry blender or fork, until mixture looks like fine crumbs. Stir in milk. Drop dough in 6 mounds onto hot peach mixture. Sprinkle 2 tablespoons sugar over dough.

3 Bake 25 to 30 minutes or until topping is golden brown. Serve warm with cream.

1 Serving Calories 260; Total Fat 7g (Saturated Fat 4g, Trans Fat 0g); Cholesterol 15mg; Sodium 370mg; Total Carbohydrate 47g (Dietary Fiber 2g); Protein 3g **Carbohydrate Choices:** 3

APPLE COBBLER: Substitute 4 cups sliced peeled tart cooking apples (Granny Smith or Rome) for the peaches.

FRESH BLUEBERRY COBBLER: Substitute 4 cups fresh blueberries for the peaches. Omit cinnamon.

FRESH CHERRY COBBLER: Substitute 4 cups pitted tart red or sweet cherries for the peaches. Increase sugar in cherry mixture to 1¼ cups for tart cherries and 1 cup for sweet cherries, and cornstarch to 3 tablespoons. Substitute ¼ teaspoon almond extract for the lemon juice.

RASPBERRY-PEACH COBBLER: Substitute 2 cups fresh raspberries for 1 cup of the peaches.

Skillet Peach-Almond Buckle

Peach Cobbler

Caramel-Maple Pears

641

Apples and Pears

Choose firm, smooth-skinned apples or pears without bruises, blemishes or musty smell. Choose apples based on how you'll use them—for eating, baking or cooking.

Golden Delicious Apple

Red Delicious Apples

Red Bartlett Pears

Cortland Apples

Bosc Pears

Pink Lady Apple

Ginger Gold Apples

Jonathan Apple

Granny Smith Apple

Bartlett Pear

Apple Pears

Honeycrisp Apple

Braeburn Apple

Seckel Pears

Gala Apple

Comice Pear

French Butter Pears

McIntosh Apples

Baked Apples

Baked apples make a perfect last-minute dessert for entertaining or family dinners. Use the larger amount of brown sugar for very tart apples.

PREP 10 Minutes **TOTAL** 50 Minutes • *4 servings*

4 large unpeeled tart cooking apples (Granny Smith or Rome)	4 teaspoons butter
	½ teaspoon ground cinnamon
2 to 4 tablespoons packed brown sugar	

1 Heat oven to 375°F. Core apples to within ½ inch of bottom. Remove 1-inch strip of peel from around middle of each apple, or peel upper half of each apple, to prevent splitting. Place apples in ungreased 8-inch square (2-quart) glass baking dish.

2 In center of each apple, place 1½ teaspoons to 1 tablespoon sugar, 1 teaspoon butter and ⅛ teaspoon cinnamon. Sprinkle with additional cinnamon if desired. Pour water into baking dish until ¼-inch deep.

3 Bake 30 to 40 minutes or until apples are tender when pierced with fork. (Time will vary depending on size and variety of apple.) Spoon syrup in dish over apples several times during baking if desired.

1 Serving Calories 190; Total Fat 4g (Saturated Fat 2.5g, Trans Fat 0g); Cholesterol 10mg; Sodium 35mg; Total Carbohydrate 38g (Dietary Fiber 5g); Protein 0g **Carbohydrate Choices:** 2½

TOP APPLE VARIETIES AND CHARACTERISTICS

VARIETY	FLAVOR	TEXTURE	BEST USED FOR
Ambrosia	Sweet	Tender	Eating, Cheese Boards, Salads
Braeburn	Sweet-Tart	Crisp	Eating, Pies
Fuji	Sweet	Crisp	Baking, Eating, Salads
Gala	Sweet	Crisp	Eating, Cheese Boards, Salads, Slaws,
Golden Delicious	Sweet-Tart	Crisp	Baking, Eating, Salads,
Honey Crisp	Sweet	Crisp	Applesauce, Baking, Eating
McIntosh	Sweet-Tart	Tender	Applesauce, Baking, Cider
Pink Lady	Sweet-Tart	Crisp	Applesauce, Cheese Boards, Salads
Red Delicious	Slightly Sweet	Slightly Crisp	Eating, Salads

NO-BAKE BAKED APPLES: Prepare apples as directed. Place each apple in 10-oz custard cup or individual microwavable casserole or bowl. Do not add water. Microwave uncovered on High 5 to 10 minutes, rotating cups a half-turn after 3 minutes, until apples are tender when pierced with fork.

Applesauce

PREP 15 Minutes **TOTAL** 15 Minutes • *3 cups*

4 medium apples (1½ lb), peeled, quartered	¼ teaspoon ground cinnamon
½ cup water	⅛ teaspoon ground nutmeg
¼ cup packed organic brown sugar or 3 to 4 tablespoons organic granulated sugar	

1 In 2-quart saucepan, heat apples and water to boiling over medium heat, stirring occasionally; reduce heat. Simmer uncovered 5 to 10 minutes, stirring occasionally to break up apples, until tender.

2 Stir in remaining ingredients. Heat to boiling; boil and stir 1 minute. Serve warm or chilled. Store covered in refrigerator.

½ Cup Calories 110; Total Fat 0g (Saturated Fat 0g, Trans Fat 0g); Cholesterol 0mg; Sodium 0mg; Total Carbohydrate 26g (Dietary Fiber 3g); Protein 0g **Carbohydrate Choices:** 2

Cranberry Sauce

The natural pectin in the cranberries thickens this easy homemade sauce. Be sure to cook the cranberries until they pop so the pectin is released and the sauce gels as it cools.

PREP 15 Minutes **TOTAL** 3 Hours 15 Minutes • *4 cups*

4 cups fresh or frozen cranberries	2 cups water
2 cups organic sugar	1 tablespoon grated orange zest, if desired

1 Wash cranberries; remove any stems and discard any blemished berries.

2 In 3-quart saucepan, heat sugar and water over medium heat until boiling, stirring occasionally. Boil 5 minutes.

3 Stir in cranberries. Heat to boiling; boil about 5 minutes or until cranberries pop. Stir in orange zest. Cover and refrigerate about 3 hours or until chilled. Store covered in refrigerator up to 1 week.

¼ Cup Calories 110; Total Fat 0g (Saturated Fat 0g, Trans Fat 0g); Cholesterol 0mg; Sodium 0mg; Total Carbohydrate 28g (Dietary Fiber 1g); Protein 0g **Carbohydrate Choices:** 2

New York Cheesecake

Cheesecake seems so special to your guests, they'll think you went all out. But don't say a word. We've worked hard to find the secrets to a perfectly baked crust and a creamy rich filling—now you will know them, too.

PREP 45 Minutes **TOTAL** 15 Hours 45 Minutes • *16 servings*

CRUST

- 1 cup all-purpose flour
- ½ cup butter, softened
- ¼ cup sugar
- 1 egg yolk

CHEESECAKE

- 5 packages (8 oz each) cream cheese, softened
- 1¾ cups sugar
- 3 tablespoons all-purpose flour
- 1 tablespoon grated orange zest, if desired
- 1 tablespoon grated lemon zest, if desired
- ¼ teaspoon salt
- ¼ cup whipping cream
- 5 whole eggs
- 2 egg yolks
- ¾ cup whipping cream
- ⅓ cup slivered almonds, toasted (see page 28), or fresh fruit, if desired

1 Heat oven to 400°F. Spray bottom and side of 9-inch springform pan with cooking spray; remove bottom. In medium bowl, mix Crust ingredients, using pastry blender or fork, until dough forms; gather into a ball. Press one-third of the dough on bottom of pan. Place on cookie sheet. Bake 8 to 10 minutes or until light golden brown; cool 10 minutes.

2 Reassemble bottom and side of pan; secure side. Press remaining dough 2 inches up side of pan. Wrap outside bottom and side of pan with heavy-duty foil to prevent leaking.

3 Increase oven temperature to 450°F. In large bowl, beat cream cheese, sugar, flour, orange zest, lemon zest and salt with electric mixer on medium speed about 1 minute or until smooth. On low speed, beat in ¼ cup whipping cream, the eggs and egg yolks just until blended. Pour into crust.

4 Bake 15 minutes. Reduce oven temperature to 200°F. Bake 1 hour 25 minutes to 1 hour 40 minutes longer or until cheesecake is set at least 2 inches from edge of pan but center of cheesecake still jiggles slightly when moved, and surface is golden brown (it will become firm during refrigeration). Do not insert knife into cheesecake because the hole may cause cheesecake to crack. Turn off oven; leave cheesecake in oven 30 minutes longer. Remove from oven and cool in pan on cooling rack away from drafts 30 minutes.

5 Without releasing side of pan, run knife around side of pan carefully to loosen cheesecake. Refrigerate uncovered about 3 hours or until chilled; cover and continue refrigerating at least 9 hours or overnight before serving.

MAKING CHEESECAKE

Press one-third of the dough evenly on bottom of springform pan. Place on cookie sheet. Bake 6 to 10 minutes.

Assemble bottom and side of pan; secure side. Press remaining dough 2 inches up side of pan.

Wrap outside and bottom of pan with foil to prevent leaking during baking.

Run knife around side of pan to loosen baked cheesecake. Then release side of pan.

Spread whipped cream over top of cheesecake. Sprinkle with almonds.

Cut with long, thin-bladed non-serrated knife. After each cut, dip knife into hot water and clean it off with towel.

New York Cheesecake

6 Run knife around side of pan to loosen cheesecake again; remove side of pan. Leave cheesecake on pan bottom to serve. In chilled medium, deep bowl, beat ¾ cup whipping cream with electric mixer on low speed until it begins to thicken. Gradually increase speed to high and beat until stiff peaks form. Spread whipped cream over top of cheesecake. Sprinkle with almonds. Store covered in refrigerator. To cut cheesecake, use long, thin-bladed, nonserrated knife. Dip knife into hot water after each cut, cleaning it off with paper towel.

1 Serving Calories 520; Total Fat 38g (Saturated Fat 22g, Trans Fat 1g); Cholesterol 195mg; Sodium 330mg; Total Carbohydrate 37g (Dietary Fiber 0g); Protein 8g **Carbohydrate Choices:** 2½

LIGHTER DIRECTIONS: For 330 calories and 19 grams fat per serving, omit Crust. Move oven rack to lowest position. Heat oven to 425°F. Lightly grease side only of 9-inch springform pan with shortening. Mix ¾ cup graham cracker crumbs, 2 tablespoons melted butter and 2 tablespoons sugar; press evenly in bottom of pan. Use reduced-fat cream cheese (Neufchâtel); increase flour to ¼ cup. Omit ¼ cup whipping cream. Substitute 1¼ cups fat-free egg product for the 5 eggs. Continue as directed in Steps 3 and 4. Omit ¾ cup whipping cream and the almonds. Serve with fruit if desired.

CHOCOLATE CHIP NEW YORK CHEESECAKE: Fold 1 cup miniature semisweet chocolate chips into cream cheese mixture before pouring into crust.

MAKE AHEAD • VEGETARIAN
English Trifle

Two packages (10.75 oz each) frozen pound cake, thawed, can be substituted for the ladyfingers. Cut each pound cake into 12 slices; spread one side of each slice with preserves and layer as directed.

PREP 30 Minutes **TOTAL** 5 Hours 30 Minutes • **10 servings**

PUDDING
- ½ cup sugar
- 3 tablespoons cornstarch
- ¼ teaspoon salt
- 3 cups milk
- ½ cup dry sherry or other dry white wine or white grape juice
- 3 egg yolks, beaten
- 3 tablespoons butter, softened
- 1 tablespoon vanilla

CAKE AND FRUIT
- 2 packages (3 oz each) ladyfingers (24 ladyfingers)
- ½ cup strawberry preserves
- 2 cups fresh strawberries, sliced, or 1 box (10 oz) frozen sliced strawberries, thawed, drained

TOPPINGS
- 1 cup heavy whipping cream
- 2 tablespoons sugar
- 2 tablespoons slivered almonds, toasted (page 28)

1 In 3-quart saucepan, mix ½ cup sugar, the cornstarch and salt. Gradually stir in milk and sherry. Heat to boiling over medium heat, stirring constantly. Boil and stir 1 minute.

Individual English Trifles

2 Gradually stir at least half of the hot mixture into egg yolks, then stir back into hot mixture in saucepan. Boil and stir 1 minute; remove from heat. Stir in butter and vanilla. Press plastic wrap on surface of pudding to prevent tough layer from forming on top. Refrigerate about 3 hours or until chilled.

3 Split ladyfingers horizontally in half. Spread cut sides with preserves. In 2-quart trifle bowl or glass serving bowl, layer one-fourth of the ladyfingers, cut sides up, half of the strawberries and half of the pudding; repeat layers. Arrange remaining ladyfingers around edge of bowl in upright position with cut sides toward center. (It may be necessary to gently ease ladyfingers down into pudding about 1 inch so they remain upright.) Cover and refrigerate at least 2 hours, but no longer than 24 hours.

4 In chilled large, deep bowl, beat whipping cream and 2 tablespoons sugar with electric mixer on low speed until mixture begins to thicken. Gradually increase speed to high and beat until stiff peaks form. Spread over trifle. Sprinkle with almonds. Cover and refrigerate any remaining trifle.

1 Serving Calories 360; Total Fat 17g (Saturated Fat 10g, Trans Fat 0g); Cholesterol 130mg; Sodium 160mg; Total Carbohydrate 43g (Dietary Fiber 1g); Protein 6g **Carbohydrate Choices:** 3

LIGHTER DIRECTIONS: For 265 calories and 5 grams of fat per serving, use fat-free (skim) milk, substitute ¼ cup fat-free egg product for the egg yolks and reduce butter to 1 tablespoon. Substitute 2 cups fat-free frozen (thawed) whipped topping for the whipping cream and 2 tablespoons sugar.

INDIVIDUAL ENGLISH TRIFLES: Prepare as directed through Step 2. Do not split ladyfingers; omit preserves. Cut ladyfingers in half crosswise; layer 3 halves in the bottom of 8 (10 oz) glasses. Divide 1 cup of the strawberries among glasses; top each with about 3 tablespoons of the pudding. Repeat layers except reserve 8 ladyfinger halves for garnish, if desired (using only 2 ladyfinger halves for second layer). Divide whipped cream and almonds among glasses. Garnish each glass with a sliced strawberry and reserved ladyfinger half.

Festive Strawberry Frozen Trifle

Chocolate Mousse

Festive Strawberry Frozen Trifle

PREP 20 Minutes TOTAL 5 Hours 20 Minutes • *6 servings*

1½ cups heavy whipping cream

1 box (4-serving size) strawberry-flavored gelatin

3 tablespoons sugar

1½ teaspoons vanilla

1 package (16 oz) frozen loaf pound cake

⅔ cup coarsely chopped fresh strawberries, patted dry, or freeze-dried strawberries, coarsely chopped

1 tablespoon multicolored sprinkles

1 In microwave-safe glass 1-cup measure, microwave ½ cup of the whipping cream on High 60 seconds; stir in gelatin until dissolved. Refrigerate 30 minutes or until almost cool and thickened; stir.

2 In chilled medium bowl, beat gelatin mixture, remaining 1 cup whipping cream, the sugar and vanilla with an electric mixer on high speed until thickened. Reserve ¾ cup whipped gelatin mixture; set aside.

3 Carefully slice frozen pound cake horizontally into 3 layers. Line pound cake loaf pan with cooking parchment paper with overhang to make removal easier. In pan, place bottom cake layer. Stir strawberries into remaining whipped gelatin mixture. Spread half of strawberry mixture over cake layer in pan; sprinkle with 1 teaspoon sprinkles; top with middle cake layer. Repeat with remaining strawberry mixture, another teaspoon of the sprinkles and top cake layer. Top with reserved whipped gelatin mixture and remaining sprinkles.

4 Loosely cover; freeze at least 4 hours or until firm but no longer than 4 days. Remove from loaf pan; fold down parchment. Cut loaf into 1¼-inch slices. Let stand at room temperature 15 minutes before serving.

1 Serving Calories 660; Total Fat 43g (Saturated Fat 23g, Trans Fat 2.5g); Cholesterol 145mg; Sodium 150mg; Total Carbohydrate 60g (Dietary Fiber 1g); Protein 7g **Carbohydrate Choices:** 4

Chocolate Mousse

PREP 20 Minutes TOTAL 2 Hours 20 Minutes • *8 servings*

4 egg yolks

¼ cup sugar

2½ cups whipping cream

8 oz semisweet or dark baking chocolate, chopped

1 In small bowl, beat egg yolks with electric mixer on high speed 3 minutes or until thick and lemon colored. Slowly beat in sugar.

2 In 2-quart saucepan, heat 1 cup of the whipping cream over medium heat just until hot. Gradually stir at least half of hot cream into egg yolk mixture, then stir back into hot cream in saucepan. Cook over low heat about 5 minutes, stirring constantly, until mixture thickens (do not boil).

3 Stir in chocolate until melted. Cover and refrigerate about 2 hours, stirring occasionally, just until chilled.

4 In chilled large deep bowl, beat remaining 1½ cups whipping cream with electric mixer on low speed until cream begins to thicken. Gradually increase speed to high and beat until stiff peaks form. Fold chocolate mixture into whipped cream.

5 Pipe or spoon mixture into 8 dessert dishes or stemmed glasses. Refrigerate until serving. Store covered in refrigerator.

1 Serving Calories 460; Total Fat 38g (Saturated Fat 23g, Trans Fat 1g); Cholesterol 175mg; Sodium 25mg; Total Carbohydrate 27g (Dietary Fiber 1g); Protein 4g **Carbohydrate Choices:** 2

LIGHTER DIRECTIONS: For 255 calories and 14 grams of fat per serving, substitute 2 whole eggs for the 4 egg yolks. Substitute half-and-half for the 1 cup whipping cream in Step 2. Substitute 3 cups frozen fat-free whipped topping, thawed, for the 1½ cups whipping cream; do not whip, just fold with chocolate mixture.

Cream Puffs

PREP 30 Minutes **TOTAL** 2 Hours 40 Minutes •
12 cream puffs

1	cup water	4	whole eggs
½	cup butter, cut into pieces		Vanilla Pudding (page 652)
1	cup all-purpose flour		Powdered sugar, if desired

1 Heat oven to 400°F. In 2-quart saucepan, heat water and butter over high heat, stirring occasionally, until boiling rapidly. Stir in flour; reduce heat to low. With wooden spoon, beat vigorously over low heat about 1 minute or until mixture forms a ball; remove from heat.

2 Add eggs one at a time, beating vigorously with whisk after each addition, until mixture is smooth and glossy. Onto ungreased cookie sheet, drop dough by slightly less than ¼-cupfuls in mounds about 3 inches apart.

3 Bake 35 to 40 minutes or until puffed and golden. Remove from cookie sheet to cooling rack; prick side of each puff with tip of sharp knife to release steam. Cool away from drafts 30 minutes.

4 Meanwhile, prepare Vanilla Pudding.

5 Using sharp knife, cut off top third of each puff; reserve tops. Pull out any strands of soft dough from puffs. Just before serving, fill bottom of each puff with about 2 rounded tablespoons pudding; replace tops. Sprinkle with powdered sugar. Store cream puffs covered in refrigerator.

1 Cream Puff Calories 210; Total Fat 13g (Saturated Fat 7g, Trans Fat 0g); Cholesterol 120mg; Sodium 140mg; Total Carbohydrate 17g (Dietary Fiber 0g); Protein 5g **Carbohydrate Choices:** 1

ECLAIRS: After dropping dough onto cookie sheet, shape each mound into finger shape, 4½x1½ inch, with metal spatula. Bake and cool as directed. Fill eclairs with Vanilla Pudding. Drizzle with Vanilla Glaze (page 602).

ICE CREAM PUFFS: Omit Vanilla Pudding. Fill puffs with your favorite flavor ice cream. Cover and freeze until serving. Serve with Chocolate Sauce, Hot Fudge Sauce or Caramel Sauce (page 661).

PROFITEROLES: Fill puffs with Vanilla Pudding or ice cream. Sprinkle with powdered sugar and drizzle with Chocolate Sauce (page 661).

WHIPPED CREAM PUFFS: Omit Vanilla Pudding. Make Sweetened Whipped Cream (page 639), using 2 cups whipping cream and ¼ cup granulated or powdered sugar and a large, deep bowl. Fill puffs with whipped cream.

DOUBLE-CHOCOLATE PUFFS: Prepare Cream Puffs— except reduce flour to ¾ cup plus 2 tablespoons. Mix flour with 2 tablespoons unsweetened baking cocoa and 1 tablespoon sugar. Continue as directed, baking puffs 35 to 40 minutes or until puffed and darker brown on top. Substitute about 2¼ cups Chocolate Mousse (opposite) for the Vanilla Pudding.

MAKING CREAM PUFFS AND ECLAIRS

Beat vigorously with wooden spoon after adding the flour until mixture forms a ball.

To shape cream puffs, drop dough by slightly less than ¼ cupfuls in mounds about 3 inches apart.

To shape éclairs, shape each mound into finger shape, 4½x1½ inch, with metal spatula

Cut off top third of each cooked puff; pull out any strands of soft dough.

Profiteroles

647

Tiramisu

Mascarpone is a rich double or triple cream cheese that originated in the Lombardy region of Italy. It has a delicate, buttery flavor with just a hint of sweetness. Look for it in the cheese case in large supermarkets, specialty cheese shops or gourmet food stores.

PREP 35 Minutes **TOTAL** 5 Hours 35 Minutes • *8 servings*

6 egg yolks	¼ cup cold brewed espresso or very strong coffee
¾ cup sugar	
⅔ cup milk	2 tablespoons rum*
2 containers (8 oz each) mascarpone cheese or 2 packages (8 oz each) cream cheese, softened	2 packages (3 oz each) ladyfingers (24 ladyfingers)**
	1½ teaspoons unsweetened baking cocoa
1¼ cups whipping cream	
½ teaspoon vanilla	

1 In 2-quart saucepan, beat egg yolks and sugar with whisk until well mixed. Beat in milk. Heat just to boiling over medium heat, stirring constantly; reduce heat to low. Boil and stir 1 minute; remove from heat. Pour into medium bowl; press plastic wrap on surface of custard to prevent tough layer from forming on top. Refrigerate about 1 hour or until chilled.

2 Add cheese to custard. Beat with electric mixer on medium speed until smooth; set aside. Wash and dry beaters. In chilled large, deep bowl, beat whipping cream and vanilla with electric mixer on low speed until mixture begins to thicken. Gradually increase speed to high and beat until stiff peaks form; set aside.

3 In small bowl, mix espresso and rum. Split ladyfingers horizontally in half.

4 In ungreased 11×7-inch (2-quart) glass baking dish, arrange half of the ladyfingers in single layer. Brush with espresso mixture (do not soak). Spread half of the cheese mixture over ladyfingers; spread with half of the whipped cream. Repeat layers with remaining ladyfingers, espresso mixture, cheese mixture and whipped cream. Sprinkle with cocoa. Cover and refrigerate at least 4 hours to develop flavors but no longer than 24 hours. Store covered in refrigerator.

1 Serving Calories 590; Total Fat 45g (Saturated Fat 27g, Trans Fat 1.5g); Cholesterol 295mg; Sodium 85mg; Total Carbohydrate 36g (Dietary Fiber 0g); Protein 8g **Carbohydrate Choices:** 2½

*⅛ teaspoon rum extract mixed with 2 tablespoons water can be substituted for the rum.

**Two packages (10.75 oz each) frozen pound cake, thawed, can be substituted for the ladyfingers. Carefully slice frozen pound cake horizontally into 3 layers. Brush each slice with espresso mixture. Arrange 3 slices crosswise in baking dish. Spread half of the cheese mixture over cake; spread with half of the whipped cream. Repeat layers with remaining pound cake, espresso mixture, cheese mixture and whipped cream.

Pavlovas with Blood Orange Curd

Beating the aquafaba with a stand mixer takes almost no time at all. If you use a hand mixer, it will take about 15 minutes.

PREP 30 Minutes **TOTAL** 3 Hours 15 Minutes • *8 pavlovas*

PAVLOVAS	BLOOD ORANGE CURD
½ cup liquid (aquafaba) from 1 can (15 oz) low-sodium garbanzo beans	¾ cup organic sugar
	3 tablespoons cornstarch
	⅛ teaspoon salt
¼ teaspoon cream of tartar	¾ cup fresh blood orange juice (about 4 blood oranges)
½ cup organic sugar	½ cup light coconut milk (from 13.5-oz can)
⅛ teaspoon almond extract	Garnishes, if desired
	Blood orange slices and fresh mint leaves

1 Heat oven to 200°F. Line cookie sheet with cooking parchment paper.

2 In large bowl, beat aquafaba and cream of tartar using electric stand mixer and whisk attachment on high until soft peaks form. Add ½ cup sugar, 1 tablespoon at a time, over 2 minutes. Add almond extract; continue beating an additional 1 minute. Do not overbeat. Mixture will be stiff. Spoon or pipe mixture forming 8 mounds, about 1 cup each, onto baking sheet. With back of spoon, shape each mound into a 4-inch round, building up sides and leaving a shallow well in the center.

3 Bake 1 hour 15 minutes. Do not open oven door. Turn oven off; cool 1 hour in oven. Remove from oven; continue cooling 30 minutes. Remove carefully from parchment paper. Store in tightly covered container until serving.

4 Meanwhile, in 2-quart saucepan, mix ¾ cup sugar, cornstarch and salt. Pour blood orange juice through small strainer to remove any pulp. Stir juice and coconut milk into cornstarch mixture. Heat to boiling over medium heat, stirring frequently with whisk; boil 1 minute, until thickened. Remove from heat; transfer to small bowl. Press plastic wrap directly on surface of curd to prevent tough layer from forming on top. Refrigerate about 2 hours or until cooled completely.

5 Just before serving, stir curd until smooth. Fill each pavlova with about 2 tablespoons curd. Garnish with blood orange slices and fresh mint leaves.

1 Pavlova Calories 160; Total Fat 1g (Saturated Fat 1g, Trans Fat 0g); Cholesterol 0mg; Sodium 40mg; Total Carbohydrate 37g (Dietary Fiber 0g); Protein 0g **Carbohydrate Choices:** 2½

Tiramisu

Baked Custard

PREP 10 Minutes **TOTAL** 1 Hour 25 Minutes • *6 servings*

3 eggs, slightly beaten	2½ cups very warm milk or half-and-half (120°F to 130°F)
⅓ cup sugar	
1 teaspoon vanilla	Ground nutmeg
Dash salt	

1 Heat oven to 350°F. In medium bowl, beat eggs, sugar, vanilla and salt with whisk or fork until combined. Gradually stir in milk.

2 Pour mixture into 6 (6-oz) ramekins or custard cups. Sprinkle with nutmeg. Place cups in 13×9-inch pan; place pan in oven. Carefully pour very hot water into pan to within ½ inch of tops of ramekins.

3 Bake about 45 minutes or until knife inserted halfway between center and edge comes out clean. Carefully remove ramekins from water using tongs or grasping tops of ramekins with pot holder. Cool about 30 minutes. Serve warm or cool. If desired, unmold custard onto individual plates. Store covered in refrigerator.

1 Serving Calories 140; Total Fat 4.5g (Saturated Fat 2g, Trans Fat 0g); Cholesterol 100mg; Sodium 105mg; Total Carbohydrate 16g (Dietary Fiber 0g); Protein 6g **Carbohydrate Choices:** 1

CARAMEL CUSTARD (CRÈME CARAMEL):

Before making custard, in heavy 1-quart saucepan, heat ½ cup sugar over low heat 10 to 15 minutes, stirring constantly with wooden spoon, until sugar is melted and golden brown. (Sugar becomes very hot and could melt a plastic spoon.) Immediately divide syrup among 6 (6-oz) custard cups before it hardens in saucepan; carefully tilt cups to coat bottoms (syrup will be extremely hot). Let syrup harden in cups about 10 minutes. Make custard as directed in Step 1; pour over syrup in cups. Bake as directed in Steps 2 and 3. Cool completely. Cover and refrigerate until serving or up to 48 hours. To unmold, carefully loosen side of custard with knife or small spatula. Place dessert dish on top of cup and, holding tightly, turn dish and cup upside down. Shake cup gently to loosen custard. Caramel syrup will drizzle over custard, forming a sauce.

Pavlovas with Blood Orange Curd

UNMOLDING CUSTARD

Run thin knife around edge of each baked custard; dip bottom of each ramekin into hot water for about 5 seconds.

Immediately place serving plate upside down onto ramekin. Turn ramekin and plate upside down; remove ramekin.

Baked Custard

649

LEARN TO MAKE CRÈME BRÛLÉE

A popular star on restaurant menus, this elegant dessert is a lovely contrast of textures—a creamy custard and brittle caramelized sugar topping. It's a great dessert to make ahead and dazzle your guests with because it's actually easy to make when you know the secrets to success.

Tips for Making Créme Brûlée

1 Use heavy whipping cream (not half-and-half or milk) to correctly set the custard and achieve the velvety-smooth texture and creamy richness crème brûlée is known for.

2 Use ceramic ramekins, not glass custard cups or glass pie plates, which may not withstand the heat from the kitchen torch or broiler and break.

3 Slightly beat the eggs with a whisk to break them up before adding to the cream mixture. Whisk eggs with cream mixture until well blended so the custard will be smooth when baked.

4 Add enough boiling water to the pan until it comes two-thirds of the height of the ramekins in order to protect the custard from the direct heat of the oven during baking.

5 Don't allow any boiling water to splash into the ramekins, which could affect the custard texture.

6 Blot any condensation from the tops of chilled custards before sprinkling with sugar.

7 Caramelize the sugar on top of the custard until sugar is melted and light golden brown—watching carefully, so the sugar doesn't burn.

MAKE AHEAD • GLUTEN FREE • VEGETARIAN

Crème Brûlée

PREP 20 Minutes TOTAL 7 Hours • *4 servings*

2 cups heavy whipping cream	6 egg yolks, slightly beaten
⅓ cup sugar	Boiling water
1 teaspoon vanilla	8 teaspoons sugar

1 Heat oven to 350°F. In large bowl, stir whipping cream, ⅓ cup sugar and the vanilla until well mixed. Add egg yolks; beat with whisk until evenly colored and well blended.

2 In 13×9-inch pan, place 4 (6-oz) ceramic ramekins.* Pour cream mixture evenly into ramekins. Carefully place pan in oven. Carefully pour boiling water into pan to within ½ inch of tops of ramekins.

3 Bake 30 to 40 minutes or until tops are light golden brown and sides are set (centers will be jiggly). Carefully transfer ramekins to cooling rack, using tongs or grasping tops of ramekins with pot holder. Cool 2 hours or until room temperature. Cover tightly with plastic wrap; refrigerate until chilled, at least 4 hours but no longer than 2 days.

4 Uncover ramekins; gently blot any condensation on custards with paper towel. Sprinkle 2 teaspoons sugar over each custard. Holding kitchen torch 3 to 4 inches from custard, caramelize sugar by heating with torch about 2 minutes, moving flame continuously over sugar in circular motion, until sugar is melted and light golden brown. (To caramelize under broiler, see below.) Serve immediately, or refrigerate up to 8 hours before serving. If served immediately, custard will be softer.

1 Serving Calories 600; Total Fat 50g (Saturated Fat 30g, Trans Fat 1.5g); Cholesterol 405mg; Sodium 45mg; Total Carbohydrate 29g (Dietary Fiber 0g); Protein 7g **Carbohydrate Choices:** 2

BROILER DIRECTIONS: Sprinkle 2 teaspoons brown sugar over each chilled custard. (Brown sugar melts much more evenly under broiler.) Place ramekins in 15×10×1-inch pan or on cookie sheet with sides. Broil with tops 4 to 6 inches from heat 5 to 6 minutes or until sugar is melted and forms a glaze.

LEMON CRÈME BRÛLÉE: Add 1 tablespoon grated lemon zest with the vanilla. After caramelizing sugar, top each ramekin with 1 tablespoon fresh raspberries, if desired.

*Do not use glass custard cups or glass pie plates; they cannot withstand the heat from the kitchen torch or broiler and may break.

CARAMELIZING SUGAR ON CRÈME BRÛLÉE

Carefully blot any condensation from tops of chilled custards with paper towel.

Caramelize sugar with kitchen torch by continuously moving torch over sugar in a circular motion.

Continue carmelizing sugar until it is melted and light golden brown.

651

Individual Meringues with Lemon Curd

Meringue Shell

A meringue shell bakes up crisp yet melts in your mouth when you bite into it. Just before serving, fill with fresh fruit, ice cream, Chocolate Mousse (page 646), Lemon Curd (page 514) or Vanilla Pudding (at right).

PREP 10 Minutes   **TOTAL** 4 Hours 40 Minutes   •   *8 servings*

3 egg whites	¾ cup sugar
¼ teaspoon cream of tartar	

1 Heat oven to 275°F. Line cookie sheet with cooking parchment paper.

2 In medium bowl, beat egg whites and cream of tartar with electric mixer on high speed until foamy. Beat in sugar, 1 tablespoon at a time; continue beating until stiff peaks form and mixture is glossy. Do not underbeat. On cookie sheet, shape meringue into 9-inch round with back of spoon, building up side.

3 Bake 1 hour 30 minutes. Turn off oven; leave meringue in oven with door closed 1 hour. Finish cooling at room temperature, about 2 hours.

1 Serving Calories 80; Total Fat 0g (Saturated Fat 0g, Trans Fat 0g); Cholesterol 0mg; Sodium 20mg; Total Carbohydrate 19g (Dietary Fiber 0g); Protein 1g **Carbohydrate Choices:** 1

CHOCOLATE MERINGUE SHELL: After beating egg white mixture, sprinkle 2 tablespoons unsweetened baking cocoa through strainer over top; fold cocoa into mixture. Bake as directed.

INDIVIDUAL MERINGUES: Drop meringue by ⅓-cupfuls onto cookie sheet. Shape into rounds, building up sides. Bake and cool as directed. Makes 8 to 10 meringues.

SHAPING MERINGUE SHELLS

Shape each meringue with back of spoon into desired shape, building up side.

Vanilla Pudding

PREP 10 Minutes   **TOTAL** 1 Hour 10 Minutes   •   *4 servings*

⅓ cup sugar	2 egg yolks, slightly beaten
2 tablespoons cornstarch	2 tablespoons butter, softened
⅛ teaspoon salt	2 teaspoons vanilla
2 cups milk	

1 In 2-quart saucepan, mix sugar, cornstarch and salt. Gradually stir in milk. Cook over medium heat, stirring constantly, until mixture thickens and boils. Boil and stir 1 minute.

2 Gradually stir at least half of hot mixture into egg yolks, then stir back into hot mixture in saucepan. Boil and stir 1 minute; remove from heat. Stir in butter and vanilla.

3 Pour pudding into dessert dishes. Cover and refrigerate about 1 hour or until chilled. Store covered in refrigerator.

1 Serving Calories 230; Total Fat 10g (Saturated Fat 6g, Trans Fat 0g); Cholesterol 115mg; Sodium 180mg; Total Carbohydrate 27g (Dietary Fiber 0g); Protein 5g **Carbohydrate Choices:** 2

BUTTERSCOTCH PUDDING: Substitute ⅔ cup packed dark or light brown sugar for the granulated sugar; reduce vanilla to 1 teaspoon.

CHOCOLATE PUDDING: Increase sugar to ½ cup; stir ⅓ cup unsweetened baking cocoa into sugar mixture. Omit butter.

Banana Split Lush

PREP 1 Hour   **TOTAL** 10 Hours   •   *16 servings*

2 batches Vanilla Pudding (above), using 3 cups milk total	1 cup powdered sugar
1 package (10 oz) shortbread cookies, crushed (about 2¼ cups)	1 can (8 oz) crushed pineapple, drained
	1 medium banana, chopped (1 cup)
⅓ cup butter, melted	2 cups thinly sliced strawberries, patted dry (8 oz)
6 cups Sweetened Whipped Cream (page 639)	½ cup chopped walnuts
	⅓ cup chocolate-flavored syrup
1 package (8 oz) cream cheese, softened	16 maraschino cherries, drained and patted dry

1 Make Vanilla Pudding as directed, using double of all ingredients. Refrigerate covered for 1 hour or until slightly thickened.

2 In medium bowl, stir cookie crumbs and butter until well mixed. Press mixture in bottom of ungreased 13×9-inch (3-quart) glass baking dish; place in refrigerator while preparing whipped cream layer.

3 Make Sweetened Whipped Cream as directed.

4 In large bowl, beat cream cheese and powdered sugar with electric mixer on medium speed until smooth, scraping down side of bowl frequently. Fold in 1½ cups of the whipped cream and the pineapple; spread over cookie crust. Top with banana and strawberries.

5 Spoon pudding evenly over fruit. Drop remaining whipped cream by spoonfuls onto pudding layer; spread to cover. Cover loosely and refrigerate at least 8 hours, but no longer than 24 hours. To serve, sprinkle with walnuts. Cut into 4 rows by 4 rows; top each piece with 1 teaspoon chocolate syrup and a cherry.

1 Serving Calories 560; Total Fat 37g (Saturated Fat 20g, Trans Fat 1g); Cholesterol 130mg; Sodium 250mg; Total Carbohydrate 48g (Dietary Fiber 1g); Protein 6g **Carbohydrate Choices:** 3

EASY BANANA SPLIT LUSH: Prepare as directed—except use 2 boxes (4-serving size) vanilla instant pudding and pie filling mix and 3 cups milk for the pudding and substitute 1 container (16 oz) frozen whipped topping, thawed, for the sweetened whipped cream.

EASY • MAKE AHEAD • CALORIE SMART • VEGETARIAN

Coconut-Lime Dip

Coconut cream can be found next to the canned coconut milk products in your grocery store. Thicker and creamier than coconut milk, you'll want to stir the contents of the can before measuring out what you need for this recipe.

PREP 10 Minutes **TOTAL** 3 Hours 10 Minutes • *1¾ cup*

½ cup coconut cream (from 13.66-oz can)	2 teaspoons poppy seed
4 oz cream cheese, softened (from 8-oz pkg)	**FRUIT, IF DESIRED** Lime slice, additional lime zest and mint leaves
1 jar (7 oz) marshmallow creme	Watermelon, cantaloupe or honeydew melon sticks
1 tablespoon grated lime zest	

In medium bowl, beat coconut cream and cream cheese with electric mixer on low speed until well mixed. Beat in marshmallow creme, lime zest and poppy seed on high speed 1 minute or until mixture is smooth. Cover and refrigerate at least 3 hours or until thickened. Top with lime slice, additional lime zest and mint leaves. Serve with fruit.

2 Tablespoons Calories 110; Total Fat 6g (Saturated Fat 4.5g, Trans Fat 0g); Cholesterol 10mg; Sodium 35mg; Total Carbohydrate 12g (Dietary Fiber 0g); Protein 1g **Carbohydrate Choices:** 1

Butterscotch, Chocolate and Vanilla Pudding

Banana Split Lush

Coconut-Lime Dip

653

Mango

Red Banana

Plantain

Dates

Coconut

Papaya

Mangosteen

Quince

Horned
Melon

Pomegranate

Lychee

Carambola
(Star Fruit)

Figs

Guayaba
(Guava)

Longan

Dragon Fruit

Kiwi

Pineapple

Cherimoya

Rambutan

654

Grapefruit

Valencia
Orange

Lime

Navel Orange

Minneola (Tangelo)

Key
Lime

Lemon

Meyer Lemon

Clementine

Tropical Fruits

Tropical fruits are available at different times of the year. Look for new and interesting varieties that are firm, with great color and a fresh aroma.

Cherimoya Creamy white flesh; sweet custard taste; inedible large black seeds. Ripen unwashed at room temperature until fruit yields to gentle pressure. For more intense flavor, chill before serving.

Dragon Fruit Pink skin (white or red flesh) or yellow skin (white flesh). Kiwi-pineapple flavor; edible seeds. Choose evenly colored skin with few blotches; avoid very dry, brown stem or brown-tipped "leaves." Fruit should yield to gentle pressure. Eat plain, in salads or smoothies.

Kiwano (Horned Melon) Bright, lime-green pulp; banana-cucumber taste; jellylike texture; edible seeds. Golden orange at peak ripeness. Store at room temperature up to 2 weeks.

Mango Golden-orange flesh; very sweet flavor; large inedible center seed. Chill before serving.

Pineapple Firm yellow flesh; very fragrant with sweet-tart flavor. Choose firm fruit with a crisp-green top and no sign of decay.

Plantain "Cooking banana" but less sweet, more firm than bananas. Popular in Latin American and some Asian and African cuisines. Avoid those with bruises. Green: mild, squash-like flavor. Ripened: soft, spongy texture. Use both types in side dishes. Store at room temperature.

Citrus

Choose fruit heavy for size, with smooth-textured skin. Store unwashed at room temperature or refrigerate up to 2 weeks.

Blood Orange (Moro Orange) Deep red; sweet, juicy flesh. Peel is smooth or pitted with red blush. Peak season: December to May. Refrigerate up to 2 weeks.

Kumquat Entirely edible; skin is sweet, pulp is tart. Peak season: December to May. Store unwashed at room temperature up to 2 days or refrigerate up to 2 weeks.

Meyer Lemon Mild, juicy. Sweeter than common lemons; rind isn't bitter. Peak season: November to May. Refrigerate in plastic bag up to 2 weeks.

Tangelo Cross between grapefruit and tangerine. Range of sizes. Yellow orange to deep orange; smooth skin. Sweet-tart; juicy; few seeds. Minneola is most common variety. Peak season: November to March. Refrigerate up to 2 weeks.

Honey-Basil Fruit Dip

Consider this your go-to holiday recipe to bring to parties. It's incredibly easy, can be made ahead and the flavor combination will bring a lot of wows!

PREP 10 Minutes **TOTAL** 2 Hours 10 Minutes • *1½ cups*

1 **package (8 oz) cream cheese, softened**	**FRUIT, IF DESIRED**
¼ **cup honey**	Strawberries, blackberries, raspberries, cantaloupe or honeydew melon
¼ **cup powdered sugar**	
2 **tablespoons finely chopped fresh basil leaves**	

1 In small bowl, beat cream cheese with electric mixer on medium speed until smooth. On low speed, beat in honey and powdered sugar until well mixed. Fold in basil.

2 Cover; refrigerate at least 2 hours to blend flavors. Dip may be made up to 3 days in advance. Remove from refrigerator 30 minutes before serving. Serve with fruit.

2 Tablespoons Calories 100; Total Fat 6g (Saturated Fat 3.5g, Trans Fat 0g); Cholesterol 20mg; Sodium 70mg; Total Carbohydrate 10g (Dietary Fiber 0g); Protein 1g **Carbohydrate Choices:** ½

Vanilla Ice Cream

PREP 10 Minutes **TOTAL** 2 Hours 40 Minutes • *1 quart*

1 **cup milk**	3 **egg yolks, slightly beaten**
½ **cup sugar**	2 **cups whipping cream**
¼ **teaspoon salt**	1 **tablespoon vanilla**

1 In 2-quart saucepan, stir milk, sugar, salt and egg yolks until well mixed. Heat just to boiling over medium heat, stirring constantly (do not allow mixture to continue to boil or it will curdle). Immediately remove from heat.

2 Pour milk mixture into chilled bowl. Refrigerate uncovered 2 to 3 hours, stirring occasionally, until room temperature. At this point, mixture can be refrigerated up to 24 hours before completing recipe, if desired.

3 Stir whipping cream and vanilla into milk mixture; pour into 1-quart ice cream freezer. Freeze according to manufacturer's directions.

½ Cup Calories 270; Total Fat 21g (Saturated Fat 12g, Trans Fat 0.5g); Cholesterol 150mg; Sodium 110mg; Total Carbohydrate 16g (Dietary Fiber 0g); Protein 3g **Carbohydrate Choices:** 1

CHOCOLATE ICE CREAM: Increase sugar to 1 cup. Beat 2 oz unsweetened baking chocolate, melted and cooled, into milk mixture before cooking. Reduce vanilla to 1 teaspoon.

FRESH PEACH ICE CREAM: Reduce vanilla to 1 teaspoon. Mash 4 or 5 peeled fresh peaches with potato masher or process in food processor until slightly chunky (not pureed) to make 2 cups; stir into milk mixture after adding vanilla.

FRESH BLUEBERRY ICE CREAM: Reduce vanilla to 1 teaspoon. Mash 2 cups fresh blueberries and an additional ⅓ cup sugar with potato masher or process in food processor until slightly chunky (not pureed); stir into milk mixture after adding vanilla.

EGGNOG ICE CREAM: Add ¼ teaspoon ground nutmeg with the sugar. Add 1 teaspoon rum extract with the vanilla.

FRESH RASPBERRY ICE CREAM: Substitute ½ teaspoon almond extract for the vanilla. Mash 2 cups fresh raspberries with potato masher or process in food processor until slightly chunky (not pureed); stir into milk mixture after adding almond extract.

FRESH STRAWBERRY ICE CREAM: Reduce vanilla to 1 teaspoon. Mash 2 cups fresh strawberries and an additional ½ cup sugar with potato masher or process in food processor until slightly chunky (not pureed); stir into milk mixture after adding vanilla. Stir in a few drops vegan red food color if desired.

Honey-Basil Fruit Dip

Vanilla Ice Cream

Blueberry "Ice Cream"

MAKE AHEAD • CALORIE SMART • GLUTEN FREE •
VEGETARIAN • VEGAN

Blueberry "Ice Cream"

PREP 35 Minutes TOTAL 3 Hours 10 Minutes • *1½ quarts*

2½ cups fresh blueberries	½ cup liquid (aquafaba) from 1 can (15 oz) chick peas or garbanzo beans, chilled
¾ cup organic sugar	
2 tablespoons water	
2 tablespoons fresh lemon juice	⅛ teaspoon cream of tartar
1 cup unsweetened coconut milk or other nut milk	

1 In 2-quart saucepan, heat 2 cups of the blueberries, the sugar, water and lemon juice over medium heat, mashing berries with potato masher or back of spoon, about 5 minutes or until mixture boils. Remove from heat; strain through fine-mesh strainer, pressing with the back of spoon, to extract all juice from skin and seeds. Discard skin and seeds. Let juice stand 15 minutes to cool; stir in coconut milk. Refrigerate at least 2 hours or until cold.

2 In large bowl, beat aquafaba and cream of tartar with electric mixer on medium-high speed about 1 minute or until frothy. Increase speed to high; beat 1 to 2 minutes longer until stiff peaks form. Fold about one-third of aquafaba mixture into blueberry mixture; fold blueberry mixture into remaining aquafaba mixture until just a few dark streaks remain.

3 Pour mixture into 1½-quart ice cream freezer and freeze according to manufacturer's directions, adding remaining ½ cup blueberries after 15 minutes.

4 For soft-serve ice cream, serve immediately. For harder ice cream, cover and freeze 4 hours.

½ Cup Calories 70; Total Fat 0g (Saturated Fat 0g, Trans Fat 0g); Cholesterol 0mg; Sodium 0mg; Total Carbohydrate 17g (Dietary Fiber 0g); Protein 0g **Carbohydrate Choices:** 1

WHAT IS AQUAFABA?

That liquid that usually gets drained away from a can of chick peas or garbanzo beans is an important ingredient that can make vegan recipes seem not-so-vegan. It can be whipped like egg whites in desserts like Pavlovas with Blood Orange Curd (page 648) and Blueberry "Ice Cream" (above) with little to no taste or textural difference.

To save the aquafaba from a can of chick peas or garbanzo beans, shake the can before opening to redistribute the starches in the liquid. Drain the chick peas or garbanzos through a fine-mesh strainer into a bowl. Keep the aquafaba in a covered container in the refrigerator for up to 1 week or freeze it in a plastic freezer storage container or resealable freezer plastic bag. Thaw frozen aquafaba in the refrigerator or microwave. Whisk the aquafaba before using it.

CHOCOLATE-PISTACHIO VEGAN "ICE CREAM": Omit blueberries, sugar, water and lemon juice. In 2-quart saucepan, place 2 tablespoons cornstarch; gradually stir in 1½ cups coconut milk and ½ cup maple syrup or agave nectar. Cook and stir over medium heat just until thickened, about 7 minutes. In medium bowl, place 3 oz chopped bittersweet chocolate; pour coconut milk mixture over chocolate and stir until melted. Refrigerate at least 2 hours or until cold. Prepare aquafaba mixture as directed above—except increase cream of tartar to ¼ teaspoon. Gently fold aquafaba into chocolate mixture as directed above. Ice Cream Freezer: Pour mixture into 2-quart ice cream freezer and freeze according to manufacturer's directions, adding ½ cup chopped salted roasted pistachio nuts after 15 minutes. Cover loosely and freeze at least 4 hours. 5 servings (½ cup). Pan Directions: Stir in pistachios after Step 2. Spread in 8-inch square pan. Cover loosely and freeze at least 4 hours. 9 servings (½ cup each).

EASY • MAKE AHEAD • CALORIE SMART • GLUTEN FREE • VEGETARIAN

Very Berry Frozen Yogurt

PREP 5 Minutes TOTAL 40 Minutes • *1½ quarts*

2 cups fresh strawberries or raspberries	⅓ cup sugar
	4 cups vanilla low-fat yogurt

1 In large bowl, mash berries with sugar. Stir in yogurt.

2 Pour mixture into 2-quart ice-cream freezer. Freeze according to manufacturer's directions.

½ Cup Calories 100; Total Fat 1g (Saturated Fat 0.5g, Trans Fat 0g); Cholesterol 0mg; Sodium 55mg; Total Carbohydrate 19g (Dietary Fiber 0g); Protein 4g **Carbohydrate Choices:** 1

Toffee-S'mores Icebox Cake

4 Sprinkle marshmallows evenly on top of cake. Set oven control to broil. Broil with cake top about 6 inches from heat about 1 minute or until marshmallows are golden brown (watch carefully so marshmallows don't burn). Freeze until firm, at least 8 hours but no longer than 1 week.

5 To serve, use foil to lift cake from pan to serving platter; remove foil. Let stand 10 minutes before serving. Drizzle each serving with 1 tablespoon hot fudge sauce.

1 Serving Calories 620; Total Fat 32g (Saturated Fat 17g, Trans Fat 1g); Cholesterol 65mg; Sodium 420mg; Total Carbohydrate 76g (Dietary Fiber 1g); Protein 6g **Carbohydrate Choices:** 5

EASY • MAKE AHEAD • CALORIE SMART • GLUTEN FREE • VEGETARIAN • VEGAN

Boozy Berry-Lemonade Pops

If you have a 4-cup measure, you can skip the bowl and just measure the ingredients right in the cup as you add them.

PREP 10 Minutes **TOTAL** 4 Hours 10 Minutes • *6 pops*

½ cup very thinly sliced small strawberries	¾ cup frozen lemonade concentrate, thawed (from 12-oz can)
6 paper drinking cups (5 oz each)	¼ cup water
1 can (12 oz) gluten-free berry-flavored hard seltzer	¼ cup gin
	6 (4-inch) squares foil
	6 wooden craft sticks

1 Divide strawberries evenly among paper cups. In 4-cup measure or medium bowl, mix all remaining ingredients except foil and sticks. Divide mixture evenly among cups. Cover cups with foil. Cut small slit in center of foil; insert stick.

2 Freeze 4 hours or overnight. Wrap hand around cup to warm slightly; remove pop from cup. Serve immediately.

1 Pop Calories 140; Total Fat 0g (Saturated Fat 0g, Trans Fat 0g); Cholesterol 0mg; Sodium 0mg; Total Carbohydrate 25g (Dietary Fiber 0g); Protein 0g **Carbohydrate Choices:** 1½

SPIRIT-FREE STRAWBERRY-LEMONADE-YOGURT POPS: Omit all ingredients except strawberries. In small bowl, combine ¾ cup vegan vanilla yogurt and ½ cup frozen strawberry-lemonade concentrate, thawed. Divide yogurt mixture evenly between 6 (3-oz) ice pop molds. Divide strawberry slices among molds, using table knife to gently push down into yogurt mixture. Insert mold tops, with sticks in each pop in center of each mold. Freeze 4 hours or overnight. Dip each mold into warm water about 20 seconds to loosen. Serve immediately.

MAKE AHEAD • VEGETARIAN

Toffee-S'mores Icebox Cake

Add another layer of flavor and texture by sprinkling servings of the cake with toasted coconut before serving—yum!

PREP 25 Minutes **TOTAL** 8 Hours 35 Minutes • *8 servings*

11 graham crackers (from 14.4 oz box)	1 cup milk chocolate toffee bits (from 8-oz pkg)
1 box (4-serving size) instant chocolate pudding and pie mix	½ cup vegan miniature marshmallows (from 10.5-oz pkg)
2 cups milk	½ cup store-bought or homemade Hot Fudge Sauce (page 661)
1½ cups heavy whipping cream	
1 cup marshmallow creme	

1 Line 9×5-inch loaf pan with foil, allowing foil to extend over edges.

2 In small bowl, crumble 2 graham crackers (reserve remaining 9 crackers); set aside. Prepare pudding mix as directed on box, using milk; set aside. In medium bowl, beat whipping cream with electric mixer on low speed until cream begins to thicken. Gradually increase speed to high and beat just until stiff peaks form; fold in marshmallow creme.

3 Line bottom of pan with 3 graham crackers, breaking in half and overlapping to fit. Spread 1 cup of the whipped cream mixture evenly over the crackers. Repeat another layer with 3 graham crackers, and spread 1 cup of the pudding evenly over crackers. Sprinkle with ½ cup toffee bits. Top with remaining 3 graham crackers, the remaining pudding and whipped cream mixtures. Sprinkle with the crumbled graham crackers and remaining ½ cup toffee bits.

Chocolate-Avocado Pudding Pops

These fudgy pops are a snap to make, but our testing showed that using wooden sticks works better than the sticks that come with most popsicle molds because they are longer, making holding the pop easier.

PREP 20 Minutes **TOTAL** 6 Hours 25 Minutes • *6 pops*

POPS
- ¾ cup milk chocolate chips
- 2 medium-size ripe avocados, pitted, peeled, coarsely chopped
- 1 cup chocolate almond milk
- 2 tablespoons unsweetened baking cocoa
- 1 tablespoon honey
- 2 teaspoons vanilla
- 6 wooden craft sticks

TOPPING
- 1 cup semisweet chocolate chips
- 1 teaspoon vegetable oil
- ⅓ cup finely chopped toasted almonds (see page 28)

1 In small microwavable bowl, microwave milk chocolate chips on High 60 to 70 seconds, stirring halfway through cooking or until chocolate can be stirred smooth. Cool slightly.

2 In blender or food processor, place melted milk chocolate chips and all remaining pop ingredients except wooden sticks. Cover and blend 1 to 2 minutes or until smooth. Divide avocado mixture among 6 ice pop molds or 5-oz paper drinking cups, pushing down with spoon to remove any air pockets. Insert wooden sticks in center of each pop (do not use sticks that come with molds). Freeze 6 hours or overnight.

3 Let pops stand at room temperature 10 minutes. Line cookie sheet with cooking parchment paper or waxed paper. Fill 2-cup measure with warm water. Dip one pop in the water about 30 seconds or until pop will release from mold. Set pop on cookie sheet. Repeat with remaining pops. Place in freezer while preparing topping.

4 In small microwavable bowl, microwave semisweet chips and oil on High 60 to 70 seconds, stirring halfway through cooking, until chocolate can be stirred smooth. Holding one pop at a time, spoon a generous tablespoon melted chocolate over top of pop. Immediately sprinkle with almonds; return to cookie sheet. Repeat with remaining pops. Place cookie sheet in freezer about 10 minutes or until chocolate is set. Serve immediately or wrap individual pops in plastic wrap and store in freezer until ready to serve.

1 Pop Calories 230; Total Fat 14g (Saturated Fat 5g, Trans Fat 0g); Cholesterol 0mg; Sodium 40mg; Total Carbohydrate 23g (Dietary Fiber 4g); Protein 2g **Carbohydrate Choices:** 1½

Watermelon Granita

Granita is the Italian term for an "ice" or frozen dessert made with fruit or fruit juice. The texture will be grainier than a sorbet—very similar to a slush.

PREP 20 Minutes **TOTAL** 4 Hours 25 Minutes • *2½ quarts*

- 1 cup water
- ½ cup organic sugar
- 3 tablespoons lime juice (2 to 3 limes)
- 6 cups 1-inch cubes seeded watermelon

1 In 1-quart saucepan, mix water, sugar and lime juice. Cook over low heat about 5 minutes, stirring occasionally, until sugar is dissolved. Cool slightly, about 5 minutes.

2 In blender or food processor, place watermelon. Cover and blend on high speed about 2 minutes or until smooth. Add lime juice mixture. Cover and blend until well mixed. Pour into 13×9-inch (3-quart) glass baking dish. Cover and freeze 1 hour.

3 Scrape with fork to distribute ice crystals evenly. Freeze at least 3 hours longer, repeating scraping procedure every 30 minutes, until mixture has consistency of fine ice crystals. To serve, scoop into chilled dessert cups.

1 Cup Calories 70; Total Fat 0g (Saturated Fat 0g, Trans Fat 0g); Cholesterol 0mg; Sodium 0mg; Total Carbohydrate 17g (Dietary Fiber 0g); Protein 0g **Carbohydrate Choices:** 1

659

Boozy Berry-Lemonade Pops and Chocolate-Avocado Pudding Pops

Watermelon Granita

Lemonade Sorbet

Raspberry Sauce

Lemonade Sorbet

PREP 5 Minutes **TOTAL** 4 Hours 5 Minutes •
About 2¾ cups

1½ cups cold water	3 tablespoons honey
1 cup thawed lemonade concentrate (from 12-oz can)	Lemon slices, if desired
	Blueberries, if desired

1 In blender or food processor, place water, lemonade concentrate and honey. Cover and blend on low speed about 30 seconds or until smooth. Pour into 8-inch square (2-quart) glass baking dish.

2 Cover and freeze about 4 hours or until firm, stirring several times to keep mixture smooth. Garnish with lemon slices and blueberries.

⅔ Cup Calories 200; Total Fat 0.5g (Saturated Fat 0g, Trans Fat 0g); Cholesterol 0mg; Sodium 10mg; Total Carbohydrate 50g (Dietary Fiber 0g); Protein 0g **Carbohydrate Choices:** 3

CRANBERRY-RASPBERRY SORBET: Substitute cranberry-raspberry concentrate for the lemonade concentrate.

LIMEADE SORBET: Substitute limeade concentrate for the lemonade concentrate.

ORANGE SORBET: Substitute orange juice concentrate for the lemonade concentrate.

PINEAPPLE SORBET: Substitute pineapple juice concentrate for the lemonade concentrate.

Raspberry Sauce

PREP 10 Minutes **TOTAL** 10 Minutes • *1 cup*

3 tablespoons organic sugar	1 box (10 oz) organic frozen raspberries in syrup, thawed, undrained
2 teaspoons cornstarch	
⅓ cup water	

1 In 1-quart saucepan, mix sugar and cornstarch. Stir in water and raspberries with syrup. Cook over medium heat, stirring constantly, until mixture thickens and boils (mixture will become translucent during cooking). Boil and stir 1 minute.

2 Strain sauce through fine-mesh strainer into bowl to remove seeds if desired. Serve sauce warm or cool. Store covered in refrigerator up to 10 days.

1 Tablespoon Calories 45; Total Fat 0g (Saturated Fat 0g, Trans Fat 0g); Cholesterol 0mg; Sodium 0mg; Total Carbohydrate 11g (Dietary Fiber 0g); Protein 0g **Carbohydrate Choices:** 1

STRAWBERRY SAUCE: Substitute organic frozen strawberries in syrup for the raspberries.

LEMON SAUCE: Increase sugar to ½ cup, cornstarch to 2 tablespoons and water to ¾ cup. Omit raspberries. Stir 1 tablespoon grated lemon zest, ¼ cup fresh lemon juice and 2 tablespoons softened vegan butter into hot sugar mixture.

MAKING RASPBERRY SAUCE

Stir water and raspberries into sugar and cornstarch.

Cook, stirring constantly, until mixture thickens and boils and becomes translucent.

Hot Fudge Sauce

PREP 10 Minutes **TOTAL** 40 Minutes • *3 cups*

1 can (12 oz) evaporated milk	½ cup sugar
2 cups semisweet or dark chocolate chips (about 12 oz)	1 tablespoon butter, softened
	1 teaspoon vanilla

1 In 2-quart saucepan, heat milk, chocolate chips and sugar over medium heat, stirring constantly, until boiling; remove from heat. Stir in butter and vanilla until mixture is smooth and creamy.

2 Cool about 30 minutes or until sauce begins to thicken. Serve warm. Store sauce, covered, in refrigerator up to 4 weeks. Sauce becomes firm when refrigerated; heat slightly before serving (sauce will become thin if overheated).

1 Tablespoon Calories 60; Total Fat 2.5g (Saturated Fat 1.5g, Trans Fat 0g); Cholesterol 0mg; Sodium 10mg; Total Carbohydrate 8g (Dietary Fiber 0g); Protein 0g **Carbohydrate Choices:** ½

Chocolate Sauce

PREP 10 Minutes **TOTAL** 10 Minutes • *1½ cups*

1½ cups light corn syrup	1 tablespoon butter, softened
3 oz unsweetened baking chocolate, chopped	¾ teaspoon vanilla

1 In 1-quart saucepan, heat corn syrup and chocolate over low heat, stirring frequently, until chocolate is melted; remove from heat. Stir in butter and vanilla.

2 Serve warm or cool. Store covered in refrigerator up to 10 days. Reheat slightly before serving if desired.

1 Tablespoon Calories 90; Total Fat 2.5g (Saturated Fat 1.5g, Trans Fat 0g); Cholesterol 0mg; Sodium 20mg; Total Carbohydrate 17g (Dietary Fiber 0g); Protein 0g **Carbohydrate Choices:** 1

Chocolate Sauce and Caramel Sauce

Rhubarb Sauce

Rhubarb varies in sweetness, so add sugar to taste. Serve it for dessert, either by itself or over pound cake or ice cream. Or serve as a sweet-tart accompaniment to pork or chicken.

PREP 20 Minutes **TOTAL** 20 Minutes • *3 cups*

½ to ¾ cup sugar	1 lb fresh or frozen rhubarb, cut into 1-inch pieces (3 cups)
½ cup water	
	Ground cinnamon, if desired

1 In 2-quart saucepan, heat ½ cup sugar and the water to boiling over medium heat, stirring occasionally. Stir in rhubarb; reduce heat to low. Simmer uncovered about 10 minutes, stirring occasionally, until rhubarb is tender and slightly transparent, adding up to ¼ cup more sugar, if desired.

2 Stir in cinnamon. Serve sauce warm or chilled. Store covered in refrigerator up to 1 week.

½ Cup Calories 80; Total Fat 0g (Saturated Fat 0g, Trans Fat 0g); Cholesterol 0mg; Sodium 0mg; Total Carbohydrate 20g (Dietary Fiber 1g); Protein 0g **Carbohydrate Choices:** 1

STRAWBERRY-RHUBARB SAUCE: Substitute 1 cup fresh strawberries, cut in half, for 1 cup of the rhubarb. After simmering rhubarb, stir in strawberries; heat just to boiling.

Caramel Sauce

What else besides ice cream is caramel sauce great on? Drizzle it over gluten-free cheesecake, or sliced bananas and sprinkle with chopped pecans. Or you can use it as a dip for apple slices or cubes of gluten-free pound cake.

PREP 10 Minutes **TOTAL** 40 Minutes • *2½ cups*

1¼ cups packed brown sugar	¼ cup butter, cut into pieces
1 cup light corn syrup	1 cup whipping cream

1 In 2-quart saucepan, heat brown sugar, corn syrup and butter over low heat, stirring constantly, until boiling. Boil 5 minutes, stirring occasionally.

2 Stir in whipping cream; heat to boiling, stirring constantly. Cool about 30 minutes. Serve warm. Store covered in refrigerator up to 10 days. Reheat slightly before serving if desired.

1 Tablespoon Calories 80; Total Fat 3.5g (Saturated Fat 2g, Trans Fat 0g); Cholesterol 10mg; Sodium 20mg; Total Carbohydrate 13g (Dietary Fiber 0g); Protein 0g **Carbohydrate Choices:** 1

Recipe Icon Index

For recipe icon definitions, see page 29.

EASY

GLUTEN FREE

General Index

Note: Page references in *italics* indicate recipe photographs.